Lecture Notes in Computer Science   13664

More information about this series at https://link.springer.com/bookseries/558

Shai Avidan · Gabriel Brostow ·
Moustapha Cissé · Giovanni Maria Farinella ·
Tal Hassner (Eds.)

Computer Vision – ECCV 2022

17th European Conference
Tel Aviv, Israel, October 23–27, 2022
Proceedings, Part IV

 Springer

Editors
Shai Avidan
Tel Aviv University
Tel Aviv, Israel

Gabriel Brostow ⓘ
University College London
London, UK

Moustapha Cissé
Google AI
Accra, Ghana

Giovanni Maria Farinella ⓘ
University of Catania
Catania, Italy

Tal Hassner ⓘ
Facebook (United States)
Menlo Park, CA, USA

ISSN 0302-9743   ISSN 1611-3349 (electronic)
Lecture Notes in Computer Science
ISBN 978-3-031-19771-0   ISBN 978-3-031-19772-7 (eBook)
https://doi.org/10.1007/978-3-031-19772-7

This Springer imprint is published by the registered company Springer Nature Switzerland AG
The registered company address is: Gewerbestrasse 11, 6330 Cham, Switzerland

Foreword

Organizing the European Conference on Computer Vision (ECCV 2022) in Tel-Aviv during a global pandemic was no easy feat. The uncertainty level was extremely high, and decisions had to be postponed to the last minute. Still, we managed to plan things just in time for ECCV 2022 to be held in person. Participation in physical events is crucial to stimulating collaborations and nurturing the culture of the Computer Vision community.

There were many people who worked hard to ensure attendees enjoyed the best science at the 16th edition of ECCV. We are grateful to the Program Chairs Gabriel Brostow and Tal Hassner, who went above and beyond to ensure the ECCV reviewing process ran smoothly. The scientific program includes dozens of workshops and tutorials in addition to the main conference and we would like to thank Leonid Karlinsky and Tomer Michaeli for their hard work. Finally, special thanks to the web chairs Lorenzo Baraldi and Kosta Derpanis, who put in extra hours to transfer information fast and efficiently to the ECCV community.

We would like to express gratitude to our generous sponsors and the Industry Chairs, Dimosthenis Karatzas and Chen Sagiv, who oversaw industry relations and proposed new ways for academia-industry collaboration and technology transfer. It's great to see so much industrial interest in what we're doing!

Authors' draft versions of the papers appeared online with open access on both the Computer Vision Foundation (CVF) and the European Computer Vision Association (ECVA) websites as with previous ECCVs. Springer, the publisher of the proceedings, has arranged for archival publication. The final version of the papers is hosted by SpringerLink, with active references and supplementary materials. It benefits all potential readers that we offer both a free and citeable version for all researchers, as well as an authoritative, citeable version for SpringerLink readers. Our thanks go to Ronan Nugent from Springer, who helped us negotiate this agreement. Last but not least, we wish to thank Eric Mortensen, our publication chair, whose expertise made the process smooth.

October 2022

Rita Cucchiara
Jiří Matas
Amnon Shashua
Lihi Zelnik-Manor

Preface

Welcome to the proceedings of the European Conference on Computer Vision (ECCV 2022). This was a hybrid edition of ECCV as we made our way out of the COVID-19 pandemic. The conference received 5804 valid paper submissions, compared to 5150 submissions to ECCV 2020 (a 12.7% increase) and 2439 in ECCV 2018. 1645 submissions were accepted for publication (28%) and, of those, 157 (2.7% overall) as orals.

846 of the submissions were desk-rejected for various reasons. Many of them because they revealed author identity, thus violating the double-blind policy. This violation came in many forms: some had author names with the title, others added acknowledgments to specific grants, yet others had links to their github account where their name was visible. Tampering with the LaTeX template was another reason for automatic desk rejection.

ECCV 2022 used the traditional CMT system to manage the entire double-blind reviewing process. Authors did not know the names of the reviewers and vice versa. Each paper received at least 3 reviews (except 6 papers that received only 2 reviews), totalling more than 15,000 reviews.

Handling the review process at this scale was a significant challenge. To ensure that each submission received as fair and high-quality reviews as possible, we recruited more than 4719 reviewers (in the end, 4719 reviewers did at least one review). Similarly we recruited more than 276 area chairs (eventually, only 276 area chairs handled a batch of papers). The area chairs were selected based on their technical expertise and reputation, largely among people who served as area chairs in previous top computer vision and machine learning conferences (ECCV, ICCV, CVPR, NeurIPS, etc.).

Reviewers were similarly invited from previous conferences, and also from the pool of authors. We also encouraged experienced area chairs to suggest additional chairs and reviewers in the initial phase of recruiting. The median reviewer load was five papers per reviewer, while the average load was about four papers, because of the emergency reviewers. The area chair load was 35 papers, on average.

Conflicts of interest between authors, area chairs, and reviewers were handled largely automatically by the CMT platform, with some manual help from the Program Chairs. Reviewers were allowed to describe themselves as senior reviewer (load of 8 papers to review) or junior reviewers (load of 4 papers). Papers were matched to area chairs based on a subject-area affinity score computed in CMT and an affinity score computed by the Toronto Paper Matching System (TPMS). TPMS is based on the paper's full text. An area chair handling each submission would bid for preferred expert reviewers, and we balanced load and prevented conflicts.

The assignment of submissions to area chairs was relatively smooth, as was the assignment of submissions to reviewers. A small percentage of reviewers were not happy with their assignments in terms of subjects and self-reported expertise. This is an area for improvement, although it's interesting that many of these cases were reviewers hand-picked by AC's. We made a later round of reviewer recruiting, targeted at the list of authors of papers submitted to the conference, and had an excellent response which helped provide enough emergency reviewers. In the end, all but six papers received at least 3 reviews.

The challenges of the reviewing process are in line with past experiences at ECCV 2020. As the community grows, and the number of submissions increases, it becomes ever more challenging to recruit enough reviewers and ensure a high enough quality of reviews. Enlisting authors by default as reviewers might be one step to address this challenge.

Authors were given a week to rebut the initial reviews, and address reviewers' concerns. Each rebuttal was limited to a single pdf page with a fixed template.

The Area Chairs then led discussions with the reviewers on the merits of each submission. The goal was to reach consensus, but, ultimately, it was up to the Area Chair to make a decision. The decision was then discussed with a buddy Area Chair to make sure decisions were fair and informative. The entire process was conducted virtually with no in-person meetings taking place.

The Program Chairs were informed in cases where the Area Chairs overturned a decisive consensus reached by the reviewers, and pushed for the meta-reviews to contain details that explained the reasoning for such decisions. Obviously these were the most contentious cases, where reviewer inexperience was the most common reported factor.

Once the list of accepted papers was finalized and released, we went through the laborious process of plagiarism (including self-plagiarism) detection. A total of 4 accepted papers were rejected because of that.

Finally, we would like to thank our Technical Program Chair, Pavel Lifshits, who did tremendous work behind the scenes, and we thank the tireless CMT team.

October 2022

Gabriel Brostow
Giovanni Maria Farinella
Moustapha Cissé
Shai Avidan
Tal Hassner

Organization

General Chairs

Rita Cucchiara   University of Modena and Reggio Emilia, Italy
Jiří Matas   Czech Technical University in Prague, Czech Republic
Amnon Shashua   Hebrew University of Jerusalem, Israel
Lihi Zelnik-Manor   Technion – Israel Institute of Technology, Israel

Program Chairs

Shai Avidan   Tel-Aviv University, Israel
Gabriel Brostow   University College London, UK
Moustapha Cissé   Google AI, Ghana
Giovanni Maria Farinella   University of Catania, Italy
Tal Hassner   Facebook AI, USA

Program Technical Chair

Pavel Lifshits   Technion – Israel Institute of Technology, Israel

Workshops Chairs

Leonid Karlinsky   IBM Research, Israel
Tomer Michaeli   Technion – Israel Institute of Technology, Israel
Ko Nishino   Kyoto University, Japan

Tutorial Chairs

Thomas Pock   Graz University of Technology, Austria
Natalia Neverova   Facebook AI Research, UK

Demo Chair

Bohyung Han   Seoul National University, Korea

Social and Student Activities Chairs

Tatiana Tommasi   Italian Institute of Technology, Italy
Sagie Benaim   University of Copenhagen, Denmark

Diversity and Inclusion Chairs

Xi Yin   Facebook AI Research, USA
Bryan Russell   Adobe, USA

Communications Chairs

Lorenzo Baraldi   University of Modena and Reggio Emilia, Italy
Kosta Derpanis   York University & Samsung AI Centre Toronto,
                         Canada

Industrial Liaison Chairs

Dimosthenis Karatzas   Universitat Autònoma de Barcelona, Spain
Chen Sagiv   SagivTech, Israel

Finance Chair

Gerard Medioni   University of Southern California & Amazon,
                         USA

Publication Chair

Eric Mortensen   MiCROTEC, USA

Area Chairs

Lourdes Agapito   University College London, UK
Zeynep Akata   University of Tübingen, Germany
Naveed Akhtar   University of Western Australia, Australia
Karteek Alahari   Inria Grenoble Rhône-Alpes, France
Alexandre Alahi   École polytechnique fédérale de Lausanne,
                         Switzerland
Pablo Arbelaez   Universidad de Los Andes, Columbia
Antonis A. Argyros   University of Crete & Foundation for Research
                         and Technology-Hellas, Crete
Yuki M. Asano   University of Amsterdam, The Netherlands
Kalle Åström   Lund University, Sweden
Hadar Averbuch-Elor   Cornell University, USA

Bohyung Han	Seoul National University, Korea
Tian Han	Stevens Institute of Technology, USA
Emily Hand	University of Nevada, Reno, USA
Bharath Hariharan	Cornell University, USA
Ran He	Institute of Automation, Chinese Academy of Sciences, China
Otmar Hilliges	ETH Zurich, Switzerland
Adrian Hilton	University of Surrey, UK
Minh Hoai	Stony Brook University, USA
Yedid Hoshen	Hebrew University of Jerusalem, Israel
Timothy Hospedales	University of Edinburgh, UK
Gang Hua	Wormpex AI Research, USA
Di Huang	Beihang University, China
Jing Huang	Facebook, USA
Jia-Bin Huang	Facebook, USA
Nathan Jacobs	Washington University in St. Louis, USA
C.V. Jawahar	International Institute of Information Technology, Hyderabad, India
Herve Jegou	Facebook AI Research, France
Neel Joshi	Microsoft Research, USA
Armand Joulin	Facebook AI Research, France
Frederic Jurie	University of Caen Normandie, France
Fredrik Kahl	Chalmers University of Technology, Sweden
Yannis Kalantidis	NAVER LABS Europe, France
Evangelos Kalogerakis	University of Massachusetts, Amherst, USA
Sing Bing Kang	Zillow Group, USA
Yosi Keller	Bar Ilan University, Israel
Margret Keuper	University of Mannheim, Germany
Tae-Kyun Kim	Imperial College London, UK
Benjamin Kimia	Brown University, USA
Alexander Kirillov	Facebook AI Research, USA
Kris Kitani	Carnegie Mellon University, USA
Iasonas Kokkinos	Snap Inc. & University College London, UK
Vladlen Koltun	Apple, USA
Nikos Komodakis	University of Crete, Crete
Piotr Koniusz	Australian National University, Australia
Philipp Kraehenbuehl	University of Texas at Austin, USA
Dilip Krishnan	Google, USA
Ajay Kumar	Hong Kong Polytechnic University, Hong Kong, China
Junseok Kwon	Chung-Ang University, Korea
Jean-Francois Lalonde	Université Laval, Canada

Ivan Laptev	Inria Paris, France
Laura Leal-Taixé	Technical University of Munich, Germany
Erik Learned-Miller	University of Massachusetts, Amherst, USA
Gim Hee Lee	National University of Singapore, Singapore
Seungyong Lee	Pohang University of Science and Technology, Korea
Zhen Lei	Institute of Automation, Chinese Academy of Sciences, China
Bastian Leibe	RWTH Aachen University, Germany
Hongdong Li	Australian National University, Australia
Fuxin Li	Oregon State University, USA
Bo Li	University of Illinois at Urbana-Champaign, USA
Yin Li	University of Wisconsin-Madison, USA
Ser-Nam Lim	Meta AI Research, USA
Joseph Lim	University of Southern California, USA
Stephen Lin	Microsoft Research Asia, China
Dahua Lin	The Chinese University of Hong Kong, Hong Kong, China
Si Liu	Beihang University, China
Xiaoming Liu	Michigan State University, USA
Ce Liu	Microsoft, USA
Zicheng Liu	Microsoft, USA
Yanxi Liu	Pennsylvania State University, USA
Feng Liu	Portland State University, USA
Yebin Liu	Tsinghua University, China
Chen Change Loy	Nanyang Technological University, Singapore
Huchuan Lu	Dalian University of Technology, China
Cewu Lu	Shanghai Jiao Tong University, China
Oisin Mac Aodha	University of Edinburgh, UK
Dhruv Mahajan	Facebook, USA
Subhransu Maji	University of Massachusetts, Amherst, USA
Atsuto Maki	KTH Royal Institute of Technology, Sweden
Arun Mallya	NVIDIA, USA
R. Manmatha	Amazon, USA
Iacopo Masi	Sapienza University of Rome, Italy
Dimitris N. Metaxas	Rutgers University, USA
Ajmal Mian	University of Western Australia, Australia
Christian Micheloni	University of Udine, Italy
Krystian Mikolajczyk	Imperial College London, UK
Anurag Mittal	Indian Institute of Technology, Madras, India
Philippos Mordohai	Stevens Institute of Technology, USA
Greg Mori	Simon Fraser University & Borealis AI, Canada

Todd Zickler   Harvard University, USA
Wangmeng Zuo   Harbin Institute of Technology, China

Technical Program Committee

Davide Abati
Soroush Abbasi
    Koohpayegani
Amos L. Abbott
Rameen Abdal
Rabab Abdelfattah
Sahar Abdelnabi
Hassan Abu Alhaija
Abulikemu Abuduweili
Ron Abutbul
Hanno Ackermann
Aikaterini Adam
Kamil Adamczewski
Ehsan Adeli
Vida Adeli
Donald Adjeroh
Arman Afrasiyabi
Akshay Agarwal
Sameer Agarwal
Abhinav Agarwalla
Vaibhav Aggarwal
Sara Aghajanzadeh
Susmit Agrawal
Antonio Agudo
Touqeer Ahmad
Sk Miraj Ahmed
Chaitanya Ahuja
Nilesh A. Ahuja
Abhishek Aich
Shubhra Aich
Noam Aigerman
Arash Akbarinia
Peri Akiva
Derya Akkaynak
Emre Aksan
Arjun R. Akula
Yuval Alaluf
Stephan Alaniz
Paul Albert
Cenek Albl

Filippo Aleotti
Konstantinos P.
    Alexandridis
Motasem Alfarra
Mohsen Ali
Thiemo Alldieck
Hadi Alzayer
Liang An
Shan An
Yi An
Zhulin An
Dongsheng An
Jie An
Xiang An
Saket Anand
Cosmin Ancuti
Juan Andrade-Cetto
Alexander Andreopoulos
Bjoern Andres
Jerone T. A. Andrews
Shivangi Aneja
Anelia Angelova
Dragomir Anguelov
Rushil Anirudh
Oron Anschel
Rao Muhammad Anwer
Djamila Aouada
Evlampios Apostolidis
Srikar Appalaraju
Nikita Araslanov
Andre Araujo
Eric Arazo
Dawit Mureja Argaw
Anurag Arnab
Aditya Arora
Chetan Arora
Sunpreet S. Arora
Alexey Artemov
Muhammad Asad
Kumar Ashutosh

Sinem Aslan
Vishal Asnani
Mahmoud Assran
Amir Atapour-Abarghouei
Nikos Athanasiou
Ali Athar
ShahRukh Athar
Sara Atito
Souhaib Attaiki
Matan Atzmon
Mathieu Aubry
Nicolas Audebert
Tristan T.
    Aumentado-Armstrong
Melinos Averkiou
Yannis Avrithis
Stephane Ayache
Mehmet Aygün
Seyed Mehdi
    Ayyoubzadeh
Hossein Azizpour
George Azzopardi
Mallikarjun B. R.
Yunhao Ba
Abhishek Badki
Seung-Hwan Bae
Seung-Hwan Baek
Seungryul Baek
Piyush Nitin Bagad
Shai Bagon
Gaetan Bahl
Shikhar Bahl
Sherwin Bahmani
Haoran Bai
Lei Bai
Jiawang Bai
Haoyue Bai
Jinbin Bai
Xiang Bai
Xuyang Bai

Yang Bai
Yuanchao Bai
Ziqian Bai
Sungyong Baik
Kevin Bailly
Max Bain
Federico Baldassarre
Wele Gedara Chaminda
  Bandara
Biplab Banerjee
Pratyay Banerjee
Sandipan Banerjee
Jihwan Bang
Antyanta Bangunharcana
Aayush Bansal
Ankan Bansal
Siddhant Bansal
Wentao Bao
Zhipeng Bao
Amir Bar
Manel Baradad Jurjo
Lorenzo Baraldi
Danny Barash
Daniel Barath
Connelly Barnes
Ioan Andrei Bârsan
Steven Basart
Dina Bashkirova
Chaim Baskin
Peyman Bateni
Anil Batra
Sebastiano Battiato
Ardhendu Behera
Harkirat Behl
Jens Behley
Vasileios Belagiannis
Boulbaba Ben Amor
Emanuel Ben Baruch
Abdessamad Ben Hamza
Gil Ben-Artzi
Assia Benbihi
Fabian Benitez-Quiroz
Guy Ben-Yosef
Philipp Benz
Alexander W. Bergman

Urs Bergmann
Jesus Bermudez-Cameo
Stefano Berretti
Gedas Bertasius
Zachary Bessinger
Petra Bevandić
Matthew Beveridge
Lucas Beyer
Yash Bhalgat
Suvaansh Bhambri
Samarth Bharadwaj
Gaurav Bharaj
Aparna Bharati
Bharat Lal Bhatnagar
Uttaran Bhattacharya
Apratim Bhattacharyya
Brojeshwar Bhowmick
Ankan Kumar Bhunia
Ayan Kumar Bhunia
Qi Bi
Sai Bi
Michael Bi Mi
Gui-Bin Bian
Jia-Wang Bian
Shaojun Bian
Pia Bideau
Mario Bijelic
Hakan Bilen
Guillaume-Alexandre
  Bilodeau
Alexander Binder
Tolga Birdal
Vighnesh N. Birodkar
Sandika Biswas
Andreas Blattmann
Janusz Bobulski
Giuseppe Boccignone
Vishnu Boddeti
Navaneeth Bodla
Moritz Böhle
Aleksei Bokhovkin
Sam Bond-Taylor
Vivek Boominathan
Shubhankar Borse
Mark Boss

Andrea Bottino
Adnane Boukhayma
Fadi Boutros
Nicolas C. Boutry
Richard S. Bowen
Ivaylo Boyadzhiev
Aidan Boyd
Yuri Boykov
Aljaz Bozic
Behzad Bozorgtabar
Eric Brachmann
Samarth Brahmbhatt
Gustav Bredell
Francois Bremond
Joel Brogan
Andrew Brown
Thomas Brox
Marcus A. Brubaker
Robert-Jan Bruintjes
Yuqi Bu
Anders G. Buch
Himanshu Buckchash
Mateusz Buda
Ignas Budvytis
José M. Buenaposada
Marcel C. Bühler
Tu Bui
Adrian Bulat
Hannah Bull
Evgeny Burnaev
Andrei Bursuc
Benjamin Busam
Sergey N. Buzykanov
Wonmin Byeon
Fabian Caba
Martin Cadik
Guanyu Cai
Minjie Cai
Qing Cai
Zhongang Cai
Qi Cai
Yancheng Cai
Shen Cai
Han Cai
Jiarui Cai

Bowen Cai
Mu Cai
Qin Cai
Ruojin Cai
Weidong Cai
Weiwei Cai
Yi Cai
Yujun Cai
Zhiping Cai
Akin Caliskan
Lilian Calvet
Baris Can Cam
Necati Cihan Camgoz
Tommaso Campari
Dylan Campbell
Ziang Cao
Ang Cao
Xu Cao
Zhiwen Cao
Shengcao Cao
Song Cao
Weipeng Cao
Xiangyong Cao
Xiaochun Cao
Yue Cao
Yunhao Cao
Zhangjie Cao
Jiale Cao
Yang Cao
Jiajiong Cao
Jie Cao
Jinkun Cao
Lele Cao
Yulong Cao
Zhiguo Cao
Chen Cao
Razvan Caramalau
Marlène Careil
Gustavo Carneiro
Joao Carreira
Dan Casas
Paola Cascante-Bonilla
Angela Castillo
Francisco M. Castro
Pedro Castro

Luca Cavalli
George J. Cazenavette
Oya Celiktutan
Hakan Cevikalp
Sri Harsha C. H.
Sungmin Cha
Geonho Cha
Menglei Chai
Lucy Chai
Yuning Chai
Zenghao Chai
Anirban Chakraborty
Deep Chakraborty
Rudrasis Chakraborty
Souradeep Chakraborty
Kelvin C. K. Chan
Chee Seng Chan
Paramanand Chandramouli
Arjun Chandrasekaran
Kenneth Chaney
Dongliang Chang
Huiwen Chang
Peng Chang
Xiaojun Chang
Jia-Ren Chang
Hyung Jin Chang
Hyun Sung Chang
Ju Yong Chang
Li-Jen Chang
Qi Chang
Wei-Yi Chang
Yi Chang
Nadine Chang
Hanqing Chao
Pradyumna Chari
Dibyadip Chatterjee
Chiranjoy Chattopadhyay
Siddhartha Chaudhuri
Zhengping Che
Gal Chechik
Lianggangxu Chen
Qi Alfred Chen
Brian Chen
Bor-Chun Chen
Bo-Hao Chen

Bohong Chen
Bin Chen
Ziliang Chen
Cheng Chen
Chen Chen
Chaofeng Chen
Xi Chen
Haoyu Chen
Xuanhong Chen
Wei Chen
Qiang Chen
Shi Chen
Xianyu Chen
Chang Chen
Changhuai Chen
Hao Chen
Jie Chen
Jianbo Chen
Jingjing Chen
Jun Chen
Kejiang Chen
Mingcai Chen
Nenglun Chen
Qifeng Chen
Ruoyu Chen
Shu-Yu Chen
Weidong Chen
Weijie Chen
Weikai Chen
Xiang Chen
Xiuyi Chen
Xingyu Chen
Yaofo Chen
Yueting Chen
Yu Chen
Yunjin Chen
Yuntao Chen
Yun Chen
Zhenfang Chen
Zhuangzhuang Chen
Chu-Song Chen
Xiangyu Chen
Zhuo Chen
Chaoqi Chen
Shizhe Chen

Xiaotong Chen
Xiaozhi Chen
Dian Chen
Defang Chen
Dingfan Chen
Ding-Jie Chen
Ee Heng Chen
Tao Chen
Yixin Chen
Wei-Ting Chen
Lin Chen
Guang Chen
Guangyi Chen
Guanying Chen
Guangyao Chen
Hwann-Tzong Chen
Junwen Chen
Jiacheng Chen
Jianxu Chen
Hui Chen
Kai Chen
Kan Chen
Kevin Chen
Kuan-Wen Chen
Weihua Chen
Zhang Chen
Liang-Chieh Chen
Lele Chen
Liang Chen
Fanglin Chen
Zehui Chen
Minghui Chen
Minghao Chen
Xiaokang Chen
Qian Chen
Jun-Cheng Chen
Qi Chen
Qingcai Chen
Richard J. Chen
Runnan Chen
Rui Chen
Shuo Chen
Sentao Chen
Shaoyu Chen
Shixing Chen

Shuai Chen
Shuya Chen
Sizhe Chen
Simin Chen
Shaoxiang Chen
Zitian Chen
Tianlong Chen
Tianshui Chen
Min-Hung Chen
Xiangning Chen
Xin Chen
Xinghao Chen
Xuejin Chen
Xu Chen
Xuxi Chen
Yunlu Chen
Yanbei Chen
Yuxiao Chen
Yun-Chun Chen
Yi-Ting Chen
Yi-Wen Chen
Yinbo Chen
Yiran Chen
Yuanhong Chen
Yubei Chen
Yuefeng Chen
Yuhua Chen
Yukang Chen
Zerui Chen
Zhaoyu Chen
Zhen Chen
Zhenyu Chen
Zhi Chen
Zhiwei Chen
Zhixiang Chen
Long Chen
Bowen Cheng
Jun Cheng
Yi Cheng
Jingchun Cheng
Lechao Cheng
Xi Cheng
Yuan Cheng
Ho Kei Cheng
Kevin Ho Man Cheng

Jiacheng Cheng
Kelvin B. Cheng
Li Cheng
Mengjun Cheng
Zhen Cheng
Qingrong Cheng
Tianheng Cheng
Harry Cheng
Yihua Cheng
Yu Cheng
Ziheng Cheng
Soon Yau Cheong
Anoop Cherian
Manuela Chessa
Zhixiang Chi
Naoki Chiba
Julian Chibane
Kashyap Chitta
Tai-Yin Chiu
Hsu-kuang Chiu
Wei-Chen Chiu
Sungmin Cho
Donghyeon Cho
Hyeon Cho
Yooshin Cho
Gyusang Cho
Jang Hyun Cho
Seungju Cho
Nam Ik Cho
Sunghyun Cho
Hanbyel Cho
Jaesung Choe
Jooyoung Choi
Chiho Choi
Changwoon Choi
Jongwon Choi
Myungsub Choi
Dooseop Choi
Jonghyun Choi
Jinwoo Choi
Jun Won Choi
Min-Kook Choi
Hongsuk Choi
Janghoon Choi
Yoon-Ho Choi

Yukyung Choi
Jaegul Choo
Ayush Chopra
Siddharth Choudhary
Subhabrata Choudhury
Vasileios Choutas
Ka-Ho Chow
Pinaki Nath Chowdhury
Sammy Christen
Anders Christensen
Grigorios Chrysos
Hang Chu
Wen-Hsuan Chu
Peng Chu
Qi Chu
Ruihang Chu
Wei-Ta Chu
Yung-Yu Chuang
Sanghyuk Chun
Se Young Chun
Antonio Cinà
Ramazan Gokberk Cinbis
Javier Civera
Albert Clapés
Ronald Clark
Brian S. Clipp
Felipe Codevilla
Daniel Coelho de Castro
Niv Cohen
Forrester Cole
Maxwell D. Collins
Robert T. Collins
Marc Comino Trinidad
Runmin Cong
Wenyan Cong
Maxime Cordy
Marcella Cornia
Enric Corona
Huseyin Coskun
Luca Cosmo
Dragos Costea
Davide Cozzolino
Arun C. S. Kumar
Aiyu Cui
Qiongjie Cui

Quan Cui
Shuhao Cui
Yiming Cui
Ying Cui
Zijun Cui
Jiali Cui
Jiequan Cui
Yawen Cui
Zhen Cui
Zhaopeng Cui
Jack Culpepper
Xiaodong Cun
Ross Cutler
Adam Czajka
Ali Dabouei
Konstantinos M. Dafnis
Manuel Dahnert
Tao Dai
Yuchao Dai
Bo Dai
Mengyu Dai
Hang Dai
Haixing Dai
Peng Dai
Pingyang Dai
Qi Dai
Qiyu Dai
Yutong Dai
Naser Damer
Zhiyuan Dang
Mohamed Daoudi
Ayan Das
Abir Das
Debasmit Das
Deepayan Das
Partha Das
Sagnik Das
Soumi Das
Srijan Das
Swagatam Das
Avijit Dasgupta
Jim Davis
Adrian K. Davison
Homa Davoudi
Laura Daza

Matthias De Lange
Shalini De Mello
Marco De Nadai
Christophe De
  Vleeschouwer
Alp Dener
Boyang Deng
Congyue Deng
Bailin Deng
Yong Deng
Ye Deng
Zhuo Deng
Zhijie Deng
Xiaoming Deng
Jiankang Deng
Jinhong Deng
Jingjing Deng
Liang-Jian Deng
Siqi Deng
Xiang Deng
Xueqing Deng
Zhongying Deng
Karan Desai
Jean-Emmanuel Deschaud
Aniket Anand Deshmukh
Neel Dey
Helisa Dhamo
Prithviraj Dhar
Amaya Dharmasiri
Yan Di
Xing Di
Ousmane A. Dia
Haiwen Diao
Xiaolei Diao
Gonçalo José Dias Pais
Abdallah Dib
Anastasios Dimou
Changxing Ding
Henghui Ding
Guodong Ding
Yaqing Ding
Shuangrui Ding
Yuhang Ding
Yikang Ding
Shouhong Ding

Haisong Ding
Hui Ding
Jiahao Ding
Jian Ding
Jian-Jiun Ding
Shuxiao Ding
Tianyu Ding
Wenhao Ding
Yuqi Ding
Yi Ding
Yuzhen Ding
Zhengming Ding
Tan Minh Dinh
Vu Dinh
Christos Diou
Mandar Dixit
Bao Gia Doan
Khoa D. Doan
Dzung Anh Doan
Debi Prosad Dogra
Nehal Doiphode
Chengdong Dong
Bowen Dong
Zhenxing Dong
Hang Dong
Xiaoyi Dong
Haoye Dong
Jiangxin Dong
Shichao Dong
Xuan Dong
Zhen Dong
Shuting Dong
Jing Dong
Li Dong
Ming Dong
Nanqing Dong
Qiulei Dong
Runpei Dong
Siyan Dong
Tian Dong
Wei Dong
Xiaomeng Dong
Xin Dong
Xingbo Dong
Yuan Dong

Samuel Dooley
Gianfranco Doretto
Michael Dorkenwald
Keval Doshi
Zhaopeng Dou
Xiaotian Dou
Hazel Doughty
Ahmad Droby
Iddo Drori
Jie Du
Yong Du
Dawei Du
Dong Du
Ruoyi Du
Yuntao Du
Xuefeng Du
Yilun Du
Yuming Du
Radhika Dua
Haodong Duan
Jiafei Duan
Kaiwen Duan
Peiqi Duan
Ye Duan
Haoran Duan
Jiali Duan
Amanda Duarte
Abhimanyu Dubey
Shiv Ram Dubey
Florian Dubost
Lukasz Dudziak
Shivam Duggal
Justin M. Dulay
Matteo Dunnhofer
Chi Nhan Duong
Thibaut Durand
Mihai Dusmanu
Ujjal Kr Dutta
Debidatta Dwibedi
Isht Dwivedi
Sai Kumar Dwivedi
Takeharu Eda
Mark Edmonds
Alexei A. Efros
Thibaud Ehret

Max Ehrlich
Mahsa Ehsanpour
Iván Eichhardt
Farshad Einabadi
Marvin Eisenberger
Hazim Kemal Ekenel
Mohamed El Banani
Ismail Elezi
Moshe Eliasof
Alaa El-Nouby
Ian Endres
Francis Engelmann
Deniz Engin
Chanho Eom
Dave Epstein
Maria C. Escobar
Victor A. Escorcia
Carlos Esteves
Sungmin Eum
Bernard J. E. Evans
Ivan Evtimov
Fevziye Irem Eyiokur
    Yaman
Matteo Fabbri
Sébastien Fabbro
Gabriele Facciolo
Masud Fahim
Bin Fan
Hehe Fan
Deng-Ping Fan
Aoxiang Fan
Chen-Chen Fan
Qi Fan
Zhaoxin Fan
Haoqi Fan
Heng Fan
Hongyi Fan
Linxi Fan
Baojie Fan
Jiayuan Fan
Lei Fan
Quanfu Fan
Yonghui Fan
Yingruo Fan
Zhiwen Fan

Zicong Fan
Sean Fanello
Jiansheng Fang
Chaowei Fang
Yuming Fang
Jianwu Fang
Jin Fang
Qi Fang
Shancheng Fang
Tian Fang
Xianyong Fang
Gongfan Fang
Zhen Fang
Hui Fang
Jiemin Fang
Le Fang
Pengfei Fang
Xiaolin Fang
Yuxin Fang
Zhaoyuan Fang
Ammarah Farooq
Azade Farshad
Zhengcong Fei
Michael Felsberg
Wei Feng
Chen Feng
Fan Feng
Andrew Feng
Xin Feng
Zheyun Feng
Ruicheng Feng
Mingtao Feng
Qianyu Feng
Shangbin Feng
Chun-Mei Feng
Zunlei Feng
Zhiyong Feng
Martin Fergie
Mustansar Fiaz
Marco Fiorucci
Michael Firman
Hamed Firooz
Volker Fischer
Corneliu O. Florea
Georgios Floros

Wolfgang Foerstner
Gianni Franchi
Jean-Sebastien Franco
Simone Frintrop
Anna Fruehstueck
Changhong Fu
Chaoyou Fu
Cheng-Yang Fu
Chi-Wing Fu
Deqing Fu
Huan Fu
Jun Fu
Kexue Fu
Ying Fu
Jianlong Fu
Jingjing Fu
Qichen Fu
Tsu-Jui Fu
Xueyang Fu
Yang Fu
Yanwei Fu
Yonggan Fu
Wolfgang Fuhl
Yasuhisa Fujii
Kent Fujiwara
Marco Fumero
Takuya Funatomi
Isabel Funke
Dario Fuoli
Antonino Furnari
Matheus A. Gadelha
Akshay Gadi Patil
Adrian Galdran
Guillermo Gallego
Silvano Galliani
Orazio Gallo
Leonardo Galteri
Matteo Gamba
Yiming Gan
Sujoy Ganguly
Harald Ganster
Boyan Gao
Changxin Gao
Daiheng Gao
Difei Gao

Chen Gao
Fei Gao
Lin Gao
Wei Gao
Yiming Gao
Junyu Gao
Guangyu Ryan Gao
Haichang Gao
Hongchang Gao
Jialin Gao
Jin Gao
Jun Gao
Katelyn Gao
Mingchen Gao
Mingfei Gao
Pan Gao
Shangqian Gao
Shanghua Gao
Xitong Gao
Yunhe Gao
Zhanning Gao
Elena Garces
Nuno Cruz Garcia
Noa Garcia
Guillermo
    Garcia-Hernando
Isha Garg
Rahul Garg
Sourav Garg
Quentin Garrido
Stefano Gasperini
Kent Gauen
Chandan Gautam
Shivam Gautam
Paul Gay
Chunjiang Ge
Shiming Ge
Wenhang Ge
Yanhao Ge
Zheng Ge
Songwei Ge
Weifeng Ge
Yixiao Ge
Yuying Ge
Shijie Geng

Zhengyang Geng
Kyle A. Genova
Georgios Georgakis
Markos Georgopoulos
Marcel Geppert
Shabnam Ghadar
Mina Ghadimi Atigh
Deepti Ghadiyaram
Maani Ghaffari Jadidi
Sedigh Ghamari
Zahra Gharaee
Michaël Gharbi
Golnaz Ghiasi
Reza Ghoddoosian
Soumya Suvra Ghosal
Adhiraj Ghosh
Arthita Ghosh
Pallabi Ghosh
Soumyadeep Ghosh
Andrew Gilbert
Igor Gilitschenski
Jhony H. Giraldo
Andreu Girbau Xalabarder
Rohit Girdhar
Sharath Girish
Xavier Giro-i-Nieto
Raja Giryes
Thomas Gittings
Nikolaos Gkanatsios
Ioannis Gkioulekas
Abhiram
    Gnanasambandam
Aurele T. Gnanha
Clement L. J. C. Godard
Arushi Goel
Vidit Goel
Shubham Goel
Zan Gojcic
Aaron K. Gokaslan
Tejas Gokhale
S. Alireza Golestaneh
Thiago L. Gomes
Nuno Goncalves
Boqing Gong
Chen Gong

Yuanhao Gong
Guoqiang Gong
Jingyu Gong
Rui Gong
Yu Gong
Mingming Gong
Neil Zhenqiang Gong
Xun Gong
Yunye Gong
Yihong Gong
Cristina I. González
Nithin Gopalakrishnan
    Nair
Gaurav Goswami
Jianping Gou
Shreyank N. Gowda
Ankit Goyal
Helmut Grabner
Patrick L. Grady
Ben Graham
Eric Granger
Douglas R. Gray
Matej Grcić
David Griffiths
Jinjin Gu
Yun Gu
Shuyang Gu
Jianyang Gu
Fuqiang Gu
Jiatao Gu
Jindong Gu
Jiaqi Gu
Jinwei Gu
Jiaxin Gu
Geonmo Gu
Xiao Gu
Xinqian Gu
Xiuye Gu
Yuming Gu
Zhangxuan Gu
Dayan Guan
Junfeng Guan
Qingji Guan
Tianrui Guan
Shanyan Guan

Denis A. Gudovskiy
Ricardo Guerrero
Pierre-Louis Guhur
Jie Gui
Liangyan Gui
Liangke Gui
Benoit Guillard
Erhan Gundogdu
Manuel Günther
Jingcai Guo
Yuanfang Guo
Junfeng Guo
Chenqi Guo
Dan Guo
Hongji Guo
Jia Guo
Jie Guo
Minghao Guo
Shi Guo
Yanhui Guo
Yangyang Guo
Yuan-Chen Guo
Yilu Guo
Yiluan Guo
Yong Guo
Guangyu Guo
Haiyun Guo
Jinyang Guo
Jianyuan Guo
Pengsheng Guo
Pengfei Guo
Shuxuan Guo
Song Guo
Tianyu Guo
Qing Guo
Qiushan Guo
Wen Guo
Xiefan Guo
Xiaohu Guo
Xiaoqing Guo
Yufei Guo
Yuhui Guo
Yuliang Guo
Yunhui Guo
Yanwen Guo

Akshita Gupta

Ankush Gupta

Kamal Gupta

Kartik Gupta

Ritwik Gupta

Rohit Gupta

Siddharth Gururani

Fredrik K. Gustafsson

Abner Guzman Rivera

Vladimir Guzov

Matthew A. Gwilliam

Jung-Woo Ha

Marc Habermann

Isma Hadji

Christian Haene

Martin Hahner

Levente Hajder

Alexandros Haliassos

Emanuela Haller

Bumsub Ham

Abdullah J. Hamdi

Shreyas Hampali

Dongyoon Han

Chunrui Han

Dong-Jun Han

Dong-Sig Han

Guangxing Han

Zhizhong Han

Ruize Han

Jiaming Han

Jin Han

Ligong Han

Xian-Hua Han

Xiaoguang Han

Yizeng Han

Zhi Han

Zhenjun Han

Zhongyi Han

Jungong Han

Junlin Han

Kai Han

Kun Han

Sungwon Han

Songfang Han

Wei Han

Xiao Han

Xintong Han

Xinzhe Han

Yahong Han

Yan Han

Zongbo Han

Nicolai Hani

Rana Hanocka

Niklas Hanselmann

Nicklas A. Hansen

Hong Hanyu

Fusheng Hao

Yanbin Hao

Shijie Hao

Udith Haputhanthri

Mehrtash Harandi

Josh Harguess

Adam Harley

David M. Hart

Atsushi Hashimoto

Ali Hassani

Mohammed Hassanin

Yana Hasson

Joakim Bruslund Haurum

Bo He

Kun He

Chen He

Xin He

Fazhi He

Gaoqi He

Hao He

Haoyu He

Jiangpeng He

Hongliang He

Qian He

Xiangteng He

Xuming He

Yannan He

Yuhang He

Yang He

Xiangyu He

Nanjun He

Pan He

Sen He

Shengfeng He

Songtao He

Tao He

Tong He

Wei He

Xuehai He

Xiaoxiao He

Ying He

Yisheng He

Ziwen He

Peter Hedman

Felix Heide

Yacov Hel-Or

Paul Henderson

Philipp Henzler

Byeongho Heo

Jae-Pil Heo

Miran Heo

Sachini A. Herath

Stephane Herbin

Pedro Hermosilla Casajus

Monica Hernandez

Charles Herrmann

Roei Herzig

Mauricio Hess-Flores

Carlos Hinojosa

Tobias Hinz

Tsubasa Hirakawa

Chih-Hui Ho

Lam Si Tung Ho

Jennifer Hobbs

Derek Hoiem

Yannick Hold-Geoffroy

Aleksander Holynski

Cheeun Hong

Fa-Ting Hong

Hanbin Hong

Guan Zhe Hong

Danfeng Hong

Lanqing Hong

Xiaopeng Hong

Xin Hong

Jie Hong

Seungbum Hong

Cheng-Yao Hong

Seunghoon Hong

Yi Hong
Yuan Hong
Yuchen Hong
Anthony Hoogs
Maxwell C. Horton
Kazuhiro Hotta
Qibin Hou
Tingbo Hou
Junhui Hou
Ji Hou
Qiqi Hou
Rui Hou
Ruibing Hou
Zhi Hou
Henry Howard-Jenkins
Lukas Hoyer
Wei-Lin Hsiao
Chiou-Ting Hsu
Anthony Hu
Brian Hu
Yusong Hu
Hexiang Hu
Haoji Hu
Di Hu
Hengtong Hu
Haigen Hu
Lianyu Hu
Hanzhe Hu
Jie Hu
Junlin Hu
Shizhe Hu
Jian Hu
Zhiming Hu
Juhua Hu
Peng Hu
Ping Hu
Ronghang Hu
MengShun Hu
Tao Hu
Vincent Tao Hu
Xiaoling Hu
Xinting Hu
Xiaolin Hu
Xuefeng Hu
Xiaowei Hu

Yang Hu
Yueyu Hu
Zeyu Hu
Zhongyun Hu
Binh-Son Hua
Guoliang Hua
Yi Hua
Linzhi Huang
Qiusheng Huang
Bo Huang
Chen Huang
Hsin-Ping Huang
Ye Huang
Shuangping Huang
Zeng Huang
Buzhen Huang
Cong Huang
Heng Huang
Hao Huang
Qidong Huang
Huaibo Huang
Chaoqin Huang
Feihu Huang
Jiahui Huang
Jingjia Huang
Kun Huang
Lei Huang
Sheng Huang
Shuaiyi Huang
Siyu Huang
Xiaoshui Huang
Xiaoyang Huang
Yan Huang
Yihao Huang
Ying Huang
Ziling Huang
Xiaoke Huang
Yifei Huang
Haiyang Huang
Zhewei Huang
Jin Huang
Haibin Huang
Jiaxing Huang
Junjie Huang
Keli Huang

Lang Huang
Lin Huang
Luojie Huang
Mingzhen Huang
Shijia Huang
Shengyu Huang
Siyuan Huang
He Huang
Xiuyu Huang
Lianghua Huang
Yue Huang
Yaping Huang
Yuge Huang
Zehao Huang
Zeyi Huang
Zhiqi Huang
Zhongzhan Huang
Zilong Huang
Ziyuan Huang
Tianrui Hui
Zhuo Hui
Le Hui
Jing Huo
Junhwa Hur
Shehzeen S. Hussain
Chuong Minh Huynh
Seunghyun Hwang
Jaehui Hwang
Jyh-Jing Hwang
Sukjun Hwang
Soonmin Hwang
Wonjun Hwang
Rakib Hyder
Sangeek Hyun
Sarah Ibrahimi
Tomoki Ichikawa
Yerlan Idelbayev
A. S. M. Iftekhar
Masaaki Iiyama
Satoshi Ikehata
Sunghoon Im
Atul N. Ingle
Eldar Insafutdinov
Yani A. Ioannou
Radu Tudor Ionescu

Umar Iqbal
Go Irie
Muhammad Zubair Irshad
Ahmet Iscen
Berivan Isik
Ashraful Islam
Md Amirul Islam
Syed Islam
Mariko Isogawa
Vamsi Krishna K. Ithapu
Boris Ivanovic
Darshan Iyer
Sarah Jabbour
Ayush Jain
Nishant Jain
Samyak Jain
Vidit Jain
Vineet Jain
Priyank Jaini
Tomas Jakab
Mohammad A. A. K.
    Jalwana
Muhammad Abdullah
    Jamal
Hadi Jamali-Rad
Stuart James
Varun Jampani
Young Kyun Jang
YeongJun Jang
Yunseok Jang
Ronnachai Jaroensri
Bhavan Jasani
Krishna Murthy
    Jatavallabhula
Mojan Javaheripi
Syed A. Javed
Guillaume Jeanneret
Pranav Jeevan
Herve Jegou
Rohit Jena
Tomas Jenicek
Porter Jenkins
Simon Jenni
Hae-Gon Jeon
Sangryul Jeon

Boseung Jeong
Yoonwoo Jeong
Seong-Gyun Jeong
Jisoo Jeong
Allan D. Jepson
Ankit Jha
Sumit K. Jha
I-Hong Jhuo
Ge-Peng Ji
Chaonan Ji
Deyi Ji
Jingwei Ji
Wei Ji
Zhong Ji
Jiayi Ji
Pengliang Ji
Hui Ji
Mingi Ji
Xiaopeng Ji
Yuzhu Ji
Baoxiong Jia
Songhao Jia
Dan Jia
Shan Jia
Xiaojun Jia
Xiuyi Jia
Xu Jia
Menglin Jia
Wenqi Jia
Boyuan Jiang
Wenhao Jiang
Huaizu Jiang
Hanwen Jiang
Haiyong Jiang
Hao Jiang
Huajie Jiang
Huiqin Jiang
Haojun Jiang
Haobo Jiang
Junjun Jiang
Xingyu Jiang
Yangbangyan Jiang
Yu Jiang
Jianmin Jiang
Jiaxi Jiang

Jing Jiang
Kui Jiang
Li Jiang
Liming Jiang
Chiyu Jiang
Meirui Jiang
Chen Jiang
Peng Jiang
Tai-Xiang Jiang
Wen Jiang
Xinyang Jiang
Yifan Jiang
Yuming Jiang
Yingying Jiang
Zeren Jiang
ZhengKai Jiang
Zhenyu Jiang
Shuming Jiao
Jianbo Jiao
Licheng Jiao
Dongkwon Jin
Yeying Jin
Cheng Jin
Linyi Jin
Qing Jin
Taisong Jin
Xiao Jin
Xin Jin
Sheng Jin
Kyong Hwan Jin
Ruibing Jin
SouYoung Jin
Yueming Jin
Chenchen Jing
Longlong Jing
Taotao Jing
Yongcheng Jing
Younghyun Jo
Joakim Johnander
Jeff Johnson
Michael J. Jones
R. Kenny Jones
Rico Jonschkowski
Ameya Joshi
Sunghun Joung

Felix Juefei-Xu
Claudio R. Jung
Steffen Jung
Hari Chandana K.
Rahul Vigneswaran K.
Prajwal K. R.
Abhishek Kadian
Jhony Kaesemodel Pontes
Kumara Kahatapitiya
Anmol Kalia
Sinan Kalkan
Tarun Kalluri
Jaewon Kam
Sandesh Kamath
Meina Kan
Menelaos Kanakis
Takuhiro Kaneko
Di Kang
Guoliang Kang
Hao Kang
Jaeyeon Kang
Kyoungkook Kang
Li-Wei Kang
MinGuk Kang
Suk-Ju Kang
Zhao Kang
Yash Mukund Kant
Yueying Kao
Aupendu Kar
Konstantinos Karantzalos
Sezer Karaoglu
Navid Kardan
Sanjay Kariyappa
Leonid Karlinsky
Animesh Karnewar
Shyamgopal Karthik
Hirak J. Kashyap
Marc A. Kastner
Hirokatsu Kataoka
Angelos Katharopoulos
Hiroharu Kato
Kai Katsumata
Manuel Kaufmann
Chaitanya Kaul
Prakhar Kaushik

Yuki Kawana
Lei Ke
Lipeng Ke
Tsung-Wei Ke
Wei Ke
Petr Kellnhofer
Aniruddha Kembhavi
John Kender
Corentin Kervadec
Leonid Keselman
Daniel Keysers
Nima Khademi Kalantari
Taras Khakhulin
Samir Khaki
Muhammad Haris Khan
Qadeer Khan
Salman Khan
Subash Khanal
Vaishnavi M. Khindkar
Rawal Khirodkar
Saeed Khorram
Pirazh Khorramshahi
Kourosh Khoshelham
Ansh Khurana
Benjamin Kiefer
Jae Myung Kim
Junho Kim
Boah Kim
Hyeonseong Kim
Dong-Jin Kim
Dongwan Kim
Donghyun Kim
Doyeon Kim
Yonghyun Kim
Hyung-Il Kim
Hyunwoo Kim
Hyeongwoo Kim
Hyo Jin Kim
Hyunwoo J. Kim
Taehoon Kim
Jaeha Kim
Jiwon Kim
Jung Uk Kim
Kangyeol Kim
Eunji Kim

Daeha Kim
Dongwon Kim
Kunhee Kim
Kyungmin Kim
Junsik Kim
Min H. Kim
Namil Kim
Kookhoi Kim
Sanghyun Kim
Seongyeop Kim
Seungryong Kim
Saehoon Kim
Euyoung Kim
Guisik Kim
Sungyeon Kim
Sunnie S. Y. Kim
Taehun Kim
Tae Oh Kim
Won Hwa Kim
Seungwook Kim
YoungBin Kim
Youngeun Kim
Akisato Kimura
Furkan Osman Kınlı
Zsolt Kira
Hedvig Kjellström
Florian Kleber
Jan P. Klopp
Florian Kluger
Laurent Kneip
Byungsoo Ko
Muhammed Kocabas
A. Sophia Koepke
Kevin Koeser
Nick Kolkin
Nikos Kolotouros
Wai-Kin Adams Kong
Deying Kong
Caihua Kong
Youyong Kong
Shuyu Kong
Shu Kong
Tao Kong
Yajing Kong
Yu Kong

Zishang Kong
Theodora Kontogianni
Anton S. Konushin
Julian F. P. Kooij
Bruno Korbar
Giorgos Kordopatis-Zilos
Jari Korhonen
Adam Kortylewski
Denis Korzhenkov
Divya Kothandaraman
Suraj Kothawade
Iuliia Kotseruba
Satwik Kottur
Shashank Kotyan
Alexandros Kouris
Petros Koutras
Anna Kreshuk
Ranjay Krishna
Dilip Krishnan
Andrey Kuehlkamp
Hilde Kuehne
Jason Kuen
David Kügler
Arjan Kuijper
Anna Kukleva
Sumith Kulal
Viveka Kulharia
Akshay R. Kulkarni
Nilesh Kulkarni
Dominik Kulon
Abhinav Kumar
Akash Kumar
Suryansh Kumar
B. V. K. Vijaya Kumar
Pulkit Kumar
Ratnesh Kumar
Sateesh Kumar
Satish Kumar
Vijay Kumar B. G.
Nupur Kumari
Sudhakar Kumawat
Jogendra Nath Kundu
Hsien-Kai Kuo
Meng-Yu Jennifer Kuo
Vinod Kumar Kurmi

Yusuke Kurose
Keerthy Kusumam
Alina Kuznetsova
Henry Kvinge
Ho Man Kwan
Hyeokjun Kweon
Heeseung Kwon
Gihyun Kwon
Myung-Joon Kwon
Taesung Kwon
YoungJoong Kwon
Christos Kyrkou
Jorma Laaksonen
Yann Labbe
Zorah Laehner
Florent Lafarge
Hamid Laga
Manuel Lagunas
Shenqi Lai
Jian-Huang Lai
Zihang Lai
Mohamed I. Lakhal
Mohit Lamba
Meng Lan
Loic Landrieu
Zhiqiang Lang
Natalie Lang
Dong Lao
Yizhen Lao
Yingjie Lao
Issam Hadj Laradji
Gustav Larsson
Viktor Larsson
Zakaria Laskar
Stéphane Lathuilière
Chun Pong Lau
Rynson W. H. Lau
Hei Law
Justin Lazarow
Verica Lazova
Eric-Tuan Le
Hieu Le
Trung-Nghia Le
Mathias Lechner
Byeong-Uk Lee

Chen-Yu Lee
Che-Rung Lee
Chul Lee
Hong Joo Lee
Dongsoo Lee
Jiyoung Lee
Eugene Eu Tzuan Lee
Daeun Lee
Saehyung Lee
Jewook Lee
Hyungtae Lee
Hyunmin Lee
Jungbeom Lee
Joon-Young Lee
Jong-Seok Lee
Joonseok Lee
Junha Lee
Kibok Lee
Byung-Kwan Lee
Jangwon Lee
Jinho Lee
Jongmin Lee
Seunghyun Lee
Sohyun Lee
Minsik Lee
Dogyoon Lee
Seungmin Lee
Min Jun Lee
Sangho Lee
Sangmin Lee
Seungeun Lee
Seon-Ho Lee
Sungmin Lee
Sungho Lee
Sangyoun Lee
Vincent C. S. S. Lee
Jaeseong Lee
Yong Jae Lee
Chenyang Lei
Chenyi Lei
Jiahui Lei
Xinyu Lei
Yinjie Lei
Jiaxu Leng
Luziwei Leng

Jan E. Lenssen
Vincent Lepetit
Thomas Leung
María Leyva-Vallina
Xin Li
Yikang Li
Baoxin Li
Bin Li
Bing Li
Bowen Li
Changlin Li
Chao Li
Chongyi Li
Guanyue Li
Shuai Li
Jin Li
Dingquan Li
Dongxu Li
Yiting Li
Gang Li
Dian Li
Guohao Li
Haoang Li
Haoliang Li
Haoran Li
Hengduo Li
Huafeng Li
Xiaoming Li
Hanao Li
Hongwei Li
Ziqiang Li
Jisheng Li
Jiacheng Li
Jia Li
Jiachen Li
Jiahao Li
Jianwei Li
Jiazhi Li
Jie Li
Jing Li
Jingjing Li
Jingtao Li
Jun Li
Junxuan Li
Kai Li

Kailin Li
Kenneth Li
Kun Li
Kunpeng Li
Aoxue Li
Chenglong Li
Chenglin Li
Changsheng Li
Zhichao Li
Qiang Li
Yanyu Li
Zuoyue Li
Xiang Li
Xuelong Li
Fangda Li
Ailin Li
Liang Li
Chun-Guang Li
Daiqing Li
Dong Li
Guanbin Li
Guorong Li
Haifeng Li
Jianan Li
Jianing Li
Jiaxin Li
Ke Li
Lei Li
Lincheng Li
Liulei Li
Lujun Li
Linjie Li
Lin Li
Pengyu Li
Ping Li
Qiufu Li
Qingyong Li
Rui Li
Siyuan Li
Wei Li
Wenbin Li
Xiangyang Li
Xinyu Li
Xiujun Li
Xiu Li

Xu Li
Ya-Li Li
Yao Li
Yongjie Li
Yijun Li
Yiming Li
Yuezun Li
Yu Li
Yunheng Li
Yuqi Li
Zhe Li
Zeming Li
Zhen Li
Zhengqin Li
Zhimin Li
Jiefeng Li
Jinpeng Li
Chengze Li
Jianwu Li
Lerenhan Li
Shan Li
Suichan Li
Xiangtai Li
Yanjie Li
Yandong Li
Zhuoling Li
Zhenqiang Li
Manyi Li
Maosen Li
Ji Li
Minjun Li
Mingrui Li
Mengtian Li
Junyi Li
Nianyi Li
Bo Li
Xiao Li
Peihua Li
Peike Li
Peizhao Li
Peiliang Li
Qi Li
Ren Li
Runze Li
Shile Li

Sheng Li
Shigang Li
Shiyu Li
Shuang Li
Shasha Li
Shichao Li
Tianye Li
Yuexiang Li
Wei-Hong Li
Wanhua Li
Weihao Li
Weiming Li
Weixin Li
Wenbo Li
Wenshuo Li
Weijian Li
Yunan Li
Xirong Li
Xianhang Li
Xiaoyu Li
Xueqian Li
Xuanlin Li
Xianzhi Li
Yunqiang Li
Yanjing Li
Yansheng Li
Yawei Li
Yi Li
Yong Li
Yong-Lu Li
Yuhang Li
Yu-Jhe Li
Yuxi Li
Yunsheng Li
Yanwei Li
Zechao Li
Zejian Li
Zeju Li
Zekun Li
Zhaowen Li
Zheng Li
Zhenyu Li
Zhiheng Li
Zhi Li
Zhong Li

Zhuowei Li
Zhuowan Li
Zhuohang Li
Zizhang Li
Chen Li
Yuan-Fang Li
Dongze Lian
Xiaochen Lian
Zhouhui Lian
Long Lian
Qing Lian
Jin Lianbao
Jinxiu S. Liang
Dingkang Liang
Jiahao Liang
Jianming Liang
Jingyun Liang
Kevin J. Liang
Kaizhao Liang
Chen Liang
Jie Liang
Senwei Liang
Ding Liang
Jiajun Liang
Jian Liang
Kongming Liang
Siyuan Liang
Yuanzhi Liang
Zhengfa Liang
Mingfu Liang
Xiaodan Liang
Xuefeng Liang
Yuxuan Liang
Kang Liao
Liang Liao
Hong-Yuan Mark Liao
Wentong Liao
Haofu Liao
Yue Liao
Minghui Liao
Shengcai Liao
Ting-Hsuan Liao
Xin Liao
Yinghong Liao
Teck Yian Lim

Che-Tsung Lin
Chung-Ching Lin
Chen-Hsuan Lin
Cheng Lin
Chuming Lin
Chunyu Lin
Dahua Lin
Wei Lin
Zheng Lin
Huaijia Lin
Jason Lin
Jierui Lin
Jiaying Lin
Jie Lin
Kai-En Lin
Kevin Lin
Guangfeng Lin
Jiehong Lin
Feng Lin
Hang Lin
Kwan-Yee Lin
Ke Lin
Luojun Lin
Qinghong Lin
Xiangbo Lin
Yi Lin
Zudi Lin
Shijie Lin
Yiqun Lin
Tzu-Heng Lin
Ming Lin
Shaohui Lin
SongNan Lin
Ji Lin
Tsung-Yu Lin
Xudong Lin
Yancong Lin
Yen-Chen Lin
Yiming Lin
Yuewei Lin
Zhiqiu Lin
Zinan Lin
Zhe Lin
David B. Lindell
Zhixin Ling

Zhan Ling
Alexander Liniger
Venice Erin B. Liong
Joey Litalien
Or Litany
Roee Litman
Ron Litman
Jim Little
Dor Litvak
Shaoteng Liu
Shuaicheng Liu
Andrew Liu
Xian Liu
Shaohui Liu
Bei Liu
Bo Liu
Yong Liu
Ming Liu
Yanbin Liu
Chenxi Liu
Daqi Liu
Di Liu
Difan Liu
Dong Liu
Dongfang Liu
Daizong Liu
Xiao Liu
Fangyi Liu
Fengbei Liu
Fenglin Liu
Bin Liu
Yuang Liu
Ao Liu
Hong Liu
Hongfu Liu
Huidong Liu
Ziyi Liu
Feng Liu
Hao Liu
Jie Liu
Jialun Liu
Jiang Liu
Jing Liu
Jingya Liu
Jiaming Liu

Jun Liu
Juncheng Liu
Jiawei Liu
Hongyu Liu
Chuanbin Liu
Haotian Liu
Lingqiao Liu
Chang Liu
Han Liu
Liu Liu
Min Liu
Yingqi Liu
Aishan Liu
Bingyu Liu
Benlin Liu
Boxiao Liu
Chenchen Liu
Chuanjian Liu
Daqing Liu
Huan Liu
Haozhe Liu
Jiaheng Liu
Wei Liu
Jingzhou Liu
Jiyuan Liu
Lingbo Liu
Nian Liu
Peiye Liu
Qiankun Liu
Shenglan Liu
Shilong Liu
Wen Liu
Wenyu Liu
Weifeng Liu
Wu Liu
Xiaolong Liu
Yang Liu
Yanwei Liu
Yingcheng Liu
Yongfei Liu
Yihao Liu
Yu Liu
Yunze Liu
Ze Liu
Zhenhua Liu

Zhenguang Liu
Lin Liu
Lihao Liu
Pengju Liu
Xinhai Liu
Yunfei Liu
Meng Liu
Minghua Liu
Mingyuan Liu
Miao Liu
Peirong Liu
Ping Liu
Qingjie Liu
Ruoshi Liu
Risheng Liu
Songtao Liu
Xing Liu
Shikun Liu
Shuming Liu
Sheng Liu
Songhua Liu
Tongliang Liu
Weibo Liu
Weide Liu
Weizhe Liu
Wenxi Liu
Weiyang Liu
Xin Liu
Xiaobin Liu
Xudong Liu
Xiaoyi Liu
Xihui Liu
Xinchen Liu
Xingtong Liu
Xinpeng Liu
Xinyu Liu
Xianpeng Liu
Xu Liu
Xingyu Liu
Yongtuo Liu
Yahui Liu
Yangxin Liu
Yaoyao Liu
Yaojie Liu
Yuliang Liu

Yongcheng Liu
Yuan Liu
Yufan Liu
Yu-Lun Liu
Yun Liu
Yunfan Liu
Yuanzhong Liu
Zhuoran Liu
Zhen Liu
Zheng Liu
Zhijian Liu
Zhisong Liu
Ziquan Liu
Ziyu Liu
Zhihua Liu
Zechun Liu
Zhaoyang Liu
Zhengzhe Liu
Stephan Liwicki
Shao-Yuan Lo
Sylvain Lobry
Suhas Lohit
Vishnu Suresh Lokhande
Vincenzo Lomonaco
Chengjiang Long
Guodong Long
Fuchen Long
Shangbang Long
Yang Long
Zijun Long
Vasco Lopes
Antonio M. Lopez
Roberto Javier
   Lopez-Sastre
Tobias Lorenz
Javier Lorenzo-Navarro
Yujing Lou
Qian Lou
Xiankai Lu
Changsheng Lu
Huimin Lu
Yongxi Lu
Hao Lu
Hong Lu
Jiasen Lu

Juwei Lu
Fan Lu
Guangming Lu
Jiwen Lu
Shun Lu
Tao Lu
Xiaonan Lu
Yang Lu
Yao Lu
Yongchun Lu
Zhiwu Lu
Cheng Lu
Liying Lu
Guo Lu
Xuequan Lu
Yanye Lu
Yantao Lu
Yuhang Lu
Fujun Luan
Jonathon Luiten
Jovita Lukasik
Alan Lukezic
Jonathan Samuel Lumentut
Mayank Lunayach
Ao Luo
Canjie Luo
Chong Luo
Xu Luo
Grace Luo
Jun Luo
Katie Z. Luo
Tao Luo
Cheng Luo
Fangzhou Luo
Gen Luo
Lei Luo
Sihui Luo
Weixin Luo
Yan Luo
Xiaoyan Luo
Yong Luo
Yadan Luo
Hao Luo
Ruotian Luo
Mi Luo

Tiange Luo
Wenjie Luo
Wenhan Luo
Xiao Luo
Zhiming Luo
Zhipeng Luo
Zhengyi Luo
Diogo C. Luvizon
Zhaoyang Lv
Gengyu Lyu
Lingjuan Lyu
Jun Lyu
Yuanyuan Lyu
Youwei Lyu
Yueming Lyu
Bingpeng Ma
Chao Ma
Chongyang Ma
Congbo Ma
Chih-Yao Ma
Fan Ma
Lin Ma
Haoyu Ma
Hengbo Ma
Jianqi Ma
Jiawei Ma
Jiayi Ma
Kede Ma
Kai Ma
Lingni Ma
Lei Ma
Xu Ma
Ning Ma
Benteng Ma
Cheng Ma
Andy J. Ma
Long Ma
Zhanyu Ma
Zhiheng Ma
Qianli Ma
Shiqiang Ma
Sizhuo Ma
Shiqing Ma
Xiaolong Ma
Xinzhu Ma

Gautam B. Machiraju
Spandan Madan
Mathew Magimai-Doss
Luca Magri
Behrooz Mahasseni
Upal Mahbub
Siddharth Mahendran
Paridhi Maheshwari
Rishabh Maheshwary
Mohammed Mahmoud
Shishira R. R. Maiya
Sylwia Majchrowska
Arjun Majumdar
Puspita Majumdar
Orchid Majumder
Sagnik Majumder
Ilya Makarov
Farkhod F.
   Makhmudkhujaev
Yasushi Makihara
Ankur Mali
Mateusz Malinowski
Utkarsh Mall
Srikanth Malla
Clement Mallet
Dimitrios Mallis
Yunze Man
Dipu Manandhar
Massimiliano Mancini
Murari Mandal
Raunak Manekar
Karttikeya Mangalam
Puneet Mangla
Fabian Manhardt
Sivabalan Manivasagam
Fahim Mannan
Chengzhi Mao
Hanzi Mao
Jiayuan Mao
Junhua Mao
Zhiyuan Mao
Jiageng Mao
Yunyao Mao
Zhendong Mao
Alberto Marchisio

Diego Marcos
Riccardo Marin
Aram Markosyan
Renaud Marlet
Ricardo Marques
Miquel Martí i Rabadán
Diego Martin Arroyo
Niki Martinel
Brais Martinez
Julieta Martinez
Marc Masana
Tomohiro Mashita
Timothée Masquelier
Minesh Mathew
Tetsu Matsukawa
Marwan Mattar
Bruce A. Maxwell
Christoph Mayer
Mantas Mazeika
Pratik Mazumder
Scott McCloskey
Steven McDonagh
Ishit Mehta
Jie Mei
Kangfu Mei
Jieru Mei
Xiaoguang Mei
Givi Meishvili
Luke Melas-Kyriazi
Iaroslav Melekhov
Andres Mendez-Vazquez
Heydi Mendez-Vazquez
Matias Mendieta
Ricardo A. Mendoza-León
Chenlin Meng
Depu Meng
Rang Meng
Zibo Meng
Qingjie Meng
Qier Meng
Yanda Meng
Zihang Meng
Thomas Mensink
Fabian Mentzer
Christopher Metzler

Gregory P. Meyer
Vasileios Mezaris
Liang Mi
Lu Mi
Bo Miao
Changtao Miao
Zichen Miao
Qiguang Miao
Xin Miao
Zhongqi Miao
Frank Michel
Simone Milani
Ben Mildenhall
Roy V. Miles
Juhong Min
Kyle Min
Hyun-Seok Min
Weiqing Min
Yuecong Min
Zhixiang Min
Qi Ming
David Minnen
Aymen Mir
Deepak Mishra
Anand Mishra
Shlok K. Mishra
Niluthpol Mithun
Gaurav Mittal
Trisha Mittal
Daisuke Miyazaki
Kaichun Mo
Hong Mo
Zhipeng Mo
Davide Modolo
Abduallah A. Mohamed
Mohamed Afham
   Mohamed Aflal
Ron Mokady
Pavlo Molchanov
Davide Moltisanti
Liliane Momeni
Gianluca Monaci
Pascal Monasse
Ajoy Mondal
Tom Monnier

Aron Monszpart
Gyeongsik Moon
Suhong Moon
Taesup Moon
Sean Moran
Daniel Moreira
Pietro Morerio
Alexandre Morgand
Lia Morra
Ali Mosleh
Inbar Mosseri
Sayed Mohammad
    Mostafavi Isfahani
Saman Motamed
Ramy A. Mounir
Fangzhou Mu
Jiteng Mu
Norman Mu
Yasuhiro Mukaigawa
Ryan Mukherjee
Tanmoy Mukherjee
Yusuke Mukuta
Ravi Teja Mullapudi
Lea Müller
Matthias Müller
Martin Mundt
Nils Murrugarra-Llerena
Damien Muselet
Armin Mustafa
Muhammad Ferjad Naeem
Sauradip Nag
Hajime Nagahara
Pravin Nagar
Rajendra Nagar
Naveen Shankar Nagaraja
Varun Nagaraja
Tushar Nagarajan
Seungjun Nah
Gaku Nakano
Yuta Nakashima
Giljoo Nam
Seonghyeon Nam
Liangliang Nan
Yuesong Nan
Yeshwanth Napolean

Dinesh Reddy
    Narapureddy
Medhini Narasimhan
Supreeth
    Narasimhaswamy
Sriram Narayanan
Erickson R. Nascimento
Varun Nasery
K. L. Navaneet
Pablo Navarrete Michelini
Shant Navasardyan
Shah Nawaz
Nihal Nayak
Farhood Negin
Lukáš Neumann
Alejandro Newell
Evonne Ng
Kam Woh Ng
Tony Ng
Anh Nguyen
Tuan Anh Nguyen
Cuong Cao Nguyen
Ngoc Cuong Nguyen
Thanh Nguyen
Khoi Nguyen
Phi Le Nguyen
Phong Ha Nguyen
Tam Nguyen
Truong Nguyen
Anh Tuan Nguyen
Rang Nguyen
Thao Thi Phuong Nguyen
Van Nguyen Nguyen
Zhen-Liang Ni
Yao Ni
Shijie Nie
Xuecheng Nie
Yongwei Nie
Weizhi Nie
Ying Nie
Yinyu Nie
Kshitij N. Nikhal
Simon Niklaus
Xuefei Ning
Jifeng Ning

Yotam Nitzan
Di Niu
Shuaicheng Niu
Li Niu
Wei Niu
Yulei Niu
Zhenxing Niu
Albert No
Shohei Nobuhara
Nicoletta Noceti
Junhyug Noh
Sotiris Nousias
Slawomir Nowaczyk
Ewa M. Nowara
Valsamis Ntouskos
Gilberto Ochoa-Ruiz
Ferda Ofli
Jihyong Oh
Sangyun Oh
Youngtaek Oh
Hiroki Ohashi
Takahiro Okabe
Kemal Oksuz
Fumio Okura
Daniel Olmeda Reino
Matthew Olson
Carl Olsson
Roy Or-El
Alessandro Ortis
Guillermo Ortiz-Jimenez
Magnus Oskarsson
Ahmed A. A. Osman
Martin R. Oswald
Mayu Otani
Naima Otberdout
Cheng Ouyang
Jiahong Ouyang
Wanli Ouyang
Andrew Owens
Poojan B. Oza
Mete Ozay
A. Cengiz Oztireli
Gautam Pai
Tomas Pajdla
Umapada Pal

Simone Palazzo
Luca Palmieri
Bowen Pan
Hao Pan
Lili Pan
Tai-Yu Pan
Liang Pan
Chengwei Pan
Yingwei Pan
Xuran Pan
Jinshan Pan
Xinyu Pan
Liyuan Pan
Xingang Pan
Xingjia Pan
Zhihong Pan
Zizheng Pan
Priyadarshini Panda
Rameswar Panda
Rohit Pandey
Kaiyue Pang
Bo Pang
Guansong Pang
Jiangmiao Pang
Meng Pang
Tianyu Pang
Ziqi Pang
Omiros Pantazis
Andreas Panteli
Maja Pantic
Marina Paolanti
Joao P. Papa
Samuele Papa
Mike Papadakis
Dim P. Papadopoulos
George Papandreou
Constantin Pape
Toufiq Parag
Chethan Parameshwara
Shaifali Parashar
Alejandro Pardo
Rishubh Parihar
Sarah Parisot
JaeYoo Park
Gyeong-Moon Park

Hyojin Park
Hyoungseob Park
Jongchan Park
Jae Sung Park
Kiru Park
Chunghyun Park
Kwanyong Park
Sunghyun Park
Sungrae Park
Seongsik Park
Sanghyun Park
Sungjune Park
Taesung Park
Gaurav Parmar
Paritosh Parmar
Alvaro Parra
Despoina Paschalidou
Or Patashnik
Shivansh Patel
Pushpak Pati
Prashant W. Patil
Vaishakh Patil
Suvam Patra
Jay Patravali
Badri Narayana Patro
Angshuman Paul
Sudipta Paul
Rémi Pautrat
Nick E. Pears
Adithya Pediredla
Wenjie Pei
Shmuel Peleg
Latha Pemula
Bo Peng
Houwen Peng
Yue Peng
Liangzu Peng
Baoyun Peng
Jun Peng
Pai Peng
Sida Peng
Xi Peng
Yuxin Peng
Songyou Peng
Wei Peng

Weiqi Peng
Wen-Hsiao Peng
Pramuditha Perera
Juan C. Perez
Eduardo Pérez Pellitero
Juan-Manuel Perez-Rua
Federico Pernici
Marco Pesavento
Stavros Petridis
Ilya A. Petrov
Vladan Petrovic
Mathis Petrovich
Suzanne Petryk
Hieu Pham
Quang Pham
Khoi Pham
Tung Pham
Huy Phan
Stephen Phillips
Cheng Perng Phoo
David Picard
Marco Piccirilli
Georg Pichler
A. J. Piergiovanni
Vipin Pillai
Silvia L. Pintea
Giovanni Pintore
Robinson Piramuthu
Fiora Pirri
Theodoros Pissas
Fabio Pizzati
Benjamin Planche
Bryan Plummer
Matteo Poggi
Ashwini Pokle
Georgy E. Ponimatkin
Adrian Popescu
Stefan Popov
Nikola Popović
Ronald Poppe
Angelo Porrello
Michael Potter
Charalambos Poullis
Hadi Pouransari
Omid Poursaeed

Shraman Pramanick
Mantini Pranav
Dilip K. Prasad
Meghshyam Prasad
B. H. Pawan Prasad
Shitala Prasad
Prateek Prasanna
Ekta Prashnani
Derek S. Prijatelj
Luke Y. Prince
Véronique Prinet
Victor Adrian Prisacariu
James Pritts
Thomas Probst
Sergey Prokudin
Rita Pucci
Chi-Man Pun
Matthew Purri
Haozhi Qi
Lu Qi
Lei Qi
Xianbiao Qi
Yonggang Qi
Yuankai Qi
Siyuan Qi
Guocheng Qian
Hangwei Qian
Qi Qian
Deheng Qian
Shengsheng Qian
Wen Qian
Rui Qian
Yiming Qian
Shengju Qian
Shengyi Qian
Xuelin Qian
Zhenxing Qian
Nan Qiao
Xiaotian Qiao
Jing Qin
Can Qin
Siyang Qin
Hongwei Qin
Jie Qin
Minghai Qin

Yipeng Qin
Yongqiang Qin
Wenda Qin
Xuebin Qin
Yuzhe Qin
Yao Qin
Zhenyue Qin
Zhiwu Qing
Heqian Qiu
Jiayan Qiu
Jielin Qiu
Yue Qiu
Jiaxiong Qiu
Zhongxi Qiu
Shi Qiu
Zhaofan Qiu
Zhongnan Qu
Yanyun Qu
Kha Gia Quach
Yuhui Quan
Ruijie Quan
Mike Rabbat
Rahul Shekhar Rade
Filip Radenovic
Gorjan Radevski
Bogdan Raducanu
Francesco Ragusa
Shafin Rahman
Md Mahfuzur Rahman
    Siddiquee
Hossein Rahmani
Kiran Raja
Sivaramakrishnan
    Rajaraman
Jathushan Rajasegaran
Adnan Siraj Rakin
Michaël Ramamonjisoa
Chirag A. Raman
Shanmuganathan Raman
Vignesh Ramanathan
Vasili Ramanishka
Vikram V. Ramaswamy
Merey Ramazanova
Jason Rambach
Sai Saketh Rambhatla

Clément Rambour
Ashwin Ramesh Babu
Adín Ramírez Rivera
Arianna Rampini
Haoxi Ran
Aakanksha Rana
Aayush Jung Bahadur
    Rana
Kanchana N. Ranasinghe
Aneesh Rangnekar
Samrudhdhi B. Rangrej
Harsh Rangwani
Viresh Ranjan
Anyi Rao
Yongming Rao
Carolina Raposo
Michalis Raptis
Amir Rasouli
Vivek Rathod
Adepu Ravi Sankar
Avinash Ravichandran
Bharadwaj Ravichandran
Dripta S. Raychaudhuri
Adria Recasens
Simon Reiß
Davis Rempe
Daxuan Ren
Jiawei Ren
Jimmy Ren
Sucheng Ren
Dayong Ren
Zhile Ren
Dongwei Ren
Qibing Ren
Pengfei Ren
Zhenwen Ren
Xuqian Ren
Yixuan Ren
Zhongzheng Ren
Ambareesh Revanur
Hamed Rezazadegan
    Tavakoli
Rafael S. Rezende
Wonjong Rhee
Alexander Richard

Christian Richardt
Stephan R. Richter
Benjamin Riggan
Dominik Rivoir
Mamshad Nayeem Rizve
Joshua D. Robinson
Joseph Robinson
Chris Rockwell
Ranga Rodrigo
Andres C. Rodriguez
Carlos Rodriguez-Pardo
Marcus Rohrbach
Gemma Roig
Yu Rong
David A. Ross
Mohammad Rostami
Edward Rosten
Karsten Roth
Anirban Roy
Debaditya Roy
Shuvendu Roy
Ahana Roy Choudhury
Aruni Roy Chowdhury
Denys Rozumnyi
Shulan Ruan
Wenjie Ruan
Patrick Ruhkamp
Danila Rukhovich
Anian Ruoss
Chris Russell
Dan Ruta
Dawid Damian Rymarczyk
DongHun Ryu
Hyeonggon Ryu
Kwonyoung Ryu
Balasubramanian S.
Alexandre Sablayrolles
Mohammad Sabokrou
Arka Sadhu
Aniruddha Saha
Oindrila Saha
Pritish Sahu
Aneeshan Sain
Nirat Saini
Saurabh Saini

Takeshi Saitoh
Christos Sakaridis
Fumihiko Sakaue
Dimitrios Sakkos
Ken Sakurada
Parikshit V. Sakurikar
Rohit Saluja
Nermin Samet
Leo Sampaio Ferraz
    Ribeiro
Jorge Sanchez
Enrique Sanchez
Shengtian Sang
Anush Sankaran
Soubhik Sanyal
Nikolaos Sarafianos
Vishwanath Saragadam
István Sárándi
Saquib Sarfraz
Mert Bulent Sariyildiz
Anindya Sarkar
Pritam Sarkar
Paul-Edouard Sarlin
Hiroshi Sasaki
Takami Sato
Torsten Sattler
Ravi Kumar Satzoda
Axel Sauer
Stefano Savian
Artem Savkin
Manolis Savva
Gerald Schaefer
Simone Schaub-Meyer
Yoni Schirris
Samuel Schulter
Katja Schwarz
Jesse Scott
Sinisa Segvic
Constantin Marc Seibold
Lorenzo Seidenari
Matan Sela
Fadime Sener
Paul Hongsuck Seo
Kwanggyoon Seo
Hongje Seong

Dario Serez
Francesco Setti
Bryan Seybold
Mohamad Shahbazi
Shima Shahfar
Xinxin Shan
Caifeng Shan
Dandan Shan
Shawn Shan
Wei Shang
Jinghuan Shang
Jiaxiang Shang
Lei Shang
Sukrit Shankar
Ken Shao
Rui Shao
Jie Shao
Mingwen Shao
Aashish Sharma
Gaurav Sharma
Vivek Sharma
Abhishek Sharma
Yoli Shavit
Shashank Shekhar
Sumit Shekhar
Zhijie Shen
Fengyi Shen
Furao Shen
Jialie Shen
Jingjing Shen
Ziyi Shen
Linlin Shen
Guangyu Shen
Biluo Shen
Falong Shen
Jiajun Shen
Qiu Shen
Qiuhong Shen
Shuai Shen
Wang Shen
Yiqing Shen
Yunhang Shen
Siqi Shen
Bin Shen
Tianwei Shen

Xi Shen
Yilin Shen
Yuming Shen
Yucong Shen
Zhiqiang Shen
Lu Sheng
Yichen Sheng
Shivanand Venkanna
    Sheshappanavar
Shelly Sheynin
Baifeng Shi
Ruoxi Shi
Botian Shi
Hailin Shi
Jia Shi
Jing Shi
Shaoshuai Shi
Baoguang Shi
Boxin Shi
Hengcan Shi
Tianyang Shi
Xiaodan Shi
Yongjie Shi
Zhensheng Shi
Yinghuan Shi
Weiqi Shi
Wu Shi
Xuepeng Shi
Xiaoshuang Shi
Yujiao Shi
Zenglin Shi
Zhenmei Shi
Takashi Shibata
Meng-Li Shih
Yichang Shih
Hyunjung Shim
Dongseok Shim
Soshi Shimada
Inkyu Shin
Jinwoo Shin
Seungjoo Shin
Seungjae Shin
Koichi Shinoda
Suprosanna Shit

Palaiahnakote
    Shivakumara
Eli Shlizerman
Gaurav Shrivastava
Xiao Shu
Xiangbo Shu
Xiujun Shu
Yang Shu
Tianmin Shu
Jun Shu
Zhixin Shu
Bing Shuai
Maria Shugrina
Ivan Shugurov
Satya Narayan Shukla
Pranjay Shyam
Jianlou Si
Yawar Siddiqui
Alberto Signoroni
Pedro Silva
Jae-Young Sim
Oriane Siméoni
Martin Simon
Andrea Simonelli
Abhishek Singh
Ashish Singh
Dinesh Singh
Gurkirt Singh
Krishna Kumar Singh
Mannat Singh
Pravendra Singh
Rajat Vikram Singh
Utkarsh Singhal
Dipika Singhania
Vasu Singla
Harsh Sinha
Sudipta Sinha
Josef Sivic
Elena Sizikova
Geri Skenderi
Ivan Skorokhodov
Dmitriy Smirnov
Cameron Y. Smith
James S. Smith
Patrick Snape

Mattia Soldan
Hyeongseok Son
Sanghyun Son
Chuanbiao Song
Chen Song
Chunfeng Song
Dan Song
Dongjin Song
Hwanjun Song
Guoxian Song
Jiaming Song
Jie Song
Liangchen Song
Ran Song
Luchuan Song
Xibin Song
Li Song
Fenglong Song
Guoli Song
Guanglu Song
Zhenbo Song
Lin Song
Xinhang Song
Yang Song
Yibing Song
Rajiv Soundararajan
Hossein Souri
Cristovao Sousa
Riccardo Spezialetti
Leonidas Spinoulas
Michael W. Spratling
Deepak Sridhar
Srinath Sridhar
Gaurang Sriramanan
Vinkle Kumar Srivastav
Themos Stafylakis
Serban Stan
Anastasis Stathopoulos
Markus Steinberger
Jan Steinbrener
Sinisa Stekovic
Alexandros Stergiou
Gleb Sterkin
Rainer Stiefelhagen
Pierre Stock

Ombretta Strafforello
Julian Straub
Yannick Strümpler
Joerg Stueckler
Hang Su
Weijie Su
Jong-Chyi Su
Bing Su
Haisheng Su
Jinming Su
Yiyang Su
Yukun Su
Yuxin Su
Zhuo Su
Zhaoqi Su
Xiu Su
Yu-Chuan Su
Zhixun Su
Arulkumar Subramaniam
Akshayvarun Subramanya
A. Subramanyam
Swathikiran Sudhakaran
Yusuke Sugano
Masanori Suganuma
Yumin Suh
Yang Sui
Baochen Sun
Cheng Sun
Long Sun
Guolei Sun
Haoliang Sun
Haomiao Sun
He Sun
Hanqing Sun
Hao Sun
Lichao Sun
Jiachen Sun
Jiaming Sun
Jian Sun
Jin Sun
Jennifer J. Sun
Tiancheng Sun
Libo Sun
Peize Sun
Qianru Sun

Shanlin Sun
Yu Sun
Zhun Sun
Che Sun
Lin Sun
Tao Sun
Yiyou Sun
Chunyi Sun
Chong Sun
Weiwei Sun
Weixuan Sun
Xiuyu Sun
Yanan Sun
Zeren Sun
Zhaodong Sun
Zhiqing Sun
Minhyuk Sung
Jinli Suo
Simon Suo
Abhijit Suprem
Anshuman Suri
Saksham Suri
Joshua M. Susskind
Roman Suvorov
Gurumurthy Swaminathan
Robin Swanson
Paul Swoboda
Tabish A. Syed
Richard Szeliski
Fariborz Taherkhani
Yu-Wing Tai
Keita Takahashi
Walter Talbott
Gary Tam
Masato Tamura
Feitong Tan
Fuwen Tan
Shuhan Tan
Andong Tan
Bin Tan
Cheng Tan
Jianchao Tan
Lei Tan
Mingxing Tan
Xin Tan

Zichang Tan
Zhentao Tan
Kenichiro Tanaka
Masayuki Tanaka
Yushun Tang
Hao Tang
Jingqun Tang
Jinhui Tang
Kaihua Tang
Luming Tang
Lv Tang
Sheyang Tang
Shitao Tang
Siliang Tang
Shixiang Tang
Yansong Tang
Keke Tang
Chang Tang
Chenwei Tang
Jie Tang
Junshu Tang
Ming Tang
Peng Tang
Xu Tang
Yao Tang
Chen Tang
Fan Tang
Haoran Tang
Shengeng Tang
Yehui Tang
Zhipeng Tang
Ugo Tanielian
Chaofan Tao
Jiale Tao
Junli Tao
Renshuai Tao
An Tao
Guanhong Tao
Zhiqiang Tao
Makarand Tapaswi
Jean-Philippe G. Tarel
Juan J. Tarrio
Enzo Tartaglione
Keisuke Tateno
Zachary Teed

Ajinkya B. Tejankar
Bugra Tekin
Purva Tendulkar
Damien Teney
Minggui Teng
Chris Tensmeyer
Andrew Beng Jin Teoh
Philipp Terhörst
Kartik Thakral
Nupur Thakur
Kevin Thandiackal
Spyridon Thermos
Diego Thomas
William Thong
Yuesong Tian
Guanzhong Tian
Lin Tian
Shiqi Tian
Kai Tian
Meng Tian
Tai-Peng Tian
Zhuotao Tian
Shangxuan Tian
Tian Tian
Yapeng Tian
Yu Tian
Yuxin Tian
Leslie Ching Ow Tiong
Praveen Tirupattur
Garvita Tiwari
George Toderici
Antoine Toisoul
Aysim Toker
Tatiana Tommasi
Zhan Tong
Alessio Tonioni
Alessandro Torcinovich
Fabio Tosi
Matteo Toso
Hugo Touvron
Quan Hung Tran
Son Tran
Hung Tran
Ngoc-Trung Tran
Vinh Tran

Phong Tran
Giovanni Trappolini
Edith Tretschk
Subarna Tripathi
Shubhendu Trivedi
Eduard Trulls
Prune Truong
Thanh-Dat Truong
Tomasz Trzcinski
Sam Tsai
Yi-Hsuan Tsai
Ethan Tseng
Yu-Chee Tseng
Shahar Tsiper
Stavros Tsogkas
Shikui Tu
Zhigang Tu
Zhengzhong Tu
Richard Tucker
Sergey Tulyakov
Cigdem Turan
Daniyar Turmukhambetov
Victor G. Turrisi da Costa
Bartlomiej Twardowski
Christopher D. Twigg
Radim Tylecek
Mostofa Rafid Uddin
Md. Zasim Uddin
Kohei Uehara
Nicolas Ugrinovic
Youngjung Uh
Norimichi Ukita
Anwaar Ulhaq
Devesh Upadhyay
Paul Upchurch
Yoshitaka Ushiku
Yuzuko Utsumi
Mikaela Angelina Uy
Mohit Vaishnav
Pratik Vaishnavi
Jeya Maria Jose Valanarasu
Matias A. Valdenegro Toro
Diego Valsesia
Wouter Van Gansbeke
Nanne van Noord

Simon Vandenhende
Farshid Varno
Cristina Vasconcelos
Francisco Vasconcelos
Alex Vasilescu
Subeesh Vasu
Arun Balajee Vasudevan
Kanav Vats
Vaibhav S. Vavilala
Sagar Vaze
Javier Vazquez-Corral
Andrea Vedaldi
Olga Veksler
Andreas Velten
Sai H. Vemprala
Raviteja Vemulapalli
Shashanka
   Venkataramanan
Dor Verbin
Luisa Verdoliva
Manisha Verma
Yashaswi Verma
Constantin Vertan
Eli Verwimp
Deepak Vijaykeerthy
Pablo Villanueva
Ruben Villegas
Markus Vincze
Vibhav Vineet
Minh P. Vo
Huy V. Vo
Duc Minh Vo
Tomas Vojir
Igor Vozniak
Nicholas Vretos
Vibashan VS
Tuan-Anh Vu
Thang Vu
Mårten Wadenbäck
Neal Wadhwa
Aaron T. Walsman
Steven Walton
Jin Wan
Alvin Wan
Jia Wan

Jun Wan

Xiaoyue Wan

Fang Wan

Guowei Wan

Renjie Wan

Zhiqiang Wan

Ziyu Wan

Bastian Wandt

Dongdong Wang

Limin Wang

Haiyang Wang

Xiaobing Wang

Angtian Wang

Angelina Wang

Bing Wang

Bo Wang

Boyu Wang

Binghui Wang

Chen Wang

Chien-Yi Wang

Congli Wang

Qi Wang

Chengrui Wang

Rui Wang

Yiqun Wang

Cong Wang

Wenjing Wang

Dongkai Wang

Di Wang

Xiaogang Wang

Kai Wang

Zhizhong Wang

Fangjinhua Wang

Feng Wang

Hang Wang

Gaoang Wang

Guoqing Wang

Guangcong Wang

Guangzhi Wang

Hanqing Wang

Hao Wang

Haohan Wang

Haoran Wang

Hong Wang

Haotao Wang

Hu Wang

Huan Wang

Hua Wang

Hui-Po Wang

Hengli Wang

Hanyu Wang

Hongxing Wang

Jingwen Wang

Jialiang Wang

Jian Wang

Jianyi Wang

Jiashun Wang

Jiahao Wang

Tsun-Hsuan Wang

Xiaoqian Wang

Jinqiao Wang

Jun Wang

Jianzong Wang

Kaihong Wang

Ke Wang

Lei Wang

Lingjing Wang

Linnan Wang

Lin Wang

Liansheng Wang

Mengjiao Wang

Manning Wang

Nannan Wang

Peihao Wang

Jiayun Wang

Pu Wang

Qiang Wang

Qiufeng Wang

Qilong Wang

Qiangchang Wang

Qin Wang

Qing Wang

Ruocheng Wang

Ruibin Wang

Ruisheng Wang

Ruizhe Wang

Runqi Wang

Runzhong Wang

Wenxuan Wang

Sen Wang

Shangfei Wang

Shaofei Wang

Shijie Wang

Shiqi Wang

Zhibo Wang

Song Wang

Xinjiang Wang

Tai Wang

Tao Wang

Teng Wang

Xiang Wang

Tianren Wang

Tiantian Wang

Tianyi Wang

Fengjiao Wang

Wei Wang

Miaohui Wang

Suchen Wang

Siyue Wang

Yaoming Wang

Xiao Wang

Ze Wang

Biao Wang

Chaofei Wang

Dong Wang

Gu Wang

Guangrun Wang

Guangming Wang

Guo-Hua Wang

Haoqing Wang

Hesheng Wang

Huafeng Wang

Jinghua Wang

Jingdong Wang

Jingjing Wang

Jingya Wang

Jingkang Wang

Jiakai Wang

Junke Wang

Kuo Wang

Lichen Wang

Lizhi Wang

Longguang Wang

Mang Wang

Mei Wang

Min Wang
Peng-Shuai Wang
Run Wang
Shaoru Wang
Shuhui Wang
Tan Wang
Tiancai Wang
Tianqi Wang
Wenhai Wang
Wenzhe Wang
Xiaobo Wang
Xiudong Wang
Xu Wang
Yajie Wang
Yan Wang
Yuan-Gen Wang
Yingqian Wang
Yizhi Wang
Yulin Wang
Yu Wang
Yujie Wang
Yunhe Wang
Yuxi Wang
Yaowci Wang
Yiwei Wang
Zezheng Wang
Hongzhi Wang
Zhiqiang Wang
Ziteng Wang
Ziwei Wang
Zheng Wang
Zhenyu Wang
Binglu Wang
Zhongdao Wang
Ce Wang
Weining Wang
Weiyao Wang
Wenbin Wang
Wenguan Wang
Guangting Wang
Haolin Wang
Haiyan Wang
Huiyu Wang
Naiyan Wang
Jingbo Wang

Jinpeng Wang
Jiaqi Wang
Liyuan Wang
Lizhen Wang
Ning Wang
Wenqian Wang
Sheng-Yu Wang
Weimin Wang
Xiaohan Wang
Yifan Wang
Yi Wang
Yongtao Wang
Yizhou Wang
Zhuo Wang
Zhe Wang
Xudong Wang
Xiaofang Wang
Xinggang Wang
Xiaosen Wang
Xiaosong Wang
Xiaoyang Wang
Lijun Wang
Xinlong Wang
Xuan Wang
Xue Wang
Yangang Wang
Yaohui Wang
Yu-Chiang Frank Wang
Yida Wang
Yilin Wang
Yi Ru Wang
Yali Wang
Yinglong Wang
Yufu Wang
Yujiang Wang
Yuwang Wang
Yuting Wang
Yang Wang
Yu-Xiong Wang
Yixu Wang
Ziqi Wang
Zhicheng Wang
Zeyu Wang
Zhaowen Wang
Zhenyi Wang

Zhenzhi Wang
Zhijie Wang
Zhiyong Wang
Zhongling Wang
Zhuowei Wang
Zian Wang
Zifu Wang
Zihao Wang
Zirui Wang
Ziyan Wang
Wenxiao Wang
Zhen Wang
Zhepeng Wang
Zi Wang
Zihao W. Wang
Steven L. Waslander
Olivia Watkins
Daniel Watson
Silvan Weder
Dongyoon Wee
Dongming Wei
Tianyi Wei
Jia Wei
Dong Wei
Fangyun Wei
Longhui Wei
Mingqiang Wei
Xinyue Wei
Chen Wei
Donglai Wei
Pengxu Wei
Xing Wei
Xiu-Shen Wei
Wenqi Wei
Guoqiang Wei
Wei Wei
XingKui Wei
Xian Wei
Xingxing Wei
Yake Wei
Yuxiang Wei
Yi Wei
Luca Weihs
Michael Weinmann
Martin Weinmann

Congcong Wen
Chuan Wen
Jie Wen
Sijia Wen
Song Wen
Chao Wen
Xiang Wen
Zeyi Wen
Xin Wen
Yilin Wen
Yijia Weng
Shuchen Weng
Junwu Weng
Wenming Weng
Renliang Weng
Zhenyu Weng
Xinshuo Weng
Nicholas J. Westlake
Gordon Wetzstein
Lena M. Widin Klasén
Rick Wildes
Bryan M. Williams
Williem Williem
Ole Winther
Scott Wisdom
Alex Wong
Chau-Wai Wong
Kwan-Yee K. Wong
Yongkang Wong
Scott Workman
Marcel Worring
Michael Wray
Safwan Wshah
Xiang Wu
Aming Wu
Chongruo Wu
Cho-Ying Wu
Chunpeng Wu
Chenyan Wu
Ziyi Wu
Fuxiang Wu
Gang Wu
Haiping Wu
Huisi Wu
Jane Wu

Jialian Wu
Jing Wu
Jinjian Wu
Jianlong Wu
Xian Wu
Lifang Wu
Lifan Wu
Minye Wu
Qianyi Wu
Rongliang Wu
Rui Wu
Shiqian Wu
Shuzhe Wu
Shangzhe Wu
Tsung-Han Wu
Tz-Ying Wu
Ting-Wei Wu
Jiannan Wu
Zhiliang Wu
Yu Wu
Chenyun Wu
Dayan Wu
Dongxian Wu
Fei Wu
Hefeng Wu
Jianxin Wu
Weibin Wu
Wenxuan Wu
Wenhao Wu
Xiao Wu
Yicheng Wu
Yuanwei Wu
Yu-Huan Wu
Zhenxin Wu
Zhenyu Wu
Wei Wu
Peng Wu
Xiaohe Wu
Xindi Wu
Xinxing Wu
Xinyi Wu
Xingjiao Wu
Xiongwei Wu
Yangzheng Wu
Yanzhao Wu

Yawen Wu
Yong Wu
Yi Wu
Ying Nian Wu
Zhenyao Wu
Zhonghua Wu
Zongze Wu
Zuxuan Wu
Stefanie Wuhrer
Teng Xi
Jianing Xi
Fei Xia
Haifeng Xia
Menghan Xia
Yuanqing Xia
Zhihua Xia
Xiaobo Xia
Weihao Xia
Shihong Xia
Yan Xia
Yong Xia
Zhaoyang Xia
Zhihao Xia
Chuhua Xian
Yongqin Xian
Wangmeng Xiang
Fanbo Xiang
Tiange Xiang
Tao Xiang
Liuyu Xiang
Xiaoyu Xiang
Zhiyu Xiang
Aoran Xiao
Chunxia Xiao
Fanyi Xiao
Jimin Xiao
Jun Xiao
Taihong Xiao
Anqi Xiao
Junfei Xiao
Jing Xiao
Liang Xiao
Yang Xiao
Yuting Xiao
Yijun Xiao

Yao Xiao
Zeyu Xiao
Zhisheng Xiao
Zihao Xiao
Binhui Xie
Christopher Xie
Haozhe Xie
Jin Xie
Guo-Sen Xie
Hongtao Xie
Ming-Kun Xie
Tingting Xie
Chaohao Xie
Weicheng Xie
Xudong Xie
Jiyang Xie
Xiaohua Xie
Yuan Xie
Zhenyu Xie
Ning Xie
Xianghui Xie
Xiufeng Xie
You Xie
Yutong Xie
Fuyong Xing
Yifan Xing
Zhen Xing
Yuanjun Xiong
Jinhui Xiong
Weihua Xiong
Hongkai Xiong
Zhitong Xiong
Yuanhao Xiong
Yunyang Xiong
Yuwen Xiong
Zhiwei Xiong
Yuliang Xiu
An Xu
Chang Xu
Chenliang Xu
Chengming Xu
Chenshu Xu
Xiang Xu
Huijuan Xu
Zhe Xu

Jie Xu
Jingyi Xu
Jiarui Xu
Yinghao Xu
Kele Xu
Ke Xu
Li Xu
Linchuan Xu
Linning Xu
Mengde Xu
Mengmeng Frost Xu
Min Xu
Mingye Xu
Jun Xu
Ning Xu
Peng Xu
Runsheng Xu
Sheng Xu
Wenqiang Xu
Xiaogang Xu
Renzhe Xu
Kaidi Xu
Yi Xu
Chi Xu
Qiuling Xu
Baobei Xu
Feng Xu
Haohang Xu
Haofei Xu
Lan Xu
Mingze Xu
Songcen Xu
Weipeng Xu
Wenjia Xu
Wenju Xu
Xiangyu Xu
Xin Xu
Yinshuang Xu
Yixing Xu
Yuting Xu
Yanyu Xu
Zhenbo Xu
Zhiliang Xu
Zhiyuan Xu
Xiaohao Xu

Yanwu Xu
Yan Xu
Yiran Xu
Yifan Xu
Yufei Xu
Yong Xu
Zichuan Xu
Zenglin Xu
Zexiang Xu
Zhan Xu
Zheng Xu
Zhiwei Xu
Ziyue Xu
Shiyu Xuan
Hanyu Xuan
Fei Xue
Jianru Xue
Mingfu Xue
Qinghan Xue
Tianfan Xue
Chao Xue
Chuhui Xue
Nan Xue
Zhou Xue
Xiangyang Xue
Yuan Xue
Abhay Yadav
Ravindra Yadav
Kota Yamaguchi
Toshihiko Yamasaki
Kohei Yamashita
Chaochao Yan
Feng Yan
Kun Yan
Qingsen Yan
Qixin Yan
Rui Yan
Siming Yan
Xinchen Yan
Yaping Yan
Bin Yan
Qingan Yan
Shen Yan
Shipeng Yan
Xu Yan

Yan Yan
Yichao Yan
Zhaoyi Yan
Zike Yan
Zhiqiang Yan
Hongliang Yan
Zizheng Yan
Jiewen Yang
Anqi Joyce Yang
Shan Yang
Anqi Yang
Antoine Yang
Bo Yang
Baoyao Yang
Chenhongyi Yang
Dingkang Yang
De-Nian Yang
Dong Yang
David Yang
Fan Yang
Fengyu Yang
Fengting Yang
Fei Yang
Gengshan Yang
Heng Yang
Han Yang
Huan Yang
Yibo Yang
Jiancheng Yang
Jihan Yang
Jiawei Yang
Jiayu Yang
Jie Yang
Jinfa Yang
Jingkang Yang
Jinyu Yang
Cheng-Fu Yang
Ji Yang
Jianyu Yang
Kailun Yang
Tian Yang
Luyu Yang
Liang Yang
Li Yang
Michael Ying Yang

Yang Yang
Muli Yang
Le Yang
Qiushi Yang
Ren Yang
Ruihan Yang
Shuang Yang
Siyuan Yang
Su Yang
Shiqi Yang
Taojiannan Yang
Tianyu Yang
Lei Yang
Wanzhao Yang
Shuai Yang
William Yang
Wei Yang
Xiaofeng Yang
Xiaoshan Yang
Xin Yang
Xuan Yang
Xu Yang
Xingyi Yang
Xitong Yang
Jing Yang
Yanchao Yang
Wenming Yang
Yujiu Yang
Herb Yang
Jianfei Yang
Jinhui Yang
Chuanguang Yang
Guanglei Yang
Haitao Yang
Kewei Yang
Linlin Yang
Lijin Yang
Longrong Yang
Meng Yang
MingKun Yang
Sibei Yang
Shicai Yang
Tong Yang
Wen Yang
Xi Yang

Xiaolong Yang
Xue Yang
Yubin Yang
Ze Yang
Ziyi Yang
Yi Yang
Linjie Yang
Yuzhe Yang
Yiding Yang
Zhenpei Yang
Zhaohui Yang
Zhengyuan Yang
Zhibo Yang
Zongxin Yang
Hantao Yao
Mingde Yao
Rui Yao
Taiping Yao
Ting Yao
Cong Yao
Qingsong Yao
Quanming Yao
Xu Yao
Yuan Yao
Yao Yao
Yazhou Yao
Jiawen Yao
Shunyu Yao
Pew-Thian Yap
Sudhir Yarram
Rajeev Yasarla
Peng Ye
Botao Ye
Mao Ye
Fei Ye
Hanrong Ye
Jingwen Ye
Jinwei Ye
Jiarong Ye
Mang Ye
Meng Ye
Qi Ye
Qian Ye
Qixiang Ye
Junjie Ye

Sheng Ye
Nanyang Ye
Yufei Ye
Xiaoqing Ye
Ruolin Ye
Yousef Yeganeh
Chun-Hsiao Yeh
Raymond A. Yeh
Yu-Ying Yeh
Kai Yi
Chang Yi
Renjiao Yi
Xinping Yi
Peng Yi
Alper Yilmaz
Junho Yim
Hui Yin
Bangjie Yin
Jia-Li Yin
Miao Yin
Wenzhe Yin
Xuwang Yin
Ming Yin
Yu Yin
Aoxiong Yin
Kangxue Yin
Tianwei Yin
Wei Yin
Xianghua Ying
Rio Yokota
Tatsuya Yokota
Naoto Yokoya
Ryo Yonetani
Ki Yoon Yoo
Jinsu Yoo
Sunjae Yoon
Jae Shin Yoon
Jihun Yoon
Sung-Hoon Yoon
Ryota Yoshihashi
Yusuke Yoshiyasu
Chenyu You
Haoran You
Haoxuan You
Yang You

Quanzeng You
Tackgeun You
Kaichao You
Shan You
Xinge You
Yurong You
Baosheng Yu
Bei Yu
Haichao Yu
Hao Yu
Chaohui Yu
Fisher Yu
Jin-Gang Yu
Jiyang Yu
Jason J. Yu
Jiashuo Yu
Hong-Xing Yu
Lei Yu
Mulin Yu
Ning Yu
Peilin Yu
Qi Yu
Qian Yu
Rui Yu
Shuzhi Yu
Gang Yu
Tan Yu
Weijiang Yu
Xin Yu
Bingyao Yu
Ye Yu
Hanchao Yu
Yingchen Yu
Tao Yu
Xiaotian Yu
Qing Yu
Houjian Yu
Changqian Yu
Jing Yu
Jun Yu
Shujian Yu
Xiang Yu
Zhaofei Yu
Zhenbo Yu
Yinfeng Yu

Zhuoran Yu
Zitong Yu
Bo Yuan
Jiangbo Yuan
Liangzhe Yuan
Weihao Yuan
Jianbo Yuan
Xiaoyun Yuan
Ye Yuan
Li Yuan
Geng Yuan
Jialin Yuan
Maoxun Yuan
Peng Yuan
Xin Yuan
Yuan Yuan
Yuhui Yuan
Yixuan Yuan
Zheng Yuan
Mehmet Kerim Yücel
Kaiyu Yue
Haixiao Yue
Heeseung Yun
Sangdoo Yun
Tian Yun
Mahmut Yurt
Ekim Yurtsever
Ahmet Yüzügüler
Edouard Yvinec
Eloi Zablocki
Christopher Zach
Muhammad Zaigham
    Zaheer
Pierluigi Zama Ramirez
Yuhang Zang
Pietro Zanuttigh
Alexey Zaytsev
Bernhard Zeisl
Haitian Zeng
Pengpeng Zeng
Jiabei Zeng
Runhao Zeng
Wei Zeng
Yawen Zeng
Yi Zeng

Yiming Zeng
Tieyong Zeng
Huanqiang Zeng
Dan Zeng
Yu Zeng
Wei Zhai
Yuanhao Zhai
Fangneng Zhan
Kun Zhan
Xiong Zhang
Jingdong Zhang
Jiangning Zhang
Zhilu Zhang
Gengwei Zhang
Dongsu Zhang
Hui Zhang
Binjie Zhang
Bo Zhang
Tianhao Zhang
Cecilia Zhang
Jing Zhang
Chaoning Zhang
Chenxu Zhang
Chi Zhang
Chris Zhang
Yabin Zhang
Zhao Zhang
Rufeng Zhang
Chaoyi Zhang
Zheng Zhang
Da Zhang
Yi Zhang
Edward Zhang
Xin Zhang
Feifei Zhang
Feilong Zhang
Yuqi Zhang
GuiXuan Zhang
Hanlin Zhang
Hanwang Zhang
Hanzhen Zhang
Haotian Zhang
He Zhang
Haokui Zhang
Hongyuan Zhang

Hengrui Zhang
Hongming Zhang
Mingfang Zhang
Jianpeng Zhang
Jiaming Zhang
Jichao Zhang
Jie Zhang
Jingfeng Zhang
Jingyi Zhang
Jinnian Zhang
David Junhao Zhang
Junjie Zhang
Junzhe Zhang
Jiawan Zhang
Jingyang Zhang
Kai Zhang
Lei Zhang
Lihua Zhang
Lu Zhang
Miao Zhang
Minjia Zhang
Mingjin Zhang
Qi Zhang
Qian Zhang
Qilong Zhang
Qiming Zhang
Qiang Zhang
Richard Zhang
Ruimao Zhang
Ruisi Zhang
Ruixin Zhang
Runze Zhang
Qilin Zhang
Shan Zhang
Shanshan Zhang
Xi Sheryl Zhang
Song-Hai Zhang
Chongyang Zhang
Kaihao Zhang
Songyang Zhang
Shu Zhang
Siwei Zhang
Shujian Zhang
Tianyun Zhang
Tong Zhang

Tao Zhang
Wenwei Zhang
Wenqiang Zhang
Wen Zhang
Xiaolin Zhang
Xingchen Zhang
Xingxuan Zhang
Xiuming Zhang
Xiaoshuai Zhang
Xuanmeng Zhang
Xuanyang Zhang
Xucong Zhang
Xingxing Zhang
Xikun Zhang
Xiaohan Zhang
Yahui Zhang
Yunhua Zhang
Yan Zhang
Yanghao Zhang
Yifei Zhang
Yifan Zhang
Yi-Fan Zhang
Yihao Zhang
Yingliang Zhang
Youshan Zhang
Yulun Zhang
Yushu Zhang
Yixiao Zhang
Yide Zhang
Zhongwen Zhang
Bowen Zhang
Chen-Lin Zhang
Zehua Zhang
Zekun Zhang
Zeyu Zhang
Xiaowei Zhang
Yifeng Zhang
Cheng Zhang
Hongguang Zhang
Yuexi Zhang
Fa Zhang
Guofeng Zhang
Hao Zhang
Haofeng Zhang
Hongwen Zhang

Hua Zhang	Zhizhong Zhang	Bowen Zhao
Jiaxin Zhang	Qilong Zhangli	Pu Zhao
Zhenyu Zhang	Bingyin Zhao	Bingchen Zhao
Jian Zhang	Bin Zhao	Borui Zhao
Jianfeng Zhang	Chenglong Zhao	Fuqiang Zhao
Jiao Zhang	Lei Zhao	Hanbin Zhao
Jiakai Zhang	Feng Zhao	Jian Zhao
Lefei Zhang	Gangming Zhao	Mingyang Zhao
Le Zhang	Haiyan Zhao	Na Zhao
Mi Zhang	Hao Zhao	Rongchang Zhao
Min Zhang	Handong Zhao	Ruiqi Zhao
Ning Zhang	Hengshuang Zhao	Shuai Zhao
Pan Zhang	Yinan Zhao	Wenda Zhao
Pu Zhang	Jiaojiao Zhao	Wenliang Zhao
Qing Zhang	Jiaqi Zhao	Xiangyun Zhao
Renrui Zhang	Jing Zhao	Yifan Zhao
Shifeng Zhang	Kaili Zhao	Yaping Zhao
Shuo Zhang	Haojie Zhao	Zhou Zhao
Shaoxiong Zhang	Yucheng Zhao	He Zhao
Weizhong Zhang	Longjiao Zhao	Jie Zhao
Xi Zhang	Long Zhao	Xibin Zhao
Xiaomei Zhang	Qingsong Zhao	Xiaoqi Zhao
Xinyu Zhang	Qingyu Zhao	Zhengyu Zhao
Yin Zhang	Rui Zhao	Jin Zhe
Zicheng Zhang	Rui-Wei Zhao	Chuanxia Zheng
Zihao Zhang	Sicheng Zhao	Huan Zheng
Ziqi Zhang	Shuang Zhao	Hao Zheng
Zhaoxiang Zhang	Siyan Zhao	Jia Zheng
Zhen Zhang	Zelin Zhao	Jian-Qing Zheng
Zhipeng Zhang	Shiyu Zhao	Shuai Zheng
Zhixing Zhang	Wang Zhao	Meng Zheng
Zhizheng Zhang	Tiesong Zhao	Mingkai Zheng
Jiawei Zhang	Qian Zhao	Qian Zheng
Zhong Zhang	Wangbo Zhao	Qi Zheng
Pingping Zhang	Xi-Le Zhao	Wu Zheng
Yixin Zhang	Xu Zhao	Yinqiang Zheng
Kui Zhang	Yajie Zhao	Yufeng Zheng
Lingzhi Zhang	Yang Zhao	Yutong Zheng
Huaiwen Zhang	Ying Zhao	Yalin Zheng
Quanshi Zhang	Yin Zhao	Yu Zheng
Zhoutong Zhang	Yizhou Zhao	Feng Zheng
Yuhang Zhang	Yunhan Zhao	Zhaoheng Zheng
Yuting Zhang	Yuyang Zhao	Haitian Zheng
Zhang Zhang	Yue Zhao	Kang Zheng
Ziming Zhang	Yuzhi Zhao	Bolun Zheng

Haiyong Zheng
Mingwu Zheng
Sipeng Zheng
Tu Zheng
Wenzhao Zheng
Xiawu Zheng
Yinglin Zheng
Zhuo Zheng
Zilong Zheng
Kecheng Zheng
Zerong Zheng
Shuaifeng Zhi
Tiancheng Zhi
Jia-Xing Zhong
Yiwu Zhong
Fangwei Zhong
Zhihang Zhong
Yaoyao Zhong
Yiran Zhong
Zhun Zhong
Zichun Zhong
Bo Zhou
Boyao Zhou
Brady Zhou
Mo Zhou
Chunluan Zhou
Dingfu Zhou
Fan Zhou
Jingkai Zhou
Honglu Zhou
Jiaming Zhou
Jiahuan Zhou
Jun Zhou
Kaiyang Zhou
Keyang Zhou
Kuangqi Zhou
Lei Zhou
Lihua Zhou
Man Zhou
Mingyi Zhou
Mingyuan Zhou
Ning Zhou
Peng Zhou
Penghao Zhou
Qianyi Zhou

Shuigeng Zhou
Shangchen Zhou
Huayi Zhou
Zhize Zhou
Sanping Zhou
Qin Zhou
Tao Zhou
Wenbo Zhou
Xiangdong Zhou
Xiao-Yun Zhou
Xiao Zhou
Yang Zhou
Yipin Zhou
Zhenyu Zhou
Hao Zhou
Chu Zhou
Daquan Zhou
Da-Wei Zhou
Hang Zhou
Kang Zhou
Qianyu Zhou
Sheng Zhou
Wenhui Zhou
Xingyi Zhou
Yan-Jie Zhou
Yiyi Zhou
Yu Zhou
Yuan Zhou
Yuqian Zhou
Yuxuan Zhou
Zixiang Zhou
Wengang Zhou
Shuchang Zhou
Tianfei Zhou
Yichao Zhou
Alex Zhu
Chenchen Zhu
Deyao Zhu
Xiatian Zhu
Guibo Zhu
Haidong Zhu
Hao Zhu
Hongzi Zhu
Rui Zhu
Jing Zhu

Jianke Zhu
Junchen Zhu
Lei Zhu
Lingyu Zhu
Luyang Zhu
Menglong Zhu
Peihao Zhu
Hui Zhu
Xiaofeng Zhu
Tyler (Lixuan) Zhu
Wentao Zhu
Xiangyu Zhu
Xinqi Zhu
Xinxin Zhu
Xinliang Zhu
Yangguang Zhu
Yichen Zhu
Yixin Zhu
Yanjun Zhu
Yousong Zhu
Yuhao Zhu
Ye Zhu
Feng Zhu
Zhen Zhu
Fangrui Zhu
Jinjing Zhu
Linchao Zhu
Pengfei Zhu
Sijie Zhu
Xiaobin Zhu
Xiaoguang Zhu
Zezhou Zhu
Zhenyao Zhu
Kai Zhu
Pengkai Zhu
Bingbing Zhuang
Chengyuan Zhuang
Liansheng Zhuang
Peiye Zhuang
Yixin Zhuang
Yihong Zhuang
Junbao Zhuo
Andrea Ziani
Bartosz Zieliński
Primo Zingaretti

Nikolaos Zioulis
Andrew Zisserman
Yael Ziv
Liu Ziyin
Xingxing Zou
Danping Zou
Qi Zou

Shihao Zou
Xueyan Zou
Yang Zou
Yuliang Zou
Zihang Zou
Chuhang Zou
Dongqing Zou

Xu Zou
Zhiming Zou
Maria A. Zuluaga
Xinxin Zuo
Zhiwen Zuo
Reyer Zwiggelaar

Contents – Part IV

Expanding Language-Image Pretrained Models for General Video Recognition

Bolin Ni[1,2], Houwen Peng[4(✉)], Minghao Chen[5], Songyang Zhang[6],
Gaofeng Meng[1,2,3(✉)], Jianlong Fu[4], Shiming Xiang[1,2], and Haibin Ling[5]

[1] NLPR, Institute of Automation, Chinese Academy of Sciences, Beijing, China
`gfmeng@nlpr.ia.ac.cn`
[2] School of Artificial Intelligence, University of Chinese Academy of Sciences,
Beijing, China
[3] CAIR, HK Institute of Science and Innovation, Chinese Academy of Sciences,
Hong Kong, China
[4] Microsoft Research Asia, Beijing, China
`houwen.peng@microsoft.com`
[5] Stony Brook University, Stony Brook, NY, USA
[6] University of Rochester, Rochester, USA

Abstract. Contrastive language-image pretraining has shown great success in learning visual-textual joint representation from web-scale data, demonstrating remarkable "zero-shot" generalization ability for various image tasks. However, how to effectively expand such new language-image pretraining methods to video domains is still an open problem. In this work, we present a simple yet effective approach that adapts the pretrained language-image models to video recognition directly, instead of pretraining a new model from scratch. More concretely, to capture the long-range dependencies of frames along the temporal dimension, we propose a cross-frame attention mechanism that explicitly exchanges information across frames. Such module is lightweight and can be plugged into pretrained language-image models seamlessly. Moreover, we propose a video-specific prompting scheme, which leverages video content information for generating discriminative textual prompts. Extensive experiments demonstrate that our approach is effective and can be generalized to different video recognition scenarios. In particular, under fully-supervised settings, our approach achieves a top-1 accuracy of 87.1% on Kinectics-400, while using 12× fewer FLOPs compared with Swin-L and ViViT-H. In zero-shot experiments, our approach surpasses the current state-of-the-art methods by +7.6% and +14.9% in terms of top-1 accuracy under two popular protocols. In few-shot scenarios, our approach outperforms previous best methods by +32.1% and +23.1% when the labeled data is extremely limited. Code and models are available at here.

Keywords: Video recognition · Contrastive language-image pretraining

B. Ni and M. Chen—Work done during internship at Microsoft Research.

Supplementary Information The online version contains supplementary material available at https://doi.org/10.1007/978-3-031-19772-7_1.

1   Introduction

Video recognition is one of the most fundamental yet challenging tasks in video understanding. It plays a vital role in numerous vision applications, such as micro-video recommendation [62], sports video analysis [40], autonomous driving [18], and so on. Over the past few years, based upon convolutional neural networks and now transformers, video recognition has achieved remarkable progress [21,62]. Most existing works follow a closed-set learning setting, where all the categories are pre-defined. Such method is unrealistic for many real-world applications, such as automatic tagging of web videos, where information regarding new video categories is not available during training. It is thus very challenging for closed-set methods to train a classifier for recognizing unseen or unfamiliar categories.

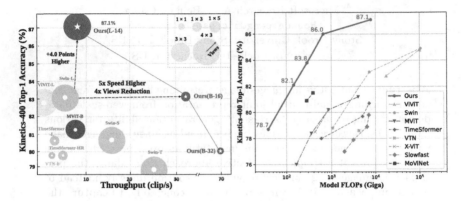

Fig. 1. Comparison with state-of-the-art methods on Kinetics-400 [22] in terms of throughput, the number of views, and FLOPs. Best viewed in color.

Fortunately, recent work in large-scale contrastive language-image pretraining, such as CLIP [36], ALIGN [19], and Florence [54], has shown great potentials in addressing this challenge. The core idea is to learn visual or visual-language representation with natural language supervision using web-scale image-text data. After pretraining, natural language is used to reference learned visual concepts (or describe new ones), thus enabling zero/few-shot transfer of the models to downstream tasks. Inspired by these works [19,36,54], we consider to use text as the supervision signals to learn a new video representation for general recognition scenarios, including zero-shot, few-shot, and fully-supervised.

However, directly training a language-video model is unaffordable for many of us, because it requires large-scale video-text pretraining data as well as a massive number of GPU resources (*e.g.*, thousands of GPU days). A feasible solution is to adapt the pretrained language-image models to video domain. Very recently, there are several studies exploring how to transfer the knowledge from the pretrained language-image models to other downstream tasks, *e.g.*, point cloud understanding [58] and dense prediction [37,59]. However, the transfer and adaptation to video recognition is not well explored. When adapting the pretrained cross-modality models from image to video domain, there are two key issues to be solved: 1) how to leverage the temporal information contained in videos, and 2) how to acquire discriminative text representation for a video.

For the first question, we present a new architecture for video temporal modeling. It consists of two key components: a cross-frame communication transformer and a multi-frame integration transformer. Specifically, the cross-frame communication transformer takes raw frames as input and provides a frame-level representation using a pretrained language-image model, while allowing information exchange between frames with message tokens. Each message token not only depicts the semantics of the current frame, but also communicates with other frames to model their dependencies. The multi-frame integration transformer then simply transfer the frame-level representations to video-level.

For the second question, we employ the text encoder pretrained in the language-image models and expand it with a video-specific prompting scheme. The key idea is to leverage video content information to enhance text prompting. The intuition behind is that appropriate contextual information can help the recognition. For example, if there is extra video content information about "in the water", the actions "swimming" and "running" will be much easier to be distinguished. In contrast to prior work manually designing a fixed set of text prompts, this work proposes a learnable prompting mechanism, which integrates both semantic labels and representation of videos for automatic prompt generation.

With the above two issues addressed, we can smoothly adapt the existing image-level cross-modality pretrained models to video domains. Without loss of generality, here we choose the available CLIP [36] and Florence [54] models and eXpand them for general video recognition, forming new model families called X-CLIP and X-Florence, respectively. Comprehensive experiments demonstrate our expanded models are generally effective. In particular, under the fully-supervised setting, X-CLIP-L/14 achieves competitive performance on Kinetics-400/600 with a top-1 accuracy of 87.1%/88.3%, surpassing ViViT-H [3] by 2.3%/2.5% while using 12× fewer FLOPs, as shown in Fig. 1. In zero-shot experiments, X-Florence surpasses the state-of-the-art ActionCLIP [48] by +7.6% and +14.9% under two popular protocols. In few-shot experiments, X-CLIP outperforms other prevailing methods by +32.1% and +23.1% when the data is extremely limited.

In summary, our contributions are three-fold:

- We propose a new cross-frame communication attention for video temporal modeling. This module is light and efficient, and can be seamlessly plugged into existing language-image pretrained models, without undermining their original parameters and performance.
- We design a video-specific prompting technique to yield instance-level textual representation automatically. It leverages video content information to enhance the textual prompt generation.
- Our work might pave a new way of expanding existing large-scale language-image pretrained models for general video recognition and other potential video tasks. Extensive experiments demonstrate the superiority and good generalization ability of our method under various learning configurations.

2   Related Work

Visual-Language Pretraining. Visual-language pretraining has achieved remarkable progress over the past few years [31,42,43,61]. In particular, contrastive language-image pretraining demonstrates very impressive "zero-shot" transfer and generalization capacities [19,36,54]. One of the most representative works is the recent CLIP [36]. A large amount of follow-up works have been proposed to leverage the pretrained models for downstream tasks. For example, CoOp [60], CLIP-Adapter [15] and Tip-Adapter [57] use the pretrained CLIP for improving the few-shot transfer, while PointCLIP [58] and DenseCLIP [37,59] transfer the knowledge to point cloud understanding and dense prediction, respectively. VideoCLIP [51] extends the image-level pretraining to video by substituting the image-text data with video-text pairs [31]. However, such video-text pretraining is computationally expensive and requires a large amount of curated video-text data which is not easy to acquire. In contrast, our method directly adapts the existing pretrained model to video recognition, largely saving the training cost.

There are two concurrent works mostly related to ours. One is ActionCLIP [48], while the other is [20]. Both of them introduce visual-language pretrained models to video understanding. ActionCLIP proposes a "pretrain, prompt and finetune" framework for action recognition, while [20] proposes to optimize a few random vectors for adapting CLIP to various video understanding tasks. In contrast, our method is more general. It supports adapting various language-image models, such as CLIP and Florence [54], from image to video. Moreover, we propose a lightweight and efficient cross-frame attention module for video temporal modeling, while presenting a new video-specific text prompting scheme.

Video Recognition. One key factor to build a robust video recognition model is to exploit the temporal information. Among many methods, 3D convolution is widely used [35,44,45,50], while it suffers from high computational cost. For efficiency purposes, some studies [35,45,50] factorize convolutions across spatial and temporal dimensions, while others insert the specific temporal modules into 2D CNNs [25,27,30]. Nevertheless, the limited receptive field of CNNs gives the rise of transformer-based methods [3,5,11,29,53], which achieve very promising performance recently. However, these transformer-based methods are either computationally intensive or insufficient in exploiting the temporal information. For example, ViViT [3] disregards the temporal information in the early stage. Video Swin [29] utilizes 3D attention while having high computational cost.

The temporal modeling scheme in our method shares a similar spirit with the recent proposed video transformers, *i.e.*, VTN [32], ViViT [3], and AVT [17]. They all use a frame-level encoder followed by a temporal encoder, but our method has two fundamental differences. 1) In [3,17,32], each frame is encoded separately, resulting in no temporal interaction before final aggregation. This late fusion strategy does not fully make use of the temporal cues. By contrast, our method replaces the spatial attention with the proposed cross-frame attention, which allows global spatio-temporal modeling for all frames. 2) Similar to previous works [5,11,12,29], both ViViT [3] and VTN [32] adopt a dense temporal sampling strategy and ensemble the predictions of multiple views at

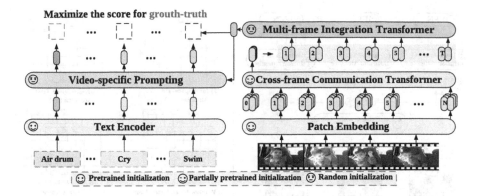

Fig. 2. An overview of our framework. The details are elaborated in Sect. 3.1.

inference, which is time-consuming. On the contrary, we empirically analyze different sampling methods for late fusion, and demonstrate that a sparse sampling is good enough, achieving better performance with fewer FLOPs than the dense strategy, as verified in Sect. 4.5 (Analysis).

3   Approach

In this section, we present our proposed framework in detail. First, we briefly overview our video-text framework in Sect. 3.1. Then, we depict the architecture of the video encoder, especially for the proposed cross-frame attention in Sect. 3.2. Finally, we introduce a video-specific prompting scheme in Sect. 3.3.

3.1   Overview

Most prior works in video recognition learn discriminative feature embeddings supervised by a one-hot label [3,5,12,47]. While in this work, inspired by the recent contrastive language-image pretraining [19,36,54], we propose to use text as the supervision, since the text provides more semantic information. As shown in Fig. 2, our method learns to align the video representation and its corresponding text representation by jointly training a video encoder and a text encoder. Rather than pretraining a new video-text model from scratch, our method is built upon prior language-image models and expands them with video temporal modeling and video-adaptive textual prompts. Such a strategy allows us to fully take advantage of existing large-scale pretrained models while transferring their powerful generalizability from image to video in a seamless fashion.

Formally, given a video clip $V \in \mathcal{V}$ and a text description $C \in \mathcal{C}$, where $\mathcal{V}$ is a set of videos and $\mathcal{C}$ is a collection of category names, we feed the video V into the video encoder f_{θ_v} and the text C into the text encoder f_{θ_c} to obtain a video representation $\mathbf{v}$ and a text representation $\mathbf{c}$ respectively, where

$$\mathbf{v} = f_{\theta_v}(V), \quad \mathbf{c} = f_{\theta_c}(C). \tag{1}$$

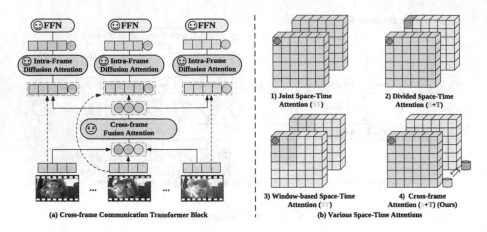

Fig. 3. (a) Cross-frame Attention. (b) compares different space-time attention mechanisms used in existing video transformer backbones [3,5,29].

Then, a video-specific prompt generator f_{θ_p} is employed to yield instance-level textual representation for each video. It takes the video representation $\mathbf{v}$ and text representation $\mathbf{c}$ as inputs, formulated as

$$\hat{\mathbf{c}} = f_{\theta_p}(\mathbf{c}, \mathbf{v}). \tag{2}$$

Finally, a cosine similarity function $\text{sim}(\mathbf{v}, \hat{\mathbf{c}})$ is utilized to compute the similarity between the visual and textual representations:

$$\text{sim}(\mathbf{v}, \hat{\mathbf{c}}) = \langle \mathbf{v}, \hat{\mathbf{c}} \rangle / (\|\mathbf{v}\| \, \|\hat{\mathbf{c}}\|). \tag{3}$$

The goal of our method is to maximize the $\text{sim}(\mathbf{v}, \hat{\mathbf{c}})$ if V and C are matched and otherwise minimize it.

3.2 Video Encoder

Our proposed video encoder is composed of two cascaded vision transformers: a cross-frame communication transformer and a multi-frame integration transformer. The cross-frame transformer takes raw frames as input and provides a frame-level representation using a pretrained language-image model, while allowing information exchange between frames. The multi-frame integration transformer then simply integrates the frame-level representations and outputs video features.

Specifically, given a video clip $V \in \mathbb{R}^{T \times H \times W \times 3}$ of T sampled frames with H and W denote the spatial resolution, following ViT [10], the t-th frame is divided into N non-overlapping patches $\{\mathbf{x}_{t,i}\}_{i=1}^{N} \in \mathbb{R}^{P^2 \times 3}$ with each of size $P \times P$ pixels, where $t \in \{1, \cdots, T\}$ denotes the temporal index, and $N = HW/P^2$. The patches $\{\mathbf{x}_{t,i}\}_{i=1}^{N}$ are then embedded into patch embeddings using a linear projection $\mathbf{E} \in \mathbb{R}^{3P^2 \times D}$. After that, we prepend a learnable embedding $\mathbf{x}_{class}$ to the sequence of embedded patches, called [class] token. Its state at the output of the encoder serves as the frame representation. The input of the cross-frame communication transformer at the frame t is denoted as:

$$\mathbf{z}_t^{(0)} = [\mathbf{x}_{class}, \mathbf{E}\mathbf{x}_{t,1}, \mathbf{E}\mathbf{x}_{t,2}, \cdots, \mathbf{E}\mathbf{x}_{t,N}] + \mathbf{e}^{spa}, \tag{4}$$

where $\mathbf{e}^{spa}$ represents the spatial position encoding.

Then we feed the patch embeddings into an L_c-layer Cross-frame Communication Transformer (CCT) to obtain the frame-level representation $\mathbf{h}_t$:

$$\begin{aligned} \mathbf{z}_t^{(l)} &= \mathrm{CCT}^{(l)}(\mathbf{z}_t^{(l-1)}), \ l = 1, \cdots, L_c \\ \mathbf{h}_t &= \mathbf{z}_{t,0}^{(L_c)}, \end{aligned} \tag{5}$$

where l denotes the block index in CCT, $\mathbf{z}_{t,0}^{(L_c)}$ represents the final output of the [class] token. CCT is built-up with the proposed cross-frame attention, as will be elaborated later.

At last, the L_m-layer Multi-frame Integration Transformer (MIT) takes all frame representation $\mathbf{H} = [\mathbf{h}_1, \mathbf{h}_2, \cdots, \mathbf{h}_T]$ as input and outputs the video-level representation $\mathbf{v}$ as following:

$$\mathbf{v} = \mathrm{AvgPool}(\mathrm{MIT}(\mathbf{H} + \mathbf{e}^{temp})), \tag{6}$$

where AvgPool and $\mathbf{e}^{temp}$ denote the average pooling and temporal position encoding, respectively. We use standard learnable absolute position embeddings [46] for $\mathbf{e}^{spa}$ and $\mathbf{e}^{temp}$. The multi-frame integration transformer is constructed by the standard multi-head self-attention and feed-forward networks [46].

Cross-Frame Attention. To enable a cross-frame information exchange, we propose a new attention module. It consists of two types of attentions, *i.e.*, cross-frame fusion attention (CFA) and intra-frame diffusion attention (IFA), with a feed-forward network (FFN). We introduce a *message token* mechanism for each frame to abstract, send and receive information, thus enabling visual information to exchange across frames, as shown in Fig. 3(a). In detail, the message token $\mathbf{m}_t^{(l)}$ for the t-th frame at the l-th layer is obtained by employing a linear transformation on the [class] token $\mathbf{z}_{t,0}^{(l-1)}$. This allows message tokens to abstract the visual information of the current frame.

Then, the cross-frame fusion attention (CFA) involves all message tokens to learn the global spatio-temporal dependencies of the input video. Mathematically, this process at l-th block can be expressed as:

$$\hat{\mathbf{M}}^{(l)} = \mathbf{M}^{(l)} + \mathrm{CFA}(\mathrm{LN}(\mathbf{M}^{(l)})), \tag{7}$$

where $\hat{\mathbf{M}}^{(l)} = [\hat{\mathbf{m}}_1^{(l)}, \hat{\mathbf{m}}_2^{(l)}, \cdots, \hat{\mathbf{m}}_T^{(l)}]$ and LN indicates layer normalization [4].

Next, the intra-frame diffusion (IFA) takes the frame tokens with the associated message token to learn visual representation, while the involved message token could also diffuse global spatio-temporal dependencies for learning. Mathematically, this process at l-th block can be formulated as:

$$[\hat{\mathbf{z}}_t^{(l)}, \bar{\mathbf{m}}_t^{(l)}] = [\mathbf{z}_t^{(l-1)}, \hat{\mathbf{m}}_t^{(l)}] + \text{IFA}(\text{LN}([\mathbf{z}_t^{(l-1)}, \hat{\mathbf{m}}_t^{(l)}])), \tag{8}$$

where $[\cdot, \cdot]$ concatenates the features of frame tokens and message tokens.

Finally, the feed-forward network(FFN) performs on the frame tokens as:

$$\mathbf{z}_t^{(l)} = \hat{\mathbf{z}}_t^{(l)} + \text{FFN}(\text{LN}(\hat{\mathbf{z}}_t^{(l)})). \tag{9}$$

Note that the message token is dropped before the FFN layer and does not pass through the next block, since it is generated online and used for frames communication within each block. Alternating the fusion and diffusion attentions through L_c blocks, the cross-frame communication transformer (CCT) can encode the global spatial and temporal information of video frames. Compared to other space-time attention mechanisms [3,5,29], as presented in Fig. 3(b), our proposed cross-frame attention models the global spatio-temporal information while greatly reducing the computational cost.

Initialization. When adapting the pretrained image encoder to the video encoder, there are two key modifications. 1) The intra-frame diffusion attention (IFA) inherits the weights directly from the pretrained models, while the cross-frame fusion attention (CFA) is randomly initialized. 2) The multi-frame integration transformer is appended to the pretrained models with random initialization.

3.3   Text Encoder

We employ the pretrained text encoder and expand it with a video-specific prompting scheme. The key idea is to use video content to enhance the text representation. Given a description C about a video, the text representation $\mathbf{c}$ is obtained by the text encoder, where $\mathbf{c} = f_{\theta_c}(C)$. For video recognition, how to generate a good text description C for each video is a challenging problem. Previous work, such as CLIP [36], usually defines textual prompts manually, such as "A photo of a {label}". However, in this work, we empirically show that such manually-designed prompts do not improve the performance for video recognition (as presented in Table 9). In contrast, we just use the "{label}" as the text description C and then propose a learnable text prompting scheme.

Video-Specific Prompting. When understanding an image or a video, human can instinctively seek helps from discriminative visual cues. For example, the extra video semantic information of "in the water" will make it easier to distinguish "swimming" from "running". However, it is difficult to acquire such visual semantics in video recognition tasks, because 1) the datasets only provide the category names, such as "swimming" and "running", which are pre-defined and fixed; and 2) the videos in the same class share the identical category name, but their visual context and content are different. To address these issues, we

Table 1. Comparison with state-of-the-art on Kinetics-400. We report the FLOPs and throughput per view. ∗ indicates video-text pretraining.

Method	Pretrain	Frames	Top-1	Top-5	Views	FLOPs(G)	Throughput
Methods with random initialization							
MViTv1-B, 64 × 3 [11]	-	64	81.2	95.1	3 × 3	455	7
Methods with ImageNet pretraining							
Uniformer-B [24]	IN-1k	32	83.0	95.4	4 × 3	259	-
TimeSformer-L [5]	IN-21k	96	80.7	94.7	1 × 3	2380	3
Mformer-HR [33]	IN-21k	16	81.1	95.2	10 × 3	959	-
Swin-L [29]	IN-21k	32	83.1	95.9	4 × 3	604	6
Swin-L (384↑) [29]	IN-21k	32	84.9	96.7	10 × 5	2107	-
MViTv2-L (312↑) [26]	IN-21k	40	86.1	97.0	5 × 3	2828	-
Methods with web-scale image pretraining							
ViViT-H/16x2 [3]	JFT-300M	32	84.8	95.8	4 × 3	8316	-
TokenLearner-L/10 [39]	JFT-300M	-	85.4	96.3	4 × 3	4076	-
CoVeR [55]	JFT-3B	-	**87.2**	-	1 × 3	-	-
Methods with web-scale language-image pretraining							
ActionCLIP-B/16 [48]	CLIP-400M	32	83.8	96.2	10 × 3	563	-
A6 [20]	CLIP-400M	16	76.9	93.5	-	-	-
MTV-H [53]	WTS∗	32	89.1	98.2	4 × 3	3705	-
X-Florence (384↑)	FLD-900M	8	86.2	96.6	4 × 3	2114	6
X-Florence	FLD-900M	32	86.5	96.9	4 × 3	2822	2
X-CLIP-B/16	IN-21k	8	81.1	94.7	4 × 3	145	33
X-CLIP-B/32	CLIP-400M	8	80.4	95.0	4 × 3	39	136
X-CLIP-B/32		16	81.1	95.5	4 × 3	75	69
X-CLIP-B/16		8	83.8	96.7	4 × 3	145	33
X-CLIP-B/16		16	84.7	96.8	4 × 3	287	17
X-CLIP-L/14		8	87.1	97.6	4 × 3	658	8
X-CLIP-L/14 (336↑)		16	87.7	97.4	4 × 3	3086	2

propose a learnable prompting scheme to generate textual representation automatically. Concretely, we design a video-specific prompting module, which takes the video content representation $\bar{\mathbf{z}}$ and text representation $\mathbf{c}$ as inputs. Each block in the video-specific prompting module is consisting of a multi-head self-attention (MHSA) [46] followed by a feed-forward network to learn the prompts,

$$\bar{\mathbf{c}} = \mathbf{c} + \text{MHSA}(\mathbf{c}, \bar{\mathbf{z}}) \text{ and } \tilde{\mathbf{c}} = \bar{\mathbf{c}} + \text{FFN}(\bar{\mathbf{c}}), \tag{10}$$

where $\mathbf{c}$ is the text embedding, $\bar{\mathbf{z}} \in \mathbb{R}^{N \times d}$ is the average of $\{\mathbf{z}_t^{(L_c)}\}_{t=1}^{T}$ along the temporal dimension, and $\tilde{\mathbf{c}}$ is the video-specific prompts. We use text representation $\mathbf{c}$ as query and the video content representation $\bar{\mathbf{z}}$ as key and value. This implementation allow the text representation to extract the related visual context from videos. We then enhance the text embedding $\mathbf{c}$ with the video-specific prompts $\tilde{\mathbf{c}}$ as follows, $\hat{\mathbf{c}} = \mathbf{c} + \alpha\tilde{\mathbf{c}}$, where α is a learnable parameter with an initial value of 0.1. The $\hat{\mathbf{c}}$ is finally used for classification in Eq. (3).

4   Experiments

In this section, we conduct experiments on different settings, *i.e.*, fully-supervised, zero-shot and few-shot, followed by the ablation studies of the proposed method.

4.1   Experimental Setup

Architectures and Datasets. We expand CLIP and Florence to derive four variants: X-CLIP-B/32, X-CLIP-B/16, X-CLIP-L/14 and X-Florence, respectively. X-CLIP-B/32 adopts ViT-B/32 as parts of the cross-frame communication transformer, X-CLIP-B/16 uses ViT-B/16, while X-CLIP-L/14 employs ViT-L/14. For all X-CLIP variants, we use a simple 1-layer multi-frame integration transformer, and the number of the video-specific prompting blocks is 2. We evaluate the efficacy of our method on four benchmarks: *Kinetics-400&600* [7,22], *UCF-101* [41] and *HMDB-51* [23]. More details about architectures and datasets are provided in the *supplementary materials*.

Table 2. Comparison with state-of-the-art on Kinetics-600.

Method	Pretrain	Frames	Top-1	Top-5	Views	FLOPs	Throughput
Methods with random initialization							
MViT-B-24, 32 × 3 [11]	-	32	83.8	96.3	5 × 1	236	-
Methods with ImageNet pretraining							
Swin-L (384↑) [29]	IN-21k	32	86.1	97.3	10 × 5	2107	-
Methods with web-scale pretraining							
ViViT-L/16x2 320 [3]	JFT-300M	32	83.0	95.7	4 × 3	3992	-
ViViT-H/16x2 [3]	JFT-300M	32	85.8	96.5	4 × 3	8316	-
TokenLearner-L/10 [39]	JFT-300M	-	86.3	97.0	4 × 3	4076	-
Florence (384↑) [54]	FLD-900M	-	87.8	97.8	4 × 3	-	-
CoVeR [55]	JFT-3B	-	**87.9**	-	1 × 3	-	-
MTV-H [53]	WTS*	32	89.6	98.3	4 × 3	3705	-
X-CLIP-B/16	CLIP-400M	8	85.3	97.1	4 × 3	145	74
X-CLIP-B/16		16	85.8	97.3	4 × 3	287	40
X-CLIP-L/14		8	88.3	97.7	4 × 3	658	20

4.2   Fully-Supervised Experiments

Training and Inference. We sample 8 or 16 frames in fully-supervised experiments. The detailed hyperparameters are showed in the *supplementary materials*.

Results. In Table 1, we report the results on Kinetics-400 and compare with other SoTA methods under different pretraining, including random initialization, IN-1k/21k [9] pretraining, web-scale image and language-image pretraining.

Compared to the methods pretrained on IN-21k [9], our X-CLIP-B/16$_{8f}$ (8 frames) surpasses Swin-L [28] by +0.7% with 4× fewer FLOPs and running 5× faster(as presented in Fig. 1). The underlying reason is that the shift-window attention in Swin is inefficient. Also, our X-CLIP-L/14$_{8f}$ outperforms MViTv2-L [26] by +1.0% with 5× fewer FLOPs. In addition, when using IN-21k pretraining, our method surpasses TimeSformer-L [5] with fewer FLOPs.

When compared to the methods using web-scale image pretraining, our X-CLIP is also competitive. For example, X-CLIP-L/14$_{8f}$ achieves +2.3% higher accuracy than ViViT-H [3] with 12× fewer FLOPs. MTV-H [53] achieves better results than ours, but it uses much more pretraining data. Specifically, MTV-H uses a 70M video-text dataset including about 17 B images, which are much larger than the 400M image-text data used in CLIP pretraining.

Moreover, compared to ActionCLIP [48], which also adopt CLIP as the pre-trained model, our X-CLIP-L/14$_{8f}$ is still superior, getting +3.3% higher accuracy with fewer FLOPs. There are two factors leading to the smaller FLOPs of our method. One is that X-CLIP does not use 3D attention like [29] and has fewer layers. The other factor is that X-CLIP samples fewer frames for each video clip, such as 8 or 16 frames, while ActionCLIP [48] using 32 frames.

Table 3. Zero-shot performances on HMDB51 [23] and UCF101 [41].

Method	HMDB-51	UCF-101
MTE [52]	19.7 ± 1.6	15.8 ± 1.3
ASR [49]	21.8 ± 0.9	24.4 ± 1.0
ZSECOC [34]	22.6 ± 1.2	15.1 ± 1.7
UR [63]	24.4 ± 1.6	17.5 ± 1.6
TS-GCN [14]	23.2 ± 3.0	34.2 ± 3.1
E2E [6]	32.7	48
ER-ZSAR [8]	35.3 ± 4.6	51.8 ± 2.9
ActionCLIP [48]	40.8 ± 5.4	58.3 ± 3.4
X-CLIP-B/16	**44.6 ± 5.2**	**72.0 ± 2.3**
	(+3.8)	(+13.7)
X-Florence	**48.4 ± 4.9**	**73.2 ± 4.2**
	(+7.6)	(+14.9)

Table 4. Zero-shot performance on Kinetics-600 [7].

Method	Top-1 Acc	Top-5 Acc
DEVISE [13]	23.8 ± 0.3	51.0 ± 0.6
ALE [1]	23.4 ± 0.8	50.3 ± 1.4
SJE [2]	22.3 ± 0.6	48.2 ± 0.4
ESZSL [38]	22.9 ± 1.2	48.3 ± 0.8
DEM [56]	23.6 ± 0.7	49.5 ± 0.4
GCN [16]	22.3 ± 0.6	49.7 ± 0.6
ER-ZSAR [8]	42.1 ± 1.4	73.1 ± 0.3
X-CLIP-B/16	**65.2 ± 0.4**	**86.1 ± 0.8**
	(+23.1)	(+13.0)
X-Florence	**68.8 ± 0.9**	**88.4 ±0.6**
	(+26.7)	(+15.3)

In addition, we report the results on Kinetics-600 in Table 2. Using only 8 frames, our X-CLIP-B/16$_{8f}$ surpasses ViViT-L, while using 27× fewer FLOPs. More importantly, our X-CLIP-L/14$_{8f}$ achieves 88.3% top-1 accuracy while using 5× fewer FLOPs compared to the current state-of-the-art method MTV-H [53].

From the above fully-supervised experiments, we can observe that, our X-CLIP method achieves very competitive performance compared to prevailing video transformer models [20,48,53–55]. This mainly attributes to two factors.

1) The proposed cross-frame attention can effectively model temporal dependencies of video frames. 2) The joint language-image representation is successfully transferred to videos, unveiling its powerful generalization ability for recognition.

4.3 Zero-Shot Experiments

Training and Inference. We pretrain X-CLIP-B/16 on Kinetics-400. More details about the evaluation protocols are provided in the *supplementary materials*.

Results. Zero-shot video recognition is very challenging, because the categories in the test set are unseen to the model during training. We report the results in Table 3 and Table 4. On HMDB-51 [23] and UCF-101 [41] benchmarks, our X-CLIP outperforms the previous best results by +3.8% and +13.7% in terms of top-1 accuracy respectively, as reported in Table 3. On Kinetics-600 [7] as presented in Table 4, our X-CLIP outperforms the state-of-the-art ER-ZSAR [8] by +23.1%. Such remarkable improvements can be attributed to the proposed video-text learning framework, which leverages the large-scale visual-text pre-training and seamlessly integrates temporal cues and textual prompts.

4.4 Few-Shot Experiments

Training and Inference. A general K-shot setting is considered, *i.e.*, K examples are sampled from each category randomly for training. We compare with some representative methods. More details about the comparison methods and evaluation protocols are provided in the *supplementary materials*.

Table 5. Few-shot results. Top-1 accuracy is reported with 32 frames.

Method	HMDB-51				UCF-101			
	$K=2$	$K=4$	$K=8$	$K=16$	$K=2$	$K=4$	$K=8$	$K=16$
TSM [27]	17.5	20.9	18.4	31.0	25.3	47.0	64.4	61.0
TimeSformer [5]	19.6	40.6	49.4	55.4	48.5	75.6	83.7	89.4
Swin-B [29]	20.9	41.3	47.9	56.1	53.3	74.1	85.8	88.7
X-CLIP-B/16	**53.0**	**57.3**	**62.8**	**64.0**	**76.4**	**83.4**	**88.3**	**91.4**
	(+32.1)	(+16.0)	(+13.4)	(+7.9)	(+23.1)	(+7.8)	(+2.5)	(+2.0)
X-Florence	**51.6**	**57.8**	**64.1**	**64.2**	**84.0**	**88.5**	**92.5**	**94.8**
	(+30.7)	(+16.5)	(+14.7)	(+8.1)	(+30.7)	(+12.9)	(+6.7)	(+5.4)

Results. Table 5 presents the results of K-shot learning. For the extreme case where $K=2$, we observe that for those single-modality methods, the performance drops significantly, demonstrating that over-fitting occurs due to the serious lack of data. In contrast, X-CLIP shows robustness by surpassing them with large margins. For example, X-CLIP-B/16 outperforms Swin-B by +32.1% and

+23.1% in terms of top-1 accuracy on HMDB-51 and UCF-101 with $K = 2$, respectively. Such large improvements are mainly due to the exploitation of the semantics in text representation. It further verifies the efficacy of transferring the knowledge of the pretrained language-image models to the few-shot models. We also observe that the performance gap between our method and others decreases as the sample size increases. It demonstrates increasing data can mitigate the over-fitting for other methods. Besides, it is noteworthy that the comparison of methods with CLIP pretraining and ImageNet pretraining is not fair enough. Hence, in Sect. 4.5, we provide an additional ablation analysis and verify the performance gains mainly comes from the use of textual information, rather than the CLIP pretraining.

4.5 Ablation and Analysis

Unless stated otherwise, the fully-supervised experiments are performed on Kinectics-400, while the few-shot experiments are conducted on HMDB-51 with $K = 2$. The zero-shot evaluation is on the first split of the validation set of UCF-101. We use X-CLIP-B/16_{8f} with single-view inference in all experiments.

Ablation. *The effects of the proposed components.* Table 6 shows the performance evolution from the pretrained image CLIP to our expanded video X-CLIP. First, we design a simple baseline that averages the CLIP features of all video frames for classification, called CLIP-Mean. It uses the text supervision but does not utilize prompting technique. We can observe that equipping the original transformer in CLIP with our proposed cross-frame communication mechanism,

Table 6. Component-wise analysis of our X-CLIP and other techniques.

Components	Top-1.(%)
Baseline(CLIP-Mean)	80.0
+ Cross-frame Communication	81.2(+1.2)
+ Multi-frame Integration	81.7(+1.7)
+ Video-specific Prompt	82.3(+2.3)
Techniques	
+ 4 × 3-views Inference	83.8(+3.8)

Table 7. Ablation study on which part to finetune. ✓means finetuning. The CUDA memory is calculated on 2 video inputs, each containing 8 frames.

Visual	Text	Zero	Few	Fully	Mem.(G)
✓	✓	**72.9**	54.6	82.4	22
✓	✗	70.0	50.8	82.3	6
✗	✓	66.8	**53.4**	79.3	20
✗	✗	64.2	47.3	79.1	4

Table 8. Ablation study on the effect of the text information.

Method	Zero-shot	Few-shot	Fully
w/o text	/	32.0	81.6
w/ text	70.0	50.8(+18.8)	82.3(+0.7)

Table 9. Comparison with different prompting methods.

Method	Fully	Few	Zero
w/o prompt	81.7	49.6	63.2
Ensemble. [36]	81.7	49.6	63.9
Vectors. [60]	82.0	49.9	63.2
Ours	**82.3**(+0.3)	**50.8**(+0.9)	**70.0**(+6.1)

i.e. Eq. (7–9), can improve the accuracy by +1.2%. Then, appending 1-layer multi-frame integration transformer (MIT) can further improve the accuracy by +0.5%. This illustrates that our X-CLIP framework can effectively leverage temporal cues in video clips. With the proposed video-specific prompting, X-CLIP can surpass the CLIP-Mean baseline by +2.3%. It demonstrates that the video-specific prompting scheme can generate more discriminative textual representation. Meanwhile, additionally using multi-view inference can boost the performance by +1.5%. Overall, with our proposed methods and all the techniques mentioned above, X-CLIP can boost the top-1 accuracy of the CLIP-Mean baseline from 80.0% to 83.8%.

Which Branch to Finetune? In order to demonstrate which branch should be finetuned when transferred to different downstream tasks, we separately freeze the parameters of the pretrained image and text encoder. Note that the randomly initialized parameters are always finetuned. From Table 7, we summarize the following observations. 1) For fully-supervised setting, finetuning the image encoder brings +3.0% improvements, while freezing the text encoder reduces the CUDA memory from 22G to 6G with minor performance loss. 2) For few-shot setting, we find the top-2 results are achieved by finetuning the text encoder. We conjecture the reason is that with few samples, the text encoder suffers less from over-fitting than the over-parameterized image model. 3) For zero-shot setting, finetuning both the image and the text encoder achieves the best results.

The Effects of Text. To evaluate the impact of text, we replace the text encoder with a randomly initialized fully-connected layer as the classification head. From Table 8, we can observe that, without the text branch, the model cannot adapt to zero-shot setting, because there is no data to initialize the head. For the few-shot and fully-supervised experiments, text information can bring +18.8% and +0.7% gains, respectively. This indicates the semantic information involved in text representation is beneficial to classification, especially for low-shot learning.

The Effects of Pretraining. In Table 10, we investigate the effects of pretraining. We use ViT-B/16 pretrained on IN-1k/21k as the video encoder in our framework. Though the pretrained image encoder and text encoder are not in a joint embedding space, the model with IN-21k and IN-1k pretraining still achieve

Table 10. Ablation study on the different pretraining.

Pretrain	Top-1 (%)	Top-5 (%)
ImageNet-1k	75.9	90.2
ImageNet-21k	79.8	94.0

Table 11. Comparison of two sampling methods.

#F	Train	Test	
		multi-view → single-view	
		Dense	Sparse
8	Dense	$81.9 \to 77.8(-4.1)$	$82.4 \to 81.1(-1.3)$
	Sparse	$82.2 \to 77.3(-4.9)$	$\mathbf{83.4} \to \mathbf{82.3}(-1.1)$
32	Dense	$82.8 \to 78.8(-4.0)$	$83.2 \to 83.0(-0.2)$
	Sparse	$83.0 \to 77.9(-5.1)$	$\mathbf{84.4} \to \mathbf{84.2}(-0.2)$

79.8% and 75.9% top-1 accuracy on Kinectics-400, yet much inferior to the original CLIP large-scale pretraining (82.3%).

Analysis. *Comparison with Other Prompting Methods.* We compare with two existing methods in Table 9: prompt ensembling [36] with 16 handcraft templates and learnable vectors [60] with length 16. It can be seen that our video-specific prompts outperforms others, especially in zero-shot setting (+6.1%). This demonstrates the efficacy of our method, which generates more adaptive prompts and better textual representation for unseen videos.

Dense v.s. Sparse Sampling. We further explore what is the best sampling strategy for our method in Table 11. We find that the dense sampling does not perform well as in previous works [3,12,29]. In contrast, the sparse sampling best matches our method. Regardless of the number of frames and views, using sparse sampling both in training and inference achieves the best performance.

Single-View v.s. Multi-view Inference. Although it can improve performance, multi-view inference takes relatively high computational cost, because the cost grows linearly with the number of views. In Table 11, we show that our multi-modality models with sparse sampling is robust to the number of views, *i.e.*, single-view can achieve comparable performance to 10 temporal views. The underlying reason is the language-image models provide robust representation.

5   Conclusion

In this work, we present a simple approach that adapts the pretrained language-image models to video recognition. To capture the temporal information, we propose a cross-frame attention mechanism that explicitly exchanges information across frames. A video-specific prompting technique is designed to yield instance-level discriminative textual representation. Extensive experiments under three different learning scenarios demonstrate the effectiveness of our method. In future work, we plan to extend our method to different video tasks beyond classification.

Acknowledgements. This research was supported in part by the National Key Research and Development Program of China under Grant No. 2018AAA0100400, and the National Natural Science Foundation of China under Grants 61976208, 62071466 and 62076242, and the InnoHK project. HL was not supported by any fund for this research.

References

1. Akata, Z., Perronnin, F., Harchaoui, Z., Schmid, C.: Label-embedding for image classification. IEEE T-PAMI **38**, 1425–1438 (2015)
2. Akata, Z., Reed, S., Walter, D., Lee, H., Schiele, B.: Evaluation of output embeddings for fine-grained image classification. In: CVPR, pp. 2927–2936 (2015)

3. Arnab, A., Dehghani, M., Heigold, G., Sun, C., Lučić, M., Schmid, C.: ViViT: a video vision transformer. In: ICCV, pp. 6836–6846 (2021)
4. Ba, J.L., Kiros, J.R., Hinton, G.E.: Layer normalization. arXiv preprint arXiv:1607.06450 (2016)
5. Bertasius, G., Wang, H., Torresani, L.: Is space-time attention all you need for video understanding? In: ICML, pp. 813–824 (2021)
6. Brattoli, B., Tighe, J., Zhdanov, F., Perona, P., Chalupka, K.: Rethinking zero-shot video classification: end-to-end training for realistic applications. In: CVPR, pp. 4613–4623 (2020)
7. Carreira, J., Noland, E., Banki-Horvath, A., Hillier, C., Zisserman, A.: A short note about kinetics-600. arXiv preprint arXiv:1808.01340 (2018)
8. Chen, S., Huang, D.: Elaborative rehearsal for zero-shot action recognition. In: ICCV, pp. 13638–13647 (2021)
9. Deng, J., Dong, W., Socher, R., Li, L.J., Li, K., Fei-Fei, L.: Imagenet: a large-scale hierarchical image database. In: CVPR, pp. 248–255. IEEE (2009)
10. Dosovitskiy, A., et al.: An image is worth 16x16 words: transformers for image recognition at scale. In: ICLR (2021)
11. Fan, H., et al.: Multiscale vision transformers. In: ICCV, pp. 6824–6835 (2021)
12. Feichtenhofer, C., Fan, H., Malik, J., He, K.: Slowfast networks for video recognition. In: ICCV, pp. 6202–6211 (2019)
13. Frome, A., et al.: Devise: a deep visual-semantic embedding model. In: NIPS, pp. 2121–2129 (2013)
14. Gao, J., Zhang, T., Xu, C.: I know the relationships: zero-shot action recognition via two-stream graph convolutional networks and knowledge graphs. In: AAAI, vol. 33, pp. 8303–8311 (2019)
15. Gao, P., et al.: Clip-adapter: better vision-language models with feature adapters. arXiv preprint arXiv:2110.04544 (2021)
16. Ghosh, P., Saini, N., Davis, L.S., Shrivastava, A.: All about knowledge graphs for actions. arXiv preprint arXiv:2008.12432 (2020)
17. Girdhar, R., Grauman, K.: Anticipative video transformer. In: ICCV (2021)
18. Herath, S., Harandi, M., Porikli, F.: Going deeper into action recognition: a survey. Image Vis. Comput. **60**, 4–21 (2017)
19. Jia, C., et al.: Scaling up visual and vision-language representation learning with noisy text supervision. In: ICML, pp. 4904–4916 (2021)
20. Ju, C., Han, T., Zheng, K., Zhang, Y., Xie, W.: Prompting visual-language models for efficient video understanding. In: CVPR (2022)
21. Karpathy, A., Toderici, G., Shetty, S., Leung, T., Sukthankar, R., Fei-Fei, L.: Large-scale video classification with convolutional neural networks. In: CVPR, pp. 1725–1732 (2014)
22. Kay, W., et al.: The kinetics human action video dataset. arXiv preprint arXiv:1705.06950 (2017)
23. Kuehne, H., Jhuang, H., Garrote, E., Poggio, T., Serre, T.: HMDB: a large video database for human motion recognition. In: ICCV, pp. 2556–2563 (2011)
24. Li, K., et al.: Uniformer: unifying convolution and self-attention for visual recognition. In: ICLR (2022)
25. Li, Y., Ji, B., Shi, X., Zhang, J., Kang, B., Wang, L.: Tea: temporal excitation and aggregation for action recognition. In: CVPR, pp. 909–918 (2020)
26. Li, Y., et al.: Improved multiscale vision transformers for classification and detection. In: CVPR (2022)
27. Lin, J., Gan, C., Han, S.: TSM: temporal shift module for efficient video understanding. In: ICCV, pp. 7083–7093 (2019)

28. Liu, Z., et al.: Swin transformer: hierarchical vision transformer using shifted windows. In: ICCV (2021)
29. Liu, Z., et al.: Video swin transformer. In: CVPR (2022)
30. Liu, Z., Wang, L., Wu, W., Qian, C., Lu, T.: TAM: temporal adaptive module for video recognition. In: ICCV, pp. 13708–13718 (2021)
31. Miech, A., Zhukov, D., Alayrac, J.B., Tapaswi, M., Laptev, I., Sivic, J.: HowTo100M: learning a text-video embedding by watching hundred million narrated video clips. In: ICCV, pp. 2630–2640 (2019)
32. Neimark, D., Bar, O., Zohar, M., Asselmann, D.: Video transformer network. arXiv preprint arXiv:2102.00719 (2021)
33. Patrick, M., et al.: Keeping your eye on the ball: trajectory attention in video transformers. In: NIPS (2021)
34. Qin, J., et al.: Zero-shot action recognition with error-correcting output codes. In: CVPR, pp. 2833–2842 (2017)
35. Qiu, Z., Yao, T., Mei, T.: Learning spatio-temporal representation with pseudo-3D residual networks. In: ICCV, pp. 5533–5541 (2017)
36. Radford, A., et al.: Learning transferable visual models from natural language supervision. In: ICML (2021)
37. Rao, Y., et al.: DenseCLIP: language-guided dense prediction with context-aware prompting. In: CVPR (2022)
38. Romera-Paredes, B., Torr, P.: An embarrassingly simple approach to zero-shot learning. In: ICML, pp. 2152–2161 (2015)
39. Ryoo, M., Piergiovanni, A., Arnab, A., Dehghani, M., Angelova, A.: Tokenlearner: adaptive space-time tokenization for videos. In: NIPS, vol. 34 (2021)
40. Selva, J., Johansen, A.S., Escalera, S., Nasrollahi, K., Moeslund, T.B., Clapés, A.: Video transformers: a survey. arXiv preprint arXiv:2201.05991 (2022)
41. Soomro, K., Zamir, A.R., Shah, M.: UCF101: a dataset of 101 human actions classes from videos in the wild. arXiv preprint arXiv:1212.0402 (2012)
42. Sun, C., Baradel, F., Murphy, K., Schmid, C.: Learning video representations using contrastive bidirectional transformer. In: ECCV (2020)
43. Sun, C., Myers, A., Vondrick, C., Murphy, K., Schmid, C.: Videobert: a joint model for video and language representation learning. In: ICCV, pp. 7464–7473 (2019)
44. Tran, D., Bourdev, L., Fergus, R., Torresani, L., Paluri, M.: Learning spatiotemporal features with 3D convolutional networks. In: ICCV, pp. 4489–4497 (2015)
45. Tran, D., Wang, H., Torresani, L., Ray, J., LeCun, Y., Paluri, M.: A closer look at spatiotemporal convolutions for action recognition. In: CVPR (2018)
46. Vaswani, A., et al.: Attention is all you need. In: NIPS, pp. 5998–6008 (2017)
47. Wang, L., et al.: Temporal segment networks: towards good practices for deep action recognition. In: Leibe, B., Matas, J., Sebe, N., Welling, M. (eds.) ECCV 2016. LNCS, vol. 9912, pp. 20–36. Springer, Cham (2016). https://doi.org/10.1007/978-3-319-46484-8_2
48. Wang, M., Xing, J., Liu, Y.: ActionCLIP: a new paradigm for video action recognition. arXiv preprint arXiv:2109.08472 (2021)
49. Wang, Q., Chen, K.: Alternative semantic representations for zero-shot human action recognition. In: ECML PKDD, pp. 87–102 (2017)
50. Xie, S., Sun, C., Huang, J., Tu, Z., Murphy, K.: Rethinking spatiotemporal feature learning: speed-accuracy trade-offs in video classification. In: ECCV, pp. 305–321 (2018)
51. Xu, H., et al.: Videoclip: contrastive pre-training for zero-shot video-text understanding. In: EMNLP (2021)

52. Xu, X., Hospedales, T.M., Gong, S.: Multi-task zero-shot action recognition with prioritised data augmentation. In: Leibe, B., Matas, J., Sebe, N., Welling, M. (eds.) ECCV 2016. LNCS, vol. 9906, pp. 343–359. Springer, Cham (2016). https://doi.org/10.1007/978-3-319-46475-6_22

53. Yan, S., et al.: Multiview transformers for video recognition. In: CVPR (2022)

54. Yuan, L., et al.: Florence: a new foundation model for computer vision. arXiv preprint arXiv:2111.11432 (2021)

55. Zhang, B., et al.: Co-training transformer with videos and images improves action recognition. arXiv preprint arXiv:2112.07175 (2021)

56. Zhang, L., Xiang, T., Gong, S.: Learning a deep embedding model for zero-shot learning. In: CVPR, pp. 2021–2030 (2017)

57. Zhang, R., et al.: Tip-adapter: training-free clip-adapter for better vision-language modeling. arXiv preprint arXiv:2111.03930 (2021)

58. Zhang, R., et al.: Pointclip: point cloud understanding by clip. In: CVPR (2021)

59. Zhou, C., Loy, C.C., Dai, B.: Denseclip: extract free dense labels from clip. arXiv preprint arXiv:2112.01071 (2021)

60. Zhou, K., Yang, J., Loy, C.C., Liu, Z.: Learning to prompt for vision-language models. arXiv preprint arXiv:2109.01134 (2021)

61. Zhu, L., Yang, Y.: Actbert: learning global-local video-text representations. In: CVPR, pp. 8746–8755 (2020)

62. Zhu, Y., et al.: A comprehensive study of deep video action recognition. arXiv preprint arXiv:2012.06567 (2020)

63. Zhu, Y., Long, Y., Guan, Y., Newsam, S., Shao, L.: Towards universal representation for unseen action recognition. In: CVPR, pp. 9436–9445 (2018)

Hunting Group Clues with Transformers for Social Group Activity Recognition

Masato Tamura[(✉)] [iD], Rahul Vishwakarma [iD], and Ravigopal Vennelakanti

Hitachi America, Ltd., White Plains, USA
masato.tamura.sf@hitachi.com,
{rahul.vishwakarma,ravigopal.vennelakanti}@hal.hitachi.com

Abstract. This paper presents a novel framework for social group activity recognition. As an expanded task of group activity recognition, social group activity recognition requires recognizing multiple sub-group activities and identifying group members. Most existing methods tackle both tasks by refining region features and then summarizing them into activity features. Such heuristic feature design renders the effectiveness of features susceptible to incomplete person localization and disregards the importance of scene contexts. Furthermore, region features are suboptimal to identify group members because the features may be dominated by those of people in the regions and have different semantics. To overcome these drawbacks, we propose to leverage attention modules in transformers to generate effective social group features. Our method is designed in such a way that the attention modules identify and then aggregate features relevant to social group activities, generating an effective feature for each social group. Group member information is embedded into the features and thus accessed by feed-forward networks. The outputs of feed-forward networks represent groups so concisely that group members can be identified with simple Hungarian matching between groups and individuals. Experimental results show that our method outperforms state-of-the-art methods on the Volleyball and Collective Activity datasets.

Keywords: Social group activity recognition · Group activity recognition · Social scene understanding · Attention mechanism · Transformer

1 Introduction

Social group activity recognition is a task of recognizing multiple sub-group activities and identifying group members in a scene. This task is derived from group activity recognition, which needs to recognize only one group activity

---

Supplementary Information The online version contains supplementary material available at https://doi.org/10.1007/978-3-031-19772-7_2.

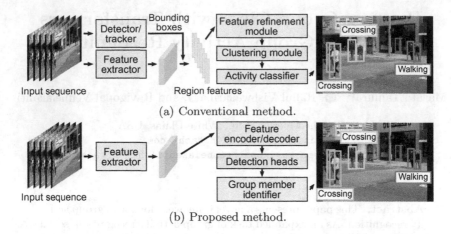

(a) Conventional method.

(b) Proposed method.

Fig. 1. Overviews of conventional and proposed social group activity recognition methods. The labels in the right image show predicted social group activities.

in a scene. Both tasks have gained tremendous attention in recent years for potential applications such as sports video analysis, crowd behavior analysis, and social scene understanding [1–5,12–14,17–19,22,24–28,34,35,37,40,43–50]. In the context of these tasks, the term "action" denotes an atomic movement of a single person, and the term "activity" refers to a more complex relation of movements performed by a group of people. Although our framework can recognize both actions and activities, we focus on group activities.

Most existing methods decompose the recognition process into two independent parts; person localization and activity recognition (See Fig. 1a) [5,12–14, 17,19,22,27,34,35,37,43,44,49,50]. Person localization identifies regions where people are observed in a scene with bounding boxes. These boxes are used to extract region features from feature maps. The region features are further refined to encode spatio-temporal relations with refinement modules such as recurrent neural networks (RNNs) [8,16], graph neural networks (GNNs) [21,42], and transformers [41]. The refined features are summarized for activity recognition.

While these methods have demonstrated significant improvement, they have several drawbacks attributed to the heuristic nature of feature design. Since region features are extracted from bounding box regions in feature maps, the effectiveness of the features is affected by the localization performance. Most existing methods ignore this effect and evaluate their performances with region features of ground truth boxes. However, several works [5,13,35,44] show that the recognition performance is slightly degraded when using predicted boxes instead of ground truth boxes. Moreover, substantial scene contexts are discarded by using region features because they are typically dominated by features of the people in the boxes. Scene contexts such as object positions and background situations are sometimes crucial to recognize group activities. For instance, the positions of sports balls are informative to recognize group activities in sports games. These features should be leveraged to enhance recognition performance.

Another challenge specific to social group activity recognition is that utilizing region features is sub-optimal to identify group members. Ehsanpour *et al.* [13] use region features as node features of graph attention networks (GATs) [42] and train them to output adjacency matrices that have low probabilities for people in different groups and high probabilities for those in the same groups. During inference, spectral clustering [32] is applied to the adjacency matrices to divide people into groups. Because adjacency matrices reflect semantic similarities of node features, this method may not work if region features of people in the same group have different semantics such as doing different actions.

To address these challenges, we propose a novel social group activity recognition method that can be applied to both social group activity recognition and group activity recognition. We leverage a transformer-based object detection framework [6,52] to obviate the need for the heuristic feature design in existing methods (See Fig. 1b). Attention modules in transformers play crucial roles in our method. We design our method in such a way that the attention modules identify and then aggregate features relevant to social group activities, generating an effective feature for each social group. Because activity and group member information is embedded into the generated features, the information can be accessed by feed-forward networks (FFNs) in the detection heads. The outputs of the detection heads are designed so concisely that group member identification can be performed with simple Hungarian matching between groups and individuals. This identification method differs from Ehsanpour *et al.*'s method [13] in that their method relies on individuals' features to divide people into groups, while our method generates features that are embedded with clues for grouping people, enabling effective group identification.

To summarize, our contributions are three-fold: (1) We propose a novel social group activity recognition method that leverages the attention modules to generate effective social group features. (2) Our method achieves better or competitive performance to state-of-the-art methods on both group activity recognition and social group activity recognition. (3) We perform comprehensive analyses to reveal how our method works with activities under various conditions.

2 Related Works

2.1 Group Member Identification and Activity Recognition

Several group member identification methods [15,33,38] were proposed independently of group activity recognition. They utilize hand-crafted features to find interactions and identify group members on the basis of their interactions.

In group activity recognition, deep-neural-network-based methods have become dominant due to the learning capability of the networks. Ibrahim *et al.* [19] proposed an RNN-based method that uses convolutional neural networks to extract region features and long short-term memories to refine the features. This architecture captures the temporal dynamics of each person between frames and the spatial dynamics of people in a scene. After their work, several RNN-based methods were proposed [5, 22, 35, 37, 43].

GNNs are also utilized to model the spatio-temporal context and relationships of people in a scene. Wu *et al.* [44] used graph convolutional networks (GCNs) [21] to capture spatio-temporal relations of people's appearances and positions between frames. Ehsanpour *et al.* [13] adopted GATs [42] to learn underlying interactions and divide people into social groups with adjacency matrices. Hu *et al.* [17] utilized both RNNs and GNNs with reinforcement learning to refine features. Yuan *et al.* [49] used person-specific dynamic graphs that dynamically change connections of GNNs for each node.

Several works introduced transformers into group activity recognition. Gavrilyuk *et al.* [14] used transformer encoders to refine region features. Li *et al.* [27] proposed spatial-temporal transformers that can encode spatio-temporal dependence and decode the group activity information. Zhou *et al.* [50] proposed multiscale spatio-temporal stacked transformers for compositional understanding and relational reasoning in group activities.

Our method differs from existing methods in that they rely on region features, while our method generates social group features with the attention modules in transformers, resulting in improving the performance.

2.2   Detection Transformer

Carion *et al.* [6] proposed a transformer-based object detector called DETR, which regards object detection as a set prediction problem. One significant difference between conventional object detectors and DETR is that conventional ones need heuristic detection points whose features are used to predict object classes and bounding boxes, while DETR obviates such heuristic components by letting queries in transformer decoders aggregate features for their target objects. DETR shows competitive performance compared with conventional state-of-the-art detectors even without such heuristic components.

To further improve the performance of DETR, several methods have been proposed [11, 39, 52]. Zhu *et al.* [52] proposed Deformable DETR that replaces standard transformers with deformable ones. Deformable attention modules in the transformers combine a sparse sampling of deformable convolution [10] and dynamic weighting of standard attention modules, which significantly reduces the computational complexity of the attention weight calculation. This reduction allows Deformable DETR to use multi-scale feature maps from backbone networks. To leverage non-heuristic designs and multi-scale feature maps, we use deformable transformers to generate social group features.

3   Proposed Method

We leverage a deformable-transformer-based object detection framework [52], whose details are omitted due to the limited space. We encourage readers to refer to the paper for more details.

3.1 Overall Architecture

Figure 2 shows the overall architecture of the proposed method. Given a frame sequence $x \in \mathbb{R}^{3 \times T \times H \times W}$, a feature extractor extracts a set of multi-scale feature maps $\mathbf{Z}_f = \{z_i^{(f)} \mid z_i^{(f)} \in \mathbb{R}^{D_i \times T \times H_i' \times W_i'}\}_{i=1}^{L_f}$, where T is the length of the sequence, H and W are the height and width of the frame, H_i' and W_i' are those of the output feature maps, D_i is the number of channels, and L_f is the number of scales. We adopt the inflated 3D (I3D) network [7] as a feature extractor to embed local spatio-temporal context into feature maps. Note that we use only the RGB stream of I3D because group members are identified by their positions, which cannot be predicted with the optical flow stream. To reduce the computational costs of transformers, each feature map $z_i^{(f)}$ is mean-pooled over the temporal dimension and input to a projection convolution layer that reduces the channel dimension from D_i to D_p. One additional projection convolution layer with a kernel size of 3×3 and stride of 2×2 is applied to the smallest feature map to further add the scale.

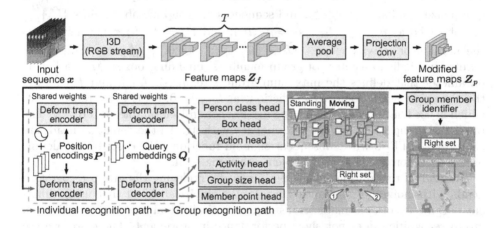

Fig. 2. Overall architecture of the proposed method.

Features in the modified feature maps are refined and aggregated with deformable transformers. Given a set of the modified multi-scale feature maps $\mathbf{Z}_p = \{z_i^{(p)} \mid z_i^{(p)} \in \mathbb{R}^{D_p \times H_i' \times W_i'}\}_{i=1}^{L_f+1}$, a set of refined feature maps $\mathbf{Z}_e = \{z_i^{(e)} \mid z_i^{(e)} \in \mathbb{R}^{D_p \times H_i' \times W_i'}\}_{i=1}^{L_f+1}$ is obtained as $\mathbf{Z}_e = f_{enc}(\mathbf{Z}_p, \mathbf{P})$, where $f_{enc}(\cdot, \cdot)$ is stacked deformable transformer encoder layers and $\mathbf{P} = \{p_i \mid p_i \in \mathbb{R}^{D_p \times H_i' \times W_i'}\}_{i=1}^{L_f+1}$ is a set of multi-scale position encodings [52], which supplement the attention modules with position and scale information to identify where each feature lies in the feature maps. The encoder helps features to acquire rich social group context by exchanging information in a feature map and between multi-scale feature maps. These enriched feature maps are fed into the deformable transformer decoder to aggregate features. Given a set of refined feature maps Z_e and learnable query embeddings $Q = \{q_i \mid q_i \in \mathbb{R}^{2D_p}\}_{i=1}^{N_q}$, a set of feature embeddings $H = \{h_i \mid h_i \in \mathbb{R}^{D_p}\}_{i=1}^{N_q}$ is obtained as $H = f_{dec}(Z_e, Q)$, where N_q is the number of query embeddings and $f_{dec}(\cdot, \cdot)$ is stacked deformable transformer decoder layers. Each decoder layer predicts locations that contain features relevant to input embeddings and aggregates the features from the locations with the dynamic weighting. We design queries in such a way that one query captures at most one social group. This design enables each query to aggregate features of its target social group from the refined feature maps.

The feature embeddings are transformed into prediction results with detection heads. Here we denote the localization results in normalized image coordinates. Social group activities are recognized by predicting activities and identifying group members. The identification is performed with a group size head and group member point head. The size head predicts the number of people in a target social group, and the point head indicates group members by localizing the centers of group members' bounding boxes. This design enables our method to identify group members with simple point matching during inference as described in Sect. 3.3. The predictions of activity class probabilities $\{\hat{v}_i \mid \hat{v}_i \in [0,1]^{N_v}\}_{i=1}^{N_q}$, group sizes $\{\hat{s}_i \mid \hat{s}_i \in [0,1]\}_{i=1}^{N_q}$, and sequences of group member points $\{\hat{U}_i\}_{i=1}^{N_q}$ are obtained as $\hat{v}_i = f_v(h_i)$, $\hat{s}_i = f_s(h_i)$, and $\hat{U}_i = f_u(h_i, r_i)$, where N_v is the number of activity classes, $\hat{U}_i = (\hat{u}_j^{(i)} \mid \hat{u}_j^{(i)} \in [0,1]^2)_{j=1}^{M}$ is a sequence of points that indicate centers of group members' bounding boxes, M is a hyperparameter that defines the maximum group size, $f_v(\cdot)$, $f_s(\cdot)$, and $f_u(\cdot, \cdot)$ are the detection heads for each prediction, and $r_i \in [0,1]^2$ is a reference point, which is used in the same way as the localization in Deformable DETR [52]. The predicted group sizes are values normalized with M. All the detection heads are composed of FFNs with subsequent sigmoid functions. We describe the details of the detection heads in the supplementary material.

Individual recognition can be performed by replacing the group recognition heads with individual recognition heads. We empirically find that using different parameters of deformable transformers for individual recognition and social group recognition does not show performance improvement. Therefore, we use shared parameters to reduce computational costs. The details of the individual recognition heads are described in the supplementary material.

3.2   Loss Calculation

We view social group activity recognition as a direct set prediction problem and match predictions and ground truths with the Hungarian algorithm [23] during training following the training procedure of DETR [6]. The optimal assignment is determined by calculating the matching cost with the predicted activity class probabilities, group sizes, and group member points. Given a ground truth set of social group activity recognition, the set is first padded with $\phi^{(gr)}$ (no activity) to change the set size to N_q. With the padded ground truth set, the matching cost of the i-th element in the ground truth set and j-th element in the prediction set is calculated as follows:

$$\mathcal{H}_{i,j}^{(gr)} = \mathbb{1}_{\{i \notin \Phi^{(gr)}\}} \left[\eta_v \mathcal{H}_{i,j}^{(v)} + \eta_s \mathcal{H}_{i,j}^{(s)} + \eta_u \mathcal{H}_{i,j}^{(u)} \right], \tag{1}$$

$$\mathcal{H}_{i,j}^{(v)} = -\frac{\boldsymbol{v}_i^T \hat{\boldsymbol{v}}_j + (1 - \boldsymbol{v}_i)^T (1 - \hat{\boldsymbol{v}}_j)}{N_v}, \tag{2}$$

$$\mathcal{H}_{i,j}^{(s)} = |s_i - \hat{s}_j|, \tag{3}$$

$$\mathcal{H}_{i,j}^{(u)} = \frac{\sum_{k=1}^{S_i} \left\| \boldsymbol{u}_k^{(i)} - \hat{\boldsymbol{u}}_k^{(j)} \right\|_1}{S_i}, \tag{4}$$

where $\boldsymbol{\Phi}^{(gr)}$ is a set of ground-truth indices that correspond to $\phi^{(gr)}$, $\boldsymbol{v}_i \in \{0, 1\}^{N_v}$ is a ground truth activity label, $s_i \in [0, 1]$ is a ground truth group size normalized with M, S_i is an unnormalized ground truth group size, $\boldsymbol{u}_k^{(i)} \in [0, 1]^2$ is a ground truth group member point normalized with the image size, and $\eta_{\{v,s,u\}}$ are hyper-parameters. Group member points in the sequence $\boldsymbol{U}_i = (\boldsymbol{u}_k^{(i)})_{k=1}^{S_i}$ are sorted in ascending order along X coordinates as seen from the image of the group recognition result in Fig. 2. We use this arrangement because group members are typically seen side by side at the same vertical positions in an image, and the order of group member points is clear from their positions, which makes the prediction easy. We evaluate the performances with other arrangements and compare the results in Sect. 4.4. Using Hungarian algorithm, the optimal assignment is calculated as $\hat{\omega}^{(gr)} = \arg\min_{\omega \in \Omega_{N_q}} \sum_{i=1}^{N_q} \mathcal{H}_{i,\omega(i)}^{(gr)}$, where Ω_{N_q} is the set of all possible permutations of N_q elements.

The training loss for social group activity recognition $\mathcal{L}_{gr}$ is calculated between matched ground truths and predictions as follows:

$$\mathcal{L}_{gr} = \lambda_v \mathcal{L}_v + \lambda_s \mathcal{L}_s + \lambda_u \mathcal{L}_u, \tag{5}$$

$$\mathcal{L}_v = \frac{1}{|\boldsymbol{\Phi}^{(gr)}|} \sum_{i=1}^{N_q} \left[\mathbb{1}_{\{i \notin \Phi^{(gr)}\}} l_f \left(\boldsymbol{v}_i, \hat{\boldsymbol{v}}_{\hat{\omega}^{(gr)}(i)} \right) + \mathbb{1}_{\{i \in \Phi^{(gr)}\}} l_f \left(\boldsymbol{0}, \hat{\boldsymbol{v}}_{\hat{\omega}^{(gr)}(i)} \right) \right], \tag{6}$$

$$\mathcal{L}_s = \frac{1}{|\boldsymbol{\Phi}^{(gr)}|} \sum_{i=1}^{N_q} \mathbb{1}_{\{i \notin \Phi^{(gr)}\}} \left| s_i - \hat{s}_{\hat{\omega}^{(gr)}(i)} \right|, \tag{7}$$

$$\mathcal{L}_u = \frac{1}{|\boldsymbol{\Phi}^{(gr)}|} \sum_{i=1}^{N_q} \sum_{j=1}^{S_i} \mathbb{1}_{\{i \notin \Phi^{(gr)}\}} \left\| \boldsymbol{u}_j^{(i)} - \hat{\boldsymbol{u}}_j^{(\hat{\omega}^{(gr)}(i))} \right\|_1, \tag{8}$$

where $\lambda_{\{v,s,u\}}$ are hyper-parameters and $l_f(\cdot, \cdot)$ is the element-wise focal loss function [29] whose hyper-parameters are described in [51].

Individual recognition is jointly learned by matching ground truths and predictions of person class probabilities, bounding boxes, and action class probabilities and calculating the losses between matched ground truths and predictions. The matching and loss calculations are performed by slightly modifying the original matching costs and losses of Deformable DETR [52]. We describe the details of these matching and loss calculations in the supplementary material.

3.3   Group Member Identification

The outputs of the detection heads represent groups in group sizes and group member points that indicate the centers of group members' bounding boxes. These values have to be transformed into values that indicate individuals. We transform the predicted values into indices that refer to the elements in the individual prediction set with the following simple process during inference. To match the group member points and individual predictions, the Hungarian algorithm [23] is used instead of just calculating the closest center of a bounding box for each group member point. Hungarian algorithm can prevent multiple group member points from matching the same individuals and thus slightly improve the performance. The matching cost between i-th group member point of k-th social group prediction and j-th individual prediction is calculated as follows:

$$\mathcal{H}_{i,j}^{(gm,k)} = \frac{\left\| \hat{\boldsymbol{u}}_i^{(k)} - f_{cent}\left(\hat{\boldsymbol{b}}_j\right) \right\|_2}{\hat{c}_j}, \tag{9}$$

where $\hat{\boldsymbol{b}}_j \in [0,1]^4$ is a predicted bounding box of an individual, $\hat{c}_j \in [0,1]$ is a detection score of the individual, and $f_{cent}(\cdot)$ is a function that calculates the center of a bounding box. By applying the Hungarian algorithm to this matching cost, the optimal assignment is calculated as $\hat{\omega}^{(gm,k)} = \arg\min_{\omega \in \Omega_{N_q}} \sum_{i=1}^{\lceil M \times \hat{s}_k \rceil} \mathcal{H}_{i,\omega(i)}^{(gm,k)}$, where $\lceil \cdot \rceil$ rounds an input value to the nearest integer. Finally, the index set of individuals for k-th social group prediction is obtained as $\boldsymbol{G}_k = \{\hat{\omega}^{(gm,k)}(i)\}_{i=1}^{\lceil M \times \hat{s}_k \rceil}$.

4   Experiments

4.1   Datasets and Evaluation Metrics

We evaluate the performance of our method on two publicly available benchmark datasets: the Volleyball dataset [19] and Collective Activity dataset [9]. The Volleyball dataset contains 4,830 videos of 55 volleyball matches, which are split into 3,493 training videos and 1,337 test videos. The center frame of each video is annotated with bounding boxes, actions, and one group activity. The number of action and activity classes are 9 and 8, respectively. Because the original annotations do not contain group member information, we use an extra annotation set provided by Sendo and Ukita [36]. We combine the original annotations with the group annotations in the extra set and use them for our experiments. Note that annotations other than the group annotations in the extra set are not used for a fair comparison. The Collective Activity dataset contains 44 videos of life scenes, which are split into 32 training videos and 12 test videos. The videos are annotated every ten frames with bounding boxes and actions. The group activity is defined as the action with the largest number in the scenes. The number of action classes is 6. Because the original annotations do not have group member information, Ehsanpour et al. [13] annotated group labels. We use their annotations for our experiments.

We divide the evaluation into two parts: group activity recognition and social group activity recognition. In the evaluation of group activity recognition, we follow the detection-based settings [5,13,35,44] and use classification accuracy as an evaluation metric. Because our method is designed to predict multiple group activities, we need to select one from them for group activity recognition. We choose the predicted activity of the highest probability and compare it with the ground truth activity. In the evaluation of social group activity recognition, different metrics are used for each dataset because each scene in the Volleyball dataset contains only one social group activity, while that in the Collective Activity dataset contains multiple social group activities. For the Volleyball dataset, group identification accuracy is used as an evaluation metric. One group prediction is first selected in the same way as group activity recognition, and then the predicted bounding boxes of the group members are compared with the ground truth boxes. The selected prediction results are correct if the predicted activity is correct and the predicted boxes have IoUs larger than 0.5 with the corresponding ground truth boxes. For the Collective Activity dataset, mAP is used as an evaluation metric. Prediction results are judged as true positives if the predicted activities are correct, and all the predicted boxes of the group members have IoUs larger than 0.5 with the corresponding ground truth boxes.

4.2   Implementation Details

We use the RGB stream of I3D [7] as a backbone feature extractor and input features from *Mixed_3c*, *Mixed_4f*, and *Mixed_5c* layers into the deformable transformers. The hyper-parameters of the deformable transformers are set in accordance with the setting of Deformable DETR [52], where $L_f = 3$, $D_p = 256$, and $N_q = 300$. We initialize I3D with the parameters trained on the Kinetics dataset [20] and deformable transformers with the parameters trained on the COCO dataset [30]. We use the AdamW [31] optimizer with the batch size of 16, the initial learning rate of 10^{-4}, and the weight decay of 10^{-4}. Training epochs are set to 120, and the learning rate is decayed after 100 epochs. We set the length of the sequence T to 9. Ground truth labels of the center frame are used to calculate the losses. To augment the training data, we randomly shift frames in the temporal direction and use bounding boxes from visual trackers as ground truth boxes when a non-annotated frame is at the center. We also augment the training data by random horizontal flipping, scaling, and cropping. Following the DETR's training [6], auxiliary losses are used to boost the performance. The maximum group size M is set to 12. The hyper-parameters are set as $\eta_v = \lambda_v = 2$, $\eta_s = \lambda_s = 1$, and $\eta_u = \lambda_u = 5$.

While evaluating performances with the Collective Activity dataset, some specific settings are used. For the evaluation of group activity recognition, training epochs are set to 10, and the learning rate is decayed after 5 epochs because the losses converge in a few epochs due to the limited diversity of the scenes in the dataset. For the evaluation of social group activity recognition, the length of the sequence T is set to 17 following the setting of Ehsanpour *et al.* [13].

4.3   Group Activity Recognition

Comparison Against State-of-the-Art. We compare our method against state-of-the-art methods on group activity recognition. Table 1 shows the comparison results. The values without the brackets demonstrate the detection-based performances, while those inside the brackets indicate the performances with ground truth bounding boxes. We show the performances of individual action recognition for future reference. Several detection-based performances are not reported because existing works typically use ground-truth boxes for the evaluation. To compare the effectiveness of our method with these methods, we evaluate GroupFormer [27], which is the strongest baseline of group activity recognition, with predicted boxes of Deformable DETR [52]. Note that Deformable DETR is fine-tuned on each dataset for a fair comparison, which demonstrates 90.8 and 90.2 mAP on the Volleyball and Collective Activity datasets, respectively.

Table 1. Comparison of group activity recognition. The values w/ and w/o the brackets show the performances in the ground-truth-based and detection-based settings, respectively. Full comparison results are in the supplementary material.

Method	Volleyball				Collective activity			
	Activity		Action		Activity		Action	
SSU [5]	86.2	(90.6)	–	(81.8)	–	(–)	–	(–)
stagNet [35]	87.6	(89.3)	–	(–)	87.9	(89.1)	–	(–)
ARG [44]	91.5	(92.5)	39.8	(83.0)	86.1	(88.1)	49.6	(77.3)
CRM [4]	–	(93.0)	–	(–)	–	(85.8)	–	(–)
Actor-Transformers [14]	–	(94.4)	–	(85.9)	–	(92.8)	–	(–)
Ehsanpour *et al.* [13]	93.0	(93.1)	41.8	(83.3)	89.4	(89.4)	55.9	(78.3)
Pramono *et al.* [34]	–	(95.0)	–	(83.1)	–	(95.2)	–	(–)
P^2CTDM [45]	–	(92.7)	–	(–)	–	(96.1)	–	(–)
DIN [49]	–	(93.6)	–	(–)	–	(95.9)	–	(–)
GroupFormer [27]	95.0*	(95.7)	–	(85.6)	85.2*	(87.5[†] /96.3)	–	(–)
Ours	**96.0**	(–)	**65.0**	(–)	**96.5**	(–)	**64.9**	(–)

* We evaluated the performance with the publicly available source codes.
[†] We evaluated but were not able to reproduce the reported accuracy because the configuration file for the Collective Activity dataset is not publicly available.

As seen from the table, our method outperforms state-of-the-art methods in the detection-based setting. We confirm that GroupFormer shows the performance degradation as well as the previous methods [5,13,35,44] when predicted bounding boxes are used. These results indicate that the latest region-feature-based method still suffers from incomplete person localization and that our feature generation has advantages over these methods. Even compared to the ground-truth-based performances, our method shows the best performance. It is worth noting that our method uses only RGB images as inputs, while Group-Former utilizes optical flows and poses in addition to RGB data. These results suggest that our features are more effective than region features and that it is not optimal to restrict regions of features to bounding boxes (Table 2).

Analysis of Group Annotations. As described in Sect. 4.1, we use the additional group annotations to fully leverage our social group activity recognition capability. We analyze the effect of the group annotations on group activity recognition by investigating the performances of both GroupFormer [27] and our method with and without the group annotations. Note that hereinafter we use the Volleyball dataset for analyses because the diversity of the scenes in the Collective Activity dataset is limited. To evaluate GroupFormer with the group annotations in the detection-based setting, we trained Deformable DETR [52] with bounding boxes of only group members, which is intended to detect only people involved in activities. The detector shows the performance of 87.1 mAP. Among all the results, GroupFormer with the group annotations in the ground-truth-based setting demonstrates the best performance. However, the performance is substantially degraded when the predicted boxes are used. This is probably because group member detection underperforms and degrades the recognition performance. As our method does not rely on bounding boxes to predict group activities, the performance does not degrade even if group members cannot be identified correctly. Accordingly, our method demonstrates the best performance in the detection-based setting.

Table 2. Analysis of the effect of the group annotations with Volleyball. The values w/ and w/o the brackets demonstrate the performances in the ground-truth-based and detection-based settings, respectively.

Method	Annotation type	Activity	
GroupFormer [27]	Original	95.0^*	(95.7)
	Group	$93.2^‡$	(96.1^*)
Ours	Original	95.0	(–)
	Group	**96.0**	(–)

*We evaluated the performance with the publicly available source codes.
‡ We trained a group member detector and evaluated the performance with publicly available source codes.

4.4 Social Group Activity Recognition

Comparison Against State-of-the-Art. To demonstrate the effectiveness, we compare our method against Ehsanpour et al.'s method [13], which is a state-of-the-art method that tackles social group activity recognition, and Group-Former [27], which is the strongest baseline on group activity recognition. Due to the unavailability of both Ehsanpour *et al.*'s source codes and their performance report on the Volleyball dataset, we implemented their algorithm based on our best understanding and evaluated the performance on the dataset. To detect group members in the evaluation of GroupFormer, we trained Deformable DETR [52] as described in the group annotation analysis section. Because this group member detection cannot be applied to multi-group detection, we evaluate GroupFormer only on the Volleyball dataset.

Table 3 shows the results of the Volleyball dataset. As shown in the table, our method yields significant performance gains over the other methods, which demonstrates the improvement in group member identification as well as in activity recognition. Our method aggregates features that are embedded with clues for grouping people from feature maps. It is highly likely that this feature aggregation contributes to the high accuracy of identifying activities with different distributions of group members in an image. We qualitatively analyze how features are aggregated depending on the distribution of group members and discuss the analysis results towards the end of the qualitative analysis section.

Table 3. Comparison of social group activity recognition with Volleyball.

Method	Accuracy	Right				Left			
		Set	Spike	Pass	Winpoint	Set	Spike	Pass	Winpoint
Ehsanpour *et al.* [13][§]	44.5	17.2	**74.0**	49.0	29.9	19.7	**79.6**	25.0	28.4
GroupFormer [27][‡]	48.8	25.0	56.6	59.0	**51.7**	31.5	55.3	58.8	51.0
Ours	**60.6**	**35.9**	68.2	**81.9**	50.6	**50.6**	53.6	**74.3**	**56.9**

[§] Because the source codes are not publicly available, we implemented their algorithm based on our best understanding and evaluated the performance.
[‡] We trained a group member detector and evaluated the performance with publicly available source codes.

Table 4. Comparison of social group activity recognition with Collective Act.

Method	mAP	Crossing	Waiting	Queueing	Walking	Talking
Ehsanpour *et al.* [13]	**51.3**	–	–	–	–	–
Ours	46.0	49.2	64.5	54.1	55.6	6.56

The comparison results on the Collective Activity dataset are listed in Table 4. As seen from the table, Ehsanpour*et al.*'s method shows better performance than our method. We find that our method demonstrates relatively low performance on the activity "Talking". This low performance is probably attributed to the number of samples in the training data. In the test data, 86% of the samples with the activity "Talking" have group sizes of four, while the training data has only 57 samples whose group sizes are four, which is 0.8% of the training data. As our method learns to predict group sizes, the number of samples in training data for each group size affects the performance. We analyze this effect in the subsequent section.

Analysis of Group Sizes. The group size prediction is one of the key factors to identify group members and thus affects social group activity recognition performance. To analyze this effect, we evaluate the performance of each group size and compare the results with Ehsanpour *et al.*'s method [13] and GroupFormer [27]. Table 5 shows the results. As shown in the table, the performances of our method are moderately correlated to the training data ratios, while the other two methods do not show the correlation. This is the drawback of our method that relies on group-size learning. However, our method shows competitive performances in both small and large group sizes if there are a certain amount of training data. In contrast, each of the other two methods shows competitive performances only in either large or small group sizes. These results imply that our method does not have the performance dependence on group sizes and thus can achieve high performance with large-scale training data.

Table 5. Analysis of group sizes with Volleyball.

Method	Group size (training data ratio)					
	1 (36%)	2 (21%)	3 (19%)	4 (6%)	5 (5%)	6 (12%)
Ehsanpour *et al.* [13]§	45.3	**48.2**	**61.2**	27.3	15.8	32.5
GroupFormer [27]‡	57.3	29.6	58.4	**28.4**	**44.7**	54.4
Ours	**83.6**	42.9	52.4	26.1	39.5	**63.8**

§ Because the source codes are not publicly available, we implemented their algorithm based on our best understanding and evaluated the performance.
‡ We trained a group member detector and evaluated the performance with publicly available source codes.

Table 6. Analysis of the order of member points with Volleyball.

Order of the group member points	Probability of changes in order	Accuracy
Ascending order in X coordinates	7.4%	**60.6**
Ascending order in Y coordinates	13%	55.5

Analysis of Group Member Point Order. As described in Sect. 3.2, group member points in a ground truth point sequence are sorted in ascending order along X coordinates. To confirm the effectiveness of this arrangement, we compare the performances with two arrangements. Table 6 shows the comparison results. As shown in the table, our method demonstrates better performance when group member points are sorted in ascending order along X coordinates than in ascending order along Y coordinates. The probabilities in the table indicate the ratio of the changes in the point order when small perturbations are added to ground-truth bounding box positions. The higher probability implies that the order of group member points changes more frequently when group members move. These results suggest that the order changes more frequently when group member points are sorted in ascending order along Y coordinates and that the order is difficult to predict with slight differences in box positions.

Qualitative Analysis. The deformable attention modules are the critical components to aggregate features relevant to social group activity recognition and generate social group features. To analyze how the attention modules aggregate features for various social group activities, we visualize the attention locations of the transformer decoder in Fig. 3. We show locations with the top four attention weights in the last layer of the decoder. The purple bounding boxes show the group members, the red circles show the predicted group member points, and the yellow circles show the attention locations. The small and large yellow circles mean that the locations are in the high and low-resolution feature maps, respectively, showing a rough range of image areas affecting the generated features. The figure shows that features are typically aggregated from low-resolution feature maps if group members are located in broad areas, and vice versa. These results indicate that the attention modules can effectively aggregate features depending on the distribution of group members and contribute to improving the performance of social group activity recognition.

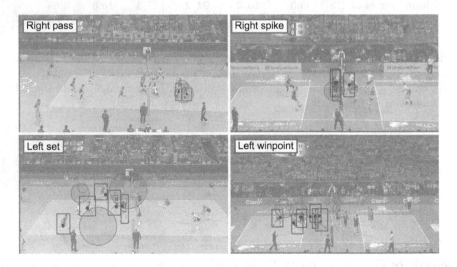

Fig. 3. Visualization of the attention locations in the deformable transformer decoder. We show the locations of the top four attention weights. The large circles mean that the locations are in the low-resolution feature maps.

5   Conclusions

We propose a novel social group activity recognition method that leverages deformable transformers to generate effective social group features. This feature generation obviates the need for region features and hence makes the effectiveness of the social group features person-localization-agnostic. Furthermore, the group member information extracted from the features is represented so concisely that our method can identify group members with simple Hungarian matching, resulting in high-performance social group activity recognition. We perform extensive experiments and show significant improvement over existing methods.

Acknowledgement. Computational resource of AI Bridging Cloud Infrastructure (ABCI) provided by National Institute of Advanced Industrial Science and Technology was used.

References

1. Amer, M.R., Lei, P., Todorovic, S.: HiRF: hierarchical random field for collective activity recognition in videos. In: Fleet, D., Pajdla, T., Schiele, B., Tuytelaars, T. (eds.) ECCV 2014. LNCS, vol. 8694, pp. 572–585. Springer, Cham (2014). https://doi.org/10.1007/978-3-319-10599-4_37
2. Amer, M.R., Todorovic, S.: Sum product networks for activity recognition. IEEE TPAMI **38**(4), 800–813 (2016)
3. Amer, M.R., Todorovic, S., Fern, A., Zhu, S.C.: Monte Carlo tree search for scheduling activity recognition. In: ICCV, December 2013
4. Azar, S.M., Atigh, M.G., Nickabadi, A., Alahi, A.: Convolutional relational machine for group activity recognition. In: CVPR, June 2019
5. Bagautdinov, T.M., Alahi, A., Fleuret, F., Fua, P.V., Savarese, S.: Social scene understanding: end-to-end multi-person action localization and collective activity recognition. In: CVPR, July 2017
6. Carion, N., Massa, F., Synnaeve, G., Usunier, N., Kirillov, A., Zagoruyko, S.: End-to-end object detection with transformers. In: Vedaldi, A., Bischof, H., Brox, T., Frahm, J.-M. (eds.) ECCV 2020. LNCS, vol. 12346, pp. 213–229. Springer, Cham (2020). https://doi.org/10.1007/978-3-030-58452-8_13
7. Carreira, J., Zisserman, A.: Quo vadis, action recognition? A new model and the kinetics dataset. In: CVPR, July 2017
8. Cho, K., et al.: Learning phrase representations using RNN encoder-decoder for statistical machine translation. In: EMNLP, October 2014
9. Choi, W., Shahid, K., Savarese, S.: What are they doing?: collective activity classification using spatio-temporal relationship among people. In: ICCVW, September 2009
10. Dai, J., et al.: Deformable convolutional networks. In: ICCV, October 2017
11. Dai, X., Chen, Y., Yang, J., Zhang, P., Yuan, L., Zhang, L.: Dynamic DETR: end-to-end object detection with dynamic attention. In: ICCV, October 2021
12. Deng, Z., Vahdat, A., Hu, H., Mori, G.: Structure inference machines: recurrent neural networks for analyzing relations in group activity recognition. In: CVPR, June 2016
13. Ehsanpour, M., Abedin, A., Saleh, F., Shi, J., Reid, I., Rezatofighi, H.: Joint learning of social groups, individuals action and sub-group activities in videos. In: Vedaldi, A., Bischof, H., Brox, T., Frahm, J.-M. (eds.) ECCV 2020. LNCS, vol. 12354, pp. 177–195. Springer, Cham (2020). https://doi.org/10.1007/978-3-030-58545-7_11
14. Gavrilyuk, K., Sanford, R., Javan, M., Snoek, C.G.M.: Actor-transformers for group activity recognition. In: CVPR, June 2020

15. Ge, W., Collins, R.T., Ruback, R.B.: Vision-based analysis of small groups in pedestrian crowds. IEEE TPAMI **34**(5), 1003–1016 (2012)
16. Hochreiter, S., Schmidhuber, J.: Long short-term memory. Neural Comput. **9**(8), 1735–1780 (1997)
17. Hu, G., Cui, B., He, Y., Yu, S.: Progressive relation learning for group activity recognition. In: CVPR, June 2020
18. Ibrahim, M.S., Mori, G.: Hierarchical relational networks for group activity recognition and retrieval. In: ECCV, September 2018
19. Ibrahim, M.S., Muralidharan, S., Deng, Z., Vahdat, A., Mori, G.: A hierarchical deep temporal model for group activity recognition. In: CVPR, June 2016
20. Kay, W., et al.: The kinetics human action video dataset, May 2017. arXiv:1705.06950
21. Kipf, T.N., Welling, M.: Semi-supervised classification with graph convolutional networks. In: ICLR, April 2017
22. Kong, L., Qin, J., Huang, D., Wang, Y., Gool, L.V.: Hierarchical attention and context modeling for group activity recognition. In: ICASSP, April 2018
23. Kuhn, H.W., Yaw, B.: The Hungarian method for the assignment problem. Naval Res. Logist. Q. **2**, 83–97 (1955)
24. Lan, T., Sigal, L., Mori, G.: Social roles in hierarchical models for human activity recognition. In: CVPR, June 2012
25. Lan, T., Wang, Y., Yang, W., Mori, G.: Beyond actions: discriminative models for contextual group activities. In: NIPS, December 2010
26. Lan, T., Wang, Y., Yang, W., Robinovitch, S.N., Mori, G.: Discriminative latent models for recognizing contextual group activities. IEEE TPAMI **34**(8), 1549–1562 (2012)
27. Li, S., et al.: GroupFormer: group activity recognition with clustered spatial-temporal transformer. In: ICCV, October 2021
28. Li, X., Chuah, M.C.: SBGAR: semantics based group activity recognition. In: ICCV, October 2017
29. Lin, T.Y., Goyal, P., Girshick, R., He, K., Dollár, P.: Focal loss for dense object detection. In: ICCV, October 2017
30. Lin, T.-Y., et al.: Microsoft COCO: common objects in context. In: Fleet, D., Pajdla, T., Schiele, B., Tuytelaars, T. (eds.) ECCV 2014. LNCS, vol. 8693, pp. 740–755. Springer, Cham (2014). https://doi.org/10.1007/978-3-319-10602-1_48
31. Loshchilov, I., Hutter, F.: Decoupled weight decay regularization. In: ICLR, May 2019
32. Ng, A., Jordan, M., Weiss, Y.: On spectral clustering: analysis and an algorithm. In: NIPS, December 2002
33. Park, H., Shi, J.: Social saliency prediction. In: CVPR, June 2015
34. Pramono, R.R.A., Chen, Y.T., Fang, W.H.: Empowering relational network by self-attention augmented conditional random fields for group activity recognition. In: Vedaldi, A., Bischof, H., Brox, T., Frahm, J.-M. (eds.) ECCV 2020. LNCS, vol. 12346, pp. 71–90. Springer, Cham (2020). https://doi.org/10.1007/978-3-030-58452-8_5
35. Qi, M., Qin, J., Li, A., Wang, Y., Luo, J., Gool, L.V.: stagNet: an attentive semantic RNN for group activity recognition. In: ECCV, September 2018
36. Sendo, K., Ukita, N.: Heatmapping of people involved in group activities. In: MVA, May 2019
37. Shu, T., Todorovic, S., Zhu, S.C.: CERN: confidence-energy recurrent network for group activity recognition. In: CVPR, July 2017

38. Shu, T., Xie, D., Rothrock, B., Todorovic, S., Zhu, S.: Joint inference of groups, events and human roles in aerial videos. In: CVPR, June 2015
39. Sun, Z., Cao, S., Yang, Y., Kitani, K.M.: Rethinking transformer-based set prediction for object detection. In: ICCV, October 2021
40. Tang, J., Shu, X., Yan, R., Zhang, L.: Coherence constrained graph LSTM for group activity recognition. IEEE TPAMI **44**(2), 636–647 (2022)
41. Vaswani, A., et al.: Attention is all you need. In: NIPS, December 2017
42. Veličković, P., Cucurull, G., Casanova, A., Romero, A., Lió, P., Bengio, Y.: Graph attention networks. In: ICLR, April 2018
43. Wang, M., Ni, B., Yang, X.: Recurrent modeling of interaction context for collective activity recognition. In: CVPR, July 2017
44. Wu, J., Wang, L., Wang, L., Guo, J., Wu, G.: Learning actor relation graphs for group activity recognition. In: CVPR, June 2019
45. Yan, R., Shu, X., Yuan, C., Tian, Q., Tang, J.: Position-aware participation-contributed temporal dynamic model for group activity recognition. IEEE TNNLS (2021)
46. Yan, R., Tang, J., Shu, X., Li, Z., Tian, Q.: Participation-contributed temporal dynamic model for group activity recognition. In: ACMMM, October 2018
47. Yan, R., Xie, L., Tang, J., Shu, X., Tian, Q.: HiGCIN: hierarchical graph-based cross inference network for group activity recognition. IEEE TPAMI (2020)
48. Yan, R., Xie, L., Tang, J., Shu, X., Tian, Q.: Social adaptive module for weakly-supervised group activity recognition. In: Vedaldi, A., Bischof, H., Brox, T., Frahm, J.-M. (eds.) ECCV 2020. LNCS, vol. 12353, pp. 208–224. Springer, Cham (2020). https://doi.org/10.1007/978-3-030-58598-3_13
49. Yuan, H., Ni, D., Wang, M.: Spatio-temporal dynamic inference network for group activity recognition. In: ICCV, October 2021
50. Zhou, H., et al.: COMPOSER: compositional learning of group activity in videos, December 2021. arXiv:2112.05892
51. Zhou, X., Wang, D., Krähenbühl, P.: Objects as points, April 2019. arXiv:1904.07850
52. Zhu, X., Su, W., Lu, L., Li, B., Wang, X., Dai, J.: Deformable DETR: deformable transformers for end-to-end object detection. In: ICLR, May 2021

Contrastive Positive Mining for Unsupervised 3D Action Representation Learning

Haoyuan Zhang[1]($\boxtimes$) , Yonghong Hou[1] , Wenjing Zhang[1] ,
and Wanqing Li[2]

[1] School of Electrical and Information Engineering, Tianjin University,
Tianjin, China
{zhy0860,houroy,zwj759}@tju.edu.cn
[2] Advanced Multimedia Research Lab, University of Wollongong,
Wollongong, Australia
wanqing@uow.edu.au

Abstract. Recent contrastive based 3D action representation learning has made great progress. However, the strict positive/negative constraint is yet to be relaxed and the use of non-self positive is yet to be explored. In this paper, a Contrastive Positive Mining (CPM) framework is proposed for unsupervised skeleton 3D action representation learning. The CPM identifies non-self positives in a contextual queue to boost learning. Specifically, the siamese encoders are adopted and trained to match the similarity distributions of the augmented instances in reference to all instances in the contextual queue. By identifying the non-self positive instances in the queue, a positive-enhanced learning strategy is proposed to leverage the knowledge of mined positives to boost the robustness of the learned latent space against intra-class and inter-class diversity. Experimental results have shown that the proposed CPM is effective and outperforms the existing state-of-the-art unsupervised methods on the challenging NTU and PKU-MMD datasets.

Keywords: Unsupervised learning · 3D action representation · Skeleton · Positive mining

1 Introduction

Human action recognition is an active research in recent years. Due to being light-weight, privacy-preserving and robust against complex conditions [2,26–28], 3D skeleton is becoming a popular modality for capturing human action dynamics [10,31,39,43]. Majority of previous skeleton-based action recognition approaches [18,35,38,42] are developed with a fully-supervised manner. However, in order to learn a good action representation, supervised methods require a huge number of labeled skeleton samples which is expensive and difficult to

© The Author(s), under exclusive license to Springer Nature Switzerland AG 2022
S. Avidan et al. (Eds.): ECCV 2022, LNCS 13664, pp. 36–51, 2022.
https://doi.org/10.1007/978-3-031-19772-7_3

obtain. It impels the exploration of learning skeleton-based action representation in an unsupervised manner [14,15,24,30]. Often unsupervised methods use pretext tasks to generate the supervision signals, such as reconstruction [7,44], auto-regression [12,30] and jigsaw puzzles [22,36]. Consequently, the learning highly relies on the quality of the designed pretext tasks, and those tasks are hard to be generalized for different downstream tasks. Recent unsupervised methods employ advanced contrastive learning [14,15,24] for instance discrimination in a latent space and have achieved promising results.

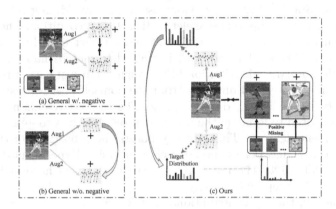

Fig. 1. Illustrations about the proposed CPM and previous contrastive methods. (a) contrastive learning methods with negative [15,24]. (b) contrastive learning methods without negative [4,6]. (c) the proposed Contrastive Positive Mining (CPM) method.

Although contrastive methods can improve the learning of skeleton representation, there are several issues, as illustrated in Fig. 1, in the current methods. Figure 1(a) shows that the conventional contrastive learning methods require negatives [15,24]. They only regard different augmentations of the same instance as positives to be drawn close during the learning, while other instances in the queue, usually formed by training samples in the previous round of epochs or batches, are all regarded as negatives and pushed apart from the current instance. Although these methods consider the correlation of current instance with others, there are inevitably instances in queue that belong to the same category as the current instance (marked with red rectangular box) and these instances are mistaken as negatives, which could degrade the learned representation. To address this issue, as shown in Fig. 1(c), this paper proposes to search for the instances in queue that are likely to be the same class of the current instance, then to consider those instances as non-self positives (marked with green rectangular box) and draw them close to current instance so as to improve the learning.

Figure 1(b) shows the conventional contrastive learning methods without negatives [4,6]. The positive setting is similar to the previous methods illustrated in Fig. 1(a). Only different augmentations of individual instance are used as positive, consistency among current instance and the non-self instances with the same class are ignored during learning, limiting the representation ability for intra-class diversity. Besides, although non-negative manner avoids the instances of same class being pushed apart, the correlation of different instances are not considered.

Notice that contrastive objective of both methods (i.e. with or without negatives) is on individual instances, which challenges learning a feature space for all instances. To overcome the above shortcomings, as illustrated in Fig. 1(c), the proposed method extends the contrastive objective from individual instances by keeping a queue of instances and mining the non-self positives in the queue to boost learning. Specifically, a novel Contrastive Positive Mining (CPM) framework is proposed for unsupervised skeleton 3D action recognition. The proposed CPM is a siamese structure with a student and a target branch, which follows the SimSiam [4]. The student network is trained to match the target network in terms of the similarity distribution of the augmented instance in reference to all instances in a contextual queue, so that the non-self positive instances with high similarity can be identified in the queue. Then a positive-enhanced learning strategy is proposed to leverage the mined non-self positives to guide the learning of the student network. This strategy boosts the robustness of the learned latent space against intra-class and inter-class diversity. Experimental results on NTU-60 [25], NTU-120 [17] and PKU-MMD [16] datasets have validated the effectiveness of the proposed strategy.

To summarize, the key contributions include:

– A novel Contrastive Positive Mining (CPM) framework for unsupervised learning of skeleton representation for 3D action recognition.
– A simple but effective non-self positive mining scheme to identify the positives in a contextual queue.
– A novel positive-enhanced leaning strategy to guide the learning of the student network via the target network.
– Extensive evaluation of the CPM on the widely used datasets, NTU and PKU-MMD, with state-of-the-art results obtained.

2   Related Works

2.1   Unsupervised Contrastive Learning

Contrastive learning is derived from noise-contrastive estimation [8], which contrasts different type of noises to estimate the latent distribution. It has been extended in different ways for unsupervised learning. Contrastive Prediction Coding (CPC) [23] develops the info-NCE to learn image representation, with an auto-regressive model used to predict future in latent space. Contrastive Multiview Coding (CMC) [34] leverages multi-view as positive samples, so that the information shared between multiple views can be captured by the learned representation. However, there often lacks of negative instances for the above methods. To solve this issue, a scheme called memory-bank [37] is developed in which the previous random representations are stored as negative instances, and each of them are regarded as an independent class. Recently, MoCo [9] utilizes a dynamic dictionary to improve the memory-bank, and introduces the momentum updated encoder to boost the representation learning. Another way to enrich the negative instances is to use large batch-size such as in SimCLR [3]. Particularly, SimCLR samples negatives from a large batch and shows that different augmentation, large batch size, and nonlinear projection head are all important for effective contrastive learning. However, these methods all regard different augmentations of the same instance as the only positives, while other instances in the queue including the ones with same category are all considered as negatives which cannot fully leverage capability of contrastive learning due to highly likely mixture of positives in the negatives.

To deal with this issue, some negative-sample-free approaches are recently developed. SimSiam [4] shows that simple siamese twin networks with a stop-gradient operation to prevent collapsing can learn a meaningful representation. Barlow Twins [41] proposes an unsupervised objective function by measuring the cross-correlation matrix between the outputs of two identical networks. BYOL [6] learns a potentially enhanced representation from an online network by predicting the representation from a given representation learned from a target network with slow updating. However, these methods do not consider consistency learning among current instances and the non-self instances with the same class.

2.2 Unsupervised 3D Action Recognition

Unsupervised methods [13,20,29] for video based action recognition are well developed, while few works are specifically for skeletons. LongT GAN (Generative adversarial network) [44] is an auto-encoder-based GAN for skeleton sequence reconstruction. P&C [30] employs an encoder-decoder learning structure, the encoder is weakened compared with decoder to learn more representative features. ASCAL [24] is a momentum LSTM with a dynamic updated memory-bank, augmented instances of the input skeleton sequence are contrasted to learn representation. MS^{2}L [15] is a multi-task learning framework, with both pretext tasks and contrastive learning. CrosSCLR [14] adopts a cross-view contrastive learning scheme and leverages multi-view complementary supervision signal. However, these methods either require pretext tasks or a large amount of negative samples, or rely on the reconstruction.

3 Proposed Method

3.1 Overview

Figure 2 shows the basic framework of CPM. CPM adopts siamese twin networks as inspired by SimSiam [4]. 3D skeleton sequences are randomly augmented. Assume that a skeleton sequence s has T frames, V joints, and C coordinate channels, which can be represented as $s \in \mathrm{R}^{C \times T \times V}$. To augment s into different versions x and x', a skeleton-specific augmentation strategy is needed. Different from the augmentations implemented for images, augmentation of skeleton

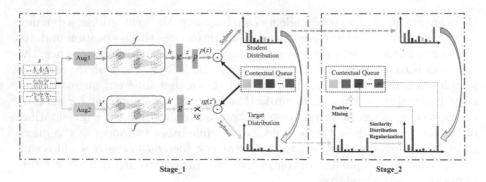

Fig. 2. Overview of the CPM framework. CPM includes two stages. In the first stage, the student branch is trained to predict the inter-skeleton similarity distribution inferred by the target network, so as to excavate non-self positive. Then in the second stage the information of mined positives is injected into the target branch through similarity distribution regularization to guide the learning of student, which achieves positive-enhanced learning (different colors in distribution and contextual queue represent the embeddings of different instances, '+' means mined positive).

sequences needs to be effective for learning spatial-temporal dynamics. In this paper, shear and crop in the spatial and temporal domain are to augment samples. Specifically, shear is applied as a spatial augmentation and is implemented as a linear transformation that displaces the skeleton joint in a fixed direction. Skeleton sequences are multiplied by a transformation matrix on the channel dimension, so as to slant the shape of 3D coordinates from body joints at a random angle. Crop is to pad a number of frames to a sequence symmetrically, then the sequence is randomly cropped into a fixed length [14,24].

The siamese encoders with identical network structure are to encode the augmented skeleton sequences, as shown in Fig. 2, in a latent feature space. One branch is referred to as the student and the other serves as the target [32]. ST-GCN [39] is adopted as the encoder networks. The siamese encoders consist of several GCN layers and embed the two augmented skeleton sequences x and x' into a latent space. In each layer, human pose in spatial-dimension and joint's motion in temporal-dimension are alternatively encoded, i.e. a spatial graph convolution is followed by a temporal convolution.

After the siamese encoders, a projection MLP g is attached to project the vector h and h' in the encoding space: $z = g(h)$, $z' = g(h')$, where z and z' are assumed to be mean-centered along the batch dimension so that each unit has 0 mean output over the batch. The projection MLP consists of two layers, the first one is followed by a batch normalization layer and rectified linear units. After the projection MLP, a prediction MLP p with same architecture of g is attached to the student branch to produce the prediction $p(z)$, while the stop-gradient operation is used in the target branch with the output $sg(z')$. In addition, a "first-in first-out" [9] contextual queue $Q = [a_1, ..., a_N]$ is used to measure how well the encoded augmented instance by student network matches that by the target network with respect to the instances in the queue.

The key idea of the proposed method is to use the output of the student network to predict the output of the target network. More specifically, our objective is to train the siamese encoders such that the student network matches the target network in terms of the similarity distribution of the augmented instance in reference to all instances in the queue.

3.2 Similarity Distribution and Positive Mining

Similarity between the encoded feature of the augmentations and the instances in queue is first calculated and similarity distribution for the student network and the target network are calculated through softmax. The learning process is to train the network so that the similarity distribution of x with respect to the instances in the queue can predict the distribution of x'. Compared with the previous methods, this strategy has the following advantages. No strict definition of positives/negatives is required and the match on similarity distribution over the instances in the queue is more reliable than that over individual instances. Since the similarity between the augmented instances and instances of the same class in the queue is expected to be high, resulting in an implicit mining of non-self positive instances in the queue.

Let $Q = [a_1, ..., a_N]$ be the queue of N instances, where a_i is the embedding of the i-th instance. The contextual queue comes from the preceding several batches of target network, which is updated in "first-in first-out" [9] strategy. Similarity distributions, d_i and d'_i, between $\bar{p}(z)$ and a_i and between $\bar{z}'$ and a_i are computed as follows, respectively,

$$d_i = \frac{e^{\bar{p}(z) \cdot a_i / \tau}}{\sum_{j=1}^{N} e^{\bar{p}(z) \cdot a_j / \tau}} \tag{1}$$

$$d'_i = \frac{e^{\bar{z}' \cdot a_i / \tau'}}{\sum_{j=1}^{N} e^{\bar{z}' \cdot a_j / \tau'}} \tag{2}$$

where $\bar{p}(z)$ and $\bar{z}'$ are l_2 normalization of $p(z)$ and z'. The overall similarity distributions, D and D' of the two arguments in the latent space with respect to the instances in the queue are,

$$D = \{d_i\}, D' = \{d'_i\}, i \in N \tag{3}$$

The idea is to training siamese encoders to match D with D'. In this paper, we adopt to minimize the Kullback-Leibler divergence between D and D', i.e.,

$$L = D_{KL}(D'||D) = H(D', D) - H(D') \tag{4}$$

By minimizing L, prediction $p(z)$ can be aligned with z'. Meanwhile, instances that belong to the same class could be pushed close in the latent space, while those from different classes are pushed apart.

The similarity measures provide information for mining the positive instance in the queue. Specifically, given one instance's embedding z and the corresponding queue Q, instances in queue with top-k high similarity are considered as positives, i.e.,

$$\Gamma(Q) = \text{Topk}(Q) \tag{5}$$

which generates the index set of positive instances,

$$D'_+ = \{d'_i\}, i \in N_+ \tag{6}$$

where N_+ is the index set of non-self positive instances. These positives can be used to facilitate a positive-enhanced learning as described below.

3.3 Positive-Enhanced Learning

The non-self positives can be used to boost the representation learning. Intuitively, it is reasonable to inject the information of mined positives into the target branch to guide the learning of the student encoder. To do this, it is proposed to regularize the similarity distribution of the target branch D' in each batch, so as to make use of the non-self positives iteratively. Specifically, we set the similarities of the K mined positive instances in target branch to 1, which means those instances are considered the same action category with current instance. This strategy is referred to as "positive-enhanced leaning". The positive-enhanced similarity distribution can be expressed as,

$$d_i^e = \begin{cases} \dfrac{e^{1/\tau'}}{\sum\limits_{j=1}^{N} e^{z' \cdot a_j / \tau'}} & , i \in N_+ \\ d'_i, \text{otherwise} \end{cases} \tag{7}$$

Then we train distribution of student to continue predicting the regularized target distribution, so that the student is guided to learn more informative intra-class diversity brought by the non-self skeleton positives knowledge we inject,

$$L' = H(D'_{NP}, D) - H(D'_{NP}) \tag{8}$$

where $D'_{NP} = \{d_i^e\}$ is the non-self positive-enhanced target distribution. Compared to Eq. (4), Eq. (8) intends to pull positive instances closer.

3.4 Learning of CPM

In the early training stage, the model is likely not stable and capable enough of providing reasonable measures of the similarity distribution to identify the positives in the queue. Therefore, a two-stage training strategy is adopted for CPM: the student branch is first trained to predict the similarity distribution inferred by the target network without enhanced positives in Eq. (4). When it is stable, the model is trained using the positive-enhanced learning strategy in Eq. (8).

4   Experiments

4.1   Datasets

NTU RGB+D 60 (NTU-60) Dataset [25]: NTU-60 is one of the widely used indoor-captured datasets for human action recognition. 56880 action clips in total are performed by 40 different actors in 60 action categories. The clips are captured by three cameras simultaneously at different horizontal angles and heights in a lab environment. Experiments are conducted on the Cross-Subject (X-Sub) and Cross-View (X-View) benchmarks.

NTU RGB+D 120 (NTU-120) Dataset [17]: NTU-120 is an extended version of NTU-60. There are totally 114480 action clips in 120 action categories. Most settings of NTU-120 follow the NTU-60. Experiments are conducted on the Cross-Subject (X-Sub) and Cross-Setup (X-Set) benchmarks.

PKU-MMD Dataset [16]: There are nearly 20,000 action clips in 51 action categories. Two subsets PKU-MMD I and PKU-MMD II are used in the experiments. PKU-MMD II is more challenging than PKU-MMD I as it has higher level of noise. Experiments are conducted on the Cross-Subject (X-Sub) benchmark for both subsets.

4.2   Implementation

Architecture: The 9-layer ST-GCN [39] network is chosen as the encoders. In each layer, the spatial graph convolution is followed by a temporal convolution, the temporal convolutional kernel size is 9. A projector of 2-layer MLP is attached to the output of both networks. The first layer is followed by a batch normalization layer and rectified linear units, with output size of 512, while the output dimension of the second layer is 128. A predictor with the same architecture is used in the student branch, while the stop-gradient operation is applied in target branch. The contextual queue size N is set to 65536, 32768 and 16384 for NTU-60/120, PKU-MMD I and PKU-MMD II datasets, respectively.

Unsupervised Pre-training: LARS [40] is utilized as optimizer and trained for 400 epochs with batch size 512, note that the positive-enhanced learning is conducted after 300 epochs. The learning rate starts at 0 and is linearly increased to 0.5 in the first 10 epochs of training and then decreased to 0.0005 by a cosine decay schedule [19]. All experiments are conducted on one Nvidia RTX3090 GPU using PyTorch.

Linear Evaluation Protocol: The pre-trained models are verified by linear evaluation. Specifically, a linear classifier (a fully-connected layer followed by a softmax layer) is trained supervisedly for 100 epochs while the pre-trained model is fixed.

4.3 Results and Comparison

Unsupervised Results: The performance of the proposed CPM is compared with the state-of-the-art supervised and unsupervised methods on the NTU and PKU-MMD datasets and results are shown in Table 1. Following the standard practice in literature the recognition performance in terms of top-1 classification accuracy is reported. Note that, if not specified, the experiments including ablation study are conducted on the joint data. 3S means the ensemble results of joint, bone and motion data. The obvious performance improvement compared with the recent advanced unsupervised counterparts [14,33] has been obtained and demonstrates the effectiveness of CPM. In addition, CPM (3S) outperforms the supervised ST-GCN [39] on both NTU and PKU-MMD datasets.

Table 1. Performance and comparison with the state-of-the-art methods on the NTU and PKU-MMD datasets.

Architectures	NTU-60 (%)		NTU-120 (%)		PKU-MMD (%)	
	X-Sub	X-View	X-Sub	X-Set	Part I	Part II
Supervised						
C-CNN + MTLN [11]	79.6	84.8	-	-	-	-
TSRJI [1]	73.3	80.3	67.9	62.8	-	-
ST-GCN [39]	81.5	88.3	70.7	73.2	84.1	48.2
Unsupervised						
LongT GAN [44]	39.1	48.1	-	-	67.7	27.0
ASCAL [24]	58.5	64.8	48.6	49.2	-	-
MS^{2}L [15]	52.6	-	-	-	64.9	27.6
P&C [30]	50.7	76.3	-	-	-	-
ISC [33]	76.3	85.2	67.9	67.1	80.9	36.0
CrosSCLR (joint) [14]	72.9	79.9	-	-	-	-
CrosSCLR (3S) [14]	77.8	83.4	67.9	66.7	84.9	-
CPM (joint)	78.7	84.9	68.7	69.6	88.8	48.3
CPM (3S)	**83.2**	**87.0**	**73.0**	**74.0**	**90.7**	**51.5**

Semi-supervised Results: The CPM is first pre-trained on all training data in an unsupervised way, then the classifier is fine-tuned with 1% and 10% annotated data respectively. Table 2 shows the semi-supervised results on the NTU-60

Table 2. Semi-supervised performance and comparison with the state-of-the-art methods on the NTU-60 dataset.

Architectures	Label fraction (%)	X-Sub (%)	X-View (%)
LongT GAN [44]	1	35.2	-
MS^{2}L [15]	1	33.1	-
ISC [33]	1	35.7	38.1
CPM	1	**56.7**	**57.5**
LongT GAN [44]	10	62.0	-
MS^{2}L [15]	10	65.2	-
ISC [33]	10	65.9	72.5
CPM	10	**73.0**	**77.1**

dataset. The results have shown the proposed CPM performs significantly better than the compared methods. Compared with MS^{2}L [15] and ISC [33], CPM improves the performance by a large margin and shows its robustness when fewer labels are available for fine-tuning.

Fully Fine-Tuned Results: The model is first unsupervisedly pre-trained, then a linear classifier is appended to the learnable encoder. Both the pre-trained model and the classifier undergo a supervised training using all training data [41], results are shown in Table 3. On both NTU-60 and NTU-120 datasets the fully fine-tuned CPM outperforms the supervised ST-GCN [39], demonstrating the effectiveness of the unsupervised pretraining.

Table 3. Fully fine-tuned performance and comparison on the NTU-60 and NTU-120 datasets.

Architectures	NTU-60 (%)		NTU-120 (%)	
	X-Sub	X-View	X-Sub	X-Set
C-CNN + MTLN [11]	79.6	84.8	-	-
TSRJI [1]	73.3	80.3	67.9	62.8
ST-GCN [39]	81.5	88.3	70.7	73.2
CPM	**84.8**	**91.1**	**78.4**	**78.9**

4.4   Ablation Study

On Positive Mining: To verify the effectiveness of positive-enhanced learning, we pre-train the CPM (w/o. PM) without identifying the positive instances and, hence, positive-enhanced learning, other settings are kept the same. Performance of CPM and CPM (w/o. PM) is shown in Table 4. On the NTU-60 X-Sub and X-View tasks, CPM improves the recognition accuracy by 3.1% points and 3.2% points, respectively. On the NTU-120 X-Sub and X-Set tasks, 3.9% points and 4.9% points improvements are obtained by CPM. This demonstrates that identification of positive instances and the positive-enhanced learning strategy do improve the representation learning.

Table 4. Benefit of positive mining.

Datasets	CPM (w/o. PM) (%)	CPM (%)
X-Sub (NTU-60)	75.6	78.7
X-View (NTU-60)	81.7	84.9
X-Sub (NTU-120)	64.8	68.7
X-Set (NTU-120)	64.7	69.6

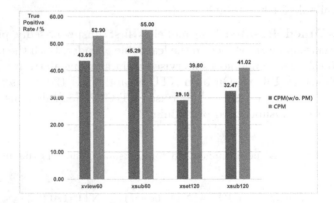

Fig. 3. Precision of positive instances identified by CPM and CPM (w/o. PM) on different datasets.

To further verify how well the non-self positives in the queue can be identified for the positive-enhanced learning, Fig. 3 shows the precision of the positives selected by CPM and CPM (w/o. PM) in one epoch in the top-100 identified positive instances. The results show that even CPM (w/o. PM) is capable of identifying many true positives. This is in significant contrast to the methods in [15,24] where all instances in the queue would be considered as negatives. When positive-enhanced learning is applied, the precision has been significantly increased and so that the learned representation is more robust against the intra-class diversity.

On the Value of K**:** Hyper-parameter K refers to the number of positives identified in the queue. This study shows how K affects the performance. Experiments have shown that when K is 100, best results are obtained on the NTU-60 and NTU-120 datasets. Results on NTU-60 X-View are shown in Fig. 4. It is found that too large or too small K both decreases the performance. A large value of K could include unexpected false positives with low similarity that misleads the learning. A small value of K might ignore too many true positives that would potentially decrease representation ability to accommodate intra-class diversity. Good performance was observed when K is 50 and 25 for PKU-MMD I and PKU-MMD II datasets, respectively. It is conjectured that choice of K may depend on the scale of the dataset.

On the Value of τ': Figure 5 shows the performance of CPM (w/o. PM) using different τ' with τ fixed to 0.1 [5], the optimal performance is obtained when τ' is 0.05. A large value of τ' could lead to a flatter target distribution so that the learned representation becomes less discriminative. A small value of τ' would suppress the difference in similarities between the positive and the negative, leading to many false positives included in the positive-enhanced learning. If

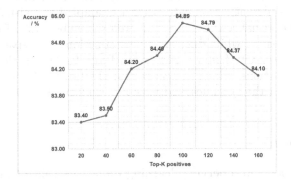

Fig. 4. Effect of the number K of top positives on the proposed CPM in the NTU-60 X-View task.

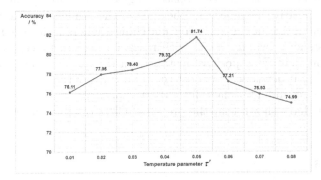

Fig. 5. Effect of different temperature τ' on the performance in the NTU-60 X-View task.

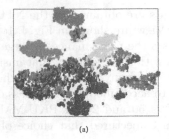 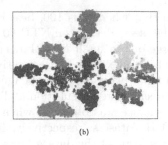

(a)   (b)

Fig. 6. t-SNE visualization of embedding for (a) CPM (w/o. PM) and (b) CPM on the NTU-60 X-View task (best view in color). (Color figure online)

τ' is too small, less positive instances could be identified and this would again adversely affect the effectiveness of learning.

Embedding Visualization: t-SNE [21] is used to visualize the embedding clustering produced by CPM (w/o. PM) and CPM as shown in Fig. 6. Note that embedding of 10 different action categories are sampled and visualized with different colors. The visual results show how well the embedding of the same type of actions form clusters while different types of actions are separated. By comparing the t-SNE of CPM and CPM (w/o. PM), CPM has clearly improved the clustering of actions, which indicates that the learned latent space is more discriminative than the space learned without using positive-enhanced learning strategy.

5 Conclusion

In this paper, a novel unsupervised learning framework called Contrastive Positive Mining (CPM) is developed for learning 3D skeleton action representation. The proposed CPM follows the SimSiam [4] structure, consisting of siamese encoders, student and target. By constructing a contextual queue and identifying non-self positive instances in the queue, the student encoder is able to learn a discriminative latent space by matching the similarity distributions of individual instance's two augments with respect to the instances in the queue. In addition, by identifying positive instances in the queue, a positive-enhanced learning strategy is developed to boost the robustness of the learned latent space against intra-class and inter-class diversity. Experiments on the NTU and PKU-MMD datasets have shown that the proposed CPM obtains the state-of-the-art results.

References

1. Caetano, C., Brémond, F., Schwartz, W.R.: Skeleton image representation for 3D action recognition based on tree structure and reference joints. In: 2019 32nd SIB-GRAPI Conference on Graphics, Patterns and Images (SIBGRAPI), pp. 16–23. IEEE (2019)

2. Chen, J., Samuel, R.D.J., Poovendran, P.: LSTM with bio inspired algorithm for action recognition in sports videos. Image Vis. Comput. **112**, 104214 (2021)
3. Chen, T., Kornblith, S., Norouzi, M., Hinton, G.: A simple framework for contrastive learning of visual representations. In: International Conference on Machine Learning, pp. 1597–1607. PMLR (2020)
4. Chen, X., He, K.: Exploring simple siamese representation learning. In: Proceedings of the IEEE/CVF Conference on Computer Vision and Pattern Recognition, pp. 15750–15758 (2021)
5. Fang, Z., Wang, J., Wang, L., Zhang, L., Yang, Y., Liu, Z.: SEED: self-supervised distillation for visual representation. arXiv preprint arXiv:2101.04731 (2021)
6. Grill, J.B., et al.: Bootstrap your own latent: a new approach to self-supervised learning. arXiv preprint arXiv:2006.07733 (2020)
7. Gui, L.Y., Wang, Y.X., Liang, X., Moura, J.M.: Adversarial geometry-aware human motion prediction. In: Proceedings of the European Conference on Computer Vision (ECCV), pp. 786–803 (2018)
8. Gutmann, M.U., Hyvärinen, A.: Noise-contrastive estimation of unnormalized statistical models, with applications to natural image statistics. J. Mach. Learn. Res. **13**(2) (2012)
9. He, K., Fan, H., Wu, Y., Xie, S., Girshick, R.: Momentum contrast for unsupervised visual representation learning. In: Proceedings of the IEEE/CVF Conference on Computer Vision and Pattern Recognition, pp. 9729–9738 (2020)
10. Hou, Y., Li, Z., Wang, P., Li, W.: Skeleton optical spectra-based action recognition using convolutional neural networks. IEEE Trans. Circuits Syst. Video Technol. **28**(3), 807–811 (2018)
11. Ke, Q., Bennamoun, M., An, S., Sohel, F., Boussaid, F.: A new representation of skeleton sequences for 3D action recognition. In: Proceedings of the IEEE Conference on Computer Vision and Pattern Recognition, pp. 3288–3297 (2017)
12. Kundu, J.N., Gor, M., Uppala, P.K., Radhakrishnan, V.B.: Unsupervised feature learning of human actions as trajectories in pose embedding manifold. In: 2019 IEEE Winter Conference on Applications of Computer Vision (WACV), pp. 1459–1467. IEEE (2019)
13. Li, J., Wong, Y., Zhao, Q., Kankanhalli, M.S.: Unsupervised learning of view-invariant action representations. arXiv preprint arXiv:1809.01844 (2018)
14. Li, L., Wang, M., Ni, B., Wang, H., Yang, J., Zhang, W.: 3D human action representation learning via cross-view consistency pursuit. In: Proceedings of the IEEE/CVF Conference on Computer Vision and Pattern Recognition, pp. 4741–4750 (2021)
15. Lin, L., Song, S., Yang, W., Liu, J.: MS2L: multi-task self-supervised learning for skeleton based action recognition. In: Proceedings of the 28th ACM International Conference on Multimedia, pp. 2490–2498 (2020)
16. Liu, J., Song, S., Liu, C., Li, Y., Hu, Y.: A benchmark dataset and comparison study for multi-modal human action analytics. ACM Trans. Multimedia Comput. Commun. Appl. (TOMM) **16**(2), 1–24 (2020)
17. Liu, J., Shahroudy, A., Perez, M., Wang, G., Duan, L.Y., Kot, A.C.: NTU RGB+D 120: a large-scale benchmark for 3D human activity understanding. IEEE Trans. Pattern Anal. Mach. Intell. **42**(10), 2684–2701 (2019)
18. Liu, M., Liu, H., Chen, C.: 3D action recognition using multiscale energy-based global ternary image. IEEE Trans. Circuits Syst. Video Technol. **28**(8), 1824–1838 (2017)
19. Loshchilov, I., Hutter, F.: SGDR: stochastic gradient descent with warm restarts. arXiv preprint arXiv:1608.03983 (2016)

20. Luo, Z., Peng, B., Huang, D.A., Alahi, A., Fei-Fei, L.: Unsupervised learning of long-term motion dynamics for videos. In: Proceedings of the IEEE Conference on Computer Vision and Pattern Recognition, pp. 2203–2212 (2017)
21. Van der Maaten, L., Hinton, G.: Visualizing data using t-SNE. J. Mach. Learn. Res. **9**(11) (2008)
22. Noroozi, M., Favaro, P.: Unsupervised learning of visual representations by solving jigsaw puzzles. In: Leibe, B., Matas, J., Sebe, N., Welling, M. (eds.) ECCV 2016. LNCS, vol. 9910, pp. 69–84. Springer, Cham (2016). https://doi.org/10.1007/978-3-319-46466-4_5
23. Oord, A.V.D., Li, Y., Vinyals, O.: Representation learning with contrastive predictive coding. arXiv preprint arXiv:1807.03748 (2018)
24. Rao, H., Xu, S., Hu, X., Cheng, J., Hu, B.: Augmented skeleton based contrastive action learning with momentum LSTM for unsupervised action recognition. Inf. Sci. **569**, 90–109 (2021)
25. Shahroudy, A., Liu, J., Ng, T.T., Wang, G.: NTU RGB+D: a large scale dataset for 3D human activity analysis. In: Proceedings of the IEEE Conference on Computer Vision and Pattern Recognition, pp. 1010–1019 (2016)
26. Shi, Z., Kim, T.K.: Learning and refining of privileged information-based RNNs for action recognition from depth sequences. In: Proceedings of the IEEE Conference on Computer Vision and Pattern Recognition, pp. 3461–3470 (2017)
27. Si, C., Chen, W., Wang, W., Wang, L., Tan, T.: An attention enhanced graph convolutional LSTM network for skeleton-based action recognition. In: Proceedings of the IEEE Conference on Computer Vision and Pattern Recognition, pp. 1227–1236 (2019)
28. Song, S., Lan, C., Xing, J., Zeng, W., Liu, J.: Spatio-temporal attention-based LSTM networks for 3D action recognition and detection. IEEE Trans. Image Process. **27**(7), 3459–3471 (2018)
29. Srivastava, N., Mansimov, E., Salakhudinov, R.: Unsupervised learning of video representations using LSTMs. In: International Conference on Machine Learning, pp. 843–852. PMLR (2015)
30. Su, K., Liu, X., Shlizerman, E.: Predict & cluster: unsupervised skeleton based action recognition. In: Proceedings of the IEEE/CVF Conference on Computer Vision and Pattern Recognition, pp. 9631–9640 (2020)
31. Sun, N., Leng, L., Liu, J., Han, G.: Multi-stream slowfast graph convolutional networks for skeleton-based action recognition. Image Vis. Comput. **109**, 104141 (2021)
32. Tarvainen, A., Valpola, H.: Mean teachers are better role models: weight-averaged consistency targets improve semi-supervised deep learning results. arXiv preprint arXiv:1703.01780 (2017)
33. Thoker, F.M., Doughty, H., Snoek, C.G.: Skeleton-contrastive 3D action representation learning. In: Proceedings of the 29th ACM International Conference on Multimedia, pp. 1655–1663 (2021)
34. Tian, Y., Krishnan, D., Isola, P.: Contrastive multiview coding. In: Vedaldi, A., Bischof, H., Brox, T., Frahm, J.-M. (eds.) ECCV 2020. LNCS, vol. 12356, pp. 776–794. Springer, Cham (2020). https://doi.org/10.1007/978-3-030-58621-8_45
35. Wang, P., Li, W., Gao, Z., Zhang, Y., Tang, C., Ogunbona, P.: Scene flow to action map: a new representation for RGB-D based action recognition with convolutional neural networks. In: Proceedings of the IEEE Conference on Computer Vision and Pattern Recognition, pp. 595–604 (2017)

36. Wei, C., et al.: Iterative reorganization with weak spatial constraints: solving arbitrary jigsaw puzzles for unsupervised representation learning. In: Proceedings of the IEEE/CVF Conference on Computer Vision and Pattern Recognition, pp. 1910–1919 (2019)
37. Wu, Z., Xiong, Y., Yu, S.X., Lin, D.: Unsupervised feature learning via nonparametric instance discrimination. In: Proceedings of the IEEE Conference on Computer Vision and Pattern Recognition, pp. 3733–3742 (2018)
38. Xiao, Y., Chen, J., Wang, Y., Cao, Z., Zhou, J.T., Bai, X.: Action recognition for depth video using multi-view dynamic images. Inf. Sci. **480**, 287–304 (2019)
39. Yan, S., Xiong, Y., Lin, D.: Spatial temporal graph convolutional networks for skeleton-based action recognition. In: Thirty-Second AAAI Conference on Artificial Intelligence (2018)
40. You, Y., Gitman, I., Ginsburg, B.: Large batch training of convolutional networks. arXiv preprint arXiv:1708.03888 (2017)
41. Zbontar, J., Jing, L., Misra, I., LeCun, Y., Deny, S.: Barlow twins: self-supervised learning via redundancy reduction. arXiv preprint arXiv:2103.03230 (2021)
42. Zhang, H., Hou, Y., Wang, P., Guo, Z., Li, W.: SAR-NAS: skeleton-based action recognition via neural architecture searching. J. Vis. Commun. Image Represent. **73**, 102942 (2020)
43. Zhang, X., Xu, C., Tao, D.: Context aware graph convolution for skeleton-based action recognition. In: Proceedings of the IEEE/CVF Conference on Computer Vision and Pattern Recognition, pp. 14333–14342 (2020)
44. Zheng, N., Wen, J., Liu, R., Long, L., Dai, J., Gong, Z.: Unsupervised representation learning with long-term dynamics for skeleton based action recognition. In: Proceedings of the AAAI Conference on Artificial Intelligence, vol. 32 (2018)

Target-Absent Human Attention

Zhibo Yang$^{(\boxtimes)}$, Sounak Mondal, Seoyoung Ahn, Gregory Zelinsky, Minh Hoai,
and Dimitris Samaras

Stony Brook University, Stony Brook, NY 11794, USA
zhibyang@cs.stonybrook.edu

Abstract. The prediction of human gaze behavior is important for
building human-computer interaction systems that can anticipate the
user's attention. Computer vision models have been developed to predict the fixations made by people as they search for target objects.
But what about when the target is not in the image? Equally important is to know how people search when they cannot find a target, and
when they would stop searching. In this paper, we propose a data-driven
computational model that addresses the search-termination problem and
predicts the scanpath of search fixations made by people searching for
targets that do not appear in images. We model visual search as an
imitation learning problem and represent the internal knowledge that
the viewer acquires through fixations using a novel state representation
that we call *Foveated Feature Maps (FFMs)*. FFMs integrate a simulated foveated retina into a pretrained ConvNet that produces an in-
network feature pyramid, all with minimal computational overhead. Our
method integrates FFMs as the state representation in inverse reinforcement learning. Experimentally, we improve the state of the art in predicting human target-absent search behavior on the COCO-Search18
dataset. Code is available at: https://github.com/cvlab-stonybrook/
Target-absent-Human-Attention.

Keywords: Visual search · Human attention · Inverse reinforcement
learning · Scanpath prediction · Termination prediction · Target absent

1 Introduction

The attention mechanism used by humans to prioritize and select visual information [35–37] has attracted the interest of computer vision researchers seeking to reproduce this selection efficiency in machines [7,8,38,43,44]. The most
often-used paradigm to study this efficiency is a visual search task, where efficiency is measured with respect to how many attention shifts (gaze fixations)
are needed to detect a target in an image. But what about when the target

Supplementary Information The online version contains supplementary material
available at https://doi.org/10.1007/978-3-031-19772-7_4.

is not there? Understanding gaze behavior during target-absent search (including search termination) would serve applications in human-computer interaction while addressing basic questions in attention research. No predictive model of human search fixations would be complete without addressing the unique problems arising from target-absent search.

The neuroanatomy of the primate foveated retina is such that visual acuity decreases with increasing distance from the high-resolution central fovea. When searching for a target, this foveated retina drives people to move their eyes selectively to image locations most likely to be the target, thereby providing the highest-resolution visual input to the target-recognition task, with each fixation movement guided by low-resolution input from peripheral vision. Recognizing the fact that the human visual input is filtered through a foveated retina is crucial to understanding and predicting human gaze behavior, and this is especially true for target-absent search where there is no clear target signal and gaze is driven instead by contextual relationships to other objects and the spatial cues that might provide about the target's location.

To simulate a foveated retina for predicting human search fixations, Zelinsky et al. [44] directly applied a pretrained ResNet [16] to foveated images [34] to extract feature maps for the state representation. Yang et al. [43] proposed DCBs that approximate a high-resolution fovea and a low-resolution periphery by using the segmentation maps of a full-resolution image and its blurred version, respectively, predicted by a pretrained Panoptic-FPN [22]. Like other models for predicting human attention [7,25,26,31,46], both approaches rely on pretrained networks to extract image features and train much smaller networks for the downstream tasks using transfer learning, usually due to the lack of human fixation data for training. Also noteworthy is that these approaches apply networks pretrained on full-resolution images (e.g., ResNets [16] trained on ImageNet [39]) on blurred images, expecting the pretrained networks to approximate how humans perceive blurred images. However, Convolutional Neural Networks (ConvNets) are highly vulnerable to image perturbation [13,17] and the visual features extracted from the model on blurred images are hardly meaningful in the context of object recognition (contrary to human vision that actively seeks guidance from low-resolution peripheral vision for target recognition).

To better represent the degraded information that humans have available from their peripheral vision and can therefore use to guide their search, we exploit the fact that modern ConvNets have an inherent hierarchical architecture such that deeper layers have progressively larger receptive fields, corresponding to the greater blurring that occurs with increasing visual eccentricity. We propose combining the feature maps at different layers in a manner that is contingent upon the human fixation locations, approximating the information available from a foveated retina[1]. We name this method *Foveated Feature Maps (FFMs)*. FFMs are computed on full-resolution images, so they can be readily applied to a wide range of pretrained ConvNets. Moreover, FFMs are a lightweight modification of

---

[1] Note that it is not our aim to perfectly approximate the information extracted by a human foveated retina.

modern ConvNets that capable of representing the subtle transition from fovea to periphery and are thus better suited for predicting human gaze movement. We find that our FFMs, when combined with inverse reinforcement learner (IQ-Learn [12]), significantly outperforms DCBs [43] and other baselines (see Sect. 4.3) in predicting both target-absent and target-present fixations.

In short, our paper makes the following contributions: (1) we introduce a data-driven computational model applicable to both the target-present and target-absent search prediction problems; (2) we propose a new state representation that dynamically integrates knowledge collected via a foveated retina, similar to humans; (3) we predict target-absent search fixations at the ceiling of human performance, and achieve superior performance in predicting target-present scanpaths compared to previous methods; and (4) We propose a novel evaluation metric called semantic sequence score that measures the object-level consistency between human scanpaths. Compared to the traditional sequence score [4], it better captures the contextual cues that people use to guide their target-absent search behavior.

2   Related Work

Visual search is one of the fundamental human goal-directed gaze behaviors that actively scan the visual environment to find any exemplar of a target-object category [11,42,45]. There is an emerging interest in modeling and predicting human gaze during visual search [7,9,38,43,44]. Yang et al. [43] first used inverse reinforcement learning to model target-present search fixations spanning 18 target categories. Most recently, [7] directly applied reinforcement learning to predict scanpaths in various visual tasks including target-present search. However, their generalizability has never been interrogated for the prediction of target-absent search scanpaths, where no strong target signal is available in the images. Early work showed that target-absent search is not random behavior [2,10] but greatly influenced by target-relevant visual features to such an extent that the target category being searched for can be decoded from one's scanpaths [47]. However, that study used only two target categories and the task was to search through only four non-targets. In this work, we study target-absent gaze behavior from a data-driven perspective.

Several recent studies have attempted to model a foveated representation of the input image for predicting human gaze behavior [38,43,44] or solving other visual tasks (e.g., object detection; [1,19]). Yang et al. [43] approximated a foveated retina by having a high-resolution center (full-resolution image) surrounded by a degraded visual periphery (a slightly blurred version of the image) at each fixation. A pretrained Panoptic-FPN [22] was applied on the full-resolution and blurred images separately to obtain the panoptic segmentation maps that were finally combined into the final state representation. Instead of approximating the foveated retina as a central-peripheral pairing of high- and low-resolution images, Zelinsky et al. [44] used a pretrained ResNet-50 [16] directly to extract feature maps from foveated images [34] for the state representation. Notably, both methods apply pretrained networks on blurred images

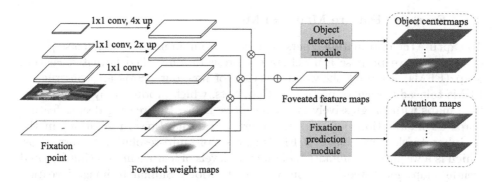

Fig. 1. Overview of the foveated feature maps (FFMs). FFMs are a set of multi-resolution feature maps constructed by combining the in-network feature pyramid produced by a pretrained ConvNet using the foveated weight maps computed based on previous fixations. The object detection module and the fixation prediction module map FFMs to a set of object center heatmaps (80 object categories in COCO [30]) and a set of attention maps for the 18 targets in COCO-Search18 [8], respectively.

whereas our FFMs are extracted from the full-resolution images, for which the pretrained networks are more robust. Rashidi *et al.* [38] proposed a method to directly estimate the foveated detectability of a target object [32] from eye tracking data. However, this approach cannot be easily extended to a larger number of target categories because it requires training multiple detectors for each target and manually creating specialized datasets by showing each target at multiple scales against different textured backgrounds. In contrast, our model is able to jointly learn the foveation process at feature level and the networks that predict human scanpaths through back-propagation from human gaze behavior.

3   Approach

Following the model of Yang *et al.* [43] for target-present data, we also propose to model visual search behavior for target absent data using Inverse Reinforcement Learning (IRL). Specifically, we assume a human viewer is a reinforcement learning agent trying to localize the target object on a given *target-absent* image (the human viewer does not know if the image contains the target or not). The viewer acquires knowledge through a sequence of gaze fixations and allocates their next gaze point based on this knowledge to search for the target (Sect. 3.1). The search is terminated when the viewer confirms there is no target in the given image (Sect. 3.2). In this framework, we assume access to ground-truth human scanpaths (expert demonstrations), and the goal is to learn a policy that mimics or predicts human gaze behavior given an image and the target (Sect. 3.2).

3.1   Foveated Feature Maps (FFMs)

To capture the information a person acquires from an image through a sequence of fixations, we propose a novel state representation, called Foveated Feature Map (FFMs). Figure 1 shows an overview of how our FFMs are constructed. FFMs take advantage of pretrained ConvNets, which produce a pyramid of feature maps with progressively larger receptive fields. By treating deeper feature maps as information obtained at larger eccentricity (lower-resolution) in the peripheral vision, we construct FFMs as a set of multi-resolution feature maps, which is a weighted combination of different levels of feature maps using foveated weight maps generated based on previous fixations. Similar to image foveation [44], in FFMs, deeper feature maps with a lower resolution (corresponding to a larger eccentricity) are more weighted at locations with increasing distance from the fixation points. Below we discuss FFMs in greater detail.

Relative Resolution Map. The human vision system is known to be foveated, meaning the visual information in the view is not processed at a uniform resolution. Rather, high spatial details are only obtained around the fixation point (i.e., the fovea) and the resolution outside of the fovea drops off as the distance between the peripheral pixels and the fovea increases. To simulate this, Perry and Geisler [34] proposed an image foveation method, which has been used in both free viewing [20] and visual search [44] tasks. Here, we extend image foveation to produce multi-resolutional feature maps to represent the foveated view of an image at the level of image features. Specifically, given a fixation $f = (x_f, y_f)$, we first define a relative resolution map contingent on f as

$$R(x, y|f) = \frac{\alpha}{\alpha + \frac{\sqrt{(x-x_f)^2 + (y-y_f)^2}}{p}}. \tag{1}$$

Here, p is the number of pixels in one degree of visual angle, which depends on the distance between the viewer and the display. α is a learnable parameter that controls the decreasing speed of resolution as the pixel (x, y) moves away from the fixation point.

For multiple fixations $\{f_1, \cdots, f_n\}$, we compute the combined resolution map by taking the maximum at every location: $R(x, y|\{f_1, \cdots, f_n\}) = \max_i R(x, y|f_i)$. In contrast to [34], which creates a Gaussian pyramid of the given image I to produce the multi-resolutional version of I, we take inspiration from the Feature Pyramid Network [28] and use the in-network feature pyramid produced by existing pretrained ConvNets and blend the feature maps at each level of the feature pyramid to construct multi-resolutional feature maps (i.e., FFMs) based on the relative resolution map $R(x, y|f)$. For brevity, we will write $R(x, y|f)$ as $R(x, y)$ in the following text.

Foveated Feature Maps (FFMs). We use a ResNet-50 [16] as the backbone (the method can be easily extended to other ConvNet backbones such as VGG nets [40]), and let the feature pyramid from the ResNet be $\{C_1 \cdots, C_5\}$, which represents the feature activation outputs from the last residual block at each stage of ResNet-50, namely the outputs of conv1, conv2, conv3, conv4, and conv5. Similar to the Gaussian pyramid of an image, a lower level of the feature pyramid contains more spatial details, while a higher-level feature map is stronger in semantics. To reduce the semantic discrepancy among different levels, we apply an 1×1 convolutional layer on every C_i to project them to the same embedding space. Then, we upsample $\{C_i\}_{i=1}^{5}$ to the same spatial dimensions of C_1, yielding 3D tensors of the same size, denoted as $\{P_1, \cdots, P_5\}$. We then compute a spatial weight map W_i for each P_i and produce a set of multi-resolution feature maps M as the weighted combination of W_i and P_i: $M = \sum_i W_i \odot P_i$, where $\odot$ denotes the element-wise multiplication at the spatial axes. We call these multi-resolution feature maps FFMs. Below we describe how to compute W_i based on the relative resolution map $R(x, y)$.

Each level of the feature pyramid P_i represents a certain eccentricity, corresponding to a fixed spatial resolution, which we denote as R_i^*. It is defined as the relative resolution where a transfer function $T_i(\cdot)$ is at its half maximum, i.e., $T_i(R_i^*) = 0.5$ [34]. The transfer function $T_i(\cdot)$ is the function that maps relative resolution r to relative amplitude, and it is defined as:

$$T_i(r) = \exp(-(2^{i-3}r/\sigma)^2/2). \tag{2}$$

It can be shown that $R_1^* > R_2^* > R_3^* > R_4^* > R_5^*$, forming four resolution bins whose boundaries are defined by R_i^* and R_{i-1}^* ($i \in \{2, 3, 4, 5\}$). To compute the weights at location (x, y), we first determine which bin pixel (x, y) falls in, according to its relative resolution $R(x, y)$ (see the supplementary material for more details). Assume pixel (x, y) falls in between layer j and $j - 1$, i.e., $R_{j-1}^* \geq R(x, y) > R_j^*$. Then, we set the weights at layer j and $j - 1$ to be the ratio of the distance between pixel (x, y) and the corresponding layer to the distance between the layer j and $j - 1$ at (x, y) in relative amplitude space:

$$W_i(x, y) = \begin{cases} \frac{0.5 - T_j(R(x,y))}{T_{j-1}(R(x,y)) - T_j(R(x,y))} & \text{if } i = j - 1, \\ 1 - \frac{0.5 - T_j(R(x,y))}{T_{j-1}(R(x,y)) - T_j(R(x,y))} & \text{if } i = j, \\ 0 & \text{otherwise.} \end{cases} \tag{3}$$

Apparently, $\sum_i W_i(x, y) = 1$ and at location (x, y) only features from layer j and layer $j - 1$ are integrated into the final FFMs. In [34], α is tuned to match human perception via physiological experiments. Here we learn the parameters of FFMs, α and σ, together with the policy from human gaze data directly.

3.2   Reward and Policy Learning

Using FFMs as our state representation, we train a policy that mimics human gaze behavior using the IRL framework [43]. However, we found that the GAIL [18] IRL algorithm used in [43] is too sensitive to its hyper-parameters, due to its adversarial learning design, which is also shown in [23]. We therefore use IQ-Learn [12] as our IRL algorithm instead. Based on soft Q-Learning [14], IQ-Learn encodes both the reward and the policy in a single Q-function, and thus is able to optimize both reward and policy simultaneously.

Let $Q(s, a)$ be the Q-function, which maps a state-action pair (s, a) to a scalar value representing the amount of future reward gained by taking action a under state s. We want to find a reward function that maximizes the expected amount of cumulative rewards that the expert policy obtains over all other possible policies. Hence, IQ-Learn trains the Q-function by minimizing the following loss:

$$\mathcal{L}_{\text{irl}} = -\mathbb{E}_{\rho_E}\left[Q(s, a) - \gamma \mathbb{E}_{s' \sim \mathcal{P}(s,a)} V(s')\right], \tag{4}$$

where $V(s) = \log \sum_a \exp(Q(s, a))$, ρ_E and $\mathcal{P}$ denote the occupancy measure of the expert policy [18] and the dynamics, respectively. We do not apply the χ^2-divergence proposed in [12] on the reward function since it did not lead to any notable improvement on our task. Given the learned Q-function Q, we can compute the reward as a function of the state and action:

$$r(s, a) = Q(s, a) - \gamma \mathbb{E}_{s' \sim \mathcal{P}(s,a)} V(s'), \tag{5}$$

and the policy as a function of the state:

$$\pi(a|s) = \frac{\exp(Q(s, a)/\tau)}{\sum_{a'} \exp(Q(s, a')/\tau)}. \tag{6}$$

τ is the temperature coefficient, controlling the entropy of the action distribution.

Action Space. Our task is to predict the next fixation given the previous fixations, the input image, and the categorical target. To predict fixations on an image, we follow [43] and discretize the image space into a 20×32 grid (action space). At each time step, the policy samples one cell out of 640 grid cells according to the predicted categorical action distribution $\pi(\cdot|s)$. For the selected grid cell, we set the predicted fixation to be the center of the cell.

Auxiliary Detection Task. A visual search task is essentially a detection task, so it is important for the state representation to capture features of the target object. Moreover, in target-absent search where the target object is absent, human behavior is driven by the expected location of the target in relation to other commonly co-occurring objects. In contrast to [43] which directly uses the output of a pretrained panoptic segmentation network, we train the Q-function with an auxiliary task of predicting the center maps of the objects. Specifically, we add a detection network module on top of FFMs. This module outputs 80 heatmaps $\hat{Y}$ for the 80 object categories in the COCO dataset [30]. Let $\hat{Y}_{xyc}$ denote the value of the c-th heatmap at location (x, y). Following CenterNet [48], we use pixel-wise focal loss [29] as an additional loss to train the whole network:

$$\mathcal{L}_{\text{det}} = -\frac{1}{N} \sum_{x,y,c} \begin{cases} (1 - \hat{Y}_{xyc})^\kappa \log(\hat{Y}_{xyc}) & \text{if } Y_{xyc} = 1, \\ (1 - Y_{xyc})^\lambda (\hat{Y}_{xyc})^\kappa \log(1 - \hat{Y}_{xyc}) & \text{otherwise,} \end{cases} \tag{7}$$

where Y is the ground-truth heatmap created by an object size dependent Gaussian kernel [27]. We set $\kappa = 2$ and $\lambda = 4$ as in [48]. Note that we do not predict the exact heights and widths of the objects in the image because we think rough estimates of the locations of different objects are sufficient to help predict the target-absent fixations. We learn the Q-function using both the IRL loss and the auxiliary detection loss:

$$\mathcal{L} = \mathcal{L}_{\mathrm{irl}} + \omega \mathcal{L}_{\mathrm{det}}, \qquad (8)$$

where ω is a weight to balance the two loss terms.

Termination Prediction. When a person will stop searching is a question intrinsic to target-absent search. Different from [7], which formulates termination as an extra action to fixation prediction in policy learning, we treat termination prediction as an additional task that occurs every step after a new fixation has been made. We found that if we treat termination as an extra action, the policy would overfit to the termination action as it appears much more frequent than other actions.

To this end, we train a binary classifier on top of the Q-function (see Sect. 3.2) for termination prediction using binary cross entropy loss. We weigh the loss computed on the termination and non-termination actions inversely proportionally to their frequencies. In addition, psychology studies [10, 41] have suggested that time could be an important ingredient in predicting stopping. However, we do not predict the duration of fixations in our model. Instead, we use the number of previous fixations as an approximation of time and concatenate it with the Q-values from the Q-function as input to train the termination classifier.

4   Experiments

We train and evaluate the proposed method and other models by using COCO-Search18 [8], which contains both target-present and target-absent human scanpaths in searching for 18 different object categories. COCO-Search18 has 3101 target-present images and 3101 target-absent images, each viewed by 10 subjects. In this paper, we mainly focus on the target-absent gaze behavior prediction. All models are only trained with target-absent images and fixations unless otherwise specified. For all models, we predict one scanpath for each testing image in a greedy manner (i.e., always selecting the action with the largest probability mass from the predicted action distribution as the next fixation) and compare them with the ground-truth scanpaths.

4.1   Semantic Sequence Score

The sequence score (SS) has often been used to quantify the success of scanpath prediction [4, 43]. The sequence score is computed by an existing string matching algorithm that compares the two fixation sequences [33] after transforming them into strings of fixation cluster IDs. The fixation clusters are computed based on the fixation locations. However, we argue that the sequence score does not capture the semantic meaning of fixations which plays an important role in analyzing goal-directed attention: it only captures "where" a person is looking at but not "what" is being looked at. To this end, we propose the *Semantic Sequence Score (SemSS)*, which transforms a fixation sequence into an *object category* sequence by leveraging the segmentation annotation provided in COCO [30]. Then, we apply the same string matching algorithm used in the traditional sequence score to measure the similarity between two scanpaths. Using the "things" versus "stuff" paradigm [6], we do not distinguish between object instances. In this paper, we focus on "thing" categories only, as we are interested in how non-target objects collectively affect human gaze behavior in visual search tasks. "Stuff" categories can be easily integrated into the semantic sequence score.

Other Metrics. We also report other scanpath prediction metrics including the traditional sequence score and conditional priority maps [24], which measure how well the model predicts a fixation when given the previous fixations using saliency metrics including information gain (IG) and normalized scanpath saliency (NSS) [5]. For clarity, we denote them by cIG and cNSS where "c" represents "conditional". cIG measures the amount of information gain the model prediction has over a task-specific fixation density map computed using the training fixations. cNSS measures the correspondence between the predicted fixation probability map and the ground-truth fixation. In addition, to measure termination prediction accuracy, we report the Mean Absolute Error (MAE) between predicted and ground-truth scanpath lengths. To compare fairly with models that do not terminate automatically such as IRL [43], we also report the truncated sequence score by truncating predicted and ground-truth scanpaths at the first 2 and 4 new fixations, denoted as SS(2) and SS(4), respectively.

4.2 Implementation Details

Network Structure. Following [43], we resize the input images to 320×512 for computational efficiency. As shown in Fig. 1, our model has three components: a set of 1×1 convolutional layers that project the feature maps in the feature pyramid to the same dimension (i.e., the number of channels in FFMs); an object detection module; and a fixation prediction module. We set the number of FFMs channels to 128. The fixation prediction module and the object detection module share the same ConvNet consisting of three consecutive convolutional blocks which reduce the spatial resolution of the input foveated feature maps (FFMs) by a factor of 8 (from 160×256 to 20×32). In between two consecutive convolutional layers of a convolutional block, we apply Layer Normalization [3] and a ReLU activation function. Finally, the fixation prediction module uses two convolutional layers to map the output of the shared ConvNet into 18 attention maps (one for each target in COCO-Search18 [8]). The object detection module has a similar structure, but outputs 80 center maps (one for each object category in COCO [30]). Note that the backbone networks of all models in this paper are kept fixed during training. Detailed network parameters are in supplementary.

Hyperparameters. We train the models in this paper by using the Adam [21] optimizer with learning rate 10^{-4}. The weight for the auxiliary detection loss ω in Eq. (8) is 0.1. In COCO-Search18 [8], the number of pixels in one degree

Table 1. Comparing target-absent scanpath prediction algorithms (rows) using multiple scanpath metrics (columns) on the target-absent test set of COCO-Search18. The best results are highlighted in bold.

	SemSS	SS	cIG	cNSS	SS(2)	SS(4)
Human consistency	0.542	0.381	–	–	0.561	0.478
Detector	0.497	0.321	−0.516	0.446	0.497	0.402
Fixation heuristic	0.484	0.298	−0.599	0.405	0.492	0.379
IRL [43]	0.476	0.319	0.032	1.202	0.508	0.407
Chen *et al.* [7]	0.484	0.331	–	–	0.516	0.434
Ours	**0.516**	**0.372**	**0.729**	**1.524**	**0.537**	**0.441**

of visual angle $p = 9.14$. We scale it according to the spatial resolution of P_1 and set $p = 4.57$. For models with a termination predictor, we set the maximum length of each predicted scanpath to 10 (excluding the initial fixation) during training and testing. For models that do not terminate automatically, we set the length of the scanpath to 6 which is approximately the average length of the target-absent scanpaths in COCO-Search18. For the IQ-Learn algorithm, the reward discount factor is set to 0.8. Following [12,15], we use target updates and a replay buffer in IQ-Learn to stabilize the training. The temperature coefficient τ in Eq. (5) is set to 0.01. We update the target Q networks for four iterations using exponential moving average with a 0.01 coefficient. The replay buffer can hold 8000 state-action pairs and is updated online during training.

4.3   Comparing Scanpath Prediction Methods

We compare our model with the following baselines: 1) *human consistency*, an oracle method where one searcher's scanpath is used to predict another searcher's scanpath; 2) *detector*, a ConvNet trained on target-present images of COCO-Search18 to output a target detection confidence map, from which we sample fixations sequentially with inhibition of return (IOR); 3) *fixation heuristic*, similar to detector, but trained to predict human fixation density maps using target-absent data; and more recent approaches including 4) *IRL* [43], and 5) *Chen et al.'s model* [7]. Note that Chen *et al.*'s model used a finer action space 30×40. For fair comparison, we rescale its predicted fixations to our action space 20×32.

As can be seen from Table 1, our method outperforms all other methods across all metrics in target-absent scanpath prediction[2]. Our method is the closest to human consistency which is regarded as the ceiling of any predictive model. In the sequence score case, our method is only inferior to human consistency by 0.09, leading the second best (Chen *et al.*[7]) by 0.41. Excluding the effect of the termination predictor, the sequence scores of the first 2 and 4 fixations also

---

[2] Both cIG and cNSS can only be computed for auto-regressive probabilistic models (our method, IRL, detector and fixation heuristic).

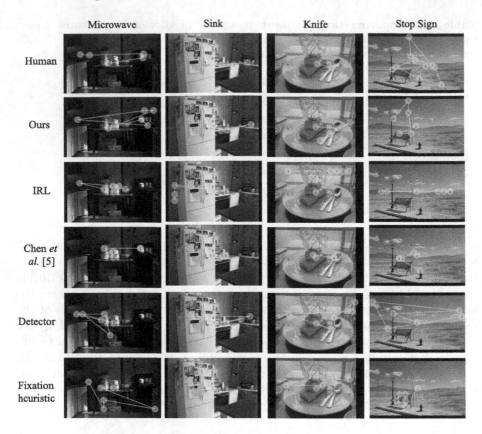

Fig. 2. Visualizing the **predicted scanpaths** of different methods (rows) for different search targets (columns). The top row shows the ground-truth human scanpaths and the other rows are predicted scanpaths from different models.

show that even without terminating the scanpaths our method is still the best compared to all other computational models. Moreover, comparing the sequence scores of truncated scanpaths and full scanpaths, we see a trend of decreasing performance as the scanpath length increases for all methods, i.e., $SS(2) > SS(4) > SS$, and this pattern is particularly pronounced in target-absent search (there is no significant difference between SS and SS(4) for target-present search, see Table 3). The fact that later fixations during target-absent search are harder to predict suggests that human eye-movements behave more randomly at the later stage of search especially when there is no target in the scene.

We also qualitatively compare different methods by visualizing their predicted scanpaths for four scenes in Fig. 2. When searching for a microwave in this scene, our method alone predicted fixations on all three table and countertop surfaces in the image where microwaves are often found (similar to how a representative human searched). Similar phenomena are observed for the sink and knife searches. This shows that our method is able to capture the contextual relations between

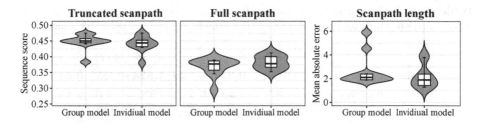

Fig. 3. Comparing group model (red) and individual model (cyan) using: (left) the sequence score of the truncated scanpath (first 4 fixations) without automatic termination, and (middle) the sequence score of the full scanpath including termination, and (right) the mean absolute error for the predicted scanpath length. We perform Wilcoxon signed-rank tests for each experimental setting. The two-sided p values are 0.012, 0.028 and 0.006, respectively. (Color figure online)

objects that play a role in driving target-absent fixations. When searching for the stop sign, our method was the only one that looked at the top of the centrally-located vertical object, despite heavy occlusion, speculatively because stop signs are usually mounted to the tops of poles. In contrast, IRL, which extracts features from blurred pixels using a pretrained ConvNet, completely failed to capture the vertical objects in this image that seem to be guiding search. This argues for the value in using our proposed FFMs to capture guiding contextual information extracted from peripheral vision.

4.4   Group Model Versus Individual Model

In target-present search, human scanpaths are very consistent due to the strong guidance provided by the target object in the image. Indeed, a model trained with fixations from a group of people generalized well for a new **unseen** person [43]. However, given that there are large individual differences in termination time for target-absent search [8], we expect that individualized modeling may be necessary for target-absent search prediction. To test this hypothesis, we compared the predictive performance of group versus individual modeling of target-absent search fixations. The group model was trained with 9 subjects' training scanpaths and tested on the testing scanpaths of the remaining subject. The individual model was trained with the training scanpaths of a single subject and tested on the same subject's testing scanpaths. We did this for all 10 subjects.

Figure 3 shows the comparison between the group model and the individual model in the sequence score of full scanpaths and truncated scanpaths (first four fixations) and the MAE of the length of the predicted scanpath. Interestingly, despite being trained with less data, the individual model shows better performance than the group model in full scanpath modeling, contrary to the group model being better in the truncated scanpath prediction. A critical difference between the modeling of truncated versus full scanpath is that the latter involves the search termination prediction. The rightmost graph in Fig. 3 also shows that

Table 2. Ablation study. We ablate the loss function (second row) and the state representation (third and fourth rows). All methods are trained using IQ-Learn.

	SemSS	SS	cIG	cNSS	SS(2)	SS(4)
FFMs	**0.516**	**0.372**	**0.729**	**1.524**	0.537	**0.441**
FFMs w/o detection loss	0.476	0.350	0.550	1.332	**0.545**	0.437
DCBs	0.508	0.355	0.212	1.129	0.514	0.426
CFI	0.504	0.352	0.518	1.252	0.506	0.426
FPN	0.508	0.338	0.018	0.881	0.408	0.351
Binary masks	0.510	0.364	0.347	1.148	0.438	0.378

Table 3. Comparing target-present scanpath prediction algorithms using multiple scanpath metrics on the COCO-Search18 test dataset.

	SemSS	SS	cIG	cNSS	SS(2)	SS(4)
Human consistency	0.624	0.478	–	–	0.486	0.480
IRL [43]	0.536	0.419	−9.709	1.977	0.437	0.421
Chen et al. [7]	**0.572**	0.445	–	–	0.429	0.319
Ours	0.562	**0.451**	**1.548**	**2.376**	**0.467**	**0.450**

the individual model generates less error (in MAE metric) in scanpath length prediction than the group model. These results altogether suggest that individualized modeling may be more suitable for target-absent search prediction. More experimental results on the termination criterion across different subjects can be found in supplementary.

4.5 Ablation Study

First, we ablate the loss (see Eq. (8)) of our model by removing the auxiliary detection loss. Second, we ablate our proposed foveated feature maps (FFMs) by comparing it with dynamic contextual beliefs (DCBs) [43] and cumulative foveated image (CFI) [44] using the same IRL algorithm (i.e., IQ-Learn). As a finer-grained ablation, we ablate FFMs by using the features extracted by the FPN backbone of a COCO-pretrained Mask R-CNN as the state representation. We use the highest-resolution feature maps of FPN P_2. We further binarize the FFMs of our model such that the values are one at the fixated locations of the finest level (fovea) and the non-fixated locations of the coarsest level (periphery) and zero elsewhere. As shown in Table 2, the proposed auxiliary detection loss improves the performance in 5 out of 6 metrics. The semantic sequence score is increased from 0.476 to 0.516, which indicates that knowing the locations of non-target objects in the image is helpful for predicting the target-absent fixations. Comparing different state representations (i.e., FFMs, DCBs, CFI, FPN and binary masks), we can see that the proposed FFMs are superior to all other state presentations in predicting target-absent fixations. This shows the superiority of FFMs in representing the knowledge a human acquires through fixations compared to DCBs and CFI, which apply pretrained ConvNets on blurred images to simulate the foveated retina.

4.6 Generalization to Target-Present Search

Despite being motivated by target-absent search, our method is also directly applicable to target-present fixation prediction. In this section, we compare our model with two competitive models, IRL [43] and Chen *et al.* [7], in target-present scanpath prediction. For fair comparison, we follow [43] and set the maximum scanpath length to be 6 (excluding the first fixation) for all models and automatically terminate the scanpath once the fixation falls in the bounding box of the target. Table 3 shows that our method achieves the best performance in 5 out of 6 metrics. Chen *et al.*'s model is slightly better than ours in semantic sequence score. They used a pretrained CenterNet [48] trained on COCO images [30] (about 118K images) to predict the bounding box of the target as input for their model, whereas we only used the target-present images in COCO-Search18 [8] (about 3K images) to train our object detection module (see Fig. 1). Despite being trained with less data, our model still outperforms Chen *et al.* [7] in the other five metrics, especially when evaluated in truncated fixed-length scanpaths (i.e., SS(2) and SS(4)). We further expect our model to perform better when using all COCO training images to train our object detection module. Table 1 and Table 3 together demonstrate that our proposed method not only excels in predicting target-absent fixations (see Sect. 4.3), but also target-present fixations.

5   Conclusions and Discussion

We have presented the first computational model for predicting target-absent search scanpaths. To represent the internal knowledge that the viewer acquires through fixations, we proposed a novel state representation, *foveated feature maps (FFMs)*. FFMs circumvent the drawbacks of directly applying pretrained ConvNets on blurred images in previous methods [43,44] by integrating the in-network feature pyramid produced by a pretrained ConvNet with a foveated retina. When trained and evaluated on the COCO-Search18 dataset, FFMs outperform previous state representations and achieve state-of-the-art performance in predicting both target-absent and target-present search fixations using the IRL framework. Moreover, we also proposed a new variant of the sequence score for measuring scanpath similarity, called semantic sequence score. It better captures the object-to-object relation used to guide target-absent search.

Future Work. Inspired by [43], our future work will involve extending our model and semantic sequence score to include "stuff" categories in COCO [6] to study the impact of background categories to target-absent search gaze behavior, and exploring using semi-supervised learning to address the lack of human gaze data by leveraging the rich annotation in COCO images [30].

Acknowledgements. The authors would like to thank Jianyuan Deng for her help in result visualization and statistical analysis. This project was partially supported by US National Science Foundation Awards IIS-1763981 and IIS-2123920, the Partner University Fund, the SUNY2020 Infrastructure Transportation Security Center, and a gift from Adobe.

References

1. Akbas, E., Eckstein, M.P.: Object detection through search with a foveated visual system. PLoS Comput. Biol. **13**(10), e1005743 (2017)
2. Alexander, R.G., Zelinsky, G.J.: Visual similarity effects in categorical search. J. Vis. **11**(8), 9–9 (2011)
3. Ba, J.L., Kiros, J.R., Hinton, G.E.: Layer normalization. arXiv preprint arXiv:1607.06450 (2016)
4. Borji, A., Tavakoli, H.R., Sihite, D.N., Itti, L.: Analysis of scores, datasets, and models in visual saliency prediction. In: Proceedings of the IEEE International Conference on Computer Vision, pp. 921–928 (2013)
5. Bylinskii, Z., Judd, T., Oliva, A., Torralba, A., Durand, F.: What do different evaluation metrics tell us about saliency models? IEEE Trans. Pattern Anal. Mach. Intell. **41**(3), 740–757 (2018)
6. Caesar, H., Uijlings, J., Ferrari, V.: Coco-stuff: thing and stuff classes in context. In: Proceedings of the IEEE Conference on Computer Vision and Pattern Recognition, pp. 1209–1218 (2018)
7. Chen, X., Jiang, M., Zhao, Q.: Predicting human scanpaths in visual question answering. In: Proceedings of the IEEE/CVF Conference on Computer Vision and Pattern Recognition, pp. 10876–10885 (2021)
8. Chen, Y., Yang, Z., Ahn, S., Samaras, D., Hoai, M., Zelinsky, G.: Coco-search18 fixation dataset for predicting goal-directed attention control. Sci. Rep. **11**(1), 1–11 (2021)
9. Chen, Y., et al.: Characterizing target-absent human attention. In: Proceedings of the IEEE/CVF Conference on Computer Vision and Pattern Recognition (CVPR) Workshops, pp. 5031–5040 (2022)
10. Chun, M.M., Wolfe, J.M.: Just say no: how are visual searches terminated when there is no target present? Cogn. Psychol. **30**(1), 39–78 (1996)
11. Eckstein, M.P.: Visual search: a retrospective. J. Vis. **11**(5), 14–14 (2011)
12. Garg, D., Chakraborty, S., Cundy, C., Song, J., Ermon, S.: IQ-learn: inverse soft-Q learning for imitation. In: Advances in Neural Information Processing Systems, vol. 34 (2021)
13. Geirhos, R., Rubisch, P., Michaelis, C., Bethge, M., Wichmann, F.A., Brendel, W.: Imagenet-trained CNNs are biased towards texture; increasing shape bias improves accuracy and robustness. In: International Conference on Learning Representations (2019). https://openreview.net/forum?id=Bygh9j09KX
14. Haarnoja, T., Tang, H., Abbeel, P., Levine, S.: Reinforcement learning with deep energy-based policies. In: International Conference on Machine Learning, pp. 1352–1361. PMLR (2017)

15. Haarnoja, T., Zhou, A., Abbeel, P., Levine, S.: Soft actor-critic: off-policy maximum entropy deep reinforcement learning with a stochastic actor. In: International Conference on Machine Learning, pp. 1861–1870. PMLR (2018)
16. He, K., Zhang, X., Ren, S., Sun, J.: Deep residual learning for image recognition. In: Proceedings of the IEEE Conference on Computer Vision and Pattern Recognition, pp. 770–778 (2016)
17. Hendrycks, D., Dietterich, T.: Benchmarking neural network robustness to common corruptions and perturbations. In: International Conference on Learning Representations (2019). https://openreview.net/forum?id=HJz6tiCqYm
18. Ho, J., Ermon, S.: Generative adversarial imitation learning. In: Advances in Neural Information Processing Systems, vol. 29 (2016)
19. Jaramillo-Avila, U., Anderson, S.R.: Foveated image processing for faster object detection and recognition in embedded systems using deep convolutional neural networks. In: Martinez-Hernandez, U., et al. (eds.) Living Machines 2019. LNCS (LNAI), vol. 11556, pp. 193–204. Springer, Cham (2019). https://doi.org/10.1007/978-3-030-24741-6_17
20. Jiang, M., Huang, S., Duan, J., Zhao, Q.: Salicon: saliency in context. In: The IEEE Conference on Computer Vision and Pattern Recognition (CVPR), June 2015
21. Kingma, D.P., Ba, J.: Adam: a method for stochastic optimization. In: ICLR (Poster) (2015)
22. Kirillov, A., Girshick, R., He, K., Dollár, P.: Panoptic feature pyramid networks. In: Proceedings of the IEEE Conference on Computer Vision and Pattern Recognition, pp. 6399–6408 (2019)
23. Kostrikov, I., Agrawal, K.K., Dwibedi, D., Levine, S., Tompson, J.: Discriminator-actor-critic: addressing sample inefficiency and reward bias in adversarial imitation learning. In: International Conference on Learning Representations (2019). https://openreview.net/forum?id=Hk4fpoA5Km
24. Kümmerer, M., Bethge, M.: State-of-the-art in human scanpath prediction. arXiv preprint arXiv:2102.12239 (2021)
25. Kümmerer, M., Theis, L., Bethge, M.: Deep gaze I: boosting saliency prediction with feature maps trained on imagenet. arXiv preprint arXiv:1411.1045 (2014)
26. Kümmerer, M., Wallis, T.S., Bethge, M.: Information-theoretic model comparison unifies saliency metrics. Proc. Natl. Acad. Sci. **112**(52), 16054–16059 (2015)
27. Law, H., Deng, J.: Cornernet: detecting objects as paired keypoints. In: Proceedings of the European Conference on Computer Vision (ECCV), pp. 734–750 (2018)
28. Lin, T.Y., Dollár, P., Girshick, R., He, K., Hariharan, B., Belongie, S.: Feature pyramid networks for object detection. In: Proceedings of the IEEE Conference on Computer Vision and Pattern Recognition, pp. 2117–2125 (2017)
29. Lin, T.Y., Goyal, P., Girshick, R., He, K., Dollár, P.: Focal loss for dense object detection. In: Proceedings of the IEEE International Conference on Computer Vision, pp. 2980–2988 (2017)
30. Lin, T.-Y., et al.: Microsoft COCO: common objects in context. In: Fleet, D., Pajdla, T., Schiele, B., Tuytelaars, T. (eds.) ECCV 2014. LNCS, vol. 8693, pp. 740–755. Springer, Cham (2014). https://doi.org/10.1007/978-3-319-10602-1_48
31. Linardos, A., Kümmerer, M., Press, O., Bethge, M.: DeepGaze IIE: calibrated prediction in and out-of-domain for state-of-the-art saliency modeling. In: Proceedings of the IEEE/CVF International Conference on Computer Vision, pp. 12919–12928 (2021)
32. Najemnik, J., Geisler, W.S.: Optimal eye movement strategies in visual search. Nature **434**(7031), 387–391 (2005)

33. Needleman, S.B., Wunsch, C.D.: A general method applicable to the search for similarities in the amino acid sequence of two proteins. J. Mol. Biol. **48**(3), 443–453 (1970)
34. Perry, J.S., Geisler, W.S.: Gaze-contingent real-time simulation of arbitrary visual fields. In: Human Vision and Electronic Imaging VII, vol. 4662, pp. 57–70. International Society for Optics and Photonics (2002)
35. Petersen, S.E., Posner, M.I.: The attention system of the human brain: 20 years after. Annu. Rev. Neurosci. **35**, 73–89 (2012)
36. Posner, M.I.: Attention: the mechanisms of consciousness. Proc. Natl. Acad. Sci. **91**(16), 7398–7403 (1994)
37. Posner, M.I., Petersen, S.E.: The attention system of the human brain. Annu. Rev. Neurosci. **13**(1), 25–42 (1990)
38. Rashidi, S., Ehinger, K., Turpin, A., Kulik, L.: Optimal visual search based on a model of target detectability in natural images. In: Advances in Neural Information Processing Systems, vol. 33 (2020)
39. Russakovsky, O., et al.: Imagenet large scale visual recognition challenge. Int. J. Comput. Vision **115**(3), 211–252 (2015)
40. Simonyan, K., Zisserman, A.: Very deep convolutional networks for large-scale image recognition. arXiv preprint arXiv:1409.1556 (2014)
41. Wolfe, J.M.: Guided search 6.0: an updated model of visual search. Psychon. Bull. Rev. **28**(4), 1060–1092 (2021)
42. Wolfe, J.: Visual search. In: Pashler, H. (ed.) Attention (1998)
43. Yang, Z., et al.: Predicting goal-directed human attention using inverse reinforcement learning. In: Proceedings of the IEEE/CVF Conference on Computer Vision and Pattern Recognition, pp. 193–202 (2020)
44. Zelinsky, G., et al.: Benchmarking gaze prediction for categorical visual search. In: Proceedings of the IEEE/CVF Conference on Computer Vision and Pattern Recognition Workshops (2019)
45. Zelinsky, G.J.: A theory of eye movements during target acquisition. Psychol. Rev. **115**(4), 787 (2008)
46. Zelinsky, G.J., et al.: Predicting goal-directed attention control using inverse-reinforcement learning. Neurons Behav. Data Anal. Theory **2021** (2021)
47. Zelinsky, G.J., Peng, Y., Samaras, D.: Eye can read your mind: decoding gaze fixations to reveal categorical search targets. J. Vis. **13**(14), 10–10 (2013)
48. Zhou, X., Wang, D., Krähenbühl, P.: Objects as points. arXiv preprint arXiv:1904.07850 (2019)

Uncertainty-Based Spatial-Temporal Attention for Online Action Detection

Hongji Guo[1], Zhou Ren[2], Yi Wu[2], Gang Hua[2], and Qiang Ji[1]($\boxtimes$)

[1] Rensselaer Polytechnic Institute, Troy, NY 12180, USA
{guoh11,jiq}@rpi.edu
[2] Wormpex AI Research, Bellevue, WA 98004, USA

Abstract. Online action detection aims at detecting the ongoing action in a streaming video. In this paper, we proposed an uncertainty-based spatial-temporal attention for online action detection. By explicitly modeling the distribution of model parameters, we extend the baseline models in a probabilistic manner. Then we quantify the predictive uncertainty and use it to generate spatial-temporal attention that focus on large mutual information regions and frames. For inference, we introduce a two-stream framework that combines the baseline model and the probabilistic model based on the input uncertainty. We validate the effectiveness of our method on three benchmark datasets: THUMOS-14, TVSeries, and HDD. Furthermore, we demonstrate that our method generalizes better under different views and occlusions, and is more robust when training with small-scale data.

Keywords: Online action detection · Spatial-temporal attention · Uncertainty modeling · Generalization · Robustness

1 Introduction

Traditional offline action detection [33,49,52] takes the entire sequence as the input to temporally localize the actions. Differently, online action detection (OAD) aims at detecting the ongoing action in a streaming video with only the previous and current frames. An illustration is shown in Fig. 1. Online action detection has many practical applications since many real world tasks do not provide future observations and require real-time responses such as autonomous driving [19], anomaly detection [37], sports analysis [38]. Online action detection is very challenging due to the following reasons: (1) the beginnings of actions are unknown; (2) the observations of actions are incomplete; (3) background and irrelevant actions in the video may cause problems to the detection of the ongoing action; (4) there is a large within-class variability and the distribution of training data is imbalanced; and (5) the training data is limited in many situations.

© The Author(s), under exclusive license to Springer Nature Switzerland AG 2022
S. Avidan et al. (Eds.): ECCV 2022, LNCS 13664, pp. 69–86, 2022.
https://doi.org/10.1007/978-3-031-19772-7_5

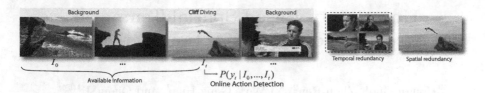

Fig. 1. An illustration of online action detection, temporal and spatial redundancy. Online action detection aims at detecting the ongoing action without seeing the future. The available information includes all the frames up to the current.

Online action detection relies on existing observations, so features selection is crucial for the task. However, both temporal and spatial domains contain redundant information as illustrated in Fig. 1, which may degenerate the performance since the prediction is made based on the irrelevant features. This problem can be alleviated by the attention mechanism, which automatically assigns weights to features according to their importance. In this way, the model performs better since the input features are more relevant and discriminative. For instance, Transformer [40] is a kind of attention model that captures the pair-wise dependency by scaled dot-product. However, when the amount of training data is limited or the model is applied to datasets with distribution shifts, traditional deterministic attention modeling methods become less robust and generalize poorly. Also, the purely learning-based attention methods are less interpretable in terms of attention generalization since the attentions are predicted to minimize the final loss function without considering the underlying dynamics.

To address these issues, we propose an uncertainty-based spatial-temporal attention for online action detection. Specifically, the model is extended in a probabilistic manner and the predictive uncertainty is quantified to compute the attention weights. The attention associated with a certain frame or region is based on its potential to reduce the prediction uncertainty of the ongoing action. In this way, the frames and regions with higher mutual information are assigned larger attention weights and the model can benefit from these discriminative features. When training data is insufficient, the model should be aware of that thanks to the quantified epistemic uncertainty in the probabilistic formulation. On the other hand, the generated attention is based on the input, thus the model can also generalize better when dealing with datasets with different distributions.

In general, our main contributions are summarized as: (1) we proposed an uncertainty-based spatial-temporal attention based on predictive uncertainty for online action detection; (2) the proposed attention mechanism can discriminate high mutual information frames and regions for better prediction of the ongoing action; (3) our proposed attention is validated on three benchmark datasets with multiple baseline methods and it shows the performance improvement; (4) we demonstrate that our proposed attention generalizes better under different views and occlusions and is more robust with small-scale training data.

2 Related Work

Online Action Detection. Online action detection [4] is an important emerging research topic on account of the requirements of many real-time applications. Here we review the online action detection methods and related works chronologically. Gao *et al.* [10] proposed an encoder-decoder network trained by reinforcement learning for online action anticipation. To distinguish ambiguous background, Shou *et al.* [32] designed a hard negative samples generation module and an adaptive sampling method is used to handle the scarcity of the important training frames around the action starts. Xu *et al.* [45] proposed temporal recurrent network (TRN) that aggregates the features from the past and the future under the LSTM framework. To specifically detect the action starts, StarNet [11] combines an action classification network and a localization network to boost the performance. To deal with background and irrelevant features from the past, Eun *et al.* [6,7] introduced information discrimination unit (IDU) and temporal filtering network (TFN) to accumulate information based on its relevance to the current action and filter out irrelevant features. Zhao *et al.* [51] proposed a learning-with-privileged framework for online action detection by combing a offline teacher model and an online student model. With only video-level annotations, Gao *et al.* [12] proposed WORD for weakly supervised online action detection by introducing a proposal generator and an action recognizer. Recently, Transformer [40] is utilized to model the pairwise dependencies among frames. Wang *et al.* introduced OadTR [42] based on the standard Transformer architecture. Further, Xu *et al.* [46] proposed long short-term Transformer (LSTR) to simultaneously capture long-range and short-term information. Besides video modality, skeleton-based online action detection was also explored in [24–26].

Spatial-Temporal Attention. In video-based action recognition and detection, spatial-temporal attention modeling aims at learning the discriminative feature representation of actions from the input. In particular, attention modeling in online action detection is crucial since the input contains a lot of redundant or irrelevant information, which may cause the degeneracy of performance. In this part, we review the recent spatial-temporal attention modeling methods. In general, attention mechanisms in video understanding can be divided into spatial attention [18,28] and temporal attention [5,8,35,48], which model the discriminative regions and frames respectively. And the joint modeling yields the spatial-temporal attention [5,8,35,48]. The Transformer [40] is a fixed attention mechanism achieved by the scaled dot-product. Wang *et al.* proposed Non-Local (NL) network [43] by modeling the dependencies between human and objects across frames. To utilize the information of interaction between actors and context, ACAR-Net [29] models the relation between the actors and the context for spatial-temporal action localization. Recently, Zhao *et al.* introduced Tubelet Transformer (TubeR) [50] that can learn tubelet-queries and capture the dynamic spatial-temporal nature of videos through tubelet-attention. To model the spatial-temporal attention for action detection by utilizing the self-attention, Dai *et al.* introduced MS-TCT [3] with a multi-scale feature mixer module under the Transformer framework to capture global and local temporal relations at multiple temporal resolutions. Existing attention modeling methods either generate the attention by a fixed mechanism such as scaled dot-product or let the neural network handle the input. These may work well when training data is sufficient but may not be robust under less training data or when generalized to different datasets. Furthermore, the attention generation process is less interpretable. When the task becomes challenging such as online action detection, these purely learning-based attention methods may confront problems. The trained model may perform poorly when generalizing to different datasets and become less robust when training data is limited. In this work, we aim at addressing these issues by generating the attention based on predictive uncertainty.

Uncertainty Modeling. In machine learning systems, uncertainty quantification is crucial for better understanding the prediction the and improving the model [20]. Under the probabilistic setting, the prediction uncertainty of the model can be quantified using various approaches such as deep ensembles [23], dropout [9] and prior network [27]. Recently, uncertainty modeling has been applied to many computer vision tasks. By explicitly modeling the epistemic and aleatoric uncertainty, the predictions can be better interpreted and further be used to guide the model for specific tasks. Subedar *et al.* [36] quantified the uncertainty in a Bayesian framework and use it for the fusion of audio data and visual data. Want *et al.* [44] computed the data uncertainty to guide the semi-supervised object detection. Specifically, the image uncertainty guides the easy data selection and the region uncertainty guides RoI re-weighting. Yang *et al.* proposed UGTR [47] to perform the weakly-supervised action detection. Arnab *et al.* proposed a probabilistic variant of Multiple Instance Learning where the uncertainty of each prediction is estimated. Guo *et al.* proposed UGPT [13] for complex action recognition by utilizing the model uncertainty. In this paper, we quantify the predictive uncertainty for online action detection.

3   Method

In this section, we first formulate the problem of online action detection and spatial-temporal attention in Sect. 3.1. Then we introduce our uncertainty quantification method in Sect. 3.2 and how to compute the spatial-temporal attention in Sect. 3.3. The mechanism of the proposed uncertainty-based attention with respect to mutual information is discussed in Sect. 3.4. Finally, we introduce our two-stream inference framework in Sect. 3.5.

3.1   Problem Setup

Online action detection (OAD) aims at identifying the ongoing action in a streaming video without seeing the future frames. Mathematically, denote an untrimmed video as $V = [I_1, I_2, ..., I_T]$, where T is the video length and I_t represents the frame at time t. The available frames at time t is $V_t = \{I_{t'}\}_{t'=1}^{t}$.

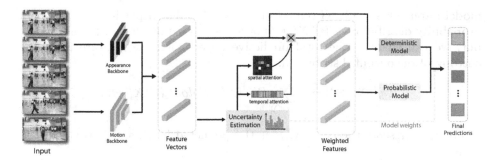

Fig. 2. Overall framework. Firstly, feature vectors are constructed by concatenating the appearance features and motion features. Then we estimate the uncertainty based on the input and use the quantified uncertainty to generate the spatial-temporal attention. Finally, the prediction is made by dynamically combining both the deterministic model and probabilistic model, whose inputs are original features and attention-weighted features respectively.

Then online action detection can be formulated as a classification problem of frame t given $\boldsymbol{V}_t$:

$$y_t^* = \text{argmax}_c \, P(\hat{y}_t = c | \boldsymbol{V}_t) \tag{1}$$

where $\hat{y}_t$ is the prediction of frame t. Class c belongs to an action set $\mathcal{Y} = \{0, 1, ..., C\}$, where 0 represents background class and C is the number of action classes.

Spatial-Temporal Attention (STA). For video-based action detection, spatial-temporal attention modeling aims at discriminating salient regions in certain frames that contain useful information for the tasks. By assigning higher weights to these regions, the model can take advantage of more discriminative features and improve the performance. Also, the spatial-temporal attention can make the model more interpretable by visualizing the attention weights. For online action detection, denote the extracted features of available frames at time t as $\boldsymbol{F}_t = \{f_{t'}\}_{t'=1}^t$, where $f_{t'}$ is the feature of frame t'. The spatial-temporal attention generates attention-weighted features $\boldsymbol{F}_t' = \{f_{t'}'\}_{t'=1}^t$, where

$$f_{t'}' = a_{t'} \times (b_{t'} \odot f_{t'}) \tag{2}$$

where $a_{t'}$ is the temporal attention weight and $b_{t'}$ is the spatial attention weight. $a_{t'}$ and $b_{t'}$ measure the temporal and spatial importance respectively. By applying the spatial-temporal attention, the impact of redundant or irrelevant information should be alleviated since they are assigned smaller weights (Fig, 2).

3.2 Uncertainty Quantification

In this part, we introduce the concepts of uncertainties and their quantification methods. Assume the problem is in classification setting. Denote the trained model parameters as Θ^*. Given a test sample $\boldsymbol{X'}$, the output is the conditional probability distribution $P(y'|\boldsymbol{X'}, \Theta^*)$ over a set of action classes. From the output, we can quantify the total predictive uncertainty. We measure it by the entropy of the output distribution:

$$\mathcal{H}[y'|\boldsymbol{X'}, \Theta^*] = - \sum_{y' \in \mathcal{Y}} P(y'|\boldsymbol{X'}, \Theta^*) log P(y'|\boldsymbol{X'}, \Theta^*) \qquad (3)$$

where $\mathcal{H}$ represents the entropy, y' is the predicted label, and $\mathcal{Y}$ is the action class set.

There are two sources of predictive uncertainty. One is the model parameters when the model is inadequately learned due to the insufficient data. We refer this kind of uncertainty as **epistemic uncertainty** [20]. Increasing the data can reduce epistemic uncertainty. On the other hand, uncertainty also comes from data. When the input data is noisy, the uncertainty is large. We refer this kind of uncertainty as **aleatoric uncertainty** [20]. It cannot be reduced by increasing data. These two kinds of uncertainties add up to the total predictive uncertainty.

In a probabilistic model, denote all the model parameters as $\Theta = \{\Theta_d, \Theta_p\}$, where Θ_d and Θ_p represent deterministic and probabilistic model parameters respectively. The epistemic uncertainty is quantified as the mutual information between the prediction and the probabilistic model parameters [34]:

$$\mathcal{U}_E = \mathcal{I}[y', \Theta_p|\boldsymbol{X'}, \Theta_d^*] \qquad (4)$$

where $\mathcal{I}$ represents the mutual information.

The aleatoric uncertainty measures the inherent noise in the observation. It is quantified as the expectation of the predictive uncertainty:

$$\mathcal{U}_A = \mathbb{E}_{p(\Theta_p|\boldsymbol{X'}, \Theta_d^*)}[\mathcal{H}[y'|\boldsymbol{X'}, \Theta_p]] \qquad (5)$$

The total uncertainty can be rewritten as the sum of epistemic uncertainty and aleatoric uncertainty as below:

$$\mathcal{H}[y'|\boldsymbol{X'}, \Theta^*] = \mathcal{I}[y', \Theta_p|\boldsymbol{X'}, \Theta_d^*] + \mathbb{E}_{p(\Theta_p|\boldsymbol{X'}, \Theta_d^*)}[\mathcal{H}[y'|\boldsymbol{X'}, \Theta_p]] \qquad (6)$$

Directly computing the uncertainty is infeasible since it is intractable to integrate over the true distribution. Thus, we generate samples and approximate the uncertainty by the sample average. After obtaining K output samples by repeating the probabilistic forward process, the epistemic uncertainty can be estimated as:

$$\mathcal{I}(y', \Theta_p|\boldsymbol{X'}, \Theta_d^*) \approx \mathcal{H}[\frac{1}{K} \sum_{k=1}^{K} P(y'|\boldsymbol{X'}, \Theta_d^*, \Theta_p^k)] - \frac{1}{K} \sum_{k=1}^{K} \mathcal{H}[y'|\boldsymbol{X'}, \Theta_d^*, \Theta_p^k] \qquad (7)$$

Notice that we rearrange Eq. (6) and the first term on the right is the entropy of the average of the sample predictions, which is the estimation of total uncertainty. The second term is the average of the entropy of the sample predictions, which is the estimation of the aleatoric uncertainty.

Motivation: For online action detection, most existing methods [10,12,45] directly take the raw features as the input without attention modeling, the drawbacks related to background and irrelevant actions are ignored. Recently, methods including IDN [6] and Transformer [42,46] model the temporal dependencies to alleviate the impacts of background and irrelevant actions. The euclidean distance between features and the scaled dot-product are used as measures for dependencies respectively. In this paper, we consider this problem from the information theory perspective: we assume the regions or frames that have large mutual information with respect to the ongoing action are more relevant and important to the current detection, which is analyzed in Sect. 3.4. Based on the assumption, the proposed uncertainty-based attention can identify high mutual information regions and frames. Also, the probabilistic extension of the framework can improve the robustness and generalization of the model.

3.3 Uncertainty-Based Spatial-Temporal Attention

Spatial Attention. Given the input $V_t = \{I_1, ..., I_t\}$ at time t, features extracted by the backbone are denoted as $F_t = \{f_t, ..., f_t\}$, where $f_{t'} \in \mathbb{R}^{h \times w}$. Spatial attention aims at identifying relevant discriminative regions within each frame. Specifically, a spatial attention mask $b_{t'} \in \mathbb{R}^{h \times w}$ is generated for the feature of each frame and is applied by the Hadamard product [15] as $f_{t'}^s = b_{t'} \odot f_{t'}$.

To model the spatial attention mask by uncertainty. We model each element of the mask with a Gaussian distribution:

$$b_{t'}^s(i,j) \sim \mathcal{N}(\mu_{ij}, \sigma_{ij}), \ i = 1, ...h; j = 1, ...w \tag{8}$$

During the training, the reparameterization trick [22] is adopted to perform the forward process: $b_{t'}^s(i,j) = \mu_{ij} + \epsilon\sigma_{ij}$, where $\epsilon \sim \mathcal{N}(0,1)$. In this way, the spatial attention mask can capture the randomness within the spatial domain of the input feature and further be utilized to quantify the predictive uncertainty. Noticed that except for these spatial attention masks, other model parameters are deterministic, which are fixed during the inference.

For inference, we estimate the predictive uncertainty to apply the attention. Based on the learned distribution of the spatial attention mask, we sample from it to generate multiple output from the input. Specifically, feature $f_{t'}$ goes through the spatial-attention mask for K times and generate K masks denoted as $\{b_{t'1}^s, ..., b_{t'K}^s\}$. From these samples, we estimate the uncertainty of each pixel (i,j) in the feature map. At time t', the epistemic uncertainty of each element can be estimated as:

$$\mathcal{I}_{t'}(i,j) = \mathcal{H}[\frac{1}{K}\sum_{k=1}^{K} P(y|x, b_{t'k}^s(i,j))] - \frac{1}{K}\sum_{k=1}^{K} \mathcal{H}[y|x, b_{t'k}^s(i,j)] \tag{9}$$

With the estimated uncertainty, we generate the spatial attention mask by a normalization:

$$b_{t'}(i,j) = 1 + \mathcal{U}_{t'}(i,j) \Big/ \sum_{i,j} \mathcal{U}_{t'}(i,j) \tag{10}$$

The equation above indicates that regions with high uncertainty are assigned large weights. Later we show these regions also have high mutual information. These attention weights are applied to the feature by $f_{t'}^s = b_{t'} \odot f_{t'}$.

Temporal Attention. Temporal attention aims at identifying important frames from the input sequence. Specifically, a temporal attention weight $\alpha_{t'}$ is generated and applied to the input sequence by multiplication with the corresponding frame: $f_{t'}' = a_{t'} \times f_{t'}$.

For online action detection, the prediction of each frame is made by a fully connected classifier with a softmax layer in the end. Similar as spatial attention, we model the parameters in these fully connected layers in a probabilistic manner [39]. In this way, all the aggregated features are considered and evaluated for the current detection. Similarly, we assume the parameters Θ follows Gaussian distribution with mean μ and covariance matrix Σ. The probabilistic parameters are computed by $\Theta = \mu + \epsilon\Sigma$, where $\epsilon \sim \mathcal{N}(\mathbf{0}, \mathbf{I})$. By learning the mean μ and covariance matrix Σ, we can estimate the distribution of Θ.

With probabilistic model parameters, we generate K samples from the input. Then the epistemic uncertainty corresponding to frame t' is estimated as:

$$\mathcal{I}_{t'} = \mathcal{H}[\frac{1}{K}\sum_{k=1}^{K} p(y_{t'}^k)] - \frac{1}{K}\sum_{k=1}^{K} \mathcal{H}[p(y_{t'}^k)] \tag{11}$$

To discriminate important frames, we make the temporal attention weight positively correlated to the epistemic uncertainty. We show this mechanism works with mutual information in Sect. 3.4. The temporal attention is computed by normalizing the weights of all considered frames as below:

$$a_{t'} = 1 + \mathcal{U}_{t'} \Bigg/ \sum_{t''=t-\tau}^{t} \mathcal{U}_{t''} \tag{12}$$

where τ is the number of past frame we consider. Then the generated weights are multiplied to the corresponding input. By modeling the temporal attention, the frames used to make the online prediction are evaluated and optimized based on their importance. So the discriminative information from the past are better utilized with less redundancy. Different from the other attention modeling methods, our proposed attention is based on the prediction uncertainty, which is more interpretable in terms of the generation process.

Spatial-Temporal Attention. To jointly model the spatial and temporal attention, we combine them to formulate a unified spatial-temporal attention using Eq. (2). The samples generated from the same input are used to estimate the predictive uncertainty for both spatial and temporal attention simultaneously. In this way, the spatial and temporal attention can be generated with the same estimated uncertainty, which is more computationally efficient. The training procedure is summarized as Algorithm 1.

Algorithm 1. Training
Input: $\mathcal{D} = \{X_n \in \mathbb{R}^{T_n \times d}, y_n \in \mathbb{R}^{T_n}\}_{n=1}^N$: training data
Output: Θ: model parameters
1: **for** $\{X_n, y_n\}$ in $\mathcal{D}$ **do**
2:    Generate K samples
3:    Compute uncertainty by Eq. (7)
4:    Compute temporal attention a and spatial attention b
5:    Generate attention-weighted feature by Eq. (2)
6:    Optimize Θ with weighted features
7: **end for**
8: **Return** Θ

Algorithm 2. Inference
Input: $\mathcal{D}' = \{X_n'\}$: testing data
Output: $\{y'\}$: predicted labels
1: **for** X_n' in $\mathcal{D}'$ **do**
2:    Generate K samples
3:    Compute uncertainty by Eq. (7)
4:    Compute temporal attention a and spatial attention b
5:    Generate attention-weighted feature by Eq. (2)
6: **end for**
7: Compute w_u and w_b by Eq. (16)
8: Make prediction $\{y'\}$ by Eq. (15)
9: **Return** $\{y'\}$

3.4 Mechanism of Uncertainty-Based Attention

In this part, we relate the predictive uncertainty with mutual information to demonstrate the underlying mechanism of our proposed attention mechanism. For online action detection, the relevant frames in the past should have high mutual information with the current frame, which can guide the generation of attention.

Uncertainty and Mutual Information. For a past time t', denote $F_{-t'} = \{F_{t-T}, ..., F_{t'-1}, F_{t'+1}, ..., F_t\}$. Then the mutual information between its feature and the current action can be written as:

$$\mathcal{I}[y_t; F_{t'}|F, \Theta_d] = \mathcal{H}\big[E_{p(\Theta_p|F_{-t'})}[P(y_t|F_{-t'}, \Theta_p, \Theta_d)]\big] \\ - \mathcal{H}\big[E_{P(\Theta_p|F)}[P(y_t|F, \Theta_p, \Theta_d)]\big] \tag{13}$$

Combining Eq. 6 and Eq. 13 yields:

$$\mathcal{I}[y_t; F_{t'}|F_{-t'}] = \mathcal{H}\big[E_{p(\Theta_p|F_{-t'})}[P(y_t|F_{-t'}, \Theta_p, \Theta_d)]\big] - \mathcal{I}[y_t; \Theta_p|F, \Theta_d] \\ - E_{(P(\Theta_p|F)}\big[\mathcal{H}[y_t|F, \Theta_p, \Theta_d]\big] \tag{14}$$

The mutual information on the left is what we desired. It is negatively correlated to the predictive uncertainty of the current action. So the features that lead to lower predictive uncertainty have higher mutual information with the ongoing action. In another words, the information that leads to low predictive uncertainty is treated higher weight.

Analysis and Insights. By explicitly modeling the distributions of model parameters, our probabilistic architecture can well capture the stochasticity of the data and model. On the other hand, deterministic methods [5,8,35] directly generate the attention from the input feature. The network for attention generation needs to be trained well with enough data. Thus, the uncertainty-based model should have better generalization ability and more robustness than the deterministic methods. To demonstrate our propositions, we perform the generalization experiments and insufficient data experiments.

3.5 Two-Stream Framework

To leverage both the probabilistic model and deterministic model, we combine the baseline model with the uncertainty-based model dynamically based on the input uncertainty. The final prediction model is formulated as:

$$P(y|\boldsymbol{X}',\Theta^*) = w_u(\boldsymbol{X}')p_u(y|\boldsymbol{X}',\Theta^*) + w_b(\boldsymbol{X}')p_b(y|\boldsymbol{X}',\Theta^*) \qquad (15)$$

where w_u and w_b are the weights of uncertainty-based model and baseline model respectively. They are computed based on the predictive uncertainty as below:

$$w_u(\boldsymbol{X}') = \sigma\left(w\frac{\mathcal{U}_{max} - \mathcal{U}(\boldsymbol{X}')}{\mathcal{U}_{max} - \mathcal{U}_{min}} + b\right), \quad w_b(\boldsymbol{X}') = 1 - w_b(\boldsymbol{X}') \qquad (16)$$

where $\mathcal{U}_{max}$ and $\mathcal{U}_{min}$ are the maximum and minimum uncertainty respectively. w and b are learnable parameters. The inference procedure is summarized as Algorithm 2.

4 Experiments

In this section, we first introduce benchmark datasets and evaluation metrics of online action detection in Sect. 4.1 and Sect. 4.2 respectively. Implementation details are provided in Sect. 4.3. The main experimental results on baseline methods are discussed in Sect. 4.4. Some qualitative results are presented in Sect. 4.5. The ablation studies are shown in Sect. 4.6.

4.1 Datasets

THUMOS-14 [16]. THUMOS-14 is a dataset of videos for temporal action localization. Following the settings in existing works [10,45], we use the 200 videos in the validation set for training and 213 videos in the test set for evaluation. There are totally 20 sports action classes as well as background in these videos. Each video contains 15.8 actions on average and the background frames occupy 71% of the video.

TVSeries [4]. TVSeries contains 27 episodes untrimmed videos from six TV series. There are totally 16 h videos and 30 daily action classes such as 'eat', 'smoke'. It is a challenging dataset due to the diversity of actions, moving cameras, and heavy occlusion. This dataset provide metadata such as viewpoints and occlusions, which are used for our generalization experiments.

HDD [31]. HDD is a dataset for driving scene understanding. It includes 104 h of real human driving in the San Francisco Bay Area collected by an instrumented vehicle. There are totally 11 goal-oriented driving actions such as passing, right turn. Following the settings in [31], we use 100 sessions for training and 37 sessions for testing.

4.2 Evaluation Metrics

mean Average Precision (mAP): following existing works [4,6,42,45], we use mAP as the evaluation metric for THUMOS-14 and HDD dataset. It is computed by taking the mean of the average precision of each action class over all frames. **mean Calibrated Average Precision (mcAP).** [4] is used as the evaluation metric for TVSeries dataset. As mAP is sensitive to the ratio of positive frames versus negative background frames, it is difficult to compare two classes with different positive vs. negative ratio. To address this issue, the mcAP is used. The calibrated precision is defined as:

$$cPrec = \frac{TP}{TP + \frac{FP}{\omega}} = \frac{\omega \times TP}{\omega \times TP + FP} \tag{17}$$

where ω is the ratio between negative frames and positive frames. Then the calibrated average precision (cAP) is computed similarly as mAP:

$$cAP = \frac{\sum_k cPrec(k) \times \mathbb{1}(k)}{P} \tag{18}$$

where P is the total number of positive frames and $\mathbb{1}(k)$ is an indicator function that is equal to 1 if frame k is a true positive. The mcAP is the mean of calibrated average precision of all action classes.

4.3 Implementation Details

Feature Extraction. We use TSN [41] for feature extraction. The video frames are extracted at 24 fps and the chunk size is set to 6. We adopt a two-stream architecture with ResNet-200 [14] for appearance features and BN-Inception [17] for motion features. Specifically, the network pretrained on ActivityNet [1] outputs 3072-dimensions features. The appearance features have 2048 dimensions and the motion features have 1024 dimension. And the network pretrained on Kinetics [2] generates 4096-dimensions features. Both appearance features and motion features have 2048 dimensions.

Settings. We implemented our proposed uncertainty-based spatial-temporal attention in PyTorch [30]. The training is conducted by the Adam optimizer [21]. For TRN, the learning rate is set to 5×10^{-5} with a weight decay rate of 5×10^{-5}. The batch size is set to 12. The number of epochs is set to 25. For OadTR, we set the learning rate to 10^{-4} with a weight decay rate of 10^{-4}. The batch size is set to 128.

4.4 Main Experimental Results

To demonstrate the effectiveness of our proposed uncertainty-based spatial-temporal attention, we apply it on three baseline methods: TRN [45], OadTR [42], and LSTR [46]. Experimental results on THUMOS-14 are shown in Table 1. Results on TVSeries and HDD are shown in Table 2 and Table 3 respectively.

Table 1. Experimental results on THUMOS-14 with ActivityNet features and Kinetics features in terms of mAP (%)

Method	ActivityNet	Kinetics
TRN [45]	47.2	62.1
TRN + Spatial	48.3	62.5
TRN + Temporal	50.1	62.8
TRN + Spatial-Temporal	51.3	63.1
OadTR [42]	58.3	65.2
OadTR + Spatial	58.9	66.9
OadTR + Temporal	59.4	66.4
OadTR + Spatial-Temporal	60.7	67.5
LSTR [46]	65.3	69.5
LSTR + Spatial	65.7	69.8
LSTR + Temporal	65.9	69.9
LSTR + Spatial-Temporal	66.0	69.9

Table 2. Experimental results on TVSeries

Method	ActivityNet	Kinetics
TRN [45]	83.7	86.2
TRN + STA	85.2	86.9
OadTR [42]	85.4	87.2
OadTR + STA	86.6	87.7
LSTR [46]	88.1	89.1
LSTR + STA	88.3	89.3

Table 3. Experimental results on HDD

Method	mAP (%)
TRN [45]	29.2
TRN + STA	29.6
OadTR [42]	29.8
OadTR + STA	30.1

From the results, our proposed uncertainty-based spatial-temporal attention improves the performance of all baseline methods on three datasets. Both spatial and temporal attention improve the online action detection, especially for the RNN-based method TRN. For Transformer-based method, LSTR, the performance gain with STA is not as significant as TRN with STA. This is because the self-attention mechanisms have already used in the baseline approach which may reduce the benefits of our proposed attention. The performance of different portions of videos on TVSeries is shown in Table 4. The methods with STA outperforms baseline methods at every stage of action instances.

Table 4. Experimental results on TVSeries of different portions of videos in terms of mcAP (%). Each portion is only used to compute mcAP after detecting the current actions on all frames in an online manner.

Method	Portion of video									
	0%–10%	10%–20%	20%–30%	30%–40%	40%–50%	50%–60%	60%–70%	70%–80%	80%–90%	90%–100%
TRN [45]	78.8	79.6	80.4	81.0	81.6	81.9	82.3	82.7	82.9	83.3
TRN+STA	81.4	80.2	80.6	81.3	83.7	85.8	84.9	83	83.5	83.7
OadTR [42]	79.5	83.9	86.4	85.4	86.4	87.9	87.3	87.3	85.9	84.6
OadTR + STA	79.9	84.4	87.2	85.7	86.5	88.4	88.0	88.2	87.4	85.1
LSTR [46]	83.6	85.0	86.3	87.0	87.8	88.5	88.6	88.9	89.0	88.9
LSTR + STA	83.7	85.2	87.2	87.1	88.3	88.7	88.6	89.2	89.5	89.0

4.5 Qualitative Results

Attention and Mutual Information. To verified the mechanism in Sect. 3.4, we plot the distribution of attention and mutual information in Fig. 3. The distributions are obtained on THUMOS-14 dataset. When computing the mutual information, we select top-k high-probability actions to reduce the impact of low-probability actions. From the visualization, the attention is approximately positively related to the mutual information, which is as expected.

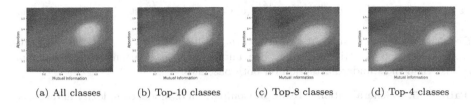

(a) All classes   (b) Top-10 classes   (c) Top-8 classes   (d) Top-4 classes

Fig. 3. Distributions of attention and mutual information. The attention is approximately positively related with the mutual information.

Temporal and Spatial Attention. Visualization of temporal and spatial attention are shown in Fig. 4. From the visualization, the action in the temporal and spatial domain are assigned with higher attention weights, which is as expected.

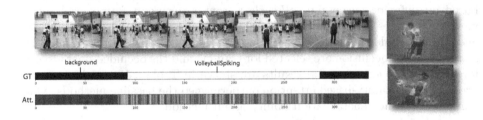

Fig. 4. Visualization of attention. The temporal attention is shown on the left and the spatial attention is shown on the right.

4.6 Ablation Studies

Training with Small-Scale Data. The amount of training data is limited in many real situations, where the data-hungry methods may not work well. To demonstrate the robustness of our proposed uncertainty-based attention, we reduce the amount of training data from 100% to 10% and compare with the deterministic baseline methods. The experimental results on two baseline methods with two features are plotted in Fig. 5. For both baseline methods with ActivityNet features and Kinetics features, our uncertainty-based attention perform better, which shows that our method is more robust. The performance gaps are obvious when the amount of training data is between 20% and 70%. When the training data is extremely limited (10%), the uncertainty estimation failed and lead to marginal improvement on the baseline methods.

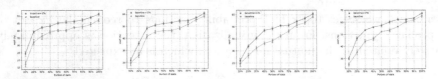

(a) TRN- ActivityNet   (b) TRN-Kinetics   (c) OadTR- ActivityNet   (d) OadTR- Kinetics

Fig. 5. Experiment results of training with small-scale data on THUMOS-14 with ActivityNet and Kinetics features. The uncertainty-based attention perform more robust than the standard attention on both baselines.

Table 5. Generalization experimental results.

Method	CV (%)	Occ. (%)
TRN [45]	65.8	85.2
TRN + STA	69.5	88.6
OadTR [42]	66.2	87.7
OadTR + STA	67.3	89.5

Table 6. Comparison of model complexity and computation cost.

Method	# of Paras	FLOPs	Per-frame speed	Memory cost
TRN [45]	357.8 M	1.4 G	0.0104 s	6479 MB
TRN + STA	379.2 M	3.1 G	0.0201 s	9662 MB
OadTR [42]	74.7 M	2.5 G	0.0069 s	1787 MB
OadTR + STA	78.5 M	5.9 G	0.0094 s	2835 MB

Generalization. Based on the meta annotations of TVSeries, we perform two kinds of generalization experiments. First, we divide the dataset into two parts based on different viewpoints. We select frontal viewpoint frames and special viewpoint frames as the training set, and side viewpoint frames as testing set. Second, we divide the dataset based on occlusion conditions in the frames. The frames without occlusion are selected for training and the occluded ones are used for testing. The experimental results are shown in Table 5. For both cases, our proposed uncertainty-based attention outperformed the baseline methods, which demonstrates the generalization ability of our method.

Computation Efficiency and Model Complexity. We made a comparison with baseline methods in Table 6. Compared with the baseline methods, our proposed uncertainty-based attention increase the computation cost of baseline methods since we need to sample from the parameter distribution and perform K times forward process. Compared with baseline ensembles, our method perform better with less computation cost and model complexity. We also make a comparison of inference speed and memory cost. The computation complexity increase linearly and our method can still achieve real-time responses.

5   Conclusion and Future Work

In this paper, we proposed uncertainty-based spatial-temporal attention for online action detection. By modeling the predictive uncertainty, the proposed attention mechanism improves the model with more discriminative features. Under the probabilistic setting, the generalization and robustness of the model are also improved. The proposed method is validated on three benchmark datasets to show the effectiveness, generalization, and robustness.

Future work may include the evaluation of different uncertainty quantification methods and improving the computation efficiency.

Acknowledgement. This project is supported in part by a gift from Wormpex AI Research to Rensselaer Polytechnic Institute.

References

1. Caba Heilbron, F., Escorcia, V., Ghanem, B., Carlos Niebles, J.: Activitynet: a large-scale video benchmark for human activity understanding. In: Proceedings of the IEEE Conference on Computer Vision and Pattern Recognition, pp. 961–970 (2015)
2. Carreira, J., Zisserman, A.: Quo vadis, action recognition? A new model and the kinetics dataset. In: Proceedings of the IEEE Conference on Computer Vision and Pattern Recognition, pp. 6299–6308 (2017)
3. Dai, R., Das, S., Kahatapitiya, K., Ryoo, M.S., Bremond, F.: MS-TCT: multi-scale temporal convtransformer for action detection. In: Proceedings of the IEEE/CVF Conference on Computer Vision and Pattern Recognition, pp. 20041–20051 (2022)
4. De Geest, R., Gavves, E., Ghodrati, A., Li, Z., Snoek, C., Tuytelaars, T.: Online action detection. In: Leibe, B., Matas, J., Sebe, N., Welling, M. (eds.) ECCV 2016. LNCS, vol. 9909, pp. 269–284. Springer, Cham (2016). https://doi.org/10.1007/978-3-319-46454-1_17
5. Du, W., Wang, Y., Qiao, Y.: Recurrent spatial-temporal attention network for action recognition in videos. IEEE Trans. Image Process. **27**(3), 1347–1360 (2017)
6. Eun, H., Moon, J., Park, J., Jung, C., Kim, C.: Learning to discriminate information for online action detection. In: Proceedings of the IEEE/CVF Conference on Computer Vision and Pattern Recognition, pp. 809–818 (2020)
7. Eun, H., Moon, J., Park, J., Jung, C., Kim, C.: Temporal filtering networks for online action detection. Pattern Recogn. **111**, 107695 (2021)
8. Fu, Y., Wang, X., Wei, Y., Huang, T.: STA: spatial-temporal attention for large-scale video-based person re-identification. In: Proceedings of the AAAI Conference on Artificial Intelligence, vol. 33, pp. 8287–8294 (2019)
9. Gal, Y., Ghahramani, Z.: Dropout as a Bayesian approximation: representing model uncertainty in deep learning. In: International Conference on Machine Learning, pp. 1050–1059. PMLR (2016)
10. Gao, J., Yang, Z., Nevatia, R.: RED: reinforced encoder-decoder networks for action anticipation. arXiv preprint arXiv:1707.04818 (2017)
11. Gao, M., Xu, M., Davis, L.S., Socher, R., Xiong, C.: Startnet: online detection of action start in untrimmed videos. In: Proceedings of the IEEE/CVF International Conference on Computer Vision, pp. 5542–5551 (2019)
12. Gao, M., Zhou, Y., Xu, R., Socher, R., Xiong, C.: Woad: weakly supervised online action detection in untrimmed videos. In: Proceedings of the IEEE/CVF Conference on Computer Vision and Pattern Recognition, pp. 1915–1923 (2021)
13. Guo, H., Wang, H., Ji, Q.: Uncertainty-guided probabilistic transformer for complex action recognition. In: Proceedings of the IEEE/CVF Conference on Computer Vision and Pattern Recognition, pp. 20052–20061 (2022)

14. He, K., Zhang, X., Ren, S., Sun, J.: Deep residual learning for image recognition. In: Proceedings of the IEEE Conference on Computer Vision and Pattern Recognition, pp. 770–778 (2016)
15. Horn, R.A.: The hadamard product. In: Proceedings of Symposia in Applied Mathematics, vol. 40, pp. 87–169 (1990)
16. Idrees, H., et al.: The THUMOS challenge on action recognition for videos "in the wild". Comput. Vis. Image Underst. **155**, 1–23 (2017)
17. Ioffe, S., Szegedy, C.: Batch normalization: accelerating deep network training by reducing internal covariate shift. In: International Conference on Machine Learning, pp. 448–456. PMLR (2015)
18. Jaderberg, M., Simonyan, K., Zisserman, A., et al.: Spatial transformer networks. Adv. Neural. Inf. Process. Syst. **28**, 2017–2025 (2015)
19. Janai, J., Güney, F., Behl, A., Geiger, A., et al.: Computer vision for autonomous vehicles: problems, datasets and state of the art. Found. Trends® Comput. Graph. Vis. **12**(1–3), 1–308 (2020)
20. Kendall, A., Gal, Y.: What uncertainties do we need in Bayesian deep learning for computer vision? In: Advances in Neural Information Processing Systems, vol. 30 (2017)
21. Kingma, D.P., Ba, J.: Adam: a method for stochastic optimization. In: ICLR (2015)
22. Kingma, D.P., Salimans, T., Welling, M.: Variational dropout and the local reparameterization trick. Adv. Neural. Inf. Process. Syst. **28**, 2575–2583 (2015)
23. Lakshminarayanan, B., Pritzel, A., Blundell, C.: Simple and scalable predictive uncertainty estimation using deep ensembles. In: Advances in Neural Information Processing Systems, vol. 30 (2017)
24. Li, Y., Lan, C., Xing, J., Zeng, W., Yuan, C., Liu, J.: Online human action detection using joint classification-regression recurrent neural networks. In: Leibe, B., Matas, J., Sebe, N., Welling, M. (eds.) ECCV 2016. LNCS, vol. 9911, pp. 203–220. Springer, Cham (2016). https://doi.org/10.1007/978-3-319-46478-7_13
25. Liu, J., Li, Y., Song, S., Xing, J., Lan, C., Zeng, W.: Multi-modality multi-task recurrent neural network for online action detection. IEEE Trans. Circuits Syst. Video Technol. **29**(9), 2667–2682 (2018)
26. Liu, J., Shahroudy, A., Wang, G., Duan, L.Y., Kot, A.C.: SSNet: scale selection network for online 3D action prediction. In: Proceedings of the IEEE Conference on Computer Vision and Pattern Recognition, pp. 8349–8358 (2018)
27. Malinin, A., Gales, M.: Predictive uncertainty estimation via prior networks. In: Advances in Neural Information Processing Systems, vol. 31 (2018)
28. Mnih, V., Heess, N., Graves, A., et al.: Recurrent models of visual attention. In: Advances in Neural Information Processing Systems, pp. 2204–2212 (2014)
29. Pan, J., Chen, S., Shou, M.Z., Liu, Y., Shao, J., Li, H.: Actor-context-actor relation network for spatio-temporal action localization. In: Proceedings of the IEEE/CVF Conference on Computer Vision and Pattern Recognition, pp. 464–474 (2021)
30. Paszke, A., et al.: Automatic differentiation in pytorch (2017)
31. Ramanishka, V., Chen, Y.T., Misu, T., Saenko, K.: Toward driving scene understanding: a dataset for learning driver behavior and causal reasoning. In: Proceedings of the IEEE Conference on Computer Vision and Pattern Recognition, pp. 7699–7707 (2018)
32. Shou, Z., et al.: Online action detection in untrimmed, streaming videos-modeling and evaluation. In: ECCV, vol. 1, p. 5 (2018)
33. Shou, Z., Wang, D., Chang, S.F.: Temporal action localization in untrimmed videos via multi-stage CNNs. In: Proceedings of the IEEE Conference on Computer Vision and Pattern Recognition, pp. 1049–1058 (2016)

34. Smith, L., Gal, Y.: Understanding measures of uncertainty for adversarial example detection. arXiv preprint arXiv:1803.08533 (2018)
35. Song, S., Lan, C., Xing, J., Zeng, W., Liu, J.: An end-to-end spatio-temporal attention model for human action recognition from skeleton data. In: Proceedings of the AAAI Conference on Artificial Intelligence, vol. 31 (2017)
36. Subedar, M., Krishnan, R., Meyer, P.L., Tickoo, O., Huang, J.: Uncertainty-aware audiovisual activity recognition using deep Bayesian variational inference. In: Proceedings of the IEEE/CVF International Conference on Computer Vision, pp. 6301–6310 (2019)
37. Sultani, W., Chen, C., Shah, M.: Real-world anomaly detection in surveillance videos. In: Proceedings of the IEEE Conference on Computer Vision and Pattern Recognition, pp. 6479–6488 (2018)
38. Thomas, G., Gade, R., Moeslund, T.B., Carr, P., Hilton, A.: Computer vision for sports: current applications and research topics. Comput. Vis. Image Underst. **159**, 3–18 (2017)
39. Tran, D., Dusenberry, M., van der Wilk, M., Hafner, D.: Bayesian layers: a module for neural network uncertainty. Adv. Neural. Inf. Process. Syst. **32**, 14660–14672 (2019)
40. Vaswani, A., et al.: Attention is all you need. In: Advances in Neural Information Processing Systems, pp. 5998–6008 (2017)
41. Wang, L., et al.: Temporal segment networks: towards good practices for deep action recognition. In: Leibe, B., Matas, J., Sebe, N., Welling, M. (eds.) ECCV 2016. LNCS, vol. 9912, pp. 20–36. Springer, Cham (2016). https://doi.org/10.1007/978-3-319-46484-8_2
42. Wang, X., et al.: OadTR: online action detection with transformers. arXiv preprint arXiv:2106.11149 (2021)
43. Wang, X., Girshick, R., Gupta, A., He, K.: Non-local neural networks. In: Proceedings of the IEEE Conference on Computer Vision and Pattern Recognition, pp. 7794–7803 (2018)
44. Wang, Z., Li, Y., Guo, Y., Fang, L., Wang, S.: Data-uncertainty guided multi-phase learning for semi-supervised object detection. In: Proceedings of the IEEE/CVF Conference on Computer Vision and Pattern Recognition, pp. 4568–4577 (2021)
45. Xu, M., Gao, M., Chen, Y.T., Davis, L.S., Crandall, D.J.: Temporal recurrent networks for online action detection. In: Proceedings of the IEEE/CVF International Conference on Computer Vision, pp. 5532–5541 (2019)
46. Xu, M., et al.: Long short-term transformer for online action detection. In: Advances in Neural Information Processing Systems, vol. 34 (2021)
47. Yang, F., et al.: Uncertainty-guided transformer reasoning for camouflaged object detection. In: Proceedings of the IEEE/CVF International Conference on Computer Vision, pp. 4146–4155 (2021)
48. Yang, J., Zheng, W.S., Yang, Q., Chen, Y.C., Tian, Q.: Spatial-temporal graph convolutional network for video-based person re-identification. In: Proceedings of the IEEE/CVF Conference on Computer Vision and Pattern Recognition, pp. 3289–3299 (2020)
49. Zhao, C., Thabet, A.K., Ghanem, B.: Video self-stitching graph network for temporal action localization. In: Proceedings of the IEEE/CVF International Conference on Computer Vision, pp. 13658–13667 (2021)

50. Zhao, J., et al.: TubeR: Tubelet transformer for video action detection. In: Proceedings of the IEEE/CVF Conference on Computer Vision and Pattern Recognition, pp. 13598–13607 (2022)
51. Zhao, P., Xie, L., Zhang, Y., Wang, Y., Tian, Q.: Privileged knowledge distillation for online action detection. arXiv preprint arXiv:2011.09158 (2020)
52. Zhao, Y., Xiong, Y., Wang, L., Wu, Z., Tang, X., Lin, D.: Temporal action detection with structured segment networks. In: Proceedings of the IEEE International Conference on Computer Vision, pp. 2914–2923 (2017)

Iwin: Human-Object Interaction Detection via Transformer with Irregular Windows

Danyang Tu[1], Xiongkuo Min[1], Huiyu Duan[1], Guodong Guo[2],
Guangtao Zhai[1(✉)], and Wei Shen[3(✉)]

[1] Institute of Image Communication and Network Engineering, Shanghai Jiao Tong
University, Shanghai, China
{danyangtu,minxiongkuo,huiyuduan,wei.shen}@sjtu.edu.cn
[2] Institute of Deep Learning, Baidu Research, Beijing, China
zhaiguangtao@sjtu.edu.cn
[3] MoE Key Lab of Artificial Intelligence, AI Institute, Shanghai Jiao Tong
University, Shanghai, China
guoguodong01@baidu.com

Abstract. This paper presents a new vision Transformer, named Iwin
Transformer, which is specifically designed for human-object interaction
(HOI) detection, a detailed scene understanding task involving a sequential process of human/object detection and interaction recognition. Iwin
Transformer is a hierarchical Transformer which progressively performs
token representation learning and token agglomeration within irregular
windows. The irregular windows, achieved by augmenting regular grid
locations with learned offsets, 1) eliminate redundancy in token representation learning, which leads to efficient human/object detection, and
2) enable the agglomerated tokens to align with humans/objects with
different shapes, which facilitates the acquisition of highly-abstracted
visual semantics for interaction recognition. The effectiveness and efficiency of Iwin Transformer are verified on the two standard HOI detection benchmark datasets, HICO-DET and V-COCO. Results show our
method outperforms existing Transformers-based methods by large margins (3.7 mAP gain on HICO-DET and 2.0 mAP gain on V-COCO) with
fewer training epochs (0.5×).

Keywords: Human-object interaction detection · Transformers ·
Irregular windows

1 Introduction

Given an image containing several humans and objects, the goal of human-
object interaction (HOI) detection is to localize each pair of human and object
as well as to recognize their interaction. It has attracted considerable research
interests recently for its great potential in the high-level human-centric scene
understanding tasks.

Recently, vision Transformers [37] have started to revolutionize the HOI
detection task, which enable end-to-end HOI detection and achieve leading

© The Author(s), under exclusive license to Springer Nature Switzerland AG 2022
S. Avidan et al. (Eds.): ECCV 2022, LNCS 13664, pp. 87–103, 2022.
https://doi.org/10.1007/978-3-031-19772-7_6

Fig. 1. An illustration of **regular windows** and **irregular windows**. For regular window, the window can be a global rectangle containing the entire image (**a**) or a local one (**b**) that might divide an object into parts. In contrast, irregular windows can align with the arbitrary shapes of objects or semantic regions. We can rearrange the tokens within an irregular window to form a rectangular window for self-attention computation

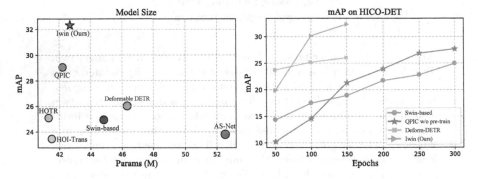

Fig. 2. Model size and **training epochs** vs. performance analysis for HOI detection on HICO-DET. Specifically, Swin-based refers to perform a Swin-T model on the output of a FPN as the encoder of a Transformer. For fair comparison, all the models in the right sub-figure are trained from scratch

performance [3,15,35,44,51]. However, they mainly adopt DETR-like [1] Transformers, which learn visual semantics by self-attention between patch tokens within rectangular windows (Fig. 1), either local or global, resulting in mixed and redundant visual semantics. Such visual semantics fail to capture object-level abstractions, which are crucial for interaction recognition.

To address the aforementioned limitation, we propose Iwin Transformer, short for Transformer with <u>i</u>rregular <u>win</u>dows, which is a new hierarchical vision Transformer specifically designed for HOI detection. The irregular windows, as illustrated in Fig. 1, are obtained by augmenting regular grid locations with learned offsets, which are expected to be aligned with humans/objects with arbitrary shapes. Iwin Transformer performs both token representation learning and token agglomeration within irregular windows. The former eliminates redundancy in self-attention computation between patch-level tokens, leading to efficient human/object detection; The latter progressively structurizes an image as a few agglomerated tokens with highly-abstracted visual semantics, the contextual relations between which can be easily captured for interaction recognition.

Iwin Transformer takes the characteristic of HOI detection into account, *i.e.*, a sequential process of human/object detection and interaction recognition, enjoying both higher efficiency and better effectiveness, as shown in Fig. 2.

It is worth emphasizing that our method is different from regular window-based Transformers as well as deformable DETR [50]. In addition to the different objectives, the former, *e.g.*, Swin Transformer [26], partitions an image into several regular windows that are not aligned with humans/objects with different shapes, leading to redundancy in self-attention computation; The latter, *i.e.*, deformable DETR, deals with a fixed number of tokens without token grouping, being weak in extracting highly-abstracted visual semantics.

Experimental results show that Iwin Transformer outperforms existing SOTA methods by large margins and is much easier to train. Specifically, Iwin achieves a 3.7 mAP gain on HICO-DET [2] and a 2.0 mAP gain on V-COCO [8] with fewer training epochs (0.5×).

2   Related Work

CNN-Based HOI Detection. CNN-based methods can be divided into two different types:1) Two-stage. Most two-stage methods [2,5–7,9,12,14,16,18,20, 24,25,31,36,38–40,42,43,46,48,49] obtain the human and object proposals by using a pre-trained object detector firstly, and then predict interaction labels by combining features from localized regions. More specifically, they first use Faster R-CNN [33] or Mask R-CNN [10] to localize targets, including humans and objects. Then, the cropped features are fed into a multi-stream network, which normally contains a human stream, an object stream and a pairwise stream. The first two process features of target humans and objects, respectively, and the last one normally processes some auxiliary features, such as spatial configurations of the targets, human poses, or the combination of them. In addition, some other methods utilize graph neural networks to refine the features [31,36,39,43,45,48]. Such methods have made impressive progress in HOI detection, but they still suffer from low efficiency and effectiveness. 2) Single-stage. Different from two-stage methods, single-stage methods detect the targets and their interactions simultaneously. In detail, UnionDet [14] predicts the interactions for each human-object union box by an anchor-based method. PPDM [21] and IPNet [41] represent the interactions as the midpoints of human-object pairs and detect them based on point detection networks. GGNet [47] further improves the performance of the point-based method by introducing a novel glance and gaze manner. These methods are simpler, but are weak in modeling long range contextual information, resulting in poor performance when human and object are far apart.

Transformers-Based HOI Detection. Recently, Transformers-based methods have been proposed to handle HOI detection as a set prediction problem. More specifically, [35,51] design the HOI instances as some learnable queries, and use a typical Transformer with encoder-decoder architectures to directly predict HOI instances in an end-to-end manner. In addition, [3,15] detect human-object instances and interaction labels with parallel decoders. In [44], human/object

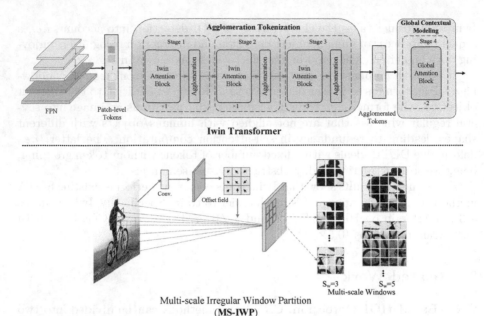

Fig. 3. An overview of Iwin Transformer. For simplicity of presentation, the decoder and matching component are omitted. The detailed illustrations about "Iwin Attention Block" and "Agglomeration" can be seen in Fig. 4

detection and interaction classification are disentangled in a cascade manner. However, these methods adopt the simple tokenization strategy to structurize an image into a sequence of local patches, which is insufficient for detailed image understanding tasks like HOI detection.

3   Method

An overview of the proposed Iwin Transformer is presented in Fig. 3. In this section, we start with a general description of the entire model, followed by a detailed technical description of each key component.

3.1   Architecture Overview

Backbone. Taking as input an image $\mathbf{x} \in \mathbb{R}^{3 \times H \times W}$, the feature maps with different spatial resolutions are firstly computed by using a ResNet [11] backbone to model local structures. Then, a feature pyramid network (FPN) is performed to get a high resolution feature map $\mathbf{z}_b \in \mathbb{R}^{C_b \times \frac{H}{4} \times \frac{W}{4}}$ by weighted merging the feature maps with different resolutions, to ensure reliable performance in detecting small objects. Here, C_b is the number of channels.

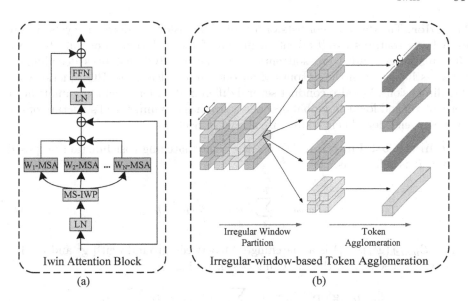

Fig. 4. Iwin attention block (a) and Irregular window-based token agglomeration (b). "LN" refers to layer normalization

Encoder. The encoder consists of two main parts: 1) agglomerative tokenization that progressively structurizes an image as a few agglomerated tokens by recursively performing irregular window-based token representation learning and agglomeration. 2) global contextual modeling for long-range context modeling. *Agglomerative Tokenization.* It consists of three "Stage"s in a cascaded manner. Each stage is composed of token representation learning and token agglomeration within irregular windows. Specifically, token representation learning is performed by stacking several attention blocks based on multi-scale irregular window partition (MS-IWP), *i.e.*, "Iwin Attention Block" in Fig. 3. We describe it in detail in the next Sect. 3.3. After token representation learning, tokens in an irregular window are agglomerated into new tokens as the inputs for the next stage, which is described in detailed in Sect. 3.4. By recursively performing irregular window-based token representation learning and agglomeration, an image can be structurized as a few agglomerated tokens with highly-abstracted semantics. *Global Contextual Modeling.* After agglomerative tokenization, we then apply two cascaded global self-attention blocks to modeling the global contextual information. Unlike Iwin attention block, the attention weights are computed among all tokens in a global self-attention block. There are two main reasons: 1) interaction recognition demands a larger and more flexible receptive field, since the human and the object he/she interacts with may be far away or very close. 2) one interaction instance can provide some clues for the recognition of another interaction category, *e.g.*, a man holding a fork is likely to be eating something. Although attention is computed in a global manner, global self-attention block does not introduce too much computation since the number of tokens has been greatly reduced after agglomerative tokenization.

Decoder. The decoder consists of 6 typical Transformer decoder layers, where each layer contains a self-attention module for correlations modeling between HOI instances, and a cross-attention module for HOI instances decoding. It takes as inputs both the outputs of encoder and N learnable HOI queries with 256 dimensions. We also conduct several different decoders, including multi-layer perceptron and local-to-global decoder which has a symmetrical structure of the proposed encoder. Their results are shown in Sect. 4.4.

Matching Cost Function. We use the same matching cost function proposed in [35]. It is defined as:

$$\mathcal{L}_{cost} = \sum_{i}^{N} \mathcal{L}_{match}(\mathbf{g}^i, \mathbf{p}^{\sigma(i)}), \tag{1}$$

where $\mathcal{L}_{match}(\mathbf{g}^i, \mathbf{p}^{\sigma(i)})$ is a matching cost between ground truth $\mathbf{g}^i$ and prediction $\mathbf{p}^{\sigma(i)}$. Specifically, the matching cost is designed as:

$$\mathcal{L}_{match}(\mathbf{g}^i, \mathbf{p}^{\sigma(i)}) = \beta_1 \sum_{j \in h,o,r} \alpha_j \mathcal{L}_{cls}^j + \beta_2 \sum_{k \in h,o} \mathcal{L}_{box}^k, \tag{2}$$

where $\mathcal{L}_{cls}^j = \mathcal{L}_{cls}(g_j^i, p_j^{\theta(i)})$ is cross-entropy loss function, $j \in \{h,o,r\}$ denotes human, object or interaction, and g_j^i represents the class label of j on ground-truth g^i. $\mathcal{L}_{box}^k$ is box regression loss for human box and object box, which is a weighted sum of GIoU [34] loss and L_1 loss. β and α are both hyper-parameters. Finally, the Hungarian algorithm [17] is used to solve the following problem to find a bipartite matching:

$$\hat{\sigma} = \arg\min_{\sigma \in \mathfrak{S}_N} \mathcal{L}_{cost}, \tag{3}$$

where $\mathfrak{S}_N$ denotes the one-to-one matching solution space.

3.2   Irregular Window Partition

Window partition is firstly proposed in [26], which splits an image into several regular windows, as illustrated in Fig. 1. Considering a feature map with resolution of $H \times W$ and dimension of C, the computational complexity of a global multi head self-attention (G-MSA) module and a window-based one (W-MSA) with window size of $S_w \times S_w$ are:

$$\Omega(\text{G-MSA}) = 4HWC^2 + 2(HW)^2C, \tag{4}$$

$$\Omega(\text{W-MSA}) = 4HWC^2 + 2S_w^2HWC, \tag{5}$$

where the former is of quadratic computation $w.r.t$ pixel numbers while the latter is of linear computation. In regular window partition scheme, the tokens are sampled by using a regular rectangle $\mathcal{R}$ over the input feature map $\mathbf{z}$, where the rectangle $\mathcal{R}$ defines the receptive field size. For example, $\mathcal{R} = \{(0,0), (0,1), ..., (3,4), (4,4)\}$ defines a window with size of 5×5. However, as shown in Fig. 1, regular windows may divide an object into parts and the tokens in a window are most likely unrelated, leading to redundancy in self-attention computing. Inspired by [4], we propose irregular window partition by augmenting the regular windows with learned offsets $\mathbf{f_o} \in \mathbb{R}^{2 \times H \times W}$. Specifically, the $\mathbf{f_o}$ is learned by performing a convolutional layer with a kernel size of 3×3 over the entire feature map. With the learned offsets $\mathbf{f_o}$, we can rearrange the tokens that are sampled from the irregular and offset locations $\mathbf{z}(\mathbf{p}_n + \Delta_{\mathbf{p}_n})$ to form a rectangular window, where $\mathbf{p}_n \in \mathcal{R}$ are the sampling locations for regular windows while $\Delta_{\mathbf{p}_n} \in \mathbf{f_o}$ are the learned offsets, $n = 1, 2, ..., |\mathcal{R}|$. Since the learned offset $\Delta_{\mathbf{p}_n}$ is usually fractional, $\mathbf{z}(\mathbf{p})$ is defined via bilinear interpolation as

$$\mathbf{z}(\mathbf{p}) = \sum_{\mathbf{q}} K(\mathbf{q}, \mathbf{p}) \cdot \mathbf{z}(\mathbf{q}), \tag{6}$$

where $\mathbf{p}$ denotes an arbitrary location $\mathbf{p}_n + \Delta_{\mathbf{p}_n}$, $\mathbf{q}$ enumerates all integral spatial locations, and $K(\cdot, \cdot)$ is the bilinear interpolation kernel. Since K is two dimensional, it can be separated into two one dimensional kernels as

$$K(\mathbf{p}, \mathbf{q}) = k(q_x, p_x) \cdot k(q_y, p_y), \tag{7}$$

where $k(a, b) = \max(0, 1 - |a - b|)$.

For convenience, we simply use the term "an irregular window with size of $S_w \times S_w$" to denote an irregular window that is generated by augmenting a regular rectangle with size of $S_w \times S_w$ in the following.

3.3   Irregular-Window-Based Token Representation Learning

Irregular-window-based token representation learning is performed by stacked several Iwin attention blocks, where self-attention is computed within irregular windows. As illustrated in Fig. 4 (a), all Iwin attention blocks have an identical structure, which contains a multi-scale irregular window partition (MS-IWP) module, several window-based multi-head self-attention (W-MSA) modules as well as a feed-forward network (FFN). Specifically, in MS-IWP, a input feature map is dynamically splitted into several irregular windows by performing irregular window partitioning. Then, we rearrange the tokens within an irregular window to form a rectangular window for self-attention computition. Moreover, the window size S_w is designed to be various since the scales of the humans/objects in an image can be different, as illustrated in Fig. 3. Specifically, $S_w \in \{5, 7\}$ for "Stage-1" and "Stage-2" and $S_w \in \{3, 5\}$ for "Stage-3". Then, we apply multi-head self-attention within each window. As shown in Fig. 4, window-based multi-head self-attention (W-MSA) is applied for N times as there are windows of N different sizes. After that, the output feature maps of different W-MSA modules are weighted summed via a convolutional layer with kernel size of 1×1. Finally, the FFN is applied to the sum of different W-MSA modules and input features, and each FFN is formed by two dense linear layers with ReLU [29] activations in between.

3.4 Irregular-window-based Token Agglomeration

As illustrated in Fig. 4 (b), we first perform irregular window partitioning with a size of 2×2, *i.e.*, every 4 related tokens are grouped into one window. Then, these 4 tokens are concatenated to generate a $4C$-dimensional feature, where C is the number of channels of one token. After that, we apply a linear layer on the $4C$-dimensional feature as

$$t_{new} = \mathbf{w} \cdot \text{concat} \left[\mathbf{z}(\mathbf{p}_n + \Delta_{\mathbf{p}_n}) | n \in 1, 2, 3, 4 \right], \tag{8}$$

where $\mathbf{w}$ denotes the learned weights of linear layer. $\mathbf{p}_n$ and $\Delta_{\mathbf{p}_n}$ are regular grid locations and learned offsets, respectively. The output dimension of the linear layer is set as $2C$.

After each stage in tokenization, the number of tokens is reduced by a factor of $2 \times 2 = 4$, and the dimension of feature map are doubled (from C to $2C$). Specifically, The number of tokens before and after "Stage-i" are $\frac{H}{2^{1+i}} \times \frac{W}{2^{1+i}}$ and $\frac{H}{2^{2+i}} \times \frac{W}{2^{2+i}}$ respectively, and the output dimensions are $64 \times 2^{i-1}$. It not only further reduces the redundancy of tokens, but also enables the newly generated tokens to be aligned with humans/objects with different shapes and to characterize higher-abstracted visual semantics.

4 Experiments

4.1 Datasets and Evaluation Metric

Datasets. We conducted experiments on HICO-DET [2] and V-COCO [8] benchmarks to evaluate the proposed method by following the standard scheme. Specifically, HICO-DET contains 38,118 and 9,658 images for training and testing, and includes 600 HOI categories (*full*) over 117 interactions and 80 objects. It has been further split into 138 Rare (*rare*) and 462 Non-Rare (*non-rare*) HOI categories based on the number of training instances. V-COCO is a relatively smaller dataset that originates from the COCO [23]. It consists of 2,533 and 2,867 images for training, validation, as well as 4,946 ones for testing. The images are annotated with 80 object and 29 action classes.

Evaluation Metric. We use the commonly used mean average precision (mAP) to evaluate model performance on both datasets. A predicted HOI instance is considered as true positive if and only if the predicted human and object bounding boxes both have IoUs larger than 0.5 with the corresponding ground-truth bounding boxes, and the predicted action label is correct.

Moreover, for HICO-DET, we evaluate model performance in two different settings following [2]: (1) *Known-object setting*. For each HOI category, we evaluate the detection only on the images containing the target object category. (2) *Default setting*. For each HOI category, we evalute the detection on the full test set, including images that may not contain the target object.

Table 1. Performance comparison on the HICO-Det test set. 'P' refers to human pose and 'L' denotes language. The Best performance are represented in red and the second best ones are shown in **blue**.

Method	Backbone	Detector	P	L	Default			Known object		
					Full↑	Rare↑	NonRare↑	Full↑	Rare↑	NonRare↑
CNN-based two-stage methods										
InteractNet [7]	ResNet-50-FPN	COCO			9.94	7.16	10.77	-	-	-
GPNN [31]	ResNet-101	COCO			13.11	9.34	14.23	-	-	-
iCAN [6]	ResNet-50	COCO			14.84	10.45	16.15	16.26	11.33	17.73
No-Frills [9]	ResNet-152	COCO		✓	17.18	12.17	18.68	-	-	-
TIN [20]	ResNet-50	COCO	✓		17.22	13.51	18.32	19.38	15.38	20.57
PMFNet [38]	ResNet-50-FPN	COCO	✓		17.46	15.65	18.00	20.34	17.47	21.20
CHG [39]	ResNet-50	COCO			17.57	16.85	17.78	21.00	20.74	21.08
Peyre et al. [30]	ResNet-50-FPN	COCO		✓	19.40	14.63	20.87	-	-	-
VSGNet [36]	ResNet152	COCO			19.80	16.05	20.91	-	-	-
FCMNet [25]	ResNet-50	COCO	✓	✓	20.41	17.34	21.56	22.04	18.97	23.12
ACP [16]	ResNet-152	COCO	✓	✓	20.59	15.92	21.98	-	-	-
PD-Net [46]	ResNet-152	COCO		✓	20.81	15.90	22.28	24.78	18.88	26.54
PastaNet [19]	ResNet-50	COCO	✓	✓	22.65	21.17	23.09	24.53	23.00	24.99
VCL [12]	ResNet101	COCO			19.43	16.55	20.29	22.00	19.09	22.87
DRG [5]	ResNet-50-FPN	COCO		✓	19.26	17.74	19.71	23.40	21.75	23.89
Zhang et al. [45]	ResNet-50-FPN	COCO			21.85	18.11	22.97	-	-	-
CNN-based single-stage methods										
UnionDet [14]	ResNet-50-FPN	HICO-DET			17.58	11.52	19.33	19.76	14.68	21.27
IPNet [41]	Hourglass	COCO			19.56	12.79	21.58	22.05	15.77	23.92
PPDM [21]	Hourglass	HICO-DET			21.73	13.78	24.10	24.58	16.65	26.84
GGNet [47]	Hourglass	HICO-DET			23.47	16.48	25.60	27.36	20.23	29.48
ATL [13]	ResNet-50	HICO-DET			23.81	17.43	25.72	27.38	22.09	28.96
Transformer-based methods										
HOI-Trans [51]	ResNet-50	HICO-DET			23.46	16.91	25.41	26.15	19.24	28.22
HOTR [15]	ResNet-50	HICO-DET			25.10	17.34	27.42	-	-	-
AS-Net [3]	ResNet-50	HICO-DET			28.87	24.25	30.25	31.74	27.07	33.14
QPIC [35]	ResNet-50	HICO-DET			29.07	21.85	31.23	31.68	24.14	33.93
Iwin-S (Ours)	ResNet-50-FPN	HICO-DET			24.33	18.50	26.04	28.41	20.67	30.17
Iwin-B (Ours)	ResNet-50-FPN	HICO-DET			**32.03**	**27.62**	**34.14**	**35.17**	28.79	**35.91**
Iwin-L (Ours)	ResNet-101-FPN	HICO-DET			32.79	27.84	35.40	35.84	28.74	36.09

4.2 Implementation Details

We implemented three variant architectures of Iwin: Iwin-S, Iwin-B, and Iwin-L, where "S", "B" and "L" refer to small, base and large, respectively. The number of blocks in these model variants are:

- Iwin-S: $D_c = 32$, block numbers = $\{1, 1, 1, 1\}$,
- Iwin-B: $D_c = 64$, block numbers = $\{1, 1, 3, 2\}$,
- Iwin-L: $D_c = 64$, block numbers = $\{1, 1, 3, 2\}$,

where we applied ResNet-50 as a backbone feature extractor for both Iwin-S and Iwin-B, and ResNet-101 was utilized for Iwin-L. Besides, the decoder contains 6 Transformers decoder layers and the hyper-parameters β_1, α and β_2 in the loss function are set as 1, 1, 2.5 for all experiments. The number of

Table 2. Performance comparison on the V-COCO test set

Method	Backbone	P	L	AP_{role}
CNN-based two-stage methods				
InteractNet [7]	ResNet-50-FPN			40.00
GPNN [31]	ResNet-101			44.00
iCAN [6]	ResNet-50			45.30
TIN [20]	ResNet-50			47.80
VSGNet [36]	ResNet152			51.80
PMFNet [38]	ResNet-50-FPN	✓		52.00
CHG [39]	ResNet-50			52.70
FCMNet [25]	ResNet-50	✓	✓	53.10
ACP [16]	ResNet-152		✓	53.23
CNN-based single-stage methods				
UnionDet [14]	ResNet-50-FPN			47.50
IPNet [41]	Hourglass			51.00
GGNet [47]	Hourglass			54.70
Transformer-based methods				
HOI-Trans [51]	ResNet-50			52.90
HOTR [15]	ResNet-50			55.20
AS-Net [3]	ResNet-50			53.90
QPIC [35]	ResNet-50			58.80
Iwin-S (Ours)	ResNet-50-FPN			51.81
Iwin-B (Ours)	ResNet-50-FPN			**60.47**
Iwin-L (Ours)	ResNet-101-FPN			60.85

Table 3. The effects of different modules. "IWP": irregular window partition, "MS": multi-scale windows, "TA": token agglomeration and "GC": global contextual modeling

FPN	IWP	MS	TA	GC	Full↑	Rare↑	NoneRare↑
	✓	✓	✓	✓	31.24	26.01	32.95
✓		✓	✓	✓	29.12	24.74	31.08
✓	✓		✓	✓	31.42	26.97	33.15
✓			✓	✓	26.33	24.05	28.21
✓	✓	✓		✓	30.16	25.68	32.49
✓	✓	✓	✓		23.05	16.50	24.62
✓	✓	✓	✓	✓	**32.03**	**27.62**	**34.14**

Table 4. Comparison between different types of token agglomeration strategy

Strategy	Full↑	Rare↑	NoneRare↑
Norm-window	27.50	24.27	29.84
K-means	28.19	24.72	30.12
Irregular-window	**32.03**	**27.62**	**34.14**

queries N was set to 50 for HICO-DET and 100 for V-COCO. Unlike existing methods that initialized the network by the parameters of DETR trained with the COCO dataset, which contains prior-information about objects, we train Iwin Transformer from scratch. We employed an AdamW [27] optimizer for 150 epochs as well as a multi-step decay learning rate scheduler. A batch size of 16, an initial learning rate of 2.5e-4 for Transformers and 1e-5 for backbone are used. The learning rate decayed by half at 50, 90, and 120 steps respectively.

4.3 Comparisons with State-of-the-Art

We first summarize the main quantitative results in terms of mAP on HICO-DET in Table 1 and AP_{role} on V-COCO in Table 2. As shown by the results, Transformers-based methods show great potential compared to the CNN-based methods. This can mainly attribute to the ability of self-attention to selectively capture long range dependence, which is essential for HOI detection. On the basis of that, our method outperforms SOTA approaches. Specifically, Iwin achieves 3.7 mAP gain compared with QPIC [35] on *Full* setting of HICO-DET dataset as well as 2.0 AP_{role} gain on V-COCO. The main reason for such results is that we conduct token representation learning and agglomeration in a more effective manner. Firstly, instead of utilizing global attention, we novelly perform self-attention in irregular windows for token representation learning. It allows Iwin effectively eliminates redundancy in self-attention while achieves a linear computational complexity. Secondly, Iwin introduces a new irregular window-based

Table 5. The effects of different position encoding strategies

Position Encoding	Full↑	Rare↑	NoneRare↑
None	20.80	17.54	22.30
Sin at input	28.74	25.83	31.07
Sin for all	28.59	25.74	30.86
Learned at attn.	31.64	27.03	32.79
Sine at attn.	**32.03**	**27.62**	**34.14**

Table 6. The effects of different types of decoder

Decoder	Full↑	Rare↑	NoneRare↑
MLP	19.39	16.41	21.85
Symmetry	26.03	24.11	29.02
Trans×2	27.31	25.07	30.28
Trans×4	29.40	26.16	31.46
Trans×6	**32.03**	**27.62**	**34.14**

token agglomeration strategy, which progressively structurizes an image as a few agglomerated tokens with highly-abstracted visual semantic, which enables the contextual relations to be more easily captured for interaction recognition. Moreover, Iwin can leverage high-resolution feature maps due to its computational efficiency, which also boosts the performance in detecting small objects.

4.4 Ablation Study

4.4.1 Model Components
In this subsection, we analyze the effectiveness of the proposed strategies and components in detail. All experiments are performed on the HICO-DET dataset and the results are reported under the *Default* setting. Due to space limitations, some other important experiments can be seen in the *supplementary material*.

FPN. Feature pyramid network [22] was first proposed to solve the problem of detecting small objects. It is also crucial for HOI detection since the objects with which a human interacts may be small, such as a cup, a spoon and a mobile phone. It has been applied in lots of CNN-based HOI detection methods [5,7,38]. However, limited by the high computational complexity, existing Transformers-based HOI detection methods can not process such high resolution feature maps, resulting in poor performance in detecting small objects. In contrast, Iwin is friendly to high resolution feature maps thanks to the strategies of irregular window-based attention and token agglomeration. As shown in Table 3, with FPN, the model obtains 0.79 mAP gain.

Multi-scale Irregular Window Partition. There are two main strategies in a MS-IWP module, including irregular window partition (IWP) and multi-scale windows (MS). Augmented by learned offsets, IWP enables the irregular windows to align with human/object with different shapes and to eliminate redundancy in token representation learning. Moreover, it allows the irregular windows to own a dynamic receptive field compared to the regular ones, leading to efficient human/object detection. As shown in Table 3, it plays an essential role in IWP and achieves 3.1 mAP gain. Besides, we encourage the window size to be diverse so that they can handle different sizes of objects. When we use neither of the two strategies, the performance of the model is severely degraded, from 32.03 to 26.33 mAP, which indicates that learning strong token representation is important for HOI detection.

Fig. 5. Visualization of irregular windows. Each **blue** point is the location of an agglomerated token obtained by agglomerative tokenization, and the red points are the locations of the tokens involved in agglomeration. The envelope line of the red points shows the shape of the irregular window for the agglomerated token. As the input of Iwin Transformer are feature maps outputted by the backbone, the locations in the original image are calculated via bilinear interpolation. Best view in color

Token Agglomeration. Irregular window-based token agglomeration progressively structurizes an image as few agglomerated tokens with highly-abstracted visual semantics. It gradually reduce the number of tokens, ensures the self-attention to be performed in a global manner. Specifically, we illustrate the learned sampling locations in Fig. 5. There are totally $4^3 = 64$ sampling points for each of the agglomerated token obtained by agglomerative tokenization, since every 4 tokens are fused in a merging layer and 3 layers are employed. It can be seen from the figure that the envelope line of the sampling locations shows the shape of the irregular window, which is aligned with a semantic region with different shapes. In addition, we have performed several other merging strategies and list the quantitative results in Table 4. The "Norm-Window" refers to fusing 4 neighbouring tokens in a regular window, *i.e.*, a rectangle with size of 2×2. "K-means" denotes using an additional k-means algorithm [28] to cluster the similar tokens. For the former, it is more of a regular downsampling operation rather than generating high-level object-level semantic information, where the performance of model is reduced to 27.5. Meanwhile, when applying k-means algorithm, it is hard to determine the value of K, and as an individual module, it has to be trained separately.

Global Contextual Modeling. Global contextual modeling consists of two global self-attention mechanisms. As an essential component, it achieves a gain of 9+ mAP. To further validate the importance of global self-attention for interaction recognition, we perform the global contextual modeling in two extra different manners: remove this module directly and replace the global attention with window-based attention. Their results are shown in Fig. 6. Specifically, on the basis of normalizing both the height and width of image, we divide the L_1 distance between a human center and an object center into three uniform parts and denote them as "close", "moderate dist." and "far", respectively. Without global contextual modeling, the model has unsatisfactory performance in all

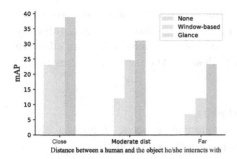

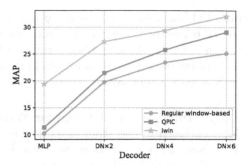

Fig. 6. Performance of different types global contextual modeling on different spatial distributions. The mAP is reported under the *Full* setting (Color figure online)

Fig. 7. Performance of different types of decoder. "DN $\times M$" refers to stacking M typical Transformer decoder layers. The mAP is reported under the *Full* setting

cases. When human and object are close, window-based attention achieves similar performance with global attention. However, as the distance increases, the performance of window-based attention is degraded seriously while the global attention can still work well. The main reason is that the ROI of interaction recognition can be diversely distributed image-wide.

Position Encoding. Position encoding is essential for Transformer architecture since it is permutation invariant. However, in Iwin, convolutional operation is also employed to learn the offsets in irregular windowing, in which position encoding is not a necessity. Therefore, we conduct more experiments to explore the effect of position encoding on convolution operation and the results are shown in Table 5. Specifically, "Sin" refers to using fixed sinusoidal functions and "Learned" denotes using learning embeddings. "At input" refers the position encoding is utilized for only one time that directly be added to the output features of backbone. "At attention" implies the position encoding is used only when computing attention weights and "For all" indicts the position encodings are employed in both attention modules and convolution operations. As the result shown, position encoding is important for attention computing but of little significant for convolution ones.

Decoder. We simply use the typical Transformers decoder for our approach. As shown in Table 6, when we replace the Transformers decoder with a simple multi-layer perceptron (MLP), the model still has a competitive performance to some recent CNN-based methods. It suggests that our encoder has the ability to effectively transform the visual information into high-level semantic space of HOI. Besides, we also design a decoder that has a symmetry structure with the encoder, where attention is conducted in both local and global manners. However, it does not achieve the desired effect. There are two different types of attention in decoder: self-attention and cross-attention. Specifically, self-attention is responsible for learning the correlation among the HOI queries. For example, a man holding a fork is more likely to be eating. Meanwhile, with self-attention, the HOI instances are decoded from the high-level semantic space generated by the encoder. As these two both require a large receptive field, it is more effective to perform the attention in a global manner. Besides, the model performs better with more decoder layers.

4.4.2   Importance of Irregular Windowing

As mentioned above, HOI detection is a sequential process of human/object detection and interaction recognition. Unlike object detection that can be performed by modeling local structures, interaction recognition demands a larger receptive field and higher-level semantic understanding. To verify the capacity of different models to extract highly-abstracted features, we employ several different types of decoder, from simple to cpmplex, the results are illustrated in Fig. 7. The relative gaps of performance between Iwin and the other methods become more evident as the decoder gets simper. There are two main reasons: 1) computing attention weights among all tokens introduces severe redundancy in self-attention for QPIC [35]. Regular window-based Transformer has the same weakness since the tokens in a regular window are most likely to be irrelevant. 2) without token agglomeration, QPIC-liked methods deal with local patch-based tokens, which can only model the local structures needed for object detection. With irregular window-based token representation learning and agglomeration, Iwin's robust highly-abstracted visual semantic extraction capability are shown in two aspects. Firstly, even using a quite simple decoder, e.g., a MLP consists of two dense-connected layers, Iwins achicves competitive performance compared to some recent CNN-based methods. Secondly, Iwin is trained from scratch to get the SOTA results while most existing methods utilize pre-trained models, such as DETR [1] and CLIP [32]. Besides, unlike existing methods, Iwin is easy to train by performing irregular window partition. As shown in Fig. 2, when training from scratch, Iwin only needs half of the training epoches compared to other methods.

5   Conclusion

In this paper, we propose Iwin transformer, a novel vision Transformer for HOI detection, which progressively performs token representation learning and token agglomeration within irregular windows. By employing irregular window partition, Iwin Transformer can eliminate redundancy in token representation and generate new tokens to align with humans/objects with different shapes, enables the extraction of highly-abstracted visual semantics for HOI detection. We validate Iwin transformer on two challenging HOI benchmarks and achieve considerable performance boost over SOTA results.

Acknowledgments. This work was supported by NSFC 61831015, National Key R&D Program of China 2021YFE0206700, NSFC 62176159, Natural Science Foundation of Shanghai 21ZR1432200 and Shanghai Municipal Science and Technology Major Project 2021SHZDZX0102.

References

1. Carion, N., Massa, F., Synnaeve, G., Usunier, N., Kirillov, A., Zagoruyko, S.: End-to-end object detection with transformers. In: Vedaldi, A., Bischof, H., Brox, T., Frahm, J.-M. (eds.) ECCV 2020. LNCS, vol. 12346, pp. 213–229. Springer, Cham (2020). https://doi.org/10.1007/978-3-030-58452-8_13
2. Chao, Y.W., Liu, Y., Liu, X., Zeng, H., Deng, J.: Learning to detect human-object interactions. In: WACV (2018)
3. Chen, M., Liao, Y., Liu, S., Chen, Z., Wang, F., Qian, C.: Reformulating hoi detection as adaptive set prediction. In: CVPR (2021)
4. Dai, J., et al.: Deformable convolutional networks. In: ICCV (2017)
5. Gao, C., Xu, J., Zou, Y., Huang, J.B.: Drg: Dual relation graph for human-object interaction detection. In: ECCV (2020)
6. Gao, C., Zou, Y., Huang, J.B.: iCAN: instance-centric attention network for human-object interaction detection. In: BMVC (2018)
7. Gkioxari, G., Girshick, R., Dollár, P., He, K.: Detecting and recognizing human-object interactions. In: CVPR (2018)
8. Gupta, S., Malik, J.: Visual semantic role labeling. arXiv preprint arXiv:1505.04474 (2015)
9. Gupta, T., Schwing, A., Hoiem, D.: No-frills human-object interaction detection: factorization, layout encodings, and training techniques. In: ICCV (2019)
10. He, K., Gkioxari, G., Dollár, P., Girshick, R.: Mask r-cnn. In: ICCV. pp. 2961–2969 (2017)
11. He, K., Zhang, X., Ren, S., Sun, J.: Deep residual learning for image recognition. In: CVPR (2016)
12. Hou, Z., Peng, X., Qiao, Yu., Tao, D.: Visual compositional learning for human-object interaction detection. In: Vedaldi, A., Bischof, H., Brox, T., Frahm, J.-M. (eds.) ECCV 2020. LNCS, vol. 12360, pp. 584–600. Springer, Cham (2020). https://doi.org/10.1007/978-3-030-58555-6_35
13. Hou, Z., Yu, B., Qiao, Y., Peng, X., Tao, D.: Affordance transfer learning for human-object interaction detection. In: CVPR (2021)
14. Kim, B., Choi, T., Kang, J., Kim, H.J.: UnionDet: union-level detector towards real-time human-object interaction detection. In: Vedaldi, A., Bischof, H., Brox, T., Frahm, J.-M. (eds.) ECCV 2020. LNCS, vol. 12360, pp. 498–514. Springer, Cham (2020). https://doi.org/10.1007/978-3-030-58555-6_30
15. Kim, B., Lee, J., Kang, J., Kim, E.S., Kim, H.J.: Hotr: end-to-end human-object interaction detection with transformers. In: CVPR (2021)
16. Kim, D.-J., Sun, X., Choi, J., Lin, S., Kweon, I.S.: Detecting human-object interactions with action co-occurrence priors. In: Vedaldi, A., Bischof, H., Brox, T., Frahm, J.-M. (eds.) ECCV 2020. LNCS, vol. 12366, pp. 718–736. Springer, Cham (2020). https://doi.org/10.1007/978-3-030-58589-1_43
17. Kuhn, H.W.: The hungarian method for the assignment problem. Naval Res. Logist. Q. **2**(1–2), 83–97 (1955)
18. Li, Y.L., et al.: Detailed 2d–3d joint representation for human-object interaction. In: CVPR (2020)
19. Li, Y.L., et al.: Pastanet: toward human activity knowledge engine. In: CVPR (2020)
20. Li, Y.L., et al.: Transferable interactiveness knowledge for human-object interaction detection. In: CVPR (2019)

21. Liao, Y., Liu, S., Wang, F., Chen, Y., Qian, C., Feng, J.: Ppdm: parallel point detection and matching for real-time human-object interaction detection. In: CVPR (2020)
22. Lin, T.Y., Dollár, P., Girshick, R., He, K., Hariharan, B., Belongie, S.: Feature pyramid networks for object detection. In: CVPR (2017)
23. Lin, T.Y., et al.: Microsoft coco: Common objects in context. In: ECCV (2014)
24. Lin, X., Zou, Q., Xu, X.: Action-guided attention mining and relation reasoning network for human-object interaction detection. In: IJCAI (2020)
25. Liu, Y., Chen, Q., Zisserman, A.: Amplifying key cues for human-object-interaction detection. In: Vedaldi, A., Bischof, H., Brox, T., Frahm, J.-M. (eds.) ECCV 2020. LNCS, vol. 12359, pp. 248–265. Springer, Cham (2020). https://doi.org/10.1007/978-3-030-58568-6_15
26. Liu, Z., et al.: Swin transformer: hierarchical vision transformer using shifted windows. In: ICCV (2021)
27. Loshchilov, I., Hutter, F.: Decoupled weight decay regularization. In: ICLR (2017)
28. MacQueen, J., et al.: Some methods for classification and analysis of multivariate observations. In: Proceedings of the fifth Berkeley Symposium on Mathematical Statistics and Probability (1967)
29. Nair, V., Hinton, G.E.: Rectified linear units improve restricted boltzmann machines. In: ICML (2010)
30. Peyre, J., Laptev, I., Schmid, C., Sivic, J.: Detecting unseen visual relations using analogies. In: ICCV (2019)
31. Qi, S., Wang, W., Jia, B., Shen, J., Zhu, S.C.: Learning human-object interactions by graph parsing neural networks. In: ECCV (2018)
32. Radford, A., et al.: Learning transferable visual models from natural language supervision. In: International Conference on Machine Learning, pp. 8748–8763. PMLR (2021)
33. Ren, S., He, K., Girshick, R., Sun, J.: Faster r-cnn: towards real-time object detection with region proposal networks. In: NIPS (2015)
34. Rezatofighi, H., Tsoi, N., Gwak, J., Sadeghian, A., Reid, I., Savarese, S.: Generalized intersection over union: a metric and a loss for bounding box regression. In: CVPR (2019)
35. Tamura, M., Ohashi, H., Yoshinaga, T.: Qpic: query-based pairwise human-object interaction detection with image-wide contextual information. In: CVPR (2021)
36. Ulutan, O., Iftekhar, A., Manjunath, B.S.: Vsgnet: spatial attention network for detecting human object interactions using graph convolutions. In: CVPR (2020)
37. Vaswani, A., et al.: Attention is all you need. In: NIPS (2017)
38. Wan, B., Zhou, D., Liu, Y., Li, R., He, X.: Pose-aware multi-level feature network for human object interaction detection. In: ICCV (2019)
39. Wang, H., Zheng, W., Yingbiao, L.: Contextual heterogeneous graph network for human-object interaction detection. In: Vedaldi, A., Bischof, H., Brox, T., Frahm, J.-M. (eds.) ECCV 2020. LNCS, vol. 12362, pp. 248–264. Springer, Cham (2020). https://doi.org/10.1007/978-3-030-58520-4_15
40. Wang, T., et al.: Deep contextual attention for human-object interaction detection. In: ICCV (2019)
41. Wang, T., Yang, T., Danelljan, M., Khan, F.S., Zhang, X., Sun, J.: Learning human-object interaction detection using interaction points. In: CVPR (2020)
42. Xu, B., Li, J., Wong, Y., Zhao, Q., Kankanhalli, M.S.: Interact as you intend: Intention-driven human-object interaction detection. In: TMM (2019)
43. Yang, D., Zou, Y.: A graph-based interactive reasoning for human-object interaction detection. In: IJCAI (2020)

44. Zhang, A., et al.: Mining the benefits of two-stage and one-stage hoi detection. NIPs **34**, 17209–17220 (2021)
45. Zhang, F.Z., Campbell, D., Gould, S.: Spatially conditioned graphs for detecting human-object interactions. In: ICCV (2021)
46. Zhong, X., Ding, C., Qu, X., Tao, D.: Polysemy deciphering network for robust human-object interaction detection. In: ICCV (2021)
47. Zhong, X., Qu, X., Ding, C., Tao, D.: Glance and gaze: inferring action-aware points for one-stage human-object interaction detection. In: CVPR (2021)
48. Zhou, P., Chi, M.: Relation parsing neural network for human-object interaction detection. In: ICCV (2019)
49. Zhou, T., Wang, W., Qi, S., Ling, H., Shen, J.: Cascaded human-object interaction recognition. In: CVPR (2020)
50. Zhu, X., Su, W., Lu, L., Li, B., Wang, X., Dai, J.: Deformable detr: deformable transformers for end-to-end object detection. In: ICLR (2020)
51. Zou, C., et al.: End-to-end human object interaction detection with hoi transformer. In: CVPR (2021)

Rethinking Zero-shot Action Recognition: Learning from Latent Atomic Actions

Yijun Qian$^{(\boxtimes)}$, Lijun Yu, Wenhe Liu, and Alexander G. Hauptmann

Carnegie Mellon University, Pittsburgh, PA 15213, USA
{yijunqia,wenhel}@andrew.cmu.edu, lijun@cmu.edu, Alex@cs.cmu.edu

Abstract. To avoid time-consuming annotating and retraining cycle in applying supervised action recognition models, Zero-Shot Action Recognition (ZSAR) has become a thriving direction. ZSAR requires models to recognize actions that never appear in training set through bridging visual features and semantic representations. However, due to the complexity of actions, it remains challenging to transfer knowledge learned from source to target action domains. Previous ZSAR methods mainly focus on mitigating representation variance between source and target actions through integrating or applying new action-level features. However, the action-level features are coarse-grained and make the learned one-to-one bridge fragile to similar target actions. Meanwhile, integration or application of features usually requires extra computation or annotation. These methods didn't notice that two actions with different names may still share the same atomic action components. It enables humans to quickly understand an unseen action given bunch of atomic actions learned from seen actions. Inspired by this, we propose Jigsaw Network (JigsawNet) which recognizes complex actions through unsupervisedly decomposing them into combinations of atomic actions and bridging group to group relationships between visual features and semantic representations. To enhance the robustness of learned group-to-group bridge, we propose Group Excitation (GE) module to model intra-sample knowledge and Consistency Loss to enforce the model learn from inter-sample knowledge. Our JigsawNet achieves state-of-the-art performance on three benchmarks and surpasses previous works with noticeable margins.

Keywords: Computer vision · Action recognition · Zero-shot learning

1 Introduction

Supervised action recognition has been a heated computer vision task and makes continuous progress thanks to the development of spatio-temporal modeling [28, 32,39] and release of large datasets [18,36]. However, while the performance of models has been boosted, the models also become deeper and deeper and require more and more annotated data for training. Meanwhile, the target actions vary in different scenes and may change or increase in real-world applications. Thus, the time-consuming cycle of gathering data, annotating, and retraining becomes

© The Author(s), under exclusive license to Springer Nature Switzerland AG 2022
S. Avidan et al. (Eds.): ECCV 2022, LNCS 13664, pp. 104–120, 2022.
https://doi.org/10.1007/978-3-031-19772-7_7

Fig. 1. The majority of actions in daily life are complicated and can be regarded as combinations of atomic actions. Complex actions with different name may still share the same atomic actions. (*e.g.* "hand stand" exists commonly in complex actions such as capoeira, cartwheeling, and vault.) To better understand the ZSAR procedure, we could regard target actions as "assembled puzzles" picture drawn on puzzle boxes, atomic actions are "puzzle pieces" and the videos are stacks of puzzle pieces. JigsawNet is determining which boxes the stacks belong to through matching the puzzle pieces in stack with the ones drawn on boxes

inevitable to use these supervised action recognition models. To alleviate such burden, Zero-Short Action Recognition (ZSAR) has become a vigorous direction which enables models the capability of recognizing actions that never appear in the training set.

These years have witnessed many successful explorations [4,8,29,46] in ZSAR. The task requires models to bridge semantic representations of actions and visual features extracted from videos. However, it remains challenging due to the complexity of videos and semantic variance between source and target actions.

Previous methods mainly focus on mitigating the representation variance between source and target actions through integrating or applying new action-level features. The first series of works [29,46] use manually designed attributes to represent video features and action semantics. Another series of works [17,22] introduce the existence of objects as attributes. Features are generated through embedding verbal objects detected in action descriptions and visual objects recognized in video clips. The last series of works [4,44] use embedding of label name as action semantics and end-to-end train a spatio-temporal modeling network to extract visual features. The most recent work [8] uses description instead of label name for semantic extraction. It also integrates both spatio-temporal features and semantics of detected verbal objects as visual representations. To the best of our knowledge, all the previous methods regard the videos and actions as single entities and enforce the model to build a one-to-one bridge between visual features and semantic representations. They project the visual features extracted from videos and semantic representations extracted from actions to a shared sphere. The models are then optimized through minimizing distance between visual features and corresponding action semantics.

Although both visual and semantic variance between source and target actions will be mitigated to a extent, the features are still coarse-grained and may not as distinct on target actions domain as learned among source actions domain. It makes the one-to-one bridge fragile and make the action classifier difficult to distinguish similar target actions. What's more, integration or application of new attributes usually requires extra computation or annotation which may limit the usage in real world scenes. In this work, we take the inspiration from how humans quickly understand a brand new action through factorizing it into combinations of atomic actions.

We use puzzles as an example to introduce the difference between our JigsawNet and previous works. As is shown in Fig. 1, complex actions like "capoeira", "cartwheeling", and "vault" can be regarded as "assembled puzzles" drawn on boxes, atomic actions like "bent over", "hand stand", and "stretch arms over head" can be regarded as "puzzle pieces", and videos can be regarded as stacks of these puzzle pieces. Then, a ZSAR task is to determine which boxes the stacks should be placed in. Previous methods [8] are trying to make the decision based on stack-level (action-level) features. For example, the number of edge puzzle pieces in stacks (number of people in videos) is a distinct stack-level feature between capoeira and cartwheeling. However, it's not as distinct between cartwheeling and vault. JigsawNet, instead, looks deeper and makes decision through matching the pieces in stacks with the ones drawn on boxes. It notices that different assembled puzzles still share the same pieces. Such piece-level features are easier to recognize and stable among different assembled puzzles. In other words, these atomic actions can be regarded as joint latent features shared by source and target actions, which are fine-grained and won't change drastically.

Given videos and descriptions of target actions crawled from wiki, the videos are split into groups of segments and the descriptions are separated into groups of verb phrases through dependency parsing. JigsawNet then recognizes unseen actions through unsupervisedly bridging a group-to-group relationship among video segments and semantics of atomic actions. JigsawNet can learn the relationship only based on target action labels assigned to the entire videos and require no extra annotation of atomic action label assigned to each segment. Meanwhile, to better model the latent features of atomic actions, we propose the Consistency Loss to learn from inter-sample knowledge and Group Excitation (GE) module to adaptively aggregate intra-sample representations. Consistency Loss enforces the model to extract similar features from segments which are predicted as the same atomic action but split from different videos. It also enforces the model to enlarge distance of similar features which are extracted from segments that are predicted as different atomic actions. For computation efficiency, a memory cache is implemented to remember past visual features grouped by atomic action labels. Visual features extracted from single segment has limited temporal receptive field. Thus, GE module will adaptively aggregate contextual spatio-temporal and object features and enables the model a better capability of understanding latent atomic actions. To the best of our knowledge, the proposed algorithm is the first to explore atomic actions as joint latent features and build group-to-group bridge between visual features and semantic representations. It is also the first exploration in making full usage of both inter and intra sample knowledge in ZSAR.

In a nutshell, the contributions of our paper are summarized as follows:

1. We propose a novel view to implement atomic actions as joint latent features which is fine-grained and stable between source and target actions for ZSAR.
2. We propose JigsawNet which recognizes unseen actions through unsupervisedly decomposing them into combinations of atomic actions and then bridging a group-to-group relationship between visual features and semantic representations.
3. We propose the Consistency Loss and the Group Excitation (GE) module to make full usage of both inter and intra sample knowledge for ZSAR.
4. Our method achieves state-of-the-art (SOTA) performance on three ZSAR benchmarks (*i.e.* KineticsZSAR, HMDB51, and UCF101) which demonstrates the superiority of our work.

2 Related Work

Supervised Action Recognition. Action Recognition has been a heated task in computer vision given its wide application in real world scenes. Given a target-centered action clip, supervised action recognition models can recognize the actions that it has seen in the training set. There are three major series of solutions.

The earliest works operate spatial-convolution independently over the temporal dimension and resort to temporal motion information like optical flow or RGB diff of adjacent frames for temporal modeling [23,35,41,49]. However, the extraction of motion features is time consuming and limits the usage in real world applications.

Later works [11,12,20,21] resort to 3D CNNs which can model spatial and temporal information simultaneously. They have achieved state-of-the-art (SOTA) results on many data sets, especially after the release of large video action data sets like Kinetics [24] and Activity Net [5]. For example, Du proposes a simple, yet effective approach for spatio-temporal feature learning using deep 3D CNN [38]. Carreira implements a two-stream inflated 3D convolution network [7]. However, 3D CNNs contain much more parameters and will easily overfit and still time consuming.

Given the drawbacks of traditional 2D CNN and 3D CNN mentioned above, most recent works [13,13,34,39,47] focus on factorizing the spatial and temporal modeling operations. For example, Du proposed R(2+1)D which factorizes the 3D convolutional filters into 2D spatial convolution kernel and 1D temporal convolution kernel [39].

Zero-shot Action Recognition. The earliest works take manual-defined attributes [29, 46] to represent the action. For example, Gan *et al.* propose multi-source domain generalization method for attribute detection. However, the attributes of actions are numerous and harder to define compared with static images. Later works [16, 17, 22] resort to objects as attributes. For example, Jain *et al.* [22] detect objects in videos then project the object features and action labels to a shared sphere and calculate the similarity. Gao *et al.* propose a graph networks based model to learn the relationship between action and objects and match them according to action prototypes. These works are pretty efficient, however, they ignore the spatio-temporal information inherited in videos. Most recent works use word embeddings of action names [4, 31, 33, 44] or action descriptions [8] to extract semantic representations. For example, Brattoli *et al* [4] propose an end-to-end pipeline which directly projects the extracted spatio-temporal features from videos and semantic representations extracted from word embeddings of action names to a shared sphere. The most similar work to ours is ER [8] which also uses description, objects, and videos as input. However ER is different from ours in that, it still recognizes the videos and actions as single entities and enforces the model to build one-to-one bridge between visual features and semantic representations. The action-level features are coarse-grained and may not as distinct among target action as learned among source actions.

3   Proposed Approach

ZSAR task requires the model to recognize actions that never appears in training set. In the rest subsections, we will present our novel Group Alignment Module, Consistency Loss, and Group Excitation Module. We will then show how to combine these modules together as Jigsaw Network.

3.1   Group Alignment (GA) Module

For each action label y^i, we crawled a short description and split it into group of verb phrases through dependency parsing. Manual correction is applied to remove typos and modify incorrect descriptions. The action y^i is then represented as $d^i = \{w_1, ..., w_k\}$, where each w_j is a verb phrase and represents an atomic action. We implement a spatio-temporal extraction backbone $\mathcal{N}_{vid}$ to extract visual features from i^{th} video v^i. $\mathcal{F}_i = \mathcal{N}_{vid}(v^i)$, where $\mathcal{F}_i = \{f_1^i, ..., f_m^i\} \in \mathbb{R}^{m \times d}$, m represents the number of segments the v^i is split into, and d is the dimension of features extracted from each video segment. A semantic extraction backbone $\mathcal{N}_{text}$ is implemented to extract semantic representations from group of verb phrases $\mathcal{G}_i = \mathcal{N}_{text}(d^i)$, where $\mathcal{G}_i = \{g_1^i, ..., g_k^i\} \in \mathbb{R}^{k \times d}$. Besides extracting spatio-temporal features, we also use object types in videos as a kind of video attribute. An object classification backbone $\mathcal{N}_{obj}$ is implemented to recognize object classes $\mathcal{W}_{obj}^i = \mathcal{N}_{obj}(v^i)$, and $\mathcal{W}_{obj}^i = \{w_{obj}^1, ..., w_{obj}^l\}$. Each w_{obj}^k represents the name of a recognized object. The object names are concatenated and forwarded to $\mathcal{N}_{text}$ to extract verbal features $\mathcal{O}_i = \mathcal{N}_{text}(\mathcal{W}_{obj}^i)$, and $\mathcal{O}_i \in \mathbb{R}^d$.

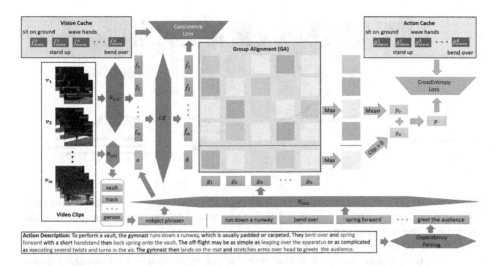

Fig. 2. Architecture of Jigsaw Network. Given videos and short descriptions of target actions, Jigsaw Network will adaptively learn to build group-to-group bridges. N_{vid} is the spatio-temporal extractor backbone, N_{text} is the semantic extractor backbone, and N_{obj} is the object recognition backbone. Green represents verbal features, blue represents visual features, and red represents fused features

Current spatio-temporal feature f_x^i extracted from each segment has limited temporal receptive field, and the complete atomic action may be split into two segments. To solve this, we propose the Group Excitation (GE) Module $\mathcal{M}$ to adaptively aggregate intra sample features.

$$\hat{\mathcal{F}}_i, \hat{\mathcal{O}}_i = \mathcal{M}(\mathcal{F}_i \oplus \mathcal{O}_i) \tag{1}$$

$$\hat{\mathcal{F}}_i = \{\hat{f}_1^i, ..., \hat{f}_m^i\} \in \mathbb{R}^{m \times d}, \hat{\mathcal{O}}_i \in \mathbb{R}^d \tag{2}$$

where $\oplus$ represents concatenate. Each output $\hat{f}_j^i \in \hat{\mathcal{F}}_i$ will contain spatio-temporal features extracted from contextual segments and object feature $\mathcal{O}_i$ of the whole video sample. The details of $\mathcal{M}$ will be presented in later subsections. We then build the group-to-group bridge between the group of video segments and the group of atomic actions.

$$p_{xy}^{ij} = \hat{f}_x^i \cdot (g_y^j)^T \tag{3}$$

$$p_a^{ij} = \frac{\sum_x (\max_y(p_{xy}^{ij}))}{m} \tag{4}$$

$$p_o^{ij} = \max_y(\hat{\mathcal{O}}_i \cdot (g_y^j)^T) \tag{5}$$

$$p^{ij} = p_a^{ij} + \max(p_o^{ij}, 0) \tag{6}$$

where p_{xy}^{ij} represents the cosine similarity between the visual feature $\hat{f}_x^i$ extracted from the xth video segment of v^i, and semantic representations g_y^j of the yth verb phrase of d^i, p^{ij} is the probability that v^i is recognized as j^{th} target action

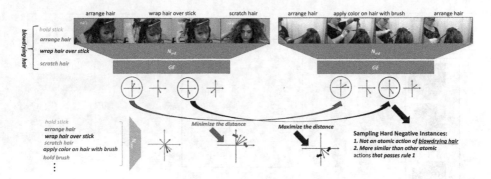

Fig. 3. Illustration of Consistency Loss. Although the first segments of the left and right video are both predicted as "arrange hair", their visual features may approaching the semantic representation in two directions and Consistency Loss will further minimize their distance. The visual features extracted from the second segments of left (seg_l) and right (seg_r) videos are similar. However, "apply color on hair with brush" is not a component of "blowdrying hair". Thus the seg_r is a hard negative sample of seg_l and there distances will be enlarged by Consistency Loss as well

(y^i=j), · denotes vector-matrix multiplication. We implement a cross entropy loss to train the GA module. $P^i = \{p^{i1}, p^{i2}, ..., p^{iB}\} \in \mathbb{R}^B$ is the probability vector of video v^i to B source actions. $Y^i = \{y^i_1, y^i_2, ..., y^i_B\} \in \mathbb{R}^B$ is the one-hot label vector extended from y^i. The cross entropy loss is shown as:

$$L(P^i, Y^i) = -\sum_{j=1}^{B} y^i_j \log \frac{\exp(p^{ij}/\lambda)}{\sum_{k=1}^{B} \exp(p^{ik}/\lambda)} \qquad (7)$$

where λ is a temperature parameter. Although P^i is already calculated by both $\hat{\mathcal{F}}_i$ and $\hat{\mathcal{O}}_i$, we intend to enforce these two features similar to the semantic representation of target action as well. $P^i_a = \{p^{i1}_a, p^{i2}_a, ..., p^{iB}_a\} \in \mathbb{R}^B$ and $P^i_o = \{p^{i1}_o, p^{i2}_o, ..., p^{iB}_o\} \in \mathbb{R}^B$ are probability vectors of video v^i to B source actions calculated by $\hat{\mathcal{F}}_i$ and $\hat{\mathcal{O}}_i$ independently. Thus, the matching loss is shown as:

$$L_{act} = \frac{1}{N} \sum_{i=1}^{N} (L(P^i, Y^i) + L(P^i_a, Y^i) + L(P^i_o, Y^i)) \qquad (8)$$

During inference stage, only P^i is used as the probability scores of v^i to C target actions.

3.2   Consistency Loss

L_{act} only uses B semantic representations of source actions for training which makes the model easily overfit. To enhance the robustness of group-to-group bridge, we propose Consistency Loss which optimizes the model unsupervisedly with inter sample knowledge. As is shown in Fig. 3, although the model doesn't have the ground truth atomic action label of each video segment, the segments should only contain atomic actions which are components of the aligned source action. Meanwhile, the same atomic action will be a joint latent feature shared by different source actions. Generally, the consistency regularization is two folded. Features extracted from segments of different videos but aligned to the same atomic action should be consistently similar. Segment features aligned to certain atomic action should be consistently different from those aligned to other atomic actions. The loss can be represented as:

$$\mathcal{F}_{mem} = \{\hat{f}_{mem}^1, \hat{f}_{mem}^2, ..., \hat{f}_{mem}^A\} \in \mathbb{R}^{A \times d} \tag{9}$$

$$\hat{j} = \text{argmax}_{j \in \{1,...,B\}} \, p^{ij} \tag{10}$$

$$s_x^i = \Phi(\text{argmax}_y \, p_{xy}^{i\hat{j}}) \tag{11}$$

$$n_x^i = \text{argmax}_{m \notin W^{\hat{j}}} \, \hat{f}_x^i \cdot \hat{f}_{mem}^m \tag{12}$$

$$L_{cons} = \frac{\sum_i \sum_x \max(1 - \hat{f}_x^i \cdot \hat{f}_{mem}^{s_x^i} + \hat{f}_x^i \cdot \hat{f}_{mem}^{n_x^i}, 0)}{N} \tag{13}$$

where $\mathcal{F}_{mem}$ is the memorized visual feature buffer grouped by atomic action types, and A is the number of unique atomic actions of all source actions. $\hat{j}$ is the predicted action id of video v^i. $s_x^i \in \{1, 2, ..., A\}$ represents the predicted atomic action id of the xth segment of v^i. Φ is a wrap function which projects the inner group id y to its global unique id in $\mathcal{F}_{mem}$. $W^{\hat{j}} = \{w_1^{\hat{j}}, w_2^{\hat{j}}, ..., w_k^{\hat{j}}\}$ is the ids of atomic actions belonging to source action $\hat{j}$, and $w_m^{\hat{j}} \in \{1, 2, ..., A\}$. Thus n_x^i represents the atomic action whose memorized feature is mostly similar to $\hat{f}_x^i$ but not a component of source action $\hat{j}$. L_{cons} minimizes the distance between $\hat{f}_x^i$ and $\hat{f}_{mem}^{s_x^i}$ and maximizes the distance between $\hat{f}_x^i$ and $\hat{f}_{mem}^{n_x^i}$. The rule of updating $\mathcal{F}_{mem}$ is:

$$\hat{f}_{mem}^{s_x^i} = \begin{cases} f_x^i & f_x^i \cdot \hat{g}_{mem}^{s_x^i} > \hat{f}_{mem}^{s_x^i} \cdot \hat{g}_{mem}^{s_x^i} \\ \hat{f}_{mem}^{s_x^i} & f_x^i \cdot \hat{g}_{mem}^{s_x^i} \le \hat{f}_{mem}^{s_x^i} \cdot \hat{g}_{mem}^{s_x^i} \end{cases} \tag{14}$$

where $\mathcal{G}_{mem} = \{\hat{g}_{mem}^1, ..., \hat{g}_{mem}^A\}$ is the memorized verbal feature buffer of atomic actions. Meanwhile, we also implemented the ER Loss [8] L_{er} which resorts to recognized objects as weak supervision. Thus, the full loss function $\mathcal{L}$ is:

$$\mathcal{L} = L_{act} + L_{er} + L_{cons} \tag{15}$$

3.3 Group Excitation (GE) Module

Different from previous methods which extract spatio-temporal features from entire videos, our $\mathcal{N}_{vid}$ only extracts spatio-temporal features from video segments with limited temporal receptive field. Meanwhile, each segment may not cover the complete atomic action. To better understand each atomic action, we propose the GE module to adaptively aggregate intra sample features. Inspired by recent success of implementing transformer [40] for both computer vision

[3,30] and NLP [10,14] tasks, we propose GE, a multi-head transformer based aggregation module to fuse intra sample features $\hat{\mathcal{F}}_i$ and $\hat{\mathcal{O}}_i$. It enables the feature $\hat{f}_j^i$ of each video segment to contain contextual spatio-temporal feature of all other inter sample segments. GE is functioned as:

$$H = \text{concat}(\mathcal{F}_i, \mathcal{O}_i)$$
$$= \{f_1^i, ..., f_m^i, \mathcal{O}_i\} \in \mathbb{R}^{(m+1) \times d} \tag{16}$$

$$head_j = \frac{HW_j^Q \cdot (HW_j^K)^T}{\sqrt{d}} HW_j^V \tag{17}$$

$$\mathcal{M}(I) = \text{concat}(head_1, ..., head_h)W^O$$
$$= \{\hat{f}_1^i, ..., \hat{f}_m^i, \hat{\mathcal{O}}_i\} \tag{18}$$
$$= \{\hat{\mathcal{F}}_i, \hat{\mathcal{O}}_i\}$$

where $W_j^Q \in \mathbb{R}^{d \times \frac{d}{h}}, W_j^K \in \mathbb{R}^{d \times \frac{d}{h}}, W_j^V \in \mathbb{R}^{d \times \frac{d}{h}}$, and $W^O \in \mathbb{R}^{d \times d}$.

3.4 Jigsaw Network (JigsawNet)

As is shown in Fig. 2, we implement the JigsawNet with modules introduced above. For efficiency, JigsawNet has an action cache to memorize semantic representations extracted from verb phrases grouped by atomic actions. In each training iteration, $\mathcal{N}_{text}$ only extracts semantic representations from verb phrases belonging to labeled source actions and concatenated verbal objects of videos in batch. Before each training or validation epoch starts, the action cache will be initialized through extracting features from all A verb phrases of atomic actions with $\mathcal{N}_{text}$. In each validation iteration, since the $\mathcal{N}_{text}$ won't be updated, so the model will directly pick semantic representations from the action cache. JigsawNet also contains a vision cache to memorize visual features extracted from video segments. The memorized visual features are also grouped by predicted atomic action types. Different from the action cache, it's difficult to initialize the vision cache, in that the model doesn't have ground truth atomic action label for each video clip. Since the model aims to bridge between visual features and semantic representations, g_y^j will then become a "perfect" expected output for initialization. A threshold ϵ is set as current distance of $\hat{f}_{mem}^{s_x^i} \cdot \hat{g}_{mem}^{s_x^i}$, it enables the memorized feature get replaced by the real extracted visual features after several iterations. The vision cache is only used for optimization during training stages.

4   Experiments

4.1 Datasets

HMDB51 and **UCF101.** HMDB51 [26] is a human motion benchmark. It contains 6,849 videos divided into 51 action categories, each category contains a minimum of 101 clips. UCF101 [37] contains 13320 videos divided into 101 sports related actions. For robust and fair comparison, we followed the evaluation procedure proposed in [44]. The model is tested 50 times with 50 randomly generated splits, the average rank1 accuracy and standard deviation are reported for evaluation. In each split, 50% classes are used for training and the rest 50% classes are preserved for testing.

KineticsZSAR. Given the size limit of previous ZSAR protocols, [8] proposes a new benchmark with videos and annotations selected from Kinetics400 [7] and Kinetics600 [6]. The 400 classes of Kinetics400 [7] are selected as seen actions and the rest 220 actions from Kinetics600 [6] are used as unseen actions for validation and testing. To be specific, we followed [8] to generate three splits. In each split, 60 actions are used for validation and the rest 160 actions are used for testing. The model will be tested three times. Many videos in the original val and test split can't be accessed, so we re-select the videos and preserve the same number of videos for each action to make a fair comparison. The average rank1 accuracy and standard deviation are reported for evaluation.

4.2   Implementation Details

For spatio-temporal extractor backbone $\mathcal{N}_{vis}$, we use a pretrained 34 layers R(2+1)D [39] model, and remove the temporal pooling layers. If not specified,

Table 1. ZSAR performance comparison on HMDB51 and UCF101. *FV* represents fisher vetor, BoW represents bag of words, O represents the model uses object as video attributes, V represents the model uses spatio-temporal features of videos, A represents manually designed attributes, W_N represents class label names, W_D represents descriptions of classes. For fair comparison, the rank1 accuracy (%) and standard deviation ($\pm$) are reported. We only list the average rank1 accuracy in table for several methods whose deviations are not provided

Method	Video input	Action input	HMDB51↑	UCF101↑
DAP [27]	FV	A	N/A	15.9 ± 1.2
IAP [27]	FV	A	N/A	16.7 ± 1.1
HAA [29]	FV	A	N/A	14.9 ± 0.8
SVE [43]	BoW	W_N	13.0 ± 2.7	10.9 ± 1.5
ESZSL [43]	FV	W_N	18.5 ± 2.0	15.0 ± 1.3
SJE [2]	FV	W_N	13.3 ± 2.4	9.9 ± 1.4
SJE [2]	FV	A	N/A	12.0 ± 1.2
MTE [45]	FV	W_N	19.7 ± 1.6	15.8 ± 1.3
ZSECOC [33]	FV	W_N	22.6 ± 1.2	15.1 ± 1.7
UR [50]	FV	W_N	24.4 ± 1.6	17.5 ± 1.6
O2A [22]	O	W_N	15.6	30.3
ASR [42]	V	W_D	21.8 ± 0.9	24.4 ± 1.0
TS-GCN [17]	O	W_N	23.2 ± 3.0	34.2 ± 3.1
E2E [4]	V	W_N	29.8	44.1
ER [8]	V+O	W_D	35.3 ± 4.6	51.8 ± 2.9
Ours	**V+O**	W_D	**38.7 ± 3.7**	**56.0 ± 3.1**

N_{vis} is initialized with weights pretrained on Kinetics400 [7] and IG65M [18] for experiments on KineticsZSAR benchmark, and initialized with weights pretrained on Kinetics605 [4] which removes all overlapped actions that appears in HMDB51 and UCF101 for experiments on these two benchmarks. For semantic extractor backbone N_{text}, we use a pretrained 12-layer Bert [10] model. For object recognition backbone N_{obj}, we use a BiT model [25] pretrained on ImageNet21K [9]. The top 5 recognized verbal objects are selected and forwarded to N_{text} to extract semantic representations. N_{obj} is frozen during the training stage. All layers of N_{vis} and last two layers of N_{text} are finetuned during training stages on KineticsZSAR. For experiments on HMDB51 and UCF101, only the last layer of N_{vis} and last two layers of N_{text} are finetuned. The dimension of shared sphere is set as $d = 768$, the threshold ϵ is set as 0.3, and the number of self-attention head $h = 8$. We use SGD with Momentum algorithm for optimization. The weight decay is 5e-4, the momentum is 0.9, and the initial learning rate is 1e-5 on Kinetics ZSAR and 1e-4 on HMDB51 and UCF101. The learning rate is updated with a plateau scheduler which monitors the rank-1 accuracy on validation set, the patience is set as 1, and the min learning rate is set as 1e-9. The model is trained 15 epochs on HMDB51 and UCF101, and 20 epochs on KineticsZSAR. All experiments are made on four TITAN RTX gpus.

4.3   Comparison with State-of-the-Art Methods

Table 2. ZSAR performance comparison on KineticsZSAR. O represents the model uses object as video attributes, V represents the model uses spatio-temporal features of videos, W_N represents class label names, W_D represents descriptions of classes

Method	Video Input	Action Input	Rank1 Acc↑	Rank5 Acc↑
DEVISE [15]	V	W_N	23.8 ± 0.3	51.0 ± 0.6
DEM [48]	V	W_N	23.6 ± 0.7	49.5 ± 0.4
ALE [1]	V	W_N	23.4 ± 0.8	50.3 ± 1.4
ESZSL [43]	V	W_N	22.9 ± 1.2	48.3 ± 0.8
SJE [2]	V	W_N	22.3 ± 0.6	48.2 ± 0.4
GCN [19]	V	W_N	22.3 ± 0.6	49.7 ± 0.6
ER [8]	V+O	W_D	42.1 ± 1.4	73.1 ± 0.3
Ours	**V+O**	W_D	**45.9 ± 1.6**	**78.8 ± 1.0**

We make experiments on three benchmarks to evaluate our method against previous SOTAs. Since the N_{vid} needs to extract spatio-temporal features from video segments which has a different temporal receptive field with all off-the-shelf pretrained weights. We need to firstly pretrain the model on Kinetics605 [4]. Kinetics605 [4] removes the overlapped actions that also appears in HMDB51 or UCF101, so there is no data leakage caused by the pretraining. As is shown in Table 1, our model consistently outperforms previous SOTAs on both

Table 3. Comparing models w or w/o GA module

GA module	Rank1 Acc	Rank5 Acc
w/o	41.7 ± 1.3	73.4 ± 0.5
w	45.9 ± 1.6	78.8 ± 1.0

Table 4. Comparing models w or w/o consistency Loss

Consistency loss	Rank1 Acc	Rank5 Acc
w/o	43.2 ± 1.9	76.2 ± 1.3
w	45.9 ± 1.6	78.8 ± 1.0

benchmarks with noticeable margins. When compared with E2E [4], which also pretrains the spatio-temporal extractor backbone on Kinetics605 [4], our method achieves significant better performance with 8.9 and 11.9 gains on HMDB51 and UCF101. When compared with ER [8], which uses the same video and action input formats (Video, Object, and Description) as ours, JigsawNet still continuously outperforms it with 3.4 and 4.2 gains on HMDB51 and UCF101.

We also compare our method against previous SOTAs on the recently released KineticsZSAR [8] benchmark. The $\mathcal{N}_{vis}$ is initialized with weights pretrained on Kinetics400, because the val and test set of KineticsZSAR have no overlap with Kinetics400. We followed the procedures mentioned in [8] to test the model three times on three splits of KineticsZSAR. The average mean and deviation is provided in Table 2 for comparison. Our method consistently outperforms all previous works in Table 2 with noticeable margins. When compared with ER [8], which uses the same input types, our model performs better with 3.8 and 5.7 gains of rank1 and rank5 accuracy.

4.4 Ablation Studies

We also make ablation studies to analyze the contribution of each module to the final performance. All experiments below in this subsection are made on Kinetics ZSAR.

Is Group-to-Group Alignment Necessary for Zero-Shot Action Recognition? Although our model already achieves SOTA performance on three benchmarks, it's natural for people to ask how much benefit it earns changing from building one-to-one bridge to establishing gorup-to-group bridge? We design a comparison experiment for evaluation. Instead of extracting visual features from groups of video segments, the visual features are now directly extracted from whole videos, which means $\mathcal{F}^i = \mathcal{N}_{vid}(V_i), \mathcal{F}^i \in \mathbb{R}^d$. For action semantic extraction, the semantics are also extracted from entire descriptions instead of groups of verb phrases, $\mathcal{G}^j = \mathcal{N}_{text}(d^j), \mathcal{G}^j \in \mathbb{R}^d$. The one-to-one relationship between i^{th} video v^i and j^{th} action is represented as $p_a^{ij} = \mathcal{F}^i \cdot (\mathcal{G}^j)^T$, $p_o^{ij} = \mathcal{O}^i \cdot (\mathcal{G}^j)^T$, $p^{ij} = p_a^{ij} + \max(p_o^{ij}, 0)$. For fair comparison, Consistency Loss and GE are preserved with slight modifications. For Consistency Loss, the memorized cache are grouped by action types instead of atomic action types. For GE, it will now directly aggregate $\mathcal{F}^i$ and $\mathcal{O}^i$. As is shown in Table 3, the group-to-group model earns 4.2 and 5.4 gains of rank1 and rank5 accuracy, which is pretty significant.

Table 5. Comparing features optimized by Consistency Loss

Optimized Features	Rank1 Acc	Rank5 Acc
spatio-temporal	45.1 ± 1.4	78.0 ± 0.8
aggregated	45.9 ± 1.6	78.8 ± 1.0

Table 6. Comparing models w or w/o GE Module

GE	Rank1 Acc	Rank5 Acc
w/o	42.7 ± 2.0	72.9 ± 1.7
w	45.9 ± 1.6	78.8 ± 1.0

Table 7. Comparing improvements brought by backbone

Model	Backbone	Rank1 Acc	Rank5 Acc
R(2+1)D [39]	ResNet18	42.9 ± 1.7	73.0 ± 1.3
R(2+1)D [39]	ResNet34	45.9 ± 1.6	78.8 ± 1.0
TSM [28]	ResNet50	45.3 ± 1.8	78.4 ± 1.2

Is the Consistency Loss Beneficial? In Table 4, we compare models trained with or without Consistency Loss. As is shown by the results, the model trained with Consistency Loss builds a more robust bridge between vision features and action semantics. It's consistent with our expectation that the model can benefit from modeling inter-sample knowledge.

Which Vision Feature should be Memorized, Spatio-Temporal Feature or Fused Feature? We have shown the benefits brought by Consistency Loss, however, we want to dig deeper and show why aggregated feature, instead of spatio-temporal features are selected in Consistency Loss. Table 5 compares models with Consistency Loss optimized on aggregated features $\hat{f}_x^i$ and vision features f_x^i. According to the results, we can easily find that the aggregated feature is a better option. We assume it because the integration of object features enables the text extractor $\mathcal{N}_{text}$ also learn from inter-sample knowledge and get optimized by gradients back propagated from Consistency Loss. Meanwhile, the integration of object features enlarges the domain variance, which may also help in this training procedure.

Is the GE Module Beneficial? Table 6 compares models with or without GE module. According to the result, GE makes noticeable contributions to the final performance. GE not only enlarges the temporal receptive field of visual features extracted from video segments, but enables both spatio-temporal and object features to gain knowledge from a different domain.

How Much Improvements are from the Pretrained R(2+1)D Model? In Table 7, we compare performance of models with different spatio-temporal extractor backbones. Compared with R(2+1)D-18, the deeper R(2+1)D-34 significantly boosts the performance and outperforms with 3.0 and 5.8 gains of rank1 and rank5 accuracy. We also notice that, when using the same sptio-temporal feature extractor [28] and the same input information types with ER [8], our model still achieves noticeable better performance with 3.2 and 5.3 gains of rank1 and rank5 accuracy.

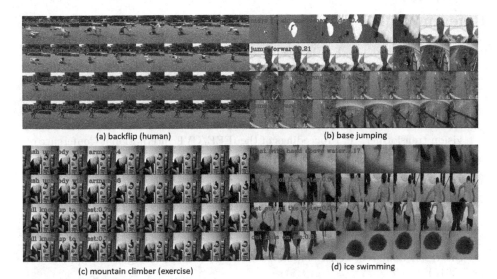

(a) backflip (human)   (b) base jumping

(c) mountain climber (exercise)   (d) ice swimming

Fig. 4. Visualization of predicted atomic action types of segments when recognizing target actions

4.5 Visualization

To better understand the group-to-group bridge, we visualize the atomic actions our model assigned to each segment. As is shown in Fig. 4, the model successfully learned the latent atomic actions unsupervisedly from source actions. For example, the model may learn "hand stand" and "jump backward" from gymnastics actions, and "push up body with arms" from fitness related actions in training set. Meanwhile, we also noticed the benefits brought by intra and inter samples modeling. In Fig. 4(c), the model can successfully distinguish between "push up body with arms" and "pull knee up to chest" whose visual features are pretty similar. In Fig. 4(d), the model still recognizes the second segment as "get out of the water" with the intra sample knowledge aggregated from contextual frames. Of course, we also found several places which can be improved by future works. For example, current strategy directly splits video into sequential segments, however, the atomic actions may locate between two segments. Although the model can still gain contextual information brought by GE, a soft temporal localization module may further improve the performance.

5   Conclusion

We propose a novel ZSAR model, JigsawNet.

Acknowledgments. This research was supported in part by the Defence Science and Technology Agency (DSTA).

References

1. Akata, Z., Perronnin, F., Harchaoui, Z., Schmid, C.: Label-embedding for image classification. IEEE Trans. Pattern Anal. Mach. Intell. **38**(7), 1425–1438 (2015)
2. Akata, Z., Reed, S., Walter, D., Lee, H., Schiele, B.: Evaluation of output embeddings for fine-grained image classification. In: Proceedings of the IEEE Conference on Computer Vision and Pattern Recognition, pp. 2927–2936 (2015)
3. Arnab, A., Dehghani, M., Heigold, G., Sun, C., Lučić, M., Schmid, C.: Vivit: a video vision transformer. In: Proceedings of the IEEE/CVF International Conference on Computer Vision, pp. 6836–6846 (2021)
4. Brattoli, B., Tighe, J., Zhdanov, F., Perona, P., Chalupka, K.: Rethinking zero-shot video classification: end-to-end training for realistic applications. In: Proceedings of the IEEE/CVF Conference on Computer Vision and Pattern Recognition, pp. 4613–4623 (2020)
5. Caba Heilbron, F., Escorcia, V., Ghanem, B., Carlos Niebles, J.: Activitynet: a large-scale video benchmark for human activity understanding. In: Proceedings of the IEEE Conference on Computer Vision and Pattern Recognition, pp. 961–970 (2015)
6. Carreira, J., Noland, E., Banki-Horvath, A., Hillier, C., Zisserman, A.: A short note about kinetics-600. arXiv preprint arXiv:1808.01340 (2018)
7. Carreira, J., Zisserman, A.: Quo vadis, action recognition? a new model and the kinetics dataset. In: Proceedings of the IEEE Conference on Computer Vision and Pattern Recognition, pp. 6299–6308 (2017)
8. Chen, S., Huang, D.: Elaborative rehearsal for zero-shot action recognition. In: Proceedings of the IEEE/CVF International Conference on Computer Vision, pp. 13638–13647 (2021)
9. Deng, J., Dong, W., Socher, R., Li, L.J., Li, K., Fei-Fei, L.: Imagenet: a large-scale hierarchical image database. In: 2009 IEEE Conference on Computer Vision and Pattern Recognition, pp. 248–255. IEEE (2009)
10. Devlin, J., Chang, M.W., Lee, K., Toutanova, K.: Bert: pre-training of deep bidirectional transformers for language understanding. arXiv preprint arXiv:1810.04805 (2018)
11. Diba, A., et al.: Temporal 3d convnets using temporal transition layer. In: Proceedings of the IEEE Conference on Computer Vision and Pattern Recognition Workshops, pp. 1117–1121 (2018)
12. Diba, A., et al.: Temporal 3d convnets: new architecture and transfer learning for video classification. arXiv preprint arXiv:1711.08200 (2017)
13. Fan, L., et al.: Rubiksnet: learnable 3d-shift for efficient video action recognition. In: Proceedings of the European Conference on Computer Vision (ECCV) (2020)
14. Floridi, L., Chiriatti, M.: Gpt-3: Its nature, scope, limits, and consequences. Minds Mach. **30**(4), 681–694 (2020)
15. Frome, A., et al.: Devise: a deep visual-semantic embedding model. Adv. Neural Inf. Process. Syst. **26** (2013)
16. Gan, C., Lin, M., Yang, Y., De Melo, G., Hauptmann, A.G.: Concepts not alone: exploring pairwise relationships for zero-shot video activity recognition. In: Thirtieth AAAI Conference on Artificial Intelligence (2016)
17. Gao, J., Zhang, T., Xu, C.: I know the relationships: zero-shot action recognition via two-stream graph convolutional networks and knowledge graphs. In: Proceedings of the AAAI Conference on Artificial Intelligence, vol. 33, pp. 8303–8311 (2019)

18. Ghadiyaram, D., Tran, D., Mahajan, D.: Large-scale weakly-supervised pre-training for video action recognition. In: Proceedings of the IEEE/CVF Conference on Computer Vision and Pattern Recognition, pp. 12046–12055 (2019)
19. Ghosh, P., Saini, N., Davis, L.S., Shrivastava, A.: All about knowledge graphs for actions. arXiv preprint arXiv:2008.12432 (2020)
20. Guo, M., Chou, E., Huang, D.A., Song, S., Yeung, S., Fei-Fei, L.: Neural graph matching networks for fewshot 3d action recognition. In: Proceedings of the European Conference on Computer Vision (ECCV), pp. 653–669 (2018)
21. Hara, K., Kataoka, H., Satoh, Y.: Can spatiotemporal 3d CNNs retrace the history of 2d CNNs and imagenet? In: Proceedings of the IEEE conference on Computer Vision and Pattern Recognition, pp. 6546–6555 (2018)
22. Jain, M., Van Gemert, J.C., Mensink, T., Snoek, C.G.: Objects2action: classifying and localizing actions without any video example. In: Proceedings of the IEEE International Conference on Computer Vision, pp. 4588–4596 (2015)
23. Karpathy, A., Toderici, G., Shetty, S., Leung, T., Sukthankar, R., Fei-Fei, L.: Large-scale video classification with convolutional neural networks. In: Proceedings of the IEEE Conference on Computer Vision and Pattern Recognition, pp. 1725–1732 (2014)
24. Kay, W., et al.: The kinetics human action video dataset. arXiv preprint arXiv:1705.06950 (2017)
25. Kolesnikov, A., et al.: Big transfer (BiT): general visual representation learning. In: Vedaldi, A., Bischof, H., Brox, T., Frahm, J.-M. (eds.) ECCV 2020. LNCS, vol. 12350, pp. 491–507. Springer, Cham (2020). https://doi.org/10.1007/978-3-030-58558-7_29
26. Kuehne, H., Jhuang, H., Garrote, E., Poggio, T., Serre, T.: HMDB: a large video database for human motion recognition. In: Proceedings of the International Conference on Computer Vision (ICCV) (2011)
27. Lampert, C.H., Nickisch, H., Harmeling, S.: Learning to detect unseen object classes by between-class attribute transfer. In: 2009 IEEE Conference on Computer Vision and Pattern Recognition, pp. 951–958. IEEE (2009)
28. Lin, J., Gan, C., Han, S.: Tsm: temporal shift module for efficient video understanding. In: Proceedings of the IEEE International Conference on Computer Vision, pp. 7083–7093 (2019)
29. Liu, J., Kuipers, B., Savarese, S.: Recognizing human actions by attributes. In: CVPR 2011, pp. 3337–3344. IEEE (2011)
30. Liu, Z., et al.: Swin transformer: Hierarchical vision transformer using shifted windows. In: Proceedings of the IEEE/CVF International Conference on Computer Vision, pp. 10012–10022 (2021)
31. Mandal, D., et al.: Out-of-distribution detection for generalized zero-shot action recognition. In: Proceedings of the IEEE/CVF Conference on Computer Vision and Pattern Recognition, pp. 9985–9993 (2019)
32. Qian, Y., Kang, G., Yu, L., Liu, W., Hauptmann, A.G.: Trm: temporal relocation module for video recognition. In: Proceedings of the IEEE/CVF Winter Conference on Applications of Computer Vision, pp. 151–160 (2022)
33. Qin, J., et al.: Zero-shot action recognition with error-correcting output codes. In: Proceedings of the IEEE Conference on Computer Vision and Pattern Recognition, pp. 2833–2842 (2017)
34. Shao, H., Qian, S., Liu, Y.: Temporal interlacing network. In: Proceedings of the AAAI Conference on Artificial Intelligence, vol. 34, pp. 11966–11973 (2020)

35. Simonyan, K., Zisserman, A.: Two-stream convolutional networks for action recognition in videos. In: Advances in neural Information Processing Systems, pp. 568–576 (2014)
36. Smaira, L., Carreira, J., Noland, E., Clancy, E., Wu, A., Zisserman, A.: A short note on the kinetics-700-2020 human action dataset. arXiv preprint arXiv:2010.10864 (2020)
37. Soomro, K., Zamir, A.R., Shah, M.: Ucf101: a dataset of 101 human actions classes from videos in the wild. arXiv preprint arXiv:1212.0402 (2012)
38. Tran, D., Bourdev, L., Fergus, R., Torresani, L., Paluri, M.: Learning spatiotemporal features with 3d convolutional networks. In: Proceedings of the IEEE International Conference on Computer Vision, pp. 4489–4497 (2015)
39. Tran, D., Wang, H., Torresani, L., Ray, J., LeCun, Y., Paluri, M.: A closer look at spatiotemporal convolutions for action recognition. In: Proceedings of the IEEE Conference on Computer Vision and Pattern Recognition, pp. 6450–6459 (2018)
40. Vaswani, A., et al.: Attention is all you need. Adv. Neural Inf. Process. Syst. **30** (2017)
41. Wang, L., et al.: Temporal segment networks: towards good practices for deep action recognition. In: Leibe, B., Matas, J., Sebe, N., Welling, M. (eds.) ECCV 2016. LNCS, vol. 9912, pp. 20–36. Springer, Cham (2016). https://doi.org/10.1007/978-3-319-46484-8_2
42. Wang, Q., Chen, K.: Alternative semantic representations for zero-shot human action recognition. In: Ceci, M., Hollmén, J., Todorovski, L., Vens, C., Džeroski, S. (eds.) ECML PKDD 2017. LNCS (LNAI), vol. 10534, pp. 87–102. Springer, Cham (2017). https://doi.org/10.1007/978-3-319-71249-9_6
43. Xu, X., Hospedales, T., Gong, S.: Semantic embedding space for zero-shot action recognition. In: 2015 IEEE International Conference on Image Processing (ICIP), pp. 63–67. IEEE (2015)
44. Xu, X., Hospedales, T., Gong, S.: Transductive zero-shot action recognition by word-vector embedding. Int. J. Comput. Vision **123**(3), 309–333 (2017)
45. Xu, X., Hospedales, T.M., Gong, S.: Multi-task zero-shot action recognition with prioritised data augmentation. In: Leibe, B., Matas, J., Sebe, N., Welling, M. (eds.) ECCV 2016. LNCS, vol. 9906, pp. 343–359. Springer, Cham (2016). https://doi.org/10.1007/978-3-319-46475-6_22
46. Zellers, R., Choi, Y.: Zero-shot activity recognition with verb attribute induction. arXiv preprint arXiv:1707.09468 (2017)
47. Zhang, H., Hao, Y., Ngo, C.W.: Token shift transformer for video classification. In: Proceedings of the 29th ACM International Conference on Multimedia, pp. 917–925 (2021)
48. Zhang, L., Xiang, T., Gong, S.: Learning a deep embedding model for zero-shot learning. In: Proceedings of the IEEE Conference on Computer Vision and Pattern Recognition, pp. 2021–2030 (2017)
49. Zhou, B., Andonian, A., Oliva, A., Torralba, A.: Temporal relational reasoning in videos. In: Proceedings of the European Conference on Computer Vision (ECCV), pp. 803–818 (2018)
50. Zhu, Y., Long, Y., Guan, Y., Newsam, S., Shao, L.: Towards universal representation for unseen action recognition. In: Proceedings of the IEEE Conference on Computer Vision and Pattern Recognition, pp. 9436–9445 (2018)

Mining Cross-Person Cues for Body-Part Interactiveness Learning in HOI Detection

Xiaoqian Wu[1] , Yong-Lu Li[1,2] , Xinpeng Liu[1] , Junyi Zhang[1] ,
Yuzhe Wu[3] , and Cewu Lu[1(✉)]

[1] Shanghai Jiao Tong University, Shanghai, China
{enlighten,yonglu_li,junyizhang,lucewu}@sjtu.edu.cn
[2] Hong Kong University of Science and Technology, Hong Kong, China
[3] DongHua University, Shanghai, China

Abstract. Human-Object Interaction (HOI) detection plays a crucial role in activity understanding. Though significant progress has been made, interactiveness learning remains a challenging problem in HOI detection: existing methods usually generate redundant negative H-O pair proposals and fail to effectively extract interactive pairs. Though interactiveness has been studied in both whole body- and part- level and facilitates the H-O pairing, previous works only focus on the *target person* once (*i.e.*, in a **local** perspective) and overlook the information of the other persons. In this paper, we argue that comparing body-parts of multi-person simultaneously can afford us more useful and supplementary interactiveness cues. That said, to learn body-part interactiveness from a **global** perspective: when classifying a target person's body-part interactiveness, visual cues are explored not only from herself/himself but also from *other persons in the image*. We construct body-part saliency maps based on self-attention to mine cross-person informative cues and learn the holistic relationships between *all* the body-parts. We evaluate the proposed method on widely-used benchmarks HICO-DET and V-COCO. With our new perspective, the holistic global-local body-part interactiveness learning achieves significant improvements over state-of-the-art. Our code is available at https://github.com/enlighten0707/Body-Part-Map-for-Interactiveness.

Keywords: Human-object interaction · Interactiveness learning · Body-part correlations

1 Introduction

Human-Object Interaction (HOI) detection retrieves human and object locations and infers the interactions simultaneously from still images. In practice, an HOI

X. Wu and Y.-L. Li—The first two authors contribute equally.
C. Lu–member of Qing Yuan Research Institute and Shanghai Qi Zhi institute.

Supplementary Information The online version contains supplementary material available at https://doi.org/10.1007/978-3-031-19772-7_8.

S. Avidan et al. (Eds.): ECCV 2022, LNCS 13664, pp. 121–136, 2022.
https://doi.org/10.1007/978-3-031-19772-7_8

Fig. 1. a) Statistics of hard cases in HOI datasets HICO-DET [1]. The images containing tiny persons, crowded scenes, and occlusion are considered. b) Our idea of learning body-part interactiveness from the same/different body-parts of other persons in the image.

instance is represented as a triplet: (*human, verb, object*). As a sub-task of visual relationship [12,28], it is crucial for activity understanding, embodied AI, etc.

Though significant progress has been made, HOI detection is still bottle-necked by interactiveness learning [22]: they fail to effectively extract interacted pairs while generating redundant negative pairs. The problem is first raised in TIN [22], where a pairwise interactiveness classifier is inserted into the HOI detection framework and the interactiveness prediction is used for non-interaction suppression. The decent gain on HOI detection performance verifies the great potential and importance of interactiveness learning.

Recently, TIN++ [17] is further proposed to utilize body-part level features to improve instance-level interactiveness learning via a hierarchical diagram. Despite the improvement in detecting positive pairs, it focuses on *local* body-part features from the targeted person only, which is not enough. We argue that when classifying the target person's body-part interactiveness, visual cues can be explored not only from himself/herself but also from *other persons in the image*. First, aside from the targeted person and object, it is also important to exploit contextual cues from the whole image [5]. Existing methods [5,32] have made efforts to learn relevant context to facilitate HOI learning. However, it is hard and **unstable** to retrieve useful information from various backgrounds without restriction. Therefore, we argue to better utilize contextual information by highlighting *all the persons* in the image because regions containing persons are usually more informative according to our prior. For instance, when recognizing a speaker giving a lecture, the audience is evidence more obviously than the stage decoration. Furthermore, as is shown in Fig. 1a, there are a large proportion of **hard cases** in HOI datasets [1], *e.g.*, tiny interactive persons, crowded scenes, and occlusion. In these cases, the cue carried by body parts of the local targeted person is very limited, while mining cues from a *global* multi-person perspective with other persons as a reference would be a good choice to alleviate the difficulty.

Following this insight, we propose to learn body-part interactiveness from the same/different body-parts of other persons in the image, which is illustrated in Fig. 1b. In the upper image, a crowd of tiny persons is rowing boats, and their lower bodies are occluded. When classifying a targeted H-O pair, aside from the targeted object, TIN++ [17] only focuses on the targeted person from the body-part level (e.g., hand), which is highlighted in the image. Nevertheless, we also emphasize other persons' hands even when classifying the targeted person's hand interactiveness, which provides a **supplementary** and **contrastive** viewpoint for interactiveness learning. Suppose another person B's hands are given as a reference which is easier to identify interactiveness, then the similarity between B's and targeted person A's hands will lead to the same prediction (both interactive or non-interactive), while discernable difference will lead to an opposite conclusion. Further, attention to different body-parts of multi-person also matters. In the bottom image, the left person is kicking a football while the right person is defending. When classifying the left person's *feet* interactiveness, the right person's *arms* would provide useful cues, since he is stretching out his arms and trying to intercept the ball. Thus, the relationship between *different* body-parts of different persons overlooked by previous works also offers supplementary information to interactiveness inference.

In light of these, we utilize a transformer for body-part interactiveness detection, where self-attention helps to capture informative cross-person visual cues. **First**, *body-part saliency maps* are constructed via image patches (*i.e.*, transformer tokens) masking, where patches not containing interested body-parts are masked and blocked from the computation. **Second**, to encode diverse visual patterns more flexibly, body-parts are *progressively masked*, where different attention mask is applied in successive transformer layers and more tokens are dropped in the late layers. **Third**, motivated by the sparsity property [17,21] of body-part interactiveness [17], the model classifies interactiveness of different body-parts via *one-time passing* to improve computation efficiency. An early filter is inserted to drop unimportant body-parts, and then the remaining saliency maps are merged. **Fourth**, we also propose a *sparsity adaptive sampling strategy* on the train set to put more emphasis on crowded scenes and guide better interactiveness knowledge. In extensive experiments, the proposed method achieves state-of-the-art. We firstly achieve all **33+** mAP on three sets of HICO-DET [1], especially the impressive improvement on Rare HOIs (**6.16** mAP improvement upon the SOTA CDN [36]) thanks to our holistic global-local interactiveness learning. Meanwhile, on the HOI hard cases, we also show our significant superiority.

Our contribution includes: 1) We propose to learn body-part interactiveness from a global perspective as an effective supplement for existing local-based methods, thus boosting interactiveness learning; 2) To mine cross-person cues, we construct body-part saliency maps based on self-attention computation and propose the progressively mask and one-time passing strategies to improve flexibility and efficiency; 3) With our proposed interactiveness detector, we achieve state-of-the-art on widely-used benchmarks HICO-DET [1] and V-COCO [8].

2   Related Work

Human-Object Interaction. Human-Object Interaction is essential to understand human-centric interaction with objects. Rapid progress has been made in HOI learning. Many large datasets [1,8,13,21] and deep learning based methods [1,5,6,9,16–18,22,23,25,26,30,32,35,36] have been proposed. They usually followed the two-stage pipeline, *i.e.*, first H-O pair detection, and then HOI classification. Chao *et al.* [1] proposed the widely-used multi-stream framework combining visual features and spatial locations, while GPNN [30] incorporated DNN and graph model to model the HOI relationship. InteractNet [6] utilized an action-specific density map to estimate the interacted object locations. DJ-RN [16] introduced 3D information and proposed a 2D-3D joint representation learning method. PaStaNet [21] inferred human part states [29] first and then reason out the activities based on part-level semantics. IDN [18] analyzed HOI from an integration and decomposition perspective. Recently, several one-stage methods have been proposed [23,32,35,36], where HOIs triplets are directly detected by parallel HOI detectors. PPDM [23] and IP-Net [35] adopted a variant of one-stage object detector for HOI detection. QPIC [32] utilized the recent transformer-based object detector DETR [38] to aggregate image-wide contextual information and facilitate HOI learning.

Interactiveness Learning. Though significant progress has been made, interactiveness learning remains challenging in HOI detection. Existing methods fail to pair interactive human and object effectively but generate redundant negative pairs. TIN and TIN++ [17,22] first raised this problem and tried to address it via an inserted pairwise interactiveness classifier. In TIN++ [17], the framework is extended to a hierarchical paradigm with jointly learning instance-level and body part-level interactiveness. Recently, CDN [36] proposed to accurately locate interactive pairs via a one-stage transformer framework disentangling human-object pair detection and interaction classification. However, it still performs not well on interactiveness detection (Sect. 5.3). Here, we point out the previously overlooked global perspective and utilize it to improve interactiveness learning.

Part-Based Action Recognition. The part-level human feature provides finer-grained visual cues to improve HOI detection. Based on the whole person and part boxes, Gkioxari *et al.* [7] developed a part-based model to make fine-grained action recognition. Fang *et al.* [3] proposed a pairwise body-part attention model which can learn to focus on crucial parts and their correlations, while TIN++ [17] utilized the human instance and body-part features together to learn interactiveness in a hierarchical paradigm and extract deeper interactive visual clues.

3   Method

3.1   Overview

As is shown in Fig. 2, our pipeline consists of three main modules: a *box detector*, an *interactiveness classifier*, and a *verb classifier*. They are all implemented as stacked transformed decoder.

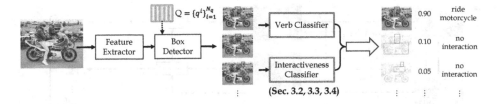

Fig. 2. The overall framework of our proposed method.

Given an input image $x \in \mathcal{R}^{3 \times H_0 \times W_0}$, we first adopt a ResNet-50 followed by a transformer encoder as our visual feature extractor. The output feature map is obtained as $z \in \mathcal{R}^{D_c \times H \times W}$, where D_c is the number of channels and H, W is the size. A fixed positional embedding $pos \in \mathcal{R}^{D_c \times H \times W}$ is additionally input to the transformer to supplement the positional information. Then based on the feature map z, the three main components are used for HOI detection.

An interactive human-object pair is mathematically defined following [32]: **1)** a human bounding box vector $b(h) \in [0,1]^4$ normalized by the image size, **2)** an object bounding box vector $b(o) \in [0,1]^4$ normalized by the image size, **3)** an object class vector $c \in \{0,1\}^{N_{obj}}$, where N_{obj} is the number of object classes, **4)** an interactiveness prediction $p_{int} \in [0,1]$, and **5)** a verb prediction $p_{verb} \in \{0,1\}^{N_v}$, where N_v is the number of verb classes. For **box detection**, a transformer decoder $f_{dec1}(\cdot,\cdot,\cdot)$ transforms a set of learnable query vectors $Q = \{q^i | q^i \in \mathcal{R}^{D_c}\}_{i=1}^{N_q}$ into a set of decoded embeddings $D = \{d^i | d^i \in \mathcal{R}^{D_c}\}_{i=1}^{N_q}$, which is obtained as $D = f_{dec1}(z, Q, pos)$. The subsequent three small feed-forward networks (FFNs): human bounding box FFN f_h, object bounding box FFN f_o, and object class FFN f_c further process the decoded embeddings D to produce N_q prediction results $\{b(h)^i\}_{i=1}^{N_q}$, $\{b(o)^i\}_{i=1}^{N_q}$, $\{c^i\}_{i=1}^{N_q}$, respectively. The decoded embeddings D are then fed into the interactiveness classifier and verb classifier as their query embeddings. For **verb classification**, another transformer decoder $f_{dec3}(\cdot,\cdot,\cdot)$ takes D as input and outputs $V = \{v^i | v^i \in \mathcal{R}^{D_c}\}_{i=1}^{N_q}$. With the verb class FFN f_v, the classification results is obtained as $p_{verb}^i = Sigmoid(f_v(v^i))$.

Our main contribution is global-local interactiveness learning based on the proposed body-part saliency map. Thus, we focus on the design of the new proposed **interactiveness classifier** (Fig. 3). In Sect. 3.2, we introduce the construction of body-part saliency map based on self-attention computation, and provide an intuitive scheme to validate its effectiveness (Fig. 3a). Then, we improve the intuitive scheme from two aspects: progressively masking to encode diverse visual patterns flexibly (Sect. 3.3), and one-time passing to improve efficiency (Sect. 3.4). The final improved model is shown in Fig. 3b.

3.2   Constructing Body-Part Saliency Map

We divide a person into six body-parts: feet, legs, hip, hands, arms, and head following HAKE [20]. To construct the body-part saliency map, *e.g.*, for hands, we utilize the attention mask matrix in the transformer. Only image patches

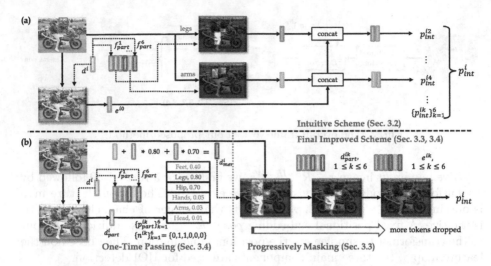

Fig. 3. The design of interactiveness classifier. a) Body-part saliency map construction and the intuitive scheme. We use legs and arms as examples. b) The final improved model. Here, we use the images to show the masking process for clarity instead of masking real images. The decoded embedding d^i is generated from the box detector and fed into the interactiveness classifier as query embeddings.

(or equally, transformer tokens) containing hands are remained for attention calculation, while other patches are masked. The attention mask is pre-calculated from body-part boxes detection results.

An Intuitive Scheme. In implementation, a transformer decoder $f_{dec2}(\cdot,\cdot,\cdot,\cdot)$ is used to transform input query embeddings D into $E = \{e^i|e^i \in \mathcal{R}^{D_c}\}_{i=1}^{N_q}$. Body-part saliency map is applied in f_{dec2} by masking partial of the feature map z via a masking matrix $M = \{m^i|m^i \in \{0,1\}^{H \times W}\}_{i=1}^{N_q}$ (1 for effective tokens and 0 for masked tokens). First, to integrate image-wide contextual information, a set of decoded embeddings are obtained as $E^0 = f_{dec2}(z, D, pos, M^0)$, where M^0 is an all-one matrix, *i.e.*, applying no mask. Next, the finer-grained body-part level features are used. The input query embeddings D_{part}^k for the k-th ($1 \leq k \leq 6$) body-part is transformed from the original query embeddings D via FFNs $\{f_{part}^k\}_{k=1}^6$, *i.e.*, $D_{part}^k = f_{part}^k(D)$. Then the decoded embeddings are calculated via $E^k = f_{dec2}(z, D_{part}^k, pos, M^k)$, where M^k is the corresponding mask matrix. In f_{dec2}, the attention masks are different for each body-part, while the learned parameters are shared. Finally, based on decoded embeddings E^0 and $\{E^k\}_{i=1}^6$, an interactiveness FFN f_{int} is used to generate body-part interactiveness prediction. For the i-th proposal and the k-th body-part, its interactiveness score is obtained via $p_{int}^{ik} = Sigmoid(f_{int}(concat(e^{ik}, e^{i0})))$. The instance-level interactiveness score is then obtained as $p_{int}^i = max_k\{p_{int}^{ik}\}$.

Attention Mask. To calculate the attention mask of all persons in the image, we first obtain the body-part boxes from the pose estimation [4,14,15] results following [17]. For the failure cases of pose estimation, we use the whole-body detection boxes from [31] as body-part boxes. With the k-th body-part boxes as $b(p)^k = \{b(p)^{kl}|b(p)^{kl} = [w_1^{kl}, h_1^{kl}, w_2^{kl}, h_2^{kl}], 1 \leq l \leq L\}$ (L is the persons count in the image), the global body-parts mask matrix m_{part}^{ik} ($\forall i, m_{part}^{ik} = m_{part}^k$) is calculated as:

$$m_{part}^{k(xy)} = \begin{cases} 1 & \exists\, l, h_1^{kl} \leq x * (H_0/H) \leq h_2^{kl}, w_1^{kl} \leq y * (W_0/W) \leq w_2^{kl} \\ 0 & otherwise \end{cases}, \quad (1)$$

where x, y is the index of the matrix. The scaling factor H_0/H and W_0/W are used here because the size of the feature map z is scaled down from that of the original image, e.g., $H_0/H = W_0/W = 32$ with ResNet-50 backbone.

Notably, although one proposal corresponds to only *one* targeted H-O pair, its body-part saliency map contains the body-parts of *all* persons in the image. Thus, the relationship between body-parts of all persons is learned from a global perspective. Here m_{part}^{ik} is a core component of the final mask m^{ik}. We briefly set $m^{ik} = m_{part}^{ik}$ for the intuitive scheme in this section, and will further modify m^{ik} in the next sections.

3.3 Progressively Body-Part Masking for Flexibility

In Sect. 3.2, an intuitive scheme with body-part saliency map is introduced, and its effectiveness is validated by experiments (Sect. 5). However, it lacks flexibility to *simply* construct body-part saliency maps to highlight all the **same** body-parts. As aforementioned in Fig. 1b, it also matters to learn attention from **different** body-parts of **different** persons. Thus, we develop a *progressively masking* strategy, where different attention masks are applied in successive transformer layers. Considering that the token representations are encoded more and more sufficiently throughout the whole network, fewer tokens are dropped in the early layers while more tokens are dropped in the late layers. In other words, the "**receptive field**" gradually becomes more focused as the computation proceeds. Attention to different body-parts of different persons is learned in the early layer, then comes the same body-parts of different persons. After encoding useful information from a global perspective, our model focuses on the targeted person in the final layer, which is similar to TIN++ [17].

Implementation. We construct the progressive masks from three components: body-part mask m_{part}^k ($1 \leq k \leq 6$, Sect. 3.2) shared by proposals, detected human mask m_{hum}^i ($1 \leq i \leq N_q$) dynamically calculated from the box detection of the i-th proposal, and detected object mask m_{obj}^i ($1 \leq i \leq N_q$) similar to m_{hum}^i. For the i-th proposal and its detected human bounding box $b(h)^i \in [0, 1]^4$, the box is first unnormalized by the image size as $b(h)^i = [w_1^i, h_1^i, w_2^i, h_2^i]$. Then

$$m_{hum}^{i(xy)} = \begin{cases} 1 & h_1^i \leq x * (H_0/H) \leq h_2^i, w_1^i \leq y * (W_0/W) \leq w_2^i \\ 0 & otherwise \end{cases}, \quad (2)$$

The detected object mask m_{obj}^i is obtained from $b(o)^i$ in a similar way.

The transformer decoder f_{dec2} for interactiveness inference has three stacked layers. The attention mask $m_j^{ik} \in \{0,1\}^{H \times W}$ for the i-th proposal, the j-th ($j = 1, 2, 3$, larger for later layer) layer and the k-th body-part is:

$$m_1^{ik} = max(m_{hum'}^i, m_{part}^k, m_{obj}^i), m_{hum'}^i = max(\max_k(m_{part}^k) - m_{hum}^i), 0), \quad (3)$$

$$m_2^{ik} = max(m_{part}^k, m_{obj}^i), \quad (4)$$

$$m_3^{ik} = max(min(m_{part}^k, m_{hum}^i), m_{obj}^i). \quad (5)$$

An example is given in Fig. 3b. The targeted object is highlighted in all layers. Specifically, the 1-st layer highlights the k-th body-part of the detected human, and the whole body of the other humans in the image ($m_{hum'}^i$), which allows attention computation from different body-parts of different persons. The 2-nd layer emphasizes the k-th body-part from all persons in the image, while the 3-rd layer focuses on the k-th body-part of the targeted person. With the progressive mask throughout transformer layers, different visual patterns are flexibly encoded to facilitate body-part interactiveness learning.

3.4   One-Time Passing via Body-Parts Filtering and Merging

In the intuitive scheme, six repeated calculations are needed for each body-part because their saliency maps are not shared. However, this is computationally redundant since body-part interactiveness has a notable property: **sparsity**. Namely, only several body-parts will get involved when people are interacting with daily objects. For instance, in "eat apple", the head and hands have stronger relationships with the apple than the lower body. Therefore, we can select the most important body-parts and only feed their visual feature into the network to classify interactiveness, i.e., the *filtering* process. Then, for the selected body-parts, there are still repeated calculations although fewer times. Thus, we spatially *merge* the saliency maps of the selected body-parts, feed them into the network, and obtain the whole-body interactiveness prediction via a one-time calculation. The rationality of merging is validated from the following two aspects. First, it seems that the spatial merging leads to "mixed-up" body-part feature, since merging all the six body-parts is equal to instance-level learning instead of body-part level. However, we emphasize that body-part level finer-grained feature remains in our model because only *several* body-parts are merged. Second, here the whole-body interactiveness prediction is directly calculated, while in the intuitive scheme we obtain it from six body-part interactiveness predictions. This does not impede interactiveness learning because most *important* body-parts are used for calculation.

Implementation. The implementation is illustrated in Fig. 3b. First, the importance of body-parts is calculated via a one-layer transformer decoder layer $h(\cdot, \cdot, \cdot)$ without mask. For the i-th proposal, it transforms d^i into $d_{part}^i =$

$h(z, d^i, pos)$, and a subsequent FFN is applied to get body-part attention score $\{p^{ik}_{part}\}^6_{k=1} = Sigmoid(FFN(d^i_{part}))$. Then, body-parts with relatively higher scores (top 25% of $\{p^{ik}_{part}|1 \leq i \leq N_q, 1 \leq k \leq 6\}$) are chosen for the following computation and others are filtered out. The result is represented as $\{n^{ik} \in \{0, 1\}\}$ (1 for chosen and 0 for dropped). After the filtering, both the mask matrix and query embeddings are merged as:

$$m^i_j = max_k(m^{ik}_j * n^{ik}), \tag{6}$$

$$d^i_{mer} = d^i + \sum_k (d^{ik}_{part} * n^{ik} * p^{ik}_{part}). \tag{7}$$

For the mask matrix, the spatial merge is equivalent to the elementwise maximum operation. For the query embeddings, the weighted sum of query embeddings d^{ik}_{part} of the selected body-parts is added to the whole-image query embeddings d^i to generate the merged embeddings d^i_{mer}. Then the decoder f_{dec2} with progressively masking transforms d^i_{mer} into embedding e^i_{mer}. Finally, the interactiveness score is obtained by a FFN via $p^i_{int} = Sigmoid(FFN(e^i_{mer}))$. Compared with the intuitive scheme, the one-time passing strategy drops unnecessary computation and improves computation efficiency.

3.5   Training and Inference

When training our model, following the set-based training process of QPIC [32], we first match predictions and ground-truths via bipartite matching, then calculate the loss for the matched pairs. For box detection, the loss is composed by three parts: box regression loss L_b, intersection-over-union loss L_u and object-class loss L_c. The loss L_{det} is obtained via $L_{det} = \lambda_1 * L_b + \lambda_2 * L_u + \lambda_3 * L_c$, where $\lambda_1, \lambda_2, \lambda_3$ are hyperparameters for adjusting the weights. The interactiveness classifier and verb classifier are supervised with classification loss L_{int} and L_{verb} respectively.

The training is divided into two stages. First, we train the box detector and interactiveness classifier along with the visual feature extractor with loss $L_1 = L_{det} + L_{int}$. Then, the box detector and verb classifier are trained along with the visual feature extractor and the loss is $L_2 = L_{det} + L_{verb}$. In inference, we use the interactiveness results to improve verb classification via non-interaction suppression (NIS) [17], where H-O pairs with lower interactiveness scores are filtered out.

4   Discussion: Sparse vs. Crowded Scene

In this section, we discuss a naturally raised question: our method focuses on crowded scenes with multi interactive pairs or multi persons/objects, then what about the sparse scenes?

First, our model is adapted to both crowded and sparse scenes. Under crowded scenes, mining cross-person cues provides more useful information of interactiveness. While for sparse scenes, our method would be operated similar to TIN++ [17]. However, our model is still superior to TIN++ [17] thanks to the integration body-part feature and DETR [38] backbone.

Next, we want to re-emphasize the importance of HOI detection in crowded scenes, especially for interactiveness learning and interactive human-object pair proposal detection. We find that crowded images occupy a large proportion of the HOI dataset, validating the effects brought by our method. Meanwhile, the performance of interactiveness learning under crowded scenes is inferior to sparse ones. We split HICO-DET [1] test set into *sparse/crowded* scenes respectively and evaluate the interactiveness AP: 16.96/9.64 AP (TIN++ [17]) and 43.62/33.10 AP (ours, Sect. 5). From the large performance gap between sparse and crowded scenes (7.32 AP for TIN++ [17] and 10.52 AP for ours, Sect. 5), we can see that interactiveness learning is mainly bottlenecked by crowded scenes, where it is usually harder to effectively extract interactive pairs. Therefore, it matters to focus on crowded scenes for interactiveness learning. Statistics are detailed in the supplementary.

Then, we further propose a novel **sparsity adaptive sampling strategy** on train set to put more emphasis on crowded scenes and facilitate interactiveness learning. The sampling probability is modified as 1:α ($\alpha >1$, in practice $\alpha = 3$) for sparse vs. crowded images, compared with the original 1:1, which guides better interactiveness knowledge to identify interactive pairs under complex scenes. Finally, the experiment (Sect. 5.3) proves that the proposed global perspective indeed boosts interactiveness learning, especially for crowded scenes.

5 Experiment

In this section, we first introduce the datasets and metrics in Sect. 5.1, and describe implementation details in Sect. 5.2. Next, we report the results on HICO-DET [1] and V-COCO [8] in Sect. 5.3. Some visualization results are given in Sect. 5.4. Finally, ablation studies are conducted in Sect. 5.5.

5.1 Dataset and Metric

Datasets. We adopt two datasets HICO-DET [1] and V-COCO [8]. HICO-DET [1] includes 47,776 images (38,118 in train set and 9658 in test set), 600 HOI categories on 80 object categories (same with [24]) and 117 verbs, and provides more than 150k annotated human-object pairs. V-COCO [8] provides 10,346 images (2,533 for training, 2,867 for validating, and 4,946 for testing) and 16,199 person instances. Each person has labels for 29 action categories (five of them have no paired object).

Metrics. We follow the settings adopted in [1], i.e., a prediction is a true positive only when the human and object bounding boxes both have IoUs larger than 0.5 with reference to ground truth, and the HOI classification result is accurate. The role mean average precision [8] is used to measure the performance. Additionally, we measure interactiveness detection in a similar setting.

5.2 Implementation Details

We adopt ResNet-50 followed by a six-layer transformer encoder as our visual feature extractor. The box detector and the verb classifier are both implemented as a six-layer transformer decoder. The interactiveness classifier is implemented as a three-layer transformer decoder, where selected tokens are masked. During training, AdamW [27] with the weight decay of 1e-4 is used. The visual feature extractor and box decoder are initialized from COCO [24] pretrained DETR [38]. The query size is set as 64 for HICO-DET [1] and 100 for V-COCO [8] following CDN [36]. The loss weight coefficients $\lambda_1, \lambda_2, \lambda_3$ are respectively set as 1, 2.5, 1, exactly the same as QPIC [32]. In 1st stage, the model is trained for 90 epochs with a learning rate of 1e-4 which is decreased by 10 times at the 60th epoch. In 2nd stage, the model is fine-tuned for 60 epochs. All experiments are conducted on four NVIDIA GeForce RTX 3090 GPUs with a batch size of 16. In inference, a pairwise NMS with a threshold of 0.6 is conducted.

5.3 Results

Interactiveness Detection. We evaluate our interactiveness detection on HICO-DET [1] and V-COCO [8]. On HICO-DET [1], we adopt the interactiveness detection AP proposed in TIN++ [17], while on V-COCO [8] we construct the benchmark in a similar way. Table 1 shows our interactiveness detection results compared with open-source state-of-the-art methods [17,23,32,36]. For TIN++ [17], the output interactiveness score is used. For PPDM [23], QPIC [32], and CDN [36], the mean of HOI scores (520 HOI categories for HICO-DET [1], and 24 for V-COCO [8]) is used as an approximation.

Table 1. Interactiveness detection results on HICO-DET [1] and V-COCO [8].

Method	HICO-DET [1]	V-COCO [8]
TIN++ [17]	14.35	29.36
PPDM [23]	27.34	–
QPIC [32]	32.96	38.33
CDN [36]	33.55	40.13
Ours	**38.74 (+5.19)**	**43.61 (+3.48)**

As is shown in Table 1, for the two-stage method TIN++ [17], the interactiveness AP is unsatisfactory. We claim that it suffers from exhaustively generated negative H-O pairs from the detector in the first stage, despite the non-interaction suppression [17]. Instead, the one-stage methods PPDM [23], QPIC [32], and CDN [36] benefit from the avoidance of exhaustive pairing and achieve better performance on interactiveness detection. With the insight of holistically modeling body-part level interactiveness, our method achieves a even better interactiveness AP of **38.74** on HICO-DET [1] and **43.61** on V-COCO [8].

Next, we evaluate the effectiveness of our method in hard cases, as is discussed in Sect. 1. We split HICO-DET [1] test set and compare the interactiveness detection performance of TIN++ [17] and our method. Compared with the local-based method TIN++ [17], our method improves an interactiveness AP gain of 26.66 (157%) / 23.46 (243%) for sparse/crowded scenes, 23.74 (147%)/23.53(263%) for normal/tiny-persons scenes, and 22.11 (134%) / 14.69 (182%) for less/more-occlusion scenes. We can see that the proposed global perspective indeed boosts interactiveness learning, especially for hard cases where interactive persons are more difficult to identify. For detailed results, please refer to our supplementary.

Body-Part Interactiveness Detection. To detail the analysis of body-part level interactiveness learning, we evaluate body-part interactiveness AP from the output body-part attention score. When trained without body-part interactiveness supervision, our method still learns body-part interactiveness well. The interactiveness APs on HICO-DET [1] are: 38.74 (whole body), 11.66 (feet), 5.31 (legs), 23.83 (hip), 23.11 (hands), 1.38 (arms), 5.51 (head). Further, we utilize annotations provided by HAKE [19,21] to apply body-part supervision, i.e., $\{p_{part}^{ik}\}_{k=1}^6$ is bound with body-part level interactiveness labels, and the loss is added to L_{int}. The results are: 38.83 (whole body), 34.89 (feet), 31.02 (legs), 38.11 (hip), 34.18 (hands), 31.32 (arms), 24.94 (head). We can see that the performance is further improved with body-part supervision, especially for "legs", "arms", and "head". Without supervision, the performance of "arms" and "head" are inferior to other body-parts. One possible reason is that "arms" suffer from relatively ambiguous definitions, and can sometimes be confused with "torso" or "hands" due to occlusion. Additionally, "head" is related to HOIs harder to identify such as "look", "smell".

HOI Detection Boosting. In Table 2 and Table 3, we evaluate how HOI learning can benefit from the interactiveness detection results of our method. Here we use instance-level supervision without annotations from HAKE [19,21] for interactiveness learning to compare with TIN++ [17]. In Table 2, the first part adopted COCO pre-trained detector. HICO-DET fine-tuned or one-stage detector is used in the second part. All the results are with ResNet-50.

Our method outperforms state-of-the-arts with **35.15/37.56** mAP (Default Full/ Known Object Full) on HICO-DET [1] and **63.0/65.1** mAP (Scenario 1/2) on V-COCO [8], verifying its effectiveness. For two-stage HOI methods, we feed the representative method iCAN [5] (human-object pairs are exhaustively paired) with our detected pairs. Table 4 reports the performance comparison on HICO-DET [1] with different pair detection results. We find that with high-quality detected interactive pairs, the performance of iCAN [5] is significantly boosted, especially from the results of our method. We leave the detailed settings in supplementary.

Table 2. Results on HICO-DET [1].

Method	Default			Known object		
	Full	Rare	Non-Rare	Full	Rare	Non-Rare
iCAN [5]	14.84	10.45	16.15	16.26	11.33	17.73
TIN [22]	17.03	13.42	18.11	19.17	15.51	20.26
PMFNet [34]	17.46	15.65	18.00	20.34	17.47	21.20
DJ-RN [16]	21.34	18.53	22.18	23.69	20.64	24.60
PPDM [23]	21.73	13.78	24.10	24.58	16.65	26.84
VCL [9]	23.63	17.21	25.55	25.98	19.12	28.03
IDN [18]	26.29	22.61	27.39	28.24	24.47	29.37
Zou et al. [39]	26.61	19.15	28.84	29.13	20.98	31.57
AS-Net [2]	28.87	24.25	30.25	31.74	27.07	33.14
QPIC [32]	29.07	21.85	31.23	31.68	24.14	33.93
FCL [10]	29.12	23.67	30.75	31.31	25.62	33.02
GGNet [37]	29.17	22.13	30.84	33.50	26.67	34.89
CDN [36]	31.78	27.55	33.05	34.53	29.73	35.96
Ours	**35.15**	**33.71**	**35.58**	**37.56**	**35.87**	**38.06**

Table 3. Results on V-COCO [8].

Method	AP_{role}(S1)	AP_{role}(S2)
iCAN [5]	45.3	52.4
TIN [22]	47.8	54.2
VSGNet [33]	51.8	57.0
PMFNet [34]	52.0	–
IDN [18]	53.3	60.3
AS-Net [2]	53.9	–
GGNet [37]	54.7	–
HOTR [11]	55.2	64.4
QPIC [32]	58.8	61.0
CDN [36]	62.3	64.4
Ours	**63.0**	**65.1**

Table 4. The performance comparison on HICO-DET [1] with different pair detection results.

Method	Full	Rare	Non-Rare
$iCAN$ [5]	14.84	10.45	16.15
$iCAN$ [5]^{QPIC}	20.36	11.14	23.11
$iCAN$ [5]^{CDN}	21.09	11.20	24.04
$iCAN$ [5]^{Ours}	**24.38**	**16.27**	**26.80**

Table 5. Results of ablation studies on HICO-DET [1].

Method	int AP	HOI mAP
Ours	**38.74**	**35.15**
w/o body-part	36.46	32.16
w/o body-part saliency map	37.43	32.60
intuitive scheme	37.91	33.12
w/o progressive mask	38.06	34.05
w/o sparsity adaptive sampling	38.29	34.37
w/o one-time passing	38.51	34.90

5.4 Visualization

Figure 4 shows some visualization results of the learned attention. Our model can effectively learn body-part attention (Fig. 4b) and extract informative cues from other persons in the image, either from the same (Fig. 4d, f) or the different (Fig. 4a, c) body-parts. Learning holistic relationship between body-parts from different persons alleviates the difficulties of interactiveness learning in hard cases, e.g., tiny interactive persons (Fig. 4e, g), crowded scenes (Fig. 4e), and occlusion (Fig. 4f). Also, our method benefits both interactive pairs and non-interactive pairs (Fig. 4d, h). For more please refer to our supplementary.

5.5 Ablation Studies

We conduct ablation studies on HICO-DET [1] and list interactiveness AP and corresponding HOI mAP results in Table 5.

We first validate the effectiveness of the body-part saliency map. In the intuitive scheme, the body-part saliency map is applied via an attention mask and

Fig. 4. Visualization results of learned attention. Number j ($j = 1, 2, 3$) in the bracket represents which layer the attention results are obtained from.

interactiveness is calculated for each body-part. The intuitive scheme achieves 37.91 interactiveness AP and 33.12 HOI mAP. In contrast, the interactiveness AP falls to 37.43 when body-part saliency map is removed, $i.e.$, for each proposal, body-part and layer, the mask matrix is set as $\mathbf{1}^{H \times W}$. It validates the effectiveness of introducing global-level visual cues and learning holistic body-part relationship. Further, if trained with only instance-level visual features without emphasis on body-parts, the interactiveness AP falls to 36.46. Thus, learning body-part interactiveness benefits instance-level interactiveness learning by introducing fine-grained visual features.

Then we evaluate the proposed modules. (1) When progressively masking is removed, all decoder layers are applied with the same attention mask of body-part saliency map, which leads to an interactiveness AP drop to 38.06. The result validates that our model indeed benefits from the progressively masking strategy, where diverse body-part oriented visual patterns are combined and integrated to facilitate interactiveness learning. (2) Without sparsity adaptive sampling, the interactiveness AP falls to 38.29. We find that the sampling augmentation on crowded-scene images helps to extract interactive pairs, especially in complex scenes. (3) Finally, we evaluate the one-time passing strategy. If removed, the interactiveness AP falls to 38.51, and computation speed is reduced by approximately 20% from 28 min/epoch to 33 min/epoch. We can see that our model benefits from it to improve performance as well as efficiency.

6   Conclusions

Currently, HOI detection is still bottlenecked by interactiveness learning. In this paper, we focus on learning human body-part interactiveness from a previously overlooked global perspective. We construct body-part saliency maps to mine informative cues from not only the targeted person, but also other persons in the image. Our method provides an effective supplement for existing local-based methods and achieves significant improvements on widely used HOI benchmarks.

Despite the improvement, we believe there is still much room left to make further progress on interactiveness learning.

Acknowledgments. This work was supported by the National Key R&D Program of China (No. 2021ZD0110700), Shanghai Municipal Science and Technology Major Project (2021SHZDZX0102), Shanghai Qi Zhi Institute, and SHEITC (2018-RGZN-02046).

References

1. Chao, Y.W., Liu, Y., Liu, X., Zeng, H., Deng, J.: Learning to detect human-object interactions. In: WACV (2018)
2. Chen, M., Liao, Y., Liu, S., Chen, Z., Wang, F., Qian, C.: Reformulating hoi detection as adaptive set prediction. In: CVPR (2021)
3. Fang, H.S., Cao, J., Tai, Y.W., Lu, C.: Pairwise body-part attention for recognizing human-object interactions. In: ECCV (2018)
4. Fang, H.S., Xie, S., Tai, Y.W., Lu, C.: Rmpe: regional multi-person pose estimation. In: ICCV (2017)
5. Gao, C., Zou, Y., Huang, J.B.: iCAN: Instance-centric attention network for human-object interaction detection. In: BMVC (2018)
6. Gkioxari, G., Girshick, R., Dollár, P., He, K.: Detecting and recognizing human-object interactions. In: CVPR (2018)
7. Gkioxari, G., Girshick, R., Malik, J.: Actions and attributes from wholes and parts. In: ICCV (2015)
8. Gupta, S., Malik, J.: Visual semantic role labeling. arXiv preprint arXiv:1505.04474 (2015)
9. Hou, Z., Peng, X., Qiao, Y., Tao, D.: Visual compositional learning for human-object interaction detection. arXiv preprint arXiv:2007.12407 (2020)
10. Hou, Z., Yu, B., Qiao, Y., Peng, X., Tao, D.: Detecting human-object interaction via fabricated compositional learning. In: CVPR (2021)
11. Kim, B., Lee, J., Kang, J., Kim, E.S., Kim, H.J.: Hotr: End-to-end human-object interaction detection with transformers. In: CVPR (2021)
12. Krishna, R., et al.: Visual genome: connecting language and vision using crowd-sourced dense image annotations. In: IJCV (2017)
13. Kuznetsova, A., et al.: The open images dataset v4: unified image classification, object detection, and visual relationship detection at scale. arXiv:1811.00982 (2018)
14. Li, J., et al.: Human pose regression with residual log-likelihood estimation. In: ICCV (2021)
15. Li, J., Wang, C., Zhu, H., Mao, Y., Fang, H.S., Lu, C.: Crowdpose: efficient crowded scenes pose estimation and a new benchmark. In: CVPR (2019)
16. Li, Y.L., et al.: Detailed 2d-3d joint representation for human-object interaction. In: CVPR (2020)
17. Li, Y.L., Liu, X., Wu, X., Huang, X., Xu, L., Lu, C.: Transferable interactiveness knowledge for human-object interaction detection. In: TPAMI (2022)
18. Li, Y.L., Liu, X., Wu, X., Li, Y., Lu, C.: Hoi analysis: integrating and decomposing human-object interaction. In: NeurIPS (2020)
19. Li, Y.L., et al.: Hake: a knowledge engine foundation for human activity understanding. arXiv preprint arXiv:2202.06851 (2022)

20. Li, Y.L., et al.: Hake: human activity knowledge engine. arXiv preprint arXiv:1904.06539 (2019)
21. Li, Y.L., et al.: Pastanet: toward human activity knowledge engine. In: CVPR (2020)
22. Li, Y.L., et al.: Transferable interactiveness knowledge for human-object interaction detection. In: CVPR (2019)
23. Liao, Y., Liu, S., Wang, F., Chen, Y., Feng, J.: Ppdm: parallel point detection and matching for real-time human-object interaction detection. In: CVPR (2020)
24. Lin, T.Y., et al.: Microsoft coco: Common objects in context. In: ECCV (2014)
25. Liu, X., Li, Y.L., Lu, C.: Highlighting object category immunity for the generalization of human-object interaction detection. In: AAAI (2022)
26. Liu, X., Li, Y.L., Wu, X., Tai, Y.W., Lu, C., Tang, C.K.: Interactiveness field in human-object interactions. In: CVPR (2022)
27. Loshchilov, I., Hutter, F.: Decoupled weight decay regularization. arXiv preprint arXiv:1711.05101 (2017)
28. Lu, C., Krishna, R., Bernstein, M., Fei-Fei, L.: Visual relationship detection with language priors. In: ECCV (2016)
29. Lu, C., Su, H., Li, Y., Lu, Y., Yi, L., Tang, C.K., Guibas, L.J.: Beyond holistic object recognition: Enriching image understanding with part states. In: CVPR (2018)
30. Qi, S., Wang, W., Jia, B., Shen, J., Zhu, S.C.: Learning human-object interactions by graph parsing neural networks. In: ECCV (2018)
31. Ren, S., He, K., Girshick, R., Sun, J.: Faster r-cnn: towards real-time object detection with region proposal networks. In: NeurIPS (2015)
32. Tamura, M., Ohashi, H., Yoshinaga, T.: QPIC: query-based pairwise human-object interaction detection with image-wide contextual information. In: CVPR (2021)
33. Ulutan, O., Iftekhar, A., Manjunath, B.: Vsgnet: spatial attention network for detecting human object interactions using graph convolutions. In: CVPR (2020)
34. Wan, B., Zhou, D., Liu, Y., Li, R., He, X.: Pose-aware multi-level feature network for human object interaction detection. In: ICCV (2019)
35. Wang, T., Yang, T., Danelljan, M., Khan, F.S., Zhang, X., Sun, J.: Learning human-object interaction detection using interaction points. In: CVPR (2020)
36. Zhang, A., et al.: Mining the benefits of two-stage and one-stage hoi detection. arXiv preprint arXiv:2108.05077 (2021)
37. Zhong, X., Qu, X., Ding, C., Tao, D.: Glance and gaze: Inferring action-aware points for one-stage human-object interaction detection. In: CVPR (2021)
38. Zhu, X., Su, W., Lu, L., Li, B., Wang, X., Dai, J.: Deformable detr: deformable transformers for end-to-end object detection. arXiv preprint arXiv:2010.04159 (2020)
39. Zou, C., et al.: End-to-end human object interaction detection with hoi transformer. In: CVPR (2021)

Collaborating Domain-Shared and Target-Specific Feature Clustering for Cross-domain 3D Action Recognition

Qinying Liu[ID] and Zilei Wang[✉][ID]

University of Science and Technology of China, Hefei, China
lydyc@mail.ustc.edu.cn, zlwang@ustc.edu.cn

Abstract. In this work, we consider the problem of cross-domain 3D action recognition in the open-set setting, which has been rarely explored before. Specifically, there is a source domain and a target domain that contain the skeleton sequences with different styles and categories, and our purpose is to cluster the target data by utilizing the labeled source data and unlabeled target data. For such a challenging task, this paper presents a novel approach dubbed CoDT to collaboratively cluster the domain-shared features and target-specific features. CoDT consists of two parallel branches. One branch aims to learn domain-shared features with supervised learning in the source domain, while the other is to learn target-specific features using contrastive learning in the target domain. To cluster the features, we propose an online clustering algorithm that enables simultaneous promotion of robust pseudo label generation and feature clustering. Furthermore, to leverage the complementarity of domain-shared features and target-specific features, we propose a novel collaborative clustering strategy to enforce pair-wise relationship consistency between the two branches. We conduct extensive experiments on multiple cross-domain 3D action recognition datasets, and the results demonstrate the effectiveness of our method. Code is at https://github.com/canbaoburen/CoDT.

Keywords: Skeleton-based action recognition · Cross-domain · Open-set

1 Introduction

Recent advances in 3D depth cameras and pose estimation algorithms have made it possible to estimate 3D skeletons quickly and accurately. In contrast to RGB images, the skeleton data only contain the coordinates of human keypoints, providing high-abstract and environment-free information. Thus, 3D action recognition (*a.k.a*, skeleton-based action recognition) is attracting more and more

Supplementary Information The online version contains supplementary material available at https://doi.org/10.1007/978-3-031-19772-7_9.

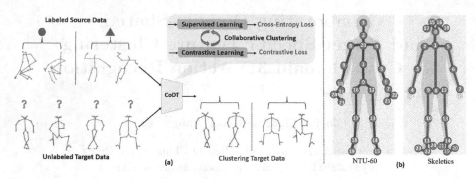

Fig. 1. (a) Illustration of CD-SAR task and our proposed CoDT method. CD-SAR aims to group the target samples into semantic clusters by virtue of labeled source data and unlabeled target data. The core idea of CoDT is to collaborate the supervised learning of source data and contrastive learning of target data. (b) Illustration of different joint definitions in the NTU-60 [58] and Skeletics [25]. The figure is modified from [75].

attentions [50,74,80]. Nevertheless, existing methods mainly focus on the traditional supervised classification. In this learning paradigm, it is assumed that the labeled training (source) dataset and unlabeled test (target) dataset have the same distribution. In practical scenarios, it is not easy to hold such assumption, because labeling a dataset with the same distribution as the target data is a laborious task. In reality, it is preferred to utilize a related public annotated skeleton or even image dataset as a source dataset. Unfortunately, there is typically discrepancy (*a.k.a*, domain gap [2]) between the source and target datasets due to various factors, including the devices (*e.g.*, 3D sensors [18,83], image-based pose estimation algorithms [5,37]), the camera setup (*e.g.*, viewpoints), the scenes (*e.g.*, in-the-lab or in-the-wild), *etc.* These factors make the skeletons of different datasets distinct in *styles* (*e.g.*, joint types, qualities, views) and action *categories*. For example, consider a very practical application that needs to recognize the action classes of the in-the-wild unlabeled 3D dataset Skeletics [25], we might seek help from the large-scale in-the-lab dataset NTU-60 [58] with high-quality skeletons and annotated labels. However, the NTU-60 and Skeletics are captured by Microsoft Kinect V2 camera [18] and the pose estimation method VIBE [37] respectively, resulting in different styles of skeletons, *e.g.*, different definitions of human joints (see Fig. 1(b)). Furthermore, NTU-60 mainly contains indoor actions, while Skeletics contains more unconstrained actions from internet videos, thereby leading to different action categories. In summary, the domain gap problem is very practical in skeleton-based action recognition but rarely studied in the literature. In this paper, we present the first systematic study to the domain gap problem in skeleton-based action recognition, where the source and target datasets have different *styles* and *categories*. Obviously, this is an open-set problem, and it is expected that the algorithm can automatically cluster the target samples into latent classes.

The labeled source dataset, although collected from a different domain from the target domain, is helpful to develop *domain-shared* representations. By training the models in the standard supervised manner, the representations are expected to be discriminative to different action categories. However, the models generally generalize poorly to the target domain due to the domain gap [24,75]. On the other hand, the target domain has many unlabeled samples, which can be used to learn more *target-specific* representations. This suggests the possibility of applying recently emerging contrastive learning [11,23,28] on target data. The contrastive learning optimizes the features by instance discrimination, *i.e.*, the features are enforced to be invariant for different transformations of an instance and distinct for different instances. By learning to attract or repel different instances, the features appear to automatically capture some extent of semantic similarity. Yet, they may not have enough discrimination to action categories.

Based on the above discussions, we consider that the domain-shared representations and target-specific representations are conceptually complementary. This motivates us to integrate the supervised learning on labeled source data and contrastive learning on unlabeled target data. Previous methods [33,56,89] commonly implement such integration through multi-task learning with a shared feature encoder. However, in our case, the two domains may differ considerably in styles and even joint types, and thus we argue that the domain-shared and target-specific features should be learned via different models in order to sufficiently exploit their respective merits. With the purpose of clustering target samples, a natural problem arises: *is it possible to collaborate the two models on feature clustering?* To achieve this goal, we need to address two key issues. The first one is how to cluster the features for a single model, which is expected to be optimized in an end-to-end manner rather than computed by some offline clustering algorithms (*e.g.*, k-means) whose usefulness is proven to be limited [6]. The second one is how to collaborate both models to jointly optimize feature clustering. It is quite challenging since the learned clusters from two models cannot be matched exactly due to the lack of labels.

In this paper, we propose a novel **Co**llaborating **D**omain-shared and **T**arget-specific features clustering (CoDT) network for the task of cross-domain skeleton-based action recognition (CD-SAR). Figure 1 illustrates the overview of the task and our method. Specifically, to address the first issue, we propose an online clustering algorithm to generate robust pseudo labels to guide feature clustering. It is built upon the teacher-student framework [64], where the clustering is optimized via the pseudo labels generated by the teacher model. Under this framework, a straightforward way to determine pseudo label is to select the cluster with which the teacher is most confident. However, due to the discrepancy between target sample clustering and source-based supervised learning (or instance-based contrastive learning), there is a risk of obtaining a trivial solution that groups most samples into only a few clusters, as observed in Sect. 4.3. To make the clusters balanced, we propose to generate uniformly distributed pseudo labels. It is non-trivial to achieve it online as we have to take into consideration the global distribution of pseudo labels. Hence, we transform it to an optimal transport problem that can be solved by linear programming [14].

As for the second issue, we propose a collaborative clustering strategy that exchanges pseudo labels across models for collaborative training (co-training). In the traditional co-training methods [4,26,57], the categories of two models are pre-defined and consistent, and thus the pseudo labels produced by one model can be directly used to train another model. In our case, however, the semantics of the learned clusters of two models are agnostic and variable during training, making it difficult to determine the correlation between the clusters of two models. To this end, we propose to perform co-training on the pair-wise relationship that represents whether a pair of samples are from the same cluster (positive pair) or distinct clusters (negative pair). Specifically, we first construct the pair-wise binary pseudo labels by comparing the instance-wise pseudo labels of samples. Thereafter, the pair-wise labels are used to train the other model, where a novel contrastive loss is particularly adopted to enforces the model to produce consistent/inconsistent predictions for the positive/negative pairs.

Our contributions are summarized as: 1) We provide a benchmark for CD-SAR. To solve this task, we propose a novel two-branch framework dubbed CoDT to collaborate domain-shared and target-specific features. 2) We propose an online clustering algorithm that can alternate the robust pseudo label generation and balanced feature clustering. 3) We propose a collaborative clustering algorithm, which enables co-training of two models to enforce their consistency in terms of pair-wise relationship. 4) We evaluate our method upon different cross-domain tasks, and the effectiveness of our method is well shown.

2   Related Work

Unsupervised Representation Learning and Visual Clustering. In the field of unsupervised learning, there are two main research topics: representation learning and image clustering. The former focuses on training the feature encoder by self-supervised learning. To achieve this, existing methods either design numerous pre-designed pretext tasks [16,52,55,81] or perform contrastive learning [11,23,28]. Despite these efforts, these approaches are mainly used for pretraining. As an alternative, image clustering methods simultaneously optimize clustering and representation learning. Previous methods train the model using the pseudo labels derived from the most confident samples [10,12,54,70], or through cluster re-assignments [6,7]. Recently, [1,8] are proposed to apply a balanced label assignment. In this work, we take advantage of the idea in [1,8] but incorporate it into the student-teacher network.

Supervised and Unsupervised 3D Action Recognition. To tackle skeleton-based action recognition, many RNN-based methods [37,61,79] and CNN-based methods [35,41] are carried out. Recently, GCN-based methods [40,50,59,74,80] have attracted increasing attention due to their outstanding performances. We adopt the widely-used ST-GCN [74] as the backbone.

There are also many unsupervised methods [44,45,53,72,86] proposed to learn the skeleton representations. In particular, many methods [38,62,63,76,88] utilize the encoder-decoder structure to reconstruct skeletons from the encoded features. CrosSCLR [44] proposes to apply contrastive learning for skeleton representation learning. A recent work [75] studies the generalizability of the models by first pretraining a model on one dataset and then finetuning it on another dataset. Our task is different from the above works, as we do not require the ground-truth labels of target data to train or finetune the model.

Close-Set and Open-Set Transfer Learning. In (close-set) unsupervised domain adaptation (UDA) [2,3,69], the source and target datasets are different in styles but have an identical label set. Many methods aim to learn domain-invariant features by adversarial learning [13,20] or explicitly reducing the distribution discrepancy [73]. For example, GVB [13] proposes a gradually vanishing bridge layer to facilitate the adversarial training. Yet, these methods are not suitable for the open-set problem [51]. Novel class discovery (NCD) [27] aims to transfer knowledge between datasets with different categories but almost the same style. UNO [19] trains the source set with ground-truth labels and the target set with pseudo labels generated by [8]. Another similar task to ours is cross-domain person re-identification (CD-ReID) [15,68]. Representative methods are based on clustering [17,82,87] or domain-invariant feature learning [31,46,49]. Among them, a series of methods [21,78,85] propose a collaborative learning scheme among multiple peer networks to alleviate the effects of label noise. However, the multiple networks are just initialized differently, making them essentially different from our method. Recently, cross-domain few-shot learning (CD-FSL) [24,65] has emerged, where the source and target datasets are drawn from different domains and classes. A few methods [32,56,77] relax the task to allow access to unlabeled target data during training. STARTUP [56] uses the model pretrained on the source dataset to produce soft pseudo labels for target samples, and then finetunes the model using target samples and their soft labels.

3   Method

3.1   Problem Formulation

Formally, we denote the labeled source domain as $\mathbb{D}^l = (x_n^s, y_n^s)|_{n=1}^{N^s}$, where x_n^s and y_n^s are the n-th training sample and its associated action label, N^s is the number of source skeleton sequences. The N^t unlabeled target skeleton sequences are denoted as $\mathbb{D}^t = \{x_n^t|_{n=1}^{N^t}\}$, which are not associated with any label. Our goal is to mine the latent classes of $\mathbb{D}^t$, which are disjoint with that of $\mathbb{D}^s$.

3.2   Overview

The framework of CoDT is depicted in Fig. 2. It is composed of two parallel branches denoted by $\mathcal{B}_0$ and $\mathcal{B}_1$, where $\mathcal{B}_0$ processes the data of both domains

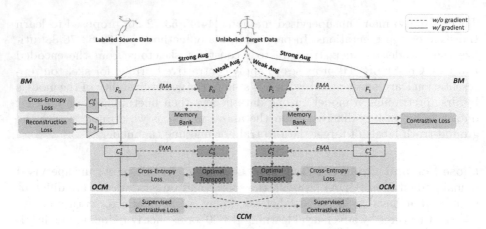

Fig. 2. Illustration of our CoDT network. It consists of two branches (left and right), each of which contains a base module (BM), and an online clustering module (OCM). The two branches are connected by a collaborative clustering module (CCM).

for exploiting domain-shared knowledge and $\mathcal{B}_1$ only processes the target data for capturing target-specific characteristics. Each branch contains a base module (BM) dubbed BM-$\mathcal{B}_0$ and BM-$\mathcal{B}_1$ to optimize the feature encoders. The BM-$\mathcal{B}_0$ is to learn discriminative information from source data via supervised learning. To make the features more domain-invariant, we add a domain-shared decoder in BM-$\mathcal{B}_0$ for skeleton reconstruction. The BM-$\mathcal{B}_1$ is to learn semantic similarity of target data with contrastive learning. Then we aim to collaboratively train the two branches and encourage their agreement on the clustering of target data. Yet, there are two problems: 1) How to optimize the feature clustering? 2) How to achieve co-training? To address the problems, we propose the online clustering module (OCM) and collaborative clustering module (CCM), respectively.

3.3   Base Module

BM-$\mathcal{B}_0$. There are two feature encoders dubbed F_0 and $\hat{F}_0$. The $\hat{F}_0$ is updated by an exponential moving average (EMA) of F_0 and used by the subsequent OCM. The encoder F_0 first embeds the input skeleton sequences into features. The features of source samples are then fed into a source classifier C_0^s and optimized by cross-entropy loss with annotated labels

$$\mathcal{L}_{sup} = \frac{1}{n^s} \sum_{i=1}^{n^s} \mathrm{CE}\left(C_0^s(F_0(\boldsymbol{x}_i^s)), y_i^s\right),\tag{1}$$

where n^s is the mini-batch size of source data, and CE is the short of Cross Entropy loss. The decoder D_0 reconstructs the input skeletons from the features for both source data and target data. The reconstruction loss is computed as

$$\mathcal{L}_{dec} = \frac{1}{n^s} \sum_{i=1}^{n^s} \mathrm{MSE}\left(D_0(F_0(\boldsymbol{x}_i^s)), \boldsymbol{x}_i^s\right) + \frac{1}{n^t} \sum_{i=1}^{n^t} \mathrm{MSE}\left(D_0(F_0(\boldsymbol{x}_i^t)), \boldsymbol{x}_i^t\right), \quad (2)$$

where n^t denotes the mini-batch size of target data, and MSE denotes Mean Square Error loss. The reconstruction enforces the representations to retain generic and meaningful human structure, which can strengthen the domain invariance of representations [22]. Note that, based on the principle of 'domain-sharing', when the source data and target data have different joints, we only keep their shared joints in $\mathcal{B}_0$.

BM-$\mathcal{B}_1$. To learn the target-specific representations from the target set, we employ the popular contrastive learning based on instance discrimination [28], where the features of the different augments of a sample are pulled together and the features of different samples are pushed apart.

Specifically, similar to BM-$\mathcal{B}_0$, BM-$\mathcal{B}_1$ contains a feature encoder F_1 and an EMA encoder $\hat{F}_1$. For a target sample, we first transform it to two augments $\left(\boldsymbol{x}_i^t, \hat{\boldsymbol{x}}_i^t\right)$ by data augmentation, and then pass them into F_1 and $\hat{F}_1$, respectively. Here we denote the outputs as $\boldsymbol{z}_i^t = F_1(\boldsymbol{x}_i^t)$, $\hat{\boldsymbol{z}}_i^t = \hat{F}_1(\hat{\boldsymbol{x}}_i^t)$. Besides, to enlarge the number of negative samples, following [28,42], we maintain a memory bank $\boldsymbol{M}^t = \{\hat{\boldsymbol{z}}_m^t\}|_m^{N^t}$ to store the features from $\hat{F}_1$ of all target samples. In each iteration, the $\boldsymbol{M}^t$ is updated by the $\hat{\boldsymbol{z}}_i^t$ in current mini-batch, and then we compute the contrastive loss as

$$\mathcal{L}_{cont} = \frac{1}{n^t} \sum_{i=1}^{n^t} - \log \frac{e^{\rho \cdot \cos(\boldsymbol{z}_i^t, \hat{\boldsymbol{z}}_i^t)}}{\sum_{m=1}^{N^t} e^{\rho \cdot \cos(\boldsymbol{z}_i^t, \hat{\boldsymbol{z}}_m^t)}}, \quad (3)$$

where $\cos(\cdot)$ denotes the cosine similarity function and ρ is the temperature.

3.4 Online Clustering Module

Pipeline of OCM. In both $\mathcal{B}_0$ and $\mathcal{B}_1$, we employ an OCM to guide the feature clustering via pseudo labels. The OCM is based on the student-teacher framework [39,64,71], where a teacher model (*e.g.*, $\hat{F}_0$, $\hat{F}_1$) is updated by EMA of a student model (*e.g.*, F_0, F_1). To learn the optimal cluster assignment, we add a target classifier to both student and teacher. The classifiers are denoted by C_0^t and $\hat{C}_0^t$ in $\mathcal{B}_0$, and C_1^t and $\hat{C}_1^t$ in $\mathcal{B}_1$. Following image clustering [34,66,70], we set the numbers of categories of the classifiers to the number of ground-truth categories for the purpose of evaluation[1]. Given a target sample $\boldsymbol{x}_i^t$, inspired by [60], a strong augmentation operator A and a weak augmentation operator a are applied to transform $\boldsymbol{x}_i^t$ into $A(\boldsymbol{x}_i^t)$ and $a(\boldsymbol{x}_i^t)$, respectively. The teacher generates the pseudo label based on its prediction on the $a(\boldsymbol{x}_i^t)$. Then the student is trained to predict the pseudo label by feeding $A(\boldsymbol{x}_i^t)$. These practices can enhance the invariance of representations to varying degrees of transformations.

---

[1] In fact, as proven in [66], even if the exact number of ground-truth categories is unknown, we can overcluster to a larger amount of clusters.

Pseudo Label Generation. Before elaborating on the details, we first review the objective of a classification task. Specifically, given a dataset with N instances $\{x_n\}|_{n=1}^{N}$ drawn from K classes, the task is to maximize the mutual information between labels and input data through minimizing the Kullback-Leibler divergence $D(Q||P)$ between the model's predictions P and labels Q:

$$D(Q||P) = \frac{1}{N}\sum_{n=1}^{N}\sum_{y=1}^{K} Q_{yn}\log\frac{Q_{yn}}{P_{yn}} = \frac{1}{N}\sum_{n=1}^{N}\sum_{y=1}^{K}\big(\underbrace{Q_{yn}\log Q_{yn}}_{-H(Q)}\underbrace{-Q_{yn}\log P_{yn}}_{E(Q||P)}\big),$$

$$(4)$$

where Q_{yn} is the (y,n) element of $Q \in \mathbb{R}^{K\times N}$ denoting the label probability of x_n being assigned to the label $y \in \{1,\ldots,K\}$. P_{yn} is the element of $P \in \mathbb{R}^{K\times N}$ that denotes the probability predicted by the model. $D(Q||P)$ can be split into a cross-entropy term $E(Q||P)$ and an entropy term $H(Q)$. Unlike the supervised task where Q is deterministic, labels are unavailable in our case, and we have to minimize $D(Q||P)$ w.r.t. both the Q and P. Further, we extend it to the student-teacher framework. Formally, it is to alternate the following steps

$$\left\{\begin{array}{l} Q \leftarrow \underset{\hat{Q}}{\arg\min}\, D(\hat{Q}||\hat{P}), \qquad\qquad\qquad (5) \\[2ex] \theta \leftarrow \theta - \epsilon\dfrac{\partial\big(D(\hat{Q}||P) + \mathcal{L}\big)}{\partial\theta}, \qquad\quad (6) \\[2ex] \hat{\theta} \leftarrow \alpha\hat{\theta} + (1-\alpha)\theta, \qquad\qquad\qquad (7) \end{array}\right.$$

where P and θ are the predictions and parameters of student. $\hat{P}$ and $\hat{\theta}$ correspond to teacher. $\hat{Q}$ represents the pseudo labels. First, $\hat{Q}$ is calculated by Eq. (5). Then, we fix $\hat{Q}$ and optimize the predictions P of student by minimizing $D(\hat{Q}||P)$ along with other auxiliary loss $\mathcal{L}$ (e.g., $\mathcal{L}_{sup}$, $\mathcal{L}_{cont}$) on a mini-batch via Eq. (6), where ϵ is the learning rate of gradient descent. Finally, the teacher is updated by an EMA of the student in Eq. (7), where α is the decay rate.

Let's first take a look at Eq. (5). Since we only consider the one-hot pseudo labels, i.e., $\hat{Q}_{yn} \in \{0,1\}$, then $H(\hat{Q}) \equiv 0$ and $D(\hat{Q}||\hat{P}) \equiv E(\hat{Q}||\hat{P})$. Thus we can obtain the solution to Eq. (5) by taking the index that has the maximum value in the prediction of teacher, i.e.,

$$\hat{Q}_{yn}^{*} = \delta\big(y - \underset{k}{argmax}\hat{P}_{Kn}\big), \qquad\qquad (8)$$

where $\delta(\cdot)$ is the Dirac delta function with $\delta(\cdot) = 0$ except $\delta(0) = 1$. The Eq. (8) is similar in spirit to the semi-supervised learning method [60]. Obviously, if $\mathcal{L} = 0$, there is a shortcut to minimize both $D(\hat{Q}||\hat{P})$ and $D(\hat{Q}||P)$ by assigning all samples to a single label, which is known as clustering degeneration. This phenomenon can be avoided in [60], since the supervised training on a few labeled samples can regularize the model via $\mathcal{L}$. However, in our case, the $\mathcal{L}$ is either the supervised loss of source dataset with a distribution different from that of target dataset, or the contrastive loss for instance discrimination rather than clustering. In other words, there are discrepancies between the objectives of $\mathcal{L}$ and the ultimate goal (*i.e.*, target sample clustering). It renders existing $\mathcal{L}$ unable to prevent clustering degeneration, as proven in Sect. 4.3. To avoid clustering degeneration, we propose to constrain the distribution of clusters to be as uniform as possible, *i.e.*, all clusters contain the same number of samples. Achieving it within Eq. (6) in an end-to-end fashion is difficult as the constraint involves the global distribution of the entire dataset. Alternatively, we propose to balance the pseudo labels generated by Eq. (5) without gradient descent. Formally, we restrict $\hat{Q}$ to be an element of transportation polytope [14]

$$\mathcal{U} = \{\hat{Q} \in \mathbb{R}_+^{K \times N} | \hat{Q}^\top 1_K = 1_N, \hat{Q} 1_N = \frac{N}{K} 1_K\}, \tag{9}$$

where 1_K denotes the vector of ones with dimension K. The Eq. (9) indicates that each class has equal number (*i.e.*, $\frac{N}{K}$) of samples. Inspired by [1,8], solving Eq. (5) subject to Eq. (9) can transformed to an optimal transport problem for mapping the N data points to the K centers, whose solution is

$$\hat{Q}^* = N \text{diag}(\mathbf{u})(\hat{P}/N)^\xi \text{diag}(\mathbf{v}), \tag{10}$$

where ξ is a pre-defined scalar, and $\mathbf{u} \in \mathbb{R}^K$, $\mathbf{v} \in \mathbb{R}^N$ are two vectors computed by the fast version of Sinkhorn-Knopp algorithm [14]. Please refer to Supplementary for more details.

Since it is costly to calculate $\hat{P}$ from scratch each iteration, we maintain the same memory bank as that used in contrastive learning, and the extra cost of computing predictions from the bank is affordable.

Objective of OCM. Thus, for a target instance x_i^t, we can obtain its pseudo labels denoted by $\hat{y}_{0,i}^t, \hat{y}_{0,i}^t \in \{1, \ldots, K\}$ in $\mathcal{B}_0$ and $\mathcal{B}_1$, respectively. Then we use the pseudo labels to train the corresponding student models by minimizing following loss function

$$\mathcal{L}_{ocm} = \frac{1}{n^t} \sum_{i=1}^{n^t} \left(\text{CE}(\hat{C}_0^t(\hat{F}_0(A(x_i^t))), \hat{y}_{0,i}^t) + \text{CE}(\hat{C}_1^t(\hat{F}_1(A(x_i^t))), \hat{y}_{1,i}^t) \right), \tag{11}$$

3.5 Collaborative Clustering Module

To make use of complementarity between $\mathcal{B}_0$ and $\mathcal{B}_1$, we propose the collaborative clustering module (CCM) to allow co-training between two branches. Since the two branches have different parameters and regularized by different losses (*e.g.*, $\mathcal{L}_{sup}$ for $\mathcal{B}_0$, $\mathcal{L}_{cont}$ for $\mathcal{B}_1$), the classes of the target classifiers of $\mathcal{B}_0$ and $\mathcal{B}_1$ are difficult to be matched exactly. Hence, the pseudo labels from one model cannot be used directly to train the other model. To overcome this challenge, we present a conceptually simple but practically effective co-training method. Instead of matching clusters between models, we propose to exchange the pair-wise relationships of samples across branches, which are explicitly matched between two branches and meanwhile can determine the performance of clustering.

Specifically, for two target instances $\boldsymbol{x}_i^t$, $\boldsymbol{x}_j^t$, we first define the binary pairwise pseudo label as $\mathcal{G}_{0,ij}^t = \delta(\hat{y}_{0,i}^t - \hat{y}_{0,j}^t)$ in $\mathcal{B}_0$ and $\mathcal{G}_{1,ij}^t = \delta(\hat{y}_{1,i}^t - \hat{y}_{1,j}^t)$ in $\mathcal{B}_1$, indicating that whether $\boldsymbol{x}_i^t$, $\boldsymbol{x}_j^t$ are from the same cluster (positive pair) or from different clusters (negative pair) in each branch. Besides, we define the pair-wise similarity of a pair of samples as the inner product of their predictions, $i.e.$, $\mathcal{P}_{0,ij}^t = \boldsymbol{p}_{0,i}^t{}^\top \boldsymbol{p}_{0,j}^t$ and $\mathcal{P}_{1,ij}^t = \boldsymbol{p}_{1,i}^t{}^\top \boldsymbol{p}_{1,j}^t$, where $\boldsymbol{p}_{0,i}^t = \mathrm{softmax}(\hat{C}_0^t(\hat{F}_0(A(\boldsymbol{x}_i^t)))) \in \mathbb{R}^K$ (likewise for $\boldsymbol{p}_{0,j}^t$, $\boldsymbol{p}_{1,i}^t$, $\boldsymbol{p}_{1,j}^t$). For co-training, we use $\mathcal{G}_{0,ij}^t$ and $\mathcal{G}_{1,ij}^t$ as the supervisions to optimize $\mathcal{P}_{1,ij}^t$ and $\mathcal{P}_{0,ij}^t$, respectively, aiming to make the similarities of positive/negative pairs increase/diminish. To achieve it, we design the objective function similar in spirit to the supervised contrastive loss [36]:

$$\mathcal{L}_{ccm} = -\frac{1}{n^t}\sum_{i=1}^{n^t}\left(\frac{\sum_{j=1}^{n^t}\mathcal{G}_{0,ij}^t \log \overline{\mathcal{P}^t}_{1,ij}}{\sum_{j=1}^{n^t}\mathcal{G}_{0,ij}^t} + \frac{\sum_{j=1}^{n^t}\mathcal{G}_{1,ij}^t \log \overline{\mathcal{P}^t}_{0,ij}}{\sum_{j=1}^{n^t}\mathcal{G}_{1,ij}^t}\right), \qquad (12)$$

where $\overline{\mathcal{P}^t}_{0,ij}$ and $\overline{\mathcal{P}^t}_{1,ij}$ are defined as $\overline{\mathcal{P}^t}_{0,ij} = \frac{\mathcal{P}_{0,ij}^t}{\sum_{j=1}^{n^t}\mathcal{P}_{0,ij}^t}$, $\overline{\mathcal{P}^t}_{1,ij} = \frac{\mathcal{P}_{1,ij}^t}{\sum_{j=1}^{n^t}\mathcal{P}_{1,ij}^t}$. Note that, to maximize the similarity ($i.e.$, the inner product of the predictions) of a positive pair, both predictions need to be one-hot and assigned to the same cluster [66]. This property enforces the two branches to be consistent in the pair-wise relationships of cluster assignments, yielding consistent clustering performance on the two branches.

Discussion. Here we discuss the vital differences between our proposed co-training method and some related methods. [8] swaps instance-wise labels of two views of the same image, forcing the (single) model to produce consistent predictions for different views. In contrast, CoDT exchanges pair-wise labels across models for co-training to utilize the complementarity of domain-shared and target-specific features. Recently, [84] proposes a mutual knowledge distillation algorithm across two different branches by comparing the feature similarity distribution between each instance and a queue of features. Differently, CoDT conducts co-training on the predictions of classifiers, leading to a direct optimization on the cluster assignments.

Apart from the idea of co-training, the objective function $\mathcal{L}_{ccm}$, to our knowledge, is also different from existing methods. To name a few, the differences between [36] and ours include: 1) [36] applies the loss on features, while our $\mathcal{L}_{ccm}$ is applied on predictions; 2) $\mathcal{L}_{ccm}$ has a simpler formula without any hyperparameter ($e.g.$, temperature). Recently, [43] proposes to adopt the instance-based contrastive loss on the predictions, showing promising performance in close-set domain adaption. Yet, [43] handles the close-set tasks with known classes, and its loss is used for instance discrimination, which is evidently different from ours. $\mathcal{L}_{ccm}$ is also different from [27,42,66] where a pair of samples is positive only when the similarity between their features meets a heuristic condition ($e.g.$, is larger than a threshold). Note that, none of the above competitors involve co-training.

3.6 Training and Test

In training phase, we first pretrain BM-$\mathcal{B}_0$ and BM-$\mathcal{B}_1$ with the loss

$$\mathcal{L}_{base} = \lambda_{sup}\mathcal{L}_{sup} + \lambda_{dec}\mathcal{L}_{dec} + \lambda_{cont}\mathcal{L}_{cont}, \tag{13}$$

where λ_* denotes the loss weight. After obtaining a good initialization, OCM and CCM are successively included for finetuning. The overall loss is

$$\mathcal{L}_{all} = \mathcal{L}_{base} + \lambda_{ocm}\mathcal{L}_{ocm} + \lambda_{ccm}\mathcal{L}_{ccm}. \tag{14}$$

In test phase, following [32,44], we use the student models for testing. Specifically, if there is a target classifier in the model, we use its predictions as cluster assignments, otherwise, we use the spherical k-means [29] to cluster the features.

4 Experiment

4.1 Datasets and Metrics

NTU-60 [58] is a 3D action recognition dataset with 60 classes. The skeletons are shot by Microsoft Kinect V2 [18]. *NTU-120* [48] is an extended version of NTU-60, containing 120 classes. Here we only take the classes of NTU-120 that are not overlapped with those of NTU-60, denoted by *NTU-60+*. *PKUMMD* [47] is a dataset for temporal action detection, where the trimmed action instances have been used for action recognition [45]. The skeletons are also collected by Kinect V2. There are 51 classes different from that of NTU-60+. Different from the above in-the-lab datasets, *Skeletics* [25] is a carefully curated dataset sourced from real-world videos [9]. The 3D poses are estimated by the pose estimation method VIBE [37]. Three cross-domain tasks are chosen to imitate various situations: NTU-60 $\rightarrow$ Skeletics (xview), Skeletics $\rightarrow$ PKUMMD (xview), and NTU-60+ $\rightarrow$ PKUMMD (xsub). Let's take NTU-60+ $\rightarrow$ PKUMMD (xsub) as an example. The NTU-60+ and PKUMMD are the source and target datasets, respectively, and 'xsub' is the evaluation protocol. The former two tasks are more challenging than the last one because the former two tasks simulate the transfer learning between an in-the-lab dataset shot by 3D sensors and a real-world dataset estimated by pose estimation algorithm, while in the last task, the two datasets are shot by similar device, and are therefore more similar in style. In the rest of the paper, we abbreviate the three tasks as N $\rightarrow$ S, S $\rightarrow$ P, and N+ $\rightarrow$ P. For evaluation, we use three widely-used clustering performance metrics [30], including Accuracy (ACC), Normalised Mutual Information (NMI), Adjusted Rand Index (ARI). Due to the space constraint, we refer readers to Supplementary for more details about datasets, metrics, implementation details.

4.2 Comparison with Different Baselines

To verify the effectiveness of CoDT, we first compare CoDT with related baselines in Table 1. Here the results of both branches are reported. For fairness, we use the pretrained weights of our base modules to initialize the weights of other baselines. The 'BM-$\mathcal{B}_0$ w/o D_0' means that the decoder D_0 is not used. Compared to 'BM-$\mathcal{B}_0$', we can see that the decoder improves the performances in most cases. We further evaluate the performance when we combine 'BM-$\mathcal{B}_0$' and 'BM-$\mathcal{B}_1$' via multi-task learning, denoted by 'BM-$\mathcal{B}_0$ + BM-$\mathcal{B}_1$'. We can see that it outperforms both 'BM-$\mathcal{B}_0$' and 'BM-$\mathcal{B}_1$', demonstrating the complementarity of 'BM-$\mathcal{B}_0$' and 'BM-$\mathcal{B}_1$'. Thereafter, we combine BM-$\mathcal{B}_0$ with other advanced methods of unsupervised skeleton/image learning [1,44]. We can see that the performances are improved. However, their performance is still far behind that of CoDT, demonstrating that multi-task framework is suboptimal for combining 'BM-$\mathcal{B}_0$' and 'BM-$\mathcal{B}_1$'. What's more, we re-implement some representative methods of other cross-domain tasks, including UDA [13], NCD [19], CD-ReID [21] and CD-FSL [56]. These methods commonly share the same feature extractor among different domains. It can be seen that our CoDT significantly outperforms all of them. CoDT achieves salient performances since it can 1) *disentangle* the learning of domain-shared and target-specific features via a two-branch framework to fully exploit their respective characteristics; 2) *coordinate* the clustering of domain-shared and target-specific features to fully utilize their complementarity. Especially, these two properties are more advantageous when the domain gaps are larger, since the domain-shared and target-specific features are more different and complementary. It makes our CoDT extremely superior in the former two tasks with large domain gaps.

Table 1. Comparison between different methods. '†' indicates that the spherical k-means is used for clustering in these methods

Methods	N → S			S → P			N+ → P		
	ACC	NMI	ARI	ACC	NMI	ARI	ACC	NMI	ARI
BM-$\mathcal{B}_0$†	17.9	22.5	6.1	40.0	58.9	30.2	54.8	73.7	44.3
BM-$\mathcal{B}_0$ w/o D_0†	16.6	20.5	6.1	38.5	55.6	27.6	53.3	73.4	43.4
BM-$\mathcal{B}_1$†	18.7	23.3	6.4	43.3	58.4	32.1	42.7	57.4	32.3
BM-$\mathcal{B}_0$ + BM-$\mathcal{B}_1$†	19.4	22.8	6.4	47.7	62.1	36.9	58.3	74.0	47.7
BM-$\mathcal{B}_0$ + CrossCLR [44]†	20.5	24.1	7.0	49.1	63.8	36.6	60.4	75.2	47.9
BM-$\mathcal{B}_0$ + Asano. *et.al.* [1]	21.2	26.1	8.4	51.4	65.4	38.4	62.3	74.4	49.4
GVB [13]†	19.3	22.2	6.0	37.8	56.9	28.4	59.5	75.6	50.0
STARTUP [56]†	19.0	22.1	5.9	48.5	63.1	38.1	59.1	72.5	47.2
MMT [21]	20.8	25.5	7.6	52.4	67.3	41.2	65.4	76.2	55.6
UNO [19]	22.5	26.4	9.1	54.1	70.0	43.2	66.8	76.9	56.7
CoDT-$\mathcal{B}_0$	25.0	28.0	10.7	**59.5**	**74.1**	50.0	**68.2**	**78.5**	**58.8**
CoDT-$\mathcal{B}_1$	**25.4**	**28.7**	**11.3**	59.4	73.9	**50.2**	67.8	78.1	58.1

4.3   Ablation Study

Effectiveness of Proposed Components. We conduct ablation studies in Table 2 to investigate the effectiveness of the proposed components, *i.e.*, OCM and CCM. After introducing OCM, the performances on all branches and tasks are substantially improved when compared to the base modules. This is because the base modules are only trained to learn good representations and an offline clustering criterion (*e.g.*, k-means) is still needed for clustering, whereas OCM is capable of optimizing both feature learning and clustering simultaneously. By taking account of CCM, $\mathcal{B}_0$ and $\mathcal{B}_1$ perform very closely. It is because CCM can enforce the consistency between $\mathcal{B}_0$ and $\mathcal{B}_1$ in terms of pair-wise relationships on cluster assignments. More importantly, after using CCM, the performances are greatly improved, verifying that CCM can effectively leverage the complementarity of domain-shared features and target-specific features. In Fig. 3, we show the evolution of the learned representations of target samples on 'N+→P'. It is shown that while the clusters overlap in the beginning, they become more and more separated as the OCM and CCM are successively involved.

Table 2. Effect of different components

Methods	$\mathcal{B}_*$	N→S			S → P			N+ → P		
		ACC	NMI	ARI	ACC	NMI	ARI	ACC	NMI	ARI
BM†	$\mathcal{B}_0$	17.9	22.5	6.1	40.0	58.9	30.2	54.8	73.7	44.3
	$\mathcal{B}_1$	18.7	23.3	6.4	43.3	58.4	32.1	42.7	57.4	32.3
BM+OCM	$\mathcal{B}_0$	22.0	26.8	9.1	55.3	70.3	45.1	63.7	80.1	53.9
	$\mathcal{B}_1$	21.8	26.4	8.7	54.7	67.5	44.3	52.6	66.1	41.9
BM+OCM+CCM	$\mathcal{B}_0$	25.0	28.0	10.7	59.5	74.1	50.0	68.1	78.5	58.8
	$\mathcal{B}_1$	25.4	28.7	11.3	59.4	73.9	50.2	67.8	78.1	58.1

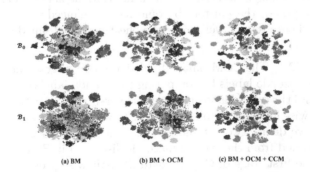

(a) BM   (b) BM + OCM   (c) BM + OCM + CCM

Fig. 3. t-SNE visualization of features learned by different methods. Different colors represent different clusters.

Table 3. Analysis of OCM, where the numbers before and after the '/' denote the results of $\mathcal{B}_0$ and $\mathcal{B}_1$, respectively.

Methods	$\mathcal{L}$	$\mathcal{U}$	ACC(%)	Uniformity
BM+OCM	✗	✗	9.0/6.9	0.70/1.09
	✓	✗	31.2/48.4	2.76/3.68
	✓	✓	55.7/54.7	3.91/3.93
BM+OCM+CCM	✗	✗	9.1/8.9	0.80/0.80
	✓	✗	48.4/48.7	3.48/3.47
	✓	✓	59.5/59.4	3.91/3.93

Table 4. Comparison between our CCM with its variants, where the numbers before and after the '/' denote the ACC of $\mathcal{B}_0$ and $\mathcal{B}_1$

Methods	N → S	N+ → P
CCM-*FP*	22.3/24.2	63.9/55.3
CCM-*PF*	22.8/24.7	64.7/55.9
CCM (ours)	25.0/25.4	68.1/67.8

Analysis of OCM. In Table 3, we give the detailed analysis of OCM, where the models with and without CCM are evaluated. Without loss of generalization, we take the task of 'S → P' as an example. Apart from 'ACC', we also report the metric of 'Uniformity' which is measured by the entropy of clustering results. The more uniform the distribution of clusters, the greater its value. It takes the maximum value of 3.93 when all clusters are equal in size. The value corresponding to the ground-truth labels is 3.88, indicating that the ground-truth distribution is not exactly uniform. The $\mathcal{L}$ in Table 3 denotes the loss regularization in Eq. (6), including $\mathcal{L}_{sup}$, $\mathcal{L}_{dec}$, and $\mathcal{L}_{con}$. The $\mathcal{U}$ represents the uniform constraint of Eq. (9). Note that, the pseudo labels are generated by Eq. (10) when $\mathcal{U}$ is used, and by Eq. (8) otherwise. From Table 3, we have following observations: 1) When neither $\mathcal{L}$ nor $\mathcal{U}$ is used, the 'Uniformity' is very small, indicating that the models encounter catastrophic clustering degeneration. 2) When $\mathcal{L}$ is used, the degeneration is alleviated and the performances increase, demonstrating that $\mathcal{L}$ is helpful to generate meaningful groups for the target data. Besides, we observe that in the row of 'BM+OCM', the 'Uniformity' of $\mathcal{B}_1$ is larger than that of $\mathcal{B}_0$. The reason may be that the features learned by the contrastive learning have the property of uniformity in instance-level [67]. Nevertheless, the clusters are still not balanced enough, indicating that using $\mathcal{L}$ alone is not enough. 3) When $\mathcal{U}$ is further imposed, the clusters become more balanced, resulting in better performances. These results well prove the effectiveness of our design.

Analysis of CCM. The CCM can be divided into two stages. The first is to construct pair-wise pseudo labels by comparing the pseudo labels of sample pairs in each branch, and the second is to optimize the pair-wise similarities of predictions using the pair-wise labels of the other branch. To verify the necessity of our design at each stage, we device two variants of CCM dubbed CCM-*PF* and CCM-*FP*, which are extended from the related methods discussed in Sect. 3.5. The CCM-*PF* modifies the first stage of CCM, where the pair-wise pseudo labels are constructed based on *the pair-wise similarities of features* (rather than the pair-wise comparisons of pseudo labels), following [27]. The CCM-*PF* changes the second stage of CCM, where the pair-wise similarities of *features* (rather than predictions) are optimized, following [36]. Please refer to the Supplementary for details about the variants. Their performances are shown in Table 4. We can see that neither CCM-*PF* nor CCM-*FP* can ensure performance consistency between two branches, showing that in these two variants, the cluster assignments are not fully inherited across branches. Due to such reason, their performances are also inferior to ours, demonstrating the effectiveness of our design.

5   Conclusion and Future Work

In this paper, we propose a novel method dubbed CoDT for CD-SAR. The main idea of CoDT is to leverage the complementarity of domain-shared and target-specific features. To this end, we introduce the OCM to obtain robust pseudo labels to guide feature clustering, and the CCM to collaborate the two kinds of features. The experimental results show that our method significantly outperforms other cross-domain training or unsupervised learning methods. In principle, our method can be adopted to other cross-domain tasks in an open-set setting (*e.g.*, CD-FSL [56], CD-ReID [68]). We leave this as our future work.

Acknowledgement. This work is supported by the National Natural Science Foundation of China under Grant No. 62176246 and No. 61836008.

References

1. Asano, Y.M., Rupprecht, C., Vedaldi, A.: Self-labelling via simultaneous clustering and representation learning. In: ICLR (2020)
2. Ben-David, S., Blitzer, J., Crammer, K., Kulesza, A., Pereira, F., Vaughan, J.W.: A theory of learning from different domains. Mach. Learn. 151–175 (2009). https://doi.org/10.1007/s10994-009-5152-4
3. Ben-David, S., Blitzer, J., Crammer, K., Pereira, F., et al.: Analysis of representations for domain adaptation. In: NIPS (2007)
4. Blum, A., Mitchell, T.: Combining labeled and unlabeled data with co-training. In: COLT, pp. 92–100 (1998)
5. Cao, Z., Simon, T., Wei, S.E., Sheikh, Y.: Realtime multi-person 2d pose estimation using part affinity fields. In: CVPR (2017)
6. Caron, M., Bojanowski, P., Joulin, A., Douze, M.: Deep clustering for unsupervised learning of visual features. In: ECCV (2018)
7. Caron, M., Bojanowski, P., Mairal, J., Joulin, A.: Unsupervised pre-training of image features on non-curated data. In: ICCV (2019)
8. Caron, M., Misra, I., Mairal, J., Goyal, P., Bojanowski, P., Joulin, A.: Unsupervised learning of visual features by contrasting cluster assignments. In: NIPS (2020)
9. Carreira, J., Noland, E., Hillier, C., Zisserman, A.: A short note on the kinetics-700 human action dataset. arXiv preprint arXiv:1907.06987 (2019)
10. Chang, J., Wang, L., Meng, G., Xiang, S., Pan, C.: Deep adaptive image clustering. In: ICCV (2017)
11. Chen, T., Kornblith, S., Norouzi, M., Hinton, G.: A simple framework for contrastive learning of visual representations. In: ICML (2020)
12. Chen, X., Fan, H., Girshick, R., He, K.: Improved baselines with momentum contrastive learning. arXiv preprint arXiv:2003.04297 (2020)

13. Cui, S., Wang, S., Zhuo, J., Su, C., Huang, Q., Tian, Q.: Gradually vanishing bridge for adversarial domain adaptation. In: CVPR (2020)
14. Cuturi, M.: Sinkhorn distances: Lightspeed computation of optimal transport. In: NIPS (2013)
15. Deng, W., Zheng, L., Ye, Q., Kang, G., Yang, Y., Jiao, J.: Image-image domain adaptation with preserved self-similarity and domain-dissimilarity for person re-identification. In: CVPR (2018)
16. Doersch, C., Gupta, A., Efros, A.A.: Unsupervised visual representation learning by context prediction. In: ICCV (2015)
17. Fan, H., Zheng, L., Yan, C., Yang, Y.: Unsupervised person re-identification: clustering and fine-tuning. ACM Trans. Multimedia Comput. Commun. Appl. **14**(4), 1–18 (2018)
18. Fankhauser, P., Bloesch, M., Rodriguez, D., Kaestner, R., Hutter, M., Siegwart, R.: Kinect v2 for mobile robot navigation: Evaluation and modeling. In: ICAR (2015)
19. Fini, E., Sangineto, E., Lathuilière, S., Zhong, Z., Nabi, M., Ricci, E.: A unified objective for novel class discovery. In: ICCV (2021)
20. Ganin, Y., et al.: Domain-adversarial training of neural networks. J. Mach. Learn. Res. **17**(1), 2030–2096 (2016)
21. Ge, Y., Chen, D., Li, H.: Mutual mean-teaching: pseudo label refinery for unsupervised domain adaptation on person re-identification. In: ICLR (2019)
22. Ghifary, M., Kleijn, W.B., Zhang, M., Balduzzi, D.: Domain generalization for object recognition with multi-task autoencoders. In: ICCV (2015)
23. Grill, J.B., et al.: Bootstrap your own latent: a new approach to self-supervised learning. In: NIPS (2020)
24. Guo, Y., et al.: A broader study of cross-domain few-shot learning. In: ECCV (2020)
25. Gupta, P., et al.: Quo vadis, skeleton action recognition? Int. J. Comput. Vision **129**(7), 2097–2112 (2021)
26. Han, B., et al.: Co-teaching: robust training of deep neural networks with extremely noisy labels. In: NIPS (2018)
27. Han, K., Rebuffi, S.A., Ehrhardt, S., Vedaldi, A., Zisserman, A.: Automatically discovering and learning new visual categories with ranking statistics. In: ICLR (2019)
28. He, K., Fan, H., Wu, Y., Xie, S., Girshick, R.: Momentum contrast for unsupervised visual representation learning. In: CVPR (2020)
29. Hornik, K., Feinerer, I., Kober, M., Buchta, C.: Spherical k-means clustering. J. Stat. Softw. **50**, 1–22 (2012)
30. Huang, J., Gong, S., Zhu, X.: Deep semantic clustering by partition confidence maximisation. In: CVPR (2020)
31. Huang, Y., Peng, P., Jin, Y., Xing, J., Lang, C., Feng, S.: Domain adaptive attention model for unsupervised cross-domain person re-identification. In: AAAI (2019)
32. Islam, A., Chen, C.F., Panda, R., Karlinsky, L., Feris, R., Radke, R.J.: Dynamic distillation network for cross-domain few-shot recognition with unlabeled data. In: NIPS (2021)
33. Islam, A., Chen, C.F., Panda, R., Karlinsky, L., Radke, R., Feris, R.: A broad study on the transferability of visual representations with contrastive learning. In: ICCV (2021)
34. Ji, X., Henriques, J.F., Vedaldi, A.: Invariant information clustering for unsupervised image classification and segmentation. In: ICCV (2019)

35. Ke, Q., Bennamoun, M., An, S., Sohel, F., Boussaid, F.: A new representation of skeleton sequences for 3d action recognition. In: CVPR (2017)
36. Khosla, P., et al.: Supervised contrastive learning. In: NIPS (2020)
37. Kocabas, M., Athanasiou, N., Black, M.J.: Vibe: Video inference for human body pose and shape estimation. In: CVPR (2020)
38. Kundu, J.N., Gor, M., Uppala, P.K., Radhakrishnan, V.B.: Unsupervised feature learning of human actions as trajectories in pose embedding manifold. In: WACV (2019)
39. Laine, S., Aila, T.: Temporal ensembling for semi-supervised learning. In: ICLR (2016)
40. Li, B., Li, X., Zhang, Z., Wu, F.: Spatio-temporal graph routing for skeleton-based action recognition. In: AAAI (2019)
41. Li, C., Zhong, Q., Xie, D., Pu, S.: Skeleton-based action recognition with convolutional neural networks. In: 2017 IEEE International Conference on Multimedia & Expo Workshops, pp. 597–600. IEEE (2017)
42. Li, J., Li, G., Shi, Y., Yu, Y.: Cross-domain adaptive clustering for semi-supervised domain adaptation. In: CVPR (2021)
43. Li, J., Zhang, Y., Wang, Z., Tu, K.: Semantic-aware representation learning via probability contrastive loss. arXiv preprint arXiv:2111.06021 (2021)
44. Li, L., Wang, M., Ni, B., Wang, H., Yang, J., Zhang, W.: 3d human action representation learning via cross-view consistency pursuit. In: CVPR (2021)
45. Lin, L., Song, S., Yang, W., Liu, J.: Ms2l: multi-task self-supervised learning for skeleton based action recognition. In: ACMMM (2020)
46. Lin, S., Li, H., Li, C.T., Kot, A.C.: Multi-task mid-level feature alignment network for unsupervised cross-dataset person re-identification. In: BMVC (2018)
47. Liu, C., Hu, Y., Li, Y., Song, S., Liu, J.: Pku-mmd: a large scale benchmark for continuous multi-modal human action understanding. arXiv preprint arXiv:1703.07475 (2017)
48. Liu, J., Shahroudy, A., Perez, M., Wang, G., Duan, L.Y., Kot, A.C.: NTU RGB+D 120: a large-scale benchmark for 3d human activity understanding. IEEE Trans. Pattern Anal. Mach. Intell. 42(10), 2684–2701 (2019)
49. Liu, X., Zhang, S.: Domain adaptive person re-identification via coupling optimization. In: ACMMM (2020)
50. Liu, Z., Zhang, H., Chen, Z., Wang, Z., Ouyang, W.: Disentangling and unifying graph convolutions for skeleton-based action recognition. In: CVPR (2020)
51. Mekhazni, D., Bhuiyan, A., Ekladious, G., Granger, E.: Unsupervised domain adaptation in the dissimilarity space for person re-identification. In: ECCV (2020)
52. Misra, I., Maaten, L.V.D.: Self-supervised learning of pretext-invariant representations. In: CVPR (2020)
53. Nie, Q., Liu, Z., Liu, Y.: Unsupervised 3d human pose representation with viewpoint and pose disentanglement. In: ECCV (2020)
54. Park, S., et al.: Improving unsupervised image clustering with robust learning. In: CVPR (2021)
55. Pathak, D., Krahenbuhl, P., Donahue, J., Darrell, T., Efros, A.A.: Context encoders: feature learning by inpainting. In: CVPR (2016)
56. Phoo, C.P., Hariharan, B.: Self-training for few-shot transfer across extreme task differences. In: ICLR (2020)
57. Qiao, S., Shen, W., Zhang, Z., Wang, B., Yuille, A.: Deep co-training for semi-supervised image recognition. In: ECCV (2018)
58. Shahroudy, A., Liu, J., Ng, T.T., Wang, G.: NTU RGB+ D: a large scale dataset for 3d human activity analysis. In: CVPR (2016)

59. Shi, L., Zhang, Y., Cheng, J., Lu, H.: Two-stream adaptive graph convolutional networks for skeleton-based action recognition. In: CVPR (2019)
60. Sohn, K., et al.: Fixmatch: simplifying semi-supervised learning with consistency and confidence. In: NIPS (2020)
61. Song, S., Lan, C., Xing, J., Zeng, W., Liu, J.: Spatio-temporal attention-based LSTM networks for 3d action recognition and detection. IEEE Trans. Image Process. **27**(7), 3459–3471 (2018)
62. Su, K., Liu, X., Shlizerman, E.: Predict & cluster: unsupervised skeleton based action recognition. In: CVPR (2020)
63. Su, Y., Lin, G., Wu, Q.: Self-supervised 3d skeleton action representation learning with motion consistency and continuity. In: ICCV (2021)
64. Tarvainen, A., Valpola, H.: Mean teachers are better role models: weight-averaged consistency targets improve semi-supervised deep learning results. In: NIPS (2017)
65. Tseng, H.Y., Lee, H.Y., Huang, J.B., Yang, M.H.: Cross-domain few-shot classification via learned feature-wise transformation. In: ICLR (2019)
66. Van Gansbeke, W., Vandenhende, S., Georgoulis, S., Proesmans, M., Van Gool, L.: Scan: learning to classify images without labels. In: ECCV (2020)
67. Wang, T., Isola, P.: Understanding contrastive representation learning through alignment and uniformity on the hypersphere. In: ICML (2020)
68. Wei, L., Zhang, S., Gao, W., Tian, Q.: Person transfer GAN to bridge domain gap for person re-identification. In: CVPR (2018)
69. Wilson, G., Cook, D.J.: A survey of unsupervised deep domain adaptation. ACM Trans. Intell. Syst. Technol. **11**(5), 1–46 (2020)
70. Xie, J., Girshick, R., Farhadi, A.: Unsupervised deep embedding for clustering analysis. In: ICML (2016)
71. Xie, Q., Luong, M.T., Hovy, E., Le, Q.V.: Self-training with noisy student improves imagenet classification. In: CVPR (2020)
72. Xu, S., Rao, H., Hu, X., Hu, B.: Prototypical contrast and reverse prediction: unsupervised skeleton based action recognition. arXiv preprint arXiv:2011.07236 (2020)
73. Yan, H., Ding, Y., Li, P., Wang, Q., Xu, Y., Zuo, W.: Mind the class weight bias: weighted maximum mean discrepancy for unsupervised domain adaptation. In: CVPR (2017)
74. Yan, S., Xiong, Y., Lin, D.: Spatial temporal graph convolutional networks for skeleton-based action recognition. In: AAAI (2018)
75. Yang, D., Wang, Y., Dantcheva, A., Garattoni, L., Francesca, G., Bremond, F.: Unik: a unified framework for real-world skeleton-based action recognition. In: BMVC (2021)
76. Yang, S., Liu, J., Lu, S., Er, M.H., Kot, A.C.: Skeleton cloud colorization for unsupervised 3d action representation learning. In: ICCV (2021)
77. Yao, F.: Cross-domain few-shot learning with unlabelled data. arXiv preprint arXiv:2101.07899 (2021)
78. Zhai, Y., Ye, Q., Lu, S., Jia, M., Ji, R., Tian, Y.: Multiple expert brainstorming for domain adaptive person re-identification. In: ECCV (2020)
79. Zhang, P., Lan, C., Xing, J., Zeng, W., Xue, J., Zheng, N.: View adaptive recurrent neural networks for high performance human action recognition from skeleton data. In: ICCV (2017)
80. Zhang, P., Lan, C., Zeng, W., Xing, J., Xue, J., Zheng, N.: Semantics-guided neural networks for efficient skeleton-based human action recognition. In: CVPR (2020)
81. Zhang, R., Isola, P., Efros, A.A.: Colorful image colorization. In: ECCV (2016)

82. Zhang, X., Cao, J., Shen, C., You, M.: Self-training with progressive augmentation for unsupervised cross-domain person re-identification. In: ICCV (2019)
83. Zhang, Z.: Microsoft kinect sensor and its effect. IEEE Multimedia **19**(2), 4–10 (2012)
84. Zhao, B., Han, K.: Novel visual category discovery with dual ranking statistics and mutual knowledge distillation. In: NIPS (2021)
85. Zhao, F., Liao, S., Xie, G.S., Zhao, J., Zhang, K., Shao, L.: Unsupervised domain adaptation with noise resistible mutual-training for person re-identification. In: ECCV (2020)
86. Zhao, L., et al.: Learning view-disentangled human pose representation by contrastive cross-view mutual information maximization. In: CVPR (2021)
87. Zheng, K., Liu, W., He, L., Mei, T., Luo, J., Zha, Z.J.: Group-aware label transfer for domain adaptive person re-identification. In: CVPR (2021)
88. Zheng, N., Wen, J., Liu, R., Long, L., Dai, J., Gong, Z.: Unsupervised representation learning with long-term dynamics for skeleton based action recognition. In: AAAI (2018)
89. Zhong, Z., Zheng, L., Luo, Z., Li, S., Yang, Y.: Invariance matters: exemplar memory for domain adaptive person re-identification. In: CVPR (2019)

Is Appearance Free Action Recognition Possible?

Filip Ilic[1]([⊠])(iD), Thomas Pock[1](iD), and Richard P. Wildes[2](iD)

[1] Graz University of Technology, Graz, Austria
filip.ilic@tugraz.at
[2] York University, Toronto, Canada

Abstract. Intuition might suggest that motion and dynamic information are key to video-based action recognition. In contrast, there is evidence that state-of-the-art deep-learning video understanding architectures are biased toward static information available in single frames. Presently, a methodology and corresponding dataset to isolate the effects of dynamic information in video are missing. Their absence makes it difficult to understand how well contemporary architectures capitalize on dynamic vs. static information. We respond with a novel Appearance Free Dataset (AFD) for action recognition. AFD is devoid of static information relevant to action recognition in a single frame. Modeling of the dynamics is necessary for solving the task, as the action is only apparent through consideration of the temporal dimension. We evaluated 11 contemporary action recognition architectures on AFD as well as its related RGB video. Our results show a notable decrease in performance for all architectures on AFD compared to RGB. We also conducted a complimentary study with humans that shows their recognition accuracy on AFD and RGB is very similar and much better than the evaluated architectures on AFD. Our results motivate a novel architecture that revives explicit recovery of optical flow, within a contemporary design for best performance on AFD and RGB.

Keywords: Action recognition · Action recognition dataset · Deep learning · Static and dynamic video representation · Human motion perception

1 Introduction

1.1 Motivation

Action recognition from video has been subject of significant effort in developing and improving both algorithms and datasets [30,63]. This interplay between algorithm and dataset advances has led to paradigm shifts in both. Algorithms have evolved from primarily hand-crafted mathematically, physically,

---

Code & Data: f-ilic.github.io/AppearanceFreeActionRecognition.

S. Avidan et al. (Eds.): ECCV 2022, LNCS 13664, pp. 156–173, 2022.
https://doi.org/10.1007/978-3-031-19772-7_10

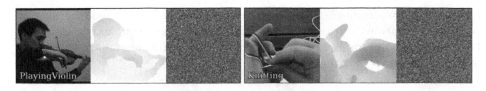

Fig. 1. Appearance Free Dataset (AFD) for Action recognition. Within each set of three images we show: a single RGB frame (left); corresponding optical flow in Middlebury colour coding [4] (middle); corresponding appearance free frame (right). When viewed as video the AFD reveals the motion in the original video even as any single frame provides no relevant discriminative information.

and heuristically driven approaches to methods based on deep-learning architectures. Datasets have evolved from relatively small, carefully selected videos to massive, web-crawled collections. As a result, current state-of-the-art algorithms for action recognition achieve impressive levels of performance on challenging datasets. In contrast, the internal representations learned by the architectures remain under explored [24]. This lack of understanding is unsatisfying both scientifically as well as pragmatically. From a scientific perspective, such detailed analysis is integral to understanding how a system operates and can guide further improvements. From a pragmatic perspective, multiple jurisdictions are beginning to require explainability as a precondition for deployment of artificial intelligence technologies [1,2]; technologies lacking such documentation may not see real-world application.

Some evidence suggests that contemporary deep-learning architectures for video understanding can perform well on the task of action recognition with little to no regard for the actual actors [9,23,59]. These studies suggest that static visual information available in a single frame (*e.g.* colour, spatial texture, contours, shape) drives performance, rather than dynamic information (*e.g.*, motion, temporal texture). While some methodologies have been aimed at understanding the representations learned by these architectures [16,39,61], none provide an approach to completely disentangle static vs. dynamic information. In response, we have developed an Appearance Free Dataset (AFD) for evaluating action recognition architectures when presented with purely dynamic information; see Fig. 1. AFD has been rendered by animating spatial noise, historically known as Random Dot Cinematographs RDCs [29], using image motion extracted from the UCF101 dataset [51] by a state-of-the-art optical flow estimator [53]. The resulting videos show no pattern relevant to action recognition in any single frame; however, when viewed as video reveal the underlying motion. We have produced AFD for the entire UCF101 dataset, evaluated a representative sample of contemporary action recognition architectures and used our results to drive development of a novel architecture that enhances performance when confronted with purely dynamic information, as present in AFD.

The ability of action recognition (and other) video architectures to work in absence of static appearance information is not only an academic exercise. Real-world deployment scenarios may require it, such as in the presence of camouflage. Two examples: Video surveillance for security should be able to cope with nefarious actors who artificially camouflage their activities; video-based wildlife monitoring must be robust to the natural camouflage that many animals possess to hide their presence.

1.2 Related Work

Datasets. A wide variety of datasets for development and evaluation of automated approaches of video understanding are available [3]. For action recognition, in particular, there is a large body ranging from a few dozen classes [31,36,38,39,51] to massively crawled datasets with classes in the hundreds [8,19,20,31]. Some work has specifically focused on curating videos where temporal modeling is particularly important for action recognition [19,33,38,48]; however, they still contain strong cues from single frame static appearance (*e.g.* colour, shape, texture). Overall, no action recognition dataset completely disentangles single frame static information from multiframe dynamic information.

Camouflaged actors would provide a way to evaluate recognition systems based primarily on dynamic information. While there are camouflage video understanding dataset available, they are of animals in the wild as selected for object segmentation (*e.g.* [5,37]). In contrast, it is unlikely that a non-trivial number of real-world videos of camouflaged actors can be found. In response, our Appearance Free Dataset (AFD) provides synthetic camouflaged action recognition videos as coherently moving patterns of spatial noise, historically known as Random Dot Cinematograms (RDCs) [29]. These patterns are defined via animation of an initial random spatial pattern, where the pixelwise intensity values of the pattern are randomly selected. By design, they reveal no information relevant to the motion in any single frame; however, when viewed as video the motion is apparent; examples are shown in the right columns of Fig. 1. Such videos have a long history in the study of motion processing in both biological [6,44] and machine [58,62] vision systems. Interestingly, humans can understand complex human body motion solely from sparse dots marking certain body points, even while merely a random dot pattern is perceived in any single frame [28].

Synthetic video, both striving for photorealism [7,11,42,45,46] and more abstracted [40,52], is a common tool in contemporary computer vision research that allows for careful control of variables of interest. Our effort adds to this body with its unique contribution of a synthetic camouflage action recognition dataset for probing a system's ability to recognize actions purely based on dynamic information. Notably, while our texture patterns are synthetic, they are animated by the motion of real-world actions [51].

Models and Action Recognition Architectures. A wide range of action recognition architectures have been developed [3]. Most contemporary architectures can be categorized as single stream 3D (x, y, t) convolutional, two-stream and attention based methods. Single stream approaches are motivated by the great success of 2D convolutional architectures on single image tasks [22,26,35,50]. In essence, the 3D architectures extend the same style of processing by adding temporal support to their operations [8, 13, 27, 55, 56]. Two-stream architectures have roots in biological vision systems [18, 25]. The idea of having separate pathways for **static** video content and **dynamic** information has been variously adopted. A key distinction in these designs is whether the pathway for dynamic information explicitly relies on optical flow estimation [15, 49] or internally computed features that are thought to emulate flow like properties [14]. Attention-based approaches rely on various forms of non-local spatiotemporal data association as manifested in transformer architectures [12, 60]. For evaluation of architectures on the new AFD, we select a representative sampling from each of these categories.

Interpretability. Various efforts have addressed the representational abilities of video understanding architectures ranging from dynamic texture recognition [21], future frame selection [17] and comparing 3D convolutional vs. LSTM architectures [41]. Other work centering on action recognition focused on visualization of learned filters in convolutional architectures [16, 61], or trying to remove scene biases for action recognition [38, 39]. Evidence also suggests that optical flow is useful exactly because it contains invariances related to single frame appearance information [47]. More closely related to our study is work that categorized various action classes as especially dependent on temporal information; however, single frame static information still remains [48]. Somewhat similarly, an approach tried to tease apart the bias of various architectures and datasets towards static vs. dynamic information by manipulating videos through stylization; however, single frame static information remained a confounding factor [34]. While insights have been gained, no previous research has been able to completely disentangle the ability of these models to capitalize on single frame static information vs. dynamic information present across multiple frames. We concentrate on the ability of these systems to capture dynamic information, with an emphasis on action recognition.

1.3   Contributions

In light of previous work, we make the following three major contributions.

1. We introduce the Appearance Free Dataset (AFD) for video-based action recognition. AFD is a synthetic derivative of UCF101 [51] having *no static* appearance cues, however, revealing real-world motion as video.
2. We evaluate 11 contemporary architectures for action recognition on AFD; *i.e.* dynamic information alone. We conduct a psychophysical study with humans on AFD, and show significanly better performance of humans than networks. These results question the ability of the tested networks to use dynamic information effectively.
3. We provide a novel improved action recognition architecture with enhanced performance on AFD, while maintaining performance on standard input.

We make AFD, associated code and our novel architecture publicly available.

2   Appearance Free Dataset

Our proposed appearance free dataset, AFD101, is built from the original UCF101 [51] by employing a state-of-the-art optical flow estimator [53] to generate the corresponding framewise flow that is used to animate spatial noise patterns. The resulting AFD101, consisting of 13,320 videos, depicts realistic motion even while any individual frame is devoid of static appearance information that is relevant for action recognition. Figure 1 and the project webpage provide illustrative examples. We use UCF101 from many possible choices [3] as the basis for AFD because it was widely used in action recognition evaluation and is large enough to support training, yet small enough to facilitate numerous experiments.

2.1   Dataset Generation Methodology

Fig. 2. Appearance free videos are created by 1) initializing noise $R0$, 2) calculating optical flow between input frame pairs, and 3) using the optical flow to warp $R0$. Steps 2 and 3 are repeated for each frame-pair in the input video.

Generation of AFD from RGB video follows three key steps; see Fig. 2.

1. Initialization: Generate a single frame of noise, with same spatial dimensions as the frames in the input video. The pixel values are sampled uniformly i.i.d. as three-channel RGB values. Let this frame be denoted as R_0.
2. Flow calculation: Generate interframe optical flow for each temporally adjacent pair of input RGB frames, $I_{t-1}, I_t, t \in [1, T]$, yielding the flow $F_{t-1,t}$, with T being the number of frames in the input video. We use RAFT [53], for the extraction of optical flow.
3. Warping: We warp the initial noise frame R_0 using $F_{t-1,t}, t \in [1, T]$, to generate the next noise frame, R_t. The output frames, R_t, are an appearance free version of the input RGB video, where at each frame all that is seen is i.i.d. noise, but whose interframe motion corresponds to that of the original video; this output video has the same spatial and temporal dimension as the input video.

2.2   Implementation Details

The details of our proposed methodology are particularly important, as all *static* discriminatory single frame information must be removed; to this end

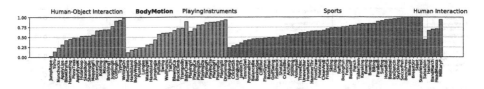

Fig. 3. ResNet50 Top-1 accuracy on single frame UCF101 by *Action Groups*.

nearest neighbor interpolation during warping is performed. For each warp, newly occluded pixels are overwritten by the new value moved to that location; de-occluded pixels are filled with R_0 values to ensure that the spatial extent of the noise is constant. Along the border where the warping leads to undefined values (*e.g.* pixel at that location moves elsewhere and no new value is warped into that location) are treated as de-occlusions as well. In preliminary experiments, we found that other choices of implementation, *e.g.* bilinear interpolation as opposed to nearest neighbor interpolation, or always estimating flow with respect to I_0 always yielded inferior results and unwanted artifacts. In the worst cases these artifacts led to revealing motion boundaries of actors in single frames.

2.3 Is Optical Flow Appearance Free?

The concept of appearance consists of multiple intertwined qualities, including texture, contour and shape. While optical flow is indeed free of texture it is not free of contour and shape induced by motion of the camera or the actor itself; this fact can be observed qualitatively in Fig. 1: The flow visualizations alone reveal violin playing and knitting. We quantify this observation as follows. We train a strong single frame recognition architecture, ResNet50 [22], on single frames from three datasets: UCF101 (the original), UCF101Flow, comprised of optical flow frames generated from UCF101 by RAFT [53], and AFD101. Top-1 recognition results for UCF101, UCF101Flow and AFD101 are 65.6%, 29.4% and 1.1%, respectively. These results show that only AFD101 contains no discriminatory information in a single frame, as only 1.1% top-1 accuracy is in line with random guessing.

2.4 AFD5: A Reduced Subset Suitable for Small Scale Exploration

To evaluate the performance of state-of-the-art architectures in the context of human performance, a reduced subset of the classes in UCF101 is needed, simply because it is not feasible to conduct an experiment with humans with the original 101 categories. We chose to have five classes as it is possible for humans to hold five action classes in working memory for a prolonged duration [43]. In the following, we refer to the reduced size version of AFD101 as AFD5 and the corresponding reduction of UCF101, *i.e.* the RGB video, as UCF5.

A defining property of the subset is that it discourages recognition from static information in single frames even within the original RGB input. To this

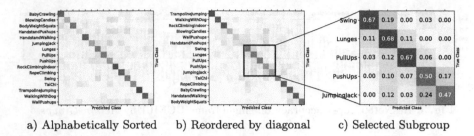

a) Alphabetically Sorted   b) Reordered by diagonal   c) Selected Subgroup

Fig. 4. Singleframe ResNet50: after finetuning on the *BodyMotion* action group of UCF101, we a) inspect the resulting confusion matrix b) reorder it by its diagonal weight so that classes that are often confused among each other get grouped together, and c) select the most prominent subgroup.

end we train a ResNet50 [22], used by many state-of-the-art architectures as inspiration for their backbone [3], on the entire UCF101 dataset in a single frame classification manner, *i.e.*, we randomly sample a frame from UCF101. By design, this procedure isolates the ability of any given class to support recognition on the basis of a single frame. UCF101 is subdivided into five action groups [51]: *Human Object Interaction, BodyMotion, PlayingInstruments, Sports* and *Human Human Interaction*; Fig. 3 has single frame recognition accuracy by group.

Our selection criterion is to choose videos with similar appearance; therefore, we select a subset of actions within a group. To select the action group we consider the following points. The *Body Motion* group is particularly attractive because it is the only category that has five or more classes with below 25% single frame recognition accuracy. The *Human Object Interaction* group is the next closest in terms of having several (albeit fewer that five) categories with such low single frame accuracy. However, its classes tend to be distinguished by featuring a prominent object and we do not want to promote categorization based on single frame object recognition. The *PlayingInstruments* group also features prominent objects and likewise is a poor choice. The remaining groups (*Sports* and *Human Human Interaction*) have generally higher single frame recognition accuracies; so, also are excluded. These considerations lead us to *Body Motion* as the group of interest for present concerns.

With the selection of *Body Motion*, we finetune the previously trained ResNet on that particular group. Given that finetuning, we perform confusion matrix reordering [54] and select the five classes that are most confused among each other in the group. More precisely we find the permutation matrix that has the highest interclass entropy, excluding classes with less than 50% accuracy; see Fig. 4. This results in the choice of the following five classes for AFD5: *Swing, Lunges, PushUps, PullUps, JumpingJack*. AFD5 consists in total of 583 videos with approximately 116 videos per class.

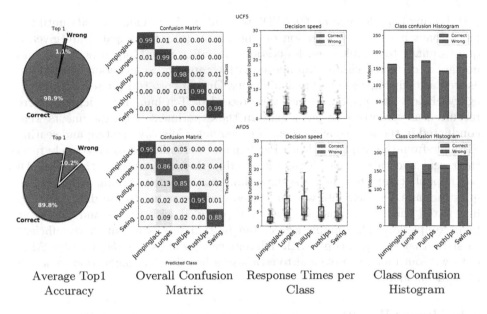

| Average Top1
Accuracy | Overall Confusion
Matrix | Response Times per
Class | Class Confusion
Histogram |

Fig. 5. Results of psychopysical study. Top row: Performance on standard RGB video, UCF5. Bottom row: Performance on appearance free data, AFD5.

3   Psychophysical Study: Human Performance on AFD5

To set a baseline for Appearance Free Data we perform a psychophysical study. The ability of humans to recognize actions from dynamic information alone, *i.e.* without any single frame static information, has been documented previously [10,28,57]. These studies are conducted with sparse dots, typically at major body joints, on otherwise blank displays. Our study appears to be unique in its use of dense noise patterns *i.e.* dense random dots.

3.1   Experiment Design

A session in the experiment consisted of the following seven phases. (i) The participant is presented with a brief slide show explaining the task. The participant is told that they will see a series of videos as well as a menu on the same display from which to indicate their perception of a human action that is depicted. (ii) Training is provided on UCF5, *i.e.*, RGB video. During this phase, four training videos from each class, totaling 20 videos, are presented with correct responses indicated in the menu. The videos are shown in randomized order. (iii) Testing is performed on 90 UCF5 test videos. Each video repeats until the participant makes their selection on the menu. (iv) A rest period of five minutes is provided. (v) Training is provided on AFD5, *i.e.* appearance free video. During this phase, four training videos from each class are presented with correct responses indicated in the menu. The videos also are shown in randomized order.

(vi) Testing is performed on 90 AFD5 test videos. Each video repeats until the participant makes their selection on the menu. (vii) Participants are given a questionnaire to complete, with questions including visual impairments (all had normal or corrected vision), familiarity with computer vision, action recognition, as well as their impression of task difficulty. During both test phases, action category choices and response times were recorded. Ten human participants were recruited as volunteers to participate in the experiment. All experiments were conducted in the same environment, *i.e.* computer/display, lighting and seating distance from the display (0.5 m). Participants were allowed to view freely from their seat and take as much time in making their responses as they like. All participants completed their session within approximately 30 min, including the questionnaire. Participants were informed and consented to the data gathered in written and signed manner, and were provided with sweets and thanks at task completion. The sample size of ten participants is in our view sufficient to show that various people with different backgrounds are *able* to solve AFD data without much trouble and to establish a baseline for comparison to action recognition architectures.

3.2   Human Results

Results of the psychophysical study are shown in Fig. 5. On average, our participants perform with an accuracy of 89.8% on AFD5 and 98.9% on UCF5. Participants report that mistakes on UCF5, the RGB videos, resulted from accidental clicks when making selections. Our analysis of AFD5 samples that were most frequently misclassified by the participants reveals that those videos typically have sudden and high speed camera movement, *e.g.* as induced by quick panning and zooming, which in turn creates very large optical flow displacement. The plots of response time show that participants take longer to make their choice on AFD5, with the exception of *JumpingJack* which remains largely unaffected. The extended time taken for AFD5 suggests that appearance free recognition requires more effort and repeated playback of the video is necessary, even though ultimate performance is high.

Overall, the psychophysical results document the strong ability of humans to recognize actions on the basis of AFD, as well as standard RGB videos.

4   Computational Study: Model Performances on AFD

We evaluate 11 state-of-the-art action recognition architectures on UCF101 and our new AFD101. We select representative examples from the currently most widely used categories of action recognition architectures, *cf.* Sect. 1.2: single stream 3D convolutional [8,13,56], two-stream convolutional [14,49] and attention-based [12,60]. We also evaluate on a standard 2D convolutional architecture (ResNet50 [22]) to verify that our AFD does not support classification based on single frame static information. Notably, our results from the psychophysical study allow us to compare the performance of the network architectures to that of humans on both UCF5 and AFD5.

4.1 Training Procedure

To guarantee a fair comparison all reported results are obtained by training and testing with our procedure, described below. Furthermore, since we want to investigate architectural benefits on Appearance Free Data, all results (except for one architecture, see below) are obtained without pretraining - concurrently often done on Kinetics400 [8] - as there is no AFD for Kinetics. Our goal is not to show how to archieve best performance on UCF101; it is to show the difference in performance of each network when presented with *only* dynamic information. We also ran preliminary experiments with pretraining on Kinetics and finetuning on AFD, but saw no significant improvement during AFD testing compared to no pretraining. Nevertheless, since all the evaluated architectures, save one, employ a ResNet-like backbone we use ImageNet pretrained versions of those to initialize our training. The exception is MViT, which needed to be initialized with Kintecs400 weights, as its performance was not increasing from baseline with the aforementioned scheme. However the Kinetics weights were only used as an intializer and we allowed for retraining of the entire backbone to make the results comparing UCF and AFD as comparable as possible. We acknowledge that our training strategy does not allow for the architectures to show state-of-the-art performance on RGB input in our experiments; however, our approach is necessary to allow for fair comparison of performance on RGB vs. AFD and measure the respective performance between the modalities.

4.2 Training Details

We train with Adam [32] using an early stopping scheme, and a base learning rate of $3e^{-4}$. The batch size is chosen as large as possible on two GPUs with 24GB memory each. Data augmentation, a staple of modern deep learning, is kept the same for all evaluated models and datasets; uniform temporal sampling with jitter, random start frame selection, and contrast, hue, and brightness jitter are applied. Random horizontal flipping of entire videos is used, as actions in UCF101 do not depend on handedness. A quite aggressive data augmentation scheme that changes over the course of every 20 epochs to a less aggressive one, and capping at 80 epochs is used. We find that this aggressive data augmentation technique is needed to achieve reasonable results when no pretraining is used. Spatial center crops of 224×224 are used as the final input to all networks with the exception of X3D XS and S, which use a spatial resolution of 160×160. The reported results are the averages of the three standard splits used on UCF101, now applied to both the original RGB as well as AFD. The results on UCF5 and AFD5 were obtained by finetuning the networks previously trained on their 101 class counterparts and using the same splits.

4.3 Architecture Results

Table 1 shows top-1 accuracy results for all evaluated architectures on UCF101, AFD101, UCF5 and AFD5. Note that the results for the single frame ResNet on

UCF101 essentially are the same as those shown in Fig. 3. The results in Table 1 also validate our claim of having removed all *static*, single frame information relevant to recognition, as the performance is equal to random choice.

For most of the action recognition architectures, it is seen that obtaining $\approx$70–80% top-1 accuracy is possible. This fact makes the sizable drop of performance on AFD data, the Δ columns in Table 1, especially striking. The average performance drops by approximately 30% almost evenly across all architectures - with two notable exceptions: The Fast stream of SlowFast and I3D OF a common I3D architecture with an optical flow estimator before the network input. These two architectures are noteworthy because their ability to maintain performance across regular and appearance free video apparently stems from their design to prioritize temporal information over spatial; although, this focus on temporal information leads them to be less competitive on the standard RGB input in comparison to the other evaluated architectures. The comparison to human performance shows X3D variations to be the best architectures, competitive with human performance on UCF5; *however*, the best architectures on AFD5 (X3D M and SlowFast) are *considerably* below human top-1 accuracy (18% below). These results show that there is room for improvement by enhancing the ability of current architectures to exploit dynamic information for action recognition. It also suggests that optical flow is *not* what is learned by these networks, when no explicit representation of flow is enforced. Importantly, TwoStream [49] and I3D [8] OF were evaluated with RAFT optical to allow for a fair comparison with each other and with our new algorithm, introduced in the next section. The summary plots below Table 1 show learnable architecture parameter counts and ordering by AFD accuracy. These plots further emphasize the fact that explicit representation of dynamic information (*e.g.* as in I3D OF and to some extent Fast) is best at closing the gap between performance on RGB and AFD. X3D M is among the top performing architectures on RGB; further, among those top RGB performers, it shows the smallest Δ. Also, it is has a relatively small number of learnable parameters, with only Fast notably smaller. These observations motivate the novel architecture that we present in the next section. It improves performance on AFD, while also slightly improving performance on RGB. This architecture is given as E2S-X3D in Table 1. Moreover, it performs on par with humans on UCF5 and AFD5.

5   Two-Stream Strikes Back

The results of our evaluation of architectures in Sect. 4 show the importance of explicit representation of dynamic information for strong performance on AFD. This result motivates us to revive the two-stream appearance plus optical flow design [49]. While state of the art when introduced, compared to more recent action recognition architectures, *e.g.* those evaluated in Sect. 4, it is no longer competitive [63]; so, we incorporate two-streams into the top performing architecture on RGB input with the smallest drop on AFD, *i.e.* X3D.

Table 1. Top-1 accuracy for the evaluated action recognition architectures. The second column indicates the number of frames and the temporal sampling rate, $f \times r$, of each network. For two-stream approaches the notation $\binom{\text{Appearance}}{\text{Motion}}\binom{f \times r}{f \times r}$ is used. A drop in performance across all networks on AFD data is observed. Plots below the table show parameter counts as well as summarize the accuracy findings, sorted by AFD performance. Absolute performance on UCF is of secondary importance; it merely gives a point of comparison with respect to AFD. The Δ columns shows the difference between UCF and AFD performance, which highlights the relative *dynamic* recognition capability of architectures.

	$f \times r$	UCF101	AFD101	Δ	UCF5	AFD5	Δ
Single Image Input							
ResNet50 [22]	1×1	65.6	1.1	64.5	74.2	20.1	54.1
Video Input							
I3D [8]	8×8	67.8	43.3	24.5	95.6	55.1	40.5
TwoStream [49]	$\binom{1 \times 1}{10 \times 1}$	76.1	29.3	46.8	78.1	62.3	15.8
C2D [60]	8×8	77.4	42.6	34.8	84.5	69.0	15.5
R2+1D [56]	16×4	68.2	28.9	39.3	80.6	67.9	12.7
Slow [14]	8×8	73.3	37.6	35.7	89.9	40.6	49.3
Fast [14]	32×2	50.5	45.9	4.6	71.4	65.7	5.7
SlowFast [14] $\binom{\text{Slow}}{\text{Fast}}$	$\binom{8 \times 8}{32 \times 2}$	82.9	55.4	27.5	91.0	70.2	20.8
I3D [8] OF	8×8	54.5	44.4	10.1	74.4	59.7	14.7
X3D XS [13]	4×12	79.8	43.2	36.6	95.2	57.0	38.2
X3D S [13]	13×6	80.8	56.9	23.9	97.3	69.8	27.5
X3D M [13]	16×5	81.5	58.2	23.3	98.8	71.5	27.3
MViT [12]	16×4	82.9	39.8	43.1	95.1	22.2	72.9
E2S-X3D **Ours** $\binom{\text{M}}{\text{S}}$	$\binom{16 \times 5}{13 \times 6}$	85.7	73.9	11.8	99.4	90.8	8.6
Human Average					98.9	89.8	9.1

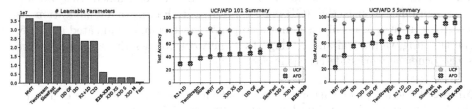

5.1   E2S-X3D: Design of a Novel Action Recognition Architecture

The design of our novel architecture, ES2-X3D, is shown in Fig. 6. Initially, optical flow fields and RGB images are processed in separate 3D convolutional streams. Both streams are versions of the X3D architecture [13], where we use the S variant for optical flow and the M variant for RGB. These two architectures differ in their spatiotemporal resolution of the input and as a consequence the activation maps. X3D M uses larger spatial and temporal extents, whereas

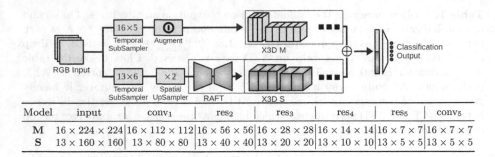

Model	input	conv₁	res₂	res₃	res₄	res₅	conv₅
M	$16 \times 224 \times 224$	$16 \times 112 \times 112$	$16 \times 56 \times 56$	$16 \times 28 \times 28$	$16 \times 14 \times 14$	$16 \times 7 \times 7$	$16 \times 7 \times 7$
S	$13 \times 160 \times 160$	$13 \times 80 \times 80$	$13 \times 40 \times 40$	$13 \times 20 \times 20$	$13 \times 10 \times 10$	$13 \times 5 \times 5$	$13 \times 5 \times 5$

Fig. 6. Our novel ES2-X3D operates with two parallel streams for processing of RGB (top stream) and optical flow (bottom stream). Late fusion via concatenation is followed by a fully connected and Softmax layer. The table shows the output sizes of each employed X3D architecture in the format T×H×W.

S has smaller spatial and temporal supports. Since the input flow field already represents the dynamic information with detail, the additional spatiotemporal extent is not needed; in contrast, the RGB stream without the optical flow benefits from larger spatial and temporal support, see Fig. 6 (bottom). We validate these choices below via ablation. The dimensionality of the layers is shown in Fig. 6. Following the separate parallel processing, late fusion is performed. We fuse the outputs via simple concatenation of the outputs of the two streams. While more sophisticated fusion schemes might be considered, *e.g.* [15], we leave that for future work. Finally, a fully connected layer followed by a Softmax layer yields the classification output, which is used with a cross-entropy loss to train the network. For optical flow input, we use a state-of-the-art optical flow estimator, RAFT [53] pretrained on Sintel [7]. We do not further train the flow extractor and only use it in its inference mode. To capture fine grained motion and to adjust for the different spatial resolution RAFT was trained with, we add an up-sampling layer to the RGB images prior to RAFT. Data augmentation, as described in Sect. 4, is only used in the appearance stream, as indicated in Fig. 6. The training, validation and testing of the network follows the same procedure as the other networks; described in Sect. 4.

Table 2. Performance of X3D architecture configurations, XS, S and M for UCF5 and AFD5. Ablation is performed for both optical flow and RGB inputs.

		UCF5					**AFD5**		
		Input					**Input**		
Architecture		$\binom{\text{RGB}}{-}$	$\binom{-}{\text{RAFT}}$	$\binom{\text{RGB}}{\text{RAFT}}$		Architecture	$\binom{\text{RGB}}{-}$	$\binom{-}{\text{RAFT}}$	$\binom{\text{RGB}}{\text{RAFT}}$
XS	4×12	95.2	82.1	—		XS	4×12 57.0	77.3	—
S	13×6	97.3	**89.5**	—		S	13×6 69.8	**80.3**	—
M	16×5	**98.8**	86.8	—		M	16×5 **71.5**	78.9	—
$\binom{\text{M}}{\text{S}}$	$\binom{16\times5}{13\times6}$	—	—	**99.4**		$\binom{\text{M}}{\text{S}}$	$\binom{16\times5}{13\times6}$ —	—	**90.8**

5.2   E2S-X3D: Empirical Evaluation

E2S-X3D outperforms all competing architectures on AFD101, with the closest competitor (singlestream X3D) trailing by 15.7%; see Table 1. It also improves performance on UCF101, albeit slightly; 2.8% points gained on MViT (MViT has around 6× more parameters). To rule out an ensembling effect, we compared our network in its default configuration (RGB in one stream, optical flow in the other) with an alternative where it inputs RGB to both streams. We find a performance drop of 10.6% on UCF101 and 30.7% on AFD101, validating our hypothesis that explicit optical flow is crucial. Moreover, it is on par with human performance on both AFD5 and UCF5. These results document the advantage of explicit modeling of motion for action recognition. Table 2 shows results of ablations across various X3D configurations for both AFD5 and UCF5. It shows that for both input modalities, best performance is achieved when the S configuration is used for optical flow and the M configuration for the RGB stream. This set of experiments empirically validates our final ES2-X3D design.

6   Conclusions

We introduce an extension to a widely used action recognition dataset that disentangles static and dynamic video components. In particular, no single frame contains any *static* discriminatory information in our apperance free dataset (AFD); the action is only encoded in the temporal dimension. We show, by means of a psychophysical study with humans, that solving AFD is possible with a high degree of certainty (~90% Top1 Accuracy). This result is especially interesting as 11 current state-of-the-art action recognition architectures show much weaker performance as well as a steep drop in performance when comparing standard RGB to AFD input. These results lend to the interpretability of the evaluated architectures, by documenting their ability to exploit dynamic information. In particular, this shows that optical flow, or a similarly descriptive representation, is not an emergent property of *any* of the tested network architectures.

We propose a novel architecture incorporating the explicit computation of optical flow and use insights from recent action recognition research. This explict form of modeling *dynamics* allows our approach to outperform all competing methods, and compete with human level performance. Given the strong performance of our architecture in our evaluation, future work could consider training and investigation of performance on larger datasets [8, 19] as well as application to other tasks where non-synthetic data is available and dynamic information plays a crucial role, *e.g.* camouflaged animal detection [37]. Alternative fusion strategies are also a potential for improvement of our present architecture.

References

1. Laying down harmonised rules on artificial intelligence (artificial intelligence act) and amending certain union legislative acts. European Commision (2021)
2. Regulating AI: Critical issues and choices. Law Council of Ontario (2021)
3. Aafaq, N., Mian, A., Liu, W., Gilani, S.Z., Shah, M.: Video description: a survey of methods, datasets, and evaluation metrics. ACM Comput. Surv. **52**(6), 1–37 (2019)
4. Baker, S., Scharstein, D., Lewis, J., Roth, S., Black, M.J., Szeliski, R.: A database and evaluation methodology for optical flow. Int. J. Comput. Vision **92**(1), 1–31 (2011)
5. Bideau, P., Learned-Miller, E.: It's moving! A probabilistic model for causal motion segmentation in moving camera videos. In: Proceedings of the European Conference on Computer Vision (2016)
6. Braddick, O.J.: Low-level and high-level processes in apparent motion. Philos. Trans. R. Soc. London B Biol. Sci. **290**(1038), 137–151 (1980)
7. Butler, D.J., Wulff, J., Stanley, G.B., Black, M.J.: A naturalistic open source movie for optical flow evaluation. In: Proceedings of the European Conference on Computer Vision (2012)
8. Carreira, J., Zisserman, A.: Quo vadis, action recognition? A new model and the kinetics dataset. In: Proceedings of the Conference on Computer Vision and Pattern Recognition (2017)
9. Choi, J., Gao, C., Messou, C.E.J., Huang, J.B.: Why can't I dance in the mall? Learning to mitigate scene bias in action recognition. In: Proceedings of the Conference on Advances in Neural Information Processing Systems (2019)
10. Dittrich, W.H.: Action categories and the perception of biological motion. Perception **22**(1), 15–22 (1993)
11. Dosovitskiy, A., et al.: FlowNet: learning optical flow with convolutional networks. In: Proceedings of the International Conference on Computer Vision (2015)
12. Fan, H., et al.: Multiscale vision transformers. In: Proceedings of the International Conference on Computer Vision (2021)
13. Feichtenhofer, C.: X3D: expanding architectures for efficient video recognition. In: Proceedings of the Conference on Computer Vision and Pattern Recognition (2020)
14. Feichtenhofer, C., Fan, H., Malik, J., He, K.: SlowFast networks for video recognition. In: Proceedings of the International Conference on Computer Vision (2019)
15. Feichtenhofer, C., Pinz, A., Wildes, R.P.: Spatiotemporal multiplier networks for video action recognition. In: Proceedings of the Conference on Computer Vision and Pattern Recognition (2017)
16. Feichtenhofer, C., Pinz, A., Wildes, R.P., Zisserman, A.: Deep insights into convolutional networks for video recognition. Int. J. Comput. Vision **128**(2), 420–437 (2020)
17. Ghodrati, A., Gavves, E., Snoek, C.G.M.: Video time: properties, encoders and evaluation. In: British Machine Vision Conference (2018)
18. Goodale, M.A., Milner, A.D.: Separate visual pathways for perception and action. Trends Neurosci. **15**(1), 20–25 (1992)
19. Goyal, R., et al.: The "something something" video database for learning and evaluating visual common sense. In: Proceedings of the International Conference on Computer Vision (2017)
20. Gu, C., et al.: AVA: a video dataset of spatio-temporally localized atomic visual actions. In: Proceedings of the Conference on Computer Vision and Pattern Recognition (2018)

21. Hadji, I., Wildes, R.P.: A new large scale dynamic texture dataset with application to convnet understanding. In: Proceedings of the European Conference on Computer Vision (2018)
22. He, K., Zhang, X., Ren, S., Sun, J.: Deep residual learning for image recognition. In: Proceedings of the Conference on Computer Vision and Pattern Recognition (2016)
23. He, Y., Shirakabe, S., Satoh, Y., Kataoka, H.: Human action recognition without human. In: Proceedings of the European Conference on Computer Vision (2016)
24. Hiley, L., Preece, A., Hicks, Y.: Explainable deep learning for video recognition tasks: a framework & recommendations. arXiv preprint arXiv:1909.05667 (2019)
25. Hubel, D.H., Wiesel, T.N.: Receptive fields of single neurones in the cat's striate cortex. J. Physiol. **148**(3), 574–591 (1959)
26. Iandola, F.N., Han, S., Moskewicz, M.W., Ashraf, K., Dally, W.J., Keutzer, K.: SqueezeNet: AlexNet-level accuracy with 50x fewer parameters and < 0.5 mb model size. arXiv preprint arXiv:1602.07360 (2016)
27. Ji, S., Xu, W., Yang, M., Yu, K.: 3D convolutional neural networks for human action recognition. IEEE Trans. Pattern Anal. Mach. Intell. **35**(1), 221–231 (2012)
28. Johansson, G.: Visual perception of biological motion and a model for its analysis. Percept. Psychophysics **14**(2), 201–211 (1973)
29. Julesz, B.: Foundations of Cyclopean Perception. U. Chicago Press, Chicago (1971)
30. Kang, S.M., Wildes, R.P.: Review of action recognition and detection methods. arXiv preprint arXiv:1610.06906 (2016)
31. Karpathy, A., Toderici, G., Shetty, S., Leung, T., Sukthankar, R., Fei-Fei, L.: Large-scale video classification with convolutional neural networks. In: Proceedings of the Conference on Computer Vision and Pattern Recognition (2014)
32. Kingma, D.P., Ba, J.: Adam: a method for stochastic optimization. arXiv preprint arXiv:1412.6980 (2014)
33. Kong, Y., Jia, Y., Fu, Y.: Interactive phrases: semantic descriptions for human interaction recognition. IEEE Trans. Pattern Anal. Mach. Intell. **36**(9), 1775–1788 (2014)
34. Kowal, M., Siam, M., Islam, A., Bruce, N.D.B., Wildes, R.P., Derpanis, K.G.: A deeper dive into what deep spatiotemporal networks encode: Quantifying static vs. dynamic information. In: Proceedings of the Conference on Computer Vision and Pattern Recognition (2022)
35. Krizhevsky, A., Sutskever, I., Hinton, G.E.: Imagenet classification with deep convolutional neural networks. In: Proceedings of the Advances in Neural Information Processing Systems (2012)
36. Kuehne, H., Jhuang, H., Garrote, E., Poggio, T., Serre, T.: HMDB: a large video database for human motion recognition. In: Proceedings of the International Conference on Computer Vision (2011)
37. Lamdouar, H., Yang, C., Xie, W., Zisserman, A.: Betrayed by motion: camouflaged object discovery via motion segmentation. In: Proceedings of the Asian Conference on Computer Vision (2020)
38. Li, Y., Li, Y., Vasconcelos, N.: Diving48 dataset. https://www.svcl.ucsd.edu/projects/resound/dataset.html
39. Li, Y., Li, Y., Vasconcelos, N.: Resound: towards action recognition without representation bias. In: Proceedings of the European Conference on Computer Vision (2018)
40. Mahmood, N., Ghorbani, N., Troje, N., Pons-Moll, G., Black, M.: AMASS: archive of motion capture as surface Shapes. In: Proceedings of the International Conference on Computer Vision (2019)

41. Manttari, J., Broomé, S., Folkesson, J., Kjellstrom, H.: Interpreting video features: a comparison of 3d convolutional networks and convolutional LSTM networks. In: Proceedings of the Asian Conference on Computer Vision (2020)
42. Mayer, N., et al.: A large dataset to train convolutional networks for disparity, optical flow, and scene flow estimation. In: Proceedings of the Conference on Computer Vision and Pattern Recognition (2016)
43. Miller, G.A.: The magical number seven, plus or minus two: Some limits on our capacity for processing information. Psychol. Rev. **63**(2), 81 (1956)
44. Nishida, S., Kawabe, T., Sawayama, M., Fukiage, T.: Motion perception: from detection to interpretation. Ann. Rev. Vis. Sci. **4**, 501–523 (2018)
45. Richter, S.R., Hayder, Z., Koltun, V.: Playing for benchmarks. In: Proceedings of the International Conference on Computer Vision (2017)
46. Ros, G., Sellart, L., Materzynska, J., Vazquez, D., Lopez, A.M.: The SYNTHIA dataset: a large collection of synthetic images for semantic segmentation of urban scenes. In: Proceedings of the Conference on Computer Vision and Pattern Recognition (2016)
47. Sevilla-Lara, L., Liao, Y., Güney, F., Jampani, V., Geiger, A., Black, M.J.: On the integration of optical flow and action recognition. In: Brox, T., Bruhn, A., Fritz, M. (eds.) GCPR 2018. LNCS, vol. 11269, pp. 281–297. Springer, Cham (2019). https://doi.org/10.1007/978-3-030-12939-2_20
48. Sevilla-Lara, L., Zha, S., Yan, Z., Goswami, V., Feiszli, M., Torresani, L.: Only time can tell: discovering temporal data for temporal modeling. In: Proceedings of the Winter Conference on Applications of Computer Vision (2021)
49. Simonyan, K., Zisserman, A.: Two-stream convolutional networks for action recognition in videos. In: Proceedings of the Conference on Advances in Neural Information Processing Systems (2014)
50. Simonyan, K., Zisserman, A.: Very deep convolutional networks for large-scale image recognition. arXiv preprint arXiv:1409.1556 (2014)
51. Soomro, K., Zamir, A.R., Shah, M.: UCF101: a dataset of 101 human actions classes from videos in the wild. arXiv preprint arXiv:1212.0402 (2012)
52. Sriastava, N., Manisomov, E., Salakhutdinov, R.: Unsupervised learning of video representations using LSTMs. In: Proceedings of the International Conference on Machine Learning (2015)
53. Teed, Z., Deng, J.: RAFT: recurrent all-pairs field transforms for optical flow. In: Proceedings of the European Conference on Computer Vision (2020)
54. Thoma, M.: Analysis and Optimization of Convolutional Neural Network Architectures. Master's thesis, University of the State of Baden-Wuerttemberg (2017)
55. Tran, D., Bourdev, L., Fergus, R., Torresani, L., Paluri, M.: Learning spatiotemporal features with 3D convolutional networks. In: Proceedings of the International Conference on Computer Vision (2015)
56. Tran, D., Wang, H., Torresani, L., Ray, J., LeCun, Y., Paluri, M.: A closer look at spatiotemporal convolutions for action recognition. In: Proceedings of the Conference on Computer Vision and Pattern Recognition (2018)
57. Troje, N.F.: Decomposing biological motion: a framework for analysis and synthesis of human gait patterns. J. Vision **2**(5), 2 (2002)
58. Ullman, S.: The Interpretation of Visual Motion. MIT Press, Cambridge (1979)
59. Vu, T.H., Olsson, C., Laptev, I., Oliva, A., Sivic, J.: Predicting actions from static scenes. In: Proceedings of the European Conference on Computer Vision (2014)
60. Wang, X., Girshick, R., Gupta, A., He, K.: Non-local neural networks. In: Proceedings of the Conference on Computer Vision and Pattern Recognition (2018)

61. Zhao, H., Wildes, R.P.: Interpretable deep feature propagation for early action recognition. arXiv preprint arXiv:2107.05122 (2021)
62. Zhou, B., Tang, X., Wang, X.: Coherent filtering: detecting coherent motions from crowd clutters. In: Proceedings of the European Conference on Computer Vision (2012)
63. Zhu, Y., et al.: A comprehensive study of deep video action recognition. arXiv preprint arXiv:2012.06567 (2020)

Learning Spatial-Preserved Skeleton Representations for Few-Shot Action Recognition

Ning Ma[1,2,3], Hongyi Zhang[1,2,3], Xuhui Li[1,2,3], Sheng Zhou[1,2,3(✉)],
Zhen Zhang[4], Jun Wen[5], Haifeng Li[6], Jingjun Gu[1,2], and Jiajun Bu[1,2,3(✉)]

[1] Zhejiang Provincial Key Laboratory of Service Robot, College of Computer Science, Zhejiang University, Hangzhou, China
{ma_ning,zhy1998,12021064,zhousheng_zju,gjj,bjj}@zju.edu.cn
[2] Alibaba-Zhejiang University Joint Institute of Frontier Technologies, Hangzhou, China
[3] Ningbo Research Institute, Zhejiang University, Ningbo, China
[4] Department of Computer Science, National University of Singapore, Singapore, Singapore
zhen@nus.edu.sg
[5] Department of Biomedical Informatics, Harvard Medical School, Boston, USA
junwen@zju.edu.cn
[6] The Children's Hospital Zhejiang University School of Medicine, Hangzhou, China
6199005@zju.edu.cn

Abstract. Few-shot action recognition aims to recognize few-labeled novel action classes and attracts growing attentions due to practical significance. Human skeletons provide explainable and data-efficient representation for this problem by explicitly modeling spatial-temporal relations among skeleton joints. However, existing skeleton-based spatial-temporal models tend to deteriorate the positional distinguishability of joints, which leads to fuzzy spatial matching and poor explainability. To address these issues, we propose a novel spatial matching strategy consisting of spatial disentanglement and spatial activation. The motivation behind spatial disentanglement is that we find more spatial information for leaf nodes (e.g., the "hand" joint) is beneficial to increase representation diversity for skeleton matching. To achieve spatial disentanglement, we encourage the skeletons to be represented in a full rank space with rank maximization constraint. Finally, an attention based spatial activation mechanism is introduced to incorporate the disentanglement, by adaptively adjusting the disentangled joints according to matching pairs. Extensive experiments on three skeleton benchmarks demonstrate that the proposed spatial matching strategy can be effectively inserted into existing temporal alignment frameworks, achieving considerable performance improvements as well as inherent explainability.

Keywords: Action recognition · Few-shot learning · Explainable AI

H. Zhang—Equal Contribution With the First Author.

Supplementary Information The online version contains supplementary material available at https://doi.org/10.1007/978-3-031-19772-7_11.

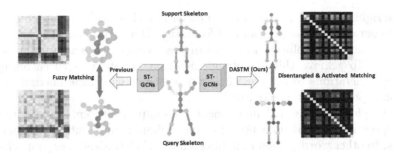

Fig. 1. The Illustration that demonstrates the fuzzy skeleton matching using degenerated spatial representation, and the disentangled skeleton matching by our spatial disentanglement and activation. The brighter grids in heatmaps denote larger similarity among intra-skeleton joints. The size of joints denotes their importance in matching.

1   Introduction

Action recognition has achieved tremendous success with developed deep learning models and abundant action recordings [21,39]. However, in many scenarios like healthcare, collecting and labeling enough medical action videos may spend several years with the efforts of multiple medical experts. To address this data scarcity, few-shot action recognition is proposed and attracts growing attentions [2,7,15,16,20,28].

Given a few labeled demonstrations of novel action classes, i.e., *support* actions, few-shot action recognition usually aims to predict the unlabeled actions, i.e., *query* actions. Existing works can be divided into video-based [2,16,28,29] and skeleton-based methods [15,25,33]. In the video-based methods, the high dimensional redundancy information such as luminance and background is usually unreliable under few-shot scenarios. In contrast, skeleton sequences provide *explainable* and *data-efficient* action representation by explicitly modeling the spatial-temporal relation of body joints. Existing methods usually perform Spatial-Temporal Graph Convolution (ST-GCN, [42]) to capture the spatial-temporal relations among skeletons. However, the over-smoothing of graph convolution tends to make the nodes representations indistinguishable, resulting in the partial loss of joints' positional information after ST-GCN. The left part of Fig. 1 illustrates the over-smoothed similarity heatmaps of intra-skeleton joints and the fuzzy spatial matching caused by the degenerated spatial representation. This fuzzy spatial matching further leads to fragile spatial-temporal matching between the query and the support skeletons in few-shot action recognition.

To address the distinguishability caused by over-smoothing, typical graph learning methods try to drop graph edges (DropEdge, [32]) or push away non-adjacent nodes (PairNorm [45]). However, in small size skeleton graphs, these methods may destroy the skeleton structure, or smoothing joints' representations as long as they are adjacent, e.g., PairNorm is prone to produce distinguishable representations between elbow joints and hand joints. Instead, the disentangled joint representations naturally produce distinguishability for spatial matching (see the right of Fig. 1). For example, the skeleton's leaf nodes (joints) like "hand" usually contain essential positional information. Hence disentangling these joints from the spatial convolution process can preserve spatial structure for skeleton matching. To achieve this disentanglement, one strategy is to encourage the joint representations to have less linear dependence with rank maximization on skeleton representation matrices.

Although this disentanglement encourages important joints to have independent representations, it does not filter out unimportant joints in the matching process. In other words, when matching a query skeleton and a support skeleton, the query skeleton should know whether one joint is significant for the support one and vice versa. Motivated by this, we design two independent cross-attention modules for query and support pairs to adaptively activate their spatial information.

Finally, this spatial matching strategy can be orthometric with popular temporal matching methods like Dynamic Time Warping (DTW, [34]), which determines the optimal temporal matching strategy for two skeleton sequences. By seamlessly inserting the proposed spatial matching into temporal matching, we propose a holistic spatial-temporal measurement for skeleton sequences. Our ablation experiments on NTU RGB+D 120 [22] and Kinetics [17] demonstrate its effectiveness on few-shot action classification tasks. Our method can be summarized as **D**isentangled and **A**daptive **S**patial-**T**emporal **M**atching (**DASTM**) for few-shot action recognition. The contributions are enumerated as follows:

- We systematically investigate skeleton-based few-shot action recognition and find the degeneration of spatial information existing in mainstream methods under data scarcity scenarios.
- To alleviate the degenerated spatial representations, we propose a novel spatial matching strategy through adaptively disentangling and activating the representations of skeleton joints.
- Extensive few-shot experiments on public action datasets demonstrate the effectiveness of our holistic spatial-temporal matching.
- Our heatmap visualizations demonstrate which joints are vital in recognition tasks, providing explainable predictions for trustworthy action recognition.

2   Related Work

2.1   Few-Shot Action Recognition

Few-shot action recognition aims to recognize novel action classes given a few labeled action examples. Due to practical significance, this recognition paradigm recently attracts enormous attentions [2,4,5,7,14,16,19,20,26,28–30,38,40,41, 43,44,46,47].

[15] demonstrates that low dimensional skeleton data may be better for capturing spatial-temporal information. For skeleton-based representation, [33] uses a temporal convolutional network [1] and computes the cosine distance between

the query and support actions. [25] construct positive and negative pairs to learn the appropriate distance of different action classes.

2.2 Graph Representation and Matching

A human skeleton can be naturally represented as a graph whose joints and bones are denoted by vertexes and edges respectively. Based on graph representation, ST-GCN [42] and its variants [8,23,35] perform graph and temporal convolution to capture the spatial and temporal features. Although the ST-GCNs have been mainstream backbones for skeleton-based action classification, it is still challenging to match the action representations after these backbones. For example, the joints' positional information may be lost or inaccurate due to over-smoothed graph convolution in ST-GCNs. This over-smoothing is an intrinsic characteristic brought by message passing mechanism [45] and is further magnified without abundant training data.

2.3 Temporal Alignment

The start time and motion speed of two actions are usually mismatched in spite of the same action labels. This temporal mismatch has drawn elastic temporal alignment methods such as Dynamic Time Warping (DTW, [10,34]). DTW calculates an optimal match between two given sequences using dynamic programming. Recently, DTW and its variants have been used to boost the alignment of temporal features in low-shot setting [5,44].

3   Preliminary

Skeleton-Based Actions. A frame of skeleton graph can be defined as $G = \{\mathbf{X}, \mathbf{A}\}$, where $\mathbf{X} \in \mathbb{R}^{n \times 3}$ is the feature matrix, $\mathbf{A} \in \mathbb{R}^{n \times n}$ is the adjacent matrix, n and 3 is the number of node (joints) and node dimension respectively. From the above definition, a skeleton-based action sequence is $\mathcal{G} = \{G_1, G_2, \cdots, G_M\}$, where M is number of the input frames.

Few-shot action recognition aims to adapt a model into novel classes and classify the unlabeled actions, i.e., *query* actions, given a few labeled actions, i.e., the *support* actions. There usually are three parts including training set $\mathcal{T}_{train}$, validation set $\mathcal{T}_{val}$, and test set $\mathcal{T}_{test}$, in which the action classes of the three parts do not overlap. In a training task, given N classes with K labeled support actions per class, the prototypical representation [36] of each class is $C_k = \frac{1}{K} \sum_{(\mathcal{G}_i^s, y_i^s)} f_\phi(\mathcal{G}_i^s) \times \mathbb{I}(y_i^s = k)$, where $\mathcal{G}_i^s$ is the support action, $\mathbb{I}$ is Indicator function. Let d denote the node's latent dimension, $f_\phi(\cdot) : \mathbb{R}^{M \times n \times 3} \to \mathbb{R}^{m \times n \times d}$ can be viewed as an action encoder with parameters ϕ. The prediction of a query action $\mathcal{G}^q$ can be formed into the following prototype method:

$$p_\phi(y = k \mid \mathcal{G}^q) = \frac{\exp\left(-dis\left(f_\phi(\mathcal{G}^q), C_k\right)\right)}{\sum_{k'} \exp\left(-dis\left(f_\phi(\mathcal{G}^q), C_{k'}\right)\right)}, \tag{1}$$

where $dis(x, y)$ is the distance of two action sequences. Compared with meta-learning methods like MAML [13], the prototype methods do not need large memory overhead to memorize multiple gradient steps, hence making it possible to incorporate larger backbones like ST-GCNs.

4   Proposed Framework

In essence, designing a distance measurement for query skeleton sequences and support skeleton sequences is the key to predict the query's categories. However, the mainstream methods like Spatial-Temporal Convolution (typically used in ST-GCN [42] and its extensions [23,35,42]) focus on learning integrated spatial-temporal representation, without considering the relation of different actions sequences. In our few-shot setting, directly measuring the integrated spatial-temporal representations are suboptimal with the following issues: 1) the degeneration of spatial representation; 2) the misalignment of temporal sequences. In the next part, we will discuss how the two issues arise and propose a holistic solution with spatial matching as well as temporal alignment.

4.1   Spatial Disentanglement and Activation

Learning Disentangled Skeleton Representation. Existing ST-GCNs get satisfying performance in capturing discriminative spatial-temporal features. However, their graph convolution operators often repeat message passing among skeleton nodes, which eventually leads to indistinguishable node embeddings. The phenomenon is also known as the over-smoothing problem, which does not seriously impact action classification once given abundant training data [45]. However, lacking sufficient data in few-shot learning, this over-smoothing is magnified, leading to the degeneration of nodes' positional representation. For example, the "elbow" node of a skeleton graph may get more spatial information of the "hand" node. If we measure the distance of two skeleton graphs, the degenerated spatial representation will result in noisy distances.

To alleviate the over-smoothing of graph convolution, some methods were proposed via directly dropping edges (DropEdge, [24,32]) or centering and rescaling node representations (PairNorm [45]). However, these methods are suboptimal for the particular skeleton structure. For example, the node "left hand" is relatively near the "left elbow" on a graph, hence is easier to have similar representations via DropEdge or PairNorm. We argue that smoothing the representation of "hands" may lose key action features. Besides that, the forced dropping edges will destroy the integrity or the symmetry of skeleton graphs. Instead, our strategy is disentangling the skeleton representations to keep the key spatial features like "hand" by reducing the dependence among skeleton nodes. In the field of matrix analysis, the rank of a matrix is a permutation invariant diversity measure indicating the maximum number of linearly independent vectors in a matrix. Given a skeleton graph representations matrix $\mathbf{H}_{bi} \in \mathbb{R}^{n \times d}$, where b denotes the b-th sequence in a batch, i denotes the i-th skeleton graph

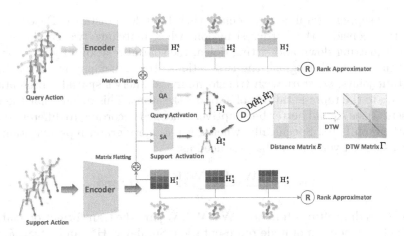

Fig. 2. The Illustration that describes 1-shot action recognition with our framework. $\mathbf{H}^q$ and $\mathbf{H}^s$ are the outputs of *identical* spatial-temporal encoder like ST-GCN [42]. The parameterized modules QA and SA denote query activation and support activation respectively. For clarity, we only demonstrate the matching process of the first skeleton representations, i.e., $\mathbf{H}_1^q$ and $\mathbf{H}_1^s$.

in the sequence, n is the number of node and d is the node's latent dimension, we can maximize its rank to reduce the dependencies among skeletons joints. Directly maximizing the rank of $\mathbf{H}_{bi}$ is a NP-hard problem [31]. A common solution is to use nuclear-norm $||\mathbf{H}_{bi}||_*$ as a surrogate for $rank(\mathbf{H}_{bi})$ [9,31]:

$$||\mathbf{H}_{bi}||_* = (\sum_{j}^{\min(n,d)} \sigma_i^j) < rank(\mathbf{H}_{bi}), \tag{2}$$

where σ_i^j is the j-th singular value of matrix $\mathbf{H}_{bi}$ and can be calculated through Singular Value Decomposition (SVD) [3]. Pytorch[1] has released a differential SVD tool for for convenient implementation. The constraint can be applied to a batch of skeleton sequences, forming the spatial disentanglement objective:

$$\mathcal{L}_{dis} = -\frac{1}{B*m} \sum_b^B \sum_i^m ||\mathbf{H}_{bi}||_*, \tag{3}$$

where B is the number of action sequences in a batch, m is the length of a sequence after temporal convolution.

Learning Spatial Activation. Recovering the spatial representations grounds the spatial matching between the query graph representation $\mathbf{H}^q \in \mathbb{R}^{n \times d}$ and the support graph representation $\mathbf{H}^s \in \mathbb{R}^{n \times d}$. A direct solution to match the query

---

[1] https://pytorch.org/.

graph and support graph is to calculate their Euclidean distance. Based on this, we further consider the harder situation: when matching two similar actions such as squatting down and sitting down, the spatial relation of joints plays an important role to distinguish the two actions. To further pay attention to the important joints, we start with transforming the query's spatial representation according to the representations of support skeletons. This means that the node representations should better be adaptively changed according to different query-support graph pairs. Specifically, when given a query graph representation $\mathbf{H^q}$, the transformed version can be produced as:

$$\hat{\mathbf{H}}^q = \mathrm{S}\left(\frac{\mathbf{W}_1^q\mathbf{H}^q \cdot [\mathbf{W}_2^q\mathbf{H}^s]^T}{\sqrt{d}}\right)\mathbf{W}_3^q\mathbf{H}^q, \tag{4}$$

where $\mathrm{S}(\cdot)$ is the Softmax function, $\mathbf{W}_1^q, \mathbf{W}_2^q, \mathbf{W}_3^q$ are the transformation matrices and d is the dimension of node representation. Similarly, $\mathbf{H^s}$ can be transformed as:

$$\hat{\mathbf{H}}^s = \mathrm{S}\left(\frac{\mathbf{W}_1^s\mathbf{H}^s \cdot [\mathbf{W}_2^s\mathbf{H}^q]^T}{\sqrt{d}}\right)\mathbf{W}_3^s\mathbf{H}^s, \tag{5}$$

then the distance of two graphs can be defined as:

$$D(\hat{\mathbf{H}}^q, \hat{\mathbf{H}}^s) = ||\hat{\mathbf{H}}^q - \hat{\mathbf{H}}^s||_F, \tag{6}$$

where $||\cdot||_F$ is the Frobenius norm. The cross-attention form Eq. (4) and Eq. (5) is inspired by the Transformer [37], but learns different inductive bias compared with popular cross-attention methods. Previous cross-attentions usually focus on one of the two parties involved in the measurement process, e.g., only learning the inductive bias for support prototype instead of query examples [11]. We suppose that the $\mathbf{H}^s$ and $\mathbf{H}^q$ have different activation patterns because of asymmetrical calculation in measurement, e.g., the $\mathbf{H}^s$ in Eq. (5) is usually a weighted average representation corresponding to $\mathbf{H}^q$. Hence learning the inductive bias each side with Eq. (4) and Eq. (5) may stimulate different activation patterns.

4.2 Temporal Matching

Given a transformed query sequence $Q = \{\hat{\mathbf{H}}_1^q, \hat{\mathbf{H}}_2^q, \cdots \hat{\mathbf{H}}_m^q\}$ and a support sequence $C_k = \{\hat{\mathbf{H}}_1^s, \hat{\mathbf{H}}_2^s, \cdots \hat{\mathbf{H}}_m^s\}$, there may be the misalignment that $\hat{\mathbf{H}}_i^q$ does not corresponding to $\hat{\mathbf{H}}_i^s$. Therefore, directly calculating the sequence distance with the sum of graph pairs $D(\hat{\mathbf{H}}_i^q, \hat{\mathbf{H}}_i^s)$ will impact the distance measurement between two action sequences. To tackle this misalignment, we introduce Dynamic Time Warping (DTW, [34]), which is a popular temporal alignment method with multiple variants [12,27]. Concretely, for a query-support pair, we can get a distance matrix $E \in \mathbb{R}^{m \times m}$, where each element E_{ij} is calculated with $D(\hat{\mathbf{H}}_i^q, \hat{\mathbf{H}}_j^s)$. Supposing the cumulative distance from a query frame i to a support frame j can be calculated with the following dynamic programming form:

$$\Gamma(i, j) = E(i, j) + \min\{\Gamma(i - 1, j - 1), \Gamma(i - 1, j), \Gamma(i, j - 1)\}, \tag{7}$$

Algorithm 1. Training Algorithm for Few-Shot Action Recognition

---

Input: The training data $\mathcal{T}_{train}$
Parameter: Model parameters θ, including action encoder parameters ϕ, spatial transformation parameters sets $\{\mathbf{W}\} = \mathbf{W}_1^q, \mathbf{W}_2^q, \mathbf{W}_3^q, \mathbf{W}_1^s, \mathbf{W}_2^s, \mathbf{W}_3^s$.
Output: The learned θ and $\{\mathbf{W}\}$.

1: **while** not convergence **do**
2:    **for** $step = 0 \to T$ **do**
3:       Sample a N-way-K-shot classification task with query actions $\{\mathcal{G}_i^q, Y_i^q\}_{i=1}^{N^q}$ and support actions $\{\mathcal{G}_i^s, Y_i^s\}_{i=1}^{N^s}$
4:       Compute all support action prototypes $\{C_k\}_{k=1}^{N}$ using $\{\mathcal{G}_i^s, Y_i^s\}_{i=1}^{N^s}$, where $C_k = \{\mathbf{H}_1^s, \mathbf{H}_2^s, \cdots \mathbf{H}_m^s\}$
5:       Compute all query action representations $\{Q_i\}_{i=1}^{N^q}$, $Q_i = \{\mathbf{H}_1^q, \mathbf{H}_2^q, \cdots, \mathbf{H}_m^q\}$
6:       for each Q_i, compute its distance with each support sequence C_k by Algorithm 2
7:       Compute the labels for all query actions with Eq. (1)
8:       For all query actions, compute $\mathcal{L}_{dis}$ with Eq. (3)
9:       Compute $\mathcal{L}_{match}$ via Eq. (8)
10:      Update θ and $\{\mathbf{W}\}$ by $\mathcal{L}_{match}$.
11:    **end for**
12: **end while**

---

hence we can utilize $d(Q, C_k) = \Gamma(m, m)$ as the sequence distance. To get a differentiable distance, the minimization function $min(\cdot, \cdot)$ can be replaced with a differentiable version [27].

4.3 The Learning Objective

According to Eq. (1) and Eq. (3), the overall learning objective can be derived:

$$\mathcal{L}_{match} = -\frac{1}{N^q} \sum_i^{N^q} \log p_\phi(\hat{y}_i = y_i \mid \mathcal{G}_i^q) + \lambda \mathcal{L}_{dis}, \tag{8}$$

where N^q is the number of query actions, $\hat{y}_i$ and y_i is the predicted label and ground truth label for $\mathcal{G}_i^q$, λ denotes the weight of $\mathcal{L}_{dis}$. Algorithm 1 and Algorithm 2 demonstrate the overall training process of our algorithm. Figure 2 illustrates the graphical framework.

5 Experiments

In this section, we will evaluate our approach and baselines on two public large scale datasets, trying to answer the following questions: (1) What's the performance of primitive baselines like using ST-GCN [42]+ProtoNet [36] without any spatial-temporal alignment? (2) Is our rank maximization strategy working better than typical methods that tackle the over-smoothness of ST-GCNs? (3) How does the activation strategy work for each part of the skeletons?

Algorithm 2. Matching Algorithm for Skeleton Sequences

Input: A query action representation $Q = \{\mathbf{H}_1^q, \mathbf{H}_2^q, \cdots, \mathbf{H}_m^q\}$, and a support prototype $C_k = \{\mathbf{H}_1^s, \mathbf{H}_2^s, \cdots \mathbf{H}_m^s\}$
Parameter: Spatial transformation parameters $\mathbf{W}_1^q, \mathbf{W}_2^q, \mathbf{W}_3^q, \mathbf{W}_1^s, \mathbf{W}_2^s, \mathbf{W}_3^s$
Output: $\Gamma(m, m)$, the distance between Q and C_k

1: Initialize distance matrix $E \in \mathbb{R}^{m \times m}$
2: **for** $i = 0 \to m$ **do**
3:     **for** $j = 0 \to m$ **do**
4:         Compute $\hat{\mathbf{H}}_i^q$ with $\mathbf{H}_i^q$ and $\mathbf{H}_j^s$ using Eq. (4)
5:         Compute $\hat{\mathbf{H}}_j^s$ with $\mathbf{H}_j^s$ and $\mathbf{H}_i^q$ using Eq. (5)
6:         $E_{ij} = D(\hat{\mathbf{H}}_i^q, \hat{\mathbf{H}}_j^s)$ with Eq. (6)
7:     **end for**
8: **end for**
9: Compute accumulation distance matrix Γ with E using Eq. (7)

5.1   Datasets

We firstly introduce the used datasets including NTU RGB+D 120 [22] and Kinetics [17].

NTU RGB+D 120 [22] is a large-scale dataset with 3D joints annotations for human action recognition tasks, containing 113,945 skeleton sequences with 25 body joints for each skeleton. In our experiments, we use 120 action categories, including 80, 20 and 20 categories as training, validation and test categories. For each category, we randomly take 60 samples and 30 samples, denoted as two subsets "**NTU-S**" and "**NTU-T**", respectively. Please see our Appendix A for more details.

Kinetics skeleton dataset [17] is sourced from YouTube videos. The dataset contains 260,232 videos over 400 classes, where each skeleton graph has 18 body joints after pose estimation, along with their 2D spatial coordinates and the prediction confidence score from OpenPose [6] as the initial joint features. In our experiments, we only use the first 120 actions with 100 samples per class. The number of training/validation/test partitions is identical to NTU RGB+D 120 (please see our Appendix A for more detailed separation).

5.2   Baselines

The baselines includes the following categories for few-shot action recognition: **ProtoNet** [36]; temporal alignment **DTW** [34]; the methods for spatial recover, such as **PairNorm** [45] and **DropEdge** [32]; spatial alignment or graph metric learning like **NGM** [15]. Note that all the above methods use ProtoNet as classifier head for few-shot action recognition. Besides that, the baselines PairNorm, DropEdge and NGM are combined with temporal alignment DTW.

ProtoNet [36] treats the representation of action sequences as vectors and computes the Euclidean similarity of the vectors without any spatial matching and temporal alignment.

DTW calculates an optimal match between two sequences using dynamic programming, and is a popular temporal alignment method adopted by previous video-based few-shot action recognition.

PairNorm [45] aims to tackle over-smoothing in graph neural networks (GNNs). By centering and rescaling node's representations, PairNorm uses a normalization after graph convolution layer to prevent all node embeddings from becoming too similar.

DropEdge [32] randomly drops a few edges in input graphs to make nodes aggregation diverse from their neighbors. Both PairNorm and DropEdge are designed to alleviate the over-smoothing problem in large noisy graphs. To the best of our knowledge, the two strategies are the first to be applied to skeleton graphs.

NGM [15] jointly learns a graph generator and a graph matching metric function in an end-to-end fashion to optimize the few-shot learning objective.

DASTM* and **DASTM**** denote our ablation models with Rank Maximization and Spatial Activation, respectively.

5.3 Implementation Details

Data Preparation. We randomly sample N classes with each class containing K actions as the support set. Correspondingly, we have N categories including K actions of query set, where the query set has the same classes as the support set. Thus each episode has a total of $N \times (K + K)$ examples as a training or test batch. For each skeleton sequence, we pre-process the skeleton sequences following pre-processing video procedure as TSN [39]. For different datasets, we uniformly sample 50 and 30 frames per skeleton sequence in Kinetics and NTU-T/S. This uniform sampling provides identical sequence lengths for the support and query actions.

Spatial-Temporal Backbones. To encode the action skeleton sequence, we adopt typical **ST-GCN** [42], **2s-AGCN** [35] and **MS-G3D** [23] as the backbones. ST-GCN proposes spatial-temporal graph convolution on skeleton sequences. 2s-AGCN uses joints and bones information to learn data-dependent graph structure. MS-G3D proposes multi-scale aggregation scheme to disentangle the importance of nodes in different neighborhoods and cross-spacetime edges to capture high-level node interaction. Appendix C provides smaller backbones and corresponding performances.

Model Training and Evaluation. All models are trained with Adam [18] optimizer, using an initial learning rate 0.001. The weight λ of $\mathcal{L}_{dis}$ is set with 0.1 according to the validation sets for all experiments. With randomly sampling 1,000 episodes in training and 500 episodes in test, each experiment is repeated **3** times to calculate mean accuracy with standard deviation. Furthermore, all experiments are constructed using Pytorch and performed on Ubuntu 18.04 with one GeForce RTX 3090 GPU. The training codes can be found here[2]. Each training task may need about 10 h.

---

[2] https://github.com/NingMa-AI/DASTM.

5.4   Results

As shown in Table 1 and Table 2, we compare our method with mentioned baselines using 3 datasets and 3 backbones. 5-way-k-shot denotes performing 5-way classification using k labeled support example per class.

Strong Baselines Are Constructed for Skeleton-Based Few-Shot Action Recognition. With the spatial-temporal convolution, only using ProtoNet classifier can produce 71.2% 1-shot classification accuracy on NTU-T (see ProtoNet baseline in Table 1), even though this dataset only contains 30 action examples per class. This performance demonstrates the potential of simply spatial-temporal convolution for skeleton-based few-shot action recognition.

Generalized Methods Coping Over-Smoothing May Harm the Few-Shot Task. We perform two comparison experiments containing DropEdge and PairNorm (denoted with DropEdge and PairNorm in Table 1 and Table 2). For DropEdge, we find only randomly dropping 4 edges already destroys the small skeleton graphs and harms the improvement brought by DTW. In contrast, PairNorm makes the adjacent nodes have similar representations with pushing away the non-adjacent nodes. However, making the adjacent nodes have similar representations may smooth the key joints' features such as "hands" and "elbows", which harms the matching process (see PairNorm and DTW in Table 1). The heatmaps in Fig. 3 also illustrate the joints' smoothness with PairNorm and DropEdge. An extreme case happens on Kinetics dataset, on

Table 1. The 5-way-1-shot action classification accuracies (%).

Backbones	ST-GCN			2s-AGCN			MS-G3D		
Methods	NTU-T	NTU-S	Kinetics	NTU-T	NTU-S	Kinetics	NTU-T	NTU-S	Kinetics
ProtoNet	71.2 ± 1.5	73.3 ± 0.3	37.4 ± 0.4	68.1 ± 0.5	72.8 ± 0.3	38.4 ± 0.2	70.1 ± 1.0	73.6 ± 0.2	39.5 ± 0.3
DTW	74.0 ± 2.1	73.5 ± 0.4	39.2 ± 0.2	70.8 ± 1.4	71.5 ± 1.2	40.9 ± 0.4	72.4 ± 0.2	73.9 ± 0.4	40.6 ± 0.2
NGM	71.8 ± 1.2	75.7 ± 0.4	39.1 ± 0.3	72.2 ± 1.0	73.2 ± 0.6	40.9 ± 0.2	73.5 ± 0.3	**76.9** ± 0.4	40.8 ± 0.3
PairNorm	72.9 ± 0.5	72.8 ± 0.4	39.3 ± 0.7	70.0 ± 0.5	70.8 ± 0.3	40.9 ± 0.3	71.0 ± 0.8	70.8 ± 0.9	40.7 ± 0.7
DropEdge	67.3 ± 1.9	70.7 ± 0.7	38.9 ± 0.9	70.1 ± 0.4	72.6 ± 0.2	39.9 ± 0.3	68.7 ± 0.4	69.5 ± 0.7	39.4 ± 0.3
DASTM*	74.5 ± 1.9	73.4 ± 0.6	39.5 ± 0.9	72.4 ± 0.9	72.9 ± 0.5	40.9 ± 0.4	72.7 ± 0.6	74.4 ± 1.6	40.7 ± 0.2
DASTM**	74.4 ± 2.9	75.9 ± 0.3	**39.8** ± 0.1	72.9 ± 1.5	**74.6** ± 0.3	**41.0** ± 0.1	74.1 ± 0.3	75.5 ± 1.7	41.0 ± 0.1
DASTM	**75.1** ± 1.8	**76.2** ± 0.3	39.3 ± 0.1	**73.3** ± 0.6	74.0 ± 0.7	40.8 ± 0.3	**75.0** ± 0.9	76.3 ± 1.2	**41.1** ± 0.2

Table 2. The 5-way-5-shot action classification accuracies (%).

Backbones	ST-GCN			2s-AGCN			MS-G3D		
Methods	NTU-T	NTU-S	Kinetics	NTU-T	NTU-S	Kinetics	NTU-T	NTU-S	Kinetics
ProtoNet	81.1 ± 0.2	84.3 ± 0.3	46.8 ± 0.4	81.9 ± 0.1	84.2 ± 0.1	50.5 ± 0.2	82.3 ± 0.2	85.3 ± 0.1	50.0 ± 0.3
DTW	81.0 ± 0.6	81.5 ± 0.5	47.9 ± 0.3	81.2 ± 0.9	82.5 ± 0.8	50.8 ± 0.3	81.3 ± 0.3	83.2 ± 0.4	50.0 ± 0.2
NGM	81.4 ± 0.5	84.2 ± 0.4	48.6 ± 0.4	83.2 ± 0.3	85.9 ± 0.4	49.8 ± 0.3	83.1 ± 0.4	86.7 ± 0.2	50.7 ± 0.3
PairNorm	81.8 ± 0.4	81.4 ± 0.3	48.6 ± 0.5	80.0 ± 0.3	80.3 ± 0.2	50.4 ± 0.4	81.6 ± 0.7	82.5 ± 0.9	50.6 ± 0.1
DropEdge	77.9 ± 1.5	78.6 ± 0.7	48.2 ± 0.2	80.5 ± 0.3	83.1 ± 0.6	50.2 ± 0.3	80.9 ± 0.4	80.2 ± 0.6	50.1 ± 0.2
DASTM*	81.8 ± 0.6	82.4 ± 0.5	48.8 ± 0.2	81.8 ± 0.3	83.6 ± 0.6	51.0 ± 0.1	81.9 ± 0.1	84.1 ± 0.6	**51.3** ± 0.2
DASTM**	82.9 ± 0.8	85.3 ± 0.7	**49.2** ± 1.0	83.5 ± 0.4	86.3 ± 0.7	**51.3** ± 0.6	84.2 ± 0.5	86.4 ± 1.6	51.1 ± 0.5
DASTM	**83.0** ± 0.1	**85.5** ± 0.3	48.9 ± 0.1	**83.8** ± 0.8	**86.8** ± 0.3	50.9 ± 0.2	**84.9** ± 0.3	**87.3** ± 1.2	51.1 ± 0.9

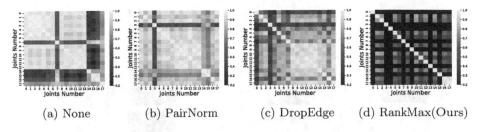

(a) None   (b) PairNorm   (c) DropEdge   (d) RankMax(Ours)

Fig. 3. The intra-skeleton joints similarity heatmaps according to different spatial pre-serving strategies (see more visualizations in our Appendix D). All the skeletons are sampled from Kinetics dataset with 18 joints per skeleton. (a). None, no spatial pre-serving strategy is used. Almost all the upper limb joints (number 0–6) and lower limb joints (number 8–13) are distinguishable. (b). PairNorm method produces similar representations for the upper limb joints (number 5–7) and lower limb joints (8–13), due to its centering and rescaling operations. (c). DropEdge, randomly dropping edges of skeleton graphs can not alleviate the smoothness representations such as lower limb joints (number 8–13). (d). Our RankMax method, the representative joints such as hands (number 4 and 7) and feet (number 13) are disentangled from other joints, providing more specific spatial features for skeleton matching.

which nearly all methods (including ours) do not get significant improvements compared with DTW. One of the reasons might be the large data noise in Kinetics, in which a large proportion of actions even can not be efficiently distinguished via skeletons. Given noisy skeleton distance, the optimal alignment path for DTW is fragile and the improvements for DTW are overwhelmed by this noise. Our method still successfully obtain gains for DTW, while there are no performance improvements or even drops over DTW by PairNorm, Dropedge on Kinetics.

Comparison with Existing Skeleton-Based Few-Shot Methods. NGM proposes the first skeleton-based few-shot recognition method with graph matching. We tried to implement an enhanced version with deeper edge-weight learning layers in ST-GCNs, adding time alignment via DTW and learning a more powerful graph tensor with Transformer's self-attention. Although these additional technics result in a strong baseline, we find that our mutual-activation between query and support skeletons still works better than the self-activation in NGM.

5.5   Ablation Studies

In this section, we demonstrate how each component contributes to the overall performances.

Analysis of Spatial Disentanglement. In our framework, the disentanglement of spatial information is achieved by maximizing the rank of skeleton representation matrix. Compared with temporal alignment baseline DTW, this disentanglement strategy achieves up to 1.4% improvements on NTU-T with 2s-AGCN (see Table 1). The reason behind is that our rank maximizing strategy

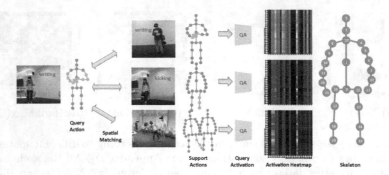

Fig. 4. The spatial activation illustration containing query-support pairs and corresponding inter-skeleton activation heatmaps on NTU-T dataset (best view in color). Each pair represents a matching process between a query action and a support action, and each heatmap is derived from the output of the Softmax function in Eq. (4). (Color figure online)

encourages skeleton joints to have independent representation, which provides more spatial information for skeleton matching. For example, in Fig. 3d, the hand joints (number 4, 7) and foot joints (number 13) are the disentangled key parts to describe one action. This result also demonstrates that the spatial information was not fully considered in previous skeleton-based few-shot action recognition.

The Explainability of Spatial Activation. To identify the intra-class and inter-class spatial activation patterns, we collect the outputs of the Softmax function in Eq. (4) and visualize them with heatmap (see Fig. 4). In the first matching pair "writing"-"writing", the query's upper limb joints (number 2–6 and 8–11) are activated. In the pair "writing"- "kicking", we can observe that the query's activation has much lower responses, which indicates the query action and support action may belong to different classes. We hope the explainability will bring more interesting works in future action recognition tasks.

Analysis of Temporal Alignment. To demonstrate the improvement of our spatial matching strategy, we also perform ablation studies on temporal alignment (see DTW in Table 1). Based on DTW, our spatial matching strategy gets up to 3.5% improvement on 1-shot tasks. However, for 5-shot tasks (see DTW in Table 2), DTW may be suboptimal compared with ProtoNet due to its sensibility to skeleton noise, which may bring suboptimal matching path in DTW. Tackling the fragility of DTW falls slightly out of the scope of this study. One of our future works is to enhance the robustness for DTW's path selection.

5.6   Hyper-Parameter Analyses

The degree of spatial disentanglement, PairNorm Scale and Drop Rate are three key hyper-parameters in our framework, PairNorm and Dropedge, respectively. Figure 5a illustrates the accuracy changing with different weight λ using DASTM* consisting of temporal alignment DTW and Rank Maximization. When $\lambda = 0.01$ is small, the model gets much lower performance due to limited spatial disentanglement. When λ is close to 1, the compulsive disentanglement of all joints damages the original spatial relation. This failed situation also verifies our claim in the previous section: only a part of joints that maintain critical positional information need to be disentangled to help skeleton matching. In practice, we find disentangling a few joints is more helpful for skeleton matching, e.g., about 7 joints are disentangled in Fig. 3d. We suggest using a small λ like 0.1 or 0.05 to encourage the model to adaptively select a part critical joints. Besides that, Fig. 5b and Fig. 5c demonstrate two baselines' hyper-parameter sensibility (please see the Appendix B for more details).

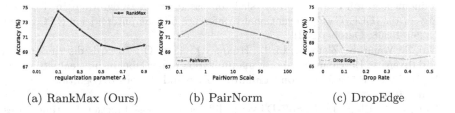

(a) RankMax (Ours)   (b) PairNorm   (c) DropEdge

Fig. 5. The hyper-parameter sensibility for RankMax(ours), PairNorm and DropEdge, respectively. All tasks are 5-way-1-shot on NTU-T using ST-GCN.

6   Conclusion and Future Works

We propose a novel skeleton representation and matching solution for few-shot action recognition. The proposed method tries to capture key joints from the disentanglement view, hence bring more explainability for concrete few-shot action recognition tasks. Compared with the well studied video-based solutions, it is the first time exploring skeleton-based few-shot action recognition with the powerful representation ability of modern ST-GCNs. We hope more skeleton-based few-shot works can be explored in the future.

Acknowledgement. This work is supported by the National Key Research and Development Program (Grant No. 2019YFF0302601), National Natural Science Foundation of China (Grant No: 61972349, 62106221) and Multi-Center Clinical Research Project in National Center (No. S20A0002).

References

1. Bai, S., Kolter, J.Z., Koltun, V.: An empirical evaluation of generic convolutional and recurrent networks for sequence modeling. arXiv:1803.01271 (2018)
2. Ben-Ari, R., Nacson, M.S., Azulai, O., Barzelay, U., Rotman, D.: TAEN: temporal aware embedding network for few-shot action recognition. In: Proceedings of the IEEE/CVF Conference on Computer Vision and Pattern Recognition (CVPR) Workshops, pp. 2786–2794, June 2021

3. Bhatia, R.: Matrix analysis (2013)
4. Cao, C., Li, Y., Lv, Q., Wang, P., Zhang, Y.: Few-shot action recognition with implicit temporal alignment and pair similarity optimization (2020)
5. Cao, K., Ji, J., Cao, Z., Chang, C.Y., Niebles, J.C.: Few-shot video classification via temporal alignment. In: 2020 IEEE/CVF Conference on Computer Vision and Pattern Recognition (CVPR), pp. 10615–10624 (2020). https://doi.org/10.1109/CVPR42600.2020.01063
6. Cao, Z., Hidalgo, G., Simon, T., Wei, S.E., Sheikh, Y.: OpenPose: realtime multi-person 2D pose estimation using part affinity fields. IEEE Trans. Pattern Anal. Mach. Intell. **43**(1), 172–186 (2019)
7. Careaga, C., Hutchinson, B., Hodas, N., Phillips, L.: Metric-based few-shot learning for video action recognition (2019)
8. Chen, Y., Zhang, Z., Yuan, C., Li, B., Deng, Y., Hu, W.: Channel-wise topology refinement graph convolution for skeleton-based action recognition. In: Proceedings of the IEEE/CVF International Conference on Computer Vision (ICCV), pp. 13359–13368, October 2021
9. Cui, S., Wang, S., Zhuo, J., Li, L., Huang, Q., Tian, Q.: Towards discriminability and diversity: Batch nuclear-norm maximization under label insufficient situations. In: IEEE/CVF Conference on Computer Vision and Pattern Recognition (CVPR), June 2020
10. Cuturi, M., Blondel, M.: Soft-DTW: a differentiable loss function for time-series. In: Proceedings of the 34th International Conference on Machine Learning, ICML 2017, vol. 70, p. 894–903. JMLR.org (2017)
11. Doersch, C., Gupta, A., Zisserman, A.: CrossTransformers: spatially-aware few-shot transfer. In: Larochelle, H., Ranzato, M., Hadsell, R., Balcan, M.F., Lin, H. (eds.) Advances in Neural Information Processing Systems, vol. 33, pp. 21981–21993. Curran Associates, Inc. (2020). https://proceedings.neurips.cc/paper/2020/file/fa28c6cdf8dd6f41a657c3d7caa5c709-Paper.pdf
12. Dvornik, N., Hadji, I., Derpanis, K.G., Garg, A., Jepson, A.D.: Drop-DTW: aligning common signal between sequences while dropping outliers. In: NeurIPS (2021)
13. Finn, C., Abbeel, P., Levine, S.: Model-agnostic meta-learning for fast adaptation of deep networks. In: Precup, D., Teh, Y.W. (eds.) Proceedings of the 34th International Conference on Machine Learning. Proceedings of Machine Learning Research, vol. 70, pp. 1126–1135. PMLR, 06–11 August 2017. https://proceedings.mlr.press/v70/finn17a.html
14. Fu, Y., Zhang, L., Wang, J., Fu, Y., Jiang, Y.G.: Depth guided adaptive meta-fusion network for few-shot video recognition. In: Proceedings of the 28th ACM International Conference on Multimedia, pp. 1142–1151 (2020)
15. Guo, M., Chou, E., Huang, D.-A., Song, S., Yeung, S., Fei-Fei, L.: Neural graph matching networks for fewshot 3D action recognition. In: Ferrari, V., Hebert, M., Sminchisescu, C., Weiss, Y. (eds.) ECCV 2018. LNCS, vol. 11205, pp. 673–689. Springer, Cham (2018). https://doi.org/10.1007/978-3-030-01246-5_40
16. Hong, J., Fisher, M., Gharbi, M., Fatahalian, K.: Video pose distillation for few-shot, fine-grained sports action recognition. In: Proceedings of the IEEE/CVF International Conference on Computer Vision (ICCV), pp. 9254–9263, October 2021
17. Kay, W., et al.: The kinetics human action video dataset. arXiv preprint arXiv:1705.06950 (2017)

18. Kingma, D.P., Ba, J.: Adam: a method for stochastic optimization. In: Bengio, Y., LeCun, Y. (eds.) 3rd International Conference on Learning Representations, ICLR 2015, San Diego, CA, USA. Conference Track Proceedings, 7–9 May 2015. https://arxiv.org/abs/1412.6980

19. Konecny, J., Hagara, M.: One-shot-learning gesture recognition using HOG-HOF features. J. Mach. Learn. Res. **15**(72), 2513–2532 (2014). https://jmlr.org/papers/v15/konecny14a.html

20. Li, S., et al.: TA2N: two-stage action alignment network for few-shot action recognition (2021)

21. Lin, J., Gan, C., Wang, K., Han, S.: TSM: temporal shift module for efficient video understanding. In: 2019 IEEE/CVF International Conference on Computer Vision (ICCV), pp. 7082–7092 (2019)

22. Liu, J., et al.: NTU RGB+D 120: a large-scale benchmark for 3D human activity understanding. IEEE Trans. Pattern Anal. Mach. Intell. **42**(10), 2684–2701 (2020)

23. Liu, Z., Zhang, H., Chen, Z., Wang, Z., Ouyang, W.: Disentangling and unifying graph convolutions for skeleton-based action recognition. In: Proceedings of the IEEE/CVF Conference on Computer Vision and Pattern Recognition, pp. 143–152 (2020)

24. Luo, D., et al.: Learning to drop: Robust graph neural network via topological denoising. In: Proceedings of the 14th ACM International Conference on Web Search and Data Mining, WSDM 2021, pp. 779–787. Association for Computing Machinery, New York (2021). https://doi.org/10.1145/3437963.3441734

25. Memmesheimer, R., Häring, S., Theisen, N., Paulus, D.: Skeleton-DML: deep metric learning for skeleton-based one-shot action recognition. arXiv preprint arXiv:2012.13823 (2020)

26. Ni, X., Song, S., Tai, Y.W., Tang, C.K.: Semi-supervised few-shot atomic action recognition (2020)

27. Nielsen, F., Sun, K.: Guaranteed bounds on information-theoretic measures of univariate mixtures using piecewise Log-Sum-Exp inequalities. Entropy **18**(12) (2016). https://doi.org/10.3390/e18120442. https://www.mdpi.com/1099-4300/18/12/442

28. Patravali, J., Mittal, G., Yu, Y., Li, F., Chen, M.: Unsupervised few-shot action recognition via action-appearance aligned meta-adaptation. In: Proceedings of the IEEE/CVF International Conference on Computer Vision (ICCV), pp. 8484–8494, October 2021

29. Perrett, T., Masullo, A., Burghardt, T., Mirmehdi, M., Damen, D.: Temporal-relational CrossTransformers for few-shot action recognition. In: Proceedings of the IEEE/CVF Conference on Computer Vision and Pattern Recognition (CVPR), pp. 475–484, June 2021

30. Qi, M., Qin, J., Zhen, X., Huang, D., Yang, Y., Luo, J.: Few-shot ensemble learning for video classification with SlowFast memory networks. In: Proceedings of the 28th ACM International Conference on Multimedia, MM 2020, pp. 3007–3015. Association for Computing Machinery, New York (2020). https://doi.org/10.1145/3394171.3416269

31. Recht, B., Fazel, M., Parrilo, P.A.: Guaranteed minimum-rank solutions of linear matrix equations via nuclear norm minimization. SIAM Rev. **52**(3), 471–501 (2010). https://doi.org/10.1137/070697835

32. Rong, Y., Huang, W., Xu, T., Huang, J.: DropEdge: towards deep graph convolutional networks on node classification. In: International Conference on Learning Representations (2020). https://openreview.net/forum?id=Hkx1qkrKPr

33. Sabater, A., Santos, L., Santos-Victor, J., Bernardino, A., Montesano, L., Murillo, A.C.: One-shot action recognition in challenging therapy scenarios. In: Proceedings of the IEEE/CVF Conference on Computer Vision and Pattern Recognition (CVPR) Workshops, pp. 2777–2785, June 2021

34. Sakoe, H., Chiba, S.: Dynamic programming algorithm optimization for spoken word recognition. IEEE Trans. Acoust. Speech Signal Process. **26**(1), 43–49 (1978). https://doi.org/10.1109/TASSP.1978.1163055

35. Shi, L., Zhang, Y., Cheng, J., Lu, H.: Two-stream adaptive graph convolutional networks for skeleton-based action recognition. In: Proceedings of the IEEE/CVF Conference on Computer Vision and Pattern Recognition, pp. 12026–12035 (2019)

36. Snell, J., Swersky, K., Zemel, R.S.: Prototypical networks for few-shot learning. arXiv preprint arXiv:1703.05175 (2017)

37. Vaswani, A., et al.: Attention is all you need. In: Guyon, I., et al. (eds.) Advances in Neural Information Processing Systems, vol. 30. Curran Associates, Inc. (2017). https://proceedings.neurips.cc/paper/2017/file/3f5ee243547dee91fbd053c1c4a845aa-Paper.pdf

38. Wang, J., Wang, Y., Liu, S., Li, A.: Few-shot fine-grained action recognition via bidirectional attention and contrastive meta-learning. In: Proceedings of the 29th ACM International Conference on Multimedia, MM 2021, pp. 582–591. Association for Computing Machinery, New York (2021). https://doi.org/10.1145/3474085.3475216

39. Wang, L., et al.: Temporal segment networks: towards good practices for deep action recognition. In: Leibe, B., Matas, J., Sebe, N., Welling, M. (eds.) ECCV 2016. LNCS, vol. 9912, pp. 20–36. Springer, Cham (2016). https://doi.org/10.1007/978-3-319-46484-8_2

40. Wang, X., et al.: Semantic-guided relation propagation network for few-shot action recognition. In: Proceedings of the 29th ACM International Conference on Multimedia, MM 2021, pp. 816–825. Association for Computing Machinery, New York (2021). https://doi.org/10.1145/3474085.3475253

41. Xian, Y., Korbar, B., Douze, M., Schiele, B., Akata, Z., Torresani, L.: Generalized many-way few-shot video classification. In: Bartoli, A., Fusiello, A. (eds.) ECCV 2020. LNCS, vol. 12540, pp. 111–127. Springer, Cham (2020). https://doi.org/10.1007/978-3-030-65414-6_10

42. Yan, S., Xiong, Y., Lin, D.: Spatial temporal graph convolutional networks for skeleton-based action recognition. In: Thirty-Second AAAI Conference on Artificial Intelligence (2018)

43. Zhang, H., Zhang, L., Qi, X., Li, H., Torr, P.H.S., Koniusz, P.: Few-shot action recognition with permutation-invariant attention. In: Vedaldi, A., Bischof, H., Brox, T., Frahm, J.-M. (eds.) ECCV 2020. LNCS, vol. 12350, pp. 525–542. Springer, Cham (2020). https://doi.org/10.1007/978-3-030-58558-7_31

44. Zhang, S., Zhou, J., He, X.: Learning implicit temporal alignment for few-shot video classification. In: IJCAI (2021)

45. Zhao, L., Akoglu, L.: PairNorm: tackling oversmoothing in GNNs. In: International Conference on Learning Representations (2020). https://openreview.net/forum?id=rkecl1rtwB

46. Zhu, L., Yang, Y.: Compound memory networks for few-shot video classification. In: Ferrari, V., Hebert, M., Sminchisescu, C., Weiss, Y. (eds.) ECCV 2018. LNCS, vol. 11211, pp. 782–797. Springer, Cham (2018). https://doi.org/10.1007/978-3-030-01234-2_46
47. Zhu, Z., Wang, L., Guo, S., Wu, G.: A closer look at few-shot video classification: A new baseline and benchmark (2021)

Dual-Evidential Learning for Weakly-supervised Temporal Action Localization

Mengyuan Chen[1,2(✉)], Junyu Gao[1,2], Shicai Yang[3], and Changsheng Xu[1,2,4]

[1] National Lab of Pattern Recognition (NLPR), Institute of Automation, Chinese Academy of Sciences (CASIA), Beijing, China
chenmengyuan2021@ia.ac.cn, {junyu.gao,csxu}@nlpr.ia.ac.cn
[2] School of Artificial Intelligence, University of Chinese Academy of Sciences (UCAS), Beijing, China
[3] Hikvision Research Institute, Hangzhou, China
yangshicai@hikvision.com
[4] Peng Cheng Laboratory, ShenZhen, China

Abstract. Weakly-supervised temporal action localization (WS-TAL) aims to localize the action instances and recognize their categories with only video-level labels. Despite great progress, existing methods suffer from severe action-background ambiguity, which mainly comes from background noise introduced by aggregation operations and large intra-action variations caused by the task gap between classification and localization. To address this issue, we propose a generalized evidential deep learning (EDL) framework for WS-TAL, called Dual-Evidential Learning for Uncertainty modeling (DELU), which extends the traditional paradigm of EDL to adapt to the weakly-supervised multi-label classification goal. Specifically, targeting at adaptively excluding the undesirable background snippets, we utilize the video-level uncertainty to measure the interference of background noise to video-level prediction. Then, the snippet-level uncertainty is further deduced for progressive learning, which gradually focuses on the entire action instances in an "easy-to-hard" manner. Extensive experiments show that DELU achieves state-of-the-art performance on THUMOS14 and ActivityNet1.2 benchmarks. Our code is available in github.com/MengyuanChen21/ECCV2022-DELU.

Keywords: Weakly-supervised temporal action localization · Evidential deep learning · Action-background ambiguity

1 Introduction

Temporal action localization is one of the most fundamental tasks of video understanding, which aims to localize the start and end timestamps of action instances and recognize their categories simultaneously in untrimmed videos [31,49,53,62]. It has attracted significant attention from both academia and industry, due to the

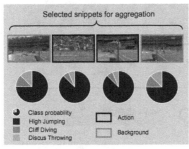
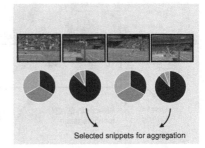

(a) Background noise   (b) Large intra-action variations

Fig. 1. Action-background ambiguity in WS-TAL. (a) Some background snippets are misclassified to the foreground, thus distracting the aggregation process under video-level supervision. (b) Due to the large intra-action variations, the learned action classifiers tend to ignore snippets which are not discriminative enough, thus easily responding to only a fraction of action snippets instead of the entire action instances

great potential for video retrieval [9,41], summarization [24], surveillance [18,51], anomaly detection [50], visual question answering [25], to name a few. In recent years, numerous action localization methods have been proposed and achieved remarkable performance under the fully-supervised setting. However, these methods require extensive manual frame-level annotations, which limits their scalability and practicability in real-world application scenarios, since densely annotating large amounts of videos is time-consuming, error-prone and extremely costly. To address this problem, weakly-supervised temporal action localization (WS-TAL) methods have been explored [13,14,42,56], which requires only easily available video-level labels.

Due to the absence of frame-wise annotations in the weakly-superwised setting, most existing WS-TAL methods adopt the localization-by-classification strategy [40,45,52,54], in which the commonly used mutiple-instance learning (MIL) strategy [35] and/or attention mechanism [42] are employed. Specifically, after dividing each untrimmed video into multiple fixed-size non-overlapping snippets, these methods apply action classifiers to predict a sequence of classification probabilities of snippets, termed as Class Activation Sequence (CAS). The top ranked snippets are then selected for aggregation, resulting in a video-level prediction for model optimization. To improve the accuracy of the learned CAS, a variety of strategies have been adopted, such as feature enhancement [13,57], pseudo label generation [56], context modeling [42], contrastive learning [58], which have achieved impressive performance.

Despite remarkable progress has been achieved, existing methods still suffer from severe action-background ambiguity due to the weakly-supervised setting, thus leading to the significant performance gap with fully-supervised methods [26,27,29]. We argue that the action-background ambiguity mainly comes from two aspects: (**1**) Background noise introduced by the aggregation operations when generating video-level predictions. As shown in Fig. 1(a), the selection of the

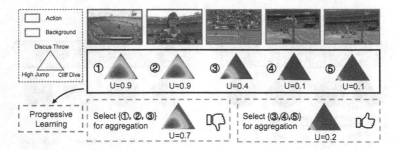

Fig. 2. A toy example of 3-class WS-TAL, which demonstrates the two-level evidential learning structure of DELU. (1) The video-level uncertainty is learned to adaptively exclude the undesirable background snippets in the aggregation process (Sect. 3.3). (2) The snippet-level uncertainty is employed to better perform foreground-background separation by progressive learning (Sect. 3.4). Each triangle in this figure represents a Dirichlet distribution of all possible prediction results(Sect. 3.1). The three vertices of the triangle represent three categories and each point in the triangle represents a particular allocation of class probabilities. When points with high values are concentrated at a certain vertex, the model classifies the sample into the corresponding category with a low uncertainty U

top action snippets for later aggregation may be inaccurate, *i.e.* some background snippets are mistakenly recognized as action snippets due to their similarity with the foreground in appearance. As a result, background noise will distract or even dominate the further video-level classification. (**2**) Large intra-action variations caused by the task gap between classification and localization. Since only video-level supervisions are provided for WS-TAL, the learned classifiers only need to focus on the most discriminative action snippets when performing video-level classification. As shown in Fig. 1(b), the model tends to ignore the action snippets that are not significant enough, *i.e.* fail to classify them into the target action category, thus easily responding to only a fraction of action snippets instead of the entire action instance. These two issues are essentially entangled with each other, jointly intensifying the action-background ambiguity in the model learning process.

Inspired by the above observation, we find that it is desirable to tackle the action-background ambiguity by considering the uncertainty of classification results in both video and snippet levels. Recently, Evidential Deep Learning (EDL) [36, 44], which can collect the evidence of each category and quantify the predictive uncertainty, has received extensive attention and achieved impressive performance in a few computer vision tasks [3, 43, 46]. However, EDL is designed for fully-supervised single-label classification tasks, which is not suitable to be directly integrated into weakly-supervised temporal action localization[1].

To address the above issues, we propose a generalized EDL framework for WS-TAL, called Dual-Evidential Learning for Uncertainty modeling (DELU), which extends the traditional paradigm of EDL to adapt to the weakly-supervised multi-label classification goal. As shown in Fig. 2, to tackle the

---

[1] In WS-TAL, multiple types of action may appear simultaneously in a video.

action-background ambiguity, DELU leverages a two-level evidential learning structure to model the predictive uncertainty in both video level and snippet level. Specifically, (1) we utilize the video-level uncertainty to measure the interference of background noise. Here, we propose a novel evidential learning objective to learn the video-level unceratinty, which can adaptively exclude the undesirable background snippets in the aggregation operations. (2) When pursuing video-level uncertainty, the snippet-level uncertainty is naturally deduced. Based on this more fine-grained information, we design a progressive learning strategy, in which the order of the snippet-level uncertainty is leveraged to gradually focus on the entire action instances in an "easy-to-hard" manner. As a result, the negative impact of intra-action variations is alleviated and the background noise can be further excluded. Our proposed DELU is optimized in an end-to-end manner, and we validate its effectiveness on two popular benchmarks [6, 15].

In conclusion, the main contributions of this work are three-fold:

1. We design a generalized EDL paradigm to better adapt to the multi-label classification setting under weak supervision. To the best of our knowledge, we are among the first to introduce the evidential deep learning to weakly-supervised temporal action localization.
2. By carefully considering both video- and snippet-level uncertainty, we propose a novel dual-evidential learning framework, which can effectively alleviates the action-background ambiguity caused by background noise and large intra-action variations.
3. We conduct extensive experiments on two public benchmarks, i.e., Thumos14 dataset and Activity1.2 dataset. On both benchmarks our proposed DELU method achieves state-of-the-art results.

2   Related Work

Weakly-supervised Temporal Action Localization (WS-TAL). In recent years, WS-TAL with various types of weak supervisions has been developed, e.g., action orders [5], web videos [11], single-frame annotation [21,34], and video-level action category labels [28,39,52], while the last one is the most commonly adopted due to its simplicity. UntrimmedNet [52] is the first work to use video-level action category labels for the WS-TAL task. To date in the literature, most existing approaches can be divided into three categories, namely attention-based methods [13,32,38,42,45,54], MIL-based methods [22,33,35,37,40], and erasing-based methods [48,59,61]. Attention-based approaches generate the foreground attention weight to suppress the background parts. CO2-Net [13] filters out the information redundancy to enhance features by cross-modal attention alignment. MIL-based approaches treat the input video as a bag in which the action clips are positive samples and the background clips are negative ones, and a top-k operation is utilized to aggregate the snippet-level prediction results. ASL [35] explores a general independent concept of action by investigating a class-agnostic actionness network. The erasing-based methods attempt to erase the most discriminative parts to highlight other less discriminative snippets. For example,

FC-CRF [61] tries to find new foreground snippets progressively via step-by-step erasion from a complete input video.

Although several methods have investigated the role of uncertainty in WS-TAL, *e.g.*, GUCT [56] estimates the uncertainty about the generated snippet-level pseudo labels to mitigate noise, Lee *et al.* [23] decompose the classification probability into the action probability and the uncertainty with a chain rule, they neglect the unique two-level uncertainty structure under the weakly-supervised setting of WS-TAL. In this paper, by carefully considering both video- and snippet-level uncertainty, we propose a novel dual-evidential learning framework to effectively alleviate the action-background ambiguity.

Evidential Deep Learning (EDL). In recent years, deep learning approaches commonly adopt softmax function as the classification head to output final predictions. However, due to the exponent operation employed on neural network outputs, there exist intrinsic deficiencies of modeling class probabilities with softmax. On the one hand, softmax-based classifiers have a tendency to be over-confident in false predictions, which brings additional difficulties to the optimization process [12]. On the other hand, since the softmax output is essentially a point estimate of the probability distribution [10], it cannot estimate the predictive uncertainty.

To overcome the above weaknesses, EDL [36,44] was gradually developed and refined based on Dempster-Shafer theory of evidence (DST) [55] and Subjective Logic theory [19]. The core idea of EDL is to collect evidence of each category and construct a Dirichlet distribution parametrized over the collected evidence to model the distribution of class probabilities. Besides the probability of each category, the predictive uncertainty can be quantified from the distribution by Subjective Logic theory. EDL has been successfully utilized in various tasks requiring uncertainty modeling, and remarkable progress has been achieved in a few computer vision tasks [3,43,46]. For example, Bao *et al.* [3] use the uncertainty obtained by EDL to distinguish between the known and unknown samples for the open set action recognition (OSAR) task.

However, current EDL models are designed for fully-supervised single-label classification tasks, which is not suitable to be directly integrated into weakly-supervised multi-label classification setting. To the best of our knowledge, we are among the first to introduce the evidential deep learning to the WS-TAL task, demonstrating favorable performance.

3 Proposed Approach

In this work, we describe our DELU framework in details. We first introduce the Evidential Deep Learning (EDL) in Sect. 3.1. The overview architecture of DELU is illustrated in Fig. 3. We firstly utilize a pre-trained feature extractor to obtain snippet-level video feature and adopt a backbone network to obtain the CAS (Sect. 3.2). Then, we propose a generalized EDL paradigm which can better adapt to the setting of WS-TAL. Specifically, the video-level uncertainty is

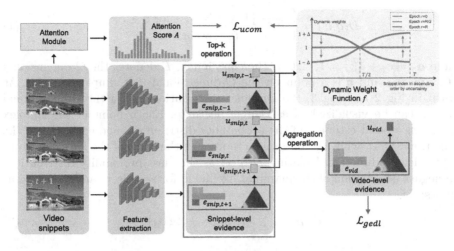

Fig. 3. Overall framework of the proposed DELU. After obtaining the snippet-level evidence, we aggregate them to generate the video-level evidence by selecting the top-k snippets according to the attention scores. The video-level evidence and uncertainty are used to generalize the EDL paradigm for WS-TAL, and the snippet-level uncertainty is employed to generate dynamic weights for progressive learning. Note that we omit the regular classification loss $\mathcal{L}_{cls}$ (Sect. 3.2) in this figure for simplicity

utilized to generalize the EDL paradigm for weakly-supervised multi-label (WS-Multi) classification (Sect. 3.3), and a progressive learning strategy is employed by leveraging the snippet-level uncertainty (Sect. 3.4). Finally, the whole framework is end-to-end learned (Sect. 3.5).

3.1 Background of Evidential Deep Learning

According to Dempster-Shafer theory of evidence [55] and Subjective Logic theory [19], evidential deep learning (EDL) [2,44] was proposed to address the deficiencies of softmax-based classifiers mentioned in Sect. 2. Instead of directly predicting the probability of each class, EDL collects evidence of each class first and then builds a Dirichlet distribution of class probabilities parametrized over the collected evidence. Based on the distribution, the predictive uncertainty can be quantified by Subjective Logic theory [19]. To represents the intensity of activation of each class, *evidence* is defined as a measure of the amount of support collected from data in favor of a sample being classified into a particular class [19,44,55].

EDL targets at predicting evidence for each category and building a Dirichlet distribution of class probability. Given a C-class classification problem, let $\boldsymbol{e} \in \mathbb{R}_+^C$ be the evidence vector predicted for a sample x, the corresponding Dirichlet distribution is given by

$$D(\boldsymbol{q}|\boldsymbol{\alpha}) = \begin{cases} \frac{1}{B(\boldsymbol{\alpha})} \prod_{j=1}^{C} q_j^{\alpha_j - 1}, & \text{for } \boldsymbol{q} \in \mathcal{S}_C \\ 0, & \text{otherwise} \end{cases} \tag{1}$$

where $\alpha_j = e_j + 1$, $j = 1, ..., C$ is the class index, B denotes the C-dimensional beta function and $\boldsymbol{q}$ is a point on the C-dimensional unit simplex $\mathcal{S}_C$ [44]. As shown in Fig. 2 and Fig. 3, the Dirichlet distribution over a three-dimensional simplex can be visualized as a triangle heatmap. Eac h point of the simplex represents a point estimate of the probability distribution, and each edge is the value range $[0, 1]$, while the brightness represents the value of the Dirichlet probability density function. Treating $D(\boldsymbol{q}|\boldsymbol{\alpha})$ as the class probability distribution, the negative logarithm of the marginal likelihood for sample x can be derived as follows:

$$\mathcal{L}_{EDL} = \sum_{j=1}^{C} y_j (\log S - \log \alpha_j), \tag{2}$$

where $\boldsymbol{y}$ is the one-hot ground-truth vector for sample x, $S = \sum_{j=1}^{C} \alpha_j$. Equation (2) is the traditional optimization objective of EDL [36,44]. Then, the predicted probablity $\hat{p}_j$ of class j and the uncertainty u of the prediction can be derived as following:

$$\hat{p}_j = \alpha_j / S, \quad u = C / S. \tag{3}$$

Note that uncertainty u is inversely proportional to the total evidence. When the total evidence is zero, the uncertainty becomes the maximum.

3.2   Notations and Preliminaries

In the following, superscript (i) is used to indicate the sample index, $i = 1, ..., N$, and subscript j is used to indicate the category index. Note that in the following, for simplicity, the superscript (i) has been omitted when there is no ambiguity. Given an untrimmed video V and its corresponding multi-hot action category label $\boldsymbol{y} \in \{0, 1\}^{C+1}$, where C is the action category number, and $C+1$ represents the non-action background class. The action instances in video V detected by WS-TAL methods can be formulated as a set of ordered quadruplets $\{c_m, t_m^s, t_m^e, \phi_m\}_{m=1}^{M}$, where M is the number of action instances in V, c_m denotes the action category, t_m^s and t_m^e denote the start and end timestamps, and ϕ_m denotes the confidence score.

Following previous works [14,42,56], we first divide the untrimmed video V into T non-overlapping 16-frame snippets, and use pre-trained networks, $e.g.$, I3D model [20], to extract features from both RGB and optical flow streams. After that, the two types of features are concatenated and then fed into an fusion module, $e.g.$, convolutional layers [13,42], to obtain the snippet-wise feature $\boldsymbol{X} = [\boldsymbol{x}_1, ..., \boldsymbol{x}_T] \in \mathbb{R}^{D \times T}$, where D is the feature dimension.

To date in the literature, existing methods mainly embrace a localization-by-classification strategy. Firstly, a classifier f_{cls} is applied to the snippet-wise features $\boldsymbol{X}$ to predict the CAS, denoted as $\boldsymbol{p} = [\boldsymbol{p}_1, ..., \boldsymbol{p}_T] \in \mathbb{R}^{T \times (C+1)}$. Meanwhile, an attention score sequence $\boldsymbol{A} = [A_1, ..., A_T] \in \mathbb{R}^T$ is predicted by an attention module to represent the probabilities of snippets belonging to the foreground. After that, the video-level classification probability $\tilde{y}$ is obtained through a top-k aggregation operation over the CAS according to the attention scores A, and the process can be formalized as:

$$\tilde{y} = \frac{1}{k} \sum_{\substack{t \in \Omega, |\Omega| = k, \\ \Omega = \arg\max_{\Omega} \sum_{t \in \Omega} A_t}} p_t, \tag{4}$$

where $p = f_{cls}(X)$. Finally, the video-level prediction $\tilde{y}$ is optimized by the ground-truth label y:

$$\mathcal{L}_{cls} = \text{Cross-entropy}(y, \tilde{y}). \tag{5}$$

3.3   Generalizing EDL for Video-level WS-Multi Classification

Although evidential deep learning has made great progress in modeling uncertainty, the traditional EDL paradigm is not suitable to be directly applied to the WS-Multi classification setting of WS-TAL. In order to extend the applicability of evidential learning methods to WS-TAL tasks, the first problem to be solved is how to predict video-level evidence $e_{vid} = [e_{vid,1}, ..., e_{vid,C}] \in \mathbb{R}^C$ from snippet-level features X. We propose to predict the snippet-level evidence $e_{snip} = [e_{snip,1}, ..., e_{snip,C}] \in \mathbb{R}^{T \times C}$ for action categories first, and then obtain the video-level evidence e_{vid} by aggregating the snippet-level evidence $e_{snip,t}$ of the snippets which are attached with the top-k attention score A_t. Note that here we jointly employ attention scores and evidence for aggregation, which makes the attention module and evidence learning enhance and complement each other. Formally, we can denote the video-level evidence collection process as following:

$$e_{vid} = \frac{1}{k} \sum_{\substack{t \in \Omega, |\Omega| = k, \\ \Omega = \arg\max_{\Omega} \sum_{t \in \Omega} A_t}} e_{snip,t}, \tag{6}$$

where $k = \lceil T/r \rceil$, r is a scaling factor, $e_{snip} = g(f(X; \theta))$, f is a DNN parameterized by θ to collect evidence, g denotes an evidence function, $e.g.$, ReLU, to keep the evidence e_{snip} non-negative. Note that here we only consider the C action categories for evidential learning since the additional background class hinders the uncertainty modeling of foreground. Following the traditional EDL method, we obtain α, S, and u_{vid} by

$$\alpha_j = e_{vid,j} + 1, S = \sum_{j=1}^{C} \alpha_j, u_{vid} = C/S, \tag{7}$$

Due to the low frequency or short duration of some action categories, the collected evidence for them tend to have a relatively low intensity, thus being easily ignored in the process of model learning. Therefore, we hope that the classifier can assign more importance to the target action categories with smaller evidence scores. With the symbols introduced in Sect. 3.2, we design a new label vector $\boldsymbol{g}$ to replace original multi-hot label $\boldsymbol{y}$:

$$g_j = \frac{y_j/e_{vid,j}}{\sum_{j=1}^{C} y_j/e_{vid,j}}, \tag{8}$$

It can be found from Eq. (8) that g_j and $e_{vid,j}$ are inversely proportional, thus the model can learn features of each target category more evenly.

Although the above modified EDL paradigm can better adapt to the multi-label classification setting, it neglects the uncertainty derived from the video-level evidential learning. We further notice that the video-level uncertainty $\boldsymbol{u}_{vid}$ can be utilized to measure the interference of background noise to video-level prediction, thus avoiding the background noise intensifying the action-background ambiguity. We argue that the selected top-k snippets are dominated by action snippets as expected only when the classifier predicts the video category correctly with a low uncertainty. Contrarily, when the prediction is accompanied by a high uncertainty, the video-level prediction is more likely to be dominated by background noise. In the latter case, we should expect the classifier to produce a trivial prediction, instead of forcing the result to be consistent with the given video-level action category label, which may lead to the action-background ambiguity further increasing. To achieve this goal, we propose to replace g_j with h_j by leveraging the video level uncertainty:

$$h_j = (1 - u_{vid})g_j, \tag{9}$$

Therefore, the samples with higher video-level uncertainties can take a smaller weight in the optimization process, thus reducing the negtive impact caused by background noise.

Based on the above derivation, our objective for generalizing EDL can be formulated to the following form:

$$\mathcal{L}_{gedl} = \sum_{i=1}^{N}(1 - u_{vid}^{(i)}) \sum_{j=1}^{C} \frac{y_j^{(i)}/e_j^{(i)}}{\sum_{j=1}^{C} y_j^{(i)}/e_j^{(i)}}(\log S^{(i)} - \log \alpha_j^{(i)}). \tag{10}$$

3.4 Snippet-level Progressive Learning

In the above section, snippet-level uncertainty is also deduced when performing video-level evidential learning. To leverage the fine-grained information, we notice that $\boldsymbol{p} \in \mathbb{R}^{T \times (C+1)}$ represents the classification probabilities of snippets, and $p_{t,c+1}$ indicates the probability of the t-th snippet belonging to the background. It is natural to think that the attention score $\boldsymbol{A}$, which represents the probability of each snippet belonging to the foreground, and the background probability $p_{t,c+1}$ should be complementary:

$$\mathcal{L}_{com} = \sum_{t=1}^{T} |A_t + p_{t,c+1} - 1|, \tag{11}$$

where $|\cdot|$ is the ℓ_1 norm.

Due to the existence of task gap between classification and localization, models tend to focus only on the most discriminative video snippets, which makes it difficult to classify other action snippets correctly. Inspired by Curriculum Learning [4], we propose a progressive learning method by leveraging snippet-level uncertainty to help the model learn the entire action instance progressively and comprehensively. Note that the snippet-level uncertainty can reflect the discriminability of itself, that is, the lower uncertainty of an action snippet means it is easier to recognize its category. Our strategy is to attach larger weights to snippets with lower uncertainty and smaller weights to ones with higher uncertainty in the beginning, and gradually reverse this allocation in the training process. During the progressively learning, the model firstly focuses on easy action snippets and then gradually pays more attention to background and difficult action snippets. As a result, the negtive impact of intra-action variation is alleviated and the background noise can be further excluded. Therefore, as shown in Fig. 3, we design a dynamic weight function $\lambda(r, t)$ as following:

$$\lambda(r, t) = \Delta \cdot \tanh\left(\delta(r)\phi(s(t))\right) + 1, \tag{12}$$

where Δ is a hyper-parameter representing the amplitude of the change of the dynamic weights. Specifically, $\delta(r) = \frac{2r}{R} - 1 \in [-1, 1]$, $r = 1, ..., R$, r is the current epoch index, R denotes the total training epoch number, and $\phi(s(t)) = \frac{2s(t)}{T} - 1 \in [-1, 1]$, $s = 1, ..., T$, $s(t)$ indicates the ordinal number of snippet t obtained by sorting the snippet-level uncertainty u_{snip} in a descending order.

Finally, after multiplying the snippet-level uncertainty guided dynamic weights to the complementary loss $\mathcal{L}_{com}$, we can gradually focus on the entire action instances in an "easy-to-hard" manner by optimizing the following objective:

$$\mathcal{L}_{ucom} = \sum_{t=1}^{T} \lambda(r, t) \cdot |A_t + p_{c+1,t} - 1|. \tag{13}$$

3.5 Learning and Inference

Training. By aggregating all the aforementioned optimization objectives, we obtain the final loss function as following

$$\mathcal{L} = \mathcal{L}_{cls} + \lambda_1 \mathcal{L}_{gedl} + \lambda_2 \mathcal{L}_{ucom}, \tag{14}$$

here, λ_1, λ_2 are balancing hyper-parameters.

Inference. In the inference phase, we first predict the CAS of the test video and then apply a threshold strategy to obtain action snippet candidates following the standard process [13]. Finally, continuous snippets are grouped into action proposals, and then non-maximum-suppression (NMS) is performed to remove duplicated proposals.

Table 1. Temporal action localization performance comparison with existing methods on the THUMOS14 dataset

Supervision	Method	mAP@t-IoU(%)									
		0.1	0.2	0.3	0.4	0.5	0.6	0.7	[0.1:0.5]	[0.3:0.7]	Avg
Fully	TAL-Net [8], CVPR2018	59.8	57.1	53.2	48.5	42.8	33.8	20.8	52.3	39.8	45.1
	GTAN [31], CVPR2019	69.1	63.7	57.8	47.2	38.8	-	-	55.3	-	-
	BU-TAL [60], ECCV2020	-	-	53.9	50.7	45.4	38.0	28.5	-	43.3	-
Weakly	UntrimmedNet [52], CVPR2017	44.4	37.7	28.2	21.1	13.7	-	-	29.0	-	-
	Hide-and-Seek [48], ICCV2017	36.4	27.8	19.5	12.7	6.8	-	-	20.6	-	-
	AutoLoc [47], ECCV2018	-	-	35.8	29.0	21.2	13.4	5.8	-	-	-
	STPN [39], CVPR2018	52.0	44.7	35.5	25.8	16.9	9.9	4.3	35.0	18.5	27.0
	W-TALC [40], ECCV2018	55.2	49.6	40.1	31.1	22.8	-	7.6	39.8	25.4	34.4
	DGAM [45], CVPR2020	60.0	54.2	46.8	38.2	28.8	19.8	11.4	45.6	29.0	37.0
	RefineLoc [1], WACV2021	-	-	40.8	32.7	23.1	13.3	5.3	-	23.0	-
	ACSNet [30], AAAI2021	-	-	51.4	42.7	32.4	22.0	11.7	-	32.0	-
	HAM-Net [16], AAAI2021	65.9	59.6	52.2	43.1	32.6	21.9	12.5	50.7	32.5	41.1
	ASL [35], CVPR2021	67.0	-	51.8	-	31.1	-	11.4	-	-	40.3
	CoLA [58], CVPR2021	66.2	59.5	51.5	41.9	32.2	22.0	13.1	50.3	32.1	40.9
	AUMN [32], CVPR2021	66.2	61.9	54.9	44.4	33.3	20.5	9.0	52.1	32.4	41.5
	UGCT [56], CVPR2021	69.2	62.9	55.5	46.5	35.9	23.8	11.4	54.0	34.6	43.6
	D2-Net [38], ICCV2021	65.7	60.2	52.3	43.4	36.0	-	-	51.5	-	-
	FAC-Net [14], ICCV2021	67.6	62.1	52.6	44.3	33.4	22.5	12.7	52.0	33.1	42.2
	ACM-Net [42], arXiv2021	68.9	62.7	55.0	44.6	34.6	21.8	10.8	53.2	33.4	42.6
	CO2-Net [13], MM2021	70.1	63.6	54.5	45.7	38.3	26.4	13.4	54.4	35.7	44.6
	ACG-Net [57], AAAI2022	68.1	62.6	53.1	44.6	34.7	22.6	12.0	52.6	33.4	42.5
	DELU(Ours)	**71.5**	**66.2**	**56.5**	**47.7**	**40.5**	**27.2**	**15.3**	**56.5**	**37.4**	**46.4**

4   Experimental Results

We evaluate our proposed DELU on two public benchmarks, *i.e.*, THUMOS14 [15] and ActivityNet1.2 [6]. The following experiments verifies the effectiveness.

4.1   Experimental Setup

THUMOS14. It contains 200 validation videos and 213 test videos annotated with temporal action boundaries from 20 action categories. Each video contains an average of 15.4 action instances, making this dataset challenging for weakly-supervised temporal action localization.

ActivityNet1.2. ActivityNet1.2 contains 4,819 training and 2,383 validation videos from 100 action categories. Since the ground-truth annotations of the test set is not yet public, we test on the validation set following the protocol in previous work [13,16,17].

Evaluation Metrics. Following previous work [13,42,52], we use mean Average Precision (mAP) under different temporal Intersection over Union (t-IoU) thresholds as evaluation metrics. The t-IoU thresholds for THUMOS14 is [0.1:0.1:0.7] and for ActivityNet is [0.5:0.05:0.95].

Implementation Details. Following existing methods, we use I3D [7] model pretrained on Kinetics [20] dataset to extract both the RGB and optical flow features. After that, we adopt CO2-Net [13] as the backbone to obtain the fused 2048 dimensional features and implement f_{cls} and $\mathcal{L}_{cls}$. The number of the sampled snippets T for THUMOS14 and ActivityNet1.2 is set to 320 and 60, and the scaling factor r is set to 7 and 5, respectively. Two convolutional layers are utilized as the evidence collector f. The amplitude Δ is set to 0.7, and the balancing hyper-parameters λ_1 and λ_2 are 1.3 and 0.4.

4.2   Comparision with State-of-the-Art Methods

Evaluation on THUMOS14. Table 1 compares DELU with existing fully and weakly-supervised TAL methods on the THUMOS14 dataset. From this table we can find that DELU outperforms all existing weakly-supervised methods in all IoU metrics. Specifically, our method achieves impressive performance of 15.3% mAP@0.7 and 46.4% mAP@Avg, and an absolute gain of 1.8% and 2.8% is obtained in terms of the average mAP when compared to the SOTA approaches CO2-Net [13] and UGCT [56]. In addition to this, we observe that our methods can even achieve comparable performance with those fully-supervised methods, especially in terms of metrics with low IoU.

Evaluation on ActivityNet1.2. Table 2 presents the comparison of experimental performance on the ActivityNet1.2 dataset. As shown, our method also achieves state-of-the-art performance under the weakly-supervised setting. Specifically, compared with the state-of-the-art method ACM-Net [42], we obtain a relative gain of 1.5% in the term of the average mAP. DELU achieves less significant performance improvement on this dataset due to the different characteristics of datasets, that THUMOS14 contains 15.4 action instances per video on average, compared with 1.6 in each video of ActivityNet. Therefore, methods that tend to treat ambiguous snippets as the foreground will perform better on ActivityNet, while methods with the opposite tendency will achieve better performance on THUMOS14. For example, ACM-Net achieves SOTA on ActivityNet, and CO2-Net achieves SOTA on THUMOS14, but neither of them can achieve the same outstanding results on the other dataset. In this paper, the proposed DELU achieves the SOTA performance on both datasets consistently.

4.3   Ablation Study

In Table 3, we investigate the contribution of each component on the THUMOS14 dataset. As introduced in Sect. 3.5, the optimization objective of our proposed DELU consists of three loss functions, $i.e.$, $\mathcal{L}_{cls}, \mathcal{L}_{gedl}$ and $\mathcal{L}_{ucom}$. Firstly, we set the baseline of the ablation study as the backbone method CO2-net [13] whose optimization objective is $\mathcal{L}_{cls}$. On this basis, we conduct experiments on each improvement scheme according to the derivation steps of $\mathcal{L}_{gedl}$, that is (T) only using the traditional EDL method optimized by Eq. (2) (B) applying the balanced improvement given by Eq. (8) on the basis of the traditional EDL,

Table 2. Comparison results on the ActivityNet1.2 dataset

Method	mAP@t-IoU(%)			
	0.5	0.75	0.95	Avg
DGAM [45], CVPR2020	41.0	23.5	5.3	24.4
RefineLoc [1], WACV2020	38.7	22.6	5.5	23.2
ACSNet [30], AAAI2021	40.1	26.1	6.8	26.0
HAM-Net [16], AAAI2021	41.0	24.8	5.3	25.1
Lee et al. [21], AAAI2021	41.2	25.6	6.0	25.9
ASL [35], CVPR2021	40.2	-	-	25.8
CoLA [58], CVPR2021	42.7	25.7	5.8	26.1
AUMN [32], CVPR2021	42.0	25.0	5.6	25.5
UGCT [56], CVPR2021	41.8	25.3	5.9	25.8
D2-Net [38], ICCV2021	42.3	25.5	5.8	26.0
ACM-Net [42], arXiv2021	43.0	25.8	**6.4**	26.5
CO2-Net [13], MM2021	43.3	26.3	5.2	26.4
ACGNet [57], AAAI2022	41.8	26.0	5.9	26.1
DELU(Ours)	**44.2**	**26.7**	5.4	**26.9**

Table 3. Ablation study of the effectiveness of our proposed EDLU on the THUMOS14 dataset. T represents the traditional EDL method (Eq. (2)). B represents the modified EDL (Eq. (8)) which balances the evidence collected for each target category. U is the generalized EDL paradigm leveraging video-level uncertainty (Eq. (10))

Exp	$\mathcal{L}_{gedl}$			$\mathcal{L}_{ucom}$	mAP@IoU(%)				
	T	B	U		0.1	0.3	0.5	0.7	mAP
1	✗	✗	✗	✗	69.7	54.7	38.2	13.2	44.5
2	✓	✗	✗	✗	68.9	54.8	39.0	14.9	44.9
3	✓	✓	✗	✗	70.4	55.4	38.9	14.7	45.2
4	✓	✓	✓	✗	70.6	56.2	39.2	14.6	45.6
5	✓	✓	✓	✓	**71.5**	**56.5**	**40.5**	**15.3**	**46.4**

and (U) optimizing the complete $\mathcal{L}_{gedl}$ which considers the video-level uncertainty (Eq. (10)). Finally, the snippet-level uncertainty guided complementary loss $\mathcal{L}_{ucom}$ is added to above components. Table 3 clearly demonstrates that every step of our method brings considerable performance improvement on the THUMOS14 dataset.

4.4 Evaluation for Insights

In this part, we provide experiment results to illustrate that **(1)** background noises and **(2)** ignoring non-salient action snippets are existing issues in WS-TAL and DELU effectively alleviates them.

The **issue (1)** does exist. Given the test videos of the THUMOS14 dataset, we select the 5% snippets with the highest target CAS, *i.e.*, the Class Activation Score of the Target (ground-truth) action category, predicted and averaged by the SOTA method CO2-Net, of which 22.54% are background snippets (this number drops to 20.92% in our DELU). This fact indicates that existing methods suffer from the background noise issue, which hinders further improvement of localization performance. To verify that DELU alleviates this issue, we utilize Area Under the Receiver Operating Characteristic (AUROC) to evaluate the action-background separation performance. Specifically, we sort snippets according to the learned attention scores and then divide them into action and background with different thresholds. Figure 4(a) presents the ROC curves of DELU and CO2-Net, which shows DELU achieves more accurate action-background separation. To be more precise, DELU has an AUROC of 85.92%, while CO2-Net has an AUROC of 83.96%.

The **issue (2)** also exists. First, we observe the following phenomenon: the target CAS predicted for action snippets in the same video are not evenly distributed. For instance, as shown in Fig. 4(b), when CO2-Net works on the

THUMOS14 dataset, 30% snippets with higher target CAS accounts for more than half of the total target CAS. In order to validate that non-salient snippets can bring performance improvement, we divide snippets in each test video into ten intervals according to the target CAS, and then manually correct the target CAS (before softmax normalization) of the snippets in each interval with a fixed amplitude (5 in our experiment). Figure 4(c) shows that the performance improvements in non-salient intervals are generally higher than those in salient ones. Note that using other amplitude values also has similar results. To verify that DELU improves this issue, we compare the target CAS distribution of DELU and CO2-Net. As shown in Fig. 4(d), the target CAS distribution of DELU is more uniform, indicating DELU does make the model more comprehensively focus on both salient and non-salient snippets and improve performance. Similar conclusions can also be found in Fig. 4(b).

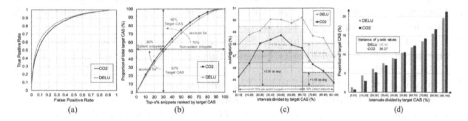

Fig. 4. Evaluation for the insights of our method

5 Conclusions

This paper proposes a generalized evidential learning framework for WS-TAL, called Dual-Evidential Learning for Uncertainty modeling. Specifically, video-level evidential learning and snippet-level progressive learning are performed to jointly alleviate the action-background ambiguity. Extensive experiments demonstrate the effectiveness of components in our proposed framework. DELU outperforms all existing methods on THUMOS14 and ActivityNet1.2 for weakly-supervised temporal action localization. Inspired by the merits of evidential learning, in the future, we plan to perform pseudo label mining or introduce single-frame annotations, to explore and widen the potential of our DELU framework.

Acknowledgments. This work was supported by the National Key Research & Development Plan of China under Grant 2020AAA0106200, in part by the National Natural Science Foundation of China under Grants 62036012, U21B2044, 61721004, 62102415, 62072286, 61720106006, 61832002, 62072455, 62002355, and U1836220, in part by Beijing Natural Science Foundation (L201001), in part by Open Research Projects of Zhejiang Lab (NO.2022RC0AB02), and in part by CCF-Hikvision Open Fund (20210004).

References

1. Alwassel, H., Heilbron, F.C., Thabet, A., Ghanem, B.: Refineloc: iterative refinement for weakly-supervised action localization. In: WACV (2019)
2. Amini, A., Schwarting, W., Soleimany, A., Rus, D.: Deep evidential regression. In: NeurIPS (2020)
3. Bao, W., Yu, Q., Kong, Y.: Evidential deep learning for open set action recognition. In: ICCV (2021)
4. Bengio, Y., Louradour, J., Collobert, R., Weston, J.: Curriculum learning. In: ICML (2009)
5. Bojanowski, P., Lajugie, R., Bach, F., Laptev, I., Ponce, J., Schmid, C., Sivic, J.: Weakly supervised action labeling in videos under ordering constraints. In: Fleet, D., Pajdla, T., Schiele, B., Tuytelaars, T. (eds.) ECCV 2014. LNCS, vol. 8693, pp. 628–643. Springer, Cham (2014). https://doi.org/10.1007/978-3-319-10602-1_41
6. Caba Heilbron, F., Escorcia, V., Ghanem, B., Carlos Niebles, J.: ActivityNet: a large-scale video benchmark for human activity understanding. In: CVPR (2015)
7. Carreira, J., Zisserman, A.: Quo vadis, action recognition? a new model and the kinetics dataset. In: CVPR (2017)
8. Chao, Y.W., Vijayanarasimhan, S., Seybold, B., Ross, D.A., Deng, J., Sukthankar, R.: Rethinking the faster R-CNN architecture for temporal action localization. In: CVPR (2018)
9. Ciptadi, A., Goodwin, M.S., Rehg, J.M.: Movement pattern histogram for action recognition and retrieval. In: Fleet, D., Pajdla, T., Schiele, B., Tuytelaars, T. (eds.) ECCV 2014. LNCS, vol. 8690, pp. 695–710. Springer, Cham (2014). https://doi.org/10.1007/978-3-319-10605-2_45
10. Gal, Y., et al.: Uncertainty in deep learning. PhD thesis, University of Cambridge (2016)
11. Gan, C., Sun, C., Duan, L., Gong, B.: Webly-supervised video recognition by mutually voting for relevant web images and web video frames. In: Leibe, B., Matas, J., Sebe, N., Welling, M. (eds.) ECCV 2016. LNCS, vol. 9907, pp. 849–866. Springer, Cham (2016). https://doi.org/10.1007/978-3-319-46487-9_52
12. Guo, C., Pleiss, G., Sun, Y., Weinberger, K.Q.: On calibration of modern neural networks. In: ICML. PMLR (2017)
13. Hong, F.T., Feng, J.C., Xu, D., Shan, Y., Zheng, W.S.: Cross-modal consensus network for weakly supervised temporal action localization. In: ACM MM (2021)
14. Huang, L., Wang, L., Li, H.: Foreground-action consistency network for weakly supervised temporal action localization. In: ICCV (2021)
15. Idrees, H., et al.: The thumos challenge on action recognition for videos "in the wild". Comput. Vis. Image Understand. **155**, 1–23 (2017)
16. Islam, A., Long, C., Radke, R.: A hybrid attention mechanism for weakly-supervised temporal action localization. In: AAAI (2021)
17. Islam, A., Radke, R.: Weakly supervised temporal action localization using deep metric learning. In: WACV (2020)
18. Ji, S., Xu, W., Yang, M., Yu, K.: 3D convolutional neural networks for human action recognition. IEEE Trans. Pattern Anal. Mach. Intell. **35**(1), 221–231 (2012)
19. Jsang, A.: Subjective Logic: A Formalism for Reasoning Under Uncertainty. Springer Verlag (2016). https://doi.org/10.1007/978-3-319-42337-1
20. Kay, W., et al.: The kinetics human action video dataset. arXiv:1705.06950 (2017)
21. Lee, P., Byun, H.: Learning action completeness from points for weakly-supervised temporal action localization. In: ICCV (2021)

22. Lee, P., Uh, Y., Byun, H.: Background suppression network for weakly-supervised temporal action localization. In: AAAI (2020)
23. Lee, P., Wang, J., Lu, Y., Byun, H.: Weakly-supervised temporal action localization by uncertainty modeling. In: AAAI (2021)
24. Lee, Y.J., Ghosh, J., Grauman, K.: Discovering important people and objects for egocentric video summarization. In: 2012 IEEE Conference on Computer Vision and Pattern Recognition, pp. 1346–1353. IEEE (2012)
25. Lei, J., Yu, L., Bansal, M., Berg, T.L.: TVQA: localized, compositional video question answering. arXiv preprint arXiv:1809.01696 (2018)
26. Li, Z., Yao, L.: Three birds with one stone: Multi-task temporal action detection via recycling temporal annotations. In: CVPR (2021)
27. Lin, C., et al.: Learning salient boundary feature for anchor-free temporal action localization. In: CVPR (2021)
28. Liu, D., Jiang, T., Wang, Y.: Completeness modeling and context separation for weakly supervised temporal action localization. In: CVPR (2019)
29. Liu, X., Hu, Y., Bai, S., Ding, F., Bai, X., Torr, P.H.: Multi-shot temporal event localization: a benchmark. In: CVPR (2021)
30. Liu, Z., et al.: ACSNet: action-context separation network for weakly supervised temporal action localization. arXiv:2103.15088 (2021)
31. Long, F., Yao, T., Qiu, Z., Tian, X., Luo, J., Mei, T.: Gaussian temporal awareness networks for action localization. In: CVPR (2019)
32. Luo, W., et al.: Action unit memory network for weakly supervised temporal action localization. In: CVPR (2021)
33. Luo, Z., et al.: Weakly-supervised action localization with expectation-maximization multi-instance learning. In: Vedaldi, A., Bischof, H., Brox, T., Frahm, J.-M. (eds.) ECCV 2020. LNCS, vol. 12374, pp. 729–745. Springer, Cham (2020). https://doi.org/10.1007/978-3-030-58526-6_43
34. Ma, F., et al.: SF-Net: single-frame supervision for temporal action localization. In: Vedaldi, A., Bischof, H., Brox, T., Frahm, J.-M. (eds.) ECCV 2020. LNCS, vol. 12349, pp. 420–437. Springer, Cham (2020). https://doi.org/10.1007/978-3-030-58548-8_25
35. Ma, J., Gorti, S.K., Volkovs, M., Yu, G.: Weakly supervised action selection learning in video. In: CVPR (2021)
36. Malinin, A., Gales, M.: Predictive uncertainty estimation via prior networks. In: NeurIPS (2018)
37. Moniruzzaman, M., Yin, Z., He, Z., Qin, R., Leu, M.C.: Action completeness modeling with background aware networks for weakly-supervised temporal action localization. In: ACM MM (2020)
38. Narayan, S., Cholakkal, H., Hayat, M., Khan, F.S., Yang, M.H., Shao, L.: D2-Net: weakly-supervised action localization via discriminative embeddings and denoised activations. In: ICCV (2021)
39. Nguyen, P., Liu, T., Prasad, G., Han, B.: Weakly supervised action localization by sparse temporal pooling network. In: CVPR (2018)
40. Paul, S., Roy, S., Roy-Chowdhury, A.K.: W-TALC: weakly-supervised temporal activity localization and classification. In: Ferrari, V., Hebert, M., Sminchisescu, C., Weiss, Y. (eds.) ECCV 2018. LNCS, vol. 11208, pp. 588–607. Springer, Cham (2018). https://doi.org/10.1007/978-3-030-01225-0_35
41. Ramezani, M., Yaghmaee, F.: A review on human action analysis in videos for retrieval applications. Artif. Intell. Rev. **46**(4), 485–514 (2016). https://doi.org/10.1007/s10462-016-9473-y

42. Qu, S., et al.: ACM-Net: action context modeling network for weakly-supervised temporal action localization. arXiv:2104.02967 (2021)
43. Sensoy, M., Kaplan, L., Cerutti, F., Saleki, M.: Uncertainty-aware deep classifiers using generative models. In: AAAI (2020)
44. Sensoy, M., Kaplan, L., Kandemir, M.: Evidential deep learning to quantify classification uncertainty. In: NeurIPS (2018)
45. Shi, B., Dai, Q., Mu, Y., Wang, J.: Weakly-supervised action localization by generative attention modeling. In: CVPR (2020)
46. Shi, W., Zhao, X., Chen, F., Yu, Q.: Multifaceted uncertainty estimation for label-efficient deep learning. In: NeurIPS (2020)
47. Shou, Z., Gao, H., Zhang, L., Miyazawa, K., Chang, S.-F.: AutoLoc: weakly-supervised temporal action localization in untrimmed videos. In: Ferrari, V., Hebert, M., Sminchisescu, C., Weiss, Y. (eds.) ECCV 2018. LNCS, vol. 11220, pp. 162–179. Springer, Cham (2018). https://doi.org/10.1007/978-3-030-01270-0_10
48. Singh, K.K., Lee, Y.J.: Hide-and-seek: forcing a network to be meticulous for weakly-supervised object and action localization. In: ICCV (2017)
49. Sridhar, D., Quader, N., Muralidharan, S., Li, Y., Dai, P., Lu, J.: Class semantics-based attention for action detection. In: ICCV (2021)
50. Sultani, W., Chen, C., Shah, M.: Real-world anomaly detection in surveillance videos. In: CVPR (2018)
51. Vishwakarma, S., Agrawal, A.: A survey on activity recognition and behavior understanding in video surveillance. Vis. Comput. **29**(10), 983–1009 (2013)
52. Wang, L., Xiong, Y., Lin, D., Van Gool, L.: Untrimmednets for weakly supervised action recognition and detection. In: CVPR (2017)
53. Xu, M., Zhao, C., Rojas, D.S., Thabet, A., Ghanem, B.: G-TAD: sub-graph localization for temporal action detection. In: CVPR (2020)
54. Xu, Y., et al.: Segregated temporal assembly recurrent networks for weakly supervised multiple action detection. In: AAAI (2019)
55. Yager, R.R., Liu, L.: Classic Works of the Dempster-Shafer Theory of Belief Functions, vol. 219, Springer (2008)
56. Yang, W., Zhang, T., Yu, X., Qi, T., Zhang, Y., Wu, F.: Uncertainty guided collaborative training for weakly supervised temporal action detection. In: CVPR (2021)
57. Yang, Z., Qin, J., Huang, D.: ACGNet: action complement graph network for weakly-supervised temporal action localization. arXiv preprint arXiv:2112.10977 (2021)
58. Zhang, C., Cao, M., Yang, D., Chen, J., Zou, Y.: Cola: weakly-supervised temporal action localization with snippet contrastive learning. In: CVPR (2021)
59. Zhang, C., et al.: Adversarial seeded sequence growing for weakly-supervised temporal action localization. In: ACM MM (2019)
60. Zhao, P., Xie, L., Ju, C., Zhang, Y., Wang, Y., Tian, Q.: Bottom-Up temporal action localization with mutual regularization. In: Vedaldi, A., Bischof, H., Brox, T., Frahm, J.-M. (eds.) ECCV 2020. LNCS, vol. 12353, pp. 539–555. Springer, Cham (2020). https://doi.org/10.1007/978-3-030-58598-3_32
61. Zhong, J.X., Li, N., Kong, W., Zhang, T., Li, T.H., Li, G.: Step-by-step erasion, one-by-one collection: a weakly supervised temporal action detector. In: ACM MM (2018)
62. Zhu, Z., Tang, W., Wang, L., Zheng, N., Hua, G.: Enriching local and global contexts for temporal action localization. In: ICCV (2021)

Global-Local Motion Transformer for Unsupervised Skeleton-Based Action Learning

Boeun Kim[1,2]([⊠]), Hyung Jin Chang[3], Jungho Kim[2], and Jin Young Choi[1]

[1] ASRI, Department of ECE., Seoul National University, Seoul, South Korea
{bony57,jychoi}@snu.ac.kr
[2] AIRC, Korea Electronics Technology Institute, Seongnam-si, South Korea
jhkim77@keti.re.kr
[3] School of Computer Science, University of Birmingham, Birmingham, UK
h.j.chang@bham.ac.uk

Abstract. We propose a new transformer model for the task of unsupervised learning of skeleton motion sequences. The existing transformer model utilized for unsupervised skeleton-based action learning is learned the instantaneous velocity of each joint from adjacent frames without global motion information. Thus, the model has difficulties in learning the attention globally over whole-body motions and temporally distant joints. In addition, person-to-person interactions have not been considered in the model. To tackle the learning of whole-body motion, long-range temporal dynamics, and person-to-person interactions, we design a global and local attention mechanism, where, global body motions and local joint motions pay attention to each other. In addition, we propose a novel pretraining strategy, multi-interval pose displacement prediction, to learn both global and local attention in diverse time ranges. The proposed model successfully learns local dynamics of the joints and captures global context from the motion sequences. Our model outperforms state-of-the-art models by notable margins in the representative benchmarks. Codes are available at *https://github.com/Boeun-Kim/GL-Transformer*.

Keywords: Unsupervised pretraining · Action recognition · Transformer

1 Introduction

In skeleton-based action recognition, to avoid expensive and time-consuming annotation for supervised learning, recent studies have focused on unsupervised learning techniques for pretraining [8,16,18,25,27,30,31,35,37,40]. For unsupervised pretraining suitable for action recognition, learning the global context

Supplementary Information The online version contains supplementary material available at https://doi.org/10.1007/978-3-031-19772-7_13.

of the entire motion sequence is essential along with learning local joint dynamics and topology. However, existing methods have limitations in effectively capturing both global context and local joint dynamics.

Several existing unsupervised pretraining methods exploit RNN-based encoder-decoder models [16,18,25,30,37,40]. However, RNN-based methods have difficulties in extracting global contexts because of the long-range dependency problem [6,10]. Other approaches utilize contrastive learning schemes [17, 27,35]. However, the performance of these methods has been reported to be highly dependent on the selection of the encoder model because the contrastive loss does not induce detailed learning in the local dynamics of the joints [17,35].

Recently, the transformer, widely used for natural language processing and image recognition, has been applied to the unsupervised pretraining of skeleton-based action recognition. The first and the only model is H-transformer [8], which learns to predict the direction of the instantaneous velocity of joints in each frame. H-transformer still has limitations in learning global attention because predicting only the instantaneous velocity induces the model to learn the local attention rather than the global context in whole-body motions. In addition, H-transformer does not consider person-to-person interactions which are important for classifying actions performed by two or more persons.

In this paper, to tackle the learning of global context, long-range temporal dynamics, and person-to-person interactions, we propose a novel transformer-based pretraining model, which is called GL-Transformer. To this end, we design the GL-Transformer architecture that contains global and local attention (GLA) mechanism. The GLA mechanism comprises spatial multi-head attention (spatial-MHA) and temporal multi-head attention (temporal-MHA) modules. Using the input body motions disentangled into global body motions and local joint motions, the spatial-MHA module performs three types of attention: local(inter-joint), global(body)-from/to-local(joint), and global(person)-to-global(person) attentions. The temporal-MHA module performs global and local attention between any two frames for sequences of every person.

In addition, a novel pretraining strategy is proposed to induce GL-Transformer to learn global attention across the long-range sequence. For the pretraining, we design a multi-task learning strategy referred to as multi-interval pose displacement prediction (MPDP). For MPDP, GL-Transformer is trained with multiple tasks to predict multiple pose displacements (angle and movement distance of every joint) over different intervals at the same time. GL-Transformer learns local attention from a small interval, as well as global attention from a large interval. To enhance performance, we add two factors to GL-Transformer. First, to learn natural joint dynamics across frames, we impose natural-speed motion sequences instead of sequences sampled to a fixed length. Next, we introduce a trainable spatial-temporal positional embedding and inject it to each GL-Transformer block repeatedly to use the order information in every block, which is the valuable information of the motion sequence.

We demonstrate the effectiveness of our method through extensive experimental evaluations on widely used datasets: NTU-60 [28], NTU-120 [19], and NW-UCLA [34]. In the linear evaluation protocol [40], the performance of GL-Transformer exceeds that of H-transformer [8] and other state-of-the-art (SOTA) methods by notable margins. Furthermore, our method even outperforms SOTA methods in semi-supervised settings. The main contributions of this study are summarized as follows:

1. We design a novel transformer architecture including global and local attention (GLA) mechanism to model local joint dynamics and capture the global context from skeleton motion sequences with multiple persons (Sect. 3.2).
2. We introduce a novel pretraining strategy, multi-interval displacement prediction (MPDP), to learn attention in diverse temporal ranges (Sect. 3.3).
3. GL-Transformer renews the state-of-the-art score in extensive experiments on three representative benchmarks: NTU-60, NTU-120, and NW-UCLA.

2   Related Works

Unsupervised Skeleton-Based Action Recognition. Earlier unsupervised learning methods for skeleton-based action recognition can be divided into two categories: using RNN-based encoder-decoders and contrastive learning schemes. Several existing methods utilize RNN-based encoder-decoder networks [16,18,25,30,37,40]. The decoder of these networks performs a pretraining task to induce the encoder to extract an appropriate representation for action recognition. The decoder of LongT GAN [40] reconstructs the randomly corrupted input sequence conditioned on the representation. MS^2L [18] learns to generate more general representations through multi-task learning, which performs tasks such as motion prediction and jigsaw puzzle recognition. Recently, Colorization [38] adopted a GCN to pretrain which regresses the temporal and spatial orders of a skeleton sequence. RNN-based models suffer from long-range dependencies, and the GCN-based models have a similar challenge because they deliver information sequentially along a fixed path [6,10,26]. Therefore, the RNN and GCN-based methods have limitations in extracting global representations from the motion sequence, especially from long motions.

Other methods exploit the contrastive learning scheme [27,31,35]. These methods augment the original motion sequence and regard it as a positive sample while considering other motion sequences as negative samples. The model is then trained to generate similar representations between the positive samples using contrastive loss. AS-CAL [27] leverages various augmentation schemes such as rotation, shear, reverse, and masking. Contrastive learning schemes have a limitation, in that all sequences other than themselves are regarded as negative samples, even sequences belonging to the same class. CrosSCLR [17] alleviates this issue by increasing the number of positive samples using representations learned from other views, such as velocity or bone sequences. Because the contrastive learning loss adjusts the distances between the final representations extracted by an encoder, it is difficult to train the encoder to reflect the local joint dynamics explicitly by the loss. To address the limitations in both categories of unsupervised action recognition, we introduce the transformer [33] architecture for modeling the local dynamics of joints and capturing the global context from motion sequences.

Transformer-Based Supervised Learning. Transformer-based models have achieved remarkable success in various supervised learning tasks using motion sequences, owing to their attention mechanism, which is suitable for handling long-range sequences. In supervised action recognition tasks, recent transformer-based methods [3,10,24,26] outperform GCN-based methods, which have limitations in yielding rich representations because of the fixed graph topology of the human body. In the motion prediction task, the method in [1,6] employs a transformer encoder to capture the spatial-temporal dependency of a given motion sequence and a transformer decoder to generate future motion sequences. In the 3D pose estimation task, the method in [39] imposes a 2D pose sequence on the spatial-temporal transformer to model joint relations and estimate the 3D pose of the center frame accurately.

Transformer-Based Pretraining. Transformer-based pretraining has become the dominant approach in natural language processing [11,20], and is being actively introduced to other research fields such as vision-language [14,23,32], images [4,7,12,13], and videos [21,36]. The H-transformer [8] is the first transformer-based pretraining method for motion sequences. The proposed pretraining strategy predicts the direction of the instantaneous velocity of the joints in each frame. This strategy focuses on learning attention from adjacent frames rather than from distant frames. The model is designed to learn spatial attention between five body part features, where global body movement is not considered. To address these limitations, we propose a GL-Transformer that contains a global and local attention mechanism and a novel pretraining strategy. We aim to train GL-Transformer to generate a representation of input motion sequences suitable for the downstream action recognition task by modeling local and global attention effectively in the pretraining process.

3 Proposed Method

3.1 Overall Scheme

Our goal is to build a transformer architecture suitable for the skeleton motion sequence (Sect. 3.2) and design a novel pretraining strategy (Sect. 3.3) for encoding both the internal dynamics and the global context of the motion sequence.

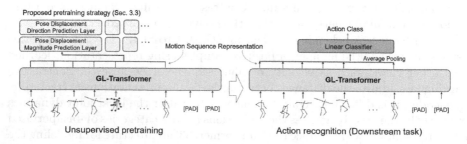

Fig. 1. Overall scheme of the proposed framework. GL-Transformer is pretrained with unlabeled motion sequences, and then evaluated in downstream action recognition task

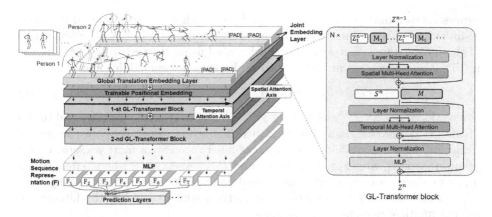

Fig. 2. Model architecture. The input motion sequence is disentangled into global translational motions (red dots) and local motions (blue dots). The proposed model comprises N stacked GL-Transformer blocks. Global and local attention mechanism is implemented in both spatial-MHA and temporal-MHA modules in each block (Color figure online)

As illustrated in Fig. 1, the proposed framework comprises two stages: unsupervised pretraining and downstream action recognition stages. In the first stage, we pretrain the proposed transformer-based model, GL-Transformer, with unlabeled motion sequences. Next, we verify that GL-Transformer generates the appropriate motion representation required for the action recognition. A single linear classifier is attached after GL-Transformer. After average pooling is applied to the motion sequence representation for the temporal axis, it is passed to the classifier.

3.2   Model Architecture

Our model comprises N stacked GL-Transformer blocks, as illustrated in Fig. 2, and each block contains spatial multi-head attention (spatial-MHA) and temporal multi-head attention (temporal-MHA) modules sequentially, as illustrated by the blue boxes on the right side in Fig. 2.

Input Motion Sequences. As illustrated at the top of the left figure in Fig. 2, the input human motion sequence is expressed by two types of information: global translational motion (red dots) of the body and local motions of the body joints (blue dots). The global translational motion represents the trajectory of the center joint of the body, and the local motions represent the relative motions of the body joints from the center joint. The center joint is defined in each dataset, for example, NTU datasets [19,28] define the spine joint as the center joint. The original 3D skeleton motion sequence is expressed by tensor $X = [X_1, X_2, \cdots, X_T]^T$, where X_t is a matrix representing the skeleton pose at the t-th frame. The pose matrix X_t is defined by $X_t = [q_t^1, q_t^2, \cdots, q_t^K]^T$, where $q_t^k \in \mathbb{R}^3$ indicates the 3-dimensional vector for the k-th joint coordinate. The relative position of the k-th joint is $r_t^k = q_t^k - q_t^c$, where q_t^c denotes the coordinate of the center joint. Using the relative joint positions, the t-th frame of local motion is expressed by a matrix $R_t = [r_t^1, \cdots, r_t^K]^T$, in which we remove $r_t^c = (0,0,0)$ and re-index it to $K-1$ dimensional matrix as $R_t = [r_t^1, \cdots, r_t^{K-1}]^T$. The t-th frame of the global translational motion is calculated using the vector $g_t = q_t^c - q_0^c$. As in Fig. 2, g_t and r_t^k are projected into D dimensional embedding vectors as

$$\bar{g}_t = W_g g_t + b_g, \quad \bar{r}_t^k = W_r r_t^k + b_r, \quad k = 1, \cdots, K-1, \tag{1}$$

where $W_g, W_r \in \mathbb{R}^{(D \times 3)}$ and $b_g, b_r \in \mathbb{R}^{(D \times 1)}$ denote trainable weights and biases of the global translation and joint embedding layers respectively. In the case of an action dataset containing the interaction between two or more persons, vector g_t and matrix R_t are expressed by $g_{t,p}$ and $R_{t,p}$ respectively, where p denotes an index of the person. Similarly, the embedding vectors are expressed as $\bar{g}_{t,p}$, and $\bar{r}_{t,p}^k$. In the following, we describe our method which considers the interaction among multiple persons in the sequence.

Trainable and Tight Positional Embedding. By extending the concept of the positional embedding matrix [33] containing the order information of a sequence, we introduce a trainable spatial-temporal positional embedding tensor $M \in \mathbb{R}^{T \times PK \times D}$ to learn the order information of both the temporal frames and spatial joints from the training data. Note that PK is the dimension for the joint indices of P persons, and D is the dimension of embedding vectors, same as D in $\bar{g}_{t,p}$ and $\bar{r}_{t,p}^k$. Joint order information plays a more important role in skeleton motion sequences than in the case of sentences or images, in that individual joint positions are not meaningful until we know which part of the body the joint belongs to. Furthermore, frame order also plays an important role in detecting the action. To this end, we propose a tight positional embedding method to use order information explicitly in every GL-Transformer block. Previous transformer-based models [11,12,39] apply positional embedding once before the first transformer block. In contrast, we apply it to the input tensors of every block, as illustrated in Fig. 2. In each GL-Transformer Block, the positional embedding is explicitly applied in both the spatial-MHA and temporal-MHA modules, as illustrated in the right figure of Fig. 2.

Global and Local Attention (GLA) Mechanism. We aim to construct a global and local attention (GLA) mechanism to extract global semantic information along with capturing the local relationships between the joints within the skeleton motion sequence. GLA is implemented in both the spatial-MHA and temporal-MHA modules. The spatial-MHA module learns spatial dependency within one frame. In the module, global(body)-from/to-local(joint) dependencies are learned by an attention operation between the features corresponding to $g_{t,p}$ and $R_{t,p}$ of each person. Likewise, person-to-person dependencies are learned by the attention among the features of multiple persons: $\{g_{t,p}, R_{t,p} | p = 1, \cdots, P\}$, where P is the number of persons. The temporal-MHA module learns the temporal dependencies across the sequence using pose features aggregated by the spatial-MHA. The temporal-MHA module learns whole-body motion information from distant frames as well as local joint dynamics from the adjacent frames.

Input pose features of the spatial-MHA module at the t-th frame in the n-th block is denoted by $Z_t^n \in \mathbb{R}^{PK \times D}$. For the first block, embeddings of multiple people are concatenated along the spatial attention axis (see Fig. 2) as

$$Z_t^0 = ||_{p=1}^{P} Z_{t,p}^0, \tag{2}$$

$$Z_{t,p}^0 = [\bar{g}_{t,p}, \bar{r}_{t,p}^1, \cdots \bar{r}_{t,p}^{K-1}]^T, \quad t = 1, \cdots, T, \tag{3}$$

where $||$ indicates the concatenation operation. The spatial-MHA in $n(\geq 2)$-th block receives the output (Z_t^{n-1}) of the previous block. The spatial-MHA module updates the pose features as

$$S_t^n = \text{spatial-MHA}(LN(Z_t^{n-1} + M_t)) + (Z_t^{n-1} + M_t), \tag{4}$$

where $M_t \in \mathbb{R}^{PK \times D}$ is t-th slice of the positional embedding tensor M. $LN(\cdot)$ denotes the layer normalization operator [2]. For the spatial-MHA$(\cdot)$, we borrow the multi-head self-attention (MHA) mechanism from [33], which is described below. For simplicity, we denote $LN(Z_t^{n-1} + M_t)$ as $\hat{Z}_t^{n-1}$. First, $\hat{Z}_t^{n-1}$ is projected to $query\,Q$, $key\,K$, $value\,V$ matrices as

$$Q = \hat{Z}_t^{n-1} W^Q, \quad K = \hat{Z}_t^{n-1} W^K, \quad V = \hat{Z}_t^{n-1} W^V, \tag{5}$$

where $W^Q, W^K, W^V \in \mathbb{R}^{D \times d}$ are weight matrices for the projection and d indicates the projection dimension. The attention mechanism is expressed as

$$\text{Attention}(Q, K, V) = softmax(QK^T/\sqrt{d})V. \tag{6}$$

Note that QK^T refers to the dot-product similarity of each projected joint vector in $query\,Q$ to $key\,K$. High attention weight is given for high similarity. In the MHA, the i-th head performs the attention mechanism in Eq.(6) with different weight matrices W_i^Q, W_i^K, W_i^V from those of other heads as

$$H_i = \text{Attention}(\hat{Z}_t^{n-1} W_i^Q, \hat{Z}_t^{n-1} W_i^K, \hat{Z}_t^{n-1} W_i^V), \quad i = 1, \cdots, h. \tag{7}$$

The concatenation of $\{H_i\}$ is projected to an aggregated pose features as

$$\text{spatial-MHA}(\hat{Z}_t^n) = (||_{i=1}^h H_i)W_H, \tag{8}$$

where $W_H \in \mathbb{R}^{dh \times dh}$ is a projection matrix.

To perform temporal-MHA in the n-th block, we vectorize the pose feature of the t-th frame $S_t^n \in R^{PK \times D}$ into $s_t^n \in R^{PK \cdot D}$. Then, the vectorized pose features are stacked to form a pose feature sequence matrix $S^n = [s_1^n, s_2^n, \ldots, s_T^n]^T \in \mathbb{R}^{T \times (PK \cdot D)}$. In the temporal-MHA module, the same MHA mechanism in Eq.(8) is used, but different weight matrices are applied. Then, the output pose sequence feature of the n-th GL-Transformer (Z^n) is obtained through MLP$(\cdot)$, that is,

$$\bar{Z}^n = \text{temporal-MHA}(LN(S^n + \bar{M})) + (S^n + \bar{M}), \tag{9}$$

$$Z^n = MLP(LN(\bar{Z}^n)) + \bar{Z}^n, \tag{10}$$

where $\bar{M} \in \mathbb{R}^{T \times (PK \cdot D)}$ is a matrix in which the dimension of the positional embedding tensor $M \in \mathbb{R}^{T \times PK \times D}$ is changed. In the N-th GL-Transformer block, the final motion sequence representation F for the input motion sequence X is obtained by passing Z^N through a 2-layer MLP as

$$F = \text{GL-Transformer}(X) = MLP(Z^N). \tag{11}$$

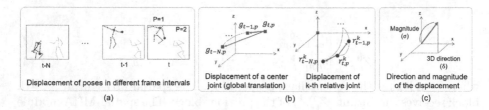

Fig. 3. Description of multi-interval pose displacement

Masked Attention for Natural-Speed Motion Sequence. Most of the existing action recognition methods [8,17,30,38] employ a fixed length of motion sequences, which overlooks the importance of the speed of the motion. To handle natural-speed motion sequences, we utilize an attention mask [33], so that our model can learn the natural joint dynamics across frames and capture speed characteristics from diverse actions. To this end, we define the maximum sequence length as T_{max}. If the length of the original sequence X_{ori} is shorter than T_{max}, the rest of the frames are filled with padding dummy tokens $[PAD] \in \mathbb{R}^{PK \times 3}$, which yields $X = [X_{ori}^T, [PAD], ..., [PAD]]^T \in \mathbb{R}^{T_{max} \times PK \times 3}$. Elements of $[PAD]$ are set to arbitrary numbers because the loss corresponding to the $[PAD]$ token is excluded. To exclude attention from the dummy values, we mask (setting to $-\infty$) columns corresponding to the $[PAD]$ tokens in the QK^T matrix.

3.3   Multi-interval Pose Displacement Prediction (MPDP) Strategy

We design a novel pretraining strategy, multi-interval pose displacement prediction (MPDP), which estimates the whole-body and joint motions at various time intervals at different scales. H-transformer [8] introduces a pretraining strategy that estimates the direction of the instantaneous joint velocity. The instantaneous velocity of the joint in a specific frame can be easily obtained from the adjacent frame so that the model is guided to learn local attention rather than long-range global attention. To overcome this limitation, we propose an MPDP strategy to effectively learn global attention as well as local attention.

As illustrated in Fig. 3(a), we first select multiple frame intervals $t-N, \cdots, t-n, \cdots, t$. GL-Transformer is trained to predict the magnitude and direction of the pose displacement between the t-th and $(t-n)$-th frame. Local motion (relative joint displacement) is predicted with the help of global motion and vice versa. In addition, the motion of other people is considered when predicting one's motion. The displacements are represented by the orange arrows in Fig. 3 (b) and (c). We design the pose displacement prediction as a classification task using *softmaxed* linear classifiers. The model is trained to predict both the direction and magnitude classes for each interval. The predictions of the t-th frame for the interval n are expressed as

$$\hat{\Delta}_{t,n} = softmax(W_n^{\delta} F_t + b_n^{\delta}), \quad \hat{\Sigma}_{t,n} = softmax(W_n^{\sigma} F_t + b_n^{\sigma}), \qquad (12)$$

where F_t denotes t-th slice of the motion sequence representation F, as shown in the left side of Fig. 2. $\hat{\Delta}_{t,n} = ||_{p=1}^{P} \hat{\Delta}_{t,p,n}$ where $\hat{\Delta}_{t,p,n} =$

$[\hat{\delta}_{t,p,n}^g, \hat{\delta}_{t,p,n}^1, \cdots, \hat{\delta}_{t,p,n}^{K-1}]^T$, and $\hat{\delta}_{t,p,n}^g, \hat{\delta}_{t,p,n}^k \in \mathbb{R}^{C_\delta}$ denotes the predicted direction class vector of global translation and k-th joints, respectively. C_δ is the number of direction classes. $\hat{\Sigma}_{t,n} = \|_{p=1}^P \hat{\Sigma}_{t,p,n}$ where $\hat{\Sigma}_{t,p,n} = [\hat{\sigma}_{t,p,n}^g, \hat{\sigma}_{t,p,n}^1, \cdots, \hat{\sigma}_{t,p,n}^{K-1}]^T$, and $\hat{\sigma}_{t,p,n}^g, \hat{\sigma}_{t,p,n}^k \in \mathbb{R}^{C_\sigma}$ denotes the predicted magnitude class vector of the global translation and k-th joints, respectively. C_σ denotes the number of magnitude classes. $W_n^\delta, W_n^\sigma, b_n^\delta$, and b_n^σ are the trainable weights and biases of the linear classifiers for interval n. To train the model parameters, we define the ground truth classes of direction δ and magnitude σ at the t-th frame for the p-th person and interval n as

$$\delta_{t,p,n}^g = class(\angle(g_{t,p} - g_{(t-n),p})), \quad \delta_{t,p,n}^k = class(\angle(r_{t,p}^k - r_{(t-n),p}^k)), \quad (13)$$

$$\sigma_{t,p,n}^g = class(\|g_{t,p} - g_{(t-n),p}\|), \quad \sigma_{t,p,n}^k = class(\|r_{t,p}^k - r_{(t-n),p}^k\|), \quad (14)$$

where we set $g_{(t-n),p} = g_{t,p}$ and $r_{(t-n),p}^k = r_{t,p}^k$ at $t \leq n$ because we do not have the information of the $(t-n)$-th frame in this case. $class(\cdot)$ denotes the class label vector of $\cdot$, where the magnitude is quantized into one of the C_σ classes, and the direction is designated as one of the $C_\delta = 27$ classes, in which each of the xyz direction has three classes: $+, -$, and no movement. The classification loss is calculated for all intervals and frames except the [PAD] tokens. The total loss is defined as follows:

$$L_{total} = \sum_{t=1}^T \sum_{p=1}^P \sum_n \left(\lambda_\delta L_\delta(t,p,n) + \lambda_\sigma L_\sigma(t,p,n) \right), \quad (15)$$

where direction loss $L_\delta(t,p,n)$ and magnitude loss $L_\sigma(t,p,n)$ are the weighted sum of cross entropy loss to train each component of $\hat{\Delta}_{t,p,n}$ and $\hat{\Sigma}_{t,p,n}$, whereas λ_δ and λ_σ denote the weighting factors of L_δ and L_σ, respectively.

4 Experiments

4.1 Datasets and Evaluation Protocol

NTU-RGB+D. NTU-RGB+D 60 (NTU-60) [28] is a large-scale dataset containing 56,880 3D skeleton motion sequences performed by up to two actors and categorized into 60 action classes. Each person has 25 joints. We follow two standard evaluation criteria: cross-subject (**xsub**) and cross-view (**xview**). In **xsub**, the training and test set are collected by different subjects. **xview** splits the training and testing set according to the camera view. NTU-RGB+D 120 (NTU-120) [19] is an extension of NTU- 60 which contains 113,945 sequences for 120 action classes. The new evaluation criterion cross-setup (**xset**) is added for NTU-120, whose training and testing sets are split by the camera setup IDs.

North-Western UCLA. North-Western UCLA (NW-UCLA) [34] contains 1,494 motion sequences captured by 10 subjects. Each sequence is performed by one actor and each person has 20 joints. The actions are categorized into 10 action classes. Following the standard evaluation protocol, the training set comprises samples from camera views 1 and 2, and the remaining samples from view 3 are arranged in the testing set.

Evaluation Protocol. We adopt linear evaluation protocol [8,16,18,25,27,37, 40] which is the standard for the evaluation of unsupervised learning tasks. Following the protocol, the weight parameters of the pretrained model are fixed, and only the attached single linear classifier is trained with the training data. In addition, we evaluate the proposed model in semi-supervised settings [17,29,31, 38]. The pretrained model is fine-tuned with 5% and 10% of the training data, and then the action recognition accuracy is evaluated.

4.2   Implementation Details

We set $T_{max} = 300$ for the NTU dataset and $T_{max} = 50$ for the NW-UCLA dataset. The sequence is augmented by applying a shear [27] and interpolation. For interpolation, the sequence is interpolated into a random length within $\pm$ 10% of the original sequence length. Since the NTU dataset includes two persons, we set it to $P = 2$. Four transformer blocks are utilized, the hidden dimension $D = 6$ for each joint, and eight heads ($h = 8$) are used for self-attention. The H-transformer [8] uses four transformer blocks with $D = 256$ for each of the five body parts. We set $\lambda_\delta, \lambda_\sigma = 1$. In the unsupervised pretraining phase, we utilize the AdamW [22] optimizer with an initial learning rate of $5e^{-4}$ and decay it by multiplying by 0.99 every epoch. The model is trained for 120 epochs for the NTU and 300 epochs for the NW-UCLA with a batch size of 128. In the linear evaluation protocol, we utilize Adam [15] optimizer with a learning rate of $3e^{-3}$. The linear layer is trained for 120 and 300 epochs for NTU and NW-UCLA, respectively, with a batch size of 1024.

4.3   Ablation Study

We conduct ablation studies using the NTU-60 dataset to demonstrate the effectiveness of the main components of our method. The final performance of GL-Transformer substantially exceeds that of the H-transformer [8] in the linear evaluation protocol, exceeding 7.0% for **xsub** and 11.0% for **xview**. The effectiveness of each component is explained as follows:

Effectiveness of GLA and MPDP. In Table 1, Experiment **(1)** exploits the original pose sequence X, Experiment **(2)** utilizes local motion $R_t(t = 1, \cdots, T)$, and Experiment **(3)** utilizes both global translational motion $g_t(t = 1, \cdots, T)$ and local motion $R_t(t = 1, \cdots, T)$. Regarding **(1)**, because global and local motions are mixed in X, it is difficult to model both global and local motions. The result of **(2)** is higher than that of **(1)** when the model learns local dynamics between the joints from local motions. The result of **(3)** is further improved demonstrating that GLA plays an important role in extracting the representation of the entire motion sequence effectively.

In Table 1, Experiment **(3)** does not adopt the displacement magnitude prediction loss, that is $\lambda_\sigma = 0$. For Experiment **(4)**, $\lambda_\sigma = 1$, and predicting both directions and magnitudes exhibits a higher performance. Experiments **(4)** to **(7)** are performed by altering the frame intervals that are utilized in MPDP.

Table 1. Ablation study for verifying the effectiveness of GLA and MPDP in the NTU-60 dataset with the linear evaluation protocol

	Displacement direction	Disentangle global translation	Displacement magnitude	Frame interval	Accuracy (%) xsub	Accuracy (%) xview
H-transformer [8]	✓			{1}	69.3	72.8
Experiment (1)	✓			{1}	71.1	73.5
Experiment (2)	✓	✓(only local motion)		{1}	74.2	81.9
Experiment (3)	✓	✓		{1}	75.4	82.8
Experiment (4)	✓	✓	✓	{1}	75.7	82.9
Experiment (5)	✓	✓	✓	{1, 5}	75.9	83.3
Experiment (6)	✓	✓	✓	{1, 5, 10}	**76.3**	**83.8**
Experiment (7)	✓	✓	✓	{1, 5, 10, 15}	75.7	83.4

Table 2. Ablation study for verifying the effectiveness of person-to-person attention in NTU-120 **xsub** (left) and trainable and tight positional embedding (right) in NTU-60 with the linear evaluation protocol

p2p attention	Accuracy(%) one person cat.	two people cat.	total
w/o	63.0	71.6	64.9
w/	**63.7**	**73.5**	**66.0**

Type	Accuracy(%) xsub	xview
Fixed (sinusoidal)	75.5	83.3
Trainable	76.0	83.6
Trainable tight	**76.3**	**83.8**

The performance gradually increases from the interval $n = \{1\}$ to $n = \{1, 5, 10\}$, demonstrating that long-range global attention is effective in aggregating the context of the entire motion sequence. The accuracy corresponding to the interval $n = \{1, 5, 10, 15\}$ is lower than that of $n = \{1, 5, 10\}$. This implies the maximum interval relies on the inter-frame dependency of the given sequence.

Effectiveness of Person-to-Person Attention. To verify the effect of person-to-person (p2p) attention, we report the model performance trained with and without p2p attention in Table 2. NTU-120 has 120 action categories, 26 among them are two-person interactions and the rest are one-person actions. The p2p attention improves the performance of both groups, especially the performance increases more in the group of two people categories.

Effectiveness of Trainable Tight Positional Embedding. For positional embedding, the performance increases when a trainable embedding is employed instead of a fixed sinusoidal embedding, as presented in the right table of Table 2. The use of tight embedding further increases the performance. We also verify that frames close to each other are trained to have similar positional embeddings. The corresponding figures are added in the supplementary material. In addition, the experiment demonstrating the effectiveness of natural-speed input is added to the supplementary material.

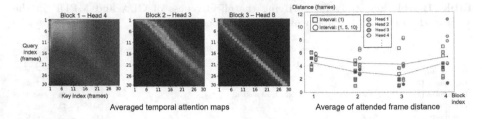

Averaged temporal attention maps   Average of attended frame distance

Fig. 4. Examples of learned temporal attention maps averaged over 300 evaluation sequences (left) and average of attended frame distance (right). Yellow color indicates a large value in the left figure. Blue (interval {1,5,10}) and red (interval {1}) lines indicate the average values over heads in each block (Color figure online)

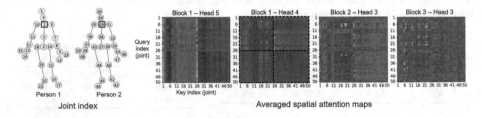

Joint index   Averaged spatial attention maps

Fig. 5. Examples of learned spatial attention maps averaged over 300 evaluation sequences. Yellow color indicates a large value

4.4   Analysis of Learned Attention

We analyze the attention map, $softmax(QK^T/\sqrt{d})$ in Eq. (6), of each pretrained GL-Transformer block. The spatial and temporal attention maps are extracted from the spatial-MHA and temporal-MHA modules, respectively. The attention maps are averaged over 300 motion sequences from the evaluation data. Each head of each transformer block indicates various types of attention maps, and representative samples are shown in Figs. 4 and 5. In Fig. 4, we indicate the averaged temporal attention map for the first 30 frames, because the length of test sequences varies from each other. The vertical and horizontal axes represent the *query* and *key* indices, respectively, and the color of each pixel indicates the degree to which the *query* attends to the *key*. Each head attends a different temporal range, for example, approximately neighboring 10 frames and 5 frames are highlighted in the attention maps of Block2-Head3 and Block3-Head8, respectively, whereas a wide range is highlighted in the attention map of Block1-Head4. The figure on the right in Fig. 4 illustrates the average attended frame distances [12] of each head. The average of the attended frame distances [12] is calculated as a weighted sum of the frame distances, where attention is regarded as the weight. Red squares indicate each head when using frame interval {1}, and blue circles indicate each head when using intervals {1, 5, 10}. In each block, more heads attend to distant frames when the model is pretrained with intervals {1, 5, 10} as compared to when the model is pretrained with interval {1}.

Table 3. Action recognition results with linear evaluation protocol in NTU-60 dataset

Method	Network	Accuracy(%)	
		xsub	xview
LongT GAN (2018) [40]	GRU (encoder-decoder)	39.1	48.1
P&C (2020) [30]	GRU (encoder-decoder)	50.7	76.3
MS^{2}L (2020) [18]	GRU (encoder-decoder)	52.6	–
PCRP (2021) [37]	GRU (encoder-decoder)	54.9	63.4
AS-CAL (2021) [27]	LSTM (contrastive learning)	58.5	64.6
CRRL (2021) [35]	LSTM (contrastive learning)	67.6	73.8
EnGAN-PoseRNN (2019) [16]	RNN (encoder-decoder)	68.6	77.8
SeBiReNet (2020) [25]	GRU (encoder-decoder)	–	79.7
'TS' Colorization (2021) [38]	GCN (encoder-decoder)	71.6	79.9
CrosSCLR-joint (2021) [17]	GCN (contrastive learning)	72.9	79.9
CrosSCLR-bone (2021) [17]	GCN (contrastive learning)	75.2	78.8
H-transformer (2021) [8]	Transformer	69.3	72.8
GL-Transformer	Transformer	**76.3**	**83.8**

An example of the spatial attention map is illustrated in Fig. 5. The 1-st and 26-th indices are utilized for the global translations corresponding to $g_{t,1}$ and $g_{t,2}$, respectively, which are represented as red squares in the left figure. In some heads, the 1-st and 26-th indices appear to be attended differently from other joints. For example, in Block1-Head5, *queries* of all joints pay attention to the 1-st and 26-th *keys* of more than *keys* of other joints. In Block1-Head4, correlations between the joints corresponding to each person are observed as 4 divisions in the attention map, as indicated in red dotted lines. Overall, the proposed model learns the global relationships at shallow blocks (i.e. Block1) and learns fine-grained relationships at deeper blocks (i.e. Block2 and Block3).

4.5   Comparison with State-of-the-Art Methods

We compared our approach with the state-of-the-art (SOTA) methods for unsupervised action recognition: methods using RNN-based encoder-decoder models [16,18,25,30,37,40], a method using GRU-based encoder-decoder model [38], methods using contrastive learning scheme [17,27], and a transformer-based method [8]. We use a linear evaluation protocol to measure the action recognition accuracy. The performance of our method substantially exceeds that of the H-transformer [8] which focuses only on the local relationship between body parts and between frames. As presented in Table 3, the performance of GL-Transformer exceeds that of the H-transformer by 7.0% in **xsub** and 11.0% in **xview** in the NTU-60 dataset. Furthermore, our method outperforms all previous methods by a notable margin.

On the NTU-120 dataset, GL-Transformer outperforms the SOTA methods with a significant margin, as presented in the left table of Table 4. It is verified that the proposed method operates robustly on datasets that include

Table 4. Action recognition results with linear evaluation protocol in the NTU-120 dataset (left) and NW-UCLA dataset (right)

Method	Accuracy(%)	
	xsub	xset
P&C (2020) [30]	41.7	42.7
PCRP (2021) [37]	43.0	44.6
AS-CAL (2021) [27]	48.6	49.2
CrosSCLR-bone (2021) [17]	53.3	50.6
CRRL (2021) [35]	56.2	57.0
CrosSCLR-joint (2021) [17]	58.8	53.3
GL-Transformer	**66.0**	**68.7**

Method	Accuracy(%)
LongT GAN (2018) [40]	74.3
MS²L (2020) [18]	76.8
SeBiReNet (2020) [25]	80.3
CRRL (2021) [35]	83.8
P&C (2020) [30]	84.9
PCRP (2021) [37]	86.1
'TS' Colorization (2021) [38]	90.1
H-transformer (2021) [8]	83.9
GL-Transformer	**90.4**

Table 5. Results with semi-supervised setting in the NTU-60 and NW-UCLA datasets

Methods	NTU-60 (xsub)		NTU-60 (xview)		NW-UCLA	
	5%	10%	5%	10%	5%	10%
MCC-ST-GCN (2021) [31]	42.4	55.6	44.7	59.9	–	–
MCC-2s-AGCN (2021) [31]	47.4	60.8	53.3	65.8	–	–
MCC-AS-GCN (2021) [31]	45.5	59.2	49.2	63.1	–	–
LongT GAN (2018) [40]	–	62.0	–	–	–	59.9
ASSL (2020) [29]	57.3	64.3	63.6	69.8	52.6	–
MS²L (2020) [18]	–	65.2	–	–	–	60.5
CrosSCLR-bone (2021) [17]	59.4	67.7	57.0	67.3	–	–
'TS' Colorization (2021) [38]	60.1	66.1	63.9	73.3	55.9	71.3
CrosSCLR-joint (2021) [17]	61.3	67.6	64.4	73.5	–	–
GL-Transformer	**64.5**	**68.6**	**68.5**	**74.9**	**58.5**	**74.3**

more detailed actions. On the NW-UCLA dataset, GL-Transformer achieved the highest performance among the previous methods, demonstrating that the proposed model is effective even with a small amount of training data, as presented in the right table of Table 4. In addition, we compare the results from the semi-supervised setting on the NTU-60 and NW-UCLA datasets in Table 5. The results of the SOTA semi-supervised action recognition methods [29,31] are also compared in conjunction with the unsupervised methods aforementioned. GL-Transformer exceeds SOTA performance in both evaluations using 5% and 10% of the training data.

5 Conclusions

We introduce a novel transformer architecture and pretraining strategy suitable for motion sequences. The proposed GL-Transformer successfully learns global and local attention, so that the model effectively captures the global context and local dynamics of the sequence. The performance of our model substantially exceeds those of SOTA methods in the downstream action recognition task in both unsupervised and self-supervised manners. In future studies, our model can be extended to a model for learning various skeleton features together, such as the position and bone, to encode richer representations. The memory usage and computation of the model are expected to be reduced by using the concept of sparse attention [5,9], which sparsely pays attention to each other among tokens. Furthermore, our model can be extended to a large-parameter model and pretrained with a large number of skeleton sequences extracted from unspecified web videos to be more generalized, and can be applied to various downstream tasks dealing with human actions.

Acknowledgement. This work was supported by IITP/MSIT [B0101-15–0266, Development of high performance visual bigdata discovery platform for large-scale realtime data analysis, 1/4; 2021–0-01343, AI graduate school program (SNU), 1/4; 2021–0-00537, Visual common sense through self-supervised learning for restoration of invisible parts in images, 1/4; 1711159681, Development of high-quality AI-AR interactive media service through deep learning-based human model generation technology, 1/4].

References

1. Aksan, E., Kaufmann, M., Cao, P., Hilliges, O.: A spatio-temporal transformer for 3D human motion prediction. In: 2021 International Conference on 3D Vision (3DV), pp. 565–574. IEEE (2021)
2. Ba, J.L., Kiros, J.R., Hinton, G.E.: Layer normalization. arXiv preprint arXiv:1607.06450 (2016)
3. Bai, R., et al.: GCsT: graph convolutional skeleton transformer for action recognition. arXiv preprint arXiv:2109.02860 (2021)
4. Bao, H., Dong, L., Wei, F.: BEiT: BERT pre-training of image transformers. arXiv preprint arXiv:2106.08254 (2021)
5. Beltagy, I., Peters, M.E., Cohan, A.: Longformer: the long-document transformer. arXiv preprint arXiv:2004.05150 (2020)
6. Cai, Y., et al.: Learning progressive joint propagation for human motion prediction. In: Vedaldi, A., Bischof, H., Brox, T., Frahm, J.-M. (eds.) ECCV 2020. LNCS, vol. 12352, pp. 226–242. Springer, Cham (2020). https://doi.org/10.1007/978-3-030-58571-6_14
7. Chen, H., et al.: Pre-trained image processing transformer. In: Proceedings of the IEEE/CVF Conference on Computer Vision and Pattern Recognition, pp. 12299–12310 (2021)
8. Cheng, Y.B., Chen, X., Chen, J., Wei, P., Zhang, D., Lin, L.: Hierarchical transformer: Unsupervised representation learning for skeleton-based human action recognition. In: 2021 IEEE International Conference on Multimedia and Expo (ICME), pp. 1–6. IEEE (2021)
9. Child, R., Gray, S., Radford, A., Sutskever, I.: Generating long sequences with sparse transformers. arXiv preprint arXiv:1904.10509 (2019)
10. Cho, S., Maqbool, M., Liu, F., Foroosh, H.: Self-attention network for skeleton-based human action recognition. In: Proceedings of the IEEE/CVF Winter Conference on Applications of Computer Vision, pp. 635–644 (2020)

11. Devlin, J., Chang, M.W., Lee, K., Toutanova, K.: BERT: pre-training of deep bidirectional transformers for language understanding. arXiv preprint arXiv:1810.04805 (2018)
12. Dosovitskiy, A., et al.: An image is worth 16x16 words: transformers for image recognition at scale. arXiv preprint arXiv:2010.11929 (2020)
13. He, K., Chen, X., Xie, S., Li, Y., Dollár, P., Girshick, R.: Masked autoencoders are scalable vision learners. arXiv preprint arXiv:2111.06377 (2021)
14. Huang, Z., Zeng, Z., Liu, B., Fu, D., Fu, J.: Pixel-BERT: aligning image pixels with text by deep multi-modal transformers. arXiv preprint arXiv:2004.00849 (2020)
15. Kingma, D.P., Ba, J.: Adam: a method for stochastic optimization. arXiv preprint arXiv:1412.6980 (2014)
16. Kundu, J.N., Gor, M., Uppala, P.K., Radhakrishnan, V.B.: Unsupervised feature learning of human actions as trajectories in pose embedding manifold. In: 2019 IEEE winter conference on applications of computer vision (WACV), pp. 1459–1467. IEEE (2019)
17. Li, L., Wang, M., Ni, B., Wang, H., Yang, J., Zhang, W.: 3D human action representation learning via cross-view consistency pursuit. In: Proceedings of the IEEE/CVF Conference on Computer Vision and Pattern Recognition, pp. 4741–4750 (2021)
18. Lin, L., Song, S., Yang, W., Liu, J.: MS2L: multi-task self-supervised learning for skeleton based action recognition. In: Proceedings of the 28th ACM International Conference on Multimedia, pp. 2490–2498 (2020)
19. Liu, J., Shahroudy, A., Perez, M., Wang, G., Duan, L.Y., Kot, A.C.: NTU RGB+D 120: a large-scale benchmark for 3D human activity understanding. IEEE Trans. Pattern Anal. Mach. Intell. **42**(10), 2684–2701 (2019)
20. Liu, Y., et al.: Roberta: a robustly optimized bert pretraining approach. arXiv preprint arXiv:1907.11692 (2019)
21. Liu, Z., et al.: Video swin transformer. arXiv preprint arXiv:2106.13230 (2021)
22. Loshchilov, I., Hutter, F.: Decoupled weight decay regularization. arXiv preprint arXiv:1711.05101 (2017)
23. Lu, J., Batra, D., Parikh, D., Lee, S.: Vilbert: pretraining task-agnostic visiolinguistic representations for vision-and-language tasks. In: Advances in Neural Information Processing Systems 32 (2019)
24. Mazzia, V., Angarano, S., Salvetti, F., Angelini, F., Chiaberge, M.: Action transformer: a self-attention model for short-time pose-based human action recognition. Pattern Recogn. **124**, 108487 (2022)
25. Nie, Q., Liu, Z., Liu, Y.: Unsupervised 3D human pose representation with viewpoint and pose disentanglement. In: Vedaldi, A., Bischof, H., Brox, T., Frahm, J.-M. (eds.) ECCV 2020. LNCS, vol. 12364, pp. 102–118. Springer, Cham (2020). https://doi.org/10.1007/978-3-030-58529-7_7
26. Plizzari, C., Cannici, M., Matteucci, M.: Spatial temporal transformer network for skeleton-based action recognition. In: Del Bimbo, A., Cucchiara, R., Sclaroff, S., Farinella, G.M., Mei, T., Bertini, M., Escalante, H.J., Vezzani, R. (eds.) ICPR 2021. LNCS, vol. 12663, pp. 694–701. Springer, Cham (2021). https://doi.org/10.1007/978-3-030-68796-0_50
27. Rao, H., Xu, S., Hu, X., Cheng, J., Hu, B.: Augmented skeleton based contrastive action learning with momentum LSTM for unsupervised action recognition. Inf. Sci. **569**, 90–109 (2021)
28. Shahroudy, A., Liu, J., Ng, T.T., Wang, G.: NTU RGB+D: a large scale dataset for 3D human activity analysis. In: Proceedings of the IEEE conference on computer vision and pattern recognition, pp. 1010–1019 (2016)

29. Si, C., Nie, X., Wang, W., Wang, L., Tan, T., Feng, J.: Adversarial self-supervised learning for semi-supervised 3D action recognition. In: Vedaldi, A., Bischof, H., Brox, T., Frahm, J.-M. (eds.) ECCV 2020. LNCS, vol. 12352, pp. 35–51. Springer, Cham (2020). https://doi.org/10.1007/978-3-030-58571-6_3
30. Su, K., Liu, X., Shlizerman, E.: Predict & cluster: Unsupervised skeleton based action recognition. In: Proceedings of the IEEE/CVF Conference on Computer Vision and Pattern Recognition, pp. 9631–9640 (2020)
31. Su, Y., Lin, G., Wu, Q.: Self-supervised 3d skeleton action representation learning with motion consistency and continuity. In: Proceedings of the IEEE/CVF International Conference on Computer Vision, pp. 13328–13338 (2021)
32. Sun, C., Myers, A., Vondrick, C., Murphy, K., Schmid, C.: VideoBERT: a joint model for video and language representation learning. In: Proceedings of the IEEE/CVF International Conference on Computer Vision, pp. 7464–7473 (2019)
33. Vaswani, A., et al.: Attention is all you need. In: Advances in Neural Information Processing Systems 30 (2017)
34. Wang, J., Nie, X., Xia, Y., Wu, Y., Zhu, S.C.: Cross-view action modeling, learning and recognition. In: Proceedings of the IEEE conference on computer vision and pattern recognition, pp. 2649–2656 (2014)
35. Wang, P., Wen, J., Si, C., Qian, Y., Wang, L.: Contrast-reconstruction representation learning for self-supervised skeleton-based action recognition. arXiv preprint arXiv:2111.11051 (2021)
36. Wang, R., et al.: BEVT: BBERT pretraining of video transformers. arXiv preprint arXiv:2112.01529 (2021)
37. Xu, S., Rao, H., Hu, X., Cheng, J., Hu, B.: Prototypical contrast and reverse prediction: unsupervised skeleton based action recognition. In: IEEE Transactions on Multimedia (2021)
38. Yang, S., Liu, J., Lu, S., Er, M.H., Kot, A.C.: Skeleton cloud colorization for unsupervised 3d action representation learning. In: Proceedings of the IEEE/CVF International Conference on Computer Vision, pp. 13423–13433 (2021)
39. Zheng, C., Zhu, S., Mendieta, M., Yang, T., Chen, C., Ding, Z.: 3D human pose estimation with spatial and temporal transformers. In: Proceedings of the IEEE/CVF International Conference on Computer Vision, pp. 11656–11665 (2021)
40. Zheng, N., Wen, J., Liu, R., Long, L., Dai, J., Gong, Z.: Unsupervised representation learning with long-term dynamics for skeleton based action recognition. In: Proceedings of the AAAI Conference on Artificial Intelligence, vol. 32 (2018)

AdaFocusV3: On Unified Spatial-Temporal Dynamic Video Recognition

Yulin Wang[1], Yang Yue[1], Xinhong Xu[1], Ali Hassani[2], Victor Kulikov[3], Nikita Orlov[3], Shiji Song[1], Humphrey Shi[2,3(✉)], and Gao Huang[1,4(✉)]

[1] Department of Automation, BNRist, Tsinghua University, Beijing, China
{wang-yl19,ley18}@mails.tsinghua.edu.cn, gaohuang@tsinghua.edu.cn
[2] University of Oregon, Eugene, USA
shihonghui3@gmail.com
[3] Picsart AI Research (PAIR), Miami, USA
[4] Beijing Academy of Artificial Intelligence (BAAI), Beijing, China

Abstract. Recent research has revealed that reducing the *temporal* and *spatial* redundancy are both effective approaches towards efficient video recognition, *e.g.*, allocating the majority of computation to a task-relevant subset of frames or the most valuable image regions of each frame. However, in most existing works, either type of redundancy is typically modeled with another absent. This paper explores the unified formulation of spatial-temporal dynamic computation on top of the recently proposed AdaFocusV2 algorithm, contributing to an improved AdaFocusV3 framework. Our method reduces the computational cost by activating the expensive high-capacity network only on some small but informative 3D video cubes. These cubes are cropped from the space formed by frame height, width, and video duration, while their locations are adaptively determined with a light-weighted policy network on a per-sample basis. At test time, the number of the cubes corresponding to each video is dynamically configured, *i.e.*, video cubes are processed sequentially until a sufficiently reliable prediction is produced. Notably, AdaFocusV3 can be effectively trained by approximating the non-differentiable cropping operation with the interpolation of deep features. Extensive empirical results on six benchmark datasets (*i.e.*, ActivityNet, FCVID, Mini-Kinetics, Something-Something V1&V2 and Diving48) demonstrate that our model is considerably more efficient than competitive baselines.

Keywords: Efficient video analysis · Dynamic neural networks · Action recognition

Y. Wang and Y. Yue—Equal contributions.

Supplementary Information The online version contains supplementary material available at https://doi.org/10.1007/978-3-031-19772-7_14.

1 Introduction

Modern deep networks have reached or even surpassed human-level performance on large-scale video recognition benchmarks [1,4,12,13,15,23,46]. Such a remarkable success is in general fueled by the rapid development of large models with high computational demands at inference time. However, the practical application of these resource-hungry models may be challenging, despite their state-of-the-art accuracy. For example, in real-world scenarios like YouTube video recommendation [8,9,17], video-based surveillance [5,7] and content-based searching engines [27], deploying computationally intensive networks significantly increases power consumption, system latency or carbon emission, all of which should be minimized due to economic and environmental concerns.

To address this issue, a number of recent works focus on reducing the inherent *temporal* or *spatial* redundancy in video analysis. For instance, for the former, several algorithms have been proposed to dynamically identify the most informative frames and allocate the majority of computation to them, yielding improvements in the overall efficiency [18,32,36,41,45,58,61]. For the latter, the recently proposed adaptive focus networks (AdaFocus) [52,56] develop dynamic models to adaptively attend to the task-relevant regions of each video frame, which considerably reduces the computational cost without sacrificing accuracy. Although both directions have been proven feasible, how to model *spatial* and *temporal* redundancy jointly and realize highly efficient spatial-temporal dynamic computation is still an under-explored topic. The preliminary results presented by AdaFocusV2+ [56] have revealed their favorable compatibility. However, AdaFocusV2+ only considers them separately in independent modules.

In this paper, we seek to explore the unified formulation that by design aims to reduce the spatial-temporal redundancy simultaneously, and thus study whether such general frameworks can lead to a more promising approach towards efficient video recognition. To implement this idea, we propose an AdaFocusV3 network. In specific, given an input video, our method first takes a quick and cheap glance at it with a light-weighted global network. A policy network will be learned on top of the obtained global information, whose training objective is to capture the most task-relevant parts of the video directly in the 3D space formed by the frame height/width and the time. This is achieved by localizing a sequence of 3D cubes inside the original video. These smaller but informative video cubes will be progressively processed using a high-capacity but computationally more expensive local network for learning discriminative representations. This procedure is dramatically more efficient than processing the whole video due to the reduced size of the cubes. As a consequence, the computation is unevenly allocated across both spatial and temporal dimensions, resulting in considerable improvements in the overall efficiency with the maximally preserved accuracy.

It is noteworthy that the operation of selecting 3D cubes from the videos is not inherently differentiable. To enable the effective training of our AdaFocusV3 framework, we propose a gradient estimation algorithm for the policy network based on deep features. Our solution significantly outperforms the pixel-based counterpart proposed by AdaFocusV2 in our problem.

In addition, an intriguing property of AdaFocusV3 is that it naturally facilitates the adaptive inference. To be specific, since the informative video cubes are processed in a sequence, the inference procedure can be dynamically terminated once the model is able to produce sufficiently reliable predictions, such that further redundant computation on relatively "easier" samples can be saved. This paradigm also allows AdaFocusV3 to adjust the computational cost online without additional training (by simply adapting the early-termination criterion). Such flexibility of our method enables it to make full use of the fluctuating computational resources or minimize the power consumption with varying performance targets. Both of them are the practical requirements of many real-world applications (*e.g.*, searching engines and mobile apps).

We validate the effectiveness of AdaFocusV3 on widely-used video recognition benchmarks. Empirical results show that AdaFocusV3 achieves a new state-of-the-art performance in terms of computational efficiency. For example, when obtaining the same accuracy, AdaFocusV3 has up to 2.6× less Multiply-Add operations compared to the recently proposed OCSampler [36] algorithm.

2   Related Works

Video Recognition. Recent years have witnessed a significant improvement of the test accuracy on large-scale automatic video recognition benchmarks [3,21,29,30,40]. This remarkable progress is largely ascribed to the rapid development of video representation learning backbones [1,4,12,13,23,35,46,51]. The majority of these works focus on modeling the temporal relationships among different frames, which is a key challenge in video understanding. Towards this direction, a representative approach is leveraging the spatial-temporal information simultaneously by expanding the 2-D convolution to 3D space [4,12,23,46]. Another line of works propose to design specialized temporal-aware architectures on top of 2-D deep networks, such as adding recurrent networks [10,33,62], temporal feature averaging [51], and temporal channel shift [11,35,42,44]. Some other works model short-term and long-term temporal relationships separately using two-stream networks [13–15,20]. Besides, since processing videos with deep networks is computationally intensive, a variety of recent works have started to focus on developing efficient video recognition models [37–39,47,48,64].

Temporal Dynamic Networks. A straightforward approach for facilitating efficient video representation learning is to leverage the inherent temporal redundancy within videos. To be specific, not all video frames are equivalently relevant to a given task, such that ideally a model should dynamically identify less informative frames and allocate less computation to them correspondingly [22]. In the context of video recognition, a number of effective approaches have been proposed under this principle [18,19,31,32,36,41,45,57,58,61]. For example, OCSampler [36] proposes a one-step framework, learning to select task-relevant frames with reinforcement learning. VideoIQ [45] processes the frames using varying precision according to their importance. FrameExit [19] performs early-termination at test time after processing sufficiently informative frames. AdaFocusV3 is more general and flexible than these works since we simultaneously model both spatial and temporal redundancy.

Spatial Dynamic Networks. In addition to the temporal dimension, considerable spatial redundancy exists when processing video frames. As a matter of fact, many works have revealed that deep networks can effectively extract representations from the image-based data via attending to a few task-relevant image regions [16,50,54,60]. Recently, the effectiveness of this paradigm has been validated in video recognition as well. As representative works, AdaFocus network V1&V2 [52,56] propose to infer the expensive high-capacity network only on a relatively small but informative patch of each frame, which is adaptively localized with a policy network, yielding a favorable accuracy-speed trade-off. An important advantage of the spatial-based approaches is that they are orthogonal to the temporal-adaptive methods. Nonetheless, in existing works, the spatial and temporal redundancy is usually modeled using independent algorithms with separate network architectures, and combined straightforwardly (e.g., AdaFocusV1&V2 [52,56]). This paper assumes that such a naive implementation may lead to sub-optimal formulation, and proposes a unified AdaFocusV3 framework to consider spatial-temporal redundancy simultaneously, which achieves significantly higher computational efficiency.

3   Method

As aforementioned, existing efficient video recognition approaches usually consider the temporal or spatial redundancy of videos with another absent. We assume that such isolated modeling of the two types of redundancy may lead to sub-optimal formulation, and propose a unified AdaFocusV3 framework. AdaFocusV3 learns to perform spatial-temporal dynamic computation simultaneously, yielding significantly improved computational efficiency compared with the state-of-the-art baselines. In the following, we introduce the details of our method.

3.1   Overview

We first describe the inference and training pipelines of AdaFocusV3, laying the basis for the detailed introduction to the network architecture, the training algorithm and the implementation details.

Inference. We start by introducing the inference procedure of AdaFocusV3, which is shown in Fig. 1. Given an input video $\mathbf{V} \in \mathbb{R}^{H \times W \times T}$ with T frames of $H \times W$ images (here we omit the RGB channels for simplicity), we first process it with a light-weighted global encoder f_{G}. The aim of this step is to obtain the coarse global information cheaply with low computational cost. Then the output features of f_{G} are fed into a policy network π, which is trained to capture the most task-relevant parts of $\mathbf{V}$ for extracting finer representations. In specific, the outputs of π localize a sequence of 3D cubes $\{\tilde{\mathbf{V}}_1, \tilde{\mathbf{V}}_2, \ldots\}$ with the size

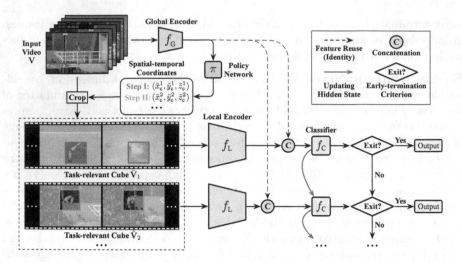

Fig. 1. Inference procedure of AdaFocusV3. The global encoder f_G first takes a quick glance at each input video in the holistic view. A policy network π is learned on top of f_G to capture the most task-relevant parts of the video with 3D spatial-temporal cubes. These cubes are processed by the high-capacity and accurate local encoder f_L for extracting discriminative deep features. A classifier π aggregates all the obtained information and dynamically outputs the prediction. Notably, the inference will be terminated once a convincing prediction (*e.g.*, with sufficiently low entropy or being adequately confident) has been produced

$H' \times W' \times T'$ ($H' < H, W' < W, T' < T$), and these cubes will be processed by a local encoder f_L. Note that f_L is designed to be high-capacity, accurate and computationally more expensive. Considerable redundant computation can be saved by only activating f_L on top of the selected informative inputs with reduced size rather than the whole video.

At last, a classifier f_C aggregates the features of all the previous inputs to produce a prediction. Importantly, the contribution of $\{\tilde{V}_1, \tilde{V}_2, \dots\}$ to recognition are formulated to be descending in the sequence (via training, details described later). They are progressively processed by f_L and f_C, while a softmax prediction $\boldsymbol{p}_t$ will be retrieved from f_C after seeing every video cube $\tilde{V}_t$. In other words, ideally, AdaFocusV3 always allocates the computation first to the most important video contents in terms of the task. The major insight behind this design is to facilitate the adaptive inference, *i.e.*, the inference can be terminated once $\boldsymbol{p}_t$ is sufficiently reliable and thus avoids further redundant computation. In the implementation, we adopt an entropy-based early-termination criterion (see Sect. 3.4 for details).

Training. AdaFocusV3 is trained by minimizing the sum of the loss corresponding to all the predictions from f_C, namely

$$\underset{f_G, f_L, f_C, \pi}{\text{minimize}} \quad \mathcal{L} = \underset{(V, y) \in \mathcal{D}_{\text{train}}}{\mathbb{E}} \left[\sum_t L_{\text{CE}}(\boldsymbol{p}_t, y) \right], \tag{1}$$

where y is the label of $\mathbf{V}$, $\mathcal{D}_{\text{train}}$ is the training set and $L_{\text{CE}}(\cdot)$ denotes the standard cross-entropy loss function. Intuitively, solving problem (1) will learn a π that enables the model to produce correct predictions with as fewer inputs as possible. The selection policy is trained to usually find the most beneficial cubes for the current model at each step.

3.2 Network Architecture

Global Encoder f_{G} and local encoder f_{L} are both deep networks (*e.g.*, ConvNets and vision Transformers) that map the input video frames to the deep feature space. However, f_{G} is exploited to take a quick glance at the videos, such that the policy network π can be activated to localize the informative video cubes. As a consequence, light-weighted architectures should be adopted. On the other hand, f_{L} is designed to extract accurate and discriminative representations from the selected important inputs. Therefore, it allows deploying computationally intensive and high-capacity models.

Policy Network π receives the global feature maps produced by f_{G}, and determines the locations of the video cubes to attend to. Notably, here we assume all the frames of $\mathbf{V}$ are fed into f_{G} at the same time, since AdaFocusV3 seeks to reduce both the temporal and spatial redundancy simultaneously. In contrast, AdaFocusV2/V1 [52,56] by design processes the videos frame by frame. To this end, we do not follow their recurrent design of π. On the contrary, we directly process the global features of the whole video, and obtain the centre coordinates of $\{\tilde{\mathbf{V}}_1, \tilde{\mathbf{V}}_2, \dots\}$ at one time.

Classifier f_{C} aggregates the information from $\{\tilde{\mathbf{V}}_1, \tilde{\mathbf{V}}_2, \dots\}$, and produces the final prediction correspondingly. The architecture of f_{C} may have various candidates, including recurrent networks [6,25,52], frame-wise prediction averaging [35,41,42], and accumulated feature pooling [19,56]. Besides, we adopt the efficient feature reuse mechanism proposed by [52,56], where the outputs of both f_{G} and f_{L} are leveraged by f_{C} (depicted using dashed lines in Fig. 1).

3.3 Training Algorithm

Naive Implementation. An obstacle towards solving problem (1) lies in that, cropping the cubes $\{\tilde{\mathbf{V}}_1, \tilde{\mathbf{V}}_2, \dots\}$ from the video $\mathbf{V}$ is not an inherently differentiable operation. Consequently, it is nontrivial to apply the standard back-propagation-based training algorithm. To address this issue, a straightforward approach is to leverage the interpolation-based cropping mechanism proposed by AdaFocusV2 [56]. Formally, given the centre coordinates $(\tilde{x}_{\text{c}}^t, \tilde{y}_{\text{c}}^t, \tilde{z}_{\text{c}}^t)$ of $\tilde{\mathbf{V}}_t$, we can obtain $\tilde{\mathbf{V}}_t$ through trilinear interpolation. In this way, the value of any pixel $\tilde{v}_{i,j,k}^t$ in $\tilde{\mathbf{V}}_t$ is calculated as the weighted combination of its surrounded eight adjacent pixels in $\mathbf{V}$, *i.e.*,

$$\tilde{v}_{i,j,k}^t = \text{Trilinear}\left(\mathbf{V}, (\tilde{x}_{i,j,k}^t, \tilde{y}_{i,j,k}^t, \tilde{z}_{i,j,k}^t)\right), \tag{2}$$

where $(\tilde{x}_{i,j,k}^t, \tilde{y}_{i,j,k}^t, \tilde{z}_{i,j,k}^t)$ corresponds to the horizontal, vertical and temporal coordinates of $\tilde{v}_{i,j,k}^t$ in $\mathbf{V}$.

In back-propagation, it is easy to obtain the gradients of the loss $\mathcal{L}$ with respect to $\tilde{v}_{i,j,k}^t$, $i.e.$, $\partial\mathcal{L}/\partial\tilde{v}_{i,j,k}^t$. With Eq. (2), we further have

$$\frac{\partial\mathcal{L}}{\partial\tilde{x}_c^t} = \sum_{i,j,k}\frac{\partial\mathcal{L}}{\partial\tilde{v}_{i,j,k}^t}\frac{\partial\tilde{v}_{i,j,k}^t}{\partial\tilde{x}_{i,j,k}^t}, \quad \frac{\partial\mathcal{L}}{\partial\tilde{y}_c^t} = \sum_{i,j,k}\frac{\partial\mathcal{L}}{\partial\tilde{v}_{i,j,k}^t}\frac{\partial\tilde{v}_{i,j,k}^t}{\partial\tilde{y}_{i,j,k}^t}, \quad \frac{\partial\mathcal{L}}{\partial\tilde{z}_c^t} = \sum_{i,j,k}\frac{\partial\mathcal{L}}{\partial\tilde{v}_{i,j,k}^t}\frac{\partial\tilde{v}_{i,j,k}^t}{\partial\tilde{z}_{i,j,k}^t}.$$

(3)

Note that Eq. (3) leverages the fact that the geometric relationship between $(\tilde{x}_{i,j,k}^t, \tilde{y}_{i,j,k}^t, \tilde{z}_{i,j,k}^t)$ and $(\tilde{x}_c^t, \tilde{y}_c^t, \tilde{z}_c^t)$ is always fixed once the size of $\tilde{\mathbf{V}}_t$ is fixed, namely we have

$$\frac{\partial\tilde{v}_{i,j,k}^t}{\partial\tilde{x}_c^t} = \frac{\partial\tilde{v}_{i,j,k}^t}{\partial\tilde{x}_{i,j,k}^t}, \quad \frac{\partial\tilde{v}_{i,j,k}^t}{\partial\tilde{y}_c^t} = \frac{\partial\tilde{v}_{i,j,k}^t}{\partial\tilde{y}_{i,j,k}^t}, \quad \frac{\partial\tilde{v}_{i,j,k}^t}{\partial\tilde{z}_c^t} = \frac{\partial\tilde{v}_{i,j,k}^t}{\partial\tilde{z}_{i,j,k}^t}.$$

(4)

Given that $\tilde{x}_c^t$, $\tilde{y}_c^t$ and $\tilde{z}_c^t$ are the outputs of $\boldsymbol{\pi}$, the regular back-propagation are capable of proceeding through Eq. (3) to compute the gradients of all the parameters and update the model.

In essence, calculating the gradients with Eqs. (2–4) follows the following logic. We change the location of $\tilde{\mathbf{V}}_t$ in an infinitesimal quantity, and measure the consequent changes on the value of each pixel in $\tilde{\mathbf{V}}_t$ via Eq. (2). These changes affect the inputs of f_L, and accordingly, have an impact on the final optimization objective.

Limitations of Pixel-Based Gradient Estimation. Although the aforementioned procedure enables the back-propagation of gradients, it suffers from some major issues. First, the change of the contents of $\tilde{\mathbf{V}}_t$ is achieved by varying the pixel values, each of which is determined only by few adjacent pixels in $\mathbf{V}$. Such a limited source of information may be too local to reflect the semantic-level changes when the location of $\tilde{\mathbf{V}}_t$ varies. However, during training, the model should ideally be informed with how the semantical contents of $\tilde{\mathbf{V}}_t$ will change with the different outputs of $\boldsymbol{\pi}$, as we hope to localize the most informative parts of the original videos. Second, performing interpolation along the temporal dimension amounts to mixing the adjacent frames in the pixel space, which is empirically observed to degrade the generalization performance of the model. We tentatively attribute this to the violation of the i.i.d. assumption, since the frames are not mixed at test time (Fig. 2).

Estimating Gradients with Deep Features. To alleviate the problems caused by the pixel-based gradient estimation, we propose a novel deep feature based approach to guide the training of the policy network $\boldsymbol{\pi}$. Our main motivation here is to enable the outputs of $\boldsymbol{\pi}$ to have a direct influence on the feature maps that are extracted by f_L. These deep representations are known to excel at capturing the task-relevant semantics of the inputs [2,49,55]. Once the gradients can explicitly tell $\boldsymbol{\pi}$ how the deep features corresponding to $\tilde{\mathbf{V}}_t$ will be affected by its outputs, $\boldsymbol{\pi}$ will receive direct supervision signals on whether $\hat{\mathbf{V}}_t$ contains valuable contents in terms of the recognition task.

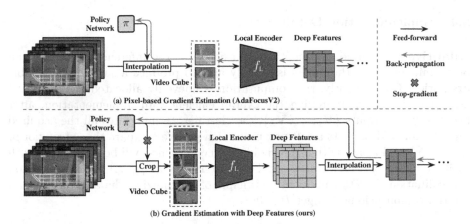

Fig. 2. Comparisons of the gradient estimation with image pixels and deep features. The back-propagation process of the policy network π is illustrated with red arrows. AdaFocusV3 proposes to guide the learning of π with deep features. In comparison with the pixel-based approach proposed in AdaFocusV2, our method not only provides more direct semantic-level supervision signals for π, but also avoids the issue that the adjacent frames are mixed in the pixel space during training. (Color figure online)

To implement this idea, assume that $e_t \in \mathbb{R}^{H^f \times W^f \times T^f}$ denotes the feature maps of $\tilde{\mathbf{V}}_t$ produced by f_L. During training, we crop a slightly larger cube $\tilde{\mathbf{V}}'_t$ at the location of $\tilde{\mathbf{V}}_t$ from the original video $\mathbf{V}$, such that the size of the feature maps e'_t corresponding to $\tilde{\mathbf{V}}'_t$ will exactly be $(H^f + 1) \times (W^f + 1) \times (T^f + 1)$. Note that here we deactivate the gradient computation and hence the back-propagation through Eqs. (2–4) will not happen. Then we obtain e_t by performing trilinear interpolation at the centre of e'_t. Formally, the value of any element $e^t_{i,j,k}$ in e_t can be solved by

$$e^t_{i,j,k} = \text{Trilinear}\left(e'_t, (x(e^t_{i,j,k}), y(e^t_{i,j,k}), z(e^t_{i,j,k}))\right). \tag{5}$$

Herein, $x(e^t_{i,j,k})$, $y(e^t_{i,j,k})$ and $z(e^t_{i,j,k})$ are the coordinates in e'_t corresponding to $e^t_{i,j,k}$. They are given by:

$$(x(e^t_{i,j,k}), y(e^t_{i,j,k}), z(e^t_{i,j,k})) = (\tilde{x}^t_c, \tilde{y}^t_c, \tilde{z}^t_c) - \text{StopGradient}(\tilde{x}^t_c, \tilde{y}^t_c, \tilde{z}^t_c) + o_{i,j,k}, \tag{6}$$

where $o_{i,j,k}$ is a vector from $(0,0,0)$ to the location of $e^t_{i,j,k}$, and it is only conditioned on i, j, k and the shape of $e^t_{i,j,k}$. When calculating the gradients with Eq. (6), the infinitesimal change on the outputs of π (*i.e.*, $\tilde{x}^t_c, \tilde{y}^t_c, \tilde{z}^t_c$) will directly act on the feature maps e_t. To sum up, in the feed-forward process, we obtain the enlarged cube $\tilde{\mathbf{V}}'_t$ in the pixel space based on outputs of π, while for back-propagation, the supervision signals for π come from the semantic-level deep feature space. In addition, it is noteworthy that only the training process is modified. At test time, we crop $\tilde{\mathbf{V}}_t$ and activate f_L as stated in Sect. 3.1.

3.4   Implementation Details

Adaptive Inference. As mentioned in Sect. 3.1, the inference procedure can be terminated once the model is already able to produce a sufficiently reliable prediction. Consequently, the computation is unevenly allocated across "easy" and "hard" videos, improving the overall efficiency. In implementation, after processing the inputs $\{\tilde{\mathbf{V}}_1, \ldots, \tilde{\mathbf{V}}_2\}$, the classifier f_C integrates all the acquired information and outputs a softmax prediction $\boldsymbol{p}_t$. We compare the entropy of $\boldsymbol{p}_t$ (*i.e.*, $-\sum_j p_{ij} \log p_{ij}$) with a threshold η_t. The inference will be terminated with $\boldsymbol{p}_t$ if we have $-\sum_j p_{ij} \log p_{ij} \leq \eta_t$. The thresholds $\{\eta_1, \eta_2, \ldots\}$ can be solved on the validation set $\mathcal{D}_{\text{val}}$, under the principle of maximizing the accuracy with a limited computational budget $B > 0$:

$$\underset{\eta_1, \eta_2, \ldots}{\text{maximize}} \ \text{Accuracy}(\eta_1, \eta_2, \ldots | \mathcal{D}_{\text{val}}) \quad \text{s.t. FLOPs}(\eta_1, \eta_2, \ldots | \mathcal{D}_{\text{val}}) \leq B. \quad (7)$$

As a matter of fact, by varying the value of B, a group of $\{\eta_1, \eta_2, \ldots\}$ can be obtained, corresponding to a variety of computational constraints. The computational cost of our proposed AdaFocusV3 framework can be online adjusted without additional training by simply adapting these termination criterion. In this paper, we solve problem (7) following the methodology proposed in [26,53,54].

Glance Step. As aforementioned, AdaFocusV3 first takes a glance at the input video with the light-weighted global encoder f_G. Although being cheap and coarse, the global representations obtained from f_G may have learned certain discriminative features of the inputs. To this end, in addition to feeding them into the policy network $\boldsymbol{\pi}$, we also activate classifier f_C to produce a quick prediction $\boldsymbol{p}_0$ only using this global information, aiming to facilitate efficient feature reuse.

4   Experiment

In this section, we present a comprehensive experimental comparison between our proposed AdaFocusV3 and state-of-the-art efficient video recognition frameworks. AdaFocusV3 significantly outperforms these competitive baselines in terms of computational efficiency. We also demonstrate that AdaFocusV3 can be deployed on the basis of recently processed light-weighted deep networks, and further improve their efficiency. The analytical results including the ablation study and visualization are provided to give additional insights into our method.

Datasets. Our experiments are based on six large-scale video recognition benchmark datasets, *i.e.*, ActivityNet [3], FCVID [29], Mini-Kinetics [30,59], Something-Something (Sth-Sth) V1&V2 [21] and Diving48 [34]. The official training-validation split is adopted for all of them. Note that these datasets are widely used in the experiments of a considerable number of recently proposed baselines. We select them for a reasonable comparison with current state-of-the-art results. Due to the spatial limitations, the detailed introductions on datasets and data pre-processing are deferred to Appendix A.

Metrics. The offline video recognition is considered, where a single prediction is required for each video. Following the common practice on the aforementioned datasets, we evaluate the performance of different methods on ActivityNet and FCVID via mean average precision (mAP), while the top-1 accuracy is adopted on Mini-Kinetics, Sth-Sth V1&V2 and Diving48. In addition, we measure the theoretical computational cost of the models using the average number of multiply-add operations required for processing a video (*i.e.*, GFLOPs/Video). To compare the practical inference speed of different methods, we report the maximal throughput (Videos/s) when a given hardware (*e.g.*, GPU) is saturated.

4.1   Comparisons with State-of-the-Art Baselines

Baselines. We first compare AdaFocusV3 with a variety of recently proposed approaches that focus on improving the efficiency of video recognition. The results on ActivityNet, FCVID and Mini-Kinetics are provided. In addition to the previous versions of AdaFocus, the following baselines are included, *i.e.*, LiteEval [59], SCSampler [32], ListenToLook [18], AR-Net [41], AdaFrame [58], VideoIQ [45], and OCSampler [36]. An introduction of them is presented in Appendix B.

Implementation Details. For a fair comparison, the design of backbone networks follows the common setups of the baselines. A MobileNet-V2 [43] and a ResNet-50 [24] are used as the global encoder f_G and local encoder f_L in AdaFocusV3. The architecture of the classifier f_C follows from [19,56]. In addition, given that the videos in ActivityNet, FCVID and Mini-Kinetics are relatively long, previous works have revealed that a single uniformly sampled frame is sufficient to represent the information within the adjacent video clip [19,36,58]. Hence, we set the cube size of AdaFocusV3 to be $96 \times 96 \times 1$ and $128 \times 128 \times 1$, which enables our method to flexibly perform spatial-temporal dynamic computation in a frame-wise fashion. The maximum number of video cubes is set to 18. During inference, we remove the frames which have been included by previous cubes. The training configurations can be found in Appendix C.

Main Results. We report the performance of AdaFocusV3 and the baselines in Table 1. The results of our method are presented when its accuracy or computational cost reaches the best records of all the baselines. It is clear that AdaFocusV3 outperforms other efficient video recognition frameworks dramatically. For example, it improves the mAP by ~2.6–3.2% compared to the competitive OCSampler [36] algorithm on ActivityNet and FCVID with the same GFLOPs. A more comprehensive comparison is depicted in Fig. 3, where we vary the computational budget and plot the ActivityNet mAP v.s. GFLOPs relationships of both AdaFocusV3 and the variants of baselines. The two black curves correspond to adopting the two sizes of video cubes. One can observed that AdaFocusV3 yields a considerably better accuracy-efficiency trade-off consistently. It reduces the demands of computation by ∼1.6–2.6× on top of the strongest baselines without sacrificing mAP.

Table 1. Performance of AdaFocusV3 and the baselines on three benchmark datasets. The comparisons are based on the same backbones, where MN2/RN denotes MobileNet-V2/ResNet and † represents adding TSM [35]. GFLOPs refer to the average computational cost for processing each video. The best two results are **bold-faced** and underlined, respectively. Blue numbers are obtained on top of the strongest baselines

Methods	Published on	Backbones	ActivityNet		FCVID		Mini-Kinetics	
			mAP	GFLOPs	mAP	GFLOPs	Top-1 Acc.	GFLOPs
LiteEval [59]	NeurIPS'19	MN2+RN	72.7%	95.1	80.0%	94.3	61.0%	99.0
SCSampler [32]	ICCV'19	MN2+RN	72.9%	42.0	81.0%	42.0	70.8%	42.0
ListenToLook [18]	CVPR'20	MN2+RN	72.3%	81.4	–	–	–	–
AR-Net [41]	ECCV'20	MN2+RN	73.8%	33.5	81.3%	35.1	71.7%	32.0
AdaFrame [58]	T-PAMI'21	MN2+RN	71.5%	79.0	80.2%	75.1	–	–
VideoIQ [45]	ICCV'21	MN2+RN	74.8%	28.1	82.7%	27.0	72.3%	20.4
OCSampler [36]	CVPR'22	MN2†+RN	<u>76.9%</u>	<u>21.7</u>	82.7%	<u>26.8</u>	<u>72.9%</u>	<u>17.5</u>
AdaFocusV3	–	MN2+RN	<u>76.9%</u>	**10.9**_{↓2.0×}	82.7%	**7.8**_{↓3.4×}	<u>72.9%</u>	**8.6**_{↓2.0×}
	–	MN2+RN	**79.5%**_{↑2.6%}	<u>21.7</u>	**85.9%**_{↑3.2%}	26.8	**75.0%**_{↑2.1%}	<u>17.5</u>

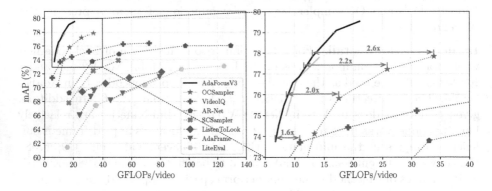

Fig. 3. AdaFocusV3 v.s. state-of-the-art baselines on ActivityNet in terms of computational efficiency. Note that the computational cost of AdaFocusV3 can be adjusted online (*i.e.*, switching within each black curve without additional training)

Comparisons of the Unified and Separate Modeling of Spatial and Temporal Redundancy. We further empirically validate whether a unified framework for spatial-temporal dynamic computation indeed outperforms the isolatedly-modeling counterpart. This is achieved by comparing AdaFocusV3 with AdaFocusV2+ [56]. The latter has the same network architecture and training procedure as AdaFocusV3, while the only difference lies in that AdaFocusV2+ models spatial and temporal redundancy independently in isolated modules. The results in Table 2 illustrate that our proposed unified framework efficiently reduce the computational cost (by ~1.3×) with preserved accuracy.

4.2 Deploying on Top of Light-weighted Models

Setups. In this subsection, we implement our framework on top of a representative efficient video analysis network, ConvNets with temporal shift module (TSM) [35], to demonstrate its effectiveness on recently proposed light-weighted models. The network architecture is not changed except for adding TSM to f_G and f_L. We uniformly sample 8 video frames for f_G. Unless otherwise specified, the size of the video cubes for f_L is set to be $128 \times 128 \times 12$, while the maximum number of cubes is 2. The training configurations can be found in Appendix C.

Table 2. Comparisons of AdaFocusV3 and AdaFocusV2+. The latter differs from AdaFocusV3 only in that it models the spatial and temporal redundancy independently in isolated modules. We report the computational cost of the two methods when they reach the same accuracy

Dataset	mAP	Computational cost (GFLOPs/video)	
		AdaFocusV2+	AdaFocusV3 (ours)
ActivityNet	77.0%	14.0	**11.1** (↓1.3×)
	78.0%	17.6	**13.6** (↓1.3×)
	79.0%	24.4	**16.8** (↓1.5×)
FCVID	83.0%	10.8	**8.3** (↓1.3×)
	84.0%	14.2	**10.5** (↓1.4×)
	85.0%	24.4	**14.4** (↓1.7×)

Table 3. Performance of AdaFocusV3 on top of TSM. MN2, R18/R34/R50 and BN-Inc. refer to MobileNet-V2, ResNet-18/34/50 and BN-Inception, respectively. TSM+ denotes the augmented TSM baseline with the same backbone network architecture as our method. The best results are **bold-faced**.

Method	Backbones	Sth-Sth V1		Sth-Sth V2		Throughput (Sth-Sth V1)
		Top-1 Acc.	GFLOPs	Top-1 Acc.	GFLOPs	(NVIDIA 3090 GPU, bs = 128)
TSN [51]	R50	19.7%	33.2	27.8%	33.2	-
AR-Net [41]	MN2+R18/34/50	18.9%	41.4	-	-	-
TRN$_{RGB/Flow}$ [63]	BN-Inc	42.0%	32.0	55.5%	32.0	-
ECO [64]	BN-Inc.+3DR18	39.6%	32.0	-	-	-
STM [28]	R50	47.5%	33.3	-	-	-
TSM [35]	R50	46.1%	32.7	59.1%	32.7	162.7 Videos/s
AdaFuse-TSM [42]	R50	46.8%	31.5	59.8%	31.3	-
TSM+ [35]	MN2+R50	47.0%	35.1	59.6%	35.1	123.0 Videos/s
AdaFocusV2	MN2+R50	47.0%	18.5 (↓1.9×)	59.6%	18.5 (↓1.9×)	197.0 Videos/s (↑1.6×)
AdaFocusV3	MN2+R50	47.0%	**14.0** (↓2.5×)	59.6%	**15.4** (↓2.3×)	**234.0 Videos/s** (↑1.9×)

Table 4. AdaFocusV3 on top of TSM with varying sizes of video cubes. MN2/R50 denotes MobileNetV2/ResNet50.

Method	Backbones	Size of 3D Video cubes	Sth-Sth V1 Acc.	GFLOPs	Sth-Sth V2 Acc.	GFLOPs	Diving48 Acc.	GFLOPs
TSM [35]	R50	–	46.1%	32.7	59.1%	32.7	77.4%	32.7
TSM+ [35]	MN2+R50	$224^2 \times 16$	47.0%	35.1	59.6%	35.1	80.4%	35.1
AdaFocusV3	MN2+R50	$128^2 \times 8$	46.1%	14.0	58.5%	15.4	79.3%	6.2
AdaFocusV3	MN2+R50	$128^2 \times 12$	**47.0%**	**14.0**	**59.6%**	**15.4**	**80.4%**	**6.2**
AdaFocusV3	MN2+R50	$128^2 \times 16$	47.0%	15.9	59.6%	17.2	80.4%	7.7

Results on Sth-Sth V1&V2 are presented in Table 3. For fair comparisons, following [56], we augment the vanilla TSM by adopting the same two backbone networks as ours, which is named as TSM+. It can be observed that AdaFocusV3 saves the computational cost by up to 2.5× compared with TSM+ when reaching the same Top-1 Acc. We also test the practical efficiency of our method on GPU devices, where the videos are fed into the model in batches, and the samples that meet the early-termination criterion will be output at each exit. The results indicate that the real speedup of AdaFocusV3 is significant as well.

Table 5. Ablation study on the learned policy and training algorithm

Gradient estimation with deep features	Learned temporal-dynamic policy	Learned spatial-dynamic policy	ActivityNet mAP after processing t video cubes (*i.e.*, with p_t)			
			$t=1$	$t=2$	$t=4$	$t=8$
–	✗ (random)	✗ (random)	44.6%	57.6%	67.4%	73.7%
✓	✓	✗ (random)	50.1%	61.3%	69.4%	74.6%
✓	✗ (random)	✓	45.5%	58.2%	68.5%	74.6%
✗ (pixel-based)	✓	✓	50.6%	61.0%	69.5%	75.0%
✓	✓	✓	**51.9%**	**62.3%**	**70.6%**	**75.4%**

Fig. 4. Visualization results on ActivityNet. Easy and hard videos refer to the samples that need a small or large number of video cubes for being correctly recognized

Fig. 5. Visualization results on Diving48. We present the examples of the task-relevant 3D video cubes localized by AdaFocusV3

Results with Varying Cube Sizes are summarized in Table 4. We find that reducing the cube size in the temporal dimension ($128^2 \times 12 \rightarrow 128^2 \times 8$) significantly degrades the accuracy on Sth-Sth/Diving48. Also interestingly, larger cubes like $128^2 \times 16$ may weaken the temporal adaptiveness, yielding inferior computational efficiency. Another interesting observation is that on Diving48, AdaFocusV3 dramatically reduces the computational cost (by 5.7×) on top of the baseline (TSM+) with the same accuracy. This phenomenon may be explained by that AdaFocusV3 will be more effective in less biased scenarios, where the background is less informative, and thus it is more sensible to attend to the task-relevant foreground parts of videos.

4.3 Analytical Results

Ablation Study. In Table 5, we test ablating the cube selection policy and the gradient estimation technique in AdaFocusV3. The results on ActivityNet with the cube size of $128^2 \times 1$ are presented. For a clean comparison, here we deactivate the glance step as well as the early-termination algorithm, and report the mAP corresponding to processing a fixed number of video cubes. One can observe that our learned policy considerably outperforms the random baselines in terms of either spatial or temporal dimensions. In addition, our gradient estimation technique based on deep features significantly outperforms the pixel-based counterpart proposed by AdaFocusV2 [56].

Visualization. In Fig. 4, the visualization on ActivityNet with the cube size of $96^2 \times 1$ is presented. The blue boxes indicate the video cubes localized by AdaFocusV3. It is shown that our method adaptively attends to the task-relevant parts of the video, such as the person, the piano and the bicycle. Figure 5 shows the examples of video cubes on Diving48. AdaFocusV3 can adaptively capture the actions of the diving athletes – the crucial contents for recognition.

5   Conclusion

In this paper, we proposed an AdaFocusV3 framework which enables the unified formulation of the efficient spatial-temporal dynamic computation in video recognition. AdaFocusV3 is trained to adaptively identify and attend to the most task-relevant video cubes in the 3D space formed by frame height/width and the time. The number of these cubes are determined conditioned on each sample under the dynamic early-termination paradigm. Extensive empirical results on six benchmark datasets validate the state-of-the-art performance of our model in terms of computational efficiency. Our work may open new avenues for the simultaneous modeling of spatial and temporal redundancy in video recognition.

Acknowledgements. This work is supported in part by National Key R&D Program of China(2020AAA0105200), the National Natural Science Foundation of China under Grants 62022048, Guoqiang Institute of Tsinghua University and Beijing Academy of Artificial Intelligence. We also appreciate the generous donation of computing resources by High-Flyer AI.

References

1. Arnab, A., Dehghani, M., Heigold, G., Sun, C., Lučić, M., Schmid, C.: ViViT: a video vision transformer. arXiv preprint arXiv:2103.15691 (2021)
2. Bengio, Y., Mesnil, G., Dauphin, Y., Rifai, S.: Better mixing via deep representations. In: ICML, pp. 552–560. PMLR (2013)
3. Caba Heilbron, F., Escorcia, V., Ghanem, B., Carlos Niebles, J.: ActivityNet: a large-scale video benchmark for human activity understanding. In: CVPR, pp. 961–970 (2015)
4. Carreira, J., Zisserman, A.: Quo Vadis, action recognition? a new model and the kinetics dataset. In: CVPR, pp. 6299–6308 (2017)
5. Chen, J., Li, K., Deng, Q., Li, K., Philip, S.Y.: Distributed deep learning model for intelligent video surveillance systems with edge computing. IEEE Trans. Ind. Inform. (2019)
6. Cho, K., et al.: Learning phrase representations using RNN encoder-decoder for statistical machine translation. In: EMNLP, pp. 1724–1734. Association for Computational Linguistics, Doha, October 2014. https://doi.org/10.3115/v1/D14-1179, www.aclweb.org/anthology/D14-1179
7. Collins, R.T., et al.: A system for video surveillance and monitoring. VSAM Final Rep. **2000**(1–68), 1 (2000)
8. Davidson, J., et al.: The Youtube video recommendation system. In: Proceedings of the Fourth ACM Conference on Recommender Systems, pp. 293–296 (2010)
9. Deldjoo, Y., Elahi, M., Cremonesi, P., Garzotto, F., Piazzolla, P., Quadrana, M.: Content-based video recommendation system based on stylistic visual features. J. Data Semant. **5**(2), 99–113 (2016)
10. Donahue, J., et al.: Long-term recurrent convolutional networks for visual recognition and description. In: CVPR, pp. 2625–2634 (2015)
11. Fan, L., et al.: RubiksNet: learnable 3D-shift for efficient video action recognition. In: Vedaldi, A., Bischof, H., Brox, T., Frahm, J.-M. (eds.) ECCV 2020. LNCS, vol. 12364, pp. 505–521. Springer, Cham (2020). https://doi.org/10.1007/978-3-030-58529-7_30

12. Feichtenhofer, C.: X3D: expanding architectures for efficient video recognition. In: CVPR, pp. 203–213 (2020)
13. Feichtenhofer, C., Fan, H., Malik, J., He, K.: Slowfast networks for video recognition. In: ICCV, pp. 6202–6211 (2019)
14. Feichtenhofer, C., Pinz, A., Wildes, R.P.: Spatiotemporal multiplier networks for video action recognition. In: Proceedings of the IEEE Conference on Computer Vision and Pattern Recognition, pp. 4768–4777 (2017)
15. Feichtenhofer, C., Pinz, A., Zisserman, A.: Convolutional two-stream network fusion for video action recognition. In: CVPR, pp. 1933–1941 (2016)
16. Figurnov, M., et al.: Spatially adaptive computation time for residual networks. In: CVPR, pp. 1039–1048 (2017)
17. Gao, J., Zhang, T., Xu, C.: A unified personalized video recommendation via dynamic recurrent neural networks. In: ACM MM, pp. 127–135 (2017)
18. Gao, R., Oh, T.H., Grauman, K., Torresani, L.: Listen to look: action recognition by previewing audio. In: CVPR, pp. 10457–10467 (2020)
19. Ghodrati, A., Bejnordi, B.E., Habibian, A.: FrameExit: conditional early exiting for efficient video recognition. In: CVPR, pp. 15608–15618 (2021)
20. Gong, X., Wang, H., Shou, M.Z., Feiszli, M., Wang, Z., Yan, Z.: Searching for two-stream models in multivariate space for video recognition. In: ICCV, pp. 8033–8042 (2021)
21. Goyal, R., et al.: The "something something" video database for learning and evaluating visual common sense. In: ICCV, pp. 5842–5850 (2017)
22. Han, Y., Huang, G., Song, S., Yang, L., Wang, H., Wang, Y.: Dynamic neural networks: a survey. IEEE Trans. Pattern Anal. Mach. Intell. (TPAMI) (2021)
23. Hara, K., Kataoka, H., Satoh, Y.: Can spatiotemporal 3D CNNs retrace the history of 2D CNNs and ImageNet? In: CVPR, pp. 6546–6555 (2018)
24. He, K., Zhang, X., Ren, S., Sun, J.: Deep residual learning for image recognition. In: CVPR, pp. 770–778 (2016)
25. Hochreiter, S., Schmidhuber, J.: Long short-term memory. Neural Comput. 9(8), 1735–1780 (1997)
26. Huang, G., Chen, D., Li, T., Wu, F., van der Maaten, L., Weinberger, K.Q.: Multi-scale dense networks for resource efficient image classification. In: ICLR (2018)
27. Ikizler, N., Forsyth, D.: Searching video for complex activities with finite state models. In: CVPR, pp. 1–8. IEEE (2007)
28. Jiang, B., Wang, M., Gan, W., Wu, W., Yan, J.: STM: spatiotemporal and motion encoding for action recognition. In: ICCV, pp. 2000–2009 (2019)
29. Jiang, Y.G., Wu, Z., Wang, J., Xue, X., Chang, S.F.: Exploiting feature and class relationships in video categorization with regularized deep neural networks. IEEE Trans. Pattern Anal. Mach. Intell. 40(2), 352–364 (2018)
30. Kay, W., et al.: The kinetics human action video dataset. arXiv preprint arXiv:1705.06950 (2017)
31. Kim, H., Jain, M., Lee, J.T., Yun, S., Porikli, F.: Efficient action recognition via dynamic knowledge propagation. In: ICCV, pp. 13719–13728 (2021)
32. Korbar, B., Tran, D., Torresani, L.: ScSampler: sampling salient clips from video for efficient action recognition. In: ICCV, pp. 6232–6242 (2019)
33. Li, D., Qiu, Z., Dai, Q., Yao, T., Mei, T.: Recurrent tubelet proposal and recognition networks for action detection. In: Ferrari, V., Hebert, M., Sminchisescu, C., Weiss, Y. (eds.) ECCV 2018. LNCS, vol. 11210, pp. 306–322. Springer, Cham (2018). https://doi.org/10.1007/978-3-030-01231-1_19

34. Li, Y., Li, Y., Vasconcelos, N.: RESOUND: towards action recognition without representation bias. In: Ferrari, V., Hebert, M., Sminchisescu, C., Weiss, Y. (eds.) ECCV 2018. LNCS, vol. 11210, pp. 520–535. Springer, Cham (2018). https://doi.org/10.1007/978-3-030-01231-1_32

35. Lin, J., Gan, C., Han, S.: TSM: temporal shift module for efficient video understanding. In: ICCV, pp. 7083–7093 (2019)

36. Lin, J., Duan, H., Chen, K., Lin, D., Wang, L.: OcSampler: compressing videos to one clip with single-step sampling. In: CVPR (2022)

37. Liu, Z., et al.: TeiNet: towards an efficient architecture for video recognition. In: AAAI, pp. 11669–11676 (2020)

38. Liu, Z., Wang, L., Wu, W., Qian, C., Lu, T.: Tam: temporal adaptive module for video recognition. In: ICCV, pp. 13708–13718 (2021)

39. Luo, C., Yuille, A.L.: Grouped spatial-temporal aggregation for efficient action recognition. In: ICCV, pp. 5512–5521 (2019)

40. Materzynska, J., Berger, G., Bax, I., Memisevic, R.: The jester dataset: a large-scale video dataset of human gestures. In: ICCVW (2019)

41. Meng, Y., et al.: AR-Net: adaptive frame resolution for efficient action recognition. In: Vedaldi, A., Bischof, H., Brox, T., Frahm, J.-M. (eds.) ECCV 2020. LNCS, vol. 12352, pp. 86–104. Springer, Cham (2020). https://doi.org/10.1007/978-3-030-58571-6_6

42. Meng, Y., et al.: AdaFuse: adaptive temporal fusion network for efficient action recognition. In: ICLR (2021)

43. Sandler, M., Howard, A., Zhu, M., Zhmoginov, A., Chen, L.C.: Mobilenetv 2: inverted residuals and linear bottlenecks. In: CVPR, pp. 4510–4520 (2018)

44. Sudhakaran, S., Escalera, S., Lanz, O.: Gate-shift networks for video action recognition. In: CVPR, pp. 1102–1111 (2020)

45. Sun, X., Panda, R., Chen, C.F.R., Oliva, A., Feris, R., Saenko, K.: Dynamic network quantization for efficient video inference. In: ICCV, pp. 7375–7385 (2021)

46. Tran, D., Bourdev, L., Fergus, R., Torresani, L., Paluri, M.: Learning spatiotemporal features with 3D convolutional networks. In: ICCV, pp. 4489–4497 (2015)

47. Tran, D., Wang, H., Torresani, L., Feiszli, M.: Video classification with channel-separated convolutional networks. In: ICCV, pp. 5552–5561 (2019)

48. Tran, D., Wang, H., Torresani, L., Ray, J., LeCun, Y., Paluri, M.: A closer look at spatiotemporal convolutions for action recognition. In: CVPR, pp. 6450–6459 (2018)

49. Upchurch, P., et al.: Deep feature interpolation for image content changes. In: CVPR, pp. 7064–7073 (2017)

50. Verelst, T., Tuytelaars, T.: Dynamic convolutions: exploiting spatial sparsity for faster inference. In: CVPR, pp. 2320–2329 (2020)

51. Wang, L., et al.: Temporal segment networks: towards good practices for deep action recognition. In: Leibe, B., Matas, J., Sebe, N., Welling, M. (eds.) ECCV 2016. LNCS, vol. 9912, pp. 20–36. Springer, Cham (2016). https://doi.org/10.1007/978-3-319-46484-8_2

52. Wang, Y., Chen, Z., Jiang, H., Song, S., Han, Y., Huang, G.: Adaptive focus for efficient video recognition. In: ICCV, October 2021

53. Wang, Y., Huang, R., Song, S., Huang, Z., Huang, G.: Not all images are worth 16x16 words: dynamic transformers for efficient image recognition. In: NeurIPS (2021)

54. Wang, Y., Lv, K., Huang, R., Song, S., Yang, L., Huang, G.: Glance and focus: a dynamic approach to reducing spatial redundancy in image classification. In: NeurIPS (2020)

55. Wang, Y., Pan, X., Song, S., Zhang, H., Huang, G., Wu, C.: Implicit semantic data augmentation for deep networks. In: NeurIPS, vol. 32 (2019)

56. Wang, Y., et al.: AdaFocus v2: end-to-end training of spatial dynamic networks for video recognition. In: CVPR (2022)

57. Wu, W., He, D., Tan, X., Chen, S., Wen, S.: Multi-agent reinforcement learning based frame sampling for effective untrimmed video recognition. In: ICCV, pp. 6222–6231 (2019a)

58. Wu, Z., Li, H., Xiong, C., Jiang, Y.G., Davis, L.S.: A dynamic frame selection framework for fast video recognition. IEEE Trans. Pattern Anal. Mach. Intell. (2020b)

59. Wu, Z., Xiong, C., Jiang, Y.G., Davis, L.S.: LiteEval: acoarse-to-fine framework for resource efficient video recognition. In: NeurIPS (2019b)

60. Xie, Z., Zhang, Z., Zhu, X., Huang, G., Lin, S.: Spatially adaptive inference with stochastic feature sampling and interpolation. In: Vedaldi, A., Bischof, H., Brox, T., Frahm, J.-M. (eds.) ECCV 2020. LNCS, vol. 12346, pp. 531–548. Springer, Cham (2020). https://doi.org/10.1007/978-3-030-58452-8_31

61. Yeung, S., Russakovsky, O., Mori, G., Fei-Fei, L.: End-to-end learning of action detection from frame glimpses in videos. In: CVPR, pp. 2678–2687 (2016)

62. Yue-Hei Ng, J., Hausknecht, M., Vijayanarasimhan, S., Vinyals, O., Monga, R., Toderici, G.: Beyond short snippets: deep networks for video classification. In: CVPR, pp. 4694–4702 (2015)

63. Zhou, B., Andonian, A., Oliva, A., Torralba, A.: Temporal relational reasoning in videos. In: Ferrari, V., Hebert, M., Sminchisescu, C., Weiss, Y. (eds.) ECCV 2018. LNCS, vol. 11205, pp. 831–846. Springer, Cham (2018). https://doi.org/10.1007/978-3-030-01246-5_49

64. Zolfaghari, M., Singh, K., Brox, T.: ECO: efficient convolutional network for online video understanding. In: Ferrari, V., Hebert, M., Sminchisescu, C., Weiss, Y. (eds.) ECCV 2018. LNCS, vol. 11206, pp. 695–712. Springer, Cham (2018). https://doi.org/10.1007/978-3-030-01216-8_43

Panoramic Human Activity Recognition

Ruize Han[1](✉) iD, Haomin Yan[1], Jiacheng Li[1] iD, Songmiao Wang[1],
Wei Feng[1](✉) iD, and Song Wang[2](✉) iD

[1] Intelligence and Computing College, Tianjin University, Tianjin, China
{han_ruize,yan_hm,threeswords,smwang,wfeng}@tju.edu.cn
[2] University of South Carolina, Columbia, USA
songwang@cec.sc.edu

Abstract. To obtain a more comprehensive activity understanding for a crowded scene, in this paper, we propose a new problem of panoramic human activity recognition (PAR), which aims to simultaneously achieve the recognition of individual actions, social group activities, and global activities. This is a challenging yet practical problem in real-world applications. To track this problem, we develop a novel hierarchical graph neural network to progressively represent and model the multi-granular human activities and mutual social relations for a crowd of people. We further build a benchmark to evaluate the proposed method and other related methods. Experimental results verify the rationality of the proposed PAR problem, the effectiveness of our method and the usefulness of the benchmark. We have released the source code and benchmark to the public for promoting the study on this problem.

Keywords: Human action · Social group · Group activity · Video surveillance

1 Introduction

Video-based human activity understanding is an important computer vision task, which has various practical applications in real world, e.g., video surveillance and social scene analysis [20,55]. In the past decade, this challenging task has been drawing much research interest in the computer-vision community. As shown in Fig. 1, previous works on human activity recognition can be divided into three categories. 1) Human action recognition aims to recognize the action categories of individual persons in a video [8,26,54]. 2) Human interaction recognition is proposed to recognize the human-human interactions [40]. 3) Group activity recognition is to recognize the overall activity of a group of people [23,48]. The last one focuses on a crowd of people while the former two commonly pay attention to the videos containing only one or a few people.

H. Yan and J. Li—Equal Contribution.

Supplementary Information The online version contains supplementary material available at https://doi.org/10.1007/978-3-031-19772-7_15.

Fig. 1. Examples of different types of activity recognition – (a) Action recognition. (b) Interaction recognition. (c–d) Group activity recognition. (e) The proposed panoramic human activity recognition (PAR), in which the labels beside each human bounding box (green) denote the individual actions, beside each human group box (pink dotted) denote the social activities, and the label at the top left corner of the image denotes the global activity (Color figure online)

In this paper, we focus on a more comprehensive human activity understanding in the crowded scenes – we are interested in not only the overall activity of the crowd in the scene, but also the instance action of each person (referred to as subject in this paper) and the social activity among a subset of subjects in the crowd. To achieve such a *comprehensive and multi-granular human activity understanding*, we propose a new problem – **P**anoramic **H**uman **A**ctivity **R**ecognition (PAR) that integrates these three sub-tasks. As shown in Fig. 1 (e), instance action recognition (Task I) aims to recognize the action of each subject in the scene, social group activity recognition (Task II) aims to divide the crowd into social groups and recognize the activity of each group, and global activity recognition (Task III) depicts the general and abstract activity according to the majority of the people. The proposed PAR problem studies the human activity understanding in multiple spatial granularity (individual, group and global) with different levels of activity categories.

The three tasks in PAR are complementary to each other and the solution of one task may benefit the others. For example, Task I recognizes the atomic action of each individual, which provides useful information for Task II of social interaction recognition, e.g., a person is talking and a person is listening may indicate the social activity of conversation if they are facing each other. Similarly, the overall activity recognition can be better achieved if we know all the individual actions and social group activities in the scene. On the contrary, the overall activity recognition provides useful priors to assist the social group activity and individual action understanding. In this paper, we aim to develop a joint framework to simultaneously address these three tasks. Compared to previous human activity understanding tasks, the proposed PAR is more challenging. A key problem is to establish a unified framework that can jointly handle all the sub tasks together, rather than address them severally or one after another. For this purpose, we expect to excavate and leverage the dependence among the different tasks and make them promote each other.

In this paper, we develop a one-stage end-to-end hierarchical graph network with a nested graph structure for PAR, in which the nodes at different hierarchies fitly represent the individual, group and global activities at different levels. Specifically, we first build a graph network by modeling each individual subject as a graph node. We then propose an AiO (all in one) feature aggregation module to aggregate individual feature nodes to group nodes in a bottom-to-up way. Similarly, the individual and group nodes are further aggregated into the global node. We further use a top-to-down feedback strategy for representation fusion and enhancement. With the hierarchical network architecture, we apply the multi-level supervisions for the multiple tasks in our problem.

The main contributions of this work are summarized as below:

1. We propose a new problem of Panoramic Human Activity Recognition (PAR), which aims to simultaneously recognize the individual human actions, social group activities and global activity in a crowded multi-person scene.

2. We develop a one-stage framework with hierarchical graph network that can effectively and collectively represent and model the activities at different level of granularities and mutual relations for multiple people in the scene.

3. We build a new video benchmark by adding new activity annotations and evaluation metrics to an existing dataset, for the proposed PAR. Experimental results verify the rationality of the proposed problem and the effectiveness of our method. We release the benchmark and code to the public at https://github. com/RuizeHan/PAR.

2   Related Work

Human Action Recognition and Localization. Human action understanding is a fundamental task in computer vision. Early works mainly focus on the task of human action recognition, which takes a video including a human with specific action as input and aims to recognize the action category. This task can be also regarded as a video classification problem. Existing methods for action recognition can be divided into two categories, i.e., the appearance based [4,5,44,56] and the skeleton-based [11,22,37,43] methods. Recent studies started to focus on the action localization (also called action segmentation) task, including temporal action localization and spatial-temporal action localization. The former is defined to localize the temporal duration of the action in untrimmed videos and then recognize the action category [26,54]. The latter not only recognizes the action and localize its duration but also provides the spatial location (in terms of a bounding box) of the corresponding actor [8,25,30,42,47]. However, the video data used in these tasks are usually collected from the actions performed by the actors in the laboratory or from the movies/website videos, e.g., UCF [39], DALY [46], Hollywood2tubes [29], and AVA [17]. Among them, the videos commonly contains only one or very few humans, and the actors usually occupy the main part of the picture in each frame. Differently, this paper is focused on the activity understanding in the crowded scenes, which is more practical in many applications, e.g., video surveillance and social analysis, in the real world.

Human Interaction Recognition. Compared to the human action recognition, the study of human-human interaction recognition is less studied. Existing human interaction recognition mainly focuses on the interactive activity involving two subjects, e.g., shaking, hugging, which occurs more in the scenarios analysis and video surveillance [15, 34, 51]. Similar to human action recognition, most works on interaction recognition focus on the videos collected from movies [27] and TV shows [32]. Some recent works begin to study the human interaction in the multi-person scenes. For example, in [55], a new problem of spatial-temporal human-human interaction detection is studied in a crowded scene. More comprehensive introduction to human interaction recognition can be found in a recent survey paper [40]. The classical human interaction as discussed above commonly considers the interactive activities involving two humans. Differently, in this paper we detect the social activities where the exact number of involved persons is priorly unknown – we first divide the people in the scene into human (social) groups with different sizes and then study the interactions in each group.

Social Group/Activity Detection. Social group detection task aims to divide a crowd of people into different (sub-)groups by the social activities or relations. Early methods for this task include the group-based methods without considering each individual person [9, 35], the individual-based methods aggregating the information of all individual subjects [2, 14, 38] and the combined methods considering both of them [1, 31]. Recently, several deep learning based methods [6, 10, 45] are developed for the group detection task. In the recent PANDA benchmark [45], human social interaction is treated as auxiliary task for group detection in the crowded scenes. Also, a couple of recent works [6, 7] aims to detect the social sub-groups in the multi-person scenes and meanwhile recognize the social activity in each sub-group. In [6, 7], the social activity in each group is simply regarded as the individual action that is performed by most humans in this group – this is not practical in many real-world cases. In this paper, the task II is focused on the social group detection and its activity recognition, which is complementary to the other two tasks for more comprehensive multi-human activity understanding.

Group Activity Recognition. Group activity recognition (GAR) is another task for human activity understanding, which aims to recognize the activity for a group of people. Early researches directly take the video recording the activity of a group of people as input, and output the activity category [23, 36], which is more like a video classification task. Recent works found that the individual human actions and the human-human interactions can help GAR. This way, several methods begin to include the individual action labels as auxiliary supervision for the GAR task [6, 23]. Several other methods [23, 48] propose to model the relations among multiple actors for better representation in the GAR task. This problem is actually the task III, i.e., the global activity recognition, in the proposed PAR. Difference lies in that we also simultaneously handle the other two tasks of the individual and social-group activity recognition.

Overall, the proposed PAR problem studies the human activity understanding in multiple spatial granules (individual, group and global) with different levels of activity categories, which is underexplored and has important applications.

3   The Proposed Method

3.1   Overview

In this work, we aim to jointly learn the individual actions, social group activities (based on the group detection) and the global activity in a unified one-stage framework. This way, we propose a hierarchical graph network that can well represent and model the multiple tasks. The architecture of the whole network is shown in Fig. 2.

Specifically, given a video recording a crowded scene, we extract the feature of each subject using a deep neural network. For each frame, we first model all the subjects appearing in the scene as a graph, in which each individual subject (feature) is modeled as a graph node, and each edge encodes relation between two subjects. Based on this graph, we propose a novel hierarchical graph network architecture. The proposed method can aggregate the *individual nodes* into the *group nodes* using the proposed bottom-to-up AiO (all in one) feature aggregation module. Similarly, the individual and group nodes are further aggregated into a *global node*. We also apply a top-to-down feedback strategy to further boost the mutual promotion among different tasks through the hierarchical network. We will elaborate on the proposed method in the following subsections.

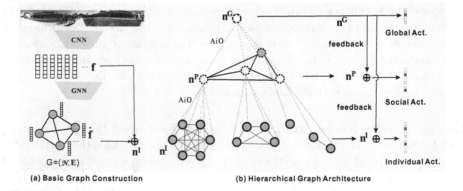

(a) Basic Graph Construction   (b) Hierarchical Graph Architecture

Fig. 2. Illustration of the framework of our method, which is mainly composed of the basic graph construction (as discussed in Sect. 3.2), and the hierarchical graph network (as discussed in Sect. 3.3)

3.2   Basic Graph Construction

We first build a fully-connected graph $G = (\mathcal{N}, \mathbf{E})$ to represent the N subjects in the scene, in which $\mathcal{N}$ denotes the node set and $\mathbf{E}$ encodes the relations for each pair of nodes.

Feature Extraction. Similar to many previous work for action recognition [48], we employ the classical CNN network, i.e., Inception-v3 [41] followed by the RoIAlign technique [21], to extract the deep appearance features of each subject and resize them into the same size. After that, we apply a fully connected (FC) layer to obtain the 1,024-dimension appearance feature for each subject. In the following, we denote the appearance feature of the subject u as $\mathbf{f}_u \in \mathbb{R}^{1,024}$. We use the GCN (Graph Convolutional Network) for the basic graph construction, which contains two parts, i.e., graph edge representation and graph node representation.

Graph Edge Representation. We use affinity matrix $\mathbf{E} \in \mathbb{R}^{N \times N}$ to learn the affinities among all the nodes in the graph, which is updated according to the node features as

$$e_{u,v} = \mathrm{F}_1(\mathbf{f}_u) \cdot (\mathrm{F}_2(\mathbf{f}_v))^\mathrm{T}, u, v \in \mathcal{N}, \tag{1}$$

where $\mathbf{f}_u$ and $\mathbf{f}_v$ denote the feature vectors of nodes u and v, respectively. F_1 and F_2 denote the MLP (multilayer perception) networks with the same structure but unshared parameters. The output vectors are multiplied into an affinity weight $e_{u,v}$, and the affinity matrix $\mathbf{E} = [e_{u,v}]_{u,v} \in \mathbb{R}^{N \times N}$ encodes the affinity weights among all node pairs. We finally apply a softmax operation on each row of $\mathbf{E}$ for normalization, since it is used as the weights for graph node representation updating.

Graph Node Representation. We then update graph node feature $\mathbf{f}_u$ through all the connected nodes weighted by the affinity matrix as

$$\hat{\mathbf{f}}_u = \mathrm{F}_\mathrm{n}(\sum_v e_{u,v}\mathbf{f}_v), u, v \in \mathcal{N}, \tag{2}$$

where F_n denotes the node update network. Finally, we take the updated feature $\hat{\mathbf{f}}_u$ together with the residual connection to the original feature $\mathbf{f}_u$ as the *individual node representation* $\mathbf{n}_u^\mathrm{I}$, i.e.,

$$\mathbf{n}_u^\mathrm{I} = \mathbf{f}_u \oplus \hat{\mathbf{f}}_u, \tag{3}$$

which embeds both the original individual feature from $\mathbf{f}_u$ and the surrounding-aware information from $\hat{\mathbf{f}}_u$, as shown in Fig. 2(a). This way, we have finished the basic graph construction.

3.3   Hierarchical Graph Network Architecture

Bottom-to-Up Aggregation (B2U). After constructing the graph with each subject as a node, we propose to build a hierarchical graph network to model the different-granularity activities in the proposed problem.

Individual to Group Aggregation. We first consider the human social group. We aim to establish the human relation matrix $\mathbf{R} \in \mathbb{R}^{N \times N}$ to represent the human social relation among the subjects, which is calculated from two aspects, i.e., the affinity matrix $\mathbf{E}$ in the basic graph and the distance-aware affinity matrix. Specifically, we first calculate the spatial distance matrix $\mathbf{D} \in \mathbb{R}^{N \times N}$ to encode the spatial distance between each two subject as

$$\mathbf{D}(u, v) = \frac{\sqrt{(x_u - x_v)^2 + (y_u - y_v)^2}}{\sqrt{S_u + S_v}}, \tag{4}$$

where x_u, y_u denote the coordinate of subject u (midpoint at bottom edge of the bounding box), S_u denotes the area of the bounding box of subject u. Here we take the bounding box area into consideration since the principle of near-large and far-small during imaging. We then get the relation matrix $\mathbf{R}$ as

$$\mathbf{R} = \lambda \mathbf{E} \odot \bar{\mathbf{D}} \oplus (1 - \lambda)\check{\mathbf{D}}, \tag{5}$$

where $\check{\mathbf{D}} = \mathrm{sigmod}(\frac{1}{\mathbf{D}})$ denotes the distance-aware affinity matrix. Similar with [48], we additionally apply a distance mask $\bar{\mathbf{D}}$ on $\mathbf{E}$ to filter the connections between two subjects that are far from each other with a threshold ρ. The distance mask matrix $\bar{\mathbf{D}}$ is computed as

$$\bar{\mathbf{D}}(x) = \begin{cases} \mathbf{D}(x), & \text{if } \mathbf{D}(x) \leq \rho, \\ -\infty, & \text{if } \mathbf{D}(x) > \rho. \end{cases} \tag{6}$$

With the human relation matrix, we can get the human group division results through a post-processing method, e.g., a clustering algorithm. As shown in Fig. 2(b), we then aggregate the individual nodes $\mathbf{n}_u^{\mathrm{I}}$ in each group $\mathcal{G}_k$ into the group node representation

$$\mathbf{n}_k^{\mathrm{P}} = \mathrm{AiO}(\mathbf{n}_u^{\mathrm{I}} \mid u \in \mathcal{G}_k), \tag{7}$$

where $\mathrm{AiO}(\cdot)$ denotes the proposed all in one (AiO) aggregation module, which will be discussed in detail later.

Group to Global Aggregation. Similar to the individual to group aggregation, as shown in Fig. 2(b), we also aggregate the individual and group nodes into a global node, as

$$\mathbf{n}^{\mathrm{G}} = \mathrm{AiO}(\mathbf{n}_u^{\mathrm{I}}, \mathbf{n}_k^{\mathrm{P}} \mid u \notin \forall \mathcal{G}, \forall k), \tag{8}$$

where we take both the individual node $\mathbf{n}_u^{\mathrm{I}}$ not in any group $\mathcal{G}$, and the aggregated group nodes $\mathbf{n}_k^{\mathrm{P}}$ in Eq. (7), as the units for aggregation. This global node can be used for representing the global activity of all subjects in the scene.

All in One (AiO) Aggregation Module. We then present the all in one (AiO) aggregation module used in the above. Take the individual to group aggregation using the AiO module in Eq. (7) for example. We assume the individual nodes $\mathbf{n}_u^I, u \in \mathcal{G}_k$ in a group $\mathcal{G}_k$ are aggregated as a group node, we first build a local GCN to get the aggregation matrix $\mathbf{W} \in \mathbb{R}^{|\mathcal{G}_k| \times |\mathcal{G}_k|}$, which is similar with the graph affinity matrix in Eq. (2), and $|\mathcal{G}_k|$ denotes the number of subjects in this group. We then accumulate the values in each column of $\mathbf{W}$ and get a weight vector $\mathbf{w} \in \mathbb{R}^{1 \times |\mathcal{G}_k|}$. We finally aggregate the individual node features with this weight vector as

$$\mathbf{n}_k^P = \sum_u (w_u \mathbf{n}_u^I \mid u \in \mathcal{G}_k), \tag{9}$$

where $\mathbf{n}_k^P$ denotes the *aggregated node feature* of group $\mathcal{G}_k$, w_u is the u-th element in $\mathbf{w}$.

The group to global aggregation in Eq. (8) takes both the individual and group nodes as input and outputs a global node, which can be similarly achieved by the above AiO module.

Top-to-Down Feedback (T2D). We use the bottom-to-up hierarchical graph network to model the multi-granular activities. To further improve the mutual promotion among different tasks, we apply a top-to-down feedback strategy. Specifically, as shown in Fig. 2(b), we integrate the group node feature together with the individual/group node feature for the final representation and action category prediction as

$$\mathbf{a}_u^I = F_i(\mathbf{n}_u^I, \mathbf{n}^G), \quad \mathbf{a}_k^P = F_p(\mathbf{n}_k^P, \mathbf{n}^G), \quad \mathbf{a}^G = F_g(\mathbf{n}^G), \tag{10}$$

where $\mathbf{a}_u^I$, $\mathbf{a}_k^P$ and $\mathbf{a}^G$ are the predicted individual, social (group) and global activities, respectively, F_i, F_p, and F_g are the corresponding readout functions implemented by the MLP neural networks.

Multi-level Multi-task Supervisions. We use the multi-level losses as supervisions for the multiple tasks in our problem. The total loss is defined as

$$\begin{aligned}
\mathcal{L} &= \mathcal{L}_i + \mathcal{L}_p + \mathcal{L}_g + \mathcal{L}_d \\
&= \sum_u L(\mathbf{a}_u^I, \tilde{\mathbf{a}}_u^I) + \sum_k L(\mathbf{a}_k^P, \tilde{\mathbf{a}}_k^P) + L(\mathbf{a}^G, \tilde{\mathbf{a}}^G) + L(\mathbf{R}, \tilde{\mathbf{R}}),
\end{aligned} \tag{11}$$

where $\mathcal{L}_i$, $\mathcal{L}_p$, $\mathcal{L}_g$, $\mathcal{L}_d$ denote the losses for the individual, social group, global activity recognition, and the group detection tasks, respectively. The notations with $\tilde{}$ denote the corresponding ground-truth labels.a $\tilde{\mathbf{R}} \in \mathbb{R}^{N \times N}$ is the human group relation matrix taking the values of 0 or 1, where 1 denotes the corresponding two subjects are in the same group.

3.4   Implementation Details

Network Details. The MLP networks F_1 and F_2 in Eq. (1), and F_n in Eq. (2) are all implemented by single-layer FC networks. The parameter λ in Eq. (5) is set as 0.5. The parameter ρ in Eq. (6) is set as the width of the input image with a ratio of 0.2. The readout function F_i, F_p in Eq. (10) are implemented by the three-layer FC networks, and F_g by a two-layer FC network. We use the binary cross entropy as the loss function in Eq. (11). As a new problem, in this work, we use the annotated human bounding boxes as input to alleviate the interference from the false human detection, which is common for the crowded scene in our problem. In our method, we do not integrate the temporal information of the individual and group along the video, since this need the multi-object tracking and group evolution detection results as auxiliaries. The challenging scenes make them not easy to be obtained, and the involved errors will have an impact on the main task.

Network Training. During the training stage, we use the ground-truth human group division for individual to group aggregation in Eq. (7). We implement the proposed network with the PyTorch framework on the GTX 3090 GPU. The batch size is set as 4 in the experiments. We use stochastic gradient descent (SGD) algorithm with Adam method for training the network, which is trained for about 50 epochs with the learning rate of 2×10^{-5} to be convergent.

Inference. During the inference stage, we get the human group division results through a post-processing method. Specifically, with the predicted human relation matrix $\mathbf{R}$, we apply a self-tuning spectral clustering algorithm [52] that uses $\mathbf{R}$ as input and automatically estimates the number of clustering groups, to obtain the group detection results.

4   Experiments

4.1   Datasets

Previous datasets for human action or group activity recognition can not meet the requirements of the proposed problem. We build a new benchmark for the proposed task. The proposed dataset is based on a state-of-the-art dataset JRDB [28] for 2D/3D person detection and tracking, which uses a mobile robot to capture the 360° RGB videos for crowded multi-person scenes , such as those at the campus, canteen, and classroom, etc. JRDB has provided the human bounding boxes with IDs as annotations. Based on it, a more recent dataset JRDB-Act [7] adds the annotations of individual human action and social group detection. The group activity label in JRDB-Act is simply defined as the combination of the involved individual action labels or the selection of them considering the occurrence frequency in the group, which seems not reasonable enough in practice. In PAR problem, the group activity is related to the individual actions but their label candidate sets are different. For example, for a two-person conversation scene, in [7] the group activity is labeled as 'listening to someone, talking to someone', which is the combination of the contained individual action labels. In our setting, we label such group activity as 'chatting', which is regarding to the whole group but not each individual. This way, we inherit the human detection annotations in JRDB and the individual action and group division annotations in JRDB-Act, and further manually annotate the social group activities and global activities for the proposed Panoramic Human Activity Recognition (PAR) task, which constitutes a new dataset – JRDB-PAR.

Fig. 3. Data distributions of social (a) and global activities (b) in JRDB-PAR

JRDB-PAR contains 27 categories of individual actions, e.g., walking, talking, which is same as JRDB-Act, and 11 categories of social group activities and 7 categories of global activities. The distributions of social/global activities are shown in Fig. 3. In total, JRDB-PAR includes 27 videos, which are splitted as 20 for training and 7 for testing, following the training/validation splitting in JRDB dataset. According to statistics, JRDB-PAR contains 27,920 frames with over 628k human bounding boxes. Following the setting in [7], we select the uniformly sampled key frames (one key frame in each 15 frames) for annotation and evaluation, which is same as previous classical activity recognition datasets like CAD [3], volleyball [24]. The numbers of frames, groups and subjects in the whole dataset and key frames are summarized in Table 1. Other details for annotated labels, e.g., the number of labels for individual actions, social activities and global activities are also shown in Table 1. Note that, we adopt the multi-class labels for the activity annotation, i.e., each individual/group/frame is with one or multiple activity labels.

Table 1. Statistics results of the panoramic human activity recognition dataset

	All frames			Key frames			Activity labels		
	Frm.	Gro.	Sub.	Frm.	Gro.	Sub.	Indiv.	Social	Global
Train.	21,724	86,949	467k	1,439	5,163	27k	57,341	7,874	2,316
Test.	6,196	31,035	160k	411	1,709	9k	18,019	2,082	735
All	27,920	117,984	628k	1,850	6,872	36k	75,360	9,956	3,051

4.2   Metrics

Protocol I. To evaluate the *individual action detection*, following the previous work [16] for multi-label classification task, we adopt the commonly used metrics - precision, recall and F_1 score (denoted as $\mathcal{P}_i$, $\mathcal{R}_i$, and $\mathcal{F}_i$) as the evaluation metrics, which measure the individual action classification accuracy for each instance in the testing dataset.

Protocol II. *Social (group) activity recognition* includes the group detection and the activity category recognition. For the group detection, we use the classical Half metrics for performance evaluation, where the group member IoU > 0.5 in the predicted group and ground-truth group is taken as the true detected group, which is followed by the general protocol in group detection task [45]. Note that, we only consider the groups containing more than one subjects in this protocol. For the true detected group under the above metric, we further consider their group activity recognition results. The true detected groups with the correct activity category prediction are taken as the true social group activity predictions. Under this protocol, we calculate the precision, recall and F_1 score (denoted as $\mathcal{P}_p$, $\mathcal{R}_p$, and $\mathcal{F}_p$) as the social activity recognition metrics.

Protocol III. *Global activity recognition* can be also taken as a multi-label classification problem, and we apply the precision, recall, and F_1 score (denoted as $\mathcal{P}_g$, $\mathcal{R}_g$, $\mathcal{F}_g$) for evaluation.

The overall metric for the panoramic activity detection task is the comprehensive results of the above three metrics. Here we simply compute the average value of the above F_1 scores, i.e., $\mathcal{F}_a = \frac{1}{3}(\mathcal{F}_i + \mathcal{F}_p + \mathcal{F}_g)$ as the overall F_1 score.

4.3   Results

Comparison Methods. For the proposed PAR problem, we can not find many methods for direct comparison. We try to include more state-of-the-art methods with necessary modifications as the comparison methods. ARG is a well-know method [48] for group activity recognition, which builds a learnable graph structure to model the human relation graph. SA-GAT [6] proposes to learn the human actions, sub-group and group activities together as a multi-stage multi-task problem, which uses the classical group activity recognition dataset CAD [3] with new sub-group activity annotations for evaluation. JRDB-Base [7] is the baseline method for the JRDB-Act dataset, which is similar to [6] and uses a progressive multi-loss strategy to recognize the different types of activities. Note that, the original version of ARG can not provide the group detection and social group activity recognition. We apply the group clustering algorithm used in our method and previous works [6], on the relation matrix generated by ARG for group detection. With the group detection results, we further employ the feature fusion method in [7] on ARG for the social group activity recognition task.

We also include several state-of-the-art methods for individual and group activity recognition for comparison, i.e., AT [13], SACRF [33], Dynamic [50], HiGCIN [49]. These methods can not provide the group detection and social activity recognition results, which also do not include the relation matrix in ARG. For comparison, we additionally provide the ground-truth group detection results as input to these methods and employ the feature fusion strategy in [7] to obtain the social group activity recognition results.

Table 2. Comparative results of the panoramic human activity recognition (%)

Method	Individual Act.			Social Act.			Global Act.			Overall
	$\mathcal{P}_i$	$\mathcal{R}_i$	$\mathcal{F}_i$	$\mathcal{P}_p$	$\mathcal{R}_p$	$\mathcal{F}_p$	$\mathcal{P}_g$	$\mathcal{R}_g$	$\mathcal{F}_g$	$\mathcal{F}_a$
ARG [48]	39.9	30.7	33.2	8.7	8.0	8.2	63.6	44.3	50.7	30.7
SA-GAT [6]	44.8	40.4	40.3	8.8	8.9	8.8	36.7	29.9	31.4	26.8
JRDB-Base [7]	19.1	34.4	23.6	14.3	12.2	12.8	44.6	46.8	45.1	27.2
Ours	51.0	40.5	43.4	24.7	26.0	24.8	52.8	31.8	38.8	35.6
AT*[13]	38.9	33.9	34.6	32.5	32.3	32.0	21.2	19.1	19.8	28.8
SACRF*[33]	31.3	23.6	25.9	25.7	24.5	24.8	42.9	35.5	37.6	29.5
Dynamic*[50]	40.7	33.4	35.1	33.5	30.1	30.9	37.5	27.1	30.6	32.2
HiGCIN*[49]	34.6	26.4	28.6	34.2	31.8	32.2	39.3	30.1	33.1	31.3
ARG*[48]	42.7	34.7	36.6	27.4	26.1	26.2	26.9	21.5	23.3	28.8
SA-GAT*[6]	39.6	34.5	35.0	32.5	32.5	30.7	28.6	24.0	25.5	30.4
JRDB-Base*[7]	21.5	44.9	27.7	54.3	45.9	48.5	38.4	33.1	34.8	37.0
Ours*	54.3	44.2	46.9	50.3	52.5	50.1	42.1	24.5	30.3	42.4

* denotes that we additional provide the ground-truth group detection results as input

Comparative Results. We show the performance of the proposed method and other comparative methods in Table 2. From the top half part, we can first see that the proposed method outperforms the comparative methods on the overall score. More specifically, we can see that the proposed method achieves particularly good performance on the individual and group activity recognition. ARG performs well on the group activity recognition task, which may benefit from its flexible actor relation graphs and sparse temporal sampling strategy.

We further compare the proposed method with other state-of-the-art methods in the bottom half part of Table 2. We can first see that, with the ground-truth group detection as input, the comparison methods perform better for the social activity detection task, which outperform the proposed method. But the overall scores of most comparison methods are still lower than our method. If we also provide the ground-truth group detection in our method, i.e., 'Ours*', the performance will be further improved as shown in the last row.

4.4 Ablation Study

We evaluate the variations of our method by removing some components.

- w/o $\mathbf{f}/\tilde{\mathbf{f}}$: For the individual node representation, we remove the original individual feature $\mathbf{f}_u$ or the surrounding-aware feature $\hat{\mathbf{f}}_u$ in Eq. (3), respectively.
- w Euclid. dist.: We replace the calculation method of subject distance in Eq. (4) with the commonly used Euclidean distance.
- w/o $\check{\mathbf{D}}/\mathbf{E}$: We remove the distance-aware matrix $\check{\mathbf{D}}$ or the edge matrix $\mathbf{E}$ in the graph network in Eq. (5), respectively.
- w/o AiO: We replace the AiO aggregation module in Eqs. (7) and (8) with the max-pooling operation used in [6,7].
- w/o G.2I./G.2P.: We remove the global node feature in the individual (G.2I.) or group (G.2P.) node feature representation in Eq. (10), respectively.

Table 3. Ablation study of the proposed method with its variations (%)

Method	Individual Act.			Social Act.			Global Act.			Overall
	$\mathcal{P}_i$	$\mathcal{R}_i$	$\mathcal{F}_i$	$\mathcal{P}_p$	$\mathcal{R}_p$	$\mathcal{F}_p$	$\mathcal{P}_g$	$\mathcal{R}_g$	$\mathcal{F}_g$	$\mathcal{F}_a$
w/o f	35.6	27.2	29.6	17.4	15.9	16.4	40.2	23.8	29.3	25.1
w/o $\tilde{\mathbf{f}}$	29.3	21.7	23.9	9.8	9.2	9.4	43.1	27.0	32.4	21.9
w Euclid. dist.	43.2	32.5	35.6	12.7	12.1	12.3	41.6	24.5	30.2	26.0
w/o $\check{\mathbf{D}}$	34.6	25.8	28.2	11.3	10.8	11.0	24.8	16.1	19.0	19.4
w/o $\mathbf{E}$	47.8	37.8	40.6	21.0	20.9	20.6	33.6	19.5	24.2	28.4
w/o AiO	19.8	14.6	16.1	18.8	16.7	17.3	34.2	30.4	31.3	21.6
w/o G.2I.	31.1	22.9	25.3	12.5	10.9	11.4	75.4	45.0	55.2	30.6
w/o G.2P.	36.4	27.5	30.0	11.9	10.4	10.9	78.4	46.8	57.3	32.7
Ours	51.0	40.5	43.4	24.7	26.0	24.8	52.8	31.8	38.8	35.6

We show the ablation study results in Table 3. We can first see that original individual feature $\mathbf{f}_u$ and the surrounding node embedded feature $\hat{\mathbf{f}}_u$ are both important for individual node representation. Especially the latter $\hat{\mathbf{f}}_u$ is very useful to the social activity recognition.

Next, in the bottom-to-up (B2U) aggregation stage, we first investigate the effect of the spatial-aware matrix $\check{\mathbf{D}}$ and the edge matrix $\mathbf{E}$ in relation matrix learning. We can see that $\check{\mathbf{D}}$ is vital in relation modeling. It is easy to explain that the social relations among the people in the crowd are highly related to the spatial distance. But the simple Euclidean distance between bounding box center performs not well enough. Also, only using the spatial-aware matrix, i.e., w/o $\mathbf{E}$, can not get the performance as using both of them. We then investigate the effectiveness of the AiO module in the proposed B2U aggregation, we can see that the aggregation method AiO is verified to be effective in our method.

Finally, in the top-to-down (T2D) feedback stage, we can see that the individual action recognition results get worse when removing the global node feature in individual node representation. Similarly, the social activity recognition performance also gets worse without the global node feature embedding. This demonstrates the effectiveness of the T2D feedback strategy in our method.

4.5 Experimental Analysis

Individual/Global Activity Recognition. We evaluate the tasks of individual action and global activity recognition, where we follow the original settings in the comparative GAR methods without modification. We show the results in Table 4. We can see that, although the margin is not very large, the proposed method performs better than the comparative methods on these two tasks. We can also find that the performance on JRDB-PAR is generally low , where is great potential for more methods to be developed.

Table 4. Comparisons of the individual action and global activity recognition (%)

Method	Individual Act.			Global Act.		
	$\mathcal{P}_i$	$\mathcal{R}_i$	$\mathcal{F}_i$	$\mathcal{P}_g$	$\mathcal{R}_g$	$\mathcal{F}_g$
AT [13]	36.8	30.1	31.7	17.4	15.7	16.1
SACRF [33]	39.2	29.4	32.2	34.8	26.2	28.4
Dynamic [50]	46.6	37.7	39.7	31.9	23.7	26.4
HiGCIN [49]	36.9	30.1	31.6	46.0	34.2	38.0
Ours	51.0	40.5	43.4	52.8	31.8	38.8

Group Detection. We further solely evaluate the group detection results in Table 5. We first use the classical Half metric used in group detection task [45], i.e., the predicted group with the group member IoU > 0.5 with the ground-truth group is taken as the true detected group, which is denoted as IOU@0.5. We extend this metric by increasing the threshold 0.5 to 1 with a step of 0.1, which means improving the criteria bar. We then plot the accuracy curve using each threshold and the corresponding accuracy. This way, we can compute the AUC (Area Under the Curve) score as the metric namely IOU@AUC. With the predicted and ground-truth binary human group relation matrices $\bar{\mathbf{R}}$ and $\tilde{\mathbf{R}}$, where 1 denotes the corresponding two subjects are in the same group, we compute the matrix IOU score as Mat.IOU $= \frac{\sum \text{AND}(\bar{\mathbf{R}}, \tilde{\mathbf{R}})}{\sum \text{OR}(\bar{\mathbf{R}}, \tilde{\mathbf{R}})}$, where AND and OR denotes the functions of element-wise logical and/or operations.

As shown in Table 5, we first apply two straightforward approaches for comparison. Here 'Dis.Mat + LP' denotes that we use the distance matrix among the subjects followed by a label propagation method [53] algorithm as the post-processing method to get the group relation matrix. 'GNN + GRU' uses a GNN to model the group relations among the subjects followed by a classical GRU model to integrate the temporal information. We also include other methods, i.e., ARG [48], SA-GAT [6], and JRDG-Base [7], that can provide the group detection results for comparison. We can see that, the proposed method outperforms the comparison methods with a large margin under all metrics.

Table 5. Comparative group detection results (%)

	IOU@0.5	IOU@AUC	Mat.IOU
Dis.Mat + LP [53]	33.4	14.1	12.9
GNN + GRU	34.5	21.7	20.1
ARG [48]	35.2	21.6	19.3
SA-GAT [6]	29.1	20.4	16.6
JRDG-Base [7]	38.4	26.3	20.6
Ours	**53.9**	**38.1**	**30.6**

5   Conclusion

In this paper, we have studied a new problem – panoramic human activity recognition (PAR), which is more comprehensive, challenging and practical than previous action recognition tasks in crowded scene video analysis. To handle this problem, we propose a novel hierarchical neural network composed of the basic graph construction, bottom-to-up node aggregation, and top-to-down feedback strategy, to model the multi-granular activities. Based on an existing dataset, we build a benchmark for this new problem. Experimental results are very promising and verify the rationality of this new problem and the effectiveness of the proposed baseline method. In the future, we plan to integrate the temporal information, e.g., the multiple object tracking [18,19] and group evolution detection, into the proposed method. An interesting problem maybe to investigate whether we can simultaneously handle the multiple object tracking [12] and PAR and make them help with each other.

Acknowledgment. This work was supported by the National Natural Science Foundation of China under Grants U1803264, 62072334, and the Tianjin Research Innovation Project for Postgraduate Students under Grant 2021YJSB174.

References

1. Bazzani, L., Cristani, M., Murino, V.: Decentralized particle filter for joint individual-group tracking. In: CVPR (2012)
2. Chang, M.C., Krahnstoever, N., Ge, W.: Probabilistic group-level motion analysis and scenario recognition. In: ICCV (2011)

3. Choi W, Shahid K, S.S.: What are they doing?: Collective activity classification using spatio-temporal relationship among people. In: ICCV (2009)
4. Diba, A., et al.: Spatio-temporal channel correlation networks for action classification. In: Ferrari, V., Hebert, M., Sminchisescu, C., Weiss, Y. (eds.) ECCV 2018. LNCS, vol. 11208, pp. 299–315. Springer, Cham (2018). https://doi.org/10.1007/978-3-030-01225-0_18
5. Du, Y., Yuan, C., Li, B., Zhao, L., Li, Y., Hu, W.: Interaction-aware spatio-temporal pyramid attention networks for action classification. In: Ferrari, V., Hebert, M., Sminchisescu, C., Weiss, Y. (eds.) ECCV 2018. LNCS, vol. 11220, pp. 388–404. Springer, Cham (2018). https://doi.org/10.1007/978-3-030-01270-0_23
6. Ehsanpour, M., Abedin, A., Saleh, F., Shi, J., Reid, I., Rezatofighi, H.: Joint learning of social groups, individuals action and sub-group activities in videos. In: Vedaldi, A., Bischof, H., Brox, T., Frahm, J.-M. (eds.) ECCV 2020. LNCS, vol. 12354, pp. 177–195. Springer, Cham (2020). https://doi.org/10.1007/978-3-030-58545-7_11
7. Ehsanpour, M., Saleh, F.S., Savarese, S., Reid, I.D., Rezatofighi, H.: JRDB-act: a large-scale dataset for spatio-temporal action, social group and activity detection. In: arXiv preprint (2021)
8. Feichtenhofer, C., Fan, H., Malik, J., He, K.: Slowfast networks for video recognition. In: ICCV (2019)
9. Feldmann, M., Fränken, D., Koch, W.: Tracking of extended objects and group targets using random matrices. IEEE Trans. Sig. Process. 59(4), 1409–1420 (2010)
10. Fernando, T., Denman, S., Sridharan, S., Fookes, C.: GD-GAN: generative adversarial networks for trajectory prediction and group detection in crowds. In: Jawahar, C.V., Li, H., Mori, G., Schindler, K. (eds.) ACCV 2018. LNCS, vol. 11361, pp. 314–330. Springer, Cham (2019). https://doi.org/10.1007/978-3-030-20887-5_20
11. Friji, R., Drira, H., Chaieb, F., Kchok, H., Kurtek, S.: Geometric deep neural network using rigid and non-rigid transformations for human action recognition. In: ICCV (2021)
12. Gan, Y., Han, R., Yin, L., Feng, W., Wang, S.: Self-supervised multi-view multi-human association and tracking. In: ACM MM (2021)
13. Gavrilyuk, K., Sanford, R., Javan, M., Snoek, C.G.: Actor-transformers for group activity recognition. In: CVPR (2020)
14. Ge, W., Collins, R.T., Ruback, R.B.: Vision-based analysis of small groups in pedestrian crowds. IEEE TPAMI 34(5), 1003–1016 (2012)
15. Gemeren, C.V., Poppe, R., Veltkamp, R.C.: Spatio-temporal detection of fine-grained dyadic human interactions. In: International Workshop on Human Behavior Understanding (2016)
16. Godbole, S., Sarawagi, S.: Discriminative methods for multi-labeled classification. In: Pacific-Asia Conference on Knowledge Discovery and Data Mining (2004)
17. Gu, C., et al.: Ava: A video dataset of spatio-temporally localized atomic visual actions. In: CVPR (2018)
18. Han, R., Feng, W., Zhang, Y., Zhao, J., Wang, S.: Multiple human association and tracking from egocentric and complementary top views. IEEE TPAMI (2021). https://doi.org/10.1109/TPAMI.2021.3070562
19. Han, R., et al.: Complementary-view multiple human tracking. In: AAAI (2020)
20. Han, R., Zhao, J., Feng, W., Gan, Y., Wan, L., Wang, S.: Complementary-view co-interest person detection. In: ACM MM (2020)
21. He, K., Gkioxari, G., Dollár, P., Girshick, R.: Mask R-CNN. In: ICCV (2017)
22. Huang, Z., Wan, C., Probst, T., Van Gool, L.: Deep learning on lie groups for skeleton-based action recognition. In: CVPR (2017)

23. Ibrahim, M.S., Mori, G.: Hierarchical relational networks for group activity recognition and retrieval. In: Ferrari, V., Hebert, M., Sminchisescu, C., Weiss, Y. (eds.) ECCV 2018. LNCS, vol. 11207, pp. 742–758. Springer, Cham (2018). https://doi.org/10.1007/978-3-030-01219-9_44

24. Ibrahim, M.S., Muralidharan, S., Deng, Z., Vahdat, A., Mori, G.: A hierarchical deep temporal model for group activity recognition. In: CVPR (2016)

25. Li, Y., Chen, L., He, R., Wang, Z., Wu, G., Wang, L.: MultiSports: a multi-person video dataset of spatio-temporally localized sports actions. In: arXiv preprint (2021)

26. Ma, F., et al.: SF-net: single-frame supervision for temporal action localization. In: Vedaldi, A., Bischof, H., Brox, T., Frahm, J.-M. (eds.) ECCV 2020. LNCS, vol. 12349, pp. 420–437. Springer, Cham (2020). https://doi.org/10.1007/978-3-030-58548-8_25

27. Marszalek, M., Laptev, I., Schmid, C.: Actions in context. In: CVPR (2009)

28. Martin-Martin, R., et al.: JRDB: a dataset and benchmark of egocentric robot visual perception of humans in built environments. IEEE TPAMI (2021). https://doi.org/10.1109/TPAMI.2021.3070543

29. Mettes, P., van Gemert, J.C., Snoek, C.G.M.: Spot on: action localization from pointly-supervised proposals. In: Leibe, B., Matas, J., Sebe, N., Welling, M. (eds.) ECCV 2016. LNCS, vol. 9909, pp. 437–453. Springer, Cham (2016). https://doi.org/10.1007/978-3-319-46454-1_27

30. Pan, J., Chen, S., Shou, M.Z., Liu, Y., Shao, J., Li, H.: Actor-context-actor relation network for spatio-temporal action localization. In: CVPR (2021)

31. Pang, S.K., Li, J., Godsill, S.J.: Detection and tracking of coordinated groups. IEEE Trans. Aerosp. Electron. Syst. **47**(1), 472–502 (2011)

32. Patron-Perez, A., Marszalek, M., Reid, I., Zisserman, A.: Structured learning of human interactions in tv shows. IEEE TPAMI **34**(12), 2441–2453 (2012)

33. Pramono, R.R.A., Chen, Y.T., Fang, W.H.: Empowering relational network by self-attention augmented conditional random fields for group activity recognition. In: Vedaldi, A., Bischof, H., Brox, T., Frahm, J.-M. (eds.) ECCV 2020. LNCS, vol. 12346, pp. 71–90. Springer, Cham (2020). https://doi.org/10.1007/978-3-030-58452-8_5

34. Ryoo, M.S., Aggarwal, J.K.: Spatio-temporal relationship match: video structure comparison for recognition of complex human activities. In: ICCV (2009)

35. Shao, J., Change Loy, C., Wang, X.: Scene-independent group profiling in crowd. In: CVPR (2014)

36. Shu, T., Todorovic, S., Zhu, S.C.: CERN: confidence-energy recurrent network for group activity recognition. In: CVPR (2017)

37. Si, C., Jing, Y., Wang, W., Wang, L., Tan, T.: Skeleton-based action recognition with spatial reasoning and temporal stack learning. In: Ferrari, V., Hebert, M., Sminchisescu, C., Weiss, Y. (eds.) ECCV 2018. LNCS, vol. 11205, pp. 106–121. Springer, Cham (2018). https://doi.org/10.1007/978-3-030-01246-5_7

38. Solera, F., Calderara, S., Cucchiara, R.: Socially constrained structural learning for groups detection in crowd. IEEE TPAMI **38**(5), 995–1008 (2015)

39. Soomro, K., Zamir, A.R., Shah, M.: Ucf101: a dataset of 101 human actions classes from videos in the wild. Comput. Sci. (2012)

40. Stergiou, A., Poppe, R.: Analyzing human-human interactions: a survey. Comput. Vision Image Underst. **188**(Nov.), 102799.1–102799.12 (2019)

41. Szegedy, C., Vanhoucke, V., Ioffe, S., Shlens, J., Wojna, Z.: Rethinking the inception architecture for computer vision. In: CVPR (2016)

42. Tang, J., Xia, J., Mu, X., Pang, B., Lu, C.: Asynchronous interaction aggregation for action detection. In: Vedaldi, A., Bischof, H., Brox, T., Frahm, J.-M. (eds.) ECCV 2020. LNCS, vol. 12360, pp. 71–87. Springer, Cham (2020). https://doi.org/10.1007/978-3-030-58555-6_5

43. Vemulapalli, R., Arrate, F., Chellappa, R.: Human action recognition by representing 3D skeletons as points in a lie group. In: CVPR (2014)

44. Wang, L., et al.: Temporal segment networks: towards good practices for deep action recognition. In: Leibe, B., Matas, J., Sebe, N., Welling, M. (eds.) ECCV 2016. LNCS, vol. 9912, pp. 20–36. Springer, Cham (2016). https://doi.org/10.1007/978-3-319-46484-8_2

45. Wang, X., et al.: Panda: a gigapixel-level human-centric video dataset. In: CVPR (2020)

46. Weinzaepfel, P., Martin, X., Schmid, C.: Towards weakly-supervised action localization. In: arXiv preprint (2016)

47. Wu, J., Kuang, Z., Wang, L., Zhang, W., Wu, G.: Context-aware RCNN: a baseline for action detection in videos. In: Vedaldi, A., Bischof, H., Brox, T., Frahm, J.-M. (eds.) ECCV 2020. LNCS, vol. 12370, pp. 440–456. Springer, Cham (2020). https://doi.org/10.1007/978-3-030-58595-2_27

48. Wu, J., Wang, L., Wang, L., Guo, J., Wu, G.: Learning actor relation graphs for group activity recognition. In: CVPR (2019)

49. Yan, R., Xie, L., Tang, J., Shu, X., Tian, Q.: HiGCIN: hierarchical graph-based cross inference network for group activity recognition. IEEE TPAMI (2020). https://doi.org/10.1109/TPAMI.2020.3034233

50. Yuan, H., Ni, D.: Learning visual context for group activity recognition. In: AAAI (2021)

51. Yun, K., Honorio, J., Chattopadhyay, D., Berg, T.L., Samaras, D.: Two-person interaction detection using body-pose features and multiple instance learning. In: CVPRW (2012)

52. Zelnik-Manor, L., Perona, P.: Self-tuning spectral clustering. In: NeurIPS (2004)

53. Zhan, X., Liu, Z., Yan, J., Lin, D., Loy, C.C.: Consensus-driven propagation in massive unlabeled data for face recognition. In: Ferrari, V., Hebert, M., Sminchisescu, C., Weiss, Y. (eds.) ECCV 2018. LNCS, vol. 11213, pp. 576–592. Springer, Cham (2018). https://doi.org/10.1007/978-3-030-01240-3_35

54. Zhang, X.Y., Shi, H., Li, C., Li, P.: Multi-instance multi-label action recognition and localization based on spatio-temporal pre-trimming for untrimmed videos. In: AAAI (2020)

55. Zhao, J., Han, R., Gan, Y., Wan, L., Feng, W., Wang, S.: Human identification and interaction detection in cross-view multi-person videos with wearable cameras. In: ACM MM (2020)

56. Zhou, Y., Sun, X., Zha, Z.J., Zeng, W.: MICT: mixed 3D/2D convolutional tube for human action recognition. In: CVPR (2018)

Delving into Details: Synopsis-to-Detail Networks for Video Recognition

Shuxian Liang[1,2], Xu Shen[2], Jianqiang Huang[2], and Xian-Sheng Hua[1(✉)]

[1] Zhejiang University, Hangzhou, China
shuxian.lsx@zju.edu.cn, huaxiansheng@gmail.com
[2] Alibaba Cloud Computing Ltd., Hangzhou, China

Abstract. In this paper, we explore the details in video recognition with the aim to improve the accuracy. It is observed that most failure cases in recent works fall on the mis-classifications among very similar actions (such as high kick *vs.* side kick) that need a capturing of fine-grained discriminative details. To solve this problem, we propose synopsis-to-detail networks for video action recognition. Firstly, a synopsis network is introduced to predict the top-k likely actions and generate the synopsis (location & scale of details and contextual features). Secondly, according to the synopsis, a detail network is applied to extract the discriminative details in the input and infer the final action prediction. The proposed synopsis-to-detail networks enable us to train models directly from scratch in an end-to-end manner and to investigate various architectures for synopsis/detail recognition. Extensive experiments on benchmark datasets, including Kinetics-400, Mini-Kinetics and Something-Something V1 & V2, show that our method is more effective and efficient than the competitive baselines. Code is available at: https://github.com/liang4sx/S2DNet.

Keywords: Video recognition · Action recognition

1 Introduction

The explosive growth of online videos requires for an automatic recognition of large-scale videos, including human actions, events or other contents within them. For example, there are more than 10^5 hours of fresh video contents uploaded to YouTube every day to be processed for ranking and recommendation. In this situation, both high accuracy and high efficiency are required for large-scale online video analysis.

Because of the strong expressive power, in recent years, deep networks become the mainstream solutions for video recognition [5, 6, 12, 24, 41, 45, 46, 51]. To model spatial and temporal patterns in videos, 2D CNNs based methods first

---

S. Liang—This work was done when the author was visiting Alibaba as a research intern.

Supplementary Information The online version contains supplementary material available at https://doi.org/10.1007/978-3-031-19772-7_16.

extract spatial features of each frame with 2D CNNs, then model the temporal patterns based on a temporal fusion of spatial features. The temporal fusion strategies consist of post-hoc fusion [6,12,15,60] or mid-level fusion [47,56,62]. These methods sacrifice the fine-grained temporal modeling at the low level for efficiency, resulting in a moderate accuracy. 3D CNNs [5,10,11,46] handles spatial and temporal dimensions jointly, which achieve higher accuracy, but the computational costs are large, making them difficult to process large-scale real-time online videos. Recently, a feasible way for high accuracy and high efficiency is to investigate better temporal modeling based on 2D CNNs [32,42,53]. In [32], parts of the 2D CNN channels are shifted along temporal dimension to merge information among neighboring frames efficiently. [42] introduces a coarse-to-fine framework, where features of multi-scale input are combined for final prediction and early exits of easy cases are adopted for higher inference speed. In [53], a policy network is used to select relevant regions and frames for better efficiency. However, there are still a number of failed cases in their results.

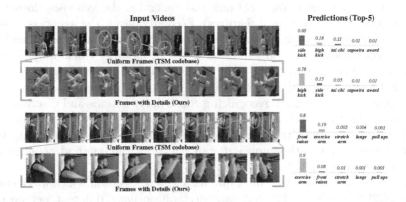

Fig. 1. Two failure cases of recent works [32,42,53]. The left shows both the input clips of uniform frames used by these works (in first/third rows), and the input clips of frames with detail sampled by our method (in second/fourth rows). The right part shows the predictions generated by [32] using these clips. The bars in red denote the probabilities of ground-truth actions. Without the details, the first case is mis-classified since the high kick moment (with the leg in front of the hip) is missing ($3^{rd}/4^{th}$ frames in the second row) and the pose ($2^{nd}/3^{rd}/4^{th}/5^{th}$ frames in the first row) of the person seems like the pose of side kick (with the leg extending out from the hip). Also, the second case is mis-classified because the motion of exercising arms (lifting the arms upward) is indistinctive and the pose of the person in earlier frames ($1^{st}/2^{nd}/3^{rd}/4^{th}$ frames in the third row) is similar to the pose of front raises (lifting the arms to the shoulder height) (Color figure online)

We investigate the failure cases in recent works and find most of these failure cases fall on the mis-classifications among very similar actions (such as high kick *vs.* side kick) that need a deep understanding of fine-grained discriminative details. Two failure cases on Kinetics-400 [5] are shown in Fig. 1. With the conventional uniform frames, we can observe that the top-5 predictions of recent works are rather reasonable and share the same scene ("martial art" for case 1 and "indoor exercise" for case 2). But without the details in the second/fourth rows, even for our human eyes, it's difficult to rank the ground-truth actions "high kick" and "exercise arm" in the first place. Intuitively, for action recognition of a video, the observation process of humans consists of two stages [2]: 1) Go through the video and identify the key frames/regions that are related to the most likely actions in consideration. 2) Slow the playback rate of key frames and zoom in the related region of each frame to obtain extra *details* for a more precise prediction. Inspired by this process, to further improve the accuracy of video recognition, we need to introduce the zoom in/out effects in both spatial and temporal dimensions for better inspection of details in the video.

Following the aforementioned analysis and motivation, we present a new perspective for accurate video recognition by proposing a novel synopsis-to-detail network (S2DNet). Firstly, a synopsis network goes through the input video, predicts the top-k most likely actions and generates the synopsis (location & scale of details and contextual features). Secondly, given the synopsis, a detail network is introduced to dynamically extract the details from the input and infer the final prediction based on the details. As all modules (including samplers, backbones and classifiers) of the synopsis/detail networks are differentiable, the synopsis-to-detail network can be trained directly from scratch in an end-to-end manner. Note that both recognizing top-k likely actions and discriminating one out of the top-k actions using details are much easier tasks than direct action recognition from the input video. As a result, despite adopting light-weighted models for both synopsis/detail networks, our method achieves both high accuracy and high efficiency.

There is another recent architecture for video recognition which has a coarse-to-fine (C2F) design [33, 42], but provides conceptually different perspectives. The C2F methods have not explored the potential of sampling details (zoom in detail regions and slow the playback rate of detail frames), which is a key concept in our method. Moreover, in C2F methods, each network shares the same task of classifying among all actions in parallel. The proposed S2DNet, however, formulates the task of action recognition as a progressive process, where the final output is generated by two simpler tasks (firstly recognizing top-k likely actions and then discriminating one out of the top-k actions using extra details).

Extensive experiments on benchmark datasets, including Kinetics-400, Mini-Kinetics and Something-Something V1 & V2, show that our method is more effective and efficient than the competitive baselines.

2   Related Works

Action Recognition. One prevalent approach to capture spatio-temporal patterns of actions adopts Convolutional Neural Networks (CNNs). Early works extract frame-level features with 2D CNNs and empower them with temporal dynamics via two-stream networks with optical flow [45], temporal averaging [51], long short-term memory [6], *etc.* The other line of works develops 3D CNNs [12,19,41,46], handling both spatial and temporal dimensions jointly. Later works on 3D CNNs leverage self-attention mechanisms [52], pathways of different framerates [11], learnable correlation operators [49], *etc.* . More recently, there have been attempts to apply vision transformers [7] for action recognition [1,3,8,39], matching or exceeding state-of-the-arts on multiple datasets.

In consideration of both accuracy and efficiency, recent efforts of efficient action recognition methods lie in two folds. The first focuses on designing light-weighted architectures, such as 2D CNNs with cost-efficient temporal modeling modules [9,30,32,34,50,54,62] and optimized 3D CNNs [10,28,35,47]. The second attempts to dynamically allocate computation along time axis [14,25,26,36,37,55,59] or in both space and time [42,53].

Coarse-to-Fine Architectures. The coarse-to-fine architectures have a long history in computer vision [13,27,48,58,61]. On the one hand, the architectures alleviate computational costs by tackling easy cases in the coarsest level [27,29]. On the other, they also help improve accuracy by fusing features of different levels [27], eliminating redundancy of input [4,58] and reducing searching space [31,44,61]. In the context of action recognition, prior works adopt coarse-to-fine architectures for early exits of easy cases [42] and multi-level feature fusion [33,42]. Our design of two-stage architecture is inspired by these prior works.

S2DNet is also similar in form to some other lines of works, *e.g.*, space-time attention and ensembling. Due to page limit, we defer discussions about the differences between these works and S2DNet to the supplementary material.

3   Synopsis-to-Detail Network

The proposed Synopsis-to-Detail Networks (S2DNet) (Fig. 2) consists of a Synopsis Network (SNet) and a Detail Network (DNet). The **synopsis** in this paper refers to a brief summary of the key factors of the input video, which is highly related to the corresponding top-k likely actions. The **details** in this paper refer to the discriminative factors that assist in differentiating the true action out of the aforementioned top-k actions.

The process of S2DNet is like: first, SNet goes through the video, predicts the top-k actions and extracts the synopsis; then, given the synopsis, DNet delves into related details of the video and infers the final precise action.

3.1   Synopsis Network (SNet)

The synopsis includes *location & scale parameters of details* (θ) and *contextual features* (m) related to the top-k likely actions. The former specifies the key frames and regions of the input video. The latter acts as task information for the extraction of discriminative features among the top-k actions. SNet learns the above information from the raw frames. It is based on a classic action recognition architecture, including a sampler, a backbone and a classifier.

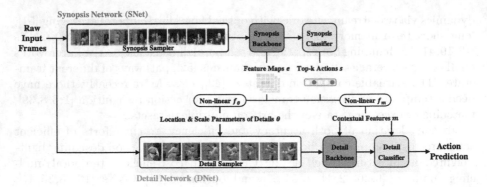

Fig. 2. Model Overview. S2DNet consists of a Synopsis Network and a Detail Network. First, the Synopsis Network goes through the video, predicts the top-k likely actions and extracts video synopsis accordingly (*location & scale of details θ and contextual features m*). Then, given the synopsis, the Detail Network delves into related details of the video and infers the final precise action

Synopsis Sampler. Consider a video with $T \times \tau$ frames totally, where T is the number of raw input frames and τ is the temporal stride of these frames. The raw input frames are denoted by $\mathcal{I} \in \mathbb{R}^{T \times H \times W}$, where H and W are height and width (the dimension of RGB channels are omitted for brevity). The synopsis sampler uniformly samples T_S frames out of the raw input frames $\mathcal{I}$, then spatially resizes them to $H_S \times W_S$. The output frames of the synopsis sampler are denoted by $\mathcal{V} \in \mathbb{R}^{T_S \times H_S \times W_S}$. Importantly, the sizes of $\mathcal{V}$ are much smaller than the sizes of $\mathcal{I}$ (*e.g.*, $16 \times 144 \times 144$ *vs.* $150 \times 224 \times 224$). This ensures a low computational cost of the following feature extraction.

Synopsis Backbone. The synopsis backbone f_s can be any 2D/3D CNNs for video recognition (*e.g.*, [10,11,32]). It takes the output frames of the synopsis sampler as input and generates spatio-temporal feature maps of the video:

$$e = f_s(\mathcal{V}), \tag{1}$$

where $e \in \mathbb{R}^{C_S \times T_S \times h_S \times w_S}$. C_S, h_S and w_S are channel size, height and width.

Synopsis Classifier. The synopsis classifier is designed to recognize the top-k likely actions of the input video. A fully-connected (FC) layer with softmax is adopted as the synopsis classifier h_s, which takes the feature maps e as input:

$$p = h_s(\text{GAP}(e)), \tag{2}$$

where GAP is global average pooling and p is the softmax predictions over all N actions. A k-hot vector s (with 1s for the top-k actions and 0s for other actions) is introduced to represent the top-k likely actions. Specifically, s is the top-k binarization of p, which takes only a single line of code[1] in PyTorch [40].

---

[1] `torch.nn.functional.one_hot(torch.topk(p,k).indices,N).sum(dim=-1)`.

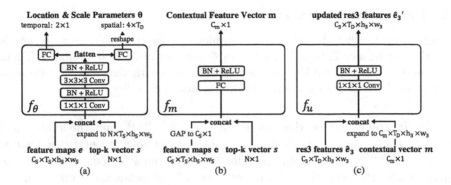

Fig. 3. Illustration of (a) generating location & scale parameters of details θ, (b) generating contextual features m, and (c) fusing contextual features m to intermediate feature maps of DNet

To ensure that the ground-truth class falls in the top-k predictions, a cross entropy loss is applied to the output of SNet:

$$\mathcal{L}_s = -\sum_{n=1}^{N} \mathbb{I}(n = y) \log p(n), \tag{3}$$

where y denotes the ground-truth class and $\mathbb{I}(\cdot)$ is an indicator function.

Synopsis I: Generating Location & Scale Parameters of Details θ (Fig. 3a). Inspired by the differentiable attention [17,18,21,57], location and scale are formulated as 6 individual parameters: $\theta = (\mu_t, \mu_y, \mu_x, \delta_t, \delta_y, \delta_x)$. These parameters will be used in the sampler of DNet and their explanations are deferred to Sect. 3.2. Taking the feature maps e and the top-k vector s as input, the parameters are generated by the module f_θ:

$$\theta = f_\theta([e, E(s)]), \tag{4}$$

where $[\cdot, \cdot]$ denotes concatenation and $E(\cdot)$ expands the vector s to the shape of e ($N \times 1 \rightarrow N \times T_S \times h_S \times w_S$). f_θ consists of one $1 \times 1 \times 1$ convolutional layer, one $3 \times 3 \times 3$ convolutional layer (both with BN [22] and ReLU [38]) and two parallel fully-connected (FC) layers. The two FC layers generate $(\mu_t, \delta_t) \in \mathbb{R}^{2 \times 1}$ for temporal sampling and $(\mu_y, \mu_x, \delta_y, \delta_x) \in \mathbb{R}^{4 \times T_D}$ for spatial sampling, respectively.

Synopsis II: Generating Contextual Features m (Fig. 3b). Given the feature maps e and the top-k vector s, m is generated by the module f_m:

$$m = f_m([\text{GAP}(e), s]), \tag{5}$$

where $m \in \mathbb{R}^{C_m \times 1}$. The module f_m is a FC layer with ReLU and BN.

3.2   Detail Network (DNet)

To delve into the details, DNet first samples a space-time volume with details from the raw frames $\mathcal{I}$, based on *location & scale parameters of details* θ. Then, it extracts discriminative features over the volume with the help of *contextual features m*. DNet has a sampler, a backbone and a classifier.

Detail Sampler. Given the raw input $\mathcal{I} \in \mathbb{R}^{T \times H \times W}$ and the real-valued parameters $\theta = (\mu_t, \mu_y, \mu_x, \delta_t, \delta_y, \delta_x)$, the detail sampler generates a volume $\hat{\mathcal{V}} \in \mathbb{R}^{T_D \times H_D \times W_D}$ that contains rich details of the top-k actions. Following the differentiable attention [17,18,21,57], an array of 3-dimensional filters is applied to the raw input $\mathcal{I}$, yielding a sequence of local patches with smoothly varying location and scale.

Specifically, given the expected output size $T_D \times H_D \times W_D$, a $T_D \times H_D \times W_D$ grid of sampling filters is applied to $\mathcal{I}$. The center of the grid is determined by the real-valued parameters (μ_t, μ_y, μ_x), which are formally time/height/width offsets to the center of $\mathcal{I}$. The time/height/width strides of the grid are controlled by the real-valued parameters $(\delta_t, \delta_y, \delta_x)$. Consequently, the grid location (p_t, p_y, p_x) at frame z, row j and column i is:

$$
\begin{aligned}
p_t(z) &= \mu_t T + (z - T_D/2 - 0.5)\delta_t, \\
p_y(j) &= \mu_y H + (j - H_D/2 - 0.5)\delta_y, \\
p_x(i) &= \mu_x W + (i - W_D/2 - 0.5)\delta_x.
\end{aligned}
\tag{6}
$$

Note that the smaller δ_t is, the slower the playback rate of detail frames will be. The smaller (δ_y, δ_x) are, the larger the resolution ratio of detail regions will be.

Previous works use Gaussian filters [18,21,57] or linear filters [21] for sampling. We have experimented with both filters and find Gaussian filters suit better for our case (discussed in the supplementary material). The coordinates specified by the grid are the mean locations of Gaussian filters. Given the variance as 1, the temporal, horizontal and vertical filtering weights $\mathcal{G}_T$ (dimensions $T_D \times T$), $\mathcal{G}_Y$ (dimensions $H_D \times H$) and $\mathcal{G}_X$ (dimensions $W_D \times W$) are defined as:

$$
\begin{aligned}
\mathcal{G}_T[z,r] &= \frac{1}{Z_T} exp(-\frac{(p_t(z) - r)^2}{2}), \\
\mathcal{G}_Y[j,v] &= \frac{1}{Z_Y} exp(-\frac{(p_y(j) - v)^2}{2}), \\
\mathcal{G}_X[i,u] &= \frac{1}{Z_X} exp(-\frac{(p_x(i) - u)^2}{2}),
\end{aligned}
\tag{7}
$$

where (z, j, i) are coordinates of a point in the output $\hat{\mathcal{V}}$ and (r, v, u) are coordinates of a point in the input $\mathcal{I}$. Z_T, Z_Y and Z_X are the normalization constants that ensure $\sum_r \mathcal{G}_T[z,r] = 1$, $\sum_v \mathcal{G}_Y[j,v] = 1$ and $\sum_u \mathcal{G}_X[i,u] = 1$.

Finally, the overall sampling operation is formulated as three 1-dimensional Gaussian filtering. The output volume $\hat{\mathcal{V}}$ from the raw input $\mathcal{I}$ is sampled via $\hat{\mathcal{V}} = \mathcal{G}_X \mathcal{G}_Y \mathcal{G}_T \mathcal{I}$, where the dimension transposition is omitted for brevity.

Detail Backbone. Similar to SNet, the detail backbone f_d can be instantiated with various video backbones. Taking the output volume of the detail sampler $\hat{\mathcal{V}}$ and the contextual features m as input, it generates detail feature maps $\hat{e} \in \mathbb{R}^{C_D \times T_S \times h_D \times w_D}$ of details by:

$$\hat{e} = f_d\left(\hat{\mathcal{V}}, m\right). \tag{8}$$

Fusing the contextual features m to detail features (Fig. 3c). Following [11], m is laterally fused into detail features via convolution. For ResNets-like architectures [10,20], we apply the lateral fusion after *res3* and *res4* (more discussions are in our supplementary material), for example,

$$\hat{e}'_3 = f_u([\hat{e}_3, E(m)]), \tag{9}$$

where $\hat{e}_3/\hat{e}'_3 \in \mathbb{R}^{C_3 \times T_D \times h_3 \times w_3}$ is the original/updated *res3* features and $E(\cdot)$ expands m to the shape of $\hat{e}_3$ ($C_m \times 1 \rightarrow C_m \times T_D \times h_3 \times w_3$). f_u is a $1 \times 1 \times 1$ convolutional layer with BN and ReLU.

Detail Classifier. The detail classifier h_d outputs the final precise predictions by generating a vector $\hat{p}$ of softmax probabilities over all classes. Taking the detail feature maps $\hat{e}$ and the contextual features m as input, a FC layer is adopted for the classification:

$$\hat{p} = h_d\left([\text{GAP}(\hat{e}), m]\right). \tag{10}$$

Notably, m conveys contextual information (the global features to refer to and the top-k actions to consider). Since DNet focuses on differentiating top-k actions, we adopt the top-k vector s as an "attention" for all output actions by multiplying $\hat{p}$ with s. Therefore, the cross entropy loss for DNet is refined as:

$$\mathcal{L}_d = -\sum_{n=1}^{N} \mathbb{I}(n = y)s(n)\log\hat{p}(n). \tag{11}$$

Finally, the overall loss of S2DNet is computed by:

$$\mathcal{L} = \alpha\mathcal{L}_s + \mathcal{L}_d, \tag{12}$$

where α weighs the task of top-k action recognition and top-1 action recognition.

3.3 Instantiations

The proposed S2DNet is generic and can be instantiated using various video backbones and implementation specifics. In this paper, we focus on action recognition for trimmed videos, and opt to instantiate S2DNet with the classic 2D/3D CNNs-based methods (*e.g.*, [10,11,32]). However, note that our method can also apply with recent Vision Transformers [1,3,7,8,39].

Specifically, to compare with state-of-the-art 2D CNNs, a TSM model with MobileNetV2 [43] is used in SNet, and a TSM model with ResNet-50 [20] is used in DNet. To compare with state-of-the-art 3D CNNs, a X3D-S [10] model is used in SNet and a X3D-M/X3D-XL model is used in DNet. The results using TSM/X3D backbones are reported in Sect. 4.2.

4   Experiments

In this section, we empirically validate the proposed method on four action recognition datasets using the standard evaluation protocols. First, in Sect. 4.2, the comparison with state-of-the-art (SOTA) methods for S2DNet is presented. Second, in Sect. 4.3, ablation results on different configurations of S2DNet are discussed. Third, in Sect. 4.4, S2DNet is also compared with efficient action recognition methods, demonstrating its merit of high efficiency. At last, we present the efficiency analysis (Sect. 4.5) and some visualization results (Sect. 4.6), to provide additional insights of S2DNet.

4.1   Setups

Datasets. Our experiments are based on four widely-used action recognition datasets. Kinetics-400 [5] is a large-scale action recognition dataset with $240k$ training and $20k$ validation videos in 400 action classes. Mini-Kinetics (assembled by [36]) is a subset of the Kinetics-400 and it contains $121k$ training and $10k$ validation videos in 200 action classes. Something-Something V1 & V2 [16] are two action recognition datasets with $98k/194k$ videos in the shared 174 classes. When compared with the SOTA methods, S2DNet is evaluated on Kinetics-400 and Something-Something V2. When compared with the efficient methods, S2DNet is evaluated on Mini-Kinetics and Something-Something V1 & V2. Following previous works, we report top-1 and/or top-5 classification accuracy (%).

Training and Inference. We use $\tau = 2$, $k = 5$, $\alpha = 0.1$ and $C_m = 256$ for all experiments in this work. During training, following [32,36,53], random scaling, 224×224 random cropping and random horizontal flipping (except Something-Something V1&V2) are adopted for data augmentation. During inference, for the spatial domain, the raw frames are first resized to 256×256. On Kinetics-400, three 224×224 patches are cropped from the resized frames, following common practice in [10,11,52]. On other datasets, only one center 224×224 cropping is used. For the temporal domain, on all datasets, we use only one clip per video. More details (*e.g.*, training hyper-parameters) are in the supplementary material.

4.2   Comparison with State-of-the-Arts

This section provides the comparison with SOTA methods on Kinetics-400 and Something-Something V2, considering both accuracy and efficiency. Kinetics-400 includes the daily actions that are highly relevant to interacting objects or scene context, thereby requiring strong spatio-temporal modeling capacity. Recent methods on this dataset are mostly based on 3D CNNs to learn space-time features jointly. Something-Something V2 pays more attention to modeling temporal relationships as pointed in [32,56,60]. Recent methods on this dataset include both 2D CNNs and 3D CNNs.

Implementation Details. To compare with SOTA methods on Kinetics-400, S2DNet is instantiated using efficient 3D CNNs (*i.e.*, X3D [10]). To compare

Table 1. Comparison with the state-of-the-arts on Kinetics-400 and Something-Something V2. "FLOPs" denotes multiply-add operations. "R50" and "R101" denote ResNet-50 and ResNet-101 [20]. "MN2" denotes MobileNetV2 [43]. "-" indicate that the numbers are not available for us. For S2DNet, "X3D-S/X3D-M" indicates that X3D-S is used in SNet and X3D-M is used in DNet

Methods	Backbone	Frames	top-1	top-5	FLOPs × Views
Kinetics400					
TSM [32]	R50	16	74.7	91.4	65G×30
C2F [42]	R50	16	76.0	-	18G×9
TANet [34]	R50	16	76.9	92.9	86G×12
SlowFast [11]	R50	8/32	75.6	92.1	36G×30
SmallBig [28]	R50	8	76.3	92.5	57G×6
CorrNet [49]	R50	32	77.2	-	115G×30
TDN [50]	R50	16	77.5	93.2	72G×30
SmallBig [28]	R101	16	77.4	93.3	418G×12
TDN [50]	R101	16	78.5	93.9	132G×30
CorrNet [49]	R101	32	79.2	-	224G×30
SlowFast [11]	R101-NL	16/64	79.8	93.9	234G×30
X3D [10]	X3D-M	16	76.0	92.3	6.2G×30
X3D [10]	X3D-XL	16	79.1	93.9	48G×30
S2DNet (ours)	X3D-S/X3D-M	16/16	78.0	93.6	**5.4G**×3
S2DNet (ours)	X3D-S/X3D-XL	16/16	**80.6**	**94.2**	39G×3
Something-Something V2					
GST [35]	R50	16	62.6	87.9	59G×6
SlowFast [11]	R50	128	63.0	88.5	-
TSM [32]	R50	16	63.4	88.5	65G×6
C2F [42]	R50	16	64.1	-	85G×6
SmallBig [28]	R50	16	63.8	88.9	105G×6
STM [23]	R50	16	64.2	89.8	67G×30
TANet [34]	R50	16	64.6	89.5	72G×6
TDN [50]	R50	16	65.3	89.5	72G×1
S2DNet (ours)	MN2/R50	16/16	**66.4**	**89.9**	35G×1

with SOTA methods on Something-Something V2, S2DNet is instantiated using efficient 2D CNNs (*i.e.*, TSM [32]). For both datasets, the input parameters are: $T_S = 16$, $T_D = 16$, $H_S = W_S = 224$ and $H_D = W_D = 144$.

Kinetics-400. The upper part of Table 1 presents the comparison with SOTA results for two S2DNet instantiations using X3D. Note that X3D-M and X3D-XL achieve similar performances to the SOTA works with ResNet-50 and ResNet-101, respectively. To make a fair comparison, we compare **S2DNet (X3D-S/X3D-M)** with ResNet-50 based works (*e.g.*, [11,28,30,32,34,49]), and compare **S2DNet (X3D-S/X3D-XL)** with ResNet-101 based works (*e.g.*, [11,28, 49,50,52]). Firstly, it is observed that S2DNet improves the X3D counterparts by a margin of 2.0%/1.5% on top-1 accuracy, while requiring fewer multiply-add operations (FLOPs). Secondly, **S2DNet (X3D-S/X3D-M)** achieves +0.5% top-1 accuracy at 13.3× fewer FLOPs than the best reported result of TDN (R50) [50]. Thirdly, **S2DNet (X3D-S/X3D-XL)** is +0.8% more accurate on top-1 accuracy and requires 6.0× fewer FLOPs than the best reported result of SlowFast (R101) [11]. The above results verify that our top-k action recognition contributes to a better performance of the final precise action prediction.

Moreover, although the top-5 results are generated by the light-weighted SNet (X3D-S), the best top-5 performance of S2DNet is still better than X3D-XL and SlowFast. This phenomenon indicates that a high-quality detail recognition help foster better top-k action recognition in return.

Something-Something V2. The lower part of Table 1 presents the comparison with SOTA results for one S2DNet instantiation using TSM. The results show that S2DNet achieves a significant improvement of 3.0%/1.4% on top-1/top-5 accuracy for TSM. Meanwhile, compared with the best reported result of TDN, our method achieves +1.1% top-1 performance at 2.0× fewer FLOPs. These results demonstrate that, by formulating action recognition into first recognizing top-k actions and then discriminating one out of the top-k actions, the task is easier to handle than the direct action recognition from input videos.

4.3   Ablation Experiments

This subsection provides ablation studies on Mini-Kinetics comparing accuracy and efficiency.

Implementation Details. In this subsection, we use TSM with MobileNetV2 in SNet and TSM with ResNet-50 in DNet. The input parameters are: $T_S = T_D = 16$, $H_S = W_S = 144$ and $H_D = W_D = 112$.

Architecture Configurations. Table 2a shows results of different architecture configurations of S2DNet. These configurations determine whether the two sub-networks (SNet and DNet) are used together or separately. Notably, to measure the standalone performance of DNet, all sampling parameters for the detail sampler are frozen, all lateral fusions in the detail backbone are canceled and the detail classifier takes as input only the detail features $\hat{e}$.

Compared with the full network ($a1$ *vs.* $a0$), SNet presents more performance drop on top-1 (-6.1%) than top-5 (-1.6%). This is because the top-5 classification is much simpler than the direct top-1 classification. Despite using a more sophisticated backbone, DNet is inferior to SNet with a performance drop of 0.5% on top-1 and 1.8% on top-5 ($a2$ *vs.* $a1$). This indicates that location & scale information provided by SNet is better than a fixed pre-defined one. By combining SNet and DNet, S2DNet achieves a significant gain of 6.1%/6.7% on top-1 accuracy ($a0$ *vs.* $a1/a2$). This result indicates that synopsis information and detail information complement each other.

Detail Network Configurations. Results of different configurations of DNet are shown in Table 2b. For $b1/b3$, location & scale parameters θ for the detail sampler are frozen. For $b1/b2$, contextual features m (Eq. 5) are not laterally

Table 2. Ablations on Mini-Kinetics. In all subtables, the bottom rows ($a0$, $b0$ and $c0$) represent the default settings of S2DNet

(a) Architecture configuration

	SNet	DNet	top-1	top-5	FLOPs
$a1$	✓		68.6	89.5	**2.2G**
$a2$		✓	68.1	87.7	15.3G
$a0$	✓	✓	**74.7**	**91.1**	18.0G

(b) Detail network configuration

	Sample	Fuse	top-1	top-5	FLOPs
$b1$			70.7	90.1	**17.5G**
$b2$	✓		73.3	90.9	17.9G
$b3$		✓	71.7	90.9	17.6G
$b0$	✓	✓	**74.7**	**91.1**	18.0G

(c) Detail sampler configuration

	Space	Time	top-1	top-5	FLOPs
$c1$			71.7	89.6	**17.6G**
$c2$	✓		72.7	89.5	17.9G
$c3$		✓	74.0	89.4	17.9G
$c0$	✓	✓	**74.7**	**91.1**	18.0G

fused to the intermediate features of the detail backbone. By incorporating location & scale parameters θ provided by SNet, DNet achieves a significant gain of 2.6% on top-1 accuracy and a gain of 0.8% on top-5 accuracy ($b2$ *vs.* $b1$). This result reveals that the detail sampler extracts more discriminative details from input video with the proposed detail sampling. The lateral fusion of contextual features in the detail backbone brings in a 1.0% improvement ($b3$ *vs.* $b1$), which indicates that contextual features boost the final prediction of actions. Finally, using all components in DNet as proposed ($b0$) leads to a further improvement, indicating that these components boost each other.

Detail Sampler Configurations. As shown in Table 2c, S2DNet is evaluated under different space-time sampling strategies. For $c1$, location & scale parameters θ are frozen, where the center croppings of uniformly sampled frames are used as the input volume $\hat{\mathcal{V}}$ for DNet. This setting leads to a performance drop of 2.8% on top-1 accuracy ($c1$ *vs.* $c0$). Only introducing spatial sampling brings in a 1.0% performance gain ($c2$ *vs.* $c1$). Only introducing temporal sampling brings in a performance gain of 2.3% ($c3$ *vs.* $c1$). These results show that both spatial sampling and temporal sampling play an important role in delving into fine-grained discriminative details from input videos.

4.4   Comparison with Efficient Action Recognition Methods

Although S2DNet is proposed to improve the accuracy, it also enjoys the merit of high efficiency. This subsection provides the comparison with efficient action recognition methods for S2DNet on three datasets: Mini-Kinetics, Something-Something V1 and Something-Something V2.

Table 3. Comparison with efficient action recognition methods. "BN-I" denotes to BN-Inception [22] and "R18" denotes ResNet-18. Only top-1 accuracy is reported since the top-5 results of many of these works are not available

(a) Mini-Kinetics

Method	Backbone	top-1	FLOPs
AR-Net [36]	MN2/R50	71.7	32G
AdaFocus [53]	MN2/R50	72.2	27G
AdaFuse [37]	R50	72.3	23G
DKP [25]	R18/R50	72.7	18G
S2DNet (ours)	MN2/R50	**74.7**	**18G**

(b) Something-Something V1/V2

Method	Backbone	top-1	FLOPs
ECO [62]	BN-I/R18	39.6/-	32G
TSM [32]	R50	45.6/59.1	33G
AdaFuse [37]	R50	46.8/59.8	31G
AdaFocus [53]	MN2/R50	48.1/60.7	34G
S2DNet (ours)	MN2/R50	**49.7/62.5**	**22G**

Implementation Details. For a fair comparison, we use the same video backbones (MobileNetV2 and ResNet-50) as [26,36,53]. To balance the trade-off between efficiency and accuracy, we adopt $T_S = T_D = 16$, $H_S = W_S = 144$ and $H_D = W_D = 112$ on Mini-Kinetics. On Something-Something V1 & V2, we adopt $T_S = 8$, $T_D = 12$, $H_S = W_S = 144$ and $H_D = W_D = 144$.

Results. Table 3 illustrates 2.0%/1.6%/1.8% better accuracy of S2DNet on the three datasets. While the gains are significant, it is also observed that S2DNet requires fewer FLOPs. This indicates that S2DNet is good at handling the trade-off between accuracy and efficiency, making it flexible to deploy in real world.

4.5   Efficiency Analysis

As in Table 4, compared with the efficient/SOTA methods [32,50], S2DNet enjoys higher accuracy (+3%/+1.1%), lower latency ($\downarrow$ 1.49×/$\downarrow$ 2.50×), lower FLOPs ($\downarrow$ 1.88×/$\downarrow$ 2.05×) with minor/less extra parameters (+15%/−8.2%). The FLOPs and latency of S2DNet are lower for two reasons. First, SNet is light-weighted and brings a small amount of extra parameters and FLOPs. Second, DNet has a smaller spatial input size (e.g., 224 → 144) by using local regions with details, which reduces the FLOPs significantly.

Table 4. Efficiency comparison on Something-Something V2. All measures use a Tesla V100 with batch size as 16. † denotes the reproduced results

Method	Backbone	Frames	FLOPs	Param.	Latency (ms)	top-1
TSM [32]	R50	16	66G	**24.3M**	15.7	63.4
TDN [50]	R50	16	72G	30.5M†	26.3†	65.3
S2DNet (ours)	MN2/R50	16/16	**35G**	28.0M	**10.5**	**66.4**

4.6   Visualization

In S2DNet, fine-grained details are sampled by a detail sampler, using *location & scale of details* from SNet. This process is visualized in Fig. 4, using the $a0$ instantiation of S2DNet in Table 2a. The upper half of the figure shows the uniform frames sampled by SNet (and also by some previous works), and the lower half shows the contents sampled by the detail sampler.

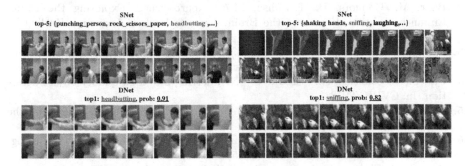

Fig. 4. Visualization of the sampled contents of S2DNet on Kinetics-400. The labels in red denote ground-truth actions (Color figure online)

In the first case, one can observe that the moment of headbutting is missing in the uniform frames while the pose of the man on the right is similar to punching person. This leads to a mis-classification of the previous works (*e.g.*, TSM). As for S2DNet, by leveraging the synopsis from SNet, it samples space-time details that are most related to the top-k actions (actions about hands/heads). Specifically, it slows the playback rate of the frames in which the two persons get close, and zooms in the regions where their moving hands/heads are conspicuous. By doing so, the action headbutting is recognized.

In the second case, one can observe that there are a lot of redundant frames in the uniform frames and the true action sniffing is indistinctive. This results in a mis-classification of the previous works. S2DNet samples space-time details that are most related to the top-k actions (actions about hands/faces). Specifically, it gets rid of the redundant frames and zooms in the regions where motions of hands/faces are conspicuous. By doing so, the action sniffing is recognized.

5   Conclusion

This paper proposes a novel network for video recognition, namely Synopsis-to-Detail Network. Inspired by the observation that recent works fail to differentiate very similar actions (such as high kick *vs.* side kick), S2DNet first predicts the top-k actions and generates the synopsis by coarsely going through the video. Then, according to the synopsis, it extracts discriminative details in the input and infers the final precise action. Extensive experiments demonstrate that our method outperforms existing works in terms of both accuracy and efficiency.

Acknowledgment. This work was partially supported by the National Key R&D Program of China under Grant 2020AAA0103901.

References

1. Arnab, A., Dehghani, M., Heigold, G., Sun, C., Lučić, M., Schmid, C.: Vivit: a video vision transformer. arXiv preprint arXiv:2103.15691 (2021)
2. Bear, M., Connors, B., Paradiso, M.A.: Neuroscience: Exploring the Brain, Enhanced Edition: Exploring the Brain. Jones & Bartlett Learning, Burlington (2020)
3. Bertasius, G., Wang, H., Torresani, L.: Is space-time attention all you need for video understanding? arXiv preprint arXiv:2102.05095 (2021)
4. Cai, Z., Vasconcelos, N.: Cascade R-CNN: delving into high quality object detection. In: CVPR (2018)
5. Carreira, J., Zisserman, A.: Quo Vadis, action recognition? A new model and the kinetics dataset. In: CVPR (2017)
6. Donahue, J., et al.: Long-term recurrent convolutional networks for visual recognition and description. In: CVPR (2015)
7. Dosovitskiy, A., et al.: An image is worth 16x16 words: transformers for image recognition at scale. arXiv preprint arXiv:2010.11929 (2020)
8. Fan, H., et al.: Multiscale vision transformers. arXiv preprint arXiv:2104.11227 (2021)
9. Fan, Q., Chen, C.F.R., Kuehne, H., Pistoia, M., Cox, D.: More is less: learning efficient video representations by big-little network and depthwise temporal aggregation. In: NeurIPS (2019)
10. Feichtenhofer, C.: X3D: expanding architectures for efficient video recognition. In: CVPR (2020)
11. Feichtenhofer, C., Fan, H., Malik, J., He, K.: Slowfast networks for video recognition. In: ICCV (2019)
12. Feichtenhofer, C., Pinz, A., Zisserman, A.: Convolutional two-stream network fusion for video action recognition. In: CVPR (2016)
13. Fleuret, F., Geman, D.: Coarse-to-fine face detection. IJCV **41**(1), 85–107 (2001)
14. Gao, R., Oh, T.H., Grauman, K., Torresani, L.: Listen to look: action recognition by previewing audio. In: CVPR (2020)
15. Girdhar, R., Ramanan, D., Gupta, A., Sivic, J., Russell, B.: ActionVLAD: learning spatio-temporal aggregation for action classification. In: CVPR (2017)
16. Goyal, R., et al.: The "something something" video database for learning and evaluating visual common sense. In: ICCV (2017)
17. Graves, A., Wayne, G., Danihelka, I.: Neural turing machines (2014)
18. Gregor, K., Danihelka, I., Graves, A., Rezende, D., Wierstra, D.: Draw: a recurrent neural network for image generation. In: ICML (2015)
19. Hara, K., Kataoka, H., Satoh, Y.: Can spatiotemporal 3D CNNs retrace the history of 2D CNNs and ImageNet? In: CVPR (2018)
20. He, K., Zhang, X., Ren, S., Sun, J.: Deep residual learning for image recognition. In: CVPR (2016)
21. Huang, Z., et al.: 3D local convolutional neural networks for gait recognition. In: ICCV (2021)
22. Ioffe, S., Szegedy, C.: Batch normalization: accelerating deep network training by reducing internal covariate shift. In: ICML (2015)

23. Jiang, B., Wang, M., Gan, W., Wu, W., Yan, J.: STM: spatiotemporal and motion encoding for action recognition. In: ICCV (2019)
24. Karpathy, A., Toderici, G., Shetty, S., Leung, T., Sukthankar, R., Fei-Fei, L.: Large-scale video classification with convolutional neural networks. In: CVPR (2014)
25. Kim, H., Jain, M., Lee, J.T., Yun, S., Porikli, F.: Efficient action recognition via dynamic knowledge propagation. In: ICCV (2021)
26. Korbar, B., Tran, D., Torresani, L.: SCSampler: sampling salient clips from video for efficient action recognition. In: ICCV (2019)
27. Li, H., Lin, Z., Shen, X., Brandt, J., Hua, G.: A convolutional neural network cascade for face detection. In: CVPR (2015)
28. Li, X., Wang, Y., Zhou, Z., Qiao, Y.: SmallBignet: integrating core and contextual views for video classification. In: CVPR (2020)
29. Li, X., Liu, Z., Luo, P., Change Loy, C., Tang, X.: Not all pixels are equal: Difficulty-aware semantic segmentation via deep layer cascade. In: CVPR (2017)
30. Li, Y., Ji, B., Shi, X., Zhang, J., Kang, B., Wang, L.: Tea: temporal excitation and aggregation for action recognition. In: CVPR (2020)
31. Li, Y., et al.: CFAD: coarse-to-fine action detector for spatiotemporal action localization. In: Vedaldi, A., Bischof, H., Brox, T., Frahm, J.-M. (eds.) ECCV 2020. LNCS, vol. 12361, pp. 510–527. Springer, Cham (2020). https://doi.org/10.1007/978-3-030-58517-4_30
32. Lin, J., Gan, C., Han, S.: TSM: temporal shift module for efficient video understanding. In: ICCV (2019)
33. Lin, W., et al.: Action recognition with coarse-to-fine deep feature integration and asynchronous fusion. In: AAAI (2018)
34. Liu, Z., Wang, L., Wu, W., Qian, C., Lu, T.: Tam: temporal adaptive module for video recognition. In: ICCV (2021)
35. Luo, C., Yuille, A.L.: Grouped spatial-temporal aggregation for efficient action recognition. In: ICCV (2019)
36. Meng, Y., et al.: AR-Net: adaptive frame resolution for efficient action recognition. In: Vedaldi, A., Bischof, H., Brox, T., Frahm, J.-M. (eds.) ECCV 2020. LNCS, vol. 12352, pp. 86–104. Springer, Cham (2020). https://doi.org/10.1007/978-3-030-58571-6_6
37. Meng, Y., et al.: AdaFuse: adaptive temporal fusion network for efficient action recognition. In: ICLR (2020)
38. Nair, V., Hinton, G.E.: Rectified linear units improve restricted Boltzmann machines. In: ICML (2010)
39. Neimark, D., Bar, O., Zohar, M., Asselmann, D.: Video transformer network. arXiv preprint arXiv:2102.00719 (2021)
40. Paszke, A., et al.: PyTorch: an imperative style, high-performance deep learning library. In: NeurIPS, vol. 32 (2019)
41. Qiu, Z., Yao, T., Mei, T.: Learning spatio-temporal representation with pseudo-3D residual networks. In: ICCV (2017)
42. Quader, N., Lu, J., Dai, P., Li, W.: Towards efficient coarse-to-fine networks for action and gesture recognition. In: Vedaldi, A., Bischof, H., Brox, T., Frahm, J.-M. (eds.) ECCV 2020. LNCS, vol. 12375, pp. 35–51. Springer, Cham (2020). https://doi.org/10.1007/978-3-030-58577-8_3
43. Sandler, M., Howard, A., Zhu, M., Zhmoginov, A., Chen, L.C.: Mobilenetv 2: inverted residuals and linear bottlenecks. In: CVPR (2018)
44. Sarlin, P.E., Cadena, C., Siegwart, R., Dymczyk, M.: From coarse to fine: robust hierarchical localization at large scale. In: CVPR (2019)

45. Simonyan, K., Zisserman, A.: Two-stream convolutional networks for action recognition in videos. In: NeurIPS (2014)
46. Tran, D., Bourdev, L., Fergus, R., Torresani, L., Paluri, M.: Learning spatiotemporal features with 3D convolutional networks. In: ICCV (2015)
47. Tran, D., Wang, H., Torresani, L., Ray, J., LeCun, Y., Paluri, M.: A closer look at spatiotemporal convolutions for action recognition. In: CVPR (2018)
48. Viola, P., Jones, M.J.: Robust real-time face detection. IJCV **57**(2), 137–154 (2004)
49. Wang, H., Tran, D., Torresani, L., Feiszli, M.: Video modeling with correlation networks. In: CVPR (2020)
50. Wang, L., Tong, Z., Ji, B., Wu, G.: TDN: temporal difference networks for efficient action recognition. In: CVPR (2021)
51. Wang, L., et al.: Temporal segment networks: towards good practices for deep action recognition. In: Leibe, B., Matas, J., Sebe, N., Welling, M. (eds.) ECCV 2016. LNCS, vol. 9912, pp. 20–36. Springer, Cham (2016). https://doi.org/10.1007/978-3-319-46484-8_2
52. Wang, X., Girshick, R., Gupta, A., He, K.: Non-local neural networks. In: CVPR (2018)
53. Wang, Y., Chen, Z., Jiang, H., Song, S., Han, Y., Huang, G.: Adaptive focus for efficient video recognition. In: ICCV (2021)
54. Weng, J., et al.: Temporal distinct representation learning for action recognition. In: Vedaldi, A., Bischof, H., Brox, T., Frahm, J.-M. (eds.) ECCV 2020. LNCS, vol. 12352, pp. 363–378. Springer, Cham (2020). https://doi.org/10.1007/978-3-030-58571-6_22
55. Wu, Z., Xiong, C., Jiang, Y.G., Davis, L.S.: LiteEval: a coarse-to-fine framework for resource efficient video recognition. In: NeurIPS (2019)
56. Xie, S., Sun, C., Huang, J., Tu, Z., Murphy, K.: Rethinking spatiotemporal feature learning: speed-accuracy trade-offs in video classification. In: Ferrari, V., Hebert, M., Sminchisescu, C., Weiss, Y. (eds.) ECCV 2018. LNCS, vol. 11219, pp. 318–335. Springer, Cham (2018). https://doi.org/10.1007/978-3-030-01267-0_19
57. Yang, J., Shen, X., Tian, X., Li, H., Huang, J., Hua, X.S.: Local convolutional neural networks for person re-identification. In: ACM MM (2018)
58. Zhang, J., Shan, S., Kan, M., Chen, X.: Coarse-to-fine auto-encoder networks (CFAN) for real-time face alignment. In: Fleet, D., Pajdla, T., Schiele, B., Tuytelaars, T. (eds.) ECCV 2014. LNCS, vol. 8690, pp. 1–16. Springer, Cham (2014). https://doi.org/10.1007/978-3-319-10605-2_1
59. Zhi, Y., Tong, Z., Wang, L., Wu, G.: MGSampler: an explainable sampling strategy for video action recognition. In: ICCV (2021)
60. Zhou, B., Andonian, A., Oliva, A., Torralba, A.: Temporal relational reasoning in videos. In: Ferrari, V., Hebert, M., Sminchisescu, C., Weiss, Y. (eds.) ECCV 2018. LNCS, vol. 11205, pp. 831–846. Springer, Cham (2018). https://doi.org/10.1007/978-3-030-01246-5_49
61. Zhu, S., Li, C., Change Loy, C., Tang, X.: Face alignment by coarse-to-fine shape searching. In: CVPR (2015)
62. Zolfaghari, M., Singh, K., Brox, T.: ECO: efficient convolutional network for online video understanding. In: Ferrari, V., Hebert, M., Sminchisescu, C., Weiss, Y. (eds.) ECCV 2018. LNCS, vol. 11206, pp. 713–730. Springer, Cham (2018). https://doi.org/10.1007/978-3-030-01216-8_43

A Generalized and Robust Framework for Timestamp Supervision in Temporal Action Segmentation

Rahul Rahaman$^{(\boxtimes)}$ (iD), Dipika Singhania (iD), Alexandre Thiery (iD), and Angela Yao (iD)

National University of Singapore, Singapore, Singapore
rahul.rahaman@u.nus.edu, {dipika16,ayao}@comp.nus.edu.sg,
a.h.thiery@nus.edu.sg

Abstract. In temporal action segmentation, Timestamp Supervision requires only a handful of labelled frames per video sequence. For unlabelled frames, previous works rely on assigning hard labels, and performance rapidly collapses under subtle violations of the annotation assumptions. We propose a novel Expectation-Maximization (EM) based approach that leverages the label uncertainty of unlabelled frames and is robust enough to accommodate possible annotation errors. With accurate timestamp annotations, our proposed method produces SOTA results and even exceeds the fully-supervised setup in several metrics and datasets. When applied to timestamp annotations with missing action segments, our method presents stable performance. To further test our formulation's robustness, we introduce the new challenging annotation setup of SkipTag Supervision. This setup relaxes constraints and requires annotations of any fixed number of random frames in a video, making it more flexible than Timestamp Supervision while remaining competitive.

Keywords: Timestamp supervision · Temporal action segmentation

1 Introduction

Temporal action segmentation partitions and classifies a sequence of actions in long untrimmed video. In a fully-supervised setting, the exact action boundaries and actions of every frame are labelled for all training videos. **Timestamp Supervision (TSS)** [22,24] is a lightweight alternative in which the annotator labels one frame from each action in the video (Fig 1). TSS requires magnitudes fewer labels than the fully-supervised setting[1], but it has a strict constraint – there must be a timestamp for **every action** in the video sequence. To fulfill

---

[1] On Breakfast Actions [15], only 0.032% of the frames need labels!.

Supplementary Information The online version contains supplementary material available at https://doi.org/10.1007/978-3-031-19772-7_17.

this constraint, annotators must watch the entire video carefully, so as not to miss any action segments. This affects the annotation efficiency and leads to only a 35% reduction in annotation time compared to full supervision. Furthermore, annotators may *mistakenly* skip actions, as observed in our user study on timestamp labelling. The annotators' slow performance and mistakes highlight the impracticality of the constraints of Timestamp Supervision.

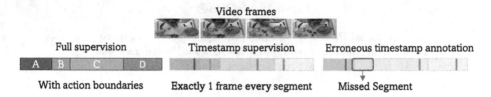

Fig. 1. Annotations levels. Full-supervision requires labels for every frame in the video. Timestamp Supervision requires labels for a *single* frame from *each* action segment, although annotators may miss some action segments.

Existing works on TSS [22, 24] are based on strong assumptions. For example, [24] directly parameterizes the position and width of action segments around the annotated timestamps, while [22] sets one action boundary with a handcrafted energy function between two annotated frames and assigns hard labels to in-between unlabelled frames. The performance of these methods collapses when annotation errors are introduced (see Fig. 4) as the errors violate the condition "*one* timestamp for *every* action segment". Note that this sort of annotation error differs from the typical annotation error of mislabelling as it emerges from the difficulty of adhering to annotation constraints.

In this work, we first propose a novel, general model formulation for Timestamp Supervision, called **EM-TSS**. EM-TSS uses the first principles of an Expectation-Maximization (E-M) formulation to model frame-wise labels conditioned on action boundary locations. We restructure the EM formulation for the temporal segmentation task so that the maximization step reduces to a frame-wise cross-entropy minimization. Unlike the heuristics of [22,24], EM-TSS has theoretical groundings and assumes only an extremely weak prior distribution on segment length. EM-TSS also makes no additional assumptions per action segment and can leverage the label uncertainty provided by the E-M formulation to avoid assigning hard labels. EM-TSS surpasses previous works [22,24] for the majority of metrics by a significant margin. For several datasets and metrics, it even outperforms the fully-supervised setting with only a handful of labels. We attribute the success to the use of more accurate (albeit fewer) labels and verify with a user study and ablations on the position of the timestamps.

Next, we generalize our EM framework into **EM-Gen** to handle errors in Timestamp Supervision due to annotators missing action segments between timestamps. EM-Gen's performance remains stable under such annotation error and can tolerate up to 20% missing segments, with a marginal drop in performance compared to the TSS methods. To further challenge the performance limits of EM-Gen, we introduce a new *SkipTag supervision* to allow for random frame annotations anywhere in the video. SkipTag supervision is far more flexible than timestamp supervision and is much less restrictive. Applying EM-Gen to SkipTag produces good results despite this weaker form of annotation.

Summarizing the **contributions** in this work,

1. We propose a novel E-M based method, EM-TSS, for action segmentation under Timestamp Supervision. EM-TSS surpasses SOTA timestamp methods by a large margin and is competitive with fully-supervised methods.
2. We generalize EM-TSS into EM-Gen, which, unlike competing works, remains robust under subtle timestamp annotation errors.
3. We push the limits of EM-Gen and apply it to the weaker SkipTag supervision, which enables the free annotation of a random selection of frames.
4. Through a user-study, we compare the annotation efforts for Timestamp and SkipTag supervision and investigate the ambiguity of boundary annotations.

2   Related Works

Temporal Action Segmentation assigns frame-wise action labels to long, untrimmed video; it is a 1-D temporal analogue of semantic segmentation. Recent approaches [4,11,12,21,30,34,38,39] have used pre-extracted I3D [32] snippet-level features as input and modelled the temporal structure using various models, such as HMMs [15], RNNs [33] or TCNs [4,18,21,38]. Temporal Convolution Networks (TCNs) [8,18,21] are shown to be the most effective, with the popular SOTA being MSTCNs [21]. We use I3D features as input and the MSTCN architecture as a backbone, similar to previous TSS work [22].

Fully-Supervised Methods [8,15,18] require action labels to be provided for all frames. To reduce the annotation costs, **weakly supervised** methods only require an ordered [3,7,19,26,29,35] or unordered list of actions [6,10,20, 28] as supervision. **Unsupervised** approaches [17,31,37] do not require any annotation and are primarily focused on clustering segments.

Timestamp Supervision (TSS) has recently emerged as a new form of weak supervision that requires a single frame annotation for each action [13,16,22, 24]. TSS thus requires segmentation methods to utilize and estimate a huge amount of unlabelled training frames. TSS is the preferred choice over other weak supervision methods due to its higher accuracy yet lower annotation cost [24].

Existing works [23,24] expand action segments' length around the annotated frames based on discriminative probability outputs. Li et al. [22] fix a boundary between two consecutive annotated frames based on similarity measures and assign the frames in between to either of the two actions. Our work emphasizes boundary localization. However, unlike solutions using hard boundaries [22] or distributional assumption [22, 24], we formulate boundary estimation and anno-tate unlabelled frames in the training videos with the principles of the E-M algorithm. Our problem formulation and derivation of the steps for the E-M algorithm stem naturally from the model assumptions of the supervised setup.

3   Preliminaries

3.1   Temporal Action Segmentation Task

Consider a video V with duration T. For fully-supervised action segmenta-tion, each frame $V[t] : t \leq T$ is labelled with the ground truth action label $y[t] \in \{1, \ldots, C\}$ of C possible action classes. The standard practice in action segmentation [21, 34, 39] is to use pre-trained frame-wise features, e.g., I3D [2] features. We denote these features as $\mathbf{f}[t] \in \mathbb{R}^d$. The TCN takes $\mathbf{f}$ as input and generates frame-wise action class probabilities $\mathbf{p}$. For frame t, the vector $\mathbf{p}[t]$ is a C-dimensional vector and $p_{t,c} := \mathbf{p}[t, c]$ is the probability value assigned to action class c. A cross-entropy loss can be used to train the model.

$$\mathcal{L}_{\text{CE}} := -\sum_{t=1}^{T} \sum_{c=1}^{C} \omega_{t,c} \cdot \log p_{t,c} \tag{1}$$

Under full supervision, ω can be set as the ground truth labels, i.e. $\omega_{t,c} = \mathbb{I}[y[t] = c]$. To use the same loss under Timestamp Supervision, however, the weights $\omega_{t,c}$ must be estimated for the unlabelled frames where $y[t]$ is unknown. Previous works [22, 24] do so by setting hard weights, i.e. $\omega_{t,c} \in \{0, 1\}$, through some rules or a ranking scheme.

3.2   E-M Algorithm

Expectation-Maximization (E-M) [5] is a classic iterative method for maximum likelihood estimation (MLE) with hidden variables and/or missing data. We consider the classical form with missing data. Formally, let X^{ob}, X^{ms} be the observed and missing parts of the data, respectively, and $\mathcal{P}(X^{ob}, X^{ms} | \Theta)$ be the data likelihood conditioned on some unknown parameter Θ, e.g., the weights of a neural network model. As X^{ob} is observed and X^{ms} is missing, directly maximizing $\mathcal{P}$ as a function of Θ, and hence obtaining the MLE of Θ^*, is not possible. The E-M algorithm provides an iterative approach to obtain the MLE of Θ under this setting through the use of a $\mathcal{Q}$-function. In simple terms, the $\mathcal{Q}$-function serves as an expected version of the log-likelihood $\mathcal{P}$ by replacing terms involving unobserved X^{ms} with the expected value based on our current estimate of the parameter. Formally, let $\Theta^{(m)}$ be the current estimate of Θ after the mth iteration. At iteration $(m + 1)$, the *Expectation step* calculates the $\mathcal{Q}$-function:

$$\mathcal{Q}(\Theta, \Theta^{(m)}) = \mathbb{E}_{\mathbf{z}}\left[\log \mathcal{P}(X^{ob}, \mathbf{z} | \Theta)\right], \tag{2}$$

where $\mathbf{z} \sim f(\mathbf{X}^{ms} \mid \mathbf{X}^{ob}, \Theta^{(m)})$, *i.e.* the posterior distribution of the unobserved data $\mathbf{X}^{ms}$ given the observed data $\mathbf{X}^{ob}$ and the current estimate of the parameters $\Theta^{(m)}$. Note that the term in Eq. 2 is a function of the parameters Θ. In the *Maximization step*, the $\mathcal{Q}$ function is then maximized with respect to the parameters Θ to obtain the new estimate

$$\Theta^{(m+1)} = \arg \max_{\Theta} \mathcal{Q}(\Theta, \Theta^{(m)}). \tag{3}$$

This process is repeated until convergence, *i.e.* $\Theta^{(m+1)}$ is desirably close to $\Theta^{(m)}$, or for a fixed number of iterations. The model (TCN) parameter learning happens during this M-step (Maximization), whereas the E-step (Expectation) iteratively updates the criteria to be optimized in the M-step.

4   Method

The assignment of hard labels to each frame may lead to some ambiguities at the action boundaries and deteriorate performance (see Sect. 5.4). To avoid the pitfalls of hard labels, we allow soft weights for ω in Eq. 1. We arrive at these soft weights using the E-M framework, as we show for Timestamp Supervision (Sect. 4.2), and extend it to the case of missing timestamps (Sect. 4.3).

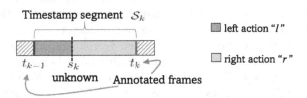

Fig. 2. Depiction of **timestamp segment** $\mathcal{S}_k$.

4.1   Segment-Based Notation

While a video is typically treated as a sequence of frames (Sect. 3.1), it can also be regarded as a sequence of action segments. Each segment is a set of contiguous frames belonging to one action, represented by a single color in Fig. 1. A video with K action segments will have action classes $c_1, \ldots, c_K$ out of C action classes. K may vary for different videos; the same action may also occur multiple times in a video. As the adjacent action segments share boundaries, $c_k \neq c_{k+1}$ for all $k < K$. We denote s_k to be the starting frame for action segment k, with $s_1 \equiv 1$ and $s_k < s_{k+1} \leq T$. Frame s_k is also the *boundary* between action segments $k-1$ and k. In the fully-supervised setup, every frame is labelled; this is equivalent to labelling start frame s_k and action class c_k for each segment k.

4.2   Timestamp Supervision

Timestamp Supervision provides one labelled frame or *'timestamp'* per action segment, resulting in K labelled frames $t_1, \ldots, t_K$ and action labels $c_1, \ldots, c_K$. There is exactly one timestamp, randomly positioned within the segment, for *every* action segment, *i.e.* $s_k \leq t_k < s_{k+1}$, or equivalently $t_{k-1} < s_k \leq t_k, \forall k$. As the action boundaries are unknown, we additionally define a *timestamp segment*; the kth timestamp segment is denoted by $\mathcal{S}_k$ and is bounded by frames $[t_{k-1}, t_k - 1]$ (see Fig. 2). Within $\mathcal{S}_k$, the label $l := y[t_{k-1}] = c_{k-1}$ denotes the *'left action'* class and $r := y[t_k] = c_k$ denotes the *'right action'* class[2].

Timestamp Segment Likelihood: If s_k is known, all the frames $[t_{k-1}, s_k)$ can be labelled with action l and frames $[s_k, t_k)$ can be labelled with action r. Hence, the likelihood of segment $\mathcal{S}_k$ given $s_k = j$, denoted as $\mathcal{P}_j(\mathcal{S}_k \mid \Theta)$, becomes

$$\mathcal{P}_j(\mathcal{S}_k \mid \Theta) := \mathcal{P}(\mathcal{S}_k \mid s_k = j, \Theta) = \prod_{i=t_{k-1}}^{j-1} p_{i,l}^{\Theta} \prod_{i=j}^{t_k-1} p_{i,r}^{\Theta}. \tag{4}$$

In Eq. 4, we add a super-script Θ to $p_{t,c}^{\Theta}$ to emphasize the dependence of the probability $p_{t,c}$ on the model parameters Θ of the temporal convolutional network. If s_k is known for each k, then maximizing the likelihood of Eq. 4 after taking the negative log and summing over all K segments simplifies to minimizing the fully-supervised frame-wise cross-entropy (CE) loss of Eq. 1. Note that Eq. 4 and fully-supervised Eq. 1 both assume independence of the frame-wise probability when conditioned on the network parameters and architecture.

In Timestamp Supervision, the boundary s_k is unknown, so we treat it as a random variable, with some prior probability of it being located at frame j, *i.e.* $\pi_k(j) := \pi(s_k = j)$. The joint likelihood of segment $\mathcal{S}_k$ and boundary s_k then becomes $\mathcal{P}(\mathcal{S}_k, s_k = j \mid \Theta) = \mathcal{P}_j(\mathcal{S}_k \mid \Theta) \cdot \pi_k(j)$. We further elaborate on the prior distribution in Subsect. 4.4. As boundary s_k can be located at any of the frames $[t_{k-1}, t_k)$, the summarized joint likelihood can be written as

$$\mathcal{P}(\mathcal{S}_k, s_k \mid \Theta) = \prod_{j=t_{k-1}}^{t_k-1} \left[\mathcal{P}_j(\mathcal{S}_k \mid \Theta) \cdot \pi_k(j) \right]^{\mathbb{I}[s_k=j]}. \tag{5}$$

$\mathcal{Q}$-**Function & Posterior.** Following Eq. 2, the $\mathcal{Q}$-function for timestamp segment $\mathcal{S}_k$ is obtained by taking the expectation of the log of the likelihood in Eq. 5 with respect to $f(s_k \mid \mathcal{D}; \Theta^{(m)})$. This represents the posterior distribution of boundary s_k given observed data $\mathcal{D}$ under the previous estimate of parameter $\Theta^{(m)}$. Here, observed data $\mathcal{D}$ contains all the training information, such as input video features $\mathbf{f}$ and the annotations $y[t_{k-1}], y[t_k]$. The $\mathcal{Q}$-function for $\mathcal{S}_k$,

---

[2] We do not discuss the first and last timestamp segments $\mathcal{S}_1 := [1, t_1)$ and $\mathcal{S}_{K+1} := [t_K, T]$ as their action labels c_1, c_K are known.

denoted by $\mathcal{Q}_k(\Theta, \Theta^{(m)})$, thus becomes

$$\mathcal{Q}_k(\Theta, \Theta^{(m)}) = \sum_{j=t_{k-1}}^{t_k-1} \mathbb{E}_{s_k}\left[\mathbb{I}[s_k = j] \cdot \log\left(\mathcal{P}_j(\mathcal{S}_k \mid \Theta) \cdot \pi_k(j)\right)\right]$$

$$= \Lambda + \sum_{j=t_{k-1}}^{t_k-1} \mathbb{P}^{(m)}[s_k = j|\mathcal{D}] \cdot \log \mathcal{P}_j(\mathcal{S}_k \mid \Theta), \tag{6}$$

where $\mathbb{P}^{(m)}[s_k = j|\mathcal{D}]$ is the posterior probability that s_k is located at frame j given the data and under the model parameter $\Theta^{(m)}$. Λ consists of the terms (prior $\pi_k(j)$) that are constant with respect to the parameter Θ and hence can be ignored during the maximization of $\mathcal{Q}$ with respect to Θ. The posterior probabilities can be obtained by

$$\mathbb{P}^{(m)}[s_k = j|\mathcal{D}] = \frac{\mathcal{P}_j(\mathcal{S}_k \mid \Theta^{(m)}) \cdot \pi_k(j)}{\sum_{i=t_{k-1}}^{t_k-1} \mathcal{P}_i(\mathcal{S}_k \mid \Theta^{(m)}) \cdot \pi_k(i)}, \tag{7}$$

where $\mathcal{P}_j(\mathcal{S}_k \mid \Theta^{(m)})$ is defined in Eq. 4. The final $\mathcal{Q}$-function for the whole video is calculated by $\mathcal{Q}(\Theta, \Theta^{(m)}) = \sum_k \mathcal{Q}_k(\Theta, \Theta^{(m)})$.

$\mathcal{Q}$-function to Frame-Wise CE Loss. The formulation of the $\mathcal{Q}$-function in Eq. 6 requires estimating two terms for each frame j. The first is $\mathbb{P}^{(m)}[s_k = j|\mathcal{D}]$, which can be calculated only once per E-step as it does not depend on Θ. The second term $\mathcal{P}_j(\mathcal{S}_k \mid \Theta)$, however, must be calculated for every iteration of the M-step. Even after obtaining frame-wise probabilities $p_{j,c}^{\Theta}$ from the model, every calculation of $\log \mathcal{P}_j(\mathcal{S}_k|\Theta)$ for each frame j (as given in Eq. 4) takes linear time with respect to video length, i.e., of complexity $\mathcal{O}(T)$ per frame j. This may make each epoch of the parameter learning in the M-step computationally expensive. To reduce the computational complexity, we simplify Eq. 6 by substituting $\log \mathcal{P}_j(\mathcal{S}_k; \Theta)$ from Eq. 4 and rearranging the sums to get

$$\mathcal{Q}_k(\Theta, \Theta^{(m)}) = \sum_{j=t_{k-1}}^{t_k-1} \sum_{c=1}^{C} \omega_{j,c}^{(m)} \cdot \log p_{j,c}^{\Theta},$$

$$\text{where} \quad \omega_{j,c}^{(m)} = \begin{cases} \sum_{i=j+1}^{t_k-1} \mathbb{P}^{(m)}[s_k = i|\mathcal{D}] &: c = l \\ 1 - \omega_{j,l}^{(m)} &: c = r \\ 0 &: \text{otherwise.} \end{cases} \tag{8}$$

This new form of $\mathcal{Q}_k(\Theta, \Theta^{(m)})$ is more intuitive than Eq. 6 and, as desired at the start of this section, reduces to a negative frame-wise CE loss (Eq. 1). Furthermore, our posterior weights $\omega^{(m)}$ are not hard labels, and the weights capture the label uncertainty of the unlabelled frames. This simplified formulation converges in very few iterations and adds negligible differences to the training time compared to a fully-supervised approach. The weights $(\omega_{j,l}^{(m)}, \omega_{j,r}^{(m)})$ are actually the posterior probabilities (given data and parameters) that frame j belongs to the left and right actions l and r, respectively. The weight $\omega_{j,l}^{(m)}$ acts as the current estimate of $\mathbb{I}[y[j] = l]$ (see Eq. 1) when $y[j]$ is unknown. Furthermore, regardless of the current parameter $\Theta^{(m)}$, the weights have the property that $\omega_{t_{k-1},l}^{(m)} = 1$ and $\omega_{j,l}^{(m)} \geq \omega_{j+1,l}^{(m)}$, $\omega_{j,r}^{(m)} \leq \omega_{j+1,r}^{(m)}$ for any $t_{k-1} \leq j < t_k$. This means the weight assigned to left action class l is 1 for frame t_{k-1} (as it should be), and it gradually decreases as j increases, with the converse being true for the action class r. These weights can be calculated during the E-step and be used in a CE loss without additional computation during the M-step.

Initialization and Overall Procedure. The E-M algorithm requires good initialization. Following [22], we initialize the TCN parameters with $\Theta^{(0)}$ derived from a '*Naive*' baseline learned with a frame-wise cross-entropy loss applied *only* to the annotated frames t_k. From this initialization, we perform the first E-step to obtain the frame-wise weights $\omega_{j,c}^{(0)}$. Thereafter, we iterate between Maximization (maximize $\mathcal{Q}$) and Expectation (update $\omega^{(m)}$) steps, which we call **EM-TSS**, to find the best estimate Θ^* (see the pseudo-code in Algorithm 1).

Algorithm 1. Our iterative procedure for EM-TSS

1: **for** *epoch* $\leq N^{init}$ **do**   ▷ *Initialization*:
2:      calculate $\mathcal{L} := -\sum_{k=1}^{K} \log p_{t_k,c_k}^{\Theta}$
3:      minimize $\mathcal{L}$, update Θ
4: set $\Theta^{(0)} = \Theta$, set $m = 0$
5: **for** $m < M$ **do**
6:      calculate $\omega^{(m)}$ using $\Theta^{(m)}$ ▷ *Expectation*:
7:      **for** *epoch* $\leq N^{max}$ **do**   ▷ *Maximization*:
8:          maximize $\mathcal{Q}(\Theta, \Theta^{(m)})$, update Θ
9:      set $\Theta^{(m+1)} = \Theta$
10: set final $\Theta^* = \Theta^{(M)}$

4.3   Timestamp Supervision Under Missed Timestamps

Timestamp Supervision places a strong constraint that there is one timestamp for *every* action segment present in the video. In practice, as revealed by our user study (see *Supplementary*), annotators may miss action segments. These missed segments, as we show later in Sect. 5, cause TSS methods to collapse rapidly.

As such, we target the impracticality of having perfectly accurate timestamps and develop a method that is more robust to such annotation errors. Specifically, we generalize our E-M framework **EM-TSS** into **EM-Gen** to accommodate possible missing segments between two consecutive annotated timestamps, as depicted in Fig. 3. The overall E-M framework remains the same as Timestamp supervision, but differs in the derivation of the associated $\mathcal{Q}$-function and weights ω. We consider the timestamp segment $[t_{k-1}, t_k]$ with the following cases.

Case 1 (C_1): Correct timestamp annotation. In this case, there will be exactly *one action boundary* s, where $t_{k-1} < s \leq t_k$ and $r \neq l$. This case is the

Correct Annotation   **Wrong Annotation (missed segment)**

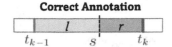 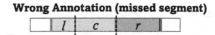

One action boundary between   Two action boundaries between
consecutive timestamps   consecutive timestamps

Fig. 3. Correct vs. Missed Segments. Timestamp segment $\mathcal{S}$ between consecutive timestamps t_{k-1}, t_k with action labels l, r respectively. When correct, there is one unknown action boundary s; when a segment is missed, there are actually two unknown boundaries, s_1 and s_2, and an unknown action c in between.

same as a typical timestamp segment of TSS; given boundary location s, the segment likelihood is the same as Eq. 4 earlier,

$$\mathcal{P}(\mathcal{S}|C_1, s, \Theta) = \prod_{i=t_{k-1}}^{s-1} p_{i,l}^{\Theta} \prod_{i=s}^{t_k-1} p_{i,r}^{\Theta}.$$

Case 2 (C_2): Missed timestamp annotation. In this case, there will be *two action boundaries* s_1, s_2, which define a middle action segment such that $t_{k-1} < s_1 < s_2 \leq t_k$. If the middle action label is c, where $c \neq l$ and $c \neq r$ (this allows for both $r \neq l$ and $r = l$), the segment likelihood is

$$\mathcal{P}(\mathcal{S}|C_2, s_1, s_2, c, \Theta) = \prod_{i=t_{k-1}}^{s_1-1} p_{i,l}^{\Theta} \prod_{i=s_1}^{s_2-1} p_{i,c}^{\Theta} \prod_{i=s_2}^{t_k-1} p_{i,r}^{\Theta}.$$

Similar to EM-TSS, to calculate the $\mathcal{Q}$-function, we now need to combine the log-likelihoods with the corresponding weights as the posterior probabilities. The $\mathcal{Q}$-function for the segment $\mathcal{S}$ is calculated as

$$\mathcal{Q}(\Theta, \Theta^{(m)}) = \sum_s \mathbb{P}^{(m)}[C_1, s|\mathcal{D}] \cdot \log \mathcal{P}(\mathcal{S}|C_1, s, \Theta) +$$
$$\sum_\tau \mathbb{P}^{(m)}[C_2, \tau|\mathcal{D}] \cdot \log \mathcal{P}(\mathcal{S}|C_2, \tau, \Theta), \qquad (9)$$

where τ indexes all valid triplets (s_1, s_2, c) of Case 2. In the first term, $\mathbb{P}^{(m)}[C_2, s|\mathcal{D}]$ denotes the posterior probability that the segment belongs to Case 1 *and* the action boundary is located at s, given the data and under parameter $\Theta^{(m)}$. The second term contains an analogous posterior for Case 2 and some triplet τ. The probabilities of Eq. 9 can be estimated in the same way as Eq. 7 of EM-TSS. A few components in the $\mathcal{Q}$-function have high computational complexity, e.g., the second sum in Eq. 9 is of $\mathcal{O}(T^2)$ where T is the video duration. However, a few rearrangements similar to the EM-TSS change the $\mathcal{Q}$-function into the same form as in Eq. 8. We defer the exact forms to the *Supplementary*.

The final posterior weights become

$$\omega_{j,l}^{(m)} = \sum_{s>j} \mathbb{P}^{(m)}[C_1, s | \mathcal{D}] + \sum_{\tau:s_1>j} \mathbb{P}^{(m)}[C_2, \tau | \mathcal{D}]$$

$$\omega_{j,c}^{(m)} = \sum_{s_1 \leq j} \sum_{s_2 > j} \mathbb{P}^{(m)}[C_2, s_1, s_2, c | \mathcal{D}] \qquad \text{if } c \neq l, c \neq r,$$

and $\omega_{j,r}^{(m)} = 1 - \omega_{j,l}^{(m)} - \sum_c \omega_{j,c}^{(m)}$. We calculate these weights during the E-step and simply apply the negative cross-entropy loss during the M-steps to perform our EM-Gen. The initialization and training are the same as algorithm 1.

4.4   Prior Distribution

We apply a prior on the position of the action boundaries s_k. Like previous works [16,27,35], we assume that the length of an action segment for action c is a random variable following a *Poisson* distribution $\text{Pois}(\mu_c)$ with a mean length $\mu_c > 0$. Using this assumption, one can arrive that $\pi(s_k = j)$ of Eq. 7 (probability of the kth action boundary s_k is located at frame j), follows a binomial distribution, *i.e.* $s_k \sim \text{Bin}(T, p_k)$, with parameters T, the video length, and $p_k = \frac{\sum_{n \leq k-1} \mu_{cn}}{\sum_{n \leq K} \mu_{cn}}$, where K is the number of action segments in the video. For EM-Gen, the prior is less straightforward and we defer it to the *Supplementary*.

4.5   Loss Function

We apply $\mathcal{L}_{\text{EM}} := -\frac{1}{T} \mathcal{Q}(\Theta, \Theta^{(m)})$ during the M-step, *i.e.* we minimize the negative $\mathcal{Q}$-function normalized by the number of frames T as a loss for learning the TCN. We also add two auxiliary losses, similar to [22]: a *transition loss* $\mathcal{L}_{\text{TR}} = \frac{1}{TC} \sum_{t,c} \min(|\delta_{t,c}|, \epsilon)$ to penalize small inter-frame differences (up to a threshold ϵ) to limit over-segmentation; and a *confidence loss* $\mathcal{L}_{\text{Conf}} = \frac{1}{T} \sum_{k=1}^{K} \sum_{t=t_{k-1}}^{t_k-1} \left(\delta_{t,y[t_{k-1}]}^+ + \delta_{t,y[t_k]}^- \right)$ to ensure peak confidence at the annotated timestamps. Here, $\delta_{t,c} := \log p_{t,c}^\Theta - \log p_{t-1,c}^\Theta$, $\delta^+ := \max(\delta, 0)$, $\delta^- := \max(-\delta, 0)$, C is the number of action classes, and K is the total number of annotated timestamps in the video. It is worth noting that our posterior weights from Eq. 8 already induce this property. The final loss function is

$$\mathcal{L} = \mathcal{L}_{\text{EM}} + \lambda_{\text{TR}} \cdot \mathcal{L}_{\text{TR}} + \lambda_{\text{Conf}} \cdot \mathcal{L}_{\text{Conf}}$$

We use the values of $\lambda_{\text{TR}}, \lambda_{\text{Conf}}$ as suggested by [22].

4.6   SkipTag Supervision

Even though TSS requires annotation of very few frames, the constraint of exactly one frame for every action segment incurs significant amounts of annotation time (see Sect. 5.4). As the EM-Gen formulation tolerates missing frames between segments, we are motivated to introduce a more flexible form of frame-wise annotation. To this end, we propose the new SkipTag Supervision. SkipTag Supervision is less restrictive and allows annotators to simply label the actions of a random set of timestamps placed somewhat evenly. However, two consecutively annotated timestamps t_{k-1} and t_k now have an unknown number of action boundaries in between, including no boundaries. As an experimental setting, SkipTag annotations are more challenging than TSS not only because of removing the TSS annotation constraint but also because the number of annotated timestamps do not correspond to the (unknown) number of action segments. TSS implicitly gives the number of segments per video since the annotations match the exact number of action segments. Thus, Skiptag annotation is a weaker form of supervision than TSS annotation.

To accommodate SkipTag annotations, EM-Gen must also handle the case of no action boundaries between timestamps t_{k-1}, t_k. We defer the formulation related to this new case to the *Supplementary*. To limit complexity, we also do not consider beyond two action boundaries between consecutive timestamps t_{k-1}, t_k. Experimentally, this occurs very infrequently (see *Supplementary*). However, this simplification is our design choice and is not a limitation of the EM-Gen framework, i.e., one can enumerate more cases in line with the same foundation.

5 Experiments

Datasets: We show our results on standard cross-validation splits of Breakfast [15] (1.7k, 3.6 mins/video, 48 actions), 50Salads [36] (50, 6.4 mins/video, 19 actions) and GTEA [9] (28, 1.5 mins/video, 11 actions). The standard evaluation criteria are the Mean-over-Frames (MoF), segment-wise edit distance (Edit), and $F1$-scores with IoU thresholds of 0.25 and 0.50 ($F1@\{25, 50\}$) (see [21]).

Implementation Details: We compare using the same modified MS-TCN as [22] as our base network. We report results on additional base networks in the *Supplementary*. To initialize $\Theta^{(0)}$, we train the base TCN for $\{30,50,50\}$ epochs (N^{init}) for Breakfast, 50Salads, and GTEA, respectively. Subsequently, we apply $\{10,20,20\}$ E-M iterations (M), fixing each M-step to 5 epochs (N^{max}) for all datasets to update $\Theta^{(m)}$. We use the Adam optimizer [14] during initialization; for each M-step we use a learning rate 5e-4 and a batch-size of 8.

Random Seeds and Variation in Annotations: All our results, including baselines, are reported for three seeds used for random selection of the annotated frames (timestamps) for both modes of supervision. Since [22] reports a single run, we report the results from that same set of timestamps in Table 3.

Baselines: We compare with two baselines: a '*Naive*' baseline trained on *only* the annotated frames (see initialization in Sect. 4.2) and a '*Uniform*' baseline (named according to [22], applicable only to TSS) that fixes the action boundary s_k to the mid-point between consecutive timestamps t_{k-1}, t_k. The action classes of unlabelled frames are then set accordingly and used during training.

Table 1. EM-TSS Posterior performance. The obtained boundaries are highly accurate with high MoF and low boundary error (*'Error %'*).

Method	50Salads		Breakfast	
	Error (%)	MoF	Error (%)	MoF
Uniform	1.23	76.3	4.69	69.2
EM-TSS	0.55	89.6	2.19	87.8

5.1 Timestamp Supervision Results

Evaluation of Formulated Posterior. Table 1 compares the performance of our boundaries estimated from EM-TSS posterior probabilities against *'Uniform'* (boundary at mid-point) for all training data. The action boundary locations s_k (unknown under Timestamp Supervision) are obtained by taking the expectation with respect to the posterior probabilities in Eq. 7. We evaluate *duration normalized* boundary error (Error (%)) as $|\widehat{s}_k - s_k^{gt}|/T$, where $\widehat{s}_k$ and s_k^{gt} are the expected and ground-truth boundary locations, respectively, and T is the video duration. We also evaluate the frame-wise posterior weights $\omega_{j,c}^{(M)}$ (obtained after the final E-step) from Eq. 8 by regarding them as probability predictions and computing the frame-wise accuracy (MoF). Our boundary errors are less than half that of the uniform baseline; for 50Salads, our EM-TSS's boundary error is less than 1%, while the MoF reaches 87% or higher for Breakfast and 50Salads.

Table 2. Timestamp Supervision. Our EM-TSS exceeds Fully-supervised (100% labels) on several metrics on 50Salads and GTEA. On Breakfast and 50Salads, EM-TSS has only 0.9% and 0.5% less MoF than Fully-supervised. We report the average results over three randomly sampled sets of annotations.

Method	50Salads			Breakfast			GTEA		
	$F1\{25,50\}$	Edit	MoF	$F1\{25,50\}$	Edit	MoF	$F1\{25,50\}$	Edit	MoF
Naive	39.4	29.3	34.2	69.9	27.6	19.5	35.4	58.0	52.4	37.5	50.0	55.3
Uniform	58.2	42.3	60.4	63.4	56.3	36.4	68.1	51.0	72.5	50.9	73.1	56.5
EM-TSS	**75.4**	**63.7**	**70.9**	77.3	63.0	49.9	67.0	67.1	81.3	66.4	**81.2**	68.6
Fully-supervised	67.7	58.6	63.8	**77.8**	64.2	51.5	69.4	68.0	82.7	69.6	79.6	**76.1**

Comparison to Baseline and Full Supervision. Table 2 compares our EM-TSS with the *'Naive'* and *'Uniform'* baselines (see Sect. 5) and a fully-supervised setup. Our EM-TSS outperforms all baselines and even the fully-supervised method in several metrics for the 50Salads and GTEA datasets. Most notable is the +7% difference in the F1{50,25} and Edit scores in 50Salads.

Table 3. Comparison with SOTA: In Timestamp Supervision (TSS), we exceed the previous SOTA by a considerable margin for almost all metrics. Our TSS results are reported for the same timestamp set as [22,24].

Method	50Salads			Breakfast			GTEA		
	$F1\{25,50\}$	Edit	MoF	$F1\{25,50\}$	Edit	MoF	$F1\{25,50\}$	Edit	MoF
Plateau [24]	68.2	56.1	62.6	73.9	59.1	43.2	65.9	63.5	68.0	43.6	72.3	52.9
Li et al. [22]	70.9	60.1	66.8	75.6	63.6	47.4	**69.9**	64.1	73.0	55.4	72.3	66.4
Our EM	**75.9**	**64.7**	**71.6**	**77.9**	**63.7**	**49.8**	67.2	**67.0**	**82.7**	**66.5**	**82.3**	**70.5**
(Inc. SOTA)	+5.0	+4.6	+4.8	+2.3	+0.1	+2.4	-2.7	+2.9	+9.7	+11.1	+10	+4.1
Fully-supervised	67.7	58.6	63.8	77.8	64.2	51.5	69.4	68.0	82.7	69.6	79.6	76.1

We discuss possible reasons behind EM-TSS exceeding full-supervision in the *Supplementary*, and in Subsect. 5.4, where the (negative) effect of boundary ambiguity is shown to be more prominent in 50Salads and GTEA than Breakfast.

SOTA **Comparison.** In Table 3, we compare our EM-TSS with [22,24]; we use the *same* set of annotated timestamps as [22,24]. Our method outperforms the previous SOTA for most metrics on all datasets, with margins of +11%, +10%, +5% in GTEA F1@50, GTEA Edit, and 50Salads F1@25, respectively.

5.2 Performance with Missed Segments

In Fig. 4, we show that existing TSS methods suffer from poor performance with missing segments, with a sharp drop in performance at 5% and at 20% missing segments. While EM-TSS fares better, it does not exhibit the robustness of EM-Gen, as EM-Gen explicitly models missing segments between two consecutive timestamps. We detail the numerical performance in the *Supplementary*.

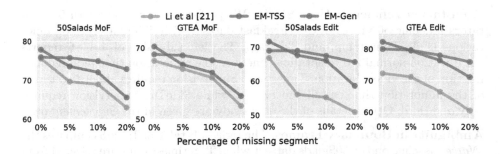

Fig. 4. Performance under (% of) missing action segments. Our EM-TSS performs significantly better than [22] under missing action segments (0% denotes no missed segment). Our EM-Gen is robust to missing segments, and with 20% missing segments, EM-Gen significantly outperforms TSS methods.

Table 4. SkipTag Supervision. Our EM-Gen provides a significant boost over *'Naive'* and [22]'s baselines. It performs close to full supervision in 50Salads, and out-performs it in few metrics. Results are averaged over three sets of annotations. (*) indicates the results reported in [22].

Method	50Salads ($\bar{K} = 19$)				Breakfast ($\bar{K} = 6$)				GTEA ($\bar{K} = 32$)			
	$F1\{25, 50\}$		Edit	MoF	$F1\{25, 50\}$		Edit	MoF	$F1\{25, 50\}$		Edit	MoF
Naive	49.2	38.1	46.3	70.4	27.0	18.8	36.4	59.8	64.2	43.4	65.8	63.1
Li et al. [22]	54.3	40.1	54.6	70.7	-	-	-	*61.7	69.4	50.0	68.9	66.0
EM-Gen	**68.1**	54.9	**64.3**	74.4	57.3	45.2	59.9	64.1	76.7	57.9	73.5	69.8
Fully-supervised	67.7	**58.6**	63.8	**77.8**	**64.2**	**51.5**	**69.4**	**68.0**	**82.7**	**69.6**	**79.6**	**76.1**

5.3   SkipTag Supervision Results

For SkipTag annotation, we annotate K number of timestamps per video. We set K to be the average number of action segments, i.e., $K = \{19, 6, 32\}$ for 50Salads, Breakfast and GTEA, respectively. Having K random frames per video results in approximately the same number of annotated frames as Timestamp Supervision, but is much easier for the annotator. Table 4 compares the performance of previous methods to EM-Gen under SkipTag Supervision and shows that EM-Gen surpasses [22] across all metrics and datasets. Moreover, in 50Salads, EM-Gen is comparable to and sometimes surpasses *Fully-supervised* (i.e., 100% labels).

5.4   Additional Results

In *Supplementary*, we provide ablation related to **(1) different priors** (see Subsect. 4.4) (section S1.1), **(2) loss-functions** (section S1.2), **(3) TCN architectures** (section S1.4), **(4) effect of timestamp position** (section S1.3), other hyper-parameters, and **(5) qualitative analysis** (section S2).

Annotation Efficiency User Study. We perform a user study with 5 annotators labelling 50 videos of the Breakfast dataset with different types of annotations (Full, Timestamp, and SkipTag). The left sub-table of Table 5 reports the duration-normalized annotation time, i.e., the annotation time required as a fraction of the video duration. Timestamp Supervision requires about two-thirds of the annotation time as full supervision, while SkipTag Supervision requires only one-third. Other details of the user study are given in the *Supplementary*.

Ambiguity in Boundary Frames. The right sub-table of Table 5 compares the *'Naive'* baseline on the 50Salads dataset when TSS timestamps are selected from different locations of the action segment. There is a $\geq 20\%$ difference in scores when trained with boundary frames (start/end frame) versus frames selected at *(Random)* or from the middle *(Mid)* of the action segment. This indicates ambiguity in boundary frame annotation (also see [1,25]). We further explain in the *Supplementary*, how EM-TSS exceeds fully-supervised results.

Table 5. *(left)* Labelling cost on Breakfast. Time (%) denotes annotation cost as a fraction of video duration. *(right)* Choosing TSS timestamps near boundaries (start or end) lowers *'Naive'* initialization performance significantly (sometimes $\geq -30\%$), indicating ambiguity in labelling the boundary frames.

Cost	Full-sup	Timestamp	SkipTag
Frames (%)	100	0.03	0.03
Time (%)	93.3	65.1	36.4

Frame Type	F1@{25,50}		Edit	MoF
Random	39.4	29.3	34.2	69.9
Mid	47.7	34.9	40.9	69.7
Start	12.5	3.2	17.5	31.9
End	12.2	2.7	21.4	29.1

5.5   Training Complexity

The M-step of our E-M, transformed into the traditional cross-entropy loss, is extremely efficient and takes the same per-epoch time as fully-supervised. We only update our weights at the E-step once every (N^{max}) 5 epochs (unlike the updates at every iteration required in [22,24]). Our EM-TSS training time is one magnitude less than [22]. Our initialization time is exactly same as [22], whereas post-initialization, on one RTX 2080 GPU, 10 epochs (50Salads) of our EM-TSS require only 5 mins vs 50 mins for [22] (official code) under the same resources.

6   Conclusion

We first tackle the problem of timestamp supervision by introducing a novel E-M algorithm based method. Our proposed framework is general and robust enough to work with timestamp supervision, even with mistakenly missed action segments. We also propose SkipTag supervision, a novel and much weaker form of annotation than TSS. Our method seamlessly applies to all the scenarios, producing *SOTA* results, and in some cases surpassing fully-supervised results.

Acknowledgment. This research is supported by the National Research Foundation, Singapore under its NRF Fellowship for AI (NRF-NRFFAI1-2019-0001). Any opinions, findings and conclusions or recommendations expressed in this material are those of the author(s) and do not reflect the views of National Research Foundation, Singapore.

References

1. Alwassel, H., Caba Heilbron, F., Escorcia, V., Ghanem, B.: Diagnosing error in temporal action detectors. In: Ferrari, V., Hebert, M., Sminchisescu, C., Weiss, Y. (eds.) ECCV 2018. LNCS, vol. 11207, pp. 264–280. Springer, Cham (2018). https://doi.org/10.1007/978-3-030-01219-9_16
2. Carreira, J., Zisserman, A.: Quo Vadis, action recognition? A new model and the kinetics dataset. In: Proceedings of the IEEE Conference on Computer Vision and Pattern Recognition, pp. 6299–6308 (2017)

3. Chang, C.Y., Huang, D.A., Sui, Y., Fei-Fei, L., Niebles, J.C.: D3TW: discriminative differentiable dynamic time warping for weakly supervised action alignment and segmentation. In: Proceedings of the IEEE/CVF Conference on Computer Vision and Pattern Recognition, pp. 3546–3555 (2019)
4. Chen, M.H., Li, B., Bao, Y., AlRegib, G., Kira, Z.: Action segmentation with joint self-supervised temporal domain adaptation. In: Proceedings of the IEEE/CVF Conference on Computer Vision and Pattern Recognition, pp. 9454–9463 (2020)
5. Dempster, A.P., Laird, N.M., Rubin, D.B.: Maximum likelihood from incomplete data via the EM algorithm. J. Roy. Stat. Soc. Ser. B (Methodol.) **39**(1), 1–38 (1977). https://www.jstor.org/stable/2984875'
6. Ding, G., Yao, A.: Temporal action segmentation with high-level complex activity labels. arXiv preprint arXiv:2108.06706 (2021)
7. Ding, L., Xu, C.: Weakly-supervised action segmentation with iterative soft boundary assignment. In: Proceedings of the IEEE Conference on Computer Vision and Pattern Recognition, pp. 6508–6516 (2018)
8. Farha, Y.A., Gall, J.: MS-TCN: multi-stage temporal convolutional network for action segmentation. In: Proceedings of the IEEE/CVF Conference on Computer Vision and Pattern Recognition, pp. 3575–3584 (2019)
9. Fathi, A., Ren, X., Rehg, J.M.: Learning to recognize objects in egocentric activities. In: CVPR 2011, pp. 3281–3288. IEEE (2011)
10. Fayyaz, M., Gall, J.: SCT: set constrained temporal transformer for set supervised action segmentation. In: Proceedings of the IEEE/CVF Conference on Computer Vision and Pattern Recognition (CVPR), June 2020
11. Gao, S.H., Han, Q., Li, Z.Y., Peng, P., Wang, L., Cheng, M.M.: Global2local: Efficient structure search for video action segmentation. In: Proceedings of the IEEE/CVF Conference on Computer Vision and Pattern Recognition. pp. 16805–16814 (2021)
12. Ishikawa, Y., Kasai, S., Aoki, Y., Kataoka, H.: Alleviating over-segmentation errors by detecting action boundaries. In: Proceedings of the IEEE/CVF Winter Conference on Applications of Computer Vision, pp. 2322–2331 (2021)
13. Ju, C., Zhao, P., Chen, S., Zhang, Y., Wang, Y., Tian, Q.: Divide and conquer for single-frame temporal action localization. In: Proceedings of the IEEE/CVF International Conference on Computer Vision, pp. 13455–13464 (2021)
14. Kingma, D.P., Ba, J.: Adam: a method for stochastic optimization. arXiv:1412.6980 (2014)
15. Kuehne, H., Arslan, A., Serre, T.: The language of actions: recovering the syntax and semantics of goal-directed human activities. In: Proceedings of the IEEE Conference on Computer Vision and Pattern Recognition, pp. 780–787 (2014)
16. Kuehne, H., Richard, A., Gall, J.: A hybrid RNN-HMM approach for weakly supervised temporal action segmentation. IEEE Trans. Pattern Anal. Mach. Intell. **42**(4), 765–779 (2018)
17. Kukleva, A., Kuehne, H., Sener, F., Gall, J.: Unsupervised learning of action classes with continuous temporal embedding. In: Proceedings of the IEEE/CVF Conference on Computer Vision and Pattern Recognition, pp. 12066–12074 (2019)
18. Lea, C., Flynn, M.D., Vidal, R., Reiter, A., Hager, G.D.: Temporal convolutional networks for action segmentation and detection. In: proceedings of the IEEE Conference on Computer Vision and Pattern Recognition, pp. 156–165 (2017)
19. Li, J., Lei, P., Todorovic, S.: Weakly supervised energy-based learning for action segmentation. In: Proceedings of the IEEE/CVF International Conference on Computer Vision, pp. 6243–6251 (2019)

20. Li, J., Todorovic, S.: Set-constrained viterbi for set-supervised action segmentation. In: Proceedings of the IEEE/CVF Conference on Computer Vision and Pattern Recognition (CVPR), June 2020
21. Li, S.J., AbuFarha, Y., Liu, Y., Cheng, M.M., Gall, J.: MS-TCN++: multi-stage temporal convolutional network for action segmentation. IEEE Trans. Pattern Anal. Mach. Intell. (2020)
22. Li, Z., Abu Farha, Y., Gall, J.: Temporal action segmentation from timestamp supervision. In: Proceedings of the IEEE/CVF Conference on Computer Vision and Pattern Recognition, pp. 8365–8374 (2021)
23. Ma, F., et al.: SF-Net: single-frame supervision for temporal action localization. In: Vedaldi, A., Bischof, H., Brox, T., Frahm, J.-M. (eds.) ECCV 2020. LNCS, vol. 12349, pp. 420–437. Springer, Cham (2020). https://doi.org/10.1007/978-3-030-58548-8_25
24. Moltisanti, D., Fidler, S., Damen, D.: Action recognition from single timestamp supervision in untrimmed videos. In: Proceedings of the IEEE/CVF Conference on Computer Vision and Pattern Recognition, pp. 9915–9924 (2019)
25. Moltisanti, D., Wray, M., Mayol-Cuevas, W., Damen, D.: Trespassing the boundaries: labeling temporal bounds for object interactions in egocentric video. In: Proceedings of the IEEE International Conference on Computer Vision, pp. 2886–2894 (2017)
26. Rashid, M., Kjellstrom, H., Lee, Y.J.: Action graphs: weakly-supervised action localization with graph convolution networks. In: Proceedings of the IEEE/CVF Winter Conference on Applications of Computer Vision (WACV), March 2020
27. Richard, A., Gall, J.: Temporal action detection using a statistical language model. In: Proceedings of the IEEE Conference on Computer Vision and Pattern Recognition. pp. 3131–3140 (2016)
28. Richard, A., Kuehne, H., Gall, J.: Action sets: weakly supervised action segmentation without ordering constraints. In: Proceedings of the IEEE Conference on Computer Vision and Pattern Recognition, pp. 5987–5996 (2018)
29. Richard, A., Kuehne, H., Iqbal, A., Gall, J.: Neuralnetwork-viterbi: a framework for weakly supervised video learning. In: Proceedings of the IEEE Conference on Computer Vision and Pattern Recognition, pp. 7386–7395 (2018)
30. Sener, F., Singhania, D., Yao, A.: Temporal aggregate representations for long-range video understanding. In: Vedaldi, A., Bischof, H., Brox, T., Frahm, J.-M. (eds.) ECCV 2020. LNCS, vol. 12361, pp. 154–171. Springer, Cham (2020). https://doi.org/10.1007/978-3-030-58517-4_10
31. Sener, F., Yao, A.: Unsupervised learning and segmentation of complex activities from video. In: Proceedings of the IEEE Conference on Computer Vision and Pattern Recognition, pp. 8368–8376 (2018)
32. Simonyan, K., Zisserman, A.: Two-stream convolutional networks for action recognition in videos. In: Advances in Neural Information Processing Systems, pp. 568–576 (2014)
33. Singh, B., Marks, T.K., Jones, M., Tuzel, O., Shao, M.: A multi-stream bi-directional recurrent neural network for fine-grained action detection, pp. 1961–1970 (2016)
34. Singhania, D., Rahaman, R., Yao, A.: Coarse to fine multi-resolution temporal convolutional network. arXiv preprint arXiv:2105.10859 (2021)
35. Souri, Y., Fayyaz, M., Minciullo, L., Francesca, G., Gall, J.: Fast weakly supervised action segmentation using mutual consistency. IEEE Trans. Pattern Anal. Mach. Intell. (2021)

36. Stein, S., McKenna, S.J.: Combining embedded accelerometers with computer vision for recognizing food preparation activities. In: Proceedings of the 2013 ACM International Joint Conference on Pervasive and Ubiquitous Computing, pp. 729–738. ACM (2013)
37. VidalMata, R.G., Scheirer, W.J., Kukleva, A., Cox, D., Kuehne, H.: Joint visual-temporal embedding for unsupervised learning of actions in untrimmed sequences. In: Proceedings of the IEEE/CVF Winter Conference on Applications of Computer Vision, pp. 1238–1247 (2021)
38. Wang, D., Yuan, Y., Wang, Q.: Gated forward refinement network for action segmentation. Neurocomputing **407**, 63–71 (2020)
39. Wang, Z., Gao, Z., Wang, L., Li, Z., Wu, G.: Boundary-aware cascade networks for temporal action segmentation. In: Vedaldi, A., Bischof, H., Brox, T., Frahm, J.-M. (eds.) ECCV 2020. LNCS, vol. 12370, pp. 34–51. Springer, Cham (2020). https://doi.org/10.1007/978-3-030-58595-2_3

Few-Shot Action Recognition with Hierarchical Matching and Contrastive Learning

Sipeng Zheng[1], Shizhe Chen[2], and Qin Jin[1(✉)]

[1] Renmin University of China, Beijing, China
{zhengsipeng,qjin}@ruc.edu.cn
[2] Inria, Paris, France
shizhe.chen@inria.fr

Abstract. Few-shot action recognition aims to recognize actions in test videos based on limited annotated data of target action classes. The dominant approaches project videos into a metric space and classify videos via nearest neighboring. They mainly measure video similarities using global or temporal alignment alone, while an optimum matching should be multi-level. However, the complexity of learning coarse-to-fine matching quickly rises as we focus on finer-grained visual cues, and the lack of detailed local supervision is another challenge. In this work, we propose a hierarchical matching model to support comprehensive similarity measure at global, temporal and spatial levels via a zoom-in matching module. We further propose a mixed-supervised hierarchical contrastive learning (HCL), which not only employs supervised contrastive learning to differentiate videos at different levels, but also utilizes cycle consistency as weak supervision to align discriminative temporal clips or spatial patches. Our model achieves state-of-the-art performance on four benchmarks especially under the most challenging 1-shot recognition setting.

Keywords: Few-shot learning · Action recognition · Contrastive learning

1 Introduction

Large-scale video datasets [5,13] have greatly accelerated the research on action recognition using deep neural networks [31], which however, is data-hungry and hard to generalize well on new classes with limited training examples. Therefore, few-shot action recognition (FSAR) [3,48] has attracted more and more attention. One of the mainstream approaches for FSAR is the metric-based method [32,41]. The key idea is to learn a generalizable metric from action classes with abundant labeled videos, and such metric can be used to measure the similarity

Supplementary Information The online version contains supplementary material available at https://doi.org/10.1007/978-3-031-19772-7_18.

between any videos. In this way, we recognize the few-shot classes by computing the similarity between the query video and the few labeled videos.

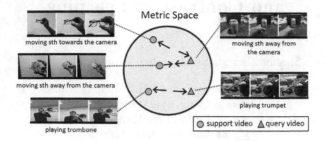

Fig. 1. Metric-based approaches for FSAR learn a metric space to measure video similarities. In addition to global cues, the video representation in the space should hierarchically capture temporal dynamics and discriminative spatial regions to correctly match query videos with support videos.

There is no doubt that an ideal metric should be learned from multi-levels for accurate video matching *e.g.*, at instance, clip, frame or even patch level. However, the matching complexity drastically rises from coarse- to fine-grained, and combining the alignment of these different granularities is quiet challenging. For example, global matching refers only to the similarity of a pair of features, while patch matching may need to deal with a large number of patch-to-patch alignment. Subject to this limitation, existing metric-based FSAR works simply compare two videos from a single granularity, mainly including global or temporal matching. The global matching approaches [11,20] encode a video as a fixed-size vector to compute similarities, which fail to differentiate different temporal dynamics such as "moving towards" or "moving away" as shown in Fig. 1. The temporal matching approaches instead leverage temporal alignment between frames [4] or clips [29]. Despite great progress, these works suffer from condensed spatial information. For example, actions "playing trombone" and "playing trumpet" in Fig. 1 have similar temporal movements. One needs to focus on discriminative spatial regions of the instrument in order to classify them correctly. Therefore, a mechanism to reliably and efficiently capture various alignment in videos is necessary.

Another challenge to learn both coarse- and fined-grained alignment simultaneously lies in the learning approach on few-shot sets. Earlier FSAR methods [3,20,41] employ cross entropy loss to train on global features, which are prone to overfit and do not generalize well for few-shot classes. More recent works [29] adopt supervised contrastive loss [17] in episodic training, where a limited number of action classes are used per training iteration. Such episodic training mimics standard N-way K-shot setting [32], but it cannot take full advantage of contrastive learning, which usually requires diverse and large number of negative examples [14,45] to learn good representations. In addition, the supervisions are only available at the video level, and it is expensive to manually annotate temporal or spatial alignment between videos to train fine-grained matching. Therefore the training becomes quite challenging without detailed annotations.

In this paper, we tackle the above challenges by comparing any two videos based on: global video representations, temporally aligned clip representations to capture temporal orders, and spatially aligned patch representations to encode detailed spatial information. To be specific, we firstly propose a hierarchical matching model to more comprehensively and efficiently measure video similarities. Our proposed model matches videos progressively from coarse-level to fine-grained level, using features of coarse level to focus on local information at finer-grained level e.g., from clip to patch. Such matching mechanism, called zoom-in matching module, alleviates the complexity of hierarchical matching to better scale up when aligning fine-grained visual cues like clips or patches. Secondly, we develop a hierarchical contrastive learning (HCL) algorithm for coarse-to-fine video representation learning. Specifically, we develop a mixed-supervised contrastive learning to avoid the limitations of previous episodic training paradigm and thus learn more discriminatively. In addition to supervised contrastive learning, we use cycle consistency to build temporal and spatial associations between videos of the same action class. It enables contrastive learning of discriminative local information via weak supervision — meaning that only class labels are given. Note that noises of irrelevant cues from contexts are unavoidable when building the local contrastive alignment, we thus incorporate a semantic attention component to suppress them. We carry out extensive experiments on four FSAR benchmarks including Kinetics, SSv2, UCF-101 and HMDB-51. Our approach achieves state-of-the-art results under various few-shot settings, and superior performance in the more challenging cross-domain evaluation as well.

In summary, our contributions are three-fold:

- We propose a hierarchical matching model for FSAR. The hierarchical architecture utilizes a zoom-in matching module to alleviate the complexity and computation cost for multi-level matching, therefore video similarities using coarse-to-fine cues can be measured.
- We propose the mixed-supervised hierarchical contrastive learning (HCL) to learn generalizable and fine-grained video representations, by using cycle consistency for weakly-supervised spatial-temporal association. Additionally, a semantic attention component is applied to suppress contextual noises.
- We carry out experiments on four benchmark datasets to validate our model, which achieve state-of-the-art performance especially under the 1-shot setup.

2   Related Work

Action Recognition has received significant improvements thanks to deep neural networks [15,18]. Early deep models [16,31,42] adopt 2D CNNs in temporal domain. 3D CNNs [38] are then proposed to encode short-range temporal dynamics in videos. Just to name a few, Carreira et al. [5] propose I3D to inflate 2D CNN to 3D CNN; Tran et al. [39] and Qiu et al. [30] decompose 3D convolution into 2D and 1D convolutions for efficiency; Wang et al. [43] insert non-local blocks into 3D CNNs. More recently, transformer architectures [1,2] are exploited in video domain to capture long-range dependency. Despite strong performance, these models are hard to generalize to new action classes with limited examples. In this work, we focus on few-shot action recognition.

Few-shot Learning approaches can be categorized into three types: generative methods [22,26], optimization-based methods [10,44], and metric-based methods [24,32,35,36,41]. The generative method synthesizes new data of few-shot classes to enlarge the training data. The optimization-based method learns a good initialization of the network, which can be easily fine-tuned to an unseen target task without sufficient labels. Instead, metric-based method aims to learn a metric to measure similarities of images or videos, and then employs nearest neighboring for classification. Most existing few-shot action recognition works [4,8,48] follow the metric-based approach. Fu *et al.* [11] employ global video features on RGB and depth modalities for similarity measure. To capture temporal dynamics in the video, Zhu *et al.* [48] use a compound memory network to reserve the representation of key frames. Zhang *et al.* [47] align short-range while discarding long-range dependencies using a permutation invariant attention with jigsaws for self-supervised training. Cao *et al.* [4] propose to minimize the temporal distance of pairwise video sequences based on the DTW algorithm. Perrett *et al.* [29] use attention mechanism to construct query-specific class prototype for clip matching. Different from previous works, we exploit a hierarchical matching to capture from coarse to fine information for comparison of videos.

Contrastive Learning has shown great capability to learn generic representations from unlabeled data [14,28] in recent years. Wu *et al.* [45] aim to push different augmentations of an instance closer in the embedding space using a memory bank to store instance vectors, which is followed by several works [27,37,46]. Khosla *et al.* [17] extend to learn contrast under class supervision. Recent works [12,34] point out that contrastive learning helps to avoid few-shot learning from limitations like over-fitting [6,21] or supervision collapse [8], which serves as auxiliary losses to learn the representation alignment.

3   Method

Problem Formulation. In few-shot action recognition (FSAR) setting, videos in a dataset are split into two sets $\mathcal{D}_{base}$ and $\mathcal{D}_{novel}$. Action classes in $\mathcal{D}_{base}$ and $\mathcal{D}_{novel}$ are disjoint. $\mathcal{D}_{base}$ contains abundant labeled videos per action class and is used for training, while $\mathcal{D}_{novel}$ is used to evaluate few-shot learning performance in a N-way K-shot manner. Such evaluation consists of a series of tasks called episodes [32]. For each episode, we randomly sample N action classes with K videos per class from $\mathcal{D}_{novel}$ as "support set". The rest videos of the N action classes in $\mathcal{D}_{novel}$ are used to sample "query set" for testing. A model is evaluated by averaging recognition performances over all episodes.

Our Idea. We follow the metric-based methods [32,41] to learn a metric space based on $\mathcal{D}_{base}$, where classification can be performed by computing similarities among videos in the query set and support set. However, previous works fail to optimize coarse-to-fine representations with multi-level alignment. In this work, we propose to leverage multi-level matching at global, temporal and spatial levels, by developing a hierarchical matching model paired with a mixed-supervised hierarchical contrastive learning (Sect. 3.3). Our hierarchical matching model consists of a video encoder to extract multi-level visual cues (Sect. 3.1) and a zoom-in matching module to measure video similarities hierarchically (Sect. 3.2).

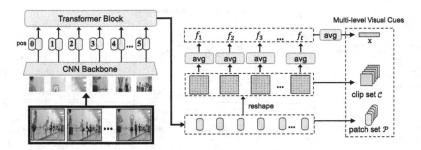

Fig. 2. Network structure of the video encoder. It firstly encodes a video into a sequence of contextualized patches and then generates global embedding x, temporal embeddings $\mathcal{C}$ and spatial embeddings $\mathcal{P}$ for the video.

3.1 Video Encoder

The video encoder contains a CNN backbone [15] and a transformer block [40] to extract contextualized video representations as shown in Fig. 2. To be specific, we uniformly sample t frames as inputs for each video. The CNN backbone extracts a feature map with size $h \times w$ for each frame. We flatten feature maps of all frames into a sequence of $t \times h \times w$ patches. Then the transformer block encodes the space-time position [2] of each patch and employs self-attention to model space-time relationships among all the patches. Let $\mathcal{P} = \{p_1, p_2, ...p_{thw}\}$ be the output embeddings of all patches, where $p_i \in \mathbb{R}^d$ and d is the dimensionality. We adopt average pooling on the spatial dimension $h \times w$ per frame to obtain frame features $\mathcal{F} = \{f_1, f_2, ...f_t\}, f_i \in \mathbb{R}^d$. In this paper, we define multi-level visual cues for the following zoom-in matching.

First, we apply average pooling over all frame embeddings to generate a global representation x for the video, which is prone to lose fine-grained temporal and spatial details. Second, to capture temporal sensitive cues, we sample N_c clips $\mathcal{C} = \{c_1, c_2, ...c_{N_c}\}$ from continuous frames to capture various temporal scales in the video similar to [29]. A clip $c_i = \{f_{i_1}, f_{i_2}, ...f_{i_{|c_i|}}\}$ is a subset of $\mathcal{F}$ with $|c_i|$ frames and its embedding is computed as follows to keep the temporal order:

$$c_i = \text{MLP}([f_{i_1}; f_{i_2}; \cdots f_{i_{|c_i|}}]), c_i \in \mathbb{R}^d \tag{1}$$

where $[;]$ denotes vector concatenation and MLP is a multi-layer perceptron. Note that we reuse c_i to denote both clip and its embedding and so does the patch p_i. Finally, we use patch embeddings $\mathcal{P}$ to provide spatial visual cues.

3.2   Zoom-in Matching Module

Given the above multi-level representations, *i.e.*, global embedding x, temporal embeddings $\mathcal{C}$ and spatial embeddings $\mathcal{P}$, we progressively zoom-in to measure similarities of a query video v and a support video $\hat{v}$ at three coarse-to-fine levels.

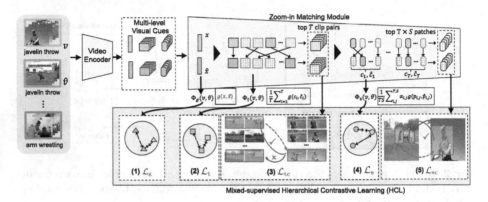

Fig. 3. Illustration of our model. *Top*: hierarchical matching with a zoom-in module to compare coarse-to-fine video similarities, using multi-level visual cues including global embedding , clip embedding and patch embedding ; *Bottom*: Mixed-supervised hierarchical contrastive learning (HCL) including five contrastive loss terms $\mathcal{L}_g$, $\mathcal{L}_t$, $\mathcal{L}_s$ and $\mathcal{L}_{tc}$, $\mathcal{L}_{sc}$ that are described in Sect. 3.3.

Global Matching. We directly compute a cosine similarity $g(.)$ between x and $\hat{x}$ for global matching, which is written by:

$$\Phi_{\mathrm{g}}(v, \hat{v}) = g(x, \hat{x}) = \frac{x}{||x||} \odot \frac{\hat{x}}{||\hat{x}||}, \tag{2}$$

where $|| \cdot ||$ means L2 norm and $\odot$ denotes inner-product operation.

Temporal Matching.   Temporal information is important to distinguish actions especially for those with similar objects but in different temporal orders, such as "open the door" and "close the door". We therefore propose to match videos in a finer-grained clip level which captures local temporal dynamics. We use clip features $\mathcal{C}, \hat{\mathcal{C}}$ to compute temporal matching scores between v and $\hat{v}$. To be specific, for each $c_i \in \mathcal{C}$, we pick its most similar clip in $\hat{\mathcal{C}}$ and form a temporally matched pair $(c_i, \hat{c}_i)$. We rank all pairs by their feature similarity and select top T pairs to compute the temporal matching score:

$$\Phi_{\mathrm{t}}(v, \hat{v}) = \frac{1}{T} \sum_{i=1}^{T} g(c_i, \hat{c}_i). \tag{3}$$

Spatial Matching. The discriminative spatial regions to differentiate actions can be small, such as "eat burger" vs. "eat doughnuts", making the spatially condensed embeddings $\mathcal{C}$ less effective to capture such fine-grained information. We further apply spatial matching between patches from the temporally aligned clip pairs $(c_i, \hat{c}_i), i \in [1, T]$ mentioned above. By doing so, we avoid to enumerate all possible patch-to-patch alignment in the entire video, which contains a numerous number of noisy information with a large burden of computation cost. Similar to temporal matching, for each picked clip pair, we align each patch $p_{i,j}$ in c_i with the most similar patch $\hat{p}_{i,j}$ in clip $\hat{c}_i$, and select top S aligned patches by the similarity score. In this way, we obtain $T \times S$ patch pairs from the video to compute the spatial matching score as follows, where $\alpha_{i,j} = 1$ if semantic attention component is not used.

$$\Phi_s(v, \hat{v}) = \frac{1}{TS} \sum_{i=1}^{T} \sum_{j=1}^{S} \alpha_{i,j} g(p_{i,j}, \hat{p}_{i,j}). \tag{4}$$

Semantic Attention Component. Not all aligned patches with high similarity are relevant to the action. For example, videos with similar backgrounds are likely to rank background patch pairs on the top. To suppress noises from semantically irrelevant patch pairs, we propose to re-weight the semantic correlation of each patch pair with the action. In particular, assume the action class of the support video $\hat{v}$ is $\hat{y}$, we use BERT [7] to obtain its class embedding as $e_{\hat{y}}$. Then the semantic attention weight of patch $p_{i,j}$ in clip c_i is reassigned as:

$$\alpha_{i,j} = \frac{\exp(p_{i,j} W e_{\hat{y}} / \sqrt{d})}{\sum_{k=1}^{N_p} \exp(p_{i,k} W e_{\hat{y}} / \sqrt{d})}, \tag{5}$$

where W denotes a projection matrix and N_p is the number of patches in clip c_i, d is the dimensionality. The $\alpha_{i,j}$ added in Eq. 4 emphasizes semantically salient patches and disregard irrelevant background noises in matching.

The final matching score $\Phi(v, \hat{v})$ between video v and $\hat{v}$ is aggregated from the three hierarchical matching scores as follows. We use $\Phi(v, \hat{v})$ to compare the similarity between any videos during the **evaluation** and **inference**.

$$\Phi(v, \hat{v}) = \Phi_g(v, \hat{v}) + \Phi_t(v, \hat{v}) + \Phi_s(v, \hat{v}). \tag{6}$$

Computation Cost Analysis. The zoom-in module mainly reduces the cost of spatial matching. Assuming we enumerate all clips with 2 frames in the video for the pairwise matching (C_t^2 clips per video). The zoom-in module applies temporal matching across video clips and then selects the top-T aligned clips for spatial matching ($T \ll C_t^2$). Hence, the computation complexity for spatial matching is $\mathcal{O}(T^2 h^2 w^2)$. The model without zoom-in module, however, applies spatial matching for all video clips instead of the top ones. Therefore, the complexity is $\mathcal{O}(t^4 h^2 w^2)$, which is more computationally expensive.

3.3   Mixed-Supervised Hierarchical Contrastive Learning

In order to learn coarse-to-fine representations, we propose mixed-supervised hierarchical contrastive learning (HCL) as shown in Fig. 3 for training visual cues of temporal and spatial levels. Apart from supervised constrastive learning to differentiate videos of different classes, our HCL further utilizes cycle consistency to enable spatio-temporal constrastive learning in a weakly-supervised manner.

Supervised Contrastive Learning. Given a mini-batch of B videos, we compute the global similarity $\Phi_g(v_i, v_j)$ between any two videos v_i and v_j in the batch. A video pair (v_i, v_j) where $i, j \in [1, B], i \neq j$ is positive only when $y_i = y_j$, otherwise it is negative. The global contrastive loss is then written as follows:

$$\mathcal{L}_g = -\frac{1}{B^2} \sum_{i \neq j} \mathbb{1}_{y_i=y_j} \log \frac{\exp(\Phi_g(v_i, v_j)/\tau)}{\sum_{k=1}^{B} \mathbb{1}_{k \neq i} \exp(\Phi_g(v_i, v_k)/\tau)}, \quad (7)$$

where τ is temperature hyper-parameter and $\mathbb{1}$ is an indicator function. To be noted, our supervised contrastive learning is different from previous works based on episodic training [32], which only allows negative examples within the N video classes in each episode. Our training instead contains more diverse negative examples, which are demonstrated to be beneficial for representation learning [6,23,25]. Similarly, we use the temporal matching score $\Phi_t(v_i, v_j)$ and spatial matching score $\Phi_s(v_i, v_j)$ to compute $\mathcal{L}_t$ and $\mathcal{L}_s$ respectively as Eq. (7).

Weakly-Supervised Contrastive Learning via Cycle Consistency. The temporal and spatial matching relies on fine-grained alignment of features at the clip and patch level respectively. To enhance such alignment, we propose to leverage cycle consistency in temporal and spatial contrastive learning. Given video v and $\hat{v}$ of the same action class, we build temporal cycle consistency [9] of their top T aligned clip pairs as supervision for training. For each clip $c_i \in \mathcal{C}$, we first compute its soft nearest neighbor $\hat{c}_{j*} \in \hat{\mathcal{C}}$, which is:

$$\hat{c}_{j*} = \sum_{j=1}^{N_c} \hat{\beta}_j \hat{c}_j, \quad \text{where} \quad \hat{\beta}_j = \frac{\exp(g(c_i, \hat{c}_j))}{\sum_{k=1}^{N_c} \exp(g(c_i, \hat{c}_k))}. \quad (8)$$

N_c is the clip number of video. Then we track back $\hat{c}_{j*}$ to find its nearest neighbor c_{i*} in v. If the alignment is well trained, the pair (c_i, c_{i*}) should satisfy the cycle consistency so that $c_i = c_{i*}$. Therefore, the temporal cycle consistency loss is:

$$\mathcal{L}_{tc}(v, \hat{v}) = -\frac{1}{T} \sum_{i=1}^{T} \log \frac{\exp(g(\hat{c}_{j*}, c_i))}{\sum_{k=1}^{T} \exp(g(\hat{c}_{j*}, c_k))}. \quad (9)$$

The temporal cycle consistency allows to learn from clip-to-clip association to improve the temporal alignment. We average such losses of all pairwise videos of the same class in a mini-batch as $\mathcal{L}_{tc}$.

It is however more challenging to extend the temporal cycle consistency in the spatial domain. Similar to challenges in spatial matching, firstly, searching all patches in videos is computationally expensive. Secondly, it is also unnecessary to enforce every patch to satisfy cycle consistency, e.g., semantically irrelevant patches. Therefore, we only build such patch-level consistency for the top T similar clip pairs from two videos of the same class. For each clip pair $(c, \hat{c})$, the spatial cycle consistency is built on top of their patch sets:

$$\mathcal{L}_{\text{sc}}(c, \hat{c}) = -\frac{1}{N_p} \sum_{i=1}^{N_p} \alpha_i \log \frac{\exp(g(\hat{p}_{j*}, p_i))}{\sum_{k=1}^{N_p} \exp(g(\hat{p}_{j*}, p_k))}, \tag{10}$$

where $\hat{p}_{j*}$ is the soft nearest neighbor computed similarly as Eq. (8), N_p is the patch number of a clip, α_i is the semantic attention weight using Eq. 5. When α_i is small, the gradient will be down weighted because it implies that the patch p_i has weak semantic association with the action. We average the loss for all selected clip pairs in a batch as $\mathcal{L}_{\text{sc}}$.

We combine all these contrastive losses and the traditional supervised cross-entropy loss $\mathcal{L}_{\text{ce}} = -\log p(y|x)$ as the following overall training objective, where λ_g, λ_t, λ_s are hyper-parameters to balance the losses for multi-scale visual cues:

$$\mathcal{L} = \mathcal{L}_{\text{ce}} + \lambda_g \mathcal{L}_{\text{g}} + \lambda_t (\mathcal{L}_{\text{t}} + \mathcal{L}_{\text{tc}}) + \lambda_s (\mathcal{L}_{\text{s}} + \mathcal{L}_{\text{sc}}), \tag{11}$$

4 Experiments

4.1 Experimental Setup

Datasets. We conduct experiments on four datasets, including Kinetics [5], Something v2 (SSv2) [13], HMDB-51 [19], and UCF-101 [33]. Kinetics and SSv2 are the most widely used benchmarks for few-shot action recognition. For Kinetics benchmark, we follow the split in [48] for fair comparison. It uses a subset of Kinetics by selecting 100 action classes with 100 videos per class from the whole dataset. The 100 classes are split into 64, 12 and 24 classes as the training, validation and testing set respectively. For SSv2 benchmark, we adopt two splits proposed in [49] and [4] denoted as SSv2[†] and SSv2[*] respectively. SSv2[*] contains nearly 70,000 training samples for 64 training classes. Each class has over 1,000 training samples on average which is 10 times larger than class samples in SSv2[†]. For HMDB-51 and UCF-101, we use the split from [47].

Implementation Details. We use ResNet-50 [15] pre-trained on ImageNet [18] as CNN backbone for fair comparison with previous works [3,8,48]. The semantic embeddings for action classes are obtained from a pretrained BERT [7]. For each video, we uniformly sample 8 frames and resize the frame scale into 224×224. The number of clips and patches selected in temporal and spatial matching is $T = 10$ and $S = 10$. During training, the weight of λ_g, λ_t and λ_s for hierarchical contrastive loss is set as 0.5, 0.3 and 0.3. We train our model for 15 epochs with 3,000 steps for each epoch. Our model is optimized via SGD with the learning rate of 0.001, which is decayed every 6 epochs by 0.5. We randomly sample 24 classes with 2 videos per class in a mini-batch. We provide more details and our codes in the supplementary material.

Evaluation Protocol. We evaluate the performance of our model under 5-way K-shot setup with $K \in \{1, 2, 3, 4, 5\}$. We randomly sample 10,000 episodes from $\mathcal{D}_{novel}$ in testing. The performance is the average of all episodes.

4.2 Ablation Study

Q1: Is Hierarchical Contrastive Learning More Effective Than Traditional Training Methods? We compare different variants of HCL training losses and the traditional cross-entropy loss in Table 1. Please note that the temporal or spatial matching will be removed during inference if the corresponding contrastive loss is not used in training. Row 1 simply adopts a pretrained ResNet-50 to extract global representations and does not involve any training on the video dataset. It already achieves 59.9% and 80.1% accuracy under 1-shot and 5-shot setups on Kinetics, which serves as a strong baseline. Row 2 adds a spatial-temporal transformer on top of the CNN backbone and fine-tunes the whole model via $\mathcal{L}_{ce}$. The temporal information and fine-tuning brings stable improvements over row 1 especially on SSv2* which focuses more on temporal orders.

Table 1. Ablation of training objectives. $\mathcal{L}_{ce}$ denotes cross entropy loss, $\mathcal{L}_g$ is global contrastive loss, $\mathcal{L}_t + \mathcal{L}_{tc}$ and $\mathcal{L}_s + \mathcal{L}_{sc}$ represent temporal/spatial contrastive loss enhanced with cycle consistency loss.

	HCL				Kinetics		SSv2*	
	$\mathcal{L}_{ce}$	$\mathcal{L}_g$	$\mathcal{L}_t + \mathcal{L}_{tc}$	$\mathcal{L}_s + \mathcal{L}_{sc}$	1-shot	5-shot	1-shot	5-shot
1	×	×	×	×	59.9	80.1	29.5	44.1
2	✓	×	×	×	62.5	81.6	37.8	55.0
3	×	✓	×	×	54.9	76.4	34.0	50.9
4	✓	✓	×	×	66.1	82.7	40.3	56.7
5	✓	✓	✓	×	70.4	83.9	45.4	62.6
6	✓	✓	×	✓	72.3	84.7	41.5	58.4
7	✓	✓	✓	✓	73.7	85.8	47.3	64.9

In row 3, we use the global contrastive loss $\mathcal{L}_g$ alone for training, which however obtains poor performance on Kinetics even compared with the model without fine-tuning in row 1. Combining $\mathcal{L}_g$ with $\mathcal{L}_{ce}$ performs better compared to using them separately, showing the two types of training objectives are complementary. $\mathcal{L}_{ce}$ alone may suffer from over-fitting especially on Kinetics while $\mathcal{L}_g$ can improve the generalization of the learned features. Both the temporal and spatial contrastive learning are beneficial as shown in row 5 and 6 respectively. Using both temporal contrastive loss and its corresponding cycle consistency loss, $\mathcal{L}_t + \mathcal{L}_{tc}$ brings significant improvements especially on SSv2* with +5.1%

for 1-shot and +5.9% for 5-shot setups. On the opposite, $\mathcal{L}_s + \mathcal{L}_{sc}$ is more effective on Kinetic dataset with +6.2% for 1-shot and +2.0% for 5-shot. The results align with our observation that SSv2* focuses more on the temporal orders and Kinetics is more discriminative in the spatial dimension. Finally, we achieve the best results by combining $\mathcal{L}_g$, $\mathcal{L}_t + \mathcal{L}_{tc}$ and $\mathcal{L}_s + \mathcal{L}_{sc}$ in row 7.

Table 2. Ablation of temporal and spatial cycle consistency losses.

	$\mathcal{L}_{tc}$	$\mathcal{L}_{sc}$	Kinetics		SSv2*	
			1-shot	5-shot	1-shot	5-shot
1	×	×	72.1	84.3	44.7	62.5
2	✓	×	72.4	84.7	46.9	64.5
3	×	✓	73.1	85.2	46.2	64.0
4	✓	✓	73.7	85.8	47.3	64.9

Table 3. Ablation of semantic attention module.

	semantic_att	Kinetics		SSv2*	
		1-shot	5-shot	1-shot	5-shot
1	×	71.3	84.4	46.3	64.2
2	✓	73.7	85.8	47.3	64.9

Q2: Is Spatio-Temporal Cycle Consistency Beneficial to Hierarchical Contrastive Learning? In Table 2, we compare models with and without temporal and spatial cycle consistency loss $\mathcal{L}_{tc}$, $\mathcal{L}_{sc}$. Without $\mathcal{L}_{tc}$, our model's performance on SSv2* decreases with −1.5% for 1-shot and −0.9% for 5-shot (row 3 vs. row 4). Significant performance degradation can also be observed on Kinetics by removing $\mathcal{L}_{sc}$ (row 2 vs. row 4). These results indicate that both temporal and spatial cycle consistency losses are beneficial to learning fine-grained association.

Q3: Does Semantic Attention Component Help Spatial Matching and Spatial Cycle Consistency Training? In Table 3, we validate the contribution of semantic attention component for spatial matching in Eq. (4). By removing the semantic attention, the performance of our model on Kinetics drops by −2.4% for 1-shot and −1.4% for 5-shot. Note that the semantic attention weight in Eq. 10 will also be removed. The results demonstrate that re-scaling semantic weight is helpful in learning spatial associations by focusing on semantically relevant patches and eliminating background noises. On SSv2*, only slight improvement can be observed due to its temporal inclination.

Q4: What is the Performance of Zoom-in Matching at Different Levels? In Table 4, we explore different combinations of zoom-in matching at test time. Table 4(a) uses $\mathcal{L}_{ce}$ for training. We can see temporal or spatial matching alone does not outperform global matching on Kinetics. Table 4(b) employs our HCL training algorithm. Instead, the temporal or spatial matching achieves superior performance on Kinetics, which proves that HCL is beneficial to learn fine-grained alignment. The two matching's improvement is more significant on SSv2* and Kinetics respectively, since SSv2* mainly focuses on temporal variation while spatial cue plays a more important role on Kinetics. In addition, the combination of global, temporal and spatial matching improves individual

Table 4. Ablation of zoom-in matching at different levels using $\mathcal{L}_{ce}$ or hierarchical contrastive loss (HCL), where G, T and S denote the global, temporal and spatial matching respectively

(a) Cross Entropy Loss $\mathcal{L}_{ce}$

	Match G T S			Kinetics 1-shot	5-shot	SSv2* 1-shot	5-shot
1	✓	×	×	62.5	81.6	37.8	55.0
2	×	✓	×	62.1	81.3	40.5	57.0
3	×	×	✓	59.0	79.8	33.2	49.5
4	✓	✓	×	62.9	81.8	40.2	56.6
5	✓	×	✓	63.8	82.2	38.5	55.4
6	✓	✓	✓	64.4	82.5	40.8	57.3

(b) Hierarchical Contrastive Loss

	Match G T S			Kinetics 1-shot	5-shot	SSv2* 1-shot	5-shot
1	✓	×	×	69.1	83.2	42.9	59.2
2	×	✓	×	71.3	84.2	45.9	62.9
3	×	×	✓	71.8	84.5	38.1	53.2
4	✓	✓	×	71.5	84.3	46.4	63.5
5	✓	×	✓	72.7	84.9	43.7	59.8
6	✓	✓	✓	73.7	85.8	47.3	64.9

performances whether using $\mathcal{L}_{ce}$ or our HCL. It shows that different levels are complementary with each other and zoom-in matching needs to equip with HCL for effective hierarchical alignment.

Table 5. Comparison with SOTA methods on Kinetics and SSv2.

Match	Method	Kinetics 1-shot	2-shot	5-shot	SSv2[†] 1-shot	2-shot	5-shot	SSv2* 1-shot	2-shot	5-shot
Global	MAML [10]	54.2	65.5	75.3	30.9	35.1	41.9	–	–	–
	ProtoNet [32]	59.1	73.6	83.5	30.9	37.2	47.2	34.0	41.2	51.7
	TARN [3]	66.6	74.6	80.7	–	–	–	–	–	–
Temporal	CMN [48]	60.5	70	78.9	36.2	42.1	48.8	–	–	–
	TAM [4]	73.0	–	85.8	–	–	–	42.8	–	52.3
	TRX [29]	64.6	76.4	85.5	34.7	43.5	**56.8**	38.1	49.1	63.9
Hierarchical	Ours	**73.7**	**79.1**	**85.8**	**38.7**	**45.5**	55.4	**47.3**	**54.5**	**64.9**

4.3 Comparison with State-of-the-Art Methods

In Table 5, we compare our method with state-of-the-art approaches on Kinetics and SSv2 benchmarks. The global matching approaches [20,32] are less competitive to temporal matching approaches [4,8] and our hierarchical model in general. Our proposed model outperforms previous temporal approaches by a large margin under 1-shot and 2-shot evaluations and is comparable under 5-shot setting on all datasets. When labels are extremely limited as in the 1-shot setting, our model achieves +9.1%, +4.0% and +9.2% improvements on Kinetics, SSv2[†] and SSv2* respectively compared to TRX [8]. The improvements from our model are more significant on SSv2 benchmarks. For example, though our model slightly outperforms TAM [4] by 0.7% under 1-shot setting on Kinetics, it beats TAM [4] by +4.5% and +12.6% under 1-shot and 5-shot settings on SSv2*, which indicates that our method has stronger capability of temporal reasoning. In addition, the performance is more encouraging on SSv2*, where we obtain significant improvements under all settings from 1-shot to 5-shot. Considering SSv2* has more training samples (more than 70,000 videos) than other datasets like Kinetics (7,600 videos), we believe that our HCL is able to benefit more from large-scale datasets compared with other approaches.

Table 6. Comparison with SOTA methods on UCF-101 and HMDB-51.

Match	Method	UCF-101		HMDB-51	
		1-shot	5-shot	1-shot	5-shot
Global	ProtoNet [32]	67.2	93.0	44.2	72.0
Temporal	TARN [3]	66.3	–	45.5	60.6
Temporal	TRX [29]	81.3	**95.9**	52.0	75.6
Hierarchical	Ours	**82.6**	94.5	**59.1**	**76.3**

We further provide comparisons on UCF-101 and HMDB-51 in Table 6, which contain much less training data than Kinetics and SSv2. Our method significantly improves over TRX [8] on HMDB-51 e.g., +7.1% for 1-shot and +0.7% for 5-shot. On UCF-101, HCL shows improvement for 1-shot but a slight decreases for 5-shot over TRX [8]. In general, our model is robust to various action categories, whether they focus on spatial information (e.g., Kinetics) or temporal orders (e.g., SSv2). Our model is more effective when the training classes have abundant samples in $\mathcal{D}_{base}$ and the test classes have extremely few samples in $\mathcal{D}_{novel}$ (e.g., SSv2*), which is exactly the situation in real applications.

Table 7. Comparison on more challenging cross-domain evaluation setting.

Method	Kinetics → UCF-101		Kinetics → HMDB-51	
	1-shot	5-shot	1-shot	5-shot
MAML [10]	62.4	80.7	43.9	59.3
ProtoNet [32]	67.8	84.2	48.5	63.0
Ours	76.1	90.6	54.2	69.5

4.4 Cross-Domain Evaluation

To further validate the generalization capability of our model, we design a new cross-domain FSAR setting similar to [6]. We use the training split in Kinetics as $\mathcal{D}_{base}$ and the testing splits in UCF-101 and HMDB-51 as $\mathcal{D}_{novel}$. Then we remove overlapped classes between Kinetics training set and the testing set. Such evaluation is more challenging, which requires the learned model not only generalizes on new action classes but also on new video domains. We compare our model with an optimization-based model MAML [10] and a metric-based model ProtoNet [32]. Table 7 presents the cross-domain results. We achieve significantly better performances than the other methods, with 8.3% and 5.7% gains under 1-shot setting on UCF-101 and HMDB-51 datasets respectively. It proves that our model can adapt well to novel actions in different domains from the base classes in the training set.

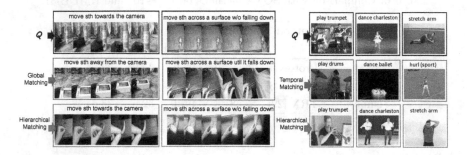

Fig. 4. Global/temporal matching vs. hierarchical matching. We show the most similar video in support sets for each query video using the matching approach.

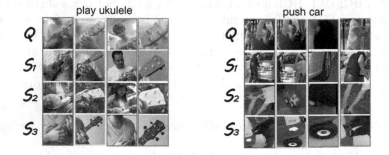

Fig. 5. Discriminative patch pairs between query and support videos. Q denotes the query, S_1, S_2 and S_3 are three distinct support videos from the same class.

4.5   Quality Analysis

Figure 4 provides qualitative comparisons for global, temporal matching with our hierarchical matching. Global matching fails to differentiate videos with similar appearances but different temporal orders, while temporal matching fails in recognizing detailed spatial information. Our hierarchical matching considers both temporal orders and discriminative spatial patches, and thus it can classify videos more accurately. Figure 5 presents examples of discriminative patch pairs between query and support videos in spatial matching with our model. First, our model is able to select semantically relevant pairs in matching. For example, it selects patches of the person's hand and the instrument in "play ukulele" action, and patches of the person and an car in "push car" action. Secondly, our model can effectively align patches with other videos in the support set.

5 Conclusion

In this paper, we propose a hierarchical matching approach for few-shot action recognition. Our model, equipped with a zoom-in matching module, hierarchically build coarse-to-fine alignment between videos without complex computation. Therefore, video similarities on few sets can be measured from multiple levels. Moreover, to learn discriminative temporal and spatial associations, we propose a mixed-supervised hierarchical contrastive learning (HCL) algorithm, which utilizes cycle consistency as weak supervision to combine with supervised learning. We carry out extensive experiments to evaluate our proposed model on four benchmark datasets. Our model achieves the state-of-the-art performances especially under 1-shot setting. It shows better generalization capacity in a more challenging cross-domain evaluation as well.

Acknowledgment. This work was partially supported by National Natural Science Foundation of China (No. 62072462), National Key R&D Program of China (No. 2020AAA0108600), and Large-Scale Pre-Training Program 468 of Beijing Academy of Artificial Intelligence (BAAI).

References

1. Arnab, A., Dehghani, M., Heigold, G., Sun, C., Lučić, M., Schmid, C.: ViViT: a video vision transformer. In: ICCV (2021)
2. Bertasius, G., Wang, H., Torresani, L.: Is space-time attention all you need for video understanding? In: ICML (2021)
3. Bishay, M., Zoumpourlis, G., Patras, I.: TARN: temporal attentive relation network for few-shot and zero-shot action recognition. In: BMVC (2019)
4. Cao, K., Ji, J., Cao, Z., Chang, C.Y., Niebles, J.C.: Few-shot video classification via temporal alignment. In: CVPR (2020)
5. Carreira, J., Zisserman, A.: Quo Vadis, action recognition? A new model and the kinetics dataset. In: CVPR (2017)
6. Chen, W.Y., Liu, Y.C., Kira, Z., Wang, Y.C.F., Huang, J.B.: A closer look at few-shot classification. In: ICLR (2019)
7. Devlin, J., Chang, M.W., Lee, K., Toutanova, K.: BERT: pre-training of deep bidirectional transformers for language understanding. In: NAACL (2019)
8. Doersch, C., Gupta, A., Zisserman, A.: CrossTransformers: spatially-aware few-shot transfer. In: NeurIPS (2020)
9. Dwibedi, D., Aytar, Y., Tompson, J., Sermanet, P., Zisserman, A.: Temporal cycle-consistency learning. In: CVPR (2019)
10. Finn, C., Abbeel, P., Levine, S.: Model-agnostic meta-learning for fast adaptation of deep networks. In: ICML (2017)
11. Fu, Y., Zhang, L., Wang, J., Fu, Y., Jiang, Y.G.: Depth guided adaptive meta-fusion network for few-shot video recognition. In: ACMMM (2020)

12. Gidaris, S., Bursuc, A., Komodakis, N., Pérez, P., Cord, M.: Boosting few-shot visual learning with self-supervision. In: ICCV (2019)
13. Goyal, R., et al.: The "something something" video database for learning and evaluating visual common sense. In: ICCV (2017)
14. Hadsell, R., Chopra, S., LeCun, Y.: Dimensionality reduction by learning an invariant mapping. In: CVPR (2006)
15. He, K., Zhang, X., Ren, S., Sun, J.: Deep residual learning for image recognition. In: CVPR (2016)
16. Karpathy, A., Toderici, G., Shetty, S., Leung, T., Sukthankar, R., Fei-Fei, L.: Large-scale video classification with convolutional neural networks. In: CVPR (2014)
17. Khosla, P., et al.: Supervised contrastive learning. arXiv preprint arXiv:2004.11362 (2020)
18. Krizhevsky, A., Sutskever, I., Hinton, G.E.: ImageNet classification with deep convolutional neural networks. In: NeurIPS (2012)
19. Kuehne, H., Jhuang, H., Garrote, E., Poggio, T., Serre, T.: HMDB: a large video database for human motion recognition. In: ICCV (2011)
20. Kumar Dwivedi, S., Gupta, V., Mitra, R., Ahmed, S., Jain, A.: ProtoGAN: towards few shot learning for action recognition. In: ICCV Workshops (2019)
21. Laenen, S., Bertinetto, L.: On episodes, prototypical networks, and few-shot learning. In: Thirty-Fifth Conference on Neural Information Processing Systems (2021)
22. Lake, B., Salakhutdinov, R., Gross, J., Tenenbaum, J.: One shot learning of simple visual concepts. In: CogSci (2011)
23. Li, W., Wang, L., Xu, J., Huo, J., Gao, Y., Luo, J.: Revisiting local descriptor based image-to-class measure for few-shot learning. In: CVPR (2019)
24. Liu, C., Xu, C., Wang, Y., Zhang, L., Fu, Y.: An embarrassingly simple baseline to one-shot learning. In: CVPR (2020)
25. Majumder, O., Ravichandran, A., Maji, S., Polito, M., Bhotika, R., Soatto, S.: Supervised momentum contrastive learning for few-shot classification. arXiv preprint arXiv:2101.11058 (2021)
26. Miller, E.G., Matsakis, N.E., Viola, P.A.: Learning from one example through shared densities on transforms. In: CVPR (2000)
27. Misra, I., Maaten, L.v.d.: Self-supervised learning of pretext-invariant representations. In: CVPR (2020)
28. Oord, A.v.d., Li, Y., Vinyals, O.: Representation learning with contrastive predictive coding. arXiv preprint arXiv:1807.03748 (2018)
29. Perrett, T., Masullo, A., Burghardt, T., Mirmehdi, M., Damen, D.: Temporal-relational crosstransformers for few-shot action recognition. In: CVPR (2021)
30. Qiu, Z., Yao, T., Mei, T.: Learning spatio-temporal representation with pseudo-3d residual networks. In: ICCV (2017)
31. Simonyan, K., Zisserman, A.: Two-stream convolutional networks for action recognition in videos. In: NeurIPS (2014)
32. Snell, J., Swersky, K., Zemel, R.S.: Prototypical networks for few-shot learning. In: NeurIPS (2017)
33. Soomro, K., Zamir, A.R., Shah, M.: UCF101: a dataset of 101 human actions classes from videos in the wild. arXiv preprint arXiv:1212.0402 (2012)
34. Su, J.-C., Maji, S., Hariharan, B.: When does self-supervision improve few-shot learning? In: Vedaldi, A., Bischof, H., Brox, T., Frahm, J.-M. (eds.) ECCV 2020. LNCS, vol. 12352, pp. 645–666. Springer, Cham (2020). https://doi.org/10.1007/978-3-030-58571-6_38
35. Sung, F., Yang, Y., Zhang, L., Xiang, T., Torr, P.H.S., Hospedales, T.M.: Learning to compare: Relation network for few-shot learning. In: CVPR (2018)

36. Sung, F., Zhang, L., Xiang, T., Hospedales, T.M., Yang, Y.: Learning to learn: Meta-critic networks for sample efficient learning. IEEE Access **7** (2019)
37. Tian, Y., Krishnan, D., Isola, P.: Contrastive multiview coding. In: Vedaldi, A., Bischof, H., Brox, T., Frahm, J.-M. (eds.) ECCV 2020. LNCS, vol. 12356, pp. 776–794. Springer, Cham (2020). https://doi.org/10.1007/978-3-030-58621-8_45
38. Tran, D., Bourdev, L., Fergus, R., Torresani, L., Paluri, M.: Learning spatiotemporal features with 3d convolutional networks. In: ICCV (2015)
39. Tran, D., Wang, H., Torresani, L., Ray, J., LeCun, Y., Paluri, M.: A closer look at spatiotemporal convolutions for action recognition. In: CVPR (2018)
40. Vaswani, A., et al.: Attention is all you need. In: NeurIPS (2017)
41. Vinyals, O., Blundell, C., Lillicrap, T., Kavukcuoglu, K., Wierstra, D.: Matching networks for one shot learning. In: NeurIPS (2016)
42. Wang, L., et al.: Temporal segment networks for action recognition in videos. TPAMI **41**, 2740–2755 (2018)
43. Wang, X., Girshick, R., Gupta, A., He, K.: Non-local neural networks. In: CVPR (2018)
44. Wang, Y.-X., Hebert, M.: Learning to learn: model regression networks for easy small sample learning. In: Leibe, B., Matas, J., Sebe, N., Welling, M. (eds.) ECCV 2016. LNCS, vol. 9910, pp. 616–634. Springer, Cham (2016). https://doi.org/10. 1007/978-3-319-46466-4_37
45. Wu, Z., Xiong, Y., Yu, S.X., Lin, D.: Unsupervised feature learning via non-parametric instance discrimination. In: CVPR (2018)
46. Ye, M., Zhang, X., Yuen, P.C., Chang, S.F.: Unsupervised embedding learning via invariant and spreading instance feature. In: CVPR (2019)
47. Zhang, H., Zhang, L., Qi, X., Li, H., Torr, P.H.S., Koniusz, P.: Few-shot action recognition with permutation-invariant attention. In: Vedaldi, A., Bischof, H., Brox, T., Frahm, J.-M. (eds.) ECCV 2020. LNCS, vol. 12350, pp. 525–542. Springer, Cham (2020). https://doi.org/10.1007/978-3-030-58558-7_31
48. Zhu, L., Yang, Y.: Compound memory networks for few-shot video classification. In: Ferrari, V., Hebert, M., Sminchisescu, C., Weiss, Y. (eds.) ECCV 2018. LNCS, vol. 11211, pp. 782–797. Springer, Cham (2018). https://doi.org/10.1007/978-3-030-01234-2_46
49. Zhu, L., Yang, Y.: Label independent memory for semi-supervised few-shot video classification. IEEE Ann. Hist. Comput. **44**, 273–2851 (2020)

PrivHAR: Recognizing Human Actions from Privacy-Preserving Lens

Carlos Hinojosa[1,2]($\boxtimes$), Miguel Marquez[1], Henry Arguello[1], Ehsan Adeli[2],
Li Fei-Fei[2], and Juan Carlos Niebles[2]

[1] Universidad Industrial de Santander, Bucaramanga, Colombia
[2] Stanford University, Stanford, USA
carlos.hinojosa@saber.uis.edu.co
https://carloshinojosa.me/project/privhar/

Abstract. The accelerated use of digital cameras prompts an increasing concern about privacy and security, particularly in applications such as action recognition. In this paper, we propose an optimizing framework to provide robust visual privacy protection along the human action recognition pipeline. Our framework parameterizes the camera lens to successfully degrade the quality of the videos to inhibit privacy attributes and protect against adversarial attacks while maintaining relevant features for activity recognition. We validate our approach with extensive simulations and hardware experiments.

Keywords: Privacy-preserving lens design · Human action recognition (HAR) · Adversarial training · Deep optics

1 Introduction

We are at the beginning of a new era of smart systems. From health care to video games, computer vision applications have provided successful solutions to real-world problems [3,24,28]. For decades, cameras have been engineered to imitate the human vision system, and machine learning algorithms are always constrained to be optimized using high-quality images as inputs. However, the abundance and growing uses of smart devices are also causing a social dilemma: we want intelligent systems (e.g., in our home) to recognize relevant events and assist us in our activities, but we also want to ensure they protect our privacy.

There have been some previous studies dealing with such a social dilemma. For instance, some early works rely on hand-crafted strategies, e.g., pixelation [52], blurring [33], face/object replacement [7], and person de-identification [1], to degrade sensitive information. More recently, Ren *et al.* [40] proposed an adversarial training strategy to learn to anonymize faces in videos and then perform activity detection. Similarly, using adversarial training, [56,57] proposed to optimize

---

Supplementary Information The online version contains supplementary material available at https://doi.org/10.1007/978-3-031-19772-7_19.

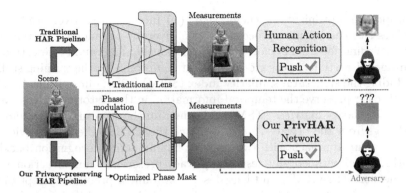

Fig. 1. Traditional HAR pipeline uses standard cameras that acquire visual details from the scene leading to privacy issues. We introduce PrivHAR, an adversarial optimization framework that learns a lens' phase mask to encode human action features and perform HAR while obscuring privacy-related attributes.

privacy attributes and recognition performance. However, all these methods rely on software-level processing of original high-resolution videos, which may already contain privacy-sensitive data. Hence, there is a possibility of these original videos being snatched by an attacker. Instead of developing new algorithms or designing software-level solutions that still rely on high-resolution images and videos as input, we believe that the privacy-preserving problem in computer vision should be addressed directly within the camera hardware, *i.e.*, sensible visual data should be protected before the images are acquired in the sensor.

Currently, few works have been developed in this direction. For instance, [41,42] proposed to use low-resolution cameras to create privacy-preserving anonymized videos and perform human action recognition. Also, Pittaluga *et al.* [37] introduced a defocusing lens to provide a certain level of privacy over a working region. On the other hand, several works used depth cameras to protect privacy and perform human action recognition [2,20]. These approaches rely on a fixed optical system; thus, their main contribution included designing an algorithm for a specific input type. More recently, [17] proposed to jointly design the lens of a camera and optimize a deep neural network to achieve two goals: privacy protection and human pose estimation. However, the formulation of the optimization in this work poses different problems: the privacy-preserving loss is not bounded as it maximizes an ℓ_2 term to enforce degradation, which may cause instability in the optimization; authors only used one human pose estimation model (OpenPose [6]) in all experiments and its not clear if the method works with other pose estimators. More importantly, to test and measure privacy, authors performed adversarial attacks after training the network; hence such attacks were not considered in the lens design.

In this paper, we address the problem of privacy-preserving human action recognition and propose a novel adversarial framework to provide robust privacy protection along the computer vision pipeline, see Fig. 1. We adopt the idea of end-to-end optimization of the camera lens and vision task [17,31,44] and propose an optimization scheme that: (**1**) Incorporates adversarial defense objectives into the learning process across a diversity of canonical privacy categories, including face, skin color, gender, relationship, and nudity detection. (**2**) Encourages distortions in the videos without compromising the training stability by including the structural similarity index (SSIM) [18] in our optimization loss. (**3**) To further preserve the temporal information in the distorted videos, we use temporal similarity matrices (TSM) and constrain the structure of the temporal embeddings from the private videos to match the TSM of the original video.

We test our approach with two popular human action recognition backbone networks. To experimentally test our privacy-preserving human action recognition network (PrivHAR) and lens design, we built a proof-of-concept optical system in our lab. Our testbed acquires distorted videos and their non-distorted version simultaneously. Our experimental results in hardware match the simulations. While we do observe a trade-off between Human Action Recognition (HAR) accuracy and image distortion level, our proposed PrivHAR system offers robust protection with reasonable accuracy.

2 Related Work

Human action recognition is a challenging task [35] and has many applications, such as video surveillance, human-computer interfaces, virtual reality, video games, and sports action analysis. Therefore, developing privacy-preserving approaches for HAR is even more challenging and has not been widely explored.

Human Action Recognition (HAR). Nowadays, there are multiple approaches in the computer vision literature for addressing the HAR problem. Some prior work relies on 2D CNNs to conduct video recognition [8,9,22,53]. A major drawback of 2D CNN approaches is not properly modeling the temporal dynamics. On the other hand, 3D CNN-based approaches use spatial and temporal convolutions over the 3D space to infer complicated spatio-temporal relationships. For instance, C3D [49] is a 3D CNN based on the VGG model that learns spatio-temporal features from a frame sequence. However, 3D CNNs are typically computationally heavy, making the deployment difficult. Therefore, many efforts on HAR focus on proposing new efficient architectures; for example, by decomposing 3D filters into separate 2D spatial and 1D temporal filters [23,50] or extending efficient 2D architectures to 3D counterparts. Moreover, RubiksNet [13] is a hardware-efficient architecture for HAR based on a shift layer that learns to perform shift operations jointly in spatial and temporal context. We build our proposed PrivHAR using both C3D and RubiksNet.

Privacy Protection in Computer Vision. Currently, few works address the privacy-preserving HAR problem. We divide prior work into software-level and hardware-level protection, where we consider the latter more robust to attacks.

Software-Level Privacy-Preserving HAR. Most prior privacy-preserving works apply different computer vision algorithms to the video data after their acquisition. The literature has relied on domain knowledge and hand-crafted

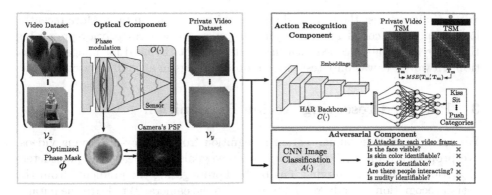

Fig. 2. Our proposed end-to-end framework. Our optical component consists of a camera with two thin convex lenses and a phase mask between them. We achieve robust privacy protection by training an adversarial framework under three goals: (1) to learn to add aberrations to the lens surface such that the acquired videos are distorted to obscure private attributes while still preserving features to (2) achieve high video action recognition accuracy, and (3) being robust to adversarial attacks.

approaches, such as pixelation, blurring, and face/object replacement, to protect sensitive information [1,7,33]. These methods can be useful in settings when we know in advance what to protect in the scene. More recent works propose a more general approach that learns privacy-preserving encodings through adversarial training [5,36,56]. These methods learn to degrade or inhibit privacy attributes while maintaining important features to perform inference tasks and provide more robust videos to adversarial attacks. Ren *et al.* [40] use adversarial training to learn a video anonymizer and remove facial features for activity detection. Similarly, Wu *et al.* [56,57] proposed an adversarial framework that learns a degradation transform for the video inputs using a 2D convolution layer. These works optimize the trade-off between action recognition performance and the associated privacy budget on the degraded video. Although these software-level approaches preserve privacy, the acquired images are not protected.

Hardware-Level Privacy-Preserving HAR. These approaches rely on the camera hardware to add an extra layer of security by removing sensitive data during the imaging sensing. Prior hardware-level privacy-preserving approaches use low-resolution cameras to anonymize videos, i.e., the videos are intentionally captured to be in special low-quality conditions that only allow for the recognition of some events or activities while avoiding the unwanted leak of the identity information for the human subjects in the video [39,42]. In [37,38], two optical designs were proposed that filter or block sensitive information directly from the incident light-field before sensor measurements acquisition, enabling k-anonymity and privacy protection by using a camera with defocusing lens. In particular, they show how to select a defocus blur that provides a certain level of privacy over a working region within the sensor size limits; however, only using optical defocus for privacy may be susceptible to reverse engineering. In addition, the authors did not test their method on the action recognition task. More recently, [55] proposed a coded aperture camera system to perform privacy-preserving HAR directly from encoded measurements without the need for image restoration. However, it was only tested for indoor settings in a small dataset.

3 Privacy-Preserving Action Recognition

We are interested in human action recognition from privacy-preserving videos. We propose a framework to accomplish three goals: 1) to learn the parameters of a robust privacy-preserving lens by backpropagating the gradients from the action recognition and adversarial branches to the camera; 2) to learn the parameters of an action recognition network to perform HAR on the private videos with high accuracy; 3) to obtain private videos that are robust to adversarial attacks. Our framework (Fig. 2) consists of three parts: optical, action recognition, and an adversarial component.

The optical component consists of a camera with two thin convex lenses and a phase mask between them. Our simulated camera takes a video $\mathbf{V_x} \in \mathbb{R}_+^{w \times h \times 3 \times T} = \{\mathbf{X}_t\}_{t=1}^T$ as input, which has $w \times h$ pixels and T frames, and outputs the corresponding distorted video $\mathbf{V_y} \in \mathbb{R}_+^{w \times h \times 3 \times T}$. Formally, $\mathbf{V_y} = O(\mathbf{V_x})$, where we denote our designed camera as the function $O(\cdot)$, which distorts every single frame $\mathbf{X}_t \in \mathbb{R}_+^{w \times h \times 3}$, and produces the respective *private* frames $\mathbf{Y}_t \in \mathbb{R}_+^{w \times h \times 3}$. Then, the distorted video $\mathbf{V_y}$ passes through the action recognition component where a convolutional neural network C predicts the class labels. Besides, $\mathbf{V_y}$ also passes through the adversarial component where an attribute estimator network A tries to predict the private information (attributes) from the distorted video. All three components consist of neural networks with trainable parameters, and the whole framework is trained adversarially. At the end of the optimization process, we obtain the optimal camera lens parameters θ_o^*, and the optimal action recognition parameters θ_c^*. Hence, the loss function of our adversarial framework is formulated as follows:

$$\theta_o^*, \theta_c^* = \arg\min_{\theta_o, \theta_c} L(O) + L(C) - L(A), \tag{1}$$

where $L(O)$, $L(C)$, and $L(A)$ are the loss functions for our optical component, action recognition component, and adversarial component, respectively.

During inference, we can construct a camera lens using the optimal parameters θ_o^* that acquires degraded images, on which our network C can perform HAR. Since we develop our protection directly in the optics (camera lens), it provides an extra layer of protection and, hence, is more difficult for a hacker to attack our system to reveal the person's identity. One could also deploy a less secure software-only approach implementing image degradation post-acquisition. A hybrid solution consists of designing an embedded chipset responsible for distorting the videos immediately after the camera sensor.

3.1   Optical Component

The main goal of the optical component in our adversarial framework PrivHAR (Fig. 2) is to design a phase mask to visually distort videos (hence obscuring privacy-sensitive attributes), encode the physical characteristics and preserve human action features to perform HAR. We adopted a similar strategy as the authors in [17,44] to couple the modeling and design of two essential operators in the imaging system: wave propagation and phase modulation.

Image Formation Model. We model the image acquisition process using the point spread function (PSF) defined in terms of the lens surface profile to emulate the wavefront propagation and train the parameters of the refractive lens. Considering by the Fresnel approximation and the paraxial regime [14], for incoherent illumination, the PSF can be described by

$$H(u', v') = |\mathcal{F}^{-1}\{\mathcal{F}\{t_L(u,v) \cdot t_\phi(u,v) \cdot W(u,v)\} \cdot T(f_u, f_v)\}|^2, \tag{2}$$

where $W(u,v)$ is the incoming wavefront, $T(\cdot)$ represents the transfer function with (f_u, f_v) as the spatial frequencies, $t_\phi(u,v) = \exp(-ik\phi(u,v))$ with $\phi(u,v)$ as the lens phase mask and $k = 2\pi/\lambda$ as the wavenumber, $t_L(\cdot)$ denotes the light wave propagation phase with $t_L(u,v) = \exp\left(-i\frac{k}{2z}(u^2 + v^2)\right)$ with z as the object-lens distance, $\mathcal{F}\{\cdot\}$ denotes the 2D Fourier transform, and (u', v') is the spatial coordinate on the camera plane. The values of $\phi(\cdot)$ are modelled via the Zernike polynomials with $\phi(u,v) = \mathcal{R}_{\bar{n}}^{\bar{m}}(\sqrt{u^2 + v^2}) \cdot \cos(\arctan(v/u))$, where $\mathcal{R}(\cdot)$ represents the radial polynomial function [27], $\bar{m}$ and $\bar{n}$ are nonnegative integers with $\bar{n} \geq \bar{m} \geq 0$. To train the phase mask values using our PrivHAR, we discretize the phase mask $\phi(\cdot)$ as:

$$\phi = \sum_{j=1}^{q} \alpha_j \mathbf{Z}_j, \tag{3}$$

where $\mathbf{Z}_j$ denotes the j-th Zernike polynomial in Noll notation, and α_j is the corresponding coefficient [4]. Each Zernike polynomial describes a wavefront aberration [27]; hence the phase mask ϕ is formed by the linear combination of all aberrations. In this regard, the optical element parameterized by ϕ can be seen as an optical encoder, where the coefficients α_j determine the data transformation. Therefore, our adversarial training finds a set of coefficients $\theta_o^* = \{\alpha_j\}_{j=1}^{q}$ that provides the maximum visual distortion of the scene but allows to extract relevant features to perform HAR. Using the defined PSF-based propagation model (assuming that image formation is a shift-invariant convolution of the image and PSF), the acquired private images for each RGB channel can be modelled as:

$$\mathbf{Y}_\ell = \mathcal{G}_\ell(\mathbf{H}_\ell * \mathbf{X}_\ell) + \boldsymbol{\eta}_\ell, \tag{4}$$

where $\mathbf{X}_\ell \in \mathbb{R}_+^{w \times h}$ represents the discrete image from the ℓ channel, with each pixel value in $[0,1]$; $\mathbf{H}_\ell$ denotes the discretized version of the PSF [14] in Eq. (2) for the channel ℓ, $\boldsymbol{\eta}_\ell \in \mathbb{R}^{w \times h}$ represents the Gaussian noise in the sensor, and

$\mathcal{G}_\ell(\cdot) : \mathbb{R}^{w \times h} \to \mathbb{R}^{w \times h}$ is the camera response function, which is modeled as a linear function. Please see our supplementary document for a schematic diagram of the light propagation in our model.

Loss Function. To encourage image degradation, we train our network to minimize the quality of the acquired image by our camera $\mathbf{Y} = \{\mathbf{Y}_\ell\}_{\ell=1}^3$ in comparison with the original image $\mathbf{X} = \{\mathbf{X}_\ell\}_{\ell=1}^3$. Instead of maximizing the ℓ_2 norm error between the two images as previous works did [17], we use the structural similarity index (SSIM) [54] in our optimization loss to measure quality. The ℓ_2 norm does not have an upper bound; hence maximizing it to enforce degradation causes instability in the optimization. On the other hand, the SSIM function is bounded, which leads to better stability during training. Specifically, the SSIM value ranges between 0 and 1, where values near 1 (better quality) indicate more perceptual similarity between the two compared images. Then, we define the loss function for our camera lens optimization as:

$$L(O) \triangleq SSIM(\mathbf{X}, \mathbf{Y}). \tag{5}$$

Since we encourage distortion in the camera's output images/videos, the $L(O)$ loss is minimized in our adversarial training algorithm, see Algorithm 1.

3.2   Action Recognition Component

We can use any neural network architecture in our adversarial framework to perform human action recognition. In this work, without loss of generality, we adopt two HAR CNN architectures: the well-known C3D [49], and the Rubkisnet [13], a more recent and efficient architecture for HAR. For a set of private videos, we assume that the output of the classifier C is a set of action class labels $\mathcal{S}_C$. Then, we can use the standard cross-entropy function $\mathcal{H}$ as the classifier's loss.

On the other hand, since our degradation model distorts each frame of the input video separately (2D convolution), part of the temporal information could be lost, decreasing the performance of the HAR CNN significantly. To preserve temporal information, we use temporal similarity matrices (TSMs). TSMs are useful representations for human action recognition and have been employed in several works [12,21,34,45] due to their robustness against dynamic view changes of the camera when paired with appropriate feature representation. Unlike previous works, we propose using TSMs as a proxy to keep the temporal information (features) similar after distortion: we build a TSM for the original and private videos and compare their structures. Specifically, we take the embeddings $\hat{e}$ from the last convolutional layer of our HAR CNN architecture and compute the TSM values using the negative of the squared euclidean distance, i.e., $(\mathbf{T_m}')_{n_1 n_2} = -\|\hat{e}_{n_1} - \hat{e}_{n_2}\|^2$. Then, we calculate the mean square error (MSE) between the $\mathbf{T_m}'$ and the TSM from the input video $\mathbf{T_m}$, which was computed similarly using the last convolutional layer of the corresponding pretrained HAR CNN (non-privacy) network. We define the action recognition objective as:

$$L(C) \triangleq \mathcal{H}(\mathcal{S}_C, C(\mathcal{V}_y)) + MSE(\mathbf{T_m}, \mathbf{T_m}'), \tag{6}$$

where $\mathcal{V}_y$ denotes the set of E private videos: $\mathcal{V}_y = \{\mathbf{V_y}^e\}_{e=1}^E = \{O(\mathbf{V_x}^e)\}_{e=1}^E$.

3.3   Adversarial Component and Training Algorithm

The attacks that an adversarial agent could perform to our privacy-preserving pipeline depends on the definition of privacy. There are different ways to measure privacy and this is, in general, not a straightforward task. For example, in smart homes with video surveillance, one might often want to avoid disclosure of the face or identity of persons. Therefore, an adversarial agent could try to attack our system by training a face detection network. However, there are other privacy-related attributes, such as race, gender, or age, that an adversarial agent could also wanted to attack too. In this work, we define the adversarial attack as a classification problem, where a CNN network A takes a private video $\mathbf{V_y}$ as input and tries to predict the corresponding private information. Therefore, the goal of our adversarial training is to try that the predictions from A diverges from the set of class labels $\mathcal{S}_A$ that describe the private information within the scene. To train the attribute estimator network, we also use the cross-entropy $\mathcal{H}$ function and define the adversarial loss as:

$$L(A) \triangleq \mathcal{H}(\mathcal{S}_A, A(\mathcal{V}_y)). \tag{7}$$

Algorithm 1 summarizes the proposed adversarial training scheme. Before performing the adversarial training, we first train each framework component separately without privacy concern to obtain the optimal performance on each task. Specifically, we train the optical component O by minimizing $1 - L(O)$ to acquire videos without distortions, i.e., $\mathbf{V_y}$ videos are very similar to the corresponding input $\mathbf{V_x}$. We also train the HAR network C by minimizing $\mathcal{H}(\mathcal{S}_C, C(\mathcal{V}_x))$, obtaining the highest action recognition accuracy (the upper bound). Finally, we train the attribute estimator network A by minimizing $\mathcal{H}(\mathcal{S}_A, A(\mathcal{V}_x))$, thus obtaining the highest classification accuracy (the upper bound). After initialization, we start the adversarial training shown in Algorithm 1, where, for each epoch and every batch, we first acquire the private videos with our camera O. Then, we update the parameters of the camera θ_o by freezing the attribute estimator network parameters θ_a and minimizing the weighted sum $L(O) + \gamma_1 L(C) - \gamma_2 L(A)$, shown on line 4 of the algorithm. Similarly, we update the parameters of the HAR network θ_c by freezing the attribute estimator network parameters and using the private videos acquired on line 3 to

---

Algorithm 1: Our Adversarial Training Algorithm.

Input   : Video Dataset $\mathcal{V}_x = \{\mathbf{V_x}^e\}_{e=1}^E$. Hyperparameters $\beta_o, \beta_c, \beta_a, \gamma_1, \gamma_2$
Output: $\theta_o, \theta_c, \theta_a$
Function $Train(\mathcal{V}_x, \beta_o, \beta_c, \beta_a, \gamma_1, \gamma_2)$

1   **for** *every epoch* **do**
2   **for** *every batch of videos* $\mathcal{V}_x^B$ **do**
3        $\mathcal{V}_y^B = O(\mathcal{V}_x^B)$ ▷ Acquire private videos
4        $\theta_o \leftarrow \theta_o - \beta_o \Delta_{\theta_o}(L(O) + \gamma_1 L(C) - \gamma_2 L(A))$
5        $\theta_c \leftarrow \theta_c - \beta_c \Delta_{\theta_c}(L(C))$
6        $\theta_a \leftarrow \theta_a - \beta_a \Delta_{\theta_a}(L(A))$
7   **return** $\mathbf{X}_e$

---

minimize $L(C)$. Finally, we perform the adversarial attack by minimizing $L(A)$ and updating the parameters of the attribute estimator network θ_a while the camera and HAR network parameters are fixed. Contrary to the prior work [17], our training scheme jointly models the privacy-preserving optics with HAR and adversarial attacks during training.

4 Experimental Results

Datasets. Given the lack of a public dataset containing both human actions and privacy attribute labels on the same videos, we follow the same approach as authors in [56] to train our proposed adversarial framework. Specifically, we perform cross-dataset training using three datasets: the HMDB51 [25], the VISPR [32], and the PA-HMDB51 [56]. The VISPR dataset contains 22,167 images annotated with 68 privacy attributes which include: semi-nudity, face, race, gender, skin color, among others. The attributes of a specific image are labeled as "present" or "not-present". The HMDB51 dataset comprises 6,849 video clips from 51 action categories, with each category containing at least 101 clips. The Privacy-annotated HMDB51 (PA-HMDB51) is a small subset of the HMDB51 dataset, containing 515 videos, with privacy attribute labels. For each video in PA-HMDB51, there are five attributes annotated on a per-frame basis: skin color, face, gender, nudity, and relationship. Similar to VISPR, the labels are binary and specify if an attribute is present or not in the frame.

Training Set. We train our models using cross-dataset training on HMDB51 and VISPR datasets. Specifically, we exclude the 515 videos in the PA-HMDB51 dataset from HMDB51 and use the remainder videos to train our action recognition component. On the other hand, we use the VISPR dataset with the same five privacy attributes available in the PA-HMDB51 dataset: skin color, face, gender, nudity, and relationship, to train our adversarial component.

Testing Set. We use PA-HMDB51 to test our action recognition and adversarial components. This dataset includes both action and privacy attribute labels.

Training Details. In Algorithm 1, we set initial learning rates $\beta_o = 3 \times 10^{-3}, \beta_c = \beta_a = 10^{-4}$, and $\gamma_1 = 0.7, \gamma_2 = 0.3$ and applied an exponential learning decay with a decay factor of 0.1 that is triggered in the epoch 25. We trained the end-to-end PrivHAR model for 50 epochs, with batch size of 8, and use the Stochastic Gradient Descent (SGD) optimizer to update parameters $\theta_o, \theta_c, \theta_a$. To perform the adversarial attacks during training (adversarial component in Fig. 2), we use the ResNet-50 architecture. Training the PrivHAR for 50 epochs took about 6 h on 8 Nvidia TITAN RTX GPU with 24 GB of memory.

4.1 Metrics and Evaluation Method

To measure the overall performance of PrivHAR, we evaluate the action recognition task and privacy protection separately. First, to test action recognition, we pass the testing videos through our designed camera lens $O(\cdot)$ to obtain the private videos. Next, we use our learned HAR backbone $C(\cdot)$ to get the predicted actions on each private video. Similarly as C3D [49], and RubiksNet [13], we report the standard average classification accuracy, denoted by A_C.

On the other hand, to evaluate privacy protection, we follow the same evaluation protocol adopted by authors in [56]. Specifically, assuming that an attacker has access to the set of private videos acquired with our $O(\cdot)$ and the corresponding privacy attribute labels, then, the attacker can train different CNNs to try to steal sensitive information from the privacy-protected videos acquired with our camera. To empirically verify that our protection is robust to this kind of attack, we separately train ten different classification networks using the private images acquired with our camera, i.e., these CNNs are different from the selected CNN used during training. To train these networks, we use the same training set defined in the previous section and fix our camera component with the optimal learned parameters θ_o^*. We use the following architectures: ResNet-$\{50, 101\}$ [16], Wide-ResNet-$\{50, 101\}$ [58], MobileNet-V2 [43], Inception-$\{V1, V3\}$ [46,47], MNASNet-$\{0.5, 0.75, 1.0\}$ [48]. Among these CNNs, eight randomly selected networks start from ImageNet-pretrained weights. The remaining two models were trained from scratch (random initialization) to eliminate the possibility that the initialization with ImageNet weights affects the correct predictions. After training, we evaluate each model on our defined testing set (videos from PA-HMDB51) and select the model with the highest performance. Similar to previous works [10,32,56,57], we adopt the Class-based Mean Average Precision (C-MAP) [32]

Table 1. Quantitative Results. (a) Multiple ablation studies of our method for two different HAR backbones, C3D and RubiksNet: each component in Fig. 2 is trained separately (No-Adversarial); not using the TSM matrices to preserve temporal information (No-TSM); 50, 100, and 200 Zernike polynomials to design our lens. (b) Comparison of our method (**PrivHAR**) with: three additional privacy-preserving approaches: defocusing, low-resolution cameras, and the lens used in [17]; and the privacy-preserving deep action recognition (PDAR) framework with different learning approaches (GRL, K-Beam, and Entropy) [56]. Accuracy values are reported in percentage.

(a) Ablation Study

C3D Backbone

Experiment	SSIM↓	A_C ↑	A_A ↓	P ↑
No-Adversarial	0.603	51.1	69.1	38.6
No-TSM	0.612	59.9	69.7	40.2
Zernike-50	0.643	58.3	70.5	39.2
Zernike-100	0.629	58.8	69.3	40.4
Zernike-200	0.612	**63.3**	**68.9**	**41.52**

RubiksNet Backbone

Experiment	SSIM↓	A_C ↑	A_A ↓	P ↑
No-Adversarial	0.592	57.6	68.2	40.9
No-TSM	0.599	72.3	67.6	44.6
Zernike-50	0.618	70.2	69.2	42.8
Zernike-100	0.601	71.9	68.4	43.9
Zernike-200	0.588	**73.8**	**66.5**	**46.1**

(b) Comparisons.

Methods	SSIM↓	A_C ↑	A_A ↓	P ↑
No-privacy (C3D)	1.0	71.1	76.1	35.8
No-privacy (RubiksNet)	1.0	85.2	76.1	37.3
Low-resolution [41]	0.686	48.3	70.9	36.3
Lens in [17]-RubiksNet	0.608	52.4	69.4	38.6
Defocus [37]	0.688	62.1	72.5	38.1
PDAR-GRL [56]	–	63.3	70.5	40.2
PDAR-K-Beam [56]	–	63.5	69.3	41.4
PDAR-Entropy [56]	–	67.3	70.3	41.2
PrivHAR-C3D	0.612	63.3	68.9	41.7
PrivHAR-RubiksNet	0.588	**73.8**	**66.5**	**46.1**

to assess the performance of the models. Specifically, we compute the Average Precision (AP) per class, which is the area under the Precision-Recall curve of the privacy-related attribute. Hence, C-MAP corresponds to the average of the AP scores across all the privacy-related attributes. We also denote C-MAP as A_A in our experiments (lower is better).

To measure image degradation, we use the structural similarity index (SSIM) metric [18]. Large values of SSIM indicate high quality. Thus, in general, we expect to achieve the minimum SSIM values while achieving high A_C and low A_A for HAR and Adversarial accuracy, respectively. Besides, we combine the two accuracy metrics (A_C and A_A) into one using the harmonic mean as:

$$P = \frac{2}{\frac{1}{A_C} + \frac{1}{1-A_A}} = \frac{2A_C(1 - A_A)}{1 - A_A + A_C}, \tag{8}$$

and we expect to achieve the maximum P value.

4.2 Simulation Experiments

Ablation Studies. We conduct multiple experiments to investigate different configurations for our adversarial approach. We show the quantitative results of our ablations studies in Table 1(a), for C3D and RubiksNet. We first train the optical and action recognition components to obtain privacy-preserving videos and perform HAR on them. Then, we fix the optical component and train the adversarial CNN to recover the privacy attributes from the videos. We refer to this experiment as 'No-adversarial' in the Table 1(a). Note that this approach is similar to the prior work [17] but on a different vision task. In our second experiment (No-TSM), we test the performance of our proposed PrivHAR with

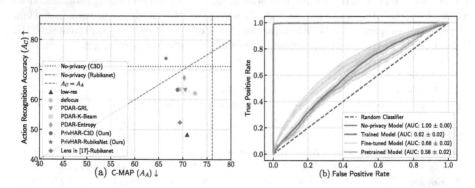

Fig. 3. (a) Trade-off between privacy protection and action recognition on PA-HMDB51. Vertical and horizontal, dashed and dotted, purple lines indicate A_A and A_C on the original non-privacy videos, using RubiksNet and C3D backbones for HAR, respectively. The red dashed line indicates where $A_A = A_C$. (b) Face recognition performance on private images (from LFW [19] dataset) acquired with our optimized lens. (Color figure online)

$q = 200$ Zernike coefficients when not using TSMs to preserve the temporal information. We can observe from the table that, in general, the A_C decreases, which evidences the importance of using TSMs to preserve temporal information. The third experiment consists of training our adversarial framework with a different number of Zernike coefficients. Specifically, we trained our PrivHAR using $q = 50$, $q = 100$, and $q = 200$ Zernike coefficients, see Eq. (3). In general, increasing the number of Zernike coefficients leads to better encoding; hence the A_C value increases while the SSIM decreases. However, memory consumption also increases since we need to store all the Zernike bases. In general, we use $q = 200$ Zernike coefficients as a default value in all other experiments. The tables show that the best HAR backbone for our proposed PrivHAR network is RubiksNet. We observed that when using RubiksNet, PrivHAR achieves higher distortions (lower SSIM) affecting the performance of the adversarial component while achieving high action recognition accuracy. We empirically verify that RubiksNet is better at preserving the temporal information than C3D; hence it performs better even with high image distortions. Besides, we observed that TSM helps more the C3D backbone, which is more affected by the distortions generated by our lens.

Attribute Estimator Network Performance. The values of A_A reported in the tables corresponds to the C-MAP obtained by the model with highest performance on our testing set, as described in Sect. 4.1. To analyze the performance of the attribute estimator networks, and hence our privacy protection, we plot the receiver operating characteristic (ROC) and Precision-Recall (PR) curves. In our supplementary document, we show the ROC and PR curves of the attribute estimator network which achieves the best performance on the privacy-preserving images/videos acquired with our camera. Specifically, considering the area under curve (AUC) of the PR curves, we obtain an average precision (AP) of 0.94, 0.72, 0.97, 0.52, 0.18 for skin color, face, gender, nudity, and relationship, respectively. These values of AP are very close to those obtained by a random classifier (null hypothesis), which are 0.95, 0.71, 0.97, 0.58, 0.17. Therefore, based on the Fisher's exact test [51], the best attribute estimator network on our privacy-protected images is not significantly different from the random classifier (p-value< 0.01).

Comparison with Other Methods. We compare our proposed PrivHAR with two traditional privacy-preserving approaches: low-resolution [42] and defocusing cameras [37]. We simulate both types of cameras and perform a similar training as shown in Fig. 2. To implement the low-resolution approach, we manually downsampled the images with a resolution of 16×16. In addition, we compare our proposed PrivHAR with the privacy-preserving deep action recognition (PDAR) framework with different learning approaches (GRL, K-Beam, and Entropy) [56]. We present the quantitative results in Table 1(b), where all methods use the C3D backbone for HAR if not otherwise specified. We also include our PrivHAR using RubiksNet for comparison. Furthermore, we use the lens designed in [17], which was optimized for human pose estimation and did not consider adversarial attacks during training, for distort the videos and then perform HAR on them. This approach obtains an $A_C = 52.4\%$ using Rubik-sNet, which is 21.4% lower than our PrivHAR-RubiksNet results. In addition, the trade-off between privacy protection and action recognition is visualized in Fig. 3(a), which shows PrivHAR obtains the best privacy while maintaining high accuracy.

Face Recognition Performance. We follow the same face recognition validation on private images acquired by the optimized lens as the prior work in [17]. Specifically, we use an implementation of the face recognition network ArcFace [11], train on Microsoft Celeb (MS-Celeb-1M) [15] and test on LFW [19] datasets. Figure 3(b) show the ROC curves for each testing approach: "No-privacy Model" uses the pretrained ArcFace model on the original (non-private) images; "Pre-trained model" uses the pretrained ArcFace model on the private version of each dataset; "Trained model" uses an ArcFace model trained from scratch using the private version of the MS-Celeb-1M dataset; "Fine-tuned Model" uses a pre-trained ArcFace model fine-tuned with the private version of the MS-Celeb-1M dataset. From the figure, we can conclude that the ArcFace model does not perform well on the images generated by our designed lens as the best performance is achieved by the fine-tuned model (AUC= 0.68), which is still close to random classifier's performance. See results with others datasets in our supplementary.

Qualitative Results. We qualitatively compare our approach with low resolution and defocusing cameras in Fig. 4. We show results on three example videos from the PA-HMDB51 dataset. The first row of the figure shows the non-privacy video acquired using a standard lens and the ground truth (GT) of the actions for reference. As observed, our lens achieves a higher distortion but still performs action recognition. The last video shows a failure case of our method.

Deconvolution Attack. Suppose the attacker has access to the camera or a large collection of acquired images with our proposed camera. In that case, the attacker could use deconvolution methods (blind and non-blind) on our distorted images to recover people's identities. To test the robustness of our designed lens to deconvolution attacks, we assume both scenarios: having access to the camera, we can easily get the PSF (by imaging a point of source light) and hence use a non-blind deconvolution method, e.g. the Wiener deconvolution; on the other hand, not having access to the camera but a large collection of our distorted images then we can train a blind deconvolution network, e.g. DeblurGAN [26]. We describe the training details in our supplementary document. In Fig. 5 we show the results with two video frames from the HMDB51 dataset with people near the camera. We observed that the distortion achieved by PrivHAR-RubiksNet (RBN) is significantly higher than C3D; hence it is more difficult for DeblurGAN and Wiener deconvolution to recover the scene. In both cases, using C3D or RBN, the distortion is sufficient to avoid recovering face details, and the people's identity is protected. However, some attributes are visible in the recovered scene when using PrivHAR-C3D. It is possible to obtain a lens with C3D that provides more distortion; however, the HAR accuracy could be affected.

Fig. 4. Qualitative Results on PA-HMDB51. Each row shows standard no-privacy videos and ground truth (GT) labels (top); and predictions from our optimized lens (PrivHAR-RubiksNet, bottom) to low-resolution (second) and defocus (third) cameras.

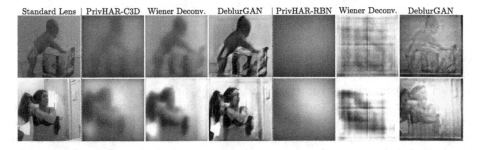

Fig. 5. Deconvolution of private images acquired with our optimized lens using C3D and RubiksNet (RBN) backbones in PrivHAR. The images acquired with our lens are robust to deconvolution, and DeblurGAN cannot recover people's identities.

4.3   Hardware Experiments

To demonstrate the PrivHAR's capability of action recognition, we conduct experimental validations acquiring four human actions: jump, clap, punch, and hair brush in our Lab. We emulate the lens designed with our PrivHAR adversarial framework using a deformable mirror-based 4f system [29,30]. We first train our system using $q = 15$ Zernike coefficients and then load the learned coefficients to the deformable mirror an calibrate the PSF. After calibration we obtained the following learned Zernike coefficients: $\{\alpha_1 = \alpha_2 = \alpha_3 = 0, \alpha_4 = -0.45, \alpha_5 = 0.36, \alpha_6 = 0.24, \alpha_7 = 0.6, \alpha_8 = -0.4, \alpha_9 = -0.11, \alpha_{10} = 0.69, \alpha_{11} = -0.31, \alpha_{12} = -0.15, \alpha_{13} = -0.70, \alpha_{14} = -0.85, \alpha_{15} = 0.38\}$. The resulting PSF and the used

Fig. 6. Experimental setup scheme and some results on acquired videos. The deformable mirror configuration and characterized PSF are shown in the upper left corner. The right column shows the non-privacy and private videos obtained with our camera.

phase mask are presented in Fig. 6(Left). Finally, we placed our proof-of-concept system on a movable table to take it out of our Lab and acquire real outdoor images. In Fig. 6(Right), we show the human action recognition for two video sequences recorded by our 4F-based system. The ground truth and the private version were illustrated in the first and second rows, respectively. Outdoor system configuration, additional qualitative and quantitative results, and detailed description of the proof-of-concept system can be found in the supplement.

5   Discussion and Conclusion

We present PrivHAR, a framework for detecting human actions from a privacy-preserving lens. Our framework consists of three components: the hardware component that comprises a camera with a privacy-preserving lens, whose parameters are learned during training and its main function is to obscure sensitive private information; the action recognition component that aims to preserve temporal information using temporal similarity matrices and performs HAR on the degraded video; and the adversarial component, which performs five attacks to the private videos seeking to recover the hidden attributes.

Limitations. One limitation of our simulated experiments is that we test our approach on a relatively small set due to the lack of a public dataset containing human actions and privacy attribute labels on the same videos. As future work, we plan to build a video dataset using our proposed optical system, which allows us to acquire both RGB and private videos. In addition, the deformable mirror is the main limitation of the proof-of-concept optical system. This device can only use $q = 15$ Zernike Polynomials, limiting the scene's level of distortion. For now, our small-scale tests show results consistent with our extensive experiments.

Conclusion. We extensively evaluated and experimentally validated our approach in simulations and a hardware prototype. Our qualitative and quantitative results indicate a trade-off between image degradation and HAR accuracy. Our optics modeling can generally be integrated into an embedded chipset or used as a software-only solution by applying the image degradation post-acquisition to deploy a less secure system. However, we show that the learned lens can be deployed as a camera, which provides a higher security layer. One could connect it to an Nvidia Jetson for real-time privacy-preserving HAR.

References

1. Agrawal, P., Narayanan, P.: Person de-identification in videos. IEEE Trans. Circuits Syst. Video Technol. **21**(3), 299–310 (2011)
2. Ahmad, Z., Illanko, K., Khan, N., Androutsos, D.: Human action recognition using convolutional neural network and depth sensor data. In: Proceedings of the 2019 International Conference on Information Technology and Computer Communications, pp. 1–5 (2019)
3. Bommasani, R., et al.: On the opportunities and risks of foundation models. arXiv preprint arXiv:2108.07258 (2021)
4. Born, M., Wolf, E.: Principles of Optics: Electromagnetic Theory of Propagation, Interference and Diffraction of Light. Elsevier, Amsterdam (2013)
5. Brkic, K., Sikiric, I., Hrkac, T., Kalafatic, Z.: I know that person: generative full body and face de-identification of people in images. In: 2017 IEEE Conference on Computer Vision and Pattern Recognition Workshops (CVPRW), pp. 1319–1328. IEEE (2017)
6. Cao, Z., Hidalgo, G., Simon, T., Wei, S.E., Sheikh, Y.: OpenPose: realtime multi-person 2d pose estimation using part affinity fields. IEEE TPAMI **43**(1), 172–186 (2019)
7. Chen, D., Chang, Y., Yan, R., Yang, J.: Tools for protecting the privacy of specific individuals in video. EURASIP J. Adv. Signal Process. **2007**, 1–9 (2007)
8. Chollet, F.: Xception: deep learning with depthwise separable convolutions. In: Proceedings of the IEEE Conference on Computer Vision and Pattern Recognition, pp. 1251–1258 (2017)
9. Christoph, R., Pinz, F.A.: Spatiotemporal residual networks for video action recognition. In: Advances in Neural Information Processing Systems, pp. 3468–3476 (2016)
10. Dave, I.R., Chen, C., Shah, M.: SPAct: self-supervised privacy preservation for action recognition. In: Proceedings of the IEEE/CVF Conference on Computer Vision and Pattern Recognition, pp. 20164–20173 (2022)
11. Deng, J., Guo, J., Xue, N., Zafeiriou, S.: ArcFace: additive angular margin loss for deep face recognition. In: Proceedings of the IEEE/CVF Conference on Computer Vision and Pattern Recognition, pp. 4690–4699 (2019)
12. Dwibedi, D., Aytar, Y., Tompson, J., Sermanet, P., Zisserman, A.: Counting out time: class agnostic video repetition counting in the wild. In: Proceedings of the IEEE/CVF Conference on Computer Vision and Pattern Recognition, pp. 10387–10396 (2020)
13. Fan, L., et al.: RubiksNet: learnable 3D-shift for efficient video action recognition. In: Vedaldi, A., Bischof, H., Brox, T., Frahm, J.-M. (eds.) ECCV 2020. LNCS, vol. 12364, pp. 505–521. Springer, Cham (2020). https://doi.org/10.1007/978-3-030-58529-7_30
14. Goodman, J.W.: Introduction to Fourier Optics, 4th edn. Macmillan Learning, New York (2017)

330 C. Hinojosa et al.

15. Guo, Y., Zhang, L., Hu, Y., He, X., Gao, J.: MS-Celeb-1M: a dataset and bench-mark for large-scale face recognition. In: Leibe, B., Matas, J., Sebe, N., Welling, M. (eds.) ECCV 2016. LNCS, vol. 9907, pp. 87–102. Springer, Cham (2016). https://doi.org/10.1007/978-3-319-46487-9_6

16. He, K., Zhang, X., Ren, S., Sun, J.: Deep residual learning for image recognition. In: Proceedings of the IEEE Conference on Computer Vision and Pattern Recognition, pp. 770–778 (2016)

17. Hinojosa, C., Niebles, J.C., Arguello, H.: Learning privacy-preserving optics for human pose estimation. In: ICCV, pp. 2573–2582, October 2021

18. Hore, A., Ziou, D.: Image quality metrics: PSNR vs. SSIM. In: 2010 20th International Conference on Pattern Recognition, pp. 2366–2369. IEEE (2010)

19. Huang, G.B., Mattar, M., Lee, H., Learned-Miller, E.: Learning to align from scratch. In: NIPS (2012)

20. Ji, X., Cheng, J., Feng, W., Tao, D.: Skeleton embedded motion body partition for human action recognition using depth sequences. Signal Process. **143**, 56–68 (2018)

21. Junejo, I.N., Dexter, E., Laptev, I., Perez, P.: View-independent action recognition from temporal self-similarities. IEEE Trans. Pattern Anal. Mach. Intell. **33**(1), 172–185 (2010)

22. Karpathy, A., Toderici, G., Shetty, S., Leung, T., Sukthankar, R., Fei-Fei, L.: Large-scale video classification with convolutional neural networks. In: Proceedings of the IEEE Conference on Computer Vision and Pattern Recognition, pp. 1725–1732 (2014)

23. Kopuklu, O., Kose, N., Gunduz, A., Rigoll, G.: Resource efficient 3d convolutional neural networks. In: Proceedings of the IEEE/CVF International Conference on Computer Vision Workshops (2019)

24. Krishna, R., Gordon, M., Fei-Fei, L., Bernstein, M.: Visual intelligence through human interaction. In: Li, Y., Hilliges, O. (eds.) Artificial Intelligence for Human Computer Interaction: A Modern Approach. HIS, pp. 257–314. Springer, Cham (2021). https://doi.org/10.1007/978-3-030-82681-9_9

25. Kuehne, H., Jhuang, H., Garrote, E., Poggio, T., Serre, T.: HMDB: a large video database for human motion recognition. In: 2011 International Conference on Computer Vision, pp. 2556–2563. IEEE (2011)

26. Kupyn, O., Martyniuk, T., Wu, J., Wang, Z.: DeblurGAN-v2: deblurring (orders-of-magnitude) faster and better. In: Proceedings of the IEEE/CVF International Conference on Computer Vision, pp. 8878–8887 (2019)

27. Lakshminarayanan, V., Fleck, A.: Zernike polynomials: a guide. J. Mod. Opt. **58**(7), 545–561 (2011)

28. Liu, B., et al.: Spatiotemporal relationship reasoning for pedestrian intent prediction. IEEE Robot. Autom. Lett. **5**(2), 3485–3492 (2020)

29. Marquez, M., Meza, P., Arguello, H., Vera, E.: Compressive spectral imaging via deformable mirror and colored-mosaic detector. Opt. Express **27**(13), 17795–17808 (2019)

30. Marquez, M., Meza, P., Rojas, F., Arguello, H., Vera, E.: Snapshot compressive spectral depth imaging from coded aberrations. Opt. Express **29**(6), 8142–8159 (2021)

31. Metzler, C.A., Ikoma, H., Peng, Y., Wetzstein, G.: Deep optics for single-shot high-dynamic-range imaging. In: Proceedings of the IEEE/CVF Conference on Computer Vision and Pattern Recognition (2020)

32. Orekondy, T., Schiele, B., Fritz, M.: Towards a visual privacy advisor: understanding and predicting privacy risks in images. In: Proceedings of the IEEE International Conference on Computer Vision, pp. 3686–3695 (2017)
33. Padilla-López, J.R., Chaaraoui, A.A., Flórez-Revuelta, F.: Visual privacy protection methods: a survey. Expert Syst. Appl. **42**(9), 4177–4195 (2015)
34. Panagiotakis, C., Karvounas, G., Argyros, A.: Unsupervised detection of periodic segments in videos. In: 2018 25th IEEE International Conference on Image Processing (ICIP), pp. 923–927. IEEE (2018)
35. Pareek, P., Thakkar, A.: A survey on video-based human action recognition: recent updates, datasets, challenges, and applications. Artif. Intell. Rev. **54**(3), 2259–2322 (2021)
36. Pittaluga, F., Koppal, S., Chakrabarti, A.: Learning privacy preserving encodings through adversarial training. In: 2019 IEEE Winter Conference on Applications of Computer Vision (WACV), pp. 791–799. IEEE (2019)
37. Pittaluga, F., Koppal, S.J.: Privacy preserving optics for miniature vision sensors. In: Proceedings of the IEEE Conference on Computer Vision and Pattern Recognition, pp. 314–324 (2015)
38. Pittaluga, F., Koppal, S.J.: Pre-capture privacy for small vision sensors. IEEE Trans. Pattern Anal. Mach. Intell. **39**(11), 2215–2226 (2016)
39. Purwanto, D., Renanda Adhi Pramono, R., Chen, Y.T., Fang, W.H.: Extreme low resolution action recognition with spatial-temporal multi-head self-attention and knowledge distillation. In: Proceedings of the IEEE/CVF International Conference on Computer Vision Workshops, p. 0 (2019)
40. Ren, Z., Lee, Y.J., Ryoo, M.S.: Learning to anonymize faces for privacy preserving action detection. In: Ferrari, V., Hebert, M., Sminchisescu, C., Weiss, Y. (eds.) ECCV 2018. LNCS, vol. 11205, pp. 639–655. Springer, Cham (2018). https://doi.org/10.1007/978-3-030-01246-5_38
41. Ryoo, M.S., Kim, K., Yang, H.J.: Extreme low resolution activity recognition with multi-Siamese embedding learning. In: Thirty-Second AAAI Conference on Artificial Intelligence (2018)
42. Ryoo, M.S., Rothrock, B., Fleming, C., Yang, H.J.: Privacy-preserving human activity recognition from extreme low resolution. In: AAAI (2017)
43. Sandler, M., Howard, A., Zhu, M., Zhmoginov, A., Chen, L.C.: MobileNetV 2: Inverted residuals and linear bottlenecks. In: Proceedings of the IEEE Conference on Computer Vision and Pattern Recognition, pp. 4510–4520 (2018)
44. Sitzmann, V., et al.: End-to-end optimization of optics and image processing for achromatic extended depth of field and super-resolution imaging. ACM TOG **37**, 1–13 (2018)
45. Sun, C., Junejo, I.N., Tappen, M., Foroosh, H.: Exploring sparseness and self-similarity for action recognition. IEEE Trans. Image Process. **24**(8), 2488–2501 (2015)
46. Szegedy, C., et al.: Going deeper with convolutions. In: Proceedings of the IEEE Conference on Computer Vision and Pattern Recognition, pp. 1–9 (2015)
47. Szegedy, C., Vanhoucke, V., Ioffe, S., Shlens, J., Wojna, Z.: Rethinking the inception architecture for computer vision. In: Proceedings of the IEEE Conference on Computer Vision and Pattern Recognition, pp. 2818–2826 (2016)
48. Tan, M., et al.: MnasNet: platform-aware neural architecture search for mobile. In: Proceedings of the IEEE/CVF Conference on Computer Vision and Pattern Recognition, pp. 2820–2828 (2019)

49. Tran, D., Bourdev, L., Fergus, R., Torresani, L., Paluri, M.: Learning spatiotemporal features with 3d convolutional networks. In: Proceedings of the IEEE International Conference on Computer Vision, pp. 4489–4497 (2015)
50. Tran, D., Wang, H., Torresani, L., Feiszli, M.: Video classification with channel-separated convolutional networks. In: Proceedings of the IEEE/CVF International Conference on Computer Vision, pp. 5552–5561 (2019)
51. Upton, G.J.: Fisher's exact test. J. R. Stat. Soc. A. Stat. Soc. **155**(3), 395–402 (1992)
52. Van Der Maaten, L., Postma, E., Van den Herik, J., et al.: Dimensionality reduction: a comparative. J. Mach. Learn. Res. **10**(66–71), 13 (2009)
53. Wang, L., et al.: Temporal segment networks: towards good practices for deep action recognition. In: Leibe, B., Matas, J., Sebe, N., Welling, M. (eds.) ECCV 2016. LNCS, vol. 9912, pp. 20–36. Springer, Cham (2016). https://doi.org/10.1007/978-3-319-46484-8_2
54. Wang, Z., Bovik, A.C., Sheikh, H.R., Simoncelli, E.P.: Image quality assessment: from error visibility to structural similarity. IEEE Trans. Image Process. **13**(4), 600–612 (2004)
55. Wang, Z.W., Vineet, V., Pittaluga, F., Sinha, S.N., Cossairt, O., Bing Kang, S.: Privacy-preserving action recognition using coded aperture videos. In: Proceedings of the IEEE/CVF Conference on Computer Vision and Pattern Recognition Workshops, p. 0 (2019)
56. Wu, Z., Wang, H., Wang, Z., Jin, H., Wang, Z.: Privacy-preserving deep action recognition: an adversarial learning framework and a new dataset. IEEE Trans. Pattern Anal. Mach. Intell. (2020)
57. Wu, Z., Wang, Z., Wang, Z., Jin, H.: Towards privacy-preserving visual recognition via adversarial training: a pilot study. In: Ferrari, V., Hebert, M., Sminchisescu, C., Weiss, Y. (eds.) ECCV 2018. LNCS, vol. 11220, pp. 627–645. Springer, Cham (2018). https://doi.org/10.1007/978-3-030-01270-0_37
58. Zagoruyko, S., Komodakis, N.: Wide residual networks. arXiv preprint arXiv:1605.07146 (2016)

Scale-Aware Spatio-Temporal Relation Learning for Video Anomaly Detection

Guoqiu Li[1], Guanxiong Cai[2], Xingyu Zeng[2(✉)], and Rui Zhao[2,3]

[1] Tsinghua University, Beijing, China
[2] SenseTime Research, Shanghai, China
zengxingyu@sensetime.com
[3] Qing Yuan Research Institute, Shanghai Jiao Tong University, Shanghai, China

Abstract. Recent progress in video anomaly detection (VAD) has shown that feature discrimination is the key to effectively distinguishing anomalies from normal events. We observe that many anomalous events occur in limited local regions, and the severe background noise increases the difficulty of feature learning. In this paper, we propose a scale-aware weakly supervised learning approach to capture local and salient anomalous patterns from the background, using only coarse video-level labels as supervision. We achieve this by segmenting frames into non-overlapping patches and then capturing inconsistencies among different regions through our patch spatial relation (PSR) module, which consists of self-attention mechanisms and dilated convolutions. To address the scale variation of anomalies and enhance the robustness of our method, a multi-scale patch aggregation method is further introduced to enable local-to-global spatial perception by merging features of patches with different scales. Considering the importance of temporal cues, we extend the relation modeling from the spatial domain to the spatio-temporal domain with the help of the existing video temporal relation network to effectively encode the spatio-temporal dynamics in the video. Experimental results show that our proposed method achieves new state-of-the-art performance on UCF-Crime and ShanghaiTech benchmarks. Code are available at https://github.com/nutuniv/SSRL.

Keywords: Scale-aware · Weakly-supervised video anomaly detection · Spatio-temporal relation modeling

1 Introduction

Video Anomaly Detection (VAD) aims to automatically recognize events that deviate from normal patterns and determine the time window in which anomalies occurred [4,6,28,30]. It is invaluable in many practical applications, such as monitoring terrorist and violent events in public places, or traffic accidents on urban roads, significantly reducing the labor costs of manual surveillance.

Most previous VAD approaches [6,28,30,32] would employ a feature encoder to extract features of video frames and then identify unusual patterns as

S. Avidan et al. (Eds.): ECCV 2022, LNCS 13664, pp. 333–350, 2022.
https://doi.org/10.1007/978-3-031-19772-7_20

Fig. 1. Samples of video anomaly detection benchmark UCF-Crime [28]. The red boxes denote the anomalous regions in frames.

anomalies. However, we found that the effect of the spatial size of anomalies was overlooked. As illustrated in Fig. 1, in the video anomaly detection datasets, many anomalous actions such as abuse and arrest occur in small areas and are difficult to be distinguished from background normal behaviors in the frame. Therefore, the extracted features of full-resolution frames, with limited local anomaly regions inside, will be dominated by the background information, increasing the recognition difficulty of subsequent classifiers.

To address the above limitation, we propose a scale-aware video anomaly detection model to efficiently capture local anomalies from the background. Specifically, we divide the input video frames into a set of non-overlapping patches by using a sliding window. Once anomalies occur, the corresponding anomaly patches will contain more salient anomalous information due to the restricted receptive field, thus suppressing the background noise. Since the patterns of anomaly patches are likely to be distinct from normal patches, we propose a patch spatial relation (PSR) module to identify the occurrence of anomalous events by capturing inconsistencies among different spatial regions.

We also observe that anomalous events vary in size, which poses a challenge to the robustness of the patch-based methods. In Fig. 1, we can see that some anomalous events such as assault or arson occur in small regions, while others, such as road accidents or explosions, span almost the entire image. To cope with this scale variation issue, we further propose a multi-scale patch aggregation (MPA) method to effectively explore anomalous regions with different scales. Since the single-scale patches are likely to suffer from size mismatch when capturing anomalous events, we gradually adjust the size of the sliding window from small to large to generate patches with a pyramidal distribution of scales. The information of these patches will eventually be integrated to give the model a pyramid-like spatial perception of the video from local to global. This improves the scale robustness in anomaly detection.

Previous studies [30,38,49] have demonstrated the significance of long-range temporal dependencies in VAD. Inspired by them, we introduce an existing video temporal relation (VTR) module [30] to extend the relation modeling from the spatial domain to the spatio-temporal domain to effectively encode the spatio-temporal dynamics in videos. The combination of our PSR module and VTR module explicitly considers the local consistency at frame level and global coherence of temporal dynamics in video sequences.

Despite the significance of spatio-temporal feature learning, the corresponding spatio-temporal level annotations are costly. For example, Liu et al. [11] have driven the network to focus on anomalous regions by using a large number of manually labeled spatio-temporal annotations as supervision. To reduce the annotation cost, we follow Sultani et al. [28] to address the VAD task in a weakly supervised multiple instance learning setting by using training samples annotated with normal or abnormal video-level labels.

Our main contributions can be summarized as follows:

- We propose a novel scale-aware weakly supervised video anomaly detection framework, which enables local-to-global spatio-temporal perception for capturing anomalous events of various scales.
- We present a multi-scale patch aggregation method to further boost the detection performance by integrating information from various scale patches.
- We introduce a separable spatio-temporal relation network. Our PSR module learns the spatial relationships among patches and the VTR module captures the temporal dependencies in the video.
- We carry out experiments on UCF-Crime and ShanghaiTech datasets to verify the effectiveness of our method, and the experimental results show that our approach achieves significant performance boosts.

2   Related Work

Weakly Supervised Video Anomaly Detection. Relevant studies on VAD can be broadly classified into two categories: unsupervised learning methods [1, 5, 6, 12, 14–19, 22, 24, 26, 29, 33, 34, 36, 40, 43, 44, 50] and weakly supervised learning methods [4, 20, 28, 30, 32, 37–39, 45, 46, 49, 51]. Most unsupervised approaches learn the usual patterns from normal videos and then identify detection targets with large prediction errors [12, 16, 26, 43, 47, 50] or reconstruction errors [3, 6, 17–19, 24, 40, 44] as anomalies.

Recently, many weakly supervised approaches have been developed. Sultani et al. [28] proposed a deep multiple instance learning (MIL) ranking framework with cheap video-level annotations to detect anomalies. Zhang et al. [46] further introduced an inner bag loss constraint. Zhong et al. [49] formulated weakly supervised anomaly detection as a label noise learning problem, and used a graph convolution neural network to filter the label noise. Wu et al. [38] explored the importance of temporal cues and feature discrimination. Tian et al. [30] proposed a feature magnitude learning approach of selecting top k snippets with the largest feature magnitude as a stronger learning signal. Feng et al. [4] proposed a two-stage scheme in which a MIL-based pseudo label generator was first trained to produce snippet-level pseudo labels, which were then used to fine-tune a task-specific feature encoder for VAD. Liu et al. [11] re-annotated the

UCF-Crime dataset, adding fully supervised anomaly location annotations to drive the model to focus on anomalous regions. Compared with previous weakly supervised methods, our approach explores the local salience of anomalous events and identifies anomalies by capturing the inconsistencies among patches, which is relatively deficient in the VAD area. Moreover, our method addresses the problem of scale variation by aggregating features of patches with different scales.

Spatio-Temporal Relation Modeling. Recently, spatio-temporal relation learning has been successfully applied in several fields, such as object detection [7], action recognition [13,21,27] and object tracking [41]. In anomaly detection, Zhao et al. [48] proposed a spatio-temporal autoencoder to learn video representation by performing 3-dimensional convolutions. Wu et al. [37] introduced a new task to localize the spatio-temporal tube of anomalous event, they used the Faster-RCNN algorithm [25] to extract tube-level instance proposals, and then adopted the multi-head self-attention method [31] to capture the relationships between video objects. However, the pre-trained object detector cannot recognize objects of unseen categories. Our method uses a separable spatio-temporal relation network to effectively capture the inconsistencies among different regions in frames and the long-range temporal dynamics in video sequences.

3 Methodology

In this section, we first present the overall pipeline of our proposed scale-aware spatio-temporal relation learning (SSRL) method in Sect. 3.1. Then we describe the patch spatial relation module in Sect. 3.2. Section 3.3 introduces the multi-scale patch aggregation method, and the video temporal relation module is described in Sect. 3.4. Finally, we introduce the loss function in Sect. 3.5.

3.1 Overview

The overall pipeline of our SSRL is shown in Fig. 2. Given an input untrimmed video V, the corresponding weak video-level label $y \in \{0,1\}$ indicates whether abnormal events exist in this video ($y = 1$ if there exist anomalous events in video V and $y = 0$ otherwise). Following the previous MIL-based frameworks [4,20, 28,30,49,51], we divide the video V into a sequence of temporal non-overlapping video snippets $\{\mathbf{v}_t\}_{t=1}^T$, here we use T to denote the number of video snippets.

We can see that given a video snippet $\mathbf{v}_t \in \mathbb{R}^{H \times W \times L \times 3}$, where H and W are the height and width of the video snippet, respectively, and L denotes the temporal length of the video snippet. The video snippet $\mathbf{v}_t$ will first be split into several sets of spatial non-overlapping patch cubes with different spatial sizes. As Fig. 3 shows, we set a number of sliding window sizes $\{(h_r, w_r)\}_{r=1}^R$ to extract patch cubes. Thus, each set of patch cubes is represented as $\mathcal{P}_t^r = \{\mathbf{p}_{t,i}^r\}_{i=1}^{N_r}$, $r \in \{1, \ldots, R\}$, where $\mathbf{p}_{t,i}^r \in \mathbb{R}^{h_r \times w_r \times L \times 3}$ denotes the extracted patch cube with spatial patch size of $h_r \times w_r$, and $N_r = \lfloor H/h_r \rfloor \times \lfloor W/w_r \rfloor$ is the number of patch cubes. Then every patch cube is fed into a pretrained feature extractor (I3D [2]) to generate features, and then features of patch cubes with the

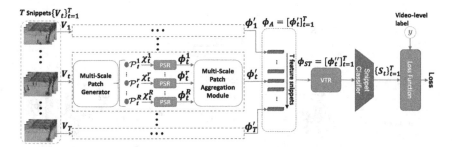

Fig. 2. The overall pipeline of our proposed SSRL. Each video snippet is first divided into several sets of patch cubes. Then, our PSR modules learn the spatial relations among patch cubes with the same size, and the multi-scale patch aggregation method further fuses the features of multi-scale patch cubes. After that, the VTR module captures the temporal dependencies among video snippets, and the snippet classifier will predict the snippet scores. Finally, the video-level label y and the snippet scores are used to compute the loss.

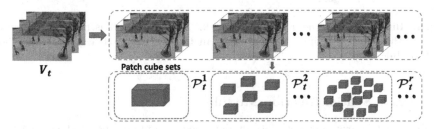

Fig. 3. Illustration of the multi-scale patch generator.

same size are stacked in horizontal dimension as $\chi_t^r \in \mathbb{R}^{N_r \times D}$, where D denotes the feature dimensions. To capture the inconsistencies between anomalous and normal patch cubes, our proposed patch spatial relation (PSR) module comes into play. It computes patch-wise correlations among patch cubes of the same size through a self-attention mechanism [35] and dilated convolutions [42] to produce spatial enhanced patch representations, denoted as $\phi_t^r \in \mathbb{R}^{N_r \times D}$. After that, we apply a multi-scale patch aggregation method to enhance the scale robustness of our model. The features of the multi-scale patch cubes will be fused to produce an aggregated snippet feature $\phi_t' \in \mathbb{R}^D$, enabling a local-to-global perception of the video snippet. Please see Sect. 3.3 for more details. After the above process, we obtain the aggregated video representation $\phi_A = [\phi_t']_{t=1}^T$ from the T video snippets, which is then fed into a video temporal relation (VTR) module to capture the temporal dependencies among video snippets, resulting in a temporal enhanced video representation $\phi_{ST} = [\phi_t'']_{t=1}^T$, where $\phi_t'' \in \mathbb{R}^D$ denotes the enhanced feature of each snippet. Finally we employ a snippet classifier [28] to generate anomaly scores $\{s_t\}_{t=1}^T$ for all video snippets.

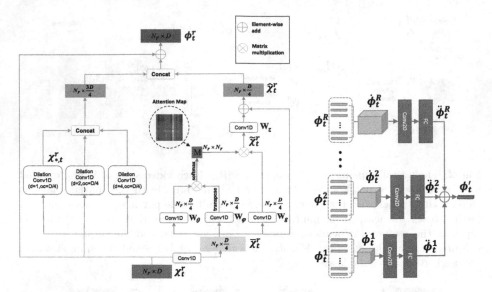

Fig. 4. Illustration of the relation network. N_r denotes the number of input patch cubes in the PSR module.

Fig. 5. Illustration of the multiscale patch aggregation method.

3.2 Patch Spatial Relation Module

Inspired by the previous work [30], which used a combined network consisting of a pyramid of dilated convolutions [42] and a temporal self-attention module [35] to capture long- and short-range temporal dependencies between video snippets, we use the same relation network in our framework, but the difference is that we employ the relation network not only to capture the temporal dependencies among video snippets but also to learn the spatial relations among patch cubes. The detailed architecture of this relation network is illustrated in Fig. 4.

Supposing an abnormal event occurs at a limited location in a video snippet, then the local feature distribution of the corresponding anomaly patch cubes should be significantly different from other normal patch cubes. Therefore, to capture the inconsistencies among different spatial regions, we propose the patch spatial relation (PSR) module. It learns the patch-wise correlations of patch cubes across different spatial regions from the pre-extracted initial patch features $\chi_t^r \in \mathbb{R}^{N_r \times D}$, where N_r denotes the number of patch cubes extracted with a particular spatial size (h_r, w_r). The right sub-network in Fig. 4 is a non-local network that aims to model the global spatial relations among patch cubes by self-attention mechanism [35]. After we feed χ_t^r into the PSR module, the non-local network first uses a 1×1 convolution to reduce the channel dimension from $\chi_t^r \in \mathbb{R}^{N_r \times D}$ to $\bar{\chi}_t^r \in \mathbb{R}^{N_r \times D/4}$, then a non-local operation is performed to model global spatial relations among patch cubes:

$$\tilde{\chi}_t^r = \text{softmax}\left(\mathbf{W}_\theta \bar{\chi}_t^r \bar{\chi}_t^{r\top} \mathbf{W}_\varphi^\top\right) \mathbf{W}_g \bar{\chi}_t^r, \tag{1}$$

$$\hat{\chi}_t^r = \mathbf{W}_z \tilde{\chi}_t^r + \bar{\chi}_t^r, \tag{2}$$

where $\bar{\chi}_t^r$ is first projected into the embedded space by three 1×1 convolutions with learnable weights $\mathbf{W}_\theta$, $\mathbf{W}_\varphi$ and $\mathbf{W}_g$. We then calculate the attention map $\mathbf{M} \in \mathbb{R}^{N_r \times N_r}$ by the dot product operation and softmax normalization, the attention map $\mathbf{M}$ is used as weights to compute the weighted sum $\tilde{\chi}_t^r$. Once the network captures an anomalous patch, its corresponding column in $\mathbf{M}$ is expected to be highlighted, thus passing the information of this anomalous patch to all patches. Our expectations coincide with the results of the later experiments (Fig. 6). Then we obtain the self-attention based representation $\hat{\chi}_t^r \in \mathbb{R}^{N \times D/4}$ by a 1×1 convolution with learnable weights $\mathbf{W}_z$ and a residual connection, shown in Eq. 2.

The left sub-network in Fig. 4 contains a pyramid of dilated convolutions to learn the local spatial dependencies of neighbouring patch cubes with multi-scale receptive fields. Specifically, we set up three 1-D dilated convolutions with different dilation factors $d \in \{1, 2, 4\}$. The input features χ_t^r will be simultaneously fed into three dilated convolutions to produce multi-scale dilation embedded representations $\chi_{*,t}^r \in \mathbb{R}^{N \times D/4}$, $* \in \{DC1, DC2, DC3\}$. Then, a concatenation operation and residual connection are applied to the outputs of two sub-networks to produce the spatial enhanced patch representations:

$$\phi_t^r = [\hat{\chi}_t^r, \chi_{*,t}^r] + \chi_t^r, \tag{3}$$

where $[.]$ denotes the concatenation operation.

3.3   Multi-scale Patch Aggregation

In the video, the spatial scales of different anomalous objects vary greatly. If we directly split the input video snippet into multiple patch cubes with a single fixed spatial size, it is likely that a large anomaly object cannot be completely divided into a single patch, while a small anomaly object still occupies only a small part of the patch region. Therefore, we propose a multi-scale patch aggregation (MPA) method to deal with this size mismatch case.

As mentioned in Sect. 3.1, we will first use sliding windows of different sizes to split the input video snippet into several sets of non-overlapping patch cubes to cover anomaly objects with different sizes. These sets of patch cubes will then be passed through the I3D feature extractor and PSR modules in parallel to obtain the spatial enhanced patch representations $\{\phi_t^r\}_{r=1}^R$, $\phi_t^r \in \mathbb{R}^{N_r \times D}$. After that, the MPA method comes into play. As Fig. 5 shows, each input patch representation ϕ_t^r will first be reconstructed into a 3-D feature vector $\dot{\phi}_t^r \in \mathbb{R}^{\lfloor H/h_r \rfloor \times \lfloor W/w_r \rfloor \times D}$ according to the initial spatial location of patch cubes. Subsequent convolutional and fully connected layers transform this 3-D feature vector into a 1-D feature vector $\ddot{\phi}_t^r \in \mathbb{R}^D$. After the above steps, the local information of the same scale patches is aggregated. Finally, the multi-scale fused patch features $\{\ddot{\phi}_t^r\}_{r=1}^R$ will be aggregated together by an element-wise add operation, resulting in an aggregated snippet feature $\phi_t' = \sum_{r=1}^R \ddot{\phi}_t^r$.

3.4 Video Temporal Relation Module

In an anomalous video, it is most likely that the motion patterns of anomalous video snippets would not follow the patterns of other normal video snippets. The existing video temporal relation (VTR) module aims to learn the temporal context of video snippets by applying the relation network in Fig. 4 over the time dimension. We formulate the VTR module as follows:

$$\tilde{\phi}_A = \text{softmax}\left(\mathbf{W}_\theta \bar{\phi}_A \bar{\phi}_A^\top \mathbf{W}_\varphi^\top\right) \mathbf{W}_g \bar{\phi}_A, \tag{4}$$

$$\hat{\phi}_A = \mathbf{W}_z \tilde{\phi}_A + \bar{\phi}_A, \tag{5}$$

$$\phi_{ST} = [\hat{\phi}_A, \phi_{*,A}] + \phi_A, \tag{6}$$

where $\phi_A = [\phi_1', \phi_2', \dots, \phi_T'] \in \mathbb{R}^{T \times D}$ represents the input aggregated features of the T video snippets, which are then fed into the 1×1 convolution layer to produce $\bar{\phi}_A \in \mathbb{R}^{T \times D/4}$. $\phi_{*,A}$ denotes the outputs of three dilated convolution layers and $\phi_{ST} \in \mathbb{R}^{T \times D}$ denotes the output spatio-temporal enhanced video representation.

3.5 Loss Function

We chose the multiple instance learning (MIL) method for weakly supervised learning. In addition, to further improve the robustness of our SSRL in detecting anomaly events, we draw on the feature magnitude learning method presented in [30], which enables better separation between anomaly and normal videos by selecting the top k snippets with largest feature magnitudes instead of the snippet with the highest anomaly score to supervise MIL model. Specifically, for the output spatio-temporal video representation $\phi_{ST} = [\phi_t'']_{t=1}^T$, where $\phi_t'' \in \mathbb{R}^D$ denotes the snippet feature, the mean feature magnitude is defined by:

$$g(\phi_{ST}) = \max_{\Omega_k(\phi_{ST}) \subseteq \{\phi_t''\}_{t=1}^T} \frac{1}{k} \sum_{\phi_t'' \in \Omega_k(\phi_{ST})} \|\phi_t''\|_2, \tag{7}$$

where $\Omega_k(\phi_{ST})$ contains k snippets selected from $\{\phi_t''\}_{t=1}^T$, the snippet feature magnitude is computed by ℓ_2 norm. After that, the feature magnitude based MIL ranking loss is formulated by:

$$\mathcal{L}_{FM} = \max\left(0, \epsilon - g(\phi_{ST}^+) + g(\phi_{ST}^-)\right), \tag{8}$$

where ϵ is a pre-defined margin, ϕ_{ST}^+ and ϕ_{ST}^- denote the anomaly and normal video representations, respectively.

We feed the top k selected snippets with largest feature magnitudes into the snippet classifier to generate the corresponding snippet anomaly scores $\{s_j\}_{j=1}^k$. Then, we apply a cross-entropy-base loss function to train the snippet classifier:

$$\mathcal{L}_{CE} = \sum_{s \in \{s_j\}_{j=1}^k} -(y \log(s) + (1 - y) \log(1 - s)). \tag{9}$$

Following the previous work [28], we add the sparsity and temporal smoothness constraints on all predicted snippet scores$\{s_t^+\}_{t=1}^T$ of the anomaly video. To sum up, the total loss function of our model is defined as follows:

$$\mathcal{L} = \mathcal{L}_{CE} + \lambda_{fm}\mathcal{L}_{FM} + \lambda_1 \sum_{t=1}^T |s_t^+| + \lambda_2 \sum_{t=1}^T (s_t^+ - s_{t-1}^+)^2, \qquad (10)$$

where λ_{fm}, λ_1 and λ_2 are weighting factors used to balance the losses of each component. $\sum_{t=1}^T |s_t^+|$ and $\sum_{t=1}^T (s_t^+ - s_{t-1}^+)^2$ denote the sparsity regularization and temporal smoothness constraint, respectively.

4 Experiments

4.1 Datasets and Metrics

We validated our SSRL on two large benchmark datasets for video anomaly detection, namely UCF-Crime [28] and ShanghaiTech [18].

UCF-Crime: UCF-Crime [28] is a large-scale dataset. It has a total of 128 h with 1900 long untrimmed videos. All videos were captured from real-world surveillance, including 13 types of anomalous events that have a significant impact on public safety. The training set consists of 1610 videos, and the testing set contains 290 videos. Both training and testing sets contain all 13 anomalies at various temporal locations in the videos.

ShanghaiTech: ShanghaiTech dataset has 437 videos, including 307 normal videos and 130 anomaly videos, all collected under 13 different scenes with complex shooting angles. However, since the original dataset [18] was proposed for semi-supervised anomaly detection, only normal videos were available in the training set. Following Zhong et al. [49], we reorganize the videos into 238 training videos and 199 testing videos, making both the training and testing sets contain anomalous videos, thus adapting to the weakly supervised setting.

Evaluation Metrics. Following previous works [4,28,30], we compute the area under the curve (AUC) of the frame-level receiver operating characteristics (ROC) as the main metric to evaluate the performance of our model and comparison methods, where a larger AUC implies higher distinguishing ability.

4.2 Implementation Details

Following previous works [28,30], for a training video, we first split the video into 32 non-overlapping video snippets ($T = 32$). Then we resize each video snippet to $480 \times 840 \times 16$ pixels ($H = 480$, $W = 840$, $L = 16$). To extract multi-scale patch cubes from the video snippet, we set four different sliding window sizes: $480 \times 840, 240 \times 280, 160 \times 168$ and 120×120, where 480×840 means that we treat the entire video frame as a patch. After that, we deploy the I3D network pretrained on Kinetic-400 dataset [8] to extract initial features. For the relation network described in Fig. 4, we use the same setting as [30]. During the multi-scale patch aggregation process, for each branch, we employ a 2-D convolutional layer with 3×3 kernel and 2×2 stride and a fully connected layer with 2048 output nodes. The snippet classifier consists of three fully connected layers with output nodes of 512, 128 and 1. For hyper-parameters, we set the margin $\epsilon = 100$ in (8) and the number of selected snippets $k = 3$ in (7), and the weighting factors λ_{fm}, λ_1 and λ_2 in (10) are set to 0.0001, 0.008 and 0.0008, respectively. All hyper-parameters are the same for both UCF-Crime and ShanghaiTech.

Training. We train our network on 8 NVIDIA Tesla V100 GPUs using PyTorch [23]. We randomly sample 32 abnormal videos and 32 normal videos per batch and use the Adam optimizer [9] with the initial learning rate of 0.001 and a weight decay of 0.0005 to train our SSRL. For the MPA module, the fusion process of multi-scale patches is difficult to optimize. To reduce the difficulty of optimization, we adopt a step-by-step training strategy. We first optimize the process of single-scale patches, and then gradually introduce new-scale patches. More details about implementation are reported in Supplementary Material.

4.3   Comparisons with Related Methods

The AUC results on two benchmarks are presented in Table 1. For the UCF-Crime dataset, our method achieves the highest AUC result of 87.43%. Compared with the existing unsupervised methods [33,34], our SSRL outperforms BODS [33] by 19.17% and GODS [34] by 16.97%. Our SSRL also surpasses existing weakly supervised methods [4,20,28,30,38,39,45,46,49,51]. In particular, when using the same I3D-RGB initial features, our model exceeds Wu et al. [39] by 4.99%, MIST [4] by 5.13%, RTFM [30] by 3.13%, Wu et al. [38] by 2.54%, MSL [10] by 2.13% and WSAL [20] by 2.05%. For the ShanghaiTech dataset, as the table indicates, the detection performance of our SSRL outperforms all previous weakly supervised methods. It is worth noting that among other models that also use I3D-RGB features, the previous best method [38] achieved an AUC result of 97.48%, which is already a fairly high result considering that only video-level anomaly labels are provided, but our method still improves further on this to 97.98%, which proves the powerful anomaly detection capability of our SSRL. We further report the result when the parameters of different PSRs are shared, with an AUC of 86.85% and 97.84% on the two datasets, respectively. Although the performance is slightly dropped, the parameter amount is much reduced (Table 6), which is more favorable for practical applications.

We also compare our SSRL with other spatio-temporal relation modeling methods on UCF-Crime. As shown in the Table 2, our approach significantly exceeds STC-Graph [29] by 14.73% and STAD [37] by 4.7%. Video swin transformer [13] is a transformer-based backbone architecture that has recently achieved strong performance on a broad range of video-based recognition tasks. We implemented it in VAD field, specifically, we used video swin transformer (tiny version, due to memory limitations) as backbone, and performed multi-instance weakly supervised learning using the classifier and loss function in this

Table 1. Quantitative comparisons with other state-of-the-art methods on UCF-Crime and ShanghaiTech. Share parameters denotes different PSRs' parameters are shared.

Method	Supervised	Feature	AUC (%)	
			UCF-Crime	ShanghaiTech
BODS [33]	Un	I3D-RGB	68.26	–
GODS [34]	Un	I3D-RGB	70.46	–
Sultani et al. [28]	Weak	C3D-RGB	75.41	86.30
Zhang et al. [46]	Weak	C3D-RGB	78.66	82.50
Motion-Aware [51]	Weak	PWC-Flow	79.00	–
Zhong et al. [49]	Weak	TSN-RGB	82.12	84.44
Wu et al. [39]	Weak	I3D-RGB	82.44	–
MIST [4]	Weak	I3D-RGB	82.30	94.83
CLAWS [45]	Weak	C3D-RGB	83.03	89.67
RTFM [30]	Weak	I3D-RGB	84.30	97.21
Wu et al. [38]	Weak	I3D-RGB	84.89	97.48
WSAL [20]	Weak	I3D-RGB	85.38	–
MSL [10]	Weak	I3D-RGB	85.30	96.08
MSL [10]	Weak	VideoSwin-RGB	85.62	97.32
Our SSRL (share parameters)	Weak	I3D-RGB	86.85	97.84
Our SSRL	Weak	I3D-RGB	**87.43**	**97.98**

Table 2. Quantitative comparisons with other spatio-temporal relation modeling methods on UCF-Crime. * indicates the result implemented by us.

Method	Supervised	AUC (%) - UCF
STC-Graph [29]	Un	72.70
STAD [37]	Weak	82.73
Video swin transformer [13]	Weak	81.62*
Our SSRL	Weak	**87.43**

paper, with the rest of the setup as in [13]. The test results on UCF-Crime show that our method outperforms video swin transformer by 5.81%, which may be due to the lack of long-range temporal dependencies in video swin transformer.

4.4 Ablation Study

In this section, we conduct ablation studies to study the impact of important designed elements in our SSRL.

Analysis of Multi-scale Patch Aggregation. To investigate the influence of our proposed multi-scale patch aggregation method, we conduct ablation studies on the UCF-Crime and ShanghaiTech datasets. The detailed comparison results are shown in Table 3. Specifically, we employ RTFM [30] as our baseline, which

Table 3. Ablation studies on the multi-scale patch aggregation method (see Sect. 3.3) on two benchmarks. * indicates we use the method in [30] as our baseline.

Patch size				AUC (%)	
480 × 840	240 × 280	160 × 168	120 × 120	UCF-Crime	ShanghaiTech
✓				84.30*	97.21*
✓	✓			86.38	97.60
✓		✓		85.69	97.69
✓			✓	85.29	97.55
✓	✓	✓		86.70	97.85
✓		✓	✓	86.32	97.77
✓	✓		✓	86.97	97.71
✓	✓	✓	✓	**87.43**	**97.98**

Table 4. Ablation studies on two benchmarks for investigating the effect of spatio-temporal relation learning. Baseline is [30] trained with video temporal relation network. SSRL is our whole model. SSRL$^{w/o\ PSR}$ is SSRL trained without patch spatial relation module but with multi-scale patch aggregation module. For the MPA module, we use all four patch sizes in Table 3.

Methods	VTR	MPA	PSR	AUC (%)	
				UCF-Crime	ShanghaiTech
Baseline	✓			84.30	97.21
SSRL$^{w/o\ PSR}$	✓	✓		85.98	97.45
SSRL	✓	✓	✓	**87.43**	**97.98**

performs anomaly detection directly on the input video snippet and achieves 84.30% and 97.21% AUC results on UCF-Crime and ShanghaiTech, respectively. Then, we set up three different patch sizes: 240 × 280, 160 × 168 and 120 × 120 for capturing anomalous events on the corresponding spatial scales. When we extract patch cubes using only one of the sizes, the corresponding experimental results are shown in the second to fourth rows of Table 3. We observe 0.99% to 2.08% and 0.34% to 0.48% improvement on the two datasets respectively. This verifies the effectiveness of patch-based feature learning. After that, we start integrating multiple sizes of patch cubes to capture anomaly events of different sizes. We report the corresponding experimental results in the fifth to the last row of the table. We observe the AUC results increase gradually as more sizes of patch cubes are introduced. The AUC increases from 86.32% to 87.43% on the UCF-Crime dataset and improves from 97.71% to 97.98% on the ShanghaiTech dataset. Our MPA module fuses patch features from multiple branches by an element-wise add operation, so that anomalies will be identified if they are captured by any of the branches. The above observations reveal the complementary effect among the patch information at multiple scales.

Analysis of Spatio-Temporal Relation Learning. The results in Table 4 verify the effect of spatio-temporal relation learning. Compared with the baseline that only considers the temporal context in the video and treats the video frame as a whole, SSRL$^{w/o\ PSR}$ achieves a significant improvement when the MPA-enabled spatial local patterns are utilized. In particular, we observe 1.68% and 0.24% improvement in AUC on two benchmarks, respectively, which shows that spatio-temporal features are more discriminatory than simple temporal features. Moreover, the PSR module also plays an important role in spatio-temporal feature learning by capturing the inconsistencies among different patches. Compared with SSRL$^{w/o\ PSR}$, with the help of the PSR module, SSRL further increases 1.45% AUC on the UCF-Crime and 0.53% AUC on the ShanghaiTech.

Analysis on Two Sub-networks in the PSR Module. The results in Table 5 verify the effect of two sub-networks in PSR. We employ the pyramid of dilated convolutions to learn the local spatial dependencies of neighboring patches with multi-scale receptive field, and it brings 0.24% and 0.18% AUC gains on UCF-Crime and ShanghaiTech, respectively. We also use the no-local network to capture the global spatial relations of different patches, and it improves the AUC by 0.69% and 0.37% on UCF-Crime and ShanghaiTech, respectively. When both sub-networks are added, we observe an increase in AUC of 1.45% and 0.53% on UCF-Crime and ShanghaiTech, respectively. This indicates that two

Table 5. Ablation studies on two benchmarks for verifying the effectiveness of subnetworks in the PSR module.

Methods	AUC (%)	
	UCF-Crime	ShanghaiTech
Full	87.43	97.98
w/o dilated convolutions	86.57	97.82
w/o no-local network	86.22	97.63
w/o PSR module	85.98	97.45

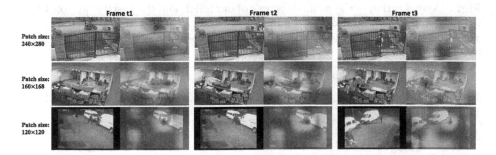

Fig. 6. Visualization results of attention heatmaps with three patch sizes on UCF-Crime (*Stealing079, Burglary017, Arson010*, from top to bottom) test videos.

sub-networks complement each other in capturing both local and global range spatial dependencies, and contribute to the overall performance.

4.5   Visual Results

To further evaluate the performance of our method, we visualize the attention map $\mathbf{M} = [w_{m,n}]_{m=1,n=1}^{N_r,N_r}$ in the PSR module. As we mentioned in Sect. 3.2, the columns corresponding to anomalous patches are expected to be highlighted in $\mathbf{M}$. We accumulate the weights $[w_{m,n}]_{m=1,n=1}^{N_r,N_r}$ row by row to generate a 1-D attention vector $[w'_n]_{n=1}^{N_r}$, $w'_n = \sum_{m=1}^{N_r} w_{m,n}$, which is normalized and then rearranged into a 2-D attention mask $\mathbf{M}' \in \mathbb{R}^{\lfloor H/h_r \rfloor \times \lfloor W/w_r \rfloor}$ according to the initial spatial location of the patches. We then use $\mathbf{M}'$ to generate the attention heatmap for spatial explanation. As Fig. 6 shows, our PSR module is able to sensitively focus on salient anomalous regions and suppress the background, even if the anomalous objects keep moving over time. In addition, the three rows in Fig. 6 correspond to three different patch sizes, and from top to bottom, we can see that as the patch size decreases, the focus of attention becomes more concentrated. This scale-aware pyramidal attentional vision can effectively improve the scale robustness of detecting anomalies. We also compare the predicted anomaly scores of our SSRL and the baseline [30] in Fig. 7. Two anomalous videos (*Shooting022*, *01_0141*) and one normal video (*Normal210*) are used. As we can see, compared with the baseline, our SSRL can effectively detect small anomalous events (e.g., *Shooting022* and *01_0141*). Moreover, our SSRL produces much less

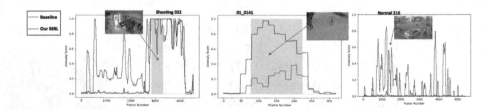

Fig. 7. Visualization of the anomaly scores of our SSRL and the baseline [30] on UCF-Crime (*Shooting022*, *Normal210*), and ShanghaiTech (*01_0141*) test videos. Pink areas are temporal ground truths of anomalies. The red boxes denote anomalous regions. (Color figure online)

Table 6. Computational complexity comparisons with other methods.

Method	Feature encoder	Param	FLOPs
RTFM [30]	I3D	28M	186.9G
Zhong et al. [49]	C3D	78M	386.2G
Our SSRL	I3D	191M	214.6G
Our SSRL (share parameters)	I3D	136M	214.6G

false positives on normal videos (e.g., *Normal210*) and anomalous videos (e.g., *Shooting022*).

4.6 Computational Complexity

We provide detailed information of parameter amount and computational cost in Table 6, and we acknowledge that large parameter amount is a potential limitation of our approach. Since our SSRL uses the same VTR module as baseline, the extra computational cost and parameters come from the PSR and MPA modules, and we can address this limitation by sharing parameters between different PSR modules. As the Table 6 shows, with a slight decrease in performance (Table 1), the parameter amount drops by 55 megabytes, which facilitates the real-world application of our method.

5 Conclusion

In this work, we propose a scale-aware weakly supervised video anomaly detection framework that uses only video-level labeled training videos to learn to focus on locally salient anomalous regions. We adopt a separable spatio-temporal relation network which explores the spatio-temporal context in the video to generate discriminative spatio-temporal features. We also introduce a multi-scale patch aggregation method to enable the local-to-global perception in frames and to enhance the scale robustness of our model. Remarkably, our proposed method achieves significant improvements on two public benchmarks.

References

1. Cai, R., Zhang, H., Liu, W., Gao, S., Hao, Z.: Appearance-motion memory consistency network for video anomaly detection. In: Thirty-Fifth AAAI Conference on Artificial Intelligence, pp. 938–946 (2021)
2. Carreira, J., Zisserman, A.: Quo Vadis, action recognition? A new model and the kinetics dataset. In: Proceedings of the IEEE/CVF Conference on Computer Vision and Pattern Recognition, pp. 4724–4733 (2017)
3. Fan, Y., Wen, G., Li, D., Qiu, S., Levine, M.D., Xiao, F.: Video anomaly detection and localization via gaussian mixture fully convolutional variational autoencoder. Comput. Vis. Image Underst. 195, 102920 (2020)
4. Feng, J., Hong, F., Zheng, W.: MIST: multiple instance self-training framework for video anomaly detection. In: Proceedings of the IEEE/CVF Conference on Computer Vision and Pattern Recognition, pp. 14009–14018 (2021)
5. Georgescu, M., Barbalau, A., Ionescu, R.T., Khan, F.S., Popescu, M., Shah, M.: Anomaly detection in video via self-supervised and multi-task learning. In: Proceedings of the IEEE/CVF Conference on Computer Vision and Pattern Recognition, pp. 12742–12752 (2021)
6. Hasan, M., Choi, J., Neumann, J., Roy-Chowdhury, A.K., Davis, L.S.: Learning temporal regularity in video sequences. In: Proceedings of the IEEE/CVF Conference on Computer Vision and Pattern Recognition, pp. 733–742 (2016)

7. He, L., et al.: End-to-end video object detection with spatial-temporal transformers. CoRR abs/2105.10920 (2021). https://arxiv.org/abs/2105.10920
8. Kay, W., et al.: The kinetics human action video dataset. arXiv preprint arXiv:1705.06950 (2017)
9. Kingma, D.P., Ba, J.: Adam: a method for stochastic optimization. In: Bengio, Y., LeCun, Y. (eds.) 3rd International Conference on Learning Representations (2015)
10. Li, S., Liu, F., Jiao, L.: Self-training multi-sequence learning with transformer for weakly supervised video anomaly detection. In: Thirty-Sixth AAAI Conference on Artificial Intelligence (2022)
11. Liu, K., Ma, H.: Exploring background-bias for anomaly detection in surveillance videos. In: Proceedings of the 27th ACM International Conference on Multimedia, pp. 1490–1499 (2019)
12. Liu, W., Luo, W., Lian, D., Gao, S.: Future frame prediction for anomaly detection - a new baseline. In: Proceedings of the IEEE/CVF Conference on Computer Vision and Pattern Recognition, pp. 6536–6545 (2018)
13. Liu, Z., et al.: Video swin transformer. arXiv preprint arXiv:2106.13230 (2021)
14. Liu, Z., Nie, Y., Long, C., Zhang, Q., Li, G.: A hybrid video anomaly detection framework via memory-augmented flow reconstruction and flow-guided frame prediction. CoRR abs/2108.06852 (2021). https://arxiv.org/abs/2108.06852
15. Lu, C., Shi, J., Jia, J.: Abnormal event detection at 150 FPS in MATLAB. In: Proceedings of the IEEE/CVF International Conference on Computer Vision, pp. 2720–2727 (2013)
16. Lu, Y., Kumar, K.M., Nabavi, S.S., Wang, Y.: Future frame prediction using convolutional VRNN for anomaly detection. In: 16th IEEE International Conference on Advanced Video and Signal Based Surveillance, pp. 1–8 (2019)
17. Luo, W., Liu, W., Gao, S.: Remembering history with convolutional LSTM for anomaly detection. In: 2017 IEEE International Conference on Multimedia and Expo, pp. 439–444 (2017)
18. Luo, W., Liu, W., Gao, S.: A revisit of sparse coding based anomaly detection in stacked RNN framework. In: Proceedings of the IEEE/CVF International Conference on Computer Vision, pp. 341–349 (2017)
19. Luo, W., et al.: Video anomaly detection with sparse coding inspired deep neural networks. IEEE Trans. Pattern Anal. Mach. Intell. **43**(3), 1070–1084 (2021)
20. Lv, H., Zhou, C., Cui, Z., Xu, C., Li, Y., Yang, J.: Localizing anomalies from weakly-labeled videos. IEEE Trans. Image Process. **30**, 4505–4515 (2021)
21. Pan, J., Chen, S., Shou, M.Z., Liu, Y., Shao, J., Li, H.: Actor-context-actor relation network for spatio-temporal action localization. In: Proceedings of the IEEE/CVF Conference on Computer Vision and Pattern Recognition, pp. 464–474 (2021)
22. Park, H., Noh, J., Ham, B.: Learning memory-guided normality for anomaly detection. In: Proceedings of the IEEE/CVF Conference on Computer Vision and Pattern Recognition, pp. 14360–14369 (2020)
23. Paszke, A., et al.: PyTorch: an imperative style, high-performance deep learning library. Adv. Neural Inf. Process. Syst. **32**, 8026–8037 (2019)
24. Ravanbakhsh, M., Nabi, M., Sangineto, E., Marcenaro, L., Regazzoni, C.S., Sebe, N.: Abnormal event detection in videos using generative adversarial nets. In: 2017 IEEE International Conference on Image Processing, pp. 1577–1581 (2017)
25. Ren, S., He, K., Girshick, R., Sun, J.: Faster R-CNN: towards real-time object detection with region proposal networks. Adv. Neural Inf. Process. Syst. **28**, 91–99 (2015)

26. Rodrigues, R., Bhargava, N., Velmurugan, R., Chaudhuri, S.: Multi-timescale trajectory prediction for abnormal human activity detection. In: IEEE Winter Conference on Applications of Computer Vision, pp. 2615–2623 (2020)

27. Song, L., Zhang, S., Yu, G., Sun, H.: TACNet: transition-aware context network for spatio-temporal action detection. In: Proceedings of the IEEE/CVF Conference on Computer Vision and Pattern Recognition, pp. 11987–11995 (2019)

28. Sultani, W., Chen, C., Shah, M.: Real-world anomaly detection in surveillance videos. In: Proceedings of the IEEE/CVF Conference on Computer Vision and Pattern Recognition, pp. 6479–6488 (2018)

29. Sun, C., Jia, Y., Hu, Y., Wu, Y.: Scene-aware context reasoning for unsupervised abnormal event detection in videos. In: MM 2020: The 28th ACM International Conference on Multimedia, pp. 184–192 (2020)

30. Tian, Y., Pang, G., Chen, Y., Singh, R., Verjans, J.W., Carneiro, G.: Weakly-supervised video anomaly detection with robust temporal feature magnitude learning. In: Proceedings of the IEEE/CVF International Conference on Computer Vision (2021)

31. Vaswani, A., et al.: Attention is all you need. In: Advances in Neural Information Processing Systems, pp. 5998–6008 (2017)

32. Wan, B., Fang, Y., Xia, X., Mei, J.: Weakly supervised video anomaly detection via center-guided discriminative learning. In: IEEE International Conference on Multimedia and Expo, pp. 1–6 (2020)

33. Wang, J., Cherian, A.: GODS: generalized one-class discriminative subspaces for anomaly detection. In: Proceedings of the IEEE/CVF International Conference on Computer Vision, pp. 8201–8211 (2019)

34. Wang, J., Cherian, A.: GODS: generalized one-class discriminative subspaces for anomaly detection. In: Proceedings of the IEEE/CVF International Conference on Computer Vision, pp. 8200–8210 (2019)

35. Wang, X., Girshick, R.B., Gupta, A., He, K.: Non-local neural networks. In: Proceedings of the IEEE/CVF Conference on Computer Vision and Pattern Recognition, pp. 7794–7803 (2018)

36. Wang, Z., Zou, Y., Zhang, Z.: Cluster attention contrast for video anomaly detection. In: MM 2020: The 28th ACM International Conference on Multimedia, pp. 2463–2471 (2020)

37. Wu, J., et al.: Weakly-supervised spatio-temporal anomaly detection in surveillance video. In: Proceedings of the Thirtieth International Joint Conference on Artificial Intelligence, pp. 1172–1178 (2021)

38. Wu, P., Liu, J.: Learning causal temporal relation and feature discrimination for anomaly detection. IEEE Trans. Image Process. 30, 3513–3527 (2021)

39. Wu, P., et al.: Not only look, but also listen: learning multimodal violence detection under weak supervision. In: Vedaldi, A., Bischof, H., Brox, T., Frahm, J.-M. (eds.) ECCV 2020. LNCS, vol. 12375, pp. 322–339. Springer, Cham (2020). https://doi.org/10.1007/978-3-030-58577-8_20

40. Xu, D., Ricci, E., Yan, Y., Song, J., Sebe, N.: Learning deep representations of appearance and motion for anomalous event detection. In: Proceedings of the British Machine Vision Conference 2015, pp. 8.1–8.12 (2015)

41. Xu, J., Cao, Y., Zhang, Z., Hu, H.: Spatial-temporal relation networks for multi-object tracking. In: Proceedings of the IEEE/CVF International Conference on Computer Vision, pp. 3987–3997 (2019)

42. Yu, F., Koltun, V.: Multi-scale context aggregation by dilated convolutions. In: 4th International Conference on Learning Representations (2016)

43. Yu, G., et al.: Cloze test helps: effective video anomaly detection via learning to complete video events. In: MM 2020: The 28th ACM International Conference on Multimedia, pp. 583–591 (2020)
44. Zaheer, M.Z., Lee, J., Astrid, M., Lee, S.: Old is gold: redefining the adversarially learned one-class classifier training paradigm. In: Proceedings of the IEEE/CVF Conference on Computer Vision and Pattern Recognition, pp. 14171–14181 (2020)
45. Zaheer, M.Z., Mahmood, A., Astrid, M., Lee, S.-I.: CLAWS: clustering assisted weakly supervised learning with normalcy suppression for anomalous event detection. In: Vedaldi, A., Bischof, H., Brox, T., Frahm, J.-M. (eds.) ECCV 2020. LNCS, vol. 12367, pp. 358–376. Springer, Cham (2020). https://doi.org/10.1007/978-3-030-58542-6_22
46. Zhang, J., Qing, L., Miao, J.: Temporal convolutional network with complementary inner bag loss for weakly supervised anomaly detection. In: 2019 IEEE International Conference on Image Processing, pp. 4030–4034 (2019)
47. Zhang, Y., Nie, X., He, R., Chen, M., Yin, Y.: Normality learning in multispace for video anomaly detection. IEEE Trans. Circuits Syst. Video Technol. 31(9), 3694–3706 (2021)
48. Zhao, Y., Deng, B., Shen, C., Liu, Y., Lu, H., Hua, X.S.: Spatio-temporal autoencoder for video anomaly detection. In: Proceedings of the 25th ACM international conference on Multimedia, pp. 1933–1941 (2017)
49. Zhong, J.X., Li, N., Kong, W., Liu, S., Li, T.H., Li, G.: Graph convolutional label noise cleaner: Train a plug-and-play action classifier for anomaly detection. In: Proceedings of the IEEE/CVF Conference on Computer Vision and Pattern Recognition, pp. 1237–1246 (2019)
50. Zhou, J.T., Zhang, L., Fang, Z., Du, J., Peng, X., Xiao, Y.: Attention-driven loss for anomaly detection in video surveillance. IEEE Trans. Circuits Syst. Video Technol. 30(12), 4639–4647 (2020)
51. Zhu, Y., Newsam, S.D.: Motion-aware feature for improved video anomaly detection. In: 30th British Machine Vision Conference 2019, p. 270 (2019)

Compound Prototype Matching
for Few-Shot Action Recognition

Yifei Huang$^{(\boxtimes)}$ ⓘ, Lijin Yang ⓘ, and Yoichi Sato ⓘ

Institute of Industrial Science, The University of Tokyo, Tokyo, Japan
{hyf,yang-lj,ysato}@iis.u-tokyo.ac.jp

Abstract. Few-shot action recognition aims to recognize novel action classes using only a small number of labeled training samples. In this work, we propose a novel approach that first summarizes each video into compound prototypes consisting of a group of global prototypes and a group of focused prototypes, and then compares video similarity based on the prototypes. Each global prototype is encouraged to summarize a specific aspect from the entire video, *e.g.*, the start/evolution of the action. Since no clear annotation is provided for the global prototypes, we use a group of focused prototypes to focus on certain timestamps in the video. We compare video similarity by matching the compound prototypes between the support and query videos. The global prototypes are directly matched to compare videos from the same perspective, *e.g.*, to compare whether two actions start similarly. For the focused prototypes, since actions have various temporal variations in the videos, we apply bipartite matching to allow the comparison of actions with different temporal positions and shifts. Experiments demonstrate that our proposed method achieves state-of-the-art results on multiple benchmarks.

Keywords: Few-shot action recognition · Compound prototype · Prototype matching

1 Introduction

Difficulty in collecting large-scale data and labels promotes the research on few-shot learning. Built upon the success of few-shot learning for image understanding tasks [10,16,26,33,36,37,53,54,62], many begin to focus on the few-shot action recognition task [28]. Once realized, such techniques could greatly alleviate the cost of video labeling [20] and promote real-world applications where the labels in certain scenarios are hard to acquire [25].

Most few-shot action recognition works determine the category of a query video using its similarity to the few labeled support videos. Many works [18,73, 74] follow ProtoNet [47] to first learn a prototype for each video and compute the

---

Y. Huang and L. Yang—Equal contribution.

Supplementary Information The online version contains supplementary material available at https://doi.org/10.1007/978-3-031-19772-7_21.

video similarity based on the similarity of the prototypes. To better consider the temporal dependencies in videos (*e.g.*, temporal ordering and relation), recent works construct sub-sequence prototypes using different parts of the videos and calculate video similarity by matching the support-query prototypes [5,44].

While temporal dependencies are considered, limitations still exist in previous methods. Firstly, without considering spatial information, previous methods cannot fully exploit the spatiotemporal relation in the videos for distinguishing actions like "put A on B" and "put A besides B" because they differ only in the relative position of the objects. Secondly, the sub-sequence prototypes come from fixed temporal locations, so that they cannot well handle the actions that happen at different speeds. Thirdly, it is computationally costly to exhaustively compute the similarity between all pairs of sub-sequence prototypes [44].

To address the limitations and achieve more robust few-shot action recognition, we explore how to: (1) better generate prototypes that can robustly encode spatiotemporal relation in the videos, (2) enable the prototypes to flexibly encode the actions done with different lengths and speeds, and (3) match the prototypes between two videos without exhaustively comparing all prototype pairs.

One straightforward way to address the first point is to use object features extracted from object bounding boxes [22]. However, we observed in our preliminary experiments only limited performance gain when previous methods [44,70] directly use them as additional inputs. In this work, we propose a multi-relation encoder to effectively encode the object features, by considering the spatiotemporal relation among objects across frames, the temporal relation between different frame-wise features, as well as the relation between object features and frame-wise features.

For the second and third points, we propose to generate *global prototypes* that consider all frames in the input video. This is done by taking advantage of the self-attention mechanism of Transformers [51]. Since it is difficult to represent a wide variety of actions by using a single prototype, we instead use a group of prototypes to represent each action. We match the support-query similarity by fixed 1-to-1 matching, *i.e.*, the i-th prototype of the query video is always matched with the i-th prototype of the support video. Thus, during training, each prototype will try to capture a certain aspect of the video. To avoid all prototypes to be the same, we apply a diversity loss when learning the prototypes, so that they are encouraged to capture different aspects of the action (*e.g.*, one prototype captures the start of the action, and another prototype captures the action evolution).

However, learning prototypes to represent different aspects of the action (*e.g.*, the start/end of the action) is a difficult task even with annotation [9,40,41]. Thus, it is not sufficient to compute video similarity only by the global prototypes. To make the similarity measurement more reliable, we generate another group of *focused prototypes*, where each prototype is encouraged to focus on certain timestamps of the video. Since actions may happen in different parts of the videos at different speeds [34], it is not correct to compare the same timestamp between two videos. We therefore use bipartite matching to match the focused prototypes between the support and query videos, so that comparison of actions with different lengths and speeds can be done.

Our method uses the compound of two groups of prototypes, which we call *compound prototypes*, for calculating video similarity. On multiple benchmark datasets, our method outperforms previous methods significantly when only one example is available, demonstrating the superiority of using our compound prototypes in similarity measurement.

To summarize, our key contributions include:

- A novel method for few-shot action recognition based on generating and matching compound prototypes.
- Our method achieves state-of-the-art performance on multiple benchmark datasets [7,19,30], outperforming previous methods by a large margin.
- A detailed ablation study showing the usefulness of leveraging object information for few-shot action recognition and demonstrating how the two groups of prototypes encode the video from complementary perspectives.

2   Related Works

Few-Shot Image Classification methods can be broadly divided into three categories. The transfer-learning based methods [14,45,57] use pre-training and fine-tuning to increase the performance of deep backbone networks on few-shot learning. The second line of works focuses on rapidly learning an optimized classifier using limited training data [1,2,17,21,46,58,67]. The third direction is based on metric learning, whose goal is to learn more generalizable feature embeddings under a certain distance metric [27,29,47,52]. The key to metric-learning based methods is to generate robust representations of data under a certain metric, so that it may generalize to novel categories with few labeled samples. Our work falls into this school of research and focus on the more challenging video setting.

Few-Shot Action Recognition methods [3,24,34,42,43,50,61,74,75] mainly fall into the metric-learning framework. Many works follow the scheme of ProtoNet [47] to compute video similarity based on generated prototypes. For learning better prototypes, ProtoGAN [32] synthesizes additional feature, CMN [72,73] uses a multi-layer memory network, while ARN [69] uses jigsaws for self-supervision and enhances the video-level representation via spatial and temporal attention. There are also methods that perform pretraining with semantic labels [56,59,60] or use additional information such as depth [18] to augment video-level prototypes. Our method uses another form of additional information: the object bounding box from pretrained object detectors [22].

The temporal variance of actions form a major challenge in few-shot action recognition task [34]. To better model temporal dependencies, recent researches put more focus on generating and matching sub-video level prototypes. OTAM [5] uses a generalized dynamic time warping technique [8] to monotonously match the prototypes between query and support videos. ITA-Net [70] first implicitly aggregates information for each frame using other frames, and conducts a 1-to-1 matching of all prototypes. However, these two methods use frame-wise prototypes, thus cannot well capture the higher-level temporal relation in multiple frames. Recently, TRX [44] constructs prototypes of different cardinalities for query and support videos, and calculate similarity by matching all prototype pairs. However, since TRX can only match prototypes with the same cardinality (*e.g.*, three-frame prototypes matches with three-frame proto-types), it is hard to align the actions with different evolving speeds (*e.g.*, one takes 2 frames while the other takes 4 frames). Also, the exhaustively matching of all pairs is computationally expensive.

We summarize three main differences compared with previous works: (1) We encode spatiotemporal object information to form more robust prototypes. (2) We generate a compound of global and focused prototypes to represent the actions from diverse perspectives. (3) The two groups of prototypes are efficiently matched to robustly compute video similarity.

Transformers [51] have recently acquired remarkable achievements in com-puter vision [6,13,15,38,64,68]. FEAT [65] represents early work that applies transformer in the few-shot learning task, and TRX [44] first introduces Trans-former [15] into the few-shot action recognition task. Different from TRX, we apply a Transformer encoder-decoder to generate compound prototypes, and show that this is more effective in the few-shot action recognition scenario.

3   Method

3.1   Problem Setting

In few-shot action recognition, a model aims to recognize an unlabeled video (query) into one of the target categories each with a limited number of labeled examples (support set) [5,44]. We follow the common practice [17,52] to use episodic training, where in each episode a C-way K-shot problem is sampled: the support set $S = \{X_s^j\}_{j=1}^{C \times K}$ is composed of $C \times K$ labeled videos from C different classes where each class contains K samples. The query set contains N unlabeled videos $Q = \{X_q^i\}_{i=1}^{N}$. The goal is to classify each video in the query set as one of the C classes.

3.2   Proposed Method

We propose a new method for few-shot action recognition by generating and matching compound prototypes between query and support videos. As shown in Fig. 1, given the video input, a feature embedding network first extracts global (frame-wise) features F_g. To better model the actions involving multiple objects, we obtain object bounding boxes by a pretrained object detector [22], and extract object features F_o using the same embedding network. Then a multi-relation encoder uses F_g and F_o to output multi-relation features F_m containing spa-tiotemporal global-object relations. Then a compound prototype decoder gen-erates global prototypes P_g and focused prototypes P_f for each video. During similarity calculation, we use fixed 1-to-1 matching on the global prototypes and bipartite matching on the focused prototypes, encouraging the similarity to be computed robustly from diverse perspectives. We introduce the details of each component below.

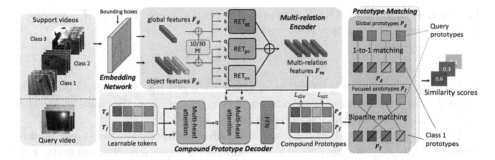

Fig. 1. Illustration of our proposed method on a 3-way 1-shot problem. First, the videos are processed by an embedding network to acquire global (frame-level) features F_g and object features F_o. Features F_g and F_o are equipped with 1D and 3D positional encoding (PE), respectively, and then used by a multi-relation encoder (Sect. 3.2) to encode global-global, global-object and object-object information into a multi-relation feature F_m. Using F_m, a Transformer-based compound prototype decoder transforms the learnable tokens T_g, T_f into compound prototypes that represent the input video (Sect. 3.2). The compound prototypes is consisted of several global prototypes P_g (green squares) and focused prototypes P_f (blue squares). They are applied with different loss and different matching strategies, so that each global prototype captures a certain aspect of the action summarized from the whole video, and each focused prototype focuses on a specific temporal location of the video. The final similarity score is calculated as the average similarity of all matched prototype pairs between support and query videos. (Color figure online)

Feature Embedding. For each input video $X \in \mathcal{S} \cup \mathcal{Q}$, we sample T frames following the sampling strategy of TSN [55]. We use an embedding network to acquire a global (frame-level) feature representation for each video $F_g \in \mathbb{R}^{T \times d}$, where d is the feature dimension. Additionally we extract object features via ROI-Align [22] using the predicted bounding boxes on each frame. We use only B most confident boxes on each frame, forming object features $F_o \in \mathbb{R}^{BT \times d}$.

Multi-relation Encoder. To better generate prototypes that are discriminative for actions involving multiple objects, we propose to use a multi-relation encoder to encode the spatiotemporal information from F_g and F_o. We specifically consider the following three relations: global-global (frame-wise) relation, global-object relation, object-object relation, and apply transformer [51] as the base architecture to allow relation modeling across frames. As shown in Fig. 1, the encoder consists of three relation encoding transformers (RETs). The global-global RET (RET_{gg}) and the object-object RET (RET_{oo}) are identical except the input. They take as input the global feature F_g and the object feature F_o respectively, and use the input to generate the query Q, key K and value V vectors for the transformer:

$$F_{gg} = RET_{gg}(Q = K = V = F_g) \tag{1}$$
$$F_{oo} = RET_{oo}(Q = K = V = F_o), \tag{2}$$

The global-object RET (RET$_{go}$) works differently, where it maps F_g as query vector, while F_o as key and value vectors:

$$F_{go} = RET_{go}(Q = F_g, \ K = V = F_o). \tag{3}$$

The output size of each RET is the same as its input query vector. Thus, each of the T frame would have $B + 2$ features with dimension d. We concatenate the three outputs into a multi-relation feature $F_m \in \mathbb{R}^{(B+2)T \times d}$.

Positional encoding (PE) is shown to be effective in transformer-based architectures [38,39,51]. We also use PE but omit in the equations for simplicity. For F_g we use 1D PE to encode the temporal location of each frame, and for F_o we apply 3D PE, encoding both spatial and temporal location of each object.

Compound Prototype Decoder. The compound prototype decoder also follows the transformer architecture [6,11,49,51], so that the prototypes can be generated by considering feature of all frames via self-attention. As shown in Fig. 1, the input to the prototype decoder are two groups of learnable tokens $T_g \in \mathbb{R}^{m_g \times d}$ and $T_f \in \mathbb{R}^{m_f \times d}$. A multi-head attention layer first encodes the tokens into $\hat{T}_g$ and $\hat{T}_f$, then another multi-head attention layer transforms them into two groups of prototypes $P_g = \{p_{g,k}\}_{k=1}^{m_g} \in \mathbb{R}^{m_g \times d}$ and $P_f = \{p_{f,k}\}_{k=1}^{m_f} \in \mathbb{R}^{m_f \times d}$. For simplicity, we omit the subscripts $_{g,f}$ and all normalization layers, thus the equation can be written as:

$$Q = \hat{T} W_Q, \quad K = F_m W_K, \quad V = F_m W_V, \tag{4}$$

where $W_Q, W_K, W_V \in \mathbb{R}^{d \times d}$ are linear projection weights, then we have

$$A = softmax(\frac{QK^T}{\sqrt{d}}), \quad P = FFN(AV), \tag{5}$$

where $A \in \mathbb{R}^{m \times (B+2)T}$ is the self-attention weights, and FFN denotes feed forward network.

To encourage the prototypes to capture different aspects of the action, we apply constraints on the two groups of prototypes individually. For the global prototypes P_g, we add a diversity loss to maximize their diversity:

$$L_{div} = \sum_{i \neq j} sim(p_{g,i}, \ p_{g,j}), \tag{6}$$

where sim denotes the cosine similarity function.

Since learning P_g to robustly represent each aspect of the action (e.g., the start of the action) is difficult even with annotation [63,66]. To increase the overall robustness, for the focused prototypes P_f, we instead add regularization on the self-attention weight A_f so that different p_f can focus on different temporal locations of the video:

$$L_{att} = \sum_{i \neq j} sim(\alpha_{f,i}, \ \alpha_{f,j}). \tag{7}$$

Here $\boldsymbol{\alpha}_{f,i} \in \mathbb{R}^{(B+2)T}$ denotes the i-th row in $\boldsymbol{A}_f$.

Compound Prototype Matching. Cooperating with the compound proto-types, we use different matching strategies to calculate the overall similarity between two videos. As shown in Fig. 1, for the global prototypes $\boldsymbol{P}_g$, we match the query and support prototypes in a 1-to-1 manner, *i.e.*, the i-th prototype of the query video is always matched with the i-th prototype of the support video. To calculate the global prototypes' overall similarity score between video a and video b, we average the similarity score of all the m_g global prototypes:

$$s_g^{a,b} = \frac{1}{m_g} \sum_{k=1}^{m_g} sim(\boldsymbol{p}_{g,k}^a, \boldsymbol{p}_{g,k}^b). \qquad (8)$$

Thus, to maximize the similarity score of correct video pairs and minimize the similarity of incorrect video pairs during episodic training, each $\boldsymbol{p}_g$ will try to encode a certain aspect of the action, *e.g.*, the start of the action. This phe-nomenon is supported by our experiments in Sect. 4.

For the focused prototypes $\boldsymbol{P}_f$, we apply a bipartite matching-based similar-ity measure. Since different actions may happen in different temporal positions in the videos, the bipartite matching enables the temporal alignment of actions, allowing the comparison between actions of different lengths and at different speeds. Formally speaking, for $\boldsymbol{P}_f^a$ of video a and $\boldsymbol{P}_f^b$ of video b, we find a bipar-tite matching between these two sets of prototypes by searching for the best permutation of m_f elements with the highest cosine similarity using the Hun-garian algorithm [31]. Denote σ as the best permutation, the similarity score of $\boldsymbol{P}_f^a$ and $\boldsymbol{P}_f^b$ is calculated by:

$$s_d^{i,j} = \frac{1}{m_f} \sum_{k=1}^{m_f} sim(\boldsymbol{p}_{f,k}^a, \boldsymbol{p}_{f,\sigma(k)}^b). \qquad (9)$$

Finally, the similarity score is computed by a weighted average of s_g and s_f: $s^{a,b} = \lambda_1 s_g^{a,b} + \lambda_2 s_f^{a,b}$. During training, this similarity score is directly regarded as logits for the cross-entropy loss L_{ce}. The total loss function is a weighted sum of three losses: $L = w_1 L_{ce} + w_2 L_{div} + w_3 L_{att}$. During inference, we assign the label of the query video as the label of the most similar video in the support set.

4   Experiments

We conduct experiments on four public datasets. **Kinetics** [7] and Something-something V2 (**SSv2**) [19] are two most frequently used benchmarks for few-shot action recognition. These two datasets are both splitted as 64/12/24 classes for train/val/test. For **SSv2**, we use both the split from CMN [72] (**SSv2°**) and the split from OTAM [5] (**SSv2♯**). Recently, Zhang *et al.* [69] proposed new splits for **HMDB** [30] and **UCF** [48] datasets. We also conduct experiments on these two datasets using the split from [69].

Since our method's performance is competitive in both standard 1-shot 5-way setting and 5-shot 5-way setting, in this section we only demonstrate 1-shot results and place 5 shot results in the supplementary due to page limitation. Following previous works, we report the average result of 10,000 test episodes in the experiments.

Baselines. We compare our method with recent works reporting state-of-the-art performance, including MatchNet [52], CMN [73], OTAM [5], TRN [71], ARN [69], TRX [44], ITA-Net [70]. Following [74], we also compare with the few-shot image classification model FEAT [65] which is also based on transformers. Specifically, since no previous works used object detector in few-shot action recognition, for a fair comparison with previous works, we conduct experiments in two settings: (1) we give baseline methods the same input (both F_g and F_o) as our method and compare the performance. We denote the baselines as "Baseline+" in this setting. (2) We discard the object detector in our method and use only F_g as input and RET_{gg} as the encoder. We denote our method in this setting as "Ours-".

To enable previous methods to take object features as input, we choose to compare with methods TRX+, FEAT+, and ITA-Net+ because they also use transformer-based architectures like our method, thus no modification on the model architecture is needed. For completeness, we also compare MatchNet+ and TRN+ without transformer architecture. For these two methods, we reshape the object features F_o to $F'_o \in \mathbb{R}^{T \times Bd}$ as input. Since these two works are not designed to input the object features, we train an ensembled network, one with F_g as input and the other with F'_o as input. We use the public implementation of TRX and implement ITA-Net by ourselves. More details about baseline implementation can be found in the supplementary material. Recently, several works [4,56,74] pretrain the backbone on the meta-training set and found this pretraining to be useful for few-shot action recognition. To compare with the majority of prior works, we do not follow this setting in our experiments.

Implementation Details. We use ResNet-50 [23] pretrained on ImageNet [12] as the backbone of embedding network, and a fixed Mask-RCNN [22] trained on COCO dataset [35] is used as the bounding box extractor. We select $B = 3$ most confident object bounding boxes per frame. The pre-processing steps follow OTAM [5] where we also sample $T = 8$ frames with random crop during training and center crop during inference. The model and the backbone is optimized using SGD with an initial learning rate of 0.001 and decaying every 20 epochs by 0.1. The embedding network except its first BatchNorm layer is fine-tuned with 1/10 learning rate. The training is stopped when the loss on the validation set is greater than the average of the previous 5 epochs. Unless otherwise stated, we report result using $m_g = m_f = 8$, $\lambda_1 = \lambda_2 = 0.5$, $w_1 = 1, w_2 = w_3 = 0.1$.

Table 1. Results of 5-way 1-shot experiments on 5 dataset splits. Methods marked with * indicates results of our implementation with the original reported results shown in parenthesis. The bottom and upper block are results with and without using object features, respectively. For ITA-Net, result on SSv2° comes from Table 5 of [70].

Method	SSv2°	SSv2#	Kinetics	HMDB	UCF
MatchNet* [52]	34.9 (31.3)	35.1	54.6 (53.3)	50.1	70.3
CMN [73]	36.2	–	60.5	–	–
ARN [69]	–	–	63.7	45.5	66.3
OTAM [5]	–	42.8	73.0	–	–
TRN* [5,71]	35.9	39.6 (38.6)	68.6 (68.4)	52.3	76.3
FEAT* [65]	38.4	45.5	73.0	56.1	75.8
ITA-Net* [70]	38.4 (38.6)	46.1	72.6	56.5	76.0
TRX* [44]	37.1 (36.0)	41.5 (42.0)	64.6 (63.6)	54.4	**77.7**
Ours-	**38.9**	**49.3**	**73.3**	**60.1**	71.4
MatchNet+*	35.6	36.5	57.6	52.8	72.8
TRN+*	38.1	41.3	71.4	55.3	79.7
FEAT+*	43.1	46.6	73.9	61.5	79.7
ITA-Net+*	43.7	48.9	74.4	61.6	79.5
TRX+*	39.4	44.2	71.8	60.1	**81.2**
Ours	**57.1**	**59.6**	**81.0**	**80.3**	79.0

4.1 Results

Table 1 shows result comparison with baseline methods. In the upper block, our model slightly outperforms previous works even without using the object detector on 4 of the 5 dataset/splits. This suggests that compared with other prototype generation methods, our proposed approach to generate and match the compound prototypes enables better similarity measurement for few-shot action recognition. From the comparison of baseline methods with their "+" variants, we can see that these methods cannot fully exploit the information brought by the object features. When object features are added as input, our full model significantly outperforms previous methods that use the same input. Compared with the performance of our method in the upper block, the object features significantly stimulates the potential of our proposed compound prototype matching scheme, by improving the accuracy on the SSv2 dataset for over 10%, the Kinetics dataset for 7.7% and the HMDB dataset for over 20%. In the ablation study, we show even better performance can be achieved by carefully adjusting the number of prototypes m_g and m_f.

Table 2. Results comparison of different methods when using/not using object information, and using/not using our proposed encoder.

Encoding	Prototype	SSv2°	SSv2♯	Kinetics
Backbone only (w/o. object features)	None	34.9	35.1	54.6
	ITA-Net	**38.4**	45.5	**72.6**
	TRX	37.1	41.5	64.6
	Ours	37.9	**48.5**	72.5
Our encoder (w/o. object features)	None	35.3	37.2	59.4
	ITA-Net	38.6	46.5	73.0
	TRX	38.2	44.4	68.9
	Ours	**38.0**	**49.3**	**73.3**
Concat (w. object features)	None	35.6	36.5	57.6
	ITA-Net+	**43.7**	48.9	74.4
	TRX+	39.4	44.2	71.8
	Ours	42.1	**49.1**	**79.2**
Our encoder (w. object features)	None	39.1	42.5	58.4
	ITA-Net+	44.0	50.7	73.3
	TRX+	46.3	48.4	73.4
	Ours	**57.1**	**59.6**	**81.0**

Table 3. Results comparison of our model using different encoding relations with different number of global prototypes and focused prototypes.

Setting	F_{gg}	F_{go}	F_{oo}	SSv2♯	Kinetics
$m_g = 8$, $m_f = 8$	✓	×	×	49.3	73.3
	×	✓	×	47.3	69.1
	×	×	✓	55.5	73.6
	✓	✓	×	49.6	75.0
	✓	×	✓	57.7	79.7
	×	✓	✓	57.8	77.1
	✓	✓	✓	**59.6**	**81.0**
$m_g = 16$, $m_f = 0$	✓	×	×	38.9	65.5
	×	✓	×	38.8	65.2
	×	×	✓	38.5	64.0
	✓	✓	✓	**39.3**	**66.1**
$m_g = 0$, $m_f = 16$	✓	×	×	41.9	72.3
	×	✓	×	34.4	73.7
	×	×	✓	29.3	61.0
	✓	✓	✓	**44.0**	**76.7**

Our method does not achieve state-of-the-art results on the UCF dataset. One reason is that classes in the UCF dataset can be easily distinguished only from appearance. This causes our multi-relation encoder to overfit. If we remove this encoder and directly use concatenation of object and global features as input to the compound prototype decoder, our method can achieve the state-of-the-art accuracy of 87.7. This reveals one limitation of our method, *i.e.*, easy to overfit on simple datasets.

4.2   Ablation Study

Effect of Object Features. While there exist previous studies that leverage additional information for few-shot action recognition [18], no work has investigated the use of object features as in our method. One may argue that the performance improvement of our method only comes from the use of object features. However, in Table 1 we find that performance gain of previous methods is limited if object features are additionally used as input. Here, we show that a boost in performance only happens when object features, our multi-relation encoder, and our decoder are used together.

We test the performance of multiple methods with and without using object information, and also with and without using our multi-relation encoder. In Table 2, the first block uses neither object feature nor our multi-relation encoder, and the second block uses our encoder but with only the global-global relation RET_{gg}. From the comparison between these two blocks, we can see that our multi-relation encoder can improve the performance of all methods, but not significantly. In the third block of Table 2, we concatenate each frame-wise feature with its corresponding object features as input. The comparison between this block and the first block shows the improvement brought by object features: around 2–5% on SSv2 dataset, and 2– 6% on Kinetics dataset. Finally, in the fourth block of Table 2, both object features and our multi-relation encoder are used. Comparing this block with the second and third blocks, all methods get more improvement. This shows that using our multi-relation encoder to consider multiple relations across frames can better leverage the information brought by the object features. Among all methods in the fourth block of Table 2, our method enjoys the most significant performance gain. This indicates that while the object features bring additional information, our method can best leverage this information to help the few-shot action recognition task.

Impact of Multi-relation Feature Encoding. To see how does the multi-relation feature encoding contribute to the performance, we conduct ablation study of our method considering only subsets of $\{F_{gg}, F_{go}, F_{oo}\}$. We also vary the number of global prototypes m_g and focused prototypes m_f to see the influence of feature encoding on each group of prototypes.

Results can be seen in Table 3. From the experiments with $m_g = m_f = 8$, the SSv2$^\sharp$ dataset gets much improvement from the use of object-object feature F_{oo}, while the Kinetics dataset benefits more from the global-global feature F_{gg}. This is reasonable since SSv2 dataset includes more actions with multiple objects. From the experiments with $m_g = 16$, the global prototypes seem to work equally well using the three encoded features on both datasets. The experiments with $m_f = 16$ suggest that focused prototypes work better with global-global relations. When using all three features (last row of each block), the comparison between different choices of m_g and m_f indicates that the two groups of prototypes capture complementary aspects of the action, since the performances got significantly improved when two groups of prototypes both present. A more detailed figure showing the accuracy difference of each action class can be found in the supplementary material.

4.3 Analysis of Compound Prototypes

The core of our proposed method is the generation and matching of compound prototypes. In this section we conduct extensive experiments to get a more comprehensive understanding of the two groups of prototypes.

What Aspect of the Action Does Each Prototype Capture? We address this question by investigating the self-attention operation that generates the prototypes. From Eq. 5, the self-attention weight $\alpha \in \mathbb{R}^{(B+2)\times T}$ on each frame represents from which part of the video does each prototype gather its information. To better understand the prototypes, we visualize this attention in Fig. 2 using two 1-shot 2-way examples. In the visualization we average the $B + 2$ attention weights in each frame, forming $\tilde{\alpha} \in \mathbb{R}^T$, and show this averaged value on each of the $T = 8$ frames. For clarity we only show 2 global prototypes and 2

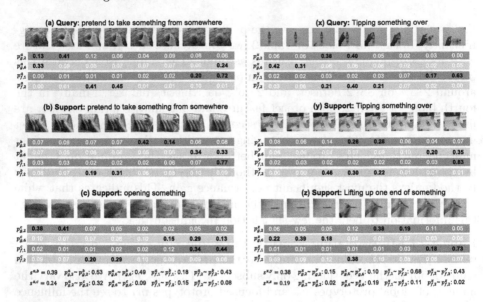

Fig. 2. Visualization of the self-attention weight of two global prototypes and two focused prototypes on each timestamp of the input. Attention weights higher than average (0.125) are marked in black. We can see the global prototypes capture a certain aspect of the action in the video, regardless of temporal location: $p_{g,2}$ - the start of the action; $p_{g,6}$ - the frames without hand. Meanwhile, the focused prototypes mainly attend on fixed timestamps of the video: $p_{f,1}$ - the end of the video; $p_{f,2}$ - the middle part of the video. Example to the left comes from the SSv2° dataset and the example to the right is from SSv2$^\sharp$. Video similarity scores s and similarity scores of matched prototypes $p_* \sim p_*$ are shown at the bottom.

focused prototypes in each video. We also show the video similarity scores and the similarity of matched prototypes at the bottom of the figure.

The visualization is shown in Fig. 2. We first analyze the attention of each prototype. In all videos, the global prototype $p_{g,2}$ have high attention weights on the start of the *action* (not the start of the *video*), and $p_{g,6}$ pays more attention to the frames that contain appearance change compared with other frames (no hand existence). This is expected since L_{div} forces each global prototype to be different, while the 1-to-1 matching encourages each global prototype to focus on similar aspects so that correct video similarity can be predicted. For the focused prototypes, $p_{f,1}$ usually gives high attention to the last few frames, and $p_{f,2}$ pays more attention on the middle frames. This is also expected since L_{att} refrains the focused prototypes to attend on similar temporal locations, and bipartite matching allows similar actions to be matched even when they are at different temporal locations of the videos. A similar phenomenon exists in the object detection task [6], where each object query focuses on detecting objects in a specific spatial location of the image.

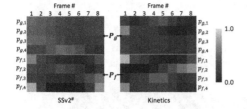

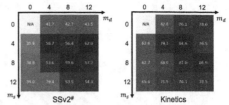

Fig. 3. Visualization of self-attention weights of P_s and P_d for all samples on the test set of SSv2$^\sharp$ and Kinetics datasets.

Fig. 4. Performance on the SSv2$^\sharp$ and Kinetics datasets when changing the number of global/focused prototypes.

In the left example, both the prototype pairs $< p_{g,2}^a, p_{g,2}^b >$ and $< p_{g,6}^a, p_{g,6}^b >$ have high similarity scores (0.53 and 0.49 shown at the bottom of the left example). This indicates that video a and b have similar starts, and the intra-video appearance change is also similar. Thus the query action is correctly classified as "Pretending to take something from somewhere". In the right example, we can see the effectiveness of the focused prototypes. By Hungarian matching, $p_{f,1}^x$ is matched with $p_{f,2}^y$. Since they both encode the frames where the hands just tip the objects over, these two prototypes give high similarities, enabling the query action of "Tipping something over" to be correctly recognized.

A statistical analysis of self-attention weights can be found in Fig. 3 showing the average response of the first 4 global prototypes and the first 4 focused prototypes on all videos of the test set. As a result of the loss functions L_{div}, L_{att} and the matching strategies, on both SSv2$^\sharp$ and Kinetics datasets, P_g (first 4 rows) have a more uniform attention distribution, while P_f have obvious temporal regions of focus. The diversity of the prototypes ensures a robust representation of the videos, thus similarity between videos can be better computed during the few-shot learning process.

How Much Does Each Group of Pprototype Contribute? To find the answer, we test our method using different numbers of prototypes (m_g and m_f) and show the results in Fig. 4. Although the best combination of m_g and m_f are different for each dataset, the performance gets better when the number of prototypes increases, and after a certain threshold, the result saturates because of the overfitting on the training data. Best results on both SSv2$^\sharp$ (62.0) and Kinetics (86.9) datasets are achieved when m_f is larger than m_g. Although $m_g = m_f = 8$ is not the optimal setting, we apply this setting in Sect. 4.1 and Sect. 4.2 since it is the most stable setting on all datasets. A method to automatically choose the number of prototypes is left for our future work.

Also, we show the class accuracy improvement when our method uses both groups of prototypes compared with our method using only one group of prototype. In Fig. 5, orange bars denote the accuracy difference between the $m_g = m_f = 8$ setting and the $m_g = 16, m_f = 0$ setting, which indicates the performance gain by introducing the focused prototypes. Blue bars, on the other hand, show the accuracy improvement brought by the global prototypes. We

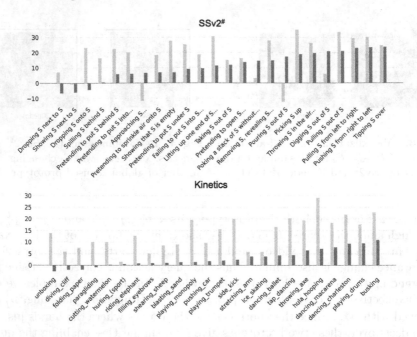

Fig. 5. Class accuracy improvement when our method uses $m_g = m_f = 8$ prototypes compared to: orange bars: $m_g = 16$, $m_f = 0$; blue bars: $m_g = 0$, $m_f = 16$. S stands for the abbreviation of "something". (Color figure online)

can see on the SSv2$^\sharp$ dataset that when combining the two groups of prototypes, some hard classes like "pulling S out of S", "pulling S from left to right" and "pushing S from right to left" can be better distinguished. From the results of the two datasets, we observe the focused prototypes are more effective in the Kinetics dataset. This is because the Kinetics dataset focuses more on appearance, which can be better captured and compared by the focused prototypes.

Will Wrong Bipartite Matching Destroy the Temporal Ordering of Actions? Although we observe great performance gain brought by P_f in Table 3 and Fig. 5, the bipartite matching will unavoidably produce some wrongly matched prototype pairs when creating the correct matchings. Our additional experiments in the supplementary show that filtering the matched prototypes with low similarity negatively affects the convergence of the model. One reason is that positional encoding implicitly encodes the temporal ordering of the frames within each prototype. During training, the similarity scores of all the wrong matching pairs are learned to be small and so that the final similarity score can be dominated by the similarity score of the correctly matched prototype pairs.

5 Conclusion

In this work, we introduce a novel method for few-shot action recognition by generating global and focused prototypes and compare video similarity based on the prototypes. When generating the prototypes, we encode spatiotemporal object relations to address the actions that involve multiple objects. The two groups of prototypes are encouraged to capture different aspects of the input by different loss functions and matching strategies. In our future work, we will explore a more flexible prototype matching strategy that can avoid the mismatch in the bipartite matching.

Acknowledgement. This work is supported by JSPS KAKENHI Grant Number JP22K17905, JP20H04205 and JST AIP Acceleration Research Grant Number JPMJCR20U1.

References

1. Andrychowicz, M., et al.: Learning to learn by gradient descent by gradient descent. In: NeurIPS (2016)
2. Antoniou, A., Edwards, H., Storkey, A.: How to train your MAML. In: ICML (2019)
3. Bishay, M., Zoumpourlis, G., Patras, I.: TARN: temporal attentive relation network for few-shot and zero-shot action recognition. In: BMVC (2019)
4. Cao, C., Li, Y., Lv, Q., Wang, P., Zhang, Y.: Few-shot action recognition with implicit temporal alignment and pair similarity optimization. In: CVIU (2021)
5. Cao, K., Ji, J., Cao, Z., Chang, C.Y., Niebles, J.C.: Few-shot video classification via temporal alignment. In: CVPR (2020)
6. Carion, N., Massa, F., Synnaeve, G., Usunier, N., Kirillov, A., Zagoruyko, S.: End-to-end object detection with transformers. In: Vedaldi, A., Bischof, H., Brox, T., Frahm, J.-M. (eds.) ECCV 2020. LNCS, vol. 12346, pp. 213–229. Springer, Cham (2020). https://doi.org/10.1007/978-3-030-58452-8_13
7. Carreira, J., Zisserman, A.: Quo Vadis, action recognition? A new model and the kinetics dataset. In: CVPR (2017)
8. Chang, C.Y., Huang, D.A., Sui, Y., Fei-Fei, L., Niebles, J.C.: D3TW: discriminative differentiable dynamic time warping for weakly supervised action alignment and segmentation. In: CVPR (2019)
9. Chao, Y.W., Vijayanarasimhan, S., Seybold, B., Ross, D.A., Deng, J., Sukthankar, R.: Rethinking the faster R-CNN architecture for temporal action localization. In: CVPR (2018)
10. Chowdhury, A., Jiang, M., Chaudhuri, S., Jermaine, C.: Few-shot image classification: just use a library of pre-trained feature extractors and a simple classifier. In: ICCV (2021)
11. Cong, Y., Liao, W., Ackermann, H., Rosenhahn, B., Yang, M.Y.: Spatial-temporal transformer for dynamic scene graph generation. In: ICCV (2021)
12. Deng, J., Dong, W., Socher, R., Li, L.J., Li, K., Fei-Fei, L.: ImageNet: a large-scale hierarchical image database. In: CVPR (2009)
13. Deng, J., Yang, Z., Chen, T., Zhou, W., Li, H.: TransVG: end-to-end visual grounding with transformers. In: ICCV (2021)
14. Dhillon, G.S., Chaudhari, P., Ravichandran, A., Soatto, S.: A baseline for few-shot image classification. In: ICLR (2019)
15. Doersch, C., Gupta, A., Zisserman, A.: CrossTransformers: spatially-aware few-shot transfer. In: NeurIPS (2020)

16. Fan, Q., Zhuo, W., Tang, C.K., Tai, Y.W.: Few-shot object detection with attention-RPN and multi-relation detector. In: CVPR (2020)

17. Finn, C., Abbeel, P., Levine, S.: Model-agnostic meta-learning for fast adaptation of deep networks. In: International Conference on Machine Learning. PMLR (2017)

18. Fu, Y., Zhang, L., Wang, J., Fu, Y., Jiang, Y.G.: Depth guided adaptive meta-fusion network for few-shot video recognition. In: ACM MM (2020)

19. Goyal, R., et al.: The "something something" video database for learning and evaluating visual common sense. In: ICCV (2017)

20. Grauman, K., Westbury, A., Byrne, E., et al.: Ego4D: around the world in 3,000 hours of egocentric video. arXiv preprint arXiv:2110.07058 (2021)

21. Gui, L.-Y., Wang, Y.-X., Ramanan, D., Moura, J.M.F.: Few-shot human motion prediction via meta-learning. In: Ferrari, V., Hebert, M., Sminchisescu, C., Weiss, Y. (eds.) ECCV 2018. LNCS, vol. 11212, pp. 441–459. Springer, Cham (2018). https://doi.org/10.1007/978-3-030-01237-3_27

22. He, K., Gkioxari, G., Dollár, P., Girshick, R.: Mask R-CNN. In: ICCV (2017)

23. He, K., Zhang, X., Ren, S., Sun, J.: Deep residual learning for image recognition. In: CVPR (2016)

24. Hong, J., Fisher, M., Gharbi, M., Fatahalian, K.: Video pose distillation for few-shot, fine-grained sports action recognition. In: ICCV (2021)

25. Huang, Y., Cai, M., Li, Z., Sato, Y.: Predicting gaze in egocentric video by learning task-dependent attention transition. In: Ferrari, V., Hebert, M., Sminchisescu, C., Weiss, Y. (eds.) ECCV 2018. LNCS, vol. 11208, pp. 789–804. Springer, Cham (2018). https://doi.org/10.1007/978-3-030-01225-0_46

26. Kang, B., Liu, Z., Wang, X., Yu, F., Feng, J., Darrell, T.: Few-shot object detection via feature reweighting. In: ICCV (2019)

27. Kang, D., Kwon, H., Min, J., Cho, M.: Relational embedding for few-shot classification. In: ICCV (2021)

28. Kliper-Gross, O., Hassner, T., Wolf, L.: One shot similarity metric learning for action recognition. In: SIMBAD (2011)

29. Koch, G., Zemel, R., Salakhutdinov, R., et al.: Siamese neural networks for one-shot image recognition. In: ICML (2015)

30. Kuehne, H., Jhuang, H., Garrote, E., Poggio, T., Serre, T.: HMDB: a large video database for human motion recognition. In: ICCV (2011)

31. Kuhn, H.W.: The Hungarian method for the assignment problem. Nav. Res. Logist. Q. **2**, 83–97 (1955)

32. Kumar Dwivedi, S., Gupta, V., Mitra, R., Ahmed, S., Jain, A.: ProtoGAN: towards few shot learning for action recognition. In: CVPRW (2019)

33. Li, H., Eigen, D., Dodge, S., Zeiler, M., Wang, X.: Finding task-relevant features for few-shot learning by category traversal. In: CVPR (2019)

34. Li, S., et al.: TA2N: two-stage action alignment network for few-shot action recognition. arXiv preprint arXiv:2107.04782 (2021)

35. Lin, T.-Y., et al.: Microsoft COCO: common objects in context. In: Fleet, D., Pajdla, T., Schiele, B., Tuytelaars, T. (eds.) ECCV 2014. LNCS, vol. 8693, pp. 740–755. Springer, Cham (2014). https://doi.org/10.1007/978-3-319-10602-1_48

36. Liu, W., Zhang, C., Lin, G., Liu, F.: CRNet: cross-reference networks for few-shot segmentation. In: CVPR (2020)

37. Liu, Y., Zhang, X., Zhang, S., He, X.: Part-aware prototype network for few-shot semantic segmentation. In: Vedaldi, A., Bischof, H., Brox, T., Frahm, J.-M. (eds.) ECCV 2020. LNCS, vol. 12354, pp. 142–158. Springer, Cham (2020). https://doi.org/10.1007/978-3-030-58545-7_9

38. Liu, Z., et al.: Swin transformer: hierarchical vision transformer using shifted windows. In: ICCV (2021)
39. Lu, Z., He, S., Zhu, X., Zhang, L., Song, Y.Z., Xiang, T.: Simpler is better: few-shot semantic segmentation with classifier weight transformer. In: ICCV (2021)
40. Luo, Z., et al.: Weakly-supervised action localization with expectation-maximization multi-instance learning. In: Vedaldi, A., Bischof, H., Brox, T., Frahm, J.-M. (eds.) ECCV 2020. LNCS, vol. 12374, pp. 729–745. Springer, Cham (2020). https://doi.org/10.1007/978-3-030-58526-6_43
41. Ma, J., Gorti, S.K., Volkovs, M., Yu, G.: Weakly supervised action selection learning in video. In: CVPR (2021)
42. Mishra, A., Verma, V.K., Reddy, M.S.K., Arulkumar, S., Rai, P., Mittal, A.: A generative approach to zero-shot and few-shot action recognition. In: WACV (2018)
43. Patravali, J., Mittal, G., Yu, Y., Li, F., Chen, M.: Unsupervised few-shot action recognition via action-appearance aligned meta-adaptation. In: ICCV (2021)
44. Perrett, T., Masullo, A., Burghardt, T., Mirmehdi, M., Damen, D.: Temporal-relational crosstransformers for few-shot action recognition. In: CVPR (2021)
45. Qiao, S., Liu, C., Shen, W., Yuille, A.L.: Few-shot image recognition by predicting parameters from activations. In: CVPR (2018)
46. Ravi, S., Larochelle, H.: Optimization as a model for few-shot learning. In: ICLR (2017)
47. Snell, J., Swersky, K., Zemel, R.S.: Prototypical networks for few-shot learning. In: NeurIPS (2017)
48. Soomro, K., Zamir, A.R., Shah, M.: UCF101: a dataset of 101 human actions classes from videos in the wild. arXiv preprint arXiv:1212.0402 (2012)
49. Sun, R., Li, Y., Zhang, T., Mao, Z., Wu, F., Zhang, Y.: Lesion-aware transformers for diabetic retinopathy grading. In: CVPR (2021)
50. Thatipelli, A., Narayan, S., Khan, S., Anwer, R.M., Khan, F.S., Ghanem, B.: Spatio-temporal relation modeling for few-shot action recognition. arXiv preprint arXiv:2112.05132 (2021)
51. Vaswani, A., et al.: Attention is all you need. In: NeurIPS (2017)
52. Vinyals, O., Blundell, C., Lillicrap, T., Wierstra, D., et al.: Matching networks for one shot learning. In: NeurIPS (2016)
53. Wang, H., Zhang, X., Hu, Y., Yang, Y., Cao, X., Zhen, X.: Few-shot semantic segmentation with democratic attention networks. In: Vedaldi, A., Bischof, H., Brox, T., Frahm, J.-M. (eds.) ECCV 2020. LNCS, vol. 12358, pp. 730–746. Springer, Cham (2020). https://doi.org/10.1007/978-3-030-58601-0_43
54. Wang, K., Liew, J.H., Zou, Y., Zhou, D., Feng, J.: PANet: few-shot image semantic segmentation with prototype alignment. In: ICCV (2019)
55. Wang, L., et al.: Temporal segment networks: towards good practices for deep action recognition. In: Leibe, B., Matas, J., Sebe, N., Welling, M. (eds.) ECCV 2016. LNCS, vol. 9912, pp. 20–36. Springer, Cham (2016). https://doi.org/10.1007/978-3-319-46484-8_2
56. Wang, X., et al.: Semantic-guided relation propagation network for few-shot action recognition. In: ACM MM (2021)
57. Wang, X., Huang, T.E., Darrell, T., Gonzalez, J.E., Yu, F.: Frustratingly simple few-shot object detection. In: ICML (2020)
58. Wei, X.S., Wang, P., Liu, L., Shen, C., Wu, J.: Piecewise classifier mappings: learning fine-grained learners for novel categories with few examples. TIP **28**, 6116–6125 (2019)

59. Xian, Y., Korbar, B., Douze, M., Schiele, B., Akata, Z., Torresani, L.: Generalized many-way few-shot video classification. In: Bartoli, A., Fusiello, A. (eds.) ECCV 2020. LNCS, vol. 12540, pp. 111–127. Springer, Cham (2020). https://doi.org/10.1007/978-3-030-65414-6_10
60. Xian, Y., Korbar, B., Douze, M., Torresani, L., Schiele, B., Akata, Z.: Generalized few-shot video classification with video retrieval and feature generation. In: TPAMI (2021)
61. Xu, B., Ye, H., Zheng, Y., Wang, H., Luwang, T., Jiang, Y.G.: Dense dilated network for few shot action recognition. In: ICMR (2018)
62. Xu, C., et al.: Learning dynamic alignment via meta-filter for few-shot learning. In: CVPR (2021)
63. Xu, M., Zhao, C., Rojas, D.S., Thabet, A., Ghanem, B.: G-TAD: sub-graph localization for temporal action detection. In: CVPR (2020)
64. Yang, J., et al.: Focal self-attention for local-global interactions in vision transformers. In: NeurIPS (2021)
65. Ye, H.J., Hu, H., Zhan, D.C., Sha, F.: Few-shot learning via embedding adaptation with set-to-set functions. In: CVPR, pp. 8808–8817 (2020)
66. Zeng, R., Huang, W., Tan, M., Rong, Y., Zhao, P., Huang, J., Gan, C.: Graph convolutional networks for temporal action localization. In: ICCV (2019)
67. Zhang, C., Cai, Y., Lin, G., Shen, C.: DeepEMD: few-shot image classification with differentiable earth mover's distance and structured classifiers. In: CVPR (2020)
68. Zhang, C., Gupta, A., Zisserman, A.: Temporal query networks for fine-grained video understanding. In: CVPR (2021)
69. Zhang, H., Zhang, L., Qi, X., Li, H., Torr, P.H.S., Koniusz, P.: Few-shot action recognition with permutation-invariant attention. In: Vedaldi, A., Bischof, H., Brox, T., Frahm, J.-M. (eds.) ECCV 2020. LNCS, vol. 12350, pp. 525–542. Springer, Cham (2020). https://doi.org/10.1007/978-3-030-58558-7_31
70. Zhang, S., Zhou, J., He, X.: Learning implicit temporal alignment for few-shot video classification. IJCAI (2021)
71. Zhou, B., Andonian, A., Oliva, A., Torralba, A.: Temporal relational reasoning in videos. In: Ferrari, V., Hebert, M., Sminchisescu, C., Weiss, Y. (eds.) ECCV 2018. LNCS, vol. 11205, pp. 831–846. Springer, Cham (2018). https://doi.org/10.1007/978-3-030-01246-5_49
72. Zhu, L., Yang, Y.: Compound memory networks for few-shot video classification. In: Ferrari, V., Hebert, M., Sminchisescu, C., Weiss, Y. (eds.) ECCV 2018. LNCS, vol. 11211, pp. 782–797. Springer, Cham (2018). https://doi.org/10.1007/978-3-030-01234-2_46
73. Zhu, L., Yang, Y.: Label independent memory for semi-supervised few-shot video classification. TPAMI **44**, 273–285 (2020)
74. Zhu, X., Toisoul, A., Perez-Rua, J.M., Zhang, L., Martinez, B., Xiang, T.: Few-shot action recognition with prototype-centered attentive learning. BMVC (2021)
75. Zhu, Z., Wang, L., Guo, S., Wu, G.: A closer look at few-shot video classification: a new baseline and benchmark. BMVC (2021)

Continual 3D Convolutional Neural Networks for Real-time Processing of Videos

Lukas Hedegaard$^{(\boxtimes)}$ ⓘ and Alexandros Iosifidis ⓘ

Department of Electrical and Computer Engineering, Aarhus University,
Aarhus, Denmark
{lhm,ai}@ece.au.dk

Abstract. We introduce *Continual* 3D Convolutional Neural Networks (*Co*3D CNNs), a new computational formulation of spatio-temporal 3D CNNs, in which videos are processed frame-by-frame rather than by clip. In online tasks demanding frame-wise predictions, *Co*3D CNNs dispense with the computational redundancies of regular 3D CNNs, namely the repeated convolutions over frames, which appear in overlapping clips. We show that *Continual* 3D CNNs can reuse preexisting 3D-CNN weights to reduce the per-prediction floating point operations (FLOPs) in proportion to the temporal receptive field while retaining similar memory requirements and accuracy. This is validated with multiple models on Kinetics-400 and Charades with remarkable results: *Co*X3D models attain state-of-the-art complexity/accuracy trade-offs on Kinetics-400 with $12.1-15.3\times$ reductions of FLOPs and $2.3-3.8\%$ improvements in accuracy compared to regular X3D models while reducing peak memory consumption by up to 48%. Moreover, we investigate the transient response of *Co*3D CNNs at start-up and perform extensive benchmarks of on-hardware processing characteristics for publicly available 3D CNNs.

Keywords: 3D CNN · Human activity recognition · Efficient · Stream processing · Online inference · Continual inference network

1 Introduction

Through the availability of large-scale open-source datasets such as ImageNet [37] and Kinetics [4,25], deep, over-parameterized Convolutional Neural Networks (CNNs) have achieved impressive results in the field of computer vision. In video recognition specifically, 3D CNNs have lead to multiple breakthroughs in the state-of-the-art [3,10,11,43]. Despite their success in competitions and benchmarks where only prediction quality is evaluated, computational cost and processing time remains a challenge to the deployment in many real-life use-cases

Supplementary Information The online version contains supplementary material available at https://doi.org/10.1007/978-3-031-19772-7_22.

with energy constraints and/or real-time needs. To combat this general issue, multiple approaches have been explored. These include computationally efficient architectures for image [17,42,48] and video recognition [10,28,49], pruning of network weights [6,13,14], knowledge distillation [16,36,47], and network quantisation [2,12,19].

The contribution in this paper is complementary to all of the above. It exploits the computational redundancies in the application of regular spatio-temporal 3D CNNs to a continual video stream in a sliding window fashion (Fig. 2). This redundancy was also explored recently [26,39] using specialised architectures. However, these are not weight-compatible with regular 3D CNNs. We present a weight-compatible reformulation of the 3D CNN and its components as a *Continual* 3D Convolutional Neural Network (*Co*3D CNN). *Co*3D CNNs process input videos frame-by-frame rather than clip-wise and can reuse the weights of regular 3D CNNs, producing identical outputs for networks without temporal zero-padding. Contrary to most deep learning papers, the work presented here needed no training; our goal was to validate the efficacy of converting regular 3D CNNs to Continual CNNs directly, and to explore their characteristics in the online recognition domain. Accordingly, we perform conversions from five 3D CNNs, each at different points on the accuracy/speed pareto-frontier, and evaluate their framewise performance. While there is a slight reduction in accuracy after conversion due to zero-padding in the regular 3D CNNs, a simple network modification of extending the temporal receptive field recovers and improves the accuracy significantly *without* any fine-tuning at a negligible increase in computational cost.

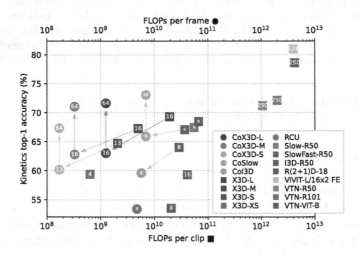

Fig. 1. Accuracy/complexity trade-off for *Continual* 3D CNNs and recent state-of-the-art methods on Kinetics-400 using 1-clip/frame testing. ■ FLOPs per *clip* are noted for regular networks, while ● FLOPs per *frame* are shown for the Continual 3D CNNs. Frames per clip/global average pool size is noted in the representative points. Diagonal and vertical arrows indicate a direct weight transfer from regular to Continual 3D CNN and an extension of receptive field.

Furthermore, we measure the transient network response at start-up, and perform extensive benchmarking on common hardware and embedded devices to gauge the expected inference speeds for real-life scenarios. Full source code is available at https://github.com/lukashedegaard/co3d.

2   Related Works

2.1   3D CNNs for Video Recognition

Convolutional Neural Networks with spatio-temporal 3D kernels may be considered the natural extension of 2D CNNs for image recognition to CNNs for video recognition. Although they did not surpass their 2D CNN + RNN competitors [7, 21] initially [20, 23, 44], arguably due to a high parameter count and insufficient dataset size, 3D CNNs have achieved state-of-the-art results on Human Action Recognition tasks [3, 11, 43] since the Kinetics dataset [25] was introduced. While recent large-scale Transformer-based methods [1, 32] have become leaders in terms of accuracy, 3D CNNs still achieve state-of-the-art accuracy/complexity trade-offs. Nevertheless, competitive accuracy comes with high computational cost, which is prohibitive to many real-life use cases.

In image recognition, efficient architectures such as MobileNet [17], ShuffleNet [48], and EfficientNet [42] attained improved accuracy-complexity trade-offs. These architectures were extended to the 3D-convolutional versions 3D-MobileNet [28], 3D-ShuffleNet [28] and X3D [10] ($\approx$3D-EfficientNet) with similarly improved pareto-frontier in video-recognition tasks. While these efficient 3D CNNs work well for offline processing of videos, they are limited in the context of online processing, where we wish to make updates predictions for each frame; real-time processing rates can only be achieved with the smallest models at severely reduced accuracy. 3D CNNs suffer from the restriction that they must process a whole "clip" (spatio-temporal volume) at a time. When predictions are needed for each frame, this imposes a significant overhead due to repeated computations. In our work, we overcome this challenge by introducing an alternative computational scheme for spatio-temporal convolutions, -pooling, and -residuals, which lets us compute 3D CNN outputs frame-wise (continually) and dispose of the redundancies produced by regular 3D CNNs.

2.2   Architectures for Online Video Recognition

A well-explored approach to video-recognition [7, 21, 22, 40] is to let each frame pass through a 2D CNN trained on ImageNet in one stream alongside a second stream of Optical Flow [9] and integrate these using a recurrent network. Such architectures requires no network modification for deployment in online-processing scenarios, lends themselves to caching [46], and are free of the computational redundancies experienced in 3D CNNs. However, the overhead of Optical Flow and costly feature-extractors pose a substantial disadvantage.

Another approach is to utilise 3D CNNs for feature extraction. In [31], spatio-temporal features from non-overlapping clips are used to train a recurrent network for hand gesture recognition. In [27], a 3D CNN processes a sliding window of the input to perform spatio-temporal action detection. These 3D CNN-based methods have the disadvantage of either not producing predictions for each input frame [31] or suffering from redundant computations from overlapping clips [27].

Massively Parallel Video Networks [5] split a DNN into depth-parallel sub-networks across multiple computational devices to improve online multi-device parallel processing performance. While their approach treats networks layers as atomic operations and doesn't tackle the fundamental redundancy of temporal convolutions, *Continual* 3D CNNs reformulate the network layers, remove redundancy, and accelerate inference on single devices as well.

Exploring modifications of the spatio-temporal 3D convolution, the Recurrent Convolutional Unit (RCU) [39] replaces the 3D convolution by aggregating a spatial 2D convolution over the current input with a 1D convolution over the prior output. Dissected 3D CNNs [26] (D3D) cache the $1 \times n_H \times n_W$ frame-level features in network residual connections and aggregate them with the current frame features via $2 \times 3 \times 3$ convolutions. Like our proposed *Continual* 3D CNNs, both RCU and D3D are causal and operate frame-by-frame. However, they are speciality architectures, which are incompatible with pre-trained 3D CNNs, and must be trained from scratch. We reformulate spatio-temporal convolutions in a one-to-one compatible manner, allowing us to reuse existing model weights.

3   Continual Convolutional Neural Networks

3.1   Regular 3D-Convolutions Lead to Redundancy

Currently, the best performing architectures (e.g., X3D [10] and SlowFast [11]) employ variations on 3D convolutions as their main building block and perform predictions for a spatio-temporal input volume (video-clip). These architectures achieve high accuracy with reasonable computational cost for predictions on clips in the offline setting. They are, however, ill-suited for online video classification, where the input is a continual stream of video frames and a class prediction is needed for each frame. For regular 3D CNNs processing clips of m_T frames to be used in this context, prior $m_T - 1$ input frames need to be stored between temporal time-steps and assembled to form a new video-clip when the next frame is sampled. This is illustrated in Fig. 2.

Recall the computational complexity for a 3D convolution:

$$\Theta([k_H \cdot k_W \cdot k_T + b] \cdot c_I \cdot c_O \cdot n_H \cdot n_W \cdot n_T), \tag{1}$$

where k denotes the kernel size, T, H, and W are time, height, and width dimension subscripts, $b \in \{0, 1\}$ indicates whether bias is used, and c_I and c_O are the number of input and output channels. The size of the output feature map is $n = (m + 2p - d \cdot (k - 1) - 1)/s + 1$ for an input of size m and a convolution with padding p, dilation d, and stride s. During online processing, every frame in the continual video-stream will be processed n_T times (once for each position in the clip), leading to a redundancy proportional with $n_T - 1$. Moreover, the memory-overhead of storing prior input frames is

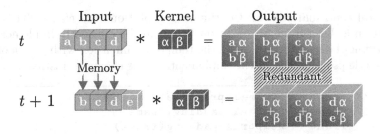

Fig. 2. Redundant computations for a temporal convolution during online processing, as illustrated by the repeated convolution of inputs (green **b, c, d**) with a kernel (blue α, β) in the temporal dimension. Moreover, prior inputs (**b, c, d**) must be stored between time-steps for online processing tasks. (Color figure online)

$$\Theta(c_I \cdot m_H \cdot m_W \cdot [m_T - 1])), \qquad (2)$$

and during inference the network has to transiently store feature-maps of size

$$\Theta(c_O \cdot n_H \cdot n_W \cdot n_T). \qquad (3)$$

3.2   Continual Convolutions

We can remedy the issue described in Sect. 3.1 by employing an alternative sequence of computational steps. In essence, we reformulate the repeated convolution of a (3D) kernel with a (3D) input-clip that continually shifts along the temporal dimension as a *Continual* Convolution (*Co*Conv), where all convolution computations (bar the final sum) for the (3D) kernel with each (2D) input-frame are performed in one time-step. Intermediary results are stored as states to be used in subsequent steps, while previous and current results are summed up to produce the output. The process for a 1D input and kernel, which corresponds to the regular convolution in Fig. 2, is illustrated in Fig. 3. In general, this scheme can be applied for online-processing of any ND input, where one dimension is

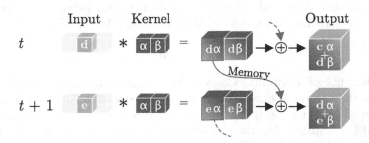

Fig. 3. Continual Convolution. An input (green **d** or **e**) is convolved with a kernel (blue α, β). The intermediary feature-maps corresponding to all but the last temporal position are stored, while the last feature map and prior memory are summed to produce the resulting output. For a continual stream of inputs, Continual Convolutions produce identical outputs to regular convolutions. (Color figure online)

a temporal continual stream. Continual Convolutions are causal [34] with no information leaking from future to past and can be efficiently implemented by zero-padding the input frame along the temporal dimension with $p = \text{floor}(k/2)$. Python-style pseudo-code of the implementation is shown in Listing 1.1.

```
def coconv3d(frame, prev_state = (mem, i)):
    frame = spatial_padding(frame)
    frame = temporal_padding(frame)
    feat = conv3d(frame, weights)
    output, rest_feat = feat[0], feat[1:]
    mem, i = prev_state or init_state(output)
    M = len(mem)
    for m in range(M):
        output += mem[(i + m) % M, M - m - 1]
    output += bias
    mem[i] = rest_feat
    i = (i + 1) % M
    return output, (mem, i)
```

Listing 1.1. Pseudo-code for Continual Convolution. Ready-to-use modules are available in the Continual Inference library [15].

In terms of computational cost, we can now perform frame-by-frame computations much more efficiently than a regular 3D convolution. The complexity of processing a frame becomes:

$$\Theta([k_H \cdot k_W \cdot k_T + b] \cdot c_I \cdot c_O \cdot n_H \cdot n_W). \tag{4}$$

This reduction in computational complexity comes at the cost of a memory-overhead in each layer due to the state that is kept between time-steps. The overhead of storing the partially computed feature-maps for a frame is:

$$\Theta(d_T \cdot [k_T - 1] \cdot c_O \cdot n_H \cdot n_W). \tag{5}$$

However, in the context of inference in a deep neural network, the transient memory usage within each time-step is reduced by a factor of n_T to

$$\Theta(c_O \cdot n_H \cdot n_W). \tag{6}$$

The benefits of Continual Convolutions include the independence of clip length on the computational complexity, state overhead, and transient memory consumption. The change from (non-causal) regular convolutions to (causal) Continual Convolutions has the side-effect of introducing a delay to the output. This is because some intermediary results of convolving a frame with the kernel are only added up at a later point in time (see Fig. 3). The delay amounts to

$$\Theta(d_T \cdot [k_T - p_T - 1]). \tag{7}$$

3.3   Continual Residuals

The delay from Continual Convolutions has an adverse side-effect on residual connections. Despite their simplicity in regular CNNs, we cannot simply add the input to a Continual Convolution with its output because the CoConv may delay the output. Residual connections to a CoConv must therefore be delayed by an equivalent amount (see Eq. 7). This produces a memory overhead of

$$\Theta(d_T \cdot [k_T - 1] \cdot c_O \cdot m_H \cdot m_W). \tag{8}$$

3.4   Continual Pooling

The associative property of pooling operations allows for pooling to be decomposed across dimensions, i.e. $\text{pool}_{T,H,W}(\mathbf{X}) = \text{pool}_T(\text{pool}_{H,W}(\mathbf{X}))$. For continual spatio-temporal pooling, the pooling over spatial dimensions is equivalent to a regular pooling, while the intermediary pooling results must be stored for prior temporal frames. For a pooling operation with temporal kernel size k_T and spatial output size $n_H \cdot n_W$, the memory consumption and delays are

$$\Theta([k_T - 1] \cdot n_H \cdot n_W), \tag{9}$$
$$\Theta(k_T - p_T - 1). \tag{10}$$

Both memory consumption and delay scale linearly with the temporal kernel size. Fortunately, the memory consumed by temporal pooling layers is relatively modest for most CNN architectures (1.5% for CoX3D-M, see Appendix A). Hence, the delay rather than memory consumption may be of primary concern for real-life applications. For some network modules it may even make sense to skip the pooling in the conversion to a Continual CNN. One such example is the 3D Squeeze-and-Excitation (SE) block [18] in X3D, where global spatio-temporal average-pooling is used in the computation of channel-wise self-attention. Discarding the temporal pooling component (making it a 2D SE block) shifts the attention slightly (assuming the frame contents change slowly relative to the sampling rate) but avoids a considerable temporal delay.

3.5   The Issue with Temporal Padding

Zero-padding of convolutional layers is a popular strategy for retaining the spatio-temporal dimension of feature-maps in consecutive CNN layers. For Continual CNNs, however, temporal zero-padding poses a problem, as illustrated in Fig. 4. Consider a 2-layer 1D CNN where each layer has a kernel size of 3 and zero padding of 1. For each new frame in a continual stream of inputs, the first layer l should produce two output feature-maps: One by the convolution of the two prior frames and the new frame, and another by convolving with one prior frame, the new frame, and a zero-pad. The next layer $l + 1$ thus receives two inputs and produces three outputs which are dependent on the new input frame of the first layer (one for each input and another from zero-padding). In

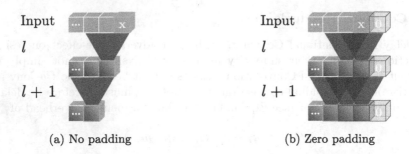

(a) No padding   (b) Zero padding

Fig. 4. Issue with temporal padding: The latest frame **x** is propagated through a CNN with (purple) temporal kernels of size 3 (a) without or (b) with zero padding. Highlighted cubes can be produced only in the latest frame, with yellow boarder indicating independence of padded zero and red boarders dependence. In the zero-padded case (b), the number of frame features dependent on **x** following a layer l increases with the number of padded zeros. (Color figure online)

effect, each zero padding in a convolution forces the next layer to retrospectively update its output for a previous time-step in a non-causal manner. Thus, there is a considerable downside to the use of padding. This questions the necessity of zero padding along the temporal dimension. In regular CNNs, zero padding has two benefits: It helps to avoid spatio-temporal shrinkage of feature-maps when propagated through a deep CNN, and it prevents information at the boarders from "washing away" [24]. The use of zero-padding, however, has the downside that it alters the input-distribution along the boarders significantly [29,33]. For input data which is a continual stream of frames, a shrinkage of the feature-size in the temporal dimension is not a concern, and an input frame (which may be considered a border frame in a regular 3D CNN) has no risk of "washing away" because it is a middle frame in subsequent time steps. Temporal padding is thus omitted in Continual CNNs. As can be seen in the experimental evaluations presented in the following, this constitutes a "model shift" in the conversion from regular to Continual 3D CNN if the former was trained with temporal padding.

3.6 Initialisation

Before a Continual CNN reaches a steady state of operation, it must have processed $r_T - p_T - 1$ frames where r_T and p_T are the aggregated temporal receptive field and padding of the network. For example, Continual X3D-{S, M, L} models have receptive fields of size {69, 72, 130}, aggregated padding {28, 28, 57}, and hence need to process {40, 43, 72} frames prior to normal operation. The initial response depends on how internal state variables are initialised. In Sect. 4.2, we explore this further with two initialisation variants: 1) Initialisation with *zeros* and 2) by repeating a *replicate* of the features corresponding to the first input-frame. The latter corresponds to operating in a steady state for a "boring video" [3] which has one frame repeated in the entire clip.

3.7   Design Considerations

Disregarding the storage requirement of model weights (which is identical between for regular and continual 3D CNNs), X3D-M has a worst-case total memory-consumption of 7,074,816 floats when prior frames and the transient feature-maps are taken into account. Its continual counterpart, CoX3D-M, has a worst case memory only 5,072,688 floats. How can this be? Since Continual 3D CNNs do not store prior input frames and have smaller transient feature maps, memory savings outweigh the cost of caching features in each continual layer. Had the clip size been four instead of sixteen, X3D-M_4 would have had a worst-case memory consumption of 1,655,808 floats and CoX3D-M_4 of 5,067,504 floats. For clip size 64, X3D-M_{64} consumes 28,449,792 floats and CoX3D-M_{64} uses 5,093,424 floats. The memory load of regular 3D CNNs is thus highly dependent on clip size, while that of Co3D CNNs is not. Continual CNNs utilise longer receptive fields much more efficiently than regular CNNs in online processing scenarios. In networks intended for embedded systems or online processing, we may increase the clip size to achieve higher accuracy with minimal penalty in computational complexity and worst-case memory.

Another consideration, which influences memory consumption is the temporal kernel size and dilation of CoConv layers. Fortunately, the trend to employ small kernel sizes leaves the memory consumption reasonable for recent 3D CNNs [3,10,11,43]. A larger temporal kernel size would not only affect the memory growth through the CoConv filter, but also for co-occuring residual connections. These consume a significant fraction of the total state-memory for real-life networks: in a Continual X3D-M model (CoX3D-M) the memory of residuals constitutes 20.5% of the total model state memory (see Appendix A).

3.8   Training

Co3D CNNs are trained with back-propagation like other neural networks. However, special care must be taken in the estimation of data statistics in normalisation layers: 1) Momentum should be adjusted to $\text{mom}_{\text{step}} = 2/(1 + \text{timesteps} \cdot (2/\text{mom}_{\text{clip}} - 1))$ to match the exponential moving average dynamics of clip-based training, where T is the clip size; 2) statistics should not be tracked for the transient response. Alternatively, they can be trained offline in their "unrolled" regular 3D-CNN form with no temporal padding. This is similar to utilising pre-trained weights from a regular 3D CNN, as we do in our experiments.

4   Experiments

The experiments in this section aim to show the characteristics and advantages of Continual 3D CNNs as compared with regular 3D CNNs. One of the main benefits of Co3D CNNs is their ability to reuse the network weights of regular 3D CNNs. As such, all Co3D CNNs in these experiments use publicly available pre-trained network weights of regular 3D CNNs [8,10,11] without further fine-tuning. Data pre-processing follows the respective procedures associated with the originating weights unless stated otherwise. The section is laid out as follows: First,

Table 1. Kinetics-400 benchmark. The noted accuracy is the single clip or frame top-1 score using RGB as the only input-modality. The performance was evaluated using publicly available pre-trained models without any further fine-tuning. For speed comparison, predictions per second denote frames per second for the CoX3D models and clips per second for the remaining models. Throughput results are the mean of 100 measurements. Pareto-optimal models are marked with bold. Mem. is the maximum allocated memory during inference noted in megabytes. [†] Approximate FLOPs derived from paper (see Appendix C).

	Model	Acc. (%)	Par. (M)	Mem. (MB)	FLOPs (G)	Throughput (preds/s)			
						CPU	TX2	Xavier	2080Ti
Clip	I3D-R50	63.98	28.04	191.59	28.61	0.93	2.54	9.20	77.15
	R(2+1)D-18_8	53.52	31.51	168.87	20.35	1.75	3.19	6.82	130.88
	R(2+1)D-18_{16}	59.29	31.51	215.44	40.71	0.83	1.82	3.77	75.81
	Slow-8×8-R50	67.42	32.45	266.04	54.87	0.38	1.34	4.31	61.92
	SlowFast-8×8-R50	68.45	66.25	344.84	66.25	0.34	0.87	2.72	30.72
	SlowFast-4×16-R50	67.06	34.48	260.51	36.46	0.55	1.33	3.43	41.28
	X3D-L	69.29	6.15	240.66	19.17	0.25	0.19	4.78	36.37
	X3D-M	67.24	3.79	126.29	4.97	0.83	1.47	17.47	116.07
	X3D-S	64.71	3.79	61.29	2.06	2.23	2.68	42.02	276.45
	X3D-XS	59.37	3.79	28.79	0.64	8.26	8.20	135.39	819.87
Frame	RCU$_8$ [39][†]	53.40	12.80	–	4.71	–	–	–	–
	CoI3D$_8$	59.58	28.04	235.87	5.68	3.00	2.41	14.88	125.59
	CoI3D$_{64}$	56.86	28.04	236.08	5.68	3.15	2.41	14.89	126.32
	CoSlow$_8$	65.90	32.45	175.98	6.90	2.80	1.60	6.18	113.77
	CoSlow$_{64}$	**73.05**	**32.45**	**176.41**	**6.90**	**2.92**	**1.60**	**6.19**	**102.00**
	CoX3D-L$_{16}$	63.03	6.15	184.29	1.25	2.30	0.99	25.17	206.65
	CoX3D-L$_{64}$	**71.61**	**6.15**	**184.37**	**1.25**	**2.30**	**0.99**	**27.56**	**217.53**
	CoX3D-M$_{16}$	62.80	3.79	68.88	0.33	7.57	7.26	88.79	844.73
	CoX3D-M$_{64}$	**71.03**	**3.79**	**68.96**	**0.33**	**7.51**	**7.04**	**86.42**	**796.32**
	CoX3D-S$_{13}$	60.18	3.79	41.91	0.17	13.16	11.06	219.64	939.72
	CoX3D-S$_{64}$	**67.33**	**3.79**	**41.99**	**0.17**	**13.19**	**11.13**	**213.65**	**942.97**

we showcase the network performance following weight transfer from regular to Continual 3D on multiple datasets for Human Activity Recognition. This is followed by a study on the transient response of Co3D CNNs at startup. Subsequently, we show how the computational advantages of Co3D CNNs can be exploited to improve accuracy by extending the temporal receptive field. Finally, we perform an extensive on-hardware benchmark of prior methods and Continual 3D CNNs, measuring the 1-clip/frame accuracy of publicly available models, as well as their inference throughput on various computational devices.

4.1 Transfer from Regular to Continual CNNs

To gauge direct transferability of 3D CNN weights, we implement continual versions of various 3D CNNs and initialise them with their publicly available weights for Kinetics-400 [25] and Charades [38]. While it is common to use an ensemble prediction from multiple clips to boost video-level accuracy on these benchmarks, we abstain from this, as it doesn't apply to online-scenarios. Instead, we report the single-clip/frame model performance.

Table 2. Charades benchmark. Noted are the FLOPs × views and video-level mean average precision (mAP) on the validation set using pre-trained model weights. [†]Results achieved using the publicly available SlowFast code [11].

	Model	FLOPs (G)× views	mAP (%)
Clip	Slow-8×8 [11]	54.9 × 30	39.0
	Slow-8×8 [11][†]	54.9 × 1	21.4
	Slow-8×8 (ours)	54.9 × 1	24.1
Fr.	CoSlow$_8$	6.9 × 1	21.5
	CoSlow$_{64}$	6.9 × 1	25.2

Kinetics-400. We evaluate the X3D network variants XS, S, M, and L on the test set using one temporally centred clip from each video. The XS network is omitted in the transfer to CoX3D, given that it is architecturally equivalent to S, but with fewer frames per clip. In evaluation on Kinetics-400, we faced the challenge that videos were limited to 10 s. Due to the longer transient response of Continual CNNs (see Sect. 4.2) and low frame-rate used for training X3D models (5.0, 6.0, 6.0 FPS for S, M, and L), the video-length was insufficient to reach steady-state for some models. As a practical measure to evaluate near steady-state, we repeated the last video-frame for a padded video length of ≈ 80% of the network receptive field as a heuristic choice. The Continual CNNs were thus tested on the last frame of the padded video and initialised with the prior frames. The results of the X3D transfer are shown in Table 1 and Fig. 1.

For all networks, the transfer from regular to Continual 3D CNN results in significant computational savings. For the S, M, and L networks the reduction in FLOPs is 12.1×, 15.1×, and 15.3× respectively. The savings do not quite reach the clip sizes since the final pooling and prediction layers are active for each frame. As a side-effect of the transfer from zero-padded regular CNN to Continual CNN without zero-padding, we see a notable reduction in accuracy. This is easily improved by using an extended pooling size for the network (discussed in Sect. 3.7 and in Sect. 4.2). Using a global average pooling with temporal kernel size 64, we improve the accuracy of X3D by 2.6%, 3.8%, and 2.3% in the Continual S, M, and L network variants. As noted, Kinetics dataset did not have sufficient frames to fill the temporal receptive field of all models in these tests. We explore this further in Sects. 4.2 and 4.2.

Charades. To showcase the generality of the approach, we repeat the above described procedure with another 3D CNN, the CoSlow network [11]. We report the video-level mean average precision (mAP) of the validation split alongside the FLOPs per prediction in Table 2. Note the accuracy discrepancy between 30 view (10 temporal positions with 3 spatial positions each) and 1 view (spatially and temporally centred) evaluation. As observed on Kinetics, the CoSlow network reduces the FLOPs per prediction proportionally with the original clip size (8 frames), and can recover accuracy by extending the global average pool size.

4.2 Ablation Experiments

As described in Sect. 3.6, Continual CNNs exhibit a transient response during their up-start. In order to gauge this response, we perform ablations on the Kinetics-400 validation set, this time sampled at 15 FPS to have a sufficient number of frames available. This corresponds to a data domain shift [45] relative to the pre-trained weights, where time advances slower.

Transient Response of Continual CNNs. Our expected upper bound is given by the baseline X3D network 1-clip accuracy at 15 FPS. The transient response is measured by varying the number of prior frames used for initialisation before evaluating a frame using the CoX3D model. Note that temporal center-crops of size $T_{\text{init}} + 1$, where T_{init} is the number of initialisation frames, are used in each evaluation to ensure that the frames seen by the network come from the centre. This precaution counters a data-bias, we noticed in Kinetics-400, namely that the start and end of a video are less informative and contribute to worse predictions than the central part. We found results to vary up to 8% for a X3D-S network evaluated at different video positions. The experiment is repeated for two initialisation schemes, "zeros" (used in other experiments) and "replicate", and two model sizes, S and M. The transient responses are shown in Fig. 5.

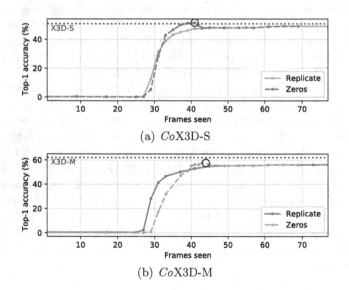

(a) CoX3D-S

(b) CoX3D-M

Fig. 5. Transient response for Continual X3D-{S,M} on the Kinetics-400 val at 15 FPS. Dotted horizontal lines denote X3D validation accuracy for 1-clip predictions. Black circles highlight the theoretically required initialisation frames.

For all responses, the first ≈25 frames produce near-random predictions, before rapidly increasing at 25−30 frames until a steady-state is reached at 49.2% and 56.2% accuracy for S and M. Relative to the regular X3D, this constitutes a steady-state error of −1.7% and −5.8%. Comparing initialisation schemes, we see that the "replicate" scheme results in a slightly earlier rise. The rise sets in later for the "zeros" scheme, but exhibits a sharper slope, topping with peaks of 51.6% and 57.6% at 41 and 44 frames seen as discussed in Sect. 3.6. This makes sense considering that the original network weights were trained with this exact amount of zero-padding. Adding more frames effectively replaces the padded zeros and causes a slight drop of accuracy in the steady state, where the accuracy settles at the same values as for the "replication" scheme.

Extended Receptive Field. Continual CNNs experience a negligible increase in computational cost when larger temporal receptive field are used (see Sect. 3.7). For CoX3D networks, this extension can be trivially implemented by increasing the temporal kernel size of the last pooling layer. In this set of experiments, we extend CoX3D-{S,M,L} to have temporal pooling sizes 32, 64, and 96, and evaluate them on the Kinetics-400 validation set sampled at 15 FPS. The Continual CNNs are evaluated at frames corresponding to the steady state.

Table 3 shows the measured accuracy and floating point operations per frame (CoX3D)/clip (X3D) as well as the pool size for the penultimate network layer (global average pooling) and the total receptive field of the network in the temporal dimension. As found in Sect. 4.1, each transfer results in significant computational savings alongside a drop in accuracy. Extending the kernel size of the global average pooling layer increases the accuracy of the Continual CNNs by $11.0-13.3\%$ for 96 frames relative the original $13-16$ frames, surpassing that of the regular CNNs. Lying at $0.017-0.009\%$, the corresponding computational increases can be considered negligible.

Table 3. Effect of extending pool size. Note that the model weights were trained at different sampling rates than evaluated at (15 FPS), resulting in a lower top-1 val. accuracy. *Italic numbers* denote measurement taken within the transient response due to a lack of frames in the video-clip.

Model	Size	Pool	Acc.	FLOPs (K)	Rec. Field
X3D	S	13	51.0	2,061,366	13
	M	16	62.1	4,970,008	16
	L	16	64.1	19,166,052	16
CoX3D	S	13	49.2	166,565	69
		16	50.1	166,567	72
		32	54.7	166,574	88
		64	59.8	166,587	120
		96	*61.8*	166,601	152
	M	16	56.3	325,456	72
		32	60.7	325,463	88
		64	64.9	325,477	120
		96	*67.3*	325,491	152
	L	16	53.0	1,245,549	130
		32	58.5	1,245,556	146
		64	*64.3*	1,245,570	178
		96	*66.3*	1,245,584	210

4.3   Inference Benchmarks

Despite their high status in activity recognition leader-boards [35], it is unclear how recent 3D CNNs methods perform in the online setting, where speed and accuracy constitute a necessary trade-off. To the best of our knowledge, there has not yet been a systematic evaluation of throughput for these video-recognition models on real-life hardware. In this set of experiments, we benchmark the FLOPs, parameter count, maximum allocated memory and 1-clip/frame accuracy of I3D [3], R(2+1)D [43], SlowFast [41], X3D [10], CoI3D, CoSlow, and CoX3D. To gauge achievable throughputs at different computational budgets, networks were tested on four hardware platforms as described in Appendix B.

As seen in the benchmark results found in Table 1, the limitation to one clip markedly lowers accuracy compared with the multi-clip evaluation published in the respective works [3,10,11,43]. Nonetheless, the Continual models with extended receptive fields attain the best accuracy/speed trade-off by a large margin. For example, CoX3D-L$_{64}$ on the Nvidia Jetson Xavier achieves an accuracy of 71.3% at 27.6 predictions per second compared to 67.2% accuracy at 17.5 predictions per second for X3D-M while reducing maximum allocated memory by 48%! Confirming the observation in [30], we find that the relation between model FLOPs and throughput varies between models, with better ratios attained for simpler models (e.g., I3D) than for complicated ones (e.g., X3D). This relates to different memory access needs and their cost. Tailor-made hardware could plausibly reduce these differences. Supplementary visualisation of the results in Table 1 are found in Appendix C.

5   Conclusion

We have introduced Continual 3D Convolutional Neural Networks (Co3D CNNs), a new computational model for spatio-temporal 3D CNNs, which performs computations frame-wise rather than clip-wise while being weight-compatible with regular 3D CNNs. In doing so, we are able dispose of the computational redundancies faced by 3D CNNs in continual online processing, giving up to a 15.1× reduction of floating point operations, a 9.2× real-life inference speed-up on CPU, 48% peak memory reduction, and an accuracy improvement of 5.6% on Kinetics-400 through an extension in the global average pooling kernel size.

While this constitutes a substantial leap in the processing efficiency of energy-constrained and real-time video recognition systems, there are still unanswered questions pertaining to the dynamics of Co3D CNNs. Specifically, the impact of extended receptive fields on the networks ability to change predictions in response to changing contents in the input video is untested. We leave these as important directions for future work.

Acknowledgement. This work has received funding from the European Union's Horizon 2020 research and innovation programme under grant agreement No 871449 (OpenDR).

References

1. Arnab, A., Dehghani, M., Heigold, G., Sun, C., Lučić, M., Schmid, C.: ViViT: a video vision transformer. In: IEEE/CVF International Conference on Computer Vision (ICCV), pp. 6836–6846 (2021)
2. Cai, Z., He, X., Sun, J., Vasconcelos, N.: Deep learning with low precision by half-wave gaussian quantization. In: 2017 IEEE Conference on Computer Vision and Pattern Recognition (CVPR), pp. 5406–5414 (2017)
3. Carreira, J., Zisserman, A.: Quo Vadis, action recognition? A new model and the kinetics dataset. In: IEEE/CVF Conference on Computer Vision and Pattern Recognition (CVPR), pp. 4724–4733 (2017)
4. Carreira, J., Noland, E., Banki-Horvath, A., Hillier, C., Zisserman, A.: A short note about kinetics-600. preprint, arXiv:1808.01340 (2018)
5. Carreira, J., Pătrăucean, V., Mazare, L., Zisserman, A., Osindero, S.: Massively parallel video networks. In: Ferrari, V., Hebert, M., Sminchisescu, C., Weiss, Y. (eds.) ECCV 2018. LNCS, vol. 11208, pp. 680–697. Springer, Cham (2018). https://doi.org/10.1007/978-3-030-01225-0_40
6. Chen, W., Wilson, J.T., Tyree, S., Weinberger, K.Q., Chen, Y.: Compressing neural networks with the hashing trick. In: International Conference on International Conference on Machine Learning (ICML), pp. 2285–2294 (2015)
7. Donahue, J., et al.: Long-term recurrent convolutional networks for visual recognition and description. In: IEEE Conference on Computer Vision and Pattern Recognition (CVPR), pp. 2625–2634 (2015)
8. Fan, H., et al.: PyTorchVideo: a deep learning library for video understanding. In: ACM International Conference on Multimedia (2021)
9. Farnebäck, G.: Two-frame motion estimation based on polynomial expansion. In: Bigun, J., Gustavsson, T. (eds.) SCIA 2003. LNCS, vol. 2749, pp. 363–370. Springer, Heidelberg (2003). https://doi.org/10.1007/3-540-45103-X_50
10. Feichtenhofer, C.: X3D: expanding architectures for efficient video recognition. In: IEEE/CVF Conference on Computer Vision and Pattern Recognition (CVPR) (2020)
11. Feichtenhofer, C., Fan, H., Malik, J., He, K.: SlowFast networks for video recognition. In: IEEE/CVF International Conference on Computer Vision (ICCV), October 2019
12. Floropoulos, N., Tefas, A.: Complete vector quantization of feedforward neural networks. Neurocomputing 367, 55–63 (2019)
13. Han, S., Mao, H., Dally, W.J.: Deep compression: compressing deep neural network with pruning, trained quantization and Huffman coding. In: International Conference on Learning Representations (ICLR) (2016)
14. He, Y., Zhang, X., Sun, J.: Channel pruning for accelerating very deep neural networks. In: 2017 IEEE International Conference on Computer Vision (ICCV), pp. 1398–1406 (2017)
15. Hedegaard, L., Iosifidis, A.: Continual inference: a library for efficient online inference with deep neural networks in pytorch. In: International Workshop on Computational Aspects of Deep Learning (2022)
16. Hinton, G., Vinyals, O., Dean, J.: Distilling the knowledge in a neural network. In: NIPS Deep Learning and Representation Learning Workshop (2015)
17. Howard, A.G., et al.: MobileNets: efficient convolutional neural networks for mobile vision applications. preprint, arXiv:1704.04861 abs/1704.04861 (2017)

18. Hu, J., Shen, L., Sun, G.: Squeeze-and-excitation networks. In: IEEE/CVF Conference on Computer Vision and Pattern Recognition (CVPR), pp. 7132–7141 (2018)
19. Hubara, I., Courbariaux, M., Soudry, D., El-Yaniv, R., Bengio, Y.: Binarized neural networks. In: Lee, D., Sugiyama, M., Luxburg, U., Guyon, I., Garnett, R. (eds.) Advances in Neural Information Processing Systems, vol. 29. Curran Associates, Inc. (2016)
20. Ji, S., Xu, W., Yang, M., Yu, K.: 3d convolutional neural networks for human action recognition. IEEE Trans. Pattern Anal. Mach. Intell. (TPAMI) 35(1), 221–231 (2013)
21. Yue-Hei Ng, J., Hausknecht, M., Vijayanarasimhan, S., Vinyals, O., Monga, R., Toderici, G.: Beyond short snippets: deep networks for video classification. In: IEEE Conference on Computer Vision and Pattern Recognition (CVPR), pp. 4694–4702 (2015)
22. Kalogeiton, V., Weinzaepfel, P., Ferrari, V., Schmid, C.: Action tubelet detector for spatio-temporal action localization. In: 2017 IEEE International Conference on Computer Vision (ICCV), pp. 4415–4423 (2017)
23. Karpathy, A., Toderici, G., Shetty, S., Leung, T., Sukthankar, R., Fei-Fei, L.: Large-scale video classification with convolutional neural networks. In: IEEE Conference on Computer Vision and Pattern Recognition (CVPR), pp. 1725–1732 (2014)
24. Karpathy, A.: CS231n convolutional neural networks for visual recognition. https://cs231n.github.io/convolutional-networks/. Accessed 26 Jan 2021
25. Kay, W., et al.: The kinetics human action video dataset. preprint, arXiv:1705.06950 (2017)
26. Köpüklü, O., Hörmann, S., Herzog, F., Cevikalp, H., Rigoll, G.: Dissected 3d CNNs: temporal skip connections for efficient online video processing. preprint, arXiv:2009.14639 (2020)
27. Köpüklü, O., Wei, X., Rigoll, G.: You only watch once: a unified CNN architecture for real-time spatiotemporal action localization. preprint, arXiv:1911.06644 (2019)
28. Köpüklü, O., Kose, N., Gunduz, A., Rigoll, G.: Resource efficient 3d convolutional neural networks. In: IEEE/CVF International Conference on Computer Vision Workshop (ICCVW), pp. 1910–1919 (2019)
29. Liu, G., et al.: Partial convolution based padding. preprint, arXiv:1811.11718, pp. 1–11 (2018)
30. Ma, N., Zhang, X., Zheng, H.-T., Sun, J.: ShuffleNet V2: practical guidelines for efficient CNN architecture design. In: Ferrari, V., Hebert, M., Sminchisescu, C., Weiss, Y. (eds.) Computer Vision – ECCV 2018. LNCS, vol. 11218, pp. 122–138. Springer, Cham (2018). https://doi.org/10.1007/978-3-030-01264-9_8
31. Molchanov, P., Yang, X., Gupta, S., Kim, K., Tyree, S., Kautz, J.: Online detection and classification of dynamic hand gestures with recurrent 3d convolutional neural networks. In: 2016 IEEE Conference on Computer Vision and Pattern Recognition (CVPR), pp. 4207–4215 (2016)
32. Neimark, D., Bar, O., Zohar, M., Asselmann, D.: Video transformer network. In: 2021 IEEE/CVF International Conference on Computer Vision Workshops (ICCVW), pp. 3156–3165 (2021)
33. Nguyen, A., Choi, S., Kim, W., Ahn, S., Kim, J., Lee, S.: Distribution padding in convolutional neural networks. In: International Conference on Image Processing (ICIP), pp. 4275–4279 (2019)
34. van den Oord, A., et al.: WaveNet: a generative model for raw audio. preprint, arXiv:1609.03499 (2016)
35. Papers with Code: Kinetics-400 leaderboard. https://paperswithcode.com/sota/action-classification-on-kinetics-400. Accessed 03 Feb 2021

36. Passalis, N., Tefas, A.: Learning deep representations with probabilistic knowledge transfer. In: Ferrari, V., Hebert, M., Sminchisescu, C., Weiss, Y. (eds.) ECCV 2018. LNCS, vol. 11215, pp. 283–299. Springer, Cham (2018). https://doi.org/10.1007/978-3-030-01252-6_17
37. Russakovsky, O., et al.: ImageNet large scale visual recognition challenge. Int. J. Comput. Vis. (ICCV) **115**(3), 211–252 (2015)
38. Sigurdsson, G.A., Varol, G., Wang, X., Farhadi, A., Laptev, I., Gupta, A.: Hollywood in homes: crowdsourcing data collection for activity understanding. In: Leibe, B., Matas, J., Sebe, N., Welling, M. (eds.) ECCV 2016. LNCS, vol. 9905, pp. 510–526. Springer, Cham (2016). https://doi.org/10.1007/978-3-319-46448-0_31
39. Singh, G., Cuzzolin, F.: Recurrent convolutions for causal 3d CNNs. In: 2019 IEEE/CVF International Conference on Computer Vision Workshop (ICCVW), pp. 1456–1465 (2019)
40. Singh, G., Saha, S., Sapienza, M., Torr, P., Cuzzolin, F.: Online real-time multiple spatiotemporal action localisation and prediction. In: 2017 IEEE International Conference on Computer Vision (ICCV), pp. 3657–3666 (2017)
41. Sovrasov, V.: Ptflops, 'github.com/sovrasov/flops-counter.pytorch'. MIT License. Accessed 02 Mar 2021
42. Tan, M., Le, Q.: EfficientNet: rethinking model scaling for convolutional neural networks. In: Proceedings of Machine Learning Research, vol. 97, pp. 6105–6114 (2019)
43. Tran, D., Wang, H., Torresani, L., Ray, J., LeCun, Y., Paluri, M.: A closer look at spatiotemporal convolutions for action recognition. In: IEEE/CVF Conference on Computer Vision and Pattern Recognition (CVPR), pp. 6450–6459 (2018)
44. Tran, D., Bourdev, L., Fergus, R., Torresani, L., Paluri, M.: Learning spatiotemporal features with 3d convolutional networks. In: IEEE International Conference on Computer Vision (ICCV), pp. 4489–4497 (2015)
45. Wang, M., Deng, W.: Deep visual domain adaptation: a survey. Neurocomputing **312**, 135–153 (2018)
46. Xu, M., Zhu, M., Liu, Y., Lin, F., Liu, X.: DeepCache: principled cache for mobile deep vision. In: International Conference on Mobile Computing and Networking (2018)
47. Yim, J., Joo, D., Bae, J., Kim, J.: A gift from knowledge distillation: Fast optimization, network minimization and transfer learning. In: 2017 IEEE Conference on Computer Vision and Pattern Recognition (CVPR), pp. 7130–7138 (2017)
48. Zhang, X., Zhou, X., Lin, M., Sun, J.: ShuffleNet: an extremely efficient convolutional neural network for mobile devices. In: IEEE/CVF Conference on Computer Vision and Pattern Recognition (CVPR), pp. 6848–6856 (2018)
49. Zhu, L., Sevilla-Lara, L., Yang, Y., Feiszli, M., Wang, H.: Faster recurrent networks for efficient video classification. In: Proceedings of the AAAI Conference on Artificial Intelligence, vol. 34, pp. 13098–13105 (2020)

Dynamic Spatio-Temporal Specialization Learning for Fine-Grained Action Recognition

Tianjiao Li[1], Lin Geng Foo[1], Qiuhong Ke[2], Hossein Rahmani[3], Anran Wang[4], Jinghua Wang[5], and Jun Liu[1(✉)]

[1] ISTD Pillar, Singapore University of Technology and Design, Singapore, Singapore
{tianjiao_li,lingeng_foo}@mymail.sutd.edu.sg,jun_liu@sutd.edu.sg
[2] Department of Data Science and AI, Monash University, Melbourne, Australia
[3] School of Computing and Communications, Lancaster University, Lancaster, UK
qiuhong.ke@monash.edu
[4] ByteDance, Beijing, China
h.rahmani@lancaster.ac.uk
[5] School of Computer Science and Technology, Harbin Institute of Technology, Harbin, China
wangjinghua@hit.edu.cn

Abstract. The goal of fine-grained action recognition is to successfully discriminate between action categories with subtle differences. To tackle this, we derive inspiration from the human visual system which contains specialized regions in the brain that are dedicated towards handling specific tasks. We design a novel Dynamic Spatio-Temporal Specialization (DSTS) module, which consists of specialized neurons that are only activated for a subset of samples that are highly similar. During training, the loss forces the specialized neurons to learn discriminative fine-grained differences to distinguish between these similar samples, improving fine-grained recognition. Moreover, a spatio-temporal specialization method further optimizes the architectures of the specialized neurons to capture either more spatial or temporal fine-grained information, to better tackle the large range of spatio-temporal variations in the videos. Lastly, we design an Upstream-Downstream Learning algorithm to optimize our model's dynamic decisions during training, improving the performance of our DSTS module. We obtain state-of-the-art performance on two widely-used fine-grained action recognition datasets.

Keywords: Action recognition · Fine-grained · Dynamic neural networks

---

T. Li and L.G. Foo—Equal contribution.

Supplementary Information The online version contains supplementary material available at https://doi.org/10.1007/978-3-031-19772-7_23.

1   Introduction

Fine-grained action recognition involves distinguishing between similar actions with only subtle differences, e.g., "cutting an apple in a kitchen" and "cutting a pear in a kitchen". This is significantly more challenging than coarse-grained classification, where the action classes can be "cutting something in a kitchen" and "playing in a gym". The higher inter-class similarity in the fine-grained setting makes it a challenging task, which coarse-grained backbones and methods struggle to overcome.

To tackle the challenging fine-grained action recognition task, we derive inspiration from the remarkable human visual system which has good fine-grained recognition capabilities. Importantly, our visual system comprises of specialized neurons that are activated only under some specific circumstances, as shown by previous works [23,33]. For example, for enhanced recognition of humans which is crucial for social behaviour, human brains have developed a set of cortical regions specialized for processing faces [23,33]. These specialized regions fire only when our attention focuses on human faces, while specific sub-regions are further specialized to fire specifically for processing face parts [25], eye gazes and expressions [12], and identity [11,27].

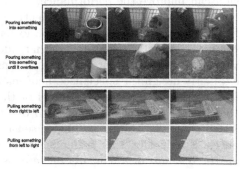

Inspired by the specialization of neurons in the human brain, we improve fine-grained recognition capabilities of a neural network by using specialized parameters that are only activated on a subset of the data. More specifically, we design a novel Dynamic Spatio-Temporal Specialization (DSTS) module which consists of *specialized neurons* that are only activated when the input is within their area of specialization (as determined by their individual *scoring kernels*). In particular, a synapse mechanism dynamically activates each specialized neuron only on a subset of samples that are highly similar, such that only fine-grained differences exist between them. During training, in order to distinguish among that particular subset of similar samples, the loss will push the specialized neurons to focus on exploiting the fine-grained differences between them. We note that previous works on fine-grained action recogni-

Fig. 1. Key frames of samples taken from the Something-Something-v2 dataset [10]. (Top) Fine-grained differences lie more in the spatial aspects of the two actions, as shown in the green box. To distinguish between these two actions, we need to focus on whether the water in the cup overflows in the final key frame, which can be quite subtle. (Bottom) Fine-grained differences lie mainly in the temporal aspects of the two actions, where we need to focus on the movement (denoted with yellow arrows) of the object across all key frames. Best viewed in colour.

tion [38,48,52] have not explicitly considered such specialization of parameters. These works [38,48,52] propose deep networks where all parameters are generally updated using all data samples, and thus, during training, the loss tends to encourage those models to pick up more common discriminative cues that apply to the more common samples, as opposed to various fine-grained cues that might be crucial to different subsets of the data.

Another interesting insight comes from the human primary visual cortex, where there are neurons that are observed to be specialized in temporal or spatial aspects [24, 43]. Magnocellular, or M cells, are observed to be specialized to detect movement, e.g., speed and direction. Parvocellular, or P cells, are important for spatial resolution, e.g., shape, size and color. Together, they effectively allow humans to distinguish between actions.

Spatial and temporal specialization has clear benefits for fine-grained action recognition. As observed in Fig 1, some fine-grained differences lie mainly in the temporal aspects of two actions, e.g., "Pulling something from right to left" and "Pulling something from left to right". In this case, a greater emphasis on the temporal dimension of each video will lead to better recognition performance. In contrast, some fine-grained differences lie more in the spatial aspects of two actions, e.g., "Pouring something into something" and "Pouring something into something and it overflows". In this case, greater emphasis on the spatial dimension can improve the performance.

To allow our module to efficiently and effectively handle fine-grained differences over a large range of spatio-temporal variations, we design a *spatio-temporal specialization* method that additionally provides specialized neurons with spatial or temporal specializations. To achieve such specialization, we explicitly design the specialized neurons to focus only on one single aspect (spatial or temporal) for each channel of the input feature map at a time, forcing the neurons to exploit fine-grained differences between similar samples in that specific aspect, leading to higher sensitivity towards these fine-grained differences. Specifically, this is implemented using *gates* that determine whether a *spatial operator* or a *temporal operator* is used to process each input channel. By adjusting their gate parameters, specialized neurons that benefit from discerning spatial or temporal patterns adapt their architectures to use the corresponding operator across more channels. Eventually, the set of specialized neurons will have diversified architectures and specializations focusing on different spatial and temporal aspects, which collectively are capable of handling a large variety of spatial and temporal fine-grained differences.

During end-to-end training of our module, we jointly train two types of parameters: *upstream parameters* (i.e., scoring kernels and gate parameters) that make dynamic decisions and *downstream parameters* (i.e., spatial and temporal operators) that process input, which can be challenging as *upstream parameters themselves also affect the training of downstream ones*. Hence, we design an Upstream-Downstream Learning (UDL) algorithm to optimize upstream parameters to learn how to make decisions that positively affect the training of downstream parameters, improving the performance of our DSTS module.

2   Related Work

2.1   Action Recognition

Action recognition involves taking an action video clip as input and predicting the class of the action. Many methods have been proposed to tackle this task, including the two-stream [30], TSN [35], TRN [51], TSM [19], TPN [44], LTC [34], I3D [3], S3D [42], SlowFast [7], X3D [6], NL [36], GST [22], Tx [9], TimeSformer [2], ViViT [1], MViT-B [5], and Swin Transformer [20].

2.2   Fine-grained Action Recognition

In comparison, fine-grained action recognition, where actions have lower inter-class differences, has been relatively less explored. Datasets such as Something-Something-v2 [10] and Diving48 [18] have been curated for this purpose.

Interaction Part Mining [52] mines mid-level parts, connects them to form a large spatio-temporal graph and mines interactions within the graph. LFB [38] employs a long-term feature bank for detailed processing of long videos that provides video-level contextual information at every time step. FineGym [28] has found that coarse-grained backbones lack the capability to capture complex temporal dynamics and subtle spatial semantics for their fine-grained dataset. TQN [48] casts fine-grained action recognition as a query-response task, where the model learns query vectors that are decoded into response vectors by a Transformer.

Different from previous works that do not explicitly consider specialized parameters, we propose a novel dynamic DSTS module that trains and selects specialized neurons for fine-grained action recognition. Furthermore, we investigate a novel spatio-temporal specialization scheme that optimizes architectures of the specialized neurons to focus more on spatial or temporal aspects, further specializing them for improved fine-grained action recognition.

2.3   Dynamic Neural Networks

Dynamic neural networks generally adapt their parameters or structures according to the input. Typical approaches include generating weights with a subnetwork, dynamically selecting network depth and dynamically selecting network widths [13,37,40,46,50]. On videos, several methods [39,41] adaptively select video frames for the sake of efficiency. GSM [31] learns to adaptively route features from a 2D-CNN through time and combine them. TANet [21] employs a dynamic video aggregation kernel that adds global video information to 2D convolutions.

Different from these methods, our DSTS module focuses on improving performance on fine-grained action recognition. We design a novel synapse mechanism that activates each specialized neuron only on samples that are highly similar, pushing them to pick up relevant fine-grained differences to distinguish between these similar samples. We further propose spatio-temporal specialization of our specialized neurons, which to the best of our knowledge, has not yet been explored in previous works.

2.4 Kernel Factorization

Kernel Factorization generally involves factorizing a 3D spatio-temporal convolution into a 2D spatial convolution plus a 1D temporal convolution, such as in P3D [26], S3D [42] and R(2+1)D [32]. In GST [22], 3D convolutions are decomposed into a fixed combination of parallel spatial and temporal convolutions. In these works, the kernel factorization leads to improved effectiveness and efficiency.

Here, we propose a novel DSTS module that dynamically activates the most relevant specialized neuron. Different from previous works, our specialized neurons learn to select a spatial or temporal operator for each channel, to better handle the corresponding fine-grained differences between similar samples, for fine-grained action recognition.

3   Proposed Method

3.1   Overview

In fine-grained action recognition, actions from different classes can be highly similar, with only fine-grained differences between them. Such fine-grained differences might not be effectively learnt by parameters that are trained on all samples, as they will tend to capture common discriminative cues that occur more commonly throughout the data, instead of various fine-grained cues, each of which might only be relevant in a small subset of the data [15]. Thus, to improve performance on fine-grained action recognition, we propose to employ specialized parameters in our model. These specialized parameters are pushed to gain specialized capabilities in identifying fine-grained differences by being trained only on a subset of the data that contains highly similar samples.

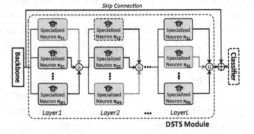

Fig. 2. Illustration of the proposed DSTS module, which processes features extracted from a backbone. There are L layers within the DSTS module, each comprising N specialized neurons (grey rectangles). When a feature map X is fed into the j-th DSTS layer, impulse values v_{ij} from each specialized neuron n_{ij} are first calculated, and the specialized neuron with the highest impulse value in that layer is activated (indicated with red arrows) using the Gumbel-Softmax technique (indicated with Ⓖ). A skip connection adds general features from the backbone to the output of the DSTS module (indicated with ⊕), before being fed into the classifier.

Our DSTS module achieves this specialization through the dynamic usage of blocks of parameters called *specialized neurons*, which can be observed in Fig. 2. For each input sample, only one specialized neuron (i.e., the neuron with the most relevant specialization) in each layer is activated to process the sample – this dynamic activation occurs in what we call the *synapse mechanism*. Crucially, we design the synapse mechanism such that each specialized neuron is only activated on a subset of samples that are similar, with only fine-grained differences between them. During training, since each specialized neuron is only trained on a subset of the data that contains similar samples, the training loss will push the specialized neuron to learn to handle the fine-grained information relevant to these samples, instead of learning more common discriminative cues that are applicable to the more common samples. Hence, each specialized neuron gains specialized capability that is highly effective at classifying a particular subset of samples, leading to improved fine-grained recognition performance.

Moreover, considering that fine-grained differences between similar samples might exist in more spatial or temporal aspects, we further propose spatio-temporal specialization in the specialized neurons, to further optimize their architectures. By explicitly forcing the specialized neurons to focus on spatial or temporal aspects for each channel of the input feature map, they are pushed to exploit fine-grained differences in that specific aspect, leading to better sensitivity towards the fine-grained differences in that aspect. Such channel-wise decisions on spatial or temporal specializations are learned in an end-to-end manner for improved performance. Lastly, we further improve the generalization capability of our DSTS module by proposing *Upstream-Downstream Learning*, where the model parameters involved in making its dynamic decisions are meta-learned.

Next, we formally introduce the DSTS module which is illustrated in Fig. 2. Setting batch size to 1 for simplicity, we assume that the pre-trained backbone outputs a feature map $X \in \mathbb{R}^{N_{in} \times N_t \times N_h \times N_w}$, where N_{in}, N_t, N_h, N_w represent the channel, temporal, height and width dimensions of the feature map, respectively. The DSTS module consists of L layers, with each layer comprising of N specialized neurons. We define the i-th specialized neuron in the j-th layer as n_{ij}, which is shown in detail in Fig. 3. Each specialized neuron n_{ij} has a scoring kernel $m_{ij} \in \mathbb{R}^{N_{out} \times N_{in} \times 1 \times 1 \times 1}$ (with the size of $1 \times 1 \times 1$ for efficiently encoding information from all channels of feature map X), a spatial operator consisting of a convolutional kernel $S_{ij} \in \mathbb{R}^{N_{out} \times N_{in} \times 1 \times 3 \times 3}$ (2D on the spatial domain), a temporal operator consisting of a convolutional kernel $T_{ij} \in \mathbb{R}^{N_{out} \times N_{in} \times 3 \times 1 \times 1}$ (1D on the temporal domain) and gates $g_{ij} \in \mathbb{R}^{N_{in}}$.

3.2 DSTS Layer

In this subsection, we describe a single DSTS layer. For clarity, we describe the first DSTS layer and omit the layer index, using n_i to represent the i-th specialized neuron (which consists of m_i, S_i, T_i and g_i) in this DSTS layer.

Synapse Mechanism. The synapse mechanism is the crucial step that dynamically activates the specialized neuron with the most relevant specialization for the given input feature map X. Importantly, similar feature maps should activate the same specialized neurons, so that each specialized neuron is pushed to specialize in fine-grained differences to distinguish between these similar feature maps during training.

To implement the synapse mechanism to achieve the above-mentioned specialization effect, we include a *scoring kernel* m_i in each specialized neuron n_i that is applied on the input feature map X in a step that we call the *scoring convolution*. The resulting output is summed to produce a relevance score (which we call an *impulse* v_i) between the input feature map X and the fine-grained specialization capabilities of the specialized neuron n_i. The higher the impulse produced by a specialized neuron, the higher the relevance of the specialized neuron's knowledge to the input feature, and the more likely it will be activated.

In the first step, to calculate the relevance scores between a specialized neuron n_i and a feature map X, we first apply a scoring convolution using the scoring kernel m_i on X:

$$q_i = m_i(X), \tag{1}$$

where we slightly abuse the notation to let $m_i(\cdot)$ denote the scoring convolution function applied to an input using scoring kernel m_i (we adopt this notation for all convolution functions in this work) and $q_i \in \mathbb{R}^{N_{out} \times Q_t \times Q_h \times Q_w}$ is an intermediate representation with Q_t, Q_h, Q_w being the resulting temporal, width and height dimensions.

We then sum all elements in q_i to get the impulse v_i of specialized neuron n_i.

$$v_i = \sum_{u_c=1}^{N_{out}} \sum_{u_t=1}^{Q_t} \sum_{u_h=1}^{Q_h} \sum_{u_w=1}^{Q_w} q_{i,u_c,u_t,u_h,u_w} \tag{2}$$

We conduct the above process (Eq. 1 and Eq. 2) for all scoring kernels $\{m_i\}_{i=1}^N$ of the N specialized neurons in the DSTS layer to obtain the complete set of impulse values $\mathcal{V}$:

$$\mathcal{V} = \{v_i\}_{i=1}^N. \tag{3}$$

Finally, we apply the Gumbel-Softmax technique [14] on $\mathcal{V}$ to select a specialized neuron to activate. The selection to activate specialized neuron n_a is made by producing a one-hot vector with a 1 at the selected index a. During training, the Gumbel-Softmax allows gradients to backpropagate through this selection mechanism. During testing, the activated specialized neuron n_a is the one with the highest impulse within $\mathcal{V}$, and has the most relevant specialization to discriminate between samples similar to the input X.

We remark that this synapse mechanism is crucial for the specialization of the specialized neurons. As convolutional filters tend to produce similar responses for similar feature maps [45,47], q_i and v_i tend to be similar for similar feature maps. Hence, during training, similar feature maps are highly likely to produce high impulse scores for (and activate) the same specialized neuron; this neuron will thus be updated using only a subset of similar samples, which pushes this neuron to specialize in fine-grained differences to distinguish between them.

Spatio-Temporal Specialization. Intuitively, after n_a is activated, we can simply apply a 3D convolution kernel (corresponding to n_a) on X to extract the spatio-temporal information. Yet, in fine-grained action recognition, the fine-grained differences between actions can exist in more spatial or temporal aspects of actions, which require emphasis along their respective dimensions for effective discrimination. Motivated by this, instead of optimizing the parameters within a 3D kernel architecture, we additionally optimize the architectures of the specialized neurons to specialize in focusing on either more spatial or more temporal fine-grained information.

More concretely, our spatio-temporal specialization method adapts the architectures of the specialized neurons to utilize either a *spatial operator* or a *temporal operator* for each input channel. The spatial operator uses a 2D convolution that focuses on the spatial aspects of the feature map while the temporal operator uses a 1D convolution that focuses on the temporal aspects. To achieve spatial or temporal specialization, we explicitly restrict the specialized neurons to choose between spatial or temporal operators for each input channel. During training, this design forces each specialized neuron to exploit fine-grained differences in each channel between similar samples in the chosen aspect, leading to better sensitivity towards these fine-grained differences. Since different channels of the input feature map can convey different information, which might lie in the spatial or temporal aspects, we let our

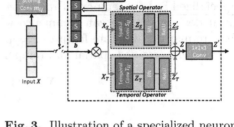

Fig. 3. Illustration of a specialized neuron n_{ij}. A scoring convolution using m_{ij}, followed by a summation, produces impulse v_{ij} that is used to determine if n_{ij} is activated. Gate parameters g_{ij} are used to generate **b** using the Improved Semhash method, which determines (using channel-wise multiplication $\otimes$) if each input channel uses the spatial operator's kernel S_{ij} (in green) or the temporal operator's kernel T_{ij} (in orange). After the processing of the spatial and temporal operators, both features Z'_S and Z'_T are added (indicated with $\oplus$) and fused using a $1 \times 1 \times 1$ convolution to get output Z'.

model adapt its architecture to select the operator in each channel that would lead to greater discriminative capability. Such architectural decisions (spatial or temporal) for each channel are learned by the *gate* parameters. When it is beneficial for the specialized neuron to focus more on a certain fine-grained aspect, the gates will learn to use the corresponding operator across more channels, pushing for higher sensitivity towards that aspect for improved discriminative capability. The efficacy of this channel-wise design for spatio-temporal specialization is investigated empirically along with other baselines in Sect. 4.3.

Spatio-temporal Architectural Decisions using Gates. This step takes place after the synapse mechanism, where a specialized neuron n_a is activated. The specialized neuron's gate parameters g_a consists of N_{in} elements, with each element corresponding to one input channel. Each gate parameter determines if the corresponding channel is processed using the spatial or temporal operator.

During the forward pass, we sample binary decisions from the gate parameters g_a using the Improved Semhash method [4,16,17], obtaining a binary vector $\mathbf{b} \in \{0,1\}^{N_{in}}$. Improved Semhash allows us to train gate parameters g_a in an end-to-end manner. We opt for the Improved Semhash instead of the Gumbel-Softmax here as we can use less parameters (N_{in} instead of $2N_{in}$). We denote the l-th element of $\mathbf{b}$ as b_l. If $b_l = 0$, then the corresponding input channel l will use the spatial operator. While if $b_l = 1$, then the corresponding input channel l will use the temporal operator. More details of Improved Semhash can be found in the Supplementary.

Specialized Spatio-Temporal Processing. After obtaining channel-wise architectural decisions $\mathbf{b}$, we can commence with the channel-wise selection of input feature map X to obtain features X_S and X_T as follows, which will be used for learning fine-grained spatial and temporal information respectively:

$$X_S = (\mathbf{1} - \mathbf{b}) \cdot X, \tag{4}$$
$$X_T = \mathbf{b} \cdot X, \tag{5}$$

where $\mathbf{1}$ is a vector of 1's of size N_{in}, and $\cdot$ refers to multiplication along the channel dimension while treating each element of $\mathbf{b}$ and $(\mathbf{1} - \mathbf{b})$ as a channel. Using X_S and X_T, spatial and temporal outputs Z_S, Z_T are obtained using the respective spatial and temporal kernels S_a, T_a within n_a:

$$Z_S = S_a(X_S), \tag{6}$$
$$Z_T = T_a(X_T), \tag{7}$$

where Z_S denotes features that capture spatial information of input feature map X, while Z_T denotes features that capture temporal information. Z_S and Z_T are then fed to a batch normalization and a ReLU activation layer. We denote the two output features as Z'_S and Z'_T. The output feature map Z is obtained by adding Z'_S and Z'_T:

$$Z = Z'_S + Z'_T \tag{8}$$

Lastly, a $1 \times 1 \times 1$ convolution is applied to Z to fuse both spatial and temporal features. These fused features Z' are then fed to the next DSTS layer or classifier.

Spatio-temporal specialization allows specialized neurons to focus on either more spatial or temporal fine-grained information. If a specialized neuron n_i is activated on a subset of similar samples with fine-grained spatial differences, encoding more spatial information by applying the spatial operator on more channels will tend to be more effective, and g_i will be trained to produce more 0's in $\mathbf{b}$. On the other hand, if the samples in the subset contain more fine-grained temporal differences, the model will learn to apply the temporal operator across more channels, by optimizing g_i to produce more 1's in **b** for better fine-grained action recognition. It is also possible that the spatial and temporal aspects are equally important to discriminate similar actions. In this case, g_i will be optimized to handle both spatial and temporal fine-grained information.

3.3   Upstream-Downstream Learning

To further improve the performance of our DSTS module, we design a UDL algorithm that better optimizes the model parameters involved in making dynamic decisions, which we call *upstream parameters*. These upstream parameters (i.e., scoring kernels m and gate parameters g) that make dynamic decisions and *downstream parameters* (i.e., spatial and temporal operators S and T) that process input, are jointly trained during our end-to-end training, which can be challenging as *upstream parameters themselves also affect the training of downstream ones*. This is because, upstream parameters determine which downstream parameters will be used, and consequently updated. Hence, we use meta-learning [8,29] to optimize upstream parameters while taking their downstream effects into account, leading to the improved learning of downstream parameters and overall improved performance.

There are three steps in our meta-learning algorithm. In the first step, we simulate an update step by updating downstream parameters while keeping upstream parameters frozen. This simulates the training process of the downstream parameters when the current set of upstream parameters are used to make dynamic decisions. In the crucial second step, we evaluate the model's performance on held-out samples in a validation set, which estimates model performance on unseen samples. The second-order gradients (with respect to upstream parameters) from this evaluation provide feedback on how upstream parameters can be updated such that their *dynamic decisions during training can improve the learning process of downstream parameters*, leading to better performance on unseen samples. In the final step, downstream parameters are optimized using the *meta-optimized upstream parameters*, which now make dynamic decisions in the model such that downstream parameters are able to benefit more from training and have improved (testing) performance.

More concretely, in each iteration, we sample two mini-batches from the training data: training samples D_{train} and validation samples D_{val}. The two mini-batches should not contain overlapping samples, as we want to use D_{val} to estimate performance on unseen samples. The algorithm proceeds in three steps:

Firstly, a **Simulated Update Step** updates downstream parameters d using supervised loss ℓ on D_{train}.

$$\hat{d} = d - \alpha \nabla_d \ell(u, d; D_{train}), \tag{9}$$

where α is a learning rate hyperparameter, while u and d denote the upstream and downstream parameters respectively. We keep upstream parameters u fixed in this step.

Secondly, a **Meta-Update Step** evaluates the updated model on D_{val}. We update upstream parameters u using the second-order gradients with respect to

u when they were used to make decisions in the first Simulated Update Step, as follows:

$$u' = u - \alpha \nabla_u \ell(\hat{u}, \hat{d}; D_{val}), \qquad (10)$$

where $\hat{u}$ is a copy of u, but no gradients are computed with respect to $\hat{u}$. We denote it this way, because the same set of u parameters are used twice (in Eq. 9 and Eq. 10), and we want to compute second-order gradients ∇_u with respect to u in Eq. 9, not first-order gradients with respect to $\hat{u}$ in Eq. 10. These second-order gradients ∇_u provide feedback on how to adjust u such that their dynamic decisions lead to better training of the downstream parameters (as simulated in the Simulated Update Step), resulting in improved performance on unseen samples. d is not updated in this step.

Finally, d is updated in the **Actual Update Step** while keeping u' frozen.

$$d' = d - \alpha \nabla_d \ell(u', d; D_{train}) \qquad (11)$$

One iteration of this algorithm concludes here, and we obtain updated parameters u' and d'. An outline of the algorithm is shown in the Supplementary.

4   Experiments

We conduct experiments using our proposed DSTS module on two popular fine-grained action recognition datasets, i.e., the Something-Something v2 dataset (SSV2) [10] and Diving48 dataset [18].

SSV2 [10] is a large dataset, containing approximately 220k videos across 174 different classes. It consists of crowd-sourced clips that show humans performing basic actions with various types of everyday objects. The difference between classes could lie in fine-grained spatial or temporal details, as depicted in Fig. 1. Following [10,20,49], we split the data into 169k training and 27k test videos.

Diving48 [18] contains approximately 18k trimmed video clips of 48 classes of competitive diving sequences. There are fine-grained differences between the 48 classes, which could exist at takeoff, in flight, at entry, or a combination of them in the diving sequences, making it a challenging classification task. Following [18,48], we split the data into 16k training and 2k test videos. Following [48], we use the cleaned (v2) labels released in Oct 2020.

4.1   Implementation Details

To evaluate the efficacy of the proposed DSTS module, Swin-B transformer [20] and TPN [44] are used as the backbone networks. In our experiments, each DSTS layer contains 10 specialized neurons ($N = 10$) and the DSTS module has 3 layers ($L = 3$). The dimensions of the input X, such as N_{in}, N_t, N_h, N_w are determined by different backbone networks, and we set $N_{out} = N_{in}$. Thus, the shape of S_{ij}, T_{ij}, g_{ij} and m_{ij} for each n_{ij} are dependent on the backbones.

The experiments are conducted on 8 Nvidia V100 GPUs with batch size $B = 8$. We follow the experimental settings of Video Swin Transformer [20], using the AdamW optimizer and setting the initial learning rate α as 3×10^{-4}. For TPN, we follow the experimental settings in [44], using the SGD optimizer and setting the initial learning rate α as 0.01. We compute cross-entropy loss as the supervised loss ℓ for classification.

During **training**, using the Gumbel-Softmax and Improved Semhash techniques for selection of specialized neurons and operators, our model is end-to-end trainable. We set Gumbel-Softmax temperature $\tau = 1$, and the noise applied to Improved SemHash is sampled from a standard Gaussian distribution.

Table 1. Top-1 and Top-5 scores (%) on SSv2. Type "C" indicates CNN-based architectures and "T" indicates Transformer-based architectures. Our DSTS module improves Top-1 accuracy of TPN by 2.5% and Swin-B by 2.2%.

Method	Type	Top-1	Top-5
SlowFast [7]	C	63.1	87.6
TPN [44]	C	64.7	88.1
ViViT-L [1]	T	65.4	89.8
TSM (Two-stream) [19]	C	66.6	91.3
MViT-B [5]	T	67.7	90.9
Swin-B [20]	T	69.6	92.7
TPN w/ DSTS	C	67.2	89.2
Swin-B w/ DSTS	T	**71.8**	**93.7**

During **testing**, given an input feature map X, impulse values $\{v_{ij}\}_{i=1}^{N}$ are computed for all N specialized neurons in each layer j. However, because we do not require gradients this time, the input X is only processed by the best-matching specialized neuron n_{aj} of each layer j, to obtain output Z'_{aj}. Notably, no noise is added to Gumbel-Softmax and Improved Semhash during inference.

4.2 Experiment Results

Results on SSv2. Following [1,19,20], we report Top-1 and Top-5 accuracy scores across all models on the test set of SSv2. Results are shown in Table 1. As both CNNs and Transformers are used to tackle action recognition, we test DSTS on a CNN-based architecture (TPN [44]) and a Transformer-based architecture (Swin-B [20]) to investigate if our DSTS module provides performance gains on both types of architectures.

Adding our DSTS module to baseline architectures leads to improved performance on both architectures. Adding DSTS to TPN (**TPN w/DSTS**), the performance of TPN improves by 2.5%, achieving a Top-1 accuracy of 67.2%. To the best of our knowledge, this performance is state-of-the-art among CNN-based architectures, surpassing even the performance of the two-stream TSM which utilizes additional optical flow information. This shows that DSTS can improve performance for CNN-based backbones on fine-grained action recognition. Adding DSTS to Swin-B (**Swin-B w/DSTS**) improves Top-1 accuracy by 2.2%, achieving a new state-of-the-art of 71.8%, showing that DSTS can help improve fine-grained action recognition on Transformer-based backbones as well. Qualitative results and visualizations have been placed in the Supplementary.

Results on Diving48. Following [48], we report Top-1 accuracy and mean accuracy per class across all models on Diving48 dataset. Results are shown in Table 2. Using DSTS module leads to significant improvements on Diving48 as well. It achieves a Top-1 improvement of 2.2% on TPN and 2.5% on Swin-B. TPN w/ DSTS achieves state-of-the-art result of 88.4% Top-1 accuracy.

Table 2. Top-1 and Class-wise accuracy scores (%) on Diving48. Our DSTS module improves Top-1 accuracy of TPN by 2.2% and Swin-B by 2.5%.

Method	Type	Top-1	Class-wise Acc
I3D [3]	C	48.3	33.2
TSM (Two-stream) [19]	C	52.5	32.7
GST [22]	C	78.9	69.5
TQN [48]	T	81.8	74.5
Swin-B [20]	T	80.5	69.7
TPN [44]	C	86.2	76.0
Swin-B w/ DSTS	T	83.0	71.5
TPN w/ DSTS	C	**88.4**	**78.2**

4.3 Ablation Studies

We conduct extensive ablation studies to evaluate the importance of certain design choices. Ablation studies are conducted on Diving48, using TPN as a backbone. More experiments are placed in the Supplementary.

1) Spatio-temporal specialization. We evaluate the impact of spatio-temporal specialization on our DSTS module, and the results are shown in Table 3. It can be observed that DSTS module with spatio-temporal specialization (**DSTS w/ STS**) performs better than DSTS without it (**DSTS w/o STS**), showing its effective-

Table 3. Evaluation results (%) on the impact of spatio-temporal specialization of DSTS modules on Diving48.

Method	Top-1	Class-wise Acc
DSTS w/o STS	87.2	76.5
DSTS w/o Gates	87.3	76.7
DSTS w/ STS	88.4	78.2

ness. For DSTS w/o STS, only one operator, i.e., a 3D convolution with batch normalization and ReLU, within each n_{ij} is employed to process X. Besides, when we remove gates g_{ij} (**DSTS w/o Gates**), and let all specialized neurons have the same factorized architecture (the channels are split into two fixed halves, to which the spatial and temporal operators are applied respectively), the performance decreases by 1.1%. This shows that our gates learn channel-wise architectures that are more specialized and effective for fine-grained recognition, compared to fixed architectures.

2) Synapse Mechanism. We investigate the impact of the synapse mechanism, and results are shown in Table 4. Following our method with the dynamic synapse mechanism and activating the

Table 4. Evaluation results (%) on the impact of the synapse mechanism on Diving48.

Method	Top-1	Class-wise Acc	Model size
Baseline TPN	86.2	76.0	63M
w/o Synapse Mechanism	86.5	76.4	75M
w/ Synapse Mechanism	88.4	78.2	75M

most relevant specialized neuron at each layer (**w/ Synapse Mechanism**) achieves better results compared to activating all specialized neurons and averaging their outputs (**w/o Synapse Mechanism**), which is a non-dynamic design with the same number of parameters as our method. This shows that the performance improvement comes from our synapse mechanism and its dynamic design, and not the additional parameters. This improvement is because, unlike w/o Synapse Mechanism which trains all neurons on all data samples and tends to learn more common discriminative cues that apply to the more common samples, our DSTS module trains each specialized neuron only on a subset of similar samples, explicitly pushing them to gain better specialized fine-grained abilities.

3) Upstream-Downstream Learning. We conduct experiments to evaluate the performance gains from our UDL method, and the results can be seen in Table 5.

We observe that our UDL method (**DSTS w/ UDL**) improves performance over using backpropagation in a single step (**DSTS w/o UDL**). We emphasize that such these performance

Table 5. Evaluation results (%) on the impact of the UDL method on Diving48.

Method	Top-1	Class-wise Acc
DSTS w/o UDL	87.4	76.7
DSTS w/ UDL	88.4	78.2

gains are achieved using only slightly more training time, which is reported in the Supplementary.

4) Number of specialized neurons in each DSTS layer. We evaluate the impact of using different numbers of specialized neurons in each DSTS layer, and the results are shown in Table 6. When N is low (e.g., $N = 5$), using more specialized neurons in each DSTS layer (e.g., $N = 10$) improves the performance, which can be explained by the increase in representational capacity. More precisely, when there are more specialized neurons,

Table 6. Evaluation results (%) for different numbers of specialized neurons N in each DSTS module on Diving48.

N	Top-1	Class-wise Acc
5	87.3	76.2
10	88.4	78.2
15	88.3	78.2

each one can afford to be more specialized towards a smaller subset of data, which improves their capability. We use $N = 10$ as this improvement effect tapers off when N is increased beyond 10.

5) Number of DSTS layers. We also evaluate the impact of varying L, i.e., stacking different numbers of DSTS layers, and results are shown in Table 7. As expected, stacking more DSTS layers leads to better performance. This is because, the DSTS module with more layers could have greater representational capacity to process more complex and fine-grained cues. When we increase L from 1 to 3, we obtain an improvement of 0.9%, and increasing L further does not lead to further improvement. We thus set $L = 3$.

Table 7. Evaluation results (%) for different numbers of DSTS layers L on Diving48.

L	Top-1	Class-wise Acc
1	87.5	76.8
3	88.4	78.2
5	88.2	78.2

5   Conclusion

In this paper, we have proposed a novel DSTS module consisting of dynamically activated specialized neurons for fine-grained action recognition. Our spatio-temporal specialization method optimizes the architectures of specialized neurons to focus more on spatial or temporal aspects. Our UDL procedure further improves the performance of our DSTS module. We obtain state-of-the-art fine-grained action recognition performance on two popular datasets by adding DSTS modules to baseline architectures.

Acknowledgement. This work is supported by National Research Foundation, Singapore under its AI Singapore Programme (AISG Award No: AISG-100E-2020-065), Ministry of Education Tier 1 Grant and SUTD Startup Research Grant. This work is also partially supported by Natural Science Foundation of China (NSFC) under the Grant no. 62172285. The research is also supported by TAILOR, a project funded by EU Horizon 2020 research and innovation programme under GA No 952215.

References

1. Arnab, A., Dehghani, M., Heigold, G., Sun, C., Lucic, M., Schmid, C.: ViViT: a video vision transformer. In: Proceedings of the IEEE/CVF International Conference on Computer Vision (ICCV), pp. 6836–6846, October 2021
2. Bertasius, G., Wang, H., Torresani, L.: Is space-time attention all you need for video understanding? (2021)
3. Carreira, J., Zisserman, A.: Quo Vadis, action recognition? A new model and the kinetics dataset. In: proceedings of the IEEE Conference on Computer Vision and Pattern Recognition, pp. 6299–6308 (2017)
4. Chen, Z., Li, Y., Bengio, S., Si, S.: You look twice: Gaternet for dynamic filter selection in CNNs. In: Proceedings of the IEEE/CVF Conference on Computer Vision and Pattern Recognition, pp. 9172–9180 (2019)
5. Fan, H., Xiong, B., Mangalam, K., Li, Y., Yan, Z., Malik, J., Feichtenhofer, C.: Multiscale vision transformers. arXiv preprint arXiv:2104.11227 (2021)
6. Feichtenhofer, C.: X3D: expanding architectures for efficient video recognition. In: Proceedings of the IEEE/CVF Conference on Computer Vision and Pattern Recognition, pp. 203–213 (2020)

7. Feichtenhofer, C., Fan, H., Malik, J., He, K.: SlowFast networks for video recognition. In: Proceedings of the IEEE/CVF International Conference on Computer Vision, pp. 6202–6211 (2019)
8. Finn, C., Abbeel, P., Levine, S.: Model-agnostic meta-learning for fast adaptation of deep networks. In: International Conference on Machine Learning, pp. 1126–1135. PMLR (2017)
9. Girdhar, R., Carreira, J., Doersch, C., Zisserman, A.: Video action transformer network. In: Proceedings of the IEEE/CVF Conference on Computer Vision and Pattern Recognition, pp. 244–253 (2019)
10. Goyal, R., et al.: The "something something" video database for learning and evaluating visual common sense. In: Proceedings of the IEEE International Conference on Computer Vision, pp. 5842–5850 (2017)
11. Haxby, J.V., Hoffman, E.A., Gobbini, M.I.: The distributed human neural system for face perception. Trends Cogn. Sci. **4**(6), 223–233 (2000)
12. Hoffman, E.A., Haxby, J.V.: Distinct representations of eye gaze and identity in the distributed human neural system for face perception. Nat. Neurosci. **3**(1), 80–84 (2000)
13. Hua, W., Zhou, Y., De Sa, C., Zhang, Z., Suh, G.E.: Channel gating neural networks (2019)
14. Jang, E., Gu, S., Poole, B.: Categorical reparameterization with Gumbel-Softmax. arXiv preprint arXiv:1611.01144 (2016)
15. Johnson, J.M., Khoshgoftaar, T.M.: Survey on deep learning with class imbalance. J. Big Data **6**(1), 1–54 (2019). https://doi.org/10.1186/s40537-019-0192-5
16. Kaiser, Ł., Bengio, S.: Discrete autoencoders for sequence models. arXiv preprint arXiv:1801.09797 (2018)
17. Kaiser, L., et al.: Fast decoding in sequence models using discrete latent variables. In: International Conference on Machine Learning, pp. 2390–2399. PMLR (2018)
18. Li, Y., Li, Y., Vasconcelos, N.: RESOUND: towards action recognition without representation bias. In: Ferrari, V., Hebert, M., Sminchisescu, C., Weiss, Y. (eds.) ECCV 2018. LNCS, vol. 11210, pp. 520–535. Springer, Cham (2018). https://doi.org/10.1007/978-3-030-01231-1_32
19. Lin, J., Gan, C., Han, S.: TSM: temporal shift module for efficient video understanding. In: Proceedings of the IEEE/CVF International Conference on Computer Vision, pp. 7083–7093 (2019)
20. Liu, Z., et al.: Video swin transformer. arXiv preprint arXiv:2106.13230 (2021)
21. Liu, Z., Wang, L., Wu, W., Qian, C., Lu, T.: TAM: temporal adaptive module for video recognition. In: Proceedings of the IEEE/CVF International Conference on Computer Vision, pp. 13708–13718 (2021)
22. Luo, C., Yuille, A.L.: Grouped spatial-temporal aggregation for efficient action recognition. In: Proceedings of the IEEE/CVF International Conference on Computer Vision, pp. 5512–5521 (2019)
23. Minxha, J., Mosher, C., Morrow, J.K., Mamelak, A.N., Adolphs, R., Gothard, K.M., Rutishauser, U.: Fixations gate species-specific responses to free viewing of faces in the human and macaque amygdala. Cell Rep. **18**(4), 878–891 (2017). https://doi.org/10.1016/j.celrep.2016.12.083
24. Nolte, J., Vanderah, T., Gould, D.: Nolte's the Human Brain: An Introduction to Its Functional Anatomy. Elsevier, Philadelphia (2016)
25. Pitcher, D., Walsh, V., Yovel, G., Duchaine, B.: TMS evidence for the involvement of the right occipital face area in early face processing. Current Biol. **17**(18), 1568–1573 (2007)

26. Qiu, Z., Yao, T., Mei, T.: Learning spatio-temporal representation with pseudo-3d residual networks. In: Proceedings of the IEEE International Conference on Computer Vision, pp. 5533–5541 (2017)

27. Rotshtein, P., Henson, R.N., Treves, A., Driver, J., Dolan, R.J.: Morphing Marilyn into Maggie dissociates physical and identity face representations in the brain. Nat. Neurosci. **8**(1), 107–113 (2005)

28. Shao, D., Zhao, Y., Dai, B., Lin, D.: FineGym: a hierarchical video dataset for fine-grained action understanding. In: Proceedings of the IEEE/CVF Conference on Computer Vision and Pattern Recognition, pp. 2616–2625 (2020)

29. Shu, J., et al.: Meta-weight-net: learning an explicit mapping for sample weighting (2019)

30. Simonyan, K., Zisserman, A.: Two-stream convolutional networks for action recognition in videos. In: Proceedings of the 27th International Conference on Neural Information Processing Systems, NIPS 2014, vol. 1, pp. 568-576. MIT Press, Cambridge (2014)

31. Sudhakaran, S., Escalera, S., Lanz, O.: Gate-shift networks for video action recognition. In: Proceedings of the IEEE/CVF Conference on Computer Vision and Pattern Recognition, pp. 1102–1111 (2020)

32. Tran, D., Wang, H., Torresani, L., Ray, J., LeCun, Y., Paluri, M.: A closer look at spatiotemporal convolutions for action recognition. In: Proceedings of the IEEE conference on Computer Vision and Pattern Recognition, pp. 6450–6459 (2018)

33. Tsao, D.Y., Moeller, S., Freiwald, W.A.: Comparing face patch systems in macaques and humans. Proc. Natl. Acad. Sci. **105**(49), 19514–19519 (2008)

34. Varol, G., Laptev, I., Schmid, C.: Long-term temporal convolutions for action recognition. IEEE Trans. Pattern Anal. Mach. Intell. **40**(6), 1510–1517 (2017)

35. Wang, L., et al.: Temporal segment networks: towards good practices for deep action recognition. In: Leibe, B., Matas, J., Sebe, N., Welling, M. (eds.) ECCV 2016. LNCS, vol. 9912, pp. 20–36. Springer, Cham (2016). https://doi.org/10.1007/978-3-319-46484-8_2

36. Wang, X., Girshick, R., Gupta, A., He, K.: Non-local neural networks. In: Proceedings of the IEEE Conference on Computer Vision and Pattern Recognition, pp. 7794–7803 (2018)

37. Wang, X., Yu, F., Dou, Z.-Y., Darrell, T., Gonzalez, J.E.: SkipNet: learning dynamic routing in convolutional networks. In: Ferrari, V., Hebert, M., Sminchisescu, C., Weiss, Y. (eds.) ECCV 2018. LNCS, vol. 11217, pp. 420–436. Springer, Cham (2018). https://doi.org/10.1007/978-3-030-01261-8_25

38. Wu, C.Y., Feichtenhofer, C., Fan, H., He, K., Krahenbuhl, P., Girshick, R.: Long-term feature banks for detailed video understanding. In: Proceedings of the IEEE/CVF Conference on Computer Vision and Pattern Recognition, pp. 284–293 (2019)

39. Wu, Z., Li, H., Xiong, C., Jiang, Y.G., Davis, L.S.: A dynamic frame selection framework for fast video recognition. IEEE Trans. Pattern Anal. Mach. Intell. **44**, 1699–1711 (2020)

40. Wu, Z., et al.: BlockDrop: dynamic inference paths in residual networks. In: CVPR, pp. 8817–8826 (2018)

41. Wu, Z., Xiong, C., Ma, C.Y., Socher, R., Davis, L.S.: AdaFrame: adaptive frame selection for fast video recognition. In: Proceedings of the IEEE/CVF Conference on Computer Vision and Pattern Recognition, pp. 1278–1287 (2019)

42. Xie, S., Sun, C., Huang, J., Tu, Z., Murphy, K.: Rethinking spatiotemporal feature learning: speed-accuracy trade-offs in video classification. In: Ferrari, V., Hebert,

M., Sminchisescu, C., Weiss, Y. (eds.) ECCV 2018. LNCS, vol. 11219, pp. 318–335. Springer, Cham (2018). https://doi.org/10.1007/978-3-030-01267-0_19

43. Xu, X., Ichida, J.M., Allison, J.D., Boyd, J.D., Bonds, A., Casagrande, V.A.: A comparison of koniocellular, magnocellular and parvocellular receptive field properties in the lateral geniculate nucleus of the owl monkey (aotus trivirgatus). J. Physiol. **531**(1), 203–218 (2001)

44. Yang, C., Xu, Y., Shi, J., Dai, B., Zhou, B.: Temporal pyramid network for action recognition. In: Proceedings of the IEEE/CVF Conference on Computer Vision and Pattern Recognition, pp. 591–600 (2020)

45. Yosinski, J., Clune, J., Nguyen, A.M., Fuchs, T.J., Lipson, H.: Understanding neural networks through deep visualization. ArXiv abs/1506.06579 (2015)

46. Zamora Esquivel, J., Cruz Vargas, A., Lopez Meyer, P., Tickoo, O.: Adaptive convolutional kernels. In: Proceedings of the IEEE/CVF International Conference on Computer Vision Workshops, p. 0 (2019)

47. Zeiler, M.D., Fergus, R.: Visualizing and understanding convolutional networks. In: Fleet, D., Pajdla, T., Schiele, B., Tuytelaars, T. (eds.) Visualizing and understanding convolutional networks. LNCS, vol. 8689, pp. 818–833. Springer, Cham (2014). https://doi.org/10.1007/978-3-319-10590-1_53

48. Zhang, C., Gupta, A., Zisserman, A.: Temporal query networks for fine-grained video understanding. In: Proceedings of the IEEE/CVF Conference on Computer Vision and Pattern Recognition, pp. 4486–4496 (2021)

49. Zhang, D.J., et al.: MorphMLP: a self-attention free, MLP-like backbone for image and video. arXiv preprint arXiv:2111.12527 (2021)

50. Zhang, J., Wang, Y., Zhou, Z., Luan, T., Wang, Z., Qiao, Y.: Learning dynamical human-joint affinity for 3d pose estimation in videos. IEEE Trans. Image Process. **30**, 7914–7925 (2021)

51. Zhou, B., Andonian, A., Oliva, A., Torralba, A.: Temporal relational reasoning in videos. In: Ferrari, V., Hebert, M., Sminchisescu, C., Weiss, Y. (eds.) ECCV 2018. LNCS, vol. 11205, pp. 831–846. Springer, Cham (2018). https://doi.org/10.1007/978-3-030-01246-5_49

52. Zhou, Y., Ni, B., Hong, R., Wang, M., Tian, Q.: Interaction part mining: a mid-level approach for fine-grained action recognition. In: Proceedings of the IEEE Conference on Computer Vision and Pattern Recognition, pp. 3323–3331 (2015)

Dynamic Local Aggregation Network with Adaptive Clusterer for Anomaly Detection

Zhiwei Yang[1], Peng Wu[2(✉)], Jing Liu[1(✉)], and Xiaotao Liu[1]

[1] Guangzhou Institute of Technology, Xidian University, Guangzhou, China
zwyang97@163.com, neouma@163.com, xtliu@xidian.edu.cn
[2] School of Computer Science, Northwestern Polytechnical University, Xi'an, China
xdwupeng@gmail.com

Abstract. Existing methods for anomaly detection based on memory-augmented autoencoder (AE) have the following drawbacks: (1) Establishing a memory bank requires additional memory space. (2) The fixed number of prototypes from subjective assumptions ignores the data feature differences and diversity. To overcome these drawbacks, we introduce **DLAN-AC**, a **D**ynamic **L**ocal **A**ggregation **N**etwork with **A**daptive **C**lusterer, for anomaly detection. First, The proposed **DLAN** can automatically learn and aggregate high-level features from the AE to obtain more representative prototypes, while freeing up extra memory space. Second, The proposed **AC** can adaptively cluster video data to derive initial prototypes with prior information. In addition, we also propose a dynamic redundant clustering strategy (**DRCS**) to enable DLAN for automatically eliminating feature clusters that do not contribute to the construction of prototypes. Extensive experiments on benchmarks demonstrate that DLAN-AC outperforms most existing methods, validating the effectiveness of our method. Our code is publicly available at https://github.com/Beyond-Zw/DLAN-AC.

Keywords: Anomaly detection · Autoencoder · Local aggregation network · Adaptive clustering

1 Introduction

Unsupervised anomaly detection is to automatically detect events that do not meet our expectations in videos [1,5,7,34,49]. This is a challenging task, its challenges mainly come from three aspects: (1) There is no clear definition of abnormal behavior, because whether the behavior is abnormal depends on the current environment. (2) Abnormal events rarely occur and cannot be exhaustively listed, which means that it is impossible to collect all abnormal samples. (3) Annotating abnormal frames in a video is an extremely time-consuming task.

Supplementary Information The online version contains supplementary material available at https://doi.org/10.1007/978-3-031-19772-7_24.

Due to the limitations of these factors, most current methods only use normal samples for training, and to learn normal behavior patterns. At inference time, samples that are far from the normal pattern are regarded as abnormal.

The video frame reconstruction and prediction based on autoencoder (AE) thus far are widely used unsupervised video anomaly detection (VAD) paradigms. Such methods have shown promising results, but there are still some limitations. The main limitation is that the generalization ability of AE is so powerful that even some abnormal frames can be reconstructed or predicted well [11], [54]. Several works are proposed to overcome the above limitation. For example, Gong et al. [11] and Park et al. [31] both proposed to record prototypes of normal data by inserting a memory bank into AE, which can enhance the ability of AE to model normal behavior patterns. These two works, to a certain extent, lessen the representation of AE for abnormal video frames, but there are two obvious shortcomings: (1) They need to build a memory bank to store the prototypes of normal data, leading to additional memory overhead. (2) Setting the number of prototypes in the memory bank based on subjective assumptions, which ignores the inherent feature differences in various scenarios, besides, simply setting the same number of prototypes for different datasets limits the features diversity. Recently, Lv et al. [27] proposed a meta-prototype network to learn normal dynamics as prototypes. This method learns normal dynamics by constructing a meta-prototype unit that contains an attention mechanism [41]. Using the attention mechanism to learn normal dynamics as prototypes instead of the previous memory bank based method, which can reduce memory overhead. However, high-level semantic information is not excavated due to only using pixel information of feature map. Besides, in this work, setting the number of normal prototypes still based on subjective assumptions.

In this paper, we introduce a novel dynamic local aggregation network with adaptive clusterer (DLAN-AC), which can adaptively cluster video data in different scenarios and dynamically aggregate high-level features to obtain prototypes of normal data. First of all, inspired by the work [2], we propose a dynamic local aggregation network (DLAN), which can automatically learn and aggregate high-level features to obtain more representative prototypes of normal data, and also solve the problem of additional memory consumption. Compared with previous memory bank based methods [11,31], DLAN can automatically learn prototypes online without additional memory consumptions. Compared with the attention mechanism based method [27], DLAN uses the weighted residual sum between all feature vectors and the cluster center to generate local aggregation features, which can mine higher-level normal features semantic information.

Setting the number of normal prototypes based on subjective assumptions limits the diversity and expressiveness of prototypes. How can we adaptively obtain a reasonable number of prototypes for normal video data according to different scenarios? Inspired by the work [18], we propose a adaptive clusterer (AC) to adaptively cluster the high-level features, which can provide a prior information for the prototypes setting. Based on AC, we can obtain different cluster numbers and corresponding cluster center vectors for different scenarios, and then use them as the initialization parameters of DLAN. AC not only solves the limitation of manually setting the number of prototypes, but also enables DLAN to be initialized based on the prior information of the data, which can speed up the training process.

In addition, we found that the background features of the high-level feature map are also clustered together by AC, and these background features cannot be used as a representative of the prototypes, because it does not contribute to judging whether the video frame is normal or abnormal. To weaken the influence of these features, drawing inspiration from the work [52], we propose a dynamic redundant clustering strategy (DRCS), that is, the final number of clusters is less than the initially set number of clusters in DLAN. Compared with the way of setting a fixed number of redundant clusters in work [52], DRCS dynamically adjusts the number of redundant clusters according to the initial number of clusters obtained by AC, which takes into account the difference of the scene. In this way, DLAN only retain the feature clusters that has important contributions to the establishment of a prototype of normal data.

The main contributions are summarized as follows:

- We propose a novel dynamic local aggregation network with adaptive clusterer (DLAN-AC), where DLAN automatically learns and aggregates high-level features to obtain more representative prototypes of the normal video data; AC adaptively clusters the high-level features of video frames according to the scene, which can provide the prior information for prototype setting.
- We propose a dynamic redundant clustering strategy (DRCS) to eliminate the unimportant feature clusters and retain the feature clusters that has important contributions to the establishment of a prototype of normal video.
- DLAN-AC is on par with or outperforms other existing methods on three benchmarks, and extensive ablation experiments demonstrate the effectiveness of DLAN-AC.

2   Related Work

Due to the inherently challenge of the VAD problem, unsupervised learning is the most commonly used method for VAD, where only normal samples are available in the training phase under the unsupervised. To determine whether an abnormal event occurs, a common method is to exploit normal patterns according to their appearance and motion in the training set. Any pattern that is inconsistent with the normal patterns is classified as an anomaly. In the early work [1,8,9,17,23,35,50], statistical models and sparse coding are commonly modeling methods that are used in VAD. For example, Adam et al. [1] characterized the normal local histograms of optical flows based on statistical monitoring of low-level observations at multiple spatial locations. Zhao et al. in [50] proposed a fully unsupervised dynamic sparse coding approach for detecting unusual events in videos based on the online sparse reconstruction. Cong et al. in [8] introduced a sparse reconstruction cost (SRC) over the normal dictionary to measure the normality of testing samples. These early methods have achieved good results in specific scenarios, but due to their poor feature expression ability, the performance is greatly reduced in some complex scenarios.

In recent years, deep learning has achieved great success in various fields [12, 14,16,19,30,32,33,35]. Video anomaly detection methods based on deep learning have begun to emerge widely [3,4,6,10,13,22,40,42–47,51]. For example, Hasan et al. in [13] used deep autoencoder to learn the temporal regularity in the videos for VAD. Luo et al. [25] presented a convolution autoencoder combined with long short-term memory (LSTM). Recently, Liu et al. [21] proposed a future frame prediction framework (FFP) for VAD. A larger difference between the predicted and the actual future frame indicates a possible abnormal event in the frame, which has achieved superior performance over previous reconstruction-based methods. The method of frame reconstruction and frame prediction based on deep learning have shown promising results. However, due to the strong generalization ability of neural networks, some abnormal frames can be also reconstructed or predicted well. This dilemma has caused their performance to encounter bottlenecks. To this end, Gong et al. [11] embedded a memory module into AE to record the prototypes of normal data, so as to enhance the ability of AE to model normal behavior patterns and weaken the reconstruction of abnormal frames. Park et al. [31] followed this trend and presented an anomaly detection method that uses multiple prototypes to consider various patterns of normal data, which can obtain more compact and sparse memory bank. Both Gong et al. [11] and Park et al. [31] have enhanced the ability of AE to model normal frames by establishing a memory bank. But the disadvantage is that, on the one hand, the memory bank for storing the prototypes of normal data leads to additional memory consumption; on the other hand, the number of prototypes in the memory bank comes from subjective assumptions and is fixed for different datasets, ignoring the scene difference, and limiting the diversity and expressiveness of prototypes. Recently, Lv et al. [27] proposed a meta-prototype network to learn normal dynamics as prototypes. This method learns normal dynamics by constructing a meta-prototype unit containing an attention mechanism to reduce the memory overhead. However, there is a lack of mining high-level semantic information of normal features, and the number of prototypes is also based on assumptions. Our method is also targeting at alleviating the excessive generalization ability of AE. However, the difference from the above-mentioned methods is that, on the one hand, our DLAN can automatically learn and aggregate data features to obtain more representative prototypes without additional memory consumption; on the other hand, our AC can adaptively cluster the high-level features of video frames according to the scene, which can provide the prior information for the prototype setting.

3   Method

Our method can be divided into four parts: an encoder, an AC, a DLAN, and a decoder. We follow the popular prediction paradigm in the filed of VAD as the main line of the method. First, the encoder extracts high-level features of four consecutive video frames from the input. Then, AC adaptively clusters the high-level features to obtain the prior cluster number and cluster center vector,

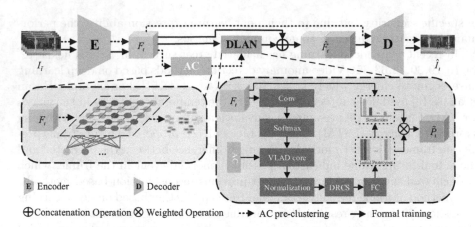

Fig. 1. An overview of our proposed DLAN-AC. Our method mainly consists of four parts: an encoder, an AC, a DLAN, and a decoder. The encoder extracts a high-level feature map F_t of size $H \times W \times D$ from an input video frame sequence $I_{\tilde{t}}$. Then, AC adaptively clusters the high-level features to obtain the prior cluster number M and cluster center vector c_l^*, which are used to initialize DLAN. Next, the F_t are further locally aggregated to obtain the prototypes $\tilde{P}_t$ by DLAN. Finally, the $\tilde{P}_t$ and the F_t are fused and fed to the decoder to predict the fifth frame $\hat{I}_t$. (Best viewed in color.) (Color figure online)

which are used to initialize DLAN. Then, DLAN further locally aggregates the high-level features to obtain the prototypes of normal video frames. Finally, the prototypes of normal video frames and the original high-level features are fused and fed to the decoder to predict the fifth frame. The overall architecture of DLAN-AC is shown in Fig. 1.

3.1   Encoder and Decoder

We use AE, a classical framework for reconstruction and prediction tasks, as the main framework of our method. AE is composed of an encoder and a decoder. Encoder is used to extract the high-level features of input video frames, which are processed by AC and DLAN, and then fed to the decoder to predict future frames. Since we follow the prediction paradigm, in order to preserve the background information of the video frame, we use a shortcut connection similar to the U-Net network. Here, we denote by $I_{\tilde{t}}$ and F_t a video frame sequence and a corresponding high-level feature map from the encoder at time t, respectively. The encoder gets the input $I_{\tilde{t}}$ and outputs F_t of size $H \times W \times D$, where H, W, D are the height, width, and number of channels, respectively. $F_t^n \in \mathbb{R}^D$ ($n = 1, 2 ... N$), where $N = H \times W$, denotes individual high-level feature vector of size $1 \times 1 \times D$ in F_t.

3.2   Adaptive Clusterer

The main function of AC is to pre-cluster the high-level features extracted by the encoder. The core of AC is Self-Organizing Maps (SOM) neural network. SOM-neural network is an unsupervised self-learning neural network, which has the characteristics of good self-organization and easy visualization. It can perform adaptive clustering by identifying the characteristics and inherent relationships between the samples. AC is a two-layer structure consisting of an input layer and output layer (competitive layer). Here, The input layer has $N = H \times W$ neurons in total, and output layer has L neurons. The two layers are connected together by means of a full connection. When AC receives an input vector, the neurons in the output layer compete for the response opportunity to the input vector, and finally the neuron closest to the input vector wins. The weight of the wining neuron and other neurons in its neighborhood will be updated. After multiple rounds of updating, each neuron in the competition layer is most sensitive to a certain type of input vector, so that the associated data in the input layer can be clustered through the competition of neurons in the output layer.

Next, we describe in detail the process of AC clustering high-level features. First, we denote by $c_l \in \mathbb{R}^D$ $(l = 1, ...L)$ the initial weight vector of neurons in the output layer. Then, for each input vector F_t^n, we calculate the Euclidean distance between it and each neuron in the output layer, and find the wining neuron that is the closest to the input vector. The distance calculation formula is as follows:

$$d_l = \sqrt{\sum_{j=1}^{D}(F_t^n(j) - c_l(j))^2}, \tag{1}$$

here, F_t^n is the n-th feature in the F_t, and c_l is the weight vector of the l-th neuron in the output layer. Then, we determine a neighborhood range of the winning neuron, which is generally determined by the neighborhood function. Here the neighborhood function $h(d_n, d_l)$ uses the Gaussian function, and is calculated as follows:

$$h(d_n, d_l) = \begin{cases} exp(-\frac{\|d_n - d_l\|^2}{2\delta(t)^2}) & d_n - d_l \leq \delta(t) \\ 0 & d_n - d_l > \delta(t) \end{cases}, \tag{2}$$

here, $\delta(t) = \delta/(1+t/(k/2))$ represents the neighborhood radius, which gradually decreases as time t increasing. δ is the initial neighborhood radius and k is the number of iterations for each feature map F_t. Next, we adjust the weight vector of winning neuron and its neighborhood to move it closer to the input vector. The weight vector is updated as follows:

$$c_l(t + 1) = c_l(t) + \eta(t)h(d_n, d_l)((F_t^n) - c_l(t)), \tag{3}$$

where $\eta(t) = \eta/(1+t/(k/2))$ represents the learning rate and η is the initial learning rate. This update process is repeated until the network converges. Finally, we obtain the updated neuron weight vector $c_l^* \in \mathbb{R}^D$ $(l = 1, ...L)$ in the output layer, and the value M of the number of clusters obtained after AC clustering. The value M is expressed follows:

$$M = \frac{\sum_{i=1}^{Q} z(F_t)}{Q}, \tag{4}$$

here, $z(F_t^n)$ represents the number of wining neurons after responding for each high-level feature map F_t in the AC competitive layer, and Q is the total number of samples in the input dataset.

3.3 Dynamic Local Aggregation Network

The Dynamic Local Aggregation Network (DLAN) is mainly composed of convolutional neural networks and a vlad [15] core, which can automatically learn and aggregate high-level features to obtain more representative prototypes of normal data, and also solve the problem of additional memory consumption. Specifically, we use the number of clusters M and the cluster center vector c_l^* output by AC as the initialization parameters of DLAN. Then DLAN automatically optimizes the location of these cluster centers and the weight of each feature vector in the F_t to the class center to which it belongs. Next, we calculate the weighted residual sum between each feature vector and the cluster center as the final video frame description vector. These description vectors are then transformed to represent prototypes. In addition, in order to enable DLAN learn to eliminate the insignificant feature clusters and retain the feature clusters that has important contributions to the establishment of a prototype of normal video data, we set dynamic redundant clustering items in DLAN, that is, the final cluster number is less than the initial number of clusters. Here, the initial number of clusters is L, namely, the number of neurons in the output layer of AC, and the number of clusters M obtained after AC clustering training is used as the final number of clusters in DLAN. The redundant cluster number is the difference $G = L - M$.

Specifically, the F_t are input into DLAN, and the weighted residual sum of the N feature points in F_t and the cluster center c_l^* is calculated as the element of the local feature matrix V. Next, we select the first M elements in the local feature matrix V, convert them into a vector form and normalize them to obtain the initial prototypes $P_m \in \mathbb{R}^D$ ($m = 1, ...M$) by a fully connected layer. The calculation formula of matrix V is as follows:

$$V(j, l) = \sum_{n=1}^{N} \beta_l(F_t^n)(F_t^n(j) - c_l^*(j)), \ 0 < j \leq D, \ 0 < l \leq L, \tag{5}$$

where $\beta_l(F_t^n)$ is the contribution weight of each feature point F_t^n to the l-th cluster center c_l^*. The calculation formula of $\beta_l(F_t^n)$ is as follows:

$$\beta_l(F_t^n) = \frac{e^{-\alpha \|F_t^n - c_l^*\|^2}}{\sum_{l'} e^{-\alpha \|F_t^n - c_{l'}^*\|^2}} = \frac{e^{W_l^T F_t^n + b_l}}{\sum_{l'} e^{W_{l'}^T F_t^n + b_{l'}}}. \tag{6}$$

Here, following [2], we replace the execution of vlad [15] with the convolutional neural network. Where $W_l = 2\alpha c_l^*$, $b_l = -\alpha\|c_l^*\|^2$, α is a positive constant that controls the decay of the response with the magnitude of the distance. Next, we fuse F_t and P_m to enable the decoder to predict the future frame using normal prototypes, which enhances the ability of AE to model normality and is the key to mitigating the overgeneralization ability of AE for anomalies. First, we calculate the cosine similarity of each F_t^n and the initial prototypes P_m, and obtain a 2-dimensional similarity matrix of size $M \times N$. Then apply a softmax function to obtain the matching probability weight vector $w_t^{n,m}$ as shown below:

$$w_t^{n,m} = \frac{exp((P_m)^T)F_t^n}{\sum_{m'=1}^{M} exp((P_{m'})^T F_t^n)}. \tag{7}$$

For the initial prototypes P_m , we multiply it with the corresponding matching probability weight $w_t^{n,m}$ to obtain the feature $\tilde{P}_t^n \in \mathbb{R}^D$ as follows:

$$\tilde{P}_t^n = \sum_{m'=1}^{M} w_t^{n,m'} P_{m'}. \tag{8}$$

For each F_t^n, we perform Eq. (7) and Eq. (8) to obtain the final prototypes $\tilde{P}_t \in \mathbb{R}^{H \times W \times D}$. Finally, $\tilde{P}_t$ and F_t are concatenated on the channel to obtain the final fusion feature $\hat{F}_t = F_t \cup \tilde{P}_t$, which is then input to decoder to predict a future frame $\hat{I}_t$.

3.4 Loss Functions

We use intensity loss and gradient loss to force AE to extract the correct high-level features of the input frame sequence, which enable the prototypes learning for normal features representation. In addition, in order to make prototypes have the characteristics of compactness and diversity, we follow the work [31] using feature compaction loss and feature separation loss to constrain prototypes.

Intensity Loss. We use the L2 distance to constrain the intensity difference between the predicted frame $\hat{I}_t$ and real frame I_t :

$$L_{int} = \left\|\hat{I}_t - I_t\right\|_2. \tag{9}$$

Gradient Loss. To improve the sharpness of the predicted image, we use gradient loss to penalize the gradient difference between the predicted frame and the real frame, where the gradient is the intensity difference between adjacent pixels in the image. The gradient loss function is given as follows:

$$L_{gd} = \sum_{i,j} \left\| \left| I_{i,j} - I_{i-1,j}\right| - \left|\hat{I}_{i,j} - \hat{I}_{i-1,j}\right| \right\|_1 + \left\| \left|I_{i,j} - I_{i,j-1}\right| - \left|\hat{I}_{i,j} - \hat{I}_{i,j-1}\right| \right\|_1, \tag{10}$$

where i, j denote the spatial index of a video frame.

Compaction Loss. The feature compactness loss urges the F_t extracted by encoder to approach the prototypes, making the prototypes more compact and reducing intra-class variations, which penalizes the discrepancies between the high-level features and their closest prototype in terms of the L2 norm as:

$$L_{cp} = \sum_t^T \sum_n^N \| F_t^n - P_a \|_2,\tag{11}$$

here a is an index of the item with the greatest probability of matching between F_t and P_m:

$$a = \arg\max_{m \in M} w_t^{n,m}.\tag{12}$$

Separation Loss. The prototypes of normal video frames should be diverse, so these prototypes should be far away from each other. To this end, we use a triplet loss function, which is defined as follows:

$$L_{sp} = \sum_t^T \sum_n^N [\| F_t^n - P_a \|_2 - \| F_t^n - P_b \|_2 + \gamma]_+,\tag{13}$$

here, high-level feature F_t^n, the item with the largest matching probability P_a, and the item with the second largest matching probability P_b, denote the anchor frame, positive example, and hard negative sample, respectively and the margin is denoted by γ. Similar to Eq. (12), b is expressed as follows:

$$b = \arg\max_{m \in M, m \neq a} w_t^{n,m}.\tag{14}$$

Overall Loss. The above four loss terms are balanced with λ_{int}, λ_{gd}, λ_{cp}, and λ_{sp} as the overall loss function:

$$L_{all} = \lambda_{int} L_{int} + \lambda_{gd} L_{gd} + \lambda_{cp} L_{cp} + \lambda_{sp} L_{sp}.\tag{15}$$

3.5   Anomaly Detection in Testing Data

After training on a large number of normal samples, DLAN-AC learns to automatically capture the normal prototype features, so it can predict well for normal frames. For abnormal frames, DLAN-AC cannot capture the abnormal features, and only excavates the normal feature parts, so there will be larger prediction errors. Therefore, we can perform anomaly detection based on the prediction error. Following the work in [28], we compute the $PSNR$ between predicted frame $\hat{I}$ and its ground truth I to evaluate the quality of the predicted frame:

$$PSNR(I, \hat{I}) = 10 log_{10} \frac{[max_{\hat{I}}]^2}{\frac{1}{K} \sum_{i=0}^{K} (I_i - \hat{I}_i)^2},\tag{16}$$

where K is the total number of image pixels and $max_{\hat{I}}$ is the maximum value of image pixels. The smaller value of $PSNR$ is, the higher probability that the test frame has abnormal behavior, and vice versa. In order to further quantify the probability of anomalies occurring, we also normalize each $PSNR$, following the work in [28], to obtain an anomaly score $S(t)$ in the ranges of $[0, 1]$ as follows:

$$S(t) = 1 - \frac{PSNR(I_t, \hat{I}_t) - min_t PSNR(I_t, \hat{I}_t)}{max_t PSNR(I_t, \hat{I}_t) - min_t PSNR(I_t, \hat{I}_t)}. \tag{17}$$

4 Experiments

4.1 Experimental Setup

Datasets. We evaluate the performance of our method on three benchmarks, which are the most commonly used in the field of VAD. (1) The UCSD Ped2 datasets [20] contains 16 training videos and 12 testing videos with 12 abnormal events, including riding a bike and driving a vehicle on the sidewalk. (2) The CUHK Avenue datasets [23] consists of 16 training videos and 21 testing videos with 47 abnormal events such as loitering, throwing stuff, and running on the sidewalk. (3) The ShanghaiTech dataset [26] contains 330 training videos and 107 testing videos with 130 abnormal events, such as affray, robbery, and fighting, etc., distributed in 13 different scenes.

Evaluation metric. Following prior works [11,21,26], we evaluate the performance of our proposed method using the Receiver Operation Characteristic curve and the Area Under the Curve (AUC). We use the frame-level AUC metrics for performance evaluation to ensure comparability between different methods.

Training Details. The training process of our proposed method contains AC pre-clustering and formal training, and the whole process can be executed end-to-end. Firstly, the size of each video frame is resized to 256×256 and the all pixels value are normalized to $[-1, 1]$. The height H and width W of the high-level feature map, and the numbers of feature channels D are set to 32, 32, and 512, respectively. During the AC pre-clustering, only the AE and AC module participate. For the AE, we use the adam optimizer with an initial learning rate of 2e-4 and decay them using a cosine annealing method. The loss function only contains intensity loss and gradient loss. For AC, the L is set to 25, the δ and the η are set to 0.5, and the k is set to 5000. In this stage, training epochs are set to 10, 10, 5 on Ped2, Avenue and ShanghaiTech, respectively, and the batch size is set to 8. In the formal training stage, AC is shielded and DLAN works. The parameter setting of AE is consistent with the above, but the separation loss and compaction loss are added and the training epochs are set to 80, 80, 20 on Ped2, Avenue and ShanghaiTech, respectively. The weights of the four loss functions are set to $\lambda_{int} = 1$, $\lambda_{gd} = 1$, $\lambda_{cp} = 0.01$, and $\lambda_{sp} = 0.01$, and the margin $\gamma = 1$. For experimental environment and hyperparameter selection, please see the supplementary materials.

Table 1. Quantitative comparison with the state of the art for anomaly detection. We measure the average AUC (%) on Ped2 [20], Avenue [23], and ShanghaiTech [26]. The comparison methods are listed in chronological order. ('R.' and 'P.' indicate the reconstruction and prediction tasks, respectively.)

	Methods	Ped2	Avenue	ShanghaiTech
–	MPPCA [17]	69.3%	N/A	N/A
	MPPC+SFA [24]	61.3%	N/A	N/A
	Unmasking [37]	82.2%	80.6%	N/A
	AMC [29]	96.2%	**86.9%**	N/A
	AnomalyNet [53]	94.9%	86.1%	N/A
	DeepOC [43]	**96.9%**	86.6%	N/A
R.	Conv-AE [13]	90.0%	70.2%	60.9%
	ConvLSTM-AE [25]	88.1%	77.0%	N/A
	Stacked RNN [26]	92.2%	81.7%	68.0%
	CDDA [53]	96.5%	86.0%	73.3%
	MemAE [11]	94.1%	83.3%	71.2%
	MNAD [31]	90.2%	82.8%	69.8%
	AMCM [6]	**96.6%**	**86.6%**	73.7%
	LNRA-P [3]	94.77%	84.91%	72.46%
	LNRA-SF [3]	96.50%	84.67%	**75.97%**
P.	FFP [21]	95.4%	84.9%	72.8%
	AnoPCN [48]	96.8%	86.2%	73.6%
	IPRAD [36]	96.3%	85.1%	73.0%
	MNAD [31]	97.0%	88.5%	70.5%
	ROADMAP [39]	96.3%	88.3%	**76.6%**
	MPN [27]	96.9%	89.5%	73.8%
	DLAN-AC	**97.6%**	**89.9%**	74.7%

4.2   Experimental Results

Comparison with Existing Methods. In Table 1, we compare the performance of our method with that of the state-of-the-art methods. It can be seen from Table 1 that our method has very strong competitiveness under the comparison of three different levels, almost surpassing most of them. In addition, MemAE [11], MNAD [31], and MPN [27], are most-related methods to our approach. They build a memory bank for storing prototypes to enhance the ability of AE to model normal behavior patterns and weaken the reconstruction of abnormal frames, but the memory bank requires additional memory storage space. Our method automatically learns to aggregate its normal pattern features directly through the neural network, which frees up extra memory space. Furthermore, the performance of our proposed method in terms of AUC on three benchmarks outperforms that of these three methods, which demonstrates the effectiveness of our method.

Fig. 2. Example of frame prediction on Ped2 dataset. The first row is a prediction example of normal event, and the second row is a prediction example of an abnormal event. Left column: the real frame. Mid column: the prediction frame. Right column: the prediction error map. (Best viewed in color.) (Color figure online)

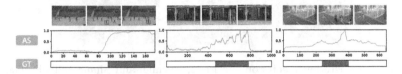

Fig. 3. Anomaly score curves of several test video clips of our method on three benchmark datasets. AS represents the anomaly score and GT represents the ground truth anomalous frame. (Best viewed in color.) (Color figure online)

Qualitative Results. Figure 2 shows the future frame prediction results of our method and the corresponding prediction error map for normal events and abnormal events. Obviously, for normal events, the future frame predicted by DLAN-AC is almost close to the actual frame, as shown by the darker error map. For abnormal events, the predicted future frame tends to be blurred and distorted compared to the real frame, and the location of the abnormality is very conspicuous in the error map. In addition, we show the fluctuations of the abnormal scores of several test videos in Fig. 3 to illustrate the effectiveness of our method for timely detection of abnormalities. It is easy to observe from Fig. 3 that the low abnormal score increases sharply with the occurrence of abnormal events, and then returns to the low level after the abnormality ends. For more qualitative results, please see the supplementary materials.

4.3 Ablation Studies

In this subsection, we conduct several ablation experiments to analyze the role played by each component of our method.

AC Analysis. To demonstrate the effectiveness of AC, we compare the performance differences between our method using AC to adaptively obtain the number of prototypes and using the pre-set fixed number of prototypes on three benchmarks in Table 2. The fixed number of setting following [27], which is taken as 10. It can be seen from Table 2 that the performance of the model with the AC is better than that of the model with a fixed number of settings. For different

Table 2. The AUC obtained by DLAN-AC with or without AC on Ped2 [20], Avenue [23] and ShanghaiTech [26] dataset. (M stands for the number of prototypes)

	Ped2	Avenue	ShanghaiTech
	M/AUC	M/AUC	M/AUC
w/o AC	10/97.1%	10/89.2%	10/74.0%
w AC	13/97.6%	13/89.9%	11/74.7%

Fig. 4. AC pre-clustering results on the Ped2, Avenue, and ShanghaiTech. The first row is the original image, and the second row is the corresponding clustering result. It can be seen that elements with similar attributes are grouped into the same category.

datasets, the number of prototypes M is different, which confirms the inherent difference of video data in different scenes. In addition, we respectively show the cluster distribution map of the high-level features obtained from above three datasets after AC clustering in Fig. 4. Taking Ped2 dataset as an example, it can be seen from Fig. 4 that grass, ground, walls, and people are clearly grouped into different categories. This shows that the adaptive clustering of video features by the AC plays a key role during the pre-clustering of our method, and is an important contributor to the prototype setup of normal data.

DLAN Analysis. In order to analyze the role of DLAN, we freeze the AC, and then set the number of central weight vectors to 10 in DLAN without using DRCS, and initialize them randomly. Next, we insert DLAN into AE as an independent module, and compare it with the AE without DLAN. The comparison results are shown in Table 3. It can be seen that even if there is no other module assistance, just inserting DLAN can increase the performance on the Ped2, Avenue and ShanghaiTech datasets by 2%, 5.3%, and 7.3%, respectively, and DLAN is completely online learning prototypes without consuming additional memory space. This fully proves the effectiveness of using DLAN for feature aggregation to build normal data prototypes.

Initialization of DLAN. In order to evaluate the effectiveness of using the cluster center vector output by AC as the initial cluster center vector of DLAN, we respectively compare the aggregation results of using the randomly initialized cluster center vector and the cluster center vector output by AC as the initialization vector. Figure 5 visualizes the aggregation results after DLAN aggregation when training to the tenth epoch. It can be clearly seen that DLAN using the

Table 3. The AUC on Ped2, Avenue and ShanghaiTech datasets with only AE or AE+DLAN.

	Ped2	Avenue	ShanghaiTech
AE	95.1%	83.9%	66.7%
AE+DLAN	97.1%	89.2%	74.0%

cluster center vector output by AC as the initial cluster center has a more compact feature aggregation under the same training epoch. This shows that the initial clustering center vector with certain prior information can make the network convergent faster than the random initialization method.

Table 4. The AUC obtained by DLAN-AC with or without Dynamic Redundant Clustering Strategy (DRCS) on Ped2, Avenue and ShanghaiTech datasets.

	Ped2	Avenue	ShanghaiTech
DLAN-AC (w/o DRCS)	97.2%	89.4%	74.1%
DLAN-AC (w DRCS)	97.6%	89.9%	74.7%

Fig. 5. t-SNE [38] visualization for the prototypes aggregated by DLAN in the 10th training epoch from Ped2 dataset. The left is the cluster center vector output by AC as the initial clustering vector, and the right is the method of random initialization.

DRCS Analysis. To verify the effectiveness of the DRCS, we respectively compare the AUC on Ped2 and Avenue datasets with and without the number of redundant clusters. It can be seen from Table 4 that the performances of the model with the number of redundant clusters set are all better than that of the unset model, which verify the effectiveness of the DRCS to eliminate insignificant feature clusters and retain the feature clusters that have important contributions to the establishment of prototypes.

5 Conclusions

We have introduced a novel dynamic local aggregation network with adaptive clusterer (DLAN-AC) for anoamly detection. To this end, we have proposed a dynamic local aggregation network (DLAN), which can automatically learn and aggregate high-level features from AE to obtain more representative normal data prototypes without consuming additional memory space. To adaptively obtain the initial information of prototypes in different scenarios, we have proposed a adaptive clusterer (AC) to perform initial clustering of high-level features to obtain the pre-cluster number and cluster center vector, which are used to initialize the DLAN. In addition, we have also proposed a dynamic redundant clustering strategy (DRCS) to enable DLAN to automatically eliminate the insignificant feature clusters. Extensive experiments on three benchmarks demonstrate that our method outperforms most existing state-of-the-art methods, validating the effectiveness of our method for anomaly detection.

Acknowledgments. This work was supported in part by the Key Project of Science and Technology Innovation 2030 supported by the Ministry of Science and Technology of China under Grant 2018AAA0101302.

References

1. Adam, A., Rivlin, E., Shimshoni, I., Reinitz, D.: Robust real-time unusual event detection using multiple fixed-location monitors. IEEE Trans. Pattern Anal. Mach. Intell. **30**(3), 555–560 (2008)
2. Arandjelovic, R., Gronat, P., Torii, A., Pajdla, T., Sivic, J.: NetVLAD: CNN architecture for weakly supervised place recognition. In: Proceedings of the IEEE Conference on Computer Vision and Pattern Recognition, pp. 5297–5307 (2016)
3. Astrid, M., Zaheer, M.Z., Lee, J.Y., Lee, S.I.: Learning not to reconstruct anomalies. arXiv preprint arXiv:2110.09742 (2021)
4. Astrid, M., Zaheer, M.Z., Lee, S.I.: Synthetic temporal anomaly guided end-to-end video anomaly detection. In: Proceedings of the IEEE/CVF International Conference on Computer Vision, pp. 207–214 (2021)
5. Benezeth, Y., Jodoin, P.M., Saligrama, V., Rosenberger, C.: Abnormal events detection based on spatio-temporal co-occurences. In: 2009 IEEE Conference on Computer Vision and Pattern Recognition, pp. 2458–2465. IEEE (2009)
6. Cai, R., Zhang, H., Liu, W., Gao, S., Hao, Z.: Appearance-motion memory consistency network for video anomaly detection. In: Proceedings of the AAAI Conference on Artificial Intelligence, pp. 938–946 (2021)
7. Chandola, V., Banerjee, A., Kumar, V.: Anomaly detection: A survey. ACM Comput. Surv. **41**(3), 1–58 (2009)
8. Cong, Y., Yuan, J., Liu, J.: Sparse reconstruction cost for abnormal event detection. In: CVPR 2011, pp. 3449–3456. IEEE (2011)
9. Dutta, J., Banerjee, B.: Online detection of abnormal events using incremental coding length. In: Proceedings of the AAAI Conference on Artificial Intelligence (2015)
10. Georgescu, M.I., Barbalau, A., Ionescu, R.T., Khan, F.S., Popescu, M., Shah, M.: Anomaly detection in video via self-supervised and multi-task learning. In: Proceedings of the IEEE/CVF Conference on Computer Vision and Pattern Recognition, pp. 12742–12752 (2021)
11. Gong, D., et al.: Memorizing normality to detect anomaly: memory-augmented deep autoencoder for unsupervised anomaly detection. In: Proceedings of the IEEE/CVF International Conference on Computer Vision, pp. 1705–1714 (2019)

12. Goodfellow, I., et al.: Generative adversarial nets. In: Advances in Neural Information Processing Systems vol. 27 (2014)
13. Hasan, M., Choi, J., Neumann, J., Roy-Chowdhury, A.K., Davis, L.S.: Learning temporal regularity in video sequences. In: Proceedings of the IEEE Conference on Computer Vision and Pattern Recognition, pp. 733–742 (2016)
14. He, K., Zhang, X., Ren, S., Sun, J.: Deep residual learning for image recognition. In: Proceedings of the IEEE Conference on Computer Vision and Pattern Recognition, pp. 770–778 (2016)
15. Jégou, H., Douze, M., Schmid, C., Pérez, P.: Aggregating local descriptors into a compact image representation. In: 2010 IEEE Computer Society Conference on Computer Vision and Pattern Recognition, pp. 3304–3311. IEEE (2010)
16. Karras, T., Laine, S., Aila, T.: A style-based generator architecture for generative adversarial networks. In: Proceedings of the IEEE/CVF Conference on Computer Vision and Pattern Recognition, pp. 4401–4410 (2019)
17. Kim, J., Grauman, K.: Observe locally, infer globally: a space-time MRF for detecting abnormal activities with incremental updates. In: 2009 IEEE Conference on Computer Vision and Pattern Recognition, pp. 2921–2928. IEEE (2009)
18. Kohonen, T.: The self-organizing map. Proc. IEEE **78**(9), 1464–1480 (1990)
19. Krizhevsky, A., Sutskever, I., Hinton, G.E.: ImageNet classification with deep convolutional neural networks. Adv. Neural. Inf. Process. Syst. **25**, 1097–1105 (2012)
20. Li, W., Mahadevan, V., Vasconcelos, N.: Anomaly detection and localization in crowded scenes. IEEE Trans. Pattern Anal. Mach. Intell. **36**(1), 18–32 (2013)
21. Liu, W., Luo, W., Lian, D., Gao, S.: Future frame prediction for anomaly detection-a new baseline. In: Proceedings of the IEEE Conference on Computer Vision and Pattern Recognition, pp. 6536–6545 (2018)
22. Liu, Z., Nie, Y., Long, C., Zhang, Q., Li, G.: A hybrid video anomaly detection framework via memory-augmented flow reconstruction and flow-guided frame prediction. In: Proceedings of the IEEE/CVF International Conference on Computer Vision, pp. 13588–13597 (2021)
23. Lu, C., Shi, J., Jia, J.: Abnormal event detection at 150 fps in MATLAB. In: Proceedings of the IEEE International Conference on Computer Vision, pp. 2720–2727 (2013)
24. Lu, C., Shi, J., Jia, J.: Abnormal event detection at 150 fps in MATLAB. In: Proceedings of the IEEE International Conference on Computer Vision, pp. 2720–2727 (2013)
25. Luo, W., Liu, W., Gao, S.: Remembering history with convolutional LSTM for anomaly detection. In: 2017 IEEE International Conference on Multimedia and Expo (ICME), pp. 439–444. IEEE (2017)
26. Luo, W., Liu, W., Gao, S.: A revisit of sparse coding based anomaly detection in stacked rnn framework. In: Proceedings of the IEEE International Conference on Computer Vision, pp. 341–349 (2017)
27. Lv, H., Chen, C., Cui, Z., Xu, C., Li, Y., Yang, J.: Learning normal dynamics in videos with meta prototype network. In: Proceedings of the IEEE/CVF Conference on Computer Vision and Pattern Recognition, pp. 15425–15434 (2021)
28. Mathieu, M., Couprie, C., LeCun, Y.: Deep multi-scale video prediction beyond mean square error. arXiv preprint arXiv:1511.05440 (2015)
29. Nguyen, T.N., Meunier, J.: Anomaly detection in video sequence with appearance-motion correspondence. In: Proceedings of the IEEE/CVF International Conference on Computer Vision, pp. 1273–1283 (2019)

30. Nie, X., Jing, W., Cui, C., Zhang, C.J., Zhu, L., Yin, Y.: Joint multi-view hashing for large-scale near-duplicate video retrieval. IEEE Trans. Knowl. Data Eng. **32**(10), 1951–1965 (2019)
31. Park, H., Noh, J., Ham, B.: Learning memory-guided normality for anomaly detection. In: Proceedings of the IEEE/CVF Conference on Computer Vision and Pattern Recognition, pp. 14372–14381 (2020)
32. Redmon, J., Divvala, S., Girshick, R., Farhadi, A.: You only look once: Unified, real-time object detection. In: Proceedings of the IEEE Conference on Computer Vision and Pattern Recognition, pp. 779–788 (2016)
33. Ren, S., He, K., Girshick, R., Sun, J.: Faster r-CNN: Towards real-time object detection with region proposal networks. Adv. Neural. Inf. Process. Syst. **28**, 91–99 (2015)
34. Sabokrou, M., Fathy, M., Hoseini, M., Klette, R.: Real-time anomaly detection and localization in crowded scenes. In: Proceedings of the IEEE Conference on Computer Vision and Pattern Recognition Workshops, pp. 56–62 (2015)
35. Shao, F., Liu, J., Wu, P., Yang, Z., Wu, Z.: Exploiting foreground and background separation for prohibited item detection in overlapping x-ray images. Pattern Recogn. **122**, 108261 (2022)
36. Tang, Y., Zhao, L., Zhang, S., Gong, C., Li, G., Yang, J.: Integrating prediction and reconstruction for anomaly detection. Pattern Recogn. Lett. **129**, 123–130 (2020)
37. Tudor Ionescu, R., Smeureanu, S., Alexe, B., Popescu, M.: Unmasking the abnormal events in video. In: Proceedings of the IEEE International Conference on Computer Vision, pp. 2895–2903 (2017)
38. Van Der Maaten, L.: Accelerating t-SNE using tree-based algorithms. J. Mach. Learn. Res. **15**(1), 3221–3245 (2014)
39. Wang, X., et al.: Robust unsupervised video anomaly detection by multipath frame prediction. IEEE Trans. Neural Netw. Learn. Syst. **33** (2021)
40. Wang, Z., Zou, Y., Zhang, Z.: Cluster attention contrast for video anomaly detection. In: Proceedings of the 28th ACM International Conference on Multimedia, pp. 2463–2471 (2020)
41. Woo, S., Park, J., Lee, J.Y., Kweon, I.S.: Cbam: Convolutional block attention module. In: Proceedings of the European conference on computer vision (ECCV). pp. 3–19 (2018)
42. Wu, P., Liu, J.: Learning causal temporal relation and feature discrimination for anomaly detection. IEEE Trans. Image Process. **30**, 3513–3527 (2021). https://doi.org/10.1109/TIP.2021.3062192
43. Wu, P., Liu, J., Shen, F.: A deep one-class neural network for anomalous event detection in complex scenes. IEEE Trans. Neural Netw. Learn. Syst. **31**(7), 2609–2622 (2019)
44. Wu, P., et al.: Not only look, but also listen: learning multimodal violence detection under weak supervision. In: Vedaldi, A., Bischof, H., Brox, T., Frahm, J.-M. (eds.) ECCV 2020. LNCS, vol. 12375, pp. 322–339. Springer, Cham (2020). https://doi.org/10.1007/978-3-030-58577-8_20
45. Xia, C., Qi, F., Shi, G.: Bottom-up visual saliency estimation with deep autoencoder-based sparse reconstruction. IEEE Trans. Neural Netw. Learn. Syst. **27**(6), 1227–1240 (2016)
46. Xu, D., Ricci, E., Yan, Y., Song, J., Sebe, N.: Learning deep representations of appearance and motion for anomalous event detection. arXiv preprint arXiv:1510.01553 (2015)
47. Yang, Z., Liu, J., Wu, P.: Bidirectional retrospective generation adversarial network for anomaly detection in videos. IEEE Access **9**, 107842–107857 (2021)

48. Ye, M., Peng, X., Gan, W., Wu, W., Qiao, Y.: AnoPCN: video anomaly detection via deep predictive coding network. In: Proceedings of the 27th ACM International Conference on Multimedia, pp. 1805–1813 (2019)
49. Zhai, S., Cheng, Y., Lu, W., Zhang, Z.: Deep structured energy based models for anomaly detection. In: International Conference on Machine Learning, pp. 1100–1109. PMLR (2016)
50. Zhao, B., Fei-Fei, L., Xing, E.P.: Online detection of unusual events in videos via dynamic sparse coding. In: CVPR 2011, pp. 3313–3320. IEEE (2011)
51. Zhao, Y., Deng, B., Shen, C., Liu, Y., Lu, H., Hua, X.S.: Spatio-temporal autoencoder for video anomaly detection. In: Proceedings of the 25th ACM International Conference on Multimedia, pp. 1933–1941 (2017)
52. Zhong, Y., Arandjelović, R., Zisserman, A.: GhostVLAD for set-based face recognition. In: Jawahar, C.V., Li, H., Mori, G., Schindler, K. (eds.) ACCV 2018. LNCS, vol. 11362, pp. 35–50. Springer, Cham (2019). https://doi.org/10.1007/978-3-030-20890-5_3
53. Zhou, J.T., Du, J., Zhu, H., Peng, X., Liu, Y., Goh, R.S.M.: Anomalynet: an anomaly detection network for video surveillance. IEEE Trans. Inf. Forensics Secur. 14(10), 2537–2550 (2019)
54. Zong, B., et al.: Deep autoencoding Gaussian mixture model for unsupervised anomaly detection. In: International Conference on Learning Representations (2018)

Action Quality Assessment with Temporal Parsing Transformer

Yang Bai[1,2], Desen Zhou[2], Songyang Zhang[3], Jian Wang[2], Errui Ding[2], Yu Guan[4], Yang Long[1], and Jingdong Wang[2(✉)]

[1] Department of Computer Science, Durham University, Durham, UK
{yang.bai,yang.long}@durham.ac.uk
[2] Department of Computer Vision Technology (VIS), Baidu Inc., Beijing, China
{zhoudesen,wangjingdong}@baidu.com
[3] Shanghai AI Laboratory, Shanghai, China
[4] University of Warwick, Coventry, UK

Abstract. Action Quality Assessment(AQA) is important for action understanding and resolving the task poses unique challenges due to subtle visual differences. Existing state-of-the-art methods typically rely on the holistic video representations for score regression or ranking, which limits the generalization to capture fine-grained intra-class variation. To overcome the above limitation, we propose a temporal parsing transformer to decompose the holistic feature into temporal part-level representations. Specifically, we utilize a set of learnable queries to represent the atomic temporal patterns for a specific action. Our decoding process converts the frame representations to a fixed number of temporally ordered part representations. To obtain the quality score, we adopt the state-of-the-art contrastive regression based on the part representations. Since existing AQA datasets do not provide temporal part-level labels or partitions, we propose two novel loss functions on the cross attention responses of the decoder: a ranking loss to ensure the learnable queries to satisfy the temporal order in cross attention and a sparsity loss to encourage the part representations to be more discriminative. Extensive experiments show that our proposed method outperforms prior work on three public AQA benchmarks by a considerable margin.

Keywords: Action quality assessment · Temporal parsing transformer · Temporal patterns · Contrastive regression

1 Introduction

Action quality assessment(AQA), which aims to evaluate how well a specific action is performed, has attracted increasing attention in research community

Y. Bai and D. Zhou—Equal contribution.
Y. Bai—Work done when Yang Bai was a research intern at VIS, Baidu.

Supplementary Information The online version contains supplementary material available at https://doi.org/10.1007/978-3-031-19772-7_25.

Fig. 1. An action consists of multiple temporally ordered key phases.

recently [17,18]. In particular, assessing the action quality accurately has great potential in a wide range of applications such as health care [34] and sports analysis [2,18–20].

In contrast to the conventional action recognition tasks [4,25], AQA poses unique challenges due to the subtle visual differences. Previous works on AQA either use ranking-based pairwise comparison between test videos [5] or estimate the quality score with regression-based methods [19,29]. However, these methods typically represent a video with its *holistic representation*, via the global pooling operation over the output of the backbone network(e.g., I3D [4]). Since the videos to be evaluated usually are from the same coarse action category (e.g., diving) in AQA, it's crucial to capture *fine-grained intra-class variation* to estimate more accurate quality scores. Thus, we propose to decompose the holistic feature into more fine-grained temporal part-level representations for AQA.

To achieve this, a promising strategy is to represent the video by using a set of atomic action patterns. For example, a diving action consists of several key phases, such as *approach, take off, flight*, etc., as illustrated in Fig. 1. The fine-grained patterns enable the model to describe the subtle differences, which is expected to improve the assessment of action quality effectively. Nevertheless, it remains challenging to learn such atomic patterns as the existing AQA datasets do not provide temporal part-level labels or partitions.

In this work, we aim to tackle the aforementioned limitations by developing a regression-based action quality assessment strategy, which enables us to leverage the fine-grained atomic action patterns without any explicit part-level supervision. Our key idea is to model the shared atomic temporal patterns, with a set of learnable queries for a specific action category. Similar to the decoding process of transformer applied in natural language modeling [24], we propose a temporal parsing transformer to decode each video into a fixed number of part representations. To obtain quality scores, we adopt the recent state-of-the-art contrastive regression framework [32]. Our decoding mechanism allows the part representations between test video and exemplar video to be implicitly aligned via a shared learnable query. Then, we generate a relative pairwise representation per part and fuse different parts together to perform the final relative score regression.

To learn the atomic action patterns without the part-level labels, we propose two novel loss functions on the cross attention responses of the decoder. Specifically, to ensure the learnable queries satisfy the temporal order in cross attention, we calculate an attention center for each query by weighted summation of the attention responses with their temporal clip orders. Then we adopt a marginal ranking loss on the attention centers to guide the temporal order. Moreover, we propose a sparsity loss for each query's attention distribution to guide the part representations to be more discriminative.

We evaluate our method, named as temporal parsing transformer(TPT), on three public AQA benchmarks: MTL-AQA [18], AQA-7 [17] and JIGSAWS [7]. As a result, our method outperforms previous state-of-the-art methods by a considerable margin. The visualization results show that our method is able to extract part-level representations with interpretable semantic meanings. We also provide abundant ablation studies for better understanding.

The main contributions of this paper are three folds:

- We propose a novel temporal parsing transformer to extract fine-grained temporal part-level representations with interpretable semantic meanings, which are optimized with the contrastive regression framework.
- We propose two novel loss functions on the transformer cross attentions to learn the part representations without the part-level labels.
- We achieve the new state-of-the-art on three public AQA benchmarks, namely MTL-AQA, AQA-7 and JIGSAWS.

2   Related Work

2.1   Action Quality Assessment

In the past years, the field of action quality assessment (AQA) has been repaid developed with a broad range of applications such as health care [34], instructional video analysis [5,6], sports video analysis [17,18], and many others [8,9]. Existing AQA methods can be categorized into two types: regression based methods and ranking based methods.

Regression Based Methods. Mainstream AQA methods formulate the AQA task as a regression task based on reliable score labels, such as scores given by expert judges of sports events. For example, Pirsiavash et al. [20] took the first steps towards applying the learning method to the AQA task and trained a linear SVR model to regress the scores of videos based on handcrafted features. Gordan et al. [8] proposed in their pioneer work the use of skeleton trajectories to solve the problem of quality assessment of gymnastic vaulting movements. Parmar et al. [19] showed that spatiotemporal features from C3D [23] can better encode the temporal representation of videos and significantly improve AQA performance. They also propose a large-scale AQA dataset and explore all-action models to better evaluate the effectiveness of models proposed by the AQA community. Xu et al. [29] proposed learning multi-scale video features by stacked LSTMs followed [19]. Pan et al. [16] proposed using spatial and temporal graphs to model the interactions between joints. Furthermore, they also propose to use I3D [4] as a stronger backbone network to extract spatiotemporal features. Parmar et al. [18] introduced the idea of multi-task learning to improve the model capacity of AQA, and collected AQA datasets with more annotations to support multi-task learning. To diminish the subjectiveness of the action score from human judges, Tang et al. [22] proposed an uncertainty-aware score distribution learning (USDL) framework Recently. However, the video's final score can only provide weak supervision concerning action quality. Because two videos with different low-quality parts are likely to share similar final scores, which means the score couldn't provide discriminative information.

Ranking Based Methods. Another branch formulates AQA task as a ranking problem. Doughty et al. [5] proposed a novel loss function that learns discriminative features when a pair of videos exhibit variance in skill and learns shared features when a pair of videos show comparable skill levels. Doughty et al. [6] used a novel rank-aware loss function to attend to skill-relevant parts of a given video. However, they mainly focus on longer, more ambiguous tasks and only predict overall rankings, limiting AQA to applications requiring some quantitative comparisons. Recently, Yu et al. [32] proposed the Contrastive Regression (CoRe) framework to learn the relative scores by pair-wise comparison, highlighting the differences between videos and guiding the models to learn the key hints for assessment.

2.2 Temporal Action Parsing

Fine-grained action parsing is also studied in the field of action segmentation or temporal parsing [1,10–13,31]. For example, Zhang et al. [33] proposed Temporal Query Network adopted query-response functionality that allows the query to attend to relevant segments. Dian et al. [21] proposed a temporal parsing method called TransParser that is capable of mining sub-actions from training data without knowing their labels. However, different from the above fields, part-level labels are not available in AQA task. Furthermore, most of the above methods focus more on frame-level feature enhancement, whereas our proposed method extracts part representations with interpretable semantic meanings.

3   Method

In this section, we introduce our temporal parsing transformer with the contrastive regression framework in detail.

3.1   Overview

The input of our network is an action video. We adopt the Inflated 3D ConvNets(I3D) [4] as our backbone, which first applies a sliding window to split the video into T overlapping clips, where each clip contains M consecutive frames. Then, each clip goes through the I3D network, resulting in time series clip level representations $V = \{v_t \in \mathbb{R}^D\}_{t=1}^T$, where D is feature dimension and T is the total number of clips. In our work, we do not explore spatial patterns, hence each clip representation v_t is obtained by average pooling across spatial dimensions. The goal of AQA is to estimate a quality score **s** based on the resulting clips representation V. In contrastive regression framework, instead of designing a network to directly estimate raw score **s**, it estimates a relative score between

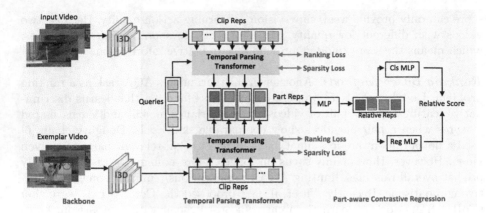

Fig. 2. Overview of our framework. Our temporal parsing transformer converts the clip-level representations into temporal part-level representations. Then the part-aware contrastive regressor first computes part-wise relative representations and then fuses them to estimate the relative score. We adopt the group-aware regression strategy, following [32]. During training, we adopt the ranking loss and sparsity loss on the decoder cross attention maps to guide the part representation learning.

the test video and an exemplar video V_0 with known quality score s_0, which is usually sampled from training set. Then, contrastive regression aims to design a network $\mathcal{F}$ that estimates the relative score Δs:

$$\Delta s = \mathcal{F}(V, V_0), \tag{1}$$

then final score can be obtained by

$$s = s_0 + \Delta s. \tag{2}$$

In our framework, we first adopt a temporal parsing transformer $\mathcal{G}$ to convert the clip level representations V into temporal part level representations, denoted by $P = \{p_k \in \mathbb{R}^d\}_{k=1}^K$, where d is the part feature dimension and K is the number of queries, i.e. temporal atomic patterns. Then for test video and exemplar video, we can have two set of aligned part representations P and $P_0 = \{p_k^0 \in \mathbb{R}^d\}_{k=1}^K$. Our new formulation can be expressed as:

$$\Delta s = \mathcal{R}(P, P_0). \tag{3}$$

where $\mathcal{R}$ is the relative score regressor, and

$$P = \mathcal{G}(V), P_0 = \mathcal{G}(V_0). \tag{4}$$

An overview of our framework is illustrated in Fig. 2. Below we describe the detailed structure of temporal parsing transformer $\mathcal{G}$ and part-aware contrastive regressor $\mathcal{R}$.

3.2   Temporal Parsing Transformer

Our temporal parsing transformer takes the clip representations as memory and exploits a set of learnable queries to decode part representations. Different from prevalent DETR architecture [3], our transformer only consists of a decoder module. We found that the encoder module does not provide improvements in our framework; it even hurts the performance. We guess it might because that clip-level self-attention smooths the temporal representations, and our learning strategy cannot decode part presentations in this way without part labels.

We perform slight modifications to the standard DETR decoder. That is, the cross attention block in our decoder has a learnable parameter, temperature, to control the amplification of the inner product. Formally, in the i-th decoder layer, the decoder part feature $\{p_k^{(i)} \in \mathbb{R}^d\}$ and learnable atomic patterns(i.e. query set) $\{q_k \in \mathbb{R}^d\}$ are first summed as a query and then perform cross attention on the embedded clip representation $\{\mathbf{v}_t \in \mathbb{R}^d\}$:

$$\alpha_{k,t} = \frac{\exp^{(\boldsymbol{p}_k^{(i)}+q_k)^T \cdot \boldsymbol{v}_t/\tau}}{\sum\limits_{j=1}^{T} \exp^{(\boldsymbol{p}_k^{(i)}+q_k)^T \cdot \boldsymbol{v}_j/\tau}}, \tag{5}$$

where $\alpha_{k,t}$ indicates the attention value for query k to clip t, $\tau \in \mathbb{R}$ indicates the learnable temperature to enhance the inner product to make the attentions more discriminative. Unlike DETR [3], in our decoder, we do not utilize position embedding of clip id to the memory $\{\boldsymbol{v}_t\}$. We expect our query to represent atomic patterns, instead of spatial anchors, as in the detection task [14, 28]. We found that adding position encoding significantly drops the performance and makes our learning strategy fail, which will be shown in the experiment section.

In our experiments, we only utilize one-head attention in our cross attention blocks. The attention values are normalized across different clips, since our goal is to aggregate clip representations into our part representation. Then the updated part representation $\boldsymbol{p}_k^{(i)'}$ has the following form:

$$\boldsymbol{p}_k^{(i)'} = \sum_{j=1}^{T} \alpha_{k,j} \boldsymbol{v}_j + \boldsymbol{p}_k^{(i)}. \tag{6}$$

We then perform standard FFN and multi-head self-attention on decoder part representations. Similar to DETR [3], our decoder also has a multi-layer structure.

3.3   Part-Aware Contrastive Regression

Our temporal parsing transformer converts the clip representations $\{\boldsymbol{v}_t\}$ into part representations $\{\boldsymbol{p}_k\}$. Given a test video and exemplar video, we can obtain two part representation sets $\{\boldsymbol{p}_k\}$ and $\{\boldsymbol{p}_k^0\}$. One possible way to estimate the relative quality score is to fuse each video's part representations and estimate the relative score. However, since our temporal parsing transformer allows the extracted part representations to be semantically aligned with the query set, we can compute the relative pairwise representation per part and then fuse them together. Formally, we utilize a multi-layer perceptron(MLP) f_r to generate the relative pairwise representation $r_k \in \mathbb{R}^d$ for k-th part:

$$r_k = f_r(Concat([p_k; p_k^0])). \tag{7}$$

The MLP f_r is shared across different parts. To balance the score distributions across the whole score range, we adopt the group-aware regression strategy to perform relative score estimation [32]. Specifically, it first calculates B relative score intervals based on all possible pairs in training set, where each interval has equal number of pair-samples. Then it generates a one-hot classification label $\{l_n\}$, where l_n indicates whether the ground truth score Δs lies in n-th interval, and a regression target $\gamma_n = \frac{\Delta s - x_{left}^n}{x_{right}^n - x_{left}^n}$, where x_{left}^n, x_{right}^n denote the left and right boundary of n-th interval. Readers can refer to [32] for more details.

We adopt average pooling[1] on the relative part representations $\{r_k\}$ and then utilize two two-layer MLPs to estimate the classification label $\{l_n\}$ and regression target $\{\gamma_n\}$. Different from [32], we do not utilize tree structure. Since we have obtained fine-grained part-level representations and hence the regression becomes simpler, we found that two-layer MLP works fine.

3.4   Optimization

Since we do not have any part-level labels at hand, it's crucial to design proper loss functions to guide the part representation learning. We have assumed that each coarse action has a set of temporally ordered atomic patterns, which are encoded in our transformer queries. To ensure that our query extracts different part representations, we constrain the attention responses in cross attention blocks for different queries. Specifically, in each cross attention process, we have calculated the normalized attention responses $\{\alpha_{k,t}\}$ by Eq. 5, then we compute an attention center $\bar{\alpha}_k$ for k-th query:

$$\bar{\alpha}_k = \sum_{t=1}^{T} t \cdot \alpha_{k,t}, \tag{8}$$

where T is the number of clips and $\sum_{t=1}^{T} \alpha_{k,t} = 1$. Then we adopt two loss functions on the attention centers: ranking loss and sparsity loss.

Ranking Loss. To encourage that each query attends to different temporal regions, we adopt a ranking loss on the attention centers. We wish our part representations have a consistent temporal order across different videos. To this

---

[1] We note that it might be better to weight each part. However, part weighting does not provide improvements during our practice. We guess that it may be during the self-attention process in the decoder, the relations between parts have already been taken into account.

end, we define an order on the query index and apply ranking losses to the corresponding attention centers. We exploit the margin ranking loss, which results in the following form:

$$L_{rank} = \sum_{k=1}^{K-1} \max(0, \bar{\alpha}_k - \bar{\alpha}_{k+1} + m) + \max(0, 1 - \bar{\alpha}_1 + m) + \max(0, \bar{\alpha}_K - T + m),$$

(9)

where m is the hyper-parameter margin controlling the penalty, the first term guides the attention centers of part k and $k+1$ to keep order: $\bar{\alpha}_k < \bar{\alpha}_{k+1}$. From Eq. 8, we have the range of attention centers: $1 \leq \bar{\alpha}_k \leq T$. To constrain the first and last part where $k = 1$ and $k = K$, we assume there is two virtual centers at boundaries: $\bar{\alpha}_0 = 1$ and $\bar{\alpha}_{K+1} = T$. The last two terms in Eq. 9 constrain the first and last attention centers not collapsed to boundaries.

Sparsity Loss. To encourage the part representations to be more discriminative, we further propose a sparsity loss on the attention responses. Specifically, for each query, we encourage the attention responses to focus on those clips around the center μ_k, resulting in the following form:

$$L_{sparsity} = \sum_{k=1}^{K} \sum_{t=1}^{T} |t - \bar{\alpha}_k| \cdot \alpha_{k,t}$$

(10)

During training, our ranking loss and sparsity loss are applied to the cross attention block in each decoder layer.

Overall Training Loss. In addition to the above auxiliary losses for cross attention, our contrastive regressor $\mathcal{R}$ generates two predictions for the group classification label $\{l_n\}$ and regression target $\{\gamma_n\}$, we follow [32] to utilize the BCE loss on each group and square error on the ground truth regression interval:

$$L_{cls} = -\sum_{n=1}^{N} l_n \log(\tilde{l}_n) + (1 - l_n) \log(1 - \tilde{l}_n)$$

(11)

$$L_{reg} = \sum_{n=1}^{N} \mathbb{1}(l_n = 1)(\gamma_n - \tilde{\gamma}_n)^2$$

(12)

where L_{reg} only supervises on the ground truth interval, $\tilde{l}_n$ and $\tilde{\gamma}_n$ are predicted classification probability and regression value. The overall training loss is given by:

$$L_{all} = \lambda_{cls} L_{cls} + \lambda_{reg} L_{reg} + \lambda_{rank} \sum_{i=1}^{L} L_{rank}^i + \lambda_{sparsity} \sum_{i=1}^{L} L_{sparsity}^i,$$

(13)

where i indicates layer id and L is the number of decoder layers, $\lambda_{cls}, \lambda_{reg}, \lambda_{rank}, \lambda_{sparsity}$ are hyper-parameter loss weights.

4   Experiment

4.1   Experimental Settup

Datasets. We perform experiments on three public benchmarks: MTL-AQA [18], AQA-7 [17], and JIGSAWS [7]. See Supplement for more details on datasets.

Evaluation Metrics. Following prior work [32], we utilize two metrics in our experiments, the Spearman's rank correlation and relative L2 distance(R-ℓ_2). **Spearman's rank correlation** was adopted as our main evaluation metric to measure the difference between true and predicted scores. The Spearman's rank correlation is defined as follows:

$$\rho = \frac{\sum_i(p_i - \bar{p})(q_i - \bar{q})}{\sqrt{\sum_i(p_i - \bar{p})^2 \sum_i(q_i - \bar{q})^2}} \qquad (14)$$

It focuses on the ranking of test samples. In contrast, **relative L2 distance** measures the numerical precision of each sample compared with ground truth. Formally, it's defined as:

$$R\text{-}\ell_2 = \frac{1}{N} \sum_{n=1}^{N} (\frac{|s_n - \hat{s}_n|}{s_{max} - s_{min}})^2 \qquad (15)$$

Implementation Details. We adopt the I3D backbone pretrained on Kinetics [4] as our local spatial-temporal feature extractor. The Adam optimizer is applied with a learning rate 1×10^{-4} for the backbone and transformer module. The learning rate for the regression head is set to 1×10^{-3}. The feature dimension is set to 512 for the transformer block. We select 10 exemplars for each test sample during the inference stage to align with previous work [32] for fair comparisons. As for the data-preprocessing on AQA-7 and MTL-AQA datasets, we sample 103 frames following previous works for all videos. Since our proposed method requires more fine-grained temporal information, unlike previous work that segmented the sample frames into 10 clips, we segment the frames into 20 overlapping clips each containing 8 continuous frames. As for the JIGSAWS dataset, we uniformly sample 160 frames following [22] and divide them into 20 non-overlapping clips as input of the I3D backbone. We select exemplars from the same difficulty degree on MTL-dataset during the training stage. For AQA-7 and JIGSAWS datasets, all exemplars come from the same coarse classes.

4.2   Comparison to State-of-the-Art

We compare our results with state-of-the-art methods on three benchmarks in Tables 1, 2 and 3. Our method outperforms priors works on all three benchmarks under all settings.

On **MTL-AQA dataset**, we evaluated our experiments with two different settings, following prior work [32]. Specifically, the MTL-AQA dataset contains

Table 1. Performance comparison on MTL-AQA dataset. 'w/o DD' means that training and test processes do not utilize difficulty degree labels, 'w/ DD' means experiments utilizing difficulty degree labels.

Method (w/o DD)	Sp. Corr	R-$\ell_2(\times 100)$
Pose+DCT [20]	0.2682	–
C3D-SVR [19]	0.7716	–
C3D-LSTM [19]	0.8489	–
MSCADC-STL [18]	0.8472	–
C3D-AVG-STL [18]	0.8960	–
MSCADC-MTL [18]	0.8612	–
C3D-AVG-MTL [18]	0.9044	–
USDL [22]	0.9066	0.654
CoRe [32]	0.9341	0.365
TSA-Net [27]	0.9422	–
Ours	**0.9451**	**0.3222**

Method (w/ DD)	Sp. Corr	R-$\ell_2(\times 100)$
USDL [22]	0.9231	0.468
MUSDL [22]	0.9273	0.451
CoRe [32]	0.9512	0.260
Ours	**0.9607**	**0.2378**

the label of difficult degree, and each video's quality score is calculated by the multiplication of the raw score with its difficulty. In the experiment setting 'w/o DD', the training and test processes do not utilize difficulty degree labels. In setting 'w/ DD', we exploit the difficulty label by comparing the test video to the exemplar videos with the same difficulty, and we estimate the raw score, which is multiplied by the difficulty to get the final quality. Our method outperforms existing works under both settings. As shown in Tables 1, under 'w/ DD', our method achieves a Sp. Corr. of 0.9607, and R-ℓ_2 of 0.2378, outperforms the tree-based CoRe [32]. Note that our model simply utilizes two shallow MLPs to perform contrastive regression instead of the tree structure as in [32]. Our transformer extracts fine-grained part representations, hence the regression becomes easier. Under 'w/o DD', out method achieves 0.9451(Sp. Corr) and 0.3222(R-ℓ_2), outperforms the CoRe and recent TSA-Net [27]. It's worth noting that TSA-Net utilizes an external VOT tracker [35] to extract human locations and then enhance backbone features, which is orthogonal to the main issue of temporal parsing addressed in our work. Consequently, we expect that our method can be further improved by incorporating the attention module as in [27].

On **AQA-7 dataset**, our method achieves state-of-the-art on 5 categories and comparable performance on the rest category, shown in Tables 2. In particular, on average, our method outperforms CoRe by 3.14 Corr.($\times 100$) and TSA-Net by 2.39 Corr.($\times 100$), and obtains a very small R-ℓ_2 of 1.68($\times 100$), demonstrating the effectiveness of our temporal parsing transformer.

Table 2. Performance comparison on AQA-7 dataset.

Sp. Corr	Diving	Gym Vault	BigSki.	BigSnow.	Sync. 3m	Sync. 10m	Avg. Corr
Pose+DCT [20]	0.5300	0.1000	–	–	–	–	–
ST-GCN [30]	0.3286	0.5770	0.1681	0.1234	0.6600	0.6483	0.4433
C3D-LSTM [19]	0.6047	0.5636	0.4593	0.5029	0.7912	0.6927	0.6165
C3D-SVR [19]	0.7902	0.6824	0.5209	0.4006	0.5937	0.9120	0.6937
JRG [16]	0.7630	0.7358	0.6006	0.5405	0.9013	0.9254	0.7849
USDL [22]	0.8099	0.7570	0.6538	0.7109	0.9166	0.8878	0.8102
CoRe [32]	0.8824	0.7746	0.7115	0.6624	0.9442	0.9078	0.8401
TSA-Net [27]	0.8379	0.8004	0.6657	0.6962	**0.9493**	0.9334	0.8476
Ours	**0.8969**	**0.8043**	**0.7336**	**0.6965**	0.9456	**0.9545**	**0.8715**
$R\text{-}\ell_2(\times 100)$	Diving	Gym Vault	BigSki.	BigSnow	Sync. 3m	Sync. 10m	Avg. $R\text{-}\ell_2$
C3D-SVR [19]	1.53	3.12	6.79	7.03	17.84	4.83	6.86
USDL [22]	0.79	2.09	4.82	4.94	0.65	2.14	2.57
CoRe [32]	0.64	1.78	3.67	3.87	0.41	2.35	2.12
Ours	**0.53**	**1.69**	**2.89**	**3.30**	**0.33**	**1.33**	**1.68**

Table 3. Performance comparison on JIGSAW dataset.

Sp. Corr	S	NP	KT	Avg.
ST-GCN [30]	0.31	0.39	0.58	0.43
TSN [26]	0.34	0.23	0.72	0.46
JRG [16]	0.36	0.54	0.75	0.57
USDL [22]	0.64	0.63	0.61	0.63
MUSDL [22]	0.71	0.69	0.71	0.70
CoRe [32]	0.84	0.86	0.86	0.85
Ours	**0.88**	**0.88**	**0.91**	**0.89**
$R\text{-}\ell_2$	S	NP	KT	Avg
CoRe [32]	5.055	5.688	2.927	4.556
Ours	**2.722**	**5.259**	**3.022**	**3.668**

On the smallest **JIGSAW dataset**, we perform 4-fold cross validation for each category, following prior work [22,32]. Our method achieves an average of 0.89 Corr. and 3.668 $R\text{-}\ell_2$, achieves new state-of-the-art.

4.3   Ablation Study

In this subsection, we perform ablation studies to evaluate the effectiveness of our proposed model components and designs. All of our ablation studies are performed on MTL-AQA dataset under 'w/ DD' setting. We build a baseline network that directly pool the clip features without transformer, and utilize the resulting holistic representation to perform contrastive regression.

Table 4. Ablation study of different components on MTL-AQA dataset.

Method	TPT	L_{rank}	$L_{sparsity}$	Sp. Corr	$R\text{-}\ell_2$
Baseline	✗	✗	✗	0.9498	0.2893
	✓	✗	✗	0.9522	0.2742
	✓	✓	✗	0.9583	0.2444
Ours	✓	✓	✓	**0.9607**	**0.2378**

Table 5. More ablation studies on MTL-AQA dataset.

(a) Different part generation strategies.

Method	Sp. Corr.	$R\text{-}\ell_2$
Baseline	0.9498	0.2893
Adaptive pooling	0.9509	0.2757
Temporal conv	0.9526	0.2758
TPT(ours)	**0.9607**	**0.2378**

(b) Effect of order guided supervision.

Method	Sp. Corr.	$R\text{-}\ell_2$
Baseline	0.9498	0.2893
Diversity loss	0.9538	0.2655
Ranking loss(ours)	**0.9607**	**0.2378**

(c) inipage Effect of positional encoding.

Pos. Encode	Memory(clip)	Query(part)	Sp. Corr.	$R\text{-}\ell_2$
	✓	✓	0.9526	0.2741
	✓	✗	0.9532	0.2651
Proposed	✗	✗	**0.9607**	**0.2378**

(d) Different relative representation generation.

Method	Sp. Corr.	$R\text{-}\ell_2$
Baseline	0.9498	0.2893
Part-enhanced holistic	0.9578	0.2391
Part-wise relative + AvgPool(ours)	**0.9607**	**0.2378**

Different Model Components. In this work, we propose a novel temporal parsing transformer(TPT), and exploit the ranking loss(L_{rank}) and sparsity loss($L_{sparsity}$) on cross attention responses to guide the part representation learning. We first perform experiments to show the effectiveness of each design, the results are shown in Tables 4. We can observe that with only TPT, the performance only improves marginally from 0.9498 Corr. to 0.9522 Corr.. With the ranking loss, the performance is significantly improved, demonstrating the importance of temporally ordered supervision strategy. The sparsity loss further improves the performance, showing that the discrimination of parts is also important.

Different Relative Representation Generation. Since we have obtained part representations from TPT for each video, we may have two options to generate relative representation for contrastive regression. For the first option, we can first fuse the part representations with a pooling operation for each video, then each video takes the part-enhanced holistic representation to estimate the relative score. For the second option, which is our proposed strategy, we first compute a part-wise relative representation and then apply the AvgPool operation over the parts. We compare the results of above options in Tables 5d. We can see that the part-wise strategy outperforms part-enhanced strategy. It's worth noting that the part-enhanced approach also outperforms our baseline network, which implies that each part indeed encodes fine-grained temporal patterns.

Different Part Generation Strategies. Our method utilizes the temporal parsing transformer to extract part representations. In this ablation study, we compare our method with the other two baseline part generation strategy, shown in Tables 5a. The first strategy utilizes the adaptive pooling operation cross temporal frames to down-sample the origin T clip representation into K part representations. The second strategy replaces the above adaptive pooling with a temporal convolution with stride $\lfloor T/K \rfloor$, resulting in a representation with K size. We found that both strategies introduce minor improvements as they can not capture fine-grained temporal patterns.

Effect of Position Encoding. Different from conventional transformer [3,24], our transformer decoding process does not rely on the temporal position encoding. We compare the results of different position encoding strategies on the memory(clip) and query(part) in Tables 5c. To embed the position encoding on queries, we add the cosine series embedding of $\lfloor T/K \rfloor \times i$ to i-th learnable query, making the queries have positional guidance uniformly distributed across temporal clips. We keep the ranking loss and sparsity for fair comparisons. From Tables 5c, we can observe that adding position encoding hurts the learning of temporal patterns.

Effect of Order Guided Training Strategy. Our ranking loss on the attention centers consistently encourages the temporal order of atomic patterns. To verify the importance of such order guided supervision, we replace the ranking loss to a diversity loss following the Associative Embedding [15] to push attention centers: $L_{div} = \sum_{i=1}^{K} \sum_{j=i+1}^{K} \exp^{-\frac{1}{2\sigma^2}(\bar{\alpha}_i - \bar{\alpha}_j)^2}$. Compared with L_{rank}, L_{div} does not encourage the order of queries, but keeps diversity of part representations. As shown in Tables 5b, the performance significantly drops from 0.9607 Corr. to 0.9538 Corr., demonstrating the effectiveness of our order guided training strategy.

4.4   Visualization Results

We provide some visualization results in Fig. 3 and Fig. 4. Samples are from MTL-AQA dataset trained under 'w/ DD' setting and AQA-7 dataset. In Fig. 3, we visualize the clip frames with the highest attention responses in cross attention maps of the last decoder layer. Since each clip consists of multiple frames, we select the middle frame of a clip as representative. We can observe that our transformer can capture semantic temporal patterns with learned queries. In Fig. 4, we visualize the cross attention maps. We can observe that the attention responses have a consistent temporal order due to our designed ranking loss, and they are also sparse due to our sparsity loss.

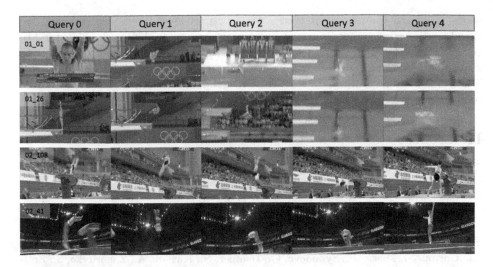

Fig. 3. Visualization of the frames with the highest attention responses in decoder cross attention maps on MTL-AQA and AQA-7 datasets. Each row represents a test video from different representative categories (diving from MTL-AQA, gymnastic vault from AQA-7), whose ID is shown in the left first frame. Different columns correspond to temporally ordered queries. The above results show that our transformer is able to capture semantic temporal patterns with learned queries.

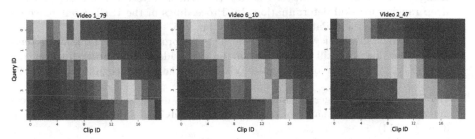

Fig. 4. Visualization of cross attention maps on three video samples from MTL-AQA dataset, where video IDs are shown on the top. In each subfigure, each row indicates one query, and each column indicates one clip. We can observe that the bright grids(with high attention responses) have a consistent temporal order due to ranking loss, and the attention maps are sparse due to our sparsity loss.

5   Conclusion

In this paper, we propose a novel temporal parsing transformer for action quality assessment. We utilize a set of learnable queries to represent the atomic temporal patterns, and exploit the transformer decoder to convert clip-level representations to part-level representations. To perform quality score regression, we exploit the contrastive regression framework that first computes the relative pairwise representation per part and then fuses them to estimate the relative score. To learn the atomic patterns without part-level labels, we propose two novel loss functions on cross attention responses to guide the queries to attend to temporally ordered clips. As a result, our method is able to outperform existing state-of-the-art methods by a considerable margin on three public benchmarks. The visualization results show that the learned part representations are semantic meaningful.

References

1. Alayrac, J.B., Laptev, I., Sivic, J., Lacoste-Julien, S.: Joint discovery of object states and manipulation actions. In: Proceedings of the IEEE International Conference on Computer Vision, pp. 2127–2136 (2017)
2. Bertasius, G., Soo Park, H., Yu, S.X., Shi, J.: Am i a baller? basketball performance assessment from first-person videos. In: Proceedings of the IEEE International Conference on Computer Vision, pp. 2177–2185 (2017)
3. Carion, N., Massa, F., Synnaeve, G., Usunier, N., Kirillov, A., Zagoruyko, S.: End-to-end object detection with transformers. In: Vedaldi, A., Bischof, H., Brox, T., Frahm, J.-M. (eds.) ECCV 2020. LNCS, vol. 12346, pp. 213–229. Springer, Cham (2020). https://doi.org/10.1007/978-3-030-58452-8_13
4. Carreira, J., Zisserman, A.: Quo vadis, action recognition? a new model and the kinetics dataset. In: proceedings of the IEEE Conference on Computer Vision and Pattern Recognition, pp. 6299–6308 (2017)
5. Doughty, H., Damen, D., Mayol-Cuevas, W.: Who's better? who's best? pairwise deep ranking for skill determination. In: Proceedings of the IEEE Conference on Computer Vision and Pattern Recognition, pp. 6057–6066 (2018)
6. Doughty, H., Mayol-Cuevas, W., Damen, D.: The pros and cons: rank-aware temporal attention for skill determination in long videos. In: Proceedings of the IEEE/CVF Conference on Computer Vision and Pattern Recognition, pp. 7862–7871 (2019)
7. Gao, Y., et al.: Jhu-isi gesture and skill assessment working set (jigsaws): a surgical activity dataset for human motion modeling. In: MICCAI workshop: M2CAI, vol. 3, p. 3 (2014)
8. Gordon, A.S.: Automated video assessment of human performance. In: Proceedings of AI-ED, vol. 2 (1995)
9. Jug, M., Perš, J., Dežman, B., Kovačič, S.: Trajectory based assessment of coordinated human activity. In: International Conference on Computer Vision Systems, pp. 534–543. Springer (2003)
10. Kuehne, H., Arslan, A., Serre, T.: The language of actions: recovering the syntax and semantics of goal-directed human activities. In: Proceedings of the IEEE Conference on Computer Vision and Pattern Recognition, pp. 780–787 (2014)
11. Lea, C., Flynn, M.D., Vidal, R., Reiter, A., Hager, G.D.: Temporal convolutional networks for action segmentation and detection. In: proceedings of the IEEE Conference on Computer Vision and Pattern Recognition, pp. 156–165 (2017)
12. Lei, P., Todorovic, S.: Temporal deformable residual networks for action segmentation in videos. In: Proceedings of the IEEE Conference on Computer Vision and Pattern Recognition, pp. 6742–6751 (2018)
13. Li, J., Lei, P., Todorovic, S.: Weakly supervised energy-based learning for action segmentation. In: Proceedings of the IEEE/CVF International Conference on Computer Vision, pp. 6243–6251 (2019)

14. Meng, D., et al.: Conditional DETR for fast training convergence. In: Proceedings of the IEEE/CVF International Conference on Computer Vision, pp. 3651–3660 (2021)
15. Newell, A., Huang, Z., Deng, J.: Associative embedding: end-to-end learning for joint detection and grouping. In: Advances in Neural Information Processing systems 30 (2017)
16. Pan, J.H., Gao, J., Zheng, W.S.: Action assessment by joint relation graphs. In: Proceedings of the IEEE/CVF International Conference on Computer Vision, pp. 6331–6340 (2019)
17. Parmar, P., Morris, B.: Action quality assessment across multiple actions. In: 2019 IEEE Winter Conference on Applications of Computer Vision (WACV), pp. 1468–1476. IEEE (2019)
18. Parmar, P., Morris, B.T.: What and how well you performed? a multitask learning approach to action quality assessment. In: Proceedings of the IEEE/CVF Conference on Computer Vision and Pattern Recognition, pp. 304–313 (2019)
19. Parmar, P., Tran Morris, B.: Learning to score olympic events. In: Proceedings of the IEEE Conference on Computer Vision and Pattern Recognition Workshops, pp. 20–28 (2017)
20. Pirsiavash, H., Vondrick, C., Torralba, A.: Assessing the quality of actions. In: Fleet, D., Pajdla, T., Schiele, B., Tuytelaars, T. (eds.) ECCV 2014. LNCS, vol. 8694, pp. 556–571. Springer, Cham (2014). https://doi.org/10.1007/978-3-319-10599-4_36
21. Shao, D., Zhao, Y., Dai, B., Lin, D.: Intra-and inter-action understanding via temporal action parsing. In: Proceedings of the IEEE/CVF Conference on Computer Vision and Pattern Recognition, pp. 730–739 (2020)
22. Tang, Y., et al.: Uncertainty-aware score distribution learning for action quality assessment. In: Proceedings of the IEEE/CVF Conference on Computer Vision and Pattern Recognition, pp. 9839–9848 (2020)
23. Tran, D., Bourdev, L., Fergus, R., Torresani, L., Paluri, M.: Learning spatiotemporal features with 3D convolutional networks. In: Proceedings of the IEEE International Conference on Computer Vision, pp. 4489–4497 (2015)
24. Vaswani, A., et al.: Attention is all you need. In: Advances in Neural Information Processing Systems 30 (2017)
25. Wang, H., Schmid, C.: Action recognition with improved trajectories. In: Proceedings of the IEEE International Conference On Computer Vision, pp. 3551–3558 (2013)
26. Wang, L., et al.: Temporal segment networks: towards good practices for deep action recognition. In: Leibe, B., Matas, J., Sebe, N., Welling, M. (eds.) ECCV 2016. LNCS, vol. 9912, pp. 20–36. Springer, Cham (2016). https://doi.org/10.1007/978-3-319-46484-8_2
27. Wang, S., Yang, D., Zhai, P., Chen, C., Zhang, L.: TSA-NET: tube self-attention network for action quality assessment. In: Proceedings of the 29th ACM International Conference on Multimedia, pp. 4902–4910 (2021)
28. Wang, Y., Zhang, X., Yang, T., Sun, J.: Anchor DETR: query design for transformer-based detector. arXiv preprint arXiv:2109.07107 (2021)
29. Xu, C., Fu, Y., Zhang, B., Chen, Z., Jiang, Y.G., Xue, X.: Learning to score figure skating sport videos. IEEE Trans. Circuits Syst. Video Technol. **30**(12), 4578–4590 (2019)
30. Yan, S., Xiong, Y., Lin, D.: Spatial temporal graph convolutional networks for skeleton-based action recognition. In: Thirty-Second AAAI Conference on Artificial Intelligence (2018)

31. Yi, F., Wen, H., Jiang, T.: AsFormer: transformer for action segmentation. arXiv preprint arXiv:2110.08568 (2021)
32. Yu, X., Rao, Y., Zhao, W., Lu, J., Zhou, J.: Group-aware contrastive regression for action quality assessment. In: Proceedings of the IEEE/CVF International Conference on Computer Vision, pp. 7919–7928 (2021)
33. Zhang, C., Gupta, A., Zisserman, A.: Temporal query networks for fine-grained video understanding. In: Proceedings of the IEEE/CVF Conference on Computer Vision and Pattern Recognition, pp. 4486–4496 (2021)
34. Zhang, Q., Li, B.: Relative hidden Markov models for video-based evaluation of motion skills in surgical training. IEEE Trans. Pattern Anal. Mach. Intell. **37**(6), 1206–1218 (2014)
35. Čehovin Zajc, L.: A modular toolkit for visual tracking performance evaluation. SoftwareX **12**, 100623 (2020). https://doi.org/10.1016/j.softx.2020.100623

Entry-Flipped Transformer for Inference and Prediction of Participant Behavior

Bo Hu[1,2]([✉]) and Tat-Jen Cham[1,2]

[1] Singtel Cognitive and Artificial Intelligence Lab (SCALE@NTU), Singapore,
Singapore
astjcham@ntu.edu.sg
[2] School of Computer Science and Engineering, Nanyang Technological University,
Singapore, Singapore
hubo@ntu.edu.sg

Abstract. Some group activities, such as team sports and choreographed dances, involve closely coupled interaction between participants. Here we investigate the tasks of inferring and predicting participant behavior, in terms of motion paths and actions, under such conditions. We narrow the problem to that of estimating how a set target participants react to the behavior of other observed participants. Our key idea is to model the spatio-temporal relations among participants in a manner that is robust to error accumulation during frame-wise inference and prediction. We propose a novel Entry-Flipped Transformer (EF-Transformer), which models the relations of participants by attention mechanisms on both spatial and temporal domains. Unlike typical transformers, we tackle the problem of error accumulation by flipping the order of query, key, and value entries, to increase the importance and fidelity of observed features in the current frame. Comparative experiments show that our EF-Transformer achieves the best performance on a newly-collected tennis doubles dataset, a Ceilidh dance dataset, and two pedestrian datasets. Furthermore, it is also demonstrated that our EF-Transformer is better at limiting accumulated errors and recovering from wrong estimations.

Keywords: Entry-flipping · Transformer · Behavior prediction

1 Introduction

The development of computer vision with machine learning has led to extensive progress in understanding human behavior, such as human action recognition and temporal action detection. Although state-of-the-art algorithms have shown promise, a majority of methods have been focused only on individuals without

---

Supplementary Information The online version contains supplementary material available at https://doi.org/10.1007/978-3-031-19772-7_26.

S. Avidan et al. (Eds.): ECCV 2022, LNCS 13664, pp. 439–456, 2022.
https://doi.org/10.1007/978-3-031-19772-7_26

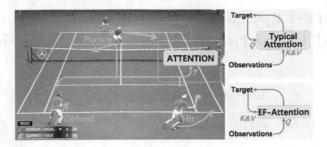

Fig. 1. This paper focuses on participants behavior prediction and inference, where the behavior of target participant from a group activity is estimated with observation of other participants. Entry-Flipping (EF) mechanism is proposed for attention function to obtain accurate prediction and inference by flipping the query, key, and value entries.

explicitly handling interaction between people. However, human behavior can span a wide range of interaction coupling, from the independence of strangers passing each other, to highly coordinated activities such as in group sports and choreographed dances.

The behavior of a person can be treated as a combination of self intention and social interaction, where the latter is more crucial in group activities. Current group-related computer vision works do not focus much on scenarios with heavy social interaction among participants. For example, in pedestrian trajectory prediction [2,40], the behavior of a pedestrian is based more on self intention than social interaction, with the latter cursorily for avoiding collisions.

To further explore the model of social interactions in group activities, we consider the tasks of inferring and predicting the behavior of some participants as they react to other participants. In these tasks, we hypothesize that the behavior of participants of a group activity are less dependent on self intentions, and instead dominated by how other participants behave. To formalize the problem, we consider a group as split into two sets of observed and target participants. For target participants, we assume that no data is provided beyond some initial states—the objective is thus to infer their behavior based *only* on the continuing data received from observed participants (see Fig. 1). We believe that this modeling of reactive human behavior in closely coupled activities such as team sports, will eventually lead to enabling more realistic agent behavior models, *e.g.* for simulation in games or sports training.

The task of inferring or predicting participant behavior is a frame-wise sequence estimation problem. There are many existing models focused on sequence estimation, such as Recurrent Neural Networks (RNN) based methods [21,25,32] and attention-based methods [26,35]. However, these methods face the problem of error accumulation, as the recurrence involves using the output estimation from the previous step as the input in the next step. While this leads to temporally smooth predictions, small errors at each step accumulate over time, leading to large final errors. Taking a typical transformer [26] as an example, the cross-attention in the decoder auto-regressively uses the previous estimate as query input. As the query is the base of an attention function, errors in subsequent queries will often grow, even if the key and value entries are accurate. This may not be a concern for *e.g.* open-ended text generation, but becomes an issue for our tasks that prioritize accurate current estimates over temporal consistency.

In this paper, we propose the Entry-Flipped Transformer (EF-Transformer), a novel framework for the inference and prediction of participant behavior. Two key properties needed are: i) good relation modeling, ii) limiting the error accumulation. To model spatio-temporal relations among all participants in different frames, we adopt a transformer-based structure with multiple layers of encoders and decoders. In every encoder, separate attentions are used for the spatial domain, *i.e.* involving different participants, and the temporal domain, *i.e.* across different frames. Each decoder contains spatio-temporal self-attention and also cross-attention to relate features of observed and target participants. To limit accumulated errors during frame-wise inference and prediction, an entry-flipped design is introduced to the cross-attention in decoders, to focus more on correctness of output than smoothness. In our method, the query, key, and value entries of decoders are flipped *w.r.t.* the typical order. As accurate information of observed participants is sent to query entry of the attention function at each step, error accumulation can be effectively suppressed.

The main contributions of this paper are as follows:

- We articulate the key considerations needed for inferring and predicting participant behavior in group activities that involve highly coupled interactions.
- A novel EF-Transformer framework is proposed for this task, where query, key, value entries are flipped in cross-attention of decoders.
- Our method achieved SOTA performance on a tennis doubles dataset and a Ceilidh dance dataset that involve highly coupled interactions, and also outperformed other methods on looser coupled pedestrian datasets.
- We show our method is more robust at limiting accumulated errors and recovering from spike errors.

2   Related Work

Relation Modeling. Participant behavior prediction involve several modules, with a core of spatio-temporal relation modeling. Probabilistic graphical models have been used to model relations, *e.g.* Dynamic Bayesian Networks (DBN) [39], Conditional Random Fields (CRF) [4], but these models heavily relied on feature engineering. With deep learning, models can directly learn the relations and find good features simultaneously. Convolutional Neural Networks (CNN) are widely employed to extract features from images and videos, while deeper layers of a CNN can be viewed as relation modeling since they summarize features from a larger image region [5,9,18,23]. Graph Convolution Networks (GCN) [34,38] are used to learn the relation among features without a fixed grid format. However, convolutions usually have limited receptive fields, and are enlarged only through many layers. RNNs, such as LSTM, have been used to model temporal relation in sequences [3,31]. Different from CNNs processing all entries in one go, RNNs are applied iteratively over time. Attention mechanisms were popularized by the Transformer [26] and became adopted for both spatial and temporal relation modeling [8,29,42]. Attention facilitates summarization for different types of input, leading to better generalization, which can be built upon backbone networks [13,15,20], or in feature learning [10]. However, the computational cost of attention is large, thus many methods [27,36,41] are hybrids involving a combination of CNN, RNN, and attention to balance efficiency and effectiveness.

Group Relevant Tasks. Group activities typically involve significant behavorial relations among group members. Group activity recognition aims to estimate video-level activity labels. In [6,16,17,30] RNN was used to model temporal relation of each person and pooled all persons together for recognition. Cross inference block has been proposed in HiGCIN [33] to capture co-occurrence spatiotemporal dependencies. In the actor transformer [12], the transformer encodes all actors after actor-level features are extracted. These frameworks are impressive but unsuitable for our proposed tasks, as they are not designed for frame-level estimation. Another related task is pedestrian trajectory prediction [19,22,28,32]. The goal is to predict moving trajectories of all pedestrians in future frames with observation of a few past frames, where interaction among pedestrians is the important cue. RNN [2,7], graph-based technique [35], and attention mechanism [11,24] have been employed for this task. In [40], LSTMs were used for single pedestrian modeling and an attention-based state refinement module designed to capture the spatial relations among different pedestrians. Graph-based attention has been proposed for spatial relation modeling [35], where the graph is built based on spatial distance among pedestrians. The difference between this task and ours is that the former aims to predict the future based on past observation for all pedestrians, while we focus more on models that can continually predict about how target participants will react to behavior of other observed participants. This is particularly important in activities that have very strongly coupled interactions. Nonetheless, existing methods can be applied to our task with minor modification, as described later.

3   Method

3.1   Problem Definition

Participants behavior inference and prediction are to estimate the behavior of a number of target participants in a group, based on information of other observed participants in that group. Supposed there are N participants in the group and they are divided into two sets, with N_{obs} observed participants and N_{tgt} target participants, where $N = N_{obs} + N_{tgt}$. Given a trimmed video clip with T frames, let $x = \{x_{i,t}\}_{i=1:N_{obs}, t=1:T}$ denote the behavior of observed participants, where the behavior comprise positions and action labels. Correspondingly, $y = \{y_{i,t}\}_{i=1:N_{tgt}, t=1:T}$ denote the behavior of target participants.

The task is to infer and predict $\{y_{i,t}\}_{i=1:N_{\text{tgt}}}$, starting from known initial states of the target participants, $\{y_{i,1}\}_{i=1:N_{\text{tgt}}}$. The estimation proceeds sequentially in time, where the observable input at time t consists of $\{x_{i,\tau}\}_{i=1:N_{\text{obs}}, \tau=1:t+K}$, where K is the number of frames *into the future* beyond t. Here, K can be interpreted as the level of (perfect) human foresight of the target participants in predicting how other participants may behave. As an ML problem, $K=0$ corresponds to participants behavior prediction, while it becomes inference for $K \geq 1$. The inference can be performed in an online manner if $K=1$, otherwise it has to be offline or with a delay.

3.2 Typical Transformer

A typical Transformer consists of multiple layers of encoder and decoder. Both encoder and decoder involve three modules: attention function, feed forward network (FFN), and normalization, where attention function is

$$X^{\text{att}} = f_o \left[\frac{S\left(f_q\left(X_q\right) f_k\left(X_k\right)^T\right)}{\sqrt{d}} f_v\left(X_v\right) \right] + X_q. \tag{1}$$

In (1), X_q, X_k, and X_v denote the input feature map of query, key, and value correspondingly, and X^{att} is the output attended feature map. $f(\cdot)$ is the fully-connected (FC) layer, $S(\cdot)$ is the softmax function on each row of the input matrix, and d is the dimension of X_q and X_k. Noted that multi-head attention scheme in [26] is also employed in all attention modules of our framework, which is ignored in (1) for simplification.

A typical transformer [26] can fit the proposed task, since the feature of observed and target participants can be treated as two different sequences. Compared with machine translation, the observed participants sequence plays the role of source language sentence and the target participants sequence plays the role of target language sentence. However, a typical transformer has a drawback that leads to error accumulation in the task of participant behavior inference and prediction. The attention function (1) takes some other feature (key and value) into consideration when maps the input (query) to the output. From another view, the attention function can be seen as a summarization of the three entries. Different from convolutions or MLP, the three entries play different roles in the attention function. Specifically, the query is the base in the attention function while key and value are the references. In the inference stage, the query of decoder comes from the previous frame estimation, which is not accurate. With a noisy or wrong query entry, it is difficult to recover the feature and provide a relative correct estimation in the next frame. Therefore, the error will accumulate over time, which may not be as relevant in open-ended tasks, *e.g.* text generation.

3.3 Entry-Flipped Transformer

To solve the error accumulation problem, an EF-Transformer is proposed. In our EF-Transformer, encoders apply spatio-temporal attention modules to encode

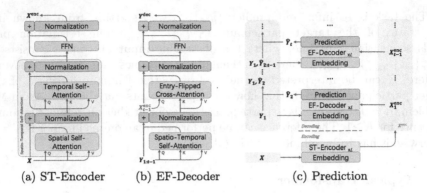

(a) ST-Encoder   (b) EF-Decoder   (c) Prediction

Fig. 2. The framework of encoder, decoder, and prediction process in the proposed EF-Transformer. For participants inference, X_t^{enc} is sent to decoder to estimate $\hat{Y}_t$.

the information from multiple participants in the whole clip. Different from typical transformers, the decoder in EF-Transformer takes the output of the encoder as the query entry. Since this does not depend as much on predictive accuracies in previous frames, it reduces the accumulation of errors. With the Spatio-Temporal Encoder (ST-Encoder) and Entry-Flipped Decoder (EF-Decoder), the proposed EF-Transformer is designed to predict the behavior of target participants frame-by-frame more from observations rather than earlier predictions.

Spatio-Temporal Encoder. An ST-Encoder employs two self-attention functions and an FFN to map the features of observed participants x to encoded features x^{enc}, as shown in Fig. 2(a). there are both spatial and temporal domains in each video clip. As the attention function has a quadratic time complexity of input size [26], the time complexity of an attention function over the combined spatio-temporal domain is $\mathcal{O}\left(N^2T^2\right)$. To reduce this, the attention over the two domains are handled separately. Spatial self-attention captures the relation among all participants in one frame, where every frame is sent to spatial self-attention independently. Subsequently, temporal self-attention captures the relation among all time frames for each participant to get the attended feature x^{att}, so that different participants across different time frames are not directly attended. By dividing the self-attention of observed participants into two domains, the time complexity is reduced to $\mathcal{O}(NT(N+T))$. Masked attention [26] is applied to avoid attending the feature beyond K frames. Following [26], a simple FFN is connected to the output of self-attention to obtain x^{enc} from x^{att}.

Entry-Flipped Decoder. In the decoding stage, an EF-Decoder module is introduced. This consists of a self-attention function, a cross-attention function, and an FFN. The self-attention in EF-Decoder is also divided into spatial and temporal domains, which has the same structure as ST-Encoder. It provides the self-attended feature of target participants y^{att}. Unlike in a typical transformer, cross-attention in the proposed EF-Decoder uses as query the encoded features of observed participants, while key and value entries are self-attended features of target participants, including both those initially observed and later predicted. This is shown in Fig. 2(b). Specifically, when predicting frame τ, $\{x^{\text{enc}}_{i,\tau-1}\}_{i=1:N_{\text{obs}}}$ is the query entry and $\{y^{\text{att}}_{i,t}\}_{i=1:N_{\text{tgt}},t=1:\tau-1}$ form the key and value entries. The key idea is that the *query only contains observed participants in the current frame*, which becomes the base for next frame inference or prediction. Keys and values only contain target participants in past frames, forming the reference bases for next frame inference or prediction. The decoded feature y^{dec} comes from an FFN stack on the cross-attention function, which is the same as the ST-Encoder.

Justification of Entry Flipping. Why is this difference between our method and a typical transformer important? For NLP translation, the most crucial word usually is the last translated word. Hence, a typical transformer uses the last translated word in the target language as the query entry of cross-attention in the decoder. However, *in scenarios where the behavior of participants are highly coupled and reactive*, such as in game sports, the most important clue for determining the behavior of a target participant in next frame would *not be the past frames of the participant*, but rather the status of *other observed participants in the current frame*. For example, the ideal movement of a tennis player highly depends on the evolving positions of her teammate and opponents, whereas rapid acceleration and direction changes mean that the historical positions of this player is not that critical as a predictor. Therefore entry-flipping is more appropriate for the proposed group behavior inference and prediction tasks.

Prediction Framework. The whole prediction (Fig. 2(c)) network includes several layers: i) feature embedding layer, ii) ST-Encoder layers, iii) EF-Decoder layers, and iv) prediction layer.

Feature Embedding. Two FC layers are separately applied on the two types of input, *i.e.* 2D coordinates and action labels of participants, to map to higher dimensional features. We first expand the 2D coordinates $(u_{i,t}, v_{i,t})$, to a normalized 7D geometric feature $x^{\text{g}}_{i,t}$ by

$$x^{\text{g}}_{i,t} = \left[uv_{i,t}, uv^{\Delta}_{i,t}, uv^{R}_{i,t}, t/T \right]^{T}, \tag{2}$$

where

$$uv_{i,t} = \left[\frac{u_{i,t}}{w}, \frac{v_{i,t}}{h} \right],$$

$$uv^{\Delta}_{i,t} = \left[\frac{u_{i,t} - u_{i,t-1}}{w}, \frac{v_{i,t} - v_{i,t-1}}{h} \right], \tag{3}$$

$$uv^{R}_{i,t} = \left[\frac{u_{i,t} - u_{i,1}}{w}, \frac{v_{i,t} - v_{i,1}}{h} \right]$$

for a video frame of width w and height h, for which $x^{\mathrm{g}}_{i,t}$ contain absolute coordinates, relative coordinates, and temporal positions, all of which are normalized. $x^{\mathrm{g}}_{i,t}$ is sent to a FC layer f_g to obtain higher dimensional geometric features. Action labels are first converted to one-hot $x^{\mathrm{s}}_{i,t}$, followed by another FC layer f_s. Both types of features are concatenated before positional encoding $x^{\mathrm{pe}}_{i,t}$ [26] is added. Thus, the feature of a participant is

$$x_{i,t} = \left[f_g(x^{\mathrm{g}}_{i,t}), f_s(x^{\mathrm{s}}_{i,t}) \right]^T + x^{\mathrm{pe}}_{i,t}. \tag{4}$$

Encoders and Decoders. L layers of ST-Encoder and EF-Decoder are stacked. The encoded feature of observed participants from output of last layer ST-Encoder is used as the query entry of all layers of EF-Decoder. The last EF-Decoder layer output is the feature that ready for target participants inference and prediction.

Prediction. A prediction layer provides a mapping of $\mathbb{R}^{N_{\mathrm{obs}} \times D} \mapsto \mathbb{R}^{N_{\mathrm{tgt}} \times D_{\mathrm{out}}}$, where D is the feature dimension of one participant in one frame. The features of N_{obs} observed participants are flattened before inference or prediction. D_{out} is dimension of output, which is 2 for trajectory estimation and number of action categories for action classification. The prediction layer consists of three FC layers, where every layer is followed by a nonlinear layer (LeakyReLU in our experiment) except the last. More implementation details can be found in the supplementary.

Loss Function. This is a simple L2 loss applied to both trajectory and action estimation:

$$L = \sum_{i=1}^{N_{\mathrm{tgt}}} \sum_{t=2}^{T} \left\| x^{\mathrm{g}^*}_{i,t} - \hat{x}^{\mathrm{g}^*}_{i,t} \right\|_2 + \lambda \left\| x^{\mathrm{s}}_{i,t} - \hat{x}^{\mathrm{s}}_{i,t} \right\|_2, \tag{5}$$

where $x^{\mathrm{g}^*}_{i,t}$ excludes the temporal coordinates t/T in $x^{\mathrm{g}}_{i,t}$ of (2). In all our experiments, $\lambda = 0.1$.

4   Experiments

4.1   Datasets and Metrics

We selected three datasets with closely coupled behavior in experiments.

Tennis Dataset. A new tennis doubles dataset was collected to evaluate our method. There are 12 videos of whole double games with resolution of 1280×720. 4905 10-frame clips were collected in total, which are downsampled to 2.5 fps and stabilized to remove camera motion. Individual-level bounding boxes and action labels were annotated, with the bottom-center point of each box representing the spatial location of the player. Coarse spatial positions of the ball were also estimated. As it is difficult to determine due to extreme motion blur when the ball was traveling fast, the ball position was only coarsely estimated by spatio-temporal linear interpolation between the locations of two players consecutively hitting the ball. Detailed information of the tennis dataset can be found in the supplemental material. In our experiments, the top-left player was selected as the target participant during testing, while the other three players and the ball were treated as observed entities.

Dance Dataset. The dance dataset [1] contains 16 videos from overhead view of Ceilidh dances by two choreographers, where every dance was performed by 10 dancers. Two videos for each choreographer were selected for testing and others for training. The raw video is 5 fps and resolution is 640 × 480. Here 3754 10-frame clips were collected. The action labels are defined as 'stand', 'walk left', 'walk right', 'walk up','walk down', and 'twirling'. No explicit information about the choreographer was provided during training.

NBA Dataset. NBA dataset [37] contains players and ball tracking data from basketball games. During pre-processing, frame rate was down-sampled to 6.25 fps and a subset of over 4000 10-frame clips was built. As actions are not provided in this dataset, we simply assigned 'defensive' and 'offensive' to players as action labels. During training, one defensive player is randomly selected as the target participant, while the first defensive player in the list is selected in testing. The 'resolution' (or court size) in this dataset is 100 × 50.

Pedestrian Datasets. ETH [19] and UCY [22] datasets are conventionally used in pedestrian trajectory prediction. Target participants were randomly selected in training, and the one with longest trajectory was picked in testing. Four nearest neighbors of the target pedestrian among all frames were selected as observed participants. We follow the leave-one-out evaluation in [14].

Metrics. To evaluate the accuracy of trajectory inference and prediction, two metrics were computed following [40]: Mean Average Displacement (MAD) is the mean distance between estimation and ground truth over all frames. Final Average Displacement (FAD) is the distance between estimation and ground truth of the last frame. Besides, metrics of short, middle, and long trajectory lengths were computed separately, where the length threshold was statistically determined over all samples to even out the number of samples across each category. For action inference and prediction, Macro F1-scores are reported.

4.2   Baseline and Other SOTA Methods

We compare with several methods in our experiments:

CNN-Based Method. This framework is based on spatial and temporal convolutional layers. The encoder consists of 2 convolutional layers while the decoder consists of 3 convolutional layers. A 5-frame sliding window is applied for input.

RNN-Based Method. This framework has encoders and decoders based on two GRU layers. At each frame, the output of the encoder is concatenated with the historical data of target participants before sending to the decoder.

Typical Transformer. The typical transformer [26] here uses the ST-encoder and a typical decoder structure, with an additional future mask added to the attention function of encoding stage.

Pedestrian Trajectory Prediction Methods. [35,40] are also compared. Modifications are made to apply them to our tasks: i) ground truth of observed pedestrians are provided for all frames in the testing stage, ii) if $K > 0$, a K-frame time shift over target participants is adopted to ensure the network has correct information of K-frame future of observed participants.

4.3   Ablation Study

In this section, we compare several ST-Encoder structures. $\mathbf{S+T}$ represents the parallel structure, where spatial and temporal self-attentions are operated on separately, with the outputs added together. $\mathbf{S{\rightarrow}T}$ and $\mathbf{T{\rightarrow}S}$ are sequential structures with different order of spatial and temporal domain. $\mathbf{S{\times}T}$ represents jointly computing attention functions over spatial and temporal domain. In addition, we evaluated the accuracy of different position estimators from among the 3 predicted components in (3), which have overlapping redundancy. Here, the

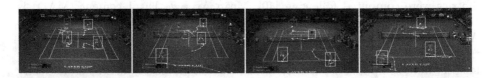

Fig. 3. Visualization of trajectory prediction results of EF-Transformer and typical transformer on tennis dataset. White rectangles and trajectories are the observed participants. Red rectangles are target participants with red trajectories for ground truth. Cyan trajectories are predicted by typical transformer and yellow ones are predicted by our method. Please zoom in to see details.

Table 1. Comparisons of different ST-Encoders and prediction types on Tennis dataset.

Encoder	Pred	MAD				FAD			
		Short	Mid	Long	Avg	Short	Mid	Long	Avg
S+T		**18.70**	31.27	44.51	28.93	**32.89**	51.56	69.15	47.74
T→S	uv^R	19.49	31.01	45.71	29.29	35.31	50.96	69.81	48.43
S×T		19.72	32.05	43.73	29.53	36.28	54.09	67.90	49.95
	uv	40.52	50.42	62.73	48.89	36.11	49.05	64.33	46.91
S→T	Σuv^Δ	20.72	32.91	49.05	31.18	40.12	57.81	78.98	54.93
	uv^R	19.40	**30.04**	**43.04**	**28.35**	35.38	**48.62**	**64.23**	**46.43**

frame-wise relative component uv^Δ is cumulatively summed to get position estimates Σuv^Δ, relative to target positions in the last fully-observed frame. Results are shown in Table 1.

Of the three components, uv^R appeared to be better predicted than the other two. Prediction of absolute coordinates uv is more difficult than only predicting the difference. However, predicting the difference of neighboring frames uv^Δ suffers from error accumulation. The output of frame t have to compensate for the error in predicting frame $t-1$, which can lead to unstable oscillations. Compared with Parallel ST-Encoder, Sequential ST-Encoder achieved better performance except on short trajectories. This is because the query of Sequential ST-Encoder is capable of attending to all other participants in all frames, while query of parallel encoders can only attend the same participants in different frames, or other participants in the same frame. Based on the results above, only predictions of uv^R are reported in the following experiments.

4.4 Trajectory Inference and Prediction

Here we focus solely on trajectory estimation, so ground truth action labels were provided for target participants. Table 2 presents the results of behavior prediction and inference on the tennis and NBA datasets. For the tennis dataset, it can be observed that our EF-Transformer achieved the best performance among compared methods, in particular significantly outperforming other methods for long trajectories. Longer trajectories provide greater risk of larger estimation errors, and our entry-flipping mechanism is effective for limiting error accumulation. Performance of SR-LSTM [40] is affected by the limited initial ground truth sequence of target participants to adequately bootstrap the LSTM cell states. Furthermore, estimated coordinates of target participants are sent to the state refinement module, so the hidden state of observed participants may become affected by past estimation errors. Similarly, STAR [35] models the spatial relations of all participants together, where the features of observed participants will also become conflated with inferred features of target participants. Comparing inference and prediction, prediction is harder for all methods as no future

Table 2. Comparisons of trajectory inference and prediction with baselines and SOTA methods on tennis dataset and NBA dataset.

		Methods	MAD				FAD			
			Short	Mid	Long	Avg	Short	Mid	Long	Avg
Inference	Tennis	CNN-based	22.61	41.63	64.43	38.54	42.97	73.27	102.78	67.22
		RNN-based	22.62	41.27	72.88	39.78	38.07	67.86	103.47	63.01
		Transformer	21.17	32.91	46.67	30.95	37.14	52.06	68.14	49.34
		SR-LSTM [40]	21.22	34.46	55.60	33.19	41.49	58.50	90.08	57.60
		STAR [35]	20.28	35.21	55.36	33.16	36.86	57.52	90.01	55.45
		EF-Transformer	**19.40**	**30.04**	**43.04**	**28.35**	**35.38**	**48.62**	**64.23**	**46.43**
Prediction		CNN-based	22.58	41.81	71.57	39.80	38.84	70.35	105.26	64.76
		RNN-based	23.84	41.99	78.97	41.57	41.34	68.29	110.63	65.58
		Transformer	20.14	33.09	50.70	31.33	35.85	52.55	71.57	49.67
		SR-LSTM [40]	20.43	43.86	85.88	42.37	39.11	75.36	117.43	69.25
		STAR [35]	23.83	43.80	83.65	43.20	37.83	70.61	117.19	66.50
		EF-Transformer	**19.24**	**30.71**	**41.98**	**28.44**	**34.97**	**50.36**	**62.60**	**46.83**
	NBA	Transformer	1.78	4.25	10.13	3.99	2.91	7.33	18.14	6.93
		SR-LSTM [40]	2.84	4.78	10.53	4.77	6.00	8.90	18.63	9.08
		STAR [35]	4.51	5.96	**10.04**	5.92	5.81	8.81	18.07	8.86
		EF-Transformer	**1.65**	**4.18**	10.05	**3.89**	**2.69**	**7.23**	**18.00**	**6.75**

information of observed participants is provided. This is especially in the tennis dataset, where the behavior of target participants involve quick reactions to observed participants, often with anticipatory foresight. Some visualizations are shown in Fig. 3, illustrating that our method can predict better trajectories than a typical transformer.

In the NBA dataset, EF-Transformer also outperformed other methods except for the MAD of long trajectories, where STAR [35] surpassed ours only by a tiny 0.01. It can be observed from Table 2 that the performance differences among compared methods are less than for the tennis dataset. We believe the main reason is that in the most of the cases, a defensive player only needs to follow the corresponding offensive player, which is a simpler reaction than the tennis scenario and usually results in a small displacement during prediction for all methods.

For the dance dataset, we evaluated the methods on a prediction task with different numbers of target participants. Results are listed in Table 3. Our method outperformed all compared methods. It can also be observed that the results of $N_{\text{tgt}} = 2$ are comparable to $N_{\text{tgt}} = 1$. Although fewer observed participants may make the prediction more difficult, it is possible that having more target participants during training provide better guidance to the network, so that the patterns of the dances are better learned. More results of inference task can be found in the supplemental material.

To evaluate the performance in pedestrian datasets, we follow the setting in [14] to provide 8-frame ground truth for the target participant, as the behavior

Table 3. Comparisons of trajectory prediction with 1 and 2 target participants with baselines and SOTA methods on dance dataset.

	Methods	MAD				FAD			
		Short	Mid	Long	Avg	Short	Mid	Long	Avg
$N_{tgt} = 1$	CNN-based	6.91	12.19	14.58	11.13	8.64	14.49	16.86	13.22
	RNN-based	8.60	15.09	20.52	14.61	10.71	17.08	20.69	16.03
	Transformer	7.29	12.75	17.33	12.35	9.63	14.83	19.43	14.53
	SR-LSTM [40]	9.50	15.67	22.48	15.76	11.56	18.16	21.82	17.05
	STAR [35]	9.25	15.34	22.34	15.52	11.76	18.93	23.70	17.99
	EF-Transformer	**6.28**	**9.99**	**12.11**	**9.39**	**7.42**	**10.83**	**12.56**	**10.20**
$N_{tgt} = 2$	CNN-based	7.24	12.55	14.99	11.49	8.78	14.86	16.97	13.42
	RNN-based	9.20	15.77	20.93	15.17	11.56	17.72	21.47	16.79
	Transformer	7.02	12.26	17.49	12.15	9.39	15.50	20.06	14.86
	SR-LSTM [40]	9.19	13.92	18.21	13.68	10.69	15.09	18.11	14.54
	STAR [35]	8.26	14.78	22.77	15.14	10.39	17.07	23.34	16.80
	EF-Transformer	**6.80**	**10.19**	**12.23**	**9.67**	**8.22**	**11.52**	**13.60**	**11.05**

of a pedestrian highly relies on self intention, which underlies one's historical trajectory. The results are shown in Table 4. Our method achieved the best performance among compared methods. As before, existing methods [35, 40] are not appropriately designed for scenarios with different sets of observed and target participants, conflating accurate observations with inaccurate past estimates. Behavior prediction with 1-frame observation for the target is also evaluated. Results and visualizations can be found in the supplementary.

Table 4. Comparisons of trajectory prediction with baselines and SOTA methods on pedestrian dataset.

Methods	Performance MAD/FAD					
	ETH	HOTEL	ZARA	ZARA2	UNIV	AVG
SR-LSTM [40]	1.09/1.76	0.69/1.31	0.79/1.70	0.88/1.85	1.23/2.32	0.94/1.79
STAR [35]	1.09/2.85	0.69/1.41	0.91/2.08	1.27/2.92	1.00/2.18	0.99/2.23
Transformer	0.73/1.40	0.52/0.93	0.63/1.24	0.68/1.46	1.00/1.96	0.71/1.40
EF-Transformer	**0.70/1.33**	**0.49/0.84**	**0.53/1.07**	**0.54/1.10**	**0.89/1.75**	**0.63/1.22**

4.5   Multi-Task Inference and Prediction

In multi-task inference and prediction, trajectories and action labels are estimated simultaneously. Different from previous experiments, estimated action

Table 5. Comparisons of multi-task prediction with baselines and SOTA methods on dance dataset.'Traj' represents the task of trajectory prediction, during which ground truth action labels are provided. 'Multi' represents the task of multi-task prediction, where both trajectories and action labels have to be predicted.

	Methods	MAD				FAD			
		Short	Mid	Long	Avg	Short	Mid	Long	Avg
Traj	Transformer	7.29	12.75	17.33	12.35	9.63	14.83	19.43	14.53
	EF-Transformer	**6.28**	**9.99**	12.11	**9.39**	**7.42**	**10.83**	12.56	**10.20**
Multi	Transformer	7.91	14.73	19.24	13.82	10.77	17.86	21.94	16.72
	EF-Transformer	6.98	10.31	**11.80**	9.63	8.28	11.65	**12.51**	10.75

labels are sent to feature embedding for next-frame inference or prediction. We only compare to a typical transformer on dance dataset here. As action labels are very tightly coupled between observed and target players in tennis, it turned out that both methods resulted in 100% action classification and only minor differences to trajectory prediction in Table 2, hence results are placed in the supplemental material.

Trajectory prediction results are shown in Table 5. Without ground truth action labels for target participants, our method achieved comparable trajectory prediction performance to results with ground truth input. In contrast, the typical transformer had worse performance when action labels for target participants had to be estimated. Action prediction confusion matrices are provided in the supplementary. The macro F1-score of our method and typical transformer are 0.99 and 0.90 correspondingly. As our method is capable of limiting accumulated errors, trajectory and action predictions occur in a virtuous cycle, where error robustness in the previous step improves action classification, which in turn improves trajectory prediction. This contrasts with a typical transformer, where error drift leads to poorer action classification and larger errors in trajectory prediction.

Table 6. Comparisons of FAD on tennis dataset with noise involved in different frames.

Noise Position	Transformer FAD				EF-Transformer FAD			
	Short	Mid	Long	Avg	Short	Mid	Long	Avg
No Noise	37.14	52.06	68.14	49.34	35.38	48.62	64.23	46.43
Noise@t = 3	75.99	103.24	141.06	99.67	37.23	56.37	84.65	54.15
Noise@t = 6	80.03	105.35	145.39	105.85	55.19	64.90	90.71	65.68
Noise@t = 9	131.76	161.07	205.26	157.81	115.93	123.30	145.31	124.29

4.6 Robustness Analysis

Robustness reflects the ability to limit error accumulation, as well as to recover from large errors (*e.g.* due to sensing failure). To evaluate robustness, the 6D prediction of one middle frame is replaced by a large noise spike of [1,1,-1,-1,-1,-1]. FAD was then computed to compare how well the methods recovered from the spike. This experiment was performed with the inference task on the tennis dataset, where the spike was added to different frames.

Table 6 shows that both methods can recover from the spike to some extent, noting that better recovery was made by the final frame for earlier spikes. Nonetheless, our method performed significantly better than the typical transformer. Even with a frame 9 spike (second-last frame), our method's FAD increased only about 78 pixels, compared to 108 pixels for the typical transformer.

4.7 Limitations

Our method assumes that a group has a fixed number of participants, all with strongly coupled behavior. Thus in *e.g.* a pedestrian scenario with varying numbers of individuals, not all of whom have correlated behavior, we need to select a fixed number of the most likely related individuals as observations for each target pedestrian (*e.g.* with k-nearest-neighbor filtering). Furthermore, although pedestrian trajectories are smoother than in tennis and dance, it turned out that prediction is also more difficult for our method. This is likely due to less behavioral coupling among pedestrians. When observations are not as informative, our method was predominantly trying to do some form of dead reckoning like other methods, which is difficult to be accurate especially for longer intervals.

5 Conclusion

In this paper, we proposed the EF-Transformer for behavior inference and prediction of target participants based on other observed participants. In our decoder, the order of query, key, and value entries of the cross-attention are flipped to effectively reduce error accumulation. EF-Transformer is evaluated in several experiments, where it outperformed all compared methods on the tennis, dance datasets and pedestrian datasets. Moreover, we demonstrate superior robustness to noise spikes. The framework of EF-Transformer can be used for application to learning realistic agent-based behavior in the future.

Acknowledgements. This study is supported under the RIE2020 Industry Alignment Fund - Industry Collaboration Projects (IAF-ICP) Funding Initiative, as well as cash and in-kind contribution from Singapore Telecommunications Limited (Singtel), through Singtel Cognitive and Artificial Intelligence Lab for Enterprises (SCALE@NTU).

References

1. Aizeboje, J.: Ceilidh dance recognition from an overhead camera, Msc, Thesis of University of Edinburgh (2016)
2. Alahi, A., Goel, K., Ramanathan, V., Robicquet, A., Fei-Fei, L., Savarese, S.: Social LSTM: human trajectory prediction in crowded spaces. In: Proceedings of the IEEE Conference on Computer Vision and Pattern Recognition, pp. 961–971 (2016)
3. Aliakbarian, M.S., Saleh, F., Salzmann, M., Fernando, B., Petersson, L., Andersson, L.: Encouraging LSTMS to anticipate actions very early. In: IEEE International Conference on Computer Vision (ICCV), pp. 280–289 (2017)
4. Amer, M.R., Lei, P., Todorovic, S.: HiRF: hierarchical random field for collective activity recognition in videos. In: Fleet, D., Pajdla, T., Schiele, B., Tuytelaars, T. (eds.) ECCV 2014. LNCS, vol. 8694, pp. 572–585. Springer, Cham (2014). https://doi.org/10.1007/978-3-319-10599-4_37
5. Azar, S.M., Atigh, M.G., Nickabadi, A., Alahi, A.: Convolutional relational machine for group activity recognition. In: Proceedings of the IEEE/CVF Conference on Computer Vision and Pattern Recognition, pp. 7892–7901 (2019)
6. Bagautdinov, T., Alahi, A., Fleuret, F., Fua, P., Savarese, S.: Social scene understanding: End-to-end multi-person action localization and collective activity recognition. In: IEEE Conference on Computer Vision and Pattern Recognition (CVPR) (2017)
7. Becker, S., Hug, R., Hübner, W., Arens, M.: RED: a simple but effective baseline predictor for the *TrajNet* benchmark. In: Leal-Taixé, L., Roth, S. (eds.) ECCV 2018. LNCS, vol. 11131, pp. 138–153. Springer, Cham (2019). https://doi.org/10.1007/978-3-030-11015-4_13
8. Carion, N., Massa, F., Synnaeve, G., Usunier, N., Kirillov, A., Zagoruyko, S.: End-to-end object detection with transformers. In: Vedaldi, A., Bischof, H., Brox, T., Frahm, J.-M. (eds.) ECCV 2020. LNCS, vol. 12346, pp. 213–229. Springer, Cham (2020). https://doi.org/10.1007/978-3-030-58452-8_13
9. Carreira, J., Zisserman, A.: Quo vadis, action recognition? a new model and the kinetics dataset. In: IEEE Conference on Computer Vision and Pattern Recognition (CVPR) (2017)
10. Dosovitskiy, A., et al.: An image is worth 16x16 words: transformers for image recognition at scale. arXiv preprint arXiv:2010.11929 (2020)
11. Fernando, T., Denman, S., Sridharan, S., Fookes, C.: Soft+hardwired attention: An LSTM framework for human trajectory prediction and abnormal event detection. Neural Netw. **108**, 466–478 (2018)
12. Gavrilyuk, K., Sanford, R., Javan, M., Snoek, C.G.: Actor-transformers for group activity recognition. In: Proceedings of the IEEE/CVF Conference on Computer Vision and Pattern Recognition, pp. 839–848 (2020)
13. Girdhar, R., Carreira, J., Doersch, C., Zisserman, A.: Video action transformer network. In: Proceedings of the IEEE/CVF Conference on Computer Vision and Pattern Recognition, pp. 244–253 (2019)
14. Gupta, A., Johnson, J., Fei-Fei, L., Savarese, S., Alahi, A.: Social GAN: socially acceptable trajectories with generative adversarial networks. In: Proceedings of the IEEE Conference on Computer Vision and Pattern Recognition, pp. 2255–2264 (2018)
15. Hu, H., Gu, J., Zhang, Z., Dai, J., Wei, Y.: Relation networks for object detection. In: IEEE Conference on Computer Vision and Pattern Recognition (CVPR) (2018)

16. Ibrahim, M.S., Mori, G.: Hierarchical relational networks for group activity recognition and retrieval. In: Ferrari, V., Hebert, M., Sminchisescu, C., Weiss, Y. (eds.) ECCV 2018. LNCS, vol. 11207, pp. 742–758. Springer, Cham (2018). https://doi.org/10.1007/978-3-030-01219-9_44

17. Ibrahim, M.S., Muralidharan, S., Deng, Z., Vahdat, A., Mori, G.: A hierarchical deep temporal model for group activity recognition. In: Proceedings of the IEEE Conference on Computer Vision and Pattern Recognition, pp. 1971–1980 (2016)

18. Lea, C., Flynn, M.D., Vidal, R., Reiter, A., Hager, G.D.: Temporal convolutional networks for action segmentation and detection. In: proceedings of the IEEE Conference on Computer Vision and Pattern Recognition, pp. 156–165 (2017)

19. Lerner, A., Chrysanthou, Y., Lischinski, D.: Crowds by example. Comput. Graph. Forum **26**(3), 655–664 (2007). https://doi.org/10.1111/j.1467-8659.2007.01089.x

20. Li, J., Liu, X., Zhang, W., Zhang, M., Song, J., Sebe, N.: Spatio-temporal attention networks for action recognition and detection. IEEE Trans. Multimedia **22**(11), 2990–3001 (2020)

21. Liang, J., Jiang, L., Carlos Niebles, J., Hauptmann, A.G., Fei-Fei, L.: Peeking into the future: Predicting future person activities and locations in videos. In: The IEEE Conference on Computer Vision and Pattern Recognition (CVPR) (2019)

22. Pellegrini, S., Ess, A., Schindler, K., Van Gool, L.: You'll never walk alone: modeling social behavior for multi-target tracking. In: 2009 IEEE 12th International Conference on Computer Vision, pp. 261–268. IEEE (2009)

23. Qiu, Z., Yao, T., Mei, T.: Learning spatio-temporal representation with pseudo-3D residual networks. In: IEEE International Conference on Computer Vision (ICCV), pp. 5534–5542. IEEE (2017)

24. Sadeghian, A., Kosaraju, V., Sadeghian, A., Hirose, N., Rezatofighi, H., Savarese, S.: Sophie: An attentive GAN for predicting paths compliant to social and physical constraints. In: Proceedings of the IEEE/CVF Conference on Computer Vision and Pattern Recognition, pp. 1349–1358 (2019)

25. Sutskever, I., Vinyals, O., Le, Q.V.: Sequence to sequence learning with neural networks. arXiv preprint arXiv:1409.3215 (2014)

26. Vaswani, A., Shazeer, N., Parmar, N., Uszkoreit, J., Jones, L., Gomez, A.N., Kaiser, Ł., Polosukhin, I.: Attention is all you need. In: Advances in Neural Information Processing Systems (NIPS), pp. 6000–6010 (2017)

27. Veličković, P., Cucurull, G., Casanova, A., Romero, A., Liò, P., Bengio, Y.: Graph attention networks. In: ICLR (2018)

28. Vemula, A., Muelling, K., Oh, J.: Social attention: modeling attention in human crowds. In: 2018 IEEE International Conference on Robotics and Automation (ICRA), pp. 4601–4607. IEEE (2018)

29. Wang, X., Girshick, R., Gupta, A., He, K.: Non-local neural networks. In: IEEE Conference on Computer Vision and Pattern Recognition (CVPR) (2018)

30. Wu, J., Wang, L., Wang, L., Guo, J., Wu, G.: Learning actor relation graphs for group activity recognition. In: Proceedings of the IEEE/CVF Conference on Computer Vision and Pattern Recognition, pp. 9964–9974 (2019)

31. Xu, M., Gao, M., Chen, Y.T., Davis, L.S., Crandall, D.J.: Temporal recurrent networks for online action detection. In: Proceedings of the IEEE/CVF International Conference on Computer Vision, pp. 5532–5541 (2019)

32. Xu, Y., Piao, Z., Gao, S.: Encoding crowd interaction with deep neural network for pedestrian trajectory prediction. In: Proceedings of the IEEE Conference on Computer Vision and Pattern Recognition, pp. 5275–5284 (2018)

33. Yan, R., Xie, L., Tang, J., Shu, X., Tian, Q.: HiGCIN: hierarchical graph-based cross inference network for group activity recognition. In: IEEE Transactions on Pattern Analysis and Machine Intelligence (2020)
34. Yan, S., Xiong, Y., Lin, D.: Spatial temporal graph convolutional networks for skeleton-based action recognition. In: Proceedings of the AAAI Conference On Artificial Intelligence (2018)
35. Yu, C., Ma, X., Ren, J., Zhao, H., Yi, S.: Spatio-temporal graph transformer networks for pedestrian trajectory prediction. In: Vedaldi, A., Bischof, H., Brox, T., Frahm, J.-M. (eds.) ECCV 2020. LNCS, vol. 12357, pp. 507–523. Springer, Cham (2020). https://doi.org/10.1007/978-3-030-58610-2_30
36. Yuan, Y., Liang, X., Wang, X., Yeung, D.Y., Gupta, A.: Temporal dynamic graph LSTM for action-driven video object detection. In: Proceedings of the IEEE International Conference On Computer Vision, pp. 1801–1810 (2017)
37. Yue, Y., Lucey, P., Carr, P., Bialkowski, A., Matthews, I.: Learning fine-grained spatial models for dynamic sports play prediction. In: 2014 IEEE International Conference on Data Mining, pp. 670–679. IEEE (2014)
38. Zeng, R., et al.: Graph convolutional networks for temporal action localization. In: Proceedings of the IEEE/CVF International Conference on Computer Vision, pp. 7094–7103 (2019)
39. Zeng, Z., Ji, Q.: Knowledge based activity recognition with dynamic Bayesian network. In: Daniilidis, K., Maragos, P., Paragios, N. (eds.) ECCV 2010. LNCS, vol. 6316, pp. 532–546. Springer, Heidelberg (2010). https://doi.org/10.1007/978-3-642-15567-3_39
40. Zhang, P., Ouyang, W., Zhang, P., Xue, J., Zheng, N.: SR-LSTM: State refinement for LSTM towards pedestrian trajectory prediction. In: CVPR (2019)
41. Zhao, R., Wang, K., Su, H., Ji, Q.: Bayesian graph convolution LSTM for skeleton based action recognition. In: Proceedings of the IEEE/CVF International Conference on Computer Vision, pp. 6882–6892 (2019)
42. Zhu, X., Su, W., Lu, L., Li, B., Wang, X., Dai, J.: Deformable DETR: deformable transformers for end-to-end object detection. In: ICLR (2021)

Pairwise Contrastive Learning Network for Action Quality Assessment

Mingzhe Li[1], Hong-Bo Zhang[1(✉)], Qing Lei[2], Zongwen Fan[2], Jinghua Liu[3], and Ji-Xiang Du[3]

[1] College of Computer Science and Technology, Huaqiao University, Xiamen, China
limingzhe@stu.hqu.edu.cn, zhanghongbo@hqu.edu.cn
[2] Xiamen Key Laboratory of Computer Vision and Pattern Recognition, Xiamen, China
{leiqing,zongwen.fan}@hqu.edu.cn
[3] Fujian Key Laboratory of Big Data Intelligence and Security, Xiamen, China
{liujinghua,jxdu}@hqu.edu.cn

Abstract. Considering the complexity of modeling diverse actions of athletes, action quality assessment (AQA) in sports is a challenging task. A common solution is to tackle this problem as a regression task that map the input video to the final score provided by referees. However, it ignores the subtle and critical difference between videos. To address this problem, a new pairwise contrastive learning network (PCLN) is proposed to concern these differences and form an end-to-end AQA model with basic regression network. Specifically, the PCLN encodes video pairs to learn relative scores between videos to improve the performance of basic regression network. Furthermore, a new consistency constraint is defined to guide the training of the proposed AQA model. In the testing phase, only the basic regression network is employed, which makes the proposed method simple but high accuracy. The proposed method is verified on the AQA-7 and MTL-AQA datasets. Several ablation studies are built to verify the effectiveness of each component in the proposed method. The experimental results show that the proposed method achieves the state-of-the-art performance.

Keywords: Action quality assessment · Pairwise contrastive learning network · Consistency constraint · Video pair · Relative score

1 Introduction

Action quality assessment (AQA) is the task of evaluating how well an action is performed. The potential value of AQA has been gradually explored in many real-world scenarios. For instance, in sports scoring [7,14,18,21,30,32,35,40], daily skill evaluation [4,8,9,25,31], and medical rehabilitation [15,16,29,34,36]. In addition, with the rapid development of the computer vision community, AQA methods are constantly emerging and improving, and the scenarios of

S. Avidan et al. (Eds.): ECCV 2022, LNCS 13664, pp. 457–473, 2022.
https://doi.org/10.1007/978-3-031-19772-7_27

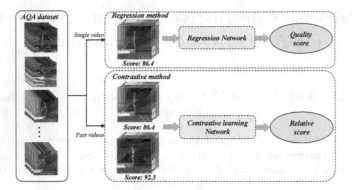

Fig. 1. An overview comparison of the contrastive learning with regression learning. In contrastive learning, the regression model is transformed into comparing the performance of a given video with another one. And the output is the relative score between video pair

AQA application are gradually enriched. In this work, we focus on the problem of AQA in sports events.

As a common solution for AQA in sports events, the score regression methods are utilized to map the input videos to quality scores [7,26,27,35]. However, this strategy ignored the subtle difference between various videos, which is the key reminder to predict action quality score. For example, in diving competition, due to the same scene and similar appearance of the athletes, the difference of an action performed by athletes is hard to discern. In addition, even the same score will also appear on actions with different difficulty degrees. It is very difficult to represent such complex changes through single regression learning. Thus, how to achieve better performance for quality score prediction in sports remains a challenge worth exploring.

An intuitive idea to solve this problem is to train a specific model to learn the difference between videos. To achieve this goal, we rethink the problem of AQA and observe that the performance ranking of different athletes plays a crucial role in AQA task. Inspired by the idea of pairwise learning to rank (LTR) task that compares each pair of data to obtain the ranking, we extend the AQA problem to the contrastive learning problem of video pairs, as shown in Fig. 1. In the proposed contrastive learning strategy, the video pair is applied as input, the relative score between these two videos is applied as the label. And a new pairwise contrastive learning network (PCLN) is designed to learn the mapping from the video pair to the relative score.

Furthermore, PCLN is fused with a basic regression network to form an end-to-end AQA model. In this work, the basic regression network is built by feature extraction network followed by multilayer perceptron (MLP). In the training stage, video pair is randomly composited from the training set. The features of these two videos are obtained by the feature extraction network. Then these extracted features are fed into MLP to predict the quality score. In PCLN, a

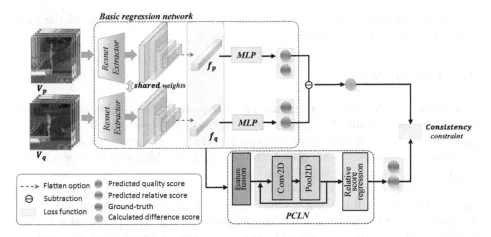

Fig. 2. Pipeline of our proposed model. The video pair is fed into the feature extractor as the input, then the score regressor is used to predict the score of these two videos, and PCLN is designed to learn the mapping from the video pair to the relative score

regression network including the feature fusion module, convolution module and fully connected layers, is applied to predict the relative score. In order to train the proposed model, three constraints are designed in this work: minimization of the error between predicted score and ground truth, minimization of the error between predicted relative score and ground truth, a new consistency constraint between basic regression network and PCLN. The overall framework of the proposed method is shown in Fig. 2.

More importantly, although the amount of computation of the proposed method in the training phase is larger than that of the basic regression network, in the testing phase, only basic regression network is employed to predict the quality score of the input video, and the PCLN module is not necessary. The computational complexity of the testing phase does not increase. Another important advantage behind the proposed method is that the combination of any two videos can expand the number and diversity of samples in the training process, resulting in better accuracy and generalization. In summary, the contributions of this work are listed as follows:

(1) We extend the quality score regression to relative score prediction and propose a new end-to-end AQA model to enhance the performance of the basic regression network. The basic regression network and PCLN are combined during the training, but in the testing, only basic regression network is employed, which makes the proposed method simple but high accuracy.

(2) A novel pairwise LTR-based model PCLN is proposed to concern the subtle difference between videos. A new consistency constraint between PCLN and basic regression network is defined.

(3) The experimental results based on the public datasets show that the proposed method achieves the better performance compared with existing methods.

Ablation experiments are also conducted to verify the effectiveness of the each component of proposed method.

2   Related Work

The purpose of AQA task is to automatically evaluate the quality of an action. In recent years, many AQA methods have been proposed and it made rapid progress in the computer vision community. Most of the previous studies used the mainstream regression method to solve AQA problem, and some works has begun to use contrastive learning methods.

In the regression-based methods, there are two kinds of methods according to the form of input data: skeleton-based methods and appearance-based methods. In skeleton-based methods, Pirsiavash et al. [27] proposed a framework for learning spatio-temporal features from human skeleton joint sequences, which extracted action features using discrete cosine transform (DCT) and predicted scores using linear support vector regression (SVR). Pan et al. [21] processed specific joint action information according to the relationship between joint locations, combined joint common module and joint difference module for human joint action learning. More recently, they continued to propose an adaptive method [20], which adaptively designed different assessment architectures for different types of actions.

Moreover, many attempts devote to acquire more detailed appearance based information to improve the assessment performance. For example, Parmar and Tran Morris [26] utilized C3D network to acquire spatio-temporal features and performed score regression using the SVR and LSTM. Later, they built an AQA dataset named MTL-AQA [24], and devoted to exploit the representation of the action and its quality to improve the performance of AQA model. Xiang et al. [37] proposed to apply P3D on each stage of diving video and then fuse the stage-wise features into P3D to regress the subscores. Tang et al. [32] proposed an uncertainty-aware score distribution learning approach, which described score as probability distribution to predict quality score. Dong et al. [3] proposed a learning and fusion network of multiple hidden substages to assess athlete performance by segmenting videos into five substages.

Furthermore, several methods defined the AQA problem as a pairwise ranking formulation. Doughty et al. [4] formulated the problem as pairwise and overall ranking of video collections, and proposed a supervised deep ranking method. They also trained [5] a rank-specific temporal attention modules, which processed higher and lower skills parts separately. Yu et al. [39] developed a group-aware regression tree to replace the traditional score regression. In addition, different from the methods which only used the vision features to assess action quality, in [32,39], the extra referee information is added to improve AQA results. Jain et al. [11] proposed a binary classification network to learn the similarities between videos. After that, it was transferred to the score regression task. In the score regression network, each input video and expert video, which has the highest score in the dataset, were combined as input for model training and score prediction. However, only selecting single expert sample as the reference is difficult to model the diversity of action scores and video differences in AQA task. This strategy adopted two-stage approach, which cannot ensure that the parameters learned from the binary classification task were applicable to the score regression network. Different from the above methods, in this work, we propose a new approach to learn the difference between video pairs, and build an end-to-end model to improve the performance of the basic regression network.

3   Approach

In this section, we introduce the proposed AQA method for sports events in details, including the feature extractor, score regressor and PCLN module.

3.1   Problem Formulation

Given a sport video $V = \{v_i\}_{i=1}^{L}$, where v_i represents the i-th frame in a video and L is the length of input video, the goal of AQA is to automatically generate the score based on the performance of athlete. It can be defined as:

$$S = \Theta(V) \tag{1}$$

where $\Theta(\cdot)$ represents the score prediction function, and S represents the predicted action quality score.

The goal of the proposed method is to find a more effective regression function $\Theta(\cdot)$. As shown in Fig. 2, in the training process of the proposed method, a pair of videos are applied as input and a multitask framework is proposed. In addition to learning the quality score of each video, we also learn the relative score between the input two videos. The AQA problem can be reformulated as:

$$[S_p, S_q, \Delta S] = \Upsilon(V_p, V_q) \tag{2}$$

where V_p and V_q represent the pair of input videos, $\Upsilon(\cdot, \cdot)$ represents the proposed algorithm, S_p and S_q represent the predicted quality score of the corresponding video respectively, and ΔS represents the predicted relative score between two videos.

In the proposed method, PCLN is built to learn the difference between videos and provide a more accurate evaluation result. To train PCLN, a video pair $<V_p, V_q>$ is generated from the original video dataset $V = \{V_1, V_2, ..., V_n\}$ by a combinations way. As shown in Eq. 3, the total number of video pairs can be reached $C(n, 2)$:

$$C(n, 2) = \frac{n!}{2! * (n-2)!} = \frac{n * (n-1)}{2} \tag{3}$$

where n represents the number of videos in the training set.

3.2 Feature Extraction and Score Regression

Given a pair of input videos $<V_p, V_q>$, the effective vision features should be extracted first. There are generally two types of methods to extract the features: 3D convolution-based methods and temporal encoder-based methods. Limited by the computational scale, 3D convolution-based methods [1,33] usually require to sample a short clip with fixed-length from the video. However, due to the randomness of the sampling strategy, the features extracted from the sampled short clip are unstable, so that the score prediction will fluctuate a lot. Therefore, we use the latter strategy to compute video features in this work.

In temporal encoder-based methods, the image feature of each video frame is extracted by the feature backbone network. In this work, we use ResNet [10] model as the feature extractor. After that, a temporal encoder network [13] is applied to encode the temporal information of the feature sequence. By doing so, the higher-level and stable video feature are obtained. The encoder network is comprised of two stacked encoding blocks, and each encoding block is composed of the 1×1 temporal convolution, specific activation function and maxpooling layer across temporal series. This feature extraction process can be defined as Eq. 4.

$$f_i = \mathbb{E}(\mathcal{F}(V_i)), i = p, q \tag{4}$$

where f_p and f_q represent the features of the input videos $<V_p, V_q>$ respectively, $\mathcal{F}(\cdot)$ represents the ResNet model and $\mathbb{E}(\cdot)$ represents the temporal encoder network.

Finally, a fully connected (FC) network is designed to regress the action quality score and form a basic regression network. Referring to the previous works [3,22,24], the FC network contains three fully connected layers: $D \times 4096$, 4096×2048 and 2048×1, where D is the dimension of the video feature. Based on the above definition, the basic regression network can be defined as:

$$S_i = \Theta(V_i) = \mathcal{R}(f_i) = \mathcal{R}(\mathbb{E}_c(\mathcal{F}(V_i))), i = p, q \tag{5}$$

where $\mathcal{R}(\cdot)$ represents the score regressor.

3.3 PCLN Model

As most of the same sport events are competed in similar environment, the differences between the same competition videos are often very subtle, and there are slight differences in how the athletes perform on the same actions. For example, in the diving competition, the referees primarily pay attention to the size of the splash, the degree of the athlete's leg bending, the execution standard of the action and so on. Although these factors are difficult to observe, they greatly affect the accuracy of scoring. In order to learn the differences between videos to assist the final scoring task, we build a separate branch for the pairwise video based LTR network named PCLN to learn the relative scores. The detailed structure of PCLN model is shown in Fig. 3.

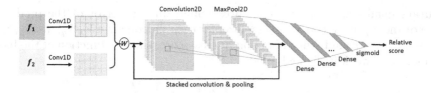

Fig. 3. Structure of PCLN model. The temporal encoded features f_1 and f_2 are applied as inputs

First, 1D convolutional layer is carried out for each encoded video feature in temporal. It can further encode features to capture higher level action information. Then the feature matrices of the two videos are connected by matrix multiplication. To be detailed, we form the fusion process as follows:

$$f'_p = \sigma(w_{(0)} \otimes f_p + b_{(0)}),$$
$$f'_q = \sigma(w_{(0)} \otimes f_q + b_{(0)}), \tag{6}$$
$$f_{(0)} = f'_p \circ f'_q$$

where f'_p and f'_q represent the output feature map of 1D convolutional layer, $w_{(0)}$ is the parameters in this layer, $\otimes$ means convolution operator and b is the corresponding bias vector, $\sigma(\cdot)$ represents the ReLU activation function, $f_{(0)}$ represents the connected matrix, $\circ$ means matrix multiplication operator.

Secondly, stacked 2D convolutional and pooling layers are performed on the connected matrix, then a high-level representation of the interaction between the two videos can be obtained. Finally, we use a general MLP module to predict the relative score of the pair videos. There are four layers in this MLP module, and the number of nodes in each layer is 64, 32, 8 and 1 subsequently. The calculation process of PCLN can be defined as follows:

$$f'_{(i)} = \sigma(w_{(i)} \otimes f_{(i-1)} + b_{(i)}),$$
$$f_{(i)} = Mp(f'_{(i)}), \tag{7}$$
$$\Delta S = \mathcal{R}_d(f_{(c)})$$

where $f'_{(i)}$ represent the output of 2D convolutional operation in i-th layer, $w_{(i)}$ and $b_{(i)}$ are the parameters and bias vector in i-th layer, and $i = 1, ..., c$, c is the number of layers in the PCLN, it is set to 2 in the experiment. $Mp(\cdot)$ represents the maxpooling operation, and $\mathcal{R}_d(\cdot)$ represents the MLP module for relative score.

3.4 Module Training and Inference

To train the proposed AQA model, we formulate three constraints to learn effective relative scores between different videos and accurate athlete quality scores simultaneously. First, the fundamental requirement of the AQA task is to obtain accurate quality scores, which requires minimizing the error of the predicted score of the input video pair. Therefore, for each video pair $<V_p, V_q>$, $<\tilde{S}_p, \tilde{S}_q>$ represents the ground truth of action quality score, the loss function of the basic regression network is defined as:

$$\mathcal{L}_{bs} = \frac{1}{2} \sum_{i=p,q}^{N} (\tilde{S}_i - S_i)^2 \tag{8}$$

Similarly, it also needs to minimize the error between the predicted relative score and the corresponding ground truth. In this task, the absolute value of two score labels between the input video pair is applied as ground truth. Therefore, the loss function of PCLN model can be defined as:

$$\mathcal{L}_{ds} = (\Delta S - |\tilde{S}_p - \tilde{S}_q|)^2 \tag{9}$$

Furthermore, a consistency constraint is defined for basic regression network and PCLN to improve the performance of the proposed AQA model. This consistency constraint confines the PCLN predicted relative score is equal to the calculated difference score from the two quality scores predicted by basic regression network. Therefore, a consistency loss function is defined as:

$$\mathcal{L}_{rs} = (\Delta S - |S_p - S_q|)^2 \tag{10}$$

Finally, the overall loss function of the proposed AQA model can be summarized as:

$$\mathcal{L} = \mathcal{L}_{bs} + \mathcal{L}_{ds} + \mathcal{L}_{rs} \tag{11}$$

In the testing phase, we only utilize the basic regression network, which includes the feature extractor, temporal encoder and regression network, to predict the quality score. No matter how many branches and constraints we add to the model during training phase, the proposed framework can still guarantee lower complexity during testing, which is different from the previous AQA studies.

4   Experimental Results and Discussion

The proposed method is evaluated on the AQA-7 [22] and MTL-AQA [24] datasets. Ablation study is applied to verify the effectiveness of each component of the method.

4.1   Datasets and Evaluation Metric

AQA-7 Dataset. The AQA-7 dataset includes 1189 videos from 7 sports captured in Summer and Winter Olympics: 370 videos from single 10m diving, 176 videos from gymnastic vault, 175 videos from big air skiing, 206 videos from big air snowboarding, 88 videos from synchronous 3m diving, 91 videos from synchronous 10m diving, and 83 videos from trampoline. All of the videos in this dataset have a fixed length of 103 frames except that trampoline videos are much longer than other sports. Thus, in this experiment, the trampoline videos are excluded according to the setting in [22]. In addition, AQA-7 dataset only provides the final score of each video as the label. The split of training set and testing set follows the official setting.

MTL-AQA Dataset. The MTL-AQA dataset is the largest diving dataset released in 2019. It contains 1412 diving videos collected from 16 different events. In addition, the dataset includes the 10m platform and 3m springboard, both male and female athletes. Different kinds of labels are provided for each video in the dataset, such as final score, difficulty degree and execution score given by the referees. We follow the split setting as [24] suggested: 1059 videos are used for training, while 353 videos are used for testing.

Evaluation Metric. To be comparable with the existing AQA methods [26, 27], the Spearman's rank correlation (SRC) is adopted to measure the rank correlation between ground-truth and predicted results. The higher the SRC, the better. The calculation can be expressed as:

$$\rho = \frac{\sum_i (h_i - h)(k_i - k)}{\sqrt{\sum_i (h_i - \bar{h})^2 \sum_i (k_i - \bar{k})^2}} \tag{12}$$

where h and k denote the rankings of the two sequences respectively. We use Fisher's z-value [6] to measure the average correlation coefficient across actions as previous work [20, 32, 39].

4.2 Implementation Details

We implement the proposed model using PyTorch, and it is trained on single Nvidia RTX 3090 GPU. ResNet-50 pretrained on ImageNet [2] is used as image feature extractor. The proposed model is trained for 200 epochs. Adam [12] optimizer with initial learning rate of 0.0001 is applied and the decay rate is set as 0.5. In the experiments on AQA-7 and MTL-AQA, all the video frames are resized to 224 × 224, and each video contains 103 frames as [22, 24] suggested.

In diving sports, the final score is generated by multiplying the execution score and the difficulty degree, and the execution score is the average score provided by judges [3, 32]. In MTL-AQA dataset, since there are difficulty degree and execution score labels for each video, we implement the proposed method in two scenarios: execution score prediction (ESP) and final score prediction (FSP). In ESP scenario, execution score is used as the training label, and in the inference stage, the predicted execution score is multiplied by the difficulty degree to obtain the final score. In the FSP scenario, the final score is predicted directly. In all experiments, the SRC of the final score is used as the evaluation metric. In addition, the final scores in both datasets are normalized with min-max normalization operation, and the execution score in MTL-AQA is divided by 30 for normalization since the range of execution score is from 0 to 30. Code is available at https://github.com/hqu-cst-mmc/PCLN.

4.3   Results on AQA-7 Dataset

Comparison with the State-of-the-Art Methods. In order to evaluate the effectiveness of the proposed method, it is compared with the existing AQA approaches. Unlike the works [3,11,19,27] that only performed experiments on part of sports to verify the robustness of the proposed method, we conduct experiments based on all the sports in the AQA-7 dataset. The experimental results are shown in Table 1. Obviously, the proposed method achieves the state-of-the-art performance in the terms of average SRC. In addition, the proposed method obtains significant improvement for all action classes except Snowboard compared to the recent USDL approach [32], which utilizes label distribution learning to replace original regression task. Another recent work Adaptive [20] reached a SRC of 0.85 for the average performance but the approach relied on human skeleton data and required different assessment architectures for different categories of sports in AQA. Compared with these two recent works, the average SRC of the proposed approach gains improvement of 0.0693 and 0.029 respectively, which clearly verifies the effectiveness of the proposed method in AQA problem.

Table 1. Comparison results of the proposed method with the state-of-the-art methods. "-" means that the result did not provide in the literature

Network	Year	Diving	Gymvault	Skiing	Snow board	Sync. 3 m	Sync. 10 m	Avg. SRC
Pose+DCT [27]	2014	0.5300	-	-	-	-	-	-
ST-GCN [38]	2018	0.3286	0.5770	0.1681	0.1234	0.6600	0.6483	0.4433
C3D-LSTM [22]	2019	0.6047	0.5636	0.4593	0.5029	0.7912	0.6927	0.6165
C3D-SVR [22]	2019	0.7902	0.6824	0.5209	0.4006	0.5937	0.9120	0.6937
JRG [21]	2019	0.7630	0.7358	0.6006	0.5405	0.9013	0.9254	0.7849
USDL [32]	2020	0.8099	0.7570	0.6538	**0.7109**	0.9166	0.8878	0.8102
DML [11]	2020	0.6900	0.4400	-	-	-	-	-
FALCONS [19]	2020	0.8453	-	-	-	-	-	-
HalluciNet [23]	2021	0.8351	-	-	-	-	-	-
EAGLE-Eye [18]	2021	0.8331	0.7411	0.6635	0.6447	0.9143	0.9158	0.8140
Adaptive [20]	2021	0.8306	0.7593	0.7208	0.6940	0.9588	0.9298	0.8500
Ours	2022	**0.8697**	**0.8759**	**0.7754**	0.5778	**0.9629**	**0.9541**	**0.8795**

Influence of Feature Extractor. As mentioned in Sect. 3, there are two methods to extract video features: 3D convolution-based (3DCNN) method and temporal encoder-based method. In order to discuss their performance for AQA task, we apply P3D [28] as the feature extraction network to replace the temporal encoder of basic regression network to build a 3DCNN regression network. And the comparison results can be found in Fig. 4. In the experiment, both of these methods are trained from the same training set, and one sample is randomly selected for testing. This sample is evaluated 10 times by two models respectively.

In Fig. 4, the green line is the predicted results using 3DCNN regression network, the yellow line is the results of basic regression network and the gray line is the ground truth, which is 83.25 for the sample "diving_007". From the comparison results, it can be observed that the predicted score of basic regression network is fixed 83.07 for 10 times testing, while the results of 3DCNN regression network is unstable. The main reason is that a random sampling process is required before feature calculation in 3DCNN, and the sampling results will affect the predicted results of the model. Therefore, in this work, we employ temporal encoder-based method to extract video features.

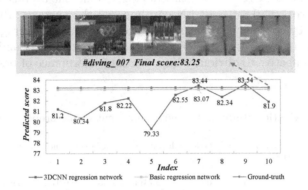

Fig. 4. Comparison results of temporal feature encoder and 3D convolution network

Table 2. Comparison results of the proposed method with different video pair number

Batch size	Video pairs	Diving	Gym vault	Skiing	Snow board	Sync. 3 m	Sync. 10 m	Avg. SRC
8	28	0.8458	0.7723	0.7311	0.5285	0.9255	0.9317	0.8276
16	120	0.8597	0.8185	0.7455	0.5750	0.9639	0.9412	0.8621
32	496	**0.8697**	**0.8759**	**0.7754**	**0.5778**	0.9629	**0.9541**	**0.8795**
64	2016	0.8189	0.8518	0.7295	0.4927	-	-	-

Influence of the Number of Video Pairs. We apply the 2-combinations method to expand the dataset. Suppose that n is the number of the selected video in each iteration, which is the batch size in the training process. According to Eq. 3, when n is set to 8, 16, 32 and 64, the number of video pairs in each iteration is 28, 120, 496 and 2016 correspondingly. In order to verify the influence of the number of video pairs, the predicted score with different batch size is reported in Table 2. The experimental results show that the number of video pairs has a positive impact on the accuracy of assessment. It means the more video pairs used, the more effectively difference information between videos can be obtained. When n is set to 32, our proposed method achieves the highest average SRC of 0.8795, and the performance in each category is the best. Since the number of training set in "sync. 3m" and "sync. 10m" are less than 64, the experiment cannot be carried out when n is set to 64.

Ablation Study for Exploring the Effectiveness of Each Module. To verify the effectiveness of each proposed component in this work, an ablation study is performed on AQA-7 dataset. The proposed method is composed of basic regression network, PCLN and consistency constraint. We discuss the contributions of PCLN and consistency constraint under basic regression network. In this experiment, the batch size is set 32. The experimental results are shown in Table 3. Without PCLN and consistency constraint, the average SRC of basic regression network is 0.8504. PCLN can improve the average SRC by 0.0217, while consistency constraint brings a 0.0174 improvement in average SRC based on PCLN. From these results, it can be observed that PCLN and consistency constraint are effective to obviously improve the performance of basic regression network.

Table 3. Ablation study of different component in the proposed method

Basic regression network	PCLN	Consistency constraint	Diving	Gym vault	Skiing	Snow board	Sync. 3 m	Sync. 10 m	Avg. SRC
✓	✗	✗	0.8604	0.8156	0.7314	0.5755	0.9432	0.9417	0.8504
✓	✓	✗	0.8656	0.8701	0.7624	0.5759	0.9547	0.9530	0.8721
✓	✓	✓	**0.8697**	**0.8759**	**0.7754**	**0.5778**	**0.9629**	**0.9541**	**0.8795**

Table 4. Comparison of our approach with existing methods on the MTL-AQA dataset

Methods	Year	Sp. corr.
Pose+DCT* [27]	2014	0.2682
C3D-SVR* [26]	2017	0.7716
C3D-LSTM* [26]	2017	0.8489
MSCADC-STL [24]	2019	0.8472
MSCADC-MTL [24]	2019	0.8612
C3D-AVG-STL [24]	2019	0.8960
C3D-AVG-MTL [24]	2019	0.9044
USDL [32]	2020	0.9066
C3D-AVG-SA&HMreg [17]	2021	0.8970
Ours(FSP)	2022	0.8798
Ours(ESP)	2022	0.9230

*These results were taken from [24].

4.4   Results on MTL-AQA Dataset

Comparison with State-of-the-Art Methods. In order to further verify the robustness and effectiveness of the proposed method, we extend the same experiment on MTL-AQA dataset. Table 4 shows the comparison results of the proposed method with the existing methods. Since the difficulty degree and execution score given by referees are available in this dataset, we further conduct experiments under two different scenarios (ESP and FSP) to verify the effectiveness of the proposed approach. The experimental results show that the proposed model in ESP scenario achieves the best SRC 0.923. In addition, it can be clearly observed that compared with FSP, using execution score as the label is more conducive to the learning of the proposed method.

Table 5. Comparison results of different video pair number on the MTL-AQA dataset

Batch size	Video pairs	Score label	
		FSP	ESP
8	28	0.8729	0.9094
16	120	0.8750	0.9118
32	496	0.8777	0.9188
64	2016	**0.8798**	**0.9230**

Table 6. Ablation study on different assessment structures on the MTL-AQA dataset, all of the models use 2016 pairs of video

Basic regression network	PCLN	Consistency constraint	Score label	
			FSP	ESP
✓	×	×	0.8745	0.9095
✓	✓	×	0.8788	0.9196
✓	✓	✓	**0.8798**	**0.9230**

Influence of the Number of Video Pairs. Similarly, we further verified the influence of the number of video pairs on MTL-AQA dataset, and the results can be found in Table 5. The experimental results show that when n is set to 64 (i.e., the number of video pairs in each batch is 2016), the proposed method achieved the highest SRC of 0.8798 and 0.9230 in FSP and ESP scenarios respectively. With the increase number of video pairs, the SRC value increases gradually in both scenarios. Therefore, in all of the ablation experiments on MTL-AQA dataset, the batch size is set to 64.

Ablation Study for Exploring the Effectiveness of Each Module. We also conduct the ablation study on the MTL-AQA dataset to further verify the effectiveness of each component in the proposed method. The experimental results are shown in Table 6. From these results, we get similar conclusions with the previous experiment based on AQA-7 dataset. When adding PCLN module with the basic regression network, the SRC value is improved by 0.0043 and 0.0101 in FSP and ESP scenarios, respectively. When consistency constraint is employed, the SRC value achieves 0.8798 and 0.923. Especially, compared with the basic regression network in ESP scenario, it is improved by 0.0135. These experimental results show that our proposed PCLN and consistency constraint can also improve the performance of basic regression network. This can further verify the effectiveness and robustness of the proposed model for AQA task.

4.5   Qualitative Evaluation

In Fig. 5, we show some exemplars of predicted scores by different methods in details to quantitatively analyze the effectiveness of the proposed method. The first video pair shows two actions that both use "Tuck Position" but the difficulty degree is different. There is a large gap between the final scores of the two videos because of the different performance of the athletes, especially the splash size in the red border frames. In the other case, these two athletes perform different actions "Tuck Position" and "Pike Position" with very close difficulty degree. But both execution scores of these two actions are equal to 24. From the comparison results in Fig. 5, it can be clearly observed that the absolute error of each module is gradually decrease, and the proposed method gives the predicted score that is closer to the ground truth. These results can further verify the effectiveness of the proposed method.

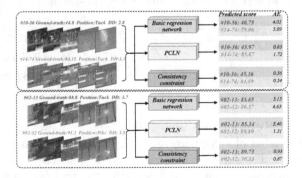

Fig. 5. Predicted results of samples. DD represents the difficulty degree. AE represents the absolute error between the predicted score and ground truth

5   Conclusions

In this paper, we propose a new contrastive learning model for AQA, which is capable of exploring the subtle difference in sports videos. In the proposed method, we adopted a more stable feature extraction strategy, a basic regression network and PCLN module were applied to predict the quality score and relative score simultaneously. Moreover, a consistency constraint was defined to train the proposed method. The experimental results showed that the proposed method has achieved the state-of-the-arts performance. However, in this work, we only use very simple score error to calculate the loss of predicted results. In the future, more assessment information, such as the scoring pattern of each referee, can be applied to improve the accuracy of the proposed method in AQA tasks.

Acknowledgements. This work was supported by the Natural Science Foundation of China (No. 61871196, 62001176); Natural Science Foundation of Fujian Province of China (No. 2019J01082, 2020J01085, 2022J01317); Scientific Research Funds of Huaqiao University (No. 21BS122) and the Promotion Program for Young and Middle-aged Teacher in Science and Technology Research of Huaqiao University (No. ZQN-YX601).

References

1. Carreira, J., Zisserman, A.: Quo vadis, action recognition? A new model and the kinetics dataset. In: Proceedings of the IEEE Conference on Computer Vision and Pattern Recognition, pp. 6299–6308 (2017)
2. Deng, J., Dong, W., Socher, R., Li, L.J., Li, K., Fei-Fei, L.: ImageNet: a large-scale hierarchical image database. In: 2009 IEEE Conference on Computer Vision and Pattern Recognition, pp. 248–255. IEEE (2009)
3. Dong, L.J., Zhang, H.B., Shi, Q., Lei, Q., Du, J.X., Gao, S.: Learning and fusing multiple hidden substages for action quality assessment. Knowl.-Based Syst. 107388 (2021). https://doi.org/10.1016/j.knosys.2021.107388, https://www.sciencedirect.com/science/article/pii/S095070512100650X
4. Doughty, H., Damen, D., Mayol-Cuevas, W.: Who's better? Who's best? Pairwise deep ranking for skill determination. In: Proceedings of the IEEE Conference on Computer Vision and Pattern Recognition, pp. 6057–6066 (2018)
5. Doughty, H., Mayol-Cuevas, W., Damen, D.: The pros and cons: rank-aware temporal attention for skill determination in long videos. In: Proceedings of the IEEE/CVF Conference on Computer Vision and Pattern Recognition, pp. 7862–7871 (2019)
6. Faller, A.J.: An average correlation coefficient. J. Appl. Meteorol. **20**(2), 203–205 (1981)
7. Farabi, S., et al.: Improving action quality assessment using resnets and weighted aggregation. arXiv preprint arXiv:2102.10555 (2021)
8. Fard, M.J., Ameri, S., Darin Ellis, R., Chinnam, R.B., Pandya, A.K., Klein, M.D.: Automated robot-assisted surgical skill evaluation: predictive analytics approach. Int. J. Med. Robot. Comput. Assist. Surg. **14**(1), e1850 (2018)
9. Gao, J., et al.: An asymmetric modeling for action assessment. In: Vedaldi, A., Bischof, H., Brox, T., Frahm, J.-M. (eds.) ECCV 2020. LNCS, vol. 12375, pp. 222–238. Springer, Cham (2020). https://doi.org/10.1007/978-3-030-58577-8_14

10. He, K., Zhang, X., Ren, S., Sun, J.: Deep residual learning for image recognition. In: Proceedings of the IEEE Conference on Computer Vision and Pattern Recognition (CVPR), June 2016
11. Jain, H., Harit, G., Sharma, A.: Action quality assessment using Siamese network-based deep metric learning. IEEE Trans. Circuits Syst. Video Technol. **31**(6), 2260–2273 (2020)
12. Kingma, D.P., Ba, J.: Adam: a method for stochastic optimization. arXiv preprint arXiv:1412.6980 (2014)
13. Lea, C., Flynn, M.D., Vidal, R., Reiter, A., Hager, G.D.: Temporal convolutional networks for action segmentation and detection. In: proceedings of the IEEE Conference on Computer Vision and Pattern Recognition, pp. 156–165 (2017)
14. Lei, Q., Du, J.X., Zhang, H.B., Ye, S., Chen, D.S.: A survey of vision-based human action evaluation methods. Sensors **19**(19), 4129 (2019)
15. Liu, D., et al.: Towards unified surgical skill assessment. In: Proceedings of the IEEE/CVF Conference on Computer Vision and Pattern Recognition, pp. 9522–9531 (2021)
16. Malpani, A., Vedula, S.S., Chen, C.C.G., Hager, G.D.: Pairwise comparison-based objective score for automated skill assessment of segments in a surgical task. In: Stoyanov, D., Collins, D.L., Sakuma, I., Abolmaesumi, P., Jannin, P. (eds.) IPCAI 2014. LNCS, vol. 8498, pp. 138–147. Springer, Cham (2014). https://doi.org/10.1007/978-3-319-07521-1_15
17. Nagai, T., Takeda, S., Matsumura, M., Shimizu, S., Yamamoto, S.: Action quality assessment with ignoring scene context. In: 2021 IEEE International Conference on Image Processing (ICIP), pp. 1189–1193. IEEE (2021)
18. Nekoui, M., Cruz, F.O.T., Cheng, L.: Eagle-eye: extreme-pose action grader using detail bird's-eye view. In: Proceedings of the IEEE/CVF Winter Conference on Applications of Computer Vision, pp. 394–402 (2021)
19. Nekoui, M., Tito Cruz, F.O., Cheng, L.: Falcons: fast learner-grader for contorted poses in sports. In: 2020 IEEE/CVF Conference on Computer Vision and Pattern Recognition Workshops (CVPRW), pp. 3941–3949 (2020). https://doi.org/10.1109/CVPRW50498.2020.00458
20. Pan, J., Gao, J., Zheng, W.: Adaptive action assessment. IEEE Trans. Pattern Anal. Mach. Intell. (01), 1 (5555). https://doi.org/10.1109/TPAMI.2021.3126534
21. Pan, J.H., Gao, J., Zheng, W.S.: Action assessment by joint relation graphs. In: Proceedings of the IEEE/CVF International Conference on Computer Vision, pp. 6331–6340 (2019)
22. Parmar, P., Morris, B.: Action quality assessment across multiple actions. In: 2019 IEEE Winter Conference on Applications of Computer Vision (WACV), pp. 1468–1476. IEEE (2019)
23. Parmar, P., Morris, B.: Hallucineting spatiotemporal representations using a 2D-CNN. Signals **2**, 604–618 (2021). https://doi.org/10.3390/signals2030037
24. Parmar, P., Morris, B.T.: What and how well you performed? A multitask learning approach to action quality assessment. In: Proceedings of the IEEE/CVF Conference on Computer Vision and Pattern Recognition, pp. 304–313 (2019)
25. Parmar, P., Reddy, J., Morris, B.: Piano skills assessment. arXiv preprint arXiv:2101.04884 (2021)
26. Parmar, P., Tran Morris, B.: Learning to score olympic events. In: Proceedings of the IEEE Conference on Computer Vision and Pattern Recognition Workshops, pp. 20–28 (2017)

27. Pirsiavash, H., Vondrick, C., Torralba, A.: Assessing the quality of actions. In: Fleet, D., Pajdla, T., Schiele, B., Tuytelaars, T. (eds.) ECCV 2014. LNCS, vol. 8694, pp. 556–571. Springer, Cham (2014). https://doi.org/10.1007/978-3-319-10599-4_36

28. Qiu, Z., Yao, T., Mei, T.: Learning spatio-temporal representation with pseudo-3D residual networks. In: Proceedings of the IEEE International Conference on Computer Vision, pp. 5533–5541 (2017)

29. Reiley, C.E., Hager, G.D.: Task versus subtask surgical skill evaluation of robotic minimally invasive surgery. In: Yang, G.-Z., Hawkes, D., Rueckert, D., Noble, A., Taylor, C. (eds.) MICCAI 2009. LNCS, vol. 5761, pp. 435–442. Springer, Heidelberg (2009). https://doi.org/10.1007/978-3-642-04268-3_54

30. Roditakis, K., Makris, A., Argyros, A.: Towards improved and interpretable action quality assessment with self-supervised alignment. In: The 14th PErvasive Technologies Related to Assistive Environments Conference. PETRA 2021, pp. 507–513. Association for Computing Machinery, New York (2021). https://doi.org/10.1145/3453892.3461624

31. Sardari, F., Paiement, A., Hannuna, S., Mirmehdi, M.: VI-net-view-invariant quality of human movement assessment. Sensors 20(18), 5258 (2020)

32. Tang, Y., et al.: Uncertainty-aware score distribution learning for action quality assessment. In: Proceedings of the IEEE/CVF Conference on Computer Vision and Pattern Recognition, pp. 9839–9848 (2020)

33. Tran, D., Bourdev, L., Fergus, R., Torresani, L., Paluri, M.: Learning spatiotemporal features with 3D convolutional networks. In: Proceedings of the IEEE International Conference on Computer Vision, pp. 4489–4497 (2015)

34. Varadarajan, B., Reiley, C., Lin, H., Khudanpur, S., Hager, G.: Data-derived models for segmentation with application to surgical assessment and training. In: Yang, G.-Z., Hawkes, D., Rueckert, D., Noble, A., Taylor, C. (eds.) MICCAI 2009. LNCS, vol. 5761, pp. 426–434. Springer, Heidelberg (2009). https://doi.org/10.1007/978-3-642-04268-3_53

35. Wang, J., Du, Z., Li, A., Wang, Y.: Assessing action quality via attentive spatio-temporal convolutional networks. In: Peng, Y., et al. (eds.) PRCV 2020. LNCS, vol. 12306, pp. 3–16. Springer, Cham (2020). https://doi.org/10.1007/978-3-030-60639-8_1

36. Wang, T., Wang, Y., Li, M.: Towards accurate and interpretable surgical skill assessment: a video-based method incorporating recognized surgical gestures and skill levels. In: Martel, A.L., et al. (eds.) MICCAI 2020. LNCS, vol. 12263, pp. 668–678. Springer, Cham (2020). https://doi.org/10.1007/978-3-030-59716-0_64

37. Xiang, X., Tian, Y., Reiter, A., Hager, G.D., Tran, T.D.: S3D: stacking segmental P3D for action quality assessment. In: 2018 25th IEEE International Conference on Image Processing (ICIP), pp. 928–932. IEEE (2018)

38. Yan, S., Xiong, Y., Lin, D.: Spatial temporal graph convolutional networks for skeleton-based action recognition. In: Thirty-second AAAI Conference on Artificial Intelligence (2018)

39. Yu, X., Rao, Y., Zhao, W., Lu, J., Zhou, J.: Group-aware contrastive regression for action quality assessment. In: Proceedings of the IEEE/CVF International Conference on Computer Vision, pp. 7919–7928 (2021)

40. Zeng, L.A., et al.: Hybrid dynamic-static context-aware attention network for action assessment in long videos. In: Proceedings of the 28th ACM International Conference on Multimedia, pp. 2526–2534 (2020)

Geometric Features Informed Multi-person Human-Object Interaction Recognition in Videos

Tanqiu Qiao[1] , Qianhui Men[2] , Frederick W. B. Li[1] , Yoshiki Kubotani[3] ,
Shigeo Morishima[3] , and Hubert P. H. Shum[1(✉)]

[1] Durham University, Durham, UK
{tanqiu.qiao,frederick.li,hubert.shum}@durham.ac.uk
[2] University of Oxford, Oxford, UK
qianhui.men@eng.ox.ac.uk
[3] Waseda Research Institute for Science and Engineering, Shinjuku, Japan
yoshikikubotani@akane.waseda.jp, shigeo@waseda.jp

Abstract. Human-Object Interaction (HOI) recognition in videos is important for analyzing human activity. Most existing work focusing on visual features usually suffer from occlusion in the real-world scenarios. Such a problem will be further complicated when multiple people and objects are involved in HOIs. Consider that geometric features such as human pose and object position provide meaningful information to understand HOIs, we argue to combine the benefits of both visual and geometric features in HOI recognition, and propose a novel Two-level Geometric feature-informed Graph Convolutional Network (2G-GCN). The geometric-level graph models the interdependency between geometric features of humans and objects, while the fusion-level graph further fuses them with visual features of humans and objects. To demonstrate the novelty and effectiveness of our method in challenging scenarios, we propose a new multi-person HOI dataset (MPHOI-72). Extensive experiments on MPHOI-72 (multi-person HOI), CAD-120 (single-human HOI) and Bimanual Actions (two-hand HOI) datasets demonstrate our superior performance compared to state-of-the-arts.

Keywords: Human-object interaction · Graph convolution neural networks · Feature fusion · Multi-person interaction

1 Introduction

The real-world human activities are often closely associated with surrounding objects. Human-Object Interaction (HOI) recognition focuses on learning and analyzing the interaction between human and object entities for activity recognition. HOI recognition involves the segmentation and recognition of individual

Supplementary Information The online version contains supplementary material available at https://doi.org/10.1007/978-3-031-19772-7_28.

Fig. 1. Two examples (*Cheering* and *Co-working*) of our collected multi-person HOI dataset. Geometric features such as skeletons and bounding boxes are annotated.

human sub-activities/object affordances in videos, such as drinking and placing, to gain an insight of the overall human activities [37]. Based on this, downstream applications such as security surveillance, healthcare monitoring and human-robot interactions can be developed.

Earlier work in HOI detection is limited to detecting interactions in one image [13,15,32]. With HOI video datasets proposed, models have been developed to learn the action representations over the spatio-temporal domain for HOI recognition [20,38]. Notably, [37] proposes a visual feature attention model to learn asynchronous and sparse HOI in videos, achieving state-of-the-art results.

A main challenge of video-based HOI recognition is that visual features usually suffer from occlusion. This is particularly problematic in real-world scenarios when multiple people and objects are involved. Recent research has shown that extracted pose features are more robust to partial occlusions than visual features [39,55]. Bottom-up pose estimators can extract body poses as long as the local image patches of joints are not occluded [4]. With advanced frameworks such as Graph Convolutional Networks (GCN), geometric pipelines generally perform better than visual ones on datasets with heavy occlusion [8]. Therefore, geometric features provide complementary information to visual ones [3,39].

In this paper, we propose to fuse geometric and visual features for HOI recognition in videos. Our research insight is that geometric features enrich fine-grained human-object interactions, as evidenced by previous research on image-based HOI detection [30,59]. We present a novel Two-level Geometric feature informed Graph Convolutional Network (2G-GCN) that extracts geometric features and fuses them with visual ones for HOI recognition in videos. We implement the network by using the geometric-level graph to model representative geometric features among humans and objects, and fusing the visual features through the fusion-level graph.

To showcase the effectiveness of our model, we further propose a multi-person dataset for Human-Object Interaction (MPHOI), which closely ensembles real-world activities that contain multiple people interacting with multiple objects. Our dataset includes common multi-person activities and natural occlusions in daily life (Fig. 1). It is annotated with the geometric features of human skeletal poses, human and object bound boxes, and ground-truth HOI activity labels, which can be used as a versatile benchmark for multiple tasks such as visual-based or skeleton-based human activity analysis or hybrid.

We outperform state-of-the-arts in multiple datasets, including our novel MPHOI-72 dataset, the single-human HOI CAD-120 [24] dataset, and the two-hand Bimanual Actions [9] dataset. We also extensively evaluate core components of 2G-GCN in ablation studies. Our main contributions are as follows:

- We propose a novel geometry-informed 2G-GCN network for HOI recognition in videos. The network consists of a two-level graph structure that models geometric features between human and object, together with the corresponding visual features.
- We present the novel problem of MPHOI in videos with a new MPHOI-72 dataset, showcasing new challenges that cannot be directly resolved by existing methods. The source code and dataset are made public[1].
- We outperform state-of-the-art HOI recognition networks in our MPHOI-72 dataset, the CAD-120 [24] dataset and the Bimanual Actions [9] dataset.

2   Related Work

2.1   HOI Detection in Images

HOI detection aims at understanding interactions between humans and objects and identifying their interdependencies within a single image. Gupta and Malik [18] first address the HOI detection task, which entails recognising human activities and the object instances they interact with in an image. Assigning distinct semantic responsibilities to items in a HOI process allows a detailed understanding of the present state of affairs. Gkioxari et al. [14] apply an action-specific density map over target object locations depending on the appearance of an identified person to the system in [18]. Multiple large-scale datasets have been presented in recent years for exploring HOI detection in images, such as V-COCO [18], HICO-DET [5] and HCVRD [61]. Specifically, Mallya and Lazebnik [32] present a simple network that fuses characteristics from a human bounding box and the entire image to detect HOIs. Gao et al. [13] exploit an instance-centric attention module to improve the information from regions of interest and assist HOI classification. These early methods focus on visual relationships between entities in images without any potential structural relationships in HOIs.

Graph Convolutional Networks (GCN) [22] can be used to assimilate valuable expressions of graph-structured data. Kato et al. [21] employ it to assemble new HOIs by using information from WordNet [35]. Xu et al. [56] also exploit a GCN to model the semantic dependencies between action and object categories. Wang et al. [51] hypothesis that it is convenient to represent the entities as nodes and the relations as the edges connecting them in HOI. They design a contextual heterogeneous graph network to deeply explore the relations between people and objects. VSGNet [48] refines the visual features from human-object pairs with

---

[1] https://github.com/tanqiu98/2G-GCN.

the spatial configuration, and exploits the structural connections between pairs through graph convolution. These approaches achieve remarkable performance in image data and can provide a basis for HOI recognition in videos.

2.2 HOI Recognition in Videos

HOI recognition in videos requires high-level spatial and temporal reasoning between humans and objects. Some earlier attempts apply spatio-temporal context to achieve rich-context for HOI recognition [17,24,29]. Recent works combine graphical models with deep neural networks (DNNs). Jain et al. [20] propose a model for integrating the strength of spatio-temporal graphs with Recurrent Neural Networks (RNNs) in sequence learning. Qi et al. [38] expand prior graphical models in DNNs for videos with learnable graph structures and pass messages through GPNN. Dabral et al. [6] analyze the effectiveness of GCNs against Convolutional Networks and Capsule Networks for spatial relation learning. Wang et al. [53] propose the STIGPN exploiting the parsed graphs to learn spatio-temporal connection development and discover objects existing in a scene. Although previous methods attain impressive improvements in specific tasks, they are all based on visual features, which are unreliable in real-life HOI activities that contain occlusions between human and object entities.

2.3 HOI Recognition Datasets

Multiple datasets are available to research HOI in videos for different tasks. CAD-120 [24], Bimanual Actions [9], Bimanual Manipulation [25], etc. are useful for single-person HOI recognition. The latter two also present bimanual HOI recognition tasks as they record human activities using both hands for object interaction. Something-Else [34], VLOG [12], EPIC Kitchens [7] are available for single-hand HOI recognition tasks, where the EPIC Kitchens dataset can be also used for bimanual HOI recognition since it captures both hands during cooking. The UCLA HHOI Dataset [45,46] focuses on human-human-object interaction, involving at most two humans and one object. As true multi-person HOI should involve multiple humans and objects, we propose a novel MPHOI dataset that collects daily activities with multiple people interacting multiple objects.

2.4 Geometric Features Informed HOI Analysis

Recent research begins to employ human pose to the HOI tasks in images, which takes the advantage of capturing structured connections in human skeletons. To focus on the important aspects of interaction, Fang et al. [10] suggest a pairwise body-part attention model. Based on semantic attention, Wan et al. [50] provide a zoom-in module for extracting local characteristics of human body joints. Zheng et al. [59] introduce a skeleton-based interactive graph network (SIGN) to capture fine-grained HOI between keypoints in human skeletons and objects.

Fig. 2. Sample video frames of three different MPHOI activities in MPHOI-72.

However, introducing geometric features such as the keypoints of human pose and objects to HOI learning in videos is challenging and underexplored for a few reasons. On the one hand, in a video, interaction definitions might be ambiguous, such as lift a cup vs. place a cup, approaching vs. retreating vs. reaching. These actions might be detected as the same image label due to their visual similarity. Videos allow the use of temporal visual cues that are not presented in images [37]. On the other hand, the model needs to consider human dynamics in the video and the shifting orientations of items in the scene in relation to humans [38]. This makes it difficult to directly extend image-based models to video that exploit the region of interest (ROI) features of human-object union [6]. We propose a novel two-level graph to refine the interactive representations; the first graph models the interdependency within the geometric key points of human and objects, and the second graph models the interdependency between the visual features and the learned geometric representations.

3   The Multi-Person HOI Dataset (MPHOI-72)

We propose a HOI dataset with multi-person activities (MPHOI-72), which is challenging due to many body occlusions among the humans and objects. We have 3 males and 2 females, aged 23–27, who are randomly combined into 8 groups with 2 people per group and perform 3 different HOI activities interacting with 2–4 objects. We also prepared 6 objects: cup, bottle, scissors, hair dryer, mouse, and laptop. 3 activities = { *Cheering, Hair cutting, Co-working*} and 13 sub-activities = { *Sit, Approach, Retreat, Place, Lift, Pour, Drink, Cheers, Cut, Dry, Work, Ask, Solve*} are defined. The dataset consists of 72 videos captured from 3 different angles at 30 fps, with totally 26,383 frames and an average length of 12 s.

Figure 2 shows some sample video frames of the three activities in our MPHOI-72 dataset, and the sub-activity label of each subject is annotated frame-wise. The top row presents *Hair cutting* from the front view, where one subject is sitting and another subject interacts with a pair of scissors and a hair dryer. Most part of the body of the subject standing at the back is invisible. The second row presents a popular human activity, *Cheering*, in which two subjects pour water from their own bottles, lift cups to cheer, and drink. The high-level occlusion exists between humans, cups and bottles during the entire activity. The bottom row presents *Co-working*, which simulates the situation of two co-workers asking and solving questions. Besides, we also consider distinct human sizes, skin colors and a balance of gender. These samples illustrate the diversity of our dataset.

We use Azure Kinect SDK to collect RGB-D videos with 3840×2160 reso-lution, and employ their Body Tracking SDK [1] to capture the full dynamics of two subject skeletons. Object bounding boxes are manually annotated frame-wise. For each video, we provide such geometric features: 2D human skeletons and bounding boxes of the subjects and objects involved in the activity (Fig. 1).

4   Two-Level Geometric Features Informed Graph Convolutional Network (2G-GCN)

To learn the correlations during human-object interaction, we propose a two-level graph structure to model the interdependency of the geometric features, known as 2G-GCN. The model consists of two key components: a geometry-level graph for modeling geometry and object features to facilitate graph convolution learn-ing, and a fusion-level graph for fusing geometric and visual features (Fig. 3).

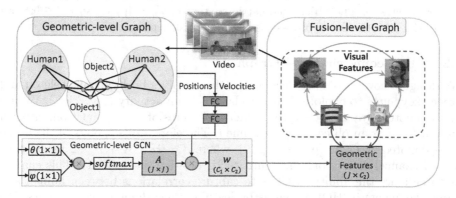

Fig. 3. Our 2G-GCN framework comprises a geometric-level and a fusion-level graph.

4.1   Geometric Features

The geometric features of humans can be represented in various ways. Human skeletons contain an explicit graph structure with joints as nodes and bones as edges. The joint position and velocity offer fine-grained dynamics in the human motion [58], while the joint angle also provides spatial cues in 3D skeleton data [43]. Alternatively, body shapes and how they deform during movement can be represented by surface models [31] or implicit models [41]. We employ human skeletons with joint position and velocity, because they are essential cues to human motion. Also, unlike body shapes, they are invariant to human appearance.

We represent human poses in an effective representation to inform HOI recognition. For human skeleton, we select specific body keypoints and denote them as a set $\mathcal{S} = \{M_t^{h,k}\}_{t=1,h=1,k=1}^{T,H,K}$, where $M_t^{h,k}$ denotes the body joint of type k in human h at time t, T denotes the total number of frames in the video, H and K denote the total number of humans and keypoints of a human body in a frame, respectively. For a given human body keypoint $M_t^{h,k}$, we define its position as $\mathbf{p}_{t,h,k} = (x_{t,h,k}, y_{t,h,k})^T \in \mathbb{R}^2$ in 2D, and the velocity as $\mathbf{v}_{t,h,k} = \mathbf{p}_{t+1,h,k} - \mathbf{p}_{t,h,k}$, which is the forward difference of neighbour frames. In the channel of each human skeleton keypoint, we concatenate its position $\mathbf{p}_{t,h,k}$, and velocity $\mathbf{v}_{t,h,k}$ in the channel domain, forming the human geometric context $\mathbf{h}_{t,h,k} = [\mathbf{p}_{t,h,k}, \mathbf{v}_{t,h,k}] \in \mathbb{R}^4$.

As objects play a crucial role in the HOI videos, we also consider their geometric features. The two diagonal points of the object bounding box are utilised to represent the object position. We define all object keypoints as $\mathcal{O} = \{B_t^{f,u}\}_{t=1,f=1,u=1}^{T,F,2}$, where $B_t^{f,u}$ denotes the object keypoint of type u in object f at time t. F denotes the maximum number of objects in a video and $u = \{1, 2\}$ is the index of the top-left and the bottom-right points of the object bounding box, respectively. The object geometric context $\mathbf{o}_{t,f,u} = [\mathbf{p}_{t,f,u}, \mathbf{v}_{t,f,u}] \in \mathbb{R}^4$ can be obtained by the same process as the human skeleton.

4.2   The Geometric-Level Graph

We design a novel geometric-level graph that involves both human skeleton and object keypoints to explore their correlations in an activity (Fig. 3 left). We use $\mathbf{g}_t$ to denote a graph node with geometric features of a keypoint from either a human $h_{t,h,k}$ or an object $o_{t,f,u}$ at frame t. Therefore, all keypoints of the frame t are denoted by $G_t = (\mathbf{g}_{t,1}; \cdots; \mathbf{g}_{t,J})$, where $J = H \times K + F \times 2$ joints, each with 4 channel dimensions including its 2D position and velocity. This enables us to enhance the ability of GCN to capture correlations between human and object keypoints in HOI activities by learning their dynamic spatial cues. We embed $\mathbf{g}_t$ using two fully connected (FC) layers following [58] as:

$$\widetilde{\mathbf{g}_t} = \sigma(W_2(\sigma(W_1\mathbf{g}_t + \mathbf{b}_1)) + \mathbf{b}_2) \in \mathbb{R}^{C_1}, \tag{1}$$

where C_1 is the dimension of the joint representation, $W_1 \in \mathbb{R}^{C_1 \times 4}$ and $W_2 \in \mathbb{R}^{C_1 \times C_1}$ are weight matrices, $\mathbf{b}_1$ and $\mathbf{b}_2$ are the bias vectors, and σ is the ReLU activation function.

We propose an adaptive adjacency matrix exploiting the similarity of the geometric features in the GCN. We employ the dot-product similarity in $\widetilde{\mathbf{g}}_t$, as it allows us to determine if and how strong a connection exists between two keypoints in the same frame t [43,54,58]. This is a better choice for our problem comparing to other strategies, e.g. the traditional adjacency matrix only represents the physical structure of the human body [57] or a fully-learned adjacency matrix without supervision of graph representations [43]. We represent the adjacency matrix A_t with $j_1{}^{th}$ and $j_2{}^{th}$ keypoints as:

$$A_t(j_1, j_2) = \theta(\widetilde{\mathbf{g}}_{t,j_1})^T \phi(\widetilde{\mathbf{g}}_{t,j_2}), \tag{2}$$

where $\theta, \phi \in \mathbb{R}^{C_2}$ denote two transformation functions, each implemented by a 1×1 convolutional layer. Then, SoftMax activation is conducted on each row of A_t to ensure the integration of all edge weights of a node equal to 1. We subsequently obtain the output of the geometry-level graph from the GCN as:

$$Y_t = A_t \widetilde{\mathbf{G}}_t W_g, \tag{3}$$

where $\widetilde{\mathbf{G}}_t = (\widetilde{\mathbf{g}}_{t,1}; \cdots ; \widetilde{\mathbf{g}}_{t,J}) \in \mathbb{R}^{J \times C_1}$ and $W_g \in \mathbb{R}^{C_1 \times C_2}$ is the transformation matrix. The size of output is $T \times J \times C_2$.

4.3   The Fusion-Level Graph

We propose a fusion-level graph to connect the geometric features learned from GCN with visual features. Previous works on CNN-based HOI recognition in videos overemphasise visual features and neglect geometric features of humans and objects [27,33]. State-of-the-arts like ASSIGN [37] also exclude geometric features. In contrast, we first extract visual features for each human or object entity by ROI pooling, and then introduce the geometric output Y_t from the GCN as the auxiliary feature to complement the visual representation. The feature vectors for all entities are then embedded by a two-layer MLP with ReLU activation function to the same hidden size.

A key design of the fusion-level graph is an attention mechanism to estimate the relevance of the interacted neighbouring entity. As illustrated in the fusion-level graph of Fig. 3, each person and object denote an entity through the time, while Y_t forms an additional entity joining the graph. All connections between the visual features of all humans and objects in the video are captured, represented by orange arrows. The blue arrows denote the connection between geometric and object visual features. Empirically, connecting the geometry-object pairs consistently performs better than applying a fully-connected graph with geometry-human connections. A possible reason is that humans are generally bigger in size and therefore have a larger chance of occlusion. Correlating such relatively noisy human visual and geometry features is a harder problem than the objects' equivalent. The fusion strategy is evaluated in the ablation studies.

The attention mechanism employed in the fusion-level graph calculates a weighted average of the contributions from neighbouring nodes, implemented by a variant of scaled dot-product attention [49] with identical keys and values:

$$\text{Att}\left(q, \{z_i\}_{i=1...n}\right) = \sum_{i=1}^{n} \text{softmax}\left(\frac{q^T z_i}{\sqrt{d}}\right) z_i, \tag{4}$$

where q is a query vector, $\{z_i\}$ is a set of keys/values vectors of size n, and d is the feature dimension.

Once fusion-level graph is constructed, we employ ASSIGN [37] as the backbone for HOI recognition. ASSIGN is a recurrent graph network that automatically detects the structure of HOI associated with asynchronous and sparse entities in videos. Our fusion-level graph is compatible with the HOI graph structure in ASSIGN, allowing us to employ the network to predict sub-activities for humans and object-affordances for objects depending on the dataset.

5 Experiments

5.1 Datasets

We have performed experiments on our MPHOI-72 dataset, the CAD-120 [24] dataset and the Bimanual Actions [9] dataset, showcasing the superior results of 2G-GCN on multi-person, single-human and two-hand HOI recognition.

CAD-120 is widely used for HOI recognition. It consists of 120 RGB-D videos of 10 different activities performed individually by 4 participants, with each activity replicated 3 times. A participant interacts with 1–5 objects in each video. There are 10 human sub-activities (*e.g.*, *eating*, *drinking*), and 12 object affordances (*e.g.*, *stationary*, *drinkable*) in total, which are annotated per frame.

Bimanual Actions is the first HOI activity dataset where subjects use two hands to interact with objects (*e.g.*, the left hand holding a piece of wood, while the right hand sawing it). It contains 540 RGB-D videos of 6 subjects performing 9 different activities, with each repeated for 10 times. There are totally 14 action labels for each hand and each entity in a video is annotated frame-wise.

5.2 Implementation Details

Network Settings. We implement 2048-dimensional ROI pooling features extracted from the 2D bounding boxes of humans and objects in the video detected by a Faster R-CNN [40] module, which is pre-trained [2] on the Visual Genome dataset [26] for entity visual features. We set the number of neurons to 64, 128 for both FC layers for the embedding and the transformation functions of Eq. 2 in the geometric-level graph, respectively (*i.e.*, $C_1 = 64$, $C_2 = 128$).

Experimental Settings. 2G-GCN is evaluated on two tasks: 1) joined segmentation, and 2) label recognition given known segmentation. The first task needs the model to segment and identifies the timeline for each entity in a video. The second task is a variant of the previous one, in which the ground-truth segmentation is known and the model requires to name the existing segments.

For the Bimanual Actions and CAD-120 datasets, we use leave-one-subject cross-validation to evaluate the generalization effort of 2G-GCN in unknown subjects. On MPHOI-72, we define a cross-validation scheme that chooses two subjects not present in the training set as the test set.

For evaluation, we report the $F_1@k$ metric [28] with the commonly used thresholds $k = 10\%$, 25% and 50%. The $F_1@k$ metric believes each predicted action segment is correct if its Intersection over Union (IoU) ratio with respect to the corresponding ground truth is at least k. Since it is more sensitive to short action classes and over-segmentation errors, F_1 is more adaptable than the frame-based metrics for joined segmentation and labelling issues, and was frequently adopted in prior segmentation researches [11,28,37].

With four Nvidia Titan RTX GPUs, training MPHOI-72, CAD-120 and Bimanual Actions takes 2 h, 8 h and 5 days, respectively. Testing the whole test set takes 2 min, 3 min and 20 min, respectively.

5.3 Quantitative Comparison

Multi-person HOIs. In our challenging MPHOI-72 dataset, 2G-GCN beats ASSIGN [37] by a considerable gap (Table 1). 2G-GCN significantly outperforms ASSIGN and has smaller standard deviation values in every F_1 configurations, reaching 68.6% in $F_1@10$ score, which is approximately 9.5% higher than ASSIGN. The performance of visual-based methods such as ASSIGN is generally ineffective, since remarkable occlusions in MPHOI typically invalids visual features to HOI recognition task. The significant gaps between the results of 2G-GCN and ASSIGN demonstrate that the application of geometric features and its fusion with visual features can motivate our model to learn stable and essential features even when significant occlusion appears in HOIs.

Table 1. Joined segmentation and label recognition on MPHOI-72.

Model	Sub-activity		
	$F_1@10$	$F_1@25$	$F_1@50$
ASSIGN [37]	59.1 ± 12.1	51.0 ± 16.7	33.2 ± 14.0
2G-GCN	$\mathbf{68.6 \pm 10.4}$	$\mathbf{60.8 \pm 10.3}$	$\mathbf{45.2 \pm 6.5}$

Single-Person HOIs. The generic formulation of 2G-GCN results in excellent performance in single-person HOI recognition. Table 2 presents the results of 2G-GCN with state-of-the-arts and two BiRNN-based baselines on CAD-120. Bidirectional GRU is used as a baseline in both cases: The Independent BiRNN models each entity individually (*i.e.*, there are no spatial messages), but the Relational BiRNN incorporates extensive spatial relations between entities.

Table 2. Joined segmentation and label recognition on CAD-120.

Model	Sub-activity			Object affordance		
	F_1@10	F_1@25	F_1@50	F_1@10	F_1@25	F_1@50
rCRF [42]	65.6 ± 3.2	61.5 ± 4.1	47.1 ± 4.3	72.1 ± 2.5	69.1 ± 3.3	57.0 ± 3.5
Independent BiRNN	70.2 ± 5.5	64.1 ± 5.3	48.9 ± 6.8	84.6 ± 2.1	81.5 ± 2.7	71.4 ± 4.9
ATCRF [23]	72.0 ± 2.8	68.9 ± 3.6	53.5 ± 4.3	79.9 ± 3.1	77.0 ± 4.1	63.3 ± 4.9
Relational BiRNN	79.2 ± 2.5	75.2 ± 3.5	62.5 ± 5.5	82.3 ± 2.3	78.5 ± 2.7	68.9 ± 4.9
ASSIGN [37]	88.0 ± 1.8	84.8 ± 3.0	73.8 ± 5.8	92.0 ± 1.1	90.2 ± 1.8	82.4 ± 3.5
2G-GCN	$\mathbf{89.5 \pm 1.6}$	$\mathbf{87.1 \pm 1.8}$	$\mathbf{76.2 \pm 2.8}$	$\mathbf{92.4 \pm 1.7}$	$\mathbf{90.4 \pm 2.3}$	$\mathbf{82.7 \pm 2.9}$

Table 3. Joined segmentation and label recognition on Bimanual Actions.

Model	Sub-activity		
	F_1@10	F_1@25	F_1@50
Dreher et al. [9]	40.6 ± 7.2	34.8 ± 7.1	22.2 ± 5.7
Independent BiRNN	74.8 ± 7.0	72.0 ± 7.0	61.8 ± 7.3
Relational BiRNN	77.7 ± 3.9	75.0 ± 4.2	64.8 ± 5.3
ASSIGN [37]	84.0 ± 2.0	81.2 ± 2.0	68.5 ± 3.3
2G-GCN	$\mathbf{85.0 \pm 2.2}$	$\mathbf{82.0 \pm 2.6}$	$\mathbf{69.2 \pm 3.1}$

Three previous works, ATCRF [23], rCRF [42] and ASSIGN [37], are fully capable of performing this task, where ASSIGN is relatively new and can improve the scores to higher levels. For both human sub-activity and object affordance labelling, 2G-GCN beats ASSIGN in every configuration of the F_1@k metric. Especially for the sub-activity labelling, 2G-GCN improves 1.5% over ASSIGN in F_1@10, and more than 2% in F_1@{25, 50} with lower standard deviation values. These findings demonstrate the benefits of using geometric features from human skeletons and object bounding boxes, rather than only using visual features like ASSIGN.

Two-Hand HOIs. For two-hand HOI recognition on the Bimanual Actions dataset, 2G-GCN outperforms ASSIGN [37] by about 1%. We compare the performance on the joined segmentation and labelling task with Dreher et al. [9], ASSIGN [37] and BiRNN baselines (Table 3). Dreher et al. [9] have the worst results due to their fairly basic graph network, which ignores hand interactions and does not account for long-term temporal context. By taking into account a larger temporal context, the BiRNN baselines outperform Dreher et al. [9]. Our 2G-GCN has made a small improvement over ASSIGN [37]. This is partly because the hand skeletons provided by the Bimanual Actions dataset are extracted by OpenPose [4], which is relatively weak on hand pose estimation.

5.4   Qualitative Comparison

We compare the visualization of 2G-GCN and relevant methods on our challenging MPHOI-72 dataset. Figure 4 shows an example of segmentation and labelling results with 2G-GCN and ASSIGN [37] approaches compared with the ground-truth for a *Cheering* activity. We highlight some major segmentation errors with red dashed boxes. Although both models have some errors, 2G-GCN is generally more robust to varying segmentation period and activity progression than ASSIGN. 2G-GCN is not particularly sensitive to the timeline of *place* and *approach*, while ASSIGN crashes for most of the activities.

Figure 5 displays an example of a *taking food* activity on the CAD-120 dataset. We highlight over-segmentation with the red dashed box and chaotic segmentation with the blue dashed box. From the figure, our 2G-GCN is able to segment and recognise both human sub-activities and object affordances more accurately than the other two models. ASSIGN [37] and Relational BiRNN fail to predict when the human opens or closes the microwave (*e.g.* the *open* and *close* sub-activities for the human, and the *openable* and *closable* affordances for the microwave).

Figure 6 depicts the qualitative visualization of a *cooking* activity on the Bimanual Actions dataset. Here, 2G-GCN performs outstandingly with precise segmentation and labelling results for the left hand, while ASSIGN [37] and Relational BiRNN have a chaotic performance when segmenting the long *stir* action. In contrast, the right hand has more complex actions, which confuses the models a lot. 2G-GCN generally performs better than ASSIGN, although both of them have some additional and missing segmentations. Relational BiRNN has the worst performance with chaotic segmentation errors in the *hold* action.

5.5   Ablation Studies

The two proposed graphs in our method contain important structural information. We ablate various essential modules and evaluate them on the CAD-120 dataset to demonstrate the role of different 2G-GCN components as shown in Table 4, where GG and FG denote the geometric-level graph and fusion-level graph, respectively.

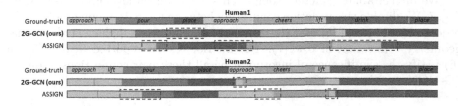

Fig. 4. Visualizing the segmentation and labels on MPHOI-72 for *Cheering*. Red dashed boxes highlights major segmentation errors. (Color figure online)

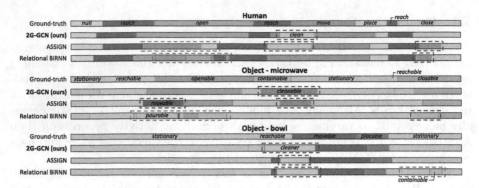

Fig. 5. Visualizing the segmentation and labels on CAD-120 for *taking food*. Red dashed boxes highlight over-segmentation. Blue ones highlight chaotic segmentation. (Color figure online)

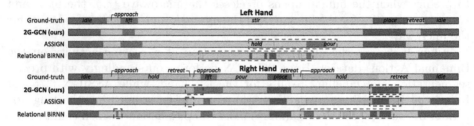

Fig. 6. Visualizing the segmentation and labels on Bimanual Actions for *cooking*. Red dashed boxes highlight extra or missing segmentation. Blue ones highlights chaotic segmentation. (Color figure online)

We firstly investigate the importance for geometric features of the human and objects. The experiments in row (1) drop the human skeleton features in the geometric-level graph, while row (2) drops the object keypoint features. Row (3) explores the effect of the embedding function on geometric features. The last component we ablated is the similarity matrix used in the GCN, the result comparison between row (4) and (8) demonstrates its significance in the model.

We further ablate different components in the fusion-level graph as shown in Fig. 7. We disable the attention connection between the pair of human-object and object-object in row (5) and (6), respectively, and also supplement the human-geometry connection in row (7). The inferior results reported in row (5) and (6) verify the significance of incorporating all these pair connections in our full 2G-GCN model.

Table 4. Ablation study on CAD-120. GG and FG denote the geometric-level graph and the fusion-level graph, respectively.

	Model	Sub-activity		Object affordance	
		F_1@10	F_1@25	F_1@10	F_1@25
(1)	GG (w/o skeletons) & FG	87.7	84.9	91.0	88.3
(2)	GG (w/o objects) & FG	88.3	85.6	90.4	88.5
(3)	GG (w/o embedding) & FG	89.4	86.4	91.5	90.0
(4)	GG (w/o similarity) & FG	88.7	85.0	90.6	89.0
(5)	GG & FG (w/o human-object)	73.4	68.8	90.3	88.4
(6)	GG & FG (w/o object-object)	88.3	84.5	90.9	88.5
(7)	GG & FG (w human-geometry)	89.0	86.6	91.4	89.3
(8)	2G-GCN	**89.5**	**87.1**	**92.4**	**90.4**

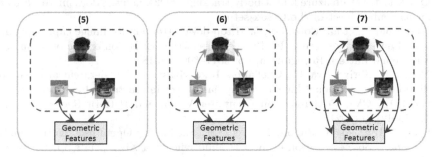

Fig. 7. Ablation study of the fusion-level graph. Human-object, object-object and geometry-human relations are ablated (rows (5), (6), (7) in Table 4 respectively).

6   Conclusions

We propose a two-level graph GCN for tackling HOIs in videos, which consists of a geometric-level graph using human skeletons and object bounding boxes, and a fusion-level graph fusing the geometric features with traditional visual features. We also propose a novel MPHOI-72 dataset to enable and motivate research in multi-person HOI recognition. Our 2G-GCN outperforms state-of-the-art HOI recognition networks in single-person, two-hand and multi-person HOI domains.

Our method is not limited to two humans; the geometric-level graph can represent multiple humans and objects. To handle an arbitrary number of entities, a graph can be constructed by only considering the k-nearest humans and objects, allowing better generalisation [36]. If there are a large number of entities, to avoid handling a large fully-connected graph, we can apply an attention mechanism to learn what nodes are related [44], thereby better recognising HOIs.

We found that the accuracy of skeleton joint detection can affect the quality of geometric features. In future work, we may employ some algorithms for noise handling. Skeleton reconstruction methods such as the lazy learning approach

[47] or motion denoising methods such as the deep learning manifold [52] would enhance the accuracy of skeleton information based on prior learning from a dataset of natural motion. One of our future directions is to employ such techniques to improve our geometric features.

Another future direction is to enrich the geometric representation of objects. While the bounding box features are powerful, it cannot represent the geometric details [60]. On the one hand, the rotation-equivariant detector [19] enriches the object representation with rotated bounding boxes, resulting in improved object detection performance. On the other hand, the recently proposed convex-hull features [16] allow representing objects of irregular shapes and layouts. They could enhance our geometric feature based HOI recognition framework significantly.

References

1. Quickstart: Set up azure kinect body tracking (2022). https://docs.microsoft.com/en-us/azure/kinect-dk/body-sdk-setup
2. Anderson, P., et al.: Bottom-up and top-down attention for image captioning and visual question answering. In: Proceedings of the IEEE Conference on Computer Vision and Pattern Recognition, pp. 6077–6086 (2018)
3. Bodla, N., Shrivastava, G., Chellappa, R., Shrivastava, A.: Hierarchical video prediction using relational layouts for human-object interactions. In: Proceedings of the IEEE/CVF Conference on Computer Vision and Pattern Recognition, pp. 12146–12155 (2021)
4. Cao, Z., Hidalgo, G., Simon, T., Wei, S.E., Sheikh, Y.: OpenPose: realtime multi-person 2D pose estimation using part affinity fields. arXiv e-prints pp. arXiv-1812 (2018)
5. Chao, Y.W., Liu, Y., Liu, X., Zeng, H., Deng, J.: Learning to detect human-object interactions. In: 2018 IEEE Winter Conference on Applications of Computer Vision (WACV), pp. 381–389. IEEE (2018)
6. Dabral, R., Sarkar, S., Reddy, S.P., Ramakrishnan, G.: Exploration of spatial and temporal modeling alternatives for HOI. In: Proceedings of the IEEE/CVF Winter Conference on Applications of Computer Vision, pp. 2281–2290 (2021)
7. Damen, D., et al.: Rescaling egocentric vision: collection, pipeline and challenges for epic-kitchens-100. Int. J. Comput. Vision (IJCV) (2021). https://doi.org/10.1007/s11263-021-01531-2
8. Das, S., Sharma, S., Dai, R., Brémond, F., Thonnat, M.: VPN: learning video-pose embedding for activities of daily living. In: Vedaldi, A., Bischof, H., Brox, T., Frahm, J.-M. (eds.) ECCV 2020. LNCS, vol. 12354, pp. 72–90. Springer, Cham (2020). https://doi.org/10.1007/978-3-030-58545-7_5
9. Dreher, C.R., Wächter, M., Asfour, T.: Learning object-action relations from bimanual human demonstration using graph networks. IEEE Robot. Autom. Lett. 5(1), 187–194 (2020)
10. Fang, H.-S., Cao, J., Tai, Y.-W., Lu, C.: Pairwise body-part attention for recognizing human-object interactions. In: Ferrari, V., Hebert, M., Sminchisescu, C., Weiss, Y. (eds.) ECCV 2018. LNCS, vol. 11214, pp. 52–68. Springer, Cham (2018). https://doi.org/10.1007/978-3-030-01249-6_4
11. Farha, Y.A., Gall, J.: MS-TCN: multi-stage temporal convolutional network for action segmentation. In: Proceedings of the IEEE/CVF Conference on Computer Vision and Pattern Recognition, pp. 3575–3584 (2019)

12. Fouhey, D.F., Kuo, W.C., Efros, A.A., Malik, J.: From lifestyle vlogs to everyday interactions. In: Proceedings of the IEEE Conference on Computer Vision and Pattern Recognition, pp. 4991–5000 (2018)
13. Gao, C., Zou, Y., Huang, J.B.: iCan: instance-centric attention network for human-object interaction detection. arXiv preprint arXiv:1808.10437 (2018)
14. Gkioxari, G., Girshick, R., Dollár, P., He, K.: Detecting and recognizing human-object interactions. In: Proceedings of the IEEE Conference on Computer Vision and Pattern Recognition, pp. 8359–8367 (2018)
15. Gkioxari, G., Girshick, R., Malik, J.: Actions and attributes from wholes and parts. In: Proceedings of the IEEE International Conference on Computer Vision, pp. 2470–2478 (2015)
16. Guo, Z., Liu, C., Zhang, X., Jiao, J., Ji, X., Ye, Q.: Beyond bounding-box: convex-hull feature adaptation for oriented and densely packed object detection. In: Proceedings of the IEEE/CVF Conference on Computer Vision and Pattern Recognition (CVPR), pp. 8792–8801, June 2021
17. Gupta, A., Kembhavi, A., Davis, L.S.: Observing human-object interactions: using spatial and functional compatibility for recognition. IEEE Trans. Pattern Anal. Mach. Intell. **31**(10), 1775–1789 (2009)
18. Gupta, S., Malik, J.: Visual semantic role labeling. arXiv preprint arXiv:1505.04474 (2015)
19. Han, J., Ding, J., Xue, N., Xia, G.S.: ReDet: a rotation-equivariant detector for aerial object detection. In: Proceedings of the IEEE/CVF Conference on Computer Vision and Pattern Recognition (CVPR), pp. 2786–2795, June 2021
20. Jain, A., Zamir, A.R., Savarese, S., Saxena, A.: Structural-RNN: deep learning on spatio-temporal graphs. In: Proceedings of the IEEE Conference on Computer Vision and Pattern Recognition, pp. 5308–5317 (2016)
21. Kato, K., Li, Y., Gupta, A.: Compositional learning for human object interaction. In: Ferrari, V., Hebert, M., Sminchisescu, C., Weiss, Y. (eds.) Computer Vision – ECCV 2018. LNCS, vol. 11218, pp. 247–264. Springer, Cham (2018). https://doi.org/10.1007/978-3-030-01264-9_15
22. Kipf, T.N., Welling, M.: Semi-supervised classification with graph convolutional networks. arXiv preprint arXiv:1609.02907 (2016)
23. Koppula, H.S., Saxena, A.: Anticipating human activities using object affordances for reactive robotic response. IEEE Trans. Pattern Anal. Mach. Intell. **38**(1), 14–29 (2016)
24. Koppula, H.S., Gupta, R., Saxena, A.: Learning human activities and object affordances from RGB-D videos. Int. J. Robot. Res. **32**(8), 951–970 (2013)
25. Krebs, F., Meixner, A., Patzer, I., Asfour, T.: The kit bimanual manipulation dataset. In: IEEE/RAS International Conference on Humanoid Robots (Humanoids) (2021)
26. Krishna, R., et al.: Visual genome: connecting language and vision using crowd-sourced dense image annotations. Int. J. Comput. Vision **123**(1), 32–73 (2017)
27. Le, H., Sahoo, D., Chen, N.F., Hoi, S.C.: BIST: bi-directional spatio-temporal reasoning for video-grounded dialogues. arXiv preprint arXiv:2010.10095 (2020)
28. Lea, C., Flynn, M.D., Vidal, R., Reiter, A., Hager, G.D.: Temporal convolutional networks for action segmentation and detection. In: Proceedings of the IEEE Conference on Computer Vision and Pattern Recognition, pp. 156–165 (2017)
29. Li, Y., Nevatia, R.: Key object driven multi-category object recognition, localization and tracking using spatio-temporal context. In: Forsyth, D., Torr, P., Zisserman, A. (eds.) ECCV 2008. LNCS, vol. 5305, pp. 409–422. Springer, Heidelberg (2008). https://doi.org/10.1007/978-3-540-88693-8_30

30. Liang, Z., Liu, J., Guan, Y., Rojas, J.: Pose-based modular network for human-object interaction detection. arXiv preprint arXiv:2008.02042 (2020)
31. Loper, M., Mahmood, N., Romero, J., Pons-Moll, G., Black, M.J.: SMPL: a skinned multi-person linear model. ACM Trans. Graph. (TOG) **34**(6), 1–16 (2015)
32. Mallya, A., Lazebnik, S.: Learning models for actions and person-object interactions with transfer to question answering. In: Leibe, B., Matas, J., Sebe, N., Welling, M. (eds.) ECCV 2016. LNCS, vol. 9905, pp. 414–428. Springer, Cham (2016). https://doi.org/10.1007/978-3-319-46448-0_25
33. Maraghi, V.O., Faez, K.: Zero-shot learning on human-object interaction recognition in video. In: 2019 5th Iranian Conference on Signal Processing and Intelligent Systems (ICSPIS), pp. 1–7. IEEE (2019)
34. Materzynska, J., Xiao, T., Herzig, R., Xu, H., Wang, X., Darrell, T.: Something-else: compositional action recognition with spatial-temporal interaction networks. In: Proceedings of the IEEE/CVF Conference on Computer Vision and Pattern Recognition, pp. 1049–1059 (2020)
35. Miller, G.A.: Wordnet: a lexical database for English. Commun. ACM **38**(11), 39–41 (1995)
36. Mohamed, A., Qian, K., Elhoseiny, M., Claudel, C.: Social-STGCNN: a social spatio-temporal graph convolutional neural network for human trajectory prediction. In: Proceedings of the IEEE/CVF Conference on Computer Vision and Pattern Recognition, pp. 14424–14432 (2020)
37. Morais, R., Le, V., Venkatesh, S., Tran, T.: Learning asynchronous and sparse human-object interaction in videos. In: Proceedings of the IEEE/CVF Conference on Computer Vision and Pattern Recognition, pp. 16041–16050 (2021)
38. Qi, S., Wang, W., Jia, B., Shen, J., Zhu, S.-C.: Learning human-object interactions by graph parsing neural networks. In: Ferrari, V., Hebert, M., Sminchisescu, C., Weiss, Y. (eds.) ECCV 2018. LNCS, vol. 11213, pp. 407–423. Springer, Cham (2018). https://doi.org/10.1007/978-3-030-01240-3_25
39. Qiu, L., et al.: Peeking into occluded joints: a novel framework for crowd pose estimation. In: Vedaldi, A., Bischof, H., Brox, T., Frahm, J.-M. (eds.) ECCV 2020. LNCS, vol. 12364, pp. 488–504. Springer, Cham (2020). https://doi.org/10.1007/978-3-030-58529-7_29
40. Ren, S., He, K., Girshick, R., Sun, J.: Faster R-CNN: towards real-time object detection with region proposal networks. IEEE Trans. Pattern Anal. Mach. Intell. **39**(6), 1137–1149 (2016)
41. Saito, S., Simon, T., Saragih, J., Joo, H.: PifuHD: multi-level pixel-aligned implicit function for high-resolution 3D human digitization. In: Proceedings of the IEEE/CVF Conference on Computer Vision and Pattern Recognition (CVPR), June 2020
42. Sener, O., Saxena, A.: RCRF: recursive belief estimation over CRFs in RGB-D activity videos. In: Robotics: Science and Systems. Citeseer (2015)
43. Shi, L., Zhang, Y., Cheng, J., Lu, H.: Two-stream adaptive graph convolutional networks for skeleton-based action recognition. In: Proceedings of the IEEE/CVF Conference on Computer Vision and Pattern Recognition, pp. 12026–12035 (2019)
44. Shi, L., et al.: SGCN: sparse graph convolution network for pedestrian trajectory prediction. In: Proceedings of the IEEE/CVF Conference on Computer Vision and Pattern Recognition, pp. 8994–9003 (2021)
45. Shu, T., Gao, X., Ryoo, M.S., Zhu, S.C.: Learning social affordance grammar from videos: transferring human interactions to human-robot interactions. In: 2017 IEEE International Conference on Robotics and Automation (ICRA), pp. 1669–1676. IEEE (2017)

46. Shu, T., Ryoo, M.S., Zhu, S.C.: Learning social affordance for human-robot interaction. arXiv preprint arXiv:1604.03692 (2016)
47. Shum, H.P., Ho, E.S., Jiang, Y., Takagi, S.: Real-time posture reconstruction for microsoft kinect. IEEE Trans. Cybern. **43**(5), 1357–1369 (2013)
48. Ulutan, O., Iftekhar, A.S.M., Manjunath, B.S.: VSGNET: spatial attention network for detecting human object interactions using graph convolutions. In: IEEE/CVF Conference on Computer Vision and Pattern Recognition (CVPR), pp. 13617–13626 (2020)
49. Vaswani, A., et al.: Attention is all you need. In: Advances in Neural Information Processing Systems, pp. 5998–6008 (2017)
50. Wan, B., Zhou, D., Liu, Y., Li, R., He, X.: Pose-aware multi-level feature network for human object interaction detection. In: Proceedings of the IEEE/CVF International Conference on Computer Vision, pp. 9469–9478 (2019)
51. Wang, H., Zheng, W., Yingbiao, L.: Contextual heterogeneous graph network for human-object interaction detection. In: Vedaldi, A., Bischof, H., Brox, T., Frahm, J.-M. (eds.) ECCV 2020. LNCS, vol. 12362, pp. 248–264. Springer, Cham (2020). https://doi.org/10.1007/978-3-030-58520-4_15
52. Wang, H., Ho, E.S.L., Shum, H.P.H., Zhu, Z.: Spatio-temporal manifold learning for human motions via long-horizon modeling. IEEE Trans. Vis. Comput. Graph. **27**(1), 216–227 (2021). https://doi.org/10.1109/TVCG.2019.2936810
53. Wang, N., Zhu, G., Zhang, L., Shen, P., Li, H., Hua, C.: Spatio-temporal interaction graph parsing networks for human-object interaction recognition. In: Proceedings of the 29th ACM International Conference on Multimedia, pp. 4985–4993 (2021)
54. Wang, X., Girshick, R., Gupta, A., He, K.: Non-local neural networks. In: Proceedings of the IEEE Conference on Computer Vision and Pattern Recognition, pp. 7794–7803 (2018)
55. Xiu, Y., Li, J., Wang, H., Fang, Y., Lu, C.: Pose flow: efficient online pose tracking. arXiv preprint arXiv:1802.00977 (2018)
56. Xu, B., Wong, Y., Li, J., Zhao, Q., Kankanhalli, M.S.: Learning to detect human-object interactions with knowledge. In: Proceedings of the IEEE/CVF Conference on Computer Vision and Pattern Recognition (2019)
57. Yan, S., Xiong, Y., Lin, D.: Spatial temporal graph convolutional networks for skeleton-based action recognition. In: Thirty-Second AAAI Conference on Artificial Intelligence (2018)
58. Zhang, P., Lan, C., Zeng, W., Xing, J., Xue, J., Zheng, N.: Semantics-guided neural networks for efficient skeleton-based human action recognition. In: Proceedings of the IEEE/CVF Conference on Computer Vision and Pattern Recognition, pp. 1112–1121 (2020)
59. Zheng, S., Chen, S., Jin, Q.: Skeleton-based interactive graph network for human object interaction detection. In: 2020 IEEE International Conference on Multimedia and Expo (ICME), pp. 1–6. IEEE (2020)
60. Zhu, M., Ho, E.S.L., Shum, H.P.H.: A skeleton-aware graph convolutional network for human-object interaction detection. In: Proceedings of the 2022 IEEE International Conference on Systems, Man, and Cybernetics. SMC 2022 (2022)
61. Zhuang, B., Wu, Q., Shen, C., Reid, I., van den Hengel, A.: Care about you: towards large-scale human-centric visual relationship detection. arXiv preprint arXiv:1705.09892 (2017)

ActionFormer: Localizing Moments of Actions with Transformers

Chen-Lin Zhang[1,2]($\boxtimes$) (iD), Jianxin Wu[1] (iD), and Yin Li[3]($\boxtimes$) (iD)

[1] State Key Laboratory for Novel Software Technology, Nanjing University,
Nanjing, China
zclnjucs@gmail.com
[2] 4Paradigm Inc., Beijing, China
[3] University of Wisconsin-Madison, Madison, USA
yin.li@wisc.edu

Abstract. Self-attention based Transformer models have demonstrated impressive results for image classification and object detection, and more recently for video understanding. Inspired by this success, we investigate the application of Transformer networks for temporal action localization in videos. To this end, we present ActionFormer—a simple yet powerful model to identify actions in time and recognize their categories in a single shot, without using action proposals or relying on pre-defined anchor windows. ActionFormer combines a multiscale feature representation with local self-attention, and uses a light-weighted decoder to classify every moment in time and estimate the corresponding action boundaries. We show that this orchestrated design results in major improvements upon prior works. Without bells and whistles, ActionFormer achieves 71.0% mAP at tIoU = 0.5 on THUMOS14, outperforming the best prior model by 14.1 absolute percentage points. Further, ActionFormer demonstrates strong results on ActivityNet 1.3 (36.6% average mAP) and EPIC-Kitchens 100 (+13.5% average mAP over prior works). Our code is available at https://github.com/happyharrycn/actionformer_release.

Keywords: Temporal action localization · Action recognition · Egocentric vision · Vision transformers · Video understanding

1 Introduction

Identifying action instances in time and recognizing their categories, known as temporal action localization (TAL), remains a challenging problem in video understanding. Significant progress has been made in developing deep models for TAL. Most previous works have considered using action proposals [32] or anchor windows [46], and developed convolutional [51,79], recurrent [6], and

---

C.-L. Zhang—Work was done when visiting UW Madison.

Supplementary Information The online version contains supplementary material available at https://doi.org/10.1007/978-3-031-19772-7_29.

graph [3,69,72] neural networks for TAL. Despite a steady progress on major benchmarks, the accuracy of existing methods usually comes at a price of modeling complexity, with increasingly sophisticated proposal generation, anchor design, loss function, network architecture, and output decoding process.

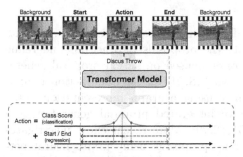

Fig. 1. An illustration of our Action-Former. We propose a Transformer based model to localize action instances in time (*top*) by (1) classifying every moment into action categories and (2) estimating their distances to action boundaries (*bottom*).

In this paper, we adopt a minimalist design and develop a Transformer based model for TAL, inspired by the recent success of Transformers in NLP [18,59] and vision [10,19,44]. Originally developed for sequence data, Transformers use self-attention to model long-range dependencies, and thus are a natural fit for TAL in untrimmed videos. Our method, illustrated in Fig. 1, adapts local self-attention to model temporal context in an input untrimmed videos, classifies every moment, and regresses their corresponding action boundaries. The result is a deep model trained using standard classification and regression loss, and can localize moments of actions in a single shot, without using action proposals or pre-defined anchor windows.

Specifically, our model, dubbed ActionFormer, integrates local self-attention to extract a feature pyramid from an input video. Each location in the output pyramid represents a moment in the video, and is treated as an action candidate. A lightweight convolutional decoder is further employed on the feature pyramid to classify these candidates into foreground action categories, and to regress the distance between a foreground candidate and its action onset and offset. The results can be easily decoded into actions with their labels and temporal boundaries. Our method thus provides a *single-stage anchor-free* model for TAL.

We show that such a simple model, with proper design, can be surprisingly powerful for TAL. In particular, ActionFormer establishes a new state of the art across several major TAL benchmarks, surpassing previous works by a significant margin. For example, ActionFormer achieves 71.0% mAP at tIoU $= 0.5$ on THUMOS14, outperforming the best prior model by 14.1 absolute percentage points. Further, ActionFormer reaches an average mAP of 36.6% on ActivityNet 1.3. More importantly, ActionFormer shows impressive results on EPIC-Kitchens 100 for egocentric action localization, with a boost of over 13.5 absolute percentage points in average mAP.

Our work is based on simple techniques, supported by favourable empirical results, and validated by extensive ablation experiments, at our best. Our main contributions are summarized as follows. First, we are among the first to propose a Transformer based model for single-stage anchor-free TAL. Second, we study key design choices of developing Transformer models for TAL, and demonstrate a simple model that works surprisingly well. Finally, our model achieves state-of-the-art results across major benchmarks and offers a solid baseline for TAL.

2   Related Works

Two-Stage TAL. These approaches first generate candidate video segments as action proposals, and further classify the proposals into actions and refine their temporal boundaries. Previous works focused on action proposal generation, by either classifying anchor windows [7,8,21] or detecting action boundaries [25,32,34,43,78], and more recently using a graph representation [3,69] or Transformers [12,54,61]. Others have integrated proposal generation and classification into a single model [13,51,52,79]. More recent effort investigates the modeling of temporal context among proposals using graph neural networks [69,74,77] or attention and self-attention mechanisms [48,53,83]. Similar to previous approaches, our method considers the modeling of long-term temporal context, yet uses a self-attention within a Transformer model. Different from previous approaches, our model detects actions without using proposals.

Single-Stage TAL. Several recent works focused on single-stage TAL, seeking to localize actions in a single shot without using action proposals. Many of them are anchor-based (*e.g.*, using anchor windows sampled from sliding windows). Lin *et al.* [33] presented the first single-stage TAL using convolutional networks, borrowing ideas from a single-stage object detector [40]. Buch *et al.* [6] presented a recurrent memory module for single-stage TAL. Long *et al.* [46] proposed to use Gaussian kernels to dynamically optimize the scale of each anchor, based on a 1D convolutional network. Yang *et al.* [71] explored the combination of anchor-based and anchor-free models for single-stage TAL, again using convolutional networks. More recently, Lin *et al.* [31] proposed an anchor-free single-stage model by designing a saliency-based refinement module incorporated in convolutional network. Similar ideas were also explored in video grounding [75].

Our model falls into the category of single-stage TAL. Indeed, our formulation follows a minimalist design of sequence labeling by classifying every moment and regressing their action boundaries, previously discussed in [31,71]. The key difference is that we design a Transformer network for action localization. The result is a single stage anchor-free model that outperforms all previous methods. A concurrent work from Liu *et al.* [42] also used Transformer for TAL, yet considered a set prediction problem similar to DETR [10].

Spatial-Temporal Action Localization. A related yet different task, known as spatial-temporal action localization, is to detect the actions both temporally and spatially, in the form of moving bounding boxes of an actor. It is possible that TAL might be used as a first step for spatial-temporal localization. Girdhar *et al.* [24] proposed to use Transformer for spatial-temporal action localization. While both our work and [24] use Transformer, the two models differ significantly. We consider a sequence of video frames as the inputs, while [24] used a set of 2D object proposals. Moreover, our work addresses a different task of TAL.

Object Detection. TAL models have been heavily influenced by the developments of object detection models. Some of our model design, including the multiscale feature representation and convolutional decoder, is inspired by feature pyramid network [35] and RetinaNet [36]. Our training using center sampling also stems from recent single-stage object detectors [20,55,76].

Vision Transformer. Transformer models were originally developed for NLP tasks [59], and has demonstrated recent success for many vision tasks. ViT [19] presented the first pure Transformer-based model that can achieve state-of-the-art performances on image classification. Subsequent works, including DeiT [56], T2T-ViT [73], Swin Transformer [44], Focal Transformer [70] and PVT [64], have further pushed the envelope, resulting in vision Transformer backbones with impressive results on classification, segmentation, and detection tasks. Transformer have also been explored in object detection [10,16,63,82], semantic segmentation [14,65,67], and video representation learning [2,22,45]. Our model builds on these developments and presents one of the first Transformer models for TAL.

3   ActionFormer: A Simple Transformer Model for Temporal Action Localization

Given an input video $\mathbf{X}$, we assume that $\mathbf{X}$ can be represented using a set of feature vectors $\mathbf{X} = \{\mathbf{x}_1, \mathbf{x}_2, \ldots, \mathbf{x}_T\}$ defined on discretized time steps $t = \{1, 2, \ldots, T\}$, where the total duration T varies across videos. For example, $\mathbf{x}_t$ can be the feature vector of a video clip at moment t extracted from a 3D convolutional network. The goal of temporal action localization is to predict the action label $\mathbf{Y} = \{\mathbf{y}_1, \mathbf{y}_2, \ldots, \mathbf{y}_N\}$ based on the input video sequence $\mathbf{X}$. $\mathbf{Y}$ consists of N action instances $\mathbf{y}_i$, where N also varies across videos. Each instance $\mathbf{y}_i = (s_i, e_i, a_i)$ is defined by its starting time s_i (onset), ending time e_i (offset) and its action label a_i, where $s_i \in [1, T]$, $e_i \in [1, T]$, $a_i \in \{1, .., C\}$ (C pre-defined categories) and $s_i < e_i$. The task of TAL is thus a challenging problem of structured output prediction.

A Simple Representation for Action Localization. Our method builds on an anchor-free representation for action localization, inspired by [31,71]. The key idea is to classify each moment as either one of the action categories or the background, and further regress the distance between this time step and the action's onset and offset. In doing so, we convert the structured output prediction problem ($\mathbf{X} = \{\mathbf{x}_1, \mathbf{x}_2, \ldots, \mathbf{x}_T\} \rightarrow \mathbf{Y} = \{\mathbf{y}_1, \mathbf{y}_2, \ldots, \mathbf{y}_N\}$) into a more approachable sequence labeling problem

$$\mathbf{X} = \{\mathbf{x}_1, \mathbf{x}_2, \ldots, \mathbf{x}_T\} \rightarrow \hat{\mathbf{Y}} = \{\hat{\mathbf{y}}_1, \hat{\mathbf{y}}_2, \ldots, \hat{\mathbf{y}}_T\}. \tag{1}$$

The output $\hat{\mathbf{y}}_t = (p(a_t), d_t^s, d_t^e)$ at time t is defined as

- $p(a_t)$ consists of C values, with each representing a binomial variable indicating the probability of action category a_t ($\in \{1, 2, \ldots, C\}$) at time t. This can be considered as the outputs of C binary classification.

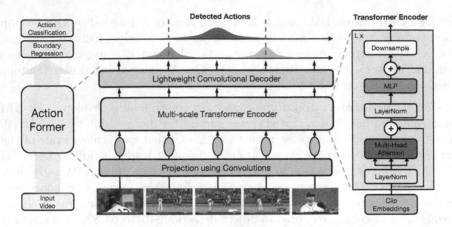

Fig. 2. Overview of our ActionFormer. Our method builds a Transformer based model to detect an action instance by classifying every moment and estimating action boundaries. Specifically, ActionFormer first extracts a sequence of video clip features, and embeds each of these features. The embedded features are further encoded into a feature pyramid using a multi-scale Transformer (right). The feature pyramid is then examined by shared classification and regression heads, producing an action candidate at every time step. Our method provides a single-stage anchor-free model for temporal action localization with strong performance across several datasets.

- $d_t^s > 0$ and $d_t^e > 0$ are the distance between the current time t to the action's onset and offset, respectively. d_t^s and d_t^e are not defined if the time step t lies on the background.

Intuitively, this formulation considers *every moment* t in the video $\mathbf{X}$ as an action candidate, recognizes the action's category a_t, and estimates the distances between current step and the action boundaries (d_t^s and d_t^e) if an action presents. Action localization results can be readily decoded from $\hat{\mathbf{y}}_t = (p(a_t), d_t^s, d_t^e)$ by

$$a_t = arg\,max\ p(a_t), \quad s_t = t - d_t^s, \quad e_t = t + d_t^e. \tag{2}$$

Method Overview. Our model—ActionFormer learns to label an input video sequence $f(\mathbf{X}) \to \hat{\mathbf{Y}}$. Specifically, f is realized using a deep model. ActionFormer follows an encoder-decoder architecture proven successful in many vision tasks, and decomposes f as $h \circ g$. Here $g \colon \mathbf{X} \to \mathbf{Z}$ encodes the input into a latent vector $\mathbf{Z}$, and $h \colon \mathbf{Z} \to \hat{\mathbf{Y}}$ subsequently decodes $\mathbf{Z}$ into the sequence label $\hat{\mathbf{Y}}$.

Figure 2 presents an overview of our model. Importantly, our encoder g is parameterized by a Transformer network [59]. Our decoder h adopts a lightweight convolutional network. To capture actions at various temporal scales, we design a multi-scale feature representation $\mathbf{Z} = \{\mathbf{Z}^1, \mathbf{Z}^2, \ldots, \mathbf{Z}^L\}$ forming a feature pyramid with varying resolutions. Note that our model operates on a temporal axis defined by feature grids rather than the absolute time, allowing it to adapt to videos with different frame rates. We now describe the details of our model.

3.1   Encode Videos with Transformer

Our model first encodes an input video $\mathbf{X} = \{\mathbf{x}_1, \mathbf{x}_2, \ldots, \mathbf{x}_T\}$ into a multiscale feature representation $\mathbf{Z} = \{\mathbf{Z}^1, \mathbf{Z}^2, \ldots, \mathbf{Z}^L\}$ using an encoder g. The encoder g consists of (1) a projection function using a convolutional network that embeds each feature $(\mathbf{x}_t)$ into a D-dimensional space; and (2) a Transformer network that maps the embedded features to the output feature pyramid $\mathbf{Z}$.

Projection. Our projection $\mathbf{E}$ is a shallow convolutional network with ReLU as the activation function, defined as

$$\mathbf{Z}^0 = [\mathbf{E}(\mathbf{x}_1), \mathbf{E}(\mathbf{x}_2), \ldots, \mathbf{E}(\mathbf{x}_T)]^T, \tag{3}$$

where $\mathbf{E}(\mathbf{x}_i) \in \mathbb{R}^D$ is the embedded feature of $\mathbf{x}_i$. Adding convolutions before a Transformer network was recently found helpful to better incorporate local context for time series data [28] and to stabilize the training of vision Transformers [66]. An position embedding [59] $\mathbf{E}_{pos} \in \mathbb{R}^{T \times D}$ can be optionally added. However, we find that doing so will decrease the performance of the model, and have thus removed position embeddings in our model by default.

Local Self-attention. The Transformer network further takes $\mathbf{Z}^0$ as input. The core of a Transformer is self-attention [59]. We briefly introduce the key idea to make the paper self-contained. Concretely, self-attention computes a weighted average of features with the weight proportional to a similarity score between pairs of input features. Given $\mathbf{Z}^0 \in \mathbb{R}^{T \times D}$ with T time steps of D dimensional features, $\mathbf{Z}^0$ is projected using $\mathbf{W}_Q \in \mathbb{R}^{D \times D_q}$, $\mathbf{W}_K \in \mathbb{R}^{D \times D_k}$, and $\mathbf{W}_V \in \mathbb{R}^{D \times D_v}$ to extract feature representations $\mathbf{Q}$, $\mathbf{K}$, and $\mathbf{V}$, referred to as query, key and value respectively with $D_k = D_q$. The outputs $\mathbf{Q}$, $\mathbf{K}$, $\mathbf{V}$ are computed as

$$\mathbf{Q} = \mathbf{Z}^0 \mathbf{W}_Q, \quad \mathbf{K} = \mathbf{Z}^0 \mathbf{W}_K, \quad \mathbf{V} = \mathbf{Z}^0 \mathbf{W}_V. \tag{4}$$

The output of self-attention is given by

$$\mathbf{S} = \text{softmax}\left(\mathbf{Q}\mathbf{K}^T / \sqrt{D_q}\right) \mathbf{V}, \tag{5}$$

where $\mathbf{S} \in \mathbb{R}^{T \times D}$ and softmax is performed *row-wise*. A multiheaded self-attention (MSA) further adds several self-attention operations in parallel.

A main advantage of MSA is the ability to integrate temporal context across the full sequence, yet such a benefit comes at the cost of computation. A vanilla MSA has a complexity of $O(T^2 D + D^2 T)$ in both memory and time, and is thus highly inefficient for long videos. There has been several recent work on efficient self-attention [4,15,62,68]. Here we adapt the local self-attention from [15] by limiting the attention within a local window. Our intuition is the temporal context beyond a certain range is less helpful for action localization. Such a local self-attention significantly reduces the complexity to $O(W^2 T D + D^2 T)$ with W the local window size ($\ll T$). Importantly, local self-attention is used in tandem with the multiscale feature representation $\mathbf{Z} = \{\mathbf{Z}^1, \mathbf{Z}^2, \ldots, \mathbf{Z}^L\}$, using the same window size on each pyramid level. With this design, a small window size (19) on a downsampled feature map (16x) will cover a large temporal range (304).

Multiscale Transformer. We now present the design of our Transformer encoder. Our Transformer has L Transformer layers with each layer consisting of alternating layers of local multiheaded self-attention (MSA) and MLP blocks. Moreover, LayerNorm (LN) is applied before every MSA or MLP block, and residual connection is added after every block. GELU is used for the MLP. To capture actions at different temporal scales, a downsampling operator $\downarrow(\cdot)$ is optionally attached. This is given by

$$\bar{\mathbf{Z}}^\ell = \alpha^\ell \, \mathrm{MSA}(\mathrm{LN}(\mathbf{Z}^{\ell-1})) + \mathbf{Z}^{\ell-1}, \quad \hat{\mathbf{Z}}^\ell = \bar{\alpha}^\ell \, \mathrm{MLP}(\mathrm{LN}(\bar{\mathbf{Z}}^\ell)) + \bar{\mathbf{Z}}^\ell,$$
$$\mathbf{Z}^\ell = \downarrow(\hat{\mathbf{Z}}^\ell), \quad \ell = 1 \ldots L, \tag{6}$$

where $\mathbf{Z}^{\ell-1}, \bar{\mathbf{Z}}^\ell, \hat{\mathbf{Z}}^\ell \in \mathbb{R}^{T^{\ell-1} \times D}$ and $\mathbf{Z}^\ell \in \mathbb{R}^{T^\ell \times D}$. $T^{\ell-1}/T^\ell$ is the downsampling ratio. α^ℓ and $\bar{\alpha}^\ell$ are learnable per-channel scaling factors as in [57].

The downsampling operator $\downarrow$ is implemented using a strided depthwise 1D convolution due to its efficiency. We use 2x downsampling for our model. Our Transformer block is shown in Fig. 2 (right). Our model further combines several Transformer blocks with downsampling in between, resulting in a feature pyramid $\mathbf{Z} = \{\mathbf{Z}^1, \mathbf{Z}^2, \ldots, \mathbf{Z}^L\}$.

3.2   Decoding Actions in Time

Next, our model decodes the feature pyramid $\mathbf{Z}$ from the encoder g into the sequence label $\hat{\mathbf{Y}} = \{\hat{\mathbf{y}}_1, \hat{\mathbf{y}}_2, \ldots, \hat{\mathbf{y}}_T\}$ using the decoder h. Our decoder is a lightweight convolutional network with a classification and a regression head.

Classification Head. Given the feature pyramid Z, our classification head examines each moment t across all L levels on the pyramid, and predicts the probability of action $p(a_t)$ at every moment t.[1] This is realized using a lightweight 1D convolutional network attached to each pyramid level with its parameters shared across all levels. Our classification network is implemented using 3 layers of 1D convolutions with kernel size=3, layer normalization (for the first 2 layers), and ReLU activation. A sigmoid function is attached to each output dimension to predict the probability of C action categories. Adding layer normalization slightly boosts the performance as we will demonstrate in our ablation.

Regression Head. Similar to our classification head, our regression head examines every moment t across all L levels on the pyramid. The difference is that the regression head predicts the distances to the onset and offset of an action (d_t^s, d_t^e), only if the current time step t lies in an action. An output regression range is pre-specified for each pyramid level. The regression head, again, is implemented using a 1D convolutional network following the same design of the classification network, except that a ReLU is attached at the end for distance estimation.

3.3   ActionFormer: Model Design

Putting things together, ActionFormer is conceptually simple: each feature on the feature pyramid $\mathbf{Z}$ outputs an action score $p(a)$ and the corresponding

---

[1] Without loss of clarity, we drop the index of the pyramid ℓ.

temporal boundaries (s, e), which are then used to decode an action candidate. Notwithstanding the simplicity, we find that several key architecture designs are important to ensure a strong performance. We discuss these design choices here.

Design of the Feature Pyramid. A critical component of our model is the design of the temporal feature pyramid $\mathbf{Z} = \{\mathbf{Z}^1, \mathbf{Z}^2, \ldots, \mathbf{Z}^L\}$. The design choices include (1) the number of levels within the pyramid; (2) the downsampling ratio between successive feature maps; and (3) the output regression range of each pyramid level. Inspired by the design of feature pyramid in modern object detectors (FPN [35] and FCOS [55]), we simplify our design choices by using a 2x downsampling of the feature maps, and roughly enlarging the output regression range by 2 accordingly. We explore different design choices in our ablation.

Loss Function. Our model outputs $(p(a_t), d_t^s, d_t^e)$ for every moment t, including the probability of action categories $p(a_t)$ and the distances to action boundaries (d_t^s, d_t^e). Our loss function, again following minimalist design, only has two terms: (1) $\mathcal{L}_{cls}$ a focal loss [36] for C way binary classification; and (2) $\mathcal{L}_{reg}$ a DIoU loss [81] for distance regression. The loss is defined for each video X as

$$\mathcal{L} = \sum_t \left(\mathcal{L}_{cls} + \lambda_{reg} \mathbb{1}_{c_t} \mathcal{L}_{reg} \right) / T_+, \tag{7}$$

where T_+ is the total number of positive samples. $\mathbb{1}_{c_t}$ is an indicator function that denotes if a time step t is within an action, *i.e.*, a positive sample. $\mathcal{L}$ is applied to all levels on the output pyramid, and averaged across all video samples during training. λ_{reg} is a coefficient balancing the classification and regression loss. We set $\lambda_{reg}{=}1$ by default and study the choice of λ_{reg} in our ablation.

Importantly, $\mathcal{L}_{cls}$ uses Focal loss [55] to recognize C action categories. Focal loss naturally handles imbalanced samples – there are much more negative samples than positive ones. Moreover, $\mathcal{L}_{reg}$ adopts a differentiable IoU loss [50]. $\mathcal{L}_{reg}$ is only enabled when the current time step contains a positive sample.

Center Sampling. During training, we find it helpful to adapt a center sampling strategy similar to [55,76], as we will show in our ablation study. Specifically, when determining the positive samples, only time steps within an interval around the center of an action are considered positive, where the duration of interval is proportional to the feature stride of the current pyramid level ℓ. More precisely, given an action centered at c, any time step $t \in [c - \alpha T/T^\ell, c + \alpha T/T^\ell]$ at the pyramid level ℓ is considered as positive, where $\alpha = 1.5$. Center sampling does not impact model inference, yet encourages higher scores around action centers.

3.4 Implementation Details

Training. Following [24], we use Adam [27] with warm-up for training. The warm-up stage is critical for model convergence and good performance, as also pointed out by [38]. When training with variable length input, we fix the maximum input sequence length, pad or cropped the input sequences accordingly, and add proper masking for operations in the model. This is equal to training with sliding windows as in [71]. Varying the maximum input sequence length during training has little impact to the performance, as shown in our ablation.

Inference. At inference time, we feed the full sequences into the model, as no position embeddings are used in the model. Our model takes the input video $\mathbf{X}$, and outputs $\{(p(a_t), d_t^s, d_t^e))\}$ for every time step t across all pyramid levels. Each time step t further decodes an action instance $(e_t = t - d_t^s, s_t = t + d_t^e, p(a_t))$. e_t and s_t are the onset and offset of the action, and $p(a_t)$ is an action confidence score. The result action candidates are further processed using Soft-NMS [5] to remove highly overlapping instances, leading to the final outputs of actions.

Network Architecture. We used 2 convolutions for projection, 7 Transformer blocks for the encoder (all using local attention and with 2x downsampling for the last 5), and separate classification and regression heads as the decoder. The regression range on each pyramid level was normalized by the stride of the features. More details are presented in the supplement.

4   Experiments and Results

We now present our experiments and results. Our main results include benchmarks on THUMOS14 [26], ActivityNet-1.3 [9] and EPIC-Kitchens 100 [17]. Moreover, we provide extensive ablation studies of our model.

Evaluation Metric. For all datasets, we report the standard mean average precision (mAP) at different temporal intersection over union (tIoU) thresholds, widely used to evaluate TAL methods. tIoU is defined as the intersection over union between two temporal windows, $i.e.$, the 1D Jaccard index. Given a tIoU threshold, mAP computes the mean of average prevision across all action categories. An average mAP is also reported by averaging across several tIoUs.

Baseline and Comparison. For our main results on THUMOS14 [26] and ActivityNet-1.3 [9]. We compare to a strong set of baselines, including both two-stage ($e.g.$, G-TAD [69], BC-GNN [3], TAL-MR [78]) and single-stage ($e.g.$, A2Net [71], GTAN [46], AFSD [31], TadTR [42]) methods for TAL. Our close competitors are those single-stage methods. Despite our best attempt for a fair comparison, we recognize some of our baselines used different setups ($e.g.$, video features). Our experiment setup follows previous works [37,78]. And our intention here is to compare our results to the best results previously reported.

4.1   Results on THUMOS14

Dataset. THUMOS14 [26] dataset contains 413 untrimmed videos with 20 categories of actions. The dataset is divided into two subsets: validation set and test set. The validation set contains 200 videos and the test set contains 213 videos. Following the common practice [32,34,69,78], we use the validation set for training and report results on the test set.

Experiment Setup. We used two-stream I3D [11] pretrained on Kinetics to extract the video features on THUMOS14, following [37,78]. mAP@[0.3:0.1:0.7]

Table 1. Results on THUMOS14 and ActivityNet1.3. We report mAP at different tIoU thresholds. Average mAP in [0.3:0.1:0.7] is reported on THUMOS14 and [0.5:0.05:0.95] on ActivityNet1.3. Best results are in **bold** and second best underlined. Our method outperforms previous methods on THUMOS14 by a large margin, and beats previous methods when using the same features on ActivityNet1.3.

Type	Model	Feature	THUMOS14						ActivityNet1.3			
			0.3	0.4	0.5	0.6	0.7	Avg.	0.5	0.75	0.95	Avg.
Two-stage	BMN [32]	TSN [60]	56.0	47.4	38.8	29.7	20.5	38.5	50.1	34.8	8.3	33.9
	DBG [30]	TSN [60]	57.8	49.4	39.8	30.2	21.7	39.8	—	—	—	—
	G-TAD [69]	TSN [60]	54.5	47.6	40.3	30.8	23.4	39.3	50.4	34.6	9.0	34.1
	BC-GNN [3]	TSN [60]	57.1	49.1	40.4	31.2	23.1	40.2	50.6	34.8	**9.4**	34.3
	TAL-MR [78]	I3D [11]	53.9	50.7	45.4	38.0	28.5	43.3	43.5	33.9	<u>9.2</u>	30.2
	P-GCN [74]	I3D [11]	63.6	57.8	49.1	—	—	—	48.3	33.2	3.3	31.1
	P-GCN [74]+TSP [1]	R(2+1)D [58]	69.1	63.3	53.5	40.4	26.0	50.5	—	—	—	—
	TSA-Net [25]	P3D [49]	61.2	55.9	46.9	36.1	25.2	45.1	48.7	32.0	9.0	31.9
	MUSES [41]	I3D [11]	68.9	64.0	56.9	46.3	31.0	—	50.0	35.0	6.6	34.0
	TCANet [48]	TSN [60]	60.6	53.2	44.6	36.8	26.7	44.3	52.3	36.7	6.9	35.5
	TCANet [48]	SlowFast [23]	—	—	—	—	—	—	54.3	**39.1**	8.4	**37.6**
	BMN-CSA [53]	TSN [60]	64.4	58.0	49.2	38.2	27.8	47.7	52.4	36.2	5.2	35.4
	ContextLoc [83]	I3D [11]	68.3	63.8	54.3	41.8	26.2	50.9	**56.0**	35.2	3.6	34.2
	VSGN [77]	TSN [60]	66.7	60.4	52.4	41.0	30.4	50.2	52.4	36.0	8.4	35.1
	VSGN [77]	I3D [11]	—	—	—	—	—	—	52.3	35.2	8.3	34.7
	VSGN [77]+TSP [1]	R(2+1)D [58]	—	—	—	—	—	—	53.3	36.8	8.1	35.9
	RTD-Net [54]	I3D [11]	68.3	62.3	51.9	38.8	23.7	49.0	47.2	30.7	8.6	30.8
Single-stage	A²Net [71]	I3D [11]	58.6	54.1	45.5	32.5	17.2	41.6	43.6	28.7	3.7	27.8
	GTAN [46]	P3D [49]	57.8	47.2	38.8	—	—	—	52.6	34.1	8.9	34.3
	PBRNet [39]	I3D [11]	58.5	54.6	51.3	41.8	29.5	—	54.0	35.0	9.0	35.0
	AFSD [31]	I3D [11]	67.3	62.4	55.5	43.7	31.1	52.0	52.4	35.3	6.5	34.4
	TadTR [42]	I3D [11]	62.4	57.4	49.2	37.8	26.3	46.6	49.1	32.6	8.5	32.3
	Ours	I3D [11]	**82.1**	**77.8**	**71.0**	**59.4**	**43.9**	**66.8**	53.5	36.2	8.2	35.6
	Ours+TSP [1]	R(2+1)D [58]	<u>73.4</u>	<u>67.4</u>	<u>59.1</u>	<u>46.7</u>	<u>31.5</u>	<u>55.6</u>	<u>54.7</u>	<u>37.8</u>	8.4	<u>36.6</u>

was used to evaluate our model. A window size of 19 was used for local self-attention based on our ablation. More implementation details are described in the supplement. To show that our method can adapt to different video features, we also consider the pre-training method from [1] using an R(2+1)D network [58].

Results. Table 1 (left) summarizes the results. Our method achieves an average mAP of 66.8% ([0.3 : 0.1 : 0.7]), with an mAP of 71.0% at tIoU = 0.5 and an mAP of 43.9% at tIoU = 0.7, outperforming all previous methods by a large margin (+14.1% mAP at tIoU = 0.5 and +12.8% mAP at tIoU = 0.7). Our results stay on top of all single-stage methods, and also beats all previous two-stage methods, including the latest ones from [29,48,53,78]. Note that our method significantly outperforms the concurrent work of TadTR [42], which also designed a Transformer model for TAL. With the combination of a simple design and a strong Transformer model, our method establishes new state of the art on THUMOS14, crossing the 65% average mAP for the first time.

4.2   Results on ActivityNet-1.3

Dataset. ActivityNet-1.3 [9] is a large-scale action dataset which contains 200 activity classes and around 20,000 videos with more than 600 h. The dataset is divided into three subsets: 10,024 videos for training, 4,926 for validation, and 5,044 for testing. Following the common practice in [32, 34, 69], we train our model on the training set and report the performance on the validation set.

Table 2. Results on EPIC-Kitchens 100 validation set. We report mAP at different tIoU thresholds and the average mAP in [0.1:0.1:0.5]. All methods used the same SlowFast features. Our method outperforms all baselines by a large margin.

Task	Method	0.1	0.2	0.3	0.4	0.5	Avg.
Verb	BMN [17,32]	10.8	9.8	8.4	7.1	5.6	8.4
	G-TAD [69]	12.1	11.0	9.4	8.1	6.5	9.4
	Ours	**26.6**	**25.4**	**24.2**	**22.3**	**19.1**	**23.5**
Noun	BMN [17,32]	10.3	8.3	6.2	4.5	3.4	6.5
	G-TAD [69]	11.0	10.0	8.6	7.0	5.4	8.4
	Ours	**25.2**	**24.1**	**22.7**	**20.5**	**17.0**	**21.9**

Experiment Setup. We used two-stream I3D [11] for feature extraction. Following [32, 34, 69], the extracted features were downsampled into a fixed length of 160 using linear interpolation. For evaluation, we used mAP@[0.5:0.05:0.95] and also reported the average mAP. A window size of 11 was used for local self-attention. Further implementation details can be found in the supplement. Moreover, we combined external classification results from [80] following [3, 69, 74, 78]. Similarly, we consider the pre-training method from [1].

Results. Table 1 (right) shows the results. With I3D features, our method reaches an average mAP of 35.6% ([0.5 : 0.05 : 0.95]), outperforming all previous methods using the same features by at least 0.6%. This boost is significant as the result is averaged across many tIoU thresholds, including those tight ones *e.g.*, 0.95. Using the pre-training method from TSP [1] largely improves our results (36.6% average mAP). Our model thus outperforms the best method with the same features [77] by a major margin (+0.7%). Again, our method outperforms TadTR [42]. Our results are worse than TCANet [48]—a latest two-stage method using stronger SlowFast features [23] that are not publicly available. We conjecture our method will also benefit from better features. Nonetheless, our model clearly demonstrates state-of-the-art results on this challenging dataset.

4.3   Results on EPIC-Kitchens 100

Dataset. EPIC-Kitchens 100 is the largest egocentric action dataset. The dataset contains 100 h of videos from 700 sessions capturing cooking activities in different kitchens. In comparison to ActivityNet-1.3, EPIC-Kitchens 100 has less number of videos, yet many more instances per video (average 128 vs. 1.5 on ActivityNet-1.3). In comparison to THUMOS14, EPIC-Kitchens is 3 times larger in terms of video hours and more than 10 times larger in terms of action instances. These egocentric videos also include significant camera motion. This dataset thus poses new challenges for TAL.

Experiment Setup. We used a SlowFast network [23] pre-trained on EPIC-Kitchens for feature extraction. This model is provided by [17]. Our model was trained on the training set and evaluated on the validation set. A window size of 9 was used for local self-attention. For evaluation, we used $mAP@[0.1:0.1:0.5]$ and report the average mAP following [17]. In this dataset, an action is defined as a combination of a verb (action) and a noun (object). As this dataset was recently released, we are only able to compare our methods to BMN [32] and G-TAD [69], both using the same SlowFast features provided by [17]. Implementation details are again described in the supplement.

Results. Table 2 presents the results. Our method achieves an average mAP ($[0.1:0.1:0.5]$) of 23.5% and 21.9% for verb and noun, respectively. Our results again largely outperform the strong baselines of BMN [32] and G-TAD [69] by over 13.5% in absolute percentage points. An interesting observation is that the gaps between our results and BMN / G-TAD are much larger on EPIC-Kitchens 100. A possible reason is that ActivityNet has a small number of actions per video (1.5), leading to imbalanced classification for our model; only a few moments (around the action center) are labeled positive while all rest are negative.

We adapt ActionFormer for EPIC-Kitchens 100 2022 Action Detection challenge. By combining features from SlowFast [23] and ViViT [2], ActionFormer achieves 21.36% / 20.95% average mAP for actions on the validation / test set. Our results ranked 2nd with a gap of 0.32 average mAP to the top solution.

4.4 Ablation Experiments

We conduct extensive ablations on THUMOS14 to understand our model design. Results are reported using I3D features with a fixed random seed for training. Further ablations on loss weight, maximum input length during training, input temporal feature resolution and error analysis can be found in the supplement.

Baseline: A Convolutional Network. Our ablation starts by re-implementing a baseline anchor-free method (AF Base) as described in [31,71] (Table 3a row 1–2). This baseline shares the same action representation as our model, yet uses a 1D convolutional network as the encoder. We roughly match the number of layers and parameters of this baseline to our model. See our supplement for more details. This baseline achieves an average mAP of 46.6% on THUMOS14 (Table 3a row 3), outperforms the numbers reported in [31] by 6.2%. We attribute the difference to variations in architectures and training schemes. This baseline, when using score fusion, reaches 52.9% average mAP (Table 3a row 4).

Transformer Network. Our next step is to simply replace the 1D convolutional network with our Transformer model using vanilla self-attention. This model

Table 3. Ablation studies on THUMOS14. We report mAP at $tIoU = 0.5$ and 0.7, and the average mAP in $[0.3 : 0.1 : 0.7]$. Results are without score fusion unless specified.

Method	Backbone	LN	CTR	PE	Fusion	0.5	0.7	Avg
AF Base [71]	Conv					36.6	15.0	34.2
AF Base [31]	Conv					31.0	19.0	40.4
AF Base (Our Impl)	Conv					48.0	29.4	46.6
AF Base (Our Impl)	Conv				✓	54.6	33.4	52.9
Ours	Trans					66.8	38.4	62.7
Ours	Trans	✓				69.0	43.0	65.4
Ours	Trans	✓	✓			70.4	43.6	66.7
Ours	Trans	✓	✓	✓		66.0	41.7	62.1
Ours	Trans	✓	✓		✓	**71.0**	**43.9**	**66.8**
Ours (win size=19)	Trans	✓	✓			**71.0**	**43.9**	**66.8**

(a) **Model Design**: We start from a baseline 1D convolutional network (AF Base), and gradually replace convolutions with our Transformer model, add layer norm to heads (LN), enable center sampling during training (CTR), explore position encoding (PE), and fuse classification scores (Fusion).

Method	Win Size	0.5	0.7	Avg	GMACs	Time
AF Base	N/A	48.0	29.4	46.6	45.6	1.0x
Ours	9	70.5	42.7	66.5	45.2	2.0x
Ours	19	**71.0**	**43.9**	**66.8**	45.3	2.0x
Ours	25	70.3	43.9	66.4	45.4	2.0x
Ours	37	71.0	43.1	66.7	45.5	2.0x
Ours	Full	71.0	43.9	66.8	57.8	2.2x

(b) **Local Window Size**: We additionally report MACs and normalized run time by varying the local window size for self-attention in our model, using an input of 2304 time steps (5 minutes on THUMOS14). Time is normalized by setting AF Base to 1.0x.

Method	# Levels	Init Range	0.5	0.7	Avg
Ours	1	$[0, +\infty)$	51.8	15.8	47.6
Ours	3	$[0, 4)$	64.4	31.5	60.1
Ours	3	$[0, 8)$	61.4	30.0	57.6
Ours	3	$[0, 16)$	54.2	19.2	50.2
Ours	4	$[0, 4)$	67.4	39.7	63.7
Ours	5	$[0, 4)$	70.2	42.2	65.5
Ours	6	$[0, 4)$	**71.0**	**43.9**	**66.8**
Ours	7	$[0, 4)$	70.6	43.2	66.2

(c) **Design of Feature Pyramid**: We vary (1) the number of pyramid levels and (2) the initial regression range, and report mAP and the average mAP.

achieves an average mAP of 62.7% (Table 3a row 5)—a major boost of 16.1%. We note that this model already outperforms the best reported results (56.9% mAP at $tIoU = 0.5$ from [41]). This result shows that our Transformer model is very powerful for TAL, and serves as the main course of performance gain.

Layer Norm, Center Sampling, Position Encoding, and Score Fusion. We further add layer norm in the classification and regression heads, apply center sampling during training, and explore position encoding as well as score fusion (Table 3a row 6–9). Adding layer norm boosts the average mAP by 2.7%, and using center sampling further improves the performance by 1.4%. The commonly used position encoding, however, does not bring performance gain. We postulate that our projection using convolutions as well as the depthwise convolutions in our Transformer blocks already leak the location information, as also pointed out in [67]. Further fusing the classification scores will decrease the largely performance. As a reference, when replacing the vanilla self-attention with a local version (window size=19), the average mAP remains the same.

Window Size for Local Self-attention. Next, we study the effects of window size for local self-attention in our model. We vary the window size, re-train the model, and present both model accuracy, complexity (in GMACs), and run time in Table 3b. All results are reported without score fusion. Due to our design of a multiscale feature pyramid, even using the global self-attention only leads to 26% increase in MACs when compared to the baseline convolutional network. Reducing the window size cuts down the MACs yet maintains a similar accuracy. In addition to MACs, we also evaluate the normalized run time of these models on GPUs, where the base convolutional model is set to 1.0x. In spite of similar

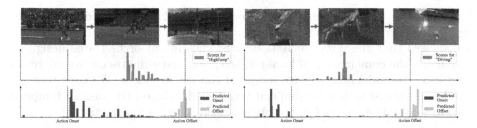

Fig. 3. Visualization of our results. From *top* to *bottom*: (1) input video frames; (2) action scores at each time step; (3) histogram of action onsets and offsets computed by weighting the regression outputs using action scores. See more in the supplement.

MACs, Transformer-based models are roughly 2x slower in run time compared to a convolution-based model (AF Base). It is known that self-attention is not easily parallelizable on GPUs. Also, our current implementation of Transformer used PyTorch primitives [47] without leveraging customized CUDA kernels.

Feature Pyramid. Further, we study the design of the feature pyramid. As discussed in Sect. 3.3, our design space is specified by (1) the number of pyramid levels and (2) an initial regression range for the first pyramid level. We vary these parameters and report results in Table 3c. We follow our best design with a local window size $= 19$ and layer norm, and center sampling.

First, we disable the feature pyramid and attach the heads to the feature map with the highest resolution. This is done by setting the number of pyramid to 1 with an initial regression range of $[0, +\infty)$, Removing the feature pyramid results in a major performance drop (-19.3% in average mAP), suggesting that using feature pyramid is critical for our model. Next, we set the number of pyramid levels to 3 and experiment with different initial regression ranges. The best results are achieved with the range of $[0, 4)$. Further increase of the range decreases the mAP scores. Finally, we fix the initial regression range to $[0, 4)$ and increase the number of pyramid levels. The performance of our method generally increases with more pyramid levels, yet is saturated when using 6 levels.

Result Visualization. Finally, we visualize the outputs of our model (before Soft-NMS) in Fig. 3, including the action scores, and the regression outputs weighted by the action scores (as a weighted histogram). Our model outputs a strong peak near the center of an action, potentially due to the employment of center sampling during training. The regression of action boundaries seems less accurate. We conjecture that our regression heads can be further improved.

5   Conclusion and Discussion

In this paper, we presented ActionFormer—a Transformer-based method for temporal action localization. ActionFormer has a simple design, falls into the category of single-stage anchor-free method, yet achieves impressive results across several major TAL benchmarks including THUMOS14, ActivityNet-1.3, and the more recent EPIC-Kitchens 100 (egocentric videos). Through our experiments, we showed that the power of ActionFormer lies in our orchestrated design, in particular the combination of local self-attention and a multiscale feature representation to model longer range temporal context in videos. We hope that our model, notwithstanding its simplicity, can shed light on the task of temporal action localization, as well as the broader field of video understanding.

References

1. Alwassel, H., Giancola, S., Ghanem, B.: TSP: Temporally-sensitive pretraining of video encoders for localization tasks. In: International Conference on Computer Vision Workshops, pp. 1–11 (2021)
2. Arnab, A., Dehghani, M., Heigold, G., Sun, C., Lučić, M., Schmid, C.: ViViT: a video vision transformer. In: International Conference on Computer Vision (2021)
3. Bai, Y., Wang, Y., Tong, Y., Yang, Y., Liu, Q., Liu, J.: Boundary content graph neural network for temporal action proposal generation. In: Vedaldi, A., Bischof, H., Brox, T., Frahm, J.-M. (eds.) ECCV 2020. LNCS, vol. 12373, pp. 121–137. Springer, Cham (2020). https://doi.org/10.1007/978-3-030-58604-1_8
4. Beltagy, I., Peters, M.E., Cohan, A.: LongFormer: the long-document transformer. arXiv:2004.05150 (2020)
5. Bodla, N., Singh, B., Chellappa, R., Davis, L.S.: Soft-NMS-improving object detection with one line of code. In: International Conference on Computer Vision, pp. 5561–5569 (2017)
6. Buch, S., Escorcia, V., Ghanem, B., Niebles Carlos, J.: End-to-end, single-stream temporal action detection in untrimmed videos. In: British Machine Vision Conference, pp. 93.1–93.12 (2017)
7. Buch, S., Escorcia, V., Shen, C., Ghanem, B., Carlos Niebles, J.: SST: Single-stream temporal action proposals. In: IEEE Conference on Computer Vision and Pattern Recognition, pp. 2911–2920 (2017)
8. Caba Heilbron, F., Carlos Niebles, J., Ghanem, B.: Fast temporal activity proposals for efficient detection of human actions in untrimmed videos. In: IEEE Conference on Computer Vision and Pattern Recognition, pp. 1914–1923 (2016)
9. Caba Heilbron, F., Escorcia, V., Ghanem, B., Carlos Niebles, J.: ActivityNet: a large-scale video benchmark for human activity understanding. In: IEEE Conference on Computer Vision and Pattern Recognition, pp. 961–970 (2015)
10. Carion, N., Massa, F., Synnaeve, G., Usunier, N., Kirillov, A., Zagoruyko, S.: End-to-end object detection with transformers. In: Vedaldi, A., Bischof, H., Brox, T., Frahm, J.-M. (eds.) ECCV 2020. LNCS, vol. 12346, pp. 213–229. Springer, Cham (2020). https://doi.org/10.1007/978-3-030-58452-8_13
11. Carreira, J., Zisserman, A.: Quo vadis, action recognition? A new model and the Kinetics dataset. In: IEEE Conference on Computer Vision and Pattern Recognition, pp. 4724–4733 (2017)
12. Chang, S., Wang, P., Wang, F., Li, H., Feng, J.: Augmented transformer with adaptive graph for temporal action proposal generation. arXiv preprint arXiv:2103.16024 (2021)
13. Chao, Y.W., Vijayanarasimhan, S., Seybold, B., Ross, D.A., Deng, J., Sukthankar, R.: Rethinking the Faster-RCNN architecture for temporal action localization. In: IEEE Conference on Computer Vision and Pattern Recognition, pp. 1130–1139 (2018)

14. Cheng, B., Schwing, A.G., Kirillov, A.: Per-pixel classification is not all you need for semantic segmentation. In: Advances in Neural Information Processing Systems (2021)
15. Choromanski, K., et al.: Rethinking attention with performers. In: International Conference on Learning Representations (2021)
16. Dai, X., Chen, Y., Yang, J., Zhang, P., Yuan, L., Zhang, L.: Dynamic DETR: end-to-end object detection with dynamic attention. In: International Conference on Computer Vision, pp. 2988–2997 (2021)
17. Damen, D., et al.: Rescaling egocentric vision. arXiv preprint arXiv:2006.13256 (2020)
18. Devlin, J., Chang, M.W., Lee, K., Toutanova, K.: BERT: pre-training of deep bidirectional transformers for language understanding. In: North American Chapter of the Association for Computational Linguistics, pp. 4171–4186 (2019)
19. Dosovitskiy, A., et al.: An image is worth 16x16 words: transformers for image recognition at scale. In: International Conference on Learning Representations (2021)
20. Duan, K., Bai, S., Xie, L., Qi, H., Huang, Q., Tian, Q.: CenterNet: keypoint triplets for object detection. In: International Conference on Computer Vision, pp. 6569–6578 (2019)
21. Escorcia, V., Caba Heilbron, F., Niebles, J.C., Ghanem, B.: DAPs: deep action proposals for action understanding. In: Leibe, B., Matas, J., Sebe, N., Welling, M. (eds.) ECCV 2016. LNCS, vol. 9907, pp. 768–784. Springer, Cham (2016). https://doi.org/10.1007/978-3-319-46487-9_47
22. Fan, H., Xiong, B., Mangalam, K., Li, Y., Yan, Z., Malik, J., Feichtenhofer, C.: Multiscale vision transformers. In: International Conference on Computer Vision (2021)
23. Feichtenhofer, C., Fan, H., Malik, J., He, K.: SlowFast networks for video recognition. In: International Conference on Computer Vision, pp. 6202–6211 (2019)
24. Girdhar, R., Carreira, J., Doersch, C., Zisserman, A.: Video action transformer network. In: IEEE Conference on Computer Vision and Pattern Recognition, pp. 244–253 (2019)
25. Gong, G., Zheng, L., Mu, Y.: Scale matters: temporal scale aggregation network for precise action localization in untrimmed videos. In: International Conference on Multimedia and Expo, pp. 1–6. IEEE (2020)
26. Idrees, H., et al.: The THUMOS challenge on action recognition for videos "in the wild". Comput. Vis. Image Under. **155**, 1–23 (2017)
27. Kingma, D.P., Ba, J.: Adam: a method for stochastic optimization. In: International Conference on Learning Representations, pp. 1–11 (2015)
28. Li, S., et al.: Enhancing the locality and breaking the memory bottleneck of transformer on time series forecasting. In: Advances in Neural Information Processing Systems, vol. 32 (2019)
29. Li, X., et al.: Deep concept-wise temporal convolutional networks for action localization. In: Proceedings of the 28th ACM International Conference on Multimedia, pp. 4004–4012 (2020)
30. Lin, C., et al.: Fast learning of temporal action proposal via dense boundary generator. In: AAAI, pp. 11499–11506 (2020)
31. Lin, C., et al.: Learning salient boundary feature for anchor-free temporal action localization. In: IEEE Conference on Computer Vision and Pattern Recognition, pp. 3320–3329 (2021)

32. Lin, T., Liu, X., Li, X., Ding, E., Wen, S.: BMN: boundary-matching network for temporal action proposal generation. In: International Conference on Computer Vision, pp. 3889–3898 (2019)

33. Lin, T., Zhao, X., Shou, Z.: Single shot temporal action detection. In: ACM International Conference on Multimedia, pp. 988–996 (2017)

34. Lin, T., Zhao, X., Su, H., Wang, C., Yang, M.: BSN: boundary sensitive network for temporal action proposal generation. In: Ferrari, V., Hebert, M., Sminchisescu, C., Weiss, Y. (eds.) ECCV 2018. LNCS, vol. 11208, pp. 3–21. Springer, Cham (2018). https://doi.org/10.1007/978-3-030-01225-0_1

35. Lin, T.Y., Dollár, P., Girshick, R., He, K., Hariharan, B., Belongie, S.: Feature pyramid networks for object detection. In: IEEE Conference on Computer Vision and Pattern Recognition, pp. 2117–2125 (2017)

36. Lin, T.Y., Goyal, P., Girshick, R., He, K., Dollár, P.: Focal loss for dense object detection. In: IEEE Conference on Computer Vision, pp. 2980–2988 (2017)

37. Liu, D., Jiang, T., Wang, Y.: Completeness modeling and context separation for weakly supervised temporal action localization. In: IEEE Conference on Computer Vision and Pattern Recognition, pp. 1298–1307 (2019)

38. Liu, L., Liu, X., Gao, J., Chen, W., Han, J.: Understanding the difficulty of training transformers. In: Proceedings of the 2020 Conference on Empirical Methods in Natural Language Processing (EMNLP), pp. 5747–5763 (2020)

39. Liu, Q., Wang, Z.: Progressive boundary refinement network for temporal action detection. In: AAAI, vol. 34, pp. 11612–11619 (2020)

40. Liu, W., et al.: SSD: single shot multibox detector. In: Leibe, B., Matas, J., Sebe, N., Welling, M. (eds.) ECCV 2016. LNCS, vol. 9905, pp. 21–37. Springer, Cham (2016). https://doi.org/10.1007/978-3-319-46448-0_2

41. Liu, X., Hu, Y., Bai, S., Ding, F., Bai, X., Torr, P.H.: Multi-shot temporal event localization: a benchmark. In: IEEE Conference on Computer Vision and Pattern Recognition, pp. 12596–12606 (2021)

42. Liu, X., Wang, Q., Hu, Y., Tang, X., Bai, S., Bai, X.: End-to-end temporal action detection with transformer. arXiv preprint arXiv:2106.10271 (2021)

43. Liu, Y., Ma, L., Zhang, Y., Liu, W., Chang, S.F.: Multi-granularity generator for temporal action proposal. In: IEEE Conference on Computer Vision and Pattern Recognition, pp. 3604–3613 (2019)

44. Liu, Z., et al.: Swin transformer: hierarchical vision transformer using shifted windows. In: IEEE Conference on Computer Vision (2021)

45. Liu, Z., et al.: Video swin transformer. arXiv preprint arXiv:2106.13230 (2021)

46. Long, F., Yao, T., Qiu, Z., Tian, X., Luo, J., Mei, T.: Gaussian temporal awareness networks for action localization. In: IEEE Conference on Computer Vision and Pattern Recognition, pp. 344–353 (2019)

47. Paszke, A., et al.: PyTorch: an imperative style, high-performance deep learning library. In: Advances in Neural Information Processing Systems, vol. 32 (2019)

48. Qing, Z., et al.: Temporal context aggregation network for temporal action proposal refinement. In: IEEE Conference on Computer Vision and Pattern Recognition, pp. 485–494 (2021)

49. Qiu, Z., Yao, T., Mei, T.: Learning spatio-temporal representation with pseudo-3D residual networks. In: IEEE Conference on Computer Vision , pp. 5533–5541 (2017)

50. Rezatofighi, H., Tsoi, N., Gwak, J., Sadeghian, A., Reid, I., Savarese, S.: Generalized intersection over union: a metric and a loss for bounding box regression. In: IEEE Conference on Computer Vision and Pattern Recognition, pp. 658–666 (2019)

51. Shou, Z., Chan, J., Zareian, A., Miyazawa, K., Chang, S.F.: CDC: convolutional-de-convolutional networks for precise temporal action localization in untrimmed videos. In: IEEE Conference on Computer Vision and Pattern Recognition, pp. 5734–5743 (2017)
52. Shou, Z., Wang, D., Chang, S.F.: Temporal action localization in untrimmed videos via multi-stage CNNs. In: IEEE Conference on Computer Vision and Pattern Recognition, pp. 1049–1058 (2016)
53. Sridhar, D., Quader, N., Muralidharan, S., Li, Y., Dai, P., Lu, J.: Class semantics-based attention for action detection. In: IEEE Conference on Computer Vision, pp. 13739–13748 (2021)
54. Tan, J., Tang, J., Wang, L., Wu, G.: Relaxed transformer decoders for direct action proposal generation. In: IEEE Conference on Computer Vision, pp. 13526–13535 (2021)
55. Tian, Z., Shen, C., Chen, H., He, T.: FCOS: fully convolutional one-stage object detection. In: IEEE Conference on Computer Vision, pp. 9627–9636 (2019)
56. Touvron, H., Cord, M., Douze, M., Massa, F., Sablayrolles, A., Jégou, H.: Training data-efficient image transformers & distillation through attention. In: International Conference on Machine Learning, pp. 10347–10357 (2021)
57. Touvron, H., Cord, M., Sablayrolles, A., Synnaeve, G., Jégou, H.: Going deeper with image transformers. In: IEEE Conference on Computer Vision (2021)
58. Tran, D., Wang, H., Torresani, L., Ray, J., LeCun, Y., Paluri, M.: A closer look at spatiotemporal convolutions for action recognition. In: IEEE Conference on Computer Vision and Pattern Recognition, pp. 6450–6459 (2018)
59. Vaswani, A., et al.: Attention is all you need. In: Advances in Neural Information Processing Systems, pp. 5998–6008 (2017)
60. Wang, L., et al.: Temporal segment networks: towards good practices for deep action recognition. In: Leibe, B., Matas, J., Sebe, N., Welling, M. (eds.) ECCV 2016. LNCS, vol. 9912, pp. 20–36. Springer, Cham (2016). https://doi.org/10.1007/978-3-319-46484-8_2
61. Wang, L., Yang, H., Wu, W., Yao, H., Huang, H.: Temporal action proposal generation with transformers. arXiv preprint arXiv:2105.12043 (2021)
62. Wang, S., Li, B., Khabsa, M., Fang, H., Ma, H.: LinFormer: self-attention with linear complexity. arXiv preprint arXiv:2006.04768 (2020)
63. Wang, T., Yuan, L., Chen, Y., Feng, J., Yan, S.: PnP-DETR: towards efficient visual analysis with transformers. In: IEEE Conference on Computer Vision, pp. 4661–4670 (2021)
64. Wang, W., et al.: Pyramid vision transformer: a versatile backbone for dense prediction without convolutions. In: IEEE Conference on Computer Vision (2021)
65. Wang, Y., et al.: End-to-end video instance segmentation with transformers. In: IEEE Conference on Computer Vision and Pattern Recognition, pp. 8741–8750 (2021)
66. Xiao, T., Singh, M., Mintun, E., Darrell, T., Dollár, P., Girshick, R.: Early convolutions help transformers see better. In: Advances in Neural Information Processing Systems (2021)
67. Xie, E., Wang, W., Yu, Z., Anandkumar, A., Alvarez, J.M., Luo, P.: SegFormer: simple and efficient design for semantic segmentation with transformers. In: Advances in Neural Information Processing Systems (2021)
68. Xiong, Y., et al.: Nyströmformer: a nyström-based algorithm for approximating self-attention. In: AAAI, vol. 35, pp. 14138–14148 (2021)

69. Xu, M., Zhao, C., Rojas, D.S., Thabet, A., Ghanem, B.: G-TAD: sub-graph localization for temporal action detection. In: IEEE Conference on Computer Vision and Pattern Recognition, pp. 10156–10165 (2020)

70. Yang, J., et al.: Focal self-attention for local-global interactions in vision transformers. In: Advances in Neural Information Processing Systems (2021)

71. Yang, L., Peng, H., Zhang, D., Fu, J., Han, J.: Revisiting anchor mechanisms for temporal action localization. IEEE Trans. Image Process. **29**, 8535–8548 (2020)

72. Yang, Z., Qin, J., Huang, D.: AcgNet: action complement graph network for weakly-supervised temporal action localization. In: AAAI, vol. 36–3, pp. 3090–3098 (2022)

73. Yuan, L., et al.: Tokens-to-token ViT: training vision transformers from scratch on ImageNet. In: IEEE Conference on Computer Vision (2021)

74. Zeng, R., et al.: Graph convolutional networks for temporal action localization. In: IEEE Conference on Computer Vision, pp. 7094–7103 (2019)

75. Zeng, R., Xu, H., Huang, W., Chen, P., Tan, M., Gan, C.: Dense regression network for video grounding. In: IEEE Conference on Computer Vision and Pattern Recognition, pp. 10287–10296 (2020)

76. Zhang, S., Chi, C., Yao, Y., Lei, Z., Li, S.Z.: Bridging the gap between anchor-based and anchor-free detection via adaptive training sample selection. In: IEEE Conference on Computer Vision and Pattern Recognition, pp. 9759–9768 (2020)

77. Zhao, C., Thabet, A.K., Ghanem, B.: Video self-stitching graph network for temporal action localization. In: IEEE Conference on Computer Vision and Pattern Recognition, pp. 13658–13667 (2021)

78. Zhao, P., Xie, L., Ju, C., Zhang, Y., Wang, Y., Tian, Q.: Bottom-up temporal action localization with mutual regularization. In: Vedaldi, A., Bischof, H., Brox, T., Frahm, J.-M. (eds.) ECCV 2020. LNCS, vol. 12353, pp. 539–555. Springer, Cham (2020). https://doi.org/10.1007/978-3-030-58598-3_32

79. Zhao, Y., Xiong, Y., Wang, L., Wu, Z., Tang, X., Lin, D.: Temporal action detection with structured segment networks. In: IEEE Conference on Computer Vision, pp. 2914–2923 (2017)

80. Zhao, Y., et al.: CUHK & ETHZ & SIAT submission to ActivityNet challenge 2017. arXiv preprint arXiv:1710.08011 (2017)

81. Zheng, Z., Wang, P., Liu, W., Li, J., Ye, R., Ren, D.: Distance-IoU loss: faster and better learning for bounding box regression. In: AAAI (2020)

82. Zhu, X., Su, W., Lu, L., Li, B., Wang, X., Dai, J.: Deformable DETR: deformable transformers for end-to-end object detection. In: International Conference on Learning Representations, pp. 1–11 (2021)

83. Zhu, Z., Tang, W., Wang, L., Zheng, N., Hua, G.: Enriching local and global contexts for temporal action localization. In: International Conference on Computer Vision, pp. 13516–13525 (2021)

SocialVAE: Human Trajectory Prediction Using Timewise Latents

Pei Xu[1,2]($\boxtimes$) (iD), Jean-Bernard Hayet[3] (iD), and Ioannis Karamouzas[1]

[1] Clemson University, South Carolina, USA
{peix,ioannis}@clemson.edu
[2] Roblox, San Mateo, USA
[3] CIMAT, A.C, Guanajuato, Mexico
jbhayet@cimat.mx
https://motion-lab.github.io/SocialVAE

Abstract. Predicting pedestrian movement is critical for human behavior analysis and also for safe and efficient human-agent interactions. However, despite significant advancements, it is still challenging for existing approaches to capture the uncertainty and multimodality of human navigation decision making. In this paper, we propose SocialVAE, a novel approach for human trajectory prediction. The core of SocialVAE is a timewise variational autoencoder architecture that exploits stochastic recurrent neural networks to perform prediction, combined with a social attention mechanism and a backward posterior approximation to allow for better extraction of pedestrian navigation strategies. We show that SocialVAE improves current state-of-the-art performance on several pedestrian trajectory prediction benchmarks, including the ETH/UCY benchmark, Stanford Drone Dataset, and SportVU NBA movement dataset.

Keywords: Human trajectory prediction · Multimodal prediction · Timewise variational autoencoder

1 Introduction

The development of autonomous agents interacting with humans, such as self-driving vehicles, indoor service robots, and traffic control systems, involves human behavior modeling and inference in order to meet both the safety and intelligence requirements. In recent years, with the rise of deep learning techniques, extracting patterns from sequential data for prediction or sequence transduction has advanced significantly in fields such as machine translation [8,46], image completion [33,45], weather forecasting [36,51], and physical simulation [25,41]. In contrast to works performing inference from regularly distributed data conforming to specific rules or physics laws, predicting human behaviors,

Supplementary Information The online version contains supplementary material available at https://doi.org/10.1007/978-3-031-19772-7_30.

e.g., body poses and socially-aware movement, still faces huge challenges due to the complexity and uncertainty in the human decision making process.

In this work, we focus on the task of human trajectory prediction from short-term historical observations. Traditional works predict pedestrian trajectories using deterministic models [7,18,19,21,34]. However, human navigation behaviors have an inherent multimodal nature with lots of randomness. Even in the same scenario, there would be more than one trajectories that a pedestrian could take. Such uncertainty cannot be captured effectively by deterministic models, especially for long-term trajectory prediction with more aleatory influences introduced. Furthermore, individuals often exhibit different behaviors in similar scenarios. Such individual differences are decided by various stationary and dynamical factors such as crowd density and scene lighting, weather conditions, social context, personality traits, etc. As such, the complexity of behaviors is hard to be consistently modeled by rule-based methods, which work under predetermined physical laws and/or social rules [18,19,21,35]. Recent works have promoted data-driven solutions based on deep generative models to perform stochastic predictions or learn the trajectory distribution directly [17,20,30,38,40,48,49,54,56]. Despite impressive results, current approaches still face the challenge of making high-fidelity predictions with a limited number of samples.

In this paper, we exploit recent advances in variational inference techniques and introduce a timewise variational autoencoder (VAE) architecture for human trajectory prediction. Similar to prior VAE-based methods [30,40,49,54,56], we rely on recurrent neural networks (RNNs) to handle trajectory data sequentially and provide stochastic predictions. However, our model uses latent variables as stochastic parameters to condition the hidden dynamics of RNNs at *each time step*, in contrast to previous solutions that condition the prior of latent variables only based on historical observations. This allows us to more accurately capture the dynamic nature of human decision making. Further, to robustly extract navigation patterns from whole trajectories, we use a backward RNN structure for posterior approximation. To cope with an arbitrary number of neighbors during observation encoding, we develop a human-inspired attention mechanism to encode neighbors' states by considering the observed social features exhibited by these neighbors.

Overall, this paper makes the following contributions:

- We propose SocialVAE, a novel approach to predict human trajectory distributions conditioned on short-term historical observations. Our model employs a *timewise* VAE architecture with a conditional prior and a posterior approximated bidirectionally from the whole trajectory, and uses an attention mechanism to capture the social influence from the neighboring agents.
- We introduce *Final Position Clustering* as an optional and easy-to-implement postprocessing technique to help reduce sampling bias and further improve the overall prediction quality when a limited number of samples are drawn from the predicted distribution.
- We experimentally show that SocialVAE captures the mutimodality of human navigation behaviors while reasoning about human-human interactions in

both everyday settings and NBA scenarios involving cooperative and adversarial agents with fast dynamics.
- We achieve state-of-the-art performance on the ETH/UCY and SDD benchmarks and SportVU NBA movement dataset, bringing more than 10% improvement and in certain test cases more than 50% improvement over existing trajectory prediction methods.

2 Related Work

Research in pedestrian trajectory prediction can be broadly classified into human-space and human-human models. The former focuses on predicting scene-specific human movement patterns [4,10,24,29,39] and takes advantage of the scene environment information, typically through the use of semantic maps. In this work, we are interested in the latter, which performs trajectory prediction by using dynamic information about human-human interactions.

Mathematical Models. Modeling human movement in human-human interaction settings typically leverages hand-tuned mathematical models to perform deterministic prediction. Such models include rule-based approaches using social forces, velocity-obstacles, and energy-based formulations [7,19,21,53]. Statistical models based on observed data such as Gaussian processes [22,44,50] have also been widely used. By nature, they cope better with uncertainty on overall trajectories but struggle on fine-grained variations due to social interactions.

Learning-Based Models. In recent years, data-driven methods using deep learning techniques for trajectory prediction have achieved impressive results. SocialLSTM [1] employs a vanilla RNN structure using long short-term memory (LSTM) units to perform prediction sequentially. SocialAttention [48] introduces an attention mechanism to capture neighbors' influence by matching the RNN hidden state of each agent to those of its neighbors. SocialGAN [17], SoPhie [38] and SocialWays [2] use generative adversarial network (GAN) architectures. To account for social interactions, SocialGAN proposes a pooling process to synthesize neighbors via their RNN hidden states, while SocialWays adopts an attention mechanism that takes into account the neighbors' social features. PEC-Net [30], Trajectron [20], Trajectron++ [40], AgentFormer [56], BiTraP [54] and SGNet [49] employ a conditional-VAE architecture [43] to predict trajectory distributions, where latent variables are generated conditionally to the given observations. Memory-based approaches for trajectory prediction have also been recently explored such as MANTRA [31] and MemoNet [52]. Though achieving impressive results, such approaches would typically suffer from slow inference speeds and storage issues when dealing with large scenes. Recent works [15,55] have also exploited Transformer architectures to perform trajectory prediction. However, as we will show in Sect. 4, Transformer-based approaches tend to have worse performance than VAE-based approaches.

Stochastic RNNs. To better model highly dynamic and multimodal data, a number of recent works [5,13,14,16] leverage VAE architectures to extend

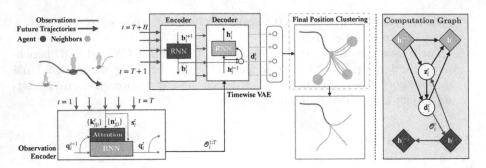

Fig. 1. Overview of SocialVAE that uses a RNN-based timewise VAE with sequentially generated stochastic latent variables for trajectory prediction. SocialVAE can be coupled with a *Final Position Clustering* postprocessing scheme (dashed box) to improve the predictions quality. The observation encoder attention mechanism considers each neighbor's state $\mathbf{n}_{j|i}$ along with its social features $\mathbf{k}_{j|i}$. The computation graph (right) shows the state transfer inside the timewise VAE. Diamonds represent deterministic states and circles represent stochastic states. Red parts are used only at training

RNNs with timewisely generated stochastic latent variables. Despite impressive performance on general sequential data modeling tasks, these approaches do not consider the interaction features appearing in human navigation tasks.

Following the literature of stochastic RNNs, we propose to use a timewise VAE as the backbone architecture for human trajectory prediction. The main motivation behind our formulation is that human decision making is highly dynamic and can lead to different trajectories at any given time. Additionally, to better extract features in human-human interactions, we employ a backward RNN for posterior approximation, which takes the *whole* ground-truth (GT) trajectory into account during learning. Neighbors are encoded through an attention mechanism that uses social features similar to [2]. A major advantage of our attention mechanism is that it relies only on the neighbors' observable states (position and velocity). In contrast, previous attention-based works use RNN hidden states as the representation of neighbors' states [2,17,38], which can only take into account neighbors that are consistently tracked during observation. As we show, our timewise VAE with the proposed attention mechanism achieves state-of-the-art performance on ETH/UCY/NBA datasets.

3   Approach

Our proposed SocialVAE approach infers the distribution of future trajectories for each agent in a scene based on given historical observations. Specifically, given a scene containing N agents, let $\mathbf{x}_i^t \in \mathbb{R}^2$ be the 2D spatial coordinate of agent i at time step t. We perform H-frame inference for the distribution over the agent's future positions $\mathbf{x}_i^{T+1:T+H}$ based on a T-frame joint observation, i.e., we estimate $p(\mathbf{x}_i^{T+1:T+H}|\mathcal{O}_i^{1:T})$ where $\mathcal{O}_i^{1:T}$ gathers the local observations from agent i to the whole scene. SocialVAE performs prediction for each agent independently, based on social features extracted from local observations, and can run with scenes having an arbitrary number of agents. This may be of particular interest in real-time and highly dynamic environments where the local neighborhood of a target agent is constantly changing or cannot be tracked consistently.

3.1 Model Architecture

Figure 1 shows the system overview of our model. Its backbone is a time-wise VAE. As in prior works [5,13,14,16], we use a RNN structure to condition the sequential predictions through an auto-regressive model relying on the state variable of the RNN structure. However, while prior works directly perform predictions over time-sequence data, we introduce the past observations as *conditional variables*. Moreover, instead of directly predicting the absolute coordinates $\mathbf{x}_i^{T+1:T+H}$, we generate a displacement sequence $\mathbf{d}_i^{T+1:T+H}$, where $\mathbf{d}_i^{t+1} \triangleq \mathbf{x}_i^{t+1} - \mathbf{x}_i^t$. The target probability distribution of the displacement sequence can be written as

$$p(\mathbf{d}_i^{T+1:T+H}|\mathcal{O}_i^{1:T}) = \prod_{\tau=1}^{H} p(\mathbf{d}_i^{T+\tau}|\mathbf{d}_i^{T+1:T+\tau-1}, \mathcal{O}_i^{1:T}). \tag{1}$$

To generate stochastic predictions, we use a conditional prior over the RNN state variable to introduce latent variables at each time step, and thus obtain a timewise VAE architecture, allowing us to model highly nonlinear dynamics during multi-agent navigation. In the following, we describe our generative model for trajectory prediction and the inference process for posterior approximation. **Generative Model.** Let $\mathbf{z}_i^t$ be the latent variables introduced at time step t. To implement the sequential generative model $p(\mathbf{d}_i^t|\mathbf{d}_i^{t-1}, \mathcal{O}_i^{1:T}, \mathbf{z}_i^t)$, we use a RNN in which the state variable $\mathbf{h}_i^t$ is updated recurrently by

$$\mathbf{h}_i^t = \overrightarrow{g}(\psi_{\mathbf{zd}}(\mathbf{z}_i^t, \mathbf{d}_i^t), \mathbf{h}_i^{t-1}), \tag{2}$$

for $t = T+1, \ldots, T+H$. In the recurrence, the initial state is extracted from historical observations, i.e., $\mathbf{h}_i^T = \psi_{\mathbf{h}}(\mathcal{O}_i^{1:T})$, where $\psi_{\mathbf{zd}}$ and $\psi_{\mathbf{h}}$ are two embedding neural networks. Developing Eq. 1 with $\mathbf{z}_i^t$, we obtain the generative model:

$$p(\mathbf{d}_i^{T+1:T+H}|\mathcal{O}_i^{1:T}) = \prod_{t=T+1}^{T+H} \int_{\mathbf{z}_i^t} p(\mathbf{d}_i^t|\mathbf{d}_i^{T:t-1}, \mathcal{O}_i^{1:T}, \mathbf{z}_i^t)p(\mathbf{z}_i^t|\mathbf{d}_i^{T:t-1}, \mathcal{O}_i^{1:T})d\mathbf{z}_i^t. \tag{3}$$

In contrast to standard VAEs that use a standard normal distribution as the prior, our prior distribution is conditioned and can be obtained from the RNN state variable. The second term of the integral in Eq. 3 can be translated into

$$p(\mathbf{z}_i^t|\mathbf{d}_i^{T:t-1}, \mathcal{O}_i^{1:T}) := p_\theta(\mathbf{z}_i^t|\mathbf{h}_i^{t-1}), \tag{4}$$

where θ are parameters for a neural network that should be optimized. This results in a parameterized conditional prior distribution over the RNN state variable, through which we can track the distribution flexibly.

The first term of the integral in Eq. 3 implies sampling new displacements from the prior distribution p, which is conditioned on the latent variable $\mathbf{z}_i^t$, and on the observations and previous displacements captured by $\mathbf{h}_i^{t-1}$, i.e.

$$\mathbf{d}_i^t \sim p_\xi(\cdot|\mathbf{z}_i^t, \mathbf{h}_i^{t-1}), \tag{5}$$

with parameters ξ. Given the displacement definition $\mathbf{d}_i^t$, we obtain

$$\mathbf{x}_i^t = \mathbf{x}_i^T + \sum_{\tau=T+1}^t \mathbf{d}_i^\tau, \tag{6}$$

as a stochastic prediction for the spatial position of agent i at time t.

Inference Model. To approximate the posterior q over the latent variables, we consider the whole GT observation $\mathcal{O}_i^{1:T+H}$ to shape the latent variable distribution via a backward recurrent network [14,16]:

$$\mathbf{b}_i^t = \overleftarrow{g}(\mathcal{O}_i^t, \mathbf{b}_i^{t+1}), \tag{7}$$

for $t = T+1, \cdots, T+H$ given the initial state $\mathbf{b}_i^{T+H+1} = \mathbf{0}$. The state variable $\mathbf{b}_i^t$ provides the GT trajectory information backward from $T + H$ to t. By defining the posterior distribution as a function of both the backward state $\mathbf{b}_i^t$ and forward state $\mathbf{h}_i^t$, the latent variable $\mathbf{z}_i^t$ is drawn implicitly during inference based on the entire GT trajectory. With ϕ denoting the parameters of the network mapping $\mathbf{b}_i^t$ and $\mathbf{h}_i^{t-1}$ to the posterior parameters, we can sample latent variables as

$$\mathbf{z}_i^t \sim q_\phi(\cdot|\mathbf{b}_i^t, \mathbf{h}_i^{t-1}). \tag{8}$$

The computation graph shown in Fig. 1 gives an illustration of the dependencies of our generative and inference models. Note that the inference model (red parts in Fig. 1) is employed only at training. During testing or evaluation, only the generative model coupled with the observation encoding module is used to perform predictions, and no information from future trajectories is considered.

Training. Similarly to the standard VAE, the learning objective of our model is to maximize the evidence lower bound (ELBO) that sums up over all time steps given the target distribution defined in Eq. 3:

$$\sum_{t=T+1}^{T+H} \mathbb{E}_{\mathbf{z}_i^t \sim q_\phi(\cdot|\mathbf{b}_i^t, \mathbf{h}_i^{t-1})} \left[\log p_\xi(\mathbf{d}_i^t|\mathbf{z}_i^t, \mathbf{h}_i^{t-1})\right] - D_{KL}\left[q_\phi(\mathbf{z}_i^t|\mathbf{b}_i^t, \mathbf{h}_i^{t-1})\|p_\theta(\mathbf{z}_i^t|\mathbf{h}_i^{t-1})\right]. \tag{9}$$

where p_ξ, q_ϕ and p_θ are parameterized as Gaussian distributions by networks.

Optimizing Eq. 9 with the GT value of $\mathbf{d}_i^t$ ignores accumulated errors when we project $\mathbf{d}_i^t$ back to $\mathbf{x}_i^t$ to get the final trajectory (Eq. 6). Hence, we replace the log-likelihood term with the squared error over $\mathbf{x}_i^t$ and optimize over $\mathbf{d}_i^t$ through reparameterization tricks [23], for prediction errors in previous time steps to be compensated in next time steps. The final training loss is

$$\mathbb{E}_i\left[\frac{1}{H} \sum_{t=T+1}^{T+H} \mathbb{E}_{\substack{\mathbf{d}_i^t \sim p_\xi(\cdot|\mathbf{z}_i^t, \mathbf{h}_i^{t-1}) \\ \mathbf{z}_i^t \sim q_\phi(\cdot|\mathbf{b}_i^t, \mathbf{h}_i^{t-1})}} \left[\|(\mathbf{x}_i^t - \mathbf{x}_i^T) - \sum_{\tau=T+1}^t \mathbf{d}_i^\tau\|^2 + q_\phi(\mathbf{z}_i^t|\mathbf{b}_i^t, \mathbf{h}_i^{t-1}) - p_\theta(\mathbf{z}_i^t|\mathbf{h}_i^{t-1})\right]\right]. \tag{10}$$

For simplicity, at training, we sample $\mathbf{z}_i^t$ and $\mathbf{d}_i^t$ only once every time, and use the reparameterization trick of Gaussian distributions to update q_ϕ, p_ξ and p_θ.

3.2   Observation Encoding

Consider a scene with an agent i being the target of our prediction process and multiple neighboring agents (their number may vary along the observation sequence of agent i). We define the local observation from agent i to the whole scene at time step $t = 2, \cdots, T$ as the vector containing the observation to the agent itself and the synthesis of all its neighbors:

$$\mathcal{O}_i^t := \left[f_{\mathbf{s}}(\mathbf{s}_i^t), \sum_j w_{j|i}^t f_{\mathbf{n}}(\mathbf{n}_{j|i}^t) \right], \tag{11}$$

where

- $\mathbf{s}_i^t := \left[\mathbf{d}_i^t, \mathbf{d}_i^t - \mathbf{d}_i^{t-1}\right] \in \mathbb{R}^4$ is the self-state of agent i, including the agent's velocity and acceleration information represented by position displacement,
- $\mathbf{n}_{j|i}^t := \left[\mathbf{x}_j^t - \mathbf{x}_i^t, \mathbf{d}_j^t - \mathbf{d}_i^t\right] \in \mathbb{R}^4$ is the local state of neighbor agent j relative to agent i, including its relative position and velocity,
- $f_{\mathbf{s}}$ and $f_{\mathbf{n}}$ are learnable feature extraction neural networks,
- $w_{j|i}^t$ is an attention weight through which features from an arbitrary number of neighbors are fused together into a fixed-length vector.

Neighbors are re-defined at every time step: agent j is a neighbor of agent i at time step t if $j \neq i$ and $\|\mathbf{x}_j^t - \mathbf{x}_i^t\| < r_i$ where r_i is the maximal observation range of agent i. Non-neighbor agents are ignored when we compose the local observation $\mathcal{O}_i^t$. Note that we use the attention mechanism only for past observations $t \leq T$. In the case of the backward recurrent network used in Eq. 7, we simply set $w_{j|i}^t = 1$ for all neighbors to form $\mathcal{O}_i^t$ for $t > T$.

To represent the past observation sequence while embedding the target agent's navigation strategy, we employ a RNN to encode the observations sequentially via the state variable $\mathbf{q}_i^t$, i.e. $\mathcal{O}_i^{1:t} := \mathbf{q}_i^t$, with $\mathbf{q}_i^t$ updated recurrently through

$$\mathbf{q}_i^{t+1} = g(\mathcal{O}_i^{t+1}, \mathbf{q}_i^t). \tag{12}$$

The initial state $\mathbf{q}_i^1$ is extracted from the agent's and its neighbors' initial positions at $t = 1$:

$$\mathbf{q}_i^1 = \sum_j f_{\mathrm{init}}(\mathbf{x}_j^1 - \mathbf{x}_i^1), \tag{13}$$

where f_{init} is a feature extraction neural network.

The attention weights, $w_{j|i}^t$, are obtained by a graph attention mechanism [47], encoding node features by learnable edge weights. To synthesize neighbors at time step t based on observations from agent i, we regard agent i and its neighbors as nodes in a graph with directed edges from the neighbor to the agent. Attention weights corresponding to the edge weights are computed by

$$w_{j|i}^t = \frac{\exp(e_{j|i}^t)}{\sum_{k \neq i} \exp(e_{k|i}^t)}, \tag{14}$$

where $e^t_{j|i}$ is the edge weight from the neighbor node j to the agent node i. To obtain the edge weights, following [2], we define the social features $\mathbf{k}^t_{j|i}$ of a neighbor j observed by the agent i at time step t using three geometric features: (1) the Euclidean distance between agents i and j, (2) the cosine value of the bearing angle from agent i to neighbor j, and (3) the minimal predicted distance [32] from agent i to j within a given time horizon.

Given the neighbor's social features $\mathbf{k}^t_{j|i}$ and the agent's navigation features $\mathbf{q}^{t-1}_i$, we compute the edge weight through the cosine similarity:

$$e^t_{j|i} = \text{LeakyReLU}(f_{\mathbf{q}}(\mathbf{q}^{t-1}_i) \cdot f_{\mathbf{k}}(\mathbf{k}^t_{j|i})), \tag{15}$$

where $f_{\mathbf{q}}$ and $f_{\mathbf{k}}$ are neural networks. This leads to a dot-product attention using social features to synthesize neighbors while modeling the observations of an agent as a graph. Here, $\mathbf{q}^{t-1}_i$, $\{\mathbf{k}^t_{j|i}\}$ and $\{f_{\mathbf{n}}(\mathbf{n}^t_{j|i})\}$ correspond to the query, key and value vectors, respectively, in the vanilla attention mechanism (cf. Fig 1).

In contrast to prior works [2,17,38] that apply attention mechanisms only on the last frame of the given observation sequence, our approach computes attention at every time step. This allows to better extract an agent's navigation strategy while always taking into account the social influence from the neighbors. While prior works use RNN hidden states to represent each neighbor, our approach relies only on the neighbors' observed states, allowing to support sparse interactions where a neighbor is not consistently tracked.

3.3   Final Position Clustering

The combination of the timewise VAE approach from 3.1 and the observation encoding from 3.2 defines our vanilla SocialVAE model. It produces as many trajectory samples from the predictive distribution as required to infer the distribution over an agent's future position. However, when only a limited number of prediction samples are drawn from the distribution, bias issues may arise as some samples may fall into low-density regions or too many samples may be concentrated in high-density regions. As such, we propose *Final Position Clustering* (FPC) as an optional

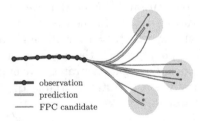

observation
prediction
FPC candidate

Fig. 2. An example of FPC to extract 3 predictions (orange) from 9 samples.

postprocessing technique to improve the prediction diversity. With FPC, we sample at a higher rate than the desired number of predictions K. Then we run a K-means clustering on the samples' final positions and for each of the K clusters, we keep only the sample whose final position is the closest to the cluster's mean. This generates K predictions in total as the final result. Figure 2 shows an example of FPC selecting 3 predictions (orange) from 9 samples. Green trajectories depict discarded prediction samples and cyan regions are the clustering result from the final positions of these 9 samples.

4   Experiments

In the following, we first give details on the implementation of SocialVAE and introduce the metrics used for evaluation. Then, we report and analyze experiments on two standard datasets: ETH/UCY [26,34] and SDD [37], and on the SportVU NBA movement dataset [27,57] which is a more challenging benchmark containing a rich set of complex human-human interactions.

Implementation Details. Our approach uses a local observation encoding and ignores agents' global coordinates. To eliminate the global moving direction preferences, we apply two types of data augmentation: flipping and rotation. We employ GRUs [12] as the RNN structure. The slope of the LeakyReLU activation layer is 0.2. The time horizon used for the minimal predicted distance is 7s. The latent variables $\mathbf{z}_i^t$ are modeled as 32-dimensional, Gaussian-distributed variables. All models are trained with 8-frame observations ($T = 8$) and 12-frame predictions ($H = 12$). The choice of sampling rate K provides a tradeoff between evaluation performance and runtime and varies per dataset. An upper bound is set at 50. We refer to our code repository for our implementation, hyperparameters values and pre-trained models. During inference, vanilla SocialVAE runs in real time on a machine equipped with a V100 GPU, performing 20 stochastic predictions within 0.05s for a batch of 1,024 observation samples.

Evaluation Metrics and Baselines. To evaluate our approach, we consider a deterministic prediction method, *Linear*, which considers agents moving with constant velocities, and the current state-of-the-art (SOTA) baselines of stochastic prediction in human-human interaction settings, as shown in Table 1. Following the literature, we use best-of-20 predictions to compute *Average Displacement Error* (ADE) and *Final Displacement Error* (FDE) as the main metrics, and also report the *Negative Log Likelihood* (NLL) estimated from 2,000 samples. We refer to the supplemental material for details about these metrics. Among the considered baselines, PECNet [30], AgentFormer [56] and MemoNet [52] rely on postprocessing to improve the model performance. The reported numbers for Trajectron++ [40], BiTraP [54] and SGNet-ED [49] were obtained by training the models from scratch using the publicly released code after fixing a recently reported issue [3,28,58] which leads to performance discrepancies compared to the numbers mentioned in the original papers.

4.1   Quantitative Evaluation

Experiments on ETH/UCY. ETH/UCY benchmark [26,34] contains trajectories of 1,536 pedestrians recorded in five different scenes. We use the same preprocessing and evaluation methods as in prior works [2,17] and apply leave-one-out cross-validation. Table 1 shows the ADE/FDE results in meters. As it can be seen, the linear model struggles to capture the complex movement patterns of pedestrians, with high errors in most test cases, though some of its results [42] are better than the GAN-based approaches of SocialGAN [17], SoPhie [38] and

Table 1. Prediction errors reported as ADE/FDE in meters for ETH/UCY and in pixels for SDD. The reported values are the mean values of ADE/FDE using the best of 20 predictions for each trajectory.

	ETH	Hotel	Univ	Zara01	Zara02	SDD
Linear	1.07/2.28	0.31/0.61	0.52/1.16	0.42/0.95	0.32/0.72	19.74/40.04
SocialGAN	0.64/1.09	0.46/0.98	0.56/1.18	0.33/0.67	0.31/0.64	27.23/41.44
SoPhie	0.70/1.43	0.76/1.67	0.54/1.24	0.30/0.63	0.38/0.78	16.27/29.38
SocialWays	0.39/0.64	0.39/0.66	0.55/1.31	0.44/0.64	0.51/0.92	-
STAR	**0.36**/0.65	0.17/0.36	0.31/0.62	0.29/0.52	0.22/0.46	-
TransformerTF	0.61/1.12	0.18/0.30	0.35/0.65	0.22/0.38	0.17/0.32	-
MANTRA	0.48/0.88	0.17/0.33	0.37/0.81	0.22/0.38	0.17/0.32	8.96/17.76
MemoNet[†]	0.40/0.61	**0.11/0.17**	0.24/0.43	0.18/0.32	0.14/0.24	8.56/12.66
PECNet[†]	0.54/0.87	0.18/0.24	0.35/0.60	0.22/0.39	0.17/0.30	9.29/15.93
Trajectron++[*]	0.54/0.94	0.16/0.28	0.28/0.55	0.21/0.42	0.16/0.32	10.00/17.15
AgentFormer[†]	0.45/0.75	0.14/0.22	0.25/0.45	0.18/0.30	0.14/0.24	-
BiTraP[*]	0.56/0.98	0.17/0.28	0.25/0.47	0.23/0.45	0.16/0.33	9.09/16.31
SGNet-ED[*]	0.47/0.77	0.21/0.44	0.33/0.62	0.18/0.32	0.15/0.28	9.69/17.01
SocialVAE	0.47/0.76	0.14/0.22	0.25/0.47	0.20/0.37	0.14/0.28	8.88/14.81
SocialVAE+FPC	0.41/**0.58**	0.13/0.19	**0.21/0.36**	**0.17/0.29**	**0.13/0.22**	**8.10/11.72**

[*]: reproduced results with a known issue fixed [†]: baselines using postprocessing

SocialWays [2]. STAR [55] and TransformerTF [15] use Transformer architectures as a model backbone. While both Transformer-based approaches outperform the listed GAN-based approaches, with STAR achieving the best performance on ETH, they tend not to be better than the VAE-based models of Trajectron++, BiTraP and SGNet-ED. Compared to conditional-VAE baselines, our model leads to better performance, both with and without FPC. Specifically, without FPC, the improvement of SocialVAE over SGNet-ED is about 12% both on ADE and FDE. With FPC, SocialVAE improves SGNet-ED by 21% and 30% in ADE and FDE, respectively. Compared to approaches that require postprocessing, SocialVAE+FPC brings an improvement around 9% on ADE and 13% on FDE over AgentFormer, and 5% on FDE over MemoNet while allowing for faster inference speeds and without requiring any extra space for memory storage. The NLL evaluation results in Table 2 further show that the SocialVAE predictive distributions have superior quality, with higher probability (lower NLL) on the GT trajectories. For a fair comparison, we restrict here our analysis on SOTA methods from Table 1 that do not rely on postprocessing.

Experiments on SDD. SDD [37] includes trajectories of 5,232 pedestrians in eight different scenes. We used the TrajNet [6] split to perform the training/testing processes and converted original pixel coordinates into spatial coordinates defined in meters for training. The related ADE/FDE and NLL results are reported in Tables 1 and 2, respectively. Following previous works, ADE and FDE are reported in pixels. As shown in Table 2, SocialVAE leads to more accurate trajectory distributions as compared to other VAE-based baselines. In addition, SocialVAE+FPC provides a significant improvement over existing baselines in terms of FDE as reported in Table 1. Given that SDD has different homographies at each scene, to draw a fair comparison with results reported in meters, we refer to additional results in the supplemental materials.

Table 2. NLL estimation on tested datasets

	ETH	Hotel	Univ	Zara01	Zara02	SDD	Rebounding	Scoring
Trajectron++	2.26	−0.52	0.32	−0.05	−1.00	1.76	2.41	2.69
BiTraP	3.68	0.48	0.71	0.49	−0.69	0.87	2.92	3.23
SGNet-ED	2.65	0.92	1.36	0.13	−0.77	1.53	3.28	3.05
SocialVAE	**0.96**	**−1.41**	**−0.49**	**−0.65**	**−2.67**	**−0.43**	**1.90**	**1.67**

Experiment on NBA Dataset. We tested SocialVAE on the SportVU NBA movement dataset focusing on NBA games from the 2015–2016 season [27,57]. Due to the large size of the original dataset, we extracted two sub-datasets to use as benchmarks named Rebounding and Scoring, consisting of 257,230 and 2,958,480 20-frame trajectories, respectively. We refer to the supplemental

Table 3. ADE/FDE on NBA Datasets

Unit: feet	Rebounding	Scoring
Linear	2.14/5.09	2.07/4.81
Trajectron++	0.98/1.93	0.73/1.46
BiTraP	0.83/1.72	0.74/1.49
SGNet-ED	0.78/1.55	0.68/1.30
SocialVAE	0.72/1.37	0.64/1.17
SocialVAE+FPC	**0.66/1.10**	**0.58/0.95**

materials for details on data acquisition. The extracted trajectories capture a rich set of agent-agent interactions and highly non-linear motions. Note that the overall frequency and the adversarial and cooperative nature of the interactions are significantly different from those in ETH/UCY and SDD, which makes trajectory prediction much more challenging [28]. This is confirmed by the rather poor performance of the Linear baseline in such scenes (Table 3). SocialVAE achieves low ADE/FDE on both datasets, much better than the ones reported in prior work [28,52], though it is unclear what training/testing data such works have used. Hence, we report our own comparisons to other VAE baselines in Tables 2 and 3. Similar to ETH/UCY and SDD, SocialVAE exhibits SOTA performance on the two NBA datasets.

4.2 Qualitative Evaluation

Case Study on ETH/UCY. Figure 3 compares trajectories generated by SocialVAE with and without FPC in the Zara scene. We show heatmaps of the predictive distributions in the 3rd row. They cover the GT trajectories very well in the first three scenarios. In the 4th scenario, the agent takes a right turn that can be hardly captured from the 8-frame observation in which he keeps walking on a straight line. Though the GT trajectory is rather far from the average

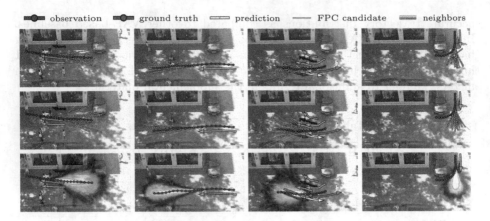

Fig. 3. Examples of predictions from SocialVAE in the UCY *Zara* scene. Observed trajectories appear in blue, predicted trajectories appear in orange, and GT is shown in red. From top to bottom: SocialVAE without FPC, SocialVAE+FPC, and heatmaps of the predicted trajectory distribution. Heatmaps are generated using 2,000 samples.

Fig. 4. Attention maps at the 1st (left) and 20th (right) frames in UCY *students003*. Trajectories of the pedestrian under prediction appear in blue. The other colored lines with arrows are the observed neighbors. Yellow dots denote stationary neighbors.

prediction, SocialVAE's output distribution still partially covers it. Using FPC improves the predictions diversity and helps to eliminate outliers. For example, the topmost predictions in the 2nd and 3rd columns and the rightmost one in the 4th column are drawn from low-probability regions and eliminated by FPC.

To better understand how the social-feature attention mechanism impacts the prediction model, we show the attention maps of scenes from *students003* in Fig. 4. The maps are generated by visualizing the attention weights (Eq. 14) with respect to each neighbor as a white circle drawn on the location of that neighbor. The opacity and the radius of the circle increases with the weight of its associated neighbor. As it can be seen, in the 1st frame, while monitoring the three neighbors on the right, much attention is paid to the green neighbor at the bottom who seems to be headed toward the pedestrian. In the 20th frame, the model ignores the green agent as it has changed its direction, and shifts its attention to the three nearby neighbors (red, purple, yellow). Among these neighbors, more attention is paid to the yellow agent walking toward the target pedestrian and less to the ones behind. In both scenes, the top-left, faraway neighbor is ignored along with the idle neighbors (yellow dots).

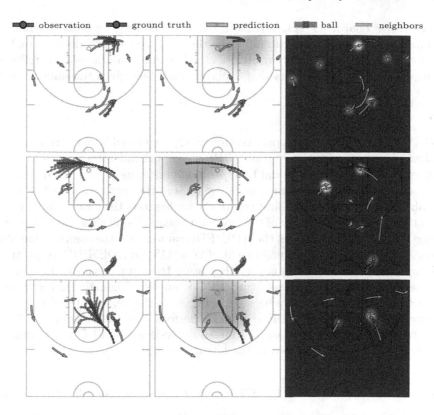

Fig. 5. Examples of predictions from SocialVAE on NBA datasets. From left to right: predicted trajectories, distribution heatmaps and attention maps. The azure lines with arrows denote trajectories of players who are in the same team as the one under prediction. The pink ones denote opposing players. The orange indicates the ball.

Case Study on NBA Datasets. The NBA scenarios contain rich interactions between players in both close and remote ranges. Players show distinct movement patterns with fast changes in heading directions. Despite such complex behaviors, SocialVAE provides high-quality predictions, with distributions covering the GT trajectories closely. In the challenging example shown in the 1st row of Fig. 5, our model successfully predicts the player's intention to change his moving direction sharply and to shake his marker and catch the ball. The predictive distribution gives several directions consistent with this intention and covers well the one that the player actually took. From the attention map, we see that the model pays more attention to the defensive player who follows the one under prediction, and, across the range from the baseline to the three-point line, to the ball. Though we do not have any semantic information about the ball, our observation encoding approach helps the model identify its importance based on historical observations. Similar behaviors are found in the examples of the 2nd and 3rd rows, where the player performs a fast move to create a passing lane and to crash the offensive board, respectively. Note that our model pays more attention to teammates and opponents who influence the predicted agent's decision making. Furthermore, the predicted trajectories clearly exhibit multimodality, reflecting multiple responding behaviors that a player could take given the same scenario.

4.3 Ablation Study

SocialVAE has four key components: timewisely generated latent variables (TL), backward posterior approximation (BP), neighborhood attention using social features (ATT), and an optional final position clustering (FPC). To understand the contributions of these components, we present the results of ablation studies in Table 4. For reference, the first row of the table shows the base performance of SocialVAE without using any of the key components. Using either the TL scheme or the BP formulation reduces the ADE/FDE values, with the combination of the two leading to an average improvement of 26%/11% on ADE/FDE, respectively. Adding the ATT mechanism can further bring the error down. In the last row, we also report the performance when FPC is applied, highlighting the value of prediction diversity. As it can be seen, using all of the four components leads to a considerable decrease in FDE and SOTA performance (cf. Tables 1 and 3). We refer to the supplementary material for an analysis on the FPC's sampling rate and explanatory visualizations of the latent space.

Table 4. Ablation studies. ETH/UCY results are the average over five tested scenes.

$\uparrow^a$ (%)	TL^b	BP^c	ATT^d	FPC	**ETH/UCY**	**SDD**	**Rebounding**	**Scoring**
	-	-	-	-	0.35/0.50	13.43/17.81	1.02/1.48	1.03/1.43
14/3	✓	-	-	-	0.32/0.48	11.08/17.50	0.81/1.46	0.84/1.40
20/6	-	✓	-	-	0.30/0.47	9.45/16.01	0.78/1.46	0.74/1.39
26/11	✓	✓	-	-	0.26/0.44	9.31/15.09	0.76/1.43	0.70/1.32
33/16	✓	✓	✓	-	0.24/0.42	8.88/14.81	0.72/1.37	0.64/1.17
38/32	✓	✓	✓	✓	0.21/0.33	8.10/11.72	0.66/1.10	0.58/0.95

[a] $\uparrow$: average performance improvement related the top row as baseline;
[b] TL: timewise latents; [c] BP: backward posterior; [d] ATT: neighborhood attention

5   Conclusion and Future Work

We introduce SocialVAE as a novel approach for human trajectory prediction. It uses an attention-based mechanism to extract human navigation strategies from the social features exhibited in short-term observations, and relies on a time-wise VAE architecture using RNN structures to generate stochastic predictions for future trajectories. Our backward RNN structure in posterior approximation helps synthesizing whole trajectories for navigation feature extraction. We also introduce FPC, a clustering method applied on the predicted trajectories final positions, to improve the quality of our prediction with a limited number of prediction samples. Our approach shows state-of-the-art performance in most of the test cases from the ETH/UCY and SDD trajectory prediction benchmarks. We also highlighted the applicability of SocialVAE to SportVU NBA data. To further improve the prediction quality and generate physically acceptable trajectories, an avenue for future work is to introduce semantic scene information as a part of the model input. By doing so, our model could explicitly take both human-space and human-agent interactions into account for prediction. This would also allow us to further evaluate SocialVAE on heterogeneous datasets [9, 11].

Acknowledgements. This work was supported by the National Science Foundation under Grant No. IIS-2047632.

References

1. Alahi, A., Goel, K., Ramanathan, V., Robicquet, A., Fei-Fei, L., Savarese, S.: Social LSTM: human trajectory prediction in crowded spaces. In: Proceedings of the IEEE Conference on Computer Vision and Pattern Recognition, pp. 961–971 (2016)
2. Amirian, J., Hayet, J.B., Pettré, J.: Social ways: learning multi-modal distributions of pedestrian trajectories with GANs. In: Proceedings of the IEEE/CVF Conference on Computer Vision and Pattern Recognition Workshops (2019)
3. Bae, I., Park, J.H., Jeon, H.G.: Non-probability sampling network for stochastic human trajectory prediction. In: Proceedings of the IEEE/CVF Conference on Computer Vision and Pattern Recognition, pp. 6477–6487 (2022)
4. Ballan, L., Castaldo, F., Alahi, A., Palmieri, F., Savarese, S.: Knowledge transfer for scene-specific motion prediction. In: Leibe, B., Matas, J., Sebe, N., Welling, M. (eds.) ECCV 2016. LNCS, vol. 9905, pp. 697–713. Springer, Cham (2016). https://doi.org/10.1007/978-3-319-46448-0_42
5. Bayer, J., Osendorfer, C.: Learning stochastic recurrent networks. arXiv preprint arXiv:1411.7610 (2014)
6. Becker, S., Hug, R., Hübner, W., Arens, M.: An evaluation of trajectory prediction approaches and notes on the TrajNet benchmark. arXiv preprint arXiv:1805.07663 (2018)
7. van den Berg, J., Guy, S.J., Lin, M., Manocha, D.: Reciprocal n-body collision avoidance. In: International Symposium of Robotics Research, pp. 3–19 (2011)
8. Brown, T., et al.: Language models are few-shot learners. Adv. Neural. Inf. Process. Syst. **33**, 1877–1901 (2020)
9. Caesar, H., et al.: nuScenes: a multimodal dataset for autonomous driving. In: IEEE/CVF Conference on Computer Vision and Pattern Recognition, pp. 11618–11628 (2020)
10. Cao, Z., Gao, H., Mangalam, K., Cai, Q.-Z., Vo, M., Malik, J.: Long-term human motion prediction with scene context. In: Vedaldi, A., Bischof, H., Brox, T., Frahm, J.-M. (eds.) ECCV 2020. LNCS, vol. 12346, pp. 387–404. Springer, Cham (2020). https://doi.org/10.1007/978-3-030-58452-8_23
11. Chandra, R., Bhattacharya, U., Bera, A., Manocha, D.: Traphic: trajectory prediction in dense and heterogeneous traffic using weighted interactions. In: Proceedings of the IEEE/CVF Conference on Computer Vision and Pattern Recognition (2019)

12. Cho, K., et al.: Learning phrase representations using RNN encoder-decoder for statistical machine translation. arXiv preprint arXiv:1406.1078 (2014)

13. Chung, J., Kastner, K., Dinh, L., Goel, K., Courville, A.C., Bengio, Y.: A recurrent latent variable model for sequential data. In: Advances in Neural Information Processing Systems 28 (2015)

14. Fraccaro, M., Sønderby, S.K., Paquet, U., Winther, O.: Sequential neural models with stochastic layers. In: Advances in Neural Information Processing Systems 29 (2016)

15. Giuliari, F., Hasan, I., Cristani, M., Galasso, F.: Transformer networks for trajectory forecasting. In: IEEE International Conference on Pattern Recognition, pp. 10335–10342 (2021)

16. Goyal, A., Sordoni, A., Côté, M.A., Ke, N.R., Bengio, Y.: Z-forcing: Training stochastic recurrent networks. In: Advances in Neural Information Processing Systems 30 (2017)

17. Gupta, A., Johnson, J., Fei-Fei, L., Savarese, S., Alahi, A.: Social GAN: socially acceptable trajectories with generative adversarial networks. In: Proceedings of the IEEE/CVF Conference on Computer Vision and Pattern Recognition, pp. 2255–2264 (2018)

18. Helbing, D., Farkas, I., Vicsek, T.: Simulating dynamical features of escape panic. Nature **407**(6803), 487–490 (2000)

19. Helbing, D., Molnar, P.: Social force model for pedestrian dynamics. Phys. Rev. E **51**(5), 4282 (1995)

20. Ivanovic, B., Pavone, M.: The trajectron: probabilistic multi-agent trajectory modeling with dynamic spatiotemporal graphs. In: Proceedings of the IEEE/CVF International Conference on Computer Vision, pp. 2375–2384 (2019)

21. Karamouzas, I., Skinner, B., Guy, S.J.: Universal power law governing pedestrian interactions. Phys. Rev. Lett. **113**(23), 238701 (2014)

22. Kim, K., Lee, D., Essa, I.: Gaussian process regression flow for analysis of motion trajectories. In: IEEE International Conference on Computer Vision, pp. 1164–1171 (2011)

23. Kingma, D.P., Welling, M.: Auto-encoding variational bayes. In: Bengio, Y., LeCun, Y. (eds.) International Conference on Learning Representations (2014)

24. Kitani, K.M., Ziebart, B.D., Bagnell, J.A., Hebert, M.: Activity forecasting. In: Fitzgibbon, A., Lazebnik, S., Perona, P., Sato, Y., Schmid, C. (eds.) ECCV 2012. LNCS, vol. 7575, pp. 201–214. Springer, Heidelberg (2012). https://doi.org/10.1007/978-3-642-33765-9_15

25. Kochkov, D., Smith, J.A., Alieva, A., Wang, Q., Brenner, M.P., Hoyer, S.: Machine learning-accelerated computational fluid dynamics. Proc. National Acad. Sci. 118(21) (2021)

26. Lerner, A., Chrysanthou, Y., Lischinski, D.: Crowds by example. In: Computer Graphics Forum, vol. 26, pp. 655–664. Wiley Online Library (2007)

27. Linou, K., Linou, D., de Boer, M.: NBA player movements. github.com/linouk23/NBA-Player-Movements (2016)

28. Makansi, O., et al.: You mostly walk alone: analyzing feature attribution in trajectory prediction. In: International Conference on Learning Representations (2022)

29. Mangalam, K., An, Y., Girase, H., Malik, J.: From goals, waypoints & paths to long term human trajectory forecasting. In: Proceedings of the IEEE/CVF International Conference on Computer Vision, pp. 15233–15242 (2021)

30. Mangalam, K., Girase, H., Agarwal, S., Lee, K.-H., Adeli, E., Malik, J., Gaidon, A.: It is not the journey but the destination: endpoint conditioned trajectory prediction. In: Vedaldi, A., Bischof, H., Brox, T., Frahm, J.-M. (eds.) ECCV 2020. LNCS, vol. 12347, pp. 759–776. Springer, Cham (2020). https://doi.org/10.1007/978-3-030-58536-5_45

31. Marchetti, F., Becattini, F., Seidenari, L., Bimbo, A.D.: Mantra: memory augmented networks for multiple trajectory prediction. In: Proceedings of the IEEE/CVF Conference on Computer Vision and Pattern Recognition, pp. 7143–7152 (2020)

32. Olivier, A.H., Marin, A., Crétual, A., Pettré, J.: Minimal predicted distance: a common metric for collision avoidance during pairwise interactions between walkers. Gait & Posture **36**(3), 399–404 (2012)

33. Van den Oord, A., Kalchbrenner, N., Espeholt, L., Vinyals, O., Graves, A., et al.: Conditional image generation with PixelCNN decoders. In: Advances in Neural Information Processing Systems 29 (2016)

34. Pellegrini, S., Ess, A., Schindler, K., Van Gool, L.: You'll never walk alone: modeling social behavior for multi-target tracking. In: IEEE International Conference on Computer Vision, pp. 261–268 (2009)

35. Pradhan, N., Burg, T., Birchfield, S.: Robot crowd navigation using predictive position fields in the potential function framework. In: Proceedings of the 2011 American control conference, pp. 4628–4633. IEEE (2011)

36. Ravuri, S., et al.: Skilful precipitation nowcasting using deep generative models of radar. Nature **597**(7878), 672–677 (2021)

37. Robicquet, A., Sadeghian, A., Alahi, A., Savarese, S.: Learning social etiquette: human trajectory understanding in crowded scenes. In: Leibe, B., Matas, J., Sebe, N., Welling, M. (eds.) ECCV 2016. LNCS, vol. 9912, pp. 549–565. Springer, Cham (2016). https://doi.org/10.1007/978-3-319-46484-8_33

38. Sadeghian, A., Kosaraju, V., Sadeghian, A., Hirose, N., Rezatofighi, H., Savarese, S.: Sophie: an attentive GAN for predicting paths compliant to social and physical constraints. In: Proceedings of the IEEE/CVF Conference on Computer Vision and Pattern Recognition, pp. 1349–1358 (2019)

39. Sadeghian, A., Legros, F., Voisin, M., Vesel, R., Alahi, A., Savarese, S.: Car-Net: clairvoyant attentive recurrent network. In: European Conference on Computer Vision, pp. 151–167 (2018)

40. Salzmann, T., Ivanovic, B., Chakravarty, P., Pavone, M.: Trajectron++: dynamically-feasible trajectory forecasting with heterogeneous data. In: Vedaldi, A., Bischof, H., Brox, T., Frahm, J.-M. (eds.) ECCV 2020. LNCS, vol. 12363, pp. 683–700. Springer, Cham (2020). https://doi.org/10.1007/978-3-030-58523-5_40

41. Sanchez-Gonzalez, A., Godwin, J., Pfaff, T., Ying, R., Leskovec, J., Battaglia, P.: Learning to simulate complex physics with graph networks. In: International Conference on Machine Learning, pp. 8459–8468 (2020)

42. Schöller, C., Aravantinos, V., Lay, F., Knoll, A.C.: What the constant velocity model can teach us about pedestrian motion prediction. IEEE Robotics Autom. Lett. **5**(2), 1696–1703 (2020)

43. Sohn, K., Lee, H., Yan, X.: Learning structured output representation using deep conditional generative models. Adv. Neural. Inf. Process. Syst. **28**, 3483–3491 (2015)

44. Trautman, P., Krause, A.: Unfreezing the robot: navigation in dense, interacting crowds. In: IEEE/RSJ International Conference on Intelligent Robots and Systems, pp. 797–803 (2010)

45. Van Oord, A., Kalchbrenner, N., Kavukcuoglu, K.: Pixel recurrent neural networks. In: International Conference on Machine Learning, pp. 1747–1756 (2016)
46. Vaswani, A., et al.: Attention is all you need. In: Advances in Neural Information Processing Systems 30 (2017)
47. Veličković, P., Cucurull, G., Casanova, A., Romero, A., Lio, P., Bengio, Y.: Graph attention networks. arXiv preprint arXiv:1710.10903 (2017)
48. Vemula, A., Muelling, K., Oh, J.: Social attention: modeling attention in human crowds. In: IEEE international Conference on Robotics and Automation, pp. 4601–4607 (2018)
49. Wang, C., Wang, Y., Xu, M., Crandall, D.: Stepwise goal-driven networks for trajectory prediction. IEEE Robot. Autom. Lett. (2022)
50. Wang, J.M., Fleet, D.J., Hertzmann, A.: Gaussian process dynamical models for human motion. IEEE Trans. Pattern Anal. Mach. Intell. **30**(2), 283–298 (2007)
51. Weyn, J.A., Durran, D.R., Caruana, R.: Can machines learn to predict weather? using deep learning to predict gridded 500-HPA geopotential height from historical weather data. J. Adv. Model. Earth Syst. **11**(8), 2680–2693 (2019)
52. Xu, C., Mao, W., Zhang, W., Chen, S.: Remember intentions: retrospective-memory-based trajectory prediction. In: Proceedings of the IEEE/CVF Conference on Computer Vision and Pattern Recognition, pp. 6488–6497 (2022)
53. Yamaguchi, K., Berg, A.C., Ortiz, L.E., Berg, T.L.: Who are you with and where are you going? In: Proceedings of the IEEE Conference on Computer Vision and Pattern Recognition, pp. 1345–1352 (2011)
54. Yao, Y., Atkins, E., Johnson-Roberson, M., Vasudevan, R., Du, X.: BiTraP: bi-directional pedestrian trajectory prediction with multi-modal goal estimation. IEEE Robot. Autom. Lett. **6**(2), 1463–1470 (2021)
55. Yu, C., Ma, X., Ren, J., Zhao, H., Yi, S.: Spatio-temporal graph transformer networks for pedestrian trajectory prediction. In: Vedaldi, A., Bischof, H., Brox, T., Frahm, J.-M. (eds.) ECCV 2020. LNCS, vol. 12357, pp. 507–523. Springer, Cham (2020). https://doi.org/10.1007/978-3-030-58610-2_30
56. Yuan, Y., Weng, X., Ou, Y., Kitani, K.: Agentformer: agent-aware transformers for socio-temporal multi-agent forecasting. arXiv preprint arXiv:2103.14023 (2021)
57. Yue, Y., Lucey, P., Carr, P., Bialkowski, A., Matthews, I.: Learning fine-grained spatial models for dynamic sports play prediction. In: IEEE International Conference on Data Mining, pp. 670–679 (2014)
58. Zamboni, S., Kefato, Z.T., Girdzijauskas, S., Norén, C., Dal Col, L.: Pedestrian trajectory prediction with convolutional neural networks. Pattern Recogn. **121**, 108252 (2022)

Shape Matters: Deformable Patch Attack

Zhaoyu Chen[1], Bo Li[2(✉)], Shuang Wu[2], Jianghe Xu[2], Shouhong Ding[2], and Wenqiang Zhang[1,3]

[1] Academy for Engineering and Technology Fudan University, Shanghai, China
[2] Youtu Lab, Tencent, Shenzhen, China
`libraboli@tencent.com`
[3] Yiwu Research Institute of Fudan University, Yiwu, China

Abstract. Though deep neural networks (DNNs) have demonstrated excellent performance in computer vision, they are susceptible and vulnerable to carefully crafted adversarial examples which can mislead DNNs to incorrect outputs. Patch attack is one of the most threatening forms, which has the potential to threaten the security of real-world systems. Previous work always assumes patches to have fixed shapes, such as circles or rectangles, and it does not consider the shape of patches as a factor in patch attacks. To explore this issue, we propose a novel Deformable Patch Representation (DPR) that can harness the geometric structure of triangles to support the differentiable mapping between contour modeling and masks. Moreover, we introduce a joint optimization algorithm, named Deformable Adversarial Patch (DAPatch), which allows simultaneous and efficient optimization of shape and texture to enhance attack performance. We show that even with a small area, a particular shape can improve attack performance. Therefore, DAPatch achieves state-of-the-art attack performance by deforming shapes on GTSRB and ILSVRC2012 across various network architectures, and the generated patches can be threatening in the real world.

Keywords: Adversarial example · Patch attack · Shape representation

1 Introduction

Despite achieving considerably excellent performance on various computer vision tasks [4, 13–17, 25, 26, 46, 52, 53, 58, 59, 61, 63, 66–68], deep neural networks (DNNs) have been shown to be susceptible and vulnerable to adversarial examples, where an adversary introduces an imperceptible perturbation to an image for inducing network misclassification [48]. Currently, adversarial examples have been found in most visual tasks, such as object detection [21, 23] and visual tracking [8, 36]. Previous attacks and defenses place emphasis on the classic setting of adversarial examples that have a global small L_p distance on the benign example [12, 22, 38, 48, 60]. However, the classic L_p setting requires global perturbation to an image, which is not always practical in the physical world.

Supplementary Information The online version contains supplementary material available at https://doi.org/10.1007/978-3-031-19772-7_31.

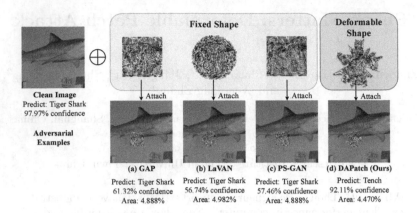

Fig. 1. Adversarial patches are generated by different methods under the untargeted attack setting. Previous work always assumes patch shapes to be circles or rectangles but our proposed DAPatch can deform the patches. As a result, DAPatch obtains a higher attack performance.

In this paper, we focus on patch attacks. It is one of the most dangerous forms of adversarial examples that an adversary can arbitrarily modify the pixels of a continuous region, and the region has to be small enough to reach the victim object in the physical world. For example, GAP [3] creates physical adversarial image patches, which cause the classifiers to ignore the other items in the scene and report a chosen target class. Then Lavan [24] shows that networks can also be fooled by much smaller patches of visible noise that cover a substantially smaller area of the image when relaxing the requirement in the digital domain.

The current patch attacks mainly consider generating robust perturbations and the shape of the patch is usually fixed, such as circles or rectangles. However, both shape and texture are shown to be essential clues for the identification of objects. Geirhos et al. [11] show that ImageNet-trained CNNs are strongly biased towards recognizing textures rather than shapes. Then Li et al. [34] find shape or texture bias has a massive impact on performance and shape-texture debiased learning can improve the accuracy and robustness. However, existing work and other physical attacks [8,10] ignore the importance of shape and assume patches to have fixed shapes, such as circles or rectangles. Specifically, adversarial patches are typically generated using gradients iteratively, and adversarial perturbations within patches could be equivalently regarded as a kind of texture. As previously mentioned, existing studies tend to concentrate on obtaining a robust adversarial texture to fool DNNs, but in this paper, we focus on another perspective of patch attacks, that is shape.

To explicitly explore the effect of shape in patch attacks, the direct approach is to deform the patch in the adversarial attack. Hence, an iterative and differentiable shape representation is required. Existing deform-related work [7,57] needs additional data for training and cannot compute differentiably during the attack patch generation. Rethinking shape modeling, we first need a deformable contour which can be represented by a point and a series of rays in the Cartesian coordinate system. Then we also need a differentiable calculation procedure to determine whether each position is outside or inside the contour.

To address this issue and explore the effect of shape on patch attacks, we propose a novel Deformable Patch Representation (DPR). The geometric structure of the triangle is used to construct a judgment point whether the point is inside or outside the contour, and the shape model can be mapped into a binary mask while ensuring the computation is differentiable. Then, to achieve a better attack performance, we propose a shape and texture joint optimization for adversarial patches. As illustrated in Fig. 1, Deformable Adversarial Patch (DAPatch) improves attack performance by deforming the shape of patches. Extensive experiments on ILSVRC2012 and GTSRB show that, under the same constraint of area, DAPatch have higher attack performance and are effective for various network architectures, such as CNNs [19,20,44,47,49] and Vision Transformer (ViT) [9,37]. Our main contributions are summarized as below:

- We propose a novel Deformable Patch Representation (DPR) that can harness the geometric structure of triangles to support the differentiable mapping between contour modeling and masks, and the shape can be differentiably deformed during patch generations.
- Based on DPR, we propose a shape and texture joint optimization algorithm for adversarial patches, named DAPatch, which can effectively optimize the shape and texture to improve attack performance.
- We show that a particular shape can improve attack performance. Extensive experiments on GTSRB and ILSVRC2012 demonstrate the adversarial threats of shapes with different networks in both digital and physical world.
- DRP first explicitly investigates the significance of shape information on DNNs' robustness through an adversarial lens and contributes to understanding and exploring the very nature of DNNs' vulnerability.

2   Related Work

Adversarial Patch. The adversarial patch currently can be mainly divided into iterative-based and generative-based methods. For the iterative-based method, GAP [3] proposes adversarial physical image patches, which cause the classifiers to predict a target class. With relaxed requirements in the digital domain, LaVAN [24] shows that networks can also be fooled by much smaller patches of visible noise that cover a much smaller area of the image. For the generative method, PS-GAN [35] refers to the patch generation via a generator as a patch-to-patch translation and simultaneously enhances both the visual fidelity and the attacking ability of the adversarial patch. Other visual tasks are also threatened by patch attacks, such as object segmentation [28–32,50,51,56,64,65], object detection [21,23] and visual tracking [8,36]. The above work can only generate patches of fixed shapes, such as circles or rectangles, without considering the impact of shape on attack performance. The generative-based method requires additional data to train a generator, which requires additional time. Furthermore, the shape of the patch cannot be deformed according to the adversarial attack. In this work, we propose Deformable Patch Representation, which can differentiably deform the patch during the adversarial attack without additional data.

Defenses Against Patch Attacks. Several empirical patch defenses are proposed such as Digital Watermark [18] and Local Gradient Smoothing [40]. However, Chiang et al. [6] demonstrate that that these empirical defenses can easily be breached by white-box attacks that take advantage of the pre-processing procedures during the optimization process. Wu et al. [54] and Sukrut et al. [42] adapt adversarial training to increase the robustness of a model against adversarial patches. Chiang et al. [6] propose the first certifiable defense against patch attacks, which gives a certificate when an output lies in the interval bound formed during the training process. Despite this, both robustness approaches require additional training and are inefficient at the ImageNet scale [6,62]. Derandomized Smoothing [27], DPGLC [33], Patchguard [55] and ECViT [5], recently proposed to improve certifiable robustness and to extend the defense to ImageNet, further improve the defense. We select patch defense that can be extended to ImageNet as the benchmark to test the effectiveness of patch attacks. Existing work has demonstrated favorable performance in defending against patch attacks. In this paper, by introducing adversarial shapes, we establish a new baseline to reflect the robustness of the defending methods against adversarial patch attacks from a novel perspective.

Shape versus Texture. Object recognition relies on two prominent and complementary cues: shape and texture. The cue that dominates object recognition has been the subject of a long-running debate. Prior to deep learning, object recognition relied on a variety of handcrafted features, such as shape [2] and texture [39]. Recently, Geirhos et al. [11] suggest that CNNs pre-trained on ImageNet exhibit a strong texture bias. Shape-based representations improve object detection and provide previously unknown robustness in the face of a range of image distortions. Furthermore, Li et al. [34] shows the benefits of shape-texture debiased neural network training on boosting both accuracy and robustness. Generating adversarial perturbations within patches could be equivalently regarded as generating a kind of texture. Previously, patch attacks consider patches more for their texture rather than their shape, so there is no deformation method in adversarial attacks. In deformable-related work, Deformable Convolution [7] and contour-based instance segmentation [57] can explicitly model deformations, but they all rely on lots of training data, and can not be differentiably mapped into a mask to participate in the generation of texture. Motivated by this dilemma, we propose the Deformable Adversarial Patch for the shape and texture joint optimization. Note that some work [42,54] has demonstrated that the positions of patches can also affect the threat of an attack, but this paper focuses on investigating the significance of shape information on DNNs' robustness. Therefore, we randomly select and fix the positions of patches to control the effect of positions on attack performance in the experiments.

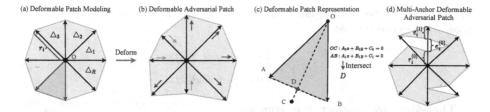

Fig. 2. Introduction of Deformable Adversarial Patch. (a) represents the contour modeling composed of one point and rays. (b) represents the deformation from (a) by updating r. (c) shows the mask obtained by differentiable calculation in a local triangle. (d) summarizes the multi-anchor mechanism on Deformable Patch Representation.

3   Method

In this section, we first introduce the problem of adversarial patch attacks on image classification and then propose our Deformable Patch Representation to deform patches during the patch generation. Then, we propose a joint optimization algorithm for improving the attack performance.

3.1   Problem Definition

For a image classifier $f : x \rightarrow y$, we denote the clean image as $x \in R^{c \times h \times w}$ and the corresponding label as y. In the traditional adversarial patch attack, adversaries attempt to find an adversarial patch δ to significantly degrade the performance of the classifier over per image. When the adversarial image at the k-th iteration is $x^k_{adv} \in R^{c \times h \times w}$, then the solving iteration will be:

$$x^k_{adv} = \delta^{k-1} \odot M + x \odot (I - M), \tag{1}$$

where $\odot$ represents the element-wise Hadmard product; $M \in \{0,1\}^{c \times h \times w}$ denotes binary masks for x^k_{adv}; I represents all-one matrices with the same dimension as M.

We denote the prediction result of x by f is $\hat{y}$. For untargeted attacks, the adversarial patch makes the model predict the wrong label, namely $\hat{y} \neq y$. For target attacks, the adversarial patch makes the model predict specified target class y_t, namely $\hat{y} = y_t$, and the target class is pre-specified.

3.2   Deformable Patch Representation

To model a deformable patch we first need a deformable contour. For simplicity, we use a polygon to represent the contour which consists of one center O and R rays in the Cartesian coordinate system, as shown in Fig. 2 (a). Then the contour deforms through the updating of the length of rays $r = \{r_1, r_2, ..., r_R\}$ during attacking. The deformation is shown in Fig. 2 (b).

Two rays and a center form a triangle and the whole patch mask can be divided into R triangles, with the angle interval $\Delta\theta = 2\pi/R$. As shown in Fig. 2

(c), for $\triangle AOB$, we define $|AO| = r_A$, $|BO| = r_B$. Therefore, for $\forall C \in x$, the mask M is expressed as:

$$M(C) = \begin{cases} 1, & C \in \triangle AOB \\ 0, & C \notin \triangle AOB. \end{cases} \tag{2}$$

Therefore, we convert the contour representation into the question of whether the point is inside or outside the contour. Next, we use the geometric properties of triangles to differentiably calculate and obtain a deformable mask. For any C falling in the area covered by $\angle AOB$, there will always be CO or the extended line of CO intersects AB at D. Note that Eq. 2 needs to be converted into computable, so we use $\frac{|CO|}{|DO|}$ to judge whether C is inside the $\triangle AOB$. Obvi-

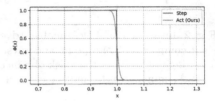

Fig. 3. The effectiveness of the activation function $\Phi(x)$. Step function represents the same effect as Eq. 3 and our activation function $\Phi(x)$ well approximates the step function.

ously, if $\frac{|CO|}{|DO|} < 1$, then $C \in \triangle AOB$ and vice versa. Since $\frac{|CO|}{|DO|} \in R^+$, we want M to be approximately binary and mapped to $\{0,1\}$. To address the issue, we choose a special activation function Φ, which is expressed as:

$$\Phi(x) = \frac{\tanh(\lambda(x-1)) + 1}{2}. \tag{3}$$

Here, λ controls the sparsity of activation function and we take $\lambda = -100$. Figure 3 reflects the effectiveness of the activation function $\Phi(x)$. In the Cartesian coordinate system, the coordinates of A and B can be calculated from the ray length r and angle intervals so D can be solved by gaussian eliminations via A, B and O. So Eq. 2 can be rephrased as:

$$M(C, r) = \Phi(\frac{|CO|}{|DO|}) \in \{0, 1\}. \tag{4}$$

By focusing on the global mask M, we pre-calculate where $\triangle_i$ belongs based on the $\angle COx$. Using the ray length r and angle interval $\triangle\theta$, we can directly calculate the coordinates of the ray endpoint $P = \{P^1, P^2, ..., P^R\}$ via triangular properties in the Cartesian coordinate system. For $\forall C \in \triangle_i$, we solve the linear equations of AB and CO, calculate the coordinates of D, and determine the corresponding mask value $M(C, r)$ according to Eq. 4. Based on parallel computing, the time complexity of calculating the global mask is $O(R)$ and the space complexity is $O(hw)$.

The proposed modeling strategy can be easily extended to more complex contours, as shown in Fig. 2 (d). This situation mainly occurs when the ray passes through the contour multiple times. Specifically, in order to enhance the

---

Algorithm 1. Deformable Patch Representation (DPR)

Input: the center O, the number of rays R, ray length array $r = \{r_1, r_2, ..., r_n\}$
Output: the mask M

1: $\Delta\theta \leftarrow 2 * \pi / R$
2: Calculate each pixel C belongs to Δ_i
3: Calculate the coordinates of the ray endpoint P by $\Delta\theta$
4: **for** $i \in [1, R]$ **do**
5:    Select the point set C in the Δ_i
6:    $A_0, B_0, C_0 \leftarrow$ Gaussian_Elimination(P^i, P^{i+1})
7:    $A_1, B_1, C_1 \leftarrow$ Gaussian_Elimination(O, C)
8:    $d \leftarrow A_0 * B_1 - A_1 * B_0$
9:    $D_x \leftarrow (B_0 * C_1 - B_1 * C_0)/d$
10:   $D_y \leftarrow (A_1 * C_0 - A_0 * C_1)/d$
11:   $M_{(x,y)\in p} = \Phi\left(\frac{|CO|}{|DO|}\right)$
12: **end for**
13: $M_O \leftarrow 1$
14: **return** M

---

modeling ability and achieve more complex contour modeling, we introduce a multi-anchor mechanism:

$$r^{(0)} = \{r_1^{(0)}, r_2^{(0)}, ..., r_R^{(0)}\}, \tag{5}$$

$$e^{(i)} = \{e_1^{(i)}, e_2^{(i)}, ..., e_R^{(i)}\}, \quad i = 0, 1, ..., R-1, \tag{6}$$

$$r^{(i+1)} = r^{(i)} + e^{(i)}, \quad i = 0, 1, ..., R-1, \tag{7}$$

where $r^{(i)}$ represents the length of the ray in the i-th anchor and $e^{(i)}$ denotes the margin between $r^{(i)}$ and $r^{(i+1)}$. In practice, Deformable Patch Representation with a single anchor can obtain promising attack performance. Due to the space limitation of the paper, we mainly elaborate the single anchor strategy in this work, and the specific implementation is illustrated in Algorithm 1.

3.3   Deformable Adversarial Patch

Although Deformable Patch Representation provides a deformation modeling, generating adversarial patches with better attack performance is still a challenging issue. In this section, we propose our Deformable Adversarial Patch by the joint optimization of shape and texture.

Area denotes the percentage of pixels of the patch relative to the image and deformation affects the area of the patch. Obviously, the larger the area, the stronger its attack performance. In order to explicitly control the area of the patch and facilitate the joint optimization of shape and texture, the loss function L can be written as:

$$L = \begin{cases} L_{adv}, & area \leq ps \\ L_{adv} + \beta \cdot L_{shape}, & area > ps \end{cases}, \tag{8}$$

where $area$ is the area of the deformable patch; ps is defined as the upper limit of the patch area; β is the hyper-parameter to limit the margin of $area$ and ps. L_{adv} is the cross-entropy loss. In order to explicitly punish patches with too large areas, we average the mask M and L_{shape} is defined as:

$$L_{shape} = \text{mean}(M^k). \tag{9}$$

Suppose the deformable mask as $M^k \in R^{c \times h \times w}$ at the k-th iteration, Eq. 1 can be re-expressed as:

$$x_{adv}^k = \delta^{k-1} \odot M^{k-1} + x_{adv}^{k-1} \odot (I - M^{k-1}). \tag{10}$$

In Eq. 4, the generation of the global mask M is controlled by r. Here, δ represents the update of texture and r represents the update of shape. Based on gradient ∇L, the updating process can be regarded as:

$$\delta^k \leftarrow \delta^{k-1} + \alpha \cdot \text{sign}(\nabla_{x_{adv}^k} L), \quad r^k \leftarrow r^{k-1} + \gamma \cdot \text{sign}(\nabla_{r^{k-1}} L). \tag{11}$$

In Eq. 3, we want M to be approximately binary. Although differentiable computation can be realized in this way, M is only close to binarization in numerical. To solve this problem, we introduce the shape ratio s (%) for perturbation tuning. Specifically, when the joint optimization of shape and texture reaches the ratio s, we sharpen the mask. The fine-tuning texture is then adapted to the sharpened mask for improving attack performance. For simplicity, we choose the binarization for sharpening. Appendix 2 summarizes the algorithm of our proposed Deformable Adversarial Patch.

4   Experiments

In this section, we evaluate our proposed DAPatch in the classification task. Firstly, we analyze the significance of shape information on DNNs' robustness through an adversarial lens. Second, we evaluate the effectiveness of the proposed DAPatch in the digital domain. Next, we verify the performance of patch attacks under patch defenses. Then, we generate patches and achieve physical attacks in the real world. Finally, we conduct ablation study for hyper-parameters in Appendix 6.

4.1   Experimental Setup

In our experiments, we use Pytorch [41] for the implementation and test on NVIDIA Tesla V100 GPUs. The proposed DAPatch compares with state-of-the-art methods, such as GAP [3], LaVAN [24] and PS-GAN [35]. Following the setting of previous work [3,24,35], we evaluate on two datasets, including German Traffic Sign Recognition Benchmark (GTSRB) and Imagenet Large Scale Visual Recognition Challenge (ILSVRC2012) [43]. We randomly select 1000 images from the ILSVRC2012 validation set and 500 images from the GTSRB test set. To

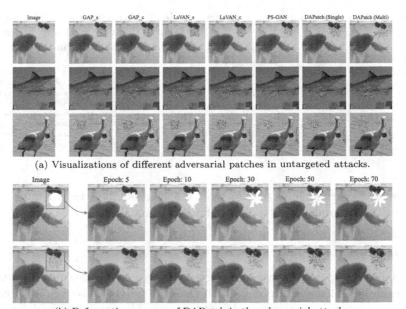

(a) Visualizations of different adversarial patches in untargeted attacks.

(b) Deformation process of DAPatch in the adversarial attack.

Fig. 4. Visualizations of patch attacks. Disabling Texture is the top of (b) and the deformation process is the bottom of (b). More details are shown in Appendix 7.

provide a fair platform for comparison, all the experimental results are reported under the white-box adversarial attack. Since attackers can design the white-box or adaptive attack according to models easily, the white-box setting can better reflect the robustness of models against patch attacks.

We explore the effectiveness of our proposed DAPatch on various model architectures. We divide the model architectures into three categories: **CNN** (VGG19 [47], Resnet-152 [19], DenseNet-161 [20] and MobileNet V2 [44]), **ViT** (ViT-B/16 [9] and Swin-B [37]), and **NAS** (EfficientNet-b7 [49]). To study the impact of different shapes on attack performance, we give patches different initial shapes. GAP_s and GAP_c represent the square and circular patch, and so does LaVAN. The initial shape of the DAPatch is the same as the circular patch. Here s is 70 and β is 200. For more details, please see the Appendix 3 and 6.

Attack Success Rate (ASR) is a quantitative metric in the attack performance. Here, we define ASR as the classification error rate. For untargeted attacks, if the predicted label $\hat{y}$ is inconsistent with the ground truth y, the attack is considered successful. For targeted attacks, we choose the most difficult setting to evaluate the attack performance. Specifically, we set the class with the smallest one in logits as the target class y_t. Only when $\hat{y} = y_t$, the attack is successful. Here, we do not consider the impact of locations on patches. All patches are randomly initialized at fixed locations for attacking 100 iterations under different areas. We select different patch areas and choose the size of squares and circles approximately close to the area. Area (%) denotes the

Table 1. A specific shape can improve ASR even if the area is small.

Network	Shape	≈0.5%		≈1%		≈2%		≈3%	
		ASR	Area	ASR	Area	ASR	Area	ASR	Area
MoblieNet v2	Circle	1.5	0.510	2.2	0.964	4.5	2.040	6.8	3.031
	Square	1.4	0.504	1.7	1.054	3.3	2.010	4.4	3.023
	Ours	**8.9**	**0.377**	**13.4**	**0.790**	**21.0**	**1.648**	**25.8**	**2.496**
Vit-B/16-224	Circle	0.9	0.510	1.4	0.964	2.2	2.040	2.2	3.031
	Square	0.5	0.504	0.7	1.054	1.1	2.010	1.6	3.023
	Ours	**8.6**	**0.355**	**12.0**	**0.789**	**16.3**	**1.563**	**20.7**	**2.507**
ResNet-152	Circle	0.9	0.510	1.2	0.964	2.6	2.040	3.3	3.031
	Square	0.5	0.504	0.6	1.054	0.8	2.010	1.3	3.023
	Ours	**5.8**	**0.371**	**10.3**	**0.776**	**18.4**	**1.618**	**23.6**	**2.449**

Table 2. Experiments on Multi-anchor DAPatch. Complex modeling can improve the attack performance in the same area.

Network	Method	≈0.5%		≈1%		≈2%		≈3%	
		ASR	Area	ASR	Area	ASR	Area	ASR	Area
MoblieNet v2	Single	65.8	0.423	88.9	0.847	97.6	1.735	99.4	2.684
	Multi	67.8	0.425	89.3	0.851	98.9	1.734	99.6	2.667
Vit-B/16-224	Single	56.9	0.417	80.9	0.849	95.0	1.717	98.3	2.676
	Multi	57.0	0.434	80.2	0.855	97.2	1.723	99.2	2.682
ResNet-152	Single	52.2	0.409	78.8	0.845	93.1	1.699	97.9	2.623
	Multi	53.2	0.421	82.3	0.832	94.5	1.711	99.4	2.636

average area percentage of patches over the successfully attacked images. The experiments are under the condition of a constrained area.

4.2 Delving into Shape and Texture

Perturbations in patch attacks can be regarded as a special texture. To evaluate the significance of shape information on DNNs' robustness through an adversarial lens, we remove the texture and fix it to white. The patch is then deformed to study only the effect of shape, as illustrated in Fig. 4 (b). As described in Table 1, placing a patch of the fixed shape on a white texture only slightly reduces accuracy. Further, we exploit the convex hull formed by deformable shapes to attack, as shown in Fig. 5. The area of the convex hull is often larger than the deformable shape, and the attack performance is not as good as the deformable shape . For example, at 3% area, ResNet-152 produces the DAPatch with an area of 2.449% and an ASR of 23.6%, but its convex hull has a larger area (5.745%) but only a lower ASR (5.0%). In DAPatch, the deformation of shape can significantly improve the attack performance, which shows that *a particular shape can improve ASR*. Please refer to Appendix 4 for more details.

The textures of the patch play a significant role in magnifying the performance of patch attack. Even if the network has a bias against texture, the shape can improve attack performance. According to the relationship between shape and texture in object recognition, the shape-biased network can be more vulnerable to the DAPatch. Furthermore, models that make predictions largely based on the shape and texture of objects in images rather than only on shape or texture can be more adversarially robust. We consider the Shape-

(a) Ours, 2.090%   (b) Convex hull, 6.178%

Fig. 5. The area of the convex hull is larger than DAPtach, but the attack performance is not as good as it, which shows that having a specific shape can improve the attack performance.

Network [11] as the most sensitive network to shape against DAPatch and Shape-Texture Debiased Network [34] is currently the best potential defense against DAPatch. The Shape-Network is supposed to be insensitive to texture, but more sensitive on shape for making predictions. ResNet50-SIN, ResNet50-SIN+IN, and ResNet50-SIN+IN-IN are proposed by Shape-Network and achieve ASR as 20.3%, 3.5% and 2.1% on randomly 1000 images before attacking. ResNet50-Debiased and ResNet152-Debiased are proposed by Shape-Texture Debiased Network and achieve ASR as 2.3% and 2.1% before attacking. The experimental results on ILSVRC2012 in Table 3 show that DAPatch easily confuses the Shape-Network and the Shape-Texture Debiased Network with basically no difference as against a normal deep network. In the untargeted attack, ResNet50-SIN increases 54.8% on ASR under 0.5% patch percentage and is much more than ResNet50-Debiased, which increases 44.3%. The same situation happens in the 1% patch area. In a larger area, the margin is not obvious because the ASR is relatively high.

We further use multi-anchor to study the effect of complex shape modeling. Here, the number of anchors is 3. The experiments show that *complex modeling can improve the attack performance in the same area, which also implies that the shape is important to the robustness of DNNs*, as shown in Table 2. In Fig. 4, we show the visualizations of DAPatch and other patches.

DAPatch is not limited to one particular type of attack. DAPatch not only evaluates the robustness of existing classification models, but also shows that a particular shape can improve the attack performance. All in all, shape information has a great impact on the robustness of DNNs, which can be seminal in understanding and exploring the very nature of DNNs' vulnerability. More details are in Appendix 4 and 7.

4.3   Digital Attacks

In this section, we evaluate the effectiveness of DAPatch in the digital domain. Before performing the attacks, the ASR (%) of the models is 0%. The experimental results in untargeted setting on ILSVRC2012 and GTSRB are summarized in Table 5 and Table 6. *Note that when the patch area is small, DAPatch always obtains a higher ASR with a smaller area. Experiments show that under different patch areas, DAPatch can always obtain better attack effects with a smaller area.* For the more challenging targeted setting, the experimental results on ILSVRC2012 are reported in Table 7. We choose the most difficult setting and the target class is the class with the smallest one in logits. According to Table 7, DAPatch also achieves stronger attack performance under different areas.

Moreover, we test them using a traditional state-of-the-art defense method known as Adversarial Training. Fast-AT trains with the Fast Gradient Sign Method (FGSM) [12], when combined with the random initialization, is as effective as training based on Projected Gradient Descent (PGD) [38] but has significantly lower cost. Feature Denoising is the state-of-the-art defense against adversarial attacks in the white-box L_p setting and PGD only decreases the accuracy to 55.7% and 45.5% after 10 and 100 iterations. Fast-AT, Adv-ResNet-152, ResNet-152-Denoise and Resnext-101-Deniose obtain ASR with 33.4%, 36.8%, 30.1% and 20.5% respectively before attacking. Our results of untargeted attacks

Table 3. Untargeted attacks on shape and texture bias.

Network	Method	≈0.5%		≈1%		≈2%		≈3%	
		ASR	Area	ASR	Area	ASR	Area	ASR	Area
ResNet50 -SIN	GAP_s	70.4	0.510	87.3	0.964	96.9	2.040	99.1	3.031
	GAP_c	70.1	0.504	88.5	1.054	96.9	2.010	99.6	3.023
	LaVAN_s	66.2	0.510	82.2	0.964	95.1	2.040	98.1	3.031
	LaVAN_c	65.6	0.504	84.2	1.054	96.0	2.010	98.7	3.023
	PS-GAN	70.0	0.510	85.3	0.964	96.8	2.040	99.5	3.031
	Ours	74.1	0.446	90.3	0.893	98.7	1.764	99.6	2.724
ResNet50 -SIN+IN	GAP_s	44.3	0.510	68.3	0.964	90.6	2.040	95.7	3.031
	GAP_c	44.7	0.504	72.4	1.054	90.9	2.010	96.3	3.023
	LaVAN_s	41.2	0.510	64.9	0.964	88.8	2.040	94.6	3.031
	LaVAN_c	42.4	0.504	69.4	1.054	89.4	2.010	96.1	3.023
	PS-GAN	44.5	0.510	68.9	0.964	90.6	2.040	95.2	3.031
	Ours	48.1	0.426	75.6	0.860	91.5	1.750	96.3	2.669
ResNet50 -SIN+IN-IN	GAP_s	41.6	0.510	62.2	0.964	85.6	2.040	93.0	3.031
	GAP_c	44.3	0.504	68.6	1.054	87.4	2.010	94.2	3.023
	LaVAN_s	38.7	0.510	58.2	0.964	83.1	2.040	92.8	3.031
	LaVAN_c	39.6	0.504	65.3	1.054	84.7	2.010	93.4	3.023
	PS-GAN	39.2	0.510	62.7	0.964	85.2	2.040	94.7	3.031
	Ours	44.3	0.420	70.1	0.845	88.9	1.729	95.1	2.651
ResNet50 -Debiased	GAP_s	42.5	0.510	64.2	0.964	85.8	2.040	93.1	3.031
	GAP_c	44.0	0.504	68.6	1.054	87.9	2.010	94.3	3.023
	LaVAN_s	38.2	0.510	59.7	0.964	83.3	2.040	90.9	3.031
	LaVAN_c	38.8	0.504	64.2	1.054	84.3	2.010	93.2	3.023
	PS-GAN	43.2	0.510	67.6	0.964	88.0	2.040	93.4	3.031
	Ours	46.6	0.438	68.6	0.852	88.1	1.744	94.7	2.665
ResNet152 -Debiased	GAP_s	33.3	0.510	53.0	0.964	81.4	2.040	91.0	3.031
	GAP_c	34.1	0.504	58.9	1.054	84.1	2.010	93.0	3.023
	LaVAN_s	30.6	0.510	49.8	0.964	77.0	2.040	88.8	3.031
	LaVAN_c	29.8	0.504	52.1	1.054	77.5	2.010	90.1	3.023
	PS-GAN	32.3	0.510	53.4	0.964	83.0	2.040	93.2	3.031
	Ours	37.4	0.422	61.8	0.850	85.3	1.735	94.5	2.626

Table 4. Untargeted attacks on networks with adversarial training. DAPatch can always obtain better attack effects on AT networks with a smaller area.

Network	Method	≈0.5%		≈1%		≈2%		≈3%	
		ASR	Area	ASR	Area	ASR	Area	ASR	Area
Adv- ResNet-152	GAP_s	61.0	0.510	74.5	0.964	86.6	2.040	90.3	3.031
	GAP_c	60.6	0.504	77.4	1.054	87.2	2.010	91.7	3.023
	LaVAN_s	58.4	0.510	71.1	0.964	83.9	2.040	88.8	3.031
	LaVAN_c	57.2	0.504	72.6	1.054	83.9	2.010	89.3	3.023
	PS-GAN	59.2	0.510	77.7	0.964	84.3	2.040	89.7	3.031
	Ours	62.5	0.472	78.4	0.948	88.2	1.921	92.4	2.791
ResNet-152- Denoise	GAP_s	59.3	0.510	74.5	0.964	86.5	2.040	92.6	3.031
	GAP_c	59.0	0.504	77.3	1.054	87.8	2.010	92.9	3.023
	LaVAN_s	59.6	0.510	72.6	0.964	84.7	2.040	91.8	3.031
	LaVAN_c	60.7	0.504	75.1	1.054	85.5	2.010	92.7	3.023
	PS-GAN	61.7	0.510	75.1	0.964	86.2	2.040	92.2	3.031
	Ours	62.3	0.464	77.4	0.959	88.0	1.835	92.9	2.853
Resnext-101- Denoise	GAP_s	50.4	0.510	66.3	0.964	83.8	2.040	90.2	3.031
	GAP_c	51.1	0.504	70.5	1.054	84.2	2.010	89.9	3.023
	LaVAN_s	49.7	0.510	65.0	0.964	80.6	2.040	87.6	3.031
	LaVAN_c	49.5	0.504	67.9	1.054	81.2	2.010	88.4	3.023
	PS-GAN	51.2	0.510	68.1	0.964	80.9	2.040	89.9	3.031
	Ours	52.9	0.471	68.9	0.949	85.5	1.928	90.2	2.814
Fast_AT	GAP_s	50.4	0.510	62.3	0.964	80.4	2.040	88.5	3.031
	GAP_c	50.6	0.504	65.5	1.054	80.3	2.010	88.8	3.023
	LaVAN_s	48.7	0.510	60.2	0.964	77.5	2.040	84.7	3.031
	LaVAN_c	48.7	0.504	62.6	1.054	78.0	2.010	85.3	3.023
	PS-GAN	48.9	0.510	63.4	0.964	79.1	2.040	85.2	3.031
	Ours	51.3	0.473	65.6	0.944	82.0	1.890	90.0	2.963

Table 5. Untargeted attacks of various network architectures on ILSVRC2012.

Model	Method	GAP_s		GAP_c		LaVan_s		LaVan_c		PS-GAN		Ours	
		ASR	Area	ASR	Area	ASR	Area	ASR	Area	ASR	Area	ASR	Area
ResNet-152	0.5%	44.3	0.510	44.8	0.504	43.7	0.510	43.5	0.504	44.5	0.510	52.2	0.409
	1%	71.0	0.964	74.4	1.054	67.5	0.964	71.2	1.054	68.9	0.964	78.8	0.845
	2%	89.5	2.040	91.2	2.010	88.3	2.040	90.4	2.010	91.3	2.040	93.1	1.699
	3%	96.5	3.031	97.8	3.023	95.9	3.031	96.8	3.023	97.4	3.031	97.9	2.623
Efficientnet-b7	0.5%	43.3	0.510	42.5	0.504	43.3	0.510	41.2	0.504	40.9	0.510	45.7	0.442
	1%	63.5	0.964	68.8	1.054	64.7	0.964	69.2	1.054	65.8	0.964	71.1	0.956
	2%	85.5	2.040	88.0	2.010	89.5	2.040	89.2	2.010	89.3	2.040	89.6	2.003
	3%	91.5	3.031	94.4	3.023	95.9	3.031	95.9	3.023	95.2	3.031	95.9	3.014
Vit-B/16-224	0.5%	47.0	0.510	45.6	0.504	47.0	0.510	46.9	0.504	45.9	0.510	56.9	0.417
	1%	72.0	0.964	77.2	1.054	71.8	0.964	74.9	1.054	71.9	0.964	80.9	0.849
	2%	92.4	2.040	93.0	2.010	93.5	2.040	93.5	2.010	90.2	2.040	95.0	1.717
	3%	97.2	3.031	97.8	3.023	98.3	3.031	98.3	3.023	97.4	3.031	98.3	2.676

are summarized in Table 4. *Note that compared with the baselines, DAPatch can always obtain better attack effects on AT networks with a smaller area.*

4.4   Attack Against Patch Defenses

We select patch defenses that can be extended to ILSVRC2012 as the benchmark to test the effectiveness of patch attacks, including Local Gradient Smoothing

Table 6. Untargeted attacks of various network architectures on GTSRB.

Network	Method	≈0.5%		≈1%		2%		≈3%	
		ASR	Area	ASR	Area	ASR	Area	ASR	Area
ResNet-152	GAP_s	13.6	0.510	21.4	0.964	37.8	2.040	56.0	3.031
	GAP_c	13.0	0.504	22.6	1.054	38.0	2.010	57.6	3.023
	LaVAN_s	14.6	0.510	22.8	0.964	41.6	2.040	60.4	3.031
	LaVAN_c	14.8	0.504	26.0	1.054	41.8	2.010	58.4	3.023
	PS-GAN	13.7	0.510	23.4	0.964	39.4	2.040	59.5	3.031
	Ours	**15.0**	**0.477**	**27.1**	**0.831**	**42.3**	**1.932**	**61.5**	**2.873**
Efficientnet-b7	GAP_s	20.4	0.510	45.0	0.964	68.0	2.040	84.0	3.031
	GAP_c	20.6	0.504	39.4	1.054	66.6	2.010	82.6	3.023
	LaVAN_s	22.2	0.510	46.2	0.964	74.0	2.040	89.2	3.031
	LaVAN_c	22.8	0.504	51.4	1.054	74.0	2.010	89.0	3.023
	PS-GAN	21.5	0.510	46.2	0.964	71.2	2.040	85.6	3.031
	Ours	**23.6**	**0.469**	**53.1**	**0.893**	**75.2**	**1.873**	**89.5**	**2.934**
Vit-B/16-224	GAP_s	28.6	0.510	61.2	0.964	90.0	2.040	97.6	3.031
	GAP_c	28.4	0.504	68.0	1.054	90.2	2.010	98.2	3.023
	LaVAN_s	28.2	0.510	61.6	0.964	91.8	2.040	98.2	3.031
	LaVAN_c	26.2	0.504	65.4	1.054	92.0	2.010	97.4	3.023
	PS-GAN	27.4	0.510	64.2	0.964	90.2	2.040	98.1	3.031
	Ours	**30.1**	**0.483**	**68.1**	**0.896**	**93.5**	**1.783**	**98.9**	**2.892**

Table 7. Targeted attacks of various network architectures on ILSVRC2012.

Network	Method	≈1%		≈3%		≈5%		≈7%	
		ASR	Area	ASR	Area	ASR	Area	ASR	Area
ResNet-152	GAP_s	5.30	0.964	41.1	3.031	68.8	4.982	87.3	6.938
	GAP_c	8.80	1.054	44.3	3.023	72.8	4.888	88.3	6.794
	LaVAN_s	3.50	0.964	22.6	3.031	45.1	4.982	61.8	6.938
	LaVAN_c	6.00	1.054	23.9	3.023	47.7	4.888	64.7	6.794
	PS-GAN	8.90	0.964	46.2	3.031	73.8	4.982	87.4	6.938
	Ours	**9.10**	**0.849**	**48.7**	**2.668**	**78.1**	**4.553**	**90.2**	**6.439**
Efficientnet-b7	GAP_s	4.40	0.964	52.1	3.031	81.9	4.982	93.7	6.938
	GAP_c	6.20	1.054	53.6	3.023	81.4	4.888	93.4	6.794
	LaVAN_s	1.50	0.964	33.1	3.031	65.0	4.982	82.2	6.938
	LaVAN_c	2.30	1.054	34.0	3.023	62.1	4.888	83.6	6.794
	PS-GAN	4.90	0.964	53.6	3.031	81.5	4.982	93.2	6.938
	Ours	**7.60**	**0.869**	**53.6**	**2.953**	**82.0**	**4.851**	**93.7**	**6.713**
Vit-B/16-224	GAP_s	6.20	0.964	48.8	3.031	85.4	4.982	97.3	6.938
	GAP_c	7.90	1.054	50.6	3.023	85.7	4.888	97.2	6.794
	LaVAN_s	3.10	0.964	25.4	3.031	52.8	4.982	78.3	6.938
	LaVAN_c	4.20	1.054	24.7	3.023	54.9	4.888	78.4	6.794
	PS-GAN	5.30	0.964	49.3	3.031	85.8	4.982	97.1	6.938
	Ours	**9.60**	**0.850**	**50.7**	**2.697**	**86.2**	**4.688**	**97.4**	**6.727**

Table 8. Patch attacks on patch defenses. A greater ASR means better.

Type	Model	Method	Clean	GAP_s		GAP_c		LaVan_s		LaVan_c		PS-GAN		Ours	
			ASR	ASR	Area	ASR	Area	ASR	Area	ASR	Area	ASR	Area	ASR	Area
Empirical	ResNet-152	Non-defense	0	89.5	2.040	91.2	2.010	88.3	2.040	90.4	2.010	91.3	2.040	**93.1**	**1.699**
		LGS	3.7	51.0	2.040	51.4	2.010	47.3	2.040	47.3	2.010	44.8	2.040	**53.9**	**2.003**
		DW	10.2	69.4	2.040	68.5	2.010	64.3	2.040	67.5	2.010	57.6	2.040	**69.5**	**1.862**
	ViT-B	Non-defense	0	92.4	2.040	93.0	2.010	93.5	2.040	93.5	2.010	90.2	2.040	**95.0**	**1.717**
		LGS	3.0	56.6	2.040	57.5	2.010	54.7	2.040	56.8	2.010	53.4	2.040	**58.1**	**1.891**
		DW	10.3	68.0	2.040	69.5	2.010	66.4	2.040	69.3	2.010	60.1	2.040	**69.8**	**2.001**
Certifiable	BagNet-17	PatchGuard	24.8	31.2	2.040	31.3	2.010	30.8	2.040	30.9	2.010	26.7	2.040	**32.7**	**1.998**
	ResNet-50	DS	7.8	13.3	2.040	13.3	2.010	13.1	2.040	12.9	2.010	10.2	2.040	**13.4**	**2.001**

(LGS) [40], Digital Watermarking (DW) [18], PatchGuard [55] and Derandomized Smoothing (DS) [27]. For empirical defenses, LGS is regarded as a differentiable pre-processing process to generate patches, and DW is added to Backward Pass Differential Approximation (BPDA) [1] to ignore the operator in backward propagation approximate gradient. For certifiable defenses, the patches are generated to attack the modified CNN model using PatchGuard and DS, which changes the forward propagation function of the CNN model.

Table 8 shows patch attacks under 2% area on patch defenses. With the help of DPR, DAPatch achieves better attack performance under all patch defense methods. We establish a new baseline to reflect the robustness of defending methods against patch attacks from the perspective of adversarial shapes.

4.5 Physical Attacks

Physical attacks are conducted to verify the effectiveness of DAPatch in real-world scenarios. We take 10 common classes from ILSVRC2012 [43] and 50 images in total are taken at five different placements (5 in each class). We conduct experiments with angles and lighting under 5% area in the untargeted setting with Total Variation (TV) loss [45]. After printing patches with CANON

(a) Envelope → Switch   (b) Pen → Ladle   (c) Ruler → Spotlight   (d) White DAPatch

Fig. 6. Physical attacks of DAPatch in the untargeted setting. When the light and shadow remain unchanged, for example, (a) is originally predicted as envelope, we use the camera to photograph and generate a patch, and attach it near the object. It is predicted as the switch after photographing again.

iR-ADV C5535, we place them next to the corresponding item and photograph via an iPhone 12. The initial ASR (%) on 50 original images is 16. Then, the ASR in these angles (−30°, 0°, and 30°) are 40, 60, and 44 in the middle lightning, respectively. The ASR (%) in different lightning (low, middle, and high lighting) are 56, 60, and 60 in 0°, respectively. Figure 6 shows some examples of physical attacks. We choose GAP and PS-GAN for comparison. Under the same experimental parameters (middle lighting, 0°), the ASR (%) is 34 and 44, which is 26 and 16 less than DAPatch (60). In general, our DAPatch is less robust to angles (since it affects the shape of patches), but still outperforms other patch attacks. We also try to use the white DAPatch to attack. Although the white DAPatch only receives 30 of the ASR, it also proves that the deformation attack is effective. Please refer to Appendix 5 for more details.

5   Conclusions

As a special form of adversarial attack, patch attacks have been extensively studied and analyzed due to their threatening nature to the real world. However, due to the lack of an effective modeling strategy, previous work has to restrict the patches to fixed shapes, such as circles or rectangles, which neglects the shape of patches as a factor in patch attacks. In this paper, we present a new Deformable Patch Representation that exploits triangle geometry and adopts a differentiable mapping process between contour modeling and masking. To further improve attack performance, we propose a joint optimization algorithm named Deformable Adversarial Patch which supports simultaneous and efficient optimization of shape and texture. Extensive experiments show that a particular shape can improve attack performance. Finally, DAPatch poses a great threat in both the digital and real-world against various DNN architectures.

Acknowledgements. This work was done when Zhaoyu Chen was an intern at Youtu Lab, Tencent. This work was supported by National Natural Science Foundation of China (No. 62072112), Scientific and Technological Innovation Action Plan of Shanghai Science and Technology Committee (No. 20511103102), Fudan University-CIOMP Joint Fund (No. FC2019-005), and Double First-class Construction Fund (No. XM03211178).

References

1. Athalye, A., Carlini, N., Wagner, D.A.: Obfuscated gradients give a false sense of security: circumventing defenses to adversarial examples. In: Dy, J.G., Krause, A. (eds.) Proceedings of the 35th International Conference on Machine Learning, ICML 2018, Stockholmsmässan, Stockholm, Sweden, 10–15 July 2018. Proceedings of Machine Learning Research, vol. 80, pp. 274–283. PMLR (2018). http:// proceedings.mlr.press/v80/athalye18a.html
2. Belongie, S.J., Malik, J., Puzicha, J.: Shape matching and object recognition using shape contexts. IEEE Trans. Pattern Anal. Mach. Intell. **24**(4), 509–522 (2002). https://doi.org/10.1109/34.993558
3. Brown, T.B., Mané, D., Roy, A., Abadi, M., Gilmer, J.: Adversarial patch (2017). http://arxiv.org/abs/1712.09665
4. Chen, C., Zhang, J., Lyu, L.: Gear: a margin-based federated adversarial training approach. In: International Workshop on Trustable, Verifiable, and Auditable Federated Learning in Conjunction with AAAI 2022 (FL-AAAI-22) (2022)
5. Chen, Z., Li, B., Xu, J., Wu, S., Ding, S., Zhang, W.: Towards practical certifiable patch defense with vision transformer. In: Proceedings of the IEEE/CVF Conference on Computer Vision and Pattern Recognition (CVPR), pp. 15148–15158, June 2022
6. Chiang, P., Ni, R., Abdelkader, A., Zhu, C., Studer, C., Goldstein, T.: Certified defenses for adversarial patches. In: 8th International Conference on Learning Representations, ICLR 2020, Addis Ababa, Ethiopia, 26–30 April 2020. OpenReview.net (2020). https://openreview.net/forum?id=HyeaSkrYPH
7. Dai, J., et al.: Deformable convolutional networks. In: IEEE International Conference on Computer Vision, ICCV 2017, Venice, Italy, 22–29 October 2017, pp. 764–773. IEEE Computer Society (2017). https://doi.org/10.1109/ICCV.2017.89
8. Ding, L., et al.: Towards universal physical attacks on single object tracking. In: Thirty-Fifth AAAI Conference on Artificial Intelligence, AAAI 2021, Thirty-Third Conference on Innovative Applications of Artificial Intelligence, IAAI 2021, The Eleventh Symposium on Educational Advances in Artificial Intelligence, EAAI 2021, Virtual Event, 2–9 February 2021, pp. 1236–1245. AAAI Press (2021). https://ojs.aaai.org/index.php/AAAI/article/view/16211
9. Dosovitskiy, A., et a.: An image is worth 16x16 words: transformers for image recognition at scale. In: 9th International Conference on Learning Representations, ICLR 2021, Virtual Event, Austria, 3–7 May 2021. OpenReview.net (2021). https://openreview.net/forum?id=YicbFdNTTy
10. Eykholt, K., et al.: Robust physical-world attacks on deep learning visual classification. In: 2018 IEEE Conference on Computer Vision and Pattern Recognition, CVPR 2018, Salt Lake City, UT, USA, 18–22 June 2018, pp. 1625–1634. IEEE Computer Society (2018). https://doi.org/10. 1109/CVPR.2018.00175, http://openaccess.thecvf.com/content_cvpr_2018/html/ Eykholt_Robust_Physical-World_Attacks_CVPR_2018_paper.html
11. Geirhos, R., Rubisch, P., Michaelis, C., Bethge, M., Wichmann, F.A., Brendel, W.: Imagenet-trained CNNs are biased towards texture; increasing shape bias improves accuracy and robustness. In: 7th International Conference on Learning Representations, ICLR 2019, New Orleans, LA, USA, 6–9 May 2019. OpenReview.net (2019). https://openreview.net/forum?id=Bygh9j09KX

12. Goodfellow, I.J., Shlens, J., Szegedy, C.: Explaining and harnessing adversarial examples. In: Bengio, Y., LeCun, Y. (eds.) 3rd International Conference on Learning Representations, ICLR 2015, San Diego, CA, USA, 7–9 May 2015, Conference Track Proceedings (2015). http://arxiv.org/abs/1412.6572
13. Gu, Z., et al.: Spatiotemporal inconsistency learning for deepfake video detection. In: Proceedings of the 29th ACM International Conference on Multimedia, pp. 3473–3481 (2021)
14. Gu, Z., Chen, Y., Yao, T., Ding, S., Li, J., Ma, L.: Delving into the local: dynamic inconsistency learning for deepfake video detection. In: Proceedings of the 36th AAAI Conference on Artificial Intelligence (2022)
15. Gu, Z., Li, F., Fang, F., Zhang, G.: A novel retinex-based fractional-order variational model for images with severely low light. IEEE Trans. Image Process. **29**, 3239–3253 (2020)
16. Gu, Z., Li, F., Lv, X.G.: A detail preserving variational model for image retinex. Appl. Math. Model. **68**, 643–661 (2019)
17. Gu, Z., Yao, T., Yang, C., Yi, R., Ding, S., Ma, L.: Region-aware temporal inconsistency learning for deepfake video detection. In: Proceedings of the 31th International Joint Conference on Artificial Intelligence (2022)
18. Hayes, J.: On visible adversarial perturbations & digital watermarking. In: 2018 IEEE Conference on Computer Vision and Pattern Recognition Workshops, CVPR Workshops 2018, Salt Lake City, UT, USA, 18–22 June 2018, pp. 1597–1604. Computer Vision Foundation/IEEE Computer Society (2018). https://doi.org/10.1109/CVPRW.2018.00210, http://openaccess.thecvf.com/content_cvpr_2018_workshops/w32/html/Hayes_On_Visible_Adversarial_CVPR_2018_paper.html
19. He, K., Zhang, X., Ren, S., Sun, J.: Deep residual learning for image recognition. In: 2016 IEEE Conference on Computer Vision and Pattern Recognition, CVPR 2016, Las Vegas, NV, USA, 27–30 June 2016, pp. 770–778. IEEE Computer Society (2016). https://doi.org/10.1109/CVPR.2016.90
20. Huang, G., Liu, Z., van der Maaten, L., Weinberger, K.Q.: Densely connected convolutional networks. In: 2017 IEEE Conference on Computer Vision and Pattern Recognition, CVPR 2017, Honolulu, HI, USA, 21–26 July 2017, pp. 2261–2269. IEEE Computer Society (2017). https://doi.org/10.1109/CVPR.2017.243
21. Huang, H., Wang, Y., Chen, Z., Tang, Z., Zhang, W., Ma, K.: Rpattack: refined patch attack on general object detectors. In: 2021 IEEE International Conference on Multimedia and Expo, ICME 2021, Shenzhen, China, 5–9 July 2021, pp. 1–6. IEEE (2021). https://doi.org/10.1109/ICME51207.2021.9428443
22. Huang, H., et al.: CMUA-watermark: a cross-model universal adversarial watermark for combating deepfakes. In: Proceedings of the AAAI Conference on Artificial Intelligence, vol. 36, pp. 989–997 (2022)
23. Huang, L., Gao, C., Zhou, Y., Xie, C., Yuille, A.L., Zou, C., Liu, N.: Universal physical camouflage attacks on object detectors. In: 2020 IEEE/CVF Conference on Computer Vision and Pattern Recognition, CVPR 2020, Seattle, WA, USA, 13–19 June 2020, pp. 717–726. Computer Vision Foundation/IEEE (2020). https://doi.org/10.1109/CVPR42600.2020.00080, https://openaccess.thecvf.com/content_CVPR_2020/html/Huang_Universal_Physical_Camouflage_Attacks_on_Object_Detectors_CVPR_2020_paper.html
24. Karmon, D., Zoran, D., Goldberg, Y.: Lavan: localized and visible adversarial noise. In: Dy, J.G., Krause, A. (eds.) Proceedings of the 35th International Conference on Machine Learning, ICML 2018, Stockholmsmässan, Stockholm, Sweden, 10–15 July 2018. Proceedings of Machine Learning Research, vol. 80, pp. 2512–2520. PMLR (2018). http://proceedings.mlr.press/v80/karmon18a.html

25. Kong, X., Liu, X., Gu, J., Qiao, Y., Dong, C.: Reflash dropout in image super-resolution. arXiv preprint arXiv:2112.12089 (2021)

26. Kong, X., Zhao, H., Qiao, Y., Dong, C.: ClassSR: a general framework to accelerate super-resolution networks by data characteristic. In: Proceedings of the IEEE/CVF Conference on Computer Vision and Pattern Recognition (CVPR), pp. 12016–12025, June 2021

27. Levine, A., Feizi, S.: (de)randomized smoothing for certifiable defense against patch attacks. In: Larochelle, H., Ranzato, M., Hadsell, R., Balcan, M., Lin, H. (eds.) Advances in Neural Information Processing Systems 33: Annual Conference on Neural Information Processing Systems 2020, NeurIPS 2020, December 2020, pp. 6–12. Virtual (2020). https://proceedings.neurips.cc/paper/2020/hash/47ce0875420b2dbacfc5535f94e68433-Abstract.html

28. Li, B., Sun, Z., Guo, Y.: SuperVAE: superpixelwise variational autoencoder for salient object detection. In: The Thirty-Third AAAI Conference on Artificial Intelligence, AAAI 2019, Honolulu, Hawaii, USA, 27 January–1 February 2019, pp. 8569–8576. AAAI Press (2019). https://doi.org/10.1609/aaai.v33i01.33018569

29. Li, B., Sun, Z., Li, Q., Wu, Y., Hu, A.: Group-wise deep object co-segmentation with co-attention recurrent neural network. In: 2019 IEEE/CVF International Conference on Computer Vision, ICCV 2019, Seoul, Korea (South), 27 October –2 November 2019, pp. 8518–8527. IEEE (2019). https://doi.org/10.1109/ICCV.2019.00861

30. Li, B., Sun, Z., Tang, L., Hu, A.: Two-b-real net: two-branch network for real-time salient object detection. In: IEEE International Conference on Acoustics, Speech and Signal Processing, ICASSP 2019, Brighton, United Kingdom, 12–17 May 2019, pp. 1662–1666. IEEE (2019). https://doi.org/10.1109/ICASSP.2019.8683022

31. Li, B., Sun, Z., Tang, L., Sun, Y., Shi, J.: Detecting robust co-saliency with recurrent co-attention neural network. In: Kraus, S. (ed.) Proceedings of the Twenty-Eighth International Joint Conference on Artificial Intelligence, IJCAI 2019, Macao, China, 10–16 August 2019, pp. 818–825. ijcai.org (2019). https://doi.org/10.24963/ijcai.2019/115

32. Li, B., Sun, Z., Wang, Q., Li, Q.: Co-saliency detection based on hierarchical consistency. In: Amsaleg, L., et al. (eds.) Proceedings of the 27th ACM International Conference on Multimedia, MM 2019, Nice, France, 21–25 October 2019, pp. 1392–1400. ACM (2019). https://doi.org/10.1145/3343031.3351016

33. Li, B., Xu, J., Wu, S., Ding, S., Li, J., Huang, F.: Detecting adversarial patch attacks through global-local consistency. In: Song, D., et al. (eds.) ADVM 2021: Proceedings of the 1st International Workshop on Adversarial Learning for Multimedia, Virtual Event, China, 20 October 2021, pp. 35–41. ACM (2021). https://doi.org/10.1145/3475724.3483606

34. Li, Y., et al.: Shape-texture debiased neural network training. In: 9th International Conference on Learning Representations, ICLR 2021, Virtual Event, Austria, 3–7 May 2021. OpenReview.net (2021). https://openreview.net/forum?id=Db4yerZTYkz

35. Liu, A., et al.: Perceptual-sensitive GAN for generating adversarial patches. In: The Thirty-Third AAAI Conference on Artificial Intelligence, AAAI 2019, The Thirty-First Innovative Applications of Artificial Intelligence Conference, IAAI 2019, The Ninth AAAI Symposium on Educational Advances in Artificial Intelligence, EAAI 2019, Honolulu, Hawaii, USA, 27 January–1 February 2019, pp. 1028–1035. AAAI Press (2019). https://doi.org/10.1609/aaai.v33i01.33011028

36. Liu, S., et al.: Efficient universal shuffle attack for visual object tracking. In: ICASSP 2022–2022 IEEE International Conference on Acoustics, Speech and Signal Processing (ICASSP), pp. 2739–2743. IEEE (2022)

37. Liu, Z., et al.: Swin transformer: hierarchical vision transformer using shifted windows (2021). https://arxiv.org/abs/2103.14030

38. Madry, A., Makelov, A., Schmidt, L., Tsipras, D., Vladu, A.: Towards deep learning models resistant to adversarial attacks. In: 6th International Conference on Learning Representations, ICLR 2018, Vancouver, BC, Canada, 30 April –3 May 2018, Conference Track Proceedings. OpenReview.net (2018). https://openreview.net/forum?id=rJzIBfZAb

39. Malik, J., Belongie, S.J., Leung, T.K., Shi, J.: Contour and texture analysis for image segmentation. Int. J. Comput. Vis. **43**(1), 7–27 (2001). https://doi.org/10.1023/A:1011174803800

40. Naseer, M., Khan, S., Porikli, F.: Local gradients smoothing: defense against localized adversarial attacks. In: IEEE Winter Conference on Applications of Computer Vision, WACV 2019, Waikoloa Village, HI, USA, 7–11 January 2019, pp. 1300–1307. IEEE (2019). https://doi.org/10.1109/WACV.2019.00143

41. Paszke, A., et al.: PyTorch: an imperative style, high-performance deep learning library. In: Wallach, H.M., Larochelle, H., Beygelzimer, A., d'Alché-Buc, F., Fox, E.B., Garnett, R. (eds.) Advances in Neural Information Processing Systems 32: Annual Conference on Neural Information Processing Systems 2019, NeurIPS 2019, pp. 8–14, December 2019. Vancouver, BC, Canada, pp. 8024–8035 (2019). https://proceedings.neurips.cc/paper/2019/hash/bdbca288fee7f92f2bfa9f7012727740-Abstract.html

42. Rao, S., Stutz, D., Schiele, B.: Adversarial training against location-optimized adversarial patches. In: Bartoli, A., Fusiello, A. (eds.) ECCV 2020. LNCS, vol. 12539, pp. 429–448. Springer, Cham (2020). https://doi.org/10.1007/978-3-030-68238-5_32

43. Russakovsky, O., et al.: ImageNet large scale visual recognition challenge. Int. J. Comput. Vision **115**(3), 211–252 (2015). https://doi.org/10.1007/s11263-015-0816-y

44. Sandler, M., Howard, A.G., Zhu, M., Zhmoginov, A., Chen, L.: MobileNetv 2: inverted residuals and linear bottlenecks. In: 2018 IEEE Conference on Computer Vision and Pattern Recognition, CVPR 2018, Salt Lake City, UT, USA, 18–22 June 2018, pp. 4510–4520. IEEE Computer Society (2018). https://doi.org/10.1109/CVPR.2018.00474, http://openaccess.thecvf.com/content_cvpr_2018/html/Sandler_MobileNetV2_Inverted_Residuals_CVPR_2018_paper.html

45. Sharif, M., Bhagavatula, S., Bauer, L., Reiter, M.K.: Accessorize to a crime: real and stealthy attacks on state-of-the-art face recognition. In: Weippl, E.R., Katzenbeisser, S., Kruegel, C., Myers, A.C., Halevi, S. (eds.) Proceedings of the 2016 ACM SIGSAC Conference on Computer and Communications Security, Vienna, Austria, 24–28 October 2016, pp. 1528–1540. ACM (2016). https://doi.org/10.1145/2976749.2978392

46. Shen, T., et al.: Federated mutual learning. arXiv preprint arXiv:2006.16765 (2020)

47. Simonyan, K., Zisserman, A.: Very deep convolutional networks for large-scale image recognition. In: Bengio, Y., LeCun, Y. (eds.) 3rd International Conference on Learning Representations, ICLR 2015, San Diego, CA, USA, 7–9 May 2015, Conference Track Proceedings (2015). http://arxiv.org/abs/1409.1556

48. Szegedy, C., et al.: Intriguing properties of neural networks. In: Bengio, Y., LeCun, Y. (eds.) 2nd International Conference on Learning Representations, ICLR 2014, Banff, AB, Canada, 14–16 April 2014, Conference Track Proceedings (2014). http://arxiv.org/abs/1312.6199

49. Tan, M., Le, Q.V.: EfficientNet: rethinking model scaling for convolutional neural networks. In: Chaudhuri, K., Salakhutdinov, R. (eds.) Proceedings of the 36th International Conference on Machine Learning, ICML 2019, 9–15 June 2019, Long Beach, California, USA. Proceedings of Machine Learning Research, vol. 97, pp. 6105–6114. PMLR (2019). http://proceedings.mlr.press/v97/tan19a.html

50. Tang, L., Li, B.: CLASS: cross-level attention and supervision for salient objects detection. In: Ishikawa, H., Liu, C.-L., Pajdla, T., Shi, J. (eds.) ACCV 2020. LNCS, vol. 12624, pp. 420–436. Springer, Cham (2021). https://doi.org/10.1007/978-3-030-69535-4_26

51. Tang, L., Li, B., Zhong, Y., Ding, S., Song, M.: Disentangled high quality salient object detection. In: 2021 IEEE/CVF International Conference on Computer Vision, ICCV 2021, Montreal, QC, Canada, 10–17 October 2021, pp. 3560–3570. IEEE (2021). https://doi.org/10.1109/ICCV48922.2021.00356

52. Wang, Y., et al.: A systematic review on affective computing: emotion models, databases, and recent advances. Inf. Fusion **83–84**, 19–52 (2022). https://doi.org/10.1016/j.inffus.2022.03.009

53. Wang, Y., et al.: Ferv39k: a large-scale multi-scene dataset for facial expression recognition in videos. In: Proceedings of the IEEE/CVF Conference on Computer Vision and Pattern Recognition (CVPR), pp. 20922–20931, June 2022

54. Wu, T., Tong, L., Vorobeychik, Y.: Defending against physically realizable attacks on image classification. In: 8th International Conference on Learning Representations, ICLR 2020, Addis Ababa, Ethiopia, 26–30 April 2020, OpenReview.net (2020). https://openreview.net/forum?id=H1xscnEKDr

55. Xiang, C., Bhagoji, A.N., Sehwag, V., Mittal, P.: PatchGuard: a provably robust defense against adversarial patches via small receptive fields and masking. In: Bailey, M., Greenstadt, R. (eds.) 30th USENIX Security Symposium, USENIX Security 2021, 11–13 August 2021, pp. 2237–2254. USENIX Association (2021). https://www.usenix.org/conference/usenixsecurity21/presentation/xiang

56. Xie, C., Wang, J., Zhang, Z., Zhou, Y., Xie, L., Yuille, A.L.: Adversarial examples for semantic segmentation and object detection. In: IEEE International Conference on Computer Vision, ICCV 2017, Venice, Italy, 22–29 October 2017, pp. 1378–1387. IEEE Computer Society (2017). https://doi.org/10.1109/ICCV.2017.153

57. Xie, E., et al.: Polarmask: single shot instance segmentation with polar representation. In: 2020 IEEE/CVF Conference on Computer Vision and Pattern Recognition, CVPR 2020, Seattle, WA, USA, 13–19 June 2020, pp. 12190–12199. IEEE (2020). https://doi.org/10.1109/CVPR42600.2020.01221

58. Zhang, J., Chen, C., Dong, J., Jia, R., Lyu, L.: QEKD: query-efficient and data-free knowledge distillation from black-box models. arXiv preprint arXiv:2205.11158 (2022)

59. Zhang, J., et al.: A practical data-free approach to one-shot federated learning with heterogeneity. arXiv preprint arXiv:2112.12371 (2021)

60. Zhang, J., et al.: Towards efficient data free black-box adversarial attack. In: Proceedings of the IEEE/CVF Conference on Computer Vision and Pattern Recognition (CVPR), pp. 15115–15125, June 2022

61. Zhang, J., Zhang, L., Li, G., Wu, C.: Adversarial examples for good: adversarial examples guided imbalanced learning. arXiv preprint arXiv:2201.12356 (2022)

62. Zhang, Z., Yuan, B., McCoyd, M., Wagner, D.A.: Clipped bagnet: defending against sticker attacks with clipped bag-of-features. In: 2020 IEEE Security and Privacy Workshops, SP Workshops, San Francisco, CA, USA, 21 May 2020, pp. 55–61. IEEE (2020). https://doi.org/10.1109/SPW50608.2020.00026

63. Zhao, H., Kong, X., He, J., Qiao, Yu., Dong, C.: Efficient image super-resolution using pixel attention. In: Bartoli, A., Fusiello, A. (eds.) ECCV 2020. LNCS, vol. 12537, pp. 56–72. Springer, Cham (2020). https://doi.org/10.1007/978-3-030-67070-2_3

64. Zhong, Y., Li, B., Tang, L., Kuang, S., Wu, S., Ding, S.: Detecting camouflaged object in frequency domain. In: Proceedings of the IEEE/CVF Conference on Computer Vision and Pattern Recognition (CVPR), pp. 4504–4513, June 2022

65. Zhong, Y., Li, B., Tang, L., Tang, H., Ding, S.: Highly efficient natural image matting. CoRR abs/2110.12748 (2021), https://arxiv.org/abs/2110.12748

66. Zhou, Q., et al.: Uncertainty-aware consistency regularization for cross-domain semantic segmentation. In: Computer Vision and Image Understanding, p. 103448 (2022)

67. Zhou, Q., Zhang, K.Y., Yao, T., Yi, R., Ding, S., Ma, L.: Adaptive mixture of experts learning for generalizable face anti-spoofing. In: Proceedings of the 30th ACM International Conference on Multimedia (2022)

68. Zhou, Q., et al.: Generative domain adaptation for face anti-spoofing. In: Avidan, S., et al. (eds.) ECCV 2022. LNCS, vol. 13665, pp. 335–356. Springer, Cham (2022). https://doi.org/10.1007/978-3-031-20065-6_20

Frequency Domain Model Augmentation for Adversarial Attack

Yuyang Long[1], Qilong Zhang[1], Boheng Zeng[1], Lianli Gao[1], Xianglong Liu[2], Jian Zhang[3], and Jingkuan Song[1(✉)]

[1] Center for Future Media, University of Electronic Science and Technology of China, Chengdu, China
yuyang.long@outlook.com, {qilong.zhang,boheng.zeng}@std.uestc.edu.cn, lianli.gao@uestc.edu.cn, jingkuan.song@gmail.com
[2] Beihang University, Beijing, China
xlliu@buaa.edu.cn
[3] Hunan University, Changsha, China
jianzh@hnu.edu.cn

Abstract. For black-box attacks, the gap between the substitute model and the victim model is usually large, which manifests as a weak attack performance. Motivated by the observation that the transferability of adversarial examples can be improved by attacking diverse models simultaneously, model augmentation methods which simulate different models by using transformed images are proposed. However, existing transformations for spatial domain do not translate to significantly diverse augmented models. To tackle this issue, we propose a novel spectrum simulation attack to craft more transferable adversarial examples against both normally trained and defense models. Specifically, we apply a spectrum transformation to the input and thus perform the model augmentation in the frequency domain. We theoretically prove that the transformation derived from frequency domain leads to a diverse spectrum saliency map, an indicator we proposed to reflect the diversity of substitute models. Notably, our method can be generally combined with existing attacks. Extensive experiments on the ImageNet dataset demonstrate the effectiveness of our method, *e.g.*, attacking nine state-of-the-art defense models with an average success rate of **95.4%**. Our code is available in https://github.com/yuyang-long/SSA.

Keywords: Adversarial examples · Model augmentation · Transferability

Supplementary Information The online version contains supplementary material available at https://doi.org/10.1007/978-3-031-19772-7_32.

1   Introduction

In recent years, deep neural networks (DNNs) have achieved a considerable success in the field of computer vision, *e.g.*, image classification [15,16,55], face recognition [40,43] and self-driving [2,34]. Nevertheless, there are still many concerns regarding the stability of neural networks. As demonstrated in prior works [12,39], adversarial examples which merely add human-imperceptible perturbations on clean images can easily fool state-of-the-art DNNs. Therefore, to help improve the robustness of DNNs, crafting adversarial examples to cover as many blind spots of DNNs as possible is necessary.

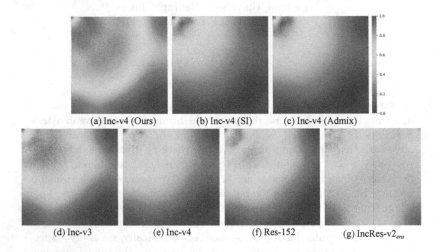

Fig. 1. Visualization of the spectrum saliency maps (average of all images) for normally trained models Inc-v3 [38], Inc-v4 [37], Res-152 [15] and defense model IncRes-v2$_{ens}$ [42]. (**a**): the result for our transformation images ($N = 5$) conducted in frequency domain. (**b∼c**): the result for scale-invariant ($m_1 = 5$) [22] and Admix ($m_1 = 5$, $m_2 = 3$) [46] transformations conducted in spatial domain. (**d∼g**): the results for raw images on four different models.

In general, settings of adversarial attacks can be divided into white-box and black-box. For the former [3,26,28,59], an adversary has access to the model, *e.g.*, model architecture and parameters are known. Therefore, adversarial examples can be directly crafted by the gradient (w.r.t. the input) of the victim model, and thus achieving a high success rate. However, white-box attack is usually impracticable in real-world applications because an adversary is impossible to obtain all information about a victim model. To overcome this limitation, a common practice of black-box attacks [4,10,53] turns to investigate the inherent cross-model transferability of adversarial examples. Typically, an adversary crafts adversarial examples via a substitute model (*a.k.a.* white-box model), and then transfers them to a victim model (*a.k.a.* black-box model) for attacking.

However, the gap between the substitute model and the victim model is usually large, which manifests as the low transferability of adversarial examples. Although attacking diverse models simultaneously can boost the transferability, collecting a large number of diverse models is difficult and training a model from scratch is also time-consuming. To tackle this issue, *model augmentation* [22] is proposed. In particular, typical model augmentation approaches [5,22,53] aim to simulate diverse models by applying loss-preserving transformations to inputs. Yet, all of existing works investigate relationships of different models in spatial domain, which may overlook the essential differences between them.

To better uncover the differences among models, we introduce the spectrum saliency map (see Sect. 3.2) from a frequency domain perspective since representation of images in this domain have a fixed pattern [1,54], *e.g.*, low-frequency components of an image correspond to its contour. Specifically, the spectrum saliency map is defined as the gradient of model loss function w.r.t. the frequency spectrum of input image. As illustrated in Fig. 1 (d~g), spectrum saliency maps of different models significantly vary from each other, which clearly reveals that each model has different interests in the same frequency component.

Motivated by this, we consider tuning the spectrum saliency map to simulate more diverse substitute models, thus generating more transferable adversarial examples. To that end, we propose a spectrum transformation based on (discrete cosine transform) DCT and (inverse discrete cosine transform) IDCT techniques [1] to diversify input images. We theoretically prove that this spectrum transformation can generate diverse spectrum saliency maps and thus simulate diverse substitute models. As demonstrated in Fig. 1 (a~c), after averaging results of diverse augmented models, only our resulting spectrum saliency map can cover almost all those of other models. This demonstrates our proposed spectrum transformation can effectively narrow the gap between the substitute model and victim model. To sum up, our main contributions are as follows:

1) We discover that augmented models derived from the spatial domain transformations are not significantly diverse, which may limit the transferability of adversarial examples.

2) To overcome this limitation, we introduce the spectrum saliency map (based on a frequency domain perspective) to investigate the differences among models. Inspired by our finds, we propose a novel Spectrum Simulation Attack to effectively narrow the gap between the substitute model and victim model.

3) Extensive experiments on the ImageNet dataset highlight the effectiveness of our proposed method. Remarkably, compared to state-of-the-art transfer-based attacks, our method improves the attack success rate by 6.3%–12.2% for normally trained models and 5.6%–23.1% for defense models.

2   Related Works

2.1   Adversarial Attacks

Since Szegedy et al. [39] discover the existence of adversarial examples, various attack algorithms [3,6,12,18,20,24,27,28,30,32,50,56–59] have been proposed to investigate the vulnerability of DNNs. Among all attack branches, FGSM-based black-box attacks [4,9–12,18,49,53] which resort to the transferability of adversarial examples are one of the most efficient families. Therefore, in this paper, we mainly focus on this family to boost adversarial attacks.

To enhance the transferability of adversarial examples, it is crucial to avoid getting trapped in a poor local optimum of the substitute model. Towards this end, Dong et al. [4] adopt the momentum term at each iteration of I-FGSM [18] to stabilize update direction. Lin et al. [22] further adapt Nesterov accelerated gradient [31] into the iterative attacks with the aim of effectively looking ahead. Gao et al. [10] propose patch-wise perturbations to better cover the discriminate region of images. In addition to considering better optimization algorithms, *model augmentation* [22] is also an effective strategy. Xie et al. [53] introduce a random transformation to the input, thus improving the transferability. Dong et al. [5] shift the input to create a series of translated images and approximately estimate the overall gradient to mitigate the problem of over-reliance on the substitute model. Lin et al. [22] leverage the scale-invariant property of DNNs and thus average the gradients with respect to different scaled images to update adversarial examples. Zou et al. [60] modify DI-FGSM [53] to promote TI-FGSM [5] by generating multi-scale gradients. Wang et al. [45] consider the gradient variance along momentum optimization path to avoid overfitting. Wang et al. [47] average the gradients with respect to feature maps to disrupt important object-aware features. Wang et al. [46] average the gradients of a set of admixed images, which are the input image admixed with a small portion of other images while maintaining the label of the input image. Wu et al. [50] utilizes an adversarial transformation network to find a better transformation for adversarial attacks in the spatial domain.

2.2 Frequency-Based Analysis and Attacks

Several works [6,36,44,48,54] have analyzed DNNs from a frequency domain perspective. Wang et al. [44] notice DNNs' ability in capturing high-frequency components of an image which are almost imperceptible to humans. Dong et al. [54] find that naturally trained models are highly sensitive to additive perturbations in high frequencies, and both Gaussian data augmentation and adversarial training can significantly improve robustness against high-frequency noises.

In addition, there also exists several adversarial attacks based on frequency domain. Guo et al. [13] propose a LF attack that only leverages the low-frequency components of an image, which shows that low-frequency components also play a significant role in model prediction as high-frequency components. Sharma et al. [36] demonstrate that defense models based on adversarial training are less sensitive to high-frequency perturbations but still vulnerable to low-frequency perturbations. Duan et al. [6] propose the AdvDrop attack which generates adversarial examples by dropping existing details of clean images in frequency domain. Unlike these works that perturb a subset of frequency components, our method aims to narrow the gap between models by frequency-based analysis.

2.3 Adversarial Defenses

To mitigate the threat of adversarial examples, numerous adversarial defense techniques have been proposed in recent years. One popular and promising way is adversarial training [12,25] which leverages adversarial examples to augment the training data during the training phase. Tramèr et al. [42] introduce ensemble adversarial training, which decouples the generation of adversarial examples from the model being trained, to yield models with stronger robustness to black-box attacks. Xie et al. [52] inject blocks that can denoise the intermediate features into the network, and then end-to-end train it on adversarial examples to learn to reduce perturbations in feature maps.

Although adversarial training is the most effective strategy to improve the robustness of the model at present, it inevitably suffers from time-consuming training costs and is expensive to be applied to large-scale datasets and complex DNNs. To avoid this issue, many works try to cure the infection of adversarial perturbations before feeding to DNNs. Guo et al. [14] utilize multiple input transformations (e.g., JPEG compression [7], total variance minimization [33] and image quilting [8]) to recover from the adversarial perturbations. Liao et al. [21] propose high-level representation guided denoiser (HGD) to suppress the influence of adversarial perturbation. Xie et al. [51] mitigate adversarial effects through random resizing and padding (R&P). Cohen et al. [17] leverage the classifier with Gaussian data augmentation to create a provably robust classifier.

In addition, researchers also try to combine the benefits of adversarial training and input pre-processing methods to further improve the robustness of DNNs. NeurIPS-r3 solution [41] propose a two-step procedure which first process images with a series of transformations (e.g., rotation, zoom and sheer) and then pass the outputs through an ensemble of adversarially trained models to obtain the overall prediction. Naseer et al. [29] design a Neural Representation Purifier (NRP) model that learns to clean adversarial perturbed images based on the automatically derived supervision.

3 Methodology

In this section, we first give the basic definition of our task in Sect. 3.1, and then introduce our motivation in Sect. 3.2. Based on the motivation, we provide a detailed description of the proposed method - Spectrum Transformation (Sect. 3.3). Finally, we introduce our overall attack algorithm in Sect. 3.4.

3.1 Preliminaries

Formally, let $f_\theta : x \to y$ denotes a classification model, where θ, x and y indicate the parameters of the model, input clean image and true label, respectively. Our goal is to craft an adversarial perturbation δ so that the resulting adversarial example $x' = x + \delta$ can successfully mislead the classifier, i.e., $f_\theta(x') \neq y$ (a.k.a. non-targeted attack). To ensure an input is minimally changed, an adversarial example should be in the ℓ_p-norm ball centered at $\boldsymbol{x}$ with radius ϵ. Following previous works [4,5,9,10,46,47,53], we focus on the ℓ_∞-norm in this paper. Therefore, the generation of adversarial examples can be formulated as the following optimization problem:

$$\arg\max_{\boldsymbol{x}'} J(\boldsymbol{x}', y; \theta), \quad \text{s.t. } \|\boldsymbol{\delta}\|_\infty \leq \epsilon, \tag{1}$$

where $J(\boldsymbol{x}', y; \theta)$ is usually the cross-entropy loss. However, it is impractical to directly optimize Eq. 1 via the victim model f_θ under the black-box manner because its parameter θ is inaccessible. To overcome this limitation, a common practice is to craft adversarial examples via the accessible substitute model f_ϕ and relying on the transferability to fool the victim model. Taking I-FGSM [18] as an example, adversarial examples at iteration $t + 1$ can be expressed as:

$$\boldsymbol{x}'_{t+1} = \text{clip}_{\boldsymbol{x},\epsilon}\{\boldsymbol{x}'_t + \alpha \cdot \text{sign}\left(\nabla_{\boldsymbol{x}'_t} J\left(\boldsymbol{x}'_t, y; \phi\right)\right)\}, \tag{2}$$

where $\text{clip}_{\boldsymbol{x},\epsilon}(\cdot)$ denotes an element-wise clipping operation to ensure $\boldsymbol{x}' \in [\boldsymbol{x} - \epsilon, \boldsymbol{x} + \epsilon]$, and α is the step size.

3.2   Spectrum Saliency Map

In order to effectively narrow the gap between models, it is important to uncover the essential differences between them. Recently, various attack methods [4,5,10,12,18,22,45,46,53,60] have been proposed to boost the transferability of adversarial examples. Among these algorithms, *model augmentation* [22] is one of the most effective strategies. However, existing works (*e.g.*, [5,22]) usually augment substitute models by applying loss-preserving transformations in the spatial domain, which might ignore essential differences among models and reduce the diversity of substitute models. Intuitively, different models usually focus on similar *spatial regions* of each input image since location of key objects in images is fixed. By contrast, as demonstrated in previous work [44,48,54], different models usually rely on different *frequency components* of each input image when making decisions.

Motivated by this, we turn to explore correlations among models from a perspective of frequency domain. Specifically, we adopt DCT to transform input images $\boldsymbol{x}$ from the spatial domain to the frequency domain. The mathematical definition of the DCT (denoted as $\mathcal{D}(\cdot)^1$ in the following) can be simplified as:

$$\mathcal{D}(\boldsymbol{x}) = \boldsymbol{A}\boldsymbol{x}\boldsymbol{A}^{\mathrm{T}}, \tag{3}$$

where $\boldsymbol{A}$ is an orthogonal matrix and thus $\boldsymbol{A}\boldsymbol{A}^{\mathrm{T}}$ is equal to the identity matrix $\boldsymbol{I}$. Formally, low-frequency components whose amplitudes are high tend to be concentrated in the upper left corner of a spectrum, and high-frequency components are located in the remaining area. Obviously, the pattern of frequency domain is more fixed compared with diverse representations of images in spatial

---

[1] In the implementation, DCT is applied to each color channel independently.

domain (more visualizations can be found in supplementary Sec. D.1). Therefore, we propose a spectrum saliency map S_ϕ to mine sensitive points of different
models f_ϕ, which is defined as:

$$S_\phi = \frac{\partial J(\mathcal{D}_\mathcal{I}(\mathcal{D}(\boldsymbol{x})), y; \phi)}{\partial \mathcal{D}(\boldsymbol{x})}, \tag{4}$$

where $\mathcal{D}_\mathcal{I}(\cdot)$ denotes the IDCT which can recover the input image from frequency
domain back to spatial domain. Note that both the DCT and the IDCT are
lossless, i.e., $\mathcal{D}_\mathcal{I}(\mathcal{D}(\boldsymbol{x})) = A^\mathsf{T} \mathcal{D}(\boldsymbol{x})A = \boldsymbol{x}$.

From the visualization result of S_ϕ shown in Fig. 1, we observe that frequency
components of interest usually varies from model to model. Hence, the spectrum
saliency map can serve as an indicator to reflect a specific model.

3.3 Spectrum Transformation

The analysis above motivates us that if we can simulate augmented models with
a similar spectrum saliency map to victim model, the gap between the substitute
model and victim model can be significantly narrowed and adversarial examples
can be more transferable.

Lemma 1. *Assume both $\boldsymbol{B}_1$ and $\boldsymbol{B}_2$ are n-by-n matrix and $\boldsymbol{B}_1$ is invertible,
then there must exist an n-by-n matrix $\boldsymbol{C}$ that can make $\boldsymbol{B}_1 \times \boldsymbol{C} = \boldsymbol{B}_2$.*

Lemma 1 shows that it is possible to make two matrices (note the essence
of spectrum saliency map is also a matrix) equal in the form of a matrix transformation. However, the spectrum saliency map of vicitm model is usually not
available under black-box setting. Moreover, spectrum saliency map of substitute model is high-dimensional and not guaranteed to be invertible. To tackle
this problem, we propose a random spectrum transformation $\mathcal{T}(\cdot)$ which decomposes matrix multiplication into matrix addition and Hadamard product to get
diverse spectrums. Specifically, in combination with the DCT/IDCT, our $\mathcal{T}(\cdot)$
can be expressed as:

$$\mathcal{T}(\boldsymbol{x}) = \mathcal{D}_\mathcal{I}((\mathcal{D}(\boldsymbol{x}) + \mathcal{D}(\boldsymbol{\xi})) \odot \boldsymbol{M}), \tag{5}$$
$$= \mathcal{D}_\mathcal{I}(\mathcal{D}(\boldsymbol{x} + \boldsymbol{\xi}) \odot \boldsymbol{M}) \tag{6}$$

where $\odot$ denotes Hadamard product, $\xi \sim \mathcal{N}(0, \sigma^2 I)$ and each element of
$M \sim \mathcal{U}(1 - \rho, 1 + \rho)$ are random variants sampled from Gaussian distribution and Uniform distribution, respectively. In practice, common DCT/IDCT
paradigm [6,19], i.e., splitting the image into several blocks before applying DCT,
not works well for boosting transferability (see the ablation study for experimental details). Therefore, we apply DCT on the whole image in our experiments and
visualization of transformation outputs can be found in supplementary Section
D.2.

Formally, $\mathcal{T}(\cdot)$ is capable of yielding diverse spectrum saliency maps (we also
provide proof in supplementary Section A) which can reflect the diversity of

substitute models, and meanwhile, narrowing the gap with the victim model. As illustrated in Fig. 1, previously proposed transformations [22,46] in the spatial domain (i.e., (b & c)) is less effective for generating diverse spectrum saliency maps, which may lead to a weaker model augmentation. In contrast, with our proposed spectrum transformation, resulting spectrum saliency map (i.e., (a)) can cover almost all those of other models.

Algorithm 1: S^2I-FGSM

Input : A classifier f with parameters ϕ; loss function J; a clean image x with ground-truth label y; iterations T; L_∞ constraint ϵ; spectrum transformation times N; tunning factor ρ; std σ of noise $\boldsymbol{\xi}$.

Output: The adversarial example x'

1 $\alpha = \epsilon/T$, $x'_0 = x$
2 **for** $t = 0 \to T - 1$ **do**
3   **for** $i = 1 \to N$ **do**
4   Get transformation output $\mathcal{T}(x'_t)$ using Eq. 6
5   Gradient calculate $g'_i = \nabla_{x'_t} J(\mathcal{T}(x'_t), y; \phi)$
6   **end**
7   Average gradient: $g' = \frac{1}{N} \sum_{i=1}^{N} g'_i$
8     $x'_{t+1} = \text{clip}_{x,\epsilon}\{x'_t + \alpha \cdot sign(g')\}$
9     $x'_{t+1} = \text{clip}(x'_{t+1}, 0, 1)$
10 **end**
11 $x' = x'_T$
12 **return** x'

3.4   Attack Algorithm

In Sect. 3.3, we have introduced our proposed spectrum transformation. This method could be integrated with any gradient-based attacks. For instance, in combination with I-FGSM [18] (i.e., Eq. 2), we propose the Spectrum Simulation Iterative Fast Gradient Sign Method (S^2I-FGSM). The algorithm is detailed in Algorithm 1. Technically, our attack can be mainly divided into three steps. First, in lines 3–6, we apply our spectrum transformation $\mathcal{T}(\cdot)$ to the input image x'_t so that the gradient g'_i obtained from the substitute model is approximately equal to the result obtained from a new model, i.e., *model augmentation*. Second, in line 7, we average N augmented models' gradients to obtain a more stable update direction g'. Finally, in line 8, we update adversarial examples x'_{t+1} of iteration $t + 1$. In short, the above process can be summarised in the following formula:

$$x'_{t+1} = \text{clip}_{x,\epsilon}\{x'_t + \alpha \cdot sign(\frac{1}{N} \sum_{i=1}^{N} \nabla_{x'_t} J(\mathcal{T}(x'_t), y; \phi))\}. \qquad (7)$$

The resulting adversarial examples are shown in Fig. 2. Compared with I-FGSM [18] and SI-FGSM [22], our proposed S^2I-FGSM can craft more threatening adversarial examples for fooling black-box models.

4   Experiments

4.1   Experiment Setup

Dataset. Following previous works [4,5,9,10], we conduct our experiments on the ImageNet-compatible dataset[2], which contains 1000 images with resolution $299 \times 299 \times 3$.

Models. We choose six popular normally trained models, including Inception-v3 (Inc-v3) [38], Inception-v4 (Inc-v4) [37], Inception-Resnet-v2 (IncRes-v2) [37], Resnet-v2-50 (Res-50), Resnet-v2-101 (Res-101) and Resnet-v2-152 (Res-152) [15]. For defenses, we consider nine defense models (i.e., Inc-v3$_{ens3}$, Inc-v3$_{ens4}$, IncRes-v2$_{ens}$ [42], HGD [21], R&P [51], NIPS-r3 [41], JPEG [14], RS [17] and NRP [29]) that are robust against black-box attacks.

Competitor. To show the effectiveness of our proposed spectrum simulation attack, we compare it with diverse state-of-the-art attack methods, including MI-FGSM [4], DI-FGSM [53], TI-FGSM [5], PI-FGSM [10], SI-NI-FGSM [22],

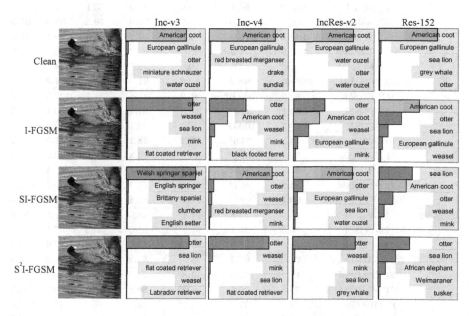

Fig. 2. The comparisons of attacks on Inc-v3 [38], Inc-v4 [37], IncRes-v2 [37] and Res152 [15]. The true label of clean image is *American coot* and marked as orange in the top-5 confidence distribution plots. The adversarial examples are crafted via Inc-v3 [38] by I-FGSM [18], SI-FGSM [22] and our proposed S^2I-FGSM, respectively. Remarkably, our method can attack the white-box model and all black-box models successfully.

---

[2] https://github.com/cleverhans-lab/cleverhans/tree/master/cleverhans_v3.1.0/examples/nips17_adversarial_competition/dataset.

VT-FGSM [45], FI-FGSM [47] and Admix [46]. Besides, we also compare the combined version of these methods, *e.g.*, TI-DIM (combined version of TI-FGSM, MI-FGSM and DI-FGSM) and SI-NI-TI-DIM.

Parameter Settings. In all experiments, the maximum perturbation $\epsilon = 16$, the iteration $T = 10$, and the step size $\alpha = \epsilon/T = 1.6$. For MI-FGSM, we set the decay factor $\mu = 1.0$. For DI-FGSM, we set the transformation probability $p = 0.5$. For TI-FGSM, we set the kernel length $k = 7$. For PI-FGSM, we set the amplification factor $\beta = 10$, project factor $\gamma = 16$ and the kernel length $k_w = 3$ for normally trained models, $k_w = 7$ for defense models. For SI-NI-FGSM, we

Table 1. The attack success rates (%) on six normally trained models. The adversarial examples are crafted via Inc-v3, Inc-v4, IncRes-v2 and Res-152, respectively. "*" indicates white-box attacks.

Model	Attack	Inc-v3	Inc-v4	IncRes-v2	Res-152	Res-50	Res-101	AVG
Inc-v3	MI-FGSM	100.0*	50.6	47.2	40.6	46.9	41.7	54.5
	DI-FGSM	99.7*	48.3	38.2	31.8	39.0	33.8	48.5
	PI-FGSM	100.0*	56.5	49.6	45.0	50.1	44.7	57.7
	S²I-FGSM(ours)	99.7*	**65.0**	**58.9**	**50.3**	**56.2**	**53.3**	**63.9**
	SI-NI-FGSM	100.0*	76.0	75.8	67.7	73.0	69.4	77.0
	VT-MI-FGSM	100.0*	75.0	69.6	62.7	67.1	63.1	72.9
	FI-MI-FGSM	98.8*	83.6	80.0	72.7	80.2	74.9	81.7
	S²I-MI-FGSM (ours)	99.6*	**88.2**	**85.8**	**81.0**	**83.4**	**81.3**	**86.6**
Inc-v4	MI-FGSM	62.0	100.0*	46.2	41.4	47.7	42.8	56.7
	DI-FGSM	54.1	99.1*	36.3	31.4	33.7	30.4	47.5
	PI-FGSM	60.3	100.0*	45.9	44.1	50.3	42.7	57.2
	S²I-FGSM (ours)	**70.2**	99.6*	**57.1**	**48.1**	**56.5**	**47.7**	**63.2**
	SI-NI-FGSM	83.8	**99.9***	78.2	73.3	77.0	73.9	81.0
	VT-MI-FGSM	77.8	99.8*	71.5	64.1	65.7	64.4	73.9
	FI-MI-FGSM	84.9	94.7*	78.0	75.4	78.0	75.7	81.1
	S²I-MI-FGSM (ours)	**90.3**	99.6*	**86.5**	**83.1**	**83.3**	**81.0**	**87.3**
IncRes-v2	MI-FGSM	60.4	52.8	99.4*	45.9	49.1	46.3	59.0
	DI-FGSM	56.5	49.1	97.8*	35.6	38.3	37.1	52.4
	PI-FGSM	62.6	57.9	**99.5***	47.0	51.4	47.9	61.1
	S²I-FGSM (ours)	**76.0**	**67.7**	98.3*	**56.2**	**59.8**	**58.4**	**69.4**
	SI-NI-FGSM	86.4	82.3	**99.8***	76.8	79.6	76.4	83.4
	VT-MI-FGSM	79.3	75.6	99.5*	66.8	69.5	69.5	76.7
	FI-MI-FGSM	81.9	77.9	89.2*	72.3	75.2	75.0	78.6
	S²I-MI-FGSM (ours)	**89.8**	**89.0**	98.4*	**84.9**	**86.0**	**84.3**	**88.7**
Res-152	MI-FGSM	54.7	50.1	45.5	99.4*	84.0	86.5	70.0
	DI-FGSM	57.3	51.5	47.2	99.3*	83.1	85.1	70.6
	PI-FGSM	63.2	55.1	47.8	**99.7***	82.8	84.8	72.2
	S²I-FGSM (ours)	**66.8**	**62.8**	**57.4**	**99.7***	**92.8**	**94.4**	**79.0**
	SI-NI-FGSM	75.3	72.9	70.2	**99.7***	94.5	94.9	84.6
	VT-MI-FGSM	73.7	69.4	66.4	99.5*	93.1	93.8	82.7
	FI-MI-FGSM	83.7	82.1	78.6	99.4*	93.6	94.2	88.6
	S²I-MI-FGSM (ours)	**88.1**	**86.9**	**86.3**	**99.7***	**97.5**	**97.6**	**92.7**

set the number of copies $m_1 = 5$. For VT-FGSM, we set the hyper-parameter β = 1.5, number of sampling examples is 20. For FI-FGSM, the drop probability $p_d = 0.3$ for normally trained models and $p_d = 0.1$ for defense models, and the ensemble number is 30. For Admix, we set number of copies $m_1 = 5^3$, sample number $m_2 = 3$ and the admix ratio $\eta = 0.2$. For our proposed S^2I-FGSM, we set the tuning factor $\rho = 0.5$ for M, the standard deviation σ of ξ is simply set to the value of ϵ, and the number of spectrum transformations $N = 20$ (discussions about ρ, σ and N can be found in supplementary Section B). The parameter settings for the combined version are the same.

4.2   Attack Normally Trained Models

In this section, we investigate the vulnerability of normally trained models. We first compare S^2I-FGSM with MI-FGSM [4], DI-FGSM [53], PI-FGSM [10] to verify the effectiveness of our method in Table 1. A first glance shows that S^2I-FGSM consistently surpasses well-known baseline attacks on all black-box models. For example, when attacking against Inc-v3, MI-FGSM, DI-FGSM and PI-FGSM only successfully transfer 47.2%, 38.2% and 49.6% adversarial examples to IncRes-v2, while our S^2I-FGSM can achieve a much higher success rate of **58.9%**. This convincingly validates the high effectiveness of our proposed method against normally trained models.

Besides, we also report the results for methods with the momentum term [4]. As displayed in Table 1, the performance gap between our proposed method and state-of-the-art approaches is still large. Notably, adversarial examples crafted by our proposed S^2I-MI-FGSM are capable of getting **88.8%** success rate on average, which outperforms SI-NI-FGSM, VT-MI-FGSM and FI-MI-FGSM by 7.3%, 12.2% and 6.3%, respectively. This also demonstrates that the combination of our method and existing attacks can significantly enhance the transferability of adversarial examples.

4.3   Attack Defense Models

Although many attack methods can easily fool normally trained models, they may fail in attacking models with the defense mechanism. To further verify the superiority of our method, we conduct a series of experiments against defense models. Given that the vanilla versions of attacks are less effective for defense models, we consider the stronger DIM, TI-DIM, PI-TI-DI-FGSM, SI-NI-TI-DIM, VT-TI-DIM, FI-TI-DIM and Admix-TI-DIM as competitors to our proposed S^2I-TI-DIM, S^2I-SI-DIM and S^2I-SI-TI-DIM.

Single-Model Attacks. We first investigate the transferability of adversarial examples crafted via a single substitute model. From the results of Table 2, we can observe that our algorithm can significantly boost existing attacks. For example, suppose we generate adversarial examples via Inc-v3, TI-DIM only

---

[3] Note that Admix is equipped with SI-FGSM by default.

Table 2. The attack success rates (%) on nine defenses. The adversarial examples are crafted via Inc-v3, Inc-v4, IncRes-v2 and Res-152, respectively.

Model	Attack	Inc-v3$_{ens3}$	Inc-v3$_{ens4}$	IncRes-v2$_{ens}$	HGD	R&P	NIPS-r3	JPEG	RS	NRP	AVG.
Inc-v3	TI-DIM	43.2	42.1	27.9	36.0	30.2	37.4	56.7	55.8	22.0	39.0
	PI-TI-DI-FGSM	43.5	46.3	35.3	33.9	35.2	39.9	47.6	74.9	37.0	43.7
	SI-NI-TI-DIM	55.0	53.0	36.5	37.0	37.9	48.5	72.3	55.2	32.7	47.6
	VT-TI-DIM	61.3	60.4	46.6	53.9	47.8	53.3	68.3	62.4	36.1	54.5
	FI-TI-DIM	61.8	59.6	49.2	51.7	48.3	55.0	71.3	64.5	38.0	55.5
	Admix-TI-DIM	75.3	72.1	56.7	65.8	59.8	66.0	83.7	70.5	45.3	66.1
	S^{2}I-TI-DIM (ours)	81.5	81.2	69.8	77.8	70.1	77.2	86.7	71.8	**56.0**	74.7
	S^{2}I-SI-DIM (ours)	83.8	81.8	64.8	71.1	68.9	77.4	**91.8**	72.6	52.3	73.8
	S^{2}I-SI-TI-DIM (ours)	**88.6**	**87.8**	**77.9**	**81.1**	**77.6**	**83.3**	91.3	71.0	55.1	**79.3**
Inc-v4	TI-DIM	38.4	38.1	27.7	33.7	29.5	33.0	51.2	55.0	19.0	36.2
	PI-TI-DI-FGSM	42.3	43.8	32.5	33.0	33.9	36.7	46.0	74.8	32.3	41.7
	SI-NI-TI-DIM	60.2	56.9	43.8	46.0	46.5	52.7	73.7	56.3	32.5	52.1
	VT-TI-DIM	57.7	57.2	46.9	55.1	48.9	50.4	63.3	59.1	34.9	52.6
	FI-TI-DIM	61.0	58.4	50.6	53.6	51.7	55.1	67.7	62.6	38.6	55.5
	Admix-TI-DIM	77.3	74.1	63.8	73.4	67.1	71.4	82.6	67.2	48.0	69.4
	S^{2}I-TI-DIM (ours)	78.7	78.0	69.9	76.6	71.9	77.1	83.5	73.4	55.0	73.8
	S^{2}I-SI-DIM (ours)	86.0	83.7	72.4	78.4	76.8	81.7	**91.2**	73.9	**60.9**	78.3
	S^{2}I-SI-TI-DIM (ours)	**88.7**	**87.7**	**81.7**	**86.1**	**83.5**	**86.3**	90.8	**75.0**	59.6	**82.2**
IncRes-v2	TI-DIM	48.0	43.6	38.9	43.9	40.5	43.2	57.3	57.3	24.7	44.2
	PI-TI-DI-FGSM	49.7	51.1	46.0	40.1	45.9	47.8	50.6	78.0	41.0	50.0
	SI-NI-TI-DIM	71.8	62.8	55.6	53.2	59.6	64.7	82.0	60.6	41.0	61.3
	VT-TI-DIM	65.9	60.1	58.2	60.3	57.6	60.1	70.1	61.2	36.9	58.9
	FI-TI-DIM	58.1	54.4	53.5	52.6	52.2	56.8	64.2	64.4	39.8	55.1
	Admix-TI-DIM	85.3	82.0	79.5	82.4	79.6	82.4	85.9	74.2	59.7	79.0
	S^{2}I-TI-DIM (ours)	82.6	79.9	79.2	79.5	79.3	81.2	86.1	74.2	61.6	78.2
	S^{2}I-SI-DIM (ours)	90.3	88.6	83.7	86.6	84.1	86.9	92.0	75.5	69.0	84.1
	S^{2}I-SI-TI-DIM (ours)	**92.1**	**91.0**	**90.6**	**90.8**	**89.2**	**90.0**	**93.3**	**79.2**	**73.4**	**87.8**
Res-152	TI-DIM	55.1	52.3	42.5	55.6	46.5	52.3	64.9	61.2	32.2	51.4
	PI-TI-DI-FGSM	54.3	56.2	45.3	43.7	46.2	48.9	55.2	78.1	47.7	52.8
	SI-NI-TI-DIM	68.6	64.0	52.4	58.9	56.8	64.2	80.1	67.5	42.3	61.6
	VT-TI-DIM	64.3	61.4	54.9	60.7	54.8	59.4	69.3	67.9	41.2	59.3
	FI-TI-DIM	70.1	66.0	59.5	63.9	60.8	66.0	77.5	71.0	47.2	64.7
	Admix-TI-DIM	83.7	81.4	73.7	81.2	77.0	80.1	87.8	75.0	59.5	77.7
	S^{2}I-TI-DIM (ours)	86.6	83.9	79.0	85.3	81.8	85.5	90.6	80.9	66.1	82.2
	S^{2}I-SI-DIM (ours)	89.3	84.4	77.9	86.6	82.7	86.3	**92.8**	76.4	65.9	82.5
	S^{2}I-SI-TI-DIM (ours)	**92.5**	**88.6**	**85.3**	**88.6**	**87.8**	**89.8**	92.4	**83.6**	**72.0**	**86.7**

Table 3. The attack success rates (%) on nine defenses. The adversarial examples are crafted via an ensemble of Inc-v3, Inc-v4, IncRes-v2 and Res-152 and the weight for each model is 1/4.

Attack	Inc-v3$_{ens3}$	Inc-v3$_{ens4}$	IncRes-v2$_{ens}$	HGD	R&P	NIPS-r3	JPEG	RS	NRP	AVG.
TI-DIM	79.2	75.3	69.3	80.4	73.9	76.7	87.5	68.3	43.1	72.6
PI-TI-DI-FGSM	75.0	76.0	67.7	69.5	68.0	72.6	77.8	83.4	60.8	72.3
SI-NI-TI-DIM	90.2	87.9	80.0	83.2	83.5	87.8	94.3	81.4	59.2	83.1
VT-TI-DIM	85.0	82.3	78.3	83.9	79.4	81.9	88.5	74.5	59.7	79.3
FI-TI-DIM	83.1	83.6	74.6	84.9	76.5	78.6	90.2	72.2	61.2	78.3
Admix-TI-DIM	93.9	92.9	90.3	94.0	91.3	92.0	95.6	82.4	76.0	89.8
S^{2}I-TI-DIM (ours)	94.6	94.3	92.5	94.3	93.1	94.3	95.8	87.4	83.5	92.2
S^{2}I-SI-DIM (ours)	96.5	96.3	94.2	95.8	94.9	96.0	**97.4**	88.2	87.3	94.1
S^{2}I-SI-TI-DIM (ours)	**96.7**	**96.7**	**95.2**	**96.3**	**95.7**	**96.5**	96.9	**92.2**	**92.2**	**95.4**

achieves an average success rate of 39.0% on the nine defense models, while our proposed S^{2}I-TI-DIM can yield about 2× transferability, i.e., outperforms TI-DIM by **35.7%**. This demonstrates the remarkable effectiveness of our proposed method against defense models.

Ensemble-Based Attacks. We also report the results for attacking an ensemble of models simultaneously [23] to demonstrate the effectiveness of our proposed method. In particular, the adversarial examples are crafted via an ensemble of Inc-v3, Inc-v4, IncRes-v2 and Res-152. Similar to the results of Table 2, our S^{2}I-SI-TI-DIM displayed in Table 3 still consistently surpass state-of-the-art approaches. Remarkably, S^{2}I-SI-TI-DIM is capable of obtaining **95.4%** success rate on average, which outperforms SI-NI-TI-DIM, VT-TI-DIM, FI-TI-DIM and Admix-TI-DIM by 23.1%, 12.4%, 16.1%, 17.1% and 5.6%, respectively. This also reveals that current defense mechanisms are still vulnerable to well-design adversarial examples and far from the need of real security.

4.4 Ablation Study

In this section, we analyze the impact of different aspects of our method:

Frequency Domain vs. Spatial Domain. For our proposed S^{2}I-FGSM, transformation is applied in the frequency domain. To verify that frequency domain transformation (i.e., our spectrum transformation) is more potent in narrowing the gap between models than spatial domain transformation (i.e., remove the DCT/IDCT in spectrum transformation), we conduction an ablation study. As depicted in Fig. 3 (left), regardless of what substitute models are attacked, the transferability of adversarial examples crafted based on frequency domain transformation is consistently higher than that of spatial domain transformation. Notably, when attacking against Inc-v3, the attack based on frequency domain transformation (i.e., S^{2}I-FGSM) outperforms the attack based on spatial domain transformation by a large margin of **15.0%**. This convincingly validates that

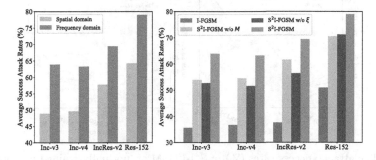

Fig. 3. The average attack success rates (%) on six normally trained models (introduced in Sect. 4.1). The adversarial examples are crafted via Inc-v3, Inc-v4, IncRes-v2 and Res-152, respectively. **Left:** Effect of frequency domain transformation. **Right:** Effect of ξ and M.

frequency domain can capture more essential differences among models, thus yielding more diverse substitute models than spatial domain.

Effect of ξ and M. To analyze the effect of each random variant (i.e., ξ and M) in our spectrum transformation, we conduct the experiment in Fig. 3 (right). From this result, we observe that both ξ and M are useful for enhancing the transferability of adversarial examples. It is because both of them can manipulate the spectrum saliency map to a certain extent, albeit from different aspects of implementation. Therefore, by leveraging them simultaneously, our proposed spectrum transformation can simulate a more diverse substitute model, thus significantly boosting attacks.

On the Block Size of DCT/IDCT. Previous works [6,19] usually started by splitting images into small blocks with size $n \times n$ and then apply DCT/IDCT. However, it is not clear that this paradigm is appropriate for our approach. Therefore, in this part, we investigate the impact of block size on the transferability. Specifically, we tune the block size from 8×8 to 299×299 (full image size) and report the attack success rates of S^2I-FGSM in Fig. 4. From this result, we observe that larger blocks are more suited to our approach. Particularly, the attack success rates reach peak when the size of the block is the same as the full image size. Therefore, in our experiment, we do not split the image beforehand and directly apply DCT/IDCT on the full image to get its spectrum (we also provide time analysis of DCT/IDCT in supplementary Sec. C).

Attention Shift. To better understand the effectiveness of our attack, we apply Grad-CAM [35] to compare attention maps of clean images with those of adversarial examples. As illustrated in Fig. 5, our proposed method can effectively shift the model's attention from the key object to other mismatched regions. Consequently, the victim model inevitably captures other irrelevant features, thus leading to misclassification.

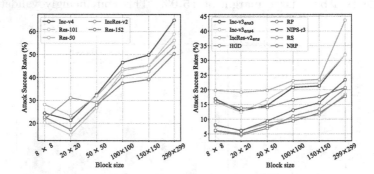

Fig. 4. The attack success rates (%) of S^2I-FGSM on normally trained models (**Left**) and defense models (**Right**) w.r.t. the block size of DCT/IDCT. Adversarial examples are generated via Inc-v3.

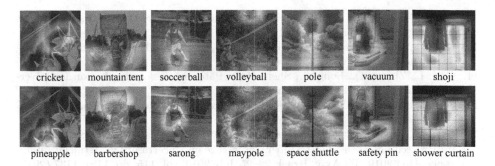

| cricket | mountain tent | soccer ball | volleyball | pole | vacuum | shoji |

| pineapple | barbershop | sarong | maypole | space shuttle | safety pin | shower curtain |

Fig. 5. Visualization for attention shift. We apply Grad-CAM [35] for Res-152 [15] to visualize attention maps of clean (1st row) and adversarial images (2nd row). Adversarial examples are crafted via Inc-v3 by our S^2I-FGSM. The result demonstrates that our adversarial examples are capable of shifting model's attention.

5   Conclusion

In this paper, we propose a Spectrum Simulation Attack to boost adversarial attacks from a frequency domain perspective. Our work gives a novel insight into model augmentation, which narrows the gap between the substitute model and victim model by a set of spectrum transformation images. We also conduct a detailed ablation study to clearly illustrate the effect of each component. Compared with traditional model augmentation attacks in spatial domain, extensive experiments demonstrate the significant effectiveness of our method, which outperforms state-of-the-art transfer-based attacks by a large margin.

Acknowledgment. This work is supported by the National Natural Science Foundation of China (Grant No. 62122018, No. 61772116, No. 61872064, No. U20B2063).

References

1. Ahmed, N., Natarajan, T.R., Rao, K.R.: Discrete cosine transform. IEEE Trans. Comput. **23**, 90–93 (1974)
2. Bojarski, M., et al.: End to end learning for self-driving cars. CoRR abs/1604.07316 (2016)
3. Carlini, N., Wagner, D.A.: Towards evaluating the robustness of neural networks. In: Symposium on Security and Privacy (2017)
4. Dong, Y., et al.: Boosting adversarial attacks with momentum. In: CVPR (2018)
5. Dong, Y., Pang, T., Su, H., Zhu, J.: Evading defenses to transferable adversarial examples by translation-invariant attacks. In: CVPR (2019)
6. Duan, R., Chen, Y., Niu, D., Yang, Y., Qin, A.K., He, Y.: AdvDrop: adversarial attack to DNNS by dropping information. In: ICCV (2021)
7. Dziugaite, Karolina, G., Ghahramani, Z., Roy., D.M.: A study of the effect of jpg compression on adversarial images. CoRR abs/1608.00853 (2016)
8. Efros, A.A., Freeman, W.T.: Image quilting for texture synthesis and transfer. In: SIGGRAPH (2001)

9. Gao, L., Cheng, Y., Zhang, Q., Xu, X., Song, J.: Feature space targeted attacks by statistic alignment. In: IJCAI (2021)
10. Gao, L., Zhang, Q., Song, J., Liu, X., Shen, H.T.: Patch-wise attack for fooling deep neural network. In: ECCV (2020)
11. Gao, L., Zhang, Q., Song, J., Shen, H.T.: Patch-wise++ perturbation for adversarial targeted attacks. CoRR abs/2012.15503 (2020)
12. Goodfellow, I.J., Shlens, J., Szegedy, C.: Explaining and harnessing adversarial examples. In: ICLR (2015)
13. Guo, C., Frank, J.S., Weinberger, K.Q.: Low frequency adversarial perturbation. In: Proceedings of the Thirty-Fifth Conference on Uncertainty in Artificial Intelligence, UAI 2019, Tel Aviv, Israel, 22–25 July 2019, vol. 115, pp. 1127–1137 (2019)
14. Guo, C., Rana, M., Cissé, M., van der Maaten, L.: Countering adversarial images using input transformations. In: ICLR (2018)
15. He, K., Zhang, X., Ren, S., Sun, J.: Deep residual learning for image recognition. In: CVPR, pp. 770–778 (2016)
16. Huang, G., Liu, Z., van der Maaten, L., Weinberger, K.Q.: Densely connected convolutional networks. In: CVPR (2017)
17. Jia, J., Cao, X., Wang, B., Gong, N.Z.: Certified robustness for top-k predictions against adversarial perturbations via randomized smoothing. In: ICLR (2020)
18. Kurakin, A., Goodfellow, I.J., Bengio, S.: Adversarial machine learning at scale. In: ICLR (2017)
19. Li, J., et al.: Projection & probability-driven black-box attack. In: CVPR (2020)
20. Li, X., et al.: QAIR: practical query-efficient black-box attacks for image retrieval. In: CVPR (2021)
21. Liao, F., Liang, M., Dong, Y., Pang, T., Hu, X., Zhu, J.: Defense against adversarial attacks using high-level representation guided denoiser. In: CVPR (2018)
22. Lin, J., Song, C., He, K., Wang, L., Hopcroft, J.E.: Nesterov accelerated gradient and scale invariance for adversarial attacks. In: ICLR (2020)
23. Liu, Y., Chen, X., Liu, C., Song, D.: Delving into transferable adversarial examples and black-box attacks. In: ICLR (2017)
24. Liu, Y., Cheng, Y., Gao, L., Liu, X., Zhang, Q., Song, J.: Practical evaluation of adversarial robustness via adaptive auto attack. CoRR abs/2203.05154 (2022)
25. Madry, A., Makelov, A., Schmidt, L., Tsipras, D., Vladu, A.: Towards deep learning models resistant to adversarial attacks. In: ICLR (2018)
26. Mao, X., Chen, Y., Wang, S., Su, H., He, Y., Xue, H.: Composite adversarial attacks. In: AAAI (2021)
27. Moosavi-Dezfooli, S., Fawzi, A., Fawzi, O., Frossard, P.: Universal adversarial perturbations. In: CVPR (2017)
28. Moosavi-Dezfooli, S., Fawzi, A., Frossard, P.: DeepFool: a simple and accurate method to fool deep neural networks. In: CVPR (2016)
29. Naseer, M., Khan, S.H., Hayat, M., Khan, F.S., Porikli, F.: A self-supervised approach for adversarial robustness. In: CVPR (2020)
30. Naseer, M., Khan, S.H., Khan, M.H., Khan, F.S., Porikli, F.: Cross-domain transferability of adversarial perturbations. In: NeurPIS (2019)
31. Nesterov, Y.: A method for unconstrained convex minimization problem with the rate of convergence $o(1/k^2)$. In: Doklady AN USSR (1983)
32. Papernot, N., McDaniel, P.D., Goodfellow, I.J., Jha, S., Celik, Z.B., Swami, A.: Practical black-box attacks against machine learning. In: Karri, R., Sinanoglu, O., Sadeghi, A., Yi, X. (eds.) Proceedings of the 2017 ACM on Asia Conference on Computer and Communications Security, ACM (2017)

33. Rudin, L.I., Osher, S., Fatemi, E.: Nonlinear total variation based noise removal algorithms. Phys. D Nonlinear Phenom. **60**, 259–268 (1992)
34. Sallab, A.E., Abdou, M., Perot, E., Yogamani, S.K.: Deep reinforcement learning framework for autonomous driving. CoRR abs/1704.02532 (2017)
35. Selvaraju, R.R., Cogswell, M., Das, A., Vedantam, R., Parikh, D., Batra, D.: Grad-cam: Visual explanations from deep networks via gradient-based localization. In: ICCV (2017)
36. Sharma, Y., Ding, G.W., Brubaker, M.A.: On the effectiveness of low frequency perturbations. In: IJCAI, pp. 3389–3396 (2019)
37. Szegedy, C., Ioffe, S., Vanhoucke, V., Alemi, A.A.: Inception-v4, inception-ResNet and the impact of residual connections on learning. In: AAAI (2017)
38. Szegedy, C., Vanhoucke, V., Ioffe, S., Shlens, J., Wojna, Z.: Rethinking the inception architecture for computer vision. In: CVPR (2016)
39. Szegedy, C., et al.: Intriguing properties of neural networks. In: ICLR (2014)
40. Taigman, Y., Yang, M., Ranzato, M., Wolf, L.: DeepFace: closing the gap to human-level performance in face verification. In: CVPR (2014)
41. Thomas, A., Elibol, O.: Defense against adversarial attacks-3rd place (2017). https://github.com/anlthms/nips-2017/blob/master/poster/defense.pdf
42. Tramèr, F., Kurakin, A., Goodfellow, I.J., Boneh, D., McDaniel, P.D.: Ensemble adversarial training: attacks and defenses. In: ICLR (2018)
43. Wang, H., et al.: CosFace: large margin cosine loss for deep face recognition. In: CVPR (2018)
44. Wang, H., Wu, X., Huang, Z., Xing, E.P.: High-frequency component helps explain the generalization of convolutional neural networks. In: CVPR, pp. 8681–8691 (2020)
45. Wang, X., He, K.: Enhancing the transferability of adversarial attacks through variance tuning. In: CVPR, pp. 1924–1933 (2021)
46. Wang, X., He, X., Wang, J., He, K.: Admix: Enhancing the transferability of adversarial attacks. In: ICCV (2021)
47. Wang, Z., Guo, H., Zhang, Z., Liu, W., Qin, Z., Ren, K.: Feature importance-aware transferable adversarial attacks. In: ICCV (2021)
48. Wang, Z., Yang, Y., Shrivastava, A., Rawal, V., Ding, Z.: Towards frequency-based explanation for robust CNN. CoRR abs/2005.03141 (2020)
49. Wu, D., Wang, Y., Xia, S., Bailey, J., Ma, X.: Skip connections matter: On the transferability of adversarial examples generated with resnets. In: ICLR (2020)
50. Wu, W., Su, Y., Lyu, M.R., King, I.: Improving the transferability of adversarial samples with adversarial transformations. In: CVPR (2021)
51. Xie, C., Wang, J., Zhang, Z., Ren, Z., Yuille, A.L.: Mitigating adversarial effects through randomization. In: ICLR (2018)
52. Xie, C., Wu, Y., van der Maaten, L., Yuille, A.L., He, K.: Feature denoising for improving adversarial robustness. In: CVPR (2019)
53. Xie, C., et al.: Improving transferability of adversarial examples with input diversity. In: CVPR (2019)
54. Yin, D., Lopes, R.G., Shlens, J., Cubuk, E.D., Gilmer, J.: A Fourier perspective on model robustness in computer vision. In: NeurIPS (2019)
55. Zhang, J., Song, J., Gao, L., Liu, Y., Shen, H.T.: Progressive meta-learning with curriculum. IEEE Trans. Circ. Syst. Video Technol. **32**, 5916 – 5930 (2022)
56. Zhang, Q., Li, X., Chen, Y., Song, J., Gao, L., He, Y., Xue, H.: Beyond imagenet attack: Towards crafting adversarial examples for black-box domains. In: ICLR (2022)

57. Zhang, Q., Zhang, C., Li, C., Song, J., Gao, L., Shen, H.T.: Practical no-box adversarial attacks with training-free hybrid image transformation. CoRR abs/2203.04607 (2022)
58. Zhang, Q., Zhu, X., Song, J., Gao, L., Shen, H.T.: Staircase sign method for boosting adversarial attacks. CoRR abs/2104.09722 (2021)
59. Zhao, Z., Liu, Z., Larson, M.A.: Towards large yet imperceptible adversarial image perturbations with perceptual color distance. In: CVPR (2020)
60. Zou, J., Pan, Z., Qiu, J., Liu, X., Rui, T., Li, W.: Improving the transferability of adversarial examples with resized-diverse-inputs, diversity-ensemble and region fitting. In: ECCV (2020)

Prior-Guided Adversarial Initialization for Fast Adversarial Training

Xiaojun Jia[1,2], Yong Zhang[3(✉)], Xingxing Wei[4], Baoyuan Wu[5], Ke Ma[6],
Jue Wang[3], and Xiaochun Cao[1,7]

[1] SKLOIS, Institute of Information Engineering, CAS, Beijing, China
`jiaxiaojun@iie.ac.cn`
[2] School of Cyber Security, University of Chinese Academy of Sciences,
Beijing, China
[3] Tencent, AI Lab, Shenzhen, China
`zhangyong201303@gmail.com`
[4] Institute of Artificial Intelligence, Beihang University, Beijing, China
`xxwei@buaa.edu.cn`
[5] School of Data Science, Secure Computing Lab of Big Data, Shenzhen Research
Institute of Big Data, The Chinese University of Hong Kong, Shenzhen, China
`wubaoyuan@cuhk.edu.cn`
[6] School of Computer Science and Technology, UCAS, Beijing, China
`make@ucas.ac.cn`
[7] School of Cyber Science and Technology, Shenzhen Campus,
Sun Yat-sen University, Shenzhen 518107, China
`caoxiaochun@mail.sysu.edu.cn`

Abstract. Fast adversarial training (FAT) effectively improves the efficiency of standard adversarial training (SAT). However, initial FAT encounters catastrophic overfitting, *i.e.*, the robust accuracy against adversarial attacks suddenly and dramatically decreases. Though several FAT variants spare no effort to prevent overfitting, they sacrifice much calculation cost. In this paper, we explore the difference between the training processes of SAT and FAT and observe that the attack success rate of adversarial examples (AEs) of FAT gets worse gradually in the late training stage, resulting in overfitting. The AEs are generated by the fast gradient sign method (FGSM) with a zero or random initialization. Based on the observation, we propose a prior-guided FGSM initialization method to avoid overfitting after investigating several initialization strategies, improving the quality of the AEs during the whole training process. The initialization is formed by leveraging historically generated AEs without additional calculation cost. We further provide a theoretical analysis for the proposed initialization method. We also propose a simple yet effective regularizer based on the prior-guided initialization, *i.e.*, the currently generated perturbation should not deviate too much from the prior-guided initialization. The regularizer adopts both historical and

---

X. Jia—Work done in an internship at Tencent AI Lab.

Supplementary Information The online version contains supplementary material available at https://doi.org/10.1007/978-3-031-19772-7_33.

S. Avidan et al. (Eds.): ECCV 2022, LNCS 13664, pp. 567–584, 2022.
https://doi.org/10.1007/978-3-031-19772-7_33

current adversarial perturbations to guide the model learning. Evaluations on four datasets demonstrate that the proposed method can prevent catastrophic overfitting and outperform state-of-the-art FAT methods. The code is released at https://github.com/jiaxiaojunQAQ/FGSM-PGI.

Keywords: Fast adversarial training · Prior-guided · Regularizer

1   Introduction

Deep neural networks (DNNs) [5,16,20,27–30,44,48,55] are vulnerable to adversarial examples (AEs) [3,4,8,12–14,17,21,31,43,51] generated by adding imperceptible perturbations to benign images. Standard adversarial training (SAT) [22,32,46] is one of the most efficient defense methods against AEs. It adopts projected gradient descent (PGD) [32], a multi-step attack method, to generate AEs for training. But, SAT requires much time to calculate gradients of the network's input multiple times.

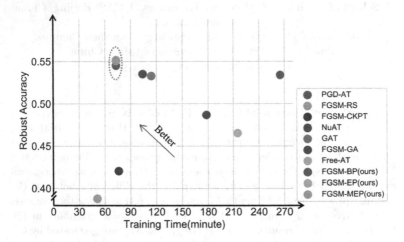

Fig. 1. PGD-10 robust accuracy and training time of different FAT methods with ResNet18 as the backbone on the CIFAR-10 dateset. *x*-axis denotes training time (lower is more efficient) and *y*-axis denotes PGD-10 accuracy (higher is more robust)

To improve efficiency, fast adversarial training (FAT) methods [15,23,35,53] have been proposed. Goodfellow *et al.* first [15] adopt FGSM to generate AEs for training, *i.e.*, FGSM-AT, but it encounters the catastrophic overfitting. Wong *et al.* [49] propose to combine FGSM-AT with random initialization along with early stopping to overcome the overfitting. Andriushchenko *et al.* [2] propose a method from the view of regularization to enhance the quality of AEs, *i.e.*, GradAlign. Kim *et al.* [25] propose a simple method to determine an appropriate step size of FGSM-AT to generate stronger AEs, *i.e.*, FGSM-CKPT. Sriramanan

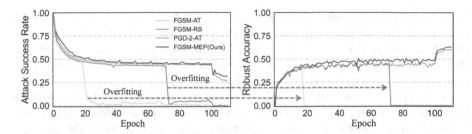

Fig. 2. The difference between the training processes of FAT and SAT methods on the CIFAR-10 dataset. Left: the attack success rate of generated AEs. Right: the PGD-10 robust accuracy of the target model. FGSM-AT and FGSM-RS encounter catastrophic overfitting after training a few epochs. But PGD-2-AT and our method can prevent the overfitting

et al. [41] introduce a relaxation term in the training loss to improve the quality of the generated AEs, *i.e.,* GAT. Then, Sriramanan *et al.* [42] propose a Nuclear-Norm regularizer to enhance the optimization of the AE generation and the model training. These methods not only prevent catastrophic overfitting but also achieve advanced defense performance by enhancing the quality of AEs. However, compared with FGSM-RS, these advanced methods require high additional calculation costs to generate stronger AEs.

As AEs are critical for adversarial training, we study the AEs of both FAT and SAT during their training processes to explore the reason for catastrophic overfitting. Surprisingly, we observe a distinct difference between the attack success rates of their AEs in the late training stage. The attack success rate of FAT drops sharply after a few training epochs while the robust accuracy decreases to 0 (see FGSM-AT and FGSM-RS in Fig. 2). This phenomenon indicates that overfitting happens when the quality of AEs becomes worse. However, the overfitting does not exist in the two-step PGD (PGD-2-AT) that can be treated as FGSM-AT with an adversarial initialization. It means adversarial initialization could be a solution to overfitting. Based on the observation, we raise a question *"can we obtain an adversarial initialization for FGSM-AT to maintain the high quality of AEs for avoiding catastrophic overfitting without additional calculation cost?"* We investigate several initialization strategies and propose a prior-guided initialization by leveraging historically generated AEs, dubbed FGSM-PGI. Specifically, we first use the buffered perturbations of AEs from the previous batch and the previous epoch as the initialization for FGSM, respectively, called FGSM-BP and FGSM-EP. The two strategies are demonstrated to be effective. To exploit complete prior information, we then propose to leverage the buffered gradients from all previous epochs via a momentum mechanism as an additional prior, dubbed FGSM-MEP, which works the best. Furthermore, we provide a theoretical analysis for the proposed initialization method.

Moreover, we also propose a simple yet effective regularizer based on the above prior-guided initialization to guide model learning for better robustness.

The current perturbation can be generated via FGSM using the prior-guided initialization. The regularizer prevents the current perturbation deviating too much from the prior-guided initialization, which is implemented by using a squared L_2 distance between the predictions of adversarial examples generated based on the current perturbation and the prior-guided initialization.

The proposed method not only prevents catastrophic overfitting but also improves the adversarial robustness against adversarial attacks. Figure 1 illustrates the robustness and training efficiency of different FAT methods. Our main contributions are in three aspects: **1)** We propose a prior-guided adversarial initialization to prevent overfitting after investigating several initialization strategies. **2)** We also propose a regularizer to guide the model learning for better robustness by considering both the currently generated perturbation and the prior-guided initialization. **3)** Extensive experiments on four datasets demonstrate that the proposed method can outperform state-of-the-art FAT methods in terms of both efficiency and robustness.

2   Related Work

2.1   Adversarial Training

Adversarial training (AT) variants [37,50,54] are effective in defending against AEs. Madry *et al.* [32] first formulate AT as a minimax optimization problem formulated as follows:

$$\min_{\mathbf{w}} \mathbb{E}_{(\mathbf{x},\mathbf{y}) \sim \mathcal{D}} [\max_{\boldsymbol{\delta} \in \Omega} \mathcal{L}(f(\mathbf{x} + \boldsymbol{\delta}; \mathbf{w}), \mathbf{y})], \tag{1}$$

where $f(\cdot; \mathbf{w})$ represents a deep neural network with parameters $\mathbf{w}$, $\mathcal{D}$ represents a joint data distribution of the benign image $\mathbf{x}$ and the GT one-hot label $\mathbf{y}$. $\mathcal{L}(f(\mathbf{x}; \mathbf{w}), \mathbf{y})$ represents the classification loss function. $\boldsymbol{\delta}$ represents the adversarial perturbation, and Ω represents a threat bound which can be defined as $\Omega = \{\boldsymbol{\delta} : \|\boldsymbol{\delta}\| \leq \epsilon\}$ with the maximum perturbation strength ϵ. Multi-step AT methods generate AEs by a multi-step adversarial attack method, *i.e.*, projected gradient ascent (PGD) [32]. It can be defined as:

$$\boldsymbol{\delta}_{t+1} = \Pi_{[-\epsilon,\epsilon]} [\boldsymbol{\delta}_t + \alpha \cdot \text{sign} (\nabla_{\mathbf{x}} \mathcal{L} (f (\mathbf{x} + \boldsymbol{\delta}_t; \mathbf{w}), \mathbf{y}))], \tag{2}$$

where $\boldsymbol{\delta}_{t+1}$ represents the perturbation at the $t+1$-th iteration, α represents the attack step size, and $\Pi_{[-\epsilon,\epsilon]}$ is the projection that maps the input to the range $[-\epsilon, \epsilon]$. This is a prime PGD-based AT framework proposed in [32]. Following this work, many advanced variants [6,24,34,38,45,47] have been proposed from different perspectives to improve model robustness. An early stopping version [37] of PGD-based AT stands out amongst them.

2.2   Fast Adversarial Training

Although multi-step AT methods can achieve good robustness, they require lots of calculation costs to generate AEs for training. Fast adversarial training variants that generate AEs by the one-step fast gradient sign method (FGSM) [15] are proposed to improve the efficiency, which can be dubbed FGSM-based AT methods. The perturbation of FGSM-AT [15] is defined as:

$$\delta = \epsilon \cdot \text{sign}\left(\nabla_{\mathbf{x}} \mathcal{L}(f(\mathbf{x}; \mathbf{w}), \mathbf{y})\right), \tag{3}$$

where ϵ is the maximal perturbation strength. Though FGSM-based AT accelerates the training speed of AT, it encounters catastrophic overfitting. Specifically, after a period of training, the trained model suddenly cannot defend against the AEs generated by PGD. Wong *et al.* [49] propose to conduct FGSM-based AT with a random initialization. Its perturbation can be defined as:

$$\delta = \Pi_{[-\epsilon, \epsilon]}\left[\boldsymbol{\eta} + \alpha \cdot \text{sign}\left(\nabla_{\mathbf{x}} \mathcal{L}(f(\mathbf{x} + \boldsymbol{\eta}; \mathbf{w}), \mathbf{y})\right)\right], \tag{4}$$

where $\boldsymbol{\eta} \in \mathbf{U}(-\epsilon, \epsilon)$ represents the random initialization, $\mathbf{U}$ is a uniform distribution, and α is set to 1.25ϵ. After that, a series of FAT methods enhances the quality of AEs to improve the defense performance. In detail, Andriushchenko *et al.* [2] demonstrate that using the random initialization cannot prevent catastrophic overfitting. They propose a regularizer to generate stronger AEs, *i.e.*, FGSM-GA. Kim *et al.* [25] reveal that FGSM-RS adopts AEs with the maximum perturbation instead of ones in the adversarial direction, resulting in the overfitting. They then propose a method to determine an appropriate step size to generate powerful AEs to improve model robustness. Sriramanan *et al.* [41] enhance the quality of the generated AEs by using a relaxation term for the classification loss, *i.e.*, GAT. Besides, Sriramanan *et al.* [42] design a Nuclear-Norm regularizer to enhance optimization of the AEs generation to improve the model robustness, *i.e.*, NuAT. Though these methods can prevent overfitting and achieve advanced defense performance, they require much additional calculation cost to conduct AT.

3   The Proposed Approach

We first present our observations of revisiting catastrophic overfitting in Sect. 3.1 and then explore several prior-guided adversarial initialization strategies for FGSM-AT to prevent the overfitting in Sect. 3.2, *i.e.*, FGSM-PGI. We propose a simple yet effective regularization method for the FGSM-PGI to further improve model robustness in Sect. 3.3. Moreover, we also provide a theoretical analysis for the proposed initialization method in Sect. 3.4.

3.1   Revisting Catastrophic Overfitting

Catastrophic overfitting is a phenomenon that the robust accuracy of FAT drops sharply to 0% in the late training stage (see the left figure of Fig. 2), which was noticed by Wong *et al.* [49]. They then found random initialization of FGSM can help avoid the overfitting with training for limited epochs. However, if the training process of FGSM-RS goes on, catastrophic overfitting still appears, as revealed in [2], which indicates that random initialization must be conducted with early stopping. Hence, FGSM-RS does not solve the overfitting fundamentally. FGSM-GA [2] proposes a method from the perspective of regularization in the loss to generate stronger AEs. FGSM-CKPT [25] proposes a method for adjusting the step size of FGSM to improve the quality of AEs in different training stages. GAT [41] adopts a relaxation term for the classification loss to generate stronger AEs during the AEs generation. NuAT [42] uses a Nuclear Norm regularizer to improve the optimization of the AEs generation. These methods prevent catastrophic overfitting by improving the quality of AEs during the training. However, FGSM-GA requires calculating gradients multiple times for regularization, FGSM-CKPT requires multiple times of forwarding propagation for step size selection, and GAT and NuAT require much more time to conduct regularization for generating powerful AEs, which significantly reduces efficiency.

We reinvestigate catastrophic overfitting by comparing the intermediate results of the training processes of FAT and SAT on the CIFAR-10 dataset [26]. For FAT, we study two methods, $i.e.$, FGSM-AT and FGSM-RS. For SAT, we study PGD-AT [32] with the iteration time of 2, $i.e.$, PGD-2-AT. As AEs are the key that distinguishes adversarial training from conventional training, we observe the quality of adversarial examples during the whole training process, $i.e.$, whether adversarial examples can successfully attack the target model. The quality is evaluated by attack success rate (ASR). Figure 2 illustrates the curves of the robust accuracy and the ASR of the above methods as well as ours. We also observe similar phenomenons on other benchmark datasets that are shown in the **supplementary material**.

We summarize the observations as follows. First, it can be observed that the ASRs of FGSM-AT and FGSM-RS drop sharply at the 20-th and 74-th epoch, respectively, leading to the dramatic decreases of the robust accuracy. This indicates that the model robustness would collapse against adversarial attacks if the generated adversarial examples fail in attacking against the model during training. Note that the investigation from the perspective of the quality of adversarial example ($i.e.$, ASR) is ignored by previous works. Second, FGSM-RS with random initialization delays the overfitting from the 20-th epoch to the 70-th epoch. Enhancing the initialization could alleviate the overfitting, but cannot essentially prevent it, which is also observed in [2]. Third, surprisingly, PGD-2-AT does not suffer from the overfitting, which draws our attention. PGD-2-AT can be treated as FGSM-AT with an adversarial initialization of FGSM for adversarial example generation. Even after 110 training epochs, there are still a portion of high-quality adversarial examples that can fool the model. It indicates that adversarial initialization can improve the quality of adversarial examples. The initialization requires additional gradient calculation, which is not desirable.

Table 1. Comparisons of clean and robust accuracy (%) and training time (minute) on the CIFAR-10 dataset. Number in bold indicates the best

Method		Clean	PGD-10	PGD-20	PGD-50	C&W	AA	Time(min)
FGSM-BP	Best	**83.15**	54.59	53.55	53.2	50.24	47.47	73
	Last	**83.09**	54.52	53.5	53.33	50.12	47.17	
FGSM-EP	Best	82.75	54.8	53.62	53.27	49.86	47.94	73
	Last	81.27	55.07	54.04	53.63	50.12	46.83	
FGSM-MEP	Best	81.72	**55.18**	**54.36**	**54.17**	**50.75**	**49.00**	73
	Last	81.72	**55.18**	**54.36**	**54.17**	**50.75**	**49.00**	

3.2 Prior-Guided Adversarial Initialization

The above three observations motivate us to dive into the question *"how to obtain adversarial initialization without additional calculation cost"*. We come up with using the adversarial perturbations of historical AEs as the initialization for FGSM to conduct adversarial training, dubbed FGSM-PGI. Such perturbations serve as the prior knowledge that we can freely obtain without additional gradient calculation except for extra storage. We explore three strategies of exploiting historical perturbations, *i.e.*, taking perturbations from the previous batch, from the previous epoch, and from the momentum of all epochs, *i.e.*, FGSM-BP, FGSM-EP, and FGSM-MEP.

Prior From the Previous Batch (FGSM-BP). We store the perturbations of AEs from the previous batch and regard them as the initialization of FGSM to generate AEs in the current batch. As the batch is randomly sampled, there is no correspondence between perturbations from the previous batch and samples from the current batch. Specifically, for a data point $\mathbf{x}$, we first add the perturbation from the previous batch onto it and then conduct FGSM based on the perturbed example. The adversarial perturbation can be defined as:

$$\delta_{B_{t+1}} = \Pi_{[-\epsilon,\epsilon]} \left[\delta_{B_t} + \alpha \cdot \text{sign} \left(\nabla_\mathbf{x} \mathcal{L}(f(\mathbf{x} + \delta_{B_t}; \mathbf{w}), \mathbf{y}) \right) \right], \tag{5}$$

where $\delta_{B_{t+1}}$ is the adversarial perturbation in the $t+1$-th batch. Compared with FGSM-RS (see Eq. 4), we replace the random initialization with the adversarial perturbation from the previous batch.

Prior From the Previous Epoch (FGSM-EP). We store the perturbations of all adversarial samples from the previous epoch and use them as initialization of FGSM to generate adversarial perturbations for the samples in the current epoch. Note that there is a correspondence between each perturbation from the previous epoch and the sample in the current epoch. The adversarial perturbation is defined as:

$$\delta_{E_{t+1}} = \Pi_{[-\epsilon,\epsilon]} \left[\delta_{E_t} + \alpha \cdot \text{sign} \left(\nabla_\mathbf{x} \mathcal{L}(f(\mathbf{x} + \delta_{E_t}; \mathbf{w}), \mathbf{y}) \right) \right], \tag{6}$$

where $\delta_{E_{t+1}}$ is the adversarial perturbation in the $t+1$-th epoch. Compared with FGSM-RS (see Eq. 4), we replace the random initialization with the adversarial perturbation from the previous epoch.

Prior From the Momentum of All Previous Epochs (FGSM-MEP). To completely leverage historical adversarial perturbations during the whole training process, we propose to compute the momentum of one sample's gradients across all previous training epochs. Then, the gradient momentum is used as the initialization of FGSM for AE generation in the current epoch. There is also a correspondence between the gradient momentum and the sample in the current epoch. The adversarial perturbation can be defined as:

$$\mathbf{g}_c = \text{sign}\left(\nabla_\mathbf{x}\mathcal{L}(f(\mathbf{x} + \boldsymbol{\eta}_{E_t}; \mathbf{w}), \mathbf{y})\right), \tag{7}$$

$$\mathbf{g}_{E_{t+1}} = \mu \cdot \mathbf{g}_{E_t} + \mathbf{g}_c, \tag{8}$$

$$\delta_{E_{t+1}} = \Pi_{[-\epsilon,\epsilon]}\left[\boldsymbol{\eta}_{E_t} + \alpha \cdot \mathbf{g}_c\right], \tag{9}$$

$$\boldsymbol{\eta}_{E_{t+1}} = \Pi_{[-\epsilon,\epsilon]}\left[\boldsymbol{\eta}_{E_t} + \alpha \cdot \text{sign}(\mathbf{g}_{E_{t+1}})\right]. \tag{10}$$

Similar to FGSM-AT (Eq. 3), $\mathbf{g}_c$ is regarded as the signed gradient and $\mathbf{g}_{E_{t+1}}$ is the signed gradient momentum in the $t+1$-th epoch. μ represents the decay factor. $\delta_{E_{t+1}}$ is the adversarial perturbation, similar to that of FGSM-EP. $\boldsymbol{\eta}_{E_{t+1}}$ is the projected perturbation, which is used as adversarial initialization in the next epoch. Compared with FGSM-EP, FGSM-MEP exploits the gradient momentum involving information of all previous epochs as initialization, instead of using only information in the previous epoch.

3.3   Prior-Guided Initialization Based Regularization

We propose an effective regularization method based on the prior-guided initialization to improve model robustness. Specifically, given the prior-guided initialization, we can generate a current perturbation via FGSM with the initialization. Both the current perturbation and the initialization can be used to create adversarial examples. Forcing the two types of adversarial examples to have similar predictions could help improve the smoothness of function. The proposed regularization term can be added into the training loss to update the model parameters $\mathbf{w}_{t+1}$, as follows:

$$\mathbf{w}_{t+1} = \arg\min_\mathbf{w}[\mathcal{L}(f(\mathbf{x} + \delta_{adv}; \mathbf{w}), \mathbf{y}) + \lambda \cdot \|f(\mathbf{x} + \delta_{adv}; \mathbf{w}) - f(\mathbf{x} + \delta_{pgi}; \mathbf{w})\|_2^2], \tag{11}$$

where δ_{pgi} represents the prior-guided initialization generated by one of the above three initialization methods. δ_{adv} represents the current adversarial perturbation generated via FGSM using δ_{pgi} as initialization. λ is a trade-off hyperparameter. The first term is the cross-entropy loss on AEs generated using the current perturbation. The second term represents the regularization, *i.e.*, the squared L_2 distance between the predictions of the two types of adversarial examples. This term makes the learned model not only robust to currently generated AEs but also historically generated AEs. In this way, the proposed regularization term explicitly enforces the function smoothness around samples to improve model robustness.

Based on the proposed prior-guided adversarial initialization and the regularization, we can establish our FAT framework. We evaluate the three prior-guided adversarial initialization approaches on CIFAR-10 (see results in Table 1) and find that they all can prevent catastrophic overfitting and achieve advanced model robustness against adversarial attacks. FGSM-MEP works the best in terms of robust accuracy under all attack scenarios. **The FGSM-EP, FGSM-BP and FGSM-MEP algorithms are presented in the supplementary material.**

3.4 Theoretical Analysis

Proposition 1. *Let δ_{pgi} be the prior-guided adversarial initialization in* ***FGSM-BP, FSGM-EP*** *or* ***FSGM-MEP***, *$\hat{\delta}_{adv}$ represents the current adversarial perturbation generated via FGSM using δ_{pgi} as initialization, and α be the step size of (5), (6), (9) and (10). If Ω is a bounded set like*

$$\Omega = \left\{ \hat{\delta}_{adv} \; : \; \|\hat{\delta}_{adv} - \delta_{pgi}\|_2^2 \leq \epsilon^2 \right\}, \tag{12}$$

and the step size α satisfies $\alpha \leq \epsilon$, it holds that

$$\mathbb{E}_{\hat{\delta}_{adv} \sim \Omega} \left[\|\hat{\delta}_{adv}\|_2 \right] \leq \sqrt{\mathbb{E}_{\hat{\delta}_{adv} \sim \Omega} \left[\|\hat{\delta}_{adv}\|_2^2 \right]}$$
$$\leq \sqrt{\frac{1}{d} \cdot \epsilon}, \tag{13}$$

where $\hat{\delta}_{adv}$ is the adversarial perturbation generated by ***FGSM-BP, FSGM-EP*** *or* ***FSGM-MEP***, *and d is the dimension of the feature space.*

The proof is deferred to the **supplementary material**. The upper bound of the proposed method is $\sqrt{\frac{1}{d}} \cdot \epsilon$ which is less than the bound $\sqrt{\frac{d}{3}} \cdot \epsilon$ of FGSM-RS provided in [2]. Due to the norm of perturbation (gradient) can be treated as the convergence criteria for the non-convex optimization problem, the smaller expectation represents that the proposed prior-guided adversarial initialization will be converged to a local optimal faster than the random initialization with the same number of iterations.

4   Experiments

4.1   Experimental Setting

Dataset Settings. To evaluate the effectiveness of the proposed FGSM-MEP, extensive experiments are conducted on four benchmark datasets that are the

Table 2. Comparisons of clean and robust accuracy (%) and training time (minute) using ResNet18 on the CIFAR-10 dataset. Number in bold indicates the best

Method		Clean	PGD-10	PGD-20	PGD-50	C&W	AA	Time(min)
PGD-AT [37]	Best	82.32	53.76	52.83	52.6	51.08	48.68	265
	Last	82.65	53.39	52.52	52.27	51.28	48.93	
FGSM-RS [49]	Best	73.81	42.31	41.55	41.26	39.84	37.07	51
	Last	83.82	00.09	00.04	00.02	0.00	0.00	
FGSM-CKPT [25]	Best	**90.29**	41.96	39.84	39.15	41.13	37.15	76
	Last	**90.29**	41.96	39.84	39.15	41.13	37.15	
NuAT [42]	Best	81.58	53.96	52.9	52.61	**51.3**	**49.09**	104
	Last	81.38	53.52	52.65	52.48	50.63	48.70	
GAT [41]	Best	79.79	54.18	53.55	53.42	49.04	47.53	114
	Last	80.41	53.29	52.06	51.76	49.07	46.56	
FGSM-GA [2]	Best	83.96	49.23	47.57	46.89	47.46	43.45	178
	Last	84.43	48.67	46.66	46.08	46.75	42.63	
Free-AT(m=8) [39]	Best	80.38	47.1	45.85	45.62	44.42	42.17	215
	Last	80.75	45.82	44.82	44.48	43.73	41.17	
FGSM-BP (ours)	Best	83.15	54.59	53.55	53.2	50.24	47.47	73
	Last	83.09	54.52	53.5	53.33	50.12	47.17	
FGSM-EP (ours)	Best	82.75	54.8	53.62	53.27	49.86	47.94	73
	Last	81.27	55.07	54.04	53.63	50.12	46.83	
FGSM-MEP (ours)	Best	81.72	**55.18**	**54.36**	**54.17**	50.75	49.00	73
	Last	81.72	**55.18**	**54.36**	**54.17**	**50.75**	**49.00**	

most widely used to evaluate adversarial robustness, *i.e.*, CIFAR-10 [26], CIFAR-100 [26], Tiny ImageNet [11], and ImageNet [11]. Following the commonly used settings in the adversarial training, we adopt ResNet18 [18] and WideResNet34-10 [52] as the backbone on CIFAR-10 and CIFAR-100, PreActResNet18 [19] on Tiny ImageNet, and ResNet50 [18] on ImageNet. We adopt the SGD optimizer [36] with a learning rate of 0.1, the weight decay of 5e-4, and the momentum of 0.9. As for CIFAR-10, CIFAR-100, and Tiny ImageNet, following the settings of [33,37], the total epoch number is set to 110. The learning rate decays with a factor of 0.1 at the 100th and 105th epoch. As for ImageNet, following the settings of [39,49], the total epoch number is set to 90. The learning rate decays with a factor of 0.1 at the 30th and 60th epoch. Experiments on ImageNet are conducted with 8 T V100 and other experiments are conducted with a single Tesla V100. For our hyper-parameters, the decay factor μ is set to 0.3 and the hyper-parameter λ is set to 8. More details are presented in the **supplementary material**.

Evaluation Metrics. For adversarial robustness evaluation, we adopt several widely used attack methods, *i.e.*, PGD [32], C&W [7], and an ensemble of diverse parameter-free attacks, AA [10] that includes APGD [10], APGD-T [10], FAB [9],

Table 3. Comparisons of clean and robust accuracy (%) and training time (minute) using ResNet18 on the CIFAR-100 dataset. Number in bold indicates the best

Method		Clean	PGD-10	PGD-20	PGD-50	C&W	AA	Time(min)
PGD-AT [37]	Best	57.52	29.6	28.99	28.87	28.85	25.48	284
	Last	57.5	29.54	29.00	28.90	27.6	25.48	
FGSM-RS [49]	Best	49.85	22.47	22.01	21.82	20.55	18.29	70
	Last	60.55	00.45	00.25	00.19	00.25	0.00	
FGSM-CKPT [25]	Best	**60.93**	16.58	15.47	15.19	16.4	14.17	96
	Last	**60.93**	16.69	15.61	15.24	16.6	14.34	
NuAT [41]	Best	59.71	27.54	23.02	20.18	22.07	11.32	115
	Last	59.62	27.07	22.72	20.09	21.59	11.55	
GAT [42]	Best	57.01	24.55	23.8	23.55	22.02	19.60	119
	Last	56.07	23.92	23.18	23.0	21.93	19.51	
FGSM-GA [2]	Best	54.35	22.93	22.36	22.2	21.2	18.88	187
	Last	55.1	20.04	19.13	18.84	18.96	16.45	
Free-AT(m=8) [39]	Best	52.49	24.07	23.52	23.36	21.66	19.47	229
	Last	52.63	22.86	22.32	22.16	20.68	18.57	
FGSM-BP (ours)	Best	57.58	30.78	30.01	28.99	26.40	23.63	83
	Last	83.82	30.56	29.96	28.82	26.32	23.43	
FGSM-EP (ours)	Best	57.74	31.01	30.17	29.93	27.37	24.39	83
	Last	57.74	31.01	30.17	29.93	27.37	24.39	
FGSM-MEP (ours)	Best	58.78	**31.88**	**31.26**	**31.14**	**28.06**	**25.67**	83
	Last	58.81	**31.6**	**31.03**	**30.88**	**27.72**	**25.42**	

and Square [1]. We set the maximum perturbation strength ϵ to 8 for all attack methods. Moreover, PGD attack is conducted with 10, 20 and, 50 iterations, i.e., PGD-10, PGD-20, and PGD-50. We report the results of the checkpoint with the best accuracy under the attack of PGD-10 as well as the results of the last checkpoint. All experiments in the manuscript are performed with the multi-step learning rate strategy. We also conduct experiments by using a cyclic learning rate strategy [40] which are presented in the **supplementary material**.

Competing Methods. We compare the proposed method with a series of state-of-the-art FAT methods, i.e., Free-AT [39], FGSM-RS [49], FGSM-GA [2], FGSM-CKPT [25], GAT [41] and NuAT [42]. We also compare with an advanced multi-step AT method, i.e., PGD-AT [37]), which is an early stopping version of the original PGD-based AT method [32].

4.2 Results on CIFAR-10

On CIFAR-10, we adopt ResNet18 as the backbone. The results are shown in Table 2. Note that the results of using WideResNet34-10 as the backbone are shown in the **supplementary material**. The proposed FGSM-MEP prevents

Table 4. Comparisons of clean and robust accuracy (%) and training time (minute) using PreActResNet18 on Tiny ImageNet. Number in bold indicates the best

Method		Clean	PGD-10	PGD-20	PGD-50	C&W	AA	Time(min)
PGD-AT [37]	Best	43.6	20.2	19.9	19.86	17.5	16.00	1833
	Last	45.28	16.12	15.6	15.4	14.28	12.84	
FGSM-RS [49]	Best	44.98	17.72	17.46	17.36	15.84	14.08	339
	Last	45.18	0.00	0.00	0.00	0.00	0.00	
FGSM-CKPT [25]	Best	**49.98**	9.20	9.20	8.68	9.24	8.10	464
	Last	**49.98**	9.20	9.20	8.68	9.24	8.10	
NuAT [42]	Best	42.9	15.12	14.6	14.44	12.02	10.28	660
	Last	42.42	13.78	13.34	13.2	11.32	9.56	
GAT [41]	Best	42.16	15.02	14.5	14.44	11.78	10.26	663
	Last	41.84	14.44	13.98	13.8	11.48	9.74	
FGSM-GA [2]	Best	43.44	18.86	18.44	18.36	16.2	14.28	1054
	Last	43.44	18.86	18.44	18.36	16.2	14.28	
Free-AT(m=8) [39]	Best	38.9	11.62	11.24	11.02	11.00	9.28	1375
	Last	40.06	8.84	8.32	8.2	8.08	7.34	
FGSM-BP (ours)	Best	45.01	21.67	21.47	21.43	17.89	15.36	458
	Last	47.16	20.62	20.16	20.07	15.68	14.15	
FGSM-EP (ours)	Best	45.01	21.67	21.47	21.43	17.89	15.36	458
	Last	46.00	20.77	20.39	20.28	16.65	14.93	
FGSM-MEP (ours)	Best	43.32	**23.8**	**23.4**	**23.38**	**19.28**	**17.56**	458
	Last	45.88	**22.02**	**21.7**	**21.6**	**17.44**	**15.50**	

catastrophic overfitting and even achieves better robustness than PGD-AT in most cases. It costs much less time than PGD-AT. Specifically, under the AA attack, PGD-AT achieves an accuracy of about 48% while the proposed FGSM-MEP achieves an accuracy of about 49%.

Compared with other FAT methods, the proposed FGSM-MEP achieves comparable robustness to the previous most potent FAT method, NuAT. But FGSM-MEP costs less time than NuAT (73 min VS 104 min). Besides, for the last checkpoint, the proposed FGSM-MEP can achieve the best robustness performance under all attack scenarios. And for the best checkpoint, the proposed FGSM-MEP also achieves the best robustness performance under the PGD-10, PGD-20, and PGD-50. In terms of efficiency, our training process is about 3 times faster than Free-AT, 2.5 times faster than FGSM-GA, and 1.4 times faster than GAT and NuAT. Previous fast adversarial training variants [2,25,41,42] improve the quality of adversarial examples in different ways. Though they can prevent catastrophic overfitting and improve model robustness, they all require much time for quality improvement. Differently, we improve adversarial example quality from the perspective of initialization and propose to adopt historically generated adversarial perturbation to initialize the adversarial examples without additional calculation cost.

Table 5. Comparisons of clean and robust accuracy (%) and training time (minute) using ResNet50 on the ImageNet dataset. Number in bold indicates the best

ImageNet	Epsilon	Clean	PGD-10	PGD-50	Time (hour)
Free-AT(m=4) [39]	ϵ =2	68.37	48.31	48.28	127.7
	ϵ =4	63.42	33.22	33.08	
	ϵ =8	52.09	19.46	12.92	
FGSM-RS [49]	ϵ =2	67.65	48.78	48.67	44.5
	ϵ =4	63.65	35.01	32.66	
	ϵ =8	53.89	0.00	0.00	
FGSM-BP (ours)	ϵ =2	**68.41**	**49.11**	**49.10**	63.7
	ϵ =4	**64.32**	**36.24**	**34.93**	
	ϵ =8	**53.96**	**21.76**	**14.33**	

4.3   Results on CIFAR-100

On CIFAR-100, we adopt ResNet18 as the backbone. The results are shown in Table 3. Compared with CIFAR-10, it is hard for the classification model to obtain robustness because the CIFAR-100 covers more classes. The proposed FGSM-MEP achieves comparable robustness to PGD-AT and costs less time than PGD-AT. Specifically, under the AA attack, PGD-AT achieves an accuracy of about 25%, while our FGSM-MEP also achieves an accuracy of about 25%. Note that our training process is about 3 times faster than PGD-AT. Compared with other FAT methods, the proposed FGSM-MEP also achieves the best robustness against AEs under all attack scenarios on the best and last checkpoints. In terms of training efficiency, we observe similar results on CIFAR-10.

4.4   Results on Tiny ImageNet and ImageNet

Results on Tiny ImageNet. Following the setting of [25,37], we adopt PreActResNet18 to conduct AT. The results are shown in Table 4. Compared with competing FAT methods, our FGSM-MEP achieves higher robust accuracy. Compared with PGD-AT, our FGSM-MEP achieves better robustness performance under all attack scenarios on the best and last checkpoints. In terms of training efficiency, we observe similar results on CIFAR-10 and CIFAR-100.

Results on ImageNet. Following the setting of [39,49], we adopt ResNet50 to conduct experiments. Specifically, ResNet50 is trained with the maximum perturbation strength $\epsilon = 2$, $\epsilon = 4$, and $\epsilon = 8$. The proposed FGSM-EP and FGSM-MEP require memory consumption to store the adversarial perturbation of the last epoch, which limits their application on ImageNet. Fortunately, FGSM-BP does not require memory consumption to conduct AT. Hence, on the ImageNet, we compare our FGSM-BP with FGSM-RS and Free-AT. The results are shown in Table 5. Compared with FGSM-RS and Free-AT, our FGSM-BP

Table 6. Ablation study of the proposed method

CIFAR-10		Clean	PGD-50	C&W	AA	Time(min)
FGSM-RS	Best	73.81	41.26	39.84	37.07	51
	Last	83.82	00.02	0.00	0.00	
FGSM-BP w/o regularizer	Best	**86.51**	45.77	44.8	43.30	51
	Last	86.57	44.39	43.82	42.08	
FGSM-EP w/o regularizer	Best	85.97	45.97	44.6	43.39	51
	Last	86.3	44.97	43.8	42.84	
FGSM-MEP w/o regularizer	Best	86.33	46.71	45.5	43.99	51
	Last	**86.61**	45.69	44.8	43.26	
FGSM-RS with regularizer	Best	84.41	50.63	48.76	46.80	73
	Last	84.41	50.63	48.76	46.80	
FGSM-BP with regularizer	Best	83.15	53.2	50.24	47.47	73
	Last	83.09	53.33	50.12	47.17	
FGSM-EP with regularizer	Best	82.75	53.27	49.86	47.94	73
	Last	81.27	53.63	50.12	46.83	
FGSM-MEP with regularizer	Best	81.72	**54.17**	**50.75**	**49.00**	73
	Last	81.72	**54.17**	**50.75**	**49.00**	

achieves the highest clean and robust accuracy. Our FGSM-BP requires a bit more calculation cost than FGSM-RS, but much less time than Free-AT.

4.5 Ablation Study

In this paper, we propose a regularization loss term to enforce function smoothness, resulting in improving model robustness. To validate the effectiveness of the proposed regularization, we adopt ResNet18 as the classification model to conduct ablation experiments on CIFAR-10. The results are shown in Table 6. It can be observed that combined with our regularization method, FGSM-BP, FGSM-EP, and FGSM-MEP can achieve better robustness performance under all attack scenarios.

5   Conclusion

In this paper, we investigate how to improve adversarial example quality from the perspective of initialization and propose to adopt historically generated adversarial perturbations to initialize adversarial examples. It can generate powerful adversarial examples with no additional calculation cost. Moreover, we also propose a simple yet effective regularizer to further improve model robustness, which prevents the current perturbation deviating too much from the prior-guided initialization. The regularizer adopts both historical and current adversarial perturbations to guide the model learning. Extensive experimental evaluations demonstrate that the proposed method can prevent catastrophic overfitting and outperform state-of-the-art FAT methods at a low computational cost.

Acknowledgement. Supported by the National Key R&D Program of China under Grant 2018AAA01 02503, National Natural Science Foundation of China (No. U2001202, U1936208, 62006217). Beijing Natural Science Foundation (No. M22006). Shenzhen Science and Technology Program under grant No.RCYX20210609103057050, and Tencent AI Lab Rhino-Bird Focused Research Program under grant No. JR202123.

References

1. Andriushchenko, M., Croce, F., Flammarion, N., Hein, M.: Square attack: a query-efficient black-box adversarial attack via random search. Computer Vision – ECCV 2020 , 484–501 (2020). https://doi.org/10.1007/978-3-030-58592-1_29
2. Andriushchenko, M., Flammarion, N.: Understanding and improving fast adversarial training. Adv. Neural. Inf. Process. Syst. **33**, 16048–16059 (2020)
3. Bai, J., et al.: Targeted attack for deep hashing based retrieval. In: Vedaldi, A., Bischof, H., Brox, T., Frahm, J.-M. (eds.) ECCV 2020. LNCS, vol. 12346, pp. 618–634. Springer, Cham (2020). https://doi.org/10.1007/978-3-030-58452-8_36
4. Bai, Y., Zeng, Y., Jiang, Y., Wang, Y., Xia, S.-T., Guo, W.: Improving query efficiency of black-box adversarial attack. In: Vedaldi, A., Bischof, H., Brox, T., Frahm, J.-M. (eds.) ECCV 2020. LNCS, vol. 12370, pp. 101–116. Springer, Cham (2020). https://doi.org/10.1007/978-3-030-58595-2_7
5. Bai, Y., Zeng, Y., Jiang, Y., Xia, S.T., Ma, X., Wang, Y.: Improving adversarial robustness via channel-wise activation suppressing. arXiv preprint arXiv:2103.08307 (2021)
6. Bai, Y., Zeng, Y., Jiang, Y., Xia, S., Ma, X., Wang, Y.: Improving adversarial robustness via channel-wise activation suppressing. In: 9th International Conference on Learning Representations, ICLR 2021, Virtual Event, Austria, 3–7 May 2021. OpenReview.net (2021)
7. Carlini, N., Wagner, D.: Towards evaluating the robustness of neural networks. In: 2017 IEEE Symposium on Security and Privacy (SP), pp. 39–57. IEEE (2017)
8. Chen, S.T., Cornelius, C., Martin, J., Chau, D.H.: Robust physical adversarial attack on faster r-CNN object detector. corr abs/1804.05810 (2018). arXiv preprint arXiv:1804.05810 (2018)
9. Croce, F., Hein, M.: Minimally distorted adversarial examples with a fast adaptive boundary attack. In: International Conference on Machine Learning, pp. 2196–2205. PMLR (2020)
10. Croce, F., Hein, M.: Reliable evaluation of adversarial robustness with an ensemble of diverse parameter-free attacks. In: International Cnnference on Machine Learning, pp. 2206–2216. PMLR (2020)
11. Deng, J., Dong, W., Socher, R., Li, L.J., Li, K., Fei-Fei, L.: ImageNet: a large-scale hierarchical image database. In: 2009 IEEE Conference on Computer Vision and Pattern Recognition, pp. 248–255. Ieee (2009)

12. Duan, R., Ma, X., Wang, Y., Bailey, J., Qin, A.K., Yang, Y.: Adversarial camouflage: Hiding physical-world attacks with natural styles. In: Proceedings of the IEEE/CVF Conference on Computer Vision and Pattern Recognition, pp. 1000–1008 (2020)
13. Duan, R., et al.: Adversarial laser beam: Effective physical-world attack to DNNS in a blink. In: Proceedings of the IEEE/CVF Conference on Computer Vision and Pattern Recognition, pp. 16062–16071 (2021)
14. Finlayson, S.G., Bowers, J.D., Ito, J., Zittrain, J.L., Beam, A.L., Kohane, I.S.: Adversarial attacks on medical machine learning. Science **363**(6433), 1287–1289 (2019)
15. Goodfellow, I.J., Shlens, J., Szegedy, C.: Explaining and harnessing adversarial examples (2014)
16. Gu, J., Tresp, V., Hu, H.: Capsule network is not more robust than convolutional network. In: Proceedings of the IEEE/CVF Conference on Computer Vision and Pattern Recognition, pp. 14309–14317 (2021)
17. Gu, J., Wu, B., Tresp, V.: Effective and efficient vote attack on capsule networks. arXiv preprint arXiv:2102.10055 (2021)
18. He, K., Zhang, X., Ren, S., Sun, J.: Deep residual learning for image recognition. In: Proceedings of the IEEE Conference on Computer Vision and Pattern Recognition, pp. 770–778 (2016)
19. He, K., Zhang, X., Ren, S., Sun, J.: Identity mappings in deep residual networks. In: Leibe, B., Matas, J., Sebe, N., Welling, M. (eds.) ECCV 2016. LNCS, vol. 9908, pp. 630–645. Springer, Cham (2016). https://doi.org/10.1007/978-3-319-46493-0_38
20. Jia, X., Wei, X., Cao, X., Foroosh, H.: ComDefend: an efficient image compression model to defend adversarial examples. In: Proceedings of the IEEE/CVF Conference on Computer Vision and Pattern Recognition, pp. 6084–6092 (2019)
21. Jia, X., Wei, X., Cao, X., Han, X.: Adv-watermark: a novel watermark perturbation for adversarial examples. In: Proceedings of the 28th ACM International Conference on Multimedia, pp. 1579–1587 (2020)
22. Jia, X., Zhang, Y., Wu, B., Ma, K., Wang, J., Cao, X.: LAS-AT: adversarial training with learnable attack strategy. In: Proceedings of the IEEE/CVF Conference on Computer Vision and Pattern Recognition. pp. 13398–13408 (2022)
23. Jia, X., Zhang, Y., Wu, B., Wang, J., Cao, X.: Boosting fast adversarial training with learnable adversarial initialization. In: IEEE Trans. Image Process. **31**, 4417–4430 (2022)
24. Kannan, H., Kurakin, A., Goodfellow, I.: Adversarial logit pairing. arXiv preprint arXiv:1803.06373 (2018)
25. Kim, H., Lee, W., Lee, J.: Understanding catastrophic overfitting in single-step adversarial training. In: Proceedings of the AAAI Conference on Artificial Intelligence, vol. 35, pp. 8119–8127 (2021)
26. Krizhevsky, A., et al.: Learning multiple layers of features from tiny images.Technical Report TR-2009 (2009)
27. LeCun, Y., Bengio, Y., Hinton, G.: Deep learning. Nature **521**(7553), 436–444 (2015)
28. Li, Y., et al.: Semi-supervised robust training with generalized perturbed neighborhood. Pattern Recogn. **124**, 108472 (2022)
29. Liang, S., Wei, X., Yao, S., Cao, X.: Efficient Adversarial attacks for visual object tracking. In: Vedaldi, A., Bischof, H., Brox, T., Frahm, J.-M. (eds.) ECCV 2020. LNCS, vol. 12371, pp. 34–50. Springer, Cham (2020). https://doi.org/10.1007/978-3-030-58574-7_3

30. Liang, S., Wu, B., Fan, Y., Wei, X., Cao, X.: Parallel rectangle flip attack: a query-based black-box attack against object detection. arXiv preprint arXiv:2201.08970 (2022)
31. Lin, J., Song, C., He, K., Wang, L., Hopcroft, J.E.: Nesterov accelerated gradient and scale invariance for adversarial attacks. arXiv preprint arXiv:1908.06281 (2019)
32. Madry, A., Makelov, A., Schmidt, L., Tsipras, D., Vladu, A.: Towards deep learning models resistant to adversarial attacks. arXiv preprint arXiv:1706.06083 (2017)
33. Pang, T., Yang, X., Dong, Y., Su, H., Zhu, J.: Bag of tricks for adversarial training. In: 9th International Conference on Learning Representations, ICLR 2021, Virtual Event, Austria, 3–7 May 2021. OpenReview.net (2021)
34. Pang, T., Yang, X., Dong, Y., Xu, K., Zhu, J., Su, H.: Boosting adversarial training with hypersphere embedding. arXiv preprint arXiv:2002.08619 (2020)
35. Park, G.Y., Lee, S.W.: Reliably fast adversarial training via latent adversarial perturbation. arXiv preprint arXiv:2104.01575 (2021)
36. Qian, N.: On the momentum term in gradient descent learning algorithms. Neural Netw. $12(1)$, 145–151 (1999)
37. Rice, L., Wong, E., Kolter, Z.: Overfitting in adversarially robust deep learning. In: International Conference on Machine Learning, pp. 8093–8104. PMLR (2020)
38. Roth, K., Kilcher, Y., Hofmann, T.: Adversarial training is a form of data-dependent operator norm regularization. arXiv preprint arXiv:1906.01527 (2019)
39. Shafahi, A., et al.: Adversarial training for free! In: 3rd Conference on Neural Information Processing Systems (NeurIPS 2019), Vancouver, Canada (2019)
40. Smith, L.N.: Cyclical learning rates for training neural networks. In: 2017 IEEE Winter Conference on Applications of Computer Vision (WACV), pp. 464–472. IEEE (2017)
41. Sriramanan, G., Addepalli, S., Baburaj, A., et al.: Guided adversarial attack for evaluating and enhancing adversarial defenses. Adv. Neural. Inf. Process. Syst. 33, 20297–20308 (2020)
42. Sriramanan, G., et al.: Towards efficient and effective adversarial training. In: 35th Conference on Neural Information Processing Systems (NeurIPS 2021), vol. 34 (2021)
43. Szegedy, C., et al.: Intriguing properties of neural networks. arXiv preprint arXiv:1312.6199 (2013)
44. Wang, X., He, K.: Enhancing the transferability of adversarial attacks through variance tuning. In: Proceedings of the IEEE/CVF Conference on Computer Vision and Pattern Recognition, pp. 1924–1933 (2021)
45. Wang, Y., Ma, X., Bailey, J., Yi, J., Zhou, B., Gu, Q.: On the convergence and robustness of adversarial training. In: Chaudhuri, K., Salakhutdinov, R. (eds.) Proceedings of the 36th International Conference on Machine Learning, ICML 2019, 9–15 June 2019, Long Beach, California, USA, pp. 6586–6595. PMLR (2019)
46. Wang, Y., Zou, D., Yi, J., Bailey, J., Ma, X., Gu, Q.: Improving adversarial robustness requires revisiting misclassified examples. In: International Conference on Learning Representations (2019)
47. Wang, Y., Zou, D., Yi, J., Bailey, J., Ma, X., Gu, Q.: Improving adversarial robustness requires revisiting misclassified examples. In: 8th International Conference on Learning Representations, ICLR 2020, Addis Ababa, Ethiopia, 26–30 April 2020. OpenReview.net (2020)
48. Wei, X., Liang, S., Chen, N., Cao, X.: Transferable adversarial attacks for image and video object detection. arXiv preprint arXiv:1811.12641 (2018)
49. Wong, E., Rice, L., Kolter, J.Z.: Fast is better than free: Revisiting adversarial training. arXiv preprint arXiv:2001.03994 (2020)

50. Wu, D., Xia, S.T., Wang, Y.: Adversarial weight perturbation helps robust generalization. In: 4th Conference on Neural Information Processing Systems (NeurIPS 2020), Vancouver, Canada, pp. 2958–2969 (2020)
51. Xie, C., et al.: Improving transferability of adversarial examples with input diversity. In: Proceedings of the IEEE/CVF Conference on Computer Vision and Pattern Recognition, pp. 2730–2739 (2019)
52. Zagoruyko, S., Komodakis, N.: Wide residual networks (2016)
53. Zhang, D., Zhang, T., Lu, Y., Zhu, Z., Dong, B.: You only propagate once: accelerating adversarial training via maximal principle. arXiv preprint arXiv:1905.00877 (2019)
54. Zhang, H., Yu, Y., Jiao, J., Xing, E., El Ghaoui, L., Jordan, M.: Theoretically principled trade-off between robustness and accuracy. In: International Conference on Machine Learning, pp. 7472–7482. PMLR (2019)
55. Zou, W., Huang, S., Xie, J., Dai, X., Chen, J.: A reinforced generation of adversarial examples for neural machine translation. arXiv preprint arXiv:1911.03677 (2019)

Enhanced Accuracy and Robustness via Multi-teacher Adversarial Distillation

Shiji Zhao[1,2], Jie Yu[1,2], Zhenlong Sun[2], Bo Zhang[2], and Xingxing Wei[1(✉)]

[1] Institute of Artificial Intelligence, Hangzhou Innovation Institute, Beihang University, Beijing, China
{zhaoshiji123,sy2106137,xxwei}@buaa.edu.cn
[2] WeChat Search Application Department, Tencent, Beijing, China
{richardsun,nevinzhang}@tencent.com

Abstract. Adversarial training is an effective approach for improving the robustness of deep neural networks against adversarial attacks. Although bringing reliable robustness, adversarial training (AT) will reduce the performance of identifying clean examples. Meanwhile, Adversarial training can bring more robustness for large models than small models. To improve the robust and clean accuracy of small models, we introduce the Multi-Teacher Adversarial Robustness Distillation (MTARD) to guide the adversarial training process of small models. Specifically, MTARD uses multiple large teacher models, including an adversarial teacher and a clean teacher to guide a small student model in the adversarial training by knowledge distillation. In addition, we design a dynamic training algorithm to balance the influence between the adversarial teacher and clean teacher models. A series of experiments demonstrate that our MTARD can outperform the state-of-the-art adversarial training and distillation methods against various adversarial attacks. Our code is available at https://github.com/zhaoshiji123/MTARD.

Keywords: Adversarial training · Knowledge distillation · DNNs

1 Introduction

Deep Neural Networks (DNNs) have become powerful tools for solving complex real-world learning problems, such as image classification [18,34], face recognition [38], and natural language processing [33]. However, Szegedy et al. [35] demonstrates that DNNs are vulnerable to adversarial attacks with imperceptible adversarial perturbations on input, which causes wrong predictions of DNNs. This phenomenon raises concerns about the robustness of DNNs in safety-related areas, such as autonomous driving [11], finance [23], and medical diagnosis [26].

To defend against adversarial attacks, adversarial training is proposed and shows effectiveness to acquire the adversarial robust DNNs [2,8,27]. In a broad sense, adversarial training can be regarded as a data augmentation method, where adversarial examples generated by the adversarial attacks are used as part of the model training set to enhance the model robustness against adversarial attacks. At the mathematical level, a min-max optimization problem can express the adversarial training process, where the inner maximization can be regarded as generating adversarial examples, and outer minimization is to train the model by adversarial examples generated in maximization.

While improving the robustness of DNNs, adversarial training has several shortcomings in some general scenes. Firstly, the robustness of models obtained from adversarial training is related to the size of models. In general, the larger model means the better robust performance [7,12,41,47,48]. However, due to the limitations of various practical factors, a large model is often not favored in actual deployment [32]. Secondly, the accuracy of identifying clean examples by adversarial trained DNNs is far worse than normal trained DNNs, which limits large-scale use in practical scenarios. Some researchers [45] try to reduce the negative effects of adversarial training bringing for clean accuracy, but the effect is still not ideal.

In this paper, we investigate the method to improve both the clean and robust accuracy of small DNNs by adversarial distillation. Adversarial Robustness Distillation (ARD) is used to boost the robustness of small models by distilling from large robust models [7,12,47], which treats large models as teachers and small models as students. Although the previous work (RSLAD) [48] improves the robustness via robust soft labels, the clean accuracy is still not ideal compared with the performance of regular training. Inspired by multi-task learning [37], we propose Multi-Teacher Adversarial Robustness Distillation (MTARD) by using different teacher models, each teacher model is responsible for what they are proficient in. To improve both robustness of the student model and the accuracy of identifying clean examples, we apply a robust teacher model and a clean teacher model to guide robustness and accuracy simultaneously. However, due to the complexity of neural networks, teacher models have different degrees of influence on student models, which can even cause catastrophic forgetting. To alleviate this phenomenon, we design a joint training algorithm to dynamically adjust the influence of the teacher models on the student network at different stages in adversarial distillation. All in all, the main contributions of this work are three-fold:

- We propose a novel adversarial robustness distillation method called Multi-Teacher Adversarial Robustness Distillation (MTARD), which applies multiple teacher models to improve student models' clean and robust accuracy by adversarial distillation.
- We design a joint training algorithm based on the proposed Adaptive Normalization Loss to balance the influence on the student model between the adversarial teacher model and the clean teacher model, which is dynamically determined by the historical training information.
- We empirically verify the effectiveness of MTARD in improving the performance of small models. For the models trained by our MTARD, the Weighted Robust Accuracy (a metric to evaluate the trade-off between the clean accuracy and robust accuracy) has been greatly improved compared with the

state-of-the-art adversarial training and distillation method against white-box and black-box attacks. Especially for black-box Square Attack, MTARD can most enhance the Weighted Robust Accuracy by 6.87% and 5.12% for MobileNet-V2 on CIFAR-10 and CIFAR-100 respectively.

2 Related Work

2.1 Adversarial Attack

Since Szegedy et al. [35] proposed that adversarial examples can mislead the deep neural network, lots of effective adversarial attack methods, such as Fast Gradient Sign Method (FGSM) [13], Projected Gradient Descent Attack (PGD) [27], Carilini and Wagner Attack (CW) [5], and Jacobian-based Saliency Map Attack (JSMA) [29] are proposed. Existing attack methods can be divided into white-box attacks and black-box attacks. White-box attacks are to know all the parameter information of the attacked model when generating adversarial examples, and black-box attacks are to know only part of the attacked model's output when generating adversarial examples. In general, black-box attacks simulate the model gradient by repeatedly querying the target model (query-based attack) [1,4,6,40,43] or searching for an alternative model similar to the target model (transfer-based attack) [9,19,24]. Since attackers hardly know the model parameters of the target model in practical applications, the model's performance against black-box attacks can better reflect the real robustness.

2.2 Adversarial Training

Adversarial Training [3,20,25,45,46] is seen as an effective way to defend against adversarial attack [48]. Madry et al. [27] formulate Adversarial Training as a minimax optimization problems formulated as follows:

$$\min_{\theta} E_{(x,y)\sim\mathcal{D}}[\max_{\delta\in\Omega} \mathcal{L}(f(x+\delta;\theta),y)], \tag{1}$$

where f represents a deep neural network, θ represents the weight of f, D represents a distribution of the clean example x and the ground truth label y. $\mathcal{L}(f(x+\delta;\theta),y)$ represents loss function of updating the training model. δ represents the adversarial perturbation, and Ω represents a bound, which can be defined as $\Omega = \{\delta : ||\delta|| \leq \epsilon\}$ with the maximum perturbation strength ϵ.

Much work has been proposed to further improve the robustness by adversarial training. Zhang et al. [45] try to make a balance between robustness and clean performance (TRADES), Wang et al. [39] further improves performance by Misclassification-Aware adveRsarial Training (MART). Wu et al. [41] believe the use of bigger models can improve the model robustness.

Previous work [21,30] use two indexes: clean accuracy and robust accuracy, as the metric to evaluate the comprehensive performance of the model. Nezihe et al. [16] proposes a metric named Weighted Robust Accuracy to balance the trade-off between clean accuracy and robust accuracy, which is used in our experiments.

2.3   Adversarial Robustness Distillation

Knowledge distillation can transfer the performance of other models to the target model. Due to the ability to transfer better model performance to other model performance, it has been widely studied in recent years and works well in some actual deployment scenarios combined with network pruning and model quantization [15,17,28]. Knowledge distillation has a wide range of practicality and can also be applied to various practical tasks such as classification [42], image detection [10], and natural language processing [36]. Knowledge distillation can briefly be formulated as the following optimization:

$$\arg\min_{\theta_S}(1 - \alpha)\mathcal{L}(S(x), y) + \alpha\tau^2 KL(S^\tau(x), (T^\tau(x)), \tag{2}$$

where KL is Kullback-Leibler divergence loss, τ is a temperature constant used in the output of network (combined with softmax operation), $\mathcal{L}$ represents the loss function of updating the training model, which can usually be regarded as cross-entropy in traditional knowledge distillation method.

In general, adversarial training can bring better robustness for the larger model [7,12,31,47,48]. RAD [12] proposes that using a bigger and stronger model as the teacher model in adversarial training allows better adversarial training methods. IAD [47] performs adversarial knowledge distillation by using the teacher model with the same structure as the student model. RSLAD [48] uses the soft label generated by the teacher model instead of the one-hot label as the label used for producing adversarial examples in the process of adversarial training, which can also improve the robustness of the student model.

3   Methodologies

In this section, we propose our MTARD method to guide the process of adversarial distillation with multiple teacher models and design a dynamic training method that controls the degree of influence between the adversarial teacher model and the clean teacher model toward the student model.

3.1   Multi-teacher Adversarial Robustness Distillation

As we mentioned before, although adversarial training is very effective in improving robustness, the improvement of standard adversarial training methods for small models is not as obvious as that for large models. Therefore, many methods on transferring the robustness of large models to small models through knowledge distillation have been proposed [12,45,48]. Although these methods can improve the robustness of small models, the adversarial training itself will hurt the ability of models to identify clean examples. Therefore, the core problem to be solved in this section is how to improve both clean and robust accuracy in the adversarial training, then our Multi-Teacher Adversarial Robustness Distillation (MTARD) is proposed (Fig. 1).

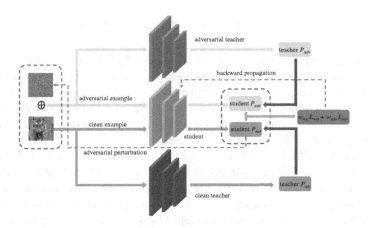

Fig. 1. The framework of our Multi-Teacher Adversarial Robustness Distillation (MTARD). In the process of MTARD, we firstly generate adversarial examples by student model. Then we produce L_{nat} and L_{adv} of the student by the guide of the clean teacher and the adversarial teacher respectively. Finally, we use Adaptive Normalization Loss to balance the influence between clean teacher and adversarial teacher and update student model.

Inspired by multi-task learning [37], we hope to not only improve the robustness of the model but also maintain the clean accuracy in Adversarial Distillation. The previous adversarial distillation method only brings a single model trained by adversarial training, which has strong robustness but weak recognition ability for clean image. As the only guide, the student model often fits the distribution of the teacher model, resulting in a lower ability to identify clean examples. Using GT one-hot labels as a learning objective to improve the clean recognition rate is still not an ideal option [48]. Therefore we additionally bring a pre-trained clean teacher model to guide the process of Adversarial Distillation.

The training of the student in MTARD is still based on adversarial training. With the guidance of an adversarial teacher and a clean teacher in knowledge distillation, we hope the student can learn robustness from the adversarial teacher and the ability to identify clean examples from the clean teacher. To produce the soft label of fulfilling the responsibilities of both teachers, the inputs of the clean teacher are initial clean examples from original datasets. In contrast, the inputs of the adversarial teacher are adversarial examples produced by the student model in the inner maximization. The student inputs are divided into clean examples and adversarial examples. The outputs of clean examples and adversarial examples will be guided by adversarial soft label and clean soft label to supervise the student model training in outer minimization. The minimax optimization framework of basic MTARD is defined as follows:

$$\arg\min_{\theta_S}(1-\alpha)KL(S(x_{nat}), T_{nat}(x_{nat})) + \alpha KL(S(x_{adv}), T_{adv}(x_{adv})), \quad (3)$$

$$x_{adv} = \arg\max_{\delta \in \Omega} CE(S(x_{nat} + \delta; \theta_S), y), \tag{4}$$

where x_{adv} are adversarial examples produced by clean examples x_{nat}, $S(x)$ are the abbreviations for $S(x; \theta_S)$, which represents student network S with parameters θ_S. T_{nat} and T_{adv} respectively represent the clean teacher model and adversarial teacher model. α is a constant in the basic proposal. The value p could be specified as different values according to the requirement. We choose cross-entropy as previous work in the maximization.

The goal of MTARD is to learn a small student network that has both robust performance as the adversarial pre-trained teacher network and clean performance as the clean pre-trained teacher network. In the actual operation process, however, the simultaneous knowledge distillation of different teacher models will affect the learning of the student model. The student's learning intensity from multiple teachers can not be easily controlled. If a teacher dominates students' learning, the student model can hardly learn the relative ability from another teacher, even causing catastrophic forgetting. So handling situations with multiple teachers becomes a problem to be solved in the next subsection.

3.2 Adaptive Normalization Loss in MTARD

In order to get both clean and robust accuracy, a strategy is needed to balance the influence between the adversarial teacher and the clean teacher. On the mathematical level, the total loss in MTARD ultimately used for the student model update at time t can be represented as $L_{total}(t)$, which can be formulated as follows:

$$L_{total}(t) = w_{adv}(t)L_{adv}(t) + w_{nat}(t)L_{nat}(t). \tag{5}$$

Since the degree of the teacher's influence on the student can be expressed as the value of the adversarial loss $L_{adv}(t)$ and clean loss $L_{nat}(t)$, the vital to control the learning degree from multiple teachers is to control the loss weight of $w_{adv}(t)$ and $w_{nat}(t)$. Inspired by gradient regularization methods in multi-task learning [2], we propose an algorithm to control the steady learning from the adversarial teacher and clean teacher, which is called as the Adaptive Normalization Loss used in our MTARD.

To better introduce the Adaptive Normalization Loss, we give a formal description from a generalized view. Suppose there are multiple teacher models to jointly guide the training process of the student network. Each teacher model is associated with a loss function L_i, and a loss weight w_i, thus the total loss L_{total} can be considered as the optimization of multiple losses as follows:

$$L_{total}(t) = \sum_{i=1}^{N} w_i(t)L_i(t), \tag{6}$$

where N represents the number of multiple losses, $L_i(t)$ and $w_i(t)$ respectively mean the i-th loss and loss weight at time t. The goal is to place $L_i(t)$ on a common scale through their relative magnitudes by dynamically adjusting $w_i(t)$ with similar rates at each update and each $L_i(t)$ has a relatively fair drop after the entire update process. The final trained model can be equally affected by various influencing factors behind the losses.

In order to choose the criterion to measure the decline of multiple losses, we choose a relative loss $\tilde{L}(t)$ following Athalye et al. [2], which is defined as follows:

$$\tilde{L}_i(t) = L_i(t)/L_i(0), \tag{7}$$

where $L_i(0)$ is the i-th loss value at time 0. Especially in our setting, we assume that the smaller value of $L_i(t)$ compared with $L_i(0)$ means the model fitting the target. $\tilde{L}_i(t)$ as a metric can reflect the change amplitude of $L_i(t)$ from begin to time t. Lower value of $\tilde{L}_i(t)$ corresponds to a relatively faster training speed for $L_i(t)$. By introducing relative loss $\tilde{L}_i(t)$, we can dynamically balance $L_i(t)$ influence toward $L_{total}(t)$ as an objective standard to get relative loss weight $r_i(t)$, which can be formulated as follows:

$$r_i(t) = [\tilde{L}_i(t)]^\beta / \sum_{i=1}^{N} [\tilde{L}_i(t)]^\beta, \tag{8}$$

where $[\tilde{L}_i(t)]^\beta$ denotes the $\tilde{L}_i(t)$ power of β, and β is set to empower the $L_i(t)$ on the disadvantaged side to control the degree of updating the loss weight. The bigger β strengthens the disadvantaged losses, which is applicable when the loss value is too different. β equal to 1 is in line with the situation that all $L_i(t)$ have similar influence abilities. We simplify the update formula for $w_i(t)$, which can be formulated as follows:

$$w_i(t) = r_w r_i(t) + (1 - r_w) w_i(t - 1), \tag{9}$$

where r_w means the learning rate of $w_i(t)$. Our MTARD can be considered as an Adaptive Normalization Loss optimization with $N = 2$, the $L_{adv}(t)$ and $L_{nat}(t)$ can be regarded as $L_1(t)$ and $L_2(t)$. In the framework of Adaptive Normalization Loss, the update process of $w_{adv}(t)$ and $w_{nat}(t)$ can be formulated as follows:

$$w_{adv}(t) = \frac{r_w[L_{adv}(t)/L_{adv}(0)]^\beta}{[L_{nat}(t)/L_{nat}(0)]^\beta + [L_{adv}(t)/L_{adv}(0)]^\beta} + (1 - r_w)w_{adv}(t - 1), \tag{10}$$

$$w_{nat}(t) = 1 - w_{adv}(t). \tag{11}$$

On a practical level, the Adaptive Normalization Loss used in MTARD can inhibit the rapid growth of a stronger teacher throughout the training cycle. If a teacher over-instructs a student compared with another teacher over a period of time, the Adaptive Normalization Loss can dynamically suppress the teacher's teaching ability by controlling the loss weight, while the ability of the other teacher will become stronger in the following period. However, this trend is not absolute. If noticing that the original strong teacher has become weaker, Adaptive Normalization Loss will make the original strong teacher stronger again.

Algorithm 1 MTARD

Require Initialize student model $S(x|\theta_S)$, pretrained teacher model T_{adv} and T_{nat}, the dataset $\mathcal{D}$ including the benign clean example x_{nat} and the label y, the threat bound Ω, the initialized perturbation δ

1: **for** $t = 0$ to *max-step* **do**
2:      Acquire adversarial example $x_{adv} = \arg\max_{\delta \in \Omega} CE(S(x_{nat} + \delta; \theta_S), y)$
3:      Compute Adversarial Loss $L_{adv}(t) = KL(S(x_{adv}), T_{adv}(x_{adv}))$
4:      Compute Clean Loss $L_{nat}(t) = KL(S(x_{nat}), T_{nat}(x_{nat}))$
5:      **if** $t = 0$ **then**
6:          Record L_{adv} and L_{nat} as $L_{adv}(0)$ and $L_{nat}(0)$ respectively
7:      **end if**
8:      Update $w_{nat}(t)$ and $w_{adv}(t)$ by Eq. 10 and Eq. 11
9:      $\theta_S \leftarrow \theta_S - \eta \nabla_{\theta_S} \left\{ w_{adv}(t) L_{adv}(t) + w_{nat}(t) L_{nat}(t) \right\}$
10: **end for**

Finally, the student can learn well from two teachers to gain both clean and robust abilities rather than appearing partial ability under the adjustment of Adaptive Normalization Loss.

The complete process of MTARD with Adaptive Normalization Loss is in Algorithm 1. Compared with other existing adversarial distillation, our method has several advantages. Firstly, the loss weights are dynamically updated without any deliberate tuning of loss weight hyper-parameters and can fit the changes as training epochs increase, which is important to fit various changing scenarios but not limited in adversarial training. Secondly, our method can fit on different teacher models and student models no matter how strong or weak the teachers' performance is, which can be controlled by Adaptive Normalization Loss. Thirdly, our method pays more attention to the performance of Weighted Robust Accuracy, which measures the trade-off between clean and robust accuracy, and thus is more valued and focused in the overall performance of the model.

4 Experiments

Initially, we describe the experimental setting, and evaluate the clean accuracy and robust accuracy of four baseline defense methods and our MTARD under prevailing white-box attack methods. Moreover, our method is evaluated under the black-box attack including transfer-based and square-based attacks. We also conduct an ablation study to demonstrate the effectiveness of our method.

4.1 Experimental Settings

We conduct our experiments on two datasets including CIFAR-10 and CIFAR-100 [22], and consider natural train method and four state-of-the-art methods of adversarial training and adversarial robustness distillation as comparison method: SAT [27], TRADES [45], ARD [12] and RSLAD [48].

Table 1. Performance of the teacher networks used in our experiments, RN and WRN are the abbreviations of ResNet and WideResNet.

Dataset	Model	Clean Acc.	FGSM	PGD$_{sat}$	PGD$_{trades}$	CW$_\infty$	Type
CIFAR-10	RN-56	**93.18%**	19.23%	0	0	0	Clean
	WRN-34-10	84.91%	**61.14%**	**55.30%**	**56.61%**	**53.84%**	Adv
CIFAR-100	WRN-22-6	**76.65%**	4.85%	0	0	0	Clean
	WRN-70-16	60.96%	**35.89%**	**33.58%**	**33.99%**	**31.05%**	Adv

Student and Teacher Networks. For the selection of models, We consider two student networks including ResNet-18 [18] and MobileNet-V2 [32] following previous work. As for teacher model, we choose two clean teacher networks including ResNet-56 for CIFAR-10 and WideResNet-22-6 [44] for CIFAR-100, and two adversarial teacher networks including WideResNet-34-10 for CIFAR-10 and WideResNet-70-16 [14] for CIFAR-100. For CIFAR-10, WideResNet-34-10 is trained using TRADES [45]; For CIFAR-100, we use the WideResNet-70-16 model provided by Gowal et al. [14], two adversarial teachers are also the teacher models used in RSLAD [48]. The whole teachers are pre-trained before adversarial distillation. The performance of the teacher models is shown in Table 1.

Training and Evaluation. We train student networks using Stochastic Gradient Descent (SGD) optimizer with an initial learning rate 0.1, momentum 0.9, and weight decay 2e-4. For our MTARD, the weight loss learning rate is initially set as 0.025. We set the total number of training epochs to 300, the learning rate is divided by 10 at 215th, 260th, and 285th epochs. We set batch size to 128, and β is set to 1. For the inner maximization of MTARD, we use a 10 step PGD (PGD-10) with random start size 0.001 and step size 2/255.

We strictly follow SAT and TRADES original settings; For ARD, we use the same adversarial teachers as RSLAD and our MTARD. The temperature constant τ of ARD is set to 30 following original settings on CIFAR-10 while set to 5 on CIFAR-100, and the α is set to 0.95 following Micah [12] on CIFAR-100. Training perturbation in the maximization process is bounded to the L_∞ norm $\epsilon = 8/255$. For natural training, we train the networks for 100 epochs on clean images, and the learning rate is divided by 10 at the 75th and 90th epochs.

The same as previous studies, we evaluate the trained model against 4 white box adversarial attacks: FGSM, PGD$_{sat}$, PGD$_{trades}$, CW$_\infty$, which are commonly used adversarial attacks in adversarial robustness evaluation. PGD$_{sat}$ is the attack proposed in Madry et al. [27], and PGD$_{trades}$ is used in Zhang [45], the step size of PGD$_{sat}$ and PGD$_{trades}$ is 2/255, and the step is 20. the total step of CW$_\infty$ is 30. Maximum perturbation is bounded to the L_∞ norm $\epsilon = 8/255$ for all attacks. Meanwhile, we also conduct a black-box evaluation, which includes the transfer-based attack and query-based attack to test the robustness of the student model in a near-real environment.

Table 2. White-box robustness of ResNet-18 on CIFAR-10 and CIFAR-100 dataset.

Attack	Defense	CIFAR-10			CIFAR-100		
		Clean	Robust	W-Robust	Clean	Robust	W-Robust
FGSM	Natural	94.57%	18.60%	56.59%	75.18%	7.96%	41.57%
	SAT	84.2%	55.59%	69.90%	56.16%	25.88%	41.02%
	TRADES	83.00%	58.35%	70.68%	57.75%	31.36%	44.56%
	ARD	84.11%	58.4%	71.26%	60.11%	33.61%	46.86%
	RSLAD	83.99%	60.41%	72.2%	58.25%	34.73%	46.49%
	MTARD	87.36%	61.2%	**74.28%**	64.3%	31.49%	**47.90%**
PGD_{sat}	Natural	94.57%	0%	47.29%	75.18%	0%	37.59%
	TRADES	83.00%	52.35%	67.68%	57.75%	28.05%	42.9%
	SAT	84.2%	45.95%	65.08%	56.16%	21.18%	38.67%
	TRADES	83.00%	52.35%	67.68%	57.75%	28.05%	42.9%
	ARD	84.11%	50.93%	67.52%	60.11%	29.4%%	**44.76%**
	RSLAD	83.99%	53.94%	68.97%	58.25%	31.19%	44.72%
	MTARD	87.36%	50.73%	**69.05%**	64.3%	24.95%	44.63%
PGD_{trades}	Natural	94.57%	0%	47.29%	75.18%	0%	37.59%
	SAT	84.2%	48.12%	66.16%	56.16%	22.02%	39.09%
	TRADES	83.00%	53.83%	68.42%	57.75%	28.88%	43.32%
	ARD	84.11%	52.96%	68.54%	60.11%	30.51%	45.31%
	RSLAD	83.99%	55.73%	69.86%	58.25%	32.05%	45.15%
	MTARD	87.36%	53.60%	**70.48%**	64.3%	26.75%	**45.53%**
CW_{∞}	Natural	94.57%	0%	47.29%	75.18%	0%	37.59%
	SAT	84.2%	45.97%	65.09%	56.16%	20.9%	38.53%
	TRADES	83.00%	50.23%	66.62%	57.75%	24.19%	40.97%
	ARD	84.11%	50.15%	67.13%	60.11%	27.56%	43.84%
	RSLAD	83.99%	52.67%	**68.33%**	58.25%	28.21%	43.23%
	MTARD	87.36%	48.57%	67.97%	64.3%	23.42%	**43.86%**

Here, we use Weighted Roubst Accuracy [16] to evaluate the trade-off between the clean and robust accuracy of the student model, it is defined as follows:

$$\mathcal{A}_f = \pi_{D_{nat}} P_{D_{nat}}[f(x) = y] + \pi_{D_{adv}} P_{D_{adv}}[f(x) = y], \qquad (12)$$

where Weighted Roubst Accuracy $\mathcal{A}_f$ are the accuracy of a model f on x drawn from either the clean distribution D_{nat} and the adversarial distribution D_{adv}. We set $\pi_{D_{nat}}$ and $\pi_{D_{adv}}$ both to 0.5, which means clean accuracy and robust accuracy are equally important for comprehensive performance in the model.

4.2   Adversarial Robustness Evaluation

White-box Robustness. The performance of ResNet-18 and MobileNet-v2 trained by our MTARD and other baseline methods under the white box attack are shown in Table 2 and 3 for CIFAR-10 and CIFAR-100. We select the best checkpoint of baseline model and MTARD based on Weighted Robust Accuracy.

The experimental results demonstrate that our method MTARD has the state-of-the-art W-Robust Accuracy on CIFAR-10 and CIFAR-100. For ResNet-18, MTARD improves W-Robust Accuracy by 1.01% compared with the best baseline method under the attack of FGSM on CIFAR-100; For MobileNet-V2, MTARD improves the W-Robust Accuracy by 1.96% against PGD_{trades}

Table 3. White-box robustness of MobileNet-V2 on CIFAR-10 and CIFAR-100 dataset.

Attack	Defense	CIFAR-10			CIFAR-100		
		Clean	Robust	W-Robust	Clean	Robust	W-Robust
FGSM	Natural	93.35%	12.22%	52.79%	74.86%	5.94%	40.4%
	SAT	83.87%	55.89%	69.88%	59.19%	30.88%	45.04%
	TRADES	77.95%	53.75%	65.85%	55.41%	30.28%	42.85%
	ARD	83.43%	57.03%	70.23%	60.45%	32.77%	46.61%
	RSLAD	83.2%	59.47%	71.34%	59.01%	33.88%	46.45%
	MTARD	89.26%	57.84%	**73.55%**	67.01%	32.42%	**49.72%**
PGD_{sat}	Natural	93.35%	0%	46.68%	74.86%	0%	37.43%
	SAT	83.87%	46.84%	65.36%	59.19%	25.64%	42.42%
	TRADES	77.95%	49.06%	63.51%	55.41%	23.33%	39.37%
	ARD	83.43%	49.5%	66.47%	60.45%	28.69%	44.57%
	RSLAD	83.2%	53.25%	**68.23%**	59.01%	30.19%	44.6%
	MTARD	89.26%	44.16%	66.71%	67.01%	25.14%	**46.08%**
PGD_{trades}	Natural	93.35%	0%	46.68%	74.86%	0%	37.43%
	SAT	83.87%	49.14%	66.51%	59.19%	26.96%	43.08%
	TRADES	77.95%	50.27%	64.11%	55.41%	28.42%	41.92%
	ARD	83.43%	51.7%	67.57%	60.45%	29.63%	45.04%
	RSLAD	83.2%	54.76%	**68.98%**	59.01%	31.19%	45.1%
	MTARD	89.26%	47.99%	68.63%	67.01%	27.1%	**47.06%**
CW_∞	Natural	93.35%	0%	46.68%	74.86%	0%	37.43%
	SAT	83.87%	46.62%	65.25%	59.19%	25.01%	42.1%
	TRADES	77.95%	46.06%	62.01%	55.41%	27.72%	41.57%
	ARD	83.43%	48.96%	66.20%	60.45%	26.55%	43.50%
	RSLAD	83.2%	51.78%	**67.49%**	59.01%	27.98%	43.50%
	MTARD	89.26%	43.42%	66.34%	67.01%	24.14%	**45.58%**

on CIFAR-100. Moreover, our method also shows relevant superiority against PGD_{sat}, CW_∞ compared with other methods.

Meanwhile, ARD, RSLAD, and MTARD outperform SAT and TRADES, which shows the adversarial robustness distillation can bring greater improvement to the small models than traditional methods. In addition, our MTARD can achieve better performance than ARD and RSLAD without artificial hyperparameters adjustment, while ARD relies on the adjustment of temperature constant τ and RSLAD relies on the adjustment of loss weight.

Black-box Robustness. In addition, we also test MTARD and other methods against black-box attacks for ResNet-18 and MobileNet-V2 on CIFAR-10 and CIFAR-100 separately. We choose the transfer-based attack and query-based attack in our evaluation. As for the transfer-based attack, we choose our adversarial teachers (WideResNet-34-10 and WideResNet-70-16) as the surrogate model to produce adversarial example against the PGD-20 (PGD_{trades}) and CW_∞ attack; As for the query-based attack, we choose the Square attack (SA) to attack these models. We select the best checkpoint of baseline model and MTARD based on Weighted Robust Accuracy. The result of ResNet-18 is showed in Table 4, while the result of MobileNet-V2 is showed in Table 5.

From the result, Our MTARD achieves better W-Robust Accuracy than any other model against all three black-box attacks in any conditions. Under the Square Attack, ResNet-18 and MobileNet-V2 trained by MTARD outperform W-

Table 4. Black-box robustness of ResNet-18 on CIFAR-10 and CIFAR-100 dataset.

Attack	Defense	CIFAR-10			CIFAR-100		
		Clean	Robust	W-Robust	Clean	Robust	W-Robust
PGD-20	SAT	84.2%	64.74%	74.47%	56.16%	38.1%	47.13%
	TRADES	83.00%	63.56%	73.28%	57.75%	38.2%	47.98%
	ARD	84.11%	63.59%	73.85%	60.11%	39.53%	49.82%
	RSLAD	83.99%	63.9%	73.95%	58.25%	39.93%	49.09%
	MTARD	87.36%	65.17%	**76.27%**	64.3%	41.39%	**52.85%**
CW_∞	SAT	84.2%	64.88%	74.54%	56.16%	39.42%	47.79%
	TRADES	83.00%	62.85%	72.93%	57.75%	38.63%	48.19%
	ARD	84.11%	62.78%	73.45%	60.11%	38.85%	49.48%
	RSLAD	83.99%	63.02%	73.51%	58.25%	39.67%	48.96%
	MTARD	87.36%	64.65%	**76.01%**	64.3%	41.03%	**52.67%**
SA	SAT	84.2%	71.3%	77.75%	56.16%	41.27%	48.72%
	TRADES	83.00%	70.33%	76.67%	57.75%	41.96%	49.86%
	ARD	84.11%	73.3%	78.71%	60.11%	48.79%	54.45%
	RSLAD	83.99%	72.1%	78.05%	58.25%	45.34%	51.80%
	MTARD	87.36%	79.99%	**83.68%**	64.3%	41.03%	**52.67%**

Table 5. Black-box results of MobileNet-V2 on CIFAR-10 and CIFAR-100 dataset.

Attack	Defense	CIFAR-10			CIFAR-100		
		Clean	Robust	W-Robust	Clean	Robust	W-Robust
PGD-20	SAT	83.87%	64.6%	74.24%	59.19%	40.7%	49.95%
	TRADES	77.95%	61.07%	69.51%	55.41%	37.76%	46.59%
	ARD	83.43%	63.34%	73.39%	60.45%	39.15%	49.8%
	RSLAD	83.2%	64.3%	73.75%	59.01%	40.32%	49.67%
	MTARD	89.26%	66.37%	**77.82%**	67.01%	43.22%	**55.12%**
CW$_\infty$	SAT	83.87%	64.16%	74.02%	59.19%	40.97%	50.08%
	TRADES	77.95%	60.68%	69.32%	55.41%	38.02%	46.72%
	ARD	83.43%	62.73%	73.08%	60.45%	38.53%	49.49%
	RSLAD	83.2%	63.61%	73.41%	59.01%	39.92%	49.47%
	MTARD	89.26%	65.67%	**77.47%**	67.01%	42.97%	**54.99%**
SA	SAT	83.87%	69.94%	76.91%	59.19%	43.35%	51.27%
	TRADES	77.95%	66.3%	72.13%	55.41%	41.39%	48.4%
	ARD	83.43%	71.82%	77.63%	60.45%	47.08%	53.77%
	RSLAD	83.2%	71.11%	77.16%	59.01%	42.95%	50.98%
	MTARD	89.26%	79.73%	**84.50%**	67.01%	50.77%	**58.89%**

Robust Accuracy by 4.97% and 6.87% respectively on CIFAR-10 compared to the second-best method; Moreover, MTARD brings 2.13% and 5.12% improvements to ResNet-18 and MobileNet-V2. In addition, MTARD has different margins in defending against attacks from PGD-20 and CW$_\infty$ transfer attack, which shows the superior performance of MTARD in defending the black-box attacks.

4.3 Ablation Study

To better understand the impact of each component in our MTARD, we conduct a set of ablation studies. Baseline denotes using one well-trained adversarial teacher (WideResNet-34-10) to guide ResNet-18 student network on CIFAR-10, and Baseline+MT denotes using an adversarial teacher (WideResNet-34-10) and a clean teacher (ResNet-56) to guide student from adversarial and clean aspects, respectively, where the weight w_{adv} and w_{nat} are constant at 0.5. Baseline+MT+ANL (MTARD) term denotes adding the Adaptive Normalization Loss to dynamically adjust the weight w_{adv} and w_{nat} based on Baseline+MT.

The final result is shown in Fig. 2. The change of total loss L_{total} is shown in Fig. 3, and the change of relative loss $\tilde{L}_{nat}$ and $\tilde{L}_{adv}$ is shown in Fig. 4. Compared to the baseline method, MTARD's improvement is remarkable, which confirms the importance of each component. Multiple teachers positively affect the student model to learn both clean and robust accuracy. However, it is not enough to use multiple teacher models without Adaptive Normalization Loss due to the poor performance of Baseline+MT.

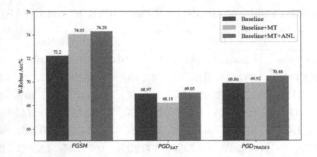

Fig. 2. Ablation study with ResNet-18 student network distilled using variants of our MTARD and Baseline method on CIFAR-10. MT and ANL are abbreviations of multi-teacher and Adaptive Normalization Loss. Baseline+MT means using multiple teachers in Baseline. Baseline+MT+ANL means our MTARD method.

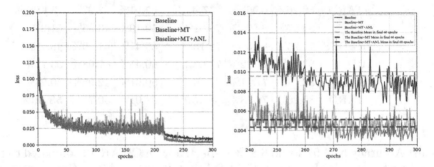

Fig. 3. The training loss with ResNet-18 student network distilled using variants of Baseline, Baseline+MT, and Baseline+MT+ANL (our MTARD) on CIFAR-10. MT and ANL are abbreviations of multi-teacher and Adaptive Normalization Loss. The y axis is the L_{total} in the training epoch x. The left is the change curve of L_{total} in the whole training process, the right is the change curve of L_{total} in final 60 epochs.

In Fig. 4, the lower $\tilde{L}$ means the student has learnt more ability from the corresponding teacher. The gap between $\tilde{L}_{nat}$ and $\tilde{L}_{adv}$ can represent the trade-off between each teacher. Compared with Baseline+MT, the MTARD's training loss is less oscillating, and relative loss can achieve a better ideal state. In the final training period, MTARD's $\tilde{L}_{nat}$ outperforms the Baseline+MT's, while $\tilde{L}_{nat}$ can reach the same level as the Baseline+MT's. Meanwhile, the MTARD's trade-off between $\tilde{L}_{nat}$ and $\tilde{L}_{adv}$ are more tiny. All the results demonstrate Adaptive Normalization Loss can better balance the influence between the adversarial teacher and the clean teacher to maximize the role of each other and obtain a more capable student with both accuracy and robustness.

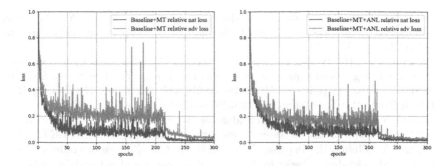

Fig. 4. The relative training loss with ResNet-18 student network distilled on CIFAR-10. The left is Baseline+MT and the right is MTARD (Baseline+MT+ANL). MT and ANL are abbreviations of multi-teacher and Adaptive Normalization Loss. The x axis means the training epochs, the y axis is the adv relative loss $\tilde{L}_{adv}$ and the adv relative loss $\tilde{L}_{nat}$ in the training epoch x.

5 Conclusion

In this paper, we investigated the problem of enhancing the accuracy and robustness of a small model via adversarial distillation. We revisited several state-of-the-art adversarial training and adversarial robustness distillation methods. To improve both the robust and clean accuracy of small models, we proposed Multi-Teacher Adversarial Robustness Distillation (MTARD) to guide the learning process of the small student models. To balance the influence toward students between adversarial teachers and clean teachers, we designed a method to use Adaptive Normalization Loss in MTARD. The effectiveness of MTARD over existing adversarial training and distillation methods were validated on both benchmark datasets. In the future, our method can be applied by other knowledge distillation tasks with multiple optimization goals, but not just limited to adversarial robustness distillation, which has greater potential to be developed.

Acknowledgement. This work was supported by National Key R&D Program of China (Grant No.2020AAA0104002) and the Project of the National Natural Science Foundation of China (No.62076018).

References

1. Andriushchenko, M., Croce, F., Flammarion, N., Hein, M.: Square attack: a query-efficient black-box adversarial attack via random search. In: Vedaldi, A., Bischof, H., Brox, T., Frahm, J.-M. (eds.) ECCV 2020. LNCS, vol. 12368, pp. 484–501. Springer, Cham (2020). https://doi.org/10.1007/978-3-030-58592-1_29
2. Athalye, A., Carlini, N., Wagner, D.: Obfuscated gradients give a false sense of security: circumventing defenses to adversarial examples. In: International Conference on Machine Learning, pp. 274–283. PMLR (2018)

3. Bai, Y., Zeng, Y., Jiang, Y., Xia, S.T., Ma, X., Wang, Y.: Improving adversarial robustness via channel-wise activation suppressing. arXiv preprint arXiv:2103.08307 (2021)
4. Bhagoji, A.N., He, W., Li, B., Song, D.: Practical black-box attacks on deep neural networks using efficient query mechanisms. In: Ferrari, V., Hebert, M., Sminchisescu, C., Weiss, Y. (eds.) ECCV 2018. LNCS, vol. 11216, pp. 158–174. Springer, Cham (2018). https://doi.org/10.1007/978-3-030-01258-8_10
5. Carlini, N., Wagner, D.: Towards evaluating the robustness of neural networks. In: 2017 IEEE Symposium on Security and Privacy (SP), pp. 39–57. IEEE (2017)
6. Chen, P.Y., Zhang, H., Sharma, Y., Yi, J., Hsieh, C.J.: Zoo: zeroth order optimization based black-box attacks to deep neural networks without training substitute models. In: Proceedings of the 10th ACM Workshop on Artificial Intelligence and Security, pp. 15–26 (2017)
7. Chen, T., Zhang, Z., Liu, S., Chang, S., Wang, Z.: Robust overfitting may be mitigated by properly learned smoothening. In: International Conference on Learning Representations (2020)
8. Croce, F., Hein, M.: Reliable evaluation of adversarial robustness with an ensemble of diverse parameter-free attacks. In: International Conference on Machine Learning, pp. 2206–2216. PMLR (2020)
9. Demontis, A., et al.: Why do adversarial attacks transfer? explaining transferability of evasion and poisoning attacks. In: 28th USENIX Security Symposium (USENIX Security 19), pp. 321–338 (2019)
10. Deng, J., Pan, Y., Yao, T., Zhou, W., Li, H., Mei, T.: Relation distillation networks for video object detection. In: Proceedings of the IEEE/CVF International Conference on Computer Vision, pp. 7023–7032 (2019)
11. Eykholt, K., et al.: Robust physical-world attacks on deep learning visual classification. In: Proceedings of the IEEE Conference on Computer Vision and Pattern Recognition, pp. 1625–1634 (2018)
12. Goldblum, M., Fowl, L., Feizi, S., Goldstein, T.: Adversarially robust distillation. In: Proceedings of the AAAI Conference on Artificial Intelligence, vol. 34, pp. 3996–4003 (2020)
13. Goodfellow, I.J., Shlens, J., Szegedy, C.: Explaining and harnessing adversarial examples. arXiv preprint arXiv:1412.6572 (2014)
14. Gowal, S., Qin, C., Uesato, J., Mann, T., Kohli, P.: Uncovering the limits of adversarial training against norm-bounded adversarial examples. arXiv preprint arXiv:2010.03593 (2020)
15. Gupta, S., Agrawal, A., Gopalakrishnan, K., Narayanan, P.: Deep learning with limited numerical precision. In: International Conference on Machine Learning, pp. 1737–1746. PMLR (2015)
16. Gürel, N.M., Qi, X., Rimanic, L., Zhang, C., Li, B.: Knowledge enhanced machine learning pipeline against diverse adversarial attacks. In: International Conference on Machine Learning, pp. 3976–3987. PMLR (2021)
17. Han, S., Mao, H., Dally, W.J.: Deep compression: compressing deep neural networks with pruning, trained quantization and huffman coding. arXiv preprint arXiv:1510.00149 (2015)
18. He, K., Zhang, X., Ren, S., Sun, J.: Deep residual learning for image recognition. In: Proceedings of the IEEE Conference on Computer Vision and Pattern Recognition, pp. 770–778 (2016)
19. Huang, Q., Katsman, I., He, H., Gu, Z., Belongie, S., Lim, S.N.: Enhancing adversarial example transferability with an intermediate level attack. In: Proceedings

of the IEEE/CVF International Conference on Computer Vision, pp. 4733–4742 (2019)

20. Ilyas, A., Santurkar, S., Tsipras, D., Engstrom, L., Tran, B., Madry, A.: Adversarial examples are not bugs, they are features. Adv. Neural Inf. Process. Syst. **32** (2019)

21. Javanmard, A., Soltanolkotabi, M., Hassani, H.: Precise tradeoffs in adversarial training for linear regression. In: Conference on Learning Theory, pp. 2034–2078. PMLR (2020)

22. Krizhevsky, A., Hinton, G., et al.: Learning multiple layers of features from tiny images (2009)

23. Kumar, R.S.S., et al.: Adversarial machine learning-industry perspectives. In: 2020 IEEE Security and Privacy Workshops (SPW), pp. 69–75. IEEE (2020)

24. Liu, Y., Chen, X., Liu, C., Song, D.: Delving into transferable adversarial examples and black-box attacks. arXiv preprint arXiv:1611.02770 (2016)

25. Ma, X., et al.: Characterizing adversarial subspaces using local intrinsic dimensionality. arXiv preprint arXiv:1801.02613 (2018)

26. Ma, X.: Understanding adversarial attacks on deep learning based medical image analysis systems. Pattern Recogn. **110**, 107332 (2021)

27. Madry, A., Makelov, A., Schmidt, L., Tsipras, D., Vladu, A.: Towards deep learning models resistant to adversarial attacks. arXiv preprint arXiv:1706.06083 (2017)

28. Mao, H., et al.: Exploring the regularity of sparse structure in convolutional neural networks. arXiv preprint arXiv:1705.08922 (2017)

29. Papernot, N., McDaniel, P., Jha, S., Fredrikson, M., Celik, Z.B., Swami, A.: The limitations of deep learning in adversarial settings. In: 2016 IEEE European Symposium on Security and Privacy (EuroS&P), pp. 372–387. IEEE (2016)

30. Raghunathan, A., Xie, S.M., Yang, F., Duchi, J., Liang, P.: Understanding and mitigating the tradeoff between robustness and accuracy. arXiv preprint arXiv:2002.10716 (2020)

31. Rice, L., Wong, E., Kolter, Z.: Overfitting in adversarially robust deep learning. In: International Conference on Machine Learning, pp. 8093–8104. PMLR (2020)

32. Sandler, M., Howard, A., Zhu, M., Zhmoginov, A., Chen, L.C.: Mobilenetv 2: inverted residuals and linear bottlenecks. In: Proceedings of the IEEE Conference on Computer Vision and Pattern Recognition, pp. 4510–4520 (2018)

33. Sarikaya, R., Hinton, G.E., Deoras, A.: Application of deep belief networks for natural language understanding. IEEE/ACM Trans. Audio Speech Lang. Process. **22**(4), 778–784 (2014)

34. Szegedy, C., Vanhoucke, V., Ioffe, S., Shlens, J., Wojna, Z.: Rethinking the inception architecture for computer vision. In: Proceedings of the IEEE Conference on Computer Vision and Pattern Recognition, pp. 2818–2826 (2016)

35. Szegedy, C., et al.: Intriguing properties of neural networks. arXiv preprint arXiv:1312.6199 (2013)

36. Tang, R., Lu, Y., Liu, L., Mou, L., Vechtomova, O., Lin, J.: Distilling task-specific knowledge from bert into simple neural networks. arXiv preprint arXiv:1903.12136 (2019)

37. Vandenhende, S., Georgoulis, S., Van Gansbeke, W., Proesmans, M., Dai, D., Van Gool, L.: Multi-task learning for dense prediction tasks: a survey. IEEE Trans. Pattern Anal. Mach. Intell. (2021)

38. Wang, H., et al.: Cosface: large margin cosine loss for deep face recognition. In: Proceedings of the IEEE Conference on Computer Vision and Pattern Recognition, pp. 5265–5274 (2018)

39. Wang, Y., Zou, D., Yi, J., Bailey, J., Ma, X., Gu, Q.: Improving adversarial robustness requires revisiting misclassified examples. In: International Conference on Learning Representations (2019)
40. Wei, X., Yan, H., Li, B.: Sparse black-box video attack with reinforcement learning. Int. J. Comput. Vision **130**(6), 1459–1473 (2022)
41. Wu, B., Chen, J., Cai, D., He, X., Gu, Q.: Do wider neural networks really help adversarial robustness? Adv. Neural Inf. Process. Syst. **34**, 7054–7067 (2021)
42. Xiang, L., Ding, G., Han, J.: Learning from multiple experts: self-paced knowledge distillation for long-tailed classification. In: Vedaldi, A., Bischof, H., Brox, T., Frahm, J.-M. (eds.) ECCV 2020. LNCS, vol. 12350, pp. 247–263. Springer, Cham (2020). https://doi.org/10.1007/978-3-030-58558-7_15
43. Yan, H., Wei, X.: Efficient sparse attacks on videos using reinforcement learning. In: Proceedings of the 29th ACM International Conference on Multimedia, pp. 2326–2334 (2021)
44. Zagoruyko, S., Komodakis, N.: Wide residual networks. arXiv preprint arXiv:1605.07146 (2016)
45. Zhang, H., Yu, Y., Jiao, J., Xing, E., El Ghaoui, L., Jordan, M.: Theoretically principled trade-off between robustness and accuracy. In: International Conference on Machine Learning, pp. 7472–7482. PMLR (2019)
46. Zhang, T., Zhu, Z.: Interpreting adversarially trained convolutional neural networks. In: International Conference on Machine Learning, pp. 7502–7511. PMLR (2019)
47. Zhu, J., et al.: Reliable adversarial distillation with unreliable teachers. arXiv preprint arXiv:2106.04928 (2021)
48. Zi, B., Zhao, S., Ma, X., Jiang, Y.G.: Revisiting adversarial robustness distillation: Robust soft labels make student better. In: International Conference on Computer Vision (2021)

LGV: Boosting Adversarial Example Transferability from Large Geometric Vicinity

Martin Gubri[1(✉)], Maxime Cordy[1], Mike Papadakis[1], Yves Le Traon[1], and Koushik Sen[2]

[1] Interdisciplinary Centre for Security, Reliability and Trust (SnT), University of Luxembourg, Luxembourg, Luxembourg
{Martin.Gubri,Maxime.Cordy,Mike.Papadakis,Yves.LeTraon}@uni.lu
[2] University of California, Berkeley, CA, USA

Abstract. We propose transferability from Large Geometric Vicinity (LGV), a new technique to increase the transferability of black-box adversarial attacks. LGV starts from a pretrained surrogate model and collects multiple weight sets from a few additional training epochs with a constant and high learning rate. LGV exploits two geometric properties that we relate to transferability. First, models that belong to a wider weight optimum are better surrogates. Second, we identify a subspace able to generate an effective surrogate ensemble among this wider optimum. Through extensive experiments, we show that LGV alone outperforms all (combinations of) four established test-time transformations by 1.8 to 59.9% points. Our findings shed new light on the importance of the geometry of the weight space to explain the transferability of adversarial examples.

Keywords: Adversarial examples · Transferability · Loss geometry · Machine learning security · Deep learning

1 Introduction

Deep Neural Networks (DNNs) can effectively solve a board variety of computer vision tasks [4] but they are vulnerable to adversarial examples, i.e., misclassified examples that result from slight alterations to an original, well-classified example [2,24]. This phenomenon leads to real-world security flaws in various computer vision applications, including road sign classification [6], face recognition [23] and person detection [30].

Algorithms to produce adversarial examples – the *adversarial attacks* – typically work in white-box settings, that is, they assume full access to the target

Supplementary Information The online version contains supplementary material available at https://doi.org/10.1007/978-3-031-19772-7_35.

DNN and its weights. In practice, however, an attacker has limited knowledge of the target model. In these black-box settings, the attacker executes the adversarial attack on a *surrogate model* to produce adversarial examples that should *transfer to* (i.e., are also misclassified by) the target DNN.

Transferability is challenging to achieve consistently, though, and the factors behind transferability (or lack thereof) remain an active field of study [3,5,17,26,27,29]. This is because adversarial attacks seek the examples that maximize the loss function of the surrogate model [8,15], whereas the target model has a different loss function. Methods to improve transferability typically rely on building diversity during optimisation [17,27,29]. While these approaches typically report significantly higher success rates than a classical surrogate, the relationships between the properties of the surrogate and transferability remain obscure. Understanding these relationships would enable the efficient construction of attacks (which would directly target the properties of interest) that effectively improve transferability.

In this paper, we propose Transferability from Geometric Vicinity (LGV), an efficient technique to increase the transferability of black-box adversarial attacks. LGV starts from a pretrained surrogate model and collects multiple weight samples from a few additional training epochs with a constant and high learning rate. Through extensive experiments, we show that LGV outperforms competing techniques by 3.1 to 59.9% points of transfer rate.

We relate this improved transferability to two properties of the weights that LGV samples. First, LGV samples weights on a wider surface of the loss landscape in the weight space, leading to wider adversarial examples in the feature space. Our observations support our hypothesis that misalignment between surrogate and target alters transferability, which LGV avoids by sampling from wider optima. Second, the span of LGV weights forms a dense subspace whose geometry is intrinsically connected to transferability, even when the subspace is shifted to other local optima.

DNN geometry has been intensively studied from the lens of natural generalization [7,10,13,14,16,28]. However, the literature on the importance of geometry to improve transferability is scarcer [3,26] and has not yielded actionable insights that can drive the design of new transferability methods (more in Appendix A).

Our main contribution is, therefore, to shed new light on the importance of the surrogate loss geometry to explain the transferability of adversarial examples, and the development of the LGV method that improves over state-of-the-art transferability techniques.

2   Experimental Settings

Our study uses standard experimental settings to evaluate transfer-based black-box attacks. The surrogates are trained ResNet-50 models from [1]. The targets are eight trained models from PyTorch [21] with a variety of architectures – including ResNet-50. Therefore, we cover both the intra-architecture and inter-architecture cases. We craft adversarial examples from a random subset of 2000

ImageNet test images that all eight targets classify correctly. We compare LGV with four test-time transformations and their combinations, all applied on top of I-FGSM. We do not consider query-based black-box attacks because the threat model of transfer attacks does not grant oracle access to the target. To select the hyperparameters of the attacks, we do cross-validation on an independent subset of well-classified training examples. We provide results for L_∞ norm bounded perturbations (results for L_2 are in Appendix C.3). We report the average and standard deviation of the attack success rate, i.e. the misclassification rate of untargeted adversarial examples, over 3 independent runs. Each run involves independent sets of examples, different surrogate models, and different random seeds. All code and models are available on GitHub[1]. More details are available in Appendix C.1.

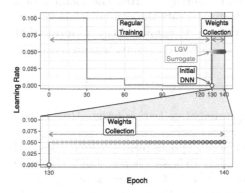

Fig. 1. Representation of the proposed approach.

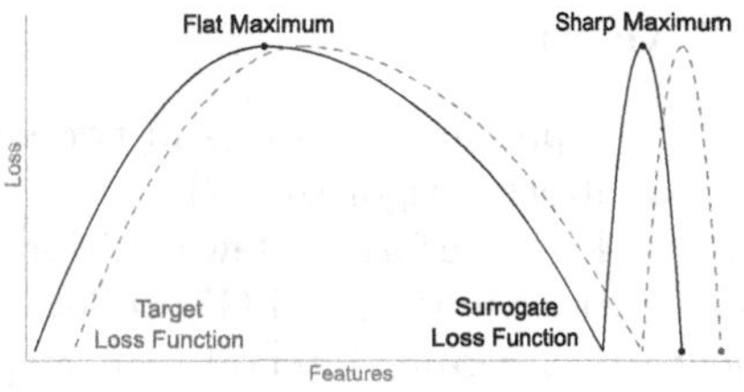

Fig. 2. Conceptual sketch of flat and sharp adversarial examples. Adapted from [14].

Notation In the following, we denote (x, y) an example in $\mathcal{X} \times \mathcal{Y}$ with $\mathcal{X} \subset \mathbb{R}^d$, w a vector of p DNN weights in $\mathbb{R}^p$, and $\mathcal{L}(x; y, w)$ the loss function at input x of a DNN parametrised by w. The weights of a regularly trained DNN are noted w_0. Our LGV approach samples K weights $w_1, \cdots, w_K$. We name *LGV-SWA* the model parametrised by the empirical average of weights collected by LGV, i.e. $w_{\text{SWA}} = \frac{1}{K} \sum_{k=1}^{K} w_k$. The dot product between two vectors u, v is noted $\langle u, v \rangle$.

3   LGV: Transferability from Large Geometric Vicinity

Preliminaries. We aim to show the importance of the geometry of the surrogate loss in improving transferability. As a first step to motivate our approach, we experimentally demonstrate that adding random directions in the weight space to a regularly trained DNN increases its transferability, whereas random directions

---

[1] https://github.com/Framartin/lgv-geometric-transferability.

in the feature space applied on gradients do not. We build a surrogate called RD (see Table 1) by adding Gaussian white noise to a DNN with weight w_0:

$$\{w_0 + e_k \mid e_k \sim \mathcal{N}(\mathbf{0}, \sigma I_p), \ k \in [\![1, K]\!]\}. \tag{1}$$

This boils down to structuring the covariance matrix of the Gaussian noise added to input gradients from local variations in the weight space (at the first order approximation, see Appendix B.1). These preliminary experiments and their results are detailed in Appendix C.2. These findings reveal that exploiting local variations in the weight space is a promising avenue to increase transferability. However, this success is sensitive to the length of the applied random vectors, and only a narrow range of σ values increase the success rate.

Based on these insights, we develop LGV (Transferability from Geometric Vicinity), our approach to efficiently build a surrogate from the vicinity of a regularly trained DNN. Despite its simplicity, it beats the combinations of four state of the art competitive techniques. The effectiveness of LGV confirms that the weight space of the surrogate is of first importance to increase transferability.

3.1   Algorithm

Our LGV approach performs in two steps: weight collection (Algorithm 1) and iterative attack (Algorithm 2).

First, LGV performs a few additional training epochs from a regularly trained model with weights w_0. LGV collects weights in a single run along the SGD trajectory at regular interval (4 per epoch). The *high constant learning rate* is key for LGV to sample in a sufficiently large vicinity. On the ResNet-50 surrogate we use in our experiments, we run SGD with half the learning rate at the start of the regular training (Fig. 1). It allows SGD to escape the basin of attraction of the initial local minimum. Appendix D.1 includes an in-depth discussion on the type of high learning rates used by LGV. Compared to adding white noise to the weights, running SGD with a high constant learning rate changes the shape of the Gaussian covariance matrix to a non-trivial one [19]. As Table 1 shows, LGV improves over random directions (RD).

Second, LGV iteratively attacks the collected models (Algorithm 2). At each iteration k, the attack computes the gradient of one collected model with weights w_k randomly sampled without replacement. If the number of iterations is greater than the number of collected models, we cycle on the models. Because the attack computes the gradient of a single model at each iteration, this step has a negligible computational overhead compared to attacking a single model.

LGV offers multiple benefits. It is efficient (requires 5 to 10 additional training epochs from a pretrained model – see Appendix D.2), and it requires only minor modifications to training algorithms and adversarial attacks. In case memory is limited, we can approximate the collected set of LGV weights by their empirical average (see Appendix B.2). The most important hyperparameter is the learning rate. In Appendix D.1, we show that LGV provides reliable transferability improvements for a wide range of learning rate.

3.2   Comparison with the State of the Art

We evaluate the transferability of LGV and compare it with four state-of-the-art techniques.

Algorithm 1 LGV Weights Collection

Input: n_{epochs} number of epochs, K number of weights, η learning rate, γ momentum, w_0 pretrained weights, $\mathcal{D}$ training dataset

Output: $(w_1, \ldots, w_K)$ LGV weights

1: $w \leftarrow w_0$ ▷ Start from a regularly trained DNN
2: **for** $i \leftarrow 1$ to K **do**
3:    $w \leftarrow \text{SGD}(w, \eta, \gamma, \mathcal{D}, \frac{n_{\text{epochs}}}{K})$
    ▷ Perform $\frac{n_{\text{epochs}}}{K}$ of an epoch of SGD with η learning rate and γ momentum on $\mathcal{D}$
4:    $w_i \leftarrow w$
5: **end for**

Algorithm 2 I-FGSM Attack on LGV

Input: (x, y) natural example, $(w_1, \ldots, w_K)$ LGV weights, n_{iter} number of iterations, ε p-norm perturbation, α step-size

Output: x_{adv} adversarial example

1: Shuffle $(w_1, \ldots, w_K)$ ▷ Shuffle weights
2: $x_{\text{adv}} \leftarrow x$
3: **for** $i \leftarrow 1$ to n_{iter} **do**
4:    $x_{\text{adv}} \leftarrow x_{\text{adv}} + \alpha \nabla_x \mathcal{L}(x_{\text{adv}}; y, w_{i \bmod K})$
    ▷ Compute the input gradient of the loss of a randomly picked LGV model
5:    $x_{\text{adv}} \leftarrow \text{project}(x_{\text{adv}}, B_\varepsilon[x])$ ▷ Project in the p-norm ball centred on x of ε radius
6:    $x_{\text{adv}} \leftarrow \text{clip}(x_{\text{adv}}, 0, 1)$ ▷ Clip to pixel range values
7: **end for**

MI [5] adds momentum to the attack gradients to stabilize them and escape from local maxima with poor transferability. Ghost Networks (**GN**) [17] use dropout or skip connection erosion to efficiently generate diverse surrogate ensembles. **DI** [29] applies transformations to inputs to increase input diversity at each attack iteration. Skip Gradient Method (**SGM**) [27] favours the gradients from skip connections rather than residual modules, and claims that the formers are of first importance to generate highly transferable adversarial examples. We discuss these techniques more deeply in Appendix A.

Table 1 reports the success rates of the ∞-norm attack (2-norm in Appendix C.3). We see that LGV alone improves over all (combinations of) other techniques (simple underline). Compared to individual techniques, LGV raises success rate by 10.1 to 59.9% points, with an average of 35.6. When the techniques are combined, LGV still outperforms them by 1.8 to 55.4% points, and 26.6 on average.

We also see that combining LGV with test-time techniques does not always improve the results and can even drastically decrease success rate. Still, LGV combined with input diversity (DI) and momentum (MI) generally outperforms LGV alone (by up to 20.5%) and ranks the best or close to the best. Indeed, both techniques tackle properties of transferability not covered by LGV: DI captures some input invariances learned by different architectures, and MI smooths the attack optimization updates in a moving average way.

The incompatibility of GN and SGM with LGV leads us to believe that their feature perturbations are cheap and bad proxies for local weight geometry.

Eroding randomly skip connection, applying dropout on all layers, or backpropagating more linearly, may (poorly) approximate sampling in the weight space vicinity. LGV does this sampling explicitly.

Table 1. Success rates of baselines, state-of-the-art and LGV under the L∞ attack. Simple underline is best without LGV combinations, double is best overall. Gray is LGV-based techniques worse than vanilla LGV. "RD" stands for random directions in the weight space. In %.

Surrogate	Target							
	RN50	RN152	RNX50	WRN50	DN201	VGG19	IncV1	IncV3
Baselines (1 DNN)								
1 DNN	45.3±2.4	29.6±0.9	28.8±0.2	31.5±1.6	17.5±0.6	16.6±0.9	10.4±0.5	5.3±1.0
MI	53.0±2.2	36.3±1.5	34.7±0.4	38.1±2.0	22.0±0.1	21.1±0.3	13.9±0.4	7.3±0.8
GN	63.9±2.4	43.8±2.4	43.3±1.3	47.4±0.9	24.8±0.3	24.1±1.0	14.6±0.3	6.8±1.2
GN+MI	68.4±2.3	49.3±2.5	47.9±1.2	52.1±1.7	28.4±0.8	28.0±0.7	17.5±0.5	8.7±0.5
DI	75.0±0.2	56.4±1.9	59.6±1.5	61.6±2.4	41.6±1.1	39.7±0.9	27.7±1.0	15.2±1.0
DI+MI	81.2±0.3	63.8±1.9	67.6±0.9	68.9±1.5	49.3±0.7	46.7±0.4	33.0±1.0	19.4±0.9
SGM	64.4±0.8	49.1±3.1	48.9±0.6	51.7±2.8	30.7±0.9	33.6±1.3	22.5±1.5	10.7±0.9
SGM+MI	66.0±0.6	51.3±3.5	50.9±0.9	54.3±2.3	32.5±1.3	35.8±0.7	24.1±1.0	12.1±1.2
SGM+DI	76.8±0.5	62.3±2.7	63.6±1.7	65.3±1.4	45.5±0.9	49.9±0.8	36.0±0.7	19.2±1.7
SGM+DI+MI	80.9±0.7	66.9±2.5	68.7±1.2	70.0±1.7	50.9±0.6	56.0±1.4	42.1±1.4	23.6±1.6
Our techniques								
RD	60.6±1.5	40.5±3.0	39.9±0.2	44.4±3.2	22.9±0.8	22.7±0.5	13.9±0.2	6.6±0.7
LGV-SWA	84.9±1.2	63.9±3.7	62.1±0.4	61.1±2.9	44.2±0.4	42.4±1.3	31.5±0.8	12.2±0.8
LGV-SWA+RD	90.2±0.5	71.7±3.4	69.9±1.2	69.1±3.3	49.9±1.0	47.4±2.0	34.9±0.3	13.5±0.9
LGV (ours)	95.4±0.1	85.5±2.3	83.7±1.2	82.1±2.4	69.3±1.0	67.8±1.2	58.1±0.8	25.3±1.9
LGV combined with other techniques								
MI	<u>97.1±0.3</u>	88.7±2.3	87.0±1.0	86.6±2.1	73.2±1.4	71.6±1.4	60.7±0.6	27.4±0.8
GN	94.2±0.2	83.0±2.2	80.8±0.7	79.5±2.4	66.9±0.7	66.6±0.7	56.2±0.5	24.4±1.4
GN+MI	96.4±0.1	87.2±2.0	85.3±0.8	84.4±2.3	70.4±1.0	71.2±0.8	59.2±0.5	26.5±0.4
DI	93.8±0.1	84.4±1.6	84.1±0.6	81.8±1.6	74.9±0.2	76.2±0.7	71.5±1.3	38.9±1.1
DI+MI	96.9±0.0	<u>89.6±1.7</u>	<u>89.6±0.4</u>	88.4±1.1	82.3±0.9	82.2±0.9	<u>78.6±0.8</u>	<u>45.4±0.5</u>
SGM	86.9±0.7	74.8±2.6	73.5±1.2	72.8±2.4	60.6±0.9	69.0±1.8	61.5±1.7	31.7±1.8
SGM+MI	89.1±0.5	77.1±2.8	76.7±1.1	75.6±2.1	62.7±1.1	72.3±1.0	64.7±2.2	34.2±1.7
SGM+DI	84.3±0.6	72.5±2.4	72.8±0.7	70.7±1.8	62.1±0.9	71.8±1.4	67.0±1.8	37.7±1.8
SGM+DI+MI	87.7±0.6	76.4±2.5	77.2±0.8	75.6±1.1	66.4±1.0	76.6±0.7	72.1±1.4	42.9±1.7

Overall, our observations lessen both the importance of skip connections to explain transferability claimed by [27], and what was believed to hurt most transferability, i.e., the optimization algorithm [5] and lack of input diversity [29]. Our results demonstrate that the diversity of surrogate models (one model per iteration) is at most importance to avoid adversarial examples overfitting to their surrogate model. LGV does so more effectively than [17].

We show that LGV consistently increases transfer-based attacks success. However, it is not trivial why sampling surrogate weights in the vicinity of a local minimum helps adversarial examples to be successful against a model from another local minimum. In the following, we analyse the LGV success with a geometrical perspective.

4   Investigating LGV Properties: On the Importance of the Loss Geometry

In the following, we relate the increased transferability of LGV to two geometrical properties of the weight space. First, we show that LGV collects weights on flatter regions of the loss landscape than where it started (the initial, pretrained surrogate). These flatter surrogates produce wider adversarial examples in feature space, and improve transferability in case of misalignment between the surrogate loss (optimized function) and the target loss (objective function). Second, the span of LGV weights forms a dense subspace whose geometry is intrinsically connected to transferability, even when the subspace is shifted to other independent solutions. The geometry plays a different role depending on the functional similarity between the target and the surrogate architectures.

4.1   Loss Flatness: The Surrogate-Target Misalignment Hypothesis

We first explain why LGV is a good surrogate through the *surrogate-target misalignment hypothesis*. We show that LGV samples from flatter regions in the weight space and, as a result, produces adversarial examples flatter in the feature space. This leads to surrogates that are more robust to misalignment between the surrogate and target prediction functions.

Sharp and flat minima have been discussed extensively in machine learning (see Appendix A). A sharp minimum is one where the variations of the objective function in a neighbourhood are important, whereas a flat minimum shows low variations [11]. Multiple studies [13,14] correlate (natural) generalization with the width of the solution in the weight space: if the train loss is shifted w.r.t. the test loss in the weight space, wide optima are desirable to keep the difference between train and test losses small.

We conjecture that a similar misalignment occurs between the surrogate model and the target model *in the feature space*. See Figure 2 for an illustration of the phenomenon. Under this hypothesis, adversarial examples at wider maxima of the surrogate loss would transfer better than sharp ones. The assumption that surrogate and target models are shifted with respect to each other seems particularly reasonable when both are the same function parametrised differently (intra-architecture transferability), or are functionally similar (same architecture family). We do not expect all types of loss flatness to increase transferability, since entirely vanished gradients would be the flatter loss surface possible and annihilate gradient-based attacks.

We provide two empirical evidences for this hypothesis. First, LGV flattens weights compared to the initial DNN. Second, LGV similarly flattens adversarial examples in the feature space.

Table 2. Sharpness metrics in the weight space, i.e., the largest eigenvalue and the rank of the Hessian, computed on three types of surrogate and 10,000 training examples.

Model	Hessian			
	Max EV		Trace	
1 DNN	558	±57	16258	±725
LGV indiv.	168	±127	4295	±517
LGV-SWA	30	±1	1837	±70

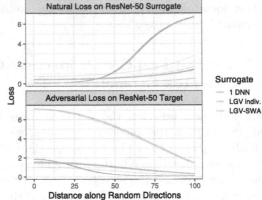

Fig. 3. L_∞ attack crafted on surrogate with natural loss (*up*), evaluated on target (*down*) with respect to the 2-norm distance along 10 random directions in the weight space from the LGV-SWA solution (*orange*), random LGV weights (*purple*), and the initial DNN (*green*).

Flatness in the Weight Space. We establish that LGV weights and their mean (LGV-SWA) are in a flatter region of the loss than the initial DNN. The reason we consider LGV-SWA is that this model lies at the center of the loss surface explored by LGV and attacking this model yields a good first-order approximation of attacking the ensemble of LGV weights (cf. Appendix B.2). First, we compute Hessian-based sharpness metrics. Second, we study the variations of the loss in the weight space along random directions from the solutions.

First, Table 2 reports two sharpness metrics in the weight space: the largest eigenvalue of the Hessian which estimates the sharpness of the sharpest direction, and the trace of the Hessian which estimates the sharpness of all directions. Both metrics conclude that the initial DNN is significantly sharper than the LGV and LGV-SWA weights.

Second, like [13], we sample a random direction vector d on the unit sphere, $d = \frac{e}{\|e\|_2}$ with $e \sim \mathcal{N}(0, I_p)$ and we study the following rays,

$$w_0(\alpha, d) = w_0 + \alpha d, \quad w_k(\alpha, d) = w_k + \alpha d, \quad w_{\text{SWA}}(\alpha, d) = w_{\text{SWA}} + \alpha d, \quad (2)$$

with $\alpha \in \mathbb{R}^+$. That is, we follow the same direction d for the three studied solutions. Figure 3 reports the intra-architecture results for 10 random directions (see Appendix C.4 for other settings). The natural loss in the weight space is wider at the individual LGV weights and at LGV-SWA than it is at the initial model weights (upper plot). When adding the random vector αd, the natural loss of LGV-SWA barely increases, while that of the initial model w_0 reaches high values: 0.40 vs. 6.67 for $\|\alpha \cdot d\|_2$ from 0 to 100. The individual LGV models are in between, with an 1.12 increase on average. As Figure 3 also reveals, the increased flatness of LGV-SWA in the weight space comes with an increased transferability. We investigate this phenomenon deeper in what follows.

Flatness in the Feature Space. Knowing that LGV (approximated via LGV-SWA) yields loss flatness in the weight space, we now connect this observation to the width of basins of attractions in the feature space when we craft adversarial examples. That is, we aim to show that flat surrogates in the weight space produce flatter adversarial examples in the feature space.

To study flatness of adversarial examples in the feature space, we consider the plane containing 3 points: the original example x, a LGV adversarial example $x_{\text{LGV}}^{\text{adv}}$, and an adversarial example crafted against the initial DNN $x_{\text{DNN}}^{\text{adv}}$. We build an orthonormal basis $(u', v') := (\frac{u}{\|u\|}, \frac{v}{\|v\|})$ using the first two steps of the Gram-Schmidt process,

$$(u, v) = \left(x_{\text{LGV}}^{\text{adv}} - x, \ (x_{\text{DNN}}^{\text{adv}} - x) - \frac{\langle x_{\text{DNN}}^{\text{adv}} - x, u \rangle}{\langle u, u \rangle} u \right). \tag{3}$$

We focus our analysis on the 2-norm attack. It constrains adversarial perturbations inside the L_2-ball centred on x of radius ε. This has the convenient property that the intersection of this ball with our previously defined plane (containing x) is a disk of radius ε.

Figure 4 shows the loss of the ensemble of LGV weights and the loss of the initial DNN in the (u', v') coordinate system. We report the average losses over 500 disks, each one centred on a randomly picked test example. It appears that LGV has a much smoother loss surface than its initial model. LGV adversarial examples are in a wide region of the LGV ensemble's loss. The maxima of the initial DNN loss is highly sharp and much more attractive for gradient ascent than the ones found by LGV – the reason why adversarial examples crafted from the initial DNN overfit.

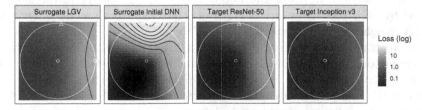

Fig. 4. Surrogate (*left*) and target (*right*) losses in the plane containing the original example (*circle*), an adversarial example against LGV (*square*) and one against the initial DNN (*triangle*), in the (u', v') coordinate system. Colours are in log-scale, contours in natural scale. The white circle represents the intersection of the 2-norm ball with the plane.

Flatness and Transferability. Figure 4 also shows the losses of two target models in the (u', v') coordinate system. The LGV loss appears particularly well aligned with the one of the ResNet-50 target (intra-architecture transferability). We observe a *shift between the contour of both models, with the same functional form*. These observations are valid for other targets and on planes defined by adversarial examples of other surrogates (see Appendix C.6). All these observations corroborate our surrogate-target misalignment hypothesis.

In Appendix C.5, we provide results of another experiment that corroborates our findings. We interpolate the weights between LGV-SWA and the initial model, i.e. moving along a non-random direction, and confirm that (i) the surrogate loss is flatter at LGV-SWA than at the initial model weights, (ii) that the adversarial loss of target models gets higher as we move from the initial model to LGV-SWA.

Section 4.1 – Conclusion. LGV weights lie in flatter regions of the loss landscape than the initial DNN weights. Flatness in the weight space correlates with flatness in the feature space: LGV adversarial examples are wider maxima than sharp adversarial examples crafted against the initial DNN. These conclusions support our surrogate-target misalignment hypothesis: if surrogate and target losses are shifted with respect to each other, a wide optimum is more robust to this shift than a sharp optimum.

4.2   On the Importance of LGV Weight Subspace Geometry

Although we have demonstrated the link between the better transferability that LGV-SWA (and in extenso, the LGV ensemble) achieves and the flatness of this surrogate's loss, additional experiments have revealed that the LGV models – taken individually – achieve lower transferability, although they also have a flatter loss than the initial model (see Appendix C.7 for details). This indicates that other factors are in play to explain LGV transferability.

In what follows, we show the importance of the geometry of the subspace formed by LGV models in increasing transferability. More precisely, deviations of LGV weights from their average spans a weight subspace which is (i) densely related to transferability (i.e., *it is useful*), (ii) composed of directions whose relative importance depends on the functional similarity between surrogate and target (i.e., *its geometry is relevant*), (iii) remains useful when shifted to other solutions (i.e., *its geometry captures generic properties*). Similarly to [12], the K-dimensional subspace of interest is defined as,

$$\mathcal{S} = \{w \mid w = w_{\mathrm{SWA}} + \mathbf{P}z\}, \tag{4}$$

where w_{SWA} is called the shift vector, $\mathbf{P} = (w_1 - w_{\mathrm{SWA}}, \ldots, w_K - w_{\mathrm{SWA}})^{\mathsf{T}}$ is the projection matrix of LGV weights deviations from their mean, and $z \in \mathbb{R}^K$.

A Subspace Useful for Transferability. First, we show that the subspace has importance for transferability. Similarly to our previous RD surrogate, we build a new surrogate "LGV-SWA + RD" by sampling random directions in the full weight space around LGV-SWA. It is defined as:

$$\{w_{\text{SWA}} + e'_k \mid e'_k \sim \mathcal{N}(\mathbf{0}, \sigma' I_p), \ k \in [\![1, K]\!]\}, \tag{5}$$

where the standard deviation σ' is selected by cross-validation in Appendix C.8.

Table 1 reports the transferability of this surrogate for the L_∞ attack (see Appendix C.3 for L_2). We observe that random deviations drawn in the entire weight space do improve the transferability of LGV-SWA (increase of 1.32 to 10.18% points, with an average of 6.90). However, the LGV surrogate systematically outperforms "LGV-SWA + RD". The differences range from 4.33 to 29.15% points, and average to 16.10. Therefore, the subspace $\mathcal{S}$ has specific geometric properties related to transferability that make this ensemble outperforms the ensemble formed by random directions around LGV-SWA.

In Appendix C.9, we also show that the subspace is densely connected to transferability by evaluating the transferability of surrogates built from $\mathcal{S}$ by sampling $z \sim \mathcal{N}(\mathbf{0}, I_K)$.

Decomposition of the LGV Projection Matrix. Second, we analyse the contribution of subspace basis vectors to transferability through a decomposition of their projection matrix. Doing so, we build alternative LGV surrogates with an increasingly reduced dimensionality, and we assess the impact of this reduction on transferability.

We decompose the matrix of LGV weights deviations $\mathbf{P}$ into orthogonal directions, using principal component analysis (PCA) since the PCA coordinate transformation diagonalises this matrix. Following [12], we apply PCA based on exact full SVD[2] to obtain a new orthonormal basis of the LGV weight subspace. We exploit the orthogonality of the components to change the basis of each w_k with the PCA linear transformation and project onto the first C principal components. We then apply the inverse map, with w_{SWA} as shift vector, to obtain a new weight vector $w_{k,C}^{\text{proj}}$. We repeat the process with different value of C, which enables us to control the amount of explained weights variance and to build LGV ensembles with a reduced dimensionality.

The eigenvalues of the LGV weights deviation matrix equal the variance of the weights along the corresponding eigenvectors. We use the ratio of explained weights variance to measure the relative loss of information that would result from removing a given direction. From an information theory perspective, if a direction in the weight space is informative of transferability, we expect the success rate to decrease with the loss of information due to dimensionality reduction. Note that the surrogate projected on the PCA zero space (i.e. $C = 0$) is LGV-SWA, whereas $C = K$ means we consider the full surrogate ensemble.

---

[2] As [12] we use the PCA implementation of sklearn [22], but here we select the full SVD solver instead of randomized SVD to keep all the singular vectors.

Figure 5 shows, for each dimensionality reduced LGV surrogates, the explained variance ratio of its lower dimensional weight subspace and the success rate that this ensemble achieves on the ResNet-50 and Inception v3 targets. To observe the trends, we add the hypothetical cases of proportionality to the variance (solid line) and equal contributions of all dimensions (dashed line).

For both targets, explained variance correlates positively with transferability. This means that our approach improves transferability more, as it samples along directions (from SWA) with higher variance. Especially in the intra-architecture case (Figure 5a), there is an almost-linear correlation between the importance of a direction in the weight space and its contribution to transferability. This conclusion can be loosely extended to the targets that belong to the same architecture family as the surrogate, i.e. ResNet-like models (Appendix C.10).

In some inter-architecture cases, we do not observe this linear trend, although the correlation remains positive. In Figure 5b, we see that the real variance ratio/transfer rate curve is close to the hypothetical case where each direction would equally improve transferability on the Inception v3 target. This means that, in this inter-architecture case, each direction contributes almost-equally to transferability regardless of their contribution to the subspace variance. In supplementary materials, we show other inter-architecture cases (e.g., DenseNet-201 and VGG19) that are intermediate between linear correlation and almost-equal dimensional contributions (Appendix C.10).

Taking together the above results, we explain the better transferability of LGV with the variance of the subspace it forms. However, this correlation is stronger as the surrogate and target architectures are more functionally similar.

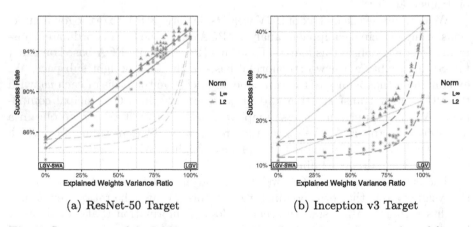

(a) ResNet-50 Target   (b) Inception v3 Target

Fig. 5. Success rate of the LGV surrogate projected on an increasing number of dimensions with the corresponding ratio of explained variance in the weight space. Hypothetical average cases of proportionality to variance (*solid*) and equal contributions of all subspace dimensions (*dashed*). Scales not shared.

Shift of LGV Subspace to Other Local Minima. Third, we demonstrate that the benefits of the LGV subspace geometry are shared across solutions in the weight space. This indicates that there are generic geometry properties that relate to transferability.

We apply LGV to another independently trained DNN w_0'. We collect K new weights w_k', which we average to obtain w_{SWA}'. We construct a new surrogate by adding the new deviations to w_{SWA},

$$\{w_{SWA} + (w_k' - w_{SWA}') \mid k \in [\![1, K]\!]\}, \tag{6}$$

and we call this new shifted surrogate "LGV-SWA + (LGV' - LGV-SWA')".

Shifting a LGV subspace to another flat solution (i.e., another LGV-SWA) yields a significantly better surrogate than sampling random directions from this solution. The difference between "LGV-SWA + (LGV' - LGV-SWA')" and "LGV-SWA + RD" varies from 3.27 to 12.32% points, with a mean of 8.61 (see Appendix C.11 for detailed results). The fact that the subspace still improves transferability (compared to a random subspace) when applied to another vicinity reveals that subspace geometry has generic properties related to transferability.

Yet, we also find a degradation of success rate between this translated surrogate and our original LGV surrogate (-7.49% points on average, with values between -1.02 and -16.80). It indicates that, though the geometric properties are shared across vicinities, the subspace is optimal (w.r.t. transferability) when applied onto its original solution.

The subspace is not solely relevant for solutions found by LGV: LGV deviations are also relevant when applied to regularly trained DNNs. For that, we build a new surrogate "1 DNN + γ (LGV' - LGV-SWA')" centred on the DNN w_0,

$$\{w_0 + \gamma(w_k' - w_{SWA}') \mid k \in [\![1, K]\!]\}, \tag{7}$$

where the LGV deviations are scaled by a factor $\gamma \in \mathbb{R}$. Scaling is essential here because DNNs are sharper than LGV-SWA. Unscaled LGV deviations exit the vicinity of low loss, which drops the success rate by 32.8% points on average compared to the optimal γ value of 0.5 (see Appendix C.11 for detailed results). When properly scaled and applied to an independently and regularly trained DNN, LGV deviations improve upon random directions by 10.0% points in average (2.87—13.88).

With all these results, we exhibit generic properties of the LGV subspace. It benefits solutions independently obtained. Applying LGV deviations on a solution of a different nature may require to scale them according to the new local flatness.

Section 4.2 – Conclusion. Taking together all our results, we conclude that the improved transferability of LGV comes from the geometry of the subspace formed by LGV weights in a flatter region of the loss. The LGV deviations spans a weight subspace whose geometry is densely and generically relevant for transferability. This subspace is key, as a single flat LGV model is not enough to succeed. This entire subspace enables to benefit from the flatness of this region, overcoming potential misalignment between the loss functions of the surrogate and that of the target model. That is, it increases the probability that adversarial examples maximizing the surrogate loss will also (near-)maximize the target loss – and thus successfully transfer.

5   Conclusion and Future Work

We show that random directions in the weight space sampled at each attack iteration increase transferability, unlike random directions in feature space. Based on this insight, we propose LGV, our approach to build a surrogate by collecting weights along the SGD trajectory with a high constant learning rate, starting from a regularly trained DNN. LGV alone beats all combinations of four state-of-the-art techniques. We analyse LGV extensively to conclude that (i) flatness in the weight space produces flatter adversarial examples which are more robust to surrogate-target misalignment; (ii) LGV weights spans a dense subspace whose geometry is intrinsically connected to transferability. Overall, we open new directions to understand and improve transferability from the geometry of the loss in the weight space. Future work may, based on the insights of [32] on natural generalization, study transferability with the perspective of volume in the weight space that leads to similar predictive function.

Acknowledgements. This work is supported by the Luxembourg National Research Funds (FNR) through CORE project C18/IS/12669767/STELLAR/LeTraon.

References

1. Ashukha, A., Lyzhov, A., Molchanov, D., Vetrov, D.: Pitfalls of in-domain uncertainty estimation and ensembling in deep learning (2020). http://arxiv.org/abs/2002.06470
2. Biggio, B., et al.: Evasion attacks against machine learning at test time. In: Lecture Notes in Computer Science, vol. 8190 LNAI, pp. 387–402 (2013). https://doi.org/10.1007/978-3-642-40994-3_25
3. Charles, Z., Rosenberg, H., Papailiopoulos, D.: A geometric perspective on the transferability of adversarial directions. In: AISTATS 2019 (2020). http://arxiv.org/abs/1811.03531
4. Dargan, S., Kumar, M., Ayyagari, M.R., Kumar, G.: A survey of deep learning and its applications: a new paradigm to machine learning. Arch. Comput. Methods Eng. **27**(4), 1071–1092 (2019)

5. Dong, Y., et al.: Boosting adversarial attacks with momentum. In: CVPR, pp. 9185–9193 (2018). https://doi.org/10.1109/CVPR.2018.00957

6. Eykholt, K., et al.: Robust physical-world attacks on deep learning models (2017). https://doi.org/10.48550/arxiv.1707.08945

7. Foret, P., Kleiner Google Research, A., Mobahi Google Research, H., Neyshabur Blueshift, B.: Sharpness-aware minimization for efficiently improving generalization (2020). http://arxiv.org/abs/2010.01412v3

8. Goodfellow, I.J., Shlens, J., Szegedy, C.: Explaining and harnessing adversarial examples (2014)

9. Gubri, M., Cordy, M., Papadakis, M., Traon, Y.L.: Efficient and transferable adversarial examples from Bayesian neural networks. UAI 2022 (2022). http://arxiv.org/abs/2011.05074

10. Gur-Ari, G., Roberts, D.A., Dyer, E.: Gradient descent happens in a tiny subspace (2018). http://arxiv.org/abs/1812.04754

11. Hochreiter, S., Schmidhuber, J.: Flat minima. Neural Comput. **9**(1), 1–42 (1997). https://doi.org/10.1162/NECO.1997.9.1.1

12. Izmailov, P., Maddox, W.J., Kirichenko, P., Garipov, T., Vetrov, D., Wilson, A.G.: Subspace inference for Bayesian deep learning. In: UAI 2019 (2019). http://arxiv.org/abs/1907.07504

13. Izmailov, P., Podoprikhin, D., Garipov, T., Vetrov, D., Wilson, A.G.: Averaging weights leads to wider optima and better generalization. In: 34th Conference on Uncertainty in Artificial Intelligence 2018, UAI 2018, vol. 2, pp. 876–885. Association For Uncertainty in Artificial Intelligence (AUAI) (2018). http://arxiv.org/abs/1803.05407

14. Keskar, N.S., Nocedal, J., Tang, P.T.P., Mudigere, D., Smelyanskiy, M.: On large-batch training for deep learning: generalization gap and sharp minima. In: ICLR 2017 (2016). http://arxiv.org/abs/1609.04836v2

15. Kurakin, A., Goodfellow, I.J., Bengio, S.: Adversarial examples in the physical world. In: 5th International Conference on Learning Representations, ICLR 2017 - Workshop Track Proceedings (2017). http://arxiv.org/abs/1607.02533

16. Li, C., Farkhoor, H., Liu, R., Yosinski, J.: Measuring the intrinsic dimension of objective landscapes. In: 6th International Conference on Learning Representations, ICLR 2018 - Conference Track Proceedings (2018). http://arxiv.org/abs/1804.08838v1

17. Li, Y., Bai, S., Zhou, Y., Xie, C., Zhang, Z., Yuille, A.: Learning transferable adversarial examples via ghost networks. In: AAAI 34(07), pp. 11458–11465 (2018). https://doi.org/10.1609/aaai.v34i07.6810, http://arxiv.org/abs/1812.03413

18. Maddox, W.J., Garipov, T., Izmailov, Vetrov, D., Wilson, A.G.: A simple baseline for Bayesian uncertainty in deep learning. In: NeurIPS, vol. 32 (2019). http://arxiv.org/abs/1902.02476

19. Mandt, S., Hof Fman, M.D., Blei, D.M.: Stochastic gradient descent as approximate Bayesian inference. J. Mach. Learn. Res. 18, 1–35 (2017). http://arxiv.org/abs/1704.04289v2

20. Papernot, N., McDaniel, P., Goodfellow, I.: Transferability in machine learning: from phenomena to black-box attacks using adversarial samples (2016). http://arxiv.org/abs/1605.07277

21. Paszke, A., et al.: PyTorch: an imperative style, high-performance deep learning library. In: NIPS, pp. 8024–8035 (2019). http://papers.neurips.cc/paper/9015-pytorch-an-imperative-style-high-performance-deep-learning-library.pdf

22. Pedregosa, F., et al.: Scikit-learn: machine learning in python. J. Mach. Learn. Res. **12**, 2825–2830 (2011)

23. Sharif, M., Bhagavatula, S., Bauer, L., Reiter, M.K.: A general framework for adversarial examples with objectives. ACM Trans. Priv. Secur. **22**(3), 30 (2017). https://doi.org/10.1145/3317611

24. Szegedy, C., et al.: Intriguing properties of neural networks (2013). http://arxiv.org/abs/1312.6199

25. Tramèr, F., Kurakin, A., Papernot, N., Goodfellow, I., Boneh, D., McDaniel, P.: Ensemble adversarial training: Attacks and defenses. In: 6th International Conference on Learning Representations, ICLR 2018 - Conference Track Proceedings (2018). http://arxiv.org/abs/1705.07204

26. Tramèr, F., Papernot, N., Goodfellow, I., Boneh, D., McDaniel, P.: The space of transferable adversarial examples (2017). http://arxiv.org/abs/1704.03453

27. Wu, D., Wang, Y., Xia, S.T., Bailey, J., Ma, X.: Skip connections matter: on the transferability of adversarial examples generated with ResNets. In: ICLR (2020). http://arxiv.org/abs/2002.05990

28. Wu, D., Xia, S.T., Wang, Y.: Adversarial weight perturbation helps robust generalization. In: Advances in Neural Information Processing Systems. Neural information processing systems foundation (2020). http://arxiv.org/abs/2004.05884v2

29. Xie, C., et al.: Improving transferability of adversarial examples with input diversity. In: Proceedings of the IEEE Computer Society Conference on Computer Vision and Pattern Recognition, vol. 2019-June, pp. 2725–2734 (2019). https://doi.org/10.1109/CVPR.2019.00284

30. Xu, K., et al.: Evading real-time person detectors by adversarial T-shirt (2019). http://arxiv.org/abs/1910.11099

31. Yao, Z., Gholami, A., Keutzer, K., Mahoney, M.W.: PyHessian: neural networks through the lens of the Hessian. Big Data 2020, pp. 581–590 (2019). https://doi.org/10.1109/BigData50022.2020.9378171

32. Zhang, S., Reid, I., Pérez, G.V., Louis, A.: Why flatness does and does not correlate with generalization for deep neural networks (2021). http://arxiv.org/abs/2103.06219

A Large-Scale Multiple-objective Method for Black-box Attack Against Object Detection

Siyuan Liang[1,2], Longkang Li[3], Yanbo Fan[4], Xiaojun Jia[1,2], Jingzhi Li[1,2(✉)], Baoyuan Wu[3(✉)], and Xiaochun Cao[5]

[1] Statrity, Institute of Information Engineering, Chinese Academy of Sciences, Beijing, China
{liangsiyuan,jiaxiaojun,lijingzhi}@iie.ac.cn
[2] School of Cyber Security, University of Chinese Academy of Sciences, Beijing, China
[3] School of Data Science, Shenzhen Research Institute of Big Data, The Chinese University of Hong Kong, Shenzhen, China
{lilongkang,wubaoyuan}@cuhk.edu.cn
[4] Tencent AI Lab, Shenzhen, China
[5] School of Cyber Science and Technology, Shenzhen Campus, Sun Yat-sen University, Shenzhen, China
caoxiaochun@mail.sysu.edu.cn

Abstract. Recent studies have shown that detectors based on deep models are vulnerable to adversarial examples, even in the black-box scenario where the attacker cannot access the model information. Most existing attack methods aim to minimize the true positive rate, which often shows poor attack performance, as another sub-optimal bounding box may be detected around the attacked bounding box to be the new true positive one. To settle this challenge, we propose to minimize the true positive rate and maximize the false positive rate, which can encourage more false positive objects to block the generation of new true positive bounding boxes. It is modeled as a multi-objective optimization (MOP) problem, of which the generic algorithm can search the Pareto-optimal. However, our task has more than two million decision variables, leading to low searching efficiency. Thus, we extend the standard **G**enetic **A**lgorithm with **R**andom **S**ubset selection and **D**ivide-and-**C**onquer, called GARSDC, which significantly improves the efficiency. Moreover, to alleviate the sensitivity to population quality in generic algorithms, we generate a gradient-prior initial population, utilizing the transferability between different detectors with similar backbones. Compared with the state-of-art attack methods, GARSDC decreases by an average 12.0 in the mAP and queries by about 1000 times in extensive experiments. Our codes can be found at https://github.com/LiangSiyuan21/GARSDC.

Supplementary Information The online version contains supplementary material available at https://doi.org/10.1007/978-3-031-19772-7_36.

Keywords: Adversarial learning · Object detection · Black-box attack

1   Introduction

With the development of deep learning, object detection [19, 20, 35, 48] has been widely applied in many practical scenarios, such as autonomous driving [21], face recognition [16], industrial detection [15], etc. In object detection, the true positive object refers to the positive object correctly and the false positive object refers to the negative object that is incorrectly marked as positive object.

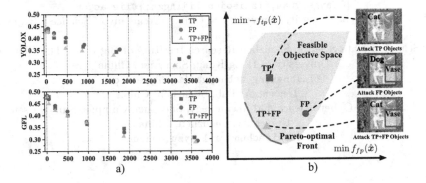

Fig. 1. *a*) We show the results of attacking two different models using three objective functions(TP, FP, 'TP+FP'). Experiments show that using 'TP+FP' can decrease the most mAP and reduce most queries. *b*) We show the difference of three objective optimizations, and the total consideration of 'TP+FP' makes the solution closer to the Pareto-optimization front.

Recently, the adversarial attack and defense around deep learning have received extensive attention [2, 17, 18, 39, 41]. Existing attacks against object detection misclassify the true positive objects from the model, which leads to attack failure. The reason is that another sub-optimal bounding box can replace the attacked bounding box successfully as the new true positive object. Another train of thought, increasing the false positive objects is also an effective attack method in some scenarios. For example, many false objects can obscure the significance of the positive object and lead to autonomous driving system [34] crashes. Therefore, we believe that is critical and desirable to simultaneously optimize true positive and false positive objects recognized by the detector for the following reasons. Firstly, optimizing the objective function with two aspects can expand the attack scenarios. Secondly, we minimize the true positive rate and maximize the false positive rate, which increases false positive objects to block the generation of the true positive object. Thirdly, considering the attack target comprehensively helps decrease the mAP. As shown in Fig. 1, through experiments on YOLOX and GFL models, we prove that optimizing the true positive or false positive objects can attack the detector successfully, and optimizing both of them will achieve better attack performance. Attacks on existing detectors are not comprehensive due to a lack of consideration of false positive objects.

Inspired by the statements above, we reformulate the adversarial attack [26, 37,38] against object detection as a large-scale multi-objective optimization problem (MOP) [7] to decrease true positive objects and increase false positive objects. Our interest focuses on the black-box settings. A large-scale MOP under the black-box setting mainly faces three challenges. Firstly, the conflict between multiple objectives makes it almost impossible to find a solution that optimizes all objectives simultaneously. Secondly, decision variables are extremely large-scaled due to the consistent dimensions of adversarial samples and images (more than two million). Nevertheless, the existing optimization algorithms w.r.t. MOP have poor scalability, and optimizing decision variables with more than one million is especially tough [14]. Thirdly, black-box attacks should reduce queries while increasing the attack rate. To address the above challenges, we use genetic algorithms to find optimal trade-off solutions for MOP, called Pareto-optimal solutions [8]. A genetic algorithm can approximate the entire set of Pareto-optimal in a single run and does not make specific assumptions about the objective functions, such as continuity or differentiability [14]. To settle the poor scalability, we propose a **G**enetic **A**lgorithm based on **R**andom **S**ubset selection and a **D**ivide-and-**C**onquer algorithm to optimize large-scale decision variables, named as GARSDC. This method aims to transform the original search space of MOP using dimensionality reduction and divide-and-conquer, improving the optimization algorithm's searchability by rebalancing exploration and exploitation. The genetic algorithm is sensitive to the population. Thus, we use gradient-based perturbations as the initial population. Moreover, we analyze more than 40 object detection backbones and find out that the perturbation is transferring well in the same backbone. Thus, we generate the chain-based and skip-based perturbations as a mixed initial population with transferability. By combining transfer and query-based attacks, our method substantially decreases the mAP and queries on eight representative detectors than the state-of-the-art method. This paper has the following contributions to the three-fold:

1. We model the adversarial attack problem against object detection as a large-scale multi-objective optimization, which can expand the attack scenarios and help understand the attack mechanism against object detection. Experiments show that this comprehensive modeling helps to decrease the mAP.
2. We design a genetic algorithm based on random subset selection and divide-and-conquer methodology for solving Pareto-optimal solutions, called GARSDC, which improves the searchability of GA by rebalancing the exploration and exploitation of the optimization problem. We generate chain-based and skip-based perturbations as a mixed initial population with gradient-prior, increasing population diversity and improving the algorithm's efficiency.
3. A large number of attack experiments based on different backbone detectors demonstrate the effectiveness and efficiency of GARSDC. Compared with

the state-of-art PRFA algorithm, GARSDC reduces by an average 12.0 in the mAP and queries by about 1000 times.

2   Related Work

2.1   Object Detection Based on Deep Learning

In recent years, the latest progress of object detectors mainly focuses on three aspects: Firstly, the improvement of the backbone network, detectors based on different backbones have produced significant differences in accuracy and inference speed. Standard models include SSD [27] based on VGG16, Centernet [10] based on ResNet18 and YOLOX [12] based on yolo-s network. Most models are based on ResNet [33] and FPN [25] series architecture, e.g., Cascade R-CNN [3], Atss [46], Fcos [36], and Freeanchor [47]. Secondly, combining the learning of instance segmentation, such as segmentation annotation in Mask R-CNN [13] and switchable atrous convolution in Detectors [32]. Thirdly, improvements of localization, such as GFL [22] based on generalized focal loss. Our research finds that detectors that focus on different improvements have significant differences in transfer attacks. In addition, compared with detectors based on different backbones, detectors with the same backbone structure are less challenging to transfer, and this phenomenon brings excellent inspiration to our model selection for transfer attacks.

2.2   Black-Box Adversarial Attack

Generally speaking, black-box adversarial attacks can be divided into transfer attacks, decision-based attacks, and score-based attacks. The transfer attack, also known as the local surrogate model attack, assumes that the attacker has access to part of the training dataset to train the surrogate model, including adaptive black-box attack [28] and data-free surrogate model attack [49]. The score-based attack allows the attacker to query the classifier and get probabilistic of the model prediction. Representative methods include the square attack [1] based on random search and the black box attack based on transfer prior. Decision-based attacks [5] can obtain less information than the above, allowing the attacker to accept label outputs instead of probabilities. By analyzing the architectural characteristics of the object detector, we improve the efficiency and accuracy of score-based attacks according to the gradient-prior.

2.3   Adversarial Attack Against Object Detection

The existing adversarial attack methods for object detection are mainly based on white-box attacks, and the attacker implements the adversarial attack by changing the predicted label of the true positive object. DAG [42], and CAP [45] mainly implement adversarial attacks by fooling the RPN network of two-stage detectors in terms of the types of attack detectors. To increase the generality of the attack algorithm, UEA [40] and TOG [6] exploit transferable adversarial perturbations to attack both the one-stage detector and the two-stage detector simultaneously. PRFA [24] first proposes a query-based black-box attack algorithm to fool existing detectors using a parallel rectangle flipping strategy. This method also provides a baseline for target detection query attacks. Our proposed algorithm not only surpasses the state-of-the-art algorithm PRFA but also attacks more representative detection models, comprehensively evaluating the robustness of existing detectors.

3 Method

3.1 Simulating Adversarial Examples Generating by MOP

We firstly introduce the background of MOP, including problem definition, non-dominant relations, and Pareto solutions. A MOP problem can be mathematically modeled as:

$$\min F(\hat{\boldsymbol{x}}) = (f_1(\hat{\boldsymbol{x}}), ..., f_K(\hat{\boldsymbol{x}})), \hat{\boldsymbol{x}} = (\hat{x}_1, ...\hat{x}_D) \in \Omega, \tag{1}$$

where there are D decision variables with respect to the decision vector $\hat{\boldsymbol{x}}$, the objective function $F : \Omega \rightarrow \mathbf{R}^K$ includes K objective functions, Ω and K represent the decision and objective spaces. Generally speaking, when the $K \geq 2$ and $D \geq 100$, when call this MOP as a large-scale MOP.

Definition 1. Given two feasible solutions $\hat{\boldsymbol{x}}_1$, $\hat{\boldsymbol{x}}_2$ and their objective functions $F(\hat{\boldsymbol{x}}_1)$, $F(\hat{\boldsymbol{x}}_2)$, $\hat{\boldsymbol{x}}_1$ dominates $\hat{\boldsymbol{x}}_2$ (denoted $\hat{\boldsymbol{x}}_1 \prec \hat{\boldsymbol{x}}_2$) if and only if $\forall i \in \{1, ..., K\}, f_i(\hat{\boldsymbol{x}}_1) \leq f_i(\hat{\boldsymbol{x}}_2)$ and $\exists j \in \{1, ..., K\}, f_j(\hat{\boldsymbol{x}}_1) < f_j(\hat{\boldsymbol{x}}_2)$.

Definition 1 describes the dominance relation in the MOP.

Definition 2. A solution $\hat{\boldsymbol{x}}^*$ is Pareto-optimal solution if and only if there exists no $\hat{\boldsymbol{x}}_1 \in \Omega$ such that $F(\hat{\boldsymbol{x}}_1) \prec F(\hat{\boldsymbol{x}}^*)$. We name the set of all Pareto-optimal solutions as the Pareto Set and the corresponding objective vector set as the Pareto front.

Given a large-scale MOP, we describes the Pareto solution in Definition 2. We have a clean image $\boldsymbol{x}$ containing a set of M recognition objects $\mathcal{O}$, that is, $\mathcal{O} = \{o_1, ..., o_M\}$. Each recognition objects o_i is assigned a groud-truth class $o_i^c \in \{1, ..., C\}$, $i \in \{1, ..., M\}$. C is the number of class, the $C = 81$ in the MS-COCO. The object detector H predict N objects as the predicted objects $\mathcal{P} = H(\boldsymbol{x})$ and the corresponding classes $\mathcal{P}^c$ in the clean image $\boldsymbol{x}$. However, limited by training datasets and complex scenes, the objects $\mathcal{P}$ predicted by the detector are not always consistent with the recognized objects $\mathcal{O}$. We define the true positive object as follows: there is a only one object o_i such that the intersection of union between p_j and o_i greater than 0.5 and p_j^c is same with o_i^c, otherwise it is a false positive object [11]. Thus, we decompose the predicted $\mathcal{P}$ objects as true positive objects $\mathcal{TP}$ and false positive objects $\mathcal{FP}$ by recognition

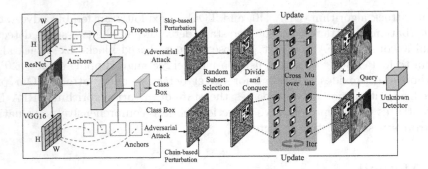

Fig. 2. To optimize multi-objective problems, we propose a **G**enetic **A**lgorithm based on **R**andom **S**ubset selection and a **D**ivide-and-**C**onquer algorithm (GARSDC). The basic flow of the GARSDC attack is shown above, which combines the transfer-based and the query-based attacks against the black-box model.

objects $\mathcal{O}$. The $|\mathcal{P}| = |\mathcal{TP}| + |\mathcal{FP}|$. Previous adversarial examples $\hat{x}$ with a small δ attack the detector by reducing the true positive objects. Figure 1 a) show that attacking the false positive objects alone can also attack the detector. Therefore, we model the adversarial attack as a large-scale MOP: reducing the true positive objects and increasing false positive object. The objective function can be represented as:

$$F(\hat{x}, H(x)) = \min(-f_{tp}(\hat{x}, \mathcal{P}), f_{fp}(\hat{x}, \mathcal{P})), s.t. \ \hat{x} = (x + \delta) \in \Omega, \ ||\hat{x} - x||_n \le \epsilon, \tag{2}$$

where n denotes norm. We solve the problem in the weighting method [44]. The Eq. (2) can be written as:

$$F(\hat{x}, H(x)) = \min(w_1 * (-f_{tp}(\hat{x}, \mathcal{P})) + w_2 * f_{fp}(\hat{x}, \mathcal{P}))$$
$$s.t. \ \hat{x} = (x + \delta) \in \Omega, \ ||\hat{x} - x||_n \le \epsilon, \tag{3}$$

where $w_i \ge 0$. We use the CW loss [4] as attack functions f_{tp} or f_{fp}:

$$f_{\{tp, fp\}}(\hat{x}, \mathcal{P}) = \sum_{i \in \{\mathcal{TP}, \mathcal{FP}\}}^{|\mathcal{P}|} \left(\max_{l \ne c}(f_{\{tp, fp\}}(\hat{x}, p_i)_l) - f_{\{tp, fp\}}(\hat{x}, p_i)_c \right), \tag{4}$$

where $i \in \mathcal{TP}$ represents the i-th predicted box, p_i is the true positive object in the predicted boxes $\mathcal{P}$. In Eq. (3), we aim to make the labels of true positive objects wrong and protect the false positive objects. Thus, we treat f_{tp} and f_{fp} as untargeted and targeted attacks, respectively.

3.2   Generating Adversarial Examples by Genetic Algorithm

Since the genetic algorithm is based on the nature of the population and does not require additional assumptions (continuous or differentiable) for objective functions, the genetic algorithm can gradually approximate the Pareto-optimal solution in the single queries [14]. We choose the genetic algorithm, which only uses the fitness function to evaluate individuals in the population and search the best individual as the adversarial perturbation. We define the initial population Δ^0 containing P individuals as $\Delta^0 = \{\boldsymbol{\delta}_1^0, ..., \boldsymbol{\delta}_p^0\}$ and the p-th individual fitness $P(\boldsymbol{x} + \boldsymbol{\delta}_p) = F(\boldsymbol{x} + \boldsymbol{\delta}_p)$. The population is iterating in the direction of greater individual fitness. Generating the i-th population Δ^i mainly relies on crossover and mutation. The greater the individual fitness, the more likely it is to be saved as the next population. For example, if $P(\boldsymbol{\delta}_1^i) > P(\boldsymbol{\delta}_2^i)$, then the next individual $\boldsymbol{\delta}_2^{i+1}$ will inherit some features (crossover) of $\boldsymbol{\delta}_1^i$ and mutate. In Fig. 2, the transfer attack generate the initial population Δ^0. The iteration stopping condition of population iteration is when reaching the maximum iteration, or the fitness is greater than a certain value. The optimal solution of the population is the individual with the greatest fitness, that is, the adversarial perturbation we need. Since our decision space is too large ($weight*height*channel$ exceeds millions), it is difficult for general genetic algorithms to converge in limited queries. Next, we will introduce the improved genetic algorithm from the gradient-prior initial population, random subset selection, and divide-and-conquer algorithm.

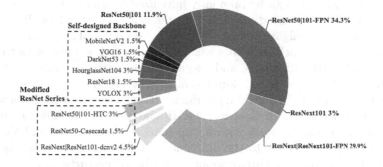

Fig. 3. The investigated results of detectors based on different backbone networks.

3.3   Mixed Initial Population Based on Gradient-prior

An excellent initial population can help the genetic algorithm converge more quickly, so finding a suitable initial population for the black-box detector is critical. Although the QAIR [23] algorithm estimates the gradient of the adversarial perturbation by stealing the image retrieval system, the cost of model stealing for the detector is too high. Because the detectors are diverse and the dataset for object detection relies on enormous annotations. Intuitively, we can generate adversarial perturbations with well transferability as an initial population against the detector.

Inspired by that transferable perturbation in image classification can attack different feature networks, we analyze more than 40 deep model-based object detectors and classify their backbone network types. In Fig. 3, detectors based on backbone networks belong to ResNet, ResNet-FPN [25], and their derivatives, e.g., ResNeXt [43], account for more than 80%. We call these backbone networks the ResNet series. The other two types of backbone networks are based on the modified ResNet series, e.g., Detectors [32], or self-designed networks, such as YOLOX [12] based on yolo-s. Therefore, we can roughly divide the current network architecture into three categories and attack against the ResNet series, the modified ResNet series, and self-designed networks. Although detection models vary widely in network structures, both of them use the cross-entropy loss of the prediction boxes. We can implement an adversarial attack by maximizing the cross-entropy loss of all prediction boxes, and the objective function is as follows:

$$D(\boldsymbol{x} + \boldsymbol{\delta}) = \sum_{i=1}^{|\mathcal{P}|} \sum_{j=1}^{|C|} y_{ij} * \log(\boldsymbol{c}_{ij}) \tag{5}$$

where y_{ij} is one when detector H classify the i-th prediction box into the j-th category, otherwise y_{ij} is zero. $\boldsymbol{c}$ represents the classification probability of the i-th prediction box. We can attack the Eq. (5) using an off-the-shelf transfer attack algorithm, such as TI-FGSM [9].

Although the input can be randomly initialized by adding noise to the clean image, adversarial perturbations based on the same detector lack diversity. To accelerate the genetic algorithm convergence, the diversity of individuals is essential. Therefore, we attack detectors with different backbone networks to generate individuals with differences, and we call this population composed of sexual individuals as the mixed initial population based on gradient-prior. Specifically, we respectively select the initial individuals attacked by the VGG16-based and ResNet-based detectors. In essence, VGG16 and ResNet are different because ResNet is a backbone network with a skip-connection structure, and VGG16 is a chain structure. We refer to the different individuals generated by these two networks as skip-based perturbation and chain-based perturbation.

3.4   Random Subset Selection

The variable space($weight*height*channel$) of the perturbation exceeds millions, and the intuitive idea for solving the large-scale MOP is to decompose high-dimensional decision variables into many low-dimensional sub-components and assign MOP to sub-components through specific strategies, which solves the MOP indirectly by optimizing a portion of the MOP. We will introduce the random subset selection for sub-components and the corresponding MOP decomposition strategy.

Since there are many decision variable combinations for sub-component selection, it is unrealistic to traverse all combinations in a limited number of queries. We use a random subset selection algorithm to sample sub-component in the decision space. We use the index vector $\boldsymbol{s} \in \{0,1\}^D$ for random subset selection. If $s_i = 1$ the i-th element of δ is selected and $s_i = 0$ otherwise. Square attack [1] achieves good black-box attack performance by generating square-shaped adversarial patches through random search in the image. It is feasible to select adversarial patches randomly to attack the detector. This process can be regarded as sampling the sub-component $\delta[s]$ in the decision space δ.

In Sect. 3.2, we introduce the individual fitness. However, the computation of individual fitness is for the overall adversarial perturbation δ rather than the sub-component $\delta[s]$. We can easily computer the coordinates s^B of sub-component $\delta[s]$ by using s, then we assign the predicted boxes $\mathcal{P}$ to the sub-component and calculate the fintess:

$$
f_{\{tp,fp\}}(\hat{x}, \mathcal{P}, s^B) = \sum_{i \in \{\mathcal{TP}, \mathcal{FP}\}}^{|\mathcal{P}|} (\max_{l \neq c}(f_{\{tp,fp\}}(\hat{x}, p_i)_l) - f_{\{tp,fp\}}(\hat{x}, p_i)_c) * IoU(p_i, s^B),
$$
(6)

where $IoU(a, b)$ denotes intersection over Union between a and b. The sub-component fitness $S(\delta[s])$ defines as follows:

$$
\begin{aligned}
S(\delta[s]) &= S(x + \delta, H(x), s^B) = S(\hat{x}, H(x), s^B) \\
&= \min(-f_{tp}(\hat{x}, \mathcal{P}, s^B), f_{fp}(\hat{x}, \mathcal{P}, s^B)).
\end{aligned}
$$
(7)

We can judge the relationship between the current sub-component and the predicted boxes by calculating the fitness of individual and sub-component. If there is no connection, we discard the current sub-component. Although PRFA has a similar operation that randomly searches for sub-components in the search space, our method has the following innovations: Firstly, we do not need a priori-guided dimension reduction but instead search the image globally, which can circumvent the risk of that the prior is terrible; secondly, we can use the window fitness to help judge whether the sub-components of random search are helpful for optimization.

3.5   Divide-and-Conquer Algorithm

Although the decision variables are greatly reduced by randomly selecting the sub-component $\delta[s]$, we can still use the divide-and-conquer method for the sub-component $\delta[s]$ to improve the optimization. In Fig. 2, we show the divide-and-conquer process of sub-component $\delta[s]$. Suppose we decompose the index vector s into i parts, that is $s = \{s_1, ..., s_i\}$. We can perform the genetic algorithm in the i-th part of the index vector s_i to find a subset u_i with a budget z. Assuming that we have two individuals δ_1 and δ_2, we can calculate the fitness of sub-components $S(\delta_1[s_i])$ and $S(\delta_2[s_i])$, respectively. If $S(\delta_1[s_i]) > S(\delta_2[s_i])$, the $\delta_2[s_i]$ gets the feature from $\delta_1[s_i]$(cross over) and mutates. The $\delta_2[s_i]$ updates and gets the new subset u_i from s_i. Merge all new subsets into a set $U = \cup_{j=1}^{i} u_i$. And we find the u_{i+1} in the set U. Then, we return the best individual fitness and the corresponding sub-component $\delta[u_{best}]$.

We will analyze the approximation of the divide-and-conquer algorithm in Lemma 1. For $1 \leq j \leq i$, let $b_j \in \arg\max_{u \subseteq s_j : |u| \leq z} P(\delta[u])$ denotes an optimal subset of s_i.

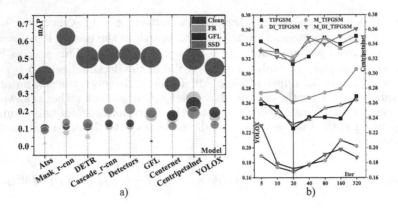

Fig. 4. *a*) We evaluate the performance of transfer attacks generated by three backbone networks on nine models, with the vertical axis representing mAP and the circle radius representing recall. *b*) We verify the effect of different attack algorithms and iterations on the YOLOX and Centripetalnet.

Lemma 1. *[29] For any partition of* **s**, *it holds that*

$$\max\{P(\boldsymbol{\delta}[\boldsymbol{b}_j])|1 \le j \le i\} \ge \{\alpha/i, \gamma_{\emptyset,z}/z\} * OPT, \tag{8}$$

where the γ*- and* α *are submodularity ratios [30]. The OPT denote the value of the objective function in Eq. (3) For any subset* $\boldsymbol{u} \subseteq \boldsymbol{s}_j$, *there exists another item, the inclusion of which can improve the individual fitness by at least a proportional to the current distance the best solution [31]. Then, we can get the approximation performance of divide-and-conquer method for random subset selection with monotone objective functions. For random subset selection with a monotone objective function* P, *our algorithm using* $\mathbb{E}[\max\{T_j|1 \le j \le i\}] = O(z^2|\boldsymbol{s}|(1 + \log i))$ *finds a subset* $\boldsymbol{u}$ *with* $\boldsymbol{u} \le z$ *and*

$$P(\boldsymbol{\delta}[\boldsymbol{u}]) \ge (1 - e^{-\gamma_{\min}}) * \max\{\alpha/i, \gamma_{\emptyset,z}/z\} * OPT, \tag{9}$$

where $\gamma_{\min} = \min_{\boldsymbol{u} \subseteq \boldsymbol{s}_j:|\boldsymbol{u}|=z-1} \gamma_{\boldsymbol{u},z}.$

The above is the complete GARSDC algorithm. Due to the limitation of the paper space, we put the proofs of Eq. (8) and Eq. (9) and the algorithm flow of GARSDC in the supplementary materials.

4   Experiments

4.1   Experiment Settings

Dataset and Evaluation. The current object detectors use the MS-COCO dataset as a benchmark for evaluating performance. For a fair comparison with PRFA, we adopt the same experimental setup as PRFA and use a part of the

MS-COCO validation set as the attack image. We use the evaluation matrix (mAP) to evaluate the detection results of the detector on adversarial examples. The lower the mean average precision, the better the attack effect. We evaluate the efficiency of the algorithm using average queries. Under the limit of 4,000 queries per image, the lower the queries, the higher the attack efficiency.

Victim Models. Section 3.2 divides the investigated object detection models into three categories. We selected two black-box models from the modified ResNet series and the self-designed backbone, GFL, Detectors, YOLOX, and Centernet. Among the object models based on the ResNet series backbone, we choose Atss, Casecade R-CNN, Free anchor and Fcos as the black-box attack model. To verify the generation of transferable perturbations, we use Faster R-CNN, GFL and SSD as the white-box attack model and add the transformer-based object detector DETR as the black-box attack model.

Table 1. An ablation study for GARSDC.

Method	GFL [22]					YOLOX [12]				
	mAP	mAP_S	mAP_M	mAP_L	AQ	mAP	mAP_S	mAP_M	mAP_L	AQ
Clean	0.59	0.36	0.62	0.79	N/A	0.52	0.27	0.55	0.76	N/A
PRFA	0.31	0.17	0.31	0.45	3571	0.31	0.15	0.34	0.51	3220
$PRFA_{TP+FP}$	0.27	0.16	0.27	0.45	3604	0.28	0.11	0.32	0.48	3109
$PRFA_{TA}$	0.21	0.07	0.20	0.33	3359	0.31	0.14	0.33	0.50	3175
GA_{TA}	0.25	0.07	0.24	0.44	3401	0.42	0.17	0.46	0.63	3600
$GARS_{TA}$	0.20	0.09	0.20	0.32	3133	0.29	0.12	0.32	0.48	3201
$GARSDC_{TA}$	0.18	0.08	0.21	0.32	3037	0.31	0.14	0.34	0.50	3170
$GARSDC_{MixTA}$	**0.16**	**0.05**	**0.16**	**0.28**	**1838**	**0.23**	**0.10**	**0.28**	**0.42**	**2691**

Experimental Parameters. The w_1 and w_2 are 0.5 in Eq. (3). For the selection of random subsets, we use a random search strategy similar to Square attack, sample patches with a size of 0.05 times the original image size in the *weight * height * channel* subspace as the initial random subset, and initial perturbation of the patch. The sampling size is reduced by half when the queries are [20, 100, 400, 1000, 2000]. In the divide-and-conquer phase, we divide the random subset into four parts and the $i = 2$. The population size is set to 2, and the adversarial perturbations respectively generated by Faster R-CNN and SSD iterations 20 times. We set the crossover and mutation rates to 0.8 and 0.3. The norm n is infinity and the budget is 0.05.

4.2 Transferable Perturbation Generation

Firstly, we verify the transferability of generative adversarial perturbations on different detectors. We chose three detectors for the white-box attack: Faster R-CNN (FR) based on ResNet50-FPN, GFL based on modified ResNet series, and SSD based on VGG16. In Fig. 4 a), we respectively show the effect of the transfer attack on nine models. The circle's radius represents the mean recall, and the height represents mAP. We have two observations: Firstly, perturbations generated on detectors of the same type perform well. Secondly, adversarial perturbations generated by detectors based on the ResNet can attack most detectors.

In Fig. 5b), we show the attack effect on Centripalnet(the red axis) and YOLOX(the black axis) of the adversarial perturbations generated by attacking the Faster R-CNN model with different transfer attack methods and different iterations. The M-TIFGSM has the best attack effect. In terms of iterations, the transfer attack has the best effect when about 20 times. As the number of iterations increases, the attack algorithm will gradually overfit. Therefore, we choose M-TIFGSM and iterate 20 times to generate the initial perturbation.

Table 2. Untargeted attacks against detectors based on different backbones.

Method	Atss [46]					Fcos [36]				
	mAP	mAP_S	mAP_M	mAP_L	AQ	mAP	mAP_S	mAP_M	mAP_L	AQ
Clean	0.54	0.32	0.58	0.74	N/A	0.54	0.33	0.56	0.74	N/A
SH	0.40	0.20	0.40	0.59	3852	0.27	0.09	0.37	0.64	3633
SQ	0.23	0.13	0.28	0.31	3505	0.21	0.14	0.20	0.37	3578
PRFA	0.20	0.12	0.25	0.30	3500	0.23	0.15	0.29	0.41	3395
GARSDC	**0.04**	**0.02**	**0.05**	**0.11**	**1837**	**0.15**	**0.09**	**0.17**	**0.28**	**3106**
Method	GFL [22]					Centernet [10]				
	mAP	mAP_S	mAP_M	mAP_L	AQ	mAP	mAP_S	mAP_M	mAP_L	AQ
Clean	0.59	0.36	0.62	0.79	N/A	0.44	0.14	0.45	0.71	N/A
SH	0.43	0.22	0.42	0.59	3904	0.35	0.08	0.33	0.56	3882
SQ	0.33	0.17	0.31	0.50	3751	0.25	0.06	0.27	0.44	3591
PRFA	0.31	0.17	0.31	0.45	3570	0.25	0.07	0.23	0.46	3697
GARSDC	**0.16**	**0.05**	**0.16**	**0.28**	**1838**	**0.12**	**0.03**	**0.13**	**0.23**	**2817**
Method	YOLOX [12]					Detectors [32]				
	mAP	mAP_S	mAP_M	mAP_L	AQ	mAP	mAP_S	mAP_M	mAP_L	AQ
Clean	0.52	0.27	0.56	0.76	N/A	0.61	0.39	0.66	0.82	N/A
SH	0.37	0.15	0.43	0.66	3651	0.51	0.27	0.48	0.72	4000
SQ	0.32	0.17	0.37	0.44	3502	0.45	0.23	0.45	0.62	3957
PRFA	0.31	0.15	0.34	0.51	3220	0.41	0.24	0.43	0.58	3925
GARSDC	**0.23**	**0.10**	**0.28**	**0.42**	**2691**	**0.28**	**0.09**	**0.27**	**0.49**	**2938**

4.3   Ablation Study

To verify the effectiveness of each component of the proposed algorithm, we perform an ablation study on GFL and YOLOX models. PRFA$_{TP+FP}$ represents replacing the optimization objective of PRFA with 'TP+FP'. The subscript TA indicates that using the skip-based perturbation as the initial perturbation. GA stands for genetic algorithm for the entire image. GARS stands for Genetic

Algorithm with random subset selection. GARSDC stands for Genetic Algorithm based on random subset selection and divide-and-conquer. $MixTA$ represents using the skip-based perturbation and chain-based perturbation as the mixed-init populations.

In Table 1, replacing the objective attack function improves the attack effect by 3 points. Replacing the initialization method of PRFA, the improvement of the attack effect is most apparent, which means that our proposed gradient-prior perturbation is better than the previous. The effect of the GA algorithm is not good because the entire image dimension space is too ample for the genetic algorithm, and it is not easy to optimize. After adding random subset selection and divide-and-conquer, the attack performance of the algorithm has been significantly improved (mAP decreased by 7 points in total). After adding the mixed perturbations mechanism, the difference between populations is more significant than that generated by a single model. Consequently, the queries for genetic algorithms are significantly reduced.

4.4   Attacks Against Detector Based on Different Backbones

In this section, we compare the attack performance of GARSDC and state-of-the-art black-box algorithms on multiple object detectors. In Table 2, we respectively select two object detectors based on three different backbones, which are ATSS based on ResNet101 structure, Fcos based on ResNeXt101 structure, GFL based on ResNeXt101 with deformable convolution, YOLOX based on yolo-s, Centernet based on ResNet18, and Detectors based on RFP and switchable atrous convolution. It is not difficult to see from the experiments that our method reduces by an average 12.0 in the mAP and 980 queries compared with the state-of-the-art algorithm PRFA. The improvement of Atss is the largest, and the attack mAP is 0.04, which may be that our generated skip-based initial perturbation works best to transfer attack against Atss. In addition, our attack effect on Atss, GFL, and Centernet has been improved by more than a half compared with PRFA.

Comparing the size of attack targets, we find that the improvement of our algorithm is mainly focused on small and medium-sized objects. The size of these targets is usually under 64∗64, which is in line with our expectations because the divide-and-conquer method decomposes the random search into smaller search areas, so the attack ability on small and medium objects will be improved. At the same time, the attack of large objects is still difficulty. Comparing the six detectors, Detectors has the most challenging attack (the mAP after the attack is still 0.28), which we think may be related to its structure(switchable atrous convolution), which may inspire us to design a robust architecture for object detection.

4.5   Visual Analysis

This section visualizes the attack results of the square attack, PRFA, and GARSDC. We show the detection results of the three attacks in Fig. 5 a) and the optimization process in Fig. 5 b). During the attack process, we find that GARSDC optimization generates many negative samples and can jump out of local optima during the perturbation iteration process. Both Square attack and PRFA are more likely to fall into local optimal solutions. In Fig. 5 c), we show the detection and segmentation results produced by the three attack methods. We generate multiple small objects and attack pixel classes in a clustered state, which means that the adversarial perturbations we generate can attack the detection and segmentation models.

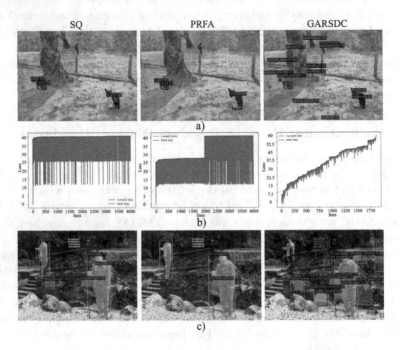

Fig. 5. The SQ [1], PRFA [24], and GARSDC respectively represent the two state-of-art attack methods and our proposed method. We show detection results after attacks in **a)**, the optimization process of three methods in **b)** and segmentation results after attacks in **c)**.

5   Conclusion

In this paper, we model the adversarial attack against object detection as a large-scale multi-objective optimization problem. Unlike the traditional attack method that reduces true positive objects, we minimize the true positive rate and maximize the false positive rate in the attack process to jointly increase the mAP and queries. We propose an efficient genetic algorithm based on random subset selection and divide-and-conquer, optimizing the Pareto-optimal solutions and conquering the challenge of the large-scale decision variables. We generate skip-based and chain-based perturbation by investigating and analyzing more than 40 detection model structures to tackle the problem that the genetic algorithm is sensitive to the population. This gradient-prior population initialization can improve the optimization efficiency of GARSDC. Many attack experiments based on different backbone detectors demonstrate the effectiveness and efficiency of GARSDC. Compared with the state-of-art PRFA algorithm, GARSDC decreases by an average 12.0 in the mAP and queries by nearly 1000 times.

Acknowledgments. Supported by the National Key R&D Program of China under Grant 2020YFB1406704, National Natural Science Foundation of China (No. 62025604), Open Project Program of State Key Laboratory of Virtual Reality Technology and Systems, Beihang University (No. VRLAB2021C06). Baoyuan Wu is supported by the National Natural Science Foundation of China under grant No.62076213, Shenzhen Science and Technology Program under grants No. RCYX20210609103057050 and No. ZDSYS20211021111415025, and Sponsored by CCF-Tencent Open Fund.

References

1. Andriushchenko, M., Croce, F., Flammarion, N., Hein, M.: Square attack: a query-efficient black-box adversarial attack via random search. In: Vedaldi, A., Bischof, H., Brox, T., Frahm, J.-M. (eds.) ECCV 2020. LNCS, vol. 12368, pp. 484–501. Springer, Cham (2020). https://doi.org/10.1007/978-3-030-58592-1_29
2. Bai, J., Chen, B., Li, Y., Wu, D., Guo, W., Xia, S.-T., Yang, E.-H.: Targeted attack for deep hashing based retrieval. In: Vedaldi, A., Bischof, H., Brox, T., Frahm, J.-M. (eds.) ECCV 2020. LNCS, vol. 12346, pp. 618–634. Springer, Cham (2020). https://doi.org/10.1007/978-3-030-58452-8_36
3. Cai, Z., Vasconcelos, N.: Cascade R-CNN: delving into high quality object detection. In: Proceedings of the IEEE Conference on Computer Vision and Pattern Recognition, pp. 6154–6162 (2018)
4. Carlini, N., Wagner, D.: Adversarial examples are not easily detected: bypassing ten detection methods. In: Proceedings of the 10th ACM workshop on artificial intelligence and security, pp. 3–14 (2017)
5. Chen, J., Jordan, M.I., Wainwright, M.J.: HopSkipJumpAttack: a query-efficient decision-based attack. In: 2020 IEEE Symposium on Security and Privacy (SP), pp. 1277–1294 (2020)
6. Chow, K.H., et al.: Adversarial objectness gradient attacks in real-time object detection systems. In: 2020 Second IEEE International Conference on Trust, Privacy and Security in Intelligent Systems and Applications (TPS-ISA), pp. 263–272 (2020)
7. Deb, K.: Multi-objective optimization. In: Search methodologies, pp. 403–449. Springer (2014). https://doi.org/10.1007/978-1-4614-6940-7_15
8. Deb, K., Gupta, H.: Searching for robust pareto-optimal solutions in multi-objective optimization. In: Coello Coello, C.A., Hernández Aguirre, A., Zitzler, E. (eds.) EMO 2005. LNCS, vol. 3410, pp. 150–164. Springer, Heidelberg (2005). https://doi.org/10.1007/978-3-540-31880-4_11
9. Dong, Y., Pang, T., Su, H., Zhu, J.: Evading defenses to transferable adversarial examples by translation-invariant attacks. In: Proceedings of the IEEE/CVF Conference on Computer Vision and Pattern Recognition, pp. 4312–4321 (2019)

10. Duan, K., Bai, S., Xie, L., Qi, H., Huang, Q., Tian, Q.: Centernet: keypoint triplets for object detection. In: Proceedings of the IEEE/CVF international conference on computer vision, pp. 6569–6578 (2019)

11. Everingham, M., et al.: The pascal visual object classes challenge 2007 (voc2007) results (2008)

12. Ge, Z., Liu, S., Wang, F., Li, Z., Sun, J.: YOLOX: exceeding yolo series in 2021. arXiv preprint arXiv:2107.08430 (2021)

13. He, K., Gkioxari, G., Dollár, P., Girshick, R.: Mask R-CNN. In: Proceedings of the IEEE International Conference on Computer Vision, pp. 2961–2969 (2017)

14. Hong, W.J., Yang, P., Tang, K.: Evolutionary computation for large-scale multi-objective optimization: a decade of progresses. Int. J. Autom. Comput. **18**(2), 155–169 (2021)

15. Hu, Y., Yang, A., Li, H., Sun, Y., Sun, L.: A survey of intrusion detection on industrial control systems. Int. J. Distrib. Sens. Netw. **14**(8), 1550147718794615 (2018)

16. Jafri, R., Arabnia, H.R.: A survey of face recognition techniques. J. Inf. Process. Syst. **5**(2), 41–68 (2009)

17. Jia, X., Zhang, Y., Wu, B., Ma, K., Wang, J., Cao, X.: LAS-AT: adversarial training with learnable attack strategy. In: Proceedings of the IEEE/CVF Conference on Computer Vision and Pattern Recognition, pp. 13398–13408 (2022)

18. Jia, X., Zhang, Y., Wu, B., Wang, J., Cao, X.: Boosting fast adversarial training with learnable adversarial initialization. IEEE Trans. Image Process. **31**, 4417–4430 (2022). https://doi.org/10.1109/TIP.2022.3184255

19. Joseph, K., Khan, S., Khan, F.S., Balasubramanian, V.N.: Towards open world object detection. In: Proceedings of the IEEE/CVF Conference on Computer Vision and Pattern Recognition, pp. 5830–5840 (2021)

20. Kong, T., Sun, F., Liu, H., Jiang, Y., Li, L., Shi, J.: Foveabox: Beyound anchor-based object detection. IEEE Trans. Image Process. **29**, 7389–7398 (2020)

21. Levinson, J., et al.: Towards fully autonomous driving: systems and algorithms. In: 2011 IEEE Intelligent Vehicles Symposium (IV), pp. 163–168 (2011)

22. Li, X., et al.: Generalized focal loss: learning qualified and distributed bounding boxes for dense object detection. Adv. Neural. Inf. Process. Syst. **33**, 21002–21012 (2020)

23. Li, X., et al.: Qair: Practical query-efficient black-box attacks for image retrieval. In: Proceedings of the IEEE/CVF Conference on Computer Vision and Pattern Recognition, pp. 3330–3339 (2021)

24. Liang, S., Wu, B., Fan, Y., Wei, X., Cao, X.: Parallel rectangle flip attack: a query-based black-box attack against object detection. arXiv preprint arXiv:2201.08970 (2022)

25. Lin, T.Y., Dollár, P., Girshick, R., He, K., Hariharan, B., Belongie, S.: Feature pyramid networks for object detection. In: Proceedings of the IEEE Conference on Computer Vision and Pattern Recognition, pp. 2117–2125 (2017)

26. Liu, A., Wang, J., Liu, X., Cao, B., Zhang, C., Yu, H.: Bias-based universal adversarial patch attack for automatic check-out. In: Vedaldi, A., Bischof, H., Brox, T., Frahm, J.-M. (eds.) ECCV 2020. LNCS, vol. 12358, pp. 395–410. Springer, Cham (2020). https://doi.org/10.1007/978-3-030-58601-0_24

27. Liu, W., Anguelov, D., Erhan, D., Szegedy, C., Reed, S., Fu, C.-Y., Berg, A.C.: SSD: single shot multibox detector. In: Leibe, B., Matas, J., Sebe, N., Welling, M. (eds.) ECCV 2016. LNCS, vol. 9905, pp. 21–37. Springer, Cham (2016). https://doi.org/10.1007/978-3-319-46448-0_2

28. Papernot, N., McDaniel, P., Goodfellow, I., Jha, S., Celik, Z.B., Swami, A.: Practical black-box attacks against machine learning. In: Proceedings of the 2017 ACM on Asia Conference on Computer and Communications Security, pp. 506–519 (2017)

29. Qian, C., Li, G., Feng, C., Tang, K.: Distributed pareto optimization for subset selection. In: IJCAI, pp. 1492–1498 (2018)

30. Qian, C., Shi, J.C., Yu, Y., Tang, K.: On subset selection with general cost constraints. In: IJCAI, vol. 17, pp. 2613–2619 (2017)

31. Qian, C., Shi, J.C., Yu, Y., Tang, K., Zhou, Z.H.: Parallel pareto optimization for subset selection. In: IJCAI, pp. 1939–1945 (2016)

32. Qiao, S., Chen, L.C., Yuille, A.: Detectors: detecting objects with recursive feature pyramid and switchable atrous convolution. In: Proceedings of the IEEE/CVF Conference on Computer Vision and Pattern Recognition, pp. 10213–10224 (2021)

33. Ren, S., He, K., Girshick, R., Sun, J.: Faster R-CNN: towards real-time object detection with region proposal networks. In: Advances in Neural Information Processing Systems 28 (2015)

34. Shim, I., et al.: An autonomous driving system for unknown environments using a unified map. IEEE Trans. Intell. Transport. Syst. **16**(4), 1999–2013 (2015)

35. Tan, M., Pang, R., Le, Q.V.: EfficientDet: scalable and efficient object detection. In: Proceedings of the IEEE/CVF Conference on Computer Vision and Pattern Recognition, pp. 10781–10790 (2020)

36. Tian, Z., Shen, C., Chen, H., He, T.: FCOS: fully convolutional one-stage object detection. In: Proceedings of the IEEE/CVF International Conference on Computer Vision, pp. 9627–9636 (2019)

37. Wang, J., Liu, A., Bai, X., Liu, X.: Universal adversarial patch attack for automatic checkout using perceptual and attentional bias. IEEE Trans. Image Process. **31**, 598–611 (2021)

38. Wang, J., Liu, A., Yin, Z., Liu, S., Tang, S., Liu, X.: Dual attention suppression attack: generate adversarial camouflage in physical world. In: Proceedings of the IEEE/CVF Conference on Computer Vision and Pattern Recognition, pp. 8565–8574 (2021)

39. Wang, X., He, K.: Enhancing the transferability of adversarial attacks through variance tuning. In: Proceedings of the IEEE Conference on Computer Vision and Pattern Recognition (2021)

40. Wei, X., Liang, S., Chen, N., Cao, X.: Transferable adversarial attacks for image and video object detection. arXiv preprint arXiv:1811.12641 (2018)

41. Wu, B., Chen, J., Cai, D., He, X., Gu, Q.: Do wider neural networks really help adversarial robustness? arXiv e-prints pp. arXiv-2010 (2020)

42. Xie, C., Wang, J., Zhang, Z., Zhou, Y., Xie, L., Yuille, A.: Adversarial examples for semantic segmentation and object detection. In: Proceedings of the IEEE International Conference on Computer Vision, pp. 1369–1378 (2017)

43. Xie, S., Girshick, R., Dollár, P., Tu, Z., He, K.: Aggregated residual transformations for deep neural networks. In: Proceedings of the IEEE Conference on Computer Vision and Pattern Recognition, pp. 1492–1500 (2017)

44. Zadeh, L.: Optimality and non-scalar-valued performance criteria. IEEE Trans. Automatic Control **8**(1), 59–60 (1963)

45. Zhang, H., Zhou, W., Li, H.: Contextual adversarial attacks for object detection. In: 2020 IEEE International Conference on Multimedia and Expo (ICME), pp. 1–6 (2020)

46. Zhang, S., Chi, C., Yao, Y., Lei, Z., Li, S.Z.: Bridging the gap between anchor-based and anchor-free detection via adaptive training sample selection. In: Proceedings

of the IEEE/CVF Conference on Computer Vision and Pattern Recognition, pp. 9759–9768 (2020)

47. Zhang, X., Wan, F., Liu, C., Ji, R., Ye, Q.: FreeAnchor: learning to match anchors for visual object detection. In: Advances in Neural Information Processing Systems 32 (2019)

48. Zhao, Z.Q., Zheng, P., Xu, S.T., Wu, X.: Object detection with deep learning: a review. IEEE Trans. Neural Netw. Learn. Syst. **30**(11), 3212–3232 (2019)

49. Zhou, M., Wu, J., Liu, Y., Liu, S., Zhu, C.: DaST: Data-free substitute training for adversarial attacks. In: Proceedings of the IEEE/CVF Conference on Computer Vision and Pattern Recognition, pp. 234–243 (2020)

GradAuto: Energy-Oriented Attack on Dynamic Neural Networks

Jianhong Pan[1], Qichen Zheng[1], Zhipeng Fan[2], Hossein Rahmani[3], Qiuhong Ke[4], and Jun Liu[1(✉)]

[1] Information Systems Technology and Design, Singapore University of Technology and Design, Singapore, Singapore
{jianhong_pan,qichen_zheng,jun_liu}@sutd.edu.sg
[2] Tandon School of Engineering, New York University, Brooklyn, NY, USA
zf606@nyu.edu
[3] School of Computing and Communications, Lancaster University, Lancaster, UK
h.rahmani@lancaster.ac.uk
[4] Department of Data Science & AI, Monash University, Melbourne, Australia
qiuhong.ke@monash.edu

Abstract. Dynamic neural networks could adapt their structures or parameters based on different inputs. By reducing the computation redundancy for certain samples, it can greatly improve the computational efficiency without compromising the accuracy. In this paper, we investigate the robustness of dynamic neural networks against energy-oriented attacks. We present a novel algorithm, named GradAuto, to attack both dynamic depth and dynamic width models, where dynamic depth networks reduce redundant computation by skipping some intermediate layers while dynamic width networks adaptively activate a subset of neurons in each layer. Our GradAuto carefully adjusts the direction and the magnitude of the gradients to efficiently find an almost imperceptible perturbation for each input, which will activate more computation units during inference. In this way, GradAuto effectively boosts the computational cost of models with dynamic architectures. Compared to previous energy-oriented attack techniques, GradAuto obtains the state-of-the-art result and recovers 100% dynamic network reduced FLOPs on average for both dynamic depth and dynamic width models. Furthermore, we demonstrate that GradAuto offers us great control over the attacking process and could serve as one of the keys to unlock the potential of the energy-oriented attack. Please visit https://github.com/JianhongPan/GradAuto for code.

1 Introduction

Deep neural networks(DNNs) have made great progress in a large variety of computer vision tasks such as image classification [12,22,26,36,37], segmentation [1,8,21,38,39] and object detection [5,16,21,33,35]. However, with the advance

---

J. Pan and Q. Zheng— Both authors contributed equally to this research.

© The Author(s), under exclusive license to Springer Nature Switzerland AG 2022
S. Avidan et al. (Eds.): ECCV 2022, LNCS 13664, pp. 637–653, 2022.
https://doi.org/10.1007/978-3-031-19772-7_37

of the research on neural architectures as well as the developments in hardware, DNNs have become deeper and deeper with millions or even billions of parameters nowadays, especially after the introduction of the Transformer [43]. The computation heavy models pose great threats to the deployment to embedded and mobile devices and motivate more researches on developing more efficient models [9,10] to accelerate the training/inference.

Dynamic Neural Network [19] renders one potential path towards acceleration in inference stage by adaptively executing a subset of layers/neurons conditioned on the properties of the input sample. Typically, gating mechanism is introduced into dynamically neural networks to adaptively determine if their corresponding layers/neurons should be executed based on the input. By skipping the redundant computations within the models on the fly, dynamic neural networks provide a better trade-off between the accuracy and the efficiency. Moreover, the adaptive mechanism enlarges the parameter space and unlocks more representation power with better interpretability [19].

Despite the fast developments in dynamic neural networks architecture and training techniques, the robustness of dynamic neural network to adversarial examples have only attracted attention [20] recently. Studying the adversarial attacks on the dynamic neural network provides an alternative view over the robustness on the efficiency of the model. As shown in ILFO [20], although dynamic neural networks offer notable advantages on accuracy, computational efficiency, and adaptiveness, these networks are highly vulnerable to energy-oriented attacks, i.e. adversarial attacks aimed at boosting the energy consumption and computation complexity.

By adding a well-designed perturbation on the input, the adversarial examples can easily activate more gates controlling the execution of the modules, therefore incuring more computations and drastically reducing the FLOPs (floating-point operations per second) saved by the state-of-the-art dynamic networks. For example, with the adversarial attack technique proposed in ILFO [20], the computation overhead of the state-of-the-art SkipNet [45] recovered by more than 84% and 81% on CIFAR-10 and ImageNet, respectively. ILFO [20] establishes a good baseline for energy-oriented adversarial attacks on dynamic depth neural networks. Nevertheless, ILFO is not evaluated on dynamic width networks. In our experiments, we adapt ILFO to attack dynamic width networks.

Furthermore, we identify two more key pitfalls of the existing energy-oriented attacks towards dynamic neural networks like ILFO, as shown in Sect. 4.1 and Sec. 4.2. First, the drastic difference between the magnitude of the gradients across the gates could potentially lead to some gates dominate the others during the training process. This imbalance between the gradient magnitude across different gates will impede the training and convergence of the model. Second, the gradients of different gates will not always in harmony. Gradients computed from inactivated gates could potentially disagree with the one that computed from activated gates, which will deactivate the already activated gates after a few updates.

To mitigate such issues at their root, we propose the GradAuto, a unified method for energy-oriented attacks on both dynamic depth and width networks. Specifically, we directly modify the gradient magnitudes to meet Lipschitz continuity, which will provide convergence guarantee during the training phase. To address the second pitfall, we make the gradient direction of the deactivated gate orthogonal to the gradient direction of the activated gates in every update step, which mitigates the influence of the gates that have already been optimized.

In summary, we propose GradAuto to perform effective energy-oriented attacks against the dynamic neural networks. The contribution of our work is three folds: (1) We provide a unified formulation to construct adversarial samples to attack both the dynamic depth and width networks. (2) To address the drastic magnitude differences among gradients as well as the disagreement in gradients for activated/inactivated gates, we propose GradAuto to rectify both of them. (3) We demonstrate the efficacy of our algorithm on multiple dynamic neural network structures as well as various datasets. Our GradAuto bumps up more computations with less perceptable perturbations.

2 Related Work

2.1 Dynamic Neural Networks

Dynamic neural network [31,44,45,48] addresses the trade-off between the accuracy and the efficiency of deep neural networks by adaptively adjusting model architectures to allocate appropriate computation conditioned on each instance. As a result, the redundant computations on those "easy" samples are reduced and the inference efficiency is improved [19]. Below we briefly review the dynamic depth networks and dynamic width networks. A more comprehensive review of dynamic neural networks can also be referred to [19].

Dynamic depth networks achieve efficient inference in two ways, early termination and conditional skipping. The early-termination based models could optionally finish the inference early from shallower layers, when high confidences on the predictions have been achieved. The conditional-skipping based models skip the execution of a few intermediate layers/blocks, while the prediction is always obtained at the end of the model. Adaptive Computation Time (ACT) [17] augments an RNN with a scalar named halting score to save computational cost. Figurnov et al. [14] further extended this idea to ResNet for vision task by applying ACT to each groups of residual blocks. SkipNet [45] attempts to skip convolutional blocks using an RL-based gating network.

Dynamic width networks selectively activate multiple components of the same layer, such as channels and neurons based on each instance. Early studies [3, 4,11] achieve dynamic width by adaptively controlling the activation of neurons. The MoE [13,27] structure builds multiple "experts" (which can be complete models or network modules) in a parallel structure, and dynamically weights the output of these "experts" to get the final prediction. Dynamic channel pruning in CNNs [25,32,34,46,47] adaptively activates different convolution channels based on different instances, thereby achieving computational efficiency improvements while maintaining model capacity.

In this paper, we propose a unified algorithm to generate adversarial samples to perform energy-oriented attacks. We showcase the efficacy of our algorithm on both the dynamic depth network (SkipNet [45] and SACT [14]) as well as dynamic width network (ManiDP [42]). Thanks to the general formulation, our algorithm could be extended to other instances of dynamic depth and width networks easily.

2.2   Energy-Oriented Attack

Although dynamic neural network is appealing in reducing the computation overhead specific to the input samples, its robustness under various adversarial attacks remains unclear. The adversarial attacks could be broadly separated into accuracy-oriented attacks and energy-oriented attacks. In accuracy-oriented attacks, the adversary aims at altering the predictions of the target models while in energy-oriented attacks, the adversary focuses on delaying the inference speed of the target model by incurring more computations within the model. With the extra computation overhead, the energy consumption of inference also increases accordingly, leaving the dynamic neural network no longer efficient and therefore defeats the whole purpose of the dynamic neural networks.

Important as it is, the study on adversarial attacks on dynamic neural networks is quite limited. ILFO [20] was the first work investigating the robustness of dynamic neural networks. Specifically, they study the energy-oriented adversarial attacks on dynamic depth networks and leverage the intermediate output within the dynamic neural network to infer the energy consumption of each layer. Deepsloth [23] attacks the early-termination based dynamic neural nets. An adversarial example crafting technique is proposed to slowdown the inference speed.

Different from existing methods that mainly focus on studying the robustness of the dynamic depth network, we provide a more universal formulation that could adapt to the attack on both the dynamic depth network and dynamic width network. Moreover, we also showcase that directly searching for the adversarial examples based on gradients could be unstable and sub-optimal. To address this, we additionally propose two remedies to rectify the gradients, leading to improved adversary performance with less perceptible perturbations.

3   Computational Complexity Attack

3.1   Introduction of Two Types of Dynamic Neural Architectures

Depth-Dynamic Neural Architecture, such as SkipNet [45], adjusts the network depth by skipping some of the network layer to reduce the computational complexity. Given a conditional skipping network, the output feature maps $x_{l+1} \in \mathbb{R}^{C_{l+1} \times H_{l+1} \times W_{l+1}}$ from the gated layer $l+1$ can be computed by

$$x_{l+1} = g_l \cdot F_l(x_l) + (1 - g_l) \cdot x_l; \tag{1}$$

where $F_l(x_l) = w_l * x_l + b_l$ denotes the output of the lth layer before the gate function $g_l \in \{0, 1\}$. $w_l \in \mathbb{R}^{C_{l+1} \times C_l \times K^l \times K^l}$ denotes the weights of the convolution kernels, and $*$ denotes the convolution operation. We omit the nonlinearity in Eq. 1 for clarity. Note that the gated function makes binary decisions (0 or 1), instead of predicting a continuous value to weightedly combine the output and the input of the layer l. This means, when $g_l = 0$, the convolution computation $F_l(x_l)$ in layer l can be skipped to reduce computation cost.

Width-Dynamic Neural Architecture, such as [2,7,15,32], employs a gate function to predict the activation status of each channel: $g_l \in \{0, 1\}^{C_{l+1}}$. The predicted activation status is then used to mask out the convolution operations on selective channels: $x_{l+1} = F_l(x_l, g_l) = (g_l \circ w_l) * x_l + g_l \circ b_l$, where $\circ$ denotes the Hadamard product over the dimension of output channel C_{l+1}. When $g_{lc} = 0$, the computation of the cth channel at the lth layer could be skipped and the corresponding computation cost could thus be saved.

Gate Generation. In many works [18,28–30,40,44,45,49], the gate is often generated by a gating network $G_l(\cdot)$ as: $g_l = \begin{cases} 1, & G_l(x_l) \geq \tau \\ 0, & G_l(x_l) < \tau \end{cases}$, where $G_l(x_l) \in (G_{\min}, G_{\max})$ is the estimated gating value of the lth layer, and $\tau \in (G_{\min}, G_{\max})$ denotes the threshold. Note that, $(G_{\min}, G_{\max})$ indicates that $G_l(\cdot)$ is bounded, e.g., $G_{\min} = 0, G_{\max} = 1$ if sigmoid is adopted as the activation function of the gating network. For dynamic width networks, the gating network predicts a vector-based mask corresponding to the activation status of each channel, which could be constructed in a similar way: $g_{lc} = \begin{cases} 1, & G_{lc}(x_l) \geq \tau \\ 0, & G_{lc}(x_l) < \tau \end{cases}$. Therefore, to perform energy-oriented attack, we could perturb the input samples to raise the intermediate gating values to go beyond the threshold τ, which leads to the corresponding gates being activated and incurs extra computational cost to the dynamic neural networks.

3.2 Overall Objective of Computational Complexity Attack

In traditional accuracy-oriented attacks, to construct an adversarial example, a human imperceptible perturbation is created to modify a given input. A specific objective function (e.g., changing the predicted logits of an image classification network yet keeping the minimum amount of changes) is often constructed to guide the search for the perturbation. After iterative updates on the perturbations, the modified input could alter the predictions of the threatened models. Similarly, we can also construct perturbed input samples to invalidate the acceleration strategy of the dynamic neural architecture, such as raising the gating value to activate more gates and accordingly computes more layers or more channels. We detail this kind of attack below:

First, we initialize a specific perturbation $\delta \in \mathbb{R}^{3 \times H \times W}$ and use it to modify the input image by:

$$x'_0 = x_0 + \delta \tag{2}$$

where H, W denote the height and width of the input image, $\boldsymbol{x}_0, \boldsymbol{x}_0' \in [0, 1]^{3 \times H \times W}$ denote the original input and modified input, respectively. The value of the input image should be in $[0, 1]$. Hence, we follow Carlini et $al.$ [6] to use $\tanh(\cdot) \in [-1, 1]$ to refine Eq. 2 to force the modified input $\boldsymbol{x}_0' \in [0, 1]^{3 \times H \times W}$ by:

$$\boldsymbol{x}_0' = \frac{1}{2} \cdot (\tanh(\boldsymbol{x}_0 + \boldsymbol{\delta}) + 1). \tag{3}$$

To make the perturbation $\boldsymbol{\delta}$ being able to increase the complexity of the network, we refer to Szegedy et $al.$ [41] and formally define the objective as:

$$\min_{\boldsymbol{\delta}} \frac{1}{3HW} \left\| \frac{1}{2} \cdot (\tanh(\boldsymbol{x}_0 + \boldsymbol{\delta}) + 1) - \boldsymbol{x}_0 \right\|_2, \quad s.t. \ G_l(\boldsymbol{x}_0, \boldsymbol{\delta}) \geq \tau, \tag{4}$$

where $\| \cdot \|_2$ denotes the L2-norm, and $\frac{1}{3HW} \| \cdot \|_2$ denotes the mean-square error, which is used to minimize the deviation between the original input and the modified input to prevent them from being differentiated. The constraint is to guarantee the gating value G_l (or G_{lc} for width-dynamic neural architecture) being above the threshold to activate the execution of the lth convolutional layer for more computational complexity. Here, we use $G_l(\boldsymbol{x}_0, \boldsymbol{\delta})$ as the gating function to indicate that it depends on both the input and the perturbation.

3.3 Complexity Loss

To increase the network complexity, we drive the gating value G_l to be larger than the threshold τ to satisfy the constraint: $G_l(\boldsymbol{x}_0, \boldsymbol{\delta}) \geq \tau$ in Eq. 4 to get the corresponding layer executed. The constraint can be considered as equivalent to $\max(\tau - G_l(\boldsymbol{x}_0, \boldsymbol{\delta}), 0) = 0$. We adopt Lagrangian relaxation to approximate Eq. 4 as:

$$\min_{\boldsymbol{\delta}} \frac{1}{3HW} \left\| \frac{1}{2} \cdot (\tanh(\boldsymbol{x}_0 + \boldsymbol{\delta}) + 1) - \boldsymbol{x}_0 \right\|_2 + \sum_l \lambda_l \cdot \max(\tau - G_l(\boldsymbol{x}_0, \boldsymbol{\delta}), 0), \tag{5}$$

where λ_l is the chosen positive weight for the lth layer. We define the right part in Eq. 5 as the Complexity Loss:

$$\mathcal{L}_C(\boldsymbol{x}_0, \boldsymbol{\delta}) = \sum_l \lambda_l \cdot \max(\tau - G_l(\boldsymbol{x}_0, \boldsymbol{\delta}), 0), \tag{6}$$

which can rise all the deactivated gating values, i.e., $G_l(\boldsymbol{x}_0, \boldsymbol{\delta}) < \tau$, until being activated, i.e., being above the threshold τ. Then, we define λ_l as: $\lambda_l = \frac{C_l}{\sum_l C_l}$, where C_l denotes the computational complexity of the lth layer, i.e., λ_l denotes the complexity proportion of lth layer to all the convolutional layers. Using different λ_l for different gating values can reweight the losses of different convolutional layers according to their corresponding complexities. For example, when $C_0 = C_1 + C_2$, then the penalty for skipping the 0th layer will be the same as the penalty for skipping both the 1th layer and the 2th layer.

For simplicity, we rewrite Eq. 5 to:

$$\min \| \frac{1}{2} \cdot [\tanh(\boldsymbol{x}_0 + \boldsymbol{\delta}) + 1] - \boldsymbol{x}_0 \|_2 + 3HW \cdot \mathcal{L}_{\mathrm{C}}(\boldsymbol{x}_0, \boldsymbol{\delta}), \tag{7}$$

as the final objective. The Complexity Loss measures the computational complexity difference between the current state and the desirable state whose complexity is maximized. The final objective leads the modified input to increase the network complexity while keeping the deviation to the original input small.

For the width-dynamic neural architecture, the Complexity Loss becomes:

$$\mathcal{L}_{\mathrm{C}}(\boldsymbol{x}_0, \boldsymbol{\delta}) = \sum_{l,c} \lambda_{lc} \cdot max(\tau - G_{lc}(\boldsymbol{x}_0, \boldsymbol{\delta}), 0), \tag{8}$$

where λ_{lc} is computed as the complexity proportion of the corresponding channel to the entire network.

4   GradAuto

In Sect. 3.3, we formulate the objective function as Eq. 7, where we minimize the combination of the overall magnitude of the perturbation $\boldsymbol{\delta}$ and the amount of gate value $G_l(\boldsymbol{x}_0, \boldsymbol{\delta})$ below the activation threshold τ. However, in practice, we found that directly optimizing the perturbation based on the gradient of Eq. 7 is suboptimal due to two main reasons: 1) The gradient becomes unstable and could change drastically when the status of the gate changes, as shown in plots A, B, and C of Fig. 1. 2) The gradient for bumping up the gate value of inactivated gates may disagree with the gradients to keep the activated gate activated, leading to previously activated gates deactivated, as shown in gate 1 in plot D of Fig. 1. These two issues impede the effective and efficient search of the optimal perturbation, leading to suboptimal attack performance as shown in our ablation studies in Sect. 5.3. To address these two issues, we propose two rectified based approaches to regularize the gradients, enabling faster and more effective energy-oriented attacks.

4.1   Rectified Magnitude of Gradient

Figure 1 shows the gating value and the gradient during adversarial training. It can be observed in the sub-figures A and B that the magnitude of the gradient, i.e., $\|\boldsymbol{g}\|$, grows very fast at around 0th, 100th and 250th iterations, which is the moment that the gating values of gate 1, gate 4, and gate 3 exceed the threshold (see sub-figure C) and we add the corresponding layer into our graph. As the result, the gradient maintains a low magnitude most of the time while occasionally grows abruptly, which leads to an unstable optimization process and sometimes even prevents the convergence of the Complexity Loss.

We suggest, there are two reasons for the gradient of dynamic neural architecture to be unstable during training: 1) The sudden change of the activation status brings discontinuities to the dynamic neural networks, leading to additional layers involved into the computation graph and drastic jumps of the gradients. 2) The range of the derivative of gating network is very large which will significantly scale up or down the gradient propagated backward. A bounded and monotonic activation function, such as sigmoid or hyperbolic tangent, is often adopted in gating network to restrict the range of its output value while their derivatives increase (or decreases) extremely fast. More specifically, the derivative of sigmoid is:

$$\sigma'(x) = \frac{1}{1 + e^{-x}} \cdot (1 - \frac{1}{1 + e^{-x}}) = \sigma(x) \cdot (1 - \sigma(x)), \tag{9}$$

where $\sigma'(0) = 2.5 \times 10^{-1}$, while $\sigma'(-5) = 6.6 \times 10^{-3}$.

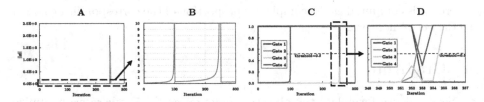

Fig. 1. Visualization of gradient and gating value. A and B show the magnitude of gradient of every training iteration. C and D show the change of gating value during adversarial training.

To stabilize the gradient, we resort to limit the change of the Complexity Loss to meet Lipschitz continuity as

$$d_{\mathcal{L}_C}(\mathcal{L}_C(\delta_1), \mathcal{L}_C(\delta_2)) \leq K d_\delta(\delta_1, \delta_2), \tag{10}$$

where $K \in \mathbb{R}_{>0}$ denotes the Lipschitz constant, and $d(\cdot)$ denotes the metric on the corresponding space of δ or $\mathcal{L}_C$. Hence, Eq. 10 can be written as:

$$\frac{|\mathcal{L}_C(\delta_1) - \mathcal{L}_C(\delta_2)|}{\|\delta_1 - \delta_2\|_2} \leq K. \tag{11}$$

According to the mean value theorem, Eq. 11 is valid if and only if the limit

$$\lim_{\|\Delta\delta\|_2 \to 0} \frac{|\mathcal{L}_C(\delta + \Delta\delta) - \mathcal{L}_C(\delta)|}{\|\Delta\delta\|_2} \leq K. \tag{12}$$

holds, where $\Delta\delta$ represents any change of the perturbation δ. Equation 12 can be formulated by directional derivative as:

$$\lim_{\|\Delta\delta\|_2 \to 0} \frac{|\langle \nabla\mathcal{L}_C(\delta), \Delta\delta \rangle|}{\|\Delta\delta\|_2} \leq K, \tag{13}$$

$$\lim_{\|\Delta\delta\|_2 \to 0} \frac{\|\nabla\mathcal{L}_C(\delta)\|_2 \cdot \|\Delta\delta\|_2 \cdot |\cos\theta|}{\|\Delta\delta\|_2} \leq K, \tag{14}$$

$$\|\nabla\mathcal{L}_C(\delta)\|_2 \cdot |\cos\theta| \leq K, \tag{15}$$

where $\langle \cdot, \cdot \rangle$ denotes inner product, and θ denotes the angle between the gradient $\nabla \mathcal{L}_C(\delta)$ and the change $\Delta \delta$ of the perturbation, which equals to zero when the $\cos \theta$ is maximized. Therefore, the sufficient condition of Eq. 15 is:

$$\left\| \frac{\nabla \mathcal{L}_C(\delta)}{K} \right\|_2 \leq 1, \tag{16}$$

Hence, we rectify the Complexity Loss in Eq. 6 to satisfy the sufficient condition Eq. 16 as:

$$\mathcal{L}_C(\delta) = K \cdot \frac{\sum_l \lambda_l \cdot max(\tau - G_l(x_0, \delta), 0)}{\| \nabla \sum_l \lambda_l \cdot max(\tau - G_l(x_0, \delta), 0) \|_2}, \tag{17}$$

This rectified version of the Complexity Loss is K-Lipschitz continuous, where we can adjust K to control the slope of the Complexity Loss as well as the magnitude of the gradient.

We further visualize the gradients and the gating values of the rectified Complexity Loss in Fig. 2. The sub-figures A and B plot the change of the gating value under the case of $K = 1$. Compared to the sub-figures C and D in Fig. 1, our AutoGrad damps the growth of the gating value and leaves room for the gates to compete with each other during the loss convergence, i.e., the activated gates would not drop to the bottom in one shot when the value of inactivated gates are growing towards the threshold. Once the values for the activated gates drop below the threshold, they will be involved into our Complexity Loss (Eq. 17) and compete against other inactivated gates.

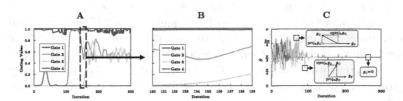

Fig. 2. Visualization of gradient and gating value after being rectified. A and B show the change of gating value during training, where the rectified magnitude of gradient is adopted (A and B can be compared to C and D in Fig. 1). C shows the change of the included angle θ between Finished Gradient and Complexity Gradient, and the gradient projection where the curves in different color represent different input image samples.

4.2 Rectified Direction of Gradient

The Complexity Loss only penalizes the inactivated gates (gate with value below the threshold) to drive them to be activated, while the already activated gates (gates with values above the threshold) are excluded. However, the gradients to boost the inactivated gates' values may not always agree with the gradients to make the activated gates keep activated. Hence some of the activated gates' value may drop and become inactivated again. This kind of disagreement will drive the gates switching back and forth between being activated and inactivated, as shown in sub-figures D of Fig. 1. While the Gate 2 increases to above the threshold, the Gate 1 drops to below the threshold and becomes inactivated. In this case, they almost cannot be activated in the same time, which limits the total number of activated gates. Below we study two ways to address this problem.

Involving Activated Gates in the Complexity Loss. In this case, we modify the Complexity Loss to encourage the gating value to rise even after activation:

$$\mathcal{L}_F(\boldsymbol{x}_0, \boldsymbol{\delta}) = \sum_l \lambda_l \cdot (\tau - G_l(\boldsymbol{x}_0, \boldsymbol{\delta})), \tag{18}$$

However, we empirically find this modification effectively leads to a tighter constraint:

$$G_l(\boldsymbol{x}_0, \boldsymbol{\delta}) = G_{\max} \tag{19}$$

for Eq. 4, while the $L2$-norm also constrains the amount of the perturbation $\boldsymbol{\delta}$. Combining these two constraints, the solution space is extremely limited. As the result, keeping the activated gate rising induces degeneracy of the solution space further, and poses greater challenges to the perturbation search process.

Gradient Projection for Complexity Loss. Keeping rising the activated gate can prevent them from switching back to some extent but always keeping them rising impedes the convergence of Complexity Loss. Moreover, encouraging higher activation values for those activate gates does not further contribute to the complexity increase, because their corresponding layer has already been counted. Hence, we further propose Finished Gradient Masking to keep them **only from dropping**. Firstly, we additionally compute the Finished Loss for those activated gates as:

$$\mathcal{L}_F(\boldsymbol{x}_0, \boldsymbol{\delta}) = -\sum_l \lambda_l \cdot max(G_l(\boldsymbol{x}_0, \boldsymbol{\delta}) - \tau, 0) \tag{20}$$

The Finished Loss $\mathcal{L}_F(\boldsymbol{x}_0, \boldsymbol{\delta})$ provides us the Finished Gradient $\boldsymbol{g}_F \in \mathbb{R}^{3 \times H \times W}$ for the perturbation $\boldsymbol{\delta}$, which is the direction to further increase the gate value for activated gates:

$$\boldsymbol{g}_F = \nabla_\delta \mathcal{L}_F(\boldsymbol{x}_0, \boldsymbol{\delta}). \tag{21}$$

Secondly, we use the Complexity Loss to calculate the Complexity Gradient $\boldsymbol{g}_C \in \mathbb{R}^{3 \times H \times W}$ by

$$\boldsymbol{g}_C = \nabla_\delta \mathcal{L}_C(\boldsymbol{x}_0, \boldsymbol{\delta}). \tag{22}$$

Thirdly, we project the Complexity Gradient onto the Finished Gradient by

$$\text{proj}_{\boldsymbol{g}_F}\boldsymbol{g}_C = \frac{\langle \boldsymbol{g}_C, \boldsymbol{g}_F \rangle}{\|\boldsymbol{g}_F\|_2} \frac{\boldsymbol{g}_F}{\|\boldsymbol{g}_F\|_2}, \tag{23}$$

and accordingly calculate the rejection of the Complexity Gradient from the Finished Gradient as:

$$\text{oproj}_{\boldsymbol{g}_F}\boldsymbol{g}_C = \boldsymbol{g}_C - \text{proj}_{\boldsymbol{g}_F}\boldsymbol{g}_C, \tag{24}$$

whose direction is orthogonal to the Finished Gradient. Hence updating with it dose not affect the gates that have already been activated. Finally, we rectify the direction of Complexity Gradient as:

$$\boldsymbol{g}'_C = \begin{cases} \text{oproj}_{\boldsymbol{g}_F}\boldsymbol{g}_C + \text{proj}_{\boldsymbol{g}_F}\boldsymbol{g}_C, & \left\langle \text{proj}_{\boldsymbol{g}_F}\boldsymbol{g}_C, \boldsymbol{g}_F \right\rangle \geq 0, \\ \text{oproj}_{\boldsymbol{g}_F}\boldsymbol{g}_C, & \left\langle \text{proj}_{\boldsymbol{g}_F}\boldsymbol{g}_C, \boldsymbol{g}_F \right\rangle < 0 \end{cases}, \tag{25}$$

which indicates that when the projection is opposite to the direction of Finished Gradient, it will be removed and only the orthogonal component of the Complexity Gradient will be updated. With this design, we update the perturbation to activate more gates and effectively avoids the activated gate from being deactivated again.

The sub-figure C in Fig. 2 visualizes the change of the angle θ between the Finished Gradient and the Complexity Gradient during training. When the angle is obtuse, the Complexity Gradient conflicts with the Finished Gradient, i.e., updating alongside the vanilla Complexity Gradient drags the activated gates toward the threshold. As shown in the plot, such conflicts occur frequently during training which drives the gate switching back and forth. Our approach of avoiding the conflict with gradient projection can be considered as a greedy algorithm to push the gate values of the remaining inactivated gates to as high as possible. Therefore, we adopt it at the later stage of the training to activate the rest of inactivated gates as much as possible.

5   Experiments

We validate our approach by using it to attack popular dynamic depth network (SkipNet [45] and SACT [14]) and dynamic width network (ManiDP [42]) on CIFAR-10 and ImageNet. For the experiments on dynamic depth network, we attack SkipNet with two different settings: SkipNet+SP and SkipNet+SP+HRL, where +SP and +HRL indicate whether supervised pre-training or hybrid reinforcement learning were used following [45]. SkipNet+SP+HRL achieves better efficiency compared to SkipNet+SP. Since ILFO only attacks SkipNet+SP, we further re-implement their code on the SkipNet+HRL and compare it with our GradAuto.

Metric. We follow the previous work [20] and evaluate the effectiveness of our attacks. We report the average percentage of the recovery in the dynamic neural

Table 1. Average recovery of the reduced FLOPs by three dynamic neural architectures: SkipNet, SACT, and ManiDP on the two datasets: CIFAR-10 and ImageNet, respectively.

Dataset	CIFAR-10			ImageNet			
Model	SkipNet	SACT	ManiDP	SkipNet	SACT	SkipNet+HRL	ManiDP
	(%)	(%)	(%)	(%)	(%)	(%)	(%)
ILFO [20]	84.29	72.49	80.3	81.36	91.06	46.9	85.6
GradAuto(ours)	100	100	100	100	100	88.9	100

network reduced FLOPs during inference following [20]. Dynamic neural networks reduced the total computation complexities at inference stage and we measure the amount of the saving computations that are invalidated by our attacks.

To measure the Quality, we adopt **peak signal-to-noise ratio (PSNR)** as the metric, which approximates the human perceptual quality and is commonly employed to evaluate image quality [24]. The PSNR can be defined as: $PSNR = 10 \cdot \log_{10}(\frac{MAX_I^2}{MSE})$, where MAX_I is the maximum possible pixel value of the image. For an original $m \times n$ image I and its corresponding adversarial example K, **mean squared error(MSE)** can be calculated by: $MSE = \frac{1}{mn}\sum_{i=0}^{m-1}\sum_{j=0}^{n-1}[I(i,j) - K(i,j)]^2$.

5.1   Attack on Dynamic Depth Network

We compare our approach with the state of the art method ILFO [20]. To ensure a fair comparison, we follow the experimental settings in [20]. Images from ImageNet and CIFAR-10 are converted into $224 \times 224 \times 3$ and $32 \times 32 \times 3$, respectively.

Quantitative Comparison. We present the comparison results in Table 1. On both CIFAR-10 and ImageNet, our GradAuto invalidates **all the reduced FLOPs**, outperforming the ILFO baseline by 15.71% & 18.64% for the SkipNet and 27.51% & 8.94% for SACT. In these experiments, our GradAuto attacks demolish the adaptive mechanism of SkipNet and SACT completely, effectively reduced them to their static counterparts, which shows the effectiveness of the proposed GradAuto.

To further evaluate the limits of our GradAuto, we additionally design and compare the ILFO on the more powerful SkipNet+HRL, i.e., the SkipNet with hybrid reinforcement learning. The original complexity reduction of SkipNet and SkipNet+HRL are 15.08% and 29.94% respectively. As shown in Table 1, our GradAuto outperforms ILFO by a large margin on attacking the SkipNet-HRL, effectively recovers 70% more reduced FLOPs compared to ILFO.

Qualitative Comparison. Figure 3 visualizes the modified input images generated by ILFO and ours GradAuto based on SkipNet-HRL. It can be observed that our method improves attack performance with lower deviation compared to ILFO. ILFO greatly changes the contrast of the image, while our GradAuto is

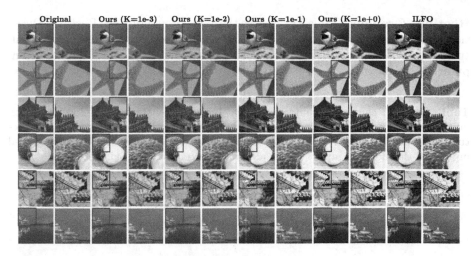

Fig. 3. The modified input images generated by our AutoGrad under different Lipschitz constant K of Lipschitz continuity. The model for the experiment is SkipNet-HRL.

more authentic to the original image. Results with different Lipschitz constant K show that on the our method generates less perceptible noise at the background.

5.2 Attack on Dynamic Width Network

We next evaluate our attack on the dynamic width network ManiDP [42]. The experimental setting of attack on ManiDP is same with the attack on SkipNet. The original computation reduction of ManiDP on ImageNet is 49%. We evaluate our approach on the ImageNet and CIFAR-10. As shown in Table 1, our GradAuto outperforms ILFO and recover ManiDP reduced FLOPs by 100% for all samples.

5.3 Ablation Study

To further validate the effect of a few important design choices of our method, we conduct ablation studies on the gains of rectified gradient, the selection of the Lipschitz constant as well as the design of rectified direction of gradient.

Table 2. Comparison for different methods. Baseline denotes ILFO. RD and RM denote Rectified Direction and Rectified Magnitude, respectively. GradAuto denotes the combination of Rectified Direction and Rectified Magnitude.

Method	Baseline	RD (Ours)	RM (Ours)	GradAuto (Ours)
Complexity Increase	46.9	52.3	86.9	88.9

Rectified Gradient. Table 2 evaluates the gains brought by the Rectified Direction and the Rectified Magnitude. Both Rectified Direction and Rectified Magnitude provide better attacking performance, incurring 5.4% and 40% more computation complexity.

Table 3. Result comparison among different Lipschitz constant K of Lipschitz continuity. Recovery denote the recovery of reduced FLOPs by the dynamic neural architecture. Baseline denotes ILFO [20]. PSNR measures the deviation between the original input and the modified input. The model for the experiment is SkipNet-HRL.

K	Baseline	$1e-3$	$1e-2$	$1e-1$	$1e+0$	$1e+1$	$1e+2$
Recovery (%)	46.9	71.0	85.2	87.0	88.9	88.9	88.9
PSNR	54.39	78.13	67.60	57.57	54.54	53.92	53.87

The Setting of K-Lipschitz. Table 3 lists the performance of Complexity Attack and the deviation of modified input images under different Lipschitz constant. A lower Lipschitz constant reduces the PSNR between the original input images and the modified input images but also drops the performance of Complexity Attack (measured by complexity increase). Note that, when the Lipschitz constant $K \in [1e-3, 1e-0]$, our AutoGrad significantly improves the performance of Complexity Attack while achieves extremely high PSNR. It can be observed that when setting the Lipschitz constant as $K = 1e-3$, the modified inputs generated by our method are hardly distinguishable from the original input images while improves the attack performance by over 20.8% compared to ILFO.

A higher Lipschitz constant accelerates the convergence of Complexity Loss which activates more gates and bring better attack performance. Meanwhile, the perturbations also becomes more noticeable. Finally, we can adjust the Lipschitz constant based on the trade off between the perceptiveness and the performance of the Complexity Attack in response to distinct needs.

6   Conclusion

In this paper, we investigate the robustness of dynamic neural network in terms of computational efficiency. We construct a framework for attacking the dynamic depth/width networks and also identify two key issues in the gradient space causing the limit success of the prior attack. First, the magnitude of the gradient is not stable. Sudden spikes in gradients make the network difficult to train. Second, gradient of different gates may have conflicting directions. To address these two issues, we proposed a new attack approach GradAuto and empirically demonstrate that it could invalidate 100% of reduced FLOPs of both dynamic depth and dynamic width model while keeping the perturbation imperceptible.

Acknowledgements. This work is supported by National Research Foundation, Singapore under its AI Singapore Programme (AISG Award No: AISG-100E-2020-065), MOE Tier 1 Grant, and SUTD Startup Research Grant. The research is also supported by TAILOR, a project funded by EU Horizon 2020 research and innovation programme under GA No 952215.

References

1. Badrinarayanan, V., Kendall, A., Cipolla, R.: SegNet: a deep convolutional encoder-decoder architecture for image segmentation. IEEE Trans. Pattern Anal. Mach. Intell. **39**(12), 2481–2495 (2017)
2. Bejnordi, B.E., Blankevoort, T., Welling, M.: Batch-shaping for learning conditional channel gated networks. arXiv preprint arXiv:1907.06627 (2019)
3. Bengio, E., Bacon, P.L., Pineau, J., Precup, D.: Conditional computation in neural networks for faster models. arXiv preprint arXiv:1511.06297 (2015)
4. Bengio, Y., Léonard, N., Courville, A.: Estimating or propagating gradients through stochastic neurons for conditional computation. arXiv preprint arXiv:1308.3432 (2013)
5. Carion, N., Massa, F., Synnaeve, G., Usunier, N., Kirillov, A., Zagoruyko, S.: End-to-end object detection with transformers. In: Vedaldi, A., Bischof, H., Brox, T., Frahm, J.-M. (eds.) ECCV 2020. LNCS, vol. 12346, pp. 213–229. Springer, Cham (2020). https://doi.org/10.1007/978-3-030-58452-8_13
6. Carlini, N., Wagner, D.: Towards evaluating the robustness of neural networks. In: 2017 IEEE Symposium on Security and Privacy (SP), pp. 39–57. IEEE (2017)
7. Chen, J., Zhu, Z., Li, C., Zhao, Y.: Self-adaptive network pruning. In: Gedeon, T., Wong, K.W., Lee, M. (eds.) ICONIP 2019. LNCS, vol. 11953, pp. 175–186. Springer, Cham (2019). https://doi.org/10.1007/978-3-030-36708-4_15
8. Chen, L.C., Papandreou, G., Kokkinos, I., Murphy, K., Yuille, A.L.: DeepLab: Semantic image segmentation with deep convolutional nets, atrous convolution, and fully connected CRFs. IEEE Trans. Pattern Anal. Mach. Intell. **40**(4), 834–848 (2017)
9. Cheng, J., Wang, P., Li, G., Hu, Q., Lu, H.: Recent advances in efficient computation of deep convolutional neural networks. arXiv preprint arXiv:1802.00939 (2018)
10. Cheng, Y., Wang, D., Zhou, P., Zhang, T.: A survey of model compression and acceleration for deep neural networks. arXiv preprint arXiv:1710.09282 (2017)
11. Cho, K., Bengio, Y.: Exponentially increasing the capacity-to-computation ratio for conditional computation in deep learning. arXiv preprint arXiv:1406.7362 (2014)
12. Dosovitskiy, A., et al.: An image is worth 16 × 16 words: Transformers for image recognition at scale. arXiv preprint arXiv:2010.11929 (2020)
13. Eigen, D., Ranzato, M., Sutskever, I.: Learning factored representations in a deep mixture of experts. arXiv preprint arXiv:1312.4314 (2013)
14. Figurnov, M., Collins, M.D., Zhu, Y., Zhang, L., Huang, J., Vetrov, D., Salakhutdinov, R.: Spatially adaptive computation time for residual networks. In: Proceedings of the IEEE Conference on Computer Vision and Pattern Recognition, pp. 1039–1048 (2017)
15. Gao, X., Zhao, Y., Dudziak, L., Mullins, R., Xu, C.Z.: Dynamic channel pruning: Feature boosting and suppression. arXiv preprint arXiv:1810.05331 (2018)
16. Girshick, R.: Fast R-CNN. In: Proceedings of the IEEE International Conference on Computer Vision pp. 1440–1448 (2015)

17. Graves, A.: Adaptive computation time for recurrent neural networks. arXiv preprint arXiv:1603.08983 (2016)
18. Guo, Q., Yu, Z., Wu, Y., Liang, D., Qin, H., Yan, J.: Dynamic recursive neural network. In: Proceedings of the IEEE/CVF Conference on Computer Vision and Pattern Recognition, pp. 5147–5156 (2019)
19. Han, Y., Huang, G., Song, S., Yang, L., Wang, H., Wang, Y.: Dynamic neural networks: a survey. IEEE Trans. Pattern Anal. Mach. Intell. (2021)
20. Haque, M., Chauhan, A., Liu, C., Yang, W.: ILFO: adversarial attack on adaptive neural networks. In: Proceedings of the IEEE/CVF Conference on Computer Vision and Pattern Recognition (CVPR) (2020)
21. He, K., Gkioxari, G., Dollár, P., Girshick, R.: Mask R-CNN. In: Proceedings of the IEEE International Conference on Computer Vision, pp. 2961–2969 (2017)
22. He, K., Zhang, X., Ren, S., Sun, J.: Deep residual learning for image recognition. In: Proceedings of the IEEE Conference on Computer Vision and Pattern Recognition, pp. 770–778 (2016)
23. Hong, S., Kaya, Y., Modoranu, I.V., Dumitras, T.: A panda? No, it's a sloth: slowdown attacks on adaptive multi-exit neural network inference. In: International Conference on Learning Representations (2021). https://openreview.net/forum?id=9xC2tWEwBD
24. Hore, A., Ziou, D.: Image quality metrics: PSNR vs. SSIM. In: 2010 20th International Conference on Pattern Recognition, pp. 2366–2369. IEEE (2010)
25. Hua, W., Zhou, Y., De Sa, C.M., Zhang, Z., Suh, G.E.: Channel gating neural networks. In: Advances in Neural Information Processing Systems 32 (2019)
26. Huang, G., Liu, Z., Van Der Maaten, L., Weinberger, K.Q.: Densely connected convolutional networks. In: Proceedings of the IEEE Conference on Computer Vision and Pattern Recognition, pp. 4700–4708 (2017)
27. Jacobs, R.A., Jordan, M.I., Nowlan, S.J., Hinton, G.E.: Adaptive mixtures of local experts. Neural Comput. 3(1), 79–87 (1991)
28. Jin, Q., Yang, L., Liao, Z.: AdaBits: Neural network quantization with adaptive bit-widths. In: Proceedings of the IEEE/CVF Conference on Computer Vision and Pattern Recognition, pp. 2146–2156 (2020)
29. Leroux, S., Molchanov, P., Simoens, P., Dhoedt, B., Breuel, T., Kautz, J.: Iamnn: iterative and adaptive mobile neural network for efficient image classification. arXiv preprint arXiv:1804.10123 (2018)
30. Li, C., Wang, G., Wang, B., Liang, X., Li, Z., Chang, X.: Dynamic slimmable network. In: Proceedings of the IEEE/CVF Conference on Computer Vision and Pattern Recognition, pp. 8607–8617 (2021)
31. Li, Y., Song, L., Chen, Y., Li, Z., Zhang, X., Wang, X., Sun, J.: Learning dynamic routing for semantic segmentation. In: Proceedings of the IEEE/CVF Conference on Computer Vision and Pattern Recognition, pp. 8553–8562 (2020)
32. Lin, J., Rao, Y., Lu, J., Zhou, J.: Runtime neural pruning. In: Advances in Neural Information Processing Systems 30 (2017)
33. Lin, T.Y., Goyal, P., Girshick, R., He, K., Dollár, P.: Focal loss for dense object detection. In: Proceedings of the IEEE International Conference on Computer Vision, pp. 2980–2988 (2017)
34. Liu, C., Wang, Y., Han, K., Xu, C., Xu, C.: Learning instance-wise sparsity for accelerating deep models. arXiv preprint arXiv:1907.11840 (2019)
35. Liu, W., Anguelov, D., Erhan, D., Szegedy, C., Reed, S., Fu, C.-Y., Berg, A.C.: SSD: single shot multibox detector. In: Leibe, B., Matas, J., Sebe, N., Welling, M. (eds.) ECCV 2016. LNCS, vol. 9905, pp. 21–37. Springer, Cham (2016). https://doi.org/10.1007/978-3-319-46448-0_2

36. Liu, Z., et al.: Swin transformer: hierarchical vision transformer using shifted windows. In: Proceedings of the IEEE/CVF International Conference on Computer Vision, pp. 10012–10022 (2021)
37. Liu, Z., Mao, H., Wu, C.Y., Feichtenhofer, C., Darrell, T., Xie, S.: A convnet for the 2020s. arXiv preprint arXiv:2201.03545 (2022)
38. Long, J., Shelhamer, E., Darrell, T.: Fully convolutional networks for semantic segmentation. In: Proceedings of the IEEE Conference on Computer Vision and Pattern Recognition, pp. 3431–3440 (2015)
39. Ronneberger, O., Fischer, P., Brox, T.: U-Net: convolutional networks for biomedical image segmentation. In: Navab, N., Hornegger, J., Wells, W.M., Frangi, A.F. (eds.) MICCAI 2015. LNCS, vol. 9351, pp. 234–241. Springer, Cham (2015). https://doi.org/10.1007/978-3-319-24574-4_28
40. Shen, J., Wang, Y., Xu, P., Fu, Y., Wang, Z., Lin, Y.: Fractional skipping: towards finer-grained dynamic CNN inference. In: Proceedings of the AAAI Conference on Artificial Intelligence, vol. 34, pp. 5700–5708 (2020)
41. Szegedy, C., et al.: Intriguing properties of neural networks. arXiv preprint arXiv:1312.6199 (2013)
42. Tang, Y., et al.: Manifold regularized dynamic network pruning. In: Proceedings of the IEEE/CVF Conference on Computer Vision and Pattern Recognition, pp. 5018–5028 (2021)
43. Vaswani, A., et al.: Attention is all you need. In: Advances in Neural Information Processing Systems 30 (2017)
44. Veit, A., Belongie, S.: Convolutional networks with adaptive inference graphs. In: Proceedings of the European Conference on Computer Vision (ECCV), pp. 3–18 (2018)
45. Wang, X., Yu, F., Dou, Z.Y., Darrell, T., Gonzalez, J.E.: SkipNet: learning dynamic routing in convolutional networks. In: Proceedings of the European Conference on Computer Vision (ECCV) (2018)
46. Wang, Y., et al.: Dual dynamic inference: enabling more efficient, adaptive, and controllable deep inference. IEEE J. Select. Top. Signal Process. 14(4), 623–633 (2020)
47. Xia, W., Yin, H., Dai, X., Jha, N.K.: Fully dynamic inference with deep neural networks. IEEE Trans. Emerg. Top. Comput. 10, 962–972 (2021)
48. Yang, B., Bender, G., Le, Q.V., Ngiam, J.: CondConv: conditionally parameterized convolutions for efficient inference. In: Advances in Neural Information Processing Systems 32 (2019)
49. Yu, H., Li, H., Shi, H., Huang, T.S., Hua, G., et al.: Any-precision deep neural networks. arXiv preprint arXiv:1911.07346 1 (2019)

A Spectral View of Randomized Smoothing Under Common Corruptions: Benchmarking and Improving Certified Robustness

Jiachen Sun[1]([✉])(iD), Akshay Mehra[2], Bhavya Kailkhura[3], Pin-Yu Chen[4](iD), Dan Hendrycks[5], Jihun Hamm[2], and Z. Morley Mao[1](iD)

[1] University of Michigan, Ann Arbor, USA
jiachens@umich.edu
[2] Tulane University, New Orleans, USA
[3] Lawrence Livermore National Laboratory, Livermore, USA
[4] IBM Research, Armonk, USA
[5] University of California, Berkeley, USA

Abstract. Certified robustness guarantee gauges a model's resistance to test-time attacks and can assess the model's readiness for deployment in the real world. In this work, we explore a new problem setting to critically examine how the adversarial robustness guarantees change when state-of-the-art randomized smoothing-based certifications encounter common corruptions of the test data. Our analysis demonstrates a previously unknown vulnerability of these certifiably robust models to low-frequency corruptions such as weather changes, rendering these models unfit for deployment in the wild. To alleviate this issue, we propose a novel data augmentation scheme, *FourierMix*, that produces augmentations to improve the spectral coverage of the training data. Furthermore, we propose a new regularizer that encourages consistent predictions on noise perturbations of the augmented data to improve the quality of the smoothed models. We show that *FourierMix* helps eliminate the spectral bias of certifiably robust models, enabling them to achieve significantly better certified robustness on a range of corruption benchmarks. Our evaluation also uncovers the inability of current corruption benchmarks to highlight the spectral biases of the models. To this end, we propose a comprehensive benchmarking suite that contains corruptions from different regions in the spectral domain. Evaluation of models trained with popular augmentation methods on the proposed suite unveils their spectral biases. It also establishes the superiority of *FourierMix* trained models in achieving stronger certified robustness guarantees under corruptions over the entire frequency spectrum.

Keywords: Certified robustness · Common corruption · Benchmark

Supplementary Information The online version contains supplementary material available at https://doi.org/10.1007/978-3-031-19772-7_38.

1 Introduction

Developing machine learning (ML) systems that are robust to adversarial variations in the test data is critical for applied domains that require ML safety [21], such as autonomous driving and cyber-security. Unfortunately, a large body of work in this direction has fallen into the cycle where new empirical defenses are proposed, followed by new adaptive attacks breaking these defenses [3,55]. Therefore, significant efforts have been dedicated to developing methods that provide provable robustness guarantees [17,42,57]. Most promising among these certified defenses are based on *randomized smoothing (RS)* based certification [9,32,33] which are scalable to deep neural networks (DNNs) and high-resolution datasets. Specifically, the RS-based certification procedure relies on a smoothed version of the original classifier, which outputs the class most likely returned by the original classifier under random noise perturbations of the input. Prediction from the RS procedure at the test time is accompanied by a *radius* in which the predictions of the smoothed classifier are guaranteed to remain constant, thereby making them resilient to adversarial attacks within the neighborhood. Training methods such as [9,47,66] have been proposed to maximize the *average certified radius (ACR)*, and models trained using these procedures achieve state-of-the-art (SOTA) adversarial robustness guarantees, all while assuming that the test data is identically distributed to the training data. In this work, we take a critical look at the current status of certifiably robust ML and consider whether these certifiably robust models are ready for deployment in the real world.

Our work takes the first steps towards answering this question by evaluating RS-based provably robust ML models under *common corruptions*, as mismatches between the training and deployment distributions are ubiquitous in the wild. Our analysis shows that **common corruptions pose a serious threat to certifiably robust models.** We, therefore, highlight a previously unrecognized threat to certifiably robust models and thereby show that these models are not ready for deployment in the real world. Specifically, we found SOTA certifiably robust models to be surprisingly brittle to low-frequency perturbations, such as weather-related corruptions (*e.g.*, fog and frost). Vulnerability to such corruptions could lead to a detrimental performance of ML models on safety-critical applications. For example, 35%–75% performance drop is observed on low-frequency corruptions rendering RS-based robustness guarantees useless (Fig. 1).

Certified Robustness Is Fragile under Common Corruptions

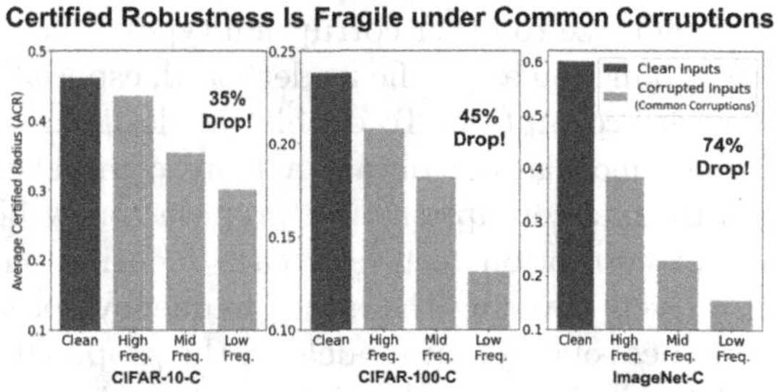

Fig. 1. Robustness guarantees of certified models [9] degrade significantly on corrupted data.

Motivated by our analysis, which shows RS-based smoothed classifiers suffer from low-frequency corruptions, we propose a novel data augmentation method that uses **spectrally diverse yet semantically consistent augmentations** of the training data. Specifically, our proposed *FourierMix* generates augmented data samples by using Fourier-based transformations on the input data to increase the spectral coverage of the training set. *FourierMix* proportionally perturbs the amplitude and phase of the images in the training data and then combines them with the affine transformations of the data, producing spectrally diverse augmentations. To encourage the model to produce consistent predictions on different data augmentations, we propose a *hierarchical consistency regularizer (HCR)*. The use of HCR as the regularizer leads to semantic consistency of representations across random noise perturbations (for RS certification) as well as *FourierMix* generated augmentations (for corruption robustness) of the same input image. *FourierMix* consistently achieves significantly better-certified robustness than existing SOTA data augmentation methods extended to build a smoothed classifier across a range of corruption benchmarks. We further analyze these smoothed models using Fourier sensitivity analysis in the spectral domain. Compared to other methods, models trained on *FourierMix* augmentations coupled with hierarchical consistency regularization are significantly more resilient to perturbations across the entire frequency spectrum.

Our evaluation of certifiably robust models on various corruption benchmark datasets uncovers another peculiar phenomenon–**even popular benchmark datasets may be biased towards certain frequency regions**. Due to the complexity of real-world data, it is extremely challenging and tedious to unveil the spectral biases of the models and identify their failure modes. Because of this, improvements in the performance of the models on these benchmarks may not generalize to other corruption types. Thus, we should be cautious and avoid over-reliance on a specific leaderboard, especially to judge the robustness of models under corruption. To enable the designers to understand the spectral biases of their models and obtain a more comprehensive view of the model robustness to data corruptions, we propose a new benchmark that includes a collection of corruption test sets, each focusing on specific frequency ranges while collectively covering the entire frequency spectrum. Evaluation of the certified robustness of different models on the proposed dataset shows that the smoothed models obtained after training with existing data augmentation schemes are indeed biased towards certain frequency regions. This justifies the observed performance (and ranking) variations across different benchmarks. On the other hand, models trained with our *FourierMix* based data augmentations perform significantly better than the competitors across the entire frequency spectrum, further demonstrating that *FourierMix* helps alleviate the spectral biases.[1]

A detailed discussion on related work is provided in Appendix A, while all the references are included in the main paper.

---

[1] The codebase and dataset of this work are available at https://github.com/jiachens/FourierMix.

2   Are Certifiably Robust Models Ready for Deployment in the Wild?

Predictions of certifiably robust ML models are guaranteed to stay constant in a neighborhood of a test point, making them provably resilient to adversaries at the test time. This feature of certified defenses makes them an attractive candidate for real-world safety-critical applications. However, progress in this area has been assessed by evaluating these models in idealistic scenarios (*i.e.*, the in-distribution setup), which is not representative of real-world data distributions. To better understand the performance of certified defenses in the real world, in this section, we evaluate SOTA certified defenses under common corruptions.

2.1   Preliminaries on SOTA Certified Defenses

Previous works have proposed different certification methods to obtain provable adversarial robustness guarantees (*e.g.*, convex polytope [57], recursive propagation [17], and linear relaxation [42,67]). However, their use is limited due to their trivial bounds derived from large-scale datasets and deep models. Recently, randomized smoothing (RS) based certification method was proposed, which is efficient and scalable to large-scale datasets and deep models. Therefore, we use RS-based certification in this study. Let us consider a base classifier $\mathcal{M}$ trained on samples $x \in \mathcal{X} \subset \mathbb{R}^{d \times d \times 3}$ and their corresponding labels $y \in \mathcal{Y} \subset \mathbb{R}^+$, obtained from an underlying data distribution $\mathcal{D}$.

Certification. The RS-based certification uses a base classifier $\mathcal{M}$ and provides certified robustness guarantees for its smoothed version defined as $\hat{\mathcal{M}}(x) = \arg\max_{c \in \mathcal{Y}} \mathbb{P}(\mathcal{M}(x + \delta) = c)$ where $\delta \sim \mathcal{N}(0, \sigma^2 \mathbf{I})$. Intuitively, $\hat{\mathcal{M}}$ returns the most probable class evaluated by $\mathcal{M}$ over a number of Gaussian perturbations of the input x. The certification guarantees that the prediction of the smoothed classifier $\hat{\mathcal{M}}$ are consistent in the ℓ_2 radius [9] of $\mathrm{CR}(\hat{\mathcal{M}}, \sigma, x; y) = \frac{\sigma}{2}(\Phi^{-1}(p_A) - \Phi^{-1}(p_B))$, where Φ^{-1} is the inverse CDF of the standard Gaussian distribution, $p_A = \mathbb{P}(\mathcal{M}(x + \delta) = c_A)$ is probability of the top class c_A and $p_B = \max_{c \neq c_A} \mathbb{P}(\mathcal{M}(x + \delta) = c)$ is the probability of the runner-up class. Monte Carlo-based sampling [18] is utilized to approximate $\underline{p_A} \leq p_A$ and $\overline{p_B} = 1 - \underline{p_A} \geq p_B$. The certified radius can still be computed using the same formula by replacing p_A and p_B with $\underline{p_A}$ and $\overline{p_B}$.

Improved Training. It has been observed empirically [9] that models trained using the standard procedure do not provide reasonable certified robustness. Therefore, there is an increasing interest in developing improved training techniques to maximize certified robustness. Several works [34] have made significant advances in the training techniques and reported impressive gains in certified radius on in-distribution test data. Specifically, new training methods such as Gaussian augmentation [9], SmoothAdv [47] and MACER [66] have been proposed. Intuitively, Cohen *et al.* [9] propose to leverage Gaussian augmentation with variance σ^2 to train the base classifier. SmoothAdv [47] and MACER [66] both use Gaussian augmentation and further improve Cohen *et al.*'s baseline

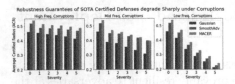

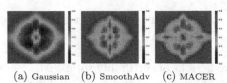

(a) Gaussian (b) SmoothAdv (c) MACER

Fig. 2. Randomized smoothing based models [9,47,66] suffer up to 54.0% decreases in their certified robustness on **mid-to-low** frequency corruptions from CIFAR-10-C. Severity 0 is in-distribution.

Fig. 3. Fourier sensitivity analysis on CIFAR-10 shows the ACR of SOTA certified defenses degrade significantly under corruptions from **mid-to-low** frequency region (interpreted in Sect. 2.2).

method by adversarial training and introducing an auxiliary objective to maximize the certified radius, respectively. However, the effect of common corruptions on the robustness guarantees of these models remains unexplored.

Evaluation Metrics. Similar to [37,47,66], we use the *average certified radius* (ACR) as our metric to evaluate the robustness:

$$\text{ACR} := \tfrac{1}{|\mathcal{D}_{test}|} \sum\nolimits_{(x,y) \in \mathcal{D}_{test}} \text{CR}(\hat{\mathcal{M}}, \sigma, x; y) \times \mathbf{1}_{\hat{\mathcal{M}}(x,\sigma)=y}$$

which is also equivalent to the area under the certified radius-accuracy curve (AUC). For performance on corruption datasets, we measure the mean ACR (mACR) as an overall metric, $\text{mACR} := \tfrac{1}{c} \sum_{i=1}^{c} \text{ACR}_i$, where c is the number of corruptions leveraged in a specific test set. For example, $c = 15$ and 10 in CIFAR-C and -C̄ datasets, respectively. Unlike previous studies on empirical defenses, we do not use the *empirical* clean and robust accuracy [9,47,66] as a metric in this work since we focus on the *certified* robustness.

2.2   Analyzing Certified Defenses Under Common Corruptions

Real-world test data often do not follow the training data distribution $\mathcal{D}$, although tangible improvements have been made in certifying the robustness of in-distribution data. Therefore, evaluating the performance of $\mathcal{M}$ under distribution shifts (*i.e.*, corrupted data) $\{(\hat{x}, y)_1, ..., (\hat{x}, y)_n\} \sim \hat{\mathcal{D}}$ becomes a major concern. We consider the impact of corrupted data on models trained using SOTA robust training methods [9,47,66] and RS-based certified defenses.

Degradation of Certified Robustness Guarantees on Common Corruptions. To measure the performance of certified defenses under data corruptions, we use the prevalent corruptions dataset CIFAR-10-C [22], which contains 15 different corruptions from four categories (with 5 severity levels): noise, blur, weather, and digital corruptions. We re-arrange the corruption dataset into three groups and evaluate the ACR by increasing the severity level of the corruption. Grouping is performed based on the visual similarity of the amplitude spectrum of corrupted images (see Appendix C). Group-H corruptions (roughly categorized as high-frequency corruption type) consist of {Gaussian noise, impulse noise, shot noise, pixelate, JPEG}; Group-M corruptions (roughly categorized as mid-frequency corruption type) consist of {defocus blur, frosted glass blur, motion blur, zoom blur, elastic}; and Group-L corruptions (roughly categorized as low-frequency corruption type) consist of {brightness, fog, frost, snow, contrast}.

The performance of SOTA certified defenses on these groups of corruptions is presented in Fig. 2. SmoothAdv and MACER achieve tangible enhancements in ACR on in-distribution CIFAR-10 data compared to the Gaussian augmentation baseline. However, all methods show a sharp performance drop in ACR as we move from Group-H (high-frequency) to Group-L (low-frequency). We see that these methods are surprisingly brittle in low-frequency corruption regimes, e.g., we see up to 54.0% drop in ACR when moving from severity 0 (i.e., in-distribution) to severity 5. We emphasize that this performance drop points to a methodological shortcoming. The degradation is not due to the corruptions in Group-L being too difficult since the empirical robust accuracy (Fig. 9 in Appendix B) remains consistently high on all the groups and severity levels for empirically robust models [23, 30, 44]. Even though the performance of any ML model is expected to suffer on test data that lies far away from the data used during training, the drastic performance degradation of RS-based certifiably robust models on low-frequency corruptions is particularly concerning. Our findings also generalize to IBP-based certification [59] (Appendix D.1), further demonstrating the vulnerability of certified defenses to low-frequency corruptions.

Validating the Brittleness of Smoothed Models Through a Spectral Lens. To highlight that the vulnerability to low-frequency corruptions is a limitation of provably robust ML models, in this section, we perform a more systematic analysis that corroborates that our finding is not limited to a specific benchmark and holds more broadly. To achieve this, we perform a spectral domain analysis of smoothed models by utilizing the Fourier sensitivity analysis [65].

A Fourier basis image in the pixel space is a real-valued matrix $U_{i,j} \in \mathbb{R}^{d \times d}$ where its $\|U_{i,j}\|_2 = 1$, and $FFT(U_{i,j})$ only has two non-zero elements at (i, j) and $(-i, -j)$ in the coordinate that views the image center as the origin. Given a test set and a smoothed model, we evaluate the $CR(\cdot)$ of $\widetilde{x}_{i,j} = x + r\epsilon U_{i,j}$ for each x in the test set and compute their ACR, where r is randomly sampled in $\{-1, 1\}$, ϵ is the perturbation in ℓ_2 norm, and we treat the RGB channels independently. Each of the evaluated ACR corresponds to a data point in the heat map located at (i, j). Figure 3 shows the heatmaps of models trained with Gaussian augmentation [9], SmoothAdv [47], and MACER [66] using $\epsilon = 4$ [65]. The center and edges of the heatmap contain the evaluation of the lowest and highest frequency perturbations, respectively. The results in Fig. 3 show that the certifiably robust classifiers achieve small ACR on corrupted data belonging to the low-frequency region (around the center of the image), whereas they achieve a high ACR in the high-frequency region (near the edges). In particular, the ACRs are always less than 0.3 for all three methods in the mid-to-low frequency range, while they perform well in a high-frequency regime. We emphasize that the

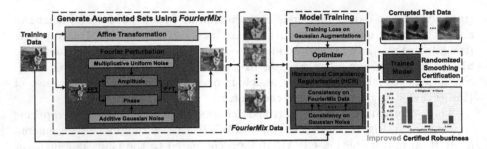

Fig. 4. Overview of our *FourierMix* pipeline for generating spectrally diverse data augmentations and training of certifiably robust models with the proposed hierarchical consistency regularization (HCR).

Fourier sensitivity analysis in Fig. 3 is general and is not specific to corruptions appearing in CIFAR-10-C. Based on our analysis, we find that certifiably robust models are biased towards high-frequency noises and perform surprisingly poor on low-frequency corrupted data.

Following this insight, we develop a data augmentation method capable of producing spectrally diverse augmentations to make certifiably robust models perform well on corrupted data across the entire frequency spectrum in Sect.3. It is also worth noting that although test-time adaptation [56] is another class of methods that improves the *empirical* corruption robustness, we demonstrate that they are ineffective when combined with certified defenses in Appendix G.

3   *FourierMix*: Data Augmentation Strategy with a Broad Spectral Coverage

To improve the certified robustness of RS-based methods under common corruptions, it is intuitively desirable to make the base classifier $\mathcal{M}$ robust against different types of corruptions and their Gaussian perturbations. Motivated by our Fourier sensitivity analysis (Sect. 2), we propose a novel data augmentation method, *FourierMix*. As opposed to existing data augmentation schemes, *FourierMix* explicitly uses *spectral coverage* as its design objective to boost the certified robustness of corrupted data. To improve the spectral coverage, we introduce Fourier-based operations that manipulate the image in the frequency domain. We also leverage randomly sampled affine transformations to enrich the augmentations in *FourierMix*. We adopt the high-level framework of AugMix [23] for chaining and mixing different augmented images. Figure 4 shows the overall pipeline and Algorithm 1 presents the pseudocode of *FourierMix*.

Fourier Operations. Two-dimensional images can be converted into the frequency domain by applying the Fourier transform and vice versa. Fourier transform has the *duality* property, which provides a unique but equivalent perspective for image analysis. We use fast Fourier transform (FFT) and inverse FFT (IFFT) for the transformation between the pixel and frequency domains. $\text{FFT}(\boldsymbol{x})$ is complex in general, $i.e.$, $\text{FFT}(\boldsymbol{x}) = \text{FFT}_{real}(\boldsymbol{x}) + i\text{FFT}_{imag}(\boldsymbol{x})$, with $\boldsymbol{A} = |\text{FFT}(\boldsymbol{x})|$ as its amplitude and $\boldsymbol{P} = \arctan(\text{FFT}_{imag}(\boldsymbol{x})/\text{FFT}_{real}(\boldsymbol{x}))$ as its phase. The amplitude spectrum of natural images generally follows a power-law distribution, $i.e.$, $\frac{1}{f^{\alpha}}$, where f is the azimuthal frequency and $\alpha \approx 2$ [5,54], resulting in extremely small power in the high-frequency areas. However, the amplitude spectrum of the I.I.D. Gaussian noise is a uniform distribution, so Gaussian augmentation biases the models toward the high-frequency regime relative to the original images. In order to have broad and unbiased spectral coverage, the core of $FourierMix$ is to allocate similar proportions of augmentations across all frequencies. We use two spectral operators in $FourierMix$ to achieve this goal:

$$\mathbf{A}(u, v) = \boldsymbol{A}_{u,v}^{\text{orig}} \cdot \text{U}(1 - s_{\mathbf{A}}, 1 + s_{\mathbf{A}}) \tag{1}$$

$$\mathbf{P}(u, v) = \boldsymbol{P}_{u,v}^{\text{orig}} + \mathcal{N}_{\text{truncated}}^{s_{\mathbf{P}}}(0, \sigma^2 \mathbf{I}) \tag{2}$$

where (u, v) is the coordinate of the 2D frequency in the spectrum, and $s_{\mathbf{A}}$ and $s_{\mathbf{P}}$ control the severity levels of two operators. Formally, the PDF of $\mathcal{N}_{\text{truncated}}^{s_{\mathbf{P}}} = \frac{\phi(x/\sigma)}{\sigma \cdot (2\Phi(s_{\mathbf{P}}/\sigma)-1)}$, where $\phi(\cdot)$ and $\Phi(\cdot)$ denote the PDF and CDF functions of a standard normal distribution, respectively. On one hand, we apply multiplicative factors sampled from a uniform distribution $\text{U}(\cdot)$ to all frequencies in the amplitude spectrum. Therefore, $\mathbf{A}(u, v)$ ensures that the proportions of augmentation are similar across all frequencies relative to the original spectrum. On the other hand, since the magnitude of the phase spectrum follows a random distribution that is not correlated with the 2D frequency [36], additive phase noises can thus assign similar proportions of augmentations across 2D frequencies. As it is widely acknowledged that the phase component retains most of the high-level semantics [29,61,64], we leverage additive truncated Gaussian to constrain $\mathbf{P}(u, v)$ so that it will not destroy the semantics of the training images. Some sample images generated using $FourierMix$ are provided in Appendix E.

Hierarchical Consistency Regularization (HCR). Motivated from [25] that enforces consistency on in-distribution data, we propose $hierarchical\ consistency\ regularization$ (HCR) to further boost the performance of $FourierMix$ in terms of the ACR on corrupted test sets:

$$\mathcal{L}_G = \frac{1}{s} \sum_{i=0}^{s} \text{KL}(\mathcal{M}(\boldsymbol{x}_j + \boldsymbol{\delta}_i) \| \overline{\mathcal{M}}(\boldsymbol{x}_j, \boldsymbol{\delta})) \tag{3}$$

$$\mathcal{L}_{HCR} = \frac{1}{k+1} \sum_{j=0}^{k} \left[\lambda \cdot \text{KL}(\overline{\mathcal{M}}(\boldsymbol{x}_j, \boldsymbol{\delta}) \| \overline{\overline{\mathcal{M}}}(\boldsymbol{x}, \boldsymbol{\delta})) + \eta \cdot \mathcal{L}_G \right] \tag{4}$$

where $\overline{\overline{\mathcal{M}}}(\boldsymbol{x}, \boldsymbol{\delta}) = \mathbb{E}_{j \in \{0,1,...,k\}}[\overline{\mathcal{M}}(\boldsymbol{x}_j, \boldsymbol{\delta})]$, $\overline{\mathcal{M}}(\boldsymbol{x}_j, \boldsymbol{\delta}) = \mathbb{E}_{i \in \{1,2,...,s\}}[\mathcal{M}(\boldsymbol{x}_j + \boldsymbol{\delta}_i)]$, $\boldsymbol{x}_0$ is the original training image, and $\text{KL}(\cdot\|\cdot)$ denotes the Kullback-Leibler divergence (KLD) [28]. We use $k = 2$ and $s = 2$ for the $FourierMix$ and Gaussian augmentation with $\boldsymbol{\delta}_i = \mathcal{N}(0, \sigma^2\mathbf{I})$, respectively. Since Jensen-Shannon divergence (JSD) [15] uses the KLD to calculate a normalized score that is symmetrical, HCR essentially stacks two levels of JSD while training the base classifier

to enforce the consistent representations over both augmentations. The first level of consistency $\mathcal{L}_G$ is applied to the Gaussian augmentation, rendering the Gaussian perturbed neighbors of $x_{0,1,2}$ have similar outputs, and the second level of consistency is on the whole $(k+1)s$ set to enforce *FourierMix* augmented images with consistent outputs. We utilize λ and η as hyper-parameters to tune the weights of two levels of consistency. The overall training loss is:
$$\mathcal{L} = \frac{1}{s}\sum_{i=1}^{s}\mathcal{L}(x_0 + \delta_i, y) + \mathcal{L}_{HCR}.$$

Algorithm 1: *FourierMix* Pseudocode

Data: Model $\mathcal{M}$, Image x_{orig}, Affine Transformation **T**, Fourier Amplitude **A** and Phase **P** Operations

Result: $x_{\text{aug}} = FourierMix(x_{\text{orig}}, k, \alpha)$

1 $x_{\text{aug}} = 0$
2 Sample mixing weights $(w_1, ..., w_k) \sim$ Dirichlet$(\alpha, ..., \alpha)$
3 **for** $i = 1, 2, ..., k$ **do**
4 $\quad$ Sample random affine transformation $\mathbf{T}_i$
5 $\quad$ $x_{\text{fourier}} = \text{FFT}(x_{\text{orig}})$
6 $\quad$ Sample severity level of operations $s_{\mathbf{A}}, s_{\mathbf{P}}$
7 $\quad$ $x_{\text{fourier}} = (\mathbf{A}_{s_{\mathbf{A}}} \circ \mathbf{P}_{s_{\mathbf{P}}})(x_{\text{fourier}})$
8 $\quad$ $x_f = \text{IFFT}(x_{\text{fourier}})$
9 $\quad$ Sample weight $t \sim \text{Beta}(\alpha, \alpha)$
10 $\quad$ $x_{\text{aug}} \mathrel{+}= w_i \cdot (t x_f + (1-t)\mathbf{T}_i^\top \cdot x_{\text{orig}})$
11 **end**
12 Sample weight $m \sim \text{Beta}(\alpha, \alpha)$
13 $x_{\text{aug}} = m x_{\text{orig}} + (1-m) x_{\text{aug}}$

Comparison with Prior Arts. There are some notable differences between *FourierMix* and prior SOTA in terms of: a) base augmentation operations, and b) data augmentation objective. These differences are later quantitatively highlighted using experimental results.

AugMix leverages the base augmentation operations from AutoAugment [11] that do not overlap with ImageNet-C. In contrast, the augmentations in *FourierMix* utilize a simpler set of generic augmentations. We compare the performance (*i.e.*, ACR) of *FourierMix* with AugMix on multiple corruption datasets in our evaluation (Sect. 4 and Sect. 5). Another key difference between *FourierMix* and prior arts is that Fourier-Mix explicitly uses spectral coverage as the data augmentation objective. For example, the recently proposed FACT [62] randomly mixes the amplitude spectra of two training samples, which has no control over the spectral coverage (results are presented in Appendix D.1). However, *FourierMix* realizes proportional assignment of augmentation across all frequencies.

4   Experiments on Popular Corruption Benchmarks

Experimental Setup. We use ACR and mACR (see Sect. 2.1) as the main evaluation metrics. We utilize the official implementation from [9] to compute the certified radius CR($\cdot$). We use the same base architectures leveraged in prior arts [9,25,47,66], *i.e.*, ResNet-110 and ResNet-50, for experiments on CIFAR-10/100 and ImageNet [19], respectively. We use Gaussian augmentation with $\sigma =$

Table 1. Models trained with *FourierMix* and HCR achieve significant improvements in the certified robustness (ACR and mACR) guarantees on all popular corruption datasets. **Bold** and <u>underline</u> denote the best and runner-up results, respectively.

Augmentation	CIFAR-10		CIFAR-10-C			CIFAR-10-C̄
	ACR	mACR	-Low	-Mid	-High	mACR
Gaussian	0.461	0.363	0.301	0.353	0.435	0.314
+JSD	**0.535**	0.439	0.346	0.451	<u>0.520</u>	0.393
+AutoAugment	0.411	0.372	0.312	0.364	0.431	0.304
+JSD	0.432	0.400	0.343	0.395	0.464	0.346
+AugMix	0.452	0.385	0.324	0.383	0.449	0.341
+JSD	0.518	0.430	0.357	0.436	0.496	0.382
+**HCR**	0.520	0.437	0.369	0.444	0.497	0.393
+*FourierMix*	0.455	0.388	0.326	0.386	0.453	0.348
+JSD	<u>0.522</u>	<u>0.444</u>	<u>0.375</u>	<u>0.454</u>	0.504	<u>0.397</u>
+**HCR**	**0.535**	**0.460**	**0.384**	**0.473**	**0.521**	**0.419**
Augmentation	CIFAR-100		CIFAR-100-C			CIFAR-100-C̄
	ACR	mACR	-Low	-Mid	-High	mACR
Gaussian	0.238	0.169	0.131	0.182	0.208	0.130
+JSD	0.291	0.232	0.167	0.248	0.280	0.196
+AutoAugment+JSD	0.265	0.225	0.175	0.234	0.265	0.176
+AugMix+JSD	0.286	0.231	0.184	0.240	0.269	0.193
+AugMix+**HCR**	<u>0.296</u>	<u>0.249</u>	<u>0.191</u>	<u>0.263</u>	<u>0.292</u>	<u>0.211</u>
+*FourierMix*+JSD	0.295	0.247	0.190	0.258	<u>0.292</u>	0.207
+*FourierMix*+**HCR**	**0.309**	**0.261**	0.199	**0.278**	**0.307**	**0.227**
Augmentation	ImageNet		ImageNet-C			ImageNet-C̄
	ACR	mACR	-Low	-Mid	-High	mACR
Gaussian	0.600	0.256	0.155	0.228	0.385	0.266
+JSD	0.736	0.395	0.220	0.382	**0.581**	0.395
+AugMix+JSD	0.717	0.391	0.238	<u>0.387</u>	0.550	0.379
+AugMix+**HCR**	0.727	0.390	0.234	0.383	0.552	0.378
+*FourierMix*+JSD	**0.751**	**0.399**	**0.242**	**0.389**	0.564	**0.413**
+*FourierMix*+**HCR**	<u>0.750</u>	<u>0.397</u>	<u>0.239</u>	<u>0.387</u>	<u>0.567</u>	<u>0.411</u>

0.25 and 0.5 for both training and certifying the CIFAR-10/100 and ImageNet models, respectively. Further training details are in Appendix D.

Baselines.   We evaluate the certified robustness of models trained with following augmentations schemes on corrupted data: Gaussian [9], AutoAugment [11], and AugMix [23]. We also compare HCR with the baseline JSD regularization [25]. We follow Cohen *et al.* [9] and Jeong *et al.* [25] to train the Gaussian and Gaussian+JSD baseline models, respectively. For other augmentation methods, we apply Gaussian noise $\mathcal{N}(0, \sigma^2 \mathbf{I})$ to half of the training samples in the mini-batch to ensure good certification performance using RS, and we follow Hendrycks *et al.*to apply JSD to these augmentation methods [23].

Datasets. For the in-distribution evaluation, we use CIFAR-10/100 [31] and ImageNet [12] datasets. CIFAR-10/100 consists of small 32×32 images belonging to 10/100 classes and ImageNet consists of 1.2 million images with 1,000 classes. We crop images in ImageNet into the same size of $224 \times 224 \times 3$ pixels. For the test data, we use the common corruptions datasets [22] (CIFAR-10/100-C and ImageNet-C) and a recently proposed dataset [38] (CIFAR-10/100-C̄ and

ImageNet-C̄) which contains human interpretable and perceptually different corruptions as compared to those contained in CIFAR-C/ImageNet-C.

4.1 Results on CIFAR-Based Corruption Benchmarks

The results in Table 1 show the overall mACR of the models trained on CIFAR-10 using different augmentation and regularization methods when evaluated on CIFAR-10-C and CIFAR-10-C̄, respectively. The results show that *FourierMix* consistently achieves the highest mACR across different corruption types. *FourierMix*+HCR significantly improves upon the baseline of Gaussian augmented training by 26.7% and 33.4% in terms of the overall mACR on CIFAR-10-C and CIFAR-10-C̄ and also improves upon the stronger baseline, AugMix+HCR, by 5.3% and 6.6% on the two datasets, respectively. We find consistency regularization to be helpful for certified robustness on corruption benchmarks. Especially, adding JSD to Gaussian augmentations significantly improves the robustness on mid- and high-frequency corrupted data. We see that combining HCR with *FourierMix* achieves SOTA ACRs on all corruption types providing significant gains even on low-frequency corruptions. This success is attributed to the spectrally diverse corruptions produced by *FourierMix*. Interestingly, we find AutoAugment overfits to corruptions in CIFAR-10-C since it suffers a major performance degradation on corruptions in CIFAR-10-C̄. We believe the large overlap between the leveraged augmentations and corruptions in CIFAR-10-C and limited spectral diversity are the primary reasons for this performance degradation of AutoAugment. Detailed results for each corruption type in CIFAR-10-C/C̄ are shown in Tables 2 and 3 in Appendix D.1.

Next, we present the mACR (Table 1) of the models trained with CIFAR-100 when evaluated on corrupted data (CIFAR-100-C and CIFAR-100-C̄). Similar to the performance of models trained with CIFAR-10, *FourierMix* achieves the highest overall mACR among all augmentation methods on both corruption datasets. Specifically, *FourierMix*+HCR outperforms the Gaussian baseline by 54.4% and 74.6% on two datasets, respectively. Compared to AugMix+HCR, *FourierMix*+HCR improves the performance by 4.8% and 7.6% on the two datasets, respectively. Detailed results for each corruption type in CIFAR-100-C/C̄ are shown in Tables 4 and 5 in Appendix D.2.

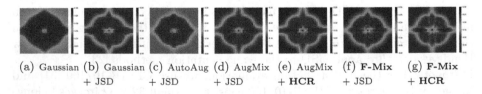

| (a) Gaussian | (b) Gaussian + JSD | (c) AutoAug + JSD | (d) AugMix + JSD | (e) AugMix + HCR | (f) **F-Mix** + JSD | (g) **F-Mix** + HCR |

Fig. 5. Fourier sensitivity analysis of models trained using different augmentations and regularizers on CIFAR-100 demonstrate their vulnerability to distribution shifts from mid-to-low frequency region (around the center of the plots). (F-Mix: *FourierMix*).

To further corroborate our findings, we carry out the Fourier sensitivity analysis of models trained on CIFAR-100 in Fig. 5. Adding a consistency loss (Gaussian+JSD) improves the ACR of the model in the high-frequency region but is still worse than the ACR achieved by the addition of consistency loss (JSD and HCR) with *FourierMix* augmentations in low-to-mid frequency regions. Similar to our quantitative results, AutoAugment does not improve much over the baseline of Gaussian augmentation which suggests that models trained with AutoAugment may be biased towards high-frequency regions. Heatmaps for CIFAR-10 models report similar findings and are presented in Fig. 7 in Appendix D.1.

4.2   Results on ImageNet-Based Corruption Benchmarks

Table 1 presents the mACR of the models trained on ImageNet when evaluated on ImageNet-C and ImageNet-C̄. We observe that distribution shifts lead to a drastic decline in the certified robustness on ImageNet. The drop between the ACR of clean data and the mACR of corrupted data is ∼57%, whereas it was ∼30% on CIFAR-10/100. Encouragingly, *FourierMix* continues to achieve the highest mACR compared to other baselines. *FourierMix* outperforms the baseline of Gaussian augmented training and AugMix+JSD by 55.9% and 2.1% in terms of the overall mACR, respectively. Detailed results and discussion for ImageNet-C/C̄ can be found in Tables 6 and 7 in Appendix D.3.

Summary. Our results in this section not only highlight the vulnerability of SOTA certified defenses to corrupted data but also uncovers spectral biases in the benchmark datasets that are used to measure corruption robustness. In particular, methods that perform well on one corrupted dataset may not work well on other datasets due to differences in the spectral signatures of the corruptions. This makes it incredibly important to obtain a comprehensive view of the model robustness to avoid issues such as leaderboard bias [39] and model overfitting to a specific benchmark [38]. To help achieve this objective, we propose a new benchmark that has a collection of spectrally diverse corruption datasets.

5   A Spectral Corruption Benchmarking Suite

Although corruptions proposed by [22] can be roughly grouped into different frequency ranges, their spectral diversity is restricted (see Figs. 10 and 11 in Appendix C). This could lead to corruption overfitting for methods that make models robust only on a limited subset of corruption types but fail on others (*e.g.*, Gaussian on ImageNet-C in Table 1). As the nature of test-time corruptions is unknown at train-time, and their form is application-dependent, models must be evaluated under diverse corruption settings. To achieve this, next we discuss the creation and evaluation of models on the proposed corruption benchmarking suite. The goal of this new suite is to complement the existing benchmark datasets and enable researchers to uncover the spectral biases of their models.

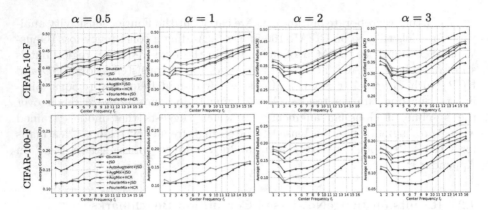

Fig. 6. ACRs on the proposed CIFAR-F dataset averaged over 3 severity levels show that *FourierMix* based models perform consistently better than other baselines across entire spectrum. Increasing α (from left to right), decreases the spread of the frequencies. Dips of ACRs in mid-frequency regions (*e.g.*, $\alpha = 2, 3$) demonstrate the vulnerability of models to low-to-mid frequency corruptions.

Protocol for Dataset Generation. The proposed benchmark is a collection of datasets each focusing on a specific frequency range while collectively covering the entire frequency spectrum. Different from the Fourier sensitivity analysis that only perturbs a single frequency using the Fourier basis, CIFAR-10/100-F leverages power law-based noise [1] to generate complex perturbations in the spectral domain [26]. Note that the power spectrum of several natural data distributions (e.g., natural images) follow power-law distribution [1]. Inspired by this, we model the amplitude perturbation as $\delta_{\text{Fourier}}(f)_{\mathbf{A}} = \frac{P(f)}{(|f-f_c|+1)^\alpha} \cdot \mathrm{U}(1 - b, 1 + b)$, where $P(f)$ approximates the tolerance of corruptions at azimuthal frequency $f = \sqrt{u^2 + v^2}$, f_c is the central frequency that the perturbation focuses on, and α denotes the power of the power law distribution. We also use a uniform distribution $\mathrm{U}(1 - b, 1 + b)$ with b as a hyper-parameter ($b = 0.2$ in our study) to diversify the perturbations.

We define $P(f) = \mathrm{clip}(\mathbf{A}_{\boldsymbol{x}}^{\text{clean}}(f), a_{\text{lower}}, a_{\text{upper}})$ which adds the amount of perturbation based on the power associated with the different frequencies in the clean image [27], *i.e.*, frequencies with higher power have larger perturbations. We leverage the $\mathrm{clip}(\cdot)$ function to bound the amount of corruption in each spatial frequency. The maximum and minimum values are chosen to ensure that perturbations do not affect the semantic content of the images. The phase perturbation is formulated as $\delta_{\text{Fourier}}(f)_{\mathbf{P}} = \mathrm{U}(0, 2\pi)$. Given each pair $(\boldsymbol{x}^i, y^i)$ in the original validation set, we synthesize CIFAR-10/100-F images as

$$\boldsymbol{x}_F^i = \boldsymbol{x}^i + \gamma \cdot \mathrm{IFFT}(\delta_{\text{Fourier}}) \tag{5}$$

where $\gamma = \frac{\epsilon}{\|\mathrm{IFFT}(\delta_{\text{Fourier}})\|_2}$ normalizes the spreading effect of the power-law distribution and, thus, controls the severity level of CIFAR-10/100-F. We create both CIFAR-10/100-F with 3 severity levels with $\epsilon \in \{8, 10, 12\}$. As the images in CIFAR-10/100 are of size 32×32, their FFT spectrum has discrete azimuthal frequencies from 0 to 16. Since zero-frequency noise is a constant in the pixel space, we set the center frequency $f_c \in \{1, 2, ..., 16\}$. We leverage $\alpha \in \{0.5, 1, 2, 3\}$ because power-law noises with $0 < \alpha \leq 3$ arise in both natural signals and in man-made processes [1]. In total, our CIFAR-10/100-F datasets are consisted of $3 \times 4 \times 16 = 192$ test sets from different regions of the frequency spectrum thereby increasing the spectral coverage of the original dataset.

Visual Effect of Varying. α **and** f_c. As shown in Fig. 12 in Appendix F, α controls the frequency dispersion of the corruption at f_c. With a smaller α, e.g., $\alpha = 0.5$, the spreading effect of the power law distribution is more significant. The corrupted images thus contain noises across all azimuthal frequencies. In contrast, for larger α, the corruptions will be focused more on a single frequency e.g., $\alpha = 3$, and higher f_c leads to a higher corruption frequency.

Results on CIFAR-10/100-F. Figure 6 reports the performance of models used in Sect. 4.1 on CIFAR-10/100-F benchmark. Our results show that both AutoAugment [11] and AugMix [23] based smoothed models are relatively biased toward low-frequency corruptions. The effect of high-frequency corruptions is more pronounced on models trained with AutoAugment which behave similarly to the simple baseline of Gaussian augmentation (Fig. 6). The intersection of the curves of AugMix+JSD and Gaussian+JSD in the mid-frequency region in CIFAR-10-F (Fig. 6), illustrates the different spectral biases introduced by different augmentation methods. Unlike CIFAR-10-F, we find that Gaussian and Gaussian+JSD perform relatively worse on CIFAR-100-F compared to other augmentation methods. In comparison to other methods, we find that models trained with *FourierMix* and HCR do not show significant spectral biases and serve as a strong baseline. Specifically, models trained with *FourierMix*+HCR, on average, outperform AugMix+HCR, by 11.8% and 16.0% on CIFAR-10/100-F, respectively. We emphasize that models trained with *FourierMix* do not overfit to CIFAR-10/100-F datasets since they have different formulations and even visual patterns (see Appendix E and F).

6 Discussion and Conclusion

Our work has shown that certified defenses are surprisingly brittle to distribution shifts such as low-frequency corruptions. To alleviate this issue, we proposed *FourierMix* augmentation to increase the spectral coverage of the training data. We also presented a benchmarking suite to understand the model's corruption robustness comprehensively. Some of our findings are consistent with past results that model evaluation under corruption is a challenging problem, and one should not rely on a single benchmark [20,38,43]. However, as opposed to the existing works that focus on *empirical* robustness, we show that these issues persist and may even be more prominent in the problem of certified adversarial defense. Even though evaluation against all possible types of corruptions is infeasible, our results highlighted that eliminating spectral biases of the models improves the certified robustness under common corruptions.

Although we have taken some first steps to address this challenging problem, many questions remain to be answered. First, bridging the gap between robustness guarantees in high-frequency and low-frequency corruption regimes is still an open problem. A deeper theoretical understanding of this phenomenon will likely motivate systematic approaches to overcome this issue. Finally, the analysis done in this work can be explored in the context of certifying other ℓ_p norms [63], spectral deformations [2], and semantic transformations [35].

Acknowledgements. This work was performed under the auspices of the U.S. Department of Energy by the Lawrence Livermore National Laboratory under Contract No. DE-AC52-07NA27344 and LLNL LDRD Program Project No. 20-ER-014. This work was partially supported by NSF under the National AI Institute for Edge Computing Leveraging Next Generation Wireless Networks, Grant # 2112562, in addition to NSF grants CMMI-2038215 and CNS-1930041.

References

1. 1/f noise (2021). http://www.scholarpedia.org/article/1/f_noise
2. Alfarra, M., Bibi, A., Khan, N., Torr, P.H., Ghanem, B.: DeformRS: certifying input deformations with randomized smoothing. Proc. AAAI Conf. Artif. Intell. **36**(6), 6001–6009 (2022). https://doi.org/10.1609/aaai.v36i6.20546, https://ojs.aaai.org/index.php/AAAI/article/view/20546
3. Athalye, A., Carlini, N., Wagner, D.: Obfuscated gradients give a false sense of security: Circumventing defenses to adversarial examples. In: International Conference on Machine Learning, pp. 274–283. PMLR (2018)
4. Bulusu, S., Kailkhura, B., Li, B., Varshney, P.K., Song, D.: Anomalous example detection in deep learning: a survey. IEEE Access **8**, 132330–132347 (2020)
5. Burton, G.J., Moorhead, I.R.: Color and spatial structure in natural scenes. Appl. Opt. **26**(1), 157–170 (1987)
6. Carlini, N., Wagner, D.: Towards evaluating the robustness of neural networks. In: 2017 IEEE Symposium on Security and Privacy (SP), pp. 39–57 (2017). https://doi.org/10.1109/SP.2017.49
7. Chen, P.Y., Sharma, Y., Zhang, H., Yi, J., Hsieh, C.J.: EAD: elastic-net attacks to deep neural networks via adversarial examples. In: Proceedings of the AAAI Conference on Artificial Intelligence, pp. 10–17 (2018)
8. Chen, P.Y., Zhang, H., Sharma, Y., Yi, J., Hsieh, C.J.: ZOO: zeroth order optimization based black-box attacks to deep neural networks without training substitute models. In: ACM Workshop on Artificial Intelligence and Security, pp. 15–26 (2017)
9. Cohen, J., Rosenfeld, E., Kolter, Z.: Certified adversarial robustness via randomized smoothing. In: International Conference on Machine Learning, pp. 1310–1320. PMLR (2019)
10. Croce, F., et al.: Robustbench: a standardized adversarial robustness benchmark. arXiv preprint arXiv:2010.09670 (2020)
11. Cubuk, E.D., Zoph, B., Mane, D., Vasudevan, V., Le, Q.V.: AutoAugment: learning augmentation strategies from data. In: Proceedings of the IEEE/CVF Conference on Computer Vision and Pattern Recognition, pp. 113–123 (2019)
12. Deng, J., Dong, W., Socher, R., Li, L.J., Li, K., Fei-Fei, L.: ImageNet: a large-scale hierarchical image database. In: 2009 IEEE Conference on Computer Vision and Pattern Recognition, pp. 248–255. IEEE (2009)

13. Dodge, S., Karam, L.: Understanding how image quality affects deep neural networks. In: 2016 Eighth International Conference on Quality of Multimedia Experience (QoMEX), pp. 1–6. IEEE (2016)
14. Fischer, M., Baader, M., Vechev, M.: Certified defense to image transformations via randomized smoothing. arXiv preprint arXiv:2002.12463 (2020)
15. Fuglede, B., Topsoe, F.: Jensen-shannon divergence and HilBERT space embedding. In: International Symposium on Information Theory, 2004. ISIT 2004. Proceedings, p. 31. IEEE (2004)
16. Gokhale, T., Anirudh, R., Kailkhura, B., Thiagarajan, J.J., Baral, C., Yang, Y.: Attribute-guided adversarial training for robustness to natural perturbations. arXiv preprint arXiv:2012.01806 (2020)
17. Gowal, S., et al.: On the effectiveness of interval bound propagation for training verifiably robust models. arXiv preprint arXiv:1810.12715 (2018)
18. Hammersley, J.: Monte Carlo methods. Springer, Singapore (2013). https://doi.org/10.1007/978-981-13-2971-5
19. He, K., Zhang, X., Ren, S., Sun, J.: Deep residual learning for image recognition. In: Proceedings of the IEEE Conference on Computer Vision and Pattern Recognition, pp. 770–778 (2016)
20. Hendrycks, D., et al.: The many faces of robustness: A critical analysis of out-of-distribution generalization. In: Proceedings of the IEEE/CVF International Conference on Computer Vision, pp. 8340–8349 (2021)
21. Hendrycks, D., Carlini, N., Schulman, J., Steinhardt, J.: Unsolved problems in ml safety. ArXiv abs/2109.13916 (2021)
22. Hendrycks, D., Dietterich, T.: Benchmarking neural network robustness to common corruptions and perturbations. arXiv preprint arXiv:1903.12261 (2019)
23. Hendrycks, D., Mu, N., Cubuk, E.D., Zoph, B., Gilmer, J., Lakshminarayanan, B.: AugMix: a simple data processing method to improve robustness and uncertainty. arXiv preprint arXiv:1912.02781 (2019)
24. Ilyas, A., Engstrom, L., Athalye, A., Lin, J.: Black-box adversarial attacks with limited queries and information. In: International Conference on Machine Learning, pp. 2137–2146. PMLR (2018)
25. Jeong, J., Shin, J.: Consistency regularization for certified robustness of smoothed classifiers. arXiv preprint arXiv:2006.04062 (2020)
26. Johnson, J.B.: The schottky effect in low frequency circuits. Phys. Rev. **26**(1), 71 (1925)
27. Joubert, O.R., Rousselet, G.A., Fabre-Thorpe, M., Fize, D.: Rapid visual categorization of natural scene contexts with equalized amplitude spectrum and increasing phase noise. J. Vis. **9**(1), 2–2 (2009)
28. Joyce, J.M.: Kullback-Leibler Divergence. In: Lovric, M. (eds.) International Encyclopedia of Statistical Science, pp. 720–722. Springer, Heidelberg (2011). https://doi.org/10.1007/978-3-642-04898-2_327
29. Kermisch, D.: Image reconstruction from phase information only. J. Opt. Soc. Am. **60**(1), 15–17 (1970)
30. Kireev, K., Andriushchenko, M., Flammarion, N.: On the effectiveness of adversarial training against common corruptions. arXiv preprint arXiv:2103.02325 (2021)
31. Krizhevsky, A., Hinton, G., et al.: Learning multiple layers of features from tiny images. Technical Report 0, University of Toronto (2009)
32. Lecuyer, M., Atlidakis, V., Geambasu, R., Hsu, D., Jana, S.: Certified robustness to adversarial examples with differential privacy. In: 2019 IEEE Symposium on Security and Privacy (SP), pp. 656–672. IEEE (2019)

33. Li, B., Chen, C., Wang, W., Carin, L.: Second-order adversarial attack and certifiable robustness (2018)
34. Li, L., Qi, X., Xie, T., Li, B.: SoK: certified robustness for deep neural networks. arXiv abs/2009.04131 (2020)
35. Li, L., et al.: TSS: transformation-specific smoothing for robustness certification. In: ACM CCS (2021)
36. Lim, J.S.: Two-Dimensional Signal and Image Processing. Prentice-Hall, Englewood Cliffs (1990)
37. Mehra, A., Kailkhura, B., Chen, P.Y., Hamm, J.: How robust are randomized smoothing based defenses to data poisoning? In: Proceedings of the IEEE/CVF Conference on Computer Vision and Pattern Recognition, pp. 13244–13253 (2021)
38. Mintun, E., Kirillov, A., Xie, S.: On interaction between augmentations and corruptions in natural corruption robustness. arXiv preprint arXiv:2102.11273 (2021)
39. Mishra, S., Arunkumar, A.: How robust are model rankings: A leaderboard customization approach for equitable evaluation. arXiv preprint arXiv:2106.05532 (2021)
40. Mohapatra, J., Ko, C.Y., Weng, T.W., Chen, P.Y., Liu, S., Daniel, L.: Higher-order certification for randomized smoothing. In: Proceedings of the 34th International Conference on Neural Information Processing Systems (2020)
41. Mohapatra, J., Weng, T.W., Chen, P.Y., Liu, S., Daniel, L.: Towards verifying robustness of neural networks against a family of semantic perturbations. In: Proceedings of the IEEE/CVF Conference on Computer Vision and Pattern Recognition, pp. 244–252 (2020)
42. Raghunathan, A., Steinhardt, J., Liang, P.: Certified defenses against adversarial examples. arXiv preprint arXiv:1801.09344 (2018)
43. Raji, I.D., Bender, E.M., Paullada, A., Denton, E., Hanna, A.: Ai and the everything in the whole wide world benchmark. arXiv preprint arXiv:2111.15366 (2021)
44. Rebuffi, S.A., Gowal, S., Calian, D.A., Stimberg, F., Wiles, O., Mann, T.: Fixing data augmentation to improve adversarial robustness. arXiv preprint arXiv:2103.01946 (2021)
45. Ruder, S.: An overview of gradient descent optimization algorithms. arXiv preprint arXiv:1609.04747 (2016)
46. Saenko, K., Kulis, B., Fritz, M., Darrell, T.: Adapting visual category models to new domains. In: Daniilidis, K., Maragos, P., Paragios, N. (eds.) ECCV 2010. LNCS, vol. 6314, pp. 213–226. Springer, Heidelberg (2010). https://doi.org/10.1007/978-3-642-15561-1_16
47. Salman, H., et al.: Provably robust deep learning via adversarially trained smoothed classifiers. arXiv preprint arXiv:1906.04584 (2019)
48. Schneider, S., Rusak, E., Eck, L., Bringmann, O., Brendel, W., Bethge, M.: Improving robustness against common corruptions by covariate shift adaptation. In: 34th Conference on Neural Information Processing Systems (NeurIPS 2020), Vancouver, Canada (2020)
49. Sun, J., Cao, Y., Chen, Q.A., Mao, Z.M.: Towards robust LiDAR-based perception in autonomous driving: General black-box adversarial sensor attack and countermeasures. In: 29th USENIX Security Symposium (USENIX Security 20), pp. 877–894. USENIX Association, August 2020. https://www.usenix.org/conference/usenixsecurity20/presentation/sun
50. Sun, J., Cao, Y., Choy, C.B., Yu, Z., Anandkumar, A., Mao, Z.M., Xiao, C.: Adversarially robust 3d point cloud recognition using self-supervisions. Adv. Neural. Inf. Process. Syst. **34**, 15498–15512 (2021)

51. Sun, J., Koenig, K., Cao, Y., Chen, Q.A., Mao, Z.M.: On adversarial robustness of 3d point cloud classification under adaptive attacks. arXiv preprint arXiv:2011.11922 (2020)
52. Sun, J., Zhang, Q., Kailkhura, B., Yu, Z., Xiao, C., Mao, Z.M.: Benchmarking robustness of 3d point cloud recognition against common corruptions. arXiv preprint arXiv:2201.12296 (2022)
53. Szegedy, C., et al.: Intriguing properties of neural networks. arXiv preprint arXiv:1312.6199 (2013)
54. Tolhurst, D., Tadmor, Y., Chao, T.: Amplitude spectra of natural images. Ophthalmic Physiol. Opt. **12**(2), 229–232 (1992)
55. Tramer, F., Carlini, N., Brendel, W., Madry, A.: On adaptive attacks to adversarial example defenses. arXiv preprint arXiv:2002.08347 (2020)
56. Wang, D., Shelhamer, E., Liu, S., Olshausen, B., Darrell, T.: Tent: fully test-time adaptation by entropy minimization. In: International Conference on Learning Representations (2021). https://openreview.net/forum?id=uXl3bZLkr3c
57. Wong, E., Kolter, Z.: Provable defenses against adversarial examples via the convex outer adversarial polytope. In: International Conference on Machine Learning, pp. 5286–5295. PMLR (2018)
58. Xiao, C., Li, B., Zhu, J.Y., He, W., Liu, M., Song, D.: Generating adversarial examples with adversarial networks. arXiv preprint arXiv:1801.02610 (2018)
59. Xu, K., et al.: Provable, scalable and automatic perturbation analysis on general computational graphs. arXiv e-prints pp. arXiv-2002 (2020)
60. Xu, K., Wang, C., Cheng, H., Kailkhura, B., Lin, X., Goldhahn, R.: Mixture of robust experts (MORE): a robust denoising method towards multiple perturbations. arXiv preprint arXiv:2104.10586 (2021)
61. Xu, Q., Zhang, R., Zhang, Y., Wang, Y., Tian, Q.: A Fourier-based framework for domain generalization. In: Proceedings of the IEEE/CVF Conference on Computer Vision and Pattern Recognition, pp. 14383–14392 (2021)
62. Xu, Q., Zhang, R., Zhang, Y., Wang, Y., Tian, Q.: A Fourier-based framework for domain generalization. In: IEEE/CVF CVPR, pp. 14383–4392, June 2021
63. Yang, G., Duan, T., Hu, J.E., Salman, H., Razenshteyn, I., Li, J.: Randomized smoothing of all shapes and sizes. In: International Conference on Machine Learning, pp. 10693–10705. PMLR (2020)
64. Yang, Y., Lao, D., Sundaramoorthi, G., Soatto, S.: Phase consistent ecological domain adaptation. In: Proceedings of the IEEE/CVF Conference on Computer Vision and Pattern Recognition, pp. 9011–9020 (2020)
65. Yin, D., Lopes, R.G., Shlens, J., Cubuk, E.D., Gilmer, J.: A fourier perspective on model robustness in computer vision. arXiv preprint arXiv:1906.08988 (2019)
66. Zhai, R., et al.: MACER: attack-free and scalable robust training via maximizing certified radius. In: International Conference on Learning Representations (2020). https://openreview.net/forum?id=rJx1Na4Fwr
67. Zhang, H., Weng, T.W., Chen, P.Y., Hsieh, C.J., Daniel, L.: Efficient neural network robustness certification with general activation functions. In: Advances in Neural Information Processing Systems, pp. 4944–4953 (2018)

Improving Adversarial Robustness of 3D Point Cloud Classification Models

Guanlin Li[1,2], Guowen Xu[1(✉)], Han Qiu[3], Ruan He[4], Jiwei Li[5,6], and Tianwei Zhang[1]

[1] Nanyang Technological University, Singapore, Singapore
{guanlin001,guowen.xu,tianwei.zhang}@ntu.edu.sg
[2] S-Lab, NTU, Singapore, Singapore
qiuhan@tsinghua.edu.cn
[3] Tsinghua University, Beijing, China
ruanhe@tencent.com
[4] Tencent, Shenzhen, China
[5] Shannon.AI, Beijing, China
jiwei_li@shannonai.com
[6] Zhejiang University, Hangzhou, China

Abstract. 3D point cloud classification models based on deep neural networks were proven to be vulnerable to adversarial examples, with a quantity of novel attack techniques proposed by researchers recently. It is of paramount importance to preserve the robustness of 3D models under adversarial environments, considering their broad application in safety- and security-critical tasks. Unfortunately, existing defenses are not general enough to satisfactorily mitigate all types of attacks. In this paper, we design two innovative methodologies to improve the adversarial robustness of 3D point cloud classification models. (1) We introduce CCN, a novel point cloud architecture which can smooth and disrupt the adversarial perturbations. (2) We propose AMS, a novel *data augmentation* strategy to adaptively balance the model usability and robustness. Extensive evaluations indicate the integration of the two techniques provides much more robustness than existing defense solutions for 3D classification models. Our code can be found in https://github.com/GuanlinLee/CCNAMS.

1 Introduction

A point cloud is a popular representation of 3D objects and shapes. It consists of a set of data points with x, y and z coordinates to describe the external surface of an object. Interpreting point cloud data becomes important in many scenarios, *e.g.*, robotics [12], manufacturing [2], construction [19], *etc.*. Recently, researchers designed new models based on Deep Neural Networks (DNNs) (*e.g.*,

Supplementary Information The online version contains supplementary material available at https://doi.org/10.1007/978-3-031-19772-7_39.

PointNet [21], DGCNN [27]) for 3D object classification, which achieve remarkable breakthrough over traditional methods.

Unfortunately, DNNs are well known to be vulnerable during training stage [31,32] and inference stage [5]. In the inference stage, DNNs are easy to be attacked by Adversarial Examples (AEs) [25] , where imperceptible perturbations on a normal sample can mislead the model to make wrong predictions. Over the years, a plethora of attacks were designed to efficiently generate AEs [9,20]. New techniques were further proposed to attack point cloud models [15,30,36]. Such vulnerabilities can significantly threaten the safe- and security-critical applications based on point cloud models.

Past works have extensively explored methods of defending 2D models against AEs. In contrast, how to enhance the robustness of 3D models is relatively less studied. The unique features of point cloud data and models increase the difficulty of model protection: (1) point clouds usually have irregular formats determined by the sensors for data collection; (2) adversaries have more choices to perform the attacks (e.g., adding or removing points) in addition to changing the coordinate values; (3) 3D point clouds have a larger perturbation space than the 2D image space, resulting in more qualified AEs. These features make existing solutions less effective: they are not general enough to cover different types of adversarial attacks [15,17,37], or can be easily bypassed by adaptive attacks [18,24]. Hence, it is urgent but challenging to have a general and comprehensive defense mechanism.

In this paper, we propose new solutions to effectively defend point cloud classification models against AEs in two aspects. First, we design Context-Consistency dynamic graph Network (CCN), a new 3D network structure with higher adversarial robustness. It is able to dilute the noise in the adversarial samples, and make them closer to the clean samples in the feature space. Second, we introduce a new data augmentation strategy, named adaptive augmentation with Adversarial and Mix-up Samples (AMS). Researchers have proposed to train 3D point cloud models with adversarial examples [15] or mix-up sampling [6,34]. However, these methods cannot achieve comprehensive protection due to the variety of techniques in crafting AEs. Hence, we propose to augment the training set with different types of adversarial examples and mix-up samples. Simply incorporating all these data samples could easily affect the model accuracy over clean samples or overfit some specific attack. To balance the trade-off between model usability and robustness, we dynamically monitor the model's behaviors during training, and adaptively select the samples that can best improve the model performance. Compared to prior solutions that mainly focus on specific attacks, our solutions can achieve the *best adversarial robustness trade-off* among all types of attacks.

To assess the adversarial robustness of our two methodologies, we leverage the mutual information theory to theoretically explain the effectiveness of the proposed network architecture and training strategy. We also perform comprehensive evaluations over two commonly-used 3D point cloud datasets (Model-Net10 and ModelNet40) against four state-of-the-art white-box attacks and one black-box attack. Experimental results show that each solution exhibits advantages compared to the baselines with the same configurations. The integration of CCN and AMS outperforms existing solutions by about 8% on average adversarial accuracy.

2   Background and Related Works

2.1   Point Cloud Models

A point cloud is formally defined as an unordered set of points $x = \{x_i\}_{i=1}^N$, where $x_i \in \mathbb{R}^3$ is a 3D point with (x, y, z) coordinates, and N is the number of points. A point cloud classification model is thus a parameterized function $f_\theta : \mathcal{X} \mapsto \mathcal{Y}$ that predicts the corresponding label from a point cloud. Researchers have proposed different deep learning algorithms and neural networks to realize this classification task. We describe three common models. (1) PointNet [21]: this network consists of single variable-functions, a max pooling layer, and a function of the max pooled features to handle unordered points with arbitrary dimensions. It converts the point cloud data to feature vectors with fixed lengths, and then learns the labels. (2) PointNet++ [22]: this is a hierarchical neural network, which recursively applies PointNet over partitioned point sets to learn the local structures. Both of PointNet and PointNet++ adopt the coordinates of the points to produce the features. (3) DGCNN [27]: this Dynamic Graph Convolutional Neural Network integrates a new module EdgeConv to point cloud models. This module captures the local geometric structures by constructing a local graph and learning the embeddings for the edges. Then the integrated model can learn to semantically group the points for more accurate classification. Different from PointNet and PointNet++, DGCNN considers the neighbors of the points and adopts high-order features, *i.e.*, distances between adjacent points, to predict the labels. As a result, it gives higher robustness than the other two models. We also validate this conclusion in Sect. 5.3.

2.2   Adversarial Attacks Against Point Clouds

The concept of adversarial examples was first proposed in [25], where the adversary tries to identify the imperceptible perturbation with the minimal scale to mislead the 2D image model. Then this attack was extended to the 3D point clouds with more techniques. Generally, these attacks can be classified into the following three categories:

Point Perturbing. Similar to 2D image attacks, the adversary can slightly perturb the coordinates of certain critical points to fool the 3D model. Conventional approaches in 2D image tasks can be applied to 3D point clouds as well. For instance, Xiang et al. [30] adopted the C&W technique [5] to identify the optimal perturbing scale. Liu et al. [15] adopted the FGSM method [25] with various perturbation constraints to craft adversarial point clouds.

Point Adding. The adversary can inject a small set of new points into the clean point cloud to attack the model. Xiang et al. [30] designed an initialize-and-shift approach to calculate the added points with their positions. Zhang et al. [35] proposed a point-wise gradient method to generate the optimal locations for point attachment.

Point Dropping. The adversary can also remove some points from the original set to alter the model output. Zheng et al. [36] constructed the saliency map to identify the critical points and then drop them for attacks. A similar idea was also proposed in [35].

2.3   Adversarial Defenses for Point Clouds

A couple of approaches were proposed to defeat adversarial attacks against point clouds. They can be briefly summarized with the following categories.

Denoising Point Clouds. The basic idea is to cleanse the point cloud data and possibly remove the adversarial perturbations. For instance, Zhou et al. [37] designed a new structure DUP-Net, with the SOR operation to drop outliers in the input samples. However, it is only effective for point perturbing attacks, but fails to thwart point adding or dropping attacks. Dong et al. [8] designed a self-robust network with the self-attention mechanism to remove adversarial local features. These defense methods have also been defeated by new adaptive attacks [18,24].

Training Robust Models. Liu et al. [15] explored how to train a 3D point cloud model with adversarial examples generated by PGD. They concluded this strategy can beat SOR and salient point removal approaches under certain attacks. Unfortunately, simple adversarial training based on PGD is not robust to cover all types of attacks, which will be demonstrated in our evaluation. Sun et al. [24] proposed a sorting-based parametric pooling operation to overcome the frangibility of default-used fixed pooling operations in point cloud models. Mix-up is a popular technique to augment training data with linear interpolations of feature vectors and labels to defeat 2D adversarial images [33]. This idea was then extended to the point cloud scenario, based on which researchers designed PointMixUP [6], and PointCutMix [34]. Our adaptive augmentation can outperform these purely mix-up strategies from the evaluation.

Certified Defenses. A couple of works designed certified defenses to defeat adversarial attacks in a theoretical way. For instance, Liu et al. [16] used a down-sampling method to give an upper bound of the number of perturbed points. However, this method is time-consuming and needs clean inputs as guides, which is not practical. Lorenz et al. [17] studied the robustness of a model with transformations (e.g., rotating, shearing). They only considered the FGSM attack while ignoring other techniques.

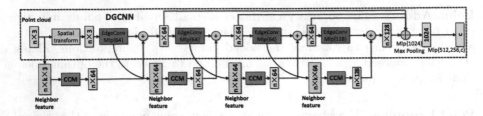

Fig. 1. Overview of CCN.

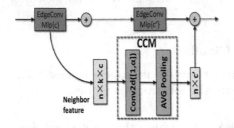

Fig. 2. The structure of CCM.

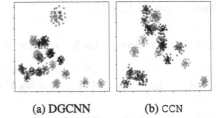

(a) DGCNN   (b) CCN

Fig. 3. Feature map visualization.

3   Methodologies

In this section, we present two methodologies to protect the point cloud models against adversarial attacks: a new model structure and training strategy. Each method can enhance the model's adversarial robustness from a different perspective, and their combination serves as an effective defense solution.

3.1   Context-Consistency Dynamic Graph Network

From the aspect of model architecture, we design Context-Consistency dynamic graph Network (CCN), a new 3D model structure for robustness enhancement. The core insight behind our architecture is to decrease feature distances between clean and noisy samples with an adaptive denoising mechanism. Figure 1 shows the structure overview. It is mainly built from the DGCNN model with the same spatial transform and EdgeConv layers. We choose DGCNN because it exhibits higher robustness than PointNet and PointNet++, due to the adoption of relation features, i.e., distances between points.

The key component of CCN is a lightweight Context-Consistency Module (CCM), which is inserted at many layers (Fig. 1). This module is responsible for collecting the features of point cloud data and diluting the potential adversarial noise, which can move the features of adversarial samples closer to that of clean ones. Since the adversarial noise in the feature space increases significantly at deeper layers (observed in Fig. 4), CCM extracts the neighbor features of every point (i.e., coordinates of each point's neighbors) before the next Edge-Conv layer, which is relatively easier for denoising. The output of CCM will be combined with the output of the next EdgeConv layer.

Figure 2 shows the detailed structure of CCM, which consists of a convolutional layer and a pooling layer. Specifically, (1) the 2D convolutional layer is used to simulate the function of the Edge layer to reduce the noise from model parameters. It has a receptive field size (i.e., kernel size) of $[1, \alpha]$ to process the context information (i.e., coordinates) in the neighbors (the closest points generated by the KNN [27]) of each point. It calculates new coordinates for the neighbors in the scope of α, which automatically learns to smooth the noise in the neighbor features. The sliding window in this convolutional layer can handle all the continuous scopes in the neighbor feature. In this way, the feature distance between adversarial and clean samples can be minimized. (2) The average pooling layer is following the convolutional layer to reduce the redundancy features. This function chooses the proper elements in the features based on their values. It can prevent noise accumulation during the model's forward propagation process by averaging elements in the features. (3) A residual connection transfers the adaptively selected context information to the output of the next EdgeConv layer. With such operation, CCM can keep the features between different layers (i.e., contexts extracted from inputs) consistent. As a result, it can prevent the adversarial noise in the features from growing quickly at deeper layers.

It is worth noting that the receptive field size α in CCM can impact the model robustness when the order of inputs changes. This is because in a point cloud, the correlation between neighbor points is less tight than the correlation between neighbor pixels in a 2D image. Visiting too many points with a big receptive field can make the noise unacceptably large. On the other hand, using a small receptive field to visit very few points can make the information from points useless to calculate the correct coordinates. Currently, there are no theoretical guidelines for determining this hyperparameter, and we figure out this optimal value empirically in Sect. 5.1.

To demonstrate the effects of CCM, we use the t-SNE method to visualize the feature map of DGCNN and our CCN with the ModelNet40 dataset, as shown in Fig. 3. We randomly select 10 classes, and each class contains 50 point clouds (Visualization results for all the 40 classes can be found in the supplementary material). Different classes are represented with different colors. We use circles and triangles to denote the clean and perturbed point clouds, respectively. From Fig. 3a, we can see that in DGCNN, some perturbed data are far from the clean data in the same class, or even overlapped with data from other classes. This implies misclassification for those data. In contrast, for CCN (Fig. 3b), the perturbed and clean data in the same class are much closer, and there is less overlap among different classes. This indicates that CCM can effectively remove the noise, making the perturbed and clean data much closer in the feature space.

3.2   Adaptive Augmentation with Adversarial and Mix-up Samples

In addition to CCN, we also introduce a novel data augmentation strategy to enhance the robustness of a point cloud model. In the conventional 2D image tasks, there are generally two types of training strategies for defeating adversarial examples. Unfortunately, they cannot achieve satisfactory performance when extended to 3D point cloud models. The first strategy is adversarial training, which augments the training set with adversarial examples crafted by the PGD technique. However, there are essentially various types of methods to generate adversarial point clouds with distinct features. Adversarial training with one type of AEs cannot provide comprehensive protection for other types of attacks [15], while simply incorporating all these sorts of AEs can significantly harm the model accuracy for clean samples. The second strategy is to mix up clean samples with different labels for model training [33]. This strategy is applied to the point cloud classification [6,34], which have limited robustness improvement.

Our adaptive augmentation strategy (AMS) considers the adversarial examples (of different types), mix-up samples as well as clean samples for model training. However, it is challenging to decide the type and quantity of samples to be used before the training task, as the training process is dynamic and relatively random. To overcome this challenge, AMS adaptively selects the desired samples in each epoch based on the current model. This dynamic selection can efficiently balance the model robustness and accuracy over clean samples for the complex 3D point cloud classification tasks.

Our training algorithm is shown in Algorithm 1. At every training epoch, for each batch (X, Y) from the training set Q, we first generate three types of batches from each sample in the batch[1]: (1) X_{drop} is a batch of AEs with the point dropping technique using the function AE-Gen^{drop}; (2) X_{perturb} is a batch of AEs with the point perturbing technique using the function AE-Gen^{perturb}; (3) X_{mix} is a batch of mix-up samples with the corresponding mix-up labels Y_{mix} using the function MS-Gen. Second, we compute the accuracy of clean and AE batches from the current model, as acc_x, acc_{drop} and acc_{perturb}, respectively. We compute $acc_{\mathrm{min}} = \min(acc_{\mathrm{drop}}, acc_{\mathrm{perturb}})$, and compare it with the weighted mean accuracy of the clean batches $acc_{\mathrm{avg}} = T * \mathrm{mean}(acc)$, where acc is a collection of clean accuracy acc_x at the current training epoch. If acc_{min} is higher than acc_{avg}, then this model is regarded as robust enough to defend against different types of AEs. So we perform *mix-up augmentation* to improve the model's generalization and utility, *i.e.*, training the model with the clean batch (X, Y) and mix-up batch $(X_{\mathrm{mix}}, Y_{\mathrm{mix}})$. Otherwise, we perform *adversarial augmentation* to improve the model's robustness, *i.e.*, training it with the clean batch (X, Y) and two types of adversarial batches (X_{drop}, Y), $(X_{\mathrm{perturb}}, Y)$.

In practice, we implement MS-Gen with the PointCutMix approach [34]. We adopt the Saliency Map Attack [36] to craft AEs by dropping points for AE-Gen^{drop}. For AE-Gen^{perturb}, we utilize the 3D L_{∞}-BIM technique [14], which

---

[1] We do not consider point adding as the generation complexity is extremely high. Experiments show the incorporation of the other two AEs can defeat the point adding AEs as well.

Algorithm 1: Adaptive Augmentation with Adversarial and Mix-up Samples.

Input : Q: point cloud training set
Output: M: robust point cloud model

1 Initialize(M);
2 **foreach** *training epoch* **do**
3    $acc = []$;
4   **foreach** *batch* $(X, Y) \sim Q$ **do**
5       $X_{\text{perturb}} = \texttt{AE-GEN}^{\texttt{perturb}}(X, Y, M)$;
6       $X_{\text{drop}} = \texttt{AE-GEN}^{\texttt{drop}}(X, Y, M)$;
7       $(X_{\text{mix}}, Y_{\text{mix}}) = \texttt{MS-GEN}(X, Y)$;
8   calculate accuracy acc_x, acc_{perturb} and acc_{drop} for X, X_{perturb} and X_{drop};
9       $acc.\text{append}(acc_x)$, $acc_{\text{min}} = \min(acc_{\text{perturb}}, acc_{\text{drop}})$;
10   **if** $acc_{\text{min}} > T * \text{mean}(acc)$ **then**
11   train M with (X, Y) and $(X_{\text{mix}}, Y_{\text{mix}})$;
12   **else**
13   train M with (X_{perturb}, Y), (X_{drop}, Y) and (X, Y);
14 **return** M

---

is a basic version of L_∞-PGD [30][2]. Besides, we calculate the averaged accuracy of acc_x for clean samples to avoid overfitting of T on a specific model and make the algorithm better generalize to other models. The optimal value of T will be empirically determined in Sect. 5.2.

For training complexity, compared to the pure adversarial training strategies, we need to generate two types of AEs for each clean sample. To keep the same training cost, we craft each AE with half the number of iterations. Our experiments in Sect. 5.2 indicate that AMS can help the model obtain higher robustness than conventional adversarial training methods under the same computational complexity constraint.

4   Explaining the Effectiveness of Our Methodologies

In this section, we perform an in-depth analysis to understand why our proposed solutions can improve the model robustness. Past works have developed frameworks to study the vulnerability of adversarial examples for 2D image models based on the mutual information theory [11,38]. Inspired by those frameworks, we aim to disclose the factors that can affect the robustness of point cloud models.

Specifically, we apply mutual information to calculate the correlation between the features of perturbed and clean point clouds. A high correlation indicates

---

[2] We do not use L_∞-PGD because when we randomly project the point cloud to an initialization position, the model has a high chance to give a wrong prediction initially, and the adversary will obtain less useful information than starting from the original position.

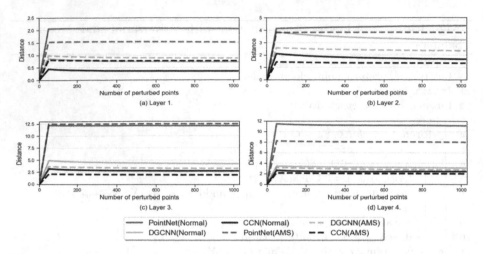

Fig. 4. Cosine distance of features between clean and perturbed samples at different layers. The perturbation is generated from a Gaussian distribution ($\mu = 0$, $\sigma = 0.05$).

the feature context of noisy data is more consistent with that of clean data, and the model is more robust to predict correct labels from noisy samples. However, it is computationally infeasible to directly calculate such mutual information, due to the high dimensions of the input space and feature space. Alternatively, we can estimate the mutual information with a substitute measurement, *i.e.*, the k-Measurement M_k. This measurement is based on the cosine distance, which can represent both the direction and magnitude of a distance in a high dimension at the same time. Formally, we have the following definition for k-Measurement:

Definition 1. (k-Measurement) Let f be a function that maps a point cloud to the feature space: $\{X_i | X_i \in R^d, i \in [N]\} \mapsto \{Y_i | Y_i \in R^D, i \in [N]\}$, where d is the dimension of the point coordinate in point clouds, D is the dimension of f's outputs for each point and N is the number of points in a point cloud. Consider a clean point cloud $S = \{X_i | X_i = (x_i, y_i, z_i), i \in [N]\}$. S_k is a perturbed point cloud with k different points compared with S, *i.e.*, $S_k = \{X_{j_i} | X_{j_i} = (x_{j_i}, y_{j_i}, z_{j_i}) \in S, j_i \in [N-k]\} \cup \{X_{h_i} + \epsilon_{h_i} | X_{h_i} = (x_{h_i}, y_{h_i}, z_{h_i}) \in S, \epsilon_{h_i} = (\epsilon_{0,h_i}, \epsilon_{1,h_i}, \epsilon_{2,h_i}), h_i \in [k]\}$. Then the k-Measurement M_k for f, S and S_k are defined as:

$$f(S) = \frac{\sum_{i=1}^{N} f(S)_i}{N}, f(S_k) = \frac{\sum_{i=1}^{N} f(S_k)_i}{N}$$

$$M_k(f, S, S_k) = 1 - \frac{f(S) \cdot f(S_k)}{\|f(S)\| \|f(S_k)\|}$$

We introduce a general theorem to prove that under the same value of k, a small $M_k(f, S, S_k)$ implies a large mutual information $I(S_K, f(S))$. The proof can be found in the supplementary material.

Theorem 1. *Let f be a function that maps a point cloud to the feature space, and Q be the distribution of clean point clouds. S is sampled from Q. $Q^k(S, \epsilon)$ is the distribution of noisy point clouds, in which each element S_k is perturbed from S with an additional noise ϵ, and the difference of numbers of points between S and S_k is smaller than a constant k, i.e., $-k \leq |S_k| - |S| \leq k$. Then for every $S \sim Q$ and $S_k \sim Q^k(S, \epsilon)$, the mutual information $I(S_k, f(S))$ has a lower bound, which is negatively correlated with the k-measurement $M_k(f, S, S_k)$.*

Theorem 1 can help us establish a connection between $M_k(f, S, S_k)$ and model robustness. A small k-measurement $M_k(f, S, S_k)$ could increase the mutual information value $I(S_k, f(S))$. According to the observation in [38], with a larger $I(S_k, f(S))$, the corresponding point cloud model is more robust, as the confidence of correctly predicting $f(S)$ from the perturbed sample S_k is higher. Therefore, *a small k-measurement $M_k(f, S, S_k)$ indicates a more robust point cloud model.*

With the above conclusion, we now explain the mechanisms of our proposed strategies. For the network architecture, as described in Sect. 3.1, the introduction of CCM is to increase the similarity of clean and perturbed samples in the feature space, which can lead to a small $M_k(f, S, S_k)$. For model training, our AMS adopts both AEs and mix-up samples for data augmentation. According to [1], training with AEs can be regarded as the process of feature purification, which can purify the non-robust direction in the features and build a tight connection between features and correct labels, i.e., increasing the mutual information between features and labels and decreasing M_k. From [33], mix-up samples can provide a generic vicinal distribution, and sampling from such a distribution can generate virtual feature-target vector pairs to force the model to minimize the Empirical Risk, which equals to minimizing M_k. We adaptively select different kinds of samples based on the model behaviors, which can take advantage of both methods and further reduce the k-measurement.

We also empirically verify the effectiveness of CCN and AMS in reducing the k-measurement. We consider three network architectures[3]: PointNet has five convolutional layers, with the first four used for feature extraction; both DGCNN and CCN have four EdgeConv layers for feature extraction. We compute the cosine distances between the features of clean and perturbed point clouds at these four layers[4]. Figure 4 compares the differences of different architectures and training strategies versus the number of perturbed points in clean point clouds. We have the following observations. (1) CCN and models trained with AMS always give smaller distances, indicating their efficacy in increasing the mutual information and enhancing the robustness. (2) For each layer, the distance decreases as the number of perturbed points increases. This is because when more points are perturbed in the point cloud, its distribution is closer to some augmented clean samples during the model training, leading to relatively smaller distance. (3) The distance increases from layer 1 to layer 3, indicating the noise is amplified

---

[3] The results for PointNet++ can be found in the supplementary material.
[4] For CCN, we choose $\alpha = 4$, which is identified in Sect. 5.1.

at deeper layers. Therefore, we adopt the neighbor features from the previous
EdgeConv instead of the current one in CCM.

5   Evaluations

We perform extensive experiments to evaluate our solutions. Below, we describe
the detailed experimental setup.

Table 1. Results for different architectures and hyperparameters (%).

Network Structure	Clean Sample	Adversarial Examples					
		SMA-40	APP	AIC	AIH	**AAUA**	**LAUA**
PointNet	90.83	63.11	**82.55**	76.14	**69.56**	72.84	63.11
DGCNN	91.88	79.91	74.88	76.01	68.47	74.82	**68.47**
CCN ($\alpha = 20$)	92.71	**82.04**	80.21	73.78	66.44	75.62	66.44
CCN ($\alpha = 16$)	92.53	80.80	78.21	73.70	64.41	74.28	64.41
CCN ($\alpha = 12$)	**92.74**	80.64	79.55	75.04	66.44	75.42	66.44
CCN ($\alpha = 8$)	92.05	81.66	78.81	71.14	63.92	73.88	63.92
CCN ($\alpha = 4$)	92.25	81.17	79.46	**76.46**	68.30	**76.35**	68.30
CCN ($\alpha = 1$)	92.37	80.60	78.45	74.88	66.60	75.13	66.60

Datasets and Models. We perform comprehensive experiments to validate
the effectiveness of CCN, AMS, and their combination. We mainly consider the
PointNet and DGCNN models. The evaluation results for PointNet++ give
the same conclusion, and can be found in the supplementary material. We adopt
the ModelNet40 dataset [29], which contains 12,311 CAD objects from 40 different classes. These objects are split into a training set of 9,843 samples and a test
set of 2,468 samples. For the training process, all the models are trained for 250
epochs with a learning rate of 0.001 and the Adam optimizer [13]. The size of
an input point cloud is 1,024 * 3, *i.e.*, there are 1,024 points in each point cloud
with three coordinates. We also perform evaluations on ModelNet10, a subset of
ModelNet40, and the results can be found in the supplementary material. Note
that there are also some more realistic point cloud datasets (e.g., ScanNet [7],
ScanObjectNN [26]). We do not consider them as currently there are no works
evaluating the attacks and defenses over them, and the feasibility of attacking
these datasets is unknown. We will consider this as future work.

Attacks. We find most of previous works only focus on the point perturbing
attack. In contrast, we also consider point adding, point dropping and black-box
adversarial attacks. We test five state-of-the-art adversarial attacks (four white-
box and one black-box). All of them are implemented as untargeted attacks.
Specifically,

- SMA−k [36] is a point dropping attack which drops $5 \times k$ points in k iterations based on the saliency map.
- APP [30] is a point perturbing attack which shifts points with 10 binary searches and 100 iterations for each search to craft AEs. Note that the $GeoA^3$ attack [28] can be regarded as APP with an external curve loss to attack models equipped with SOR. Since our CCN and AMS do not adopt SOR, evaluations on APP and $GeoA^3$ will be the same. So we do not specifically consider $GeoA^3$.
- AIC [30] is a point adding attack which conducts 10 binary searches and 100 iterations for each search to add 512 points to the point cloud. Chamfer distance is adopted to measure the point locations.
- AIH [30] is similar as AIC with the Hausdorff distance.
- BIM−k^5 is a point perturbing attack using the L_∞ basic iterative method: each sample is generated with k iterations, $\epsilon = 0.03$ and step size $= 0.0005$. We do not adopt the PGD attack as the adversarial point cloud will get disrupted at the beginning of sample generation. Different from 2D image attacks, a little perturbation in 3D point cloud can change the shape of the original object significantly. We find when $\epsilon = 0.03$ under L_∞-norm, the point clouds are difficult for humans to recognize, so we do not use the PGD attack to avoid the disruption of point clouds at the start.
- AdvPC [10] is a state-of-the-art black-box attack with higher transferability than others. We follow the same hyperparameters in the original paper, and use a larger number of iterations (500) to improve its performance.

It is also worth noting that there are some physical attacks against point cloud models (e.g., attacking the LiDAR sensor in autonomous driving [3,4]). Those attacks are very different from our focus with physical constraints. The defenses against them are beyond the scope of this paper.

Baselines. We select a couple of baseline methods to compare with our solution. (1) For the ablation study of CCN, we choose the conventional PointNet and DGCNN as the baselines. (2) For the ablation study of AMS, we compare it with normal training, adversarial training and mix-up training. For adversarial training, we consider two strategies: AT-BIM trains the model using the 3D L_∞-BIM point perturbing technique [14], with the configurations of 20 iterations, $\epsilon = 0.02$ and step $= 0.005$; AT-SMA trains the model using the point dropping technique [36], with the configurations of 20 iterations and 5 points dropped in each iteration. For mix-up training, we select PointCutMix-K [34], as it achieves the highest robustness in the white-box scenario. (3) For evaluating the integration of the two techniques, we consider the following state-of-the-art solutions: adversarial training (AT-BIM and AT-SMA); mix-up training (PointCutMix-R and PointCutMix-R [34]), SRS [35], SOR with the configuration of $k = 2$ and $\alpha = 1.1$ [23] and DUP-Net [37]. Since these solutions target different phases in the model pipeline, some of them can be integrated to further enhance the model robustness, which we will consider as well in our evaluations.

---

[5] Results can be found in supplementary materials.

Metrics. We measure the model accuracy over clean samples and different types of adversarial examples for its usability and robustness, respectively. For adversarial robustness, (1) **AAUA** measures the Average Accuracy Under Attacks in our consideration; (2) **LAUA** measures the Lowest Accuracy Under Attacks, which is the worst situation. Formally, we consider n different attacks. For each attack i, we measure the model's accuracy over the generated AEs as acc_i. The two metrics can be calculated as:

$$\text{AAUA} = \frac{\sum_{i=1}^{n} acc_i}{n}, \quad \text{LAUA} = \min\{acc_i\}, i \in [n]$$

5.1 Ablation Study of CCN

As discussed in Sect. 3.1, the size α of the receptive field in CCM can affect the model's robustness against different types of attacks. We first perform ablation studies on the hyperparameter α. We compare the performance of our CCN for different α values with PointNet and DGCNN under four white-box attacks. Each model is trained with PointCutMix-K, which gives the best results compared to other training strategies except our AMS. Table 1 presents the results. First, we observe that PointNet has the best robustness against the point perturbing attack (APP) and adding attack (AIH), as it only uses individual points to generate features, avoiding the noise accumulation. However, it has very bad performance for the point dropping attack (SMA−40). Second, our CCN provides

Table 2. Results for different training methods and hyperparameters with PointNet (%).

Training Strategy	Clean Sample	Adversarial Examples					
		SMA−40	APP	AIC	AIH	**AAUA**	**LAUA**
Normal	88.76	41.88	55.64	49.68	43.43	47.66	41.88
PointCutMix-K	**90.83**	63.11	82.55	76.14	69.56	72.84	63.11
AT-BIM	88.23	45.41	85.39	84.98	86.36	75.54	45.41
AT-SMA	87.38	**67.37**	79.79	75.73	74.92	74.45	**67.37**
AMS $(T=0.7)$	88.64	51.30	86.69	85.31	85.96	77.32	51.30
AMS $(T=0.5)$	89.45	48.99	87.01	**86.49**	**87.26**	**77.44**	48.99
AMS $(T=0.3)$	89.65	46.02	**87.30**	86.00	86.77	76.52	46.02
AMS $(T=0.1)$	89.20	42.98	80.24	79.87	81.01	71.03	42.98

Table 3. Results for different training strategies with CCN (%).

Network Structure	Training Strategy	Clean Sample	Adversarial Examples					
			SMA-40	APP	AIC	AIH	**AAUA**	**LAUA**
CCN	Normal	90.87	67.94	57.47	61.04	53.37	59.96	53.37
	AT-SMA	90.75	**84.17**	74.51	70.05	64.98	73.43	64.98
	AT-BIM	90.05	67.37	88.80	83.77	79.75	79.92	67.37
	PointCutMix-K	92.25	81.17	79.46	76.46	68.30	76.35	68.30
	AMS	**92.41**	77.72	**90.50**	**86.09**	**84.05**	**84.74**	**77.72**

more satisfactory accuracy for both clean and adversarial examples. The accuracy values for different AEs change with the hyperparameters, and $\alpha = 4$ can give the best trade-off considering all the point adding, dropping and perturbing attacks. For **AAUA**, it is 3.51% higher than PointNet, and 1.53% higher than DGCNN. For **LAUA**, it is 5.19% higher than PointNet, and only 0.17% lower than DGCNN. **We conclude that CCN is a more robust architecture than PointNet and DGCNN when we comprehensively consider all the types of attacks.**

5.2 Ablation Study of AMS

Next, we focus on the evaluation of our adaptive augmentation strategy. One important hyperparameter in AMS is T, which determines the kind of batch samples for training. We perform an ablation study to select the optimal T value. We use the PointNet model, which is simple and easy to obtain the results. We generate X_{drop} using the Saliency Map Attack (10 iterations, 10 points dropped in each iteration) and X_{perturb} using the 3D L_∞-BIM attack (10 iterations, $\epsilon = 0.02$ and step $= 0.005$). $(X_{\text{mix}}, Y_{\text{mix}})$ are generated by PointCutMix-K. Four white-box attacks are used for evaluation. Table 2 presents the accuracy of models trained with different strategies.

From Table 2, we observe that PointCutMix-K can achieve high accuracy over clean samples and AEs generated from SMA-40. However, it behaves much worse under the other three attacks. For AMS, the value of T can affect the model accuracy over different types of samples. With $T = 0.5$, the model has the highest robustness against AIC and AIH attacks. Although **LAUA** in this

Table 4. Results for different solutions under the white-box attacks (%). *Data of SRS and DUP-Net are adopted from [37].

Defense Solutions	Clean Sample	Adversarial Examples					
		SMA-40	APP	AIC	AIH	**AAUA**	**LAUA**
PointNet + Normal	88.76	41.88	55.64	49.68	43.43	47.66	41.88
PointNet + PointCutMix-K	90.83	63.11	82.55	76.14	69.56	72.84	63.11
PointNet + AT-BIM	88.23	45.41	85.39	84.98	86.36	75.54	45.41
PointNet + AT-SMA	87.38	67.37	79.79	75.73	74.92	74.45	67.37
DGCNN + Normal	91.03	65.87	46.10	54.06	48.78	53.70	46.10
DGCNN + PointCutMix-R	90.91	72.65	71.63	62.26	56.53	65.77	56.53
DGCNN + PointCutMix-K	91.88	79.91	74.88	76.01	68.47	74.82	68.47
DGCNN + AT-BIM	91.27	66.68	89.98	81.37	76.99	78.76	66.68
DGCNN + AT-SMA	91.80	**84.66**	72.00	71.75	64.25	73.17	64.25
DGCNN + SOR + Normal	91.00	66.00	86.83	51.82	54.38	64.76	51.82
DGCNN + SOR + AT-BIM	91.77	65.52	84.97	58.59	58.27	66.84	58.27
DGCNN + SOR + AT-SMA	91.05	80.59	86.91	59.85	60.25	71.90	59.85
SRS*	83.00	35.10	64.70	59.50	58.80	54.53	35.10
DUP-Net*	86.30	43.70	84.50	61.40	62.70	63.08	43.70
PointNet + AMS	89.45	48.99	87.01	**86.49**	**87.26**	77.44	48.99
DGCNN + AMS	92.21	75.41	**90.83**	85.47	83.93	83.91	75.41
CCN + AMS	**92.41**	77.72	90.50	86.09	84.05	**84.74**	**77.72**

configuration is lower than PointCutMix-K and AT-SMA (due to the bad performance in SMA−40), the average accuracy **AAUA** is still the highest. This validates the advantage of AMS, and we will adopt $T = 0.5$ for the following experiments. Table 3 shows the similar comparisons of training strategies with the CCN architecture. AMS gives much higher **AAUA** and **LAUA** than others.

5.3 End-to-End Evaluations and Comparisons

After identifying the optimal hyperparameters, we comprehensively compare our two methodologies and their integration with existing works of different network architectures (PointNet, DGCNN, DGCNN with SOR, SRS and DUP-Net) and training strategies (Normal, PointCutMix-R, PointCutMix-K, AT-BIM, AT-SMA).

Table 4 summarizes the comparison results for white-box attacks. There can be a lot of combinations with these solutions. Since PointNet has the least robustness among these architectures, we mainly compare the DGCNN architecture. First, we observe that our solution achieves the highest accuracy over clean samples. Second, for adversarial attacks, our solution also gives the best result for APP and AIC attacks. For SMA−40, our solution is worse than DGCNN+AT-SMA; for AIH, our solution is slightly worse than PointNet + AT-BIM. Nevertheless, it still gives the highest **AAUA** and **LAUA**, due to its comprehensive robustness.

Table 5. Results for different solutions under the black-box attacks (%).

Target Model	Defense	Source Model					
		PointNet		DGCNN		CCN	
		$\epsilon = 0.18$	$\epsilon = 0.45$	$\epsilon = 0.18$	$\epsilon = 0.45$	$\epsilon = 0.18$	$\epsilon = 0.45$
PointNet	Normal	84.50	84.50	86.27	86.27	86.98	85.56
	Normal + SRS	81.61	82.48	82.99	84.32	83.88	85.65
	Normal + SOR	65.46	65.90	67.64	67.90	68.08	69.78
	AT-BIM	86.11	84.70	87.88	87.88	85.76	86.82
	AT-BIM + SRS	80.52	83.93	83.05	84.55	81.17	84.26
	AT-BIM + SOR	74.36	74.26	73.38	73.67	72.06	74.11
	AMS	86.59	85.51	88.02	86.95	88.02	88.02
DGCNN	Normal	89.21	89.21	87.02	86.30	83.38	85.57
	Normal + SRS	61.88	60.97	63.72	59.61	62.97	58.24
	Normal + SOR	39.13	34.58	33.67	35.95	33.67	35.95
	AT-BIM	89.08	90.54	**89.81**	89.08	88.71	89.08
	AT-BIM + SRS	63.32	63.78	57.36	63.43	63.43	63.25
	AT-BIM + SOR	38.54	38.54	37.63	40.38	39.15	40.62
	AMS	88.89	89.26	89.63	89.63	90.00	**90.73**
CCN	Normal	89.42	88.33	89.05	88.33	85.42	85.42
	Normal + SRS	70.42	65.88	64.52	66.79	64.97	67.24
	Normal + SOR	41.80	43.16	41.80	40.95	42.71	42.25
	AT-BIM	88.61	88.61	88.61	88.25	88.25	88.97
	AT-BIM + SRS	64.53	64.39	60.78	63.04	63.94	68.85
	AT-BIM + SOR	47.25	46.38	45.48	46.83	43.22	45.90
	AMS	**90.93**	**90.56**	89.45	**90.19**	**90.56**	90.19

Furthermore, PointNet and DGCNN trained with our AMS can outperform other defense solutions when using the same model.

We further evaluate our methodologies against a black-box attack (AdvPC). The adversary crafts AEs from a different source model, and then leverages the transferability to attack the target victim model. We consider two constraints to generate AEs for testing. The results are shown in Table 5. We observe that for the source model of DGCNN with $\epsilon = 0.18$, the integration (CCN + AMS) is slightly worse than DGCNN + AT-BIM. For the source model of DGCNN with $\epsilon = 0.45$, our solution is slightly worse than DGCNN + AMS. For the rest of cases, it gives the highest accuracy. This indicates the effectiveness of our proposed solution under the black-box attack.

We compare our methodologies with more baselines, model architectures and attack configurations. The results can be found in the supplementary material. All the results confirm that our proposed CCN trained with AMS has the best robustness against different types of AEs.

6   Conclusion

Numerous research works have been done to increase our understanding about the inherent features of adversarial examples and model robustness in 2D image tasks. However, studies of adversarial defenses in the point cloud domain are still at an early stage. We advance this research direction with two contributions. For network architecture, we propose CCN, which can denoise the adversarial point clouds and smooth the perturbations in the feature space. For model training, we propose AMS, which can adaptively select clean, mix-up or adversarial samples to balance the model utility and robustness. Comprehensive evaluations show that our solution outperforms a variety of baselines under different types of white-box and black-box attacks.

Acknowledgement. This work is supported under the RIE2020 Industry Alignment Fund-Industry Collaboration Projects (IAF-ICP) Funding Initiative, as well as cash and in-kind contributions from the industry partner(s). It is also supported in part by Singapore Ministry of Education (MOE) AcRF Tier 2 MOE-T2EP20121-0006 and AcRF Tier 1 RS02/19.

References

1. Allen-Zhu, Z., Li, Y.: Feature purification: How adversarial training performs robust deep learning. CoRR abs/2005.10190 (2020)
2. Soltani, A.A., Huang, H., Wu, J., Kulkarni, T.D., Tenenbaum, J.B.: Synthesizing 3d shapes via modeling multi-view depth maps and silhouettes with deep generative networks. In: Proceedings of the Computer Vision and Pattern Recognition, pp. 1511–1519 (2017)
3. Cao, Y., et al.: Invisible for both camera and lidar: Security of multi-sensor fusion based perception in autonomous driving under physical-world attacks. In: 2021 IEEE Symposium on Security and Privacy (SP), pp. 176–194. IEEE (2021)

4. Cao, Y., et al.: Adversarial sensor attack on lidar-based perception in autonomous driving. In: Proceedings of the 2019 ACM SIGSAC Conference on Computer and Communications Security, pp. 2267–2281 (2019)

5. Carlini, N., Wagner, D.: Towards Evaluating the Robustness of Neural Networks. In: Proceedings of the S&P, pp. 39–57 (2017)

6. Chen, Y., et al.: PointMixup: augmentation for point clouds. In: Vedaldi, A., Bischof, H., Brox, T., Frahm, J.-M. (eds.) ECCV 2020. LNCS, vol. 12348, pp. 330–345. Springer, Cham (2020). https://doi.org/10.1007/978-3-030-58580-8_20

7. Dai, A., Chang, A.X., Savva, M., Halber, M., Funkhouser, T., Nießner, M.: ScanNet: richly-annotated 3D reconstructions of indoor scenes. In: Proceedings of the IEEE Conference on Computer Vision and Pattern Recognition, pp. 5828–5839 (2017)

8. Dong, X., Chen, D., Zhou, H., Hua, G., Zhang, W., Yu, N.: Self-robust 3D point recognition via gather-vector guidance. In: 2020 IEEE/CVF Conference on Computer Vision and Pattern Recognition (CVPR), pp. 11513–11521. IEEE (2020)

9. Goodfellow, I.J., Shlens, J., Szegedy, C.: Explaining and harnessing adversarial examples. In: Proceedings of the ICLR (2015)

10. Hamdi, A., Rojas, S., Thabet, A., Ghanem, B.: AdvPC: transferable adversarial perturbations on 3D point clouds. In: Vedaldi, A., Bischof, H., Brox, T., Frahm, J.-M. (eds.) ECCV 2020. LNCS, vol. 12357, pp. 241–257. Springer, Cham (2020). https://doi.org/10.1007/978-3-030-58610-2_15

11. Hjelm, R.D., et al.: Learning deep representations by mutual information estimation and maximization. arXiv preprint arXiv:1808.06670 (2018)

12. Kim, P., Chen, J., Cho, Y.K.: Slam-driven robotic mapping and registration of 3D point clouds. Autom. Constr. **89**, 38–48 (2018)

13. Kingma, D.P., Ba, J.: Adam: a method for stochastic optimization. In: Proceedings of the ICLR (2015)

14. Kurakin, A., Goodfellow, I.J., Bengio, S.: Adversarial examples in the physical world. In: Proceedings of the ICLR (Workshop) (2017)

15. Liu, D., Yu, R., Su, H.: Extending adversarial attacks and defenses to deep 3D point cloud classifiers. In: Proceedings of the ICIP (2019)

16. Liu, H., Jia, J., Gong, N.Z.: PointGuard: provably robust 3D point cloud classification. In: Proceedings of the IEEE/CVF Conference on Computer Vision and Pattern Recognition, pp. 6186–6195 (2021)

17. Lorenz, T., Ruoss, A., Balunović, M., Singh, G., Vechev, M.: Robustness certification for point cloud models. arXiv preprint arXiv:2103.16652 (2021)

18. Ma, C., Meng, W., Wu, B., Xu, S., Zhang, X.: Efficient joint gradient based attack against SOR defense for 3D point cloud classification. In: Proceedings of the MM, pp. 1819–1827 (2020)

19. Macher, H., Landes, T., Grussenmeyer, P.: From point clouds to building information models: 3D semi-automatic reconstruction of indoors of existing buildings. Appl. Sci. **7**(10), 1030 (2017)

20. Madry, A., Makelov, A., Schmidt, L., Tsipras, D., Vladu, A.: Towards deep learning models resistant to adversarial attacks. In: Proceedings of the ICLR (2018)

21. Qi, C.R., Su, H., Mo, K., Guibas, L.J.: PointNet: deep Learning on Point Sets for 3D Classification and Segmentation. In: Proceedings of the CVPR (2017)

22. Qi, C.R., Yi, L., Su, H., Guibas, L.J.: Pointnet++: deep hierarchical feature learning on point sets in a metric space. In: Proceedings of the NIPS, pp. 5099–5108 (2017)

23. Rusu, R.B., Marton, Z.C., Blodow, N., Dolha, M.E., Beetz, M.: Towards 3D Point cloud based object maps for household environments. Robotics Auton. Syst. **56**(11), 927–941 (2008)
24. Sun, J., Koenig, K., Cao, Y., Chen, Q.A., Mao, Z.M.: On adversarial robustness of 3D point cloud classification under adaptive attacks. arXiv preprint arXiv:2011.11922 (2020)
25. Szegedy, C., et al.: Intriguing properties of neural networks. In: Proceedings of the ICLR (2014)
26. Uy, M.A., Pham, Q.H., Hua, B.S., Nguyen, T., Yeung, S.K.: Revisiting point cloud classification: a new benchmark dataset and classification model on real-world data. In: Proceedings of the IEEE/CVF International Conference on Computer Vision, pp. 1588–1597 (2019)
27. Wang, Y., Sun, Y., Liu, Z., Sarma, S.E., Bronstein, M.M., Solomon, J.M.: Dynamic graph cnn for learning on point clouds. ACM Trans. Graph. **38**(5), 1–12 (2019)
28. Wen, Y., Lin, J., Chen, K., Jia, K.: Geometry-aware generation of adversarial and cooperative point clouds. CoRR abs/1912.11171 (2019)
29. Wu, Z., Song, S., Khosla, A., Yu, F., Zhang, L., Tang, X., Xiao, J.: 3D ShapeNets: a deep representation for volumetric shapes. In: Proceedings of the CVPR (2015)
30. Xiang, C., Qi, C.R., Li, B.: Generating 3d adversarial point clouds. In: Proceedings of the CVPR (2019)
31. Xu, G., Li, H., Liu, S., Yang, K., Lin, X.: VerifyNet: secure and verifiable federated learning. IEEE Trans. Inf. Forensics Secur. **15**, 911–926 (2020)
32. Xu, G., Li, H., Zhang, Y., Xu, S., Ning, J., Deng, R.H.: Privacy-preserving federated deep learning with irregular users. IEEE Trans. Dependable Secure Comput. **19**(2), 1364–1381 (2022)
33. Zhang, H., Cissé, M., Dauphin, Y.N., Lopez-Paz, D.: Mixup: beyond empirical risk minimization. In: Proceedings of the ICLR (2018)
34. Zhang, J., et al.: PointCutMix: regularization strategy for point cloud classification. CoRR abs/2101.01461 (2021)
35. Zhang, Q., Yang, J., Fang, R., Ni, B., Liu, J., Tian, Q.: Adversarial attack and defense on point sets. CoRR abs/1902.10899 (2019)
36. Zheng, T., Chen, C., Yuan, J., Li, B., Ren, K.: PointCloud saliency maps. In: Proceedings of the ICCV (2019)
37. Zhou, H., Chen, K., Zhang, W., Fang, H., Zhou, W., Yu, N.: DUP-Net: Denoiser and upsampler network for 3D adversarial point clouds defense. In: Proceedings of the ICCV (2019)
38. Zhu, S., Zhang, X., Evans, D.: Learning adversarially robust representations via worst-case mutual information maximization. In: Proceedings of the ICML, pp. 11609–11618 (2020)

Learning Extremely Lightweight and Robust Model with Differentiable Constraints on Sparsity and Condition Number

Xian Wei[1], Yangyu Xu[2,3], Yanhui Huang[4], Hairong Lv[5], Hai Lan[2],
Mingsong Chen[1], and Xuan Tang[6(✉)]

[1] MoE Engineering Research Center of Hardware/Software Co-design Technology
and Application, East China Normal University, Shanghai, China
{xwei,mschen}@sei.ecnu.edu.cn

[2] Fujian Institute of Research on the Structure of Matter,
Chinese Academy of Sciences, Beijing, China
xuyangyu20@mails.ucas.ac.cn, lanhai09@fjirsm.ac.cn

[3] University of Chinese Academy of Sciences, Beijing, China

[4] Fuzhou University, Fuzhou, China

[5] Tsinghua University, Beijing, China
lvhairong@tsinghua.edu.cn

[6] School of Communication and Electronic Engineering,
East China Normal University, Shanghai, China
xtang@cee.ecnu.edu.cn

Abstract. Learning lightweight and robust deep learning models is an enormous challenge for safety-critical devices with limited computing and memory resources, owing to robustness against adversarial attacks being proportional to network capacity. The community has extensively explored the integration of adversarial training and model compression, such as weight pruning. However, lightweight models generated by highly pruned over-parameterized models lead to sharp drops in both robust and natural accuracy. It has been observed that the parameters of these models lie in ill-conditioned weight space, i.e., the condition number of weight matrices tend to be large enough that the model is not robust. In this work, we propose a framework for building extremely lightweight models, which combines tensor product with the differentiable constraints for reducing condition number and promoting sparsity. Moreover, the proposed framework is incorporated into adversarial training with the min-max optimization scheme. We evaluate the proposed approach on VGG-16 and Visual Transformer. Experimental results on datasets such as ImageNet, SVHN, and CIFAR−10 show that we can achieve an overwhelming advantage at a high compression ratio, e.g., 200 times.

Keywords: Lightweight model · Adversarial robustness · Condition number · Tensor product · Convolutional neural networks · Visual transformer

Supplementary Information The online version contains supplementary material available at https://doi.org/10.1007/978-3-031-19772-7_40.

1   Introduction

Deep Neural Networks (DNNs) have achieved impressive achievements on large-scale machine learning tasks from computer vision to speech recognition and natural language processing [3,38,42]. However, existing over-parameterized deep learning models, including convolutional neural networks(CNNs) and Vision Transformers [8], are challenged by the following issues when they are deployed on safety-critical resource-constrained devices. On the one hand, to fully exploit the useful information hidden in the data, most deep learning models increase the capacity of their networks, either by widening the existing layers or by adding more layers [15,34,40]. Models with good performance usually require millions of parameters to be estimated during training. However, many real-time devices such as smartphones, wearable medical devices, self-driving cars and unmanned aerial vehicles are highly resource-limited, thus cannot handle such large models. Hence, the model size of DNNs is an enormous challenge for applications of deep learning. Another related issue arises from the fact that DNNs are vulnerable to perturbations from noisy environments or adversarially crafted attacks [9,20,27,47]. Such vulnerability is unacceptable and potentially dangerous for safety-critical systems such as critical infrastructure. Therefore, it is necessary to develop deep learning models that are both **lightweight** in terms of the number of parameters, and **robust** to various perturbations.

Recent studies have shown that it is difficult to simultaneously achieve high levels of natural accuracy and robustness for lightweight models [11,52]. On the one hand, most of the existing lightweight technologies, such as pruning [13] and low-rank based factorization [7,18], tend to either decrease the rank of weight matrices or cause ill-conditioned matrices, which may result in the models being vulnerable to perturbations from the environment. On the other hand, the strategies focused on robust training are likely to limit the success of achieving a lightweight model, as deep and wide model capacities contribute to the robustness [26,51].

In this work, we propose a framework for building extremely lightweight models (e.g., compression ratio >10 for CNNs) that combines tensor product with the differentiable constraints for reducing condition number and promoting sparsity. Unlike the well-known low-rank based factorization, tensor product preserves the rank of the matrix, maintaining impressive performance on highly lightweight models. Furthermore, the proposed framework is incorporated into adversarial training with the min-max optimization scheme. Note that the proposed approach trains a lightweight and robust network from scratch instead of compressing over-parameterized pre-trained models.

The main contributions of this paper are summarized as follows.

1. We proposed an extremely lightweight and robust model framework without significantly sacrificing the model robustness and the classification accuracy. Although our method focuses on the performance of extremely lightweight models, it also achieves competitive results at low compression ratios.
2. We developed differentiable constraints on promoting the sparsity and reducing the condition number, which can be imposed on each sub-matrix to

control condition numbers of these matrices and further reduce the number of parameters. We theoretically prove that the sparsity and condition number of original large-scale weight matrix are equivalent to the product of the sparsity and condition number of these decomposed sub-matrices, respectively.

3. The proposed extremely lightweight and robust framework can be incorporated into the well-known adversarial training framework associated with the min-max optimization scheme, so as to improve the robustness of the model against hand-crafted adversarial attacks.

2   Related Work

2.1   Adversarial Training

Conventional methods to improve model robustness against adversarial noise include adversarial training [26], ensemble training [43], obfuscated gradients identification [2] and defensive distillation [29,30]. Among them, adversarial training has been empirically proven to be the most effective way to defend adversarial attacks.

The key objective of adversarial training is to minimize the training loss on adversarial examples by optimizing the following min-max empirical risk problem:

$$\min_{\mathcal{A}} \mathbb{E}_{(\mathcal{X},y)\sim\mathfrak{D}} \left[\max_{\|\delta\|_p \leq \epsilon} L(\mathcal{A}, \mathcal{X} + \delta, y) \right] \tag{1}$$

where pairs of input tensor signals $\mathcal{X} \in \mathbb{R}^{I_1 \times I_2 \times \cdots \times I_N}$ and the corresponding labels $y \in [k]$ follow an underlying data distribution $\mathfrak{D}$; $\| \cdot \|_p$ with $p \geq 0$ denotes the ℓ_p norm of a tensor, δ is the adversarial perturbation added to each input tensor signal $\mathcal{X}$, belonging to perturbations set $\epsilon \subseteq \mathbb{R}^d$; $\mathcal{A} \in \mathbb{R}^p$ represents the set of weight parameters to be optimized and $L(\mathcal{A}, \mathcal{X} + \delta, y)$ is the loss function used to train the adversarial model, e.g., cross-entropy loss for classification models.

In Eq.(1), the goal of the outer minimization problem is to retrain model parameters so that the adversarial loss given by the inner attack problem is minimized; the inner maximization problem aims to generate adversarial examples that can mislead the model. Therein, adversarial examples can be obtained by iterative adversarial attacks, such as Projected Gradient Descent (PGD) based attacks [26], under the following formulation:

$$\mathcal{X}^{t+1} = \Pi_{\mathcal{X}+\epsilon}(\mathcal{X}^t + \alpha sign(\nabla_{\mathcal{X}} L(\mathcal{A}, \mathcal{X}, y))) \tag{2}$$

where α is the step size, t is the iterations, and $sign(\cdot)$ returns the sign of gradient during back-propagation.

2.2   Lightweight Model

Since embedded devices such as mobile terminals are limited in terms of computing power and storage resources, the mobile terminal model must meet the conditions of small-size, low computational complexity, and flexible deployment environments. Therefore, lightweight models are of increasing interest among researchers in the machine learning community.

Popular techniques for implementing lightweight models include network pruning [13,45], quantization [12,46], low-rank factorization [36,50], and knowledge distillation [16,33]. Network pruning was early proposed by Han et al. [13], which prunes some connections with low weight magnitudes under the assumption that they provide less effective information for the model output. The most common practice is a three-step compression pipeline, which consists of pre-training a network, pruning and fine-tuning afterwards. Since pruning the pre-trained network will bring extra computational cost, pruning could be performed during training [24]. The low-rank factorization [36,50] is under the assumption that weight vectors are mostly distributed in low-rank subspace, so that a few basis vectors can reconstruct the weight matrix. However, the matrix decomposition involves massive computation, and the layer-by-layer decomposition is not conducive to global parameter compression. In addition, the model needs to be retrained to achieve convergence. Knowledge distillation [16] refers to using the trained large model as a teacher model, which has learned a wealth of valuable information from the data, to guide the training of small-sized student model. While transferring knowledge from the teacher model to the student model enables the student model to obtain comparable performance, it is generally used for classification tasks with a softmax loss function. Quantization is often used in conjunction with other compression methods, for example, the combination of quantization and distillation [33], or pruning and quantization [12], and the integration of pruning, factorization, and quantization [10]. Furthermore, some other researchers compress model using Neural Architecture Search (NAS) [22], which requires a pre-defined search space and can only search for optimal structures in this space. However, the effect of this method is limited by the search space, search strategy and performance evaluation strategy.

The strategies mentioned above have been quite successful in learning lightweight models to a certain degree. However, the extremely lightweight models generated by these techniques, such as pruning and low-rank factorization, will result in ill-conditioned weight matrix. Linear systems with ill-conditioned matrices could amplify the instability of the gradients over multiple layers, resulting in the networks being vulnerable to perturbations from the environment. In a word, many of the current lightweight strategies may degrade model robustness.

2.3 Learning both Robust and Lightweight Models

Some recent works have attempted to build models that are both robust and lightweight by incorporating techniques for implementing lightweight models into adversarial defense framework. Sehwag et al. [37] formulated the pruning process as an empirical risk minimization problem within adversarial loss objectives. Madaan et al. [25] proposed to suppress vulnerability by pruning the latent features with high vulnerability. Ye et al. [48] incorporated the weight pruning into the framework of adversarial training associated with min-max optimization, to enable model compression while preserving robustness. Other than weight pruning, Lin et al. [23] proposed a novel defensive quantization method by controlling the neural network's Lipschitz constant during quantization. Recently, Gui et al. [10] proposed a unified framework for adversarial training with pruning, factorization and quantization being the constraints.

The aforementioned methods combine techniques for generating lightweight models and adversarial defense strategies, with the main focus on achieving adversarially robust models. While quantization reduces storage space, it does not reduce the computational complexity required for model inference. Pruning does reduce the number of parameters in the network, but it is impossible to achieve an extremely lightweight model in order to ensure the accuracy and robustness. In pursuit of models that are both lightweight and robust, it is important to resolve the inherent contradictions between model compression and robustness [52].

3   Learning Extremely Lightweight and Robust Model

In this section, we propose a novel framework for joint tensor product with the differentiable constraints for reducing condition number and promoting sparsity, to achieve extremely lightweight and robust models. Different from tensor factorization based methods [32,49], the tensor product preserves the rank of the matrix so that the expressiveness of the weight matrix is not degraded.

3.1   The Model Pruning and the Condition Number

Most deep learning models consist of L hidden layers, including linear transformations, pooling layers and activation functions, associated with a task-driven loss function. Considering that most pooling and activation functions are predefined with fixed policies, the aforementioned learning capabilities are highly dependent on the following linear transformation (omitting the bias term):

$$\begin{aligned} \boldsymbol{y} &= \boldsymbol{W}_{L+1}\boldsymbol{x}_l, \\ \boldsymbol{x}_l &= \sigma(\boldsymbol{W}_l\boldsymbol{x}_{l-1} + \boldsymbol{b}_l), \forall l = 1, \cdots, L. \end{aligned} \tag{3}$$

with $\boldsymbol{x}_l \in \mathbb{R}^m$, $\boldsymbol{y} \in \mathbb{R}^d$, $\boldsymbol{W}_l \in \mathbb{R}^{d \times m}$ and $\boldsymbol{b}_l \in \mathbb{R}^d$ being the output of hidden layers, output response, the corresponding linear transformation matrix and bias vector. We define the input tensor $\boldsymbol{x}$ as $\boldsymbol{x}_0$. The linear system in Eq. (3) covers prominent deep learning models. For example, for the Fully-Connnected (FC) layer of CNNs or attention network layer, $\boldsymbol{W}_l$ is a common linear transformation matrix.

Generally, given a multi-dimensional input signal $\mathcal{X}$, one common practice is to reshape $\mathcal{X}$ into one-dimensional tensor $\boldsymbol{x}$ and feed it into the system in Eq. (3). This results in a large dimension of the corresponding linear transformation matrix $\boldsymbol{W}_l$, which increases the computational cost and memory load during model inference. In order to reduce the computational complexity, one common approach is to prune small weights that contribute little to the output of model.

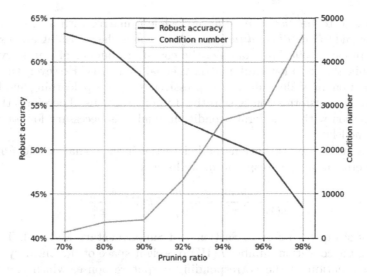

Fig. 1. Condition number and robust accuracy for different pruning ratios based on unstructured pruning. This example shows that compressing the VGG-16 network based on unstructured pruning causes the condition number of weight matrix to become ill-conditioned when pruning exceeds a certain threshold (such as 90%), which is the reason for the sharp drop in robust accuracy.

Definition 1. *(s−sparse tensor) Given a tensor $\mathcal{X} \in \mathbb{R}^{I_1 \times I_2 \times \cdots \times I_N}$ satisfies sparsity condition $\|\mathcal{X}\|_0 \leq s$, for $s \in \mathbb{Z}^+$, we call the tensor $\mathcal{X}$ is s-sparse. Here, $\|\mathcal{X}\|_0$ denotes the number of non-zero elements in $\mathcal{X}$.*

In practice, the pruned weights are set to zero, i.e., the connections between these corresponding neurons are disconnected, resulting in a sparse weight matrix. For the convenience of description, W refers to the linear transformation matrix of each layer unless otherwise specified.

However, an example shown in Fig. 1 demonstrates that robust accuracy are drastically decreased following the increase of the pruning ratio. Additionally, Fig. 1 also shows that the high pruning rate (more than 90%) leads to the sharp increase in the condition number of the weight matrix of networks, which is known as an indicator of model robustness [6]. In this case, small perturbations added to the input tensor, i.e., adversarial examples, can produce undesired outputs when fed into the model.

Definition 2. *(ℓ_2−norm condition number [6]) The ℓ_2−norm condition number of a full-rank matrix $\mathbf{A} \in \mathbb{R}^{K \times I}$ is defined as: $\kappa(\mathbf{A}) = \sigma_{\max}(\mathbf{A})/\sigma_{\min}(\mathbf{A})$, where $\sigma_{\max}(\mathbf{A})$ and $\sigma_{\min}(\mathbf{A})$ are maximal and minimal singular values of $\mathbf{A}$, respectively.*

Condition number of a matrix is commonly used to measure the sensitive of the matrix's operation in the event of how much error in the output results from an error in the input. A matrix with the condition number being close to one is said to be *"well-conditioned"*, while a matrix with a large condition number is said to be *"ill-conditioned"*, which causes the vanishing and exploding gradient problem [39]. For example, the condition number of a unitary matrix is one, while that of a low-rank matrix is equal to infinity. However, the unitary transformation may degrade the expressiveness of deep learning models and the low-rank transformation is sensitive to perturbations. Therefore, the linear transformation with a moderate condition number is necessary for robust deep learning models.

Let δx be the perturbations added to the input signal x and δy be the resulting error in output response y, we have

$$\frac{1}{k(W)}\frac{\|\delta x\|}{\|x\|} \leq \frac{\|\delta y\|}{\|y\|} \leq k(W)\frac{\|\delta x\|}{\|x\|}. \tag{4}$$

The proof of Eq. (4) refers to Section 1 of Supplementary Material. Therefore, improving the condition number $k(W)$ of weight space of the linear system will limit the variation of the corresponding output response, which can be seen from Eq. (4). That is, improving the condition number promotes the robustness of the system to the adversarial noise. In summary, to develop a both robust and lightweight deep learning model, we expect the linear transformation in Eq. (3) to have the following properties: i) W has small data sizes such as in lower dimensions, and its entries are sparse or quantized in a reduced data format. ii) W is a well-conditioned matrix with robustness to perturbations. Before introducing the proposed framework for building extremely lightweight models, we first introduce separable linear transformations.

3.2   Separable Linear Transformations

We recall the two properties of linear transformation matrix W mentioned in the previous subsection. In order to achieve a transformation with both properties at the same time, the crucial idea is to allow the transformation to have a separable structure, where separable structure means that linear transformation W can be replaced by the tensor product of several smaller weight matrices. Therefore, we can effectively impose the condition number and the sparsity constraints on these separable linear transformations. To interpret the product of a high-order signal tensor and separable matrices, we first define the $n-$mode product as follows, by referring to the concept of tensor operation in [5,44].

Definition 3. *($n-$mode product) The $n-$mode matrix product of a tensor $\mathcal{X} \in \mathbb{R}^{I_1 \times \cdots \times I_N}$ with a matrix $A \in \mathbb{R}^{K_n \times I_n}$ is denoted by $\mathcal{X} \times_n A$, which is an $N-$ order tensor. The elements of the tensor $\mathcal{X} \times_n A \in (I_1 \times \cdots \times I_{n-1} \times K_n \times I_{n+1} \times \cdots \times I_N)$ are defined as*

$$(\mathcal{X} \times_n A)_{i_1 \cdots i_{n-1} k_n i_{n+1} \cdots i_N} = \sum_{i_n=1}^{I_n} \mathcal{X}_{i_1 i_2 \cdots i_N} A_{k_n i_n} \tag{5}$$

with $\mathcal{X}_{i_1 i_2 \cdots i_N}$, $A_{k_n i_n}$ being entries in $\mathcal{X}$ and A, respectively.

For more detailed introduction of $n-$mode products, we refer the interested reader to [5, 44].

Suppose a tensor signal $\mathcal{X} \in \mathbb{R}^{I_1 \times I_2 \times \cdots \times I_N}$ is multiplied by T separable linear transformation matrices. The response $\mathcal{Y} \in \mathbb{R}^{K_1 \times K_2 \times \cdots \times K_N}$ is formulated as the $n-$mode product of $\mathcal{X}$ and these separable transformation matrices,

$$\mathcal{Y} = \mathcal{X} \times_1 \boldsymbol{A}^{(1)} \times_2 \boldsymbol{A}^{(2)} \times_3 \cdots \times_T \boldsymbol{A}^{(T)}. \tag{6}$$

The linear transformation in Eq. (6) can be conveniently converted to the one-dimensional model of Eq. (3) as follows:

$$\mathrm{vec}(\mathcal{Y}) = \left(\boldsymbol{A}^{(1)} \otimes \boldsymbol{A}^{(2)} \otimes \cdots \otimes \boldsymbol{A}^{(T)} \right) \mathrm{vec}(\mathcal{X}), \tag{7}$$

where the vector space isomorphism $\mathrm{vec} : \mathbb{R}^{a \times b} \to \mathbb{R}^{ab}$ is defined as the operation that stacks the columns on top of each other, e.g., $\boldsymbol{x} = \mathrm{vec}(\mathcal{X})$ and $\boldsymbol{y} = \mathrm{vec}(\mathcal{Y})$. Therein, $\otimes$ denotes the tensor product operator [44].

We refer to a large linear transformation matrices $\boldsymbol{W}$ that can be represented as a concatenation of smaller matrices $\mathcal{A} := \{\boldsymbol{A}^{(1)} \in \mathbb{R}^{K_1 \times I_1}, \boldsymbol{A}^{(2)} \in \mathbb{R}^{K_2 \times I_2}, \cdots, \boldsymbol{A}^{(T)} \in \mathbb{R}^{K_T \times I_T}\}$ as a separable linear transformation,

$$\boldsymbol{W} = \boldsymbol{A}^{(1)} \otimes \boldsymbol{A}^{(2)} \otimes \cdots \otimes \boldsymbol{A}^{(T)}. \tag{8}$$

Therefore, we can equivalently convert $\boldsymbol{W}$ into the tensor product of a chain of small separable matrices.

The increase of T reduces the computational load of the model, however, it may also degrade the expressiveness of the parameters [41]. This phenomenon can be explained as the gradient flow vanishing in the chain of tensor matrices during back-propagation. Hence, for the convenience of training lightweight model, we replace the original large linear transformation matrix with the tensor product of two small matrices. By regarding $\boldsymbol{x} \in \mathbb{R}^m$, $\boldsymbol{y} \in \mathbb{R}^d$, $\boldsymbol{W} \in \mathbb{R}^{d \times m}$ in Eq. (3), its two-dimensional system with separable linear transformations can be rewritten as

$$\boldsymbol{y} = \boldsymbol{W} \boldsymbol{x} = (\boldsymbol{A}^{(1)} \otimes \boldsymbol{A}^{(2)}) \boldsymbol{x} \Rightarrow \boldsymbol{Y} = \boldsymbol{A}^{(2)} \boldsymbol{X} \boldsymbol{A}^{(1)^\top}, \tag{9}$$

where $\boldsymbol{A}^{(1)} \in \mathbb{R}^{K_1 \times I_1}$ and $\boldsymbol{A}^{(2)} \in \mathbb{R}^{K_2 \times I_2}$. $\boldsymbol{X} \in \mathbb{R}^{I_2 \times I_1}$ and $\boldsymbol{Y} \in \mathbb{R}^{K_2 \times K_1}$ are reshaped two-dimensional matrices from $\boldsymbol{x}$ and $\boldsymbol{y}$. An example of replacing fully-connected layers with Separable Linear Transformation is introduced in Section 2 of Supplementary Material.

3.3   Extremely Lightweight and Robust Model

Although the separable linear transformations proposed in Sect. 3.2 greatly reduces the number of parameters and computational complexity, it is far from enough for some devices with extremely limited resources. In this subsection, we combine the separable linear transformation with sparsity constraint to develop an extremely lightweight model. Moreover, we also propose two condition number constraints to guarantee the proper condition number of model weights.

Given the multi-dimensional tensor operations in the model, it is difficult to directly impose constraints on the linear system. However, the common transformation between multi-dimensional model and one-dimensional model enables solving multi-dimensional transformation problems to take advantage of the classical and efficient algorithms of the one-dimensional model. In order to develop a learning paradigm for combining separable parameter matrices with sparsity to construct an extremely lightweight model, we now derive the following propositions between the multi-dimensional model and the one-dimensional model, and hence construct appropriate regularizers.

Differentiable Constraint on Sparsity Promotion. The linear transformation with a collection of separable parameters $\mathcal{A}$ does drastically reduce the number of parameters. In order to further reduce the computation and complexity to achieve extreme model compression, one approach is to sparse the separable linear transformation matrices.

Proposition 1. *Given* $\mathbf{W} = \mathbf{A}^{(1)} \otimes \mathbf{A}^{(2)}$ *with* $\mathbf{W} \in \mathbb{R}^{K_1 K_2 \times I_1 I_2}$, $\mathbf{A}^{(1)} \in \mathbb{R}^{K_1 \times I_1}$ *being* $s_A -sparse$ *and* $\mathbf{A}^{(2)} \in \mathbb{R}^{K_2 \times I_2}$ *being* $s_B -sparse$, *the sparsity of* $\mathbf{W}$ *is* $s_A s_B$.

The weight pruning is to make T separable matrices $\mathbf{A}^{(T)}$ with few nonzero elements, while ensuring the the matrices set $\mathcal{A}$ without reducing expressiveness. As shown in Proposition 1, the sparsity of the whole system is determined by that of each separable matrix. Therefore, a nature way for pruning is to promote the sparsity of each element in $\mathbf{A}^{(t)}$,

$$g(\mathcal{A}) = \sum_{t=1}^{T} \sum_{i_n k_n} g\left(\mathbf{A}^{(t)}_{i_n, k_n}\right) \tag{10}$$

with $\mathbf{A}^{(t)}_{i_n k_n}$ being an element of $\mathbf{A}^{(t)}$. However, this sparse penalty term is non-differentiable and cannot update parameters during gradient back-propagation. In practice, we use the following penalty term to enforce the sparsity of $\mathbf{A}^{(T)}$ by minimizing ℓ_p norm with $0 \leq p \leq 1$ instead of Eq. (10) ,

$$g(\mathcal{A}) = \frac{1}{2k_1} \sum_{t=1}^{T} \sum_{i=1}^{k_1} (\frac{1}{p} \| \mathbf{A}^{(t)}_{i,:} \|_p^p)^2, \tag{11}$$

with $\mathbf{A}^{(T)}_{i,:}$ being the ith row of $\mathbf{A}^{(T)}$. It is known that above ℓ_p norm is non-smooth. In order to make the global cost function differentiable, we exchange Eq. (11) with a smooth approximation that is concretely given as

$$g(\mathcal{A}) = \frac{1}{2k_1} \sum_{t=1}^{T} \sum_{i=1}^{k_1} (\sum_{j=1}^{k_2} (\mathbf{A}^{(t)^2}_{ij} + \varpi)^{p/2})^2, \tag{12}$$

with $0 < \varpi < 1$ being a smoothing parameter. Therein, the sparsity measurement function g is chosen to be separable, i.e., its evaluation is computed as the sum of functions of the individual components of its argument.

Differentiable Constraints on Reducing Condition Number. A robust linear system like Eq. (3) often requires the transformation matrix is as "*well-conditioned*" as possible. The key question is whether the condition number of the tensor product of separable matrices is equivalent to that of the original linear transformation matrix. In other words, does the tensor product change the condition number of the original linear transformation matrix? If the tensor product does not change the condition number of the matrix, we can impose condition number constraints on these separable small matrices, which is equivalent to improving the robustness of the original matrix.

Theorem 1. (Theorem 4.2.12 in [17])   *Let $\mathbf{A} \in \mathbb{R}^{K_1 \times I_1}$, $\mathbf{B} \in \mathbb{R}^{K_2 \times I_2}$. Furthermore, let $\lambda \in \sigma(A)$ with corresponding eigenvector $\mathbf{x}$, and let $\mu \in \sigma(B)$ with corresponding eigenvector $\mathbf{y}$. Then $\lambda\mu$ is an eigenvalue of $\mathbf{A} \otimes \mathbf{B}$ with corresponding eigenvector $\mathbf{x} \otimes \mathbf{y}$. Every eigenvalue of $\mathbf{A} \otimes \mathbf{B}$ arises as such a product of eigenvalues of $\mathbf{A}$ and $\mathbf{B}$.*

Proof: Suppose $\mathbf{Ax} = \lambda\mathbf{x}$ and $\mathbf{Bx} = \mu\mathbf{y}$ with $\mathbf{x}, \mathbf{y} \neq \mathbf{0}$, then $(\mathbf{A} \otimes \mathbf{B})(\mathbf{x} \otimes \mathbf{y}) = \lambda\mathbf{x} \otimes \mu\mathbf{y} = \lambda\mu(\mathbf{x} \otimes \mathbf{y})$. Schur's unitary triangularization theorem ensures that there are unitary matrices $\mathbf{U} \in \mathbb{R}^{K_1 \times I_1}$ and $\mathbf{V} \in \mathbb{R}^{K_2 \times I_2}$ such that $\mathbf{U}^\top \mathbf{AU} = \Delta_\mathbf{A}$ and $\mathbf{V}^\top \mathbf{BU} = \Delta_\mathbf{B}$. Then

$$(\mathbf{U} \otimes \mathbf{V})^\top (\mathbf{A} \otimes \mathbf{B})(\mathbf{U} \otimes \mathbf{V}) = (\mathbf{U}^\top \mathbf{AU}) \otimes (\mathbf{V}^\top \mathbf{BU}) = \Delta_\mathbf{A} \Delta_\mathbf{B}$$

is upper triangular and is similar to $\mathbf{A} \otimes \mathbf{B}$. The eigenvalues of $\mathbf{A}, \mathbf{B}$ and $\mathbf{A} \otimes \mathbf{B}$ are exactly the main diagonal entries of $\Delta_\mathbf{A}, \Delta_\mathbf{B}$ and $\Delta_\mathbf{A} \otimes \Delta_\mathbf{B}$, respectively, and the main diagonal of $\Delta_\mathbf{A} \otimes \Delta_\mathbf{B}$ consist of the n^2 pairwise products of the entries on the main diagonals of $\Delta_\mathbf{A}$ and $\Delta_\mathbf{B}$.

According to *Theorem 1*, we can get

$$\kappa(\boldsymbol{W}) = \kappa(\boldsymbol{A}^{(1)} \otimes \boldsymbol{A}^{(2)} \otimes \cdots \otimes \boldsymbol{A}^{(T)}) = \kappa(\boldsymbol{A}^{(1)})\kappa(\boldsymbol{A}^{(2)} \cdots \kappa(\boldsymbol{A}^{(T)}). \qquad (13)$$

As shown in Eq. (13), the condition number of whole tensor linear system are heavily depending on the construction of each separable matrix $\boldsymbol{A}^{(t)}$. Therefore, imposing condition number constraints on each separable small matrix $\boldsymbol{A}^{(t)}$ to keep an appropriate condition number is equivalent to limiting the condition number of the original large matrix. We review the definition of ℓ_2-norm condition number, one feasible way is to develop some smooth regularization terms to prevent every singular values from being essentially small and extremely large.

Let $\{\sigma_i\}_{i=1}^k, k = \min\{a, b\}$ denote the singular values of a separable matrix $\boldsymbol{A}^{(t)} \in \mathbb{R}^{a \times b}$ arranged in descending order, and $\sigma_{\max}(\boldsymbol{A}^{(t)})$ denote the largest one. It is known that $\|\boldsymbol{A}^{(t)}\|_F^2 = \sum_{i=1}^k \sigma_i^2 \geq \sigma_{\max}(\boldsymbol{A}^{(t)})^2$. Thus, we propose the following regularization term to prevent $\sigma_{\max}(\boldsymbol{A}^{(t)})$ from being too large,

$$\rho(\mathcal{A}) = \frac{1}{2Tk^2} \sum_{t=1}^T \|\boldsymbol{A}^{(t)}\|_F^2, \qquad (14)$$

Furthermore, the Gram matrix $\boldsymbol{A}^{(t)\top}\boldsymbol{A}^{(t)}$ is positive definite, which implies $\det(\boldsymbol{A}^{(t)\top}\boldsymbol{A}^{(t)}) = \prod \sigma_i^2 > 0$. Therefore, the constraint term in Eq. (15) is provided to avoid the worst case of $\det(\boldsymbol{A}^{(t)\top}\boldsymbol{A}^{(t)})$ being exponentially small or large.

$$h(\mathcal{A}) = \frac{1}{4Tk\log(k)} \sum_{t=1}^{T} \left(\log\left[\nu + \frac{1}{k}\det(\boldsymbol{A}^{(t)\top}\boldsymbol{A}^{(t)}) \right] \right)^2 \tag{15}$$

with $0 < \nu \ll 1$ being a small smoothing parameter. Additionally, the penalty $h(\mathcal{A})$ also promotes the full rank of $\boldsymbol{A}^{(t)}$, as well as the full rank of $\mathcal{A}$ in matrix-vector-product, shown in Eq. (9). More Details of Eq. (15) refers to Section 3 of Supplementary Material. Such two constraints $\rho(\mathcal{A})$ and $h(\mathcal{A})$ work together to achieve a moderate condition number for the whole tensor system.

3.4   Adversarial Training for Lightweight and Robust Model

As introduced in Sect. 3.3, the separable linear transformations and the sparsity promotion reduces the computational load of model. Furthermore, the settings for condition number within the framework of adversarial training associated with min-max optimization could exactly improve the robustness against various perturbations. By combining the regularizers discussed above, we construct the following cost function to jointly learn robust and lightweight parameters with separable structures, as

$$\min_{\mathcal{A}} \left\{ \mathbb{E}_{(\mathcal{X},y)\sim\mathfrak{D}}[\max_{\|\delta\|_p \leq \epsilon} L(\mathcal{A}, \mathcal{X} + \delta, y)] + \mu_1\rho(\mathcal{A}) + \mu_2 h(\mathcal{A}) + \mu_3 g(\mathcal{A}) \right\}, \tag{16}$$

with the three hyperparameters $\mu_1, \mu_2, \mu_3 > 0$, control the impact of the three regularizers on the final solution. In this work, we refer to it as the Adversarially Robust and Lightweight model with Separable Transformations (**ARLST**).

4   Experimental Results

In this section, we investigate the performance of the proposed $ARLST$ from two aspects: the size of model parameters and robustness against different perturbations. Our method is validated by experiments on image datasets, such as SVHN [28],Yale-B [31], MNIST [21], CIFAR-10 [19], CIFAR-100 [19] and ImageNet (ILSVRC2012) [35]. Three well-known and most related methods, ADMM [48], ATMC [10], and HYDRA [37] are used for the comparison. All networks are trained with 100 epochs for all experiments in this paper, and they are conducted on NVIDIA RTX 2080Ti GPU (10 GB memory for each GPU). Unless otherwise specified, the results of all tables are presented in percent.

Implementation Settings. We report the model performance on robustness under the Fast Gradient Sign Method (FGSM) [9], Projected Gradient Descent (PGD) [26], AutoAttack (AA) [4] and the Square Attack (SA) [1]. The PGD attack is known as the strong first-order attack, and AA is an ensemble of

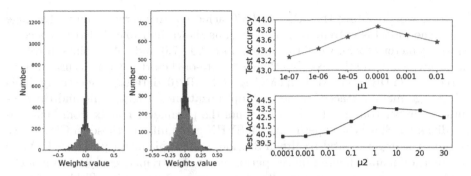

Fig. 2. (a) Weight distribution of two separable linear transformation matrices in the last FC layer of VGG-16 with (yellow part) and without (dark part) sparsity constraint; (b) Impact of condition number constraints on robust accuracy of CIFAR-10.

complementary attacks which combine the PGD with SA. The SA is a black-box attack, which is an adversary attack without any internal knowledge of the targeted network. Unless otherwise specified, we set the PGD attack and the AA attack with the perturbation magnitude $\epsilon = 8/255$, iteration numbers $t = 10$, and step size $\alpha = 2/255$. For FGSM, we set $\epsilon = 4/255$, and the number of queries in SA to 100. We evaluate the model performance by using the following metrics, i) **Compression Ratio (CR)**: compression ratio refers to the ratio of the model size before compression to that after compression; ii) **Natural Accuracy (NA)**: the accuracy on classifying benign images; iii) **Robustness Accuracy (RA)**: the accuracy on classifying images corrupted by adversarial attack.

Ablation Study of Regularization Term. We investigate the impact of the three regularizers g, ρ and h on the performance of the $ARLST$ under the PGD attack on the CIFAR-10 dataset. Firstly, we evaluate the impact of sparse regularization term on the weight distribution. As shown in the Fig. 2(a), two separable linear transformation matrices in the last fully-connected layer of VGG-16 with sparse constraint($\mu_3 = 0.00001$) are more sparser than these without constraint. In other words, the sparse regularization term can further reduce the number of parameters on the basis of tensor product of sub-matrices. Then we test the effect of two condition number constraints on robust accuracy, as shown in Fig. 2(b). Experimental results show that suitable choices of μ_1 and μ_2 can improve the performance of the $ARLST$ method, e.g., $\mu_1 = 0.0001$ and $\mu_2 = 1$ achieve the superior performance.

4.1   ARLST with VGG-16

In this experiment[1], we compare the proposed $ARLST$ with aforementioned baseline methods on the CIFAR-10, SVHN and ImageNet datasets. We selected the VGG-16 network for experiment. For more details on this experiment refer to Section 4 of Supplementary Material.

---

[1] https://github.com/MVPR-Group/ARLST.

It is worth noting that the *ARLST* achieved an overwhelming advantage when the model is extremely compressed, as shown in Table. 1. Even at a compression factor of 200, we obtain gains up to 2.0, 7.0 and 1.4% points in robust accuracy, while simultaneously achieving state-of-the-art natural accuracy, compared to HYDRA, ADMM, ATMC for CIFAR-10 dataset, respectively. This advantage may be traced to the joint optimization of the pruning and the condition number constraint, which prevents the parameter matrix from being ill-conditioned. Since the experiments on SVHN are similar to those on CIFAR, we present the experimental results in Section 4 of Supplementary Material. While our method mainly focuses on the performance of extremely compressed models, it also achieves competitive results at low compression ratios. Table 1 gives a simple comparison on the ImageNet-1K dataset at low compression ratios.

Table 1. Comparison of our approach with other pruning-based baseline methods. We use CIFAR-10 and ImageNet dataset with VGG-16 networks, iterative adversarial training from [51] for this experiment.

	Method	HYDRA	ADMM	ATMC	ARLST
	CR	NA/RA	NA/RA	NA/RA	NA/RA
CIFAR − 10	10×	75.7/46.2	75.9/44.8	75.6/44.8	**76.6/46.3**
	20×	74.5/44.9	74.7/43.7	73.9/42.9	**75.8/45.6**
	100×	69.8/40.2	68.8/40.4	69.8/41.1	**70.0/41.3**
	200×	62.4/35.5	60.6/30.5	64.0/36.1	**64.3/37.5**
ImageNet − 1K	5×	43.2/28.7	41.2/27.9	45.1/29.5	**45.4/30.0**
	10×	41.6/27.0	40.1/26.0	42.9/27.8	**43.9/28.7**

In previous experiments, we tested *ARLST* and other baselines against the PGD attack at certain fixed perturbation levels. Furthermore, we tested these models against the FGSM attack, Square Attack (SA) and AutoAttack (AA) on CIFAR-100 dataset when the compression ratio is 100×. As shown in Table 2, our proposed method shows the best performance against various attacks.

Table 2. Comparison of our approach with other pruning-based baseline methods against various adversarial attacks. We use CIFAR-100 dataset and VGG-16 networks for this experiment.

	HYDRA	ADMM	ATMC	ARLST
Attacks	NA/RA	NA/RA	NA/RA	NA/RA
FGSM	44.9/29.7	41.1/27.7	46.2/31.5	**47.1/32.1**
PGD	33.3/19.9	32.2/17.7	36.6/21.3	**37.6/22.1**
SA	43.0/31.7	41.9/30.3	42.9/33.6	**44.1/34.7**
AA	31.9/17.7	30.9/16.9	35.0/19.9	**35.2/20.8**

4.2   ARLST with Visual Transformer

To the best of our knowledge, there are few existing studies on the robustness of lightweight Transformers. In this experiment, we conduct a simple set of experiments based on Compact Convolutional Transformer (CCT) [14], comparing our method with HYDRA on CIFAR-10 dataset. We apply FGSM attack to generate adversarial examples. We set the perturbation magnitude $\epsilon = 4/255$ and all models are trained on CIFAR-10 dataset for 100 epochs. As shown in Table 3, our *ARLST* achieves the best natural and robust accuracy on CIFAR-10 dataset at the same compression ratio. Note that the model completely loses its expressiveness when compressed by 20× based on the HYDRA. Experimental results show the overwhelming advantage of our proposed method, especially on high compression ratio. This is because our method prevents the condition number from being too large, while HYDRA leads to be not full-rank at high compression ratio.

Table 3. Comparison of HYDRA with our methods for CCT trained on CIFAR-10 dataset with adversarial training. Δ represents the difference in accuracy.

Method	HYDRA	ARLST (Ours)	Δ
CR	NA/RA	NA/RA	
5×	74.43/55.54	**83.11/61.04**	+8.38/ + 5.50
10×	54.56/36.45	**80.52/56.98**	+25.96/ + 20.53
20×	–	**73.39/49.24**	> +50.0

5   Conclusions

In this work, we proposed a novel framework for learning extremely lightweight and robust models, which combines tensor product with the constraints on sparsity and condition number. Moreover, we theoretically prove that the sparsity of original large-scale weight matrix is equivalent to the product of sparsity of these sub-matrices, as well as the condition number. The proposed extremely lightweight and robust framework is incorporated into adversarial training with the min-max optimization scheme, to further improve the robustness of model against hand-crafted adversarial attacks. Experimental results performed on VGG-16 and Compact Convolutional Transformer showed that our *ARLST* surpasses several baseline methods, achieving better robustness to various adversarial perturbations with very fewer network parameters.

Acknowledgment. This work was supported by National Key Research and Development Program of China (No. 2018YFB2101300), and Natural Science Foundation of China (No. 61872147).

References

1. Andriushchenko, Maksym, Croce, Francesco, Flammarion, Nicolas, Hein, Matthias: Square attack: a query-efficient black-box adversarial attack via random search. In: Vedaldi, Andrea, Bischof, Horst, Brox, Thomas, Frahm, Jan-Michael. (eds.) ECCV 2020. LNCS, vol. 12368, pp. 484–501. Springer, Cham (2020). https://doi.org/10.1007/978-3-030-58592-1_29
2. Athalye, A., Carlini, N., Wagner, D.: Obfuscated gradients give a false sense of security: circumventing defenses to adversarial examples. In: International Conference on Learning Representations (ICLR) (2018)
3. Chollet, F.: Xception: Deep learning with depthwise separable convolutions. In: IEEE Conference on Computer Vision and Pattern Recognition (CVPR), pp. 1800–1807. IEEE (2017)
4. Croce, F., Hein, M.: Reliable evaluation of adversarial robustness with an ensemble of diverse parameter-free attacks. In: International Conference on International Conference on Machine Learning (ICML) (2020)
5. De Lathauwer, L., De Moor, B., Vandewalle, J.: A multilinear singular value decomposition. SIAM J. Matrix Anal. Appl. **21**(4), 1253–1278 (2000)
6. Demmel, J.W.: Applied Numerical Linear Algebra, vol. 56. SIAM, Philadelphia (1997)
7. Denton, E.L., Zaremba, W., Bruna, J., LeCun, Y., Fergus, R.: Exploiting linear structure within convolutional networks for efficient evaluation. In: Conference on Advances in Neural Information Processing Systems (NeurIPS) (2014)
8. Dosovitskiy, A., et al.: An image is worth 16x16 words: transformers for image recognition at scale. In: International Conference on Learning Representations (ICLR) (2020)
9. Goodfellow, I.J., Shlens, J., Szegedy, C.: Explaining and harnessing adversarial examples. In: International Conference on Learning Representations (ICLR) (2014)
10. Gui, S., Wang, H., Yang, H., Yu, C., Wang, Z., Liu, J.: Model compression with adversarial robustness: a unified optimization framework. In: Proceedings of the 33rd International Conference on Neural Information Processing Systems (NeurIPS), vol. 32 (2019)
11. Guo, Y., Zhang, C., Zhang, C., Chen, Y.: Sparse dnns with improved adversarial robustness. In: Proceedings of the Advances in Neural Information Processing Systems (NeurIPS). pp. 242–251 (2018)
12. Han, S., Mao, H., Dally, W.J.: Deep compression: Compressing deep neural networks with prunning, trained quantization and huffman coding. In: International Conference on Learning Representations (ICLR) (2016)
13. Han, S., Pool, J., Tran, J., Dally, W.: Learning both weights and connections for efficient neural network. In: Proceedings of the Advances in Neural Information Processing Systems (NeurIPS) (2015)
14. Hassani, A., Walton, S., Shah, N., Abuduweili, A., Li, J., Shi, H.: Escaping the big data paradigm with compact transformers. arXiv preprint arXiv:2104.05704 (2021)
15. He, Z., Gao, S., Xiao, L., Liu, D., He, H., Barber, D.: Wider and deeper, cheaper and faster: Tensorized LSTMs for sequence learning. In: Conference: Advances In Neural Information Processing System(NeurIPS), vol. 30 (2017)
16. Hinton, G., Vinyals, O., Dean, J.: Distilling the knowledge in a neural network. Statistics **9** 1050 (2015)

17. Horn, R.A., Horn, R.A., Johnson, C.R.: Topics in Matrix Analysis. Cambridge University Press, Cambridge (1994)
18. Khrulkov, V., Hrinchuk, O., Mirvakhabova, L., Oseledets, I.: Tensorized embedding layers for efficient model compression. In: 8th International Conference on Learning Representations (ICLR) (2020)
19. Krizhevsky, A., et al.: Learning multiple layers of features from tiny images. Master Thesis (2009)
20. Kurakin, A., Goodfellow, I., Bengio, S.: Adversarial machine learning at scale. In: International Conference on Learning Representations (ICLR) (2016)
21. LeCun, Y., Bottou, L., Bengio, Y., Haffner, P.: Gradient-based learning applied to document recognition. Proc. IEEE **86**(11), 2278–2324 (1998)
22. Lee, E., Lee, C.Y.: NeuralScale: efficient scaling of neurons for resource-constrained deep neural networks. In: Proceedings of the IEEE/CVF Conference on Computer Vision and Pattern Recognition (CVPR), pp. 1478–1487 (2020)
23. Lin, J., Gan, C., Han, S.: Defensive quantization: when efficiency meets robustness. In: International Conference on Learning Representations. International Conference on Learning Representations (ICLR) (2019)
24. Lin, J., Rao, Y., Lu, J., Zhou, J.: Runtime neural pruning. In: Proceedings of the 31st International Conference on Neural Information Processing Systems (NeurIPS), pp. 2178–2188 (2017)
25. Madaan, D., Shin, J., Hwang, S.J.: Adversarial neural pruning with latent vulnerability suppression. In: International Conference on Machine Learning (ICML), pp. 6575–6585. PMLR (2020)
26. Madry, A., Makelov, A., Schmidt, L., Tsipras, D., Vladu, A.: Towards deep learning models resistant to adversarial attacks. In: 6th International Conference on Learning Representations (ICLR). Vancouver, Canada (2018)
27. Moosavi-Dezfooli, S.M., Fawzi, A., Frossard, P.: DeepfOol: a simple and accurate method to fool deep neural networks. In: Proceedings of the IEEE Conference on Computer Vision and Pattern Recognition (CVPR), pp. 2574–2582 (2016)
28. Netzer, Y., Wang, T., Coates, A., Bissacco, A., Wu, B., Ng, A.Y.: Reading digits in natural images with unsupervised feature learning. In: Advances in Neural Information Processing Systems (NeurIPS) (2011)
29. Papernot, N., McDaniel, P., Jha, S., Fredrikson, M., Celik, Z.B., Swami, A.: The limitations of deep learning in adversarial settings. In: 2016 IEEE European Symposium on Security and Privacy (EuroS&P), pp. 372–387. IEEE (2016)
30. Papernot, N., McDaniel, P., Wu, X., Jha, S., Swami, A.: Distillation as a defense to adversarial perturbations against deep neural networks. In: 2016 IEEE Symposium on Security and Privacy (SP), pp. 582–597. IEEE (2016)
31. Peng, X., Zhang, L., Yi, Z., Tan, K.K.: Learning locality-constrained collaborative representation for robust face recognition. Pattern Recogn. **47**(9), 2794–2806 (2014)
32. Phan, Anh-Huy., Sobolev, Konstantin, Sozykin, Konstantin, Ermilov, Dmitry, Gusak, Julia, Tichavský, Petr, Glukhov, Valeriy, Oseledets, Ivan, Cichocki, Andrzej: Stable low-rank tensor decomposition for compression of convolutional neural network. In: Vedaldi, Andrea, Bischof, Horst, Brox, Thomas, Frahm, Jan-Michael. (eds.) ECCV 2020. LNCS, vol. 12374, pp. 522–539. Springer, Cham (2020). https://doi.org/10.1007/978-3-030-58526-6_31
33. Polino, A., Pascanu, R., Alistarh, D.: Model compression via distillation and quantization. In: International Conference on Learning Representations (ICLR) (2018)
34. Rolnick, D., Tegmark, M.: The power of deeper networks for expressing natural functions. In: International Conference on Learning Representations (ICLR) (2018)

35. Russakovsky, D., et al.: ImageNet large scale visual recognition challenge. Int. J. Comput. Vis. **115**(3), 211–252 (2015)
36. Sainath, T.N., Kingsbury, B., Sindhwani, V., Arisoy, E., Ramabhadran, B.: Low-rank matrix factorization for deep neural network training with high-dimensional output targets. In: IEEE International Conference on Acoustics, Speech and Signal Processing (ICASSP), pp. 6655–6659. IEEE (2013)
37. Sehwag, V., Wang, S., Mittal, P., Jana, S.: HYDRA: pruning adversarially robust neural networks. In: Advances in Neural Information Processing Systems (NeurIPS), vol. 33, pp. 19655–19666 (2020)
38. Simonyan, K., Zisserman, A.: Very deep convolutional networks for large-scale image recognition. In: International Conference on Learning Representations (ICLR) (2015)
39. Sinha, Abhishek, Singh, Mayank, Krishnamurthy, Balaji: Neural networks in an adversarial setting and ill-conditioned weight space. In: Alzate, C., et al. (eds.) ECML PKDD 2018. LNCS (LNAI), vol. 11329, pp. 177–190. Springer, Cham (2019). https://doi.org/10.1007/978-3-030-13453-2_14
40. Tan, M., Le, Q.: EfficientNet: rethinking model scaling for convolutional neural networks. In: International Conference on Machine Learning (ICML), pp. 6105–6114 (2019)
41. Thakker, U., et al.: Pushing the limits of RNN compression. In: 2019 Fifth Workshop on Energy Efficient Machine Learning and Cognitive Computing-NeurIPS Edition (EMC2-NeurIPS), pp. 18–21. IEEE (2019)
42. Tolstikhin, I.O., et al.: MLP-mixer: an all-MLP architecture for vision. In: Advances in Neural Information Processing Systems (NeurIPS), vol. 34, pp. 24261–2427a2 (2021)
43. Tramèr, F., Kurakin, A., Papernot, N., Goodfellow, I., Boneh, D., McDaniel, P.: Ensemble adversarial training: attacks and defenses. In: International Conference on Learning Representations (ICLR) (2018)
44. Van Loan, C.F.: The ubiquitous kronecker product. J. Comput. Appl. Math. **123**(1–2), 85–100 (2000)
45. Wen, W., Wu, C., Wang, Y., Chen, Y., Li, H.: Learning structured sparsity in deep neural networks. In: Proceedings of the 30th International Conference on Neural Information Processing Systems, pp. 2074–2082 (2016)
46. Wu, J., Leng, C., Wang, Y., Hu, Q., Cheng, J.: Quantized convolutional neural networks for mobile devices. In: Proceedings of the IEEE Conference on Computer Vision and Pattern Recognition (CVPR). pp. 4820–4828 (2016)
47. Xu, K., et al.: Structured adversarial attack: Towards general implementation and better interpretability. In: International Conference on Learning Representations (ICLR) (2019)
48. Ye, S., et al.: Adversarial robustness vs. model compression, or both? In: Proceedings of the IEEE/CVF International Conference on Computer Vision (ICCV), pp. 111–120 (2019)
49. Yin, M., Sui, Y., Liao, S., Yuan, B.: Towards efficient tensor decomposition-based DNN model compression with optimization framework. In: Proceedings of the IEEE/CVF Conference on Computer Vision and Pattern Recognition (CVPR), pp. 10674–10683 (2021)
50. Yu, X., Liu, T., Wang, X., Tao, D.: On compressing deep models by low rank and sparse decomposition. In: Proceedings of the IEEE Conference on Computer Vision and Pattern Recognition (CVPR), pp. 7370–7379 (2017)

51. Zhang, H., Yu, Y., Jiao, J., Xing, E., El Ghaoui, L., Jordan, M.I.: Theoretically principled trade-off between robustness and accuracy. In: International Conference on Machine Learning (ICML), pp. 7472–7482 (2019)
52. Zhao, Y., Shumailov, I., Mullins, R., Anderson, R.: To compress or not to compress: Understanding the interactions between adversarial attacks and neural network compression. In: Proceedings of Machine Learning and Systems (MLSys), pp. 230–240 (2019)

RIBAC: Towards Robust and Imperceptible Backdoor Attack against Compact DNN

Huy Phan[1]([✉]), Cong Shi[1], Yi Xie[1], Tianfang Zhang[1], Zhuohang Li[2], Tianming Zhao[3], Jian Liu[2], Yan Wang[3], Yingying Chen[1], and Bo Yuan[1]

[1] Rutgers University, New Jersey, USA
huy.phan@rutgrs.edu
[2] The University of Tennessee, Tennessee, USA
[3] Temple University, Pennsylvania, USA

Abstract. Recently backdoor attack has become an emerging threat to the security of deep neural network (DNN) models. To date, most of the existing studies focus on backdoor attack against the uncompressed model; while the vulnerability of compressed DNNs, which are widely used in the practical applications, is little exploited yet. In this paper, we propose to study and develop Robust and Imperceptible Backdoor Attack against Compact DNN models (RIBAC). By performing systematic analysis and exploration on the important design knobs, we propose a framework that can learn the proper trigger patterns, model parameters and pruning masks in an efficient way. Thereby achieving high trigger stealthiness, high attack success rate and high model efficiency simultaneously. Extensive evaluations across different datasets, including the test against the state-of-the-art defense mechanisms, demonstrate the high robustness, stealthiness and model efficiency of RIBAC. Code is available at https://github.com/huyvnphan/ECCV2022-RIBAC.

Keywords: Backdoor attack · Deep neural networks · Model security

1 Introduction

Deep neural networks (DNNs) have obtained widespread applications in many important artificial intelligence (AI) tasks. To enable the efficient deployment of DNNs in resource-constrained scenarios, especially on embedded and mobile devices, *model compression* has been widely used in practice to reduce memory footprint and accelerate inference speed [41, 42, 45]. In particular, *network pruning* is the most popular compression technique that has been extensively studied and adopted in both academia and industry [7, 8, 32].

Although model compression indeed brings promising benefits to *model efficiency*, it meanwhile raises severe issues on *model security*. In general, because

---

Supplementary Information The online version contains supplementary material available at https://doi.org/10.1007/978-3-031-19772-7_41.

of introducing additional compression process, the originally tested and verified security of the uncompressed DNNs may be altered and compromised after model compression, and thereby significantly increasing the vulnerability for the compressed models. Motivated by this challenging risk, in recent years the research community has conducted active investigations on the security issues of the compressed DNNs, and most of these existing efforts focus on the scenario of adversarial attack [15,20,24,33,38,39,43].

Despite the current prosperity of exploring adversarial robustness on the compact neural networks, the security challenges of the compressed models against *backdoor attack* [2,25], as another important and common attack strategy, are still very little explored yet. In principle, because producing a compressed DNN typically needs to first pre-train a large model and then compress it, such two-stage flow, by its nature, significantly extends the attack surface and increases the security risks. Consequently, compared with their uncompressed counterparts, it is very likely that the compressed DNN models may suffer more vulnerability and fragility against the backdoor attack when the compression is performed by third-party compression services or outsourcing.

Motivated by this emerging challenge and the corresponding insufficient investigation, this paper proposes to perform a systematic study on the vulnerability of compressed DNNs with the presence of backdoor attack. To be specific, we aim to explore the feasibility of high-performance backdoor attack against the pruned neural networks. Here this targeted *high-performance* attack is expected to exhibit the following three characteristics:

- **High Trigger Stealthiness.** The injected trigger patterns should be highly imperceptible and unnoticeable to bypass both visual inspection and state-of-the-art defense mechanisms.
- **High Attack Success Rate.** With the presence of the malicious inputs that contain the hidden triggers, the success rate of the launched attack should achieve very high level.
- **High Model Efficiency.** When receiving the benign inputs, the backdoored compressed DNN models should still demonstrate strong compression capabilities with respect to high compression ratio and minor accuracy drop.

Note the among the above three criteria, the first two are the general needs for any strong backdoor attack methods. In addition to them, the strict performance requirement on model efficiency, which is even challenging for many existing model compression-only approaches, is a specific but very critical demand that the compressed model-oriented backdoor attack must satisfy.

Technical Preview and Contributions. In this paper we propose to study and develop Robust and Imperceptible Backdoor Attack against Compact DNN models (RIBAC). By performing systematic analysis and exploration on the important design knobs for the high-performance backdoor attack, we further propose and develop a framework that can learn the proper trigger patterns, model parameters and pruning masks in an efficient way, thereby achieving high trigger stealthiness, high attack success rate and high model efficiency simultaneously. Overall, the contributions of this paper are summarized as follows:

- We systematically investigate and analyze the important design knobs for performing backdoor attack against the prune DNN models, such as the operational sequence of pruning and trigger injection as well as the pruning criterion, to understand the key factors for realizing high attack and compression performance.
- Based on the understanding obtained from the analysis, we further develop a robust and stealthy pruning-aware backdoor attack. By formulating the attack to a constrained optimization problem, we propose to solve it via a two-step scheme to learn the proper importance scored masks, trigger patterns and model weights, thereby simultaneously achieving high pruning performance and attack performance.
- We evaluate RIBAC for different models across various datasets. Experimental results show that RIBAC attack exhibits high trigger stealthiness, high attack success rate and high model efficiency simultaneously. In addition, it is also a very robust attack that can pass the tests with the presence of several state-of-the-art backdoor defense methods.

Threat Model. This paper assumes that the backdoor injection occurs during the model compression stage; in other words, the original uncompressed model is clean without embedded backdoor. We believe such an assumption is reasonable and realistic because of two reasons. First, in real-world scenarios the large-scale pre-trained models are typically provided by the trusted developers (e.g., public companies) or under very careful examination and test; while the review and scrutiny at the compression stage are much relaxed and less strict. Second, since model compression lies in the last stage of an entire model deployment pipeline, it is more likely that the backdoor injection at this stage can achieve the desired attack outcomes since the compressed model will then be directly deployed on the victim users' devices.

2   Related Works

In the backdoor attack scenario [2,6], the adversary embeds the backdoor on the DNN models via injecting the hidden triggers to a small amount of training data. Then in the inference phase the affected model will output the maliciously changed results if and only if receiving the trigger-contained inputs.

Backdoor Attack at Data Collection Stage. [2] Proposes to inject only a smaller number of poison data into the training set to create a backdoor model. Both [30] and [27] further propose methods to generate poison data consisting of the perturbed images and the corresponding correct labels. [44] investigates the property of backdoor triggers in the frequency domain.

Backdoor Attack at Model Training Stage. BadNet [6] demonstrates that the outsourced training can cause security risk via altering training data. In general, the imperceptibility of the trigger patterns are critical to the success of backdoor attack. To date, many different types of trigger generation approaches [4,21,

22] have been proposed. In particular, some state-of-the-art works [3,4,13,22] proposes that more powerful backdoor should have capability of launching the attacks with visual indistinguishable poisoned samples from their benign counterparts to evade human inspection. For instance, WaNet [22] is proposed to generate backdoor images via subtle image warping, leading to a much stealthier attack setting. [4] designs a novel backdoor attack framework, LIRA, which learns the optimal imperceptible trigger injection function to poison the input data. A more recent work, WB [3], achieves high attack success rate via generating imperceptible input noise which is stealthy in both the input and latent spaces.

Backdoor Attack at Model Compression Stage. Performing backdoor attack on the compressed model is not well studied until very recently. To date only very few papers investigate the interplay between model compression and backdoor attacks. [34] proposes a method to inject inactive backdoor to the full-size model, and the backdoor will be activated after the model is compressed. [19] discovers that the standard quantization operation can be abused to enable backdoor attacks. [10] propose to use quantization-aware backdoor training to ensure the effectiveness of backdoor if model is further quantized. The quantization effect of the backdoor injected models is also analyzed and studied in [23]. Notice that all of these existing works are based on the assumption that the pre-trained model is already infected by the backdoor; while the threat model of this paper is to inject backdoor during the compression process of the originally clean pre-trained models.

Backdoor Defense. The threat of backdoor attacks can be mitigated via different types of defensive mechanisms. The detection-style methods [1,35] aim to identify the potential malicious training samples via statistically analyzing some important behaviors of models, such as the activation values [5] or the predictions [16]. In addition, by performing pre-processing of the input, data mitigation-style strategy [14,17] targets to eliminate or mitigate the affect of the backdoor triggers, so the infected model can still behave normally with the presence of trigger-contained inputs. On the other hand, model correction-style approaches directly modify the weight parameters to alleviate the threat of backdoor attack. A series of model modification approaches, such as re-training on clean data [46] and pruning the infected neurons, [16,37], have been proposed in the existing literature.

Network Pruning for Backdoor Defense. In [16,37], network pruning serves as a model correction method for backdoor defense. Different from these pruning-related works, this paper focuses on the attack side. Our goal is to develop pruning-aware backdoor attack against a large-scale clean pre-trained DNN, thereby generating a backdoor-infected pruned model.

3 Methodology

In this section we propose to develop high-performance backdoor attack against the pruned DNN models. As outlined in Sect. 1, such attack, if possible and feasible, should exhibit high trigger stealthiness, high attack success rate and

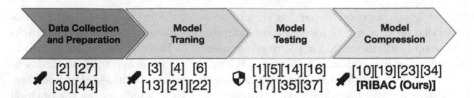

Fig. 1. Backdoor attack and defense in the DNN model deployment pipeline. RIBAC attack is performed at model compression stage. Different from other attacks launched at this stage, RIBAC assumes that the to-be-compressed model has passed model testing, and it is clean without infection.

high model efficiency simultaneously. To that end, a proper perspective that can represent and unify the requirements from both attack performance and compression performance should be identified.

Problem Formulation. In general, given a pre-trained DNN classifier function f with weight parameters $\mathcal{W}_{\mathrm{pt}}$ such that $f_{\mathcal{W}_{\mathrm{pt}}} : x \mapsto y$, where x and y are the clean input images and ground truth labels, respectively, and let $\mathcal{C}$ be the compression function that satisfy the target compression ratio, we can then formulate the behavior of injecting backdoor into the compressed models as:

$$\mathcal{W} = \mathcal{C}(\mathcal{W}_{\mathrm{pt}}) \quad s.t. \quad \begin{cases} f_{\mathcal{W}} : x \mapsto y \\ f_{\mathcal{W}} : \mathcal{B}(x) \mapsto t, \end{cases} \tag{1}$$

where $\mathcal{B}(\cdot)$ is the function that generates Trojan images from clean images x, and t is the target class chosen by the attacker. Without loss of generality, we choose weight pruning as the compression method, and patch-based to be the backdoor injection method. Then Eq. 1 is specified as:

$$\mathcal{W} = \mathcal{W}_{\mathrm{pt}} \odot \mathcal{M} \quad s.t. \quad \begin{cases} f_{\mathcal{W}} : x \mapsto y \\ f_{\mathcal{W}} : \mathtt{clip}(x + \tau) \mapsto t \end{cases} \tag{2}$$

where $\odot$, τ and $\mathtt{clip}(\cdot)$ represent element-wise multiplication, trigger pattern and clipping operation, respectively. For each attack target t_i there is the corresponding backdoor trigger τ_i. Also, $\mathcal{M}$ is the binary pruning mask with the same size of $\mathcal{W}_{\mathrm{pt}}$.

Questions to be Answered. As indicated by Eq. 2, a backdoored and pruned DNN model is jointly determined by the selection of the network pruning and backdoor trigger generation schemes. Considering the complicated interplay between these two schemes as well as their multiple design options, next we explore to answer the following three important questions towards developing high-performance pruned model-oriented backdoor attack.

   Question #1: *What is the proper operational sequence when jointly performing network pruning and injecting backdoor triggers?*

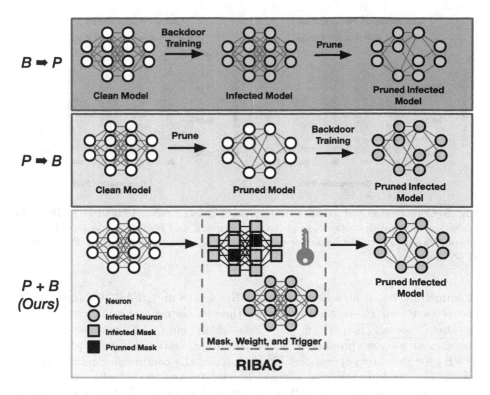

Fig. 2. Different operational sequences for obtaining backdoored pruned model. Given a clean model, $B \rightarrow P$ first injects the backdoor and then performs pruning; $P \rightarrow B$ first prunes the model and then performs backdoor training on the pruned networks; Our proposed $P + B$ learns the pruning masks, model weights and trigger patterns simultaneously.

Analysis. In general, imposing both network sparsity and backdoor triggers on the benign and uncompressed DNN models can be realized in different ways. The most straightforward solution is to perform network pruning and backdoor injection *sequentially*. As illustrated in Fig. 2, we can either "prune-then-inject" or "inject-then-prune" to alter the original uncompressed and benign model to the desired compressed and backdoored one. For simplicity, we denote these two sequential schemes as $B \rightarrow P$ and $P \rightarrow B$, where B, P represent the operation of injecting backdoor and pruning network, respectively.

Evidently, the above two-stage schemes enjoy the benefit of convenient deployment since they can be easily implemented via simply combining the existing network pruning and backdoor attack approaches. However, we argue that they are not the ideal solutions when aiming for simultaneous high compression performance and attack performance. To be specific, because the current schemes for B and P are designed to optimize these two operations individually, the simple combination of these two locally optimal strategies does not necessarily bring globally optimal solution. For instance, as shown in Fig. 3, when aiming

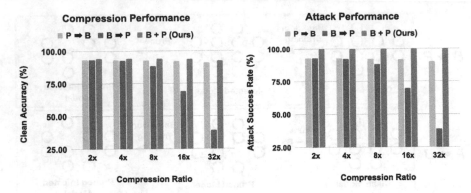

Fig. 3. Compression and Attack Performance of Preact ResNet-18 model on CIFAR-10 via using different operational sequences for pruning and backdoor injection. Here we adopt WaNet [22] as the backdoor training method B used in the $B \to P$ and $P \to B$ schemes.

to launch backdoor attacks on a Preact ResNet-18 on CIFAR-10 dataset, both the $B \to P$ and $P \to B$ fail to achieve the satisfactory performance.

Our Proposal. To perform joint network pruning and backdoor attack in an efficient way, we propose to adopt *parallel* operational scheme (denoted as $P+B$) for these two operations. To be specific, the compression-related design knobs, i.e., masking selection and weight update, and the attack-related design knobs, i.e., trigger pattern, will be determined together. To that end, Eq. 2 is reformulated to the format with a unified objective function as follows:

$$\min_{\mathcal{W},\mathcal{M},\tau} \mathcal{J} = \min_{\mathcal{W},\mathcal{M},\tau} [\underbrace{\mathcal{L}(\mathcal{W} \odot \mathcal{M}, x, y)}_{\text{clean data loss}} + \beta \cdot \underbrace{\mathcal{L}(\mathcal{W} \odot \mathcal{M}, \text{clip}(x + \tau), t)}_{\text{Trojan data loss}}],$$
$$\text{s.t. } ||\mathcal{M}||_0 \leq s \text{ and } ||\tau||_\infty \leq \epsilon,$$

$$(3)$$

where s is the sparsity constraint, and ϵ the the trigger stealthiness constraint. Here the overall loss consists of the clean data loss and Trojan data loss, which measure the model compression performance (in term of clean accuracy) and attack performance (in term of attack success rate), respectively. With such unified loss function, the backdoor triggers τ, pruning masks $\mathcal{M}$ and model weights $\mathcal{W}$ can be now learned in an end-to-end and simultaneous way. Notice that β is a hyper-parameter to control the balance between two loss terms.

Question #2: *Which pruning criterion is more suitable for producing the backdoored sparse DNN models?*

Analysis. Consider pruning serves as a key component of the compression-aware attack, the proper selection of the pruning mask $\mathcal{M}$ is very critical. To date, weight magnitude-based pruning, which aims to remove the connections that have the least weights, is the most popular pruning method used in practice. In particular, several prior works [28,40] that co-explore the sparsity and adversarial robustness of DNN models are also built on this pruning strategy.

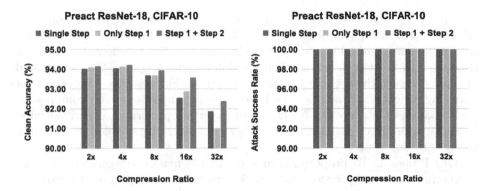

Fig. 4. Compression and Attack Performance of Preact ResNet-18 model on CIFAR-10 via using different schemes for training weights $\mathcal{W}$, triggers τ and importance scores $\mathcal{S}$. **Single Step** means to train all of them simultaneously. **Only Step 1** means to only train τ and $\mathcal{S}$. **Step 1 + Step 2** means to first train τ and $\mathcal{S}$, and then train τ and $\mathcal{W}$.

However, we argue that the weight magnitude-based pruning is not the ideal solution towards producing a backdoored pruned model. Recall that the design philosophy for this pruning criterion is that the smaller weights intend to exhibit less importance. Although this assumption heuristically works when the overall task focuses on improving compression performance, it does not hold if other requirement, such as achieving high attack performance, needs to be satisfied. More specifically, the weights with less magnitudes does not necessarily mean that they are less important for the vulnerability of the model with the presence of backdoor attack. Consequently, if a DNN model is pruned via such pruning criterion ignoring the impacts on vulnerability, the resulting backdoor attack performance is likely to be very limited.

Our Proposal. To address this issue, we propose to perform pruning in an attack-aware way. To that end, we choose to apply the philosophy of importance score [26] to the pruning process. More specifically, the trainable importance score, which measures the impact of the specific weight for the attack performance, is assigned to each neuron. Assume that $\mathcal{S}$ be the set of importance scores of the weights, and let m_i and s_i be the ith element in the flatten $\mathcal{M}$ and $\mathcal{S}$, respectively. Then in the forward pass the mask $\mathcal{M} = h(\mathcal{S})$ is generated as:

$$m_i = h(s_i) = \begin{cases} 1 & \text{if } s_i \in \texttt{topK}(\mathcal{S}, k, l), \\ 0 & \text{otherwise} \end{cases} \qquad (4)$$

where $\texttt{topK}(\cdot, \cdot, \cdot)$ is the function that returns top $k\%$ highest score in layer l. During the training $\mathcal{S}$ can be then updated with learning rate α_1 as:

$$\mathcal{S} \leftarrow \mathcal{S} - \alpha_1 \cdot \nabla_{\mathcal{S}}[\mathcal{J}(\mathcal{W}, h(\mathcal{S}), \tau, x, y)]. \qquad (5)$$

Question #3: *What is the proper learning scheme to perform the end-to-end training on pruning masks, trigger patterns and model weights?*

Analysis. Eq. 3 shows that injecting backdoor trigger to the pruned model can be interpreted as the joint learning of masks, triggers and weights. To that end, a straightforward method is to directly optimize the unified loss described in Eq. 3. However, this strategy is not an ideal solution because it ignores the complicated interplay among these three learnable objectives. For instance, the efforts for updating weights and masks may have opposite impacts on the compression performance, which may also further affect the attack performance. As illustrated in Fig. 4, such direct optimization strategy does not bring satisfied performance on compression aspect.

Our Proposal. To properly learn the suitable masks, triggers and weights to maximize the compression and attack performance, we propose to learn the masks and weights in two separate steps with always keeping the update of triggers. This idea is build on a key observation. As shown in Fig. 4, when we only train the importance score and trigger pattern (**Only Step 1**), even the weights are frozen to the initial values, very high attack success rate can already be obtained with slightly dropped clean accuracy. An intuitive explanation for this phenomenon is that since the initialization of weights inherit from the pre-trained model, as long as the masks and triggers are properly trained, the drop of clean accuracy is not very significant because of the existence of clean data loss in the overall loss (Eq. 3). Motivated by this observation, we can first focus on learning the masks and triggers to achieve the desired attack performance, and then "fine-tune" the weights to further improve the compression performance. In general, this two-step scheme can be described as follows:

$$\textbf{Step} - \textbf{1} : \min_{\mathcal{S},\tau} \mathcal{L}(\mathcal{W}_{\mathrm{pt}} \odot h(\mathcal{S}), x, y) + \beta \cdot \mathcal{L}(\mathcal{W}_{\mathrm{pt}} \odot h(\mathcal{S}), \mathtt{clip}(x + \tau), t), \quad (6)$$

$$\textbf{Step} - \textbf{2} : \min_{\mathcal{W},\tau} \mathcal{L}(\mathcal{W} \odot \mathcal{M}, x, y) + \beta \cdot \mathcal{L}(\mathcal{W} \odot \mathcal{M}, \mathtt{clip}(x + \tau), t). \quad (7)$$

The Overall Algorithm. Built upon the above analysis and proposals, we then integrate them together and develop the overall algorithm for training a pruned model to achieve simultaneous high compression performance and backdoor attack performance. The details of this procedure are described in Algorithm 1.

4   Experiments

4.1   Experiment Setup

Datasets and Models. Following the prior works WaNet [22], LIRA [4] and WB [3], we evaluate our method on four commonly used datasets for backdoor attacks: CIFAR-10 [11], GTSRB [31], CelebA [18], and Tiny ImageNet [12]. We select Pre-Activate ResNet-18 [9] for evaluation on CIFAR-10 and GTSRB datasets, and ResNet-18 [9] for evaluation on CelebA and Tiny ImageNet datasets.

Hyperparameter and Attack Setting. We train the models for 60 epochs via using Adam optimizer with the learning rate of 0.0003. All the experiments

---

Algorithm 1: The Procedure of RIBAC Algorithm

---

1 **Input:** Pre-trained model $\mathcal{W}_{\text{pt}}$, sparsity s, clean images x, labels y, targets t, learning rates $\alpha_1, \alpha_2, \alpha_3$, balancing factor β.

2 **Output:** Fine-tuned backdoored sparse model $\mathcal{W}_{\text{ft}}$, optimized triggers τ.

3 $\mathcal{S} \leftarrow \mathcal{W}_{\text{pt}}; \tau \leftarrow \text{random}(x.\text{shape}) \triangleright$ *initialize scores and triggers.*

4 **for** *(x_i, y_i, t_i) in (x, y, t)* **do** $\triangleright$ *Step #1. Optimize masks and triggers.*

5       $\mathcal{M} \leftarrow \text{generate\_mask}(\mathcal{S}, 1-s) \triangleright$ *via Equation (4).*

6       $\hat{y}_{\text{clean}}, \hat{y}_{\text{bd}} \leftarrow f_{\mathcal{W}_{\text{pt}} \odot \mathcal{M}}(x_i), f_{\mathcal{W}_{\text{pt}} \odot \mathcal{M}}(\text{clip}(x_i + \tau)) \triangleright$ *forward pass.*

7       $\mathcal{J} = \text{cross\_entropy}(\hat{y}_{\text{clean}}, y_i) + \beta \cdot \text{cross\_entropy}(\hat{y}_{\text{bd}}, t_i)$

8       $\mathcal{S} \leftarrow \mathcal{S} - \alpha_1 \cdot \nabla_{\mathcal{S}}[\mathcal{J}] \triangleright$ *update scores via Equation (5).*

9       $\tau \leftarrow \Pi_\epsilon(\tau - \alpha_2 \cdot \nabla_\tau[\mathcal{J}]) \triangleright$ *update triggers using projected SGD.*

10 $\mathcal{W} \leftarrow \mathcal{W}_{\text{pt}} \triangleright$ *Load pre-trained weight for fine-tuning.*

11 **for** *(x_i, y_i, t_i) in (x, y, t)* **do** $\triangleright$ *Step #2. Optimize weights and triggers.*

12       $\hat{y}_{\text{clean}}, \hat{y}_{\text{bd}} \leftarrow f_{\mathcal{W} \odot \mathcal{M}}(x_i), f_{\mathcal{W} \odot \mathcal{M}}(\text{clip}(x_i + \tau)) \triangleright$ *forward pass.*

13       $\mathcal{J} = \text{cross\_entropy}(\hat{y}_{\text{clean}}, y_i) + \beta \cdot \text{cross\_entropy}(\hat{y}_{\text{bd}}, t_i)$

14       $\mathcal{W} \leftarrow \mathcal{W} - \alpha_3 \cdot \nabla_{\mathcal{W}}[\mathcal{J}] \triangleright$ *update weight using SGD.*

15       $\tau \leftarrow \Pi_\epsilon(\tau - \alpha_2 \cdot \nabla_\tau[\mathcal{J}]) \triangleright$ *update triggers using projected SGD.*

16 $\mathcal{W}_{\text{ft}} \leftarrow \mathcal{W} \odot \mathcal{M} \triangleright$ *finalize the weight.*

---

are performed using Pytorch on Nvidia RTX 3090 GPU. To generate the target classes t for backdoor attacks, we adopt the two common all-to-one and all-to-all settings. For all-to-one configuration, we choose the first class as our target: $t_i = 0 \; \forall \; i$; for all-to-all configuration, the targets are the correct labels offset by 1: $t_i = y_i + 1 \bmod c \; \forall i$, where c is the number of classes. To ensure the stealthiness of our triggers τ, we use the operation Π_ϵ to clip the values of τ that are outside the limit of $\epsilon = 4/255$.

4.2   Attack Performance and Compression Performance

Comparison with Simple Combination of Pruning & Backdoor Injection. We compared the performance of RIBAC with other alternatives for obtaining the backdoored pruned model. Here we design three baseline methods: 1) Randomly initialize a sparse model, then train it using the state-of-the-art WaNet backdoor training [22]; 2) prune a clean pre-trained network, then train it using WaNet backdoor training; 3) train a full-size model using WaNet backdoor training, then prune the model to achieve the target compression ratio. As shown in Table 1, all three baseline methods fail to achieve the satisfied performance. On the other hand, RIBAC can consistently achieve high clean accuracy and high attack success rate even at high compression ratio. In particular RIBAC can achieve up to 46.22% attack success rate increase with 32× compression ratio on Tiny ImageNet dataset.

Comparison with Standard Pruning Methods on Clean Accuracy. We also compare the compression performance of RIBAC with two standard pruning approaches: L_1 global pruning [8] and importance score-based

Table 1. Simple combination of pruning and backdoor injection versus RIBAC with respect to clean accuracy/attack success rate. C.R. means compression ratio.

C.R.	P → B (Random Init.)	P → B (Clean Pre-trained)	B → P	P + B (RIBAC)
	Preact ResNet-18 on CIFAR-10 dataset			
2×	93.97 / 93.63	93.45 / 93.03	93.24 / 92.89	**94.16 / 100.00**
4×	94.18 / 93.91	93.11 / 92.55	92.56 / 92.24	**94.22 / 100.00**
8×	93.29 / 92.95	92.73 / 92.22	88.33 / 88.23	**93.94 / 100.00**
16×	92.53 / 92.18	92.21 / 91.57	68.95 / 69.50	**93.58 / 100.00**
32×	89.25 / 88.59	90.90 / 89.99	39.14 / 38.93	**92.39 / 100.00**
	ResNet-18 on CelebA dataset			
2×	79.67 / 79.61	79.32 / 79.34	77.00 / 76.95	**81.87 / 100.00**
4×	79.54 / 79.50	79.26 / 79.17	75.43 / 75.40	**81.52 / 100.00**
8×	79.83 / 79.74	79.07 / 79.06	51.38 / 51.63	**81.57 / 100.00**
16×	79.75 / 79.59	78.36 / 78.25	27.16 / 27.16	**81.68 / 100.00**
32×	79.69 / 79.75	79.28 / 78.77	27.16 / 27.16	**81.68 / 100.00**
	ResNet-18 on Tiny ImageNet dataset			
2×	61.85 / 60.97	58.83 / 58.25	59.84 / 59.29	**60.19 / 99.31**
4×	60.72 / 60.04	57.46 / 56.40	40.81 / 40.56	**60.76 / 99.64**
8×	59.04 / 58.64	57.04 / 56.37	1.64 / 1.53	**60.41 / 99.07**
16×	56.13 / 54.51	56.28 / 55.19	0.50 / 0.50	**59.11 / 99.40**
32×	50.16 / 49.28	54.28 / 53.06	0.50 / 0.50	**54.99 / 99.28**

pruning [26]. As reported in Table 2, RIBAC can achieve the similar clean accuracy to the standard pruning approach with different pruning ratio, and meanwhile RIBAC can still achieve very high attack success rate. In other words, RIBAC does not trade compression performance for attack performance.

Comparison with State-of-the-Art Backdoor Attack Methods. We also compare RIBAC with the state-of-the-art backdoor attacks approaches WaNet [22], LIRA [4], WB [3]. Notice that these existing methods cannot compress models. As shown in Table 3, on CIFAR-10 and GTSRB datasets, RIBAC can achieve very similar or higher clean accuracy and attack success rate while providing additional compression benefits. On Tiny ImageNet dataset RIBAC outperforms the state-of-the-art backdoor attack methods with up to 2.76% clean accuracy and 40.64% attack success rate increase.

4.3   Performance Against Defense Methods

To demonstrate the robustness and stealthiness of the backdoor attack enabled by our proposed RIBAC, we evaluate its performance against several state-of-the-art backdoor defense methods.

Fine-Pruning [16] argues that in a backdoored neural network there exist two groups of neurons that are associated with the clean images and backdoor triggers, respectively. Based on this assumption and with a small set of clean images,

Table 2. RIBAC vs Pruning-only Approach. Here for pruning-only baseline only clean accuracy is reported, and the clean accuracy/attack success rate is listed for RIBAC.

C.R	L1 Prune	Important Score Prune	RIBAC (all-to-one)	RIBAC (all-to-all)
Preact ResNet-18 (Pretrain 94.61) on CIFAR-10 dataset				
2×	94.51	94.61	94.35 / 100.00	94.16 / 100.00
4×	94.74	94.60	94.57 / 100.00	94.22 / 100.00
8×	94.86	94.31	94.36 / 100.00	93.94 / 100.00
16×	94.01	94.07	94.29 / 100.00	93.58 / 100.00
32×	91.51	93.05	91.77 / 100.00	92.39 / 100.00
Preact ResNet-18 (Pretrain 99.07) on GTSRB dataset				
2×	98.87	99.11	98.85 / 100.00	99.03 / 99.98
4×	98.86	98.50	98.48 / 100.00	98.96 / 99.97
8×	98.39	98.74	98.36 / 100.00	98.48 / 100.00
16×	98.86	98.65	98.80 / 100.00	98.00 / 99.02
32×	97.33	97.91	98.04 / 100.00	96.92 / 98.34
ResNet-18 (Pre-train 60.08) on Tiny ImageNet dataset				
2×	60.70	61.05	60.45 / 99.98	60.19 / 99.31
4×	60.86	61.25	60.70 / 99.95	60.76 / 99.64
8×	60.19	61.40	60.48 / 99.70	60.41 / 99.07
16×	59.20	60.25	59.65 / 99.92	59.11 / 99.40
32×	55.64	53.42	53.98 / 99.72	54.99 / 99.28

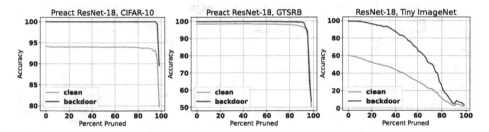

Fig. 5. Performance of RIBAC against Fine-Pruning.

Fine-Pruning records the activation maps of the neurons in last convolution layer, and then gradually prunes these neurons based on activation magnitude to remove the backdoor. Figure 5 shows the performance of Fine-Pruning on the model generated by RIBAC. As the number of pruned neuron increases, both the clean accuracy and attack success rate gradually drop. However, the attack success rate of RIBAC is always higher than the clean accuracy, thereby making Fine-Pruning fail to mitigate the backdoor.

STRIP [5] focuses on analyzing the entropy of the prediction. Its key idea is to perform perturbation on the input image via using a set of benign inputs from different classes. If the predictions of these perturbed inputs are persistent, which corresponds to low entropy, the potential presence of backdoor will be

Table 3. Comparison with different backdoor attack methods with respect to clean accuracy/attack success rate. C.R. means compression ratio.

Method	C.R.	Preact ResNet-18 CIFAR-10	Preact ResNet-18 GTSRB	ResNet-18 Tiny ImageNet
All-to-one Backdoor Attacks				
WaNet[22]	n/a	94.15/ 99.55	98.97/98.78	57.00/99.00
LIRA[4]	n/a	94.00/ 100.00	99.00/100.00	58.00/100.00
WB[3]	n/a	94.00/ 99.00	99.00/99.00	57.00/100.00
RIBAC	2×	94.35/100.00	98.85/100.00	60.45/99.98
RIBAC	4×	94.57/100.00	98.48/100.00	60.70/99.95
RIBAC	8×	94.36/100.00	98.36/100.00	60.48/99.70
RIBAC	16×	94.29/100.00	98.80/100.00	59.65/99.92
RIBAC	32×	91.77/100.00	98.04/100.00	53.98/99.72
All-to-all Backdoor Attacks				
WaNet[22]	n/a	94.00/ 93.00	99.00/98.00	58.00/58.00
LIRA[4]	n/a	94.00/ 94.00	99.00/100.00	58.00/59.00
WB[3]	n/a	94.00/ 94.00	99.00/98.00	58.00/58.00
RIBAC	2×	94.16/100.00	99.03/99.98	60.19/99.31
RIBAC	4×	94.22/100.00	98.96/99.97	60.76/99.64
RIBAC	8×	93.94/100.00	98.48/100.00	60.41/99.07
RIBAC	16×	93.58/100.00	98.00/99.02	59.11/99.40
RIBAC	32×	92.39/100.00	96.92/98.34	54.99/99.28

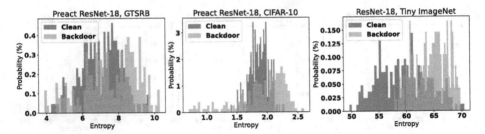

Fig. 6. Performance of RIBAC against STRIP.

alarmed. For RIBAC, because the learned backdoor triggers are imperceptible and extremely stealthy ($\|\tau\|_\infty \leq 4/255$), the perturbation operation adopted in STRIP effectively modifies the triggers, making our backdoored model behave like a clean model with similar entropy range (see Fig. 6).

Neural Cleanse [36] assumes that there exists patch-based pattern causing the misclassification. Based on this assumption, Neural Cleanse performs optimization to calculate the patch pattern that can altering the clean input to the target label. If a significant smaller pattern exists for any class label, a sign of potential backdoor will be alarmed. Such decision is quantified via using Abnormally Index with a threshold = 2.0, which determines the existence of backdoor or not. As shown in Fig. 7, our RIBAC passes all the Neural Cleanse tests across

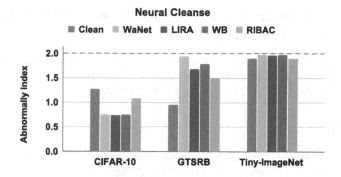

Fig. 7. Performance of RIBAC against Neural Cleanse.

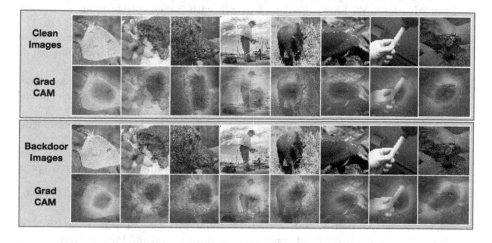

Fig. 8. Visualization of heatmap via GradCAM.

different datasets. For the test on CIFAR-10 and Tiny ImageNet, RIBAC can even achieve similar scores to the clean model.

GradCAM [29], as a method to visualize the network attention for the input image, can serve as an inspection tool to check the potential presence of backdoor. Figure 8 shows the visualization of the network's attention for both clean and trigger-contained images. It is seen that the heat map of RIBAC looks similar to the one from clean model, thereby making it passes the GradCAM-based inspection.

5 Conclusion

In this paper, we propose RIBAC, a robust and imperceptible backdoor attack against compact DNN models. The proper trigger patterns, model weights and pruning masks are simultaneously learned in an efficient way. Experimental results across different datasets show that RIBAC attack exhibits high stealthiness, high robustness and high model efficiency.

Acknowledgement. This work was partially supported by National Science Foundation under Grant CNS2114220, CCF1909963, CCF2211163, CNS2114161, CCF-2000480, CCF-2028858, CNS-2120276, and CNS-2145389.

References

1. Chen, B., et al.: Detecting backdoor attacks on deep neural networks by activation clustering. arXiv preprint arXiv:1811.03728 (2018)
2. Chen, X., Liu, C., Li, B., Lu, K., Song, D.: Targeted backdoor attacks on deep learning systems using data poisoning. arXiv preprint arXiv:1712.05526 (2017)
3. Doan, K., Lao, Y., Li, P.: Backdoor attack with imperceptible input and latent modification. In: Advances in Neural Information Processing Systems 34 (2021)
4. Doan, K., Lao, Y., Zhao, W., Li, P.: LIRA: learnable, imperceptible and robust backdoor attacks. In: Proceedings of the IEEE/CVF International Conference on Computer Vision, pp. 11966–11976 (2021)
5. Gao, Y., Xu, C., Wang, D., Chen, S., Ranasinghe, D.C., Nepal, S.: Strip: a defence against trojan attacks on deep neural networks. In: Proceedings of the 35th Annual Computer Security Applications Conference, pp. 113–125 (2019)
6. Gu, T., Liu, K., Dolan-Gavitt, B., Garg, S.: BadNets: Evaluating backdooring attacks on deep neural networks. IEEE Access **7**, 47230–47244 (2019)
7. Han, S., Mao, H., Dally, W.J.: Deep compression: compressing deep neural networks with pruning, trained quantization and huffman coding. arXiv preprint arXiv:1510.00149 (2015)
8. Han, S., Pool, J., Tran, J., Dally, W.J.: Learning both weights and connections for efficient neural networks. arXiv preprint arXiv:1506.02626 (2015)
9. He, K., Zhang, X., Ren, S., Sun, J.: Deep residual learning for image recognition. In: Proceedings of the IEEE Conference on Computer Vision and Pattern Recognition, pp. 770–778 (2016)
10. Hong, S., Panaitescu-Liess, M.A., Kaya, Y., Dumitras, T.: QU-ANTI-zation: exploiting quantization artifacts for achieving adversarial outcomes. In: Advances in Neural Information Processing Systems 34 (2021)
11. Krizhevsky, A., Hinton, G., et al.: Learning multiple layers of features from tiny images (2009)
12. Le, Y., Yang, X.: Tiny imagenet visual recognition challenge. CS 231N **7**(7), 3 (2015)
13. Li, S., Xue, M., Zhao, B., Zhu, H., Zhang, X.: Invisible backdoor attacks on deep neural networks via steganography and regularization. IEEE Trans. Depend. Secure Comput. (2020)
14. Li, Y., Zhai, T., Wu, B., Jiang, Y., Li, Z., Xia, S.: Rethinking the trigger of backdoor attack. arXiv preprint arXiv:2004.04692 (2020)
15. Li, Z., Shi, C., Xie, Y., Liu, J., Yuan, B., Chen, Y.: Practical adversarial attacks against speaker recognition systems. In: Proceedings of the 21st International Workshop on Mobile Computing Systems and Applications, pp. 9–14 (2020)
16. Liu, K., Dolan-Gavitt, B., Garg, S.: Fine-Pruning: defending against backdooring attacks on deep neural networks. In: Bailey, M., Holz, T., Stamatogiannakis, M., Ioannidis, S. (eds.) RAID 2018. LNCS, vol. 11050, pp. 273–294. Springer, Cham (2018). https://doi.org/10.1007/978-3-030-00470-5_13

17. Liu, Y., Xie, Y., Srivastava, A.: Neural trojans. In: 2017 IEEE International Conference on Computer Design (ICCD), pp. 45–48. IEEE (2017)

18. Liu, Z., Luo, P., Wang, X., Tang, X.: Deep learning face attributes in the wild. In: Proceedings of the IEEE International Conference on Computer Vision, pp. 3730–3738 (2015)

19. Ma, H., et al.: Quantization backdoors to deep learning models. arXiv preprint arXiv:2108.09187 (2021)

20. Madry, A., Makelov, A., Schmidt, L., Tsipras, D., Vladu, A.: Towards deep learning models resistant to adversarial attacks. arXiv preprint arXiv:1706.06083 (2017)

21. Nguyen, T.A., Tran, A.: Input-aware dynamic backdoor attack. Adv. Neural. Inf. Process. Syst. **33**, 3454–3464 (2020)

22. Nguyen, T.A., Tran, A.T.: WaNet-imperceptible warping-based backdoor attack. In: International Conference on Learning Representations (2021)

23. Pan, X., Zhang, M., Yan, Y., Yang, M.: Understanding the threats of trojaned quantized neural network in model supply chains. In: Annual Computer Security Applications Conference, pp. 634–645 (2021)

24. Phan, H., Xie, Y., Liao, S., Chen, J., Yuan, B.: Cag: a real-time low-cost enhanced-robustness high-transferability content-aware adversarial attack generator. In: Proceedings of the AAAI Conference on Artificial Intelligence, vol. 34, pp. 5412–5419 (2020)

25. Phan, H., Xie, Y., Liu, J., Chen, Y., Yuan, B.: Invisible and efficient backdoor attacks for compressed deep neural networks. In: ICASSP 2022–2022 IEEE International Conference on Acoustics, Speech and Signal Processing (ICASSP), pp. 96–100. IEEE (2022)

26. Ramanujan, V., Wortsman, M., Kembhavi, A., Farhadi, A., Rastegari, M.: What's hidden in a randomly weighted neural network? In: Proceedings of the IEEE/CVF Conference on Computer Vision and Pattern Recognition, pp. 11893–11902 (2020)

27. Saha, A., Subramanya, A., Pirsiavash, H.: Hidden trigger backdoor attacks. In: Proceedings of the AAAI conference on artificial intelligence, vol. 34, pp. 11957–11965 (2020)

28. Sehwag, V., Wang, S., Mittal, P., Jana, S.: Towards compact and robust deep neural networks. arXiv preprint arXiv:1906.06110 (2019)

29. Selvaraju, R.R., Cogswell, M., Das, A., Vedantam, R., Parikh, D., Batra, D.: Grad-cam: visual explanations from deep networks via gradient-based localization. In: Proceedings of the IEEE International Conference on Computer Vision, pp. 618–626 (2017)

30. Shafahi, A., et al.: Poison frogs! targeted clean-label poisoning attacks on neural networks. In: Advances in neural information processing systems 31 (2018)

31. Stallkamp, J., Schlipsing, M., Salmen, J., Igel, C.: Man vs. computer: benchmarking machine learning algorithms for traffic sign recognition. Neural Netw. **32**, 323–332 (2012)

32. Sui, Y., Yin, M., Xie, Y., Phan, H., Aliari Zonouz, S., Yuan, B.: Chip: channel independence-based pruning for compact neural networks. In: Advances in Neural Information Processing Systems 34 (2021)

33. Szegedy, C., et al.: Intriguing properties of neural networks. arXiv preprint arXiv:1312.6199 (2013)

34. Tian, Y., Suya, F., Xu, F., Evans, D.: Stealthy backdoors as compression artifacts. arXiv preprint arXiv:2104.15129 (2021)

35. Tran, B., Li, J., Madry, A.: Spectral signatures in backdoor attacks. In: Advances in Neural Information Processing Systems 31 (2018)

36. Wang, B., et al.: Neural cleanse: identifying and mitigating backdoor attacks in neural networks. In: 2019 IEEE Symposium on Security and Privacy (SP), pp. 707–723. IEEE (2019)
37. Wu, D., Wang, Y.: Adversarial neuron pruning purifies backdoored deep models. In: Advances in Neural Information Processing Systems 34 (2021)
38. Xie, Y., Li, Z., Shi, C., Liu, J., Chen, Y., Yuan, B.: Enabling fast and universal audio adversarial attack using generative model. In: Proceedings of the AAAI Conference on Artificial Intelligence, vol. 35, pp. 14129–14137 (2021)
39. Xie, Y., Shi, C., Li, Z., Liu, J., Chen, Y., Yuan, B.: Real-time, universal, and robust adversarial attacks against speaker recognition systems. In: ICASSP 2020–2020 IEEE International Conference on Acoustics, Speech and Signal Processing (ICASSP), pp. 1738–1742. IEEE (2020)
40. Ye, S., et al.: Adversarial robustness vs. model compression, or both? In: Proceedings of the IEEE/CVF International Conference on Computer Vision, pp. 111–120 (2019)
41. Yin, M., Liao, S., Liu, X.Y., Wang, X., Yuan, B.: Towards extremely compact RNNS for video recognition with fully decomposed hierarchical tucker structure. In: Proceedings of the IEEE/CVF Conference on Computer Vision and Pattern Recognition, pp. 12085–12094 (2021)
42. Yin, M., Sui, Y., Liao, S., Yuan, B.: Towards efficient tensor decomposition-based DNN model compression with optimization framework. In: Proceedings of the IEEE/CVF Conference on Computer Vision and Pattern Recognition, pp. 10674–10683 (2021)
43. Zang, X., Xie, Y., Chen, J., Yuan, B.: Graph universal adversarial attacks: a few bad actors ruin graph learning models. arXiv preprint arXiv:2002.04784 (2020)
44. Zeng, Y., Park, W., Mao, Z.M., Jia, R.: Rethinking the backdoor attacks' triggers: a frequency perspective. In: Proceedings of the IEEE/CVF International Conference on Computer Vision, pp. 16473–16481 (2021)
45. Zhang, X., Zou, J., He, K., Sun, J.: Accelerating very deep convolutional networks for classification and detection. IEEE Trans. Pattern Anal. Mach. Intell. **38**(10), 1943–1955 (2015)
46. Zhao, P., Chen, P.Y., Das, P., Ramamurthy, K.N., Lin, X.: Bridging mode connectivity in loss landscapes and adversarial robustness. arXiv preprint arXiv:2005.00060 (2020)

Boosting Transferability of Targeted Adversarial Examples via Hierarchical Generative Networks

Xiao Yang[1], Yinpeng Dong[1,2], Tianyu Pang[3], Hang Su[1,4], and Jun Zhu[1,2,4](✉)

[1] Department of Computer Science and Technology, Institute for AI,
Tsinghua-Bosch Joint ML Center, THBI Lab, BNRist Center,
Tsinghua University, Beijing, China
{yangxiao19,dyp17}@mails.tsinghua.edu.cn,
{suhangss,dcszj}@tsinghua.edu.cn
[2] RealAI, Beijing, China
[3] Sea AI Lab, Singapore, Singapore
tianyupang@sea.com
[4] Peng Cheng Laboratory; Pazhou Laboratory, Huangpu, Guangzhou, China

Abstract. Transfer-based adversarial attacks can evaluate model robustness in the black-box setting. Several methods have demonstrated impressive untargeted transferability, however, it is still challenging to efficiently produce *targeted* transferability. To this end, we develop a simple yet effective framework to craft targeted transfer-based adversarial examples, applying a hierarchical generative network. In particular, we contribute to amortized designs that well adapt to multi-class targeted attacks. Extensive experiments on ImageNet show that our method improves the success rates of targeted black-box attacks by a significant margin over the existing methods—it reaches an average success rate of 29.1% against six diverse models based only on one substitute white-box model, which significantly outperforms the state-of-the-art gradient-based attack methods. Moreover, the proposed method is also more efficient beyond an order of magnitude than gradient-based methods.

1 Introduction

Recent progress in adversarial machine learning demonstrates that deep neural networks (DNNs) are highly vulnerable to adversarial examples [13,47], which are maliciously generated to mislead a model to produce incorrect predictions. It has been demonstrated that adversarial examples possess an intriguing property of transferability [4,19,50]—the adversarial examples crafted for a white-box model can also mislead other unknown models, making *black-box attacks* feasible. The threats of adversarial examples have raised severe concerns in numerous security-sensitive applications, such as autonomous driving [10] and face recognition [53–55].

Supplementary Information The online version contains supplementary material available at https://doi.org/10.1007/978-3-031-19772-7_42.

Tremendous efforts have been made to develop more effective black-box attacking methods based on transferability, since they can serve as an important surrogate to evaluate the model robustness in real-world scenarios [8,32]. The current methods have achieved impressive performance of untargeted black-box attacks, intending to cause misclassification of the black-box models. However, *targeted* black-box attacks, aiming at misleading the black-box models by outputting the adversary-desired target class, perform unsatisfactorily or require computation scaling with number of classes [7,57]. Technically, the inefficiency of targeted adversarial attacks could result in an over-estimation of model robustness under the challenging black-box attack setting [16].

Existing efforts on targeted black-box attacks can be categorized as *instance-specific* and *instance-agnostic* attacks. Specifically, the instance-specific attack methods [8,12,25,27,34] craft adversarial examples by performing gradient updates iteratively, which obtain unsatisfactory performance for targeted black-box attacks due to easy overfitting to a white-box model [8,51]. Recently, [58] propose several improvements for instance-specific targeted attacks, thus we treat the method in [58] as one of the strong instance-specific baselines compared in our experiments.

On the other hand, the instance-agnostic attack methods learn a universal perturbation [57] or a universal function [35,43] on the data distribution independent of specific instances. They can promote more general and transferable adversarial examples since the universal perturbation or function can alleviate the data-specific overfitting problem by training on an unlabeled dataset. CD-AP [35], as one of the effective instance-agnostic methods, adopts a generative model as a universal function to obtain an acceptable performance when facing one specified target class. However, CD-AP needs to learn a generative model for each target class while performing multi-target attack [14], i.e., crafting adversarial examples targeted at different classes. Thus it is not scalable to the increasing number of targets such as hundreds of classes, limiting practical efficiency.

To address the aforementioned issues and develop a targeted black-box attack in the practical scenario, in this paper we propose a conditional generative model as the universal adversarial function to craft adversarial perturbations. Thus we can craft adversarial perturbations targeted at different classes, using a single model backbone with different class embeddings. The proposed generative method is simple yet practical to obtain superior performance of targeted black-box attacks, meanwhile with two technical improvements including (i) smooth projection mechanism that better helps the generator probe targeted semantic knowledge from the classifier; (ii) adaptive Gaussian smoothing with the focus of making generated results obtain adaptive ability against adversarially trained models. Therefore, our approach have several advantages over existing generative attacks [35,38,39], as described in the followings.

One Model for Multiple Target Classes. The previous generative methods [35,38] require costly training N models while performing a multi-target attack with N classes. However, ours only trains one model and reaches an average success rate of 51.1% against six naturally trained models and 36.4% against three adversarially trained models based only on one substitute white-box model in ImageNet dataset, which outperforms CD-AP by a large margin of 6.0% and 31.3%, respectively.

Hierarchical Partition of Classes. While handling plenty of classes (e.g., 1,000 classes in ImageNet), the effectiveness of generating targeted adversarial examples will be affected by a single generative model due to the difficulty of loss convergence in adversarial learning [1,52]. Thus we train a feasible number of models (e.g., 10–20 models on ImageNet) to further promote the effectiveness beyond the single model backbone. Specifically, each model is learned from a subset of classes specified by a designed hierarchical partition mechanism by considering the diversity property among subsets, for seeking a balance between effectiveness and scalability. It reaches an average success rate of 29.1% against six different models, outperforming the state-of-the-art gradient-based methods by a large margin, based only on one substitute white-box model. Moreover, the proposed method achieves substantial speedup over the mainstream gradient-based methods.

Strong Semantic Patterns. We experimentally find that these adversarial perturbations generated by the proposed Conditional Generative models can arise as a result of strong Semantic Pattern (C-GSP) as shown in Fig. 1(a). Furthermore, we present more valuable analyses in Sect. 4.6, illustrating that the generated semantic pattern itself achieves well-generalizing performance among the different models and is robust to the influence of data. These analyses are very instructive for the understanding and design of adversarial examples.

Technically, our main contributions can be summarized as:

- We propose a simple yet practical conditional generative targeted attack with a scalable hierarchical partition mechanism, which can generate targeted adversarial examples without tuning the parameters.
- Extensive experiments demonstrate that our method significantly improves the success rates of targeted black-box attacks over the existing methods.
- As a by-product, our baseline experiments provide a systematical evaluation on previous targeted black-box attacks, either instance-specific or instance-agnostic, on the ImageNet dataset with plenty of classes and face recognition.

2   Related Work

In this section, we review related work on adversarial attacks belonging to different types.

Instance-Specific Attacks. Some recent works [34,58] adopt gradient-based optimization methods to generate the data-dependent perturbations. MIM [8] introduces the momentum term into the iterative attack process to improve the black-box transferability. DIM [51] and TI [9] aim to achieve the better transferability by input or gradient diversity. Recent works [20,21] also attempt to costly train the multiple auxiliary classifiers to improve the black-box performance of iterative methods. In contrast, we improve the transferability performance over instance-specific methods simultaneously with the inference-time efficiency.

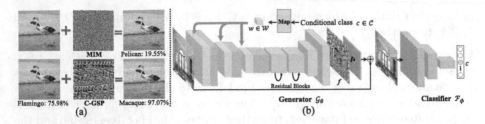

Fig. 1. (a) shows the targeted adversarial examples crafted by MIM [8] and C-GSP given the target class *Viaduct* with the maximum perturbation $\epsilon = 16$. The predicted labels and probabilities are shown by another black-box model. (b) presents an overview of our proposed generative method for crafting C-GSP, including modules of conditional generator and classifier. The generator integrates the image and conditional class vector from Map network into a hidden incorporation. The generator is only trained in the whole pipeline to probe the target boundaries of the classifier.

Instance-Agnostic Attacks. Different from instance-specific attacks, instance-agnostic attacks belong to image-independent (universal) methods. The first pipeline is to learn a universal perturbation. UAP [33] proposes to fool a model by adding a learned universal noise vector. Another pipeline of attacks introduces learned generative models to craft adversarial examples. GAP [38] and AAA [39] craft adversarial perturbations based on target data directly and compress impressions, respectively. Previous methods, including universal perturbation and function, require costly training the same number of models for multiple target classes. Our method is capable of simultaneously generating adversarial samples for specifying multiple targets with better attack performance.

Multi-target Attacks. Instance-specific attacks have the ability for specifying any target in the optimization phase. As elaborated in the introduction, these methods have degraded transferability and time-consuming iterative procedures. MAN [14] trains a generative model in the ImageNet under the constraint of ℓ_2 norm to explore the targeted attacks, which specifies all 1,000 categories from ImageNet for seeking extreme speed and storage. However, MAN does not fully compare multi-target black-box performance with previous instance-specific or instance-agnostic attacks, and the authors also claim that too many categories make it hard to transfer to another model. Recent approaches [36,57] reveal better single-target transferability by learning universal perturbation or function, whereas they require to train multiple times while specifying multiple targets. As a comparison, our method can generate adversarial samples for specifying multiple targets, meanwhile generated strong semantic patterns can outperform existing attacks by a significant margin.

3   Method

In this section, we introduce a conditional generative model to learn a universal adversarial function, which can achieve effective multi-target black-box attacks.

While handing plenty of classes, we design a hierarchical partition mechanism to make the generative model capable of specifying any target class under a feasible number of models, regarding both the effectiveness and scalability.

3.1 Problem Formulation

We use x_s to denote an input image belonging to an unlabeled training set $\mathcal{X}_s \subset \mathbb{R}^d$, and use $c \in \mathcal{C}$ to denote a specific target class. Let $\mathcal{F}_\phi : \mathcal{X}_s \to \mathbb{R}^K$ denote a classification network that outputs a class probability vector with K classes. To craft a targeted adversarial example x_s^* from a real example x_s, the targeted attack aims to fool the classifier $\mathcal{F}_\phi$ by outputting a specific label c as $\arg\max_{i \in \mathcal{C}} \mathcal{F}_\phi(x_s^*)_i = c$, meanwhile the ℓ_∞ norm of the adversarial perturbation is required to be no more than a threshold ϵ as $\|x_s^* - x_s\|_\infty \leq \epsilon$.

Although some generative methods [35,38] can learn targeted adversarial perturbation, they do not take into account the effectiveness of multi-target generation, thus leading to inconvenience. To make the generative model learn how to specify multiple targets, we propose a conditional generative network $\mathcal{G}_\theta$ that effectively crafts multi-target adversarial perturbations by modeling class-conditional distribution. Different from previous single-target methods [35,38], the target label c is regarded as a discrete variable rather than a constant. As illustrated in Fig. 1(b), our model contains a conditional generator $\mathcal{G}_\theta$ and a classification network $\mathcal{F}_\phi$ parameterized by θ and ϕ, respectively. The conditional generative model $\mathcal{G}_\theta : (\mathcal{X}_s, \mathcal{C}) \to \mathcal{P}$ learns a perturbation $\delta = \mathcal{G}_\theta(x_s, c) \in \mathcal{P} \subset \mathbb{R}^d$ on the training data. The output δ of $\mathcal{G}_\theta$ is projected within the fixed ℓ_∞ norm, thus generating the perturbed image $x_s^* = x_s + \delta$.

Given a pretrained network $\mathcal{F}_\phi$ parameterized by ϕ, we propose to generate the targeted adversarial perturbations by solving

$$\min_\theta \mathbb{E}_{(x_s \sim \mathcal{X}_s, c \sim \mathcal{C})}[\mathbb{CE}(\mathcal{F}_\phi(\mathcal{G}_\theta(x_s, c) + x_s), c)], \text{ s.t. } \|\mathcal{G}_\theta(x_s, c)\|_\infty \leq \epsilon, \qquad (1)$$

where $\mathbb{CE}$ is the cross-entropy loss. By solving problem (1), we can obtain a targeted conditional generator by minimizing the loss of specific target class in the unlabeled training dataset. Note that we only optimize the parameter θ of the generator $\mathcal{G}_\theta$ using the training data $\mathcal{X}_s$, then the targeted adversarial example x_t^* can be crafted by $x_t^* = x_t + \mathcal{G}_\theta(x_t, c)$ for any given image x_t in the test data $\mathcal{X}_t$, which only requires an inference for this targeted image x_t.

We experimentally find that the objective (1) can enforce the transferability for the generated perturbation δ. A reasonable explanation is that δ can arise as a result of **strong** and **well-generalizing** *semantic pattern* inherent to the target class, which is robust to the influence of any training data. In Sect. 4.5, we illustrate and corroborate our claim by directly feeding scaled adversarial perturbations[1] from different methods into the classifier. Indeed, we find that our semantic pattern can be classified as the target class with a high degree of confidence while the perturbation from MIM [8] performs like the noise, meanwhile

---

[1] The perturbation is linearly scaled from [-ϵ, ϵ] to [0, 255].

the scaled semantic pattern performs well transferability in different black-box models.

3.2 Network Architecture

We now present the details of the conditional generative model for targeted attack, as illustrated in Fig. 1(b). Specifically, we design a mapping network to generate a target-specific vector in the implicit space of each target and train conditional generator $\mathcal{G}_\theta$ to reflect this vector by constantly misleading the classifier $\mathcal{F}_\phi$.

Mapping Network. Given the one-hot class encoding $\mathbb{1}_c \in \mathbb{R}^K$ from target class c, the mapping network aims to generate the targeted latent vector $w = \mathcal{W}(\mathbb{1}_c)$, where $w \in \mathbb{R}^M$ and $\mathcal{W}(\cdot)$ consists of a multi-layer perceptron (MLP) and a normalization layer, which can construct diverse targeted vectors w for a given target class c. Thus $\mathcal{W}$ is capable of learning effective targeted latent vectors by randomly sampling different classes $c \in \mathcal{C}$ in training phase.

Generator. Given an input image x_s, the encoder first calculates the feature map $F \in \mathbb{R}^{N \times H \times W}$, where N, H and W refer to the number of channels, height and width of the feature map, respectively. The target latent vector w, derived from the mapping network $\mathcal{W}$ by introducing a specific target class c, is expanded along height and width directions to obtain the label feature map $w_s \in \mathbb{R}^{M \times H \times W}$. Then the above two feature maps are concatenated along the channels to obtain $F' \in \mathbb{R}^{(N+M) \times H \times W}$. The obtained mixed feature map is then fed to the subsequent network. Therefore, our generator $\mathcal{G}_\theta$ translates an input image x_s and latent target vector w into an output image $\mathcal{G}_\theta(x_s, w)$, which enables $\mathcal{G}_\theta$ to synthesize adversarial images of a series of targets. For the output of feature map $f \in \mathbb{R}^d$ in the decoder, we adopt a **smooth projection** $P(\cdot)$ to perform a change of variables over f rather than directly minimizing its ℓ_2 norm as [14] or clipping values outside the fixed norm [35], which can be denoted as

$$\delta = P(f) = \epsilon \cdot \tanh(f), \tag{2}$$

where ϵ is the strength of perturbation. Since $-1 \leq \tanh(f) \leq 1$, δ can automatically satisfy the ℓ_∞-ball bound with perturbation budget ϵ. This transformation can be regarded as a better smoothing of gradient than directly clipping values outside the fixed norm, which is also instrumental for $\mathcal{G}_\theta$ to probe and learn the targeted semantic knowledge from $\mathcal{F}_\phi$.

Training Objectives. The training objectives seek to minimize the classification error on the perturbed image of the generator as

$$\theta^* \leftarrow \arg\min_\theta \mathbb{CE}\Big(F_\phi\big(x_s + \mathcal{G}_\theta(x_s, \mathcal{W}(\mathbb{1}_c))\big), c\Big), \tag{3}$$

which adopts an end-to-end training paradigm with the goal of generating adversarial images to mislead the classifier the target label, and $\mathbb{CE}$ is the cross entropy loss. Previous studies attempt different classification losses in their works [35,57], and we found that cross-entropy loss works well in our settings. The detailed optimization procedure is summarized in Algorithm 1.

Algorithm 1. Training Algorithm for the Conditional Generative Attack

---

Require: Training Data $\mathcal{D}_s$; a generative network $\mathcal{G}_\theta$; a classification network $\mathcal{F}_\phi$; a mapping network $\mathcal{W}$.

Ensure: Adversarial perturbations θ.

1: **for** iter in MaxIterations T **do**
2:     Randomly sample B images $\{x_{s_i}\}_{i=1}^B$;
3:     Randomly sample B target classes $\{c_i\}_{i=1}^B$;
4:     Forward pass c_i into $\mathcal{W}$ to compute the targeted latent vectors w_i;
5:     Obtain the perturbed images by $x_{s_i}^* = \epsilon \cdot \tanh(\mathcal{G}(x_{s_i}, w_i)) + x_{s_i}$;
6:     Forward pass $x_{s_i}^*$ to $\mathcal{F}_\phi$ and compute loss in Eq. (3);
7:     Backward pass and update the $\mathcal{G}_\theta$;
8: **end for**

3.3 Hierarchical Partition for Classes

While handling plenty of classes, the effectiveness of a conditional generative model will decrease as illustrated in Fig. 4, because the representative capacity is limited with a single generator. Therefore, we propose to divide all classes into a feasible number of subsets to train models when the class number K is large, e.g., 1,000 classes in ImageNet, with the aim of seeking the effectiveness of targeted black-box attack. To obtain a good partition, we introduce a representative target class space, which is nearly equivalent to the original class space $\mathcal{C}$. Specifically, we utilize the weights $\phi_{cls} \in \mathbb{R}^{D \times K}$ in the classifier layer for the classification network $\mathcal{F}_\phi$. Therefore, ϕ_{cls} can be regarded as the alternative class space since the weight vector $d_c \in \mathbb{R}^D$ from ϕ_{cls} can represent a class center of the feature embeddings of input images with same class c.

Note that once those subsets with closer metric distance (e.g., larger cosine similarity) in the target class space ϕ_{cls} are regarded as conditional inputs of generative network, they obtain worse loss convergence and transferability than diverse them due to mutual influence among these input conditions, as illustrated in Fig. 5. Thus we focus on selecting target classes that do not tend to overlap or be close to each other as accessible subsets. To capture more diverse examples in a given sampling space, we adopt K-determinantal point processes (DPP) [23,24] to achieve a hierarchical partition, which can take advantage of the diversity property among subsets by assigning subset probabilities proportional to determinants of a kernel matrix.

First, we compute the RBF kernel matrix L of ϕ_{cls} and eigendecomposition of L, and a random subset V of the eigenvectors is chosen by regarding the eigenvalues as sampling probability. Second, we select a new class c_i to add to the set and update V in a manner that de-emphaseizes items similar to the one selected. Each successive point is selected and V is updated by Gram-Schmidt orthogonalization, and the distribution shifts to avoid points near those already chosen. By performing the above procedure, we can obtain a subset with k size. Thus while handling the conditional classes with K, we can hierarchically adopt this algorithm to get the final K/k subsets, which are regarded as conditional variables of generative models to craft adversarial examples. The details are presented in Appendix A.

4 Experiments

In this section, we present extensive experiments to demonstrate the effectiveness of proposed method for targeted black-box attacks[2].

4.1 Experimental Settings

Datasets. We consider the following datasets for training, including a widely used object detection dataset MS-COCO [30] and ImageNet training set [5]. We focus on standard and comprehensive testing settings, thus the inference is performed on ImageNet validation set (50k samples), a subset (5k) of ImageNet proposed by [28] and ImageNet-NeurIPS (1k) proposed by [37].

Networks. We consider some naturally trained networks, i.e., Inception-v3 (Inv3) [46], Inception-v4 (Inv4) [44], Resnet-v2-152 (R152) [15] and Inception-Resnet-v2 (IR-v2) [44], which are widely used for evaluating transferability. Besides, we supplement DenseNet-201 (DN) [17], GoogleNet (GN) [45] and VGG-16 (VGG) [42] to fully evaluate the transferability. Some adversarially trained networks [48] are also selected to evaluate the performance, i.e., ens3-adv-Inception-v3 ($Inv3_{ens3}$), ens4-adv-Inception-v3 ($Inv3_{ens4}$) and ens-adv-Inception-ResNet-v2 ($IR-v2_{ens}$).

Implementation Details. As for instance-specific attacks, we compare our method with several attacks, including MIM [8], DIM [51], TI [9], SI [29] and the state-of-the-art targeted attack named Logit [58]. All instance-specific attacks adopt optimal hyperparameters provided in their original work. Specifically, the attack iterations M of MIM, DIM and Logit are set as $10, 20, 300$, respectively. And $\|W\|_1 = 5$ is used for TI [9] as suggested by [11,58]. We choose the same ResNet autoencoder architecture in [22,35] as the basic generator networks, which consists of downsampling, residual and upsampling layers. We initialize the learning rate as 2e–5 and set the mini-batch size as 32. Smoothing mechanism is proposed to improve the transferability against adversarially trained models [9]. Instead of adopting smoothing for generated perturbation while the training is completed as CD-AP [35], we introduce adaptive Gaussian smoothing kernel to compute δ from Eq. (2) in the training phase, named **adaptive Gaussian smoothing**, with the focus of making generated results obtain adaptive ability. More implementation details and discussion with other networks (e.g., BigGAN [2]) are illustrated in Appendix B.

4.2 Transferability Evaluation

We consider 8 different target classes from [57] to form the multi-target black-box attack testing protocol with 8k times in 1k ImageNet NeurIPS set.

---

[2] Code at https://github.com/ShawnXYang/C-GSP

Table 1. Transferability comparison for multi-target attacks on ImageNet NeurIPS validation set (1k images) with the perturbation budget of $\ell_\infty \leq 16$. The results are averaged on 8 different target classes. Note that CD-AP† indicates that training **8 models** can obtain results, while our method only train **one** conditional generative model. * indicates white-box attacks.

	Method	Time (ms)	ModelNumber	Naturally Trained							Adversarially Trained		
				Inv3	Inv4	IR-v2	R152	DN	GN	VGG-16	Inv3$_{ens3}$	Inv3$_{ens4}$	IR-v2$_{ens}$
Inv3	MIM	~130	-	99.9*	0.8	1.0	0.4	0.2	0.2	0.3	<0.1	0.1	< 0.1
	TI-MIM	~130	-	99.9*	0.9	1.1	0.4	0.4	0.3	0.5	0.1	0.2	0.1
	SI-MIM	~130	-	99.8*	1.5	2.0	0.8	0.7	0.7	0.5	0.3	0.3	0.1
	DIM	~260	-	95.6*	4.0	4.8	1.3	1.9	0.8	1.3	0.1	0.2	0.1
	TI-DIM	~260	-	96.0*	4.4	5.1	1.4	2.4	1.1	1.8	0.3	0.4	0.2
	SI-DIM	~260	-	98.4*	5.6	5.9	2.8	3.0	2.3	1.6	0.9	0.9	0.3
	Logit	~3900	-	99.6*	5.6	6.5	1.7	3.0	0.8	1.5	0.2	0.3	0.1
	CD-AP†	~15	8	94.2*	57.6	60.1	37.1	41.6	32.3	41.7	1.5	2.2	1.2
	CD-AP-gs†	~15	8	69.7*	31.3	30.8	18.6	20.1	14.8	20.2	5.0	5.8	4.5
	Ours	~15	1	93.4*	**66.9**	**66.6**	**41.6**	**46.4**	**40.0**	**45.0**	**39.7**	**37.2**	**32.2**
R152	MIM	~185	-	0.5	0.4	0.6	99.7*	0.3	0.3	0.2	0.1	0.1	< 0.1
	TI-MIM	~185	-	0.3	0.3	1.0	96.5*	0.5	0.3	0.3	0.3	0.2	0.3
	SI-MIM	~185	-	1.3	1.2	1.6	99.5*	1.0	1.4	0.7	0.3	0.4	0.2
	DIM	~370	-	2.8	3.1	5.0	93.6*	3.5	1.7	1.3	0.4	0.4	0.3
	TI-DIM	~370	-	4.3	4.1	5.8	92.9*	4.3	2.1	1.4	0.8	0.7	0.4
	SI-DIM	~370	-	7.2	8.4	10.4	97.4*	7.6	6.4	2.6	0.8	0.7	1.3
	Logit	~5550	-	10.1	10.7	12.8	95.7*	12.4	3.7	3.5	1.1	0.9	0.4
	CD-AP†	~10	8	33.3	43.7	42.7	96.6*	53.8	36.6	34.1	15.7	15.2	12.0
	CD-AP-gs†	~10	8	7.8	11.3	10.0	53.6*	20.4	8.7	12.5	4.9	6.4	6.2
	Ours	~10	1	**37.7**	**47.6**	**45.1**	93.2*	**64.2**	**41.7**	**45.9**	**31.6**	**32.0**	**29.9**

Efficiency of Multi-target Black-Box Attack. Among comparable methods, instance-specific methods, i.e., MIM, DIM, and Logit, require iterative mechanism with M steps by computing gradients to obtain adversarial examples. Given the cost t_C^{FP} and t_C^{BP} of forward and backward passing the classifier, computing cost T^{IS} of single data can be defined as $T^{IS} = t_C^{FP} * M + t_C^{BP} * M$ in Table 1. Instance-agnostic methods only require the inference cost from the trained generator as $T^{IA} = t_G^{FP}$, thus possessing the priority for those attack scenarios within limited time. However, instance-agnostic methods require to train 8 models to obtain all predictions from 8 different classes. Due to time-consuming training and more storage, we only reproduce an excellent generative method CD-AP [35] as a baseline, which already fully demonstrate the superior performance than other generative methods such as GAP [38] in their work. As a comparison, our conditional generative method only trains one model to inference the results and outperforms other methods w.r.t *efficiency*.

Effectiveness of Multi-target Black-Box Aattack. Table 1 shows the transferability comparison of different methods on both naturally and adversarially trained models. The success rate of instance-specific attacks are very unsatisfactory, possibly explained by the data-point overfitting that makes it hard to transfer another model. The instance-agnostic attack CD-AP obtains acceptable performance, yet inferior to proposed method w.r.t black-box transferability.

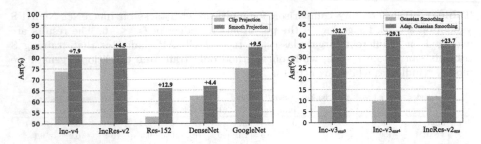

Fig. 2. Comparison of different projection functions and modes of Gaussian Smoothing. Results are reported with Inv3 network on ImageNet NeurIPS validation set.

Table 2. The untargeted fooling ratio (UT-FR) and targeted fooling ratio (T-FR) for adversarial attacks on ImageNet validation set (50k images) with the perturbation budget of $\ell_\infty \leq 10$. The attack is performed in same setting [57] with the target class 'sea lion' and the training dataset MS-COCO. * indicates white-box attacks.

	Method	VGG-16		VGG-19		R152	
		UT-FR	T-FR	UT-FR	T-FR	UT-FR	T-FR
VGG-16	UAE [57] Ours	93.62*95.30*	82.90*83.54*	82.9990.13	13.6938.59	36.0335.15	0.010.14
VGG-19	UAE [57] Ours	83.4088.20	44.5348.96	92.53*92.69*	75.61*73.96*	35.3635.96	0.010.14
R152	UAE [57] Ours	55.0583.90	1.6329.81	55.1283.24	1.0524.81	82.58*91.14*	70.20*80.47*

The **primary reason** for such a trend lies in some distinctions as 1) direct clip projection in CD-AP and our smooth projection in Eq. (2) and 2) their Gaussian Smoothing and our adaptive Gaussian Smoothing, as described in Sect. 4.1 and Appendix B. Figure 2 empirically shows the comparison results of single-target black-box attacks based on the CD-AP framework. Thus proposed conditional generative method can be a reliable baseline w.r.t targeted black-box attacks, regarding both *effectiveness* and *efficiency*.

Results of Single-Target Black-Box Attack. Recent related works, e.g., UAE [57] and TTP [36] report excellent single-target black-box performances based on universal perturbations or functions. We obtain single-target degraded version of our model by specifying an input target label during the training process. The performance of black-box targeted attack between different methods is presented in Table 2. Besides, we also make some analyses about TTP and present compared results in Appendix C. Furthermore, some other instance-agnostic adversarial methods, e.g., UAP [33], GAP [38] and RHP [28], have tendency towards the untargeted black-box problem. Despite this, we also follow the corresponding untargeted setting and compare these methods in Appendix C. Our method is steadily improved under black-box targeted and untargeted black-box manner.

Table 3. Transferability comparison with the perturbation budget of $\ell_\infty \leq 16$. White-box substitute model is Inv3 for all attacks, following the standard protocol [9] with **1,000 stochastic target classes**.

Targeted Black-box Attack in NeurIPS 2017 Competition (1,000 target classes)						
Method	Inv4	IRv2	R152	DN	GN	VGG-16
MIM	0.1	<0.1	<0.1	0.3	0.1	<0.1
TI-MIM	0.3	0.3	<0.1	0.4	<0.1	0.1
SI-MIM	0.6	0.6	0.1	0.4	0.3	0.1
DIM	2.9	2.5	0.6	1.2	0.2	0.6
TI-DIM	2.9	2.5	0.5	1.7	0.3	1.0
SI-DIM	4.3	4.1	1.7	1.9	1.8	1.1
Logit	4.7	2.4	1.2	2.4	0.4	0.8
Ours	**35.9**	**37.4**	**25.0**	**26.8**	**22.9**	**26.6**

Table 4. The success rate of black-box *impersonation* attacks on face verification with the perturbation budget of $\ell_\infty \leq 16$. ArcFace is chosen as white-box model.

Black-box Impersonation Attack in Face Recognition					
Protocol	Method	FaceNet	CosFace	SphereFace	MobileFace
I	MIM DIM Ours	34.4 38.8 **65.2**	16.6 21.2 **56.2**	22.4 27.4 **52.2**	35.0 44.3 **83.5**
II	MIM DIM Ours	31.3 36.1 **66.8**	13.6 16.4 **49.1**	21.1 24.4 **47.9**	22.3 31.9 **67.8**

4.3 Effectiveness on NeurIPS 2017 Competition

To illustrate the effectiveness of our proposed attack methods in practical 1,000 classification, we here follow the official setting from NeurIPS 2017 adversarial competition [26] for testing targeted black-box transferability. Considering limited resource, previous instance-agnostic attacks are not required as comparable methods due to training 1,000 models, thus we focus on various excellent instance-specific attacks for comparison, including official top attack methods in NeurIPS 2017 adversarial competition. Compared with other instance-agnostic attacks, our hierarchical partition mechanism can make conditional generative networks be capable of specifying any target class via a feasible number of models for the scalability. Specifically, we consider 20 models, with each specifying 50 diverse classes from k-DPP hierarchical partition in this setting, to implement targeted attack by only once inference for each target image. As shown in Table 3, our method can obviously outperform all other methods. In addition, these trained generative models can directly be applied to craft adversarial examples, which is more convenient and efficient when required to handle large-scale (e.g., millions of images) datasets than instance-specific attacks.

Fig. 3. Generative examples of adversarial images with perturbation budget of $\ell_\infty \leq$ 16. We separately adopt the ImageNet and MS-COCO dataset as the training dataset to implement the generation of targeted perturbations. Our method can generate semantic pattern independent of training dataset.

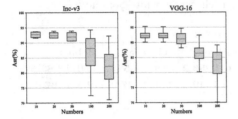

Fig. 4. Asr vs. *numbers of conditional targets* curve against Inv3 and VGG-16 models.

Fig. 5. Comparison of loss convergence and transferability between diverse and close conditional subset.

4.4 Effectiveness on Realistic Face Recognition

Adversarial perturbations added to original face images have ability to evade being recognized or impersonate another individual [41,56]. In this section, we consider the transferability of impersonation attack to further illustrate the generalization of our method, which is also corresponding to targeted attack in the image classification task.

Dataset and Models. We conduct the experiments on Labeled Faces in the Wild (LFW) [18] and introduce two test protocols. For *Protocol I* defined as single-target impersonation attack, we choose 1 target identity and 1k source face images belonging with different identities from LFW as the attackers, thus forming 1k pairs. For *Protocol II* named multi-target impersonation attack, 5 target identities and 1k source face images are selected to form 1k attack pairs, meaning that we need to implement 5k attacks. We involve some excellent face recognition models for conducting black-box testing, including Sphereface [31], CosFace [49], FaceNet [40] and MobileFace [3]. These models lie in different model architectures and training objectives. In all experiments, we only use one

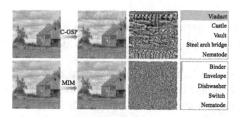

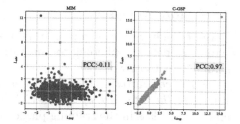

Fig. 6. We show the adversarial examples and extracted perturbation scaled in image-pixel space in the second column and the third column. The predictive confidence is presented by **directly feeding** extracted perturbation into the classifier in the last column.

Fig. 7. Plots of logit vectors from the adversarial image L_{img} and scaled crafted perturbation L_{adv} of MIM and proposed generative method, with their respective PCC values.

model ArcFace [6] as substitute model to craft adversarial samples, and test attack performance against other unknown models.

Evaluation Metrics. We first compute the optimal threshold of every face recognition models from LFW dataset by following standard protocols. If the similarity of a pair of images exceeds the threshold, we regard them as same identity, otherwise different identities.

Black-Box Attack Results. We adjust the optimization object function to adapt face recognition for chosen attack methods (detailed in Appendix C), and report the success rate of black-box *impersonation* attacks in Table 4, which illustrates that our method can achieve nearly two times of the success rates than DIM in *Protocol I* and *Protocol II*. The results indicate that our method is superior to other methods not only in image classification.

4.5   Comparison Study About Target Classes

We conduct an extensive study to investigate two key points about target classes.

Different Numbers of Target Classes. We conduct effectiveness for different numbers of target classes in Fig. 4. It can be seen that the results perform well within a feasible number of targets, whereas to a certain extent effectiveness tend to decay. Therefore, the effectiveness of conditional generative networks is influenced by the number of conditional classes, due to the representative capacity of single generator. We aim to divide all classes into a feasible number of set while handling plenty of classes.

Comparison of Different Multi-target Conditions. We select closer conditional classes with larger cosine similarity in the target class space ϕ_{cls} and diverse conditional classes from k-DPP method. In Fig. 5, closer conditional classes have worse loss convergence and transferability than diverse them due to mutual influence among conditions.

4.6   More Analyses

Targeted adversarial samples from proposed generative method can produce semantic pattern inherent to the target class in Fig. 3. Why does generative semantic pattern work?

First, *generative methods can produce strong targeted semantic pattern that is robust to the influence of data*, which is obtained by minimizing the loss of specific target class in the training phase. To corroborate our claim, we directly feed scaled crafted perturbations by instance-specific attack MIM and our generative method into the classifier. Indeed, we find that our generative perturbation is considered as target class with a high degree of confidence whereas the perturbation from MIM performs like the noise, as shown in Fig. 6. Furthermore, we plot the logit relationship by computing PCC (Pearson correlation coefficient) values from scaled crafted perturbation and adversarial image in Fig. 7. The numerical performance is also consistent with our mentioned claim.

Second, *the generated adversarial semantic pattern achieves well-generalizing performance among the different models*. We feed 1k images from ImageNet test set into the generator trained by Inv3 model to obtain 1k semantic patterns, which are scaled to image pixel space and then fed into different classifiers. We compute the mean confidence of **0.46** for DN, **0.44** for Inv4, and **0.35** for R152, whereas the perturbation from MIM is lower than 0.01. The results show that our scaled semantic pattern can directly achieve well-generalizing performance among models, possibly explained by utilizing similar feature knowledge from the same class on different classifiers trained on same training data distribution. Thus similar pattern can be instrumental for transferability among models.

5   Discussion and Conclusion

Transferability of targeted black-box attack is simultaneously affected by data and model. Therefore, instance-specific methods easily overfit the data point and white-box model, resulting in weak transferability. As a comparison, the proposed generative method with powerful learning capacity reduces the dependency for data point by adopting the unlabeled training data, thus enabling the model to learn semantic pattern and improve the transferability of targeted black-box attack. Extensive experiments demonstrate that proposed generative method can significantly improve the success rates of targeted black-box attacks against various models, meanwhile achieving faster speedup beyond an order of magnitude than gradient-based methods. Therefore, this method can be regarded as a new baseline method in terms of targeted black-box attacks, which provides a novel framework to explore the vulnerabilities of DNNs.

Acknowledgment. This work was supported by the National Key Research and Development Program of China (Nos. 2020AAA0104304, 2017YFA0700904), NSFC Projects (Nos. 62061136001, 61621136008, 62076147, U19B2034, U19A2081, U1811461), the major key project of PCL (No. PCL2021A12), Tsinghua-Alibaba Joint Research Program, Tsinghua-OPPO Joint Research Center, and the High Performance Computing Center, Tsinghua University.

References

1. Berthelot, D., Schumm, T., Metz, L.: Began: Boundary equilibrium generative adversarial networks. arXiv preprint arXiv:1703.10717 (2017)
2. Brock, A., Donahue, J., Simonyan, K.: Large scale GAN training for high fidelity natural image synthesis. arXiv preprint arXiv:1809.11096 (2018)
3. Chen, S., Liu, Y., Gao, X., Han, Z.: MobileFaceNets: efficient CNNs for accurate real-time face verification on mobile devices. In: Zhou, J., et al. (eds.) CCBR 2018. LNCS, vol. 10996, pp. 428–438. Springer, Cham (2018). https://doi.org/10.1007/978-3-319-97909-0_46
4. Demontis, A., et al.: Why do adversarial attacks transfer? Explaining transferability of evasion and poisoning attacks. In: 28th USENIX Security Symposium (USENIX Security 2019), pp. 321–338 (2019)
5. Deng, J., Dong, W., Socher, R., Li, L.J., Li, K., Fei-Fei, L.: ImageNet: a large-scale hierarchical image database. In: 2009 IEEE Conference On Computer Vision and Pattern Recognition. pp. 248–255. IEEE (2009)
6. Deng, J., Guo, J., Xue, N., Zafeiriou, S.: ArcFace: additive angular margin loss for deep face recognition. In: Proceedings of the IEEE Conference on Computer Vision and Pattern Recognition, pp. 4690–4699 (2019)
7. Dong, Y., et al.: Benchmarking adversarial robustness. In: The IEEE Conference on Computer Vision and Pattern Recognition (CVPR) (2020)
8. Dong, Y., Liao, F., Pang, T., Su, H., Zhu, J., Hu, X., Li, J.: Boosting adversarial attacks with momentum. In: Proceedings of the IEEE Conference on Computer Vision and Pattern Recognition (CVPR) (2018)
9. Dong, Y., Pang, T., Su, H., Zhu, J.: Evading defenses to transferable adversarial examples by translation-invariant attacks. In: Proceedings of the IEEE Conference on Computer Vision and Pattern Recognition (CVPR) (2019)
10. Eykholt, K., et al.: Robust physical-world attacks on deep learning visual classification. In: IEEE Conference on Computer Vision and Pattern Recognition, pp. 1625–1634 (2018)
11. Gao, L., Zhang, Q., Song, J., Liu, X., Shen, H.T.: Patch-Wise attack for fooling deep neural network. In: Vedaldi, A., Bischof, H., Brox, T., Frahm, J.-M. (eds.) ECCV 2020. LNCS, vol. 12373, pp. 307–322. Springer, Cham (2020). https://doi.org/10.1007/978-3-030-58604-1_19
12. Goodfellow, I., Bengio, Y., Courville, A.: Deep Learning. MIT Press, London (2016). http://www.deeplearningbook.org
13. Goodfellow, I.J., Shlens, J., Szegedy, C.: Explaining and harnessing adversarial examples. In: International Conference on Learning Representations (ICLR) (2015)
14. Han, J., et al.: Once a man: towards multi-target attack via learning multi-target adversarial network once. In: Proceedings of the IEEE International Conference on Computer Vision, pp. 5158–5167 (2019)
15. He, K., Zhang, X., Ren, S., Sun, J.: Identity mappings in deep residual networks. In: Leibe, B., Matas, J., Sebe, N., Welling, M. (eds.) ECCV 2016. LNCS, vol. 9908, pp. 630–645. Springer, Cham (2016). https://doi.org/10.1007/978-3-319-46493-0_38
16. Hendrycks, D., Carlini, N., Schulman, J., Steinhardt, J.: Unsolved problems in ml safety. arXiv preprint arXiv:2109.13916 (2021)
17. Huang, G., Liu, Z., Van Der Maaten, L., Weinberger, K.Q.: Densely connected convolutional networks. In: Proceedings of the IEEE Conference on Computer Vision and Pattern Recognition, pp. 4700–4708 (2017)

18. Huang, G.B., Mattar, M., Berg, T., Learned-Miller, E.: Labeled faces in the wild: A database forstudying face recognition in unconstrained environments. Technical report (2007)

19. Huang, Q., Katsman, I., He, H., Gu, Z., Belongie, S., Lim, S.N.: Enhancing adversarial example transferability with an intermediate level attack. In: Proceedings of the IEEE/CVF International Conference on Computer Vision, pp. 4733–4742 (2019)

20. Inkawhich, N., et al.: Perturbing across the feature hierarchy to improve standard and strict blackbox attack transferability. Adv. Neural. Inf. Process. Syst. **33**, 20791–20801 (2020)

21. Inkawhich, N., Liang, K.J., Carin, L., Chen, Y.: Transferable perturbations of deep feature distributions. arXiv preprint arXiv:2004.12519 (2020)

22. Johnson, J., Alahi, A., Fei-Fei, L.: Perceptual losses for real-time style transfer and super-resolution. In: Leibe, B., Matas, J., Sebe, N., Welling, M. (eds.) ECCV 2016. LNCS, vol. 9906, pp. 694–711. Springer, Cham (2016). https://doi.org/10.1007/978-3-319-46475-6_43

23. Kulesza, A., Taskar, B.: k-DPPS: fixed-size determinantal point processes. In: ICML (2011)

24. Kulesza, A., Taskar, B.: Determinantal point processes for machine learning. arXiv preprint arXiv:1207.6083 (2012)

25. Kurakin, A., Goodfellow, I., Bengio, S.: Adversarial examples in the physical world. In: International Conference on Learning Representations (ICLR) Workshops (2017)

26. Kurakin, A., et al.: Adversarial attacks and defences competition. In: Escalera, S., Weimer, M. (eds.) The NIPS '17 Competition: Building Intelligent Systems. TSSCML, pp. 195–231. Springer, Cham (2018). https://doi.org/10.1007/978-3-319-94042-7_11

27. Li, M., Deng, C., Li, T., Yan, J., Gao, X., Huang, H.: Towards transferable targeted attack. In: Proceedings of the IEEE/CVF Conference on Computer Vision and Pattern Recognition, pp. 641–649 (2020)

28. Li, Y., Bai, S., Xie, C., Liao, Z., Shen, X., Yuille, A.L.: Regional homogeneity: towards learning transferable universal adversarial perturbations against defenses. arXiv preprint arXiv:1904.00979 (2019)

29. Lin, J., Song, C., He, K., Wang, L., Hopcroft, J.E.: Nesterov accelerated gradient and scale invariance for adversarial attacks. In: International Conference on Learning Representations (2019)

30. Lin, T., et al.: Microsoft COCO: common objects in context. In: Fleet, D., Pajdla, T., Schiele, B., Tuytelaars, T. (eds.) ECCV 2014. LNCS, vol. 8693, pp. 740–755. Springer, Cham (2014). https://doi.org/10.1007/978-3-319-10602-1_48

31. Liu, W., Wen, Y., Yu, Z., Li, M., Raj, B., Song, L.: SphereFace: deep hypersphere embedding for face recognition. In: Proceedings of the IEEE Conference on Computer Vision and Pattern Recognition, pp. 212–220 (2017)

32. Liu, Y., Chen, X., Liu, C., Song, D.: Delving into transferable adversarial examples and black-box attacks. In: ICLR (2017)

33. Moosavi-Dezfooli, S.M., Fawzi, A., Fawzi, O., Frossard, P.: Universal adversarial perturbations. In: Proceedings of the IEEE Conference on Computer Vision and Pattern Recognition, pp. 1765–1773 (2017)

34. Moosavi-Dezfooli, S.M., Fawzi, A., Frossard, P.: DeepFool: a simple and accurate method to fool deep neural networks. In: Proceedings of the IEEE Conference on Computer Vision and Pattern Recognition (CVPR) (2016)

35. Naseer, M.M., Khan, S.H., Khan, M.H., Khan, F.S., Porikli, F.: Cross-domain transferability of adversarial perturbations. In: Proceedings of the Advances in Neural Information Processing Systems, pp. 12905–12915 (2019)

36. Naseer, M., Khan, S., Hayat, M., Khan, F.S., Porikli, F.: On generating transferable targeted perturbations. In: Proceedings of the IEEE/CVF International Conference on Computer Vision, pp. 7708–7717 (2021)

37. Kaggle: NeurIPS (2017). http://www.kaggle.com/c/nips-2017-defense-against-adversarial-attack/data

38. Poursaeed, O., Katsman, I., Gao, B., Belongie, S.: Generative adversarial perturbations. In: Proceedings of the IEEE Conference on Computer Vision and Pattern Recognition, pp. 4422–4431 (2018)

39. Reddy Mopuri, K., Krishna Uppala, P., Venkatesh Babu, R.: Ask, acquire, and attack: data-free UAP generation using class impressions. In: Proceedings of the European Conference on Computer Vision (ECCV), pp. 19–34 (2018)

40. Schroff, F., Kalenichenko, D., Philbin, J.: Facenet: A unified embedding for face recognition and clustering. In: Proceedings of the IEEE Conference on Computer Vision and Pattern Recognition, pp. 815–823 (2015)

41. Sharif, M., Bhagavatula, S., Bauer, L., Reiter, M.K.: Accessorize to a crime: real and stealthy attacks on state-of-the-art face recognition. In: Proceedings of the 2016 ACM SIGSAC Conference on Computer and Communications Security, pp. 1528–1540 (2016)

42. Simonyan, K., Zisserman, A.: Very deep convolutional networks for large-scale image recognition. arXiv preprint arXiv:1409.1556 (2014)

43. Song, Y., Shu, R., Kushman, N., Ermon, S.: Constructing unrestricted adversarial examples with generative models. In: Proceedings of the 32nd International Conference on Neural Information Processing Systems (2018)

44. Szegedy, C., Ioffe, S., Vanhoucke, V., Alemi, A.: Inception-v4, inception-resnet and the impact of residual connections on learning. In: AAAI (2017)

45. Szegedy, C., et al.: Going deeper with convolutions. In: Proceedings of the IEEE Conference on Computer Vision and Pattern Recognition, pp. 1–9 (2015)

46. Szegedy, C., Vanhoucke, V., Ioffe, S., Shlens, J., Wojna, Z.: Rethinking the inception architecture for computer vision. In: Proceedings of the IEEE Conference on Computer Vision and Pattern Recognition (CVPR) (2016)

47. Szegedy, C., et al.: Intriguing properties of neural networks. In: International Conference on Learning Representations (ICLR) (2014)

48. Tramèr, F., Kurakin, A., Papernot, N., Boneh, D., McDaniel, P.: Ensemble adversarial training: attacks and defenses. In: International Conference on Learning Representations (ICLR) (2018)

49. Wang, H., et al.: CosFace: large margin cosine loss for deep face recognition. In: Proceedings of the IEEE Conference on Computer Vision and Pattern Recognition, pp. 5265–5274 (2018)

50. Wu, D., Wang, Y., Xia, S.T., Bailey, J., Ma, X.: Skip connections matter: On the transferability of adversarial examples generated with resnets. arXiv preprint arXiv:2002.05990 (2020)

51. Xie, C., et al.: Improving transferability of adversarial examples with input diversity. In: Proceedings of the IEEE Conference on Computer Vision and Pattern Recognition (CVPR) (2019)

52. Xu, K., Li, C., Zhu, J., Zhang, B.: Understanding and stabilizing GANs' training dynamics with control theory. arXiv preprint arXiv:1909.13188 (2019)

53. Yang, X., Dong, Y., Pang, T., Xiao, Z., Su, H., Zhu, J.: Controllable evaluation and generation of physical adversarial patch on face recognition. arXiv e-prints pp. arXiv-2203 (2022)
54. Yang, X., Dong, Y., Pang, T., Zhu, J., Su, H.: Towards privacy protection by generating adversarial identity masks. arXiv preprint arXiv:2003.06814 (2020)
55. Yang, X., Wei, F., Zhang, H., Zhu, J.: Design and interpretation of universal adversarial patches in face detection. In: Vedaldi, A., Bischof, H., Brox, T., Frahm, J.-M. (eds.) ECCV 2020. LNCS, vol. 12362, pp. 174–191. Springer, Cham (2020). https://doi.org/10.1007/978-3-030-58520-4_11
56. Yang, X., Yang, D., Dong, Y., Yu, W., Su, H., Zhu, J.: Delving into the adversarial robustness on face recognition. arXiv preprint arXiv:2007.04118 (2020)
57. Zhang, C., Benz, P., Imtiaz, T., Kweon, I.S.: Understanding adversarial examples from the mutual influence of images and perturbations. In: Proceedings of the IEEE/CVF Conference on Computer Vision and Pattern Recognition, pp. 14521–14530 (2020)
58. Zhao, Z., Liu, Z., Larson, M.: On success and simplicity: a second look at transferable targeted attacks. In: Proceedings of 34th Iinternational Conference on Advances in Neural Information Processing Systems (2021)

Author Index

Printed in the United States
by Baker & Taylor Publisher Services